Responses to Marx's *Capital*

Historical Materialism Book Series

The Historical Materialism Book Series is a major publishing initiative of the radical left. The capitalist crisis of the twenty-first century has been met by a resurgence of interest in critical Marxist theory. At the same time, the publishing institutions committed to Marxism have contracted markedly since the high point of the 1970s. The Historical Materialism Book Series is dedicated to addressing this situation by making available important works of Marxist theory. The aim of the series is to publish important theoretical contributions as the basis for vigorous intellectual debate and exchange on the left.

The peer-reviewed series publishes original monographs, translated texts, and reprints of classics across the bounds of academic disciplinary agendas and across the divisions of the left. The series is particularly concerned to encourage the internationalization of Marxist debate and aims to translate significant studies from beyond the English-speaking world.

For a full list of titles in the Historical Materialism Book Series available in paperback from Haymarket Books, visit:
https://www.haymarketbooks.org/series_collections/1-historical-materialism

Responses to Marx's *Capital*

From Rudolf Hilferding to Isaak Illich Rubin

Edited by
Richard B. Day
Daniel F. Gaido

Haymarket Books
Chicago, IL

First published in 2017 by Brill Academic Publishers, The Netherlands
© 2017 Koninklijke Brill NV, Leiden, The Netherlands

Published in paperback in 2018 by
Haymarket Books
P.O. Box 180165
Chicago, IL 60618
773-583-7884
www.haymarketbooks.org

ISBN: 978-1-60846-999-4

Trade distribution:
In the US, Consortium Book Sales, www.cbsd.com
In Canada, Publishers Group Canada, www.pgcbooks.ca
In the UK, Turnaround Publisher Services, www.turnaround-uk.com
All other countries, Ingram Publisher Services International, ips_intlsales@ingramcontent.com

Cover design by Jamie Kerry and Ragina Johnson.

This book was published with the generous support of Lannan Foundation and the Wallace Action Fund.

10 9 8 7 6 5 4 3 2 1

Library of Congress Cataloging-in-Publication data is available.

Contents

Introduction: The Early Reception of Marx's Economic Works   1

Why Does Marx Matter?   39
    Richard B. Day

1   Karl Marx's Point of View in his Political-Economic Critique: A Review of Karl Marx, *Capital: A Critique of Political Economy* (1872)   100
    Illarion Ignat'evich Kaufman

2   The History of a Book [On the Fortieth Anniversary of the Publication of *Capital*, Vol. I] (1907)   112
    Otto Bauer

3   '*The Poverty of Philosophy*' and '*Capital*' (1886)   129
    Karl Kautsky

4   A Contribution to the Critique of Karl Marx's Economic System (1894)   162
    Werner Sombart

5   *Theories of Surplus Value* (1905)   212
    Heinrich Cunow

6   Marx's Critique of Ricardo (1906)   246
    Gustav Eckstein

7   The Prehistory of Marxian Economics (1911–12)   273
    Rudolf Hilferding

8   *Theories of Surplus Value* (1910)   328
    Otto Bauer

9   A Contribution to the Understanding of Marx's Research Method (1910)   340
    Heinrich Cunow

10   On the History of the Theory of Value (1903)   353
    Rudolf Hilferding

11   Karl Marx's Formulation of the Problem of Theoretical Economics (1905)   362
     Rudolf Hilferding

12   Back to Adam Smith! (1900)   378
     Rosa Luxemburg

13   Werner Sombart's *Modern Capitalism* (1903)   390
     Rudolf Hilferding

14   The Psychological Tendency in Recent Political Economy (1892)   405
     Conrad Schmidt

15   The Austrian School (1926)   429
     Isaak Illich Rubin

16   Marx's Teaching on Production and Consumption (1930)   448
     Isaak Illich Rubin

17   Fundamental Features of Marx's Theory of Value and How it Differs from Ricardo's Theory (1924)   536
     Isaak Illich Rubin

18   Towards a History of the Text of the First Chapter of Marx's *Capital* (1929)   583
     Isaak Illich Rubin

19   Essays on Marx's Theory of Money (1926–8)   619
     Isaak Illich Rubin

20   The Dialectical Development of Categories in Marx's Economic System (1929)   728
     Isaak Illich Rubin

Appendix: Pages from the Life and Creative Work of Economist I.I. Rubin (1992)   819
     Lyudmila L. Vasina and Yakov G. Rokityansky

References   837
Index   854

INTRODUCTION

The Early Reception of Marx's Economic Works

During most of the 1840s, Marx and Engels were making their way from the Hegelian philosophy of consciousness to the fundamental principles of historical materialism. Their writings from these years abound with creative energy, but in many respects they were also experimental and provisional in their conclusions. Ideas were in motion, and the final consequences would begin to appear only from the late 1850s onwards. Along the way to political economy, Marx first made his break with the left Hegelian group,[1] then undertook a provisional philosophical critique of economic life based on the concept of alienation in the *1844 Manuscripts*, next went beyond Feuerbach's humanism in the form of a more active concept of human *praxis*, and then finally debated economic issues directly in his polemic against Pierre-Joseph Proudhon's *Système des contradictions économiques, ou, Philosophie de la misère* (1846).

Marx's response to Proudhon first appeared in 1847 as *Misère de la philosophie*, the book that English-language readers know as *The Poverty of Philosophy*. In 1885 a German edition of the book was published after being translated by Eduard Bernstein and Karl Kautsky. In a preface to that edition, dated 13 October 1884, Engels pointed out that 'the terminology used in this work does not entirely coincide with that in *Capital*. Thus this work still speaks of *labour* as a commodity, of the purchase and sale of labour, instead of labour *power*'.[2] In a subsequent footnote Engels also criticised the original thesis 'that the "natural," i.e., normal, price of labour power coincides with the wage minimum, i.e., with the equivalent in value of the means of subsistence absolutely indispensable for the life and procreation of the worker', indicating that 'in *Capital*, Marx has put the above thesis right'.[3]

---

1 The best overview of the rise and fall of the Hegelian left, culminating in Marx and Engels's *The German Ideology* (1846), is Cornu 1955–70.
2 Marx 1977, p. 19.
3 Marx 1977, p. 45. In Volume I of *Capital* Marx wrote: 'His means of subsistence must therefore be sufficient to maintain him in his normal state as a working individual. His natural needs, such as food, clothing, fuel and housing vary according to the climatic and other physical peculiarities of his country. On the other hand, the number and extent of his so-called necessary requirements, as also the manner in which they are satisfied, are themselves products of history, and depend therefore to a great extent on the level of civilization attained by a country; in particular they depend on the conditions in which, and consequently on the

Engels faced similar issues when preparing a new edition of Marx's *Wage-Labour and Capital*, a series of lectures delivered before the German Workingmen's Club of Brussels in 1847 and first published in several instalments in *Die Neue Rheinische Zeitung*, beginning on 4 April 1849. In his introduction to the new edition, dated 30 April 1891, Engels again noted that, contrary to what Marx had originally said, workers do not sell their labour in exchange for wages but rather their *labour power*:

> Marx, in the 1840s, had not yet completed his criticism of political economy. This was not done until toward the end of the fifties. Consequently, such of his writings as were published before the first instalment of his *Critique of Political Economy* was finished, deviate in some points from those written after 1859, and contain expressions and whole sentences which, viewed from the standpoint of his later writings, appear inexact, and even incorrect.[4]

Even *A Contribution to the Critique of Political Economy* (1859), Marx's first mature economic work, stands out today mainly for the unsurpassed exposition of the general principles of historical materialism in its extraordinary preface. There Marx described existing society as the last stage in the 'prehistory' of humanity, beyond which producers would no longer be dominated by the products of their own labour. Capitalism would create the technical and social preconditions for transition to a superior social formation, in which people would exert conscious control over the production process, shortening the working day and thus making it possible to overcome the division between manual and intellectual labour. But even this work was still incomplete in terms of its exposition of the form of value, as Isaak Rubin comprehensively demonstrates in his essay 'Towards a History of the Text of the First Chapter of Marx's *Capital*' (Document 18 of this volume). As a consequence, Marx ended up rewriting the material from the *Critique* and incorporating it in the first volume of *Capital* as 'Part One: Commodities and Money'.

The problem that later Marxists repeatedly encountered was that Marx's work was forever in progress and never really completed. In the Preface to *A*

---

habits and expectations with which, the class of free workers has been formed. In contrast, therefore, with the case of other commodities, the determination of the value of labour-power contains a historical and moral element. Nevertheless, in a given country at a given period, the average amount of the means of subsistence necessary for the worker is a known *datum*' (Marx 1976, p. 275).

4 Marx 2006, p. 5.

Contribution to the Critique of Political Economy Marx stated that he intended to examine the system of bourgeois economy in six books (capital, landed property, wage-labour; the state, foreign trade, world market), yet only the first volume of the first book was actually published during Marx's lifetime. For several decades after Marx's death in 1883 major new manuscripts appeared, including the second and third volumes of *Capital*, the three parts of *Theories of Surplus-Value* and the *1844 Manuscripts*, all of which were essential for a complete understanding of Marx's project, how it developed, and what it aimed to accomplish. As a result, Marx's followers continuously had to adapt their interpretations of his work as these new materials became available. The story of this ongoing process of discovery is reconstructed in this volume. We have included a total of 20 documents, beginning with the initial response to Volume I of *Capital* and ending with six remarkable essays from Isaak Rubin that were written in the later 1920s and appear here for the first time in English translation.

The Response to the First Volume of *Capital* (1867)

In a letter to Ludwig Kugelmann, dated 11 February 1869, Marx blamed the 'cowardice of the experts, on the one side, and the conspiracy of silence of the bourgeois and reactionary press, on the other' for the limited circulation of the first volume of *Capital*.[5] However, by the autumn of 1871 the first edition had been sold out, and in the postface to the second edition, dated 24 January 1873, Marx replied to two Russian commentaries on his work: Nikolai Ivanovich Sieber's book, *David Ricardo's Theory of Value and Capital in Connection with the Latest Contributions and Interpretations*;[6] and a review by Illarion Ignat'evich Kaufman, 'Karl Marx's Point of View in his Political-Economic Critique', which we have translated for this volume as Document 1.

Kaufman struggled in his review with the relation between science and philosophy, arguing that Marx imposed Hegelian terminology on a work that in fact adopted the scientific approach of the biological sciences. In his postface to the second edition of *Capital*, Marx translated part of Kaufman's description of his research method in order to show that, despite Kaufman's aversion to dialectics, what he actually depicted in his review of *Capital* was nothing other than the dialectical method of analysis once it had been shorn of the

---

5 MECW, Vol. 43, pp. 213–14.
6 The chapter on 'Marx's Theory of Value and Money' has been translated (see Sieber 1871).

mystifying influence of Hegelian idealism. Marx regarded the dialectical movement of concepts, discovered through historical and logical analysis, as forms of thought reflecting the development of the real world. All of the ensuing documents in this volume elaborate the issues first raised by Kaufman's review and Marx's response, with the methodological relation between Marx and Hegel as a continuous theme.

Apart from its theoretical importance, the first volume of *Capital* also had a profound effect upon the tactics of German Social Democracy, encouraging the struggle for a normal (eight-hour) working day and the development of trade-unionist politics. For instance, in an article on Rodbertus, written in 1884, Karl Kautsky declared:

> As long as labour is a commodity, it is subject to the laws of supply and demand, and the only means of improving its situation is the reduction of supply and the increase of demand. To the extent that that is at all possible, it can be done through a *solid trade-union organisation* and a short *normal working-day*. Those are the goals that the workers must *initially* set themselves.[7]

This comment comes from one of Kautsky's earliest economic essays, entitled 'Rodbertus' *Capital*', which defended the originality of Marx's theories against accusations of plagiarism arising from posthumous publication of Rodbertus's fourth 'Social Letter' to Kirchmann.[8] Kautsky had no difficulty in demonstrating Rodbertus's ahistorical method, his legalistic (i.e. idealistic) approach to political economy, and his nationalistic notions of how capitalism might be 'regulated' in order to avoid periodic crises.

At the same time, Kautsky's essay revealed the limitations of his own (and by extension Social Democracy's) grasp of Marx's categories at that time, and the tendency to confuse them with Lassallean terminology. In one passage, for instance, Kautsky wrote: 'The *lack of planning* of today's mode of production and the circumstance that the working class does not receive the *full product of its labour* make possible the economic crises'.[9] An end to this confusion only came in 1891, when Marx's 'Critique of the Gotha Programme' and its Lassallean influences was published in *Die Neue Zeit*.[10]

---

7   Kautsky 1884, p. 400.
8   Robertus-Jagetzow 1884.
9   Kautsky 1884, p. 398.
10 Marx 1891.

One of the most important early commentaries on the first volume of *Capital* came in 1907 when Otto Bauer marked the fortieth anniversary of its publication with his essay 'The History of a Book' (see Document 2). Bauer was writing in the aftermath of the revisionist controversy of 1898–1903, during which time revolutionaries within the Second International were forced onto the defensive by Bernstein's attempt to convert Social Democracy into a party of reform within the framework of bourgeois parliamentary democracy. Bauer lamented the fact that, in order to defend Marx against revisionism, he and his co-thinkers were forced to appear as merely the 'orthodox' upholders of a received truth.[11]

Perhaps under the influence of Marx's notes on the method of political economy – available today as the introduction to the *Grundrisse* but first published by Kautsky in *Die Neue Zeit* in 1903 as the 'Introduction to a Critique of Political Economy'[12] – Bauer made an important advance beyond previous expositions of *Capital* by noting its links with the categories of Hegel's *Science of Logic*:

> The great fact underlying Hegel's logic, as well as his criticism of Kant, is the natural sciences. Hegel, too, does not fail to recognise their empirical character, and he has no doubt 'that all our knowledge begins with experience'; but he characteristically calls the empirical 'the immediate', and the logical conceptual processing of the experience, the 'negation of an immediately given'. Behind the immediate, Hegel looks for the true and the real. He finds the true and the real in the 'realm of shadows, the world of simple essentialities, freed of all sensuous concretion'. In *Existence* [*Dasein*], the determinacy [*Bestimmtheit*] – the concrete empirical *qualitative* condition [*Beschaffenheit*] – is one with Being [*Sein*]; but only if this condition is sublated [*aufgehoben*], posited as indifferent, only then do we get to *pure Being*, which is nothing but *quantity*. But quantity [*Quantum*], to which an existence or a quality is bound, is *measure* [*Maß*]. Measure is the concrete truth of being; in it lies the idea of essence [*Wesen*]. 'The *truth* of *being* is *essence*. Being is the immediate. Since the goal of knowledge is the truth, what being is *in and for itself*, knowledge does not stop at the immediate and its determinations, but penetrates beyond it on the presupposition that *behind* this being there still is something other than being itself, and that this background con-

---

11 See the early documents of the revisionist controversy in Tudor 1988. For books summing up the controversy, see Kautsky 1899, Bernstein 1993, Luxemburg 1989.
12 Marx 1903.

stitutes the truth of being.' That background, that essence of being, is measure; we get to it by positing the determinations of being as indifferent, when we turn from qualitatively determined existence to pure being as pure quantity.

Bauer called Hegel's terminology 'strange' and 'mystical-sounding', but he went on to show that Hegel's categories were essential for understanding the logic of Marx's *Capital*:

> Marx certainly imitates Hegel's method. He also looks behind the 'appearance of competition' for the true and real. And he also wants to find behind immediacy the truth of being – by sublating the qualitative determination of being in its empirical existence, positing it as indifferent and turning to being as pure quantity. Thus, in the famous opening chapters of the first volume of *Capital*, the concrete commodities are stripped of their determination (as a frock, or 20 yards of linen) and posited as mere quantities of social labour. In the same way, the concrete individual labour is deprived of its determination and regarded as a mere 'form of manifestation' of general social labour. Thus, even economic subjects, these men of flesh and blood, eventually lose their apparent existence and become mere 'organs of labour' and 'agents of production', one the embodiment of a certain quantity of social capital, the other the personification of a quantity of social labour-power. The quantity, to which existence or quality is bound as Hegel's *measure*, is here social labour. It is the *essence* of economic phenomena, which, as Hegel said, not only passes through its determinations – let us recall Marx's account of the circulation of capital, which makes the same value assume the ever-changing forms of money, commodity, money, money capital, productive capital, commodity capital! – but also rules them as their law. Social labour becomes finally – and it would be an enticing task to develop this idea in detail – what Hegel calls *substance*, absolute activity-of-form [*Formtätigkeit*], absolute power, from which all accidents emerge.

Though Bauer, under the influence of the neo-Kantianism then prevalent in Vienna's intellectual circles, added that 'Hegel's ontology today looks like a hardly understandable aberration after Kant's critique of reason', he was sufficiently versed in classical German philosophy to realise that 'we should not regard as a meaningless coincidence the fact that Marx owes his logical training to Hegel'. Hegel represented 'a significant advance beyond Kant' because, 'while

Kant's critique of knowledge was still mainly oriented towards the mathematical natural sciences, in Hegel human history appears at the heart of his system'.

Bauer returned to methodological issues in response to capitalism's development into the new phase of imperialism, which dragged humanity into world war a few years later. He rightly felt that Marxists could not merely defend Marx's revolutionary heritage but also had to rediscover his use of Hegel's dialectical method in order to apply it to the new circumstances of economic and political life. In June 1910, Bauer wrote a review of Rudolf Hilferding's book, *Finance Capital: A Study of the Latest Phase of Capitalist Development*, in which he agreed with Kautsky's description of it as 'a continuation of Marx's *Capital*'.[13] Marxist economics had made little progress since Karl Marx's death, mainly because 'orthodox' Marxists had been preoccupied with defending *Capital* against revisionism. In the meantime, a new world had arisen, and the former presentations of the developmental tendencies of capitalism no longer sufficed. Bauer concluded that 'the gaps resulting from this situation have now finally been filled at least in part. Rudolf Hilferding's *Finance Capital* gives us what we have long needed'.[14]

The Reception of the Second Volume of *Capital* (1885)

The second volume of *Capital* was published in 1885 and reviewed by Kautsky in *Die Neue Zeit*, together with the first German edition of *The Poverty of Philosophy*. Kautsky remarked that readers of *Capital* usually assumed that Marx was unique in ascribing value to the activity of labour. In fact, Kautsky noted, bourgeois economists had long ago made this connection. Marx's unique contribution was to associate the category of value with commodity production as a historically developed system of *social relations*:

> What is peculiar in Marx's theory of value is not the reduction of value to labour but the presentation of value as an historical category, on the one hand, and as a social relation, on the other, which can only be derived from the social functions and not from the natural properties of the commodity. That is what nobody before Marx had done, and that is what we regard as the distinguishing trait peculiar to Marx.[15]

---

13 Kautsky 1911a, p. 765.
14 Bauer 1910, in Day and Gaido 2011, p. 415.
15 Kautsky 1886, p. 57.

Kautsky clarified by offering the following description of Marx's 'characteristic method':

> We clearly see in *Capital* his conception of economic categories as historical, on the one hand, and as purely social relations, on the other, sharply distinguishing them from their underlying natural forms and deducing their peculiarities from the observation of their *movement*, their functions, not from their respective outward manifestations: in a word, his development of economic categories from the development and movement of social relations. As against the fetishism peculiar to *bourgeois* economics, which turns the social, economic character that things get stamped with in the social production process into a *natural character* springing from the material nature of those things, Marx declares: 'What is at issue here is not a set of definitions under which things are to be subsumed. They are rather definite functions that are expressed in specific categories'.[16]

Recapitulating Marx's arguments in the first volume of *Capital*, Kautsky traced this twofold character of commodities to the twofold nature of the labour expended in producing them:

> After Marx rigorously distinguished the social character of the commodity from the natural form of the good, he sets about to make an equally important distinction in labour itself: on the one hand the [concrete] labour that determines the natural form of the substance, and on the other hand [abstract] labour as a social element in its social context. Only in the latter sense does labour generate value.[17]

While the first volume of *Capital* dealt with the *creation* of surplus value in the production process, and therefore with the division between variable and fixed capital, the second volume investigated its *realisation* in the circulation process and the consequent division between fixed and circulating capital.[18] Kautsky highlighted the following passage from the second volume as particularly revealing of Marx's method:

---

16   Kautsky 1886, p. 50, citing Marx 1978, p. 303.
17   Kautsky 1886, p. 51.
18   Kautsky 1886, pp. 54–5, 193–4.

Capital, as self-valorizing value, does not just comprise class relations, a definite social character that depends on the existence of labour as wage-labour. It is a movement; a circulatory process through different stages, which itself in turn includes three different forms of the circulatory process [namely, the circuit of money, productive capital and commodity capital]. Hence it can only be grasped as a movement, and not as a static thing.[19]

One of the most important contributions of Volume II of *Capital*, as Kautsky explains in his review, was Marx's novel account of the reproduction and circulation of the total social capital. While analysis of the reproduction of individual capitals could set aside the natural form of products, reproduction of the total capital is affected not only by the value determinations of the products but also by their material content. A macroeconomic model of the production of exchange-values necessarily presupposes, as Marx demonstrated, that use-values are produced in objectively determined proportions.

The second volume of *Capital* had a strange fortune. In a letter to Friedrich Sorge, dated 3 June 1885, Engels worried that its complex subject matter would attract few readers:

> The second volume will cause great disappointment, being a purely scientific work with little in the way of agitation. By contrast the third volume will again have the effect of a thunderbolt, since the whole of capitalist production is dealt with in context for the first time and all official bourgeois economics rejected out of hand.[20]

In fact, however, the second volume of *Capital* did become the subject of much critical scrutiny for two main reasons: first, because its analysis of the circulation process of the total social capital provided essential tools for investigating cyclical crises;[21] and secondly because its reproduction schemes played a central part both in Lenin's dispute with Russian Narodniks (who denied that capitalism could create its own domestic market in a predominantly agrarian country)[22] and also in Rosa Luxemburg's theory of imperialism, which likewise

---

19 Marx 1978, p. 185.
20 MECW, Vol. 47, pp. 296–7.
21 See, for instance, Bauer 1904 and Hilferding 1981, pp. 239–98.
22 See Lenin's response to the Narodniks in *The Development of Capitalism in Russia: The Process of the Formation of a Home Market for Large-Scale Industry*, published in 1899 (Lenin 1899a).

claimed that capitalism could not experience continuous expanded reproduction without conquering external markets.[23]

The Reception of the Third Volume of *Capital* (1894)

The third volume of *Capital* was reviewed in *Die Neue Zeit* by none other than the future theoretician of revisionism in the SPD, Eduard Bernstein.[24] His long commentary, published in seven separate instalments, emphasised that the transformation of values into production prices was not only a categorical stage in Marx's analysis but also an actual historical stage in the development of commodity production, marking its transition to fully developed capitalist production.[25] In the final paragraph of his review, Bernstein wrote:

> When the first volume of *Capital* appeared, someone who personally was thoroughly opposed to Marx and had been bitterly criticised by him – Johann Baptist von Schweitzer – had to say to himself after reading that work: socialism *is* a science. Nobody will finish this third volume without feeling the same.[26]

Despite this positive summary, however, only two years later Bernstein commented in a letter to Kautsky, written on 1 September 1897, that he had long entertained some doubts regarding *Capital* and that the third volume was 'the last straw': 'It is an anti-climax vis-à-vis the first volume, not only as regards the form, but also because of its content'.[27] Although Bernstein was close to Engels at the time, Engels had his own misgivings and spoke of Bernstein's review as being 'very confused'.[28] Much of Bernstein's work consisted of lengthy quotations from Marx, and he neglected even to consider the final chapters on the theory of ground rent, which he promised to deal with in a subsequent essay.

A much more substantive review of the third volume of *Capital* came from Werner Sombart, one of the most prominent economic sociologists of the day

---

23 On Luxemburg's *The Accumulation of Capital: A Contribution to the Economic Explanation of Imperialism* (1913), see Day 1980, Day and Gaido 2011, pp. 675–752, 913–26, Gaido and Quiroga 2013.
24 Bernstein 1895a.
25 Bernstein 1895a, p. 485.
26 Bernstein 1895a, p. 632.
27 Roth 2004, pp. 937–8.
28 MECW, Vol. 50, p. 468.

and a leader, together with Max Weber, of the third generation of the German 'historical school' of political economy. We have translated Sombart's review as Document 4. Engels took Sombart's comments quite seriously. He responded in his 'Supplement and Addendum' to the third volume of *Capital* and in a personal letter (Engels to Werner Sombart in Breslau, London, 11 March 1895), which we include as an appendix to Document 4.

When Sombart's article appeared in 1894, Eugen von Böhm-Bawerk, then the most famous proponent of the Austrian School of marginalist economic theory, considered it to be an apology for Marxism.[29] From a political point of view this was nonsense: Sombart was never a socialist, and his later works were extensively criticised by Rosa Luxemburg, Ernest Belfort Bax and Max Adler.[30] Yet Böhm-Bawerk's reaction was quite understandable, coming from a representative of the subjective theory of value, for Sombart spoke of political economy as being divided into 'two worlds of ... thought [that] exist side by side, almost independently of each other; two kinds of scientific observation, which have nothing more than the name in common'.

On the one hand, the subjectivist school concentrated on price determination through individual judgements of utility in the act of exchange, an approach that Sombart said 'naturally empties into psychologism'. Marx's economic system, on the contrary, was characterised by an *extreme objectivism*, with the result that 'all the partial and complete, more or less justified, more or less clear, more or less hackneyed contradictions in our schools, which have come up for discussion so often lately, will ultimately resolve themselves in this methodologically paramount opposition of objectivism and subjectivism'.[31]

Sombart noted that, in contrast to Böhm-Bawerk and the subjectivist school, Marx emphasised the 'economic conditions which are *independent*' of the individual's will, in order to determine what 'goes on behind his back, by virtue of relations *independent* of him':

> [Marx's] train of thought was this: prices are formed by competition ... But competition itself is regulated by the rate of profit, the profit rate by the rate of surplus-value, and this by value, which is itself the expression of a socially determined fact, of the social productivity [of labour]. [This succession] now presents itself in Marx's system in reverse order: value – surplus-value – profit – competition – prices [of production], etc. If we

---

29 'An apologist of Marx, as intelligent as he is ardent, has lately appeared in the person of Werner Sombart' (Böhm-Bawerk 1896, p. 102).
30 Luxemburg 1900b, Bax 1900, Adler 1903, Luxemburg 1903.
31 Sombart 1894.

wanted a catchphrase, we could say: the question for Marx is never the motivation, but always the limitation of the individual caprice of economic agents.

Sombart's review included a detailed – and, according to Engels, 'quite excellent'[32] – rendering of the main arguments in the third volume of *Capital*. Where Sombart differed from Marx was in regarding value (and therefore surplus value) as merely a heuristic concept intended to 'give to the technical concept of productivity, or productive power, an adequate economic form, thus making it suitable for economic thinking'. According to Sombart, *'the value of the commodities is the specific historical form in which the social productivity of labour, determining all the economic processes, ultimately asserts itself'* in a society based upon exchanges between private producers. While Engels thought highly of Sombart's review in general terms, he rejected his conclusion that *'value is not an empirical but a conceptual fact'*.[33]

Sombart's tendency to regard value as a theoretical construct was also evident in his view of the equalisation of the rate of profit by competition among capitals: 'Those "equalisations" of high and low rates of profit, among capitals of different organic composition, into an average rate of profit are mental operations, but no events of real life'.[34] In his letter of response, Engels pointed out that Marx had in mind neither heuristic concepts nor mental operations but a real historical process:

> How has the equalisation been brought about in reality? ... When commodity exchange began, when products gradually turned into commodities, they were exchanged approximately *according to their value*. It was the amount of labour expended on two objects which provided the only

---

[32] 'In Braun's *Archiv für soziale Gesetzgebung*, VII, no. 4, Werner Sombart gives an outline presentation of Marx's system which is quite excellent on the whole. This is the first time that a German university professor has managed to see by and large in Marx's writings what Marx actually said, and he further declares that criticism of the Marxian system should consist not in a refutation ("that can be left to someone with political ambition"), but rather in a further development' (Engels, 'Supplement to Volume 3 of *Capital*,' in Marx 1992, p. 1031).

[33] In a letter to Conrad Schmidt, Engels remarked: 'In Sombart's otherwise very good article on Volume III I also find this tendency to dilute the theory of value: he had also obviously expected a somewhat different solution?' (Engels to Conrad Schmidt in Zurich, 12 March 1895, in *MECW*, vol. 50, p. 466).

[34] Sombart 1894.

standard for their quantitative comparison. Thus value had a *direct and real existence* at that time. We know that this direct realisation of value in exchange ceased and that now it no longer happens. And I believe that it won't be particularly difficult for you to trace the intermediate links, at least in general outline, that lead from directly real value to the value of the capitalist mode of production, which is so thoroughly hidden that our economists can calmly deny its existence. A genuinely historical exposition of these processes, which does indeed require thorough research but in return promises amply rewarding results, would be a very valuable supplement to *Capital*.

Engels insisted that 'The law of value has a far greater and more definite importance for capitalist production than that of a mere hypothesis, let alone a necessary fiction'.[35] The transformation of values into production prices involved 'not just a logical process but a historical one, and its explanatory reflection in thought, the logical following-up of its internal connections'.[36] Engels summarised this way:

> ... Marx's law of value applies universally, as much as any economic laws do apply, for the entire period of simple commodity production, i.e. up to the time at which this undergoes a modification by the onset of the capitalist form of production. Up till then, prices gravitate to the values determined by Marx's law and oscillate around these values, so that the more completely simple commodity production develops, the more do average prices coincide with values for longer periods when not interrupted by external violent disturbances, and with the insignificant variations we mentioned earlier. Thus the Marxian law of value has a universal economic validity for an era lasting from the beginning of the exchange that transforms products into commodities down to the fifteenth century of our epoch. But commodity exchange dates from a time before any written history, going back to at least 3500 B.C. in Egypt, and 4000 B.C. or maybe even 6000 B.C. in Babylon; thus the law of value prevailed for a period of some five to seven millennia.[37]

---

35 Engels, 'Supplement to Volume 3 of *Capital*', in Marx 1992, pp. 1032–3. According to Engels, Conrad Schmidt's review of the third volume of *Capital*, not included in this volume but available online in French, suffered from the same mystification (Schmidt 1895). See also Engels's letter to Conrad Schmidt in Zurich, 12 March 1895, in *MECW*, Vol. 50, pp. 462–7.
36 Engels, 'Supplement to Volume 3 of *Capital*', in Marx 1992, p. 1033.
37 Engels, 'Supplement to Volume 3 of *Capital*', in Marx 1992, p. 1037. A response to the third

The Reception of *Theories of Surplus-Value*

It is only due to historical circumstance (the fact that Engels died before completing his task of editing Marx's manuscripts) that Marx's history of political economy did not appear as the fourth volume of *Capital*. Instead, it was edited and published in rough form by Kautsky[38] as three separate volumes and under a different title, *Theories of Surplus-Value*.[39]

The first volume of *Theories of Surplus-Value* was reviewed by Heinrich Cunow (1862–1936), one of the editors of *Die Neue Zeit* and *Vorwärts*, respectively the SPD's theoretical journal and its central press organ (see Document 5).[40] Cunow would later make a spectacular volte-face during the First World War and become a strident social-patriot, but for the moment he was a member of the 'orthodox' camp, and in 1907 he became a lecturer at the SPD party school in Berlin, teaching alongside Franz Mehring, Rudolf Hilferding and Rosa Luxemburg. His theoretical works include several studies in anthropology, a history of the revolutionary press during the French Revolution and two pioneering analyses of imperialism, in which he emphasised the central role of banks and finance capital in imperialist expansionism.[41]

Cunow's review summarised Marx's assessment of the English mercantilists,[42] Physiocracy and Adam Smith, pointing out how the focus of economic inquiry had moved from the sphere of circulation in mercantilism to the sphere of production in the Physiocrats, then to the concept of productive and unpro-

---

volume of *Capital* which, for reasons of space, falls beyond the scope of the present work, is the application of Marx's theory of ground rent to the analysis of the agrarian crisis of the last quarter of the nineteenth century in Europe by Parvus and Kautsky. See Parvus 1896 and the laudatory review of the Russian edition by Lenin 1899a, as well as Kautsky 1988 and its review by Lenin, who called Kautsky's book, *The Agrarian Question*, 'the most important event in present-day economic literature since the third volume of *Capital*' (Lenin 1899b, p. 94).

38   Marx 1905–10.
39   Rubin later managed to summarise Marx's arguments and give them a cogent expression in a single volume (Rubin 1979). Unfortunately, he left out Marx's informative exposition of Richard Jones in the third volume of *Theories of Surplus-Value*; see Hilferding's remarks on this author in Document 6.
40   See also Franz Mehring's review of the first volume of *Theories of Surplus-Value* in Mehring 1905.
41   Heinrich Cunow, 'Trade-Agreements and Imperialist Expansion Policy' (May 1900), and 'American Expansionist Policy in East Asia' (June–July 1902), in Day and Gaido 2011, pp. 177–210.
42   See also Hilferding's assessment of Thomas Mun and mercantilism in Hilferding 1911.

ductive labour in Adam Smith and, finally, to the critique of capitalism in Marx's economic system. The only point where he differed from Marx was in his appraisal of Sir James Steuart. Cunow thought Marx's assessment of Steuart as a late mercantilist was mistaken and that Marx had underestimated Steuart's theoretical achievements.

But the main issue that Cunow emphasised was the distinction between productive and unproductive labour. He explained that the concept of productive labour is determined by the character of each social formation, with the result that there is no productive labour, abstractly understood, that can be treated apart from historically given modes of production. In the capitalist context, '*productive labour is labour purchased by a capitalist with a portion of his capital and employed in production in order to extract from it surplus-value, while unproductive labour, on the other hand, is labour that supplies someone with services or use-values for the satisfaction of his needs and is paid for from his income*'.[43]

The second volume of *Theories of Surplus-Value* was reviewed by Gustav Eckstein (1874–1916), later a prominent member of the Kautskyist 'centre', whom Leon Trotsky referred to in his obituary as 'one of the most outstanding Austro-German Marxists'.[44] We have included Eckstein's review because of the importance it attached to Marx's critique of the theory of rent as it appeared in the works of Smith, Ricardo and Rodbertus (see Document 6).

The Physiocrats saw agricultural labour as the only productive labour, and they therefore regarded agriculture as the source of the social surplus – although they also drew a progressive bourgeois corollary (advocacy of a 'single tax' on ground rent) from their ostensibly backward-looking analysis. Thomas Malthus had claimed that luxurious consumption by landlords was essential to ensure an adequate market for industry. Adam Smith and David Ricardo cast landlords in a different role, seeing rent as a diversion of social revenue from productive purposes. Smith wrote that 'as soon as the land of any country has all become private property, the landlords, like all other men, love to reap where they never sowed, and demand a rent even for its natural produce'.[45] Ricardo, in turn, derived ground rent from the diminishing returns obtained from increasingly less productive parcels of land brought under cultivation, and he explained the declining tendency of the rate of profit by means of this constantly increasing rent. The prospect of a declining rate of profit became

---

43   It is only to be regretted that Cunow's review omitted the best short comment in the first volume of *Theories of Surplus-Value*, namely Linguet's sardonic reference to Montesquieu: *L'esprit des lois, c'est la propriété* ('The spirit of the laws is property').
44   Trotsky 1918.
45   Smith 2007, p. 32.

the principal argument against Britain's Corn Laws, or the taxation of grain imports, which were repealed in 1846. Ricardo's analysis laid bare the class antagonism between landowners and capitalists, showing ground rent to be unearned income, a mere deduction from profit, causing his most radical disciples to conclude that land should be nationalised.

Marx criticised Ricardo for focusing on differential rent and excluding the possibility of absolute rent, a point that Gustav Eckstein elaborated in his review. Eckstein demonstrated that absolute rent, arising from the surplus-profit obtained by the excess of market prices over prices of production, presupposed a distinction between values and production prices not contemplated in Ricardo's system. With free competition, capitals will typically move from branches with a higher organic composition than the average into those with a lower organic composition, in the hope of capturing a larger return of surplus value. Eckstein noted that industries 'with low organic composition cannot, as a rule, avoid the influx of new capital and realise for themselves the surplus value exceeding the rate of profit'. However, since the owners of land enjoy a monopoly over a non-renewable means of production, the movement of capital into agriculture, with its typically low organic composition, will not occur without a 'special compensation' being paid to landowners in the form of absolute rent; that is, an element of the total rent that cannot be explained in terms of differing productivity of the land. But this analysis also showed that absolute rent was a purely historical fact, which belonged to a certain stage of development of agriculture and could disappear at a higher stage. Eckstein remarked that this possibility was already materialising in 1906:

> Before the introduction of machinery into industry, the role of living labour was even greater in industry than in primary production. Since then, however, this relation has changed completely: with the blossoming of agricultural chemistry and the penetration of machinery [into agriculture], a change of tendency has recently occurred also in this field; the difference between values and prices of production has been reduced in agriculture, and with it also absolute ground rent.

Eckstein concluded that, 'as regards methodological clarity, the presentation of ground rent, and particularly of absolute rent, is superior in this work compared to the third volume of *Capital*'.

The third volume of *Theories of Surplus-Value* was reviewed by Rudolf Hilferding in a *tour de force* of theoretical penetration and conceptual clarity (see Document 6). Since Ricardo did not distinguish between constant and variable capital, he could not develop the concept of what Marx called the organic composition of capital, i.e. the ratio between the constant and variable elements. Borrowing the Austrian physicist Ernst Mach's ideas on how and why science progresses, Hilferding attributed the eventual disintegration of the Ricardian system – the subject of the third volume of *Theories of Surplus-Value* – to its inability to accommodate a fundamentally new fact of the industrial revolution; namely, that machinery was increasingly displacing living labour and producing a rising organic composition of capital, which in turn implied a falling rate of profit since only living labour can produce surplus value.

Among the thinkers whose work Marx reviewed in portraying the breakdown of the Ricardian system, the most prominent were Thomas Malthus, James Mill, John Ramsay McCulloch and Richard Jones. Hilferding surveyed Marx's account of how Mill sought to uphold the logical consistency of Ricardo's system by explaining away new realities; how McCulloch confused the 'actions' of machinery with living labour and fetishised capital; and finally, how Jones criticised Ricardo's method from an historicist point of view.

Hilferding considered Richard Jones (1790–1855), an Anglican priest and politically conservative lecturer at Cambridge University, to be 'one of the most important *precursors of the materialist conception of history*'. Of all the economists who preceded Marx, 'Jones was the one who most clearly recognised and enunciated the historical character of capitalism'. Jones wrote that 'the general principles of political economy have hitherto been laid down by English writers with an especial and exclusive view to the peculiar form and structure of society existing in Great Britain' – a society characterised by the fact that the majority of labourers, in both industry and agriculture, were wage-workers, employed by a class of capitalists owning the means of production and different from the possessors of the soil.[46] Such a disposition of classes, Jones argued in 1833, could be seen only in England and the Low Countries, and in certain places in Western Europe and America. It did not describe the social structure of humanity during most of its history and certainly not that of most of the globe at the time when he was writing.

In his commentary on Jones in *Theories of Surplus-Value*, Marx wrote that 'The real science of political economy ends by regarding the bourgeois production relations as merely *historical* ones, leading to higher relations in which the antagonism on which they are based is resolved'.[47] In Hilferding's terms, this meant that

---

46 Jones 1859, p. 1.
47 Marx 1975, p. 429.

> With Jones, political economy arrives at the point where its previous conscious or unconscious assumption – the necessity, or the implicitly assumed existence, of the bourgeois form of production – had to be dropped in order to make possible further progress of the science. It is the point from which economics goes backwards towards vulgar economy or forwards to scientific socialism.[48]

Hilferding shared Kautsky's conclusion that 'Karl Marx starts where Richard Jones stopped', to which he added that 'Marx also begins where Ricardo stops'. The '*fundamentally* new element in Marx' was his attempt 'to combine the historical conception that Jones counterposes to Ricardo's "abstract method" with the latter, and in that way to complete it and revolutionise it'. Jones had not gone 'beyond *historical description* to *theoretical comprehension*. That is precisely Marx's achievement'. Hilferding concluded that '*The economic theory of scientific Marxism grew out of the specifically Marxist union of the "inductive method" of Jones and the abstract method of Ricardo*. And the economic categories, once discovered, *remained* historical'. From this followed a political conclusion: 'The distinguishing feature of scientific socialism is precisely that socialism is nothing but the result of the full development of the capitalist economy'.

The next document in this collection is an overview of all three volumes of *Theories of Surplus-Value* by Otto Bauer, who in 1910 wrote that only after a lapse of 51 years 'do we get to know the final part of the work – the part that Friedrich Engels intended to publish as a fourth volume of *Capital* – whose first part Karl Marx published in 1859'. As in his previous essay marking the fortieth anniversary of the first volume of *Capital* (Document 2), Bauer explored the relation between Marx and Hegel, in this case between *Theories of Surplus-Value* and the method Hegel employed in his *Lectures on the History of Philosophy*:

> Just as Hegel arranges all the older philosophical systems as integral parts of his own, as phases of its development, identifying this development with the self-development of Spirit in general, so Marx looks not only for the basic ideas of his theory, but also for each one of its component parts in the economists of the two preceding centuries, and he shows the internal development of those elements until their systematic organisation in his own doctrine reflects the development of bourgeois society.[49]

---

48 Document 7.
49 Document 8.

Whereas Cunow, Eckstein and Hilferding had explored particular authors and specific theoretical problems, Bauer summarised the whole of Marx's history of political economy by explaining how the key issues were integrated in Marx's fundamental concepts of historical materialism:

> The development of the productive forces finds its specific economic expression in the progress to a higher organic composition of capital. Thus theory passes over from the old static problem of value distribution to the problem of exploring the laws of motion of the capitalist economy. The problems of accumulation and the rate of profit, already posed by the older economists, now took on new shape.

As contradictions and antagonisms developed together with the productive forces, the analysis of the capitalist mode of production turned into its criticism and led to the discovery that capitalist relations must be replaced by other relations of production. In this connection, Bauer concurred with Hilferding in his assessment of Richard Jones, who

> regarded the capitalist mode of production as a transient phase in the development of mankind, a stage of development that can be followed by another in which the workers themselves will be the owners of the means of production and of the stocks necessary for labour. As he surveyed the changes in the productive forces and in the relations of production, he also recognised that the *ideological superstructure* changed with them. Thus Jones already enunciated the fundamental ideas of the materialist conception of history.

The Method of Political Economy

The next essay in our collection, Document 9, was written by Heinrich Cunow in 1905 and returns to fundamental questions of methodology. Whereas revisionists were rejecting Marx's conclusions because capitalism appeared not to conform to the predictions in *Capital*, Cunow responded that they were simply imitating empirical political economy, which 'seeks to provide explanations for the economic processes taking place before our eyes, and often only for the outward form of those processes', paying no regard to implicit logical patterns. Cunow pointed out that Marx's understanding of economic laws involved the same approach as in any of the physical sciences. The law of gravity is not an illusion because it is contradicted by centrifugal forces. Similarly, the law of the falling rate of profit is not an illusion because profits temporarily rise during the expanding phase of a business cycle. The laws of capitalist development, rather than being contradicted by passing phenomena, are the real explanation of such contradictions. And to account for contradictions was the purpose of all science, which would *'be superfluous if the form of appearance of things directly coincided with their essence'.*[50]

Following Cunow's essay on the essential principles of Marx's research method, we turn to Rudolf Hilferding's review of Wilhelm Liebknecht's *The History of the Theory of Value in England*.[51] The issue that Hilferding addresses involved the social determination of forms of human labour. On the one hand, labour is a physiological fact (the expenditure of human energy in production), but value-creating labour is simultaneously a specific economic category of capitalist society. Liebknecht understood 'the concept of labour, as the value-principle, in physiological terms', to which Hilferding replied that capitalist production and the labour spent upon it must be regarded 'not as a natural but as a social fact':

> Labour is a social and especially an economic category only when individual labour is regarded in its specific social *form*, in its social function. This happens when the total labour of society is regarded as a unit, of which each individual labour represents only the aliquot part. Only as part of a unit, of the total labour, are the individual labours mutually comparable; and their common measure is simple average labour – an historically, not a physiologically, determined magnitude, which changes with alterations of the historical circumstances.[52]

The universal abstraction of *labour as value* logically presupposed generalised commodity exchange. The social form of *wage-labour*, in turn, presupposed private ownership of the means of production. The labour that concerned Marx was not a matter of physiology but rather the social category of *wage-labour*, whose value is the objective cost of reproducing labour power (means of subsistence and the educational costs involved in the reproduction of skilled labour, according to prevailing social standards), which in turn determines the value of commodities, the rate of surplus value, the tendency towards the social average rate of profit, and thus ultimately the distribution of all the productive

---

50   Marx 1992, p. 956.
51   [Liebknecht, Wilhelm 1902, *Zur Geschichte der Werttheorie in England*, Jena: Fischer].
52   Document 10.

forces of capitalist society. Wage-labour, Hilferding wrote, is 'an *historical form*, through which the proportional distribution of the total labour of society, required for production [*Herstellung*] of the social product, asserts itself in a society characterised by the fact that the connection of social labour takes place through the private exchange of individual labour products'.

Document 11, also written by Hilferding, is a review of Isaiah Rosenberg's *Ricardo and Marx as Value Theorists*.[53] Its theme is 'Marx's formulation of the problem of theoretical economics', and Hilferding's argument again turns on the distinction between what is natural and what is social. Classical political economy had taken the social form of wealth in capitalist society to be a natural and pre-given fact, whereas Marx focused on the historically changing circumstances in which production occurs. The problem for theoretical economics, therefore, was not to explain wealth but rather the particular form of commodity production.

Marx wrote that 'The wealth of societies, in which the capitalist mode of production prevails, appears as an "immense collection of commodities"; the individual commodity appears as its elementary form. Our investigation therefore begins with the analysis of the commodity'.[54] As an object that has no use-value for its owner but only for someone who purchases it, the commodity becomes the mediator of production relations between people. Analysis of the commodity revealed how use-values take on the form of exchange-values, which in turn regulate the distribution of labour between the different branches of production. The task of political economy was to discover in the exchange act, as the basic process in which social relations manifest themselves, the law that makes commodity production possible. As Hilferding commented, 'The law that shows how the exchange is regulated is therefore, at the same time, the law of motion of society. Finding that law of motion was the task that Marx posited as the problem of theoretical economics'. Only then, Hilferding wrote, 'could Marx arrive at the basic distinction between concrete labour, creating use-value, and abstract, social, value-creating labour, and thus show the starting-point of political economy'.

> By identifying the 'social substance' of the commodity, by demonstrating that the question under consideration, behind the seemingly material relations of the commodities, is actually human relationships, moreover,

---

53   [Rosenberg, Isaiah 1904, *Ricardo und Marx als Werttheoretiker: Eine Kritische Studie*, Wien: Ignaz Brand].
54   Marx 1976, p. 125.

human relationships within very specific relations of production in commodity-producing society – i.e. through the discovery of the fetish character of the commodity – the 'mystery' of society was then resolved.[55]

Marxism and the German Historical School

In Documents 12 and 13, written by Rosa Luxemburg and Rudolf Hilferding, we turn to another aspect of methodological debate, this time involving the historical school of political economy, which developed chiefly in Germany in the last half of the nineteenth century. The writers of this school had no quarrel with Marx's emphasis upon the historical context of economic theory. But while they embraced the historical method, they just as enthusiastically disputed any claim that history is governed by discernible economic laws. Instead, they emphasised the significance of specific institutions and 'ethical values' that prevail at particular times and in particular places, thereby effectively denying that political economy could ever become a science with general validity. The founding generation of the school, including Wilhelm Roscher, Bruno Hildebrand and Karl Knies, was followed by a younger one, which included Gustav von Schmoller, Karl Bücher, Adolph Wagner, Georg Friedrich Knapp and Lujo Brentano, and then by a third generation that counted among its most famous members Werner Sombart and Max Weber.[56]

The so-called *Methodenstreit*, or 'dispute over method', between the historical school and marginalism, which broke out when Carl Menger attacked Schmoller and the German historical school in his *Investigations into the Method of the Social Sciences with Special Reference to Economics* (1883), was actually a tempest in an academic teapot compared to the common hostility of both groups to Marxism. In 1886 Eugen von Böhm-Bawerk, a leading promoter of marginalist theory, wrote a book-length criticism of Marxist economics shortly after the appearance of the third volume of *Capital*;[57] and Lujo Brentano, associated with the historical school, made the struggle against Marxism a leitmotif of his entire academic career.[58]

The ambition of members of the historical school to appear as *Sozialpolitiker*, or progressive advocates of reform, was commonly dismissed by Marxists and economic liberals alike as *Kathedersozialismus*. Rosa Luxemburg, in the

---

55 Document 11.
56 Shionoya 2005.
57 Böhm-Bawerk 1896, refuted by Hilferding 1904.
58 Engels 1891, Kautsky 1891, Marx-Aveling 1895, Kautsky 1900.

second edition to her brochure *Social Reform or Revolution* (1908), added this footnote:

> In 1872, Professors Wagner, Schmoller, Brentano, and others held a Congress at Eisenach at which they proclaimed noisily and with much publicity that their goal was the introduction of social reforms for the protection of the working class. These gentlemen, whom the liberal, Oppenheimer, calls *Kathedersozialisten* ['Socialists of the Chair' or 'Academic Socialists'] formed a *Verein für Sozialreform* [Association for Social Reform]. Only a few years later, when the fight against Social Democracy grew sharper, as representatives in the Reichstag these pygmies of '*Kathedersozialismus*' voted for the extension of the Antisocialist Law. Beyond this, all of the activity of the Association consists in its yearly general assemblies, at which a few professorial reports on different themes are read. Further, the Association has published over one hundred thick volumes on economic questions. Not a thing has been done for social reform by the professors – who, in addition, support protective tariffs, militarism, etc. Finally, the Association has given up social reforms and occupies itself with the problem of crises, cartels, and the like.[59]

In 1888 Karl Kautsky wrote a review of Lujo Brentano's brochure *Classical Political Economy*, pointing out that the historical school had no alternative to offer in lieu of the classical economic theory it rejected. Brentano claimed that 'economists no longer had to be thinkers, but photographers'. Kautsky replied that science does not consist of 'a mere description of *facts* and *processes*. These provide only the foundations from which *laws* can be inferred. And it is not just a question of a mere description, but of a methodical *investigation*, which again is only possible on the basis of an adequate and thoroughly thought-out *theory*'. The historical school's rejection of coherent theory actually threw its members back to the theories they rejected, because, Kautsky said, 'as long as they are unable to replace classical theory ... they continue to suffer its influence. Modern eclecticism does not kill classical political economy, but only theoretical sense, and in doing so it hinders the development of theory'.[60]

In 1900 Rosa Luxemburg reviewed Richard Schüler's book *The Economic Policy of the Historical School*, which called for repudiation of the historical-inductive approach of the historical school and a return to the deductive meth-

---

59   Luxemburg 1971, p. 88.
60   Kautsky 1888.

odology of the classics. She argued that the issue was not one of inductive versus deductive method, but rather of the state of capitalist development and of the class antagonisms to which it gave rise. The historical school was 'the only real national product of the German bourgeoisie in the field of economic theory', and it was therefore a true reflection of that class's own history. It had arisen as a reaction against the socialist doctrine of political economy. 'Classical political economy had everywhere, with invincible logic, turned into self-criticism, into criticism of the bourgeois order'; and in Marx the transformation of classical economics into its opposite, into the socialist analysis of capitalism, had been completed. It followed that

> The socialist critique, i.e. the consequence, could only be denied if the starting point, classical economics, was overcome. The results of the investigation of bourgeois commodity economy, as offered by classical economics in a coherent system, could not simply be negated or corrected. There was no other way but to fight the investigation itself, the method [of classical political economy]. If the purpose of classical economics was to understand the principles and basic laws of bourgeois economy, the historical school, by contrast, set itself the task of mystifying the inner workings of this economy.[61]

Just three years after Richard Schüler challenged the historical school to return to the deductive method of classical political economy – or, as Rosa Luxemburg put it, issued the call 'Back to Adam Smith' – Werner Sombart turned the debate in a novel direction with his monumental two-volume study of the origins and development of *Modern Capitalism* (1902). Drawing upon economic history and his own sociological insight, Sombart reformulated one of the enduring questions of historiography: Where is causality to be found, in the consciousness or 'spirit' of an era or in changing objective circumstances? For Sombart, the transition to modern capitalism came when the spirit of economic activity changed and 'the pursuit of profit, the prevalent motive of capitalist economic subjects, replaced the motive of the craftsman, his striving to gain a livelihood befitting his social status'.

Sombart effectively skirted the debate over induction or deduction, but his attempt to create a unifying theory of social causality foundered, according to Hilferding, at the point where it began. Sombart convincingly documented the relation between economic motives and economic history, but he failed to

---

61   Document 12.

explain how or why one motive gave way to another. The result was that he provided *theories*, not 'a general social theory'. The emergence of motivation, which should have been historically determined, remained unexplained.

> Sombart claims that the motivations of living people are the ultimate, primary active causes we can go back to. In order not to fall into an extremely idealistic conception that does violence to the facts, Sombart tries to understand those motives historically. But since he sees them as the primary factors, he is forced to leave them just to follow one another, while the task of a theory of development should be to derive them from one another.[62]

The Marxist Encounter with the Subjective Theory of Value

Hilferding's complaint against Werner Sombart was certainly one that could not be levelled against the Austrian School of economic theory, to which we turn in Documents 14 and 15. Marxists met no serious challenge from the historical school in Germany, but the Austrian economists were another matter. The theory of marginal utility presented itself as the final word in economic science – a universal principle of choice, rooted in human psychology, that based itself upon a single foundational premise: the 'value' of any good derives exclusively from its ability to satisfy a human need. A good that is abundant will be used in less important ways and will therefore have a lower price; conversely, a scarce good will fetch a higher price because it will satisfy needs of higher priority. The more of any good an individual possesses, the less will he value the next, or marginal, unit. Value, in this case, becomes nothing but price, and price has no objective anchor in a single determinant of cost – the expenditure of living labour and embodied labour in the forms of fixed and circulating capital.

In an article that Isaak Rubin wrote for the *Great Soviet Encyclopaedia* in 1926, he recounted that the rudiments of marginal utility theory had already been developed in the eighteenth century, but

> It was in the 1870s that works appeared almost simultaneously by Carl Menger, [William Stanley] Jevons and Léon Walras, the founders of the new school, among whom Menger developed most thoroughly the psy-

---

62   Document 13.

chological foundation of the theory and Walras the mathematical. During the 1880s [Friedrich von] Wieser and [Eugen von] Böhm-Bawerk, students of Menger (all three of them lived in Austria), worked out in detail the psychological theory that is also frequently called the Austrian theory. By the end of the nineteenth century it became widespread in bourgeois university science in almost all countries of the world.[63]

The new economics that grew out of early marginalism, and that generally prevails to this day, ignores the structurally specific features of capitalism as a whole and aims instead to predict particular prices, interest rates, GNP or other such data in order to formulate practical business decisions and social policy. The purpose of theory, in this context, is strictly instrumental, whereas Marxist political economy, as Rubin notes, is a study of history, social relations, and even philosophy all coherently integrated. Marxism regards 'value' and all its ramifications as determinate categories of a passing historical phase of commodity production, whereas 'economics', in its current bourgeois-academic meaning, treats commodity production as a natural order that is beyond the scope of inquiry. Capitalist commodity production simply 'is', and there is nothing more to be said.

With such fundamental issues in contention, it was to be expected that Marxists would mount a vigorous response. One of the earliest to do so was Conrad Schmidt in 1892, with his essay in *Die Neue Zeit* on 'The Psychological Tendency in Recent Political Economy'.[64] Hypothetically adopting the perspective of a consumer, Schmidt agreed that if a single individual *already has* determinate quantities of two goods at his disposal, he will surely judge the utility of an additional unit of one good or the other on the basis of his subjective expectation of relative satisfaction. But if the same individual must also *produce* the goods in question, then 'the greater or lesser difficulty in replacing the goods would manifest itself in the larger or smaller quantity of labour which the individual would have to expend in reproducing those goods'. The isolated *individual* then gives way to individual *commodity producers*, whose own self-interest leads them to produce and exchange according to the labour expended in production.

In 1892, the same year when Schmidt's article appeared, Parvus (under the pseudonym J.H.) also published a review of Böhm-Bawerk's book *Kapital und*

---

63   Document 15.
64   Document 14.

Kapitalzins.⁶⁵ Parvus called marginalism 'the "new" tendency in vulgar political economy' because, instead of explaining the actions of the individual from his social conditions, it explained social conditions from the conduct of the individual. In reality, Parvus commented, 'the laws of economic phenomena are neither in the individual things, nor in the individuals, but in the *relations* into which people enter with regard to each other and to things – in the economic structure of society'.⁶⁶

In 1902, the Austro-Marxist Gustav Eckstein also published a satirical review of the main works of Böhm-Bawerk and Carl Menger under the rather extravagant title of 'The Fourfold Root of the Principle of Insufficient Reason of Marginal Utility Theory: A Robinsonade' – a reference to Arthur Schopenhauer's doctoral dissertation *On the Fourfold Root of the Principle of Sufficient Reason*. Schmidt showed that marginalist theory suffered from a number of limitations, particularly its inability to account for the dynamics of the capitalist economy as a whole. But his main purpose was to demonstrate, through a series of humorous examples – Robinson starves in his attempt to sell his goods by persuading potential buyers with the help of quotations from Böhm-Bawerk's *Capital and Interest* – the impossibility of exchanging goods under the 'law' of subjective value, because it offered no objective measure of needs.

The better-known early Marxist critiques of marginalism are, of course, Hilferding's essay on *Böhm-Bawerk's Criticism of Marx*⁶⁷ and Nikolai Bukharin's *The Economic Theory of the Leisure Class*, written in 1914,⁶⁸ both of which are readily available online and in print. To summarise these works would be beyond the scope of this introductory essay, just as a serious examination of Austrian theory would require another book. Since our concern in this anthology is the historical development of Marxist political economy, we will limit ourselves to referring readers to our Document 15 by Isaak Rubin, which discusses the key issues of concern to Marxists, and to which we have added an appendix drawn from Rubin's *Essays on Marx's Theory of Value*.

The significance of Rubin's appendix is twofold. First, he demonstrates that Marx himself, not to mention Adam Smith, was perfectly familiar with the fact that total demand falls with a rise in price and that supply increases, the consequence being a diagrammatic representation of what are commonly known as the 'curves' of supply and demand. None of this, Rubin points out, would have been the least bit unfamiliar to Marx. The second distinction of Rubin's

---

65 Parvus 1892.
66 Parvus 1892, p. 594.
67 Hilferding 1904.
68 Bukharin 1927.

essay, however, is that he explains these phenomena strictly in terms of the Marxist theory of value. Rubin notes that writers in the marginalist school neglect to ask *why* prices change, dealing only with *how*. To ask why is to return to the categories of Marx's labour theory of value. Since marginalist subjectivism adds nothing to our understanding of 'why-questions', Rubin concluded that its real significance must be explained in class-political terms. The Austrian school of economics, he concluded, is

> a theoretical tendency that corresponds with the ideology of the bourgeoisie in the epoch of capitalism's decline, a time when any objective study of the tendencies of social development leads to the conclusion of capitalist economy's inevitable destruction. In this epoch the objective, social and historical method (the nucleus of which was established by the classics, as the leading ideologists of a young and progressive bourgeoisie) becomes the exclusive property of Marxist economic theory, while bourgeois science appeals to the subjective, psychological and anti-historical method. The allegedly unchanging psychological 'nature' of man comes to serve as the starting point for theoretical research and as an argument for the impossibility of a socialist economy. It is not surprising that the Austrian school has come out with a zealous polemic against Marxism and has enjoyed rapid and clamorous success amongst bourgeois scholars, who have seen in it ... an acute theoretical weapon for the struggle against Marxism and socialism.[69]

Isaak Illich Rubin's Dialectical Reading of Marx's Economic Works

Readers will recall that in the first document translated for this book, Illarion Kaufman had difficulty understanding how Marx could be 'more realistic than all of his predecessors', despite the fact that the 'external form of his presentation' was so suggestive of German idealist philosophy. In his dialectical reading of Marx's economic works, Isaak Illich Rubin shows that Marx was able to achieve that realism precisely because of his ability to draw upon Hegel in a *philosophically* inspired *science* of political economy.

Rubin is known among readers of Western European languages for his extraordinary exposition of Marx's theory of value,[70] to which should be added

---

69   Document 15.
70   Rubin 1990.

his masterful overview of the history of political economy from the mercantilists to John Stuart Mill.[71] In this volume we have included six previously untranslated essays by Rubin, including his account of Marx's theory of money, which survived in manuscript form following his assassination by Stalin's regime and has only recently been published in the original Russian. To take into account the tragic fate of this remarkable Marxist scholar, our collection closes with an essay on Rubin's life and work by Lyudmila L. Vasina and Yakov G. Rokityansky.[72]

In his essay on 'Marx's Teaching on Production and Consumption',[73] Rubin pointed out Marx had often been accused of ignoring the process of consuming products and forgetting the existence of use-value. Rubin dismissed this argument and attributed it to the critics' preoccupation with individual judgements of utility, which, according to marginalism, determine a commodity's value. Marx, in contrast, always regarded exchange-value in objective terms and treated consumption as one moment in the reproduction process as a whole. Basing himself on Marx's *1844 Manuscripts* and on the first chapter of *The German Ideology*, both recently published by his friend and colleague David Ryazanov, Rubin emphasised that human 'needs' cannot be understood merely as the subjective whims of consumers. Marx saw needs developing with the social division of labour, which, in commodity-producing society, entails satisfaction of needs through exchange. In other words, as with the developing means of production and the changing forms of production relations, 'needs' are always a product of history. Rubin regarded the instrument of labour as 'the mediating link between man and nature': 'the enormous importance of the instrument of labour is emphasised both in the process of development of man's productive activity and in the process of development of human needs'.[74]

In a commodity-producing society, the immediate purpose of production becomes exchange-value rather than use-value. Production and consumption begin to separate at the same time as they remain connected. The primacy of exchange-value over use-value becomes all the more evident in capitalist

---

71 Rubin 1979.
72 We would like to thank Professor Vasina for kindly supplying us with a bibliography of Rubin's writings, as well as Professor Rolf Hecker for generously sending us a copy of the special issue of *Beiträge zur Marx-Engels-Forschung* dealing with Rubin, which includes a German version of Rubin's 'Essays on Marx's Theory of Money': *Isaak Il'jič Rubin. Marxforscher – Ökonom – Verbannter (1886–1937)*, Hamburg: Argument Verlag, 2012 (*MEF Neue Folge, Sonderband 4*).
73 Document 16.
74 Document 16.

society. At this point, the two moments of the reproduction process are further separated at the same time as they remain necessarily connected through market demand. Demand, in turn, assumes a determinate character depending upon the class distribution of incomes. The development of production creates growing needs for both items of consumption and means of production, yet there is a 'law inherent in capitalist economy that keeps the workers' consumption at a low level despite the gigantic growth of labour productivity'. Consumption remains determined by production and the social forms within which it occurs, not 'by the needs and arbitrary will of separate individuals'.

Rubin then recounts the various ways in which use-value figures in the 'determinations of economic form', such as the constant and variable forms of capital, or the natural form of products that had to be considered in the reproduction schemes of Volume II of *Capital*. But again Rubin emphasises that Marx was concerned principally with the *social structure* of the reproduction process, not with concrete use-values. Rubin's theme throughout this essay is that use-value, while never absent from Marx's work, must always be considered in historical context and cannot be regarded as 'an independent object for research in theoretical economics':

> The capitalist production process is a unity of the labour process (i.e. the process of producing use-values) and the process of the production and expansion of value. Political economy takes the latter aspect of the production process, i.e. the process of the production and expansion of value, to be the special subject matter of its investigation. But the process of the expansion of value represents the form in which the process of the production of products, or of use-values, occurs. Thus, the latter process is always a part of our investigation, although not as an independent object for analysis by this science but rather as another side of the single process of reproduction, which we study as the 'social structure of production' (Lenin). It follows that use-value is included within the ambit of our investigation only insofar as this is necessary in order to understand the process of the production and expansion of value.[75]

In his essay 'Fundamental Features of Marx's Theory of Value and How it Differs from Ricardo's Theory',[76] Rubin argues that Ricardo studied the material-technical process of production, and particularly the result of changes in labour

---

75   Document 16.
76   Document 17.

productivity, without reference to the particular 'social form' of capitalist production relations, because he took capitalist relations to be fixed and beyond the scope of inquiry. Marx, on the contrary, emphasised that political economy presupposes capitalist society as its subject matter, and that the resulting economic categories are exclusively those of the capitalist social formation.

Thus, while Marx was Ricardo's successor in terms of seeing labour as the *content* of value, he also advanced far beyond Ricardo in his differentiation between *concrete* and *abstract* labour, and in the resulting treatment of value as a specific historical *form*. As Rubin writes, 'the dual character of labour reflects the difference between the *material-technical* process of production and its *social form*. This difference ... is the basis of the whole of Marxist economic theory, including the theory of value'.[77]

Marx showed that all the contradictions of capitalism are implicit in the fundamental contradiction of the commodity. 'Value' is a social form, whose content is concrete labour that has been abstracted.

> The equalisation of all types of labour through market equalisation of all the products of labour as values – this is what Marx means by the concept of abstract labour. And since the equalisation of labour through the equalisation of things results from the social form of commodity economy, in which there is no direct social organisation and equalisation of labour, it follows that abstract labour is a social and historical concept. *Abstract labour does not express a physiological equality of the various types of labour, but rather the social equalisation of various types of labour that occurs in the specific form of market equalisation of the products of labour as values*.[78]

Value, money, capital, and the various other categories of political economy are, on the one hand, relations between people; but they are simultaneously 'things' that have acquired a social-functional existence. Exchange-value is not the inherent property of a useful product of human labour, nor is wage-labour the natural form of human productive activity. Nevertheless, the requirement that labour become abstract in order to appear as social labour also entails the consequence that the resulting social forms appear to be real and concrete. 'This "reification" consists of the fact that the thing, with respect to which people enter into a certain relation between themselves, fulfils a special *social*

---

77 Document 17.
78 Document 17.

function of linking people together, the function of mediator or "bearer" of the particular production relation between people'. Marx believed that reification would only end when the associated producers socialise the means of production and consciously plan their own labour activities. Thus, with his elaboration of the 'dual character' of both labour and value, Marx, rather than completing the theory of the classics, became the originator of an entirely new economic theory.

Rubin's next essay, 'Towards a History of the Text of the First Chapter of Marx's *Capital*',[79] provides a detailed analysis of the development of Marx's theory of value from his *Contribution to the Critique of Political Economy* to *Capital*. The problem that Rubin poses is why the two works *differ* so substantially in terms of Marx's exposition of his theory of value. The reason, explains Rubin, is that 'in the *Critique* Marx did not yet draw a sharp distinction between value and exchange-value ... The *Critique* still lacks any teaching on the development of the poles of value (i.e. the relative and equivalent forms of value) and on development of the forms of value (i.e. the simple, expanded, general and monetary forms of value)'.

In the *Critique*, Marx did not yet strictly distinguish the *content* of value from the *form*; he treated value *quantitatively*, whereas in *Capital* he added a *qualitative* dimension. Rubin demonstrates this point by reference to the distinction between the 'value relation' (*Wertverhältnis*) – relating the quantity of materialised labour in one commodity to that in another, or their identity *as values* – and the 'value expression' (*Wertausdruck*), in which the value of one commodity is expressed in terms of the use-value of another commodity. In the latter case, the first commodity takes the 'relative form' and the second the 'equivalent form', a qualitative difference that points to exchange-value itself as a distinct value 'form'. Both sides of the equation still contain the same quantity of materialised labour, their 'common denominator', but Rubin emphasises that the change of form in the 'value expression' sets in motion 'the dialectical (logical and historical) transformation of one form of value into the other'. It is the 'polar' distinction in *Capital* between the 'relative' and 'equivalent' forms of value that points to the emergence of money, as the universal equivalent, and to Marx's distinction between concrete and abstract labour.

The need for such distinction arose from the fact that Ricardo did not differentiate between value and exchange-value. As Rubin comments, 'the conversion of commodities into money seemed to him to be a purely formal and external act'. The result, however, was to create an 'impassable abyss'

---

79   Document 18.

between value and exchange-value, leading Samuel Bailey, a critic of Ricardo, to argue that the labour theory of value makes no sense. Rubin explained that the structure of Marx's argument in *Capital*, as distinct from the *Critique*, resulted from the need to address two challenges simultaneously. First, Marx had to respond to Bailey's criticism of Ricardo; second, he had to clear up the confusion left by Ricardo in the first place. The difference between Ricardo and Bailey was that 'the former ignored the form of value, while the latter thought it possible to manage without the concept of value'.

In his concluding paragraph, Rubin provides a concise summary of his argument:

> While the classics concentrated their attention on value and regarded the form of value as something external and inconsequential, Bailey fell into the opposite error. He turned his attention mainly to the *multiplicity* of value expressions and imagined that 'by pointing to the multiplicity of the relative expressions of the same commodity-value he had obliterated any possibility of a conceptual determination of value'. In order to deflect Bailey's attacks, which threatened the entire theory of labour value, Marx had to draw a sharp distinction between 'value' and 'value expressions', from which logically followed the need to provide separate analyses of value and exchange-value. But it was only possible finally to overcome Bailey's criticism by filling the gap left by Ricardo ... As distinct from the classics, [Marx] supplements the doctrine of value with the [separate] doctrine of 'the form of value, or exchange-value' ... The need to arrange the investigation in these two opposing directions is what explains the unique structure of the first chapter of *Capital*.[80]

Rubin's 'Essays on Marx's Theory of Money'[81] emphasises that Marx begins by setting aside the subjective intentions of exchange participants. Although the theory of money results from the theory of value, the theory of value in turn cannot be constructed without the theory of money. If Marx had not presupposed money as the medium of developed commodity circulation, he would have had to begin with the exchange of two items *in natura* – that is, with two *non-commodities* – in which case it would have made sense to say, together with the marginal utility school, that 'such exchange may be regulated by the individual requirements of the participants and by their subjective

80 Document 18.
81 Document 19.

appraisal of the relative usefulness of products'. Only by explicitly beginning with commodity production – the production of *useful* things *for sale* – was it possible for Marx 'to eliminate in advance the individual-psychological way of posing the question (i.e. use-value) and *from the very beginning to define the subject matter of his investigation, exchange-value, as an object belonging to the social world*, as a social function or form of the product of labour'. The commodity, being an attribute of a particular 'social world', is also necessarily one of the latter's forms: it is a 'social form' of production relations between people, the theme that runs through all of Rubin's work.

All commodities are qualitatively equal in terms of the unity of their social function as products of labour, but for exchange to occur they must overcome their quantitative inequality as use-values: they must be equalised in terms of the abstract, socially necessary labour that they represent, or their common property as exchange-value. Thus 'the investigation leads from social labour (or the content of value) to the form of value; ... from the form of value to money; and ... [to] money as the finished result'.[82]

Rubin describes the link between the theories of value and money as follows:

> Examination of *the mechanism of social dependence between the equation of labour and the equation of commodities ... constitutes the theme of the Marxist theory of value*, or the first stage of our investigation. After showing how the equation of labour takes the form of the generalised equation of commodities, Marx turns to analysis of the latter process, showing that the *generalised equation of commodities is only possible in the form of them all being equated with one and the same designated commodity*, which acquires the character of money. This is the theory of *the origin and social function of money*, or the second stage of the study. Only after that is it possible to turn to consideration of the *individual properties of money as finished results of the process of circulation*, which at first appear to be independent of the latter and to inhere in money itself. This is the theory of the *separate functions of money*, or the third stage of the investigation. In other words, these three stages of the investigation can be characterised as the doctrine 1) of value, or of the commodity; 2) of the transformation of the commodity into money; and 3) of money itself.[83]

---

82 Document 19.
83 Document 19.

Rubin explains that the allegedly 'metaphysical' doctrine concerning the dual nature of the commodity contains 'a sociological analysis of the production relations between commodity producers'. The general form of exchangeability entails money, as the universal measure of abstract labour and exchange-value. And money, in turn, now appears as the true *reified* 'carrier' of the economic relation: 'The commodity that *fulfils the function of active initiator of the production relations of exchange between commodity producers, i.e. that possesses the capacity for direct universal exchangeability for any other commodity, is money*'.[84]

With a comprehensive analysis of the history and categories of money and exchange, Rubin guides his reader through the first three chapters of *Capital*, ending at the point where Marx turns from the accumulation of money – as a hoard – to the transition to the next higher category, *capital*. It is only to be regretted that the manuscript, after analysing the functions of money as measure of values, means of circulation, hoarding and means of payment, breaks off when it was about to describe its function as world money – an omission which should be added to Stalin's long list of crimes.

We close our selection of primary documents with the crowning glory of the collection: Rubin's essay 'The Dialectical Development of Categories in Marx's Economic System'.[85] The issue of methodology has reappeared throughout the documents that we have translated, but nowhere is it more central than in this essay by Rubin. There is no question that this essay represents a theoretical triumph on Rubin's part that far surpassed the insight of almost all of his predecessors and contemporaries.

Lenin noted in his *Philosophical Notebooks* that

> In his *Capital*, Marx first analyses the simplest, most ordinary and fundamental, most common and everyday *relation* of bourgeois (commodity) society, a relation encountered billions of times, viz., the exchange of commodities. In this very simple phenomenon (in this 'cell' of bourgeois society) analysis reveals *all* the contradictions (or the germs of *all* contradictions) of modern society. The subsequent exposition shows us the development (*both* growth *and* movement) of these contradictions and of this society in the Σ [the sum] of its individual parts. From its beginning to its end.[86]

---

84 Document 19.
85 Document 20.
86 Lenin 1915b, pp. 360–1.

In his essay on Marx's dialectical method, Rubin completed the undertaking that Lenin projected: he began with the initial 'cell' of bourgeois society and then followed Marx in dialectically (that is, logically and historically) revealing all the fundamental contradictions of capitalist society, culminating in the category of crisis.

Rubin stresses the 'dual character of the law of the unity of opposites', showing how, through a process of gradual development, different social forms arise from unity, gradually separating and becoming externally independent of one another. As in Hegel's *Logic*, Rubin's analysis moves within a dialectical circle of necessity – from the immediacy of a simple category (the commodity, for example) through its internal differentiation (the poles of value) to a new self-identity in a higher category (in this case money serving as universal equivalent for the circulation of commodities) – which again proves contradictory (money as a private hoard or means of settling private credit obligations, each with the capacity to disrupt circulation) and thereby necessitates further movement. Rubin shows that in the entire dialectical movement of the three volumes of *Capital*, there is a sequential process of immediacy dissolving into contradiction and then returning in the immediacy of a more complex, but also transitory, self-identity – all of which expresses continuously changing production relations between people. Each group of phenomena, which constitutes a unity, gives way to polarisation and difference; and each group, which appears to be contradictory, constitutes a unity within whose limits the phenomena are antitheses.

In Marx's analysis, phenomena that have 'become detached' are revealed as 'alienated' production relations between people, or social forms of human relations that have, as Rubin says, 'coalesced' with things. The reified 'determinations of form', at each level of analysis, are shown confronting one another in a condition of contradiction and struggle, yet ultimately the entire system points beyond itself to the restoration of human community. Marx's understanding of history begins with the patriarchal family and primitive community; it ends with the projection of a restored community that transcends class divisions but also retains the wealth of history. As Rubin writes, a history of class struggle, culminating in the conflict between those who own and those who create the means of production, prepares the ground

> for a real 'removal' of the alienated and detached forms of social life and for a genuine revelation of the unity that lies at their basis. The more the power of 'alienated' labour (capital) grows over living labour, the more the conditions are created for the elimination of this alienation. It is precisely because capital develops the powerful productive forces of labour, which

can no longer operate within the limits of capitalist production relations, that it also prepares its own end.[87]

The Critique of Political Economy as the Scientific Foundation of Communism

The last part of the third volume of *Capital*, entitled 'The Revenues and Their Sources', closes with an unfinished last chapter called 'Classes', in which Marx shows the economic roots of the antagonism between wage-workers, capitalists and landowners. Thus, at the very pinnacle of this imposing intellectual construction 'we have the *class struggle*, as the conclusion in which the movement and disintegration' of capitalist society 'resolves itself'.[88] The repeated attempts to replace Marx's policy of class struggle by different forms of class collaboration, ranging from Millerand's 'government of republican defence' to Stalin's 'anti-fascist popular front' to Enrico Berlinguer's 'historic compromise', show that Marx's leading ideas have to be stressed again and again, not only against obfuscations by bourgeois ideologists, but also against the policies of the putative political representatives of the working class.

But laying bare the economic foundations of the class antagonisms of present-day society was only part of Marx's research project. Another and even more important aim was to show how the developmental tendencies of capitalism revealed it to be a transitory stage in the history of humankind, pointing beyond itself to a higher stage in which class antagonisms would be transcended. The whole of history has been one of the gradual appropriation of nature by human labour and of the progressive enslavement of the majority of humanity by an ever smaller minority of exploiters. The concentration and centralisation of the means of production, as well as the international division of labour brought forth by capitalism, have created the foundations for a new social formation, an association of free and equal producers who will exert conscious control over their production and reproduction processes and thus regulate the course of social development in order to secure the widest possible scope for the development of human personality. Only then, under genuine communism, will humanity finally be able to pass to the kingdom of freedom. Concrete labour, with which Marx began the first

---

87   Document 20.
88   Letter from Marx to Engels, 30 April 1868, in *MECW*, Vol. 43, p. 25.

volume of *Capital*, will return from abstraction to the concrete universal of self-determined labour in the form of a social plan determined by the associated producers.

Why Does Marx Matter?

Richard B. Day

The common theme of the documents in this volume is the methodological uniqueness of Karl Marx's writings in political economy. Marx set out to transform political economy from a rationalisation of existing capitalist society into a scientific criticism of that same society and its dehumanising effects in terms of exploitation and commodity fetishism. It is a fact, however, that Marx's major economic works – *A Contribution to the Critique of Political Economy*, the three volumes of *Capital*, the *Grundrisse* (notebooks for *Capital*) and the three parts of *Theories of Surplus-Value* – also have much in common with philosophy, particularly with questions of how we know, and what we can hope to know, of the prospects for a civilised life in human community.

Karl Marx's debt to Hegel is generally acknowledged. Marx himself spoke of being a pupil of that 'mighty thinker'.[1] Marx's analysis of political economy originated in his critique of Hegelian philosophy, just as Hegel's system was a critical response to the epistemology and moral philosophy of Immanuel Kant. This means that to appreciate Marx's work, as a totality, presupposes some familiarity with both Hegel and Kant. Hegel spoke of his dialectical method as a 'circle of necessity'.[2] Marx replied that the 'rational kernel' of Hegel's method must be separated from its 'mystical shell'. In the theory of historical materialism, Marx severed Hegelian dialectics from ethical idealism. He began with Feuerbach's humanism in the *1844 Manuscripts*; he ended, particularly in the *Grundrisse*, with the practical prospect of human community through the rational self-determination of an agreed economic plan.

For Marx, the critique of philosophy involved transcendence, not mere repudiation. To transcend philosophical ideals required that the ideals be made real: 'The philosophers have only *interpreted* the world, in various ways; the point is to *change* it'.[3] In that sense, Marx's work moved in its own 'circle of necessity' – from the critical evaluation of Hegelian philosophy, through the economic analysis of capitalist contradictions, to the prospect of fulfilling the human potential in communism. To outline that movement, and thus to provide a larger context for Marx's specific contributions to political economy, will be the pur-

---

1   Marx 1976, p. 103.
2   Hegel 1967, p. 105.
3   Marx, 'Theses on Feuerbach', in Tucker (ed.) 1978, p. 145.

pose of this essay, beginning with the pre-history of market philosophy and then proceeding to Smith, Kant, Hegel and Marx.

The 'Spiritual' Pre-History of Adam Smith's Market Philosophy

In the hierarchical order of medieval Europe, everyone and everything had an appointed place. Economic life, apart from famine, plague or plunder, was essentially static; the seasons governed agriculture, and the notion of unlimited economic growth would have been regarded as madness. The economic problem was conceived not in terms of expanding production but rather in terms of safeguarding the right to life in tenuous circumstances. This meant that distribution of the social product was a central issue. In the thirteenth century, St. Thomas Aquinas reconciled Christian theology with the teachings of Aristotle, writing that 'man is naturally a social animal',[4] with the consequence that 'the good of one man is not a final end but is directed toward the common good, and the good of a single household is ordered to the good of the state that is a perfect community'.[5] Aristotle had said that 'Friends' goods are goods in common',[6] to which Aquinas added that 'a man should not possess external things as his alone but for the community, so that he is ready to share them with others in case of necessity. Thus the Apostle Paul says in I Timothy, "Command the rich of the world to be ready to share and to give"'.[7]

Aquinas taught that the good of the community circumscribed the individual right of property. Since each had the God-given right to life, it followed that 'when a person is in imminent danger and cannot be helped in any other way – then a person may legitimately supply his need from the property of someone else, whether openly or secretly. Strictly speaking such a case is not theft or robbery'.[8] The rich had a Christian duty of charity to the poor as a condition of their own salvation, and the doctrine of the 'just price' rationalised regulation of local markets in order to stabilise food prices. Church doctrine treated markets as a threat to social order, and Aquinas specifically condemned both usury and money-making trade as morally corrupting, for their sole end was 'greed for money which has no limit'.[9] Describing the practical effect upon

---

4   Lewis 1954, p. 226.
5   Aquinas 1988, p. 45.
6   Aristotle 1952, p. 49.
7   Aquinas 1988, p. 72.
8   Aquinas 1988, p. 73.
9   Ibid.

commerce in the fourteenth century, the economic historian Henri Pirenne wrote that 'The liberty of the individual was ruthlessly curtailed, and the sale of foodstuffs [was] subjected to a regulation almost as despotic and inquisitorial as that which was applied ... to small-scale industry'.[10] While St. Thomas condemned usury, Pirenne also noted that the Church was in fact the indispensable moneylender of the medieval world. Without credit, society could not survive the periodic disaster of famine. The Church

> possessed a liquid capital which made it a financial power of the first order. Chronicles are full of details about the wealth of the monastic shrines, teeming with reliquaries, candlesticks, censers and sacred vessels made of the precious metals, offerings both great and small, which the piety of the faithful lavished on the earthly representatives of those all-powerful saints, whose intervention was most surely to be obtained by generosity to their servants. Every church of any reputation had thus at its disposal treasures, which not only increased the pomp of its services, but were an abundant hoard of capital.[11]

Since the Church claimed to mediate between God and man, there was an obvious temptation for its adherents to attempt to purchase the remission of sin. Thomas Gascoigne (Chancellor of Cambridge University from 1443–5) complained that sinners say: 'I care not how many evils I do in God's sight, for I can easily get plenary remission of all guilt and penalty by an absolution and indulgence granted me by the Pope, whose written grant I can have for four or six pence ...'.[12] The involvement of the Church in financing the growth of mercantile capitalism, which was accelerated in the sixteenth century by Europe's colonial expansion and the influx of gold from the Americas, intensified the contradictions between medieval doctrine and commercial development, provoking Martin Luther's charge in 1517 that the Church itself was guilty of avarice and the sale of salvation.

Luther initiated the Protestant Reformation, but John Calvin provided the new world of commerce with its most coherent rationalisation. While the radical Anabaptists practised communism, in his *Institutes of the Christian Religion* (1536) Calvin reconciled business with theology by articulating what Max Weber called 'the spirit of capitalism'.[13] Aquinas had spoken of the responsib-

---

10   Pirenne 1937, p. 174.
11   Pirenne 1937, pp. 118–19.
12   Durant 1980, p. 23.
13   Weber 1958.

ility of Church and state for the common good, but for Calvin a major purpose of civil authority was to ensure 'that the public tranquillity may not be disturbed; that every person may enjoy his property without molestation; that men may transact their business together without fraud or injustice'.[14] Private property, including inheritance, was a blessing from God: 'Though some seem to enrich themselves by vigilance it is nevertheless God who blesses and cares for them. Though others are rich before they are born and their fathers have acquired great possessions, this is nevertheless not by accident but the providence of God rules over it'.[15] Just as 'gifts of the Spirit' were variously distributed, Calvin believed that civil authorities must secure to every individual 'the exclusive enjoyment of his property, as it is necessary for the preservation of the peace of society that men should have peculiar and distinct possessions'.[16]

If a principal responsibility of civil government was to protect property and commerce, money-making and the pursuit of wealth likewise had to be reinterpreted as part of the Divine plan, which for Calvin included the doctrine of pre-destination. If God was all-knowing, Calvin reasoned that He must have known from the beginning of time who would be saved and who was condemned. God could not be persuaded either by prayer or by gifts to the Church to change His mind. Some had been 'elected' for glory, others for damnation. God said to Moses: 'I will have mercy on whom I have mercy, and I will have compassion on whom I have compassion' (Romans 9:15, 21). The result of the Protestant Reformation, as Hegel later observed in his *Philosophy of History*, was that 'Men became the victims of a tormenting uncertainty as to whether the good Spirit has an abode in them, and it was deemed indispensable that the entire process of spiritual transformation should become perceptible to the individual himself'.[17]

With the separation of personal salvation from institutionalised mediation through the priesthood, Hegel saw in Calvinism the spiritual birthplace of the modern principle of 'subjective freedom'. In the Protestant view, a one-to-one relationship with God meant each was responsible for his own soul, and God speaks directly to each through the voice of conscience. Hegel wrote:

> ... there is no longer a distinction between priests and laymen; we no longer find one class in possession of the substance of the Truth, as of

---

14   Calvin 1844, Vol. II, p. 635.
15   Calvin, 'Sermon on Deuteronomy', cited by Niebuhr 1944, p. 94.
16   Calvin 1844, Vol. II, p. 223.
17   Hegel 1900, p. 425.

all the spiritual and temporal treasures of the Church ... Each has to accomplish the work of reconciliation in his own soul. – Subjective Spirit has to receive the Spirit of Truth into itself, and give it a dwelling place there ... Thus Christian Freedom is actualized.[18]

The problem was: How could one know one's place in the Divine plan? Lack of faith was clear evidence that one was *not* predestined for salvation, but economic success helped to confirm faith and implicitly linked wealth with grace. Max Weber concluded that, by pursuing wealth, the Protestant Christian 'creates his own salvation, or, as would be more correct, the conviction of it'.[19] In Calvinist theology, each was responsible for multiplying God's assets in his particular calling. But God's assets could not be squandered in self-indulgence. The moral opprobrium attached to ostentatious consumption lent spiritual significance to self-denial and the accumulation of capital. In his *Contribution to the Critique of Political Economy*, Marx later wrote that the hoarder of money is 'intrinsically a Protestant by religion and still more a Puritan'.[20] Marx described the hoarder as a 'martyr to exchange-value' and a 'holy ascetic',[21] although he added that the 'monetary soul'[22] of a hoard demanded its reinvestment for continuous accumulation. Max Weber came to the same conclusion:

> ... the religious valuation of restless, continuous, systematic work in a worldly calling, as ... the surest and most evident proof of rebirth and genuine faith, must have been the most powerful conceivable lever for the expansion of that attitude toward life which we have ... called the spirit of capitalism. When the limitation of consumption is combined with this release of acquisitive energy, the inevitable practical result is obvious: accumulation of capital through ascetic compulsion to save.[23]

The Reformation reflected in social consciousness the beginnings of what Marx called the 'primitive' accumulation of capital, which was accompanied from the late fifteenth century onwards by the growing commercialisation

---

18   Hegel 1900, p. 416.
19   Weber 1958, p. 115.
20   Marx 1970, p. 130.
21   Marx 1970, p. 134.
22   Marx 1970, p. 131.
23   Weber 1958, p. 172.

of agriculture and separation of peasants from the soil. In *Capital*, Marx began his chapter on primitive accumulation with this comment:

> The proletariat created by the breaking-up of the bands of feudal retainers and by the forcible expropriation of the people from the soil, this free and rightless proletariat could not possibly be absorbed by the nascent manufactures as fast as it was thrown upon the world. On the other hand, these men, suddenly dragged from their accustomed mode of life, could not immediately adapt themselves to the discipline of their new condition. They were turned ... into beggars, robbers and vagabonds, partly from inclination, in most cases under the force of circumstances. Hence at the end of the fifteenth and during the whole of the sixteenth centuries, a bloody legislation against vagabondage was enforced throughout Western Europe. The fathers of the present working class were chastised for their enforced transformation into vagabonds and paupers. Legislation treated them as 'voluntary' criminals, and assumed that it was entirely within their powers to go on working under the old conditions which in fact no longer existed.[24]

The dissolution of manorial life was reflected in an individualistic view of the world that eventually penetrated every dimension of social consciousness. Just as Calvinism held each accountable for his own soul, the market held each responsible for his own economic fate. Hence the 'victims' of economic transformation were damned both by God's law and by the civil authorities. To provide charity to 'idle' beggars was merely to encourage them in their idle wickedness. The more wealth became associated with godliness, the more poverty became contemptible. For Protestants, as Hegel remarked in *The Philosophy of History*, 'It is more consonant with justice that he who has money should spend it even in luxuries, than that he should give it away to idlers and beggars'.[25] The historian R.H. Tawney made a similar observation in *Religion and the Rise of Capitalism*: 'A society which reverences the attainment of riches as the supreme felicity will naturally be disposed to regard the poor as damned in the next world, if only to justify itself for making their life a hell in this'.[26]

---

24 Marx 1976, p. 896.
25 Hegel 1900, p. 423.
26 Tawney 1961, p. 265.

Adam Smith's Market Philosophy

Writing in Presbyterian Glasgow in the mid-eighteenth century, Adam Smith reinterpreted Protestant theology in terms of sociological secularism and came to totally different conclusions. Calvin had explained the role of 'conscience' in terms of the etymology of the word: it meant each individual *knowing together* with God.[27] Smith's *Theory of Moral Sentiments* (1759) emphasised instead the role of conscience as mediator between the individual will and community standards of proper conduct. Sir Isaac Newton had explained the universe as a system of 'natural laws' and bodies in motion, and Smith believed that the natural order allowed neither for Divine intervention nor for a Divine plan in the Calvinist sense: a rational Providence, the Author and Judge of the World, had designed a rational world that operates according to its own laws, of which conscience, representing the *natural* basis of moral order, was an integral part.

Smith began his moral philosophy with the proposition that the nature of man, as a naturally social being, includes the capacity for 'sympathy' with others. The opening sentence of *The Theory of Moral Sentiments* declared:

> How selfish soever man may be supposed, there are evidently some principles in his nature, which interest him in the fortune of others, and render their happiness necessary to him, though he derives nothing from it except the pleasure of seeing it. Of this kind is pity or compassion, the emotion which we feel for the misery of others ...[28]

Smith claimed that morality originates in every individual sympathetically imagining both the pain and the pleasures of other people. Such is the 'constitution of nature', and 'It is thus that man, who can subsist only in society, was fitted by nature to that situation for which he was made. All the mem-

---

27 'For as, when men apprehend the knowledge of things in the mind and understanding, they are thence said *scire*, "to know," whence is derived the word *scientia*, "science" or "knowledge," so when they have a sense of Divine justice, as an additional witness, which permits them not to conceal their sins or to elude accusation at the tribunal of the supreme Judge, this sense is termed *conscientia*, "conscience." For it is a kind of medium between God and man, because it does not suffer a man to suppress what he knows within himself, but pursues him till it brings him to conviction ... This sentiment, therefore, which places man before the Divine tribunal is appointed ... to watch over man, to observe and examine all his secrets, that nothing may remain enveloped in darkness. Hence the old proverb, "Conscience is as a thousand witnesses"' (Calvin 1844, Vol. II, pp. 74–5).

28 Smith 1976, p. 9.

bers of human society stand in need of each other's assistance, and are likewise exposed to mutual injuries'.[29] Properly informed consciences become the subjective bond of human community when each judges the actions of others – and of oneself – on the basis of whether it is possible to sympathise with a particular conduct and its consequences. Conscience is the internal 'third party' that imposes self-restraint: 'We endeavour to examine our own conduct as we imagine any other fair and impartial spectator would examine it'.[30] Rules of moral judgement result, therefore, from the reciprocal adjustments of individual behaviour;[31] they are neither God-given nor exclusively a product either of reason or of custom. Instead, they spontaneously emerge from everyday experience. To be a rational individual, for Smith, meant to possess a *fully socialised conscience*, that is, the facility of *knowing together* with other members of the community what moral propriety demands. Among the fundamental virtues of socially responsible individuals, Smith attached the highest priority to prudence, justice and benevolence.

In a dialectic of the inner and outer, Smith's theory anticipated Hegel's concept of subjective freedom. Autonomous individual judgments would take into account the legitimate expectations of what the sociologist George Herbert Mead later called 'the generalised other'.[32] But socialised individuals, attuned to what others think and experience, would also seek admiration along with moral approval. The result was that the virtue of prudence, or responsible management of one's personal affairs, might grow over into the vice of avarice. Smith retained a Protestant disdain for conspicuous wealth in the belief that human needs are by nature limited. He worried, however, that two elements of human nature pointed to the possible corruption of our moral sentiments: 1) we are all victims of the deception that wealth brings happiness; and 2) as social beings, we all believe that others will respect and envy us because, imagining themselves in our place, they will be impressed with the happiness that our wealth must bestow. In a passage reminiscent of Calvin, Smith wrote:

> The rich man glories in his riches, because he feels that they naturally draw upon him the attention of the world ... At the thought of this, his heart seems to swell and dilate itself within him, and he is fonder of his wealth, upon this account, than for all the advantages it procures him. The poor man, on the contrary, is ashamed of his poverty ... The poor

---

29   Smith 1976, p. 85.
30   Smith 1976, p. 110.
31   Smith 1976, p. 159.
32   Mead 1934, p. 152.

man goes out and comes in unheeded, and when in the midst of a crowd is in the same obscurity as if shut up in his own hovel. Those humble cares and painful attentions which occupy those in his situation, afford no amusement to the dissipated and the gay. They turn their eyes away from him, or if the extremity of his distress forces them to look at him, it is only to spurn so disagreeable an object from among them. The fortunate and the proud wonder at the insolence of human wretchedness, that it should dare to present itself before them, and with the loathsome aspect of its misery presume to disturb the serenity of their happiness. The man of rank and distinction, on the contrary, is observed by all the world.[33]

Social order and prosperity required that wealth and greatness be respected, for admiration is a powerful incentive to productive activity. But the result, Smith said, is that wealth often receives the respect properly due to virtue, while poverty is treated with the contempt that vice and folly deserve.[34] Smith believed that the virtue of justice would encourage restraint, both as an internal moral rule and as the external force of positive law. But if wealth disposes the rich to 'turn their eyes away' from the poor, how could Smith expect that the rich and powerful, who *write* the laws, would not be the exclusive beneficiaries? He answered that the order of nature includes an 'invisible hand' that causes the excesses even of the landlord class, the idlest of the rich, ultimately to benefit the poor. Since 'the eye is larger than the belly', landlords redistribute their surplus to hire others who entertain and serve them:

> The pleasures of wealth and greatness ... strike the imagination as something grand and beautiful and noble ... It is this deception which rouses and keeps in continual motion the industry of mankind ... [But] the rich only select from the heap what is most precious and agreeable. They consume little more than the poor ... in spite of their natural selfishness and rapacity ... They are led by an invisible hand to make nearly the same distribution of the necessaries of life, which would have been made, had the earth been divided into equal proportions among all its inhabitants, and thus without intending it, without knowing it, advance the interest of society, and afford means to the multiplication of the species.[35]

---

33 Smith 1976, pp. 50–1.
34 Smith 1976, pp. 61–2.
35 Smith 1976, pp. 183–5.

With this reference to the 'invisible hand', *The Theory of Moral Sentiments* pointed the way to analysis of the capitalist market in *The Wealth of Nations*, in which Smith replaced Calvin's Divine plan with objective market laws. Convinced that individual responsibility is a moral advance over feudal hierarchy, Smith found in the market the natural order that he believed must realise his philosophic ideal. The market was morally justifiable because it was the only alternative that history provided in which individuals acquire both the liberty and the responsibility to make their own decisions. The economic theory of *The Wealth of Nations* was Smith's practical elaboration of moral philosophy.

Smith began *The Wealth of Nations* with reference to a natural propensity to 'truck, barter, and exchange one thing for another'.[36] Trade and economic cooperation, through the division of labour, appeared to be 'the necessary consequence of the faculties of reason and of speech ... It is common to all men, and to be found in no other race of animals'.[37] But the decisive change in Smith's thinking involved recognition that businessmen are guided immediately by profit – or self-love – not by benevolence or the fellow-feeling of conscience. In the pursuit of profit, the capitalist 'intends only his own gain', yet he is 'led by an invisible hand to promote an end which was no part of his intention'.[38] Through the invisible hand of market prices, self-love promotes social well-being: 'It is not from the benevolence of the butcher, the brewer, or the baker, that we expect our dinner, but from their regard to their own interest. We address ourselves, not to their humanity but to their self-love'.[39] In order to maximise profit, every businessman, in a competitive market, will try to sell the best possible product at the lowest possible price.

Self-love is beneficial because it increases social income and, at the same time, is assumed to be restrained by moral consciousness and public laws. The laws also define the property rights that make accumulation and social advance possible:

> Among nations of hunters, as there is scarce any property, or at least none that exceeds the value of two or three days labour, so there is seldom any established magistrate, or any regular administration of justice. Men who have no property, can injure one another only in their persons or reputations ... Wherever there is great property, there is great inequality ... It is only under the shelter of the civil magistrate, that the owner of that

---

36 Smith 1937, p. 13.
37 Ibid.
38 Smith 1937, p. 423.
39 Smith 1937, p. 14.

valuable property ... can sleep a single night in security ... The acquisition of valuable and extensive property, therefore, necessarily requires the establishment of civil government. Where there is no property ... civil government is not so necessary.[40]

Smith was perfectly aware that 'Civil government, so far as it is instituted for the security of property, is, in reality, instituted for the defence of the rich against the poor, or of those who have some property against those who have none at all'.[41] But property was necessary for accumulation, and accumulation was necessary for raising living standards. When capital is accumulated, the division of labour is extended and workers become more productive. As a result, the self-seeking behaviour of society's parts efficiently maximises the income of the whole. Given the presupposition of moral self-restraint and positive law, the market would benefit the whole of society and do so in conformity with the objective requirements of justice. The system of 'natural liberty' would reconcile efficiency with justice.

The problem remained, of course, that employers would always try to escape competition and monopolise the market. As a group, they also shared a special interest in suppressing wages:

> Masters are always and everywhere in a sort of tacit, but constant and uniform, combination, not to raise the wages of labour above their actual rate ... We seldom, indeed, hear of this combination, because it is the usual, and, one may say, the natural state of things, which nobody ever hears of. Masters, too, sometimes enter into particular combinations to sink the wages of labour even below this rate. These are always conducted with the utmost silence and secrecy ...[42]

Workers may respond by attempting to create their own defensive combinations, but the law forbids them to do so, and the masters 'call aloud for the assistance of the civil magistrate'. And since workmen depend upon employment for their subsistence, any attempts to resist the suppression of wages 'generally end in nothing but the punishment and ruin of the ringleaders'.[43] If the laws favour the rich, where is the justification for Smith's conviction that economic growth would be to the advantage of all? The answer, Smith believed,

---

40   Smith 1937, pp. 669–70.
41   Smith 1937, p. 674.
42   Smith 1937, pp. 66–7.
43   Smith 1937, p. 67.

is that there must be a competitive market not merely for the sale of goods but also for the hiring of wage-labourers. That condition would prevail with a rapid accumulation of capital:

> When in any country the demand for those who live by wages ... is continually increasing; when every year furnishes employment for a greater number than had been employed the year before, the workmen have no occasion to combine in order to raise their wages. The scarcity of hands occasions a competition among masters, who bid against one another in order to get workmen, and thus voluntarily break through the natural combination of masters not to raise wages ... The demand for those who live by wages, therefore, necessarily increases with the increase of the revenue and stock of every country, and cannot possibly increase without it. The increase of revenue and stock is the increase of national wealth. The demand for those who live by wages, therefore, naturally increases with the increase of national wealth, and cannot possibly increase without it.[44]

In his chapter on the accumulation of capital, Smith concluded that every 'frugal man', who saves and invests his net revenue, is objectively a 'public benefactor'.[45] The market system transforms private accumulation into beneficence with or without the corresponding subjective intention. The capitalist pursues his own gain, but he is led by 'an invisible hand' of competitive market prices to promote the public interest.[46] The objective design of nature makes the market an inherently moral and moralising order. The virtues of prudence, justice and benevolence, enunciated in Smith's *Theory of Moral Sentiments*, are therefore ensured through the activity of self-love, and the seeming contradiction between greed and godliness disappears. *The Wealth of Nations*, as a practical extension of moral philosophy, gives way to the science of political economy, which demonstrates that to do 'good' in the world is to accumulate capital.

Immanuel Kant: Moral Duty and Political Philosophy

While Adam Smith began by searching for the natural-social origin of good intentions, he ended by justifying capitalism in terms of its objective con-

---

44   Smith 1937, pp. 68–9.
45   Smith 1937, p. 324.
46   Smith 1937, p. 423.

sequences. Immanuel Kant took exactly the opposite approach, believing that there is no connection whatever between economic consequences and moral judgements. Smith thought moral rules result from everyday experience, which logically implied that they are dependent upon time and place. Kant, to the contrary, held that the moral law is universal and accessible only to *a priori* reason. Despite the differences in their final conclusions, however, Kant's view of history was in many respects suggestive of the type of reasoning found in Smith's *Wealth of Nations*.

Adam Smith was aware of historical stages, moving from the Age of Hunters to that of Shepherds, then to Agriculture and eventually to Commerce,[47] which he regarded as most appropriate for the flourishing of human nature. Kant also believed that history suggested direction and purpose. Whereas Smith referred to the 'invisible hand', Kant spoke of a 'hidden plan of nature', involving progress through moral individuation to purely rational self-discipline. In his *Idea for a Universal History with a Cosmopolitan Purpose* (1784), he wrote that men are 'unwittingly guided in their advance along a course intended by nature. They are unconsciously promoting an end which, even if they knew what it was, would scarcely arouse their interest'.[48] In a subsequent passage, he sounded even more like Smith:

> *The means which nature employs to bring about the development of innate capacities is that of antagonism within society, in so far as this antagonism* [Smith would say competition] *becomes in the long run the cause of a law-governed social order*. By antagonism, I mean ... the *unsocial sociability* of man that is ... obviously rooted in human nature. Man has an inclination to *live in society* ... But he also has a great tendency to *live as an individual* ... [T]he desire for honour, power or property ... drives him to seek status among his fellows ... Nature should thus be thanked for fostering social incompatibility, enviously competing vanity, and insatiable desires for possession or even power. Without these desires, all man's excellent natural capacities would never be roused to develop ... They would thus seem to indicate the design of a wise creator ....[49]

Kant thought the 'hidden plan of nature' is to produce law-governed social order. Competition for power and property results in external laws to prevent

---

47   Smith 1982, p. 27.
48   Kant 1970, p. 41.
49   Kant 1970, p. 44–5.

mutual destruction. The laws of the state enable each to pursue his or her own ends while assuring the same freedom to all others. When self-seeking energies are lawfully opposed to one another, the destructive effects are neutralised, and 'the result is the same as if man's selfish tendencies were non-existent'.[50] Freedom under external laws is the highest task that nature and historical experience set for humankind:

> The mechanical [i.e. unconscious] process of nature visibly exhibits the purposive plan of producing concord among men, even against their will and indeed by means of their very discord. This design, if we regard it as a compelling cause whose laws of operation are unknown to us, is called *fate*. But if we consider its purposive function ... we call it *providence*.[51]

Empirical history culminates in a civil culture of *legal discipline*, which is the external condition in which we acquire the habits of mind that allow us to lay down the moral law to ourselves. The end or purpose of humankind – the 'idea' of history – is the universal rule of reason. This distinction between empirical history and its ideal significance is the beginning of a dualism in Kant's thinking that clearly distinguishes him from Smith. Kant replaced Smith's unifying concept of human nature with a distinction between the 'noumenal' and the 'phenomenal'. As phenomenal beings we *experience* the self as part of nature and as governed by natural causality: we have biological needs that must be satisfied. But as noumenal beings we *conceive* the self as a 'free will' that transcends biology: we find freedom in the duty to obey no master but our own moral reason. Like the Christian soul or the Calvinist conscience, Kant's noumenal being has no empirical existence.

Given this dualism, Kant's moral philosophy replays the logic of history – the emergence of law-governed order – as an internal drama within each consciousness. The result is an internal moral order that co-exists with external laws. Kant explained the requirements of moral law this way:

> Everyone must admit that if a law is to have moral force, i.e. to be the basis of an obligation, it must carry with it absolute necessity [otherwise it would not be a law]; ... therefore, the basis of obligation must not be sought in the nature of man [for nature is a realm of particular needs and appetites rather than rational necessity], or in the circumstances of the

---

50   Kant 1970, p. 112.
51   Kant 1970, p. 108.

world in which he is placed [a universal law cannot be determined by particular circumstances], but a priori simply in the conception of pure reason ... moral philosophy ... does not borrow the least thing from the knowledge of man himself (anthropology), but gives laws a priori to him as a rational being.[52]

An a priori law is logically prior to time and place; that is to say, it is universally valid – always and everywhere. Moral law is analogous to the laws of physics insofar as it is universal in scope and binds all without exception. But moral law is also radically different in that it determines wills that determine themselves. To apply always and everywhere, the moral law must be strictly formal, telling us *how* to judge, not *what* judgements to make (which will always pertain to a particular time and place). In the *Fundamental Principles of the Metaphysic of Morals*, Kant said: 'The conception of an objective [universally valid] principle, insofar as it is obligatory for a will, is called a command (of reason), and the formula of the command is called an imperative'.[53] The 'categorical imperative' is a meta-rule, or supreme rational principle, for all individual judgements of moral duty. The 'matter' that it 'forms' is the personal maxims, or precepts, that we each prescribe to the self.[54]

Kant gave several formulations of the categorical imperative: 1) 'Act only on that maxim whereby thou canst at the same time will that it should become a universal law';[55] 2) 'So act as to treat humanity, whether in thine own person or in that of any other, in every case as an end withal, never as means only';[56] 3) 'So act as if thy maxim were to serve likewise as the universal law (of all rational beings)'.[57] Kant's second formulation categorically forbids use of oneself or of another human being merely as a means to one's own end; all rational beings must be respected as ends in themselves, whose uniquely human attribute is the capacity for autonomous moral judgements. The third formulation, which ultimately reappears in Hegel's political philosophy and is even echoed – indirectly, by way of his critique of Hegel – in Marx's anticipation of communism, points to the logical prospect of what Kant called a universal 'kingdom of ends', meaning a self-governing whole, a community of autonom-

---

52 Kant 2008, p. 7.
53 Kant 2008, p. 31.
54 In turn, the 'matter' formed by our maxims involves the 'ends' or purposes that serve as our motives.
55 Kant 2008, p. 39.
56 Kant 2008, p. 47.
57 Kant 2008, p. 56.

ous individual wills cohering through universal laws that are identical for all, speak to each from within, and result purely from the requirements of reason. Kant explained:

> By a kingdom I understand the union of different rational beings in a system by common laws. Now since it is by laws that ends are determined as regards their universal validity, hence, if we abstract from the personal differences of rational beings and likewise from all the content of their private ends, we shall be able to conceive all ends combined in a systematic whole (including both rational beings as ends in themselves, and also the special ends which each may propose to himself), that is to say, we can conceive a kingdom of ends, which on the preceding principles is possible.[58]

Adam Smith said conscience speaks to us on behalf of our particular community; Kant replied that conscience speaks the universal, and the universal is in each of us. The insurmountable contradiction in Kant is that while the kingdom of ends is a logical imperative, it is also a practical impossibility. As part of nature, we have needs and passions that thwart moral perfection, which is why compliance with the categorical imperative is our rational *duty*; perfect beings would *spontaneously* do what ought to be done. The kingdom of ends is a rational utopia, yet Kant insists that reasoning beings must do everything possible to approach it. How can rational beings rationally pursue the impossible? Kant answered that unless reason itself is a contradiction, we must have faith in an immortal soul (only immortals could hope to achieve perfection) and in God as the lawgiver of an ethical community.

> There must ... be someone other than the people whom we can declare the public lawgiver of an ethical community. But this is the concept of God as a moral ruler of the world. Hence an ethical community is conceivable only as a people under divine commands, i.e. as a *people of God*, and indeed *in accordance with the laws of virtue*.[59]

Only God, in His perfection, could produce perfect laws that speak to each from within, yet Kant said it is our rational duty to strive for the ideal. The question then becomes: How might we aspire, in everyday life, to produce a

---

58   Kant 2008, p. 51.
59   Kant 1998, pp. 109–10.

general Will out of a plurality of individual wills? Marx will tell us that the answer lies in communal self-determination through an agreed economic plan, which coordinates all of our ends in a common purpose. For Kant, however, the answer appeared to lie in a *social contract* as the concept (or principle) of any rational constitution in which only the 'united and consenting Will of all'[60] can legislate, creating a sovereignty in which reason alone must prevail.

Kant suggested that beyond empirical history lies a rational history that we might consciously make for ourselves. History might be created a priori in the same way as a priori reason specifies moral duty: '... how is it possible to have history a priori? The answer is that it is possible if the prophet himself occasions and produces the events he predicts'.[61] The French Revolution suggested 'that man has the quality or power of being the cause and ... the author of his own improvement': 'It cannot ... have been caused by anything other than a moral disposition within the human race'.[62] This implied that the ideal might be made real: '*A philosophical attempt to work out a universal history of the world in accordance with a plan of nature aimed at a perfect civil union of mankind, must be regarded as possible and even as capable of furthering the purpose of nature itself*'.[63]

At this point, however, Kant's political philosophy ran aground on the same issue that confronted Adam Smith: the inequality of wealth and power and its effect upon the determination of public law. Each individual has the rational capacity to 'legislate' *moral precepts for the self*, but Kant was convinced that not all are capable of rational *political judgements*. Formal law might ensure that all 'are free and equal under existing public law ... but not as regards the right to make these laws'.[64] Particular wills could not finally converge as a 'general Will' – or the 'united Will of the people' – *because of the institution of private property*. In order to exercise rational judgement in political life, and thus to have a 'civil personality', one first had to have 'civil independence', which, in turn, required *economic independence*. To be a citizen, one must 'have some

---

60   Kant 1965, p. 78.
61   Kant 1970, p. 177.
62   Kant 1970, pp. 181–2. It is worth noting that while Kant praised the French Revolution after the fact, he also argued against revolution on the grounds that 'external' laws are implicitly rational and must be obeyed (Kant 1970, p. 55). The Social Contract and General Will were ideals of Reason, but he believed actual democracy was 'necessarily a despotism' (Kant 1970, p. 101).
63   Kant 1970, p. 51.
64   Kant 1970, p. 77.

property (which can include any skill, trade, fine art or science) to support himself'.[65] The self-employed and the independently wealthy – artisans and landowners – were qualified to be active citizens, but not women or day-labourers, whose judgement would be distorted by their condition of economic dependence.

> Fitness for voting is a prerequisite of being a citizen. To be fit to vote, a person must be independent ... This qualification leads to the distinction between an active and a passive citizen ... The following examples [of passive citizens] may serve to clear up this difficulty: an apprentice of a merchant or artisan; a servant (not in the service of the state); a minor ...; all women; and generally anyone who must depend for his support (subsistence and protection) ... on arrangements by others ... – all such people lack civic personality ...[66]

Kant concluded that the ideal of the social contract 'is in fact merely an *idea* of reason'.[67] Its practical significance lay solely in the conviction that legislators are rationally obligated to consider whether any proposed law *could be* agreed to by the entire people, were they in a position to express a rational judgement. But since most of them were not, the phenomenal republic could never become the noumenal republic. 'Any true republic', Kant decided, 'is and cannot be anything other than a *representative system* of the people whereby the people's rights are looked after on their behalf by deputies who represent the united will of the citizens'.[68] Landless peasants, day labourers and vagabonds – the victims, as Marx said, of primitive capitalist accumulation – would have to depend upon the wisdom and virtue of the great and powerful.

The dualism in Kant's political philosophy resulted from his inability to see beyond the existing economic order. The Marxist philosopher Lucien Goldmann wrote that Kantian man is condemned to a tragic and divided existence, 'torn between a material but atomistic and egoistic aspiration towards happiness and a purely formal morality. That is why the moral law is an imperative, an "ought", and not an "is" ...'.[69]

Kant would reply, of course, that what merely 'is', is not the point: the proper concern of philosophy is the subjective *intention* that precedes the action. 'An

---

65 Kant 1970, p. 78.
66 Kant 1965, p. 120.
67 Ibid.
68 Kant 1970, p. 163.
69 Goldmann 1971, p. 168.

action done from duty derives its moral worth ... from the maxim by which it is determined, and therefore does not depend on the realization of the object of the action, but merely on the principle of volition by which the action has taken place ...'.[70] The highest end, the ultimate end in itself, is a 'good will', which acts upon nothing but the good intention never to treat other people solely as means to our own end: 'the worth of such a will is above everything'.[71]

In *The German Ideology* (1845), Marx and Engels dismissed such thoughts as a reflection of the miserable circumstances of the German bourgeoisie in Kant's day:

> The state of Germany at the end of the last century is fully reflected in Kant's *Kritik der Practischen Vernunft* [*Critique of Practical Reason*]. While the French bourgeoisie, by means of the most colossal revolution that history has ever known, was achieving domination and conquering the Continent of Europe, while the already politically emancipated English bourgeoisie was revolutionising industry and subjugating India politically, and all the rest of the world commercially, the impotent German burghers did not get any further than 'good will'. Kant was satisfied with 'good will' alone, even if it remained entirely without result, and he transferred the *realisation* of this good will, the harmony between it and the needs and impulses of individuals, to *the world beyond* [the kingdom of ends]. Kant's good will fully corresponds to the impotence, depression and wretchedness of the German burghers, whose petty interests were never capable of developing into the common, national interests of a class and who were, therefore, constantly exploited by the bourgeois of all other nations.[72]

---

70 Kant 2008, p. 18.
71 Kant 2008, p. 12. On the same page Kant wrote: 'A good will is good not because of what it performs or effects, not by its aptness for the attainment of some proposed end, but simply by virtue of the *volition*; that is, it is good in itself, and considered by itself is to be esteemed much higher than all that can be brought about by it in favour of any inclination, nay even of the sum total of all inclinations. Even if it should happen that, owing to special disfavour of fortune, or the niggardly provision of a step-motherly nature, this will should wholly lack power to accomplish its purpose, if with its greatest efforts it should yet achieve nothing, and there should remain only the good will (not, to be sure, a mere wish, but the summoning of all means in our power), then, like a jewel, it would still shine by its own light, as a thing which has its whole value in itself. Its usefulness or fruitfulness can neither add nor take away anything from this value' (Ibid.).
72 Marx and Engels 1964, p. 207.

The characteristic form which French liberalism, based on real class interests, assumed in Germany we find again in Kant. Neither he, nor the German middle class, whose whitewashing spokesman he was, noticed that these theoretical ideas of the bourgeoisie had as their basis material interests and a *will* that was conditioned and determined by the material relations of production. Kant, therefore, separated this theoretical expression from the interests which it expressed; he made the materially motivated determinations of the will of the French bourgeois into *pure* self-determinations of *'free will'*, of the will in and for itself, of the human will, and so converted it into purely ideological conceptual determinations and moral postulates. Hence the German petty bourgeois recoiled in horror from the practice of this energetic bourgeois liberalism as soon as this practice showed itself, both in the Reign of Terror and in shameless bourgeois profit-making.[73]

Marx despised Kant's political philosophy because he thought it represented the most insipid sort of bourgeois self-deception. For thinkers such as Adam Smith and David Ricardo, Marx had much greater respect. They at least made a contribution to economic science. There is much irony, however, in the fact that numerous subsequent Marxists, who for one reason or another despaired of the prospect for proletarian revolution, ended up reverting to some form of neo-Kantianism. Kant's name, for that reason, often recurs in this volume. To disillusioned Marxists, Kant provided a comfortable haven: he expressed confidence in the ability of human reason if not to resolve class contradictions, then perhaps to promote gradual improvement. Unlike the Calvinist disdain for the poor, Kant believed that the principle of the modern state included the responsibility to redistribute wealth, through taxation, to the benefit of those who could not secure their own subsistence.[74] To later Social Democrats, such

---

73 Marx and Engels 1964, p. 209.
74 In the *Metaphysical Elements of Justice*, Kant wrote: '[The sovereign] possesses the right to levy taxes ... in particular for the relief of the poor, foundling hospitals, and churches; in other words, for what are called charitable and pious institutions ... it follows from the nature of the state that the government is authorized to require the wealthy to provide the means of sustenance to those who are unable to provide the most necessary needs of nature to themselves ... [In order to fulfil this function, the state may] tax the property of the citizens or their commerce to establish funds and use the interest from them ... for the needs of the people. The money should not be raised merely through voluntary contributions, but by compulsory exactions as political burdens ... but lotteries ought not to be permitted because they increase the number of the poor ...' (Kant 1965, p. 93).

as Eduard Bernstein and several Austro-Marxists of the early twentieth century, this sort of reformism had considerable appeal.[75]

From Kant's 'Good Will' to Hegel's Reason of History

G.W.F. Hegel, on the other hand, saw in Kant's work the ultimate frustration of Reason and Enlightenment. Whereas Kant was widely respected for his logical rigour, Hegel thought it was precisely Kant's formal logic that led to the cul-de-sac of his political theory. Hegel embraced elements of Kant's epistemology at the same time as he repudiated its inherent dualism. He took Kant's frustrating conclusions as the starting point for his own dramatically more ambitious enterprise: to replace Kantian subjective idealism with the dialectical philosophy of objective idealism. To move beyond the dualism of *what* Kant thought, first required a philosophical critique of *how* he thought. Before turning to Hegel's response to Kant, therefore, a brief commentary on the general form of Kantian thought is in order.

We have already considered Kant's view of how moral judgements must be made. Equally important was his view of objective empirical judgements. In both types of judgement, Kant aspired to a Copernican revolution in philosophy. Copernicus had shown that the apparent movement of heavenly bodies is partly due to the movement of the earth-bound observer. Kant claimed that what we know of the world is likewise dependent on the internal movement of thought. We experience through the senses, but sense impressions acquire meaning only through the activity of mind.

Kant began with space and time. All experience occurs in space and time, yet we cannot experience space or time as such. Pure space would be nothingness, and nothingness cannot be experienced. Space and time are a priori pure forms of intuition, wholes that make it possible to situate specific parts of experience in a meaningful way.[76] Every empirical judgement likewise presupposes the logical categories of *quantity, quality, relation and modality*,[77] and it is the mental activity of applying these categories that synthesises appearances into knowledge of phenomena. If all knowledge of the world is 'formed' by logical categories, then the world, as we know it, must be a product of our *own consciousness*.

---

75 Kant's philosophy continues today to have the same effect upon important philosophers such as John Rawls and Jürgen Habermas.
76 Kant 1998a, pp. 157–85.
77 See Kant's diagram in Kant 1998a, p. 206.

The result is a fundamental similarity between moral and empirical judgements. Practical reason makes moral judgements according to the universal moral law, which we know a priori, and theoretical reason judges phenomena by reference to its own rules for the coherent application of logical categories. The origin of natural laws, therefore, as with the moral law, must be mind itself: 'The understanding is thus not merely a faculty for making rules through the comparison of the appearances; it is itself the legislation for nature, i.e., without understanding there would not be any nature at all'.[78]

The necessary result of this argument is another dualism. If all that we know of the natural world is formed by our own understanding, we can never have direct knowledge of ultimate reality, only of our own experience of the world, which is mediated through the activity of our empirical judgements. The price that Kant pays for moral autonomy is the impossibility of the kingdom of ends: some will always choose to violate ethical duty. Similarly, the price paid for the activity of mind in empirical judgements is that the thing-in-itself, as the *cause* of sense perceptions, is inaccessible. A noumenon – whether it be God or the thing-in-itself – does not exist in space and time[79] and can never be 'an object of the senses'.[80] It is as if the world were in darkness, and we experience its movements only through the 'radar' of our own minds.[81] But even though we cannot directly know noumena, Kant believed we can know that the world has a moral purpose. The human being, a being with moral consciousness, exists *in* the world and thus imparts purpose to it. This is why reason can hope to improve the world. The 'pure idea' of freedom is a supersensible concept that proves its objective reality in nature by its 'possible' effect there.[82]

The purpose of Hegel's dialectical logic was to transcend these limits that Kant imposed upon reason. Hegel aimed to prove that the ideals of reason are actually realised (objectified) in the phenomenal world, and that reasoning beings can therefore know the reason of history. The kingdom of ends would then be both possible and necessary, for reasoning beings would make the

---

78 Kant 1998a, p. 242.
79 '... nothing that is intuited in space is a thing in itself, and ... space is not a form that is proper to anything in itself, ... objects in themselves are not known to us at all and what we call outer objects are nothing other than mere representations of our sensibility, whose form is space, but whose true correlate, i.e., the thing in itself, is not and cannot be cognized through them, [and] is also never asked after in experience' (Kant 1998a, pp. 161–2).
80 Kant 1998a, p. 350.
81 This analogy is made by Justus Hartnack in Hartnack 1968, p. 27.
82 Kant 2002, p. 338.

world rational. Kant's 'hidden plan of nature' would then become reason's own plan, and history would become a movement towards the rule of reason.

Kant said the unknowable thing-in-itself is the cause of sensations. Hegel replied that if cause itself is a category of thought, then the very notion of a thing-in-itself made no sense. In *The Philosophy of Right* he ironically commented that 'Even an animal has gone beyond this ... philosophy since it devours things and so proves that they are not absolutely self-subsistent'.[83] In the *Logic* he wrote:

> Thoughts, according to Kant, are *only our* thoughts – separated by an impassable gulf from the thing, as it exists apart from our knowledge ... But the true objectivity of thinking means that the thoughts, far from being merely ours, must at the same time be the real essence of things ...[84]

For Kant, the proper standard for reasoning was consistency – the law of non-contradiction.[85] Contradiction was evidence of faulty reasoning.[86] But if thoughts and things are different – yet at the same time *essentially* the same – they must somehow be dialectically joined. For Hegel, contradiction pointed to the need for a higher logic, not of what *is* but of the *movement* from what is to what reason ultimately *requires*.

The decisive step in Hegel's dialectical logic was to transform Kant's epistemology into ontology, which addresses the properties and relations of being; that is, of everything that has existed, does exist, or ever might exist. Whereas Kantian judgement always involves separation of thought from what is being judged, Hegel said that reason restores their unity. This meant that the Kantian categories of thought – quantity, quality, relation, modality and all of their subcategories – must in fact be the forms not of *experience* but of *being* itself. The categories, in other words, 'form' being, not just our sense impressions. If the

---

83   Hegel 1967, p. 236.
84   Hegel 1975, pp. 67–8.
85   Kant saw no contradiction between the noumenal and phenomenal. The separation resulted from correctly understanding the limitations inherent in practical and theoretical reason.
86   Faulty reasoning searches for factual knowledge of Absolutes (e.g. empirical knowledge of noumena: we have 'faith' in God, not knowledge). When we confuse the two – the empirical and the ideal – we arrive at dialectical contradictions and metaphysical illusions. We cannot have metaphysical knowledge of the empirical or empirical knowledge of the metaphysical.

world is *formed* by the categories of reason, then it must ultimately *conform* to the requirements of reason.[87] The phenomenal republic must then become the noumenal republic; the real must become the ideal.

Hegel described Kantian dualism this way:

> On one side there is the Ego ... But next to it there is an infinity of sensations and ... of things in themselves. Once it is abandoned by the categories, this realm cannot be anything but a formless lump ... A formal idealism, which in this way sets an absolute Ego-point and its intellect on one side, and an absolute manifold, or sensation on the other, is a dualism.[88]

Hegel objected that it is impossible for being to be merely a formless lump. If being had no determinate characteristics, it would be nothing (no-thing). Being and nothing are abstract opposites, but their opposition sets in motion the dialectical movement of becoming. Dualism, the end of Kant's theory, then becomes the beginning of Hegel's. In Hegel's *Logic*, The Doctrine of Being derives all forms of being from one another (the movement from Quality to Quantity to Measure). When categories of thought are thus shown to be the real essence of things, the Doctrine of Essence deals with paired opposites in their unity. What holds being and essence together is the force of thought, which Hegel explains in the Doctrine of the Notion. The realised end of the *Logic*, therefore, *is* 'the overt unity of subjective and objective',[89] which is the Idea, or the whole of being as it is formed by dialectical logic.

> The Idea may be described in many ways. It may be called reason ...; subject-object; the unity of the ideal and the real, of the finite and the infinite, of soul and body; the possibility which has its actuality in its own self ... the Idea contains all the relations of understanding ... in their infinite self-return and self-identity ... *The Idea itself is the dialectic* ...[90]

---

87 To say that all knowledge is conceptual means that the object is what thought makes of it: being *means* being for consciousness, so that subject and object are distinct but at the same time identical. In the *Logic* Hegel differentiated between Understanding, which believes that opposites exclude each other (the doctrine of Essence), and Reason, which says they are identical (the doctrine of the Notion).

88 Hegel, cited by Paul Guyer, 'Thought and Being: Hegel's Critique of Kant's theoretical philosophy', in Beiser 1993, p. 191.

89 Hegel 1975, p. 273.

90 Hegel 1975, p. 277, my emphasis.

In his *Philosophy of Nature*, Hegel turned from logic to the forms of sensuous existence. Nature was 'mind asleep', since on its own it has no ethical consciousness. But since nature is implicitly rational, reason must consciously make the natural world conform to its own standards. Kant said nature has moral purpose because it includes humanity; Hegel added that humanity's purpose it to make the natural world into a habitat in which reasoning beings enjoy the objective reality – not merely the Kantian ideal – of self-determination. This means that history also becomes a kind of logic; not a 'hidden plan' (Kant), but a process whose meaning is both revealed and determined through conscious reason.

Hegel's *Phenomenology of Spirit* is a logic of the appearance of reason (or Spirit) in the world. Consciousness first appears as the consciousness of an individual (Kant). When one individual cancels (or negates) the other, the result is the master-slave dialectic, which was Hegel's model of the antagonistic egoism described by both Smith and Kant. In Kant's 'hidden plan', history brings civility through external laws, meaning that history happens to us. Hegel says history is the 'story' of our own consciousness and its active role in making a civilised world.

The process begins when Spirit (consciousness) asserts its superiority by risking mere biological life (its opposite) in mortal combat. When one self enslaves the other, the master wins recognition of his autonomy by negating the slave. The problem is that the master in fact remains dependent upon the labour of the slave, while the slave regains his sense of self by imposing his will upon nature. Through work, consciousness comes to itself, yet the slave remains a slave. For each to gain self-possession – the autonomy of will that Kant described as freedom – requires mutual recognition. Each consciousness must assert itself while also restraining itself, the condition that Kant described in terms of a 'good will' and Smith in terms of a socialised conscience. Unlike Kant, however, Hegel argued that a good will is formed *within history*, not by an a priori command of reason. The 'hidden plan' of nature must then be our own plan. By recognising all others as ends, we move towards the end of history, which is an ethical world of objective spirit, consciously formed by reason. The reason of history thus turns out to be the emergence of Kant's ethical community through lived experience.

Hegel's Philosophy of the Modern State

Kant said the end in itself is a good will. Virtue involves a continuous and deliberate effort on the part of every individual to purify moral consciousness in the face of repeated temptation.[91] Hegel replied that culture is historically cumulative, and the specific content of a good will is objectively determined within the ethical life of the modern state: 'If men are to act, they must not only will the good, but they must also *know* whether this or that is good ... that question is answered by the laws and customs of a state'.[92] When Kant said freedom means laying down the law to ourselves, Hegel concluded that the modern state of self-determined laws is both the condition for human freedom and the actual *existence* of Kant's ethical commonwealth. The ambition of Hegel's project was expressed in his *Introduction to the Philosophy of History*:

> The State is the Divine Idea, as it *exists* on earth ... the State is the precise object of world history in general. It is in the State that freedom attains its objectivity ... For the law of the State is the objectification of Spirit; it is will in its true form. Only the will that is obedient to the law is free, for it obeys itself and, being self-sufficient, it is free. Insofar as the State ... constitutes a community of *existence* [rather than Kant's noumenal kingdom], and insofar as the subjective will of human beings submits to laws, the antithesis between freedom and necessity disappears. The rational is the necessary, the substantiality of a shared existence ... The objective and the subjective will are then reconciled, as one and the same serene whole.[93]

The problem that political philosophy now faced was this: How might freedom be reconciled with private property, with the capitalist market, with social classes and with the modern division of labour – all of which presupposed using others as mere 'means' to our own ends? How could Kant's ethical commonwealth be realised in face of the limitations upon the ideal of a social contract that Kant himself saw in poverty and economic inequality? Hegel

---

91   In *The Metaphysic of Morals*, Kant wrote: 'Virtue is always *in progress* and yet always starts *from the beginning* ... because, considered *objectively*, it is an ideal and unattainable, while yet constant approximation to it is a duty. [The fact] that it always starts from the beginning has a *subjective* basis in human nature, which is affected by inclinations because of which virtue can never settle down in peace and quiet with its maxims adopted once and for all ... For moral maxims, unlike technical ones, cannot be based on habit ...; on the contrary, if the practice of virtue were to become a habit the subject would suffer loss to that *freedom* in adopting his maxims which distinguishes an action done from duty' (Kant 1991, pp. 209–10).
92   Hegel 1988, p. 31, my emphasis.
93   Hegel 1988, p. 42, my emphasis.

undertook to answer these questions in *The Philosophy of Right*. He began with right as purely abstract – that is, one-sidedly objective (in property) – then proceeded dialectically to right as abstractly subjective (in morality), which then ultimately issues, through the mediating associations of civil society, in political life as the concrete unity of objective and subjective freedom.

The discussion of Abstract Right began with the individual ego that represents consciousness in itself, abstracted from family, civil society and the state. Ego is like abstract being in the *Logic*: it is potentiality without determinate existence and must therefore determine itself through an act of will, which is 'thinking as the urge to give itself existence'.[94] Thinking must objectify itself in the thing, which, rather than being 'in itself' – as Kant thought – exists to be appropriated as property.[95] Property, at this stage, has nothing to do with economics: 'The rationale of property is to be found not in the satisfaction of needs but in the supersession of the pure subjectivity of personality. In his property a person exists for the first time as reason'.[96] Consciousness gives itself properties (determines itself) through appropriating things, thereby becoming an object to itself.[97] No free will is conceivable without property.

The result must then be movement beyond the immediacy of individual property through a continuing dialectic of property owners. Property entails the power of disposal over the thing, so that each owner relates to others through transferring property in accordance with contracts, each of which posits a common will.[98] The problem is that when property owners are still abstract persons, and there is yet no law, each can act capriciously and expose the contract to 'wrong'. Wrong is a negation of the posited common will that must in turn be negated.

Each party to the contract knows that the Right ought to be restored, but the problem is to define one's duty, which at this level of abstraction is still indeterminate. Consciousness can appeal only to its own 'abstract inwardness',[99] making clear the futility of Kant's moral philosophy. Kant tells us to do 'good' to others whenever we can; but what is the 'good' when the contract is in dispute?

---

94 Hegel 1967, p. 226.
95 'A person has as his substantive end the right of putting his will into any and every thing and thereby making it his, because it has no such end in itself and derives its destiny and soul from his will. This is the absolute right of appropriation which man has over all "things"' (Hegel 1967, p. 41).
96 Hegel 1967, pp. 235–6.
97 Hegel 1967, p. 42.
98 Hegel 1967, p. 38.
99 Hegel 1967, p. 254.

Moral judgement, in these circumstances, is merely an internal monologue as to whether one's own maxim, in Kantian terms, could apply universally. But if each acts according to a purely subjective and individual judgement, the result will be revenge and a replay of the master-slave dialectic, in which neither party will be a self-determining subject. Subjective morality must therefore point beyond itself to ethical life, or ethics institutionalised. 'Ethical life,' says Hegel, 'is the Idea of freedom ... it is the good become alive ... the concept of freedom developed into the existing world ...'.[100] At the very beginning of Hegel's argument, the logic of Abstract Right demonstrates that the existence of property already presupposes the whole, the state of laws that defines the rights and the duties of property and thereby makes it serve the purpose of reason.

The unity of subjective and objective morality, or ethical substance, originates in the family. Abstract means one-sided, but the family is a community of consciousness, whose bond is not yet law (universal reason), only the immediate 'feeling' of love.[101] The objective embodiment of this subjective bond is property that has now become the 'family capital'.[102] Capital is possession that has been 'specifically determined as permanent and secure'.[103] What makes the family capital 'ethical' is that it serves the good of a whole rather than the 'arbitrariness of a single owner's particular needs'.[104] 'This capital is common property so that, while no member of the family has property of his own, each has his right in the common stock'.[105] Capital embodies the family's ethical 'spirit', and immediate ethicality supersedes the self-interest of abstract individuality.

Movement beyond the immediate community of the family occurs, however, when children become persons in their own right and inheritance occurs, involving 'the transfer to private ownership of property which is in principle common'.[106] Marriages create new families, each of which again behaves as 'a self-subsistent concrete person'.[107] The unity of the family dissolves into difference, which is the transition to civil society, the association of burghers 'whose

---

100   Hegel 1967, p. 142.
101   Hegel 1967, p. 262.
102   Hegel 1967, p. 116.
103   Ibid.
104   Ibid.
105   Ibid.
106   Hegel 1967, p. 119.
107   Hegel 1967, p. 122.

end is their own interest'[108] and among whom the ethical spirit appears once more to be lost. 'In civil society, the Idea is lost in particularity and has fallen asunder with the separation of inward and outward'.[109]

The social bond is no longer immediately apparent in love, yet Hegel claims that 'ethical life' remains the 'essence' of market relations. For that insight he credits Adam Smith, who demonstrated that subjective, individual self-seeking also *objectively* benefits the whole community. Even as they use each other as mere means, the individuals of civil society are mediated through the market to serve each other's needs (as they do immediately in the family). Hegel congratulates Smith for proving that while civil society appears to be merely 'a mass of accidents',[110] in fact it is governed by its own rational laws:

> Political economy is the science which starts from … needs and labour but then has the task of explaining mass-relationships and mass-movements in their complexity and their qualitative and quantitative character. This is one of the sciences which have arisen out of the conditions of the modern world. Its development affords the interesting spectacle (as in Smith, Say, and Ricardo) of thought working upon the endless mass of details which confront it at the outset and extracting therefrom the simple principles of the thing, the Understanding effective in the thing and directing it.[111]

Hegel calls civil society 'the external state, the state based on need, the state as the Understanding envisages it'.[112] The external state is an order that happens to us, as in Kant's 'hidden plan'.[113] It is the association of economic actors 'brought about by their needs, by the legal system – the means to security of person and property – and by an external organization for attaining their particular and common interests'.[114] It includes police, courts and Corporations, or legally

---

108   Hegel 1967, p. 124.
109   Hegel 1967, p. 145.
110   Hegel 1967, p. 268.
111   Hegel 1967, pp. 126–7.
112   Hegel 1967, p. 123. 'Understanding' is abstract thinking that characterises mathematical and empirical sciences or formal logic. It is to be distinguished from Reason, which grasps relations in their concrete totality.
113   Hegel says this external state must be 'brought back to and welded into unity in the *Constitution of the State* which is the end and actuality of both the substantial universal order and the public life devoted thereto' (Hegel 1967, p. 110).
114   Ibid.

recognised communities of shared economic interest. In the external state, the laws do not yet speak to us from within; externality means there is as yet no universal community of consciousness that binds the whole.

From economic life within civil society, new forms of community emerge. 'The family is the first precondition of the state, but class divisions are the second. The importance of the latter is due to the fact that although private persons are self-seeking, they are compelled to direct their attention to others'.[115] Since Hegel's dialectic is throughout a movement of consciousness, social classes are determined by the particular forms of consciousness that characterise their members. Classes are a rational necessity as a further step from the abstract towards the concrete whole. Hegel speaks of three classes. The agricultural class has an immediate relation to the soil; its consciousness is characterised by 'family relationship and trust'. The business class includes both employers and workers engaged in crafts, manufacturing and trade; its consciousness involves the application of technical Understanding, using the laws of nature to transform natural material into useful things. The universal class is the civil service, which is consciously committed to the work of Reason in 'the universal interests of the community'.[116]

Classes and Corporations extend the horizons of consciousness. They create an *esprit de corps* that transcends – that is to say, goes beyond but also affirms – individual self-interest. The right of the Corporation, Hegel says, 'is to come on the scene like a second family for its members'.[117] But since Corporations each represent a particular interest, the contradictions between them must in turn be transcended at the higher level of political representation. The state, for Hegel, is the concrete universal, the whole that lives through its parts, or Reason that becomes concrete through the final unity of subject and object.

The mediation that makes this possible occurs through the Estates, where the activity of determining the laws occurs. Kant thought property owners must represent the economically dependent, but Hegel declared that 'all the associations, communities and Corporations',[118] or all the particular communities of civil society, must represent themselves. All citizens, through political representation, are thereby 'in' the state. The Estates form the laws at the same time as the laws form the ethical consciousness of citizens in a mediated whole that constitutes a universal community of consciousness: 'The real significance

---

115   Hegel 1967, p. 270.
116   Hegel 1967, pp. 131–2.
117   Hegel 1967, p. 270.
118   Hegel 1967, p. 200.

of the Estates lies in the fact that it is through them that the state enters the subjective consciousness of the people and that the people begins to participate in the state'.[119]

Through institutionalised mediation, the 'external' state of civil society has now become 'internal', and the abstraction (one-sidedness) of Kantian philosophy and political life is transcended. The laws, determined by 'our' representatives, are genuinely 'our' laws. The ethicality of Corporations is affirmed when political labour makes their particular wills congruent through determining the laws in common and affirming the whole through *mutual recognition* of the parts. The result is that particular wills 'pass over of their own accord into the interest of the universal'.[120] 'The state is actual only when its members have a feeling of their own self-hood and it is stable only when public and private ends are identical'.[121] The principle of the modern state 'requires that the whole of an individual's activity shall be mediated through his will',[122] that is, through a concrete unity of subjective and objective self-determination. Compliance with self-imposed rational necessity is the objective fulfilment of self-determined freedom.

In place of a Kantian good will, Hegel regarded the state as the end-in-itself that makes all other ends possible. It is the universal as the self-determining individual (the community as a whole). In the state 'mind is objective and actual to itself as an organic totality in laws and institutions which are its will in terms of thought'.[123] Common property in things can never achieve such an end, for things are by nature particular and can never be possessed universally. Laws, however, are thoughts, and all can think the same thoughts simultaneously.[124] The state is a spiritual second nature. It transcends natural-empirical history as 'the world which mind has made for itself'.[125] The state is Objective Spirit, beyond which lies the dialectical fulfilment of Absolute Spirit, or thought contemplating thought, which is *logic*. Hegel's *Logic* is the beginning of his system, but also its end. In logic, the dialectic completes and at the same time renews its circle of rational necessity. The end is the beginning. The parts presuppose the whole, but the whole simultaneously objectifies itself in each and every part.

---

119 Hegel 1967, p. 292.
120 Hegel 1967, p. 155.
121 Hegel 1967, p. 281.
122 Hegel 1967, p. 292.
123 Hegel 1967, p. 155.
124 Hegel 1967, p. 156.
125 Hegel 1967, p. 285.

From Hegel to Marx: Property and Poverty

Despite the imposing edifice of Hegel's system, a fundamental problem lay in his treatment of property. 'In his property' he wrote, when discussing Abstract Right, 'a person exists for the first time as reason'.[126] But the right of property also entailed the right of *alienation*. Through contracts, individuals affirm the will's independence of any and every particular thing by alienating their property. This is why contractual exchange is inherent in 'the Idea of the real existence of free personality, "real" here meaning "present in the will alone"'.[127] To alienate the thing is the most concrete way of asserting one's will over it and thus one's independence of it.

> ... alienation proper is an expression of my will ... no longer to regard the thing as mine ... alienation is seen to be a true mode of taking possession. To take possession of the thing directly is the first moment in property. Use is likewise a way of acquiring property. The third moment ... is ... taking possession of the thing by alienating it.[128]

Since alienation of the thing is necessary in order to affirm self-determination, it also follows that there are limits to what may be alienated, including one's 'freedom of will' and 'ethical life', the substantive elements of personality.[129] Reason cannot tolerate slavery or serfdom. On the other hand, day-labourers, in accordance with their own will, may 'for a restricted period' alienate products of their 'particular skill' and their 'power to act'.[130] The wage contract, in other words, conforms to the requirements of reason. The problem is one of degree. How much might a worker alienate before ceasing to exist both for himself and as a citizen?

Even more problematic was the issue of unemployment. Hegel published *The Philosophy of Right* in 1821, six years after the end of the Napoleonic wars and in the midst of capitalism's first cyclical depression. Hegel looked anxiously for a solution to unemployment. One way to mitigate the increase of poverty was through price controls.[131] Unemployment might also be met with private or public charity, financed by taxes on the wealthy (as Kant had suggested).

---

126 Hegel 1967, pp. 235–6.
127 Hegel 1967, p. 57.
128 Hegel 1967, p. 241.
129 Hegel 1967, p. 53.
130 Hegel 1967, p. 54.
131 Hegel 1967, p. 147.

But the problem with charity was that 'the needy would receive subsistence directly, not by means of their work, and this would violate the principle of civil society and the feeling of individual independence and self-respect in its individual members'.[132]

By analogy with the family capital, Hegel thought the social means of production might serve as a kind of common property, 'the universal permanent capital which gives each the opportunity, by the exercise of his education and skill, to draw from it and so be assured of his livelihood, while what he thus earns by means of his work maintains and increases the general capital'.[133] When citizens find themselves impoverished by 'factors grounded in external circumstances', the public authority 'takes the place of the family'.[134] But if public resources were used to provide productive employment to the poor, the problem of post-war over-production would simply be compounded. The attempt to alleviate unemployment would create more unemployment:

> In this event the volume of production would be increased, but the evil consists precisely in an excess of production and in the lack of a proportionate number of consumers who are themselves also producers, and thus it is simply intensified ... It hence becomes apparent that despite an excess of wealth civil society is not rich enough, i.e. its own resources are insufficient to check excessive poverty and the creation of a penurious rabble.[135]

Hegel had no doubt that poverty was a 'wrong' that must be made 'right'. 'The important question of how poverty is to be abolished is one of the most disturbing problems which agitate modern society'.[136] Moreover, poverty was not simply an economic issue; it was a *spiritual sickness*, involving destruction of civic consciousness and 'loss of the sense of right and wrong, of honesty and the self-respect which makes a man insist on maintaining himself by his own work and effort'.[137] Mere physical need, on its own, does not create the rabble: 'a rabble is created only when there is joined to poverty a disposition of mind, an inner indignation against the rich, against society, against the gov-

---

132   Hegel 1967, p. 150.
133   Hegel 1967, p. 130.
134   Hegel 1967, p. 149.
135   Hegel 1967, p. 150.
136   Hegel 1967, p. 278.
137   Hegel 1967, p. 150.

ernment etc.'.[138] Impoverishment of wage-workers, accompanied by 'concentration of disproportionate wealth in a few hands',[139] also raised the threat of class struggle: 'Against nature man can claim no right, but once society is established, poverty immediately takes the form of a wrong done to one class by another'.[140]

Unable to resolve the problem of poverty *within* his political philosophy, Hegel in effect expelled it. What Reason required was renewal of the dialectical 'circle of necessity'. Hegel concluded that mature civil society is driven to colonising activity 'by which it supplies to a part of its population a return to life on the family basis in a new land and so also supplies itself with a new demand and field for its industry'.[141] The solution to capitalist unemployment turned out to be *imperialism*:

> This inner dialectic of civil society thus drives it – or at any rate drives a specific civil society – to push beyond its own limits and seek markets, and so its necessary means of subsistence, in other lands which are either deficient in the goods it has overproduced, or else generally backward in industry, etc.[142]

Marx's Response to the *Philosophy of Right*

In his *Critique of Hegel's Philosophy of Right* (1843), Marx immediately saw the loose ends of Hegel's argument: 1) 'the political constitution is the constitution of private property';[143] 2) 'the actuality of the Ethical Idea appears as the religion of private property';[144] 3) 'the class in need of immediate labour, of concrete labour, forms less a class of civil society than the basis upon which the spheres of civil society rest and move'.[145] Hegel spoke of the constitution as 'essentially a system of mediation',[146] but the propertyless could *never* be mediated into Hegel's state, for they belonged, by definition, to no Corporation.

---

138 Hegel 1967, p. 277.
139 Hegel 1967, p. 150.
140 Hegel 1967, pp. 277–8.
141 Hegel 1967, p. 152.
142 Hegel 1967, p. 151.
143 Marx 2009, p. 99; cf. p. 109.
144 Marx 2009, p. 103.
145 Marx 2009, p. 81.
146 Hegel 1967, p. 292.

Marx concluded that *immediate and direct democracy* must be the first true unity of the universal and the particular:

> In democracy, the constitution, the law, the state, so far as it is [a] *political constitution*, is itself only a self-determination of the people, and a determinate content of the people ... all forms of state have democracy for their truth, and for that reason are false to the extent that they are not democracy.[147]

Immediate democracy meant that the political state must disappear as the institutionalised 'other' of the people. 'Democracy is *human existence*, while in the other political forms man has only *legal* existence'.[148] In the immediacy of democracy, the people *are* the state, and nothing more remains to be said. A 'true' state would have neither classes, corporations, nor a bureaucratic civil service – pretending to be what Hegel called the 'universal class' – only the direct expression of the people's will.[149]

In *On the Jewish Question*, also written in 1843, Marx claimed that all political institutions express an irreconcilable contradiction, a double existence that made nonsense both of Hegel's unity of objective spirit and of Kant's categorical imperative:

> Where the political state [i.e. the institutionalised state] has attained to its full development, man leads, not only in thought, in consciousness, but in *reality*, in *life*, a double existence ... He lives in the *political community*, where he regards himself as a *communal being*, and in *civil society*, where he acts simply as a *private individual*, treats other men as means, degrades himself to the role of mere means, and becomes the plaything of alien powers.[150]

In the schemes of both Hegel and Kant, Marx saw man as merely 'the imaginary member of an imaginary sovereignty, divested of his real, individual life, and infused with an unreal universality'.[151] The state was Hegel's abstract form of pure spirit, while civil society was the sphere of active egoism. The demand for universal suffrage pointed to transcendence of this contradiction. If every

---

147 Marx 2009, p. 31, my emphasis.
148 Marx 2009, p. 30.
149 Marx 2009, p. 65.
150 Marx, in Tucker (ed.) 1978, p. 34.
151 Ibid.

individual were in the state immediately, the state's otherness in relation to civil society would disappear. Marx summarised in his *Critique of Hegel's Philosophy of Right*:

> ... the vote is the immediate, the direct, the existing and not simply imagined relation of civil society to the political state ... In unrestricted suffrage, ... civil society has actually raised itself for the first time to an abstraction of itself, to political existence as its *true universal and essential existence*. But the full achievement of this abstraction is at once [without any institutional mediation] also the transcendence [*Aufhebung*] of the abstraction. In actually establishing its political existence as its true existence, civil society has simultaneously established its civil existence [the existence of private property owners] ... as inessential ... Within the abstract political state the reform of voting advances the dissolution [*Aufhebung*] of this political state, but also the dissolution of civil society.[152]

Universal suffrage points beyond the institutional state. It also points beyond private property because it abolishes the property qualification for political life. But if property is politically inessential – and if political existence is, indeed, the 'true, universal and essential existence', then it must also follow that property is inessential in all other respects. True human community must then lie beyond not only the institutional state but also private property. The philosophical critique of Hegel's state necessarily pointed to a critique of the property foundations of civil society itself.

The Encounter with Feuerbach: Anthropology and Alienation

To posit the immediate universality of political life was the beginning of a response to Hegel, but it failed to address the larger philosophical claims of Hegel's system. Marx put the manuscript of his *Critique of Hegel's Philosophy of Right* aside, and it remained unpublished until David Ryazanov rediscovered it in the 1920s. By the spring of 1844, Marx was attracted to the more ambitious anthropological critique of Hegel initiated by the philosopher Ludwig Feuerbach.

---

152   Marx 2009, p. 121, my emphasis.

In 1841 Feuerbach published a classic work of philosophical humanism with the title *The Essence of Christianity*. Describing himself as 'a natural philosopher in the domain of mind',[153] Feuerbach explained that God is merely the externalised projection of man's own inner consciousness of the infinite. The idea of God is a response to the reality of human limitation, which results in man, the subject, projecting upon God (the predicate and thought object), the noblest elements of his own nature. Man is the 'mystery of religion', who 'projects his being into objectivity, and then again makes himself an object to this projected image of himself thus converted into an object'.[154] Men create God and then humble themselves before their own fantasy. Religion was 'the dream of the human mind',[155] and the commandments of God were the expression of man's own need to fulfil his essential, yet frustrated, human potential.[156]

Feuerbach decisively put man at the centre of the universe in place of the Hegelian Idea. In his *Principles of the Philosophy of the Future* (1843), he declared that the task of the modern era had become 'the humanization of God' and the 'dissolution of theology into anthropology'.[157] Protestantism had replaced Catholic contemplation of God – that is, of God in Himself – with 'religious anthropology', or what God is 'for man'. But Hegel's philosophy had the reactionary effect of restoring theology. Hegel cast man as playing an active role in his own history, but in reality man turned out to be God's proxy. Thus Hegel ended with the state as objective Spirit, or 'the march of God in the world'.[158] 'The secret of Hegel's dialectic', Feuerbach declared, 'lies ultimately in this alone, that it negates theology through philosophy in order then to negate

---

153 Feuerbach 1855, p. 5.
154 Feuerbach 1855, pp. 52–3.
155 Feuerbach 1855, p. 10.
156 In his discussion of conscience, Feuerbach spoke in terms similar to those of Adam Smith: 'My fellow-man is my objective conscience; he makes my failings a reproach to me, even when he does not expressly mention them, he is my personified feeling of shame. The consciousness of the moral law, of right, of propriety, of truth itself, is indissolubly united with my consciousness of another than myself ... That which I think only according to the standard of my individuality is not binding on another; it can be conceived otherwise; it is an accidental, merely subjective view. But that which I think according to the standard of the species, I think as man in general only can think, and consequently as every individual must think if he thinks normally, in accordance with law, and therefore truly' (Feuerbach 1855, p. 209).
157 Feuerbach 1986, p. 5.
158 Hegel 1967, p. 279.

philosophy through theology ... the negation of the negation is again theology. At first everything is overthrown, but then everything is reinstated in its old place'.[159]

When Marx turned in the *1844 Manuscripts* from political philosophy to his first critique of economic life, the influence of Feuerbach was readily apparent. Feuerbach's account of man's self-objectification in the fantasy of God provided new insight for an anthropological critique of the relation between the worker and his product in the form of capital. Hegel had said that self-fulfilment begins through objectification and simultaneous appropriation: 'In his property a person exists for the first time as reason'.[160] Marx replied that the activity of production in bourgeois society was the living practice of *human alienation*. The propertyless worker objectified his labour, but the other – the capitalist – did the appropriating: '... if the product of labour is alienation, production itself must be active alienation – the alienation of activity and the activity of alienation'.[161] The propertyless worker does not appropriate nature for himself. Instead, he creates capital as an alien object. Hegel's account of alienation as self-determination was therefore a mockery of the worker's dehumanisation.

> ... the more the worker expends himself in work the more powerful becomes the world of objects which he creates in face of himself, the poorer he becomes in his inner life, and the less he belongs to himself. It is just the same as in religion. The more of himself man attributes to God the less he has left in himself. The worker puts his life into the object, and his life then belongs no longer to himself but to the object. The greater his activity, therefore, the less he possesses. What is embodied in the product of his labor is no longer his own. The greater this product is, therefore, the more he is diminished. The *alienation* of the worker in his product means not only that his labor becomes an object, assumes *an external* existence, but that it exists independently, *outside himself*, and alien to him, and that it stands opposed to him as an autonomous power. The life which he has given to the object sets itself against him as an alien and hostile force.[162]

Hegel had said that *community* is founded upon property. Marx responded that labour's creation of capital, as an alien object, necessarily means the

---

159 Feuerbach 1986, pp. 33–4. Marx makes the same point (see Fromm 1961, p. 184).
160 Hegel 1967, pp. 235–6.
161 Fromm 1961, p. 97.
162 Fromm 1961, p. 95.

estrangement of man from man. The master-slave relationship was therefore inherent in the process of capitalist production, with no prospect of mutual recognition:

> ... the relation of man to himself is first realized, objectified, through his relation to other men. If therefore he is related to the product of his labor, his objectified labor, as to an *alien*, hostile, powerful and independent object, he is related in such a way that another alien, hostile, powerful and independent man is the lord of this object. If he is related to his own activity as to unfree activity, then he is related to it as activity in the service, and under the domination, coercion and yoke, of another man.[163]

In Hegel's account of the master and slave, consciousness risks biological life to establish its own superiority. But in the real activity of production, the worker is even less than the master's slave. He is effectively an animal, labouring not to develop his body and mind but merely to survive and satisfy the most elementary biological needs of 'eating, drinking and procreating'. The animal, Marx said, 'is one with its life activity. It does not distinguish the activity from itself. It is *its activity*. But man makes his life activity itself an object of his will and consciousness'. In the state of dehumanisation, however, the opposite occurs. What is human – labour, which by nature is the conscious process of self-creation – is reduced to animal-like toil; and what is animal – the preoccupation with mere biological functions – appears to be human.[164]

Alienated from the object of his labour, from other human beings, from his essential human capacity for 'free, conscious activity',[165] and from nature itself, which has been carved into private properties, the worker must negate his own negation. Hegel said: 'A slave can have no duties; only a free man has them';[166] 'It is in the nature of the case that a slave has an absolute right to free himself ...'.[167] 'Communism', Marx concluded in the *Manuscripts*, 'is the phase of negation of the negation and is, consequently, for the next stage of historical development, a real and necessary factor in the emancipation and rehabilitation of man'.[168] Borrowing Kant's terminology, Marx wrote that communism must fulfil the

---

163   Fromm 1961, pp. 103–4.
164   Fromm 1961, p. 98.
165   Fromm 1961, p. 100.
166   Hegel 1967, p. 261.
167   Hegel 1967, p. 241.
168   Fromm 1961, p. 139.

'categorical imperative' to replace all relations 'in which man is a humiliated, enslaved, abandoned, contemptible being'.[169]

> Communism as a fully developed naturalism is humanism and as a fully-developed humanism is naturalism. It is the *definitive* resolution of the antagonism between man and nature, and between man and man. It is the true solution of the conflict between existence and essence, between objectification and self-affirmation, between freedom and necessity, between individual and species. It is the solution of the riddle of history and knows itself to be this solution.[170]

The problem at this point was that Marx had no clear idea of exactly what communism must entail. When Hegel looked for the beginning of community in his *Philosophy of Right*, he spoke of the family, with its subjective bond of love and shared property in the 'family capital'. In *The Essence of Christianity*, Feuerbach likewise wrote of love, starting with love between the sexes, as 'the reality of the species': '... in love, man declares himself unsatisfied in his individuality taken by itself, he postulates the existence of another as a need of the heart; he reckons another as part of his own being; he declares the life which he has through love to be the truly human life, corresponding to the idea of man, i.e., of the species'.[171] As in his critique of Hegel's political philosophy, Marx decided that the *natural immediacy* of the man-woman relationship represented the paradigm of human community. In natural love, the bourgeois institution of marriage – 'which is incontestably *a form of exclusive private property*'[172] – is replaced by spontaneous bonds of mutual affection, the consummated oneness of man and nature:

> The immediate, natural and necessary relation of human being to human being is ... the *relation* of *man* to *woman*. In this *natural* species relationship man's relation to nature is directly his relation to man, and his relation to man is directly his relation to nature, to his own *natural* function. Thus, in this relation is *sensuously revealed*, reduced to an observable *fact*, the extent to which human nature has become nature for man and to which nature has become human nature for him. From this relationship man's whole level of development can be assessed ... It also shows

---

169 Fromm 1961, p. 209.
170 Fromm 1961, p. 126.
171 Feuerbach 1885, p. 100.
172 Fromm 1961, p. 124.

> how far man's *needs* have become *human* needs, and consequently how far the other person, as a person, has become one of his needs, and to what extent he is in his individual existence at the same time a social being.[173]

The man-woman relation provided a model for mutual recognition in the bonds of shared consciousness, but what of the activity of production? How would the anthropological concept of universality relate to appropriation of the products of labour? At this point Marx provided no clear answer beyond the common socialist aim of collective control of the social means of production. A truly satisfactory answer could only come much later, in the *Grundrisse*, his notebooks for *Capital*. He did, however, indicate what communism *is not*, and he did so in a way completely consistent with his concern – deriving from the entire tradition that we have been considering – to treat rational beings, including oneself, as self-determining ends, and thus to reconcile objective with subjective freedom.

In the *Manuscripts* he warned against replacing the abstract ideal of the Hegelian state with the even more repugnant one-sidedness of a 'crude' and 'unreflective' communism that would regard immediate *physical* possession as 'the unique goal of life and existence'. Utopian communism, detached from the ideals of philosophy, would be the ultimate dystopia: it would 'destroy everything which is incapable of being possessed by everyone as private property', eliminate differences of talent and achievement by force, and embrace 'envy and levelling' as its constitutive principle. Crude communism would reduce everyone to a means in service of the community as *universal capitalist*. Marx summarised this way:

> How little this abolition of private property represents a genuine appropriation is shown by the abstract negation of the whole world of culture and civilization, and the regression to the *unnatural* simplicity of the poor and wantless [i.e. uncultured] individual who has not only not surpassed private property but has not yet even attained to it. The community is only a community of *work* and of *equality of wages* paid out by the communal capital, by the *community* as universal capitalist. The two sides of the relation are raised to a *supposed* universality; labor as a condition in which everyone is placed, and *capital* as the acknowledged universality and power of the community.

---

173 Fromm 1961, p. 125.

Unreflective communism was the illusion of the unenlightened. What Marx expected from communism was the opposite: universal enlightenment in economic circumstances that would make the ideals of philosophy real. The standpoint of Marx's humanism, as he remarked in his *Theses on Feuerbach* (1845), was '*human* society, or socialised humanity',[174] not the mere socialisation of things. A community that regarded itself exclusively in economic terms would merely universalise the tyranny of things at the expense of Hegel's ideal of subjective and objective freedom.

Reason and Natural Science: Making Philosophy Real

If reason is to prevail in the world, it must make philosophy real by transcending philosophy's own inclination to abstraction. In the *1844 Manuscripts* Marx began the transition from economic philosophy to economic science when he reappraised the significance of what Hegel had called the Understanding. This involved moving beyond Feuerbach's philosophical anthropology – with its focus on the *nature of man* – to emphasise the historical-material achievements of *natural science* and their effect upon the practical activity of human labour.[175]

In his *Logic*, Hegel had spoken of reason in terms of three dimensions: '(a) the Abstract side, or that of understanding; (b) the Dialectical, or that of negative reason; (c) the Speculative, or that of positive reason'.[176] 'Thought, as *Understanding*, sticks to the fixity of characters and their distinctness from one another: every such limited abstract it treats as having a subsistence and being of its own'.[177] 'In the Dialectical stage these finite characterizations or formulae supersede themselves, and pass into their opposites'.[178] 'The Speculative stage, or stage of Positive Reason, apprehends the unity of terms (propositions) in their opposition ...'.[179] In other words, understanding sees the 'parts'; dialectic sees the parts in relation one to the other; and positive reason comprehends

---

174 Marx, in Tucker (ed.) 1978, p. 145.
175 In his 'Theses on Feuerbach', Marx wrote: 'Feuerbach, not satisfied with *abstract thinking*, appeals to *sensuous contemplation*; but he does not conceive sensuousness as practical, human-sensuous activity' (Marx, in Tucker (ed.) 1978, p. 144).
176 Hegel 1975, p. 113.
177 Ibid.
178 Hegel 1975, p. 114.
179 Hegel 1975, p. 119.

the parts in the totality of the 'whole'. 'The truth is the whole ... reaching its completeness through the process of its own development'.[180]

In Hegel's view, positive reason clearly ranked far higher than mere understanding, which is pre-dialectical. Philosophy is the highest of human activities, for it deals with universal truth. Empirical science, in contrast, moves within the limitations of experience; its facts 'have the aspect of a vast conglomerate, one thing coming side by side with another ... devoid of all essential or necessary connection'.[181] When science produces laws and classifications of phenomena, they can then be received into philosophy. But insofar as science follows the *analytic* method, it

> can never do more than separate the given concrete objects into their abstract elements, and then consider these elements in their isolation ... Thus the chemist, e.g. places a piece of flesh in his retort, tortures it in many ways, and then informs us that it consists of nitrogen, carbon, hydrogen, etc. True, but these abstract matters have ceased to be flesh ... The object which is subjected to analysis is treated as a sort of onion from which one coat is peeled off after another.[182]

In the *1844 Manuscripts* Marx had a far higher regard for natural science. If, as anthropology emphasised, man is inescapably a part of nature, and if he survives by working upon nature, then natural sciences are not simply 'intellectual means' but also, in practical terms, 'a part of human life and activity'. Nature, from this perspective, is much more than 'property', or an embodiment of consciousness, as Hegel thought; it is the inorganic body of man '(1) as a direct means of life; and equally (2) as the material object and instrument of his life activity'.[183]

> To say that man *lives* from nature means that nature is his *body* with which he must remain in a continuous interchange in order not to die. The statement that the physical and mental life of man, and nature, are interdependent means simply that nature is interdependent with itself, for man is a part of nature.[184]

---

180 Hegel 2001, p. 17.
181 Hegel 1874, p. 15.
182 Hegel 1874, p. 316.
183 Fromm 1961, p. 99.
184 Fromm 1961, p. 100.

The anthropological point of view imparted an altogether new significance to tools and industry, for it is through them that man not only appropriates but also transforms the natural world to make it serve human ends. This meant that the natural sciences are not mere 'theory', as distinct from human practice; they are in fact a joining of theory and practice, or truly practical and transformative knowledge.[185] Whereas Hegel interpreted history as the emergence of Spirit in the world, already in the *1844 Manuscripts* Marx saw that the real history of the human species is the history of industry. 'Everyday material industry ... shows us, in the form of *sensuous useful objects*, in an alienated form, the *essential human faculties* transformed into objects'.[186] The history of industry is therefore the history of man's own self-creation, the creation of his own second nature, whereas Hegel's philosophy relegated the whole of economic activity to civil society, in which 'this great wealth of human activity' is dismissively reduced to the satisfaction of ' "need", "common need" '.[187]

The decisive turning point in Marx's movement from philosophical critique towards a dialectical science of *historical materialism* came in the *1844 Manuscripts* when he attributed the fundamental flaw of philosophy to its ignorance of, and indifference to, the natural sciences and their contribution to human industry.

> The *natural sciences* have developed a tremendous activity and have assembled an ever-growing mass of data. But philosophy has remained alien to these sciences just as they have remained alien to philosophy ... Historiography itself only takes natural science into account incidentally, regarding it as a factor making for enlightenment, for practical utility and for particular great discoveries. But natural science has penetrated all the more *practically* into human life through industry. It has transformed human life and prepared the emancipation of humanity even though its immediate effect was to accentuate the dehumanization of man. *Industry* is the actual historical relationship of nature, and thus of natural science, to man. If industry is conceived as the *exoteric* manifestation of the essential human *faculties*, the *human* essence of nature and the *natural* essence of man can also be understood. Natural science will then abandon its abstract materialist, or rather idealist, orientation, and will become the basis of a *human* science, just as it has already become –

---

185 In *Grundrisse* Marx expressed the same idea: science is 'ideal and at the same time practical wealth' (Marx 1993, p. 540).
186 Fromm 1961, p. 134.
187 Fromm 1961, p. 135.

> though in an alienated form – the basis of actual human life. One basis for life and another for science is *a priori* a falsehood. Nature, as it develops in human history, in the act of genesis of human society, is the *actual* nature of man; thus nature, as it develops through industry, though in an *alienated* form, is truly *anthropological* nature. Sense experience (see Feuerbach) must be the basis of all science ... History itself is a *real* part of *natural history*, of the development of nature into man. Natural science will one day incorporate the science of man, just as the science of man will incorporate natural science; there will be a *single* science.[188]

If the highest expression of human activity is the practical-theoretical activity of labour, informed by the growth of science, then Hegel's *Phenomenology of Spirit* – the logic of the appearance of Spirit in the phenomenal world – must be reinterpreted as a logic (or, as Marx would say, as the real historical laws) of the appearance and development of human labour. The problem with Hegel's *Phenomenology* was that Hegel regarded the question of human freedom as '*merely* a theoretical one': he found only 'an *abstract, logical* and *speculative* expression of the historical process, which is not yet the *real* history of man'. He treated wealth, state power, etc. as 'phases of *mind, entities of thought*', and thus produced what Marx called the 'the dialectic of pure thought'.[189] The philosophical dialectic of thought reflecting upon thought was a 'pure, *unceasing* revolving within itself',[190] whose only possible outcome was that the 'whole of nature ... reiterates ... the logical abstractions'.[191]

Despite all of Hegel's philosophical 'abstractions', however, Marx never doubted that his dialectical *method* was essentially correct. The hidden subtext of Hegel's theory of the movement of history was actually the movement of man himself in making both nature and his own history.

> The outstanding achievement of Hegel's *Phenomenology* – the dialectic of negativity as the moving and creating principle – is, first, that Hegel grasps the self-creation of man as a process, objectification as loss of the object, as alienation and transcendence of this alienation, and that he therefore grasps the nature of *labor*, and conceives objective man (true, because real man) as the result of his *own labor*.[192]

---

188   Fromm 1961, pp. 136–7.
189   Fromm 1961, p. 175.
190   Fromm 1961, p. 189.
191   Fromm 1961, p. 193.
192   Fromm 1961, pp. 175–6.

Since Hegel's method was essentially correct, and since 'industry as it *objectively* exists is an *open* book of the *human faculties*',[193] or the 'comprehended and conscious process of [man's] becoming',[194] Marx's road ahead now became clear: the way beyond philosophy was to re-read the 'open book' in order to determine the economic laws of history, which in turn would lead to a critical reassessment of the laws of political economy. The *1844 Manuscripts* constituted Marx's *philosophical* critique of economic life, which in turn issued in the *scientific* critique of political economy in the *Grundrisse* and *Capital*.

Marx's Scientific Critique of Political Economy

Marx moved from economic philosophy to scientific critique by way of his reinterpretation of Hegelian dialectic, which Hegel had left 'standing on its head. It must be inverted, in order to discover the rational kernel within the mystical shell'.[195] The mystical shell was the ontology of Hegel's *Logic*; the rational kernel was 'the self-creation of man as a process', which was implicit in Hegel's *Phenomenology*. The 'inversion' had to do with what is *abstract* and what is *concrete*. For Marx, as for Hegel, the concrete is ultimately the whole, the concrete universal as the self-mediated unity of subject and object. But whereas each dialectical advance, in Hegel's *Philosophy of Right*, represented the increasing 'concreteness' of Spirit in a widening consciousness of unity in diversity, in Marx's dialectic a different movement occurs. It is *value* that expands; the expanded reproduction of capital, as value, involves movement towards the concrete through a succession of economic categories, each of which is more universal than its predecessor (more internally diverse and thus more concrete) but also more abstract (in the sense of being further removed from the concrete human activity of social labour). The dialectical movement of value categories continues until an entire society of self-seeking capitals, *unconsciously mediated* through reified relations of production and exchange, ultimately leads to total negation and transcendence in communist community, where self-determining labour returns to itself in the concrete universal of a social plan determined by the associated producers. Of the articles that we have translated for this anthology, the most comprehensive in

---

193 Fromm 1961, p. 134.
194 Fromm 1961, p. 126.
195 Marx 1976, p. 103.

treating this dialectical movement of the forms of value is Isaak Rubin's 'The Dialectical Development of Categories in Marx's Economic System'.

Since the activity of social labour was central, rather than the Hegelian activity of thought, Marx began with the labour of individual commodity producers that must first be *abstracted* before it can ever be evaluated as 'socially necessary'. In pre-capitalist economies, individual labour was immediately a part of social labour. It was concrete because it was part of the whole. But in conditions of commodity production, the labour of each producer only becomes part of the total social labour when the product is equated as *exchange-value* with that of all other producers in terms of money, the universal measure of value and medium of exchange. Apart from this initial abstraction, the labour expended in production cannot possibly be determined as socially necessary. The contradiction here is that *society itself* plays no conscious role in determining what is, and what is not, socially necessary. That question is objectively answered by the 'law of value', which specifies that socially necessary labour, in the capitalist mode of production, is labour that creates profit for capital. The result is that the fate of the worker (and also of each individual capitalist) depends entirely upon the external force of the market. In the *Grundrisse* Marx wrote:

> ... the exchange relation establishes itself as a power external to and independent of the producers. What originally appeared as a means to promote production [exchange through the division of labour] becomes a relation alien to the producers. As the producers become more dependent on exchange, exchange appears to become more independent of them ... Money does not create these antitheses and contradictions; it is, rather, the development of these contradictions and antitheses which creates the seemingly transcendental power of money.[196]

The real world of capitalism is the inverted opposite of Hegel's portrayal of ethical life in the state; it is one of commodity fetishism and reification – a world in which human relations are objectively mediated by the movement of things and the worker himself is a commodity, a thing produced for sale. Money is the reified objectification of the 'social bond' and the 'dead pledge of society'.[197] 'Circulation is the movement in which the general alienation appears as general appropriation and general appropriation as alienation'.[198]

---

196 Marx 1993, p. 146; see also pp. 469–70.
197 Marx 1993, p. 160.
198 Marx 1993, p. 196.

In the self-expansion of capital, the Hegelian right of property 'is inverted, to become, on the one side, the right [of capital] to appropriate alien labour, and, on the other, the duty of respecting the product of one's own labour, and one's own labour itself, as values belonging to others'.[199] The result is 'an *alien* social power',[200] presiding over a world in which the laws of the market operate 'behind the backs of the producers',[201] and *things* lay down the law to their *creators*. The very notion of self-determination appears to be an absurdity. In the first chapter of *Capital*, Marx elaborated upon the theme of alienation first set out in the *1844 Manuscripts*, showing how the 'commodity-form' inverts human relations into relations between things and drawing once again upon Feuerbach's anthropological insight into religion.

> It is nothing but the definite social relation between men themselves which assumes here ... the fantastic form of a relation between things. In order, therefore, to find an analogy we must take flight into the misty realm of religion. There the products of the human brain appear as autonomous figures endowed with a life of their own, which enter into relations both with each other and with the human race. So it is in the world of commodities with the products of men's hands. I call this the fetishism which attaches itself to the products of labour as soon as they are produced as commodities ... This fetishism of the world of commodities arises from the peculiar social character of the labour which produces them.[202]

Behind all of capitalism's contradictions, however, Marx also found – in a way that reminds us of Smith, Kant and Hegel – a hidden lawfulness that not only regulates the apparent anarchy of the market but also points beyond it to a rational economic plan. Capitalism is a moving system of contradictions, but 'the most extreme form of alienation ... is a necessary point of transition – and therefore already contains in *itself*, in a still only inverted form, turned on its head, the dissolution of all *limited presuppositions of production*, and moreover creates ... the full material conditions for the total, universal development of the productive forces of the individual'.[203]

---

199   Marx 1993, p. 458.
200   Marx 1993, pp. 196–7; see also pp. 469–70.
201   Marx 1976, p. 135.
202   Marx 1976, pp. 164–5.
203   Marx 1993, p. 515.

Since capital's sole ambition is profit, the concern of every capitalist is to increase the exploitation of workers. Marx first discussed the source of profit in *Wage-Labour and Capital* (1847). His explanation turned on the distinction between labour and all other commodities. When the latter are consumed (either directly or as fixed capital that gradually wears out) they lose their value, whereas the activity of labour not only reproduces the value of the wage that the worker receives but also a surplus in the form of profit.[204] In *Wage-Labour and Capital*, Marx distinguished the value components of commodity production in the analytical terms that would reappear throughout all his later works:

> The selling price of the commodities produced by the worker is divided, from the point of view of the capitalist, into three parts: first, the replacement of the price of the raw materials advanced by him, in addition to the replacement of the wear and tear of the tools, machines, and other instruments of labour ... [designated in *Capital* as 'c' for constant capital]; second, the replacement of the wages advanced ['v', for variable capital]; and third, the surplus left over, i.e., the profit of the capitalist ['s', for surplus value].[205]

Hegel had thought the parties to a contract always relate on the basis of equality: each simultaneously alienates and appropriates an identical sum of value.[206] Marx's analysis of the elements of value showed that the wage contract

---

204   Marx 2006, p. 31, my emphasis. In the *Grundrisse* and *Capital*, Marx refined the distinction by differentiating between *labour* and *labour power*. The latter represents the *quality* of human creative activity, which is sold to the capitalist and then, in the course of production, is transformed into a determinate quantity, the number of hours actually worked. See Marx 1976, pp. 270–80; see also Marx 1993, pp. 282 et seq. The English translation of *Wage-Labour and Capital* incorporates this distinction, but this resulted from an editorial change that Engels made in 1891 and that he explains in the introduction.
205   Marx 2006, p. 36.
206   In *The Philosophy of Right*, Hegel also spoke of commodity exchange in terms of a dialectic of value. Money, Hegel said, represents 'any and every thing' and makes all things commensurable (Hegel 1967, p. 59). 'Utility' (or use-value) was the qualitative and subjective aspect of value (Hegel 1967, p. 51), while the quantitative aspect (what Adam Smith called 'value in exchange') was measured by money, the universal, which has no utility in itself but 'counts as value alone' (Hegel 1967, pp. 62–3). Since Hegel thought of Nature as freely given, he concluded, as Marx did later, that what gives commodities their value must be *human labour*: 'Through work the raw material directly supplied by nature is specifically adapted to ... numerous ends .... Now this formative change *confers value on means and gives them their utility ... It is the product of human effort which man consumes*' (Hegel 1967,

is fundamentally different; it involves *formal* equality but its *content* is exploitation. Having distinguished these value components of each individual commodity – and thus of the social product as a whole – Marx could then examine the decisive quantitative relations that determine the system's overall movement: the rate of surplus value (s/v), the rate of profit (s/c+v) and the organic composition of capital (c/v).

In the rivalry of the market, every capitalist endeavours to increase his individual rate of profit by raising labour productivity, which generally involves adopting more advanced means of production relative to his competitors.[207] The result is that some capitalists survive and others perish. Each capital aspires to universalise itself as monopoly, but 'A universal capital, one without alien capitals confronting it ... is ... a non-thing'.[208] Competition points towards monopoly, but monopoly invites new competition, and competition then moves again in the direction of monopoly. In terms of aggregate outcome, the historical tendency is for one capitalist to strike down many,[209] a process that Marx characterised in terms of *the law of centralisation of existing capital and the concentration of new accumulation*.[210]

Capitalist production can never be rational because it can never meet the dialectical standard of concreteness, that is, the conscious unity of a self-determining subject. The inability to achieve *ex ante* coordination – or the inability to plan – also means that the system can never be in equilibrium.[211] 'In

---

p. 129, my emphasis). In Hegel's terms, there was no more injustice in the wage relation than in any other contractual exchange, since the worker is assumed to receive a wage equivalent to the value of his labour. With the theory of surplus value, Marx demonstrated that in capitalist production that outcome is impossible. The wage contract is always one of structured exploitation.

207 In the *Grundrisse*, Marx referred to 'the law of the rising productivity of labour time' (Marx 1993, p. 139).
208 Marx 1993, p. 421.
209 Marx 1976, p. 929.
210 Marx 1976, p. 777.
211 If equilibrium prevailed, all capitals would earn the same rate of profit and commodities would sell at their 'price of production' as distinct from fluctuating market prices. But the price of production is a conceptual norm about which market prices always fluctuate. Labour expenditure is the 'essence' of value that 'exists' as market prices: *'Price* therefore is distinguished from value ... because the latter appears as the law of motions which the former runs through. But the two are constantly different and never balance out, or balance only coincidentally or exceptionally. The price of a commodity constantly stands above or below the value of the commodity, and the value of a commodity exists only in this up-and-down movement of commodity prices. Supply and demand constantly

capitalist society ... where any kind of social rationality asserts itself only *post festum*, major disturbances can and must occur constantly'.[212] In the absence of rational foresight, Hegel's 'circle of necessity' repeats itself continuously in the expansions and crises of the market, the sort of movement that Hegel called a 'bad infinity' and which, for Marx, took the form of the capitalist business cycle.

Typically, a cyclical expansion raises wages at the expense of profit due to capital's increased demand for exploitable labour power.[213] Rising labour costs then help to precipitate the crisis, curtailing profits and deterring further investment until labour costs can be reduced through mass unemployment. The consequence is another fundamental law of capitalism's motion, 'a law of population peculiar to the capitalist mode of production',[214] which periodically renders part of the population 'relatively superfluous'. Hegel had seen the 'pauperised rabble' as an inexplicable affront to reason. Marx explained in *Capital* that the 'reserve army' of the unemployed is objectively necessary in order to restructure the market for labour power and thus resume the expanded reproduction of capital:

> ... a surplus population of workers is a necessary product of accumulation ... a condition for the existence of the capitalist mode of production. It forms a disposable industrial reserve army, which belongs to capital ... a mass of human material always ready for exploitation ... The path characteristically described by modern industry, which takes the form of a decennial cycle (interrupted by smaller oscillations) of periods of average activity, production at high pressure, crisis and stagnation, depends on the constant formation, the greater or less absorption, and the re-formation of the industrial reserve army or surplus population. In their turn, the varying phases of the industrial cycle recruit the surplus population, and become one of the most energetic agencies for its reproduction.[215]

---

determine the prices of commodities; [they] never balance, or only coincidentally ... labour time as the measure of value exists only as an ideal, it cannot serve as the matter of price-comparisons ... Price as distinct from value is necessarily money price' (Marx 1993, pp. 137–40).

212 Marx 1978, p. 390.
213 Recall that Adam Smith originally justified competitive capital accumulation in precisely these terms.
214 Marx 1976, pp. 783–4.
215 Marx 1976, pp. 784–5.

Capitalist crises involve commodities with obvious use-value losing their exchange-value and thereby becoming worthless (socially unnecessary) from the standpoint of capital. When commodity prices fall, due to cyclical unemployment and the consequent over-production in relation to demand, capitalists are compelled to reduce unit production costs in order to survive. Recovery requires the renovation of fixed capital in order to raise labour productivity and the rate of surplus value. The self-expansion of capital thus moves in another contradiction: a portion of the existing fixed capital, which has become technologically obsolescent, must be prematurely destroyed. Destruction of existing capital, both physically and through bankruptcy, is necessary in order to resume the accumulation of capital. 'Catastrophes, crises, etc. are the principal causes that compel such premature renewals of equipment on a broad social scale'.[216] 'A crisis is always the starting-point of a large volume of new investment', and compulsive replacement of machinery then provides the 'material basis for the next turnover cycle'.[217]

The renewal of capital investment, by increasing employment and creating new demand, causes prices to rise once more, beginning in the sectors that produce means of production. As employment recovers, rising prices spread outwards into the consumer-goods industries. But now the problem is that every individual capitalist, motivated by *today's* rise in prices, aspires to capture the entire *future* increase of expected social demand. When today's investments actually become operational, causing a steadily expanding stream of commodities to enter the market, the result turns out once more to be general over-production and disproportions between various branches of the economy. Today's prices can never be a rational guide to future production, but individual capitalists are incapable of making coherent investments that would anticipate the future on the basis of a social plan.[218] Capital moves from crisis to recovery, from recovery to over-production, and from over-production back to crisis.

Behind the surface of repeated cyclical crises, however, another contradiction, even more profound in its implications, is at work. Each recovery involves the advance of technology, but technological advance also tends to displace living labour and raise the 'organic composition of capital' (designated by the ratio c/v). The problem is that *only living labour can create surplus value*. Machinery and materials merely transfer their value to the commodity as costs

---

216 Marx 1976, p. 250.
217 Marx 1976, p. 264.
218 For a comprehensive commentary on the relation between prices and the reproduction of capital, see Maksakovsky 2004.

of production. 'Things' cannot be exploited to create surplus value. But if capitalism involves a long-run replacement of living labour with machinery, the result is another objective law that points to the ultimate transcendence of the capitalist mode of production; that is, the tendency for the social average rate of profit to fall.[219]

Through cyclical waves of technological advance, capitalism raises productivity and necessarily points beyond itself to the potential elimination of scarcity. At the same time, however, capitalism makes this outcome objectively impossible on its own terms. The greater is the potential for growth, the greater still are the obstacles. Capital 'frees' labour from toil, but the 'freedom' occurs in the form of labour displacement, dehumanisation and enforced cyclical unemployment. Marx summarised the consequences in Volume III of *Capital*:

> Here we have once again the characteristic barrier to capitalist production, and we see how this is in no way an absolute form for the development of the productive forces and the creation of wealth, but rather comes into conflict with it at a certain point in its development. One aspect of this conflict is presented by the periodic crises that arise when one or another section of the working population is made superfluous in its old employment. The barrier to capitalist production is the surplus time [i.e. enforced redundancy] of the workers. The absolute spare time that the society gains is immaterial to capitalist production. The development of productivity is only important to it in so far as it increases the surplus labour-time of the working class and ... not just ... the labour-time needed for material production in general; in this way it moves in a contradiction ... Capital shows itself more and more to be ... an alienated social power which has gained an autonomous position and confronts society as a thing, and as the power that the capitalist has through this thing ... [But] this development also contains the solution to this situation, in that it simultaneously raises the conditions of production into general, communal, social conditions.[220]

Capitalism reduces socially necessary labour time, which simultaneously curtails the capacity for extracting surplus value, and thus ultimately capitalism itself. This outcome is inevitable because particular capitals – each trying to

---

219 Theoretically, the increase in labour productivity might offset this tendency – were it not for the fact that the increased output could not be sold into a market that has experienced a relative decline of employment and thus of effective demand.

220 Marx 1992, pp. 372–3.

raise its particular rate of profit through higher labour productivity – contradict the fundamental need of the capitalist system to sustain the social rate of profit.

Communism: Self-Determination and Economy of Time

As a student of Hegel, Marx expected that long before capitalism collapsed of its own accord, revolutionary class consciousness would intervene as the spirit of revolution. The workers are reduced to things – commodities at the disposal of capital – but they are also *thinking things*.[221] When workers know themselves as a living contradiction, they will also know what must be done with capitalism: 'The coincidence of the changing of circumstances and of human activity can be conceived and rationally understood only as revolutionising practice'.[222]

But what follows the revolution? Marx tells us remarkably little about communist community. In the *Manuscripts* he indicated what communism must not be – a 'crude' community of labour and possession – but his only other comments on what might directly follow the revolution came in 'The Civil War in France' – his essay on the Paris Commune of 1871 – and in the 'Critique of the Gotha Program', which was adopted by the German Social Democratic Party in 1875. Both of these documents provoked widespread discussion at the time of the Russian Revolution, particularly following Lenin's famous essay in 1917 on 'The State and Revolution'. The early Bolsheviks hoped that the Soviet state might reproduce, on a far grander scale, the measures adopted nearly fifty years earlier in Paris: suppression of the standing army and its replacement by the armed people; election of all public officials, who would also be subject to recall when voters so chose; all public service to be done at workmen's wages; education that would be accessible to all, and so forth – all expressions of a 'good will' that was crushed by Stalinism.

Marx had no inhibition when it came to interpreting political events of his own time. He wrote countless such articles. But he also faced an obvious methodological constraint when it came to anticipating the future. In a society

---

221 This was the argument of the philosopher Georg Lukács in *History and Class Consciousness*: '… when the worker knows himself as a commodity his knowledge is practical. *That is to say, this knowledge brings about an objective structural change in the object of knowledge*'. When the worker knows himself, 'it becomes possible to recognise the fetish character of *every commodity* …' (Lukács 1968, p. 169).

222 Marx, in Tucker (ed.) 1978, p. 144.

beyond the contradictions of capitalism, there would be several possible variants of a future, one of which must be *made* through conscious human choice. Unless complete determinism prevails, a philosopher cannot undertake to predict what free people will do with their freedom, and Marx was a dialectician, not an abstract determinist. On the other hand, as a dialectician he could certainly assess the principal contradictions of the present and thereby come to some general conclusions as to how they might be transcended. In this respect, his most important insights are to be found in the *Grundrisse*.

First published in full in 1953, the *Grundrisse* abounds with references to the themes of alienation and reification that we have already encountered. Marx speaks of machinery that 'objectifies the scientific idea' and then becomes an 'animated monster', using the worker as its 'living isolated accessory'.[223] He says labour is deprived of skills when those same skills are transferred to 'the dead forces of nature'.[224] The machine 'possesses skill and strength in place of the worker'.[225] 'The accumulation of knowledge and of skill, of the general productive forces of the social brain, is ... absorbed into capital, as opposed to labour ...'.[226] Many more such comments could be cited.

It is worth noting that even Adam Smith had shared such concerns, worrying that machines would dehumanise and destroy the working class.[227] And Hegel, having read Smith, also warned in his unpublished manuscripts that machines dehumanise, deskill, and devalue labour at the same time as they create the prospect of alleviating toil.[228] Hegel said we deceive nature by harnessing its forces, but nature exacts its revenge by impoverishing human consciousness:

---

[223] Marx 1993, p. 470.
[224] Marx 1993, p. 587.
[225] Marx 1993, p. 693.
[226] Marx 1993, p. 694.
[227] Smith 1937, pp. 734–5. Speaking of the specialisation of labour in manufacturing, Smith wrote:
> 'The man whose whole life is spent in performing a few simple operations, of which the effects too are, perhaps, always the same, or very nearly the same, has no occasion to exert his understanding, or to exercise his invention in finding out expedients for removing difficulties which never occur. He naturally loses, therefore, the habit of such exertion, and generally becomes as stupid and ignorant as it is possible for a human creature to become ... His dexterity at his own particular trade seems, in this manner, to be acquired at the expense of his intellectual, social, and martial virtues. But in every improved and civilized society this is the state into which the labouring poor, that is, the great body of the people, must necessarily fall, unless government takes some pains to prevent it'.

[228] Hegel 1979, p. 117.

... this deceit that he practices against nature [mechanical appropriation that displaces skilled living labour] ... takes its revenge upon him; what he gains from nature, the more he subdues it, the lower he sinks himself. When he lets nature be worked over by a variety of machines, he does not cancel the necessity for his own laboring, but only postpones it, and makes it more distant from nature; ... the laboring that remains to man becomes itself *more machinelike*; man *diminishes* labor only for the whole, not for the single [laborer]; for him it is increased rather; for the more machinelike labor becomes, the less it is worth, and the more one must work in that mode.[229]

Marx would have found Hegel's remarks intriguing. In the *Grundrisse* he wrote that 'The principle of developed capital is to make special skill superfluous ... to transfer skill ... into the dead forces of nature'.[230] The difference, however, between Marx and Hegel, is that Hegel was anticipating the industrial revolution, whereas Marx saw enough of it to extrapolate its potential contribution to human emancipation. Capital, he wrote in the *Grundrisse*, 'reduces human labour, expenditure of energy, to a minimum. This will redound to the benefit of emancipated labour, and is the condition of its emancipation'.[231] With its thirst for profit, capital is compelled to replace living labour with the 'technological application of natural sciences', but since science and fixed capital cannot be 'an independent source of value, independent of labour time',[232] capital is also involved in a fatal contradiction that 'works towards its own dissolution as the force dominating production'.[233] Since the capitalist law of value measures

---

229   Hegel 1979, p. 246. In response to Adam Smith's example of rising productivity through division of labour in the pin factory, Hegel remarked: '... in the same ratio that the number [of pins] produced rises, the value of the labor falls; ... the labor becomes that much deader, it becomes machine work, the skill of the single laborer is infinitely limited, and the consciousness of the factory laborer is impoverished to the last extreme of dullness; ... the *coherence of the singular kind* of labor with the whole infinite mass of needs is quite unsurveyable, and a [matter of] *blind dependence*, so that some far-off operation often suddenly cuts off the labor of a whole class of men who were satisfying their needs by it, and makes it superfluous and useless ...' (Hegel 1979, p. 248).
230   Marx 1993, p. 587.
231   Marx 1993, p. 701.
232   Marx 1993, p. 702.
233   Marx 1993, p. 700. On p. 706 of the *Grundrisse* Marx writes: 'Capital itself is the moving contradiction [in] that it presses to reduce labour time to a minimum, while it posits labour time, on the other side, as sole measure and source of wealth ... On the one side

value in terms of labour expended, the gradual displacement of living labour necessarily negates the law of value.

> The *theft of alien labour time, on which the present wealth is based*, appears a miserable foundation in face of this new one, created by large-scale industry itself. As soon as labour in the direct form has ceased to be the great well-spring of wealth, labour time ceases and must cease to be its measure, and hence exchange value [must cease to be the measure] of use value. The *surplus labour of the mass* has ceased to be the condition for the development of general wealth, just as the *non-labour of the few*, for the development of the general powers of the human head. With that, production based on exchange value breaks down, and the direct, material production process is stripped of the form of penury and antithesis. The free development of individualities and ... the general reduction of the necessary labor of society to a minimum ... then corresponds to the artistic, scientific, etc. development of the individuals in the time set free, and with the means created, for all of them.[234]

In *Capital* and the *Grundrisse*, Marx formulated the question in terms of the 'realm of necessity' and the 'realm of freedom', which coexist in a dialectical unity at the same time as technology frames and alters their relationship. On the one hand, man is inextricably a part of nature and must work to satisfy natural needs; on the other hand, rising productivity creates the material basis for extending the realm of freedom. Movement from the former towards the latter involves the satisfaction of needs beyond those that are merely natural. The 'cultivation of all the qualities of the social human being' involves a 'constantly enriched system of need'. In a community beyond capitalism, citizens 'rich in qualities and relations', and 'cultured to a high degree', will 'take gratification in a many-sided way'. The 'social human being', in that case, will be 'the most total and universal ... social product'.[235] In Volume III of *Capital* Marx wrote:

---

then, it calls to life all the powers of science and of nature ... in order to make the creation of wealth independent (relatively) of the labour time employed in it. On the other side, it wants to use labour time as the measuring rod for the giant social forces thereby created, and to confine them within the limits required to maintain the already created value as value' (Marx 1993, p. 706).

234   Marx 1993, pp. 705–6.
235   Marx 1993, p. 409.

> The real wealth of society and the possibility of a constant expansion of its reproduction process does not depend on the length of surplus labour but rather on its productivity and on the more or less plentiful conditions of production in which it is performed. The realm of freedom really begins only where labour determined by necessity and external expediency ends; it lies by its very nature beyond the sphere of material production proper. Just as the savage must wrestle with nature to satisfy his needs, to maintain and reproduce his life, so must civilized man, and he must do so in all forms of society and under all possible modes of production. This realm of natural necessity expands with his development, because his needs do too; but the productive forces to satisfy these expand at the same time. Freedom, in this sphere, can consist only in this, that socialized man, the associated producers, govern the human metabolism with nature in a rational way, bringing it under their collective control instead of being dominated by it as a blind power; accomplishing it with the least expenditure of energy and in conditions most worthy and appropriate for their human nature. But this always remains a realm of necessity. The true realm of freedom, the development of human powers as an end in itself, begins beyond it, though it can only flourish with this realm of necessity as its basis. The reduction of the working day is the basic prerequisite.[236]

Capitalism 'frees' workers from labour, but it does so in the dehumanising form of *enforced unemployment*. Marx anticipated that communist community will replace externally imposed idleness with a working day deliberately shortened for all. A shorter working day will transform surplus labour time (in capitalist terms) into disposable time during which citizens might work out of themselves their own creative powers. The highest end, the end in itself, will then be self-development of the social individual. Communism will transcend capitalism by harnessing technological forces of production to enable 'the absolute working out of creative potentialities ... which makes ... the development of all human powers as such the end in itself'.[237]

Recognising that capitalism initially deskills labour, Marx saw that the advance of technology also presupposes reskilling. An unskilled worker cannot be the master of modern machinery. With the continuing and even accelerated development of scientific means of production, the rigid division of labour

---

236 Marx 1992, pp. 958–9.
237 Marx 1993, p. 488.

must ultimately give way to development of multiple talents and 'the universal development of the individual' – 'Not an ideal or imagined universality, but the universality of his real and ideal relations'.[238] Marx expected that universal workers will be capable of doing many things at many different times. Labour will acquire an altogether 'new use-value, the development of a constantly expanding system of different kinds of labour ... to which a constantly expanding and constantly enriched system of needs corresponds'.[239] The capitalist division of labour will be replaced by a flexibly planned 'organization of labour'.[240] If the essential human character is the capacity for 'free, conscious activity', as Marx said in the *1844 Manuscripts*, then human 'existence' must finally conform with human 'essence':

> Free time – which is both idle time and time for higher activity – has naturally transformed its possessor into a different subject, and he then enters into the direct production process as this different subject. This process is then both discipline, as regards the human being in the process of becoming; and, at the same time, practice [*Ausübung*], experimental science, materially creative and objectifying science, as regards the human being who has become, in whose head exists the accumulated knowledge of society.[241]

Knowledge, objectified in sophisticated means of production,[242] means that 'Labour no longer appears so much to be included within the production process; rather, the human being comes to relate more as watchman and regulator of the production process itself ... He steps to the side of the production process instead of being its chief actor'.[243] In a community where the realm of physical

---

238   Marx 1993, p. 542.
239   Marx 1993, p. 409.
240   Marx 1993, p. 172.
241   Marx 1993, p. 712.
242   'Nature builds no machines, no locomotives, railways, electric telegraphs, self-acting mules, etc. These are products of human industry ... They are *organs of the human brain, created by the human hand*; the power of knowledge, objectified. The development of fixed capital indicates to what degree social knowledge has become a *direct force of production*, and to what degree, hence, the conditions of the process of social life itself have come under the control of the general intellect and been transformed in accordance with it' (Marx 1993, p. 706).
243   Marx 1993, p. 705. When machines give way to 'an automatic system of machines', Marx says the worker 'supervises it and guards it against interruptions' (Marx 1993, p. 692).

necessity contracts, the need to invest in things will also diminish, creating the increasing opportunity to invest in the creative potential of human beings:

> Real economy – saving – consists of the saving of labour time ... but this saving [is] identical with development of the productive force[s] ... The saving of labour time [is] equal to an increase of free time, i.e. time for the full development of the individual, which in turn reacts back upon the productive power of labour as itself the greatest productive power. From the standpoint of the direct production process it can be regarded as the production of *fixed capital*, this fixed capital being man himself.[244]

Hegel said the consciousness that bonds society is shared ethical knowledge, articulated in the laws of the state. In the *Grundrisse* Marx placed far greater emphasis upon scientific knowledge and 'the law of the rising productivity of labour time',[245] presupposing that humans will recognise the inherent dignity of other reasoning beings when capital no longer reduces workers to things. Hegel regarded the laws of the state as 'our' laws, on the supposition that all are mediated into political life through representation in the Estates. For Marx, the analogue of Hegel's laws would be 'our' plan – not a plan that happens to us, externally imposed by a state authority, but one that might emerge from workers' associations that would be directly involved in the planning process.[246] In the *1844 Manuscripts* Marx had looked for a way beyond capitalism by way of immediacy of political life and human relations. In the *Grundrisse* he saw that

---

244 Marx 1993, pp. 711–12. On p. 708 Marx writes that development of fixed capital is '... instrumental in creating the means of social disposable time, in order to reduce labour time for the whole of society to a diminishing minimum, and thus to free everyone's time for their own development. But its tendency [is] always, on the one side, *to create disposable time, on the other, to convert it into surplus labour*. If it succeeds too well at the first, then it suffers from surplus production ... because *no surplus labour can be realized by capital*. The more this contradiction develops, the more does it become evident that ... the mass of workers must themselves appropriate their own surplus labour. Once they have done so, and *disposable time* thereby ceases to have an *antithetical* existence – then, on one side, necessary labour time will be measured by the needs of the social individual, and, on the other, the development of the power of social production will grow so rapidly that ... *disposable time* will grow for all. For real wealth is the developed productive power of all individuals. The measure of wealth is then not any longer, in any way, labour time, but rather disposable time' (Marx 1993, p. 708).

245 Marx 1993, p. 139.

246 Among Soviet Marxists, the writer who saw most clearly the possible similarity between Hegelian Corporations and worker's trade unions was Leon Trotsky. See Day 1987 and 1988.

'Mediation must, of course, take place'.[247] The purpose of a socially determined plan would be to mediate the activity of all in the pursuit of common ends.

Marx did not presume to tell future generations exactly how to plan, but he was quite certain of what a rational plan must achieve. Whereas capitalism counts labour time as 'value', in a community beyond capitalism the purpose of a plan will be to reduce labour time to a minimum. The most 'valuable' product will not be the one incorporating the most labour – as measured by the capitalist 'law of value' – but rather the one involving the least labour. Real wealth will be non-labour time, and to maximise non-labour time will be the paramount law of planning:

> Economy of time, to this all economy ultimately reduces itself ... Thus, economy of time, along with the planned distribution of labour time among the various branches of production, remains the first economic law on the basis of communal production. It becomes law, there, to an even higher degree. However, this is essentially different from a measurement of exchange values (labour or products) by labour time.[248]

If the social plan replaces the laws of Hegel's state, and if, as Kant said, we lay down the law of the plan (the economy of time) to ourselves, then communist community must finally comply with the philosophical requirements of Kant's ethical commonwealth and kingdom of ends; that is, a social plan that will, as Kant put it, 'conceive all ends combined in a systematic whole'. The activity of planning will then become the universal-practical activity of social reason. The plan will replace 'conscience', for we shall now 'know together' in a way that neither John Calvin nor Adam Smith could possibly conceive. It will also replace Hegel's Absolute Spirit – the thought of thought as creator of a world – when an emancipated human community creates its own world. The ideals of philosophy will finally be realised when Hegel's 'circle of necessity' issues in a fully human community of rational self-determination. Communism will not merely repudiate capitalism; it will transcend it by incorporating the powers of science, first harnessed by capital, to accomplish a future that capitalism objectively anticipates but can never realise.

---

247 Marx 1993, p. 171.
248 Marx 1993, p. 173.

DOCUMENT 1

Karl Marx's Point of View in his Political-Economic Critique: A Review of Karl Marx, *Capital: A Critique of Political Economy* (1872)

*Illarion Ignat'evich Kaufman**

Source: I.-Kn, 'Kapital. Kritika politicheskoi ekonomii', *Vestnik Evropy*, No. 5, May 1872, pp. 427–37.

Introduction by the Editors

We begin this anthology with Illarion I. Kaufman's review of the first Russian-language edition of Volume I of *Capital*, which appeared in 1872. The following year, writing the preface to the second edition of *Capital*, Marx quoted Kaufman's review at considerable length, commenting that the author 'pictures what he takes to be my own actual method, in a striking and, as far as concerns my own application of it, generous way'.[1]

Kaufman wrote approvingly of Marx's emphasis upon the primacy of material production in determining the movement of history and its reflection in forms of consciousness. But what he took to be Marx's method was not completely accurate. He thought Marx's distinction lay in rejecting the notion of universally valid economic laws in favour of a study of political economy by analogy with sciences such as physiology or biology. What Kaufman did not understand, with his allusion to an evolutionary process, was Marx's appropriation of the Hegelian dialectic. It seemed to him that Marx's 'external form of presentation' was dialectical 'in the bad sense of the word', yet behind the idealist veneer lay a truly scientific analysis of *factual* material. Marx's real achievement was to allow the facts to speak for themselves, in terms of objective economic laws, as if holding a perfect mirror to economic history. He did not superimpose – upon his historical research at least – any *a priori* 'criterion' of

---

* I.I. Kaufman (1848–1916) was Professor of Political Economy at the University of St. Petersburg. He published numerous works on questions of currency, loans and state debt.
1 Marx 1976, p. 100.

factual selection. Instead, Kaufman wrote: 'he does not even consider the question of what will be his criterion in the project he is undertaking. He believes this question will provide its own answer if the investigation is scientific'.

Kaufman's comments puzzled Marx. How, he wondered, could Kaufman find 'my method of inquiry severely realistic, but my method of presentation, unfortunately, German-dialectical'?[2] What the reviewer missed was Marx's conviction that the facts themselves develop through dialectical contradictions, so that what may seem to be an *a priori* conceptual packaging was really the objective movement of history. Thus, when Kaufman summarised Marx's work so sympathetically, Marx commented with obvious frustration: 'what else is he depicting but the dialectical method?'[3] The difficulty was that Kaufman knew Marx's published work, but only Marx knew what he had written in his unpublished manuscripts concerning 'The Method of Political Economy'.[4]

In his notes on method, Marx began by pointing out that when economists undertook, for example, to study 'a given country', they typically began with aspects of the 'whole social process of production'. To begin with the whole, however, treating it as some sort of self-evident fact, would be misleading. The whole was an 'abstraction' if one disregarded the parts 'of which it is composed'. Population was an abstraction if taken apart from social classes; social classes were abstractions if separated from 'the factors on which they depend, e.g. wage-labour, capital and so on', which in turn could not be separated from 'exchange, division of labour, prices, etc.'. 'A very vague notion of a complex whole' could only be made concrete by analysing the parts that constituted it, and then by making 'the journey again in the opposite direction'. In other words, the method of political economy involved *analytical* pursuit of the facts, followed by their *conceptual reconstruction* in logical form. 'The concrete concept' of the whole, Marx noted, 'is concrete because it is a synthesis of many definitions, thus representing the unity of diverse aspects'.[5]

The problem was that *conceptually* re-assembling the facts may suggest – as Marx thought it did to Hegel – that the concepts themselves actually *constitute* the world rather than reflecting it. In this connection Marx wrote: 'The concrete, regarded as a conceptual totality, as a mental fact, is indeed a product of thinking, of comprehension, but it is by no means a product of the idea which

---

2   Ibid.
3   Marx 1976, p. 102.
4   See Marx 1970, pp. 188–217. These notes were first published in *Die Neue Zeit* in 1903.
5   Marx 1970, pp. 205–6.

evolves spontaneously ...'.⁶ The conceptual totality results from mind's 'assimilation and transformation of perceptions and images into concepts', whose movement reflects the material of history in terms of successive forms of production and exchange. In other words, science separates significant facts from meaningless data by *logically* reconstructing history in order to grasp it *concretely* – 'as a concrete mental category', or a 'whole' that ceases to be abstract when it exists, and is comprehended objectively, through its 'parts'. The facts do not speak for themselves. If they did, history would be incoherent and meaningless. Thus, Kaufman understood and appreciated Marx's scientific conclusions, but he did not see that Marx arrived at them, and could only do so, through his materialist reinterpretation of the Hegelian dialectic.

Immediately following his long quotation from Kaufman in the preface to the second edition of *Capital*, Marx hoped to clarify these methodological issues with a brief but famous passage:

> Of course the method of presentation must differ in form from that of inquiry. The latter has to appropriate the material in detail, to *analyse* its different forms of development and to track down their inner connection. Only after this work has been done can the *real movement* be appropriately presented. If this is done successfully, if the life of the subject-matter is now *reflected back in the ideas*, then it may *appear* as if we have before us an *a priori* construction.
>
> My dialectical method is, in its foundations, not only different from the Hegelian, but exactly opposite to it. For Hegel, the process of thinking, which he even transforms into an independent subject, under the name of 'the Idea', is the creator of the real world, and the real world is only the external appearance of the idea. With me the reverse is true: the ideal is nothing but the material world reflected in the mind of man, and translated into forms of thought.⁷

Marx appropriated from Hegel's *Logic* and other writings the dialectical movement of concepts (or categories). He regarded concepts – not imposed *a priori* but discovered through historical analysis – as forms of thought reflecting the real world. What he denied was Hegel's conviction that the real world *begins with and is created by the movement of thought*. His two short paragraphs cited above provide both the context and the theme of many of the documents that

---

6   Marx 1970, p. 207.
7   Marx 1976, p. 102, my emphasis.

we include in this volume. Later Marxists frequently struggled with the same interpretive issues as Kaufman did in 1872, culminating in the study of Marxist political economy, in the works of Isaak Il'ich Rubin, as a 'dialectical development of categories'.

∴

Karl Marx's Point of View in his Political-Economic Critique: A Review of Karl Marx, *Capital: A Critique of Political Economy*

In 1859 Karl Marx published a short book with the title *A Contribution to the Critique of Political Economy*. The book was to serve as the beginning of a larger study of the same subject. Marx's illness interfered, however, and it was only after an eight-year interruption that he was able, in the autumn of 1871, to release the completed first volume of his broadly conceived work. Marx's goal is a critical analysis of the economic foundations of bourgeois – or, as he puts it, capitalist – society. But he is not content with the economic literature concerning these foundations. He undertakes his own investigation of the capitalist order of economic life, seeks out its foundations and, having found them, subjects them to his own critique. With a mass of notes showing enormous erudition, Marx critically follows his predecessors in examining the laws of the modern economic system, subjecting them to ruthless scrutiny and, in passing, bestowing upon them [his predecessors] witty and scathing epithets that are occasionally crude and undeserved. Thus Marx's work has three objectives: first, it provides new and independent conclusions that the author reaches by investigating questions that have not previously been addressed; second, it provides a systematic critique of the principal foundations of the modern economic system; third, and finally, it provides an enormous body of historical-literary and cultural-historical information that aptly characterises the development of capitalism.

In a book whose main content is critique, a paramount question concerns the viewpoint from which the undertaking begins. In most cases the initial views, which provide the basis for the critique, include their own significant share of arbitrariness and preconceptions. If the critique has ideas and beliefs as its subject matter, then the guarantee of its scientific character must be precise methods of re-examination. But what is to be done when it is a matter of criticising not the ideas of one or another scholar but rather the facts themselves, which are the source of the ideas? In such a case, where can one find criteria for determining what is normal and what is pathological? This question is sometimes answered by saying that the needs of man can be the criterion: what must be recognised as normal, according to this view, is what accords with human needs, while that which contradicts them is abnormal. But in that case, one has to ask: What is to be done if the critique aims to deal with the needs themselves?

It would appear, judging by the external form of his presentation, that Marx is the most idealist of philosophers, and indeed in the German, i.e. the bad sense of the word. But in point of fact he is infinitely more realistic than all of his predecessors in the business of economic criticism, and that is why he does not even consider the question of what will be his criterion in the project he is undertaking. He believes this question will provide its own answer if the investigation is scientific. Only one thing is important to him: to find the *law* behind the kinds of phenomena that he is concerned to investigate. And what concerns him is not a single law, one that governs phenomena while they have a certain form and relationship that can presently be observed. Most important is the law of their *changeability*, of their development, i.e. of the transition from one form to another, from one pattern of relationships to another. Once he has discovered this law, he examines in detail the consequences through which the law manifests itself in social life. These consequences, as they emerge from their predecessors, turn out to have the peculiarity that, for the mass of people, they are desirable and represent progress. In that case, the critique is not arbitrary in its analysis but involves a scientific comparison of the preceding and ensuing stages of development and a simple enumeration and statement of the facts in which these stages of development are expressed.

Accordingly, Marx is concerned only with one thing: to show, with precise scientific research, the necessity of certain definite types of social relations and, so far as possible, to give a precise statement of the facts that are his starting points and his basis. It is quite enough for him if, having demonstrated the necessity of the modern order, he has also shown the necessity of another order towards which a transition will inevitably occur, whether or not one thinks about it or is conscious of it. Marx regards the social movement as a natural-historical process, governed by laws that are not only independent of human will, consciousness and intentions, but rather themselves determine human will, consciousness and intentions.

Let us listen to what Marx himself has to say on how his point of view developed. Here are his words from the preface of the short book from 1859 that we previously mentioned:

> The first work which I undertook to dispel the doubts assailing me was a critical re-examination of the Hegelian philosophy of law ... My inquiry

led me to the conclusion that neither legal relations nor political forms could be comprehended whether by themselves or on the basis of a so-called general development of the human mind, but that on the contrary they originate in the material conditions of life, the totality of which Hegel, following the example of English and French thinkers of the eighteenth century, embraces within the term 'civil society'; that the anatomy of this civil society, however, has to be sought in political economy ... The general conclusion at which I arrived ... can be summarised as follows. In the social production of their existence, men inevitably enter into definite relations, which are independent of their will, namely relations of production appropriate to a given stage in the development of their material forces of production. The totality of these relations of production constitutes the economic structure of society, the real foundation, on which arises a legal and political superstructure and to which correspond definite forms of social consciousness. The mode of production of material life conditions the general process of social, political and intellectual life. It is not the consciousness of men that determines their existence, but their social existence that determines their consciousness. At a certain stage of development, the material productive forces of society come into conflict with the existing relations of production or – this merely expresses the same thing in legal terms – with the property relations within the framework of which they have operated hitherto. From forms of development of the productive forces these relations turn into their fetters. Then begins an era of social revolution. The changes in the economic foundation lead sooner or later to the transformation of the whole immense superstructure. In studying such transformations it is always necessary to distinguish between the material transformation of the economic conditions of production, which can be determined with the precision of natural science, and the legal, political, religious, artistic or philosophic – in short, ideological forms in which men become conscious of this conflict and fight it out. Just as one does not judge an individual by what he thinks about himself, so one cannot judge such a period of transformation by its consciousness, but, on the contrary, this consciousness must be explained from the contradictions of material life, from the conflict existing between the social forces of production and the relations of production. No social order is ever destroyed before all the productive forces for which it is sufficient have been developed, and new superior relations of production never replace older ones before the material conditions for their existence have matured within the framework of the old society. Mankind thus inevitably sets itself only such tasks as it is able to solve, since closer examination will always show that the problem itself arises only when the material conditions for its solution are already present or at least in the course of formation. In broad outline, the Asiatic, ancient, feudal and modern bourgeois modes of production may be designated as epochs marking progress in the economic development of society. The bourgeois mode of production is the last antagonistic form of the social process of production – antagonistic not in the sense of individual antagonism but of an antagonism that emanates from the individuals' social conditions of existence – but the productive forces developing within bourgeois society create also the material conditions for a solution of this antagonism.[8]

For Marx, therefore, the fundamental cause that is mainly responsible for conditioning the phenomena of economic life is found in the forces of production that operate in the economic world. Development of these forces is for him a natural-historical phenomenon that he traces with the aim mainly of capturing the forms that it first assumes and then leaves behind in different periods. He regards the increase of productivity as an almost mechanical fact, at least as mechanical as any physical growth. Consciousness only reflects this growth and its consequences, which occur for the reason mentioned and are independent of consciousness. The change in the relation of man to nature, which is the main content of productivity, conditions changes in the economic relations between people; these changes, in turn, bring with them change in the juridical, political and daily relations of people with each other. When these changes have actually occurred in life itself – or insofar as they are occurring in life and in fact – human consciousness gradually absorbs them and reflects them, so that the conscious man becomes accustomed to them and then seeks to express them in words, images, customs and law.

If the conscious element in cultural history plays such a subordinate role, then it is understandable that criticism, whose subject matter is culture itself, will be even less able to base itself upon some form or result of consciousness. That is to say, only external phenomena, not ideas, can serve as the starting point. A critique will consist of comparing, compiling and collating a fact not with an idea but with another fact. All that matters is that the two facts be investigated as thoroughly as possible and that they actually represent different stages of development; and, most importantly, that an equally thorough invest-

---

8   [Kaufman's translation of the preface differs in minor details from the one given in Marx 1970, pp. 20–1, which we follow here].

igation be made of the shapes, sequence and connections within which these stages of development appear.

We think it appropriate to characterise Marx's general point of view in order to help eliminate any misunderstanding that might arise for the reader who is becoming familiar with Marx for the first time by way of his book, which has now appeared in the Russian language. In the first place, he does not discuss his fundamental points of view in this book. Secondly, he is frequently quite abusive in his treatment of just about everyone. Thus he sees Comte as 'up to his knees in Catholicism', and Comte's positive system as merely a disciple's exercise, a pallid imitation of Hegel's Encyclopaedia, of no interest except for a history of the development of French philosophical views. Yet one cannot conclude from this that Marx is opposed to what we call a realist worldview. Our earlier presentation of his views is enough to convince one of that. He can in no sense be called an idealist. Finally, a Russian reader might be misled on this account by Marx's method of exposition (as distinct from his research). His exposition is dialectical, which ostensibly follows strictly from thought alone but in fact must always return to phenomena. It is precisely when Marx presents and discusses the facts that he is most difficult to read. To a Russian reader, who may be unfamiliar with the German art of developing ideas, he must be translated from the outset into a more comprehensible language in order to be understood.

The very character of his fundamental viewpoints obliges Marx to assign a very important place in his work to the facts. In this respect, his work surpasses any systematic studies that have appeared in the past 25 years, including both socialist literature and the literature coming from economists in the narrow sense of the word. In terms of dogma, Marx's book can be compared to Proudhon's *System of Economic Contradictions*. In terms of his wealth of historical material and enormous erudition, Marx might be compared to Roscher,[9] yet he surpasses him in force and depth of analysis and in comprehension of the factual material that he collects. The order in which Marx initially planned to outline the bourgeois system of economic life was the following: capital, landed property, hired labour; the state, foreign trade, and the world market. Under the first three rubrics, he wanted to investigate the economic conditions of life for the three large classes into which bourgeois society is divided.[10] Today he has somewhat modified that system. The entire project is to involve three

---

9 [The reference is to Wilhelm Georg Friedrich Roscher (1817–94), often regarded as founder of the German historical school of political economy].
10 [See the preface to Marx 1970, p. 19].

volumes. His present work appears with the general heading *Capital*. In the first volume he presents the foundations of the capitalist system of production (Book I); the second volume will deal with the capitalist system of circulation (Book II) and the general foundations of the entire capitalist economy (Book III); and a third volume will be devoted to the historical development of ideas concerning capital and the forms based upon it.[11] Accordingly, the whole of contemporary economic theory is to be included in the theory of capital. This idea is closely connected with Marx's general worldview, which we outlined previously. Since capital is presently the dominant phenomenon of real life; since it now represents the principal and practically the sole source of wealth and prosperity; since it is the starting point and the destination, the central point of all other economic processes; and since every economic phenomenon today only has practical and vital significance insofar as from one side or the other, either positively or negatively, it involves capital – it is perfectly understandable that a theory that aims to comprehend the latter must embrace the whole of modern economic life, including its causes and consequences.

It might occur to another reader to ask: What sort of science is this, in the strict sense of the word, when it intends from the outset not to investigate the general laws that regulate a given order of phenomena but rather to explain only a certain portion of the facts of this order? After all, that is not science but only a practical appendage to it, the purpose being to apply existing scientific results in order to explain phenomena that are not understood by the general public. Are not the general laws of economic life one and the same, whether they are applied to the present or to the past? But that is precisely where Marx disagrees. For him no such universal laws exist. One must conclude from his work that a direct investigation of the economic phenomena belonging to different historical stages of economic development led him to deny the existence of any economic laws common to all stages. In his opinion, to the contrary, every major historical period has its own laws, which govern life only so long as that period lasts. And just as soon as it passes through a given period of development, leaves one stage behind and enters into another, it begins to be governed by different laws. In a word, economic life, from this perspective, turns out to be a phenomenon perfectly analogous to what we observe in other orders of biological phenomena that we discuss in terms of a history of development.

---

11 [This is the project that Marx outlined in the original preface to Volume I of *Capital*. The projected third volume eventually appeared as *Theories of Surplus-Value*, edited by Karl Kautsky and frequently discussed by various authors in this anthology].

The lower organisms, while they remain at that level, are subject to their laws of structure, growth, nourishment, etc. When we turn to organisms at ensuing stages of development, we encounter such extensive anatomical refinements and physiological facts that quantitative difference becomes qualitative, with new qualities also entailing new laws. Observation of economic life reveals exactly the same thing. Close analysis of the internal structure and properties of actual phenomena has time and again persuaded numerous researchers, ever since the forties, of the error in the view of earlier economists, who regarded the nature of economic law as being identical to the laws of physics and chemistry. Analysis has led them, to the contrary, to conclude that if an analogy is to be made, it is between social laws and the laws of biology. In social life, as in physiological life, the history of development, i.e. the changeability and perfection of forms, represents the most distinguishing characteristic of phenomena. A direct and more penetrating analysis of phenomena has shown that social organisms differ one from the other no less profoundly than do botanical and zoological ones. The social organism of Asiatic despotism; the organism that could be observed among classical peoples; the organism represented by feudal society; and finally, the organism of modern capitalist society – all of them differ one from the other such that any laws, based upon observing features common to all of them, would not explain their most interesting features. One and the same phenomenon, because of differences in the structure of these organisms, of their diverse organs, and of the conditions within which the organs must function, etc., can therefore be subject to completely different laws according to the different stages of development that different social organisms represent. For example, Marx refuses to recognise a law of population growth that is one and the same, always and everywhere, for all times and all places. He claims, on the contrary, that every stage of development has its own law of reproduction. He does not reject the Malthusian law on these grounds, but he does strictly define the limits within which it retains its force, i.e. the conditions in which the phenomena governed by it occur. What happens in economic life depends upon the degree of productivity of the economic forces, i.e. their capacity to produce one consequence or another. With differences in productivity, the consequences will also differ along with the laws that govern them.

Thus, in undertaking to examine and explain the capitalist economic order, Marx formulated in strictly scientific terms the objective that a precise investigation of economic life might have. A study that has in view neither the interests of archaeology nor those of a purely contemplative love of wisdom can focus only upon real life itself. However, such a study is far from having merely a popularising significance. Its scientific purpose is to reveal the particular laws that govern the emergence, existence, development and death of a given social organism and its replacement by another, higher one. And that is the genuine value of Marx's book.

It is obvious that, as a purely scientific study, the book presupposes that the reader knows not only how to receive unfamiliar ideas but also how to follow them critically' throughout the entire research that gives rise to them. In this regard, as we have already noted, the work by Marx presents greater difficulties than those from other socialists. He presupposes a well-prepared reader, one who is familiar not just with the history of culture in general and of economic culture in particular, but, more importantly, one who has mastered the findings of economic science. Marx himself indicates that he expects a reader who wishes to learn something *new*, and therefore one who already knows all that is *old*, and for whom Marx's theory will be not be new simply because the reader is generally unfamiliar with the science of political economy.

The volume that has now appeared begins with analysis of exchange processes. By analysing the different forms that exchange assumes at different stages of development, Marx demonstrates that there is a continuous internal connection between these forms, that one form gives rise to another that contains within it the nucleus of elements whose development gives rise to a higher and more complex form. Thus, the simplest form of exchange, during the period of so-called natural economy, already contains within itself the nucleus whose development gives birth to the complex phenomena of monetary exchange.[12] Ascertaining the general law of exchange, Marx shows that commodity circulation, insofar as it involves the exchange of products, is unable to provide the capitalist with any surpluses beyond his expenditures. In order to achieve such surpluses, circulation must expand to include human labour power that is bereft of any economic independence. Application of the general law of exchange to labour power, as a commodity, enables the capitalist

---

12   [It might be noted here that in his comments on method, Marx made it clear that successive historical forms actually co-exist in numerous combinations *within a single prevalent mode of production*, so that the stages of history are not so sharply defined as Kaufman seemed to think was the case with biological organisms. Not only can the past portend the present, but the present can also provide the key to understanding the past. In the notes on method, Marx provided numerous examples of such coexistence (Marx 1970, pp. 207–14). Similar ideas later reappeared in the theories of Lenin and Trotsky, who saw in pre-revolutionary Russia a unique combination of advanced and primitive forms of economy. For Trotsky, this insight was the beginning of the theory of 'Permanent Revolution', which he systematically presented in his book *Results and Prospects*, written in 1905–6].

to acquire from circulation more than he spends, to receive a profit. The point is that, according to the law of exchange, every commodity is paid for according to the average and necessary costs of its production, expressed in terms of the labour expended. But labour power produces more than is required for its production (i.e. its sustenance). Consequently, paying labour according to the same norm that applies to any other commodity, the capitalist can acquire for his own use the difference between the value of labour and the value of the products of labour. Marx calls this difference *surplus value* (*Mehrwert*). These surpluses in excess of expenditures, and the pursuit of them, constitute the principal distinguishing characteristic of the capitalist order of economic life. To acquire profit at the expense of wages, to spend as little as possible on labour and to acquire as much as possible from it – that is capitalism's practical slogan. Corresponding to the fundamental significance that, according to Marx's doctrine, capital and its profit from wage expenditures have in our day, the main part of the first volume is devoted to a detailed portrayal and analysis of the phenomena involved in the exploitation of labour by capital, and of the conditions in which it occurs and develops or else is delayed in its development. Marx initially portrays the capitalist's endeavour to acquire profit on his capital, in the form of the previously mentioned surplus value, by means of lengthening the working day. Here he outlines the development of English law concerning the length of the working day in the factory. Then Marx turns to successive main ways of acquiring the greatest possible difference between the value of labour and the value of its products. These include increasing the productivity of labour and curtailing the costs of its maintenance relative to what it produces. Simple cooperation of a large mass of homogeneous labour; division of labour, or cooperation of large masses of dissimilar labour; and finally, extensive application of machinery – such are the main ways adopted. In the closing chapter Marx analyses the historical conditions of capital's formation and clearly demonstrates the process of its formation in the theory and practice of colonisation.

I. K-n.

DOCUMENT 2

The History of a Book [On the Fortieth Anniversary of the Publication of *Capital*, Vol. I] (1907)

Otto Bauer

Source: Otto Bauer, 'Die Geschichte eines Buches', *Die Neue Zeit*, 26. 1907–8, 1. Bd. (1907), H. 1, pp. 23–33.

Introduction by the Editors

In this article Otto Bauer appears to express a sense of *fin de siècle*, an awareness that great theoretical accomplishments were made in the past, but time had taken its toll. The vast new developments of capitalism – expansion into new continents and continuous technological change – now required a rejuvenation of critical Marxism. The 'orthodox', among whom Bauer counted himself, had defended the foundations of Marx's system against 'the pranksters, columnists and archival scholars', but new challenges required new and creative responses. The alternative, Bauer evidently feared, was that theoretical 'revisionism' – the thinking associated with Eduard Bernstein, who believed Marxism had become redundant in face of modern novelties – would condemn the workers' movement to gradual stagnation.[1]

---

1 For Bernstein's criticism of the conclusions in *Capital*, see *The Preconditions of Socialism* (Cambridge: Cambridge University Press, 1973). The principal themes of Bernstein's argument can be summarised briefly: 1) Marx's labour theory of value was mistaken, since the rate of profit had not fallen nor had unemployment significantly increased (pp. 53–4); 2) the emergence of trusts and cartels facilitated more rational control of economic phenomena, thereby diminishing the prospect of a general crisis of capitalism for 'purely economic' reasons (p. 96); 3) joint-stock ownership also contributed to social stability by expanding the number of members of the possessing classes 'both absolutely *and* relatively' (p. 61); 4) greater economic stability and the extension of ownership discouraged class consciousness (p. 104); and 5) if socialism was, therefore, neither economically nor politically inevitable, it could only come about by virtue of its ethical superiority over capitalism. Bernstein concluded that universal suffrage represented the alternative to violent revolution, for in a democracy 'the parties, and the classes supporting them soon learn to recognise the limits of their power

Bauer wrote this article at a time of renascent neo-Kantianism, characterised by the conviction that the *real* can never be reconciled with the *ideal*. If the end could never be reached, Kant said duty still demanded a continuous effort to move towards it. Bernstein captured exactly this sentiment when he famously commented, 'what is usually termed the final goal of socialism is nothing to me, the movement is everything'.[2] Since modern events seemed to render classical Marxism redundant – there was no sign of impending revolution or capitalist collapse – Bernstein and his co-thinkers typically regarded socialism in terms of 'organised liberalism',[3] or steady democratic progress towards a rational compromise between rival social classes. In legislation, Bernstein argued,

> the intellect governs emotion ...; in a revolution, emotion governs the intellect ... As soon as a nation has reached a political state of affairs where the rights of the propertied minority have ceased to be a serious impediment to social progress, where the negative tasks of political action take second place to the positive, the appeal to violent revolution becomes pointless.[4]

Bauer does not refer directly to Bernstein, but his summary of Marxism's current state of affairs speaks in terms of 'revisionism' and 'dogmatism' – of those who would abandon classical Marxism and those who rigidly defended it while adding no new ideas. Bauer's worry is that something must be done by orthodox Marxists, although he specifies neither what nor how. What he proposes, therefore, is a reconsideration of Marx's method, beginning with the problematic relation between Marx and Hegel. Was Marxism a 'science', in which case return to Marx's method was the way to respond creatively to new historical circumstances, or was it simply a version of Hegelian philosophy, in which case Kant appeared to many to provide the better practical answers?

Marx's personal notes on the method of political economy had finally been published in 1903,[5] but, as Bauer remarked, Marx spoke 'in a language that is

---

and, on each occasion, to undertake only as much as they can reasonably hope to achieve under the circumstances. Even if they make their demands rather higher than they seriously intend in order to have room for concessions in the inevitable compromise – and democracy is the school of compromise – it is done with moderation' (p. 144).

2 Bernstein 1993, p. 190.
3 Bernstein 1993, p. 150.
4 Bernstein 1993, p. 205.
5 See Marx 1903.

almost incomprehensible to us, i.e., outwardly according to Hegel's teachings'. In the famous postface to the second edition of *Capital*, published in 1873, Marx had commented that Hegel's dialectic was 'standing on its head. It must be inverted, in order to discover the rational kernel within the mystical shell'.[6] In this article Bauer argues, quite correctly, that the 'mystical shell' was Hegel's ontological system, while the rational kernel was his dialectic. To establish Marxism's claim to be a science, and therefore of timeless validity in methodological terms, Bauer explained that Marx's categorial language, although borrowed from Hegel, was in fact an expression of objective laws no different from those in the mathematical and natural sciences.

To make this argument, one had to begin with fundamentals, with the Hegelian categories of Being, Quality, Quantity and Measure. This was exactly what Marx had done in rethinking political economy. The analogue of indeterminate Being, for Marx, was the commodity, the simplest, undifferentiated category of an economy characterised by production for sale. Quality referred to 'use-value', or the natural properties distinguishing particular commodities. Quantity, which for Hegel involved many units of similar quality, led Marx to labour as the source of all value. And Measure, in turn, led to 'abstract' socially necessary labour as the synthesis of Quantity and Quality that made universal exchange possible. With these initial categories, borrowed from Hegel and reformulated in terms of political economy, Marx set in motion the dialectic that moved through successive stages of complexity in the three volumes of *Capital*.

Marx believed that Hegel had found the door to human self-understanding but then had closed it with his metaphysical ontology. In the *1844 Manuscripts* Marx wrote that Hegel provided only 'an *abstract, logical* and *speculative* expression of the historical process'.[7] He conceived 'wealth, the power of the state, etc. ... only in their thought form'[8] ending with 'the dialectic of pure thought',[9] 'a pure, *unceasing* revolving within itself'.[10] The problem with Hegel was that he believed that consciousness not merely apprehends the *forms of the world*, but in fact *forms the world* through its own activity of thought. Marx and Engels reopened the door to human self-understanding by re-reading Hegel's dialectic in historical-materialist terms, with the result that Marxist political economy emerged as a 'social theory' that was simultaneously an 'exact science'. The

---

6   Marx 1976, p. 103.
7   Marx, cited in Fromm 1961, p. 171.
8   Marx, cited in Fromm 1961, p. 173.
9   Marx, cited in Fromm 1961, p. 175.
10 Marx, cited in Fromm 1961, p. 189.

theme of Bauer's article is that Marx used Hegelian tools 'to grasp the concrete empirical intellectually and to reproduce it in science', in which case Marxism transcended both 'absolute idealism' and 'naïve empiricism'. *Capital* introduced a radically new method of historical analysis, to which Marxists must continuously return in response to new times and new circumstances. Bauer hoped that by returning to its origins, Marxism might find a new beginning appropriate to a new century.

It is worth noting that Bauer wrote this article on the eve of the great Marxist works on imperialism, which only a few years later reconceived capitalism in terms of an entirely new stage of historical development. Three years later, in June 1910, Bauer wrote a review of Rudolf Hilferding's new book, *Finance Capital*, and welcomed the first signs of the Marxist renaissance he had long been anticipating. In that review he repeated the worries expressed in the document published here and, at the same time, described Hilferding's work, which many considered to be the most important work of Marxist scholarship since Volume III of *Capital*, as 'what we have long needed'. Here are Bauer's opening thoughts in his review of Hilferding's work:

> Marxist economics made little progress after Karl Marx's death. Marxists rightly considered the popularisation of Marx's doctrines and their defence against the attacks of opponents as their most important task. Little time remained to us for the upgrading and continuation of Karl Marx's economic teachings. Ultimately, the work of popularisation also began to suffer from this situation. The capitalism described in most of our propaganda literature is that of the 1860s and 1870s, not the capitalism of our own day. The newest phenomena in economic life were certainly dealt with in many valuable articles and brochures, but we lacked a systematic theoretical presentation. Even in the most significant and independent economic work hitherto produced by the Marxist school, apart from those of Marx and Engels themselves, even in Kautsky's *Agrarian Question*, the immediate political purpose and the needs of popularisation thrust the historic-descriptive exposition into the foreground and the theoretical part into the background. Meanwhile, a new world has arisen in the economic life of all developed nations: the old presentations of the developmental tendencies of capitalism no longer suffice. The gaps resulting from this situation have now finally been filled at least in part. Rudolf Hilferding's *Finance Capital* gives us what we have long needed.

∴

The History of a Book (Otto Bauer)

Since Karl Marx published the first volume of his major economic work, 40 years of violent upheavals have passed, 40 years that have completely changed the face of the earth. During these four decades, capitalism, whose laws were revealed by that book, has created a new world. It has itself become something different from what it formerly was: what are the mills of Lancashire, which Marx described in the first volume of *Capital*, compared to the giant enterprises of our iron industry, which unite collieries and blast furnaces, steel works and rolling mills into a vast well-articulated whole? What are Marx's capitalists, who ruled over a few hundred workers, compared to the owners of modern cartels and trusts, who control entire industrial branches with hundreds of thousands of workers, and to the modern major banks, which hold in bondage the industry of whole countries? And the circle over which capital rules is constantly expanding. Karl Marx described British capitalism; now German and American capitalism stretch their arms so powerfully that they are progressively narrowing the freedom of movement of their elder British brother. In the Far East, a new capitalist island kingdom, a younger England, [Japan] has arisen. In Russia, capitalism revolutionised the conditions of existence of the old social order; capitalist industry is developing in the middle and lower Danube. Capitalism is again submitting to its power Italy, the country it first mastered and to which it subsequently proved unfaithful. Egypt, Algeria, the Congo are subject to it; rivers of gold flow to its coffers from South Africa; today, it is subjugating Morocco with blood and iron; and it is already preparing to add the ancient cultured lands of the Near East to its kingdom. Its laws prevail in Canada and Mexico, and it threateningly announces the revolutionising of the age-old economic constitution of China and India. It has driven Polish farm workers to the iron works of Westphalia, Hungarian Slovaks to the coal mines of Pennsylvania, Chinese coolies to the gold mines of South Africa. It has awakened countless nations from their deep slumber to a new life. Everywhere it shakes up the labouring and suffering masses, kindling in them new desires and driving the classes to struggle. And wherever its kingdom arises, the ideas of Marx's incomparable book, proclaimed for the first time 40 years ago, also become the property of the struggling working class. The triumph of capitalism carries Marx's work to the masses of all nations.

But just as capitalism, by continuously expanding its territory, seems to have become different from its former self, shrouded in ever-new and ever-changing forms, the doctrine that Marx bestowed four decades ago upon learning and struggling humanity has also undergone changes due to the steady expansion of its circle of operation. To be sure, it still stands intact in all its monumental size and unity, just as its creator forged it four decades ago, and far-sighted and sagacious men long ago foresaw what we now witness today. What Schweitzer and Dietzgen wrote concerning the first volume of *Capital* shortly after its publication, what Engels and Kautsky later wrote on Marx's economic doctrines,[11] is still a source of rich instruction for us today. But the way in which an individual comprehends a new doctrine reflects his *individual* knowledge and personal maturity; *public* opinion, however, looks at Marx's book today differently from the way it did 30 or 20, or even 10 years ago. Now the situation is different in the minds of journalists and popularisers, critics and apologists, politicians and scholars.

How we ourselves read *Capital* as youngsters, when we first ventured into the great master's work! Attempting, with feverish curiosity, to grasp the great overview of the history of mankind, it was only with difficulty that we overcame our impatience at having to linger on the difficult theoretical models, but how deeply shaken we were when Marx's master hand then revealed to us the development of suffering humanity! We saw how capitalism was built on the ruins of a collapsing world, dripping with the sweat and blood of generations; how it had risen over the bodies of children and women, of starved and declining peoples; how it had expanded and organised its power, revealing nature's secrets and putting its forces at the service of an insatiable greed. We saw vividly the class antagonisms; how private property became the means to produce, out of the suffering and hardship of one class, the swelling wealth, the splendid culture of the other. We understood for the first time the workers' terrible suffering, and we accompanied them into battle against the employers; we learned to hate with them the social constitution that turns every achievement of man, in the struggle with nature, into a bulwark of the servitude of man by man; but we also learned that we could hope for the final liberation of humanity from the growth of the always-expanding, gigantic productive forces and from the power of the united working class. Thus, we discovered in *Capital* not just a science, but also a sweeping historical canvas that moved and seized us, taught us to love and hate, to negate and hope.

And our personal experience was not unique: in this case, too, the development of the individual repeated the history of the species. At first, Marx's contemporaries read *Capital* as an historical work, which revealed to them the bloody history of capitalism and showed them the horrors of capitalist exploit-

---

11   [A reference to Karl Kautsky 1887, *Karl Marx' oekonomische Lehren: Gemeinverständlich dargestellt und erläutert*, Stuttgart: J.H.W. Dietz, a book frequently re-edited in the following years].

ation, the bitter reality of class antagonisms, and the hard necessity of the class struggle. And this terrible picture sparked moral outrage against capitalism in thousands of readers, awakening in them an ethical resolution to struggle for the liberation of the proletariat. Hermann Cohen must have been thinking about this effect of the first volume of *Capital* when he called its author an 'envoy of the God of history'.[12]

The first critics of Marx's work clung to its historical and descriptive parts. They asked whether exploitation is really as horrible and extensive as Marx described it; whether the fact that the worker only receives a part of the produce of his labour is merely a consequence of our social order, or a law of nature that no social order can abolish. Marx's own peculiar views, however, remained as unknown to them as to the mass of those who were under the spell of his work. In the critical as in the apologetic Marx-literature of that time, elements of Marx's thinking are still inextricably blended with ideas taken from the older rationalist socialism. Marxism had not yet freed itself of the confusion of run-of-the-mill [*Allerwelts*: all-purpose] socialism.

First, a series of excellent popularisers had to turn the gold bars of Marx's thought into usable coin, which now runs from hand to hand, before the basic ideas of Marx's work could enter, by many channels, into the consciousness of broader classes of people. Friedrich Engels's articles against Dühring, which appeared in the Leipzig *Vorwärts*, were dedicated to the solution of that problem more than 30 years ago. Collected in a book, they were the most fertile popularisation of Marx's theory.[13] The clarity of its thoughts, the gracious humour of their author, made them eminently suitable to introduce Marx's difficult arguments [*Schlussreihen*] to broader circles. The effect was all the more lasting because Engels followed Marx's opponents into all the areas of knowledge, driving them out of their last hiding places. To be sure, Engels's book also has vices as well as virtues, but those who read it today will not argue over details. Despite some mistakes and shortcomings, it remains an historical fact. It is one of our best introductions to Marx's great theoretical edifice, and the people to whom it opened up Marx's intellectual world have continued Engels's work diligently. They were the teachers of the younger generation of Marxists.

---

12 [*'Pedantisch ist es, einem solchen Gesandten des Gottes der Geschichte die Sprüchlein der spirituellen Moral vor zuhalten; und ihm zu bedeuten, daß er die Urkraft des Ich verkannt und verleumdet habe'* (Cohen 1904, p. 296). ('It is pedantic to confront such an envoy of the god of history with a little speech on spiritual morality, and to tell him that he misjudged and slandered the primal force of self')].

13 [A reference to Friedrich Engels 1878, *Herrn Eugen Dührings Umwälzung der Wissenschaft*, Leipzig: Genossenschafts-Buchdruckerei].

However, neither Engels's writings nor the works of his disciples have been able to exploit the whole richness of *Capital*. The chatter of dilettantes should not obscure the fact that no science can be popularised for the layman without losing many of its best elements in the process. But if popular presentations of Marx's theory still showed, albeit in broad outline, the master's whole intellectual system, what could become of it in the consciousness of the masses, who now began to take possession of it? How could the untrained masses grasp Marx's peculiar *method*, which can only be understood by those who know the great work of thought accomplished by German classical philosophy out of the rich material made available to it by the development of the exact sciences? Thus the method was lost; the masses stuck to the *results*. But they could not understand the propositions in which Marx summarised the results of his research, in their interdependence, into a *system*, or in their interrelation with the whole bustle of social life; they juxtaposed Marx's propositions abruptly and categorically. 'The mode of production of material life conditions the social, political and intellectual life process in general. It is not the consciousness of men that determines their being, but, on the contrary, their social being that determines their consciousness'.[14] 'The history of all hitherto existing society is the history of class struggles'.[15] 'The value of every commodity is determined by the socially necessary labour time required for its production'.[16] 'The wealth of the propertied classes stems from the surplus-value, from the unpaid labour of the working class'.[17] 'Capitalist society has the tendency to impoverish the working class more and more'.[18] 'Small businesses are destroyed, control over the means of production falls into the hands of a constantly diminishing number of large capitalists'.[19] 'The monopoly of capital

---

14 Marx 1970, p. 21.
15 Marx and Engels 1962, p. 34.
16 ['Whether the coat is expressed as the equivalent and the linen as relative value, or, inversely, the linen is expressed as equivalent and the coat as relative value, the magnitude of the coat's value is determined, as ever, by the labour-time necessary for its production, independently of its value-form' (Marx 1976, p. 147). 'We began with the assumption that labour-power is bought and sold at its value. Its value, like that of all other commodities, is determined by the labour-time necessary to produce it' (Marx 1976, p. 340)].
17 [A paraphrase of this passage in *Capital*: '... the appropriation of unpaid labour is the secret of making a profit' (Marx 1976, p. 743)].
18 [A paraphrase of this passage in *Capital*: 'Along with the constant decrease in the number of capitalist magnates, who usurp and monopolize all the advantages of this process of transformation, the mass of misery, oppression, slavery degradation and exploitation grows' (Marx 1976, p. 929)].
19 [A paraphrase of these passages in *Capital*: 'It is concentration of capitals already formed,

becomes a fetter upon the mode of production which has flourished alongside and under it. The centralization of the means of production and the socialization of labour reach a point at which they become incompatible with their capitalist integument. This integument is burst asunder. The knell of capitalist private property sounds. The expropriators are expropriated'.[20] These and a few similar sentences, immediately juxtaposed – that is the idea that the general public has of Marxism. It is that *vulgar Marxism* that the masses are acquainted with in the popular presentations of Marx's theory, and which they must necessarily be acquainted with given the inadequacy of their educational background and methodological training. It is only about that vulgar Marxism that the wider circles of the public debate whenever the question of 'Marxism' is posed.

To complain about the emergence and spread of vulgar Marxism would only testify to a deplorable lack of historical sense, because the acquisition of a new science by the masses is an historical process, in the course of which the masses change at every moment the ideas they want to take possession of, in order to adapt them to their comprehension at a particular time. Abundant examples from the history of the natural sciences and philosophy could be adduced, showing that the simplification and trivialisation of a new doctrine is nothing but a stage in its triumphal march, its road towards prevalence. And as poor as vulgar Marxism appears in comparison with the enormous wealth of Marx's thought, it stands much higher than the confused ideas about social life replaced by it. But [vulgar Marxism] is, for the masses of the workers, not just a tremendous advance in their *knowledge*; it is also one of the driving forces of their *will*. By showing them – if only in rough outline – the development of capitalist society, it has been of great help in turning proletarian class instinct into clear class consciousness, a clear recognition of the position and tasks of the working class in bourgeois society. Even in the impoverished and stunted version in which the ideas of the first volume of *Capital* have so far penetrated the consciousness of the masses, they not only enriched the knowledge of the working masses; they were also the most effective way to develop the unity, clarity and purposefulness of their will.

---

destruction of their individual independence, expropriation of capitalist by capitalist, transformation of many small into few large capitals ... The battle of competition is fought by the cheapening of commodities. The cheapness of commodities depends, all other circumstances remaining the same, on the productivity of labour, and this depends in turn on the scale of production. Therefore the larger capitals beat the smaller' (Marx 1976, p. 777)].

20   Marx 1976, p. 929.

Vulgar Marxism certainly offered to the Marx-critique welcome points of attack. This criticism did not care about Marx's method, or about the coherence of his system, but only about those individual – and in their isolation misleading – propositions that the great public takes as the quintessence of Marxism. The Marx-critique focused its attack upon them. *Theoretical revisionism is nothing but the counterpart of vulgar Marxism*, the necessary consequence of the equally necessary atrophy of Marx's theory as it seriously penetrated wider and less educated classes of people.

But precisely the attacks of revisionism had to turn us Marxists back to our sources. Since the individual propositions, in their misleading isolation, appeared shaken by the attacks of revisionism, and their validity was called into question, we had to remind ourselves again of their interconnection in the system. Since the results were disputed, we had to re-examine the method. The popularisations were no longer sufficient; and if we wanted to answer the questions with which we were overwhelmed from all sides, we had to appropriate intellectually the whole richness of the new science developed in Marx's works. The changing historical situation forced the latest generation of Marxist scholars to work in a completely different way; it set us tasks different from those of our predecessors, which we had to approach with a mental disposition totally different from that of our teachers of a quarter of a century ago.

In the year 1885 appeared the second, and in 1894 the third volume of *Capital*. They were already available to us when we started the study of Marx's economics, and for that reason alone we had to read the first volume differently [from our predecessors]. We did not have to add to the results of the first volume of *Capital* those of the second and third, but instead we had to read the entire work in one go at the beginning of our studies. For us, the question of whether the third volume stood in contradiction with the first, or whether the theory of value was overridden by the theory of production prices, could not arise. We would never have become Marxists if we had not seen, from the first day, all the component parts of the system at work in their mutual interdependence. Since the completed building was shown to us from the beginning, we recognised its plan much more easily than did our predecessors, who saw it in the making.

At the same we were assailed by countless new economic phenomena described and catalogued for us by the *historical school*: the myriad forms of indirect dependence of handicrafts [on capital]; the stupendous revolution in the character of the farm; the formation of new social strata in the advanced industrial nations; the changing forms of concentration of capital, which vary from country to country and from decade to decade. We had to overcome all that intellectually; before we could ever commit ourselves to Marx's school, we had to explain how those countless new phenomena could be classified according to Marx's broad guidelines. Thus we learned to understand Marx's theory about the developmental trends [of society] in its deepest sense, in all its richness, and we were prevented from letting that doctrine, which grasps the transformation of thousands of intricate and interconnected economic relations of people in their conformity to law, wither into mere prophecies about purely outward phenomena, which is all that can be gleaned from business statistics.

Thus we first mastered the *content*, the *substance* of Marx's system, consciously assimilating it as a lasting intellectual acquisition. It could be no mystery to us that the *first* abstractions, with which Marx's deductions begin in the first volume of *Capital*, were actually the *last* results of his intellectual work. Indeed, we experienced in our actual research work the fact that we cannot do without those ultimate and most general concepts in order to recreate in our consciousness, through their interaction, the concrete empirical facts of economic experience. But again we faced scepticism. Was the procedure that we learned from Marx, that whole tedious intellectual work, not an aberration of the human mind? In 1896, Rudolf Stammler again brought up for discussion the method of the social sciences.[21] Dilthey, Windelband, Rickert sought to reinstate naïve empiricism in the historical sciences.[22] Thus, all the results again became uncertain for us, for the *method* itself seemed to be called into question.

Marx's conception of history is an exact *science*. It is not a critique of knowledge, *not a philosophy*. The uncritical mixing up of the philosophical consideration of the limits of science with actual scientific work in the spheres of action [*Arbeitsfelde*] and experience can only cause harm in the social sciences, just as it wrought disasters in the field of the natural sciences. In itself, Marx's social theory does not require any more instruction from philosophy than, for instance, mechanics or astronomy. Philosophy does not have to provide science with its procedure; [on the contrary,] philosophy rests on science's research method. Philosophy singles out, from a given science, those elements of recognising consciousness that are 'necessary and sufficient to establish and stabilize the fact of science'.[23] Despite that fact, social theory, from an historical and

---

21 Stammler 1896.
22 [Rudolf Stammler (1856–1938) was a German jurist. The German philosopher Wilhelm Dilthey (1833–1911) is best known for the way he distinguished between the natural and human sciences (*Geisteswissenschaften*: literally, 'spiritual sciences'). Wilhelm Windelband (1848–1915) and Heinrich Rickert (1863–1936) were prominent representatives of the Baden school of Neo-Kantians, or the Southwest German school of philosophy].
23 Cohen 1885, p. 77.

psychological point of view, is much more intimately linked with philosophy than with the natural sciences, because the latter separated themselves from the crushing embrace of philosophy two centuries earlier. The natural sciences have developed their methods in such a way that, however differently they may be rated by philosophers, their practical application and general validity can no longer be challenged. But their younger sisters, the social sciences, must still defend themselves today against philosophy's desire to dominate. Confused by party hatred and patronage, none of its working methods can secure undisputed advantage. That is why social science cannot do without epistemological justification and defence of its methods.

Marx has done the methodological work of justifying his own approach himself, but he put it in a language that is almost incomprehensible to us, i.e. outwardly according to Hegel's teachings. In his work, of course, Hegel's trains of thought have become something quite different and new; the words taken over from Hegel express very different concepts. For that reason, we have to translate Marx's methodological justification of his work into the language of our own time in order to forearm ourselves against the attacks of scepticism.

The great fact underlying Hegel's logic, as well as his criticism of Kant, is the natural sciences. Hegel, too, does not fail to recognise their empirical character, and he has no doubt 'that all our knowledge begins with experience'; but he characteristically calls the empirical 'the immediate',[24] and the logical conceptual processing of the experience, the 'negation of an immediately given'.[25] Behind the immediate, Hegel looks for the true and the real. He finds the true and the real in the 'realm of shadows, the world of simple essentialities, freed of all sensuous concretion'.[26] In *Existence* [*Dasein*], the determinacy [*Bestimmtheit*] – the concrete empirical *qualitative* condition [*Beschaffenheit*] – is one with Being [*Sein*]; but only if this condition is sublated [*aufgehoben*], posited as indifferent, only then do we get to *pure Being*, which is nothing but *quantity*. But quantity [*Quantum*], to which an existence or a quality is bound, is *measure* [*Maß*].[27] Measure is the concrete truth of being; in it lies the idea of essence [*Wesen*]. 'The *truth* of *being* is *essence*. Being is the immediate. Since

---

24 [Hegel 2010a, Part One. III. Third Attitude of Thought to Objectivity: Immediate or Intuitive Knowledge].

25 ['As a matter of fact, thinking is always the negation of what we have immediately before us' (Hegel 2010a, Part One. I. Introduction, §12)].

26 ['The system of logic is the realm of shadows, the world of simple essentialities, freed of all sensuous concretion' (Hegel 2010b, p. 37)].

27 ['Measure is ... a quantum, to which a determinate being or a quality is attached' (Hegel 2010a, Part One. First Subdivision. VII. Being. C. Measure, §107)].

the goal of knowledge is the truth, what being is *in and for itself*, knowledge does not stop at the immediate and its determinations, but penetrates beyond it on the presupposition that *behind* this being there still is something other than being itself, and that this background constitutes the truth of being'.[28] That background, that essence of being, is measure; we get to it by positing the determinations of being as indifferent, when we turn from qualitatively determined existence to pure being as pure quantity.

What Hegel thus describes, in his strange and mystical-sounding way, is none other than the method of *mathematical science*, which seeks to understand the manifold empirical phenomena of nature according to their law-governed determination, by relating them to mathematical laws of motion. But those concepts, which can only find justification in the fact that they first make possible [consideration of] the objects of nature as objects of science, that they are the constitutive conditions of the possibility of science itself, become in Hegel independent essences, compared to which the empirical appears as something unreal. That is the ontological character of Hegel's logic.

Marx certainly imitates Hegel's method. He also looks behind the 'appearance of competition' for the true and real. And he also wants to find behind immediacy the truth of being – by sublating the qualitative determination of being in its empirical existence, positing it as indifferent and turning to being as pure quantity. Thus, in the famous opening chapters of the first volume of *Capital*, the concrete commodities are stripped of their determination (as a frock, or 20 yards of linen) and posited as mere quantities of social labour. In the same way, the concrete individual labour is deprived of its determination and regarded as a mere 'form of manifestation' of general social labour. Thus, even economic subjects, these men of flesh and blood, eventually lose their apparent existence and become mere 'organs of labour' and 'agents of production', one the embodiment of a certain quantity of social capital, the other the personification of a quantity of social labour power. The quantity, to which existence or quality is bound as Hegel's *measure*, is here social labour. It is the *essence* of economic phenomena, which, as Hegel said, not only passes through its determinations – let us recall Marx's account of the circulation of capital, which makes the same value assume the ever-changing forms of money, commodity, money, money capital, productive capital, commodity capital! – but also rules them as their law. Social labour becomes finally – and it would be an enticing task to develop this idea in detail – what Hegel calls *substance*, absolute activity-of-form (*Formtätigkeit*), absolute power, from

---

28 Hegel 2010b, p. 337.

which all accidents emerge.[29] But if Marx's method thus mimics Hegel's procedure, and if Marx uses Hegel's terminology to describe his own mode of research [*Arbeitsweise*], he strips this method of its *ontological* character. In many methodological remarks, scattered throughout his work, he argues that his concepts do not – as Hegel's do – pretend to be real entities, but are only tools to grasp the concrete empirical consciously and to reproduce it in science: 'The method of ascending from the abstract to the concrete is simply the way in which thought appropriates the concrete, reproduces it as a concrete in the mind. But this is by no means the process of origination of the concrete itself'.[30]

When we recognise that Marx takes from Hegel nothing but the method of mathematical natural science, disguised ontologically by Hegel and again disrobed by Marx from its ontological disguise, we recognise the essence of Marx's work as *science*: Marx has conquered a new field for the method of mathematical natural science. If we understand that Marx, in his methodological remarks, not only uses Hegel's terminology but also takes over from Hegel's logic the idea, common to all idealistic philosophy, of the determination of our knowledge by the conformity to law of our consciousness (rejecting, however, the ontological concealment of this idea by Hegel), we can understand Marx's *methodological* description of his own working method and see him as the heir of our classical philosophy. We see him equally remote from the ontological metaphysics of absolute idealism as from the illusion of naïve empiricism, which does not recognise human consciousness's own achievement in science, degrading and devaluing human knowledge into a mere image of the 'immediate'.

Marx's legacy from our classical philosophy is the concept of science. We think that the concept of science, as it was developed by idealism through a critical examination of mathematical natural science, can be found in its purest form in *Kant's* epistemology. But Marx, like the whole age in which he received his philosophical training, was too alien to Kant to take his view of science directly from critical philosophy. His historical starting point was rather the 'absolute idealism' of Hegel. And in Hegelian philosophy Marx could also find the concept of science common to all idealism, but only in a form cloaked in Hegel's ontological view. By freeing the concept of science from that shell, Marx essentially restored it to that form in which it was and is the foundation and starting point of critical philosophy – albeit in a different language.

---

29   Hegel 1991, p. 225, § 150.
30   Marx 1970, p. 206.

But for that reason we should not regard as a meaningless coincidence the fact that Marx owes his logical training to Hegel. Even if Hegel's ontology today looks like a hardly understandable aberration after Kant's critique of reason, it should not be forgotten, for that reason, that in other respects Hegel also represents a significant advance beyond Kant. For while Kant's critique of knowledge was still mainly oriented towards the mathematical natural sciences, in Hegel human history appears at the heart of his system.[31] If the historical facts of human social life were arranged by Hegel as forms of self-development of spirit, this means, when translated from the ontological language into the methodological, as in Marx, nothing but *the demand for such a logical treatment of historical phenomena that they may be understood as individual cases of a law of motion in a lawful science,*[32] *which, according to the method of the mathematical natural sciences, relates qualitative determinations to quantitative changes.* For Hegel, the concrete, individual historical representation [*Vorstellung*] is just a *metaphor* of the concept, and for that reason everything transient is only an illusion,[33] but Marx demands that the historical [material] should be understood as an *instance* of a law – not as if, for instance, there were laws somewhere outside history that rule over it, but so that the historical connection partakes that character of universality and necessity, which can only be given to it by the relation [of historical facts] to a law. Marx's political economy includes the material of economic history, processed in this sense. Economic history is the starting point of all economic research; in an accomplished economic system,

---

31 [Although Bauer evidently holds Kant's critical epistemology in higher regard than Hegel's ontology, he overlooks the decisive fact that Hegel thought the real could in fact *become* the ideal, which Hegel found fulfilled in the form of the modern state described in his *Philosophy of Right*. This totalising process, which ended in the concrete universal of a state of self-imposed laws, would surely have been a great deal more attractive to Marx, with his anticipation of the planned economy of communism, than Kant's conviction that the *phenomenal* could never be finally reconciled with the *noumenal*].

32 [A reference to Wilhelm Wundt's contrast between *Gesetzwissenschaft* (lawful science) and *Geschichtswissenschaft* (historical science), which adopted the Kantian philosopher Wilhelm Windelband's distinction between nomothetic and idiographic sciences. Nomothetic is based on what Kant described as a tendency to generalise, and is typical for the natural sciences. It describes the effort to derive laws that explain objective phenomena in general. Idiographic is based on what Kant described as a tendency to specify, and is typical for the humanities. It describes the effort to understand the meaning of contingent, unique, and often subjective phenomena].

33 [*Alles Vergängliche ist nur ein Gleichnis*: a quote from Goethe's *Faust*. *Gleichnis* also means 'allegory' or 'simile'].

however, the facts of economic history must appear as single instances of a developed economic law. What is psychologically the starting point is logically the result.

Marx performed the great task of providing an exact scientific treatment of history in the three volumes of *Capital*. He saw in the countless qualitative changes of the human *productive forces* simple quantitative changes [changes of Measure in Hegel's terms], understanding them as changes in the *organic composition of capital*. From these quantitative changes follow, with that strict universality and necessity that only the realm of mathematics knows, the laws of motion of the *rate of surplus value*, the *rate of profit* and the *accumulation of capital*, which allow us to understand the specific historical events of our time in conformity with their lawful determination. Thus Marx gave us the first *mathematical law of motion of history*.

Thus we secured Marx's doctrine against the assaults of scepticism; it is now no less secure than mathematical natural science. In Marx himself we discovered the critique of knowledge that Marxism had to overcome. And if historicism rejects the ultimate results of Marx's abstractions because they are not copies of empirical events, we respond to it, with the words of Kant, that also in this case the object does not create the concept, but the concept brings forth the object as object of our knowledge.[34]

Thus, it has not really been easy for us – the 'dogmatists', the 'Orthodox' – to secure possession of Marx's doctrine through struggle with a world of doubt, and we know very well that the way we had to pass through was not harmless for ourselves. We had to defend the boundaries of the new science against the incursions of scepticism and with the weapons of the critique of knowledge. We must now guard ourselves all the more anxiously against the danger of considering our real job to be the cherished philosophical defence of the new science as a whole, and to forget the further development of the new doctrine in particular areas. We had to appropriate all the wealth of Marx's research results,

---

34 [A reference to Kant's *Critique of Pure Reason*: 'There are only two possible cases in which synthetic representation and its objects can come together, necessarily relate to each other, and, as it were, meet each other: Either if the object alone makes the representation possible, or if the representation alone makes the object possible. If it is the first, then this relation is only empirical, and the representation is never possible *a priori*. And this is the case with appearance in respect of that in it which belongs to sensation. But if it is the second, then since representation in itself (for we are not here talking about its causality by means of the will) does not produce its object as far as its *existence* is concerned, the representation is still determinant of the object *a priori* if it is possible through it alone to *cognize something as an object*' (Kant 1998a, p. 224, B 125, emphasis in the original)].

but for that reason we must not avoid the task of applying Marx's fertile method to the ever new and broader fields of work, because the ultimate and most general abstractions only find their justification in the fact that we can explain by their interaction the concrete problems of each historical epoch and the individual characteristics of each country. What the pranksters, the columnists, and the archival scholars can only imagine as a dogma must be a creative method for us. We have to penetrate deeply into the basic structures of Marx's work, but this should not distract us from carrying out the more important task of bringing the certain knowledge thus won, piece by piece, to the masses, in this way continuing the work of permeating the masses with Marx's ideas; a work that our teachers and predecessors have begun so successfully and with such a great impact on the history of the peoples. We – the 'dogmatists' – have not ventured to intervene in the history of our people before we checked again and again the theoretical views lying at the basis of practical action, and before we related it to all the knowledge of our time. But of what use would all of our knowledge be if we did not implement it in active practical work for the goal theoretically proven to be the right? We cannot follow with slavish mindlessness every advice that Marx gave in another country, at another time and under different conditions to the struggling working class, but we must use Marx's method to understand the specific practical problems of our country and our time. We have wrested a commitment to Marx's theory by heavy struggle ourselves, and for that reason it cannot be for us a scheme that dominates us, but only a method that we control.

Thus each generation, each age group and level of education has *its own* Marx. What they are able to appropriate from the inexhaustible wealth of the master reflects their whole spiritual being. The history of *Capital* is interwoven into the whole intellectual history of recent decades. And for each generation the knowledge thus acquired becomes a determining destiny that shapes their practical actions; a personal experience that leaves indelible marks on their character. What at first is just knowledge becomes, in the living reality of creation, a never-ending source of enthusiasm, passion and energy.

DOCUMENT 3

'The Poverty of Philosophy' and 'Capital' (1886)

Karl Kautsky

Source: Karl Kautsky, ' "*Das Elend der Philosophie*" und *"Das Kapital"* ', *Die Neue Zeit*, 4 (1886), H. 1–5, pp. 7–19, 49–58, 117–29, 157–65 (Parts III and IV).

Introduction by the Editors

The second volume of *Capital* was published in 1885 and reviewed by Karl Kautsky in *Die Neue Zeit*, together with the first German edition of *The Poverty of Philosophy*, which had been translated from the original French edition by Kautsky and Eduard Bernstein. Readers of *Capital* usually assumed that the distinguishing trait of Marx's system was ascription of value to labour. In fact, Kautsky argued, bourgeois economists, from Adam Smith onwards, had already traced the origin of value back to labour. Marx's unique contribution was to associate the category of value with commodity production, exchange-value and the social relations connected with abstract labour:

> What is peculiar in Marx's theory of value is not the reduction of value to labour but the presentation of value as an historical category, on the one hand, and as a social relation, on the other, which can only be derived from the social functions and not from the natural properties of the commodity. That is what nobody before Marx had done, and that is what we regard as the distinguishing trait peculiar to Marx.[1]

Kautsky offered the following description of Marx's 'characteristic method':

> We clearly see in *Capital* his conception of economic categories as historical, on the one hand, and as purely social relations, on the other, sharply distinguishing them from their underlying natural forms and deducing their peculiarities from the observation of their *movement*, their functions, not from their respective outward manifestations: in a word, his

---

1 Kautsky 1886, p. 57.

development of economic categories from the development and movement of social relations. As against the fetishism peculiar to *bourgeois* economics, which turns the social, economic character that things get stamped with in the social production process into a *natural character* springing from the material nature of those things, Marx declares: 'What is at issue here is not a set of definitions under which things are to be subsumed. They are rather definite functions that are expressed in specific categories'.[2]

Recapitulating Marx's arguments in the first volume of *Capital*, Kautsky traced this twofold character of commodities to the twofold nature of the labour invested in producing them:

After Marx rigorously distinguished the social character of the commodity from the natural form of the good, he sets about to make an equally important distinction in labour itself: on the one hand the [concrete] labour that determines the natural form of the substance, and on the other hand [abstract] labour as a social element in its social context. Only in the latter sense does labour generate value.[3]

Kautsky also emphasised that the development of economic categories in Marx follows both a logical and an historical order:

The development that he offers in *Capital* is not merely a *logical* but also an *historical* one. The simple, the expanded, the general form of value and finally money follow one another not only logically, but also historically.[4]

Our translation of Kautsky's essay begins with his review of the second volume of *Capital*, which Frederick Engels edited and published after Marx's death in 1883. Working from Marx's manuscripts, Engels completed the work as he believed Marx had intended, but he was also the first to admit that the second volume lacked the high drama of the first. In private correspondence, Engels commented that 'The second volume is purely scientific, only dealing with questions *from one bourgeois to another*', that is, with the circulation of commodities rather than with production. In 1885 he wrote in another letter: 'The

---

2   Kautsky 1886, p. 50, citing Marx 1978, p. 303.
3   Kautsky 1886, p. 51.
4   Kautsky 1886, p. 52.

second volume will provoke great disappointment, being a purely scientific work with little in the way of agitation'.⁵

Karl Kautsky shared Engels's reaction. In his review he wrote that 'the remarks of the second volume leave us partly dissatisfied: they provide us with the solutions to many riddles, but at the same time they show us new problems. If the first volume is, in a sense, a self-contained whole, the second volume is just an introduction for the third, a fragment, a torso, which has many attractions but which also awakens the desire to get to know the whole'. At the end of his review, Kautsky repeated these misgivings:

> Even those whom Marx primarily addressed in his writings, the workers, will not greet the second volume with the same enthusiasm as the first. The scene for the investigations of the first volume is the *factory*, that of the second is the *comptoir* [cashier's desk]. The first volume dealt for the most part with conditions close to the workers, with which they are intimately familiar. The second volume deals with abstractions from facts that are distant from the workers, and which arouse in them relatively little interest. What they first of all experience is the way in which surplus-value is *produced* [the theme of the first volume]. The kind of transformations that surplus-value experiences, and how it is realised – these are questions much closer to the capitalists than to the workers.

Kautsky, like many other readers, was particularly distressed by the fact that Volume II did not address the problem of the transformation of surplus value into profit. This meant that the work was still written at a level of abstraction several steps removed from concrete capitalism. In terms of Marx's comments on methodology, written when he was preparing his *Contribution to the Critique of Political Economy*, Volume II had yet to complete the journey 'in the opposite direction' – back from such fundamental categories as commodity, abstract labour and exchange-value to capitalism as a concrete whole.

Although Volume II did not complete that journey, it did, as Kautsky was quite aware, set out the conceptual framework for doing so. Most importantly, Marx's analysis of the 'metamorphoses' and 'turnover' of capital provided numerous important insights into the causes and inevitability of cyclical crises – a 'welcome haven', as Kautsky commented, in a book that otherwise 'makes the greatest demands on the reader's attention and power of abstraction'.

---

5 *MECW*, Vol. 47, p. 296.

Marx was the first to provide the elements of a systematic theory of the capitalist business cycle, even though he did not ultimately tie them together in a single coherent work. His schemes of reproduction – in Section III of the second volume of *Capital*, and particularly in chapter 21, dealing with 'Accumulation and Reproduction on an Expanded Scale' – explained the requirements for crisis-free reproduction of the total social capital and, *by implication*, the numerous possibilities of critical 'disproportions' between capital's various components. In this context, Marx returned from exchange-value in general to the question of use-values, or what Kautsky described as 'the natural properties of the commodity'. Reproduction of the total social capital involved *what* is produced in different sectors of the economy and how the latter relate to one another, not simply the *value* of what is produced. While the analysis still dealt with values rather than prices, Volume II had lasting effects that Kautsky could not anticipate.

Besides providing some of the essential tools for investigating cyclical crises – see, for example, part IV of Rudolf Hilferding's *Finance Capital*[6] – the second volume of *Capital* also provoked some of the great Marxist debates in the years preceding World War I. Lenin cited the reproduction schemes in his quarrel with Russian Narodniks over the development of capitalism in Russia. In the same debate, Lenin also anticipated the principal theme of one of the most famous contributions to the theory of imperialism, Rosa Luxemburg's *The Accumulation of Capital* (1913). Luxemburg's book originated in her own critique of Marx's argument, in the second volume of *Capital*, that it was *theoretically* possible to realise the entire social product within a self-contained capitalist whole, without reliance on 'third parties' as non-capitalist sources of effective demand.[7] Luxemburg denied that possibility and instead explained imperialist expansion in terms of capitalism's compulsive need to conquer new markets for the sale of commodities.

∴

---

6 Hilferding 1981, pp. 239–98.
7 Luxemburg 2003. In his debate with the Narodniks Lenin wrote that 'the limits of the development of the market ... are set by the limits of the specialisation of social labour. But this specialisation, by its very nature, is as infinite as technical developments' (Lenin 1893, p. 100). Once commodity production was established, each article would be broken into its component parts and made the object of specialised manufacturing and new investments. In Lenin's view, 'Marx proved ... that capitalist production is quite conceivable without foreign markets, with the growing accumulation of wealth, and without any "third persons"' (Lenin 1894, pp. 498–9).

'The Poverty of Philosophy' and 'Capital' (Karl Kautsky)

III

> Capital, as self-valorizing value, does not just comprise class relations, a definite social character that depends on the existence of labour as wage-labour. It is a movement, a circulatory process through different stages, which itself in turn includes three different forms of the circulatory process. Hence it can only be grasped as a movement, and not as a static thing.[8]

This sentence, which is found in the second volume of *Capital*, is highly characteristic of the work. Here we find, in conformity with the subject matter, the peculiarities of the Marxian method expressed perhaps even more sharply than in the first volume. Everything is in constant flux, constant motion, and can only be seen as a movement.

But again, any economic movement can itself be understood only as a *historically determined* movement. The exchange of products (simple commodity circulation), mediated by money, developed commodity circulation, trade, and circulation of capital, are different processes with some common but also many quite different characteristics. Vulgar economy throws them all together. Just as it derives the functions of capital in the production process from the stock of the isolated imaginary savage, so it deduces the functions of capital in the circulation process from primitive exchange. Marx not only keeps these two functions of capital and simple commodity circulation strictly separate; in the second volume he also gives us the historical development and the historical tendencies of capital's circulation process.

Logically and historically, the circulation process of capital developed from the circulation of commodities: in order to understand it, we must therefore go back to the third chapter of the first section of the first volume, which deals with the circulation of commodities. If we denote the commodity by C and money by M, we find its formula to be C–M–C. People sell one commodity to buy another. The farmer, who sold grain to buy some clothes from the proceeds, provides an example of this simple commodity circulation.

Simple commodity circulation leads to developed commodity circulation, to trade. Now people no longer sell in order to buy, but buy in order to sell. The merchant buys commodities, such as grain, to sell them again. The formula for circulation is now M–C–M.

---

8   Marx 1978, p. 185.

This formula seems pointless. In the circuit C–M–C the physical body of the commodity that concludes it is different from the one that begins it. The *value* of the latter is, under normal circumstances, the same as the former, but its use-value is different. 'Consumption, the satisfaction of needs, in short *use-value*, is therefore the final goal' of this circuit.[9] To this circuit applies, under certain conditions (namely when both parties buy goods from each other, so that everyone is both a buyer and a seller), what vulgar economics unconditionally asserts about every commodity circuit: that both buyers and sellers gain by it. Both sell commodities useless to them as use-values, and obtain goods that they need to use. It is otherwise, however, with the circuit M–C–M. I give away money and eventually get the money back. This operation is meaningless if the M at the end is not quantitatively different from the M at the beginning; the merchant buys cheap to sell dear. For the formula M–C–M not to be pointless, it must, therefore, strictly speaking, be M–C–M', where M' = M + g, the original sum of money plus an increment (*Zuwachs*: growth). This increment, which Marx, as is well known, called surplus value, turns the originally advanced amount of money M into capital.

M–C–M' is thus the formula of the circulation of money capital. Originally it was the formula of the merchant's capital, which can only appropriate surplus value by purchasing under the value or selling above the value [of the commodities], i.e. by a violation of the law of value peculiar to commodity production. That is why Franklin said: 'war is robbery, commerce is cheating'.[10] But then a new commodity comes into the market, *labour power*, which during its activity not only reproduces its own value, but produces more surplus value. Whoever buys this commodity and productively consumes it, that is, applies it to the production of commodities, therewith has the opportunity to produce surplus value, even if everything takes place normally, that is, even if all commodities, including the commodity labour power, are bought and sold exactly at their value. The surplus value no longer arises, as in commercial capital, by a violation of the basic law of commodity circulation and exchange, according to which equal values are exchanged against each other, but precisely on the foundations of that law. With the development of industrial capital, therefore,

---

9 Marx 1976, p. 250.
10 A quotation from Marx 1976, p. 267, in turn taken from Benjamin Franklin, *Positions to be Examined, Concerning National Wealth*, in *Works*, Vol. 2, ed. Sparks, p. 376. The paragraph reads: 'There seem to be but three ways for a nation to acquire wealth. The first is by war, as the Romans did, in plundering their conquered neighbors. This is robbery. The second by commerce, which is generally cheating. The third by agriculture, the only honest way'.

begins the kingdom of eternal justice and equality, after trade and usury defied it so disdainfully.

Here is the point where Marx, in the first volume of *Capital*, turns to investigate the production process of capital, the production of surplus value. He continues the investigation in the second volume, where he describes the circulation process of capital.

Marx again proceeds from the formula M–C–M', but this has now been expanded through the inclusion of the production process. C, the commodities which the money capitalist buys, are, if he is an industrial capitalist, L, labour power, and MP, means of production. Through their productive consumption in the production process P, there emerges a sum of new physical bodies of commodities C', whose value is equal to M + m, i.e. the value of the means of production and the labour power employed, plus the surplus value created by the latter. The formula for the circuit of money capital now reads:

$$M - C < {}^{L}_{MP} \ldots P \ldots C' (C + c) - M' (M + m)$$

This formula assumes that labour power is a commodity, otherwise the transaction M–L is impossible. The class relation between capitalist and wage-worker is not created by money, but the existence of this class relationship makes it possible for a function of money to become a capital function.[11] Money does not

---

11   Marx 1978, p. 115. ['The class relation between capitalist and wage-labourer is thus already present, already presupposed, the moment that the two confront each other in the act M–L (L–M from the side of the worker). This is a sale and purchase, a money relation, but a sale and purchase in which it is presupposed that the buyer is a capitalist and the seller a wage-labourer; and this relation does in fact exist, because the conditions for the realization of labour-power, i.e. means of subsistence and means of production, are separated, as the property of another, from the possessor of labour-power.

'We are not concerned here with how this separation arises. If M–L takes place, it already exists. What is important here is that, if M–L appears as a function of money capital, or money appears here as a form of existence of capital, then this is in no way simply because money is involved here as the means of payment for a human activity with a useful effect, for a service; thus in no way because of money's function as means of payment. Money can be spent in this form only because labour-power is found in a state of separation from its means of production (including the means of subsistence as means of production of labour-power itself); and because this separation is abolished only through the sale of labour-power to the owner of the means of production, a sale which signifies that the buyer is now in control of the continuous flow of labour-power, a flow which by no means has to stop when the amount of labour necessary to reproduce the price of labour-power has been performed. The capital relation arises only in the production process

turn labour power into a commodity, but the commodity character of labour power turns money into capital. If money is not the cause of the class relationship between capitalists and wage-workers, mere changes in the monetary system cannot bring about the abolition of this relationship.

But if money did not create the class relation between capital and labour, money capital is the form in which capital always confronts labour.

> The normal form of advance for wages is payment in money; this process must be steadily repeated at short intervals, as the worker lives from hand to mouth. Hence the worker must constantly come face to face with the capitalist as money capitalist, and with his capital as money capital. Here there can be no question, as in the purchase of means of production and the sale of productive commodities, of a direct or indirect balancing of accounts.[12]

Thus it is understandable that money often appears to the workers, if they lack theoretical insight, to be the main cause of their oppression.[13]

But money also appears to the capitalists to be the driving force of the whole capitalist circulation process, if they regard it from the standpoint of the formula described above. Money-making, as the force driving the capitalists, appears most clearly in that formula; production seems to be only a necessary evil for that purpose. 'All nations characterized by the capitalist mode of production are periodically seized by fits of giddiness in which they try to accomplish the money-making without the mediation of the production process'.[14]

The formula M–C ... P ... C′–M′, considered as the exclusive formula of the circulation of capital, underlay the mercantile system, which put the main emphasis on M′. The more money came into the country and remained in it, the better. So [the mercantilist policy was] sell as much as possible, buy as little as possible.

---

because it exists implicitly in the act of circulation, in the basically different economic conditions in which buyer and seller confront one another, in their class relation. It is not the nature of money that gives rise to this relation; it is rather the existence of the relation that can transform a mere function of money into a function of capital' (Marx 1978, p. 115)].

12 Marx 1978, pp. 140–1.
13 [Marx discussed the futility of monetary reform in Marx 1970, pp. 83–6. In Engels's preface to the 1885 German edition of *The Poverty of Philosophy*, he writes at some length concerning the 'labour money exchange utopia' of Johann Karl Rodbertus].
14 Marx 1978, p. 137.

We therefore find among the exponents of the Mercantile System (which is based on the formula M–C ... P ... C′–M′) long sermons to the effect that the individual capitalist should consume only in his capacity as a worker, and that a capitalist nation should leave the consumption of its commodities and the consumption process in general to other more stupid nations, while making productive consumption into its own life's work. These sermons are often reminiscent in both form and content of analogous ascetic exhortations by the Fathers of the Church.[15]

The circuit of capital, however, does not take place just once; it is a constantly recurring circuit. If we posit the formula of the repeating circuit:

M–C ... P ... C′–M′. M–C ... P ... C′–M′. M–C ... P ... etc.

we see that it contains two other circuits, that of productive capital P ... C′–M′. M–C ... P, and that of commodity capital C′–M′. M–C ... P ... C′.

Let us start by considering the first circuit. It denotes the production process as a recurrent one, as a reproduction process; it shows not a singular but a periodic production of surplus value. In the form M ... M′ the production process appears merely as an interruption of the circulation process, and the latter as the main thing. In the form P ... P the circulation process appears only as an interruption of the production process, circulation being only a means to maintain ever-renewed production.

The acceptance of the formula M ... M′ as the exclusive form of the circuit of capital shows us the beginnings of the capitalist mode of production, when the merchant began to become an industrial capitalist and the *production of commodities* was for him a secondary matter. By contrast, as soon as the capitalist mode of production became more developed, it was natural to regard the formula P ... P as the exclusive form of the circuit of capital. The main focus of the capitalist class was now directed to production; it seemed more important to *produce* surplus value than to *realise* it, to monetise it. This seems to us to be the reason (Marx did not touch on this question) why classical economics adopted the formula P ... P, which includes the other forms of the circuit. Even if one is forced under certain circumstances, for the purposes of scientific investigation, to consider one of these forms on its own, we still must never forget their unity with the other two.

---

15   Marx 1978, p. 139.

Each capital-value passes *successively* through the forms of money capital, productive and commodity capital. But each individual industrial capital is also *simultaneously* in all three forms. The production process of capital is necessarily, as much as possible, a continuous, uninterrupted one; it does not take place in fits and starts. The capitalist does not use his entire money capital at once to purchase means of production and labour power in order to produce commodities, and then stop production in order to go to market with the commodities and wait until they are sold, whereupon the circuit begins anew. Wherever possible he produces without interruption, constantly having a stock of produced commodities and just as constantly having a certain sum of money capital. And it is not up to him to decide the proportions between these three forms of capital, or what should be their magnitudes. They are determined not only by the technical conditions of production, but also by a series of conditions belonging to the circulation process.

The economists are very much inclined to overlook all that. 'It is particularly the part always present as money capital that the economists forget, although precisely this circumstance is very necessary for the understanding of the bourgeois economy, and makes itself felt as such in practice as well'.[16]

The sums of money capital required for a particular operation are not all used at the same time. M–C is usually not a single purchase, but a sum of successive purchases, just as C'–M' is a sum of successive sales. Money must also be hoarded for the renewal and expansion of fixed capital, a subject to which we shall return later. Money must be ready as a reserve fund for adjusting to disturbances, such as, for instance, the disorders caused by an abnormal extension of the period C'–M'. These reasons and a number of others, discussed in the second volume in the further course of the investigation, ensure that the sum of money that the capitalists must temporarily accumulate as hoards increases as the capitalist mode of production develops. This is also one of the reasons why the function of the industrial capitalist turns increasingly into a monopoly of the big money capitalists. But this also makes the capitalists all the more inclined, instead of piling money up as a hoard until it is needed, to let their money participate in the circuit of other capitals, to invest it as interest-bearing capital. That is the reason for the development of the *credit system*.

Just as important and fundamental in this respect are the remarks, scattered throughout the second volume, concerning economic *crises*.

The economists assume that over-production is impossible because products are always exchanged against other products, and thus every purchase

---

16   Marx 1978, p. 333.

is a sale.¹⁷ But already in the first volume of *Capital* Marx pointed out that, although no one can usually sell without someone else buying, no one has to buy immediately after he has sold. Under certain circumstances, the capitalist mode of production forces the capitalist to hoard, i.e. not to buy after he has sold. On the other hand, he can sell products that are not immediately consumed.

> The volume of the mass of commodities brought into being by capitalist production is determined by the scale of this production and its needs for constant expansion, and not by a predestined ambit of supply and demand, of needs to be satisfied. Besides other industrial capitalists, mass production can have only wholesale merchants as its immediate purchasers. Within certain bounds, the reproduction process may proceed on the same or on an expanded scale, even though the commodities ejected from it do not actually enter either individual or productive consumption. The consumption of commodities is not included in the circuit of the capital from which they emerge. As soon as the yarn is sold, for example, the circuit of the capital value represented in the yarn can begin anew, at first irrespective of what becomes of the yarn when sold. As long as the product is sold, everything follows its regular course, as far as the capitalist producer is concerned. The circuit of the capital value that he represents is not interrupted. And if this process is expanded (which includes an expansion of the productive consumption of the means of production), then this reproduction of capital can be accompanied by a more expanded individual consumption (and thus demand) on the part of the workers, since this is introduced and mediated by productive consumption. The production of surplus-value and with it also the individual consumption of the capitalist can thus grow, and the whole reproduction process find itself in the most flourishing condition, while in fact a great part of the commodities have only apparently gone into consumption, and are actually lying unsold in the hands of retail traders, thus being still on the market. One stream of commodities now follows another, and it finally emerges that the earlier stream had only seemed to be swallowed up by consumption. Commodity capitals now vie with each other for space on the market. The late-comers sell below the price in order to sell

---

17   ['Marx rejected the idea that capitalist production was in equilibrium by ridiculing the then widely accepted Say's law (named after the French economist Jean-Baptiste Say). This law asserts that every purchase is a sale and that supply creates its own demand' (Carver 1991, p. 284)].

at all. The earlier streams have not yet been converted into ready money, while payment for them is falling due. Their owners must declare themselves bankrupt, or sell at any price in order to pay. This sale, however, has absolutely nothing to do with the real state of demand. It has only to do with the *demand for payment*, with the absolute necessity of transforming commodities into money. At this point the crisis breaks out. It first becomes evident not in the direct reduction of consumer demand, the demand for individual consumption, but rather in a decline in the number of exchanges of capital for capital, in the reproduction process of capital.[18]

We see here that Marx dos not explain crises by the under-consumption of the working class. Later, in another context, he explicitly rejects that theory. We would also like to quote that passage in full, because this crisis theory is currently kicking up a lot of dust.[19]

It is a pure tautology to say that crises are provoked by a lack of effective demand or effective consumption. The capitalist system does not recognize any forms of consumer other than those who can pay, if we exclude the consumption of paupers and swindlers. The fact that commodities are unsaleable means no more than that no effective buyers have been

---

18   Marx 1978, pp. 156–7.
19   [Kautsky also kicked up considerable 'dust' on this issue in 1892, with his work *The Class Struggle*, where he spoke of crises in terms of 'chronic' over-production and insufficient markets (Kautsky 1910, pp. 81–7), much as Rosa Luxemburg would do later in *The Accumulation of Capital* (1913). His comments there are difficult to reconcile with the passages he quotes in this review from Volume II of *Capital*: 'The wonderful development of transportation renders from year to year a [more complete] exploitation of the market possible; but this tendency is counteracted by the circumstance that the market steadily undergoes a change in those very countries whose population has reached a certain degree of civilization. Everywhere the introduction of the goods of capitalist large production extinguishes the domestic system of small production and transforms the industrial and agricultural laborers into proletarians. This produces two important results ...: first, it lowers the purchasing power of the population and thereby counteracts the effect of the extension of the market; and, second, and more important, it lays there the foundation for the capitalist system of production by calling into existence a proletarian class. Thus capitalist large production digs its own grave. From a certain point onward in its development every new extension of the market means the rising of a new competitor ... But this would mean the bankruptcy of the whole capitalist system ... The intervals of prosperity become ever shorter; the length of the crises ever longer' (Kautsky 1910, pp. 83–5)].

found for them, i.e. no consumers (no matter whether the commodities are ultimately sold to meet the needs of productive or individual consumption). If the attempt is made to give this tautology the semblance of greater profundity, by the statement that the working class receives too small a portion of its own product, and that the evil would be remedied if it received a bigger share, i.e. if its wages rose, we need only note that crises are always prepared by a period *in which wages generally rise*, and the working class actually does receive a greater share in the part of the annual product destined for consumption. From the standpoint of these advocates of sound and simple (!) common sense, such periods should rather avert the crisis. It thus appears that capitalist production involves certain conditions independent of people's good or bad intentions, which permit the relative prosperity of the working class only temporarily, and moreover always as a harbinger of crisis.[20]

The more capitalist production develops, the more complex it becomes: opportunities for disturbances become more frequent and increasingly noticeable. This historical tendency of the capitalist mode of production is examined more closely in a number of places of the second volume, especially in Parts Two and Three.

These remarks on crises, in their topicality and vitality, offer a welcome haven in the theoretical development of the book, which makes the greatest demands on the reader's attention and power of abstraction. We sorely miss the fact that Marx did not have the opportunity to season the second volume with his comments, as he did with the first one.

Further passages dealing with crises and the foundations of the credit system, as well as the excellent comments in Part One on the three circuits of capital, reveal the historical character of [the analyses contained in] the second volume.[21] The other parts deal with the functions and movements of capital in their simultaneous action, rather than with their development.

Above all, we are confronted with the distinction between *fixed and circulating capital*. The distinction has long been common, but it has done little to further the knowledge of capital. On the contrary, it has only created confusion because bourgeois economists here, as elsewhere, randomly mix up the determinations resulting from natural forms with those caused by peculiar

---

20   Marx 1978, pp. 486–7.
21   [Some of Marx's most interesting commentary on economic crises can be found in Chapter 17 of *Theories of Surplus-Value*, see Marx 1975, pp. 470–546].

social functions. They declare machines, buildings, etc. – as such – to be fixed capital, on account of certain material properties, such as immobility, regardless of the particular social form of the labour process, and all other capital, including money- and commodity-capital, to be circulating capital. Ricardo increased the confusion created by Adam Smith rather than putting an end to it, by mixing up fixed with constant capital, and variable with circulating capital.[22] Thus the discovery of the origin of surplus value was made impossible. The latter was derived from circulation, rather than from the production process. Naturally, the vulgar economists cling to this confusion; indeed, they have increased it as much as possible.

Marx not only provides a brilliant critique of the economists' theories of fixed and circulating capital – incidentally contrasting Quesnay's correct approach with Smith's and Ricardo's – but also gives us, for the first time, a sharp and clear definition of fixed and circulating capital.

First, Marx clearly distinguishes circulating capital from circulation capital, i.e. money- and commodity-capital. The difference between fixed and circulating capital may only spring from the *sphere of production*; it can only mean a distinction within productive capital. But this latter form of capital also splits up into *constant* and *variable* capital.

Constant capital is that productive capital, such as raw materials, tools, etc., whose value reappears unchanged in the product. Variable capital is that productive capital that not only transfers its own value to the product, but adds new value to it during the production process. There is only one type of capital that has this property: the labour power purchased by the capitalists. Labour power is a commodity as long as the wage-worker disposes of it. It is capital as soon as the capitalist buys it – in order to pay for it only after he has consumed it.

To illustrate the difference between fixed and circulating capital, we need to touch briefly on the turnover of capital. We have already considered the three forms of the circuit of capital. This circuit that includes production time and circulation time is called the *turnover* of capital if it is defined not as a singular but as a periodic process, as it actually is. The appropriate forms for investigating the turnover [of capital] are M ... M', or P ... P, but not C ... C'. The year is the natural measure of the turnover of capital. The capitalist calculates

---

22   That is, Ricardo equates circulating capital with 'capital that is to support labour'. ['The proportions, too, in which the capital that is to support labour, and the capital that is invested in tools, machinery, and buildings, may be variously combined' (Ricardo 1821, p. 25)]. The latter category coincides with Marx's category of variable capital, which we will discuss later.

how many turnovers his capital makes in a *year*. He proceeds in his calculations from M, the money capital he must advance. In this calculation, however, he finds that the number of turnovers made by the different parts of his capital during a year is very different. A portion of the capital value advanced by him, such as labour power, raw material, certain auxiliary materials – oil for lubrication, coal for heating, gas for lighting, etc. – goes totally into the product generated during a production period. Another part of the advanced capital value functions through several production periods in the same natural forms in which it is embodied (such as machines, buildings, etc.), transferring only a part of its value to the product in every production period. The turnover of the former capital value is naturally much more rapid than that of the second. The turnover of the latter includes several turnovers of the former. The first is *circulating*, the second is *fixed* capital.

The sharp distinction between fixed and circulating capital, according to their different behaviours as parts of the productive capital in terms of their turnover, on the one hand, and the distinguishing of both from constant and variable capital, on the other hand, is of the utmost importance in political economy in the explanation of the origin of surplus value. But if we are not mistaken, this distinction is also important in the elucidation of the transformation of surplus value into profit, which will appear in the third volume of *Capital*.

> According to the Ricardian law of value, (Engels wrote in this respect in his preface to the second volume), two capitals which employ the same amount of living labour at the same rate of pay, assuming all other circumstances to be also the same, produce in the same period of time products of the same value, and similarly the same amount of surplus-value or profit. If they employ unequal amounts of living labour, then they cannot produce the same surplus-value, or profit as the Ricardians say. However, the contrary is the case. In point of fact, equal capitals produce, on average, equal profits in the same time, irrespective of how much or how little living labour they employ. This contradiction to the law of value was already known to Ricardo, but neither he nor his followers were able to resolve it. Even Rodbertus could not ignore the contradiction, but instead of resolving it, he makes it one of the starting-points for his utopia (*Zur Erkenntnis* ..., p. 131). Marx had already resolved this contradiction in his manuscript '*Zur Kritik*';[23] in the plan of *Capital*, the solution is to be included in Volume 3.[24]

---

23 [See Marx 1975, Part II, Chapter VIII, 3a and 6, and Chapter X].
24 Engels's preface to Marx 1978, p. 101.

The Ricardian school could not solve this problem because of its identification of *surplus value* and *profit*. The preparation for this solution must therefore consist of singling out the factors that determine the differences between surplus value and profit.

The question seems to us to be touched upon already in the first volume, on the occasion of the investigation of the rate of surplus value. The latter can only be measured by comparing the magnitude of the surplus value with the magnitude of value of that part of capital which produces it, i.e. with variable capital. By contrast, the capitalist calculates profit by comparing the size of the *realised* surplus value – we abstract here from the differences between value and price – with the magnitude of the *total capital* advanced by him. This circumstance seems to us to determine, on the one hand, that equal rates of surplus value will yield different profit rates if different amounts of constant capital are employed, all other circumstances being equal; but it also makes it possible for different rates of surplus value to yield equal profit rates if, according to the different [rates of] exploitation of the labour power, different amounts of constant capital are used. Whether or not this fact plays a role in the equalisation of the profit rates, we do not dare to say.[25]

Other circumstances determining a difference between the rate of surplus value and the rate of profit seem to us, on the one hand, to be the differences in the *turnover time* of individual capitals and, on the other hand, the all-important difference between *advanced* and *employed* capital. In addition, the *circulation costs* should also be noticed in particular. We get to know all this in the second volume.

If surplus value is created in the production process and does not originate in the circulation process, then only the amount of the *variable* capital *employed*

---

25   Marx himself gives us no hints about it. He just says: 'Of course, the ratio of surplus-value not only to that portion of the capital from which it directly arises, and whose change in value it represents, but also to the sum total of the capital advanced, is economically of very great importance. We shall therefore deal exhaustively with this ratio in our third book' (Marx 1976, p. 323). In a note, Marx states that 'we will see in the third book that the average profit rate of the different production spheres is not affected by the division of capital into a constant and variable element peculiar to each one of them, and also that this phenomenon only seemingly contradicts the laws we have developed on the nature and production of surplus value' (Marx 1867, p. 594, note 61). [Kautsky is quoting from the first German edition. Marx's explanation of the equalisation of profit rates, given in Volume III of *Capital*, differed from Kautsky's suggestion and depended upon the transfer of surplus value between capitals through some commodities selling above, and others below, their value. This issue is discussed by Werner Sombart in the following document].

in the former determines the mass of surplus value – assuming its rate is to be a fixed magnitude. But the capitalist calculates his rate of profit according to the ratio of the profit he made to the magnitude of the *advanced* capital.

However, the capital advanced and the capital employed in the production process are by no means identical magnitudes. In the second volume, Marx developed a number of circumstances that determine the ratio between employed and advanced capital.

In general, of course, one can say that under otherwise equal conditions, the amount of capital to be advanced is all the greater, the longer is its turnover. But the total turnover of the advanced capital is the average turnover of its various constituent parts. That total turnover comprises a period all the longer, the greater is the fixed capital in proportion to the circulating capital, and the longer is the lifespan of the former. In both respects – lifespan and magnitude of value – the fixed capital increases with development of the capitalist mode of production. But this also increases the turnover time of the advanced capital.

On this occasion, Marx makes a very interesting comment on the relationship of the turnover time of fixed capital with the ten-year period of the crises.

> We can assume that, for the most important branches of large-scale industry, this life cycle [of fixed capital] is now on average a ten-year one. The precise figure is not important here. The result is that the cycle of related turnovers, extending over a number of years, within which the capital is confined by its fixed component, is one of the material foundations for the periodic cycle in which business passes through successive periods of stagnation, moderate activity, overexcitement and crisis. The periods for which capital is invested certainly differ greatly, and do not coincide in time. But a crisis is always the starting-point of a large volume of new investment. It is also, therefore, if we consider the society as a whole, more or less a new material basis for the next turnover cycle.[26]

The physical lifespan of the fixed capital is, as I said, an ever longer one. But this tendency is offset by an opposite one: with the capitalist mode of production, technological advances also develop, with upheavals of the means of production, so that the latter often have morally come to the end of their life[27] and must be replaced, even though they still stand in very good physical condition.

---

26 Marx 1978, p. 264.
27 ['Moral' wear refers to technological obsolescence].

The turnover time of fixed capital is determined by its physical and moral lifespan. The turnover time of circulating capital, by contrast, is determined by its production time and circulation time – here production time must not be understood as the time required to produce it, but as the time it must spend in the production process in order to supply a particular product. Not to be confused with the production time is the working period, which is a part of the former. 'The working period ... means the number of interrelated working days that are required, in a particular line of business, to complete a finished product'.[28] How long the working period is depends partly on technical and natural conditions, for products that constitute an independent unit in themselves (for example, ships, locomotives, buildings), or on social conditions, for products that do not constitute such a unit and whose weight and volume are, to a certain extent, divisible at will without losing their use-value (for instance yarn, coal, etc.). For such products, it is in particular the supply contracts and delivery dates that determine the length of the working period.

The production time must always be at least as long as the working period, but it can also be much longer. Many products require their production to be subjected to natural processes for longer or shorter periods of time, without the simultaneous intervention of the labour process. Thus wine must ferment, fabrics bleach, etc. During the time when the unfinished product is left to the working of natural processes, without going through the labour process, no surplus value is added to it. But this time also prolongs the turnover time, increasing the necessary amount of capital to be advanced and reducing profits. One of the keenest worries of the capitalists is therefore to reduce as much as possible the production period during which no surplus value is added [to the product], for example, by replacing natural by chemical bleaching. This can usually be done only by increasing the fixed capital. Thus, shortening of the working period is also usually associated with an increase in the invested capital (improvement and enlargement of the machinery and work space, increase in the number of workers, etc.). Where the excess of production time over the working period is very significant and cannot be artificially reduced, the operation is often unprofitable, the clearest example being forest husbandry. Forestry is not profitable; therefore, wherever capitalism penetrates, forests disappear.

Finally, the turnover time, and with it the magnitude of the advanced capital, is determined by the duration of the circulation time. The improvement of the

---

28 Marx 1978, p. 308.

means of transportation can abbreviate the duration of the turnover period, but generally it tends to prolong it because the improvement of the means of transportation entails the possibility and necessity of seeking ever more distant markets, both in order to sell the products and, on the other hand, to obtain raw materials.

The capitalist and the theoretical representatives of his interests usually really believe that capital continuously functions in the production process, that the capital employed in it and the advanced capital are equal magnitudes. However, this is not so. Let us take a case in which, for simplicity's sake, we disregard all the complicating circumstances, the surplus value, fixed capital, etc.

The working period (which we assume coincides with the production time) amounts to nine weeks, the circulation time to three weeks. The weekly outlay on wages and raw and auxiliary materials amounts to 1,000 marks, so that the capitalist must advance 9,000 marks in order to keep the labour process going during the whole period. After nine weeks, this capital is transformed into commodity capital; before it is sold and new raw materials, etc. are purchased with the proceeds, three weeks pass by. But the capitalist production process does not tolerate an interruption. It can only continue during these three weeks by the application of an additional capital of 3,000 marks (we abstract here from the possibility of limiting production in order that the 9,000 marks might last for 12 weeks, because this case offers no new peculiarities). The advanced capital does not therefore amount to 9,000 marks but rather to 12,000 marks, without the scale of production having expanded. 1,000 marks are still used every week, and if we include the production of surplus value, the same amount of surplus value is generated every week as before. The shorter the circulation time, the more of his capital the capitalist can apply in the production process, and the more surplus value he can produce. The opposite applies when the circulation time is longer. The rate of surplus value may remain the same, compared to the variable capital *employed* in the production process, and yet change with respect to the variable capital *advanced*. Since the capitalist and the bourgeois economist are concerned only with the latter, it seems to them as if the process of circulation were the source from which surplus value flows.

But one more thing should be noted: the capitalist calculates his profits in proportion to the advanced capital not for each one of its turnovers, but for the *whole year*. Marx does not deal in the second volume, any more than in the first, with *profit*, but rather with *surplus value*. He therefore does not deal [in the second volume] with the annual rate of profit, but with the annual rate of surplus value, which has to be related to the advanced variable capital and not to the total capital.

Let us assume two capitalists, one of whom has a company with a turnover time of 5 weeks, thus making about 10 turnovers per year. The company of the other has a turnover time of one year; the number of its turnovers is thus equal to 1. Each one of the two applies the same amount of variable capital; let us say 100 marks a week. Thus each one of them spends, assuming that the year has 50 weeks, 5,000 marks annually. The rate of surplus value amounts to 100 percent for both, so that each one of them will reap 5,000 marks in surplus value. But here a difference occurs: the capitalist whose capital turns over only once must advance a variable capital of 5,000 marks, while the other has to advance merely 500 marks. The annual rate of surplus value of the first is 100 percent; that of the other 1,000 percent. This seems to show that the surplus value is derived from the sphere of circulation: in fact, both have used the same amount of labour power and yet have achieved two different annual rates of surplus value, because the number of turnovers of their capitals is different. However, this contradiction of the Marxist theory of value and surplus value is only apparent: it is generated by the difference between the *employed* and the *advanced* capital. Both have *employed* the same amount of capital and pocketed the same amount of surplus value.

Although the contradiction is only apparent, the Ricardian school could not solve it. Today it is one of the main arguments of Professor Lexis[29] against the Marxian theory of value and surplus value in his review of the second volume of *Capital* published in the *Jahrbücher für Nationalökonomie und Statistik*.[30] But in making this objection, Mr. Lexis overlooks not only the difference between employed and advanced capital, but also the difference between surplus value and profit from capital.

On this occasion, an error on the part of that critic should also be pointed out. On page 461, he assumes that Marx equated exchange-value with the average price of commodities. 'If Marx wanted to say afterwards (probably in the third volume), that he means by the value of individual commodities *not* the monetary expression of their exchange-value, as it is normally formed in the existing economic order, but an ideal value that is not at all empirically expressed, he would thus contradict his earlier remarks, in a way making a mockery of his readers with his value secret'. Regarding this claim, it should be

---

29 [In his preface to Volume III of *Capital*, Friedrich Engels provides his own commentary on the review of Volume II by Wilhelm Lexis. See Marx 1992, pp. 98–100].

30 1885, 5. Heft, p. 459.

pointed out that in the first volume of *Capital* Marx already explicitly alluded to the fact that value and average price do not at all coincide. If he also wanted to keep them apart 'afterwards', the only people being mocked would be those for whom his value theory remained a mystery. But Marx is innocent of the charges levelled against him. He explicitly stated in a note to vol. I:

> How can we account for the origin of capital on the assumption that prices are regulated by the average price, *i.e. ultimately* by the value of the commodities? I say 'ultimately' *because average prices do not directly coincide with the values of commodities*, as Adam Smith, Ricardo, and others believe.[31]

Marx also gives examples of commodities whose price is constantly below their value: 'Jacob questions whether gold has ever been paid for at its full value. This applies still more to diamonds'.[32] Marx says this at the beginning of his investigation, as if to warn the reader not to confuse average price and value.

One can perhaps ask: what is the use of such an ideal value, which does not necessarily coincide with the average price? One might just as well ask, and with even better reason: what is the value of a law of falling bodies that only takes into consideration the force of gravity, completely disregarding disturbing circumstances such as air resistance, the rotation of the earth around its axis, etc., and whose theoretical results are therefore never in accord with the 'average' results of the bodies' fall? But the actual phenomena of falling can only be explained on the basis of the law of falling bodies, and average prices are only explained by the law of value.[33]

---

31 Marx 1976, p. 269, note 24.
32 Marx 1976, p. 130.
33 [Marx was also quite explicit on this point in *Grundrisse*: 'Price therefore is distinguished from *value* ... because the latter appears as the law of motions which the former runs through. But the two are constantly different and never balance out, or balance only coincidentally or exceptionally. The price of a commodity constantly stands above or below the value of the commodity, and the value of a commodity exists only in this up- and-down movement of commodity prices. Supply and demand constantly determine the prices of commodities; [they] never balance, or only coincidentally' (Marx 1973, pp. 137–8). On page 140 Marx added: 'Because labor time as the measure of value exists only as an ideal, it cannot serve as the matter of price-comparisons ... Price as distinct from value is necessarily money price'].

What Marx said about surplus value and profit also holds good for value and price:

> We shall see in Volume 3 that the rate of profit is no mystery, when one knows the laws of surplus-value. But if one works in the reverse direction, one comprehends neither the one nor the other.[34]

So much for the criticism from Professor Lexis and his assumption that Marx 'made a mockery of his readers with his value secret'.

IV

So far we have not, for reasons of brevity, adhered strictly in our review to the course of development of the original text, but have rather grouped together non-adjacent but objectively related sections, such as chapters 5, 14 and 15, dealing with the influence of the turnover time on the magnitude and self-valorisation of the advanced capital.

Following the same rule, we shall now deal for the first time with a chapter located at the beginning of the investigations of the second volume: chapter 6, dealing with the *costs of circulation*. There we find that the labour that goes into buying and selling, as well as into bookkeeping, creates no value. Wage-workers who are employed in these sectors can indeed yield surplus *labour*, but not surplus value. The expenses arising from bookkeeping and from buying and selling do not increase the value of the product; they must be paid out of the surplus value. The unpaid surplus labour of the wage-labourers employed on those activities creates no surplus value, but rather reduces the deduction from the surplus value of the capitalist caused by the circulation costs.[35]

According to the plan of his work, Marx will not deal with merchants' capital until the third volume. To anyone who knows these gentlemen, it will be no surprise that the academic and non-academic demagogues of the current edition

---

34 Marx 1976, p. 324, note 3.
35 [In *Theories of Surplus-Value*, Marx wrote that the labour of servants and trades people 'will not increase (material) wealth by a single farthing' (Marx 1969–72, Vol. I, p. 298). Marx was influenced by Adam Smith, who defined productive labour as that which 'realizes itself in some ... vendible commodity, which lasts for some time ... It is, as it were, a certain quantity of labour stocked and stored up to be employed, if necessary, upon some other occasion' (Smith 1937, p. 314). Marx thought Smith's view was too restrictive (Marx 1969–72, Vol. I, pp. 171–2). His own definition treated all labour in capitalist society as productive that 'produces surplus-value for the capitalist, or in other words contributes to the self-valorization of capital' (Marx 1978, p. 644)].

of 'true German socialism' explained Marx's previous disregard of merchants' capital in terms of demagogic rather than scientific reasons. Furthermore, they could have found, had they wanted to, some places in the first volume where Marx did make mention of the merchant.

> Since, however, it is impossible, by circulation alone, to explain the transformation of money into capital, and the formation of surplus-value, merchants' capital appears to be an impossibility, as long as equivalents are exchanged; it appears, therefore, that it can only be derived from the twofold advantage gained, over both the selling and the buying producers, by the merchant who parasitically inserts himself between them.[36]

This applies to the pre-capitalist circulation of commodities. It is complemented by the remarks in the second volume on the costs of circulation of capital. To be sure, Marx still abstracts here from the merchant as capitalist, but we already see the source from which his profit flows: the produced surplus value. Hence the moral indignation of the industrial capitalists, who produce the surplus value, concerning the immoral intermediaries with whom they must share it!

A more important item of the social overhead costs of the circulation of capital is formed by the cost of production and reproduction of *money*. Marx talks about it on page 112 [of the German edition] in connection with the circulation costs. But he also deals with this issue later and in another context, on pages 420–1. This passage seems to us particularly important. It says:

> The sum of labour-power and social means of production that is spent in the annual production of gold and silver as instruments of circulation forms a heavy item of *faux frais* (overhead costs) for the capitalist mode of production, or more generally for a mode of production based on commodity circulation. It withdraws from social use a corresponding sum of possible additional means of production and consumption, i.e. of real wealth. To the extent that the costs of this expensive machinery of circulation are reduced, with the scale of production remaining the same, i.e. at a given level of its extension, the productive forces of social labour are correspondingly heightened. Thus in as much as the auxiliary means that develop with credit have this effect, they directly increase capitalist wealth, whether this is because a greater part of the social production

---

36 Marx 1978, pp. 266–7.

and labour process is thereby accomplished without the intervention of real money, or because the capacity of the actually functioning quantity of money to fulfil its function is thereby increased.

This also disposes of the pointless question of whether capitalist production on its present scale would be possible without credit (even considered from this standpoint alone), i.e. with a merely metallic circulation. It would clearly not be possible. It would come up against the limited scale of precious-metal production. On the other hand, we should not get any mystical ideas about the productive power of the credit system, just because this makes money capital available or fluid.[37]

The overhead costs that arise from the labour of buying and selling and from bookkeeping are a burden on surplus value; by contrast, the overhead costs resulting from the production of gold and silver as means of circulation are a burden on society as a whole.

Due to considerations of space, we must pass over the investigation of the circulation costs arising from the storage and transportation of goods, and the circumstances under which they add value to the commodities or reduce the surplus value. We can already see, from the few indications we have given, that in the second volume of *Capital* a number of factors are investigated that have an influence on shaping the outward forms of surplus value. But the series of these factors is not yet complete; the volume does not deal, for instance, with ground rent; we have not received any indication of the way in which these different factors interact; even the goal of the investigation has so far been pointed out only a few times. No wonder that the remarks of the second volume leave us partly dissatisfied: they provide us with the solutions to many riddles, but at the same time they show us new problems. If the first volume is, in a sense, a self-contained whole, the second volume is just an introduction for the third, a fragment, a torso, which has many attractions but which also awakens the desire to get to know the whole.

The third volume of *Capital* will also be important for the *theory of value*, as the basis of the whole work.

Among those currently established in science, Marx's theory of value and surplus value is the only one that makes possible a sufficient explanation of economic processes. All other related theories either prove to be wrong from the outset or do not explain what they should explain. That is the case with

---

37 Marx 1978, pp. 420–1.

the theory according to which prices are determined by supply and demand. Supply and demand can explain *price fluctuations*, not the *conformity to law* in the prices of the different commodities, which comes to light most clearly when demand and supply are balanced. It is the same with the theory according to which profit does not spring from the surplus value originating in the production process, but from a surcharge on the cost of the product. This view is defended by Mr. Lexis in the aforementioned review. But since nobody profits if everyone sells dearer than he bought, because when buying everyone loses what he gained on the sale, Mr. Lexis finds himself constrained to believe that the workers occupy an exceptional position. They are forced by circumstances to sell their commodity (which he, like his colleagues, calls labour instead of labour power) as cheaply as possible, that is to say, without a surcharge on its cost price. So they have to buy dearer than they sell. The question for Mr. Lexis, as he himself says, is to offer a *justification* of the interest on capital. What does he gain by his explanation? Marx's theory explains the [origin of] surplus value itself under the assumption that the worker sells his labour power for its full value, in the same way as any other commodity owner sells his wares. Surplus value does not appear because the workers are cheated, but because of the peculiar nature of the commodity labour power, which is able to generate more value during its productive consumption than its own value amounts to. Mr. Lexis assumes, by contrast, that all capitalists cheat their neighbours, and that profits therefore come from the fact that workers are unable, for their part, to cheat the capitalists. And Mr. Lexis calls that a 'justification of the interest on capital'! According to Marx's theory, surplus value originates in a highly moral way – on the foundation of today's ruling ethics of justice and equality, corresponding to a commodity-producing society, in which each commodity is exchanged for its value. According to the theory of vulgar economy, improved upon by Lexis, profit has its source in a constant violation of the moral principles of commodity production, and the workers are the only moral people – though admittedly only out of necessity – for they are the only ones who do not cheat their fellows.

But aside from this strange 'justification of interest on capital', the scientific benefit of Lexis's theory seems to us problematic. The cheating of the workers might explain where profit comes from, but definitely not its *conformity to law*. It does not explain why the surcharge on price should, under certain circumstances, be of a certain size. The theory that profit *fluctuations* are balanced out by the fact that in the more profitable lines of business more capital is invested, tells us no more about the laws regulating the magnitude of the rate of profit than the knowledge that the crest of the wave is higher than the wave trough, and that both have a tendency to level out, acquaints us with the depths of the sea.

Only the rate of surplus value, as Marx has developed it, offers a *specific* magnitude, out of which, under certain conditions, a *specific* rate of profit must develop. Likewise, only the value theory that Marx took over from Ricardo, developing and defining it more precisely, offers a *definite* foundation from which one can deduce the magnitude of prices. Marx's theory of value and surplus value is therefore today the only scientifically satisfactory one. Only one objection can still be raised against it, a single one. Marx has still not shown us the transformation of surplus value into profit; he has not yet proved how this development proceeds and how its necessary result conforms to the facts of experience.

There is, consequently, still an apparent contradiction (which we already touched upon above) between the surplus value developed by Marx and the actual profit. This argument is far from being a proof of the falsity of the Marxian theory, but it means that its correctness has not yet been proven with scientific certainty.

The third volume promises to solve this apparent contradiction, and thus to prove scientifically the accuracy of the theory of value and of the whole structure erected upon it, to the extent that we can speak of certainty in science in general. The revolution of political economy, [accomplished] by Marx, will then be completed. This science must then follow the path marked out by Marx, or else abdicate as a science and declare that it is nothing more than the spiritual bodyguard of the profit of capital – including ground rent.

We can see the importance that the third volume of *Capital* promises to have, as well as the significance of the second volume, which is so closely associated with the third. But the more we recognise this significance, the more important appear to be the problems – whose solution is partly continued from the first volume to the second and partly set out anew – and the greater is the desire to get to know Marx's last word on political economy.

The final section of the second volume deals with the reproduction and circulation of the total social capital. We see in the following passage the standpoint from which Marx sets out to do that:

> In speaking of the social point of view, i.e. in considering the total social product, which includes both the reproduction of the social capital and individual consumption, it is necessary to avoid falling into the habits of bourgeois economics, as imitated by Proudhon, i.e. to avoid looking at things as if a society based on the capitalist mode of production lost its specific historical and economic character when considered en bloc, as

a totality. This is not the case at all. What we have to deal with is the collective capitalist. The total capital appears as the share capital of all individual capitalists together. This joint-stock company has in common with many other joint-stock companies that everyone knows what they put into it, but not what they will get out of it.[38]

Seen as a whole, the modern mode of production shows the same capitalist character as the process of reproduction of each individual capital. But in the social approach various factors come into play, whose operation could not be included in the course of the previous investigation – especially the *use-value* of the commodities produced. When considering the individual capitals, the natural forms of the products could be overlooked, so that only their magnitude of value was considered. Whether the capitalist produced shoe polish or prayer books or steam engines did not alter the laws of valorisation and circulation of individual capitals. In the societal perspective of the reproduction process of capital, however, we find that it is determined not only by the mutual value relation of the constituent parts of the social product, but also by their use-value, their material form. The capitalist process of production cannot take place if the means of production and the articles of consumption for workers and capitalists are not present in the proper proportions.

But the social perspective on the reproduction process of capital also shows us the *worker* in a new role. Until now we saw him only as commodity seller – the seller of his commodity, labour power. Now he is an important figure also as commodity buyer, as buyer of articles of consumption. For the capitalist mode of production to keep functioning, it is not only necessary for the workers to produce surplus value and to receive [the value of] their own labour power; it is also necessary for them to buy their share of the commodities from the capitalist, so that the money the capitalist gave them as wages flows back to him and can function again as capital in his hands.

On the other hand, the capitalists now appear not only as buyers of means of production, but also as buyers of means of consumption, as consumers of surplus value; and the way in which this happens turns out to be very important.

In our previous remarks we have already mentioned the division of the mass of products according to their natural form. According to this distinction, production must also be divided into *means of production* and *means of consumption*. The value of the total product of each one of these branches of

---

38   Marx 1978, p. 509.

production is divided into a portion of value that represents constant capital c, which merely transfers its value to the product, then into the variable capital v and the surplus value s; the annual product is $= c + v + s$.

However, Adam Smith, together with the economists who followed him, assumed that the value of the annual product is equal to $v + s$, i.e. that the price of each product can be resolved in the last instance into wages and surplus value. Mr. Lexis also defends this view in the article mentioned above, in which he equates constant and fixed capital. That could only be justified if, in primeval production, only labour but no constant capital (tools, etc.) were involved. Mr. Lexis adds: 'However, there is no impediment to continuing these series (of means of production, of which one contributes to generate the others) until we come to an initial state in which only labour and natural products – i.e. no fixed capital – were employed in the production of the first elements of constant capital'.[39] There is 'no impediment' to this reasoning, except the fatal fact that in the entire range of capitalist commodity production – and that is all we can be talking about if we speak about constant capital, wages and surplus value – a capitalist undertaking without means of production does not exist. Professor Lexis surely does not assume, for instance, that children looking for strawberries and flowers in the wild, in order to sell them, are the ones who furnish the elements of constant capital.[40]

Mr. Lexis's view is nothing but a hazy reference to the law that labour is the source of all commodity values – a law against which Mr. Lexis fought so resolutely. The sum of the *values newly created* in a year, the annual *value product* [*Wertprodukt des Jahres*], can certainly be resolved into $v + s$, but not the sum of the values of the products whose production was completed that year, the *value of the annual product* [*jährlichen Produktenwert*]. The latter always contains value elements that were created in previous years, means of production, whose value reappears in the product.[41]

So we must identify the value of the annual product, both in the category of means of production and in that of consumption, as being equal to $c + v + s$.

We shall consider only the simplest of the schemes underlying Marx's investigations; that in which he disregards both the portion of value that is transferred due to wear and tear from the *fixed* (not to be confused with constant) capital to the annual product, without being immediately replaced *in natura*,

---

39 Marx 1978, p. 463.
40 See the detailed critique of Adam Smith in Marx 1978, pp. 438–65.
41 ['The value product (*Wertprodukt*) of the current year, the value newly created during the year in the commodity form, is smaller than the value of the product (*Produktenwert*), the total value of the mass of commodities produced during the year' (Marx 1978, p. 513)].

and the accumulation of surplus value. We assume that the latter is wholly consumed [by the capitalists].

Marx's scheme is:

I. Means of production.
   Capital: $4{,}000\ c + 1{,}000\ v = 5{,}000$
   Commodity product: $4{,}000\ c + 1{,}000\ v + 1{,}000\ s = 6{,}000$

II. Means of consumption.
   Capital: $2{,}000\ c + 500\ v = 2{,}500$
   Commodity product: $2{,}000\ c + 500\ v + 500\ s = 3{,}000$[42]

The rate of surplus value is therefore assumed to be 100 percent. The total value of the annual product amounts to 9,000; the total value of variable capital and surplus value in both department amounts to 3,000 (let us say a million marks).

Wages and surplus value are spent on articles of consumption: the 500 v and 500 s of the second department are therefore spent within it. For purposes of this study, they need not be considered further. The constant capital c, which has been used up, must be replaced again in both departments. Department I produces the means of production required by both departments. The 4,000 c that this department requires, it has produced itself; they are sold within department I itself, so that here we can disregard them too.

1,000 v + 1,000 s of the first department must be converted into means of consumption. 2,000 c in means of production have been used up in the second department, and their value has passed to a corresponding portion of the annual product of means of consumption. For continuation of the production process, these 2,000 c in articles of consumption must be exchanged for 1,000 v + 1,000 c of the first department – sums of value that are embedded in a corresponding part of the annual product of means of production.

The capitalists of department I have paid 1,000 v in the form of money to their workers, after they used up 1,000 v in the form of labour power. With this 1,000 v in cash, the workers buy articles of consumption from the capitalists of department II, equivalent to 1,000 c. In that way, the capitalists of department II acquire the money to buy 1,000 in means of production from the capitalists of department I. Thus a capital-value of 1,000 v is converted into cash by the capitalists of department I, who can use it to buy labour power. The surplus value 1,000 s of department I is realised partly through the fact that the capitalists

---

42 [See Marx 1978, p. 473].

of department II (who possess money stocks as a condition for any capitalist production) throw money into circulation in order to purchase means of production, which converts into cash a part of the surplus value of department I. That money is used by the capitalists of department I, who are also human beings and want to live, to purchase means of consumption for themselves. In that way it flows back to the capitalists of department II. However, because the capitalist cannot always wait until he has sold his commodities in order to live from the realised surplus value, one of the requirements for being a capitalist is to have enough money not only to continue the production and circulation process, but also to be able to advance to himself as much as he needs for his own consumption, and as appears in accordance with the expected profit. The capitalists of department I thus advance money to buy means of consumption from department II, and in that way they supply money to the capitalists of department II, which in turn uses it to buy means of production from department I.

From these circumstances follows the law, later confirmed, which reads:

> The general conclusion that follows, as far as concerns the money that the industrial capitalists cast into circulation to mediate their own commodity circulation, is that whether this is advanced on the account of the constant value portion of their commodities, or on the account of the surplus-value existing in these commodities in so far as it is spent as revenue, the same amount flows back to the respective capitalists as they themselves advanced for the monetary circulation.[43]

Similarly, only in a roundabout way, the money returns to the hands of the capitalists who spent it in the payment of wages.

The precondition for the whole circulation, however, is that $v + s$ in department I $= c$ in department II.

Also, it is clear that no element can change in value, in any of the two departments, without bringing about a change in the value dimension of all the other elements. The mechanism is even more complicated if we take into consideration the division of the articles of consumption into necessities and luxury goods, as well as the fact that fixed capital only transfers a fragment of its value to the annual product, while the worn out part of fixed capital must be entirely replaced [in kind]. If – all other circumstances being equal – the proportion of the value of the functioning fixed capital that annually becomes defunct, [rel-

---

43   Marx 1978, p. 477.

ative] to the annual value transferred by the fixed capital to the product, is not constant, stoppages occur in the reproduction and circulation process. Finally, the accumulation of surplus value, the expansion of the production process, causes further complications. A wealth of new observations and remarks on the causes of crises can be found in the relevant sections, which, however, cannot be reproduced without entering into details, any more than the observations accompanying them about the role of money capital and the foundations of the credit system.

We hope to have the opportunity to come back to the third section and to compare it with Quesnay's *Tableau économique*, which set itself a task similar to that of the third section of the second volume. The latter answers the question: 'How is the *capital* consumed in production replaced in its value out of the annual product, and how is the movement of this replacement intertwined with the consumption of surplus-value by the capitalists and of wages by the workers?'.[44] Quesnay's *Tableau économique* also wanted to show the manner in which the annual total product circulates, on the one hand in order to keep the reproduction process going, and on the other hand to make possible the consumption of rents and wages. Quesnay assumed that only agricultural labour supplies a surplus, while the industrial workers merely add to the product as much value as they consume themselves. The surplus value goes first of all to the landowners in the form of ground rent; and finally, for Quesnay, the industrial capitalists and workers together constitute only a single class. As is well-known, Marx's scheme proceeds, as regards these three points, from entirely different presuppositions. However, both Quesnay's scheme and Marx's have one thing in common: that the circuit C ... C′, not M ... M′ or P ... P′, underlies them both.

Quesnay's system was the economic lodestar of the French Revolution of 1789, Mirabeau being its most important representative. The second volume of *Capital* deals with most of the questions to which Quesnay's answer was so significant for the course of the French Revolution. But in Marx, in accordance with the changed circumstances, the capitalist industrialist steps to the foreground in place of the capitalist farmer.

Already these considerations clearly indicate that the volume under review deals with more than mere doctoral questions and barren subtleties. As scant and incomplete as our sketch of the content naturally has to be – given the strict logical structure of the work and Marx's concise and compact language, which make it almost impossible to give a faithful reproduction of the content in

---

44   Marx 1978, p. 469.

abbreviated form – one still hopes that it has managed to show the importance of the problems whose solution is partly provided in the second volume or else partly initiated there.

But despite the significance of the volume under review, we believe that we are not mistaken if we assume that it is often very disappointing. It will disappoint all those who saw in *Capital* a handbook for social-democratic agitators; in the theory of value, the basis for a utopia; and in the theory of surplus value, a mere attempt to incite the proletariat against the capitalists, an appeal to eternal justice and equality. The second volume shows clearly that *Capital* has only one purpose: to further the knowledge of the mechanism of the capitalist mode of production. That is the only purpose of the study and its presentation.

But those who think it is impossible to write about political economy without demagogic and ulterior motives will not be the only ones disappointed. Even those whom Marx primarily addressed in his writings, the workers, will not greet the second volume with the same enthusiasm as the first. The scene for the investigations of the first volume is the *factory*, that of the second is the *comptoir* [cashier's desk]. The first volume dealt for the most part with conditions close to the workers, with which they are intimately familiar. The second volume deals with abstractions from facts that are distant from the workers, and which arouse in them relatively little interest. What they first of all experience is the way in which surplus value is *produced*. The kind of transformations that surplus value experiences, and how it is realised – these are questions much closer to the capitalists than to the workers.

Nevertheless, we expect the working class to greet the second volume of *Capital* if not with the same enthusiasm, then at least with the same interest as the first. The workers, especially in Germany, know perfectly well how to appreciate the value of theoretical knowledge. And this appreciation of knowledge by no means contradicts the materialist conception of historical development, which they have accepted.

It is true that the labour movement is automatically generated by the circumstances. Historical development is nowadays necessarily determined by the contradictions of interest between the different classes; and among these contradictions, the antagonism between capital and labour is daily becoming more decisive.

It is also true that the goal of the labour movement is not arbitrary, but is given by the circumstances.

But for the *course* of the labour movement and the *way* in which it reaches its goal, it is obviously not a matter for indifference whether it clearly understands this goal and always keeps it in mind, or whether it allows itself to be carried along by the circumstances, changing its direction according to the daily needs. In this field lies the task of the socialist parties. They can neither *make* the labour movement nor *prescribe* to it their own goal. They have to *recognise* that goal and to assume the *leadership* of the labour movement until it is reached. They can do that only on the basis of theoretical knowledge of the actual conditions, of the development, purpose and functioning of the capitalist mode of production. Wherever this knowledge is lacking, a socialist movement decays either into a doctrinaire utopianism or into opportunism, taking its momentary ideas and their 'scientific' foundations wherever it finds them and wherever they are cheapest.

The German workers have recognised this, and that is why they will study the second volume of *Capital*.

DOCUMENT 4

A Contribution to the Critique of Karl Marx's Economic System (1894)

Werner Sombart

Source: Werner Sombart, 'Zur Kritik des ökonomischen Systems von Karl Marx,' *Archiv für soziale Gesetzgebung und Statistik*, Vol. VII, Berlin, 1894, pp. 555–94.

Karl Marx, *Das Kapital. Kritik der politischen Oekonomie*. Dritter Band, erster Teil, 8°, XXVIII. und 448 s.; zweiter Teil, 422 S. Hamburg: Meissner 1894.

Introduction by the Editors

Volume III of *Capital* appeared in 1894, nine years after Volume II. As with Volume II, the third volume was laboriously edited and put together from Marx's manuscripts by Frederick Engels. In his preface to the new volume, Engels recounted the difficulties he faced and the extent to which he had to supplement fragmentary manuscripts with his own commentary and insertions.[1] In addition to explaining these editorial challenges, Engels also discussed the attempts of several writers, prior to the appearance of Volume III, to address the seeming contradiction between the law of value and the formation of an equal average rate of profit on capitals with different organic compositions. In that effort, he thought, Conrad Schmidt and Peter Fireman had made commendable efforts, but Wilhelm Lexis had distinguished himself as a 'vulgar economist', and Achille Loria proved to be 'a conscious sophist, paralogist, braggart and charlatan'. In light of those comments, it was with evident relief that Engels greeted the review of Volume III by Werner Sombart. In a supplement to Volume III, from which we include three excerpts, Engels remarked that 'Werner Sombart gives an outline presentation of Marx's system which is quite excellent on the whole'.[2]

Readers will recall that when Illarion Kaufman reviewed Volume I of *Capital* in 1872, he struggled with the question of how Marx's Hegelian terminology

---

1 For a sceptical commentary on Engels's editorial work, see Heinrich 1996.
2 Supplement by Engels in Marx 1981, p. 1031.

might be reconciled with his scientific analysis of factual material. Kaufman concluded that Marx's system of scientific economics was more closely related to the biological sciences than to the Hegelian dialectic. The significance of this question reappeared in the review of Volume III by Sombart. Whereas Kaufman wrote that Marx could 'in no sense be called an idealist', Sombart was more emphatic, declaring that 'Marx's economic system is characterised by an *extreme objectivism*'.

Sombart certainly did not mean that Marx was an empiricist. The new volume, he wrote, 'does not deal with the phenomena of real economic activity', for '"value" does not exist in the phenomenal world ... *value is not an empirical but a conceptual fact* ... the value-concept is a tool of our thinking, which we use to comprehend the phenomena of economic life; it is a logical fact'. As Engels pointed out, this statement was 'too generalized': before the arrival of capitalism, simple commodity producers had exchanged commodities at prices that generally approximated values. But apart from that reservation he was satisfied that Sombart had given a fair and worthy summary of Marx's thinking.

The question that Sombart asked was whether there was an irreconcilable contradiction between the following two assertions: first, 'that "value" in Marx is only a "tool of thought"'; and second, 'that the "law of value", as a "natural law", ultimately determines the entire economic life of humankind'. His answer was: 'I think not'. Although value does not *exist* in phenomenal terms, it remains the *essence* of price. In this connection Sombart quoted Marx: 'all science would be superfluous if the form of the appearance of things directly coincided with their essence', and therefore 'it is one of the tasks of science to reduce the visible and merely apparent movement to the actual inner movement'.

Sombart saw that Marx's method was the direct opposite of the 'subjectivist tendency' in economic theory, which undertakes to explain prices by starting from individual judgements of marginal utility – the same price theory that undergraduates begin with today in university economics departments. Marx, in contrast, was intent on discovering the 'economic conditions which are *independent*' of the individual's will, in order to determine what 'goes on behind his back, by virtue of relations *independent* of him'. Sombart withheld judgement on 'whether subjectivist economics (described as historical, ethical, organic, abstract, traditional or otherwise) has a bright future, or whether it stands at the end of its development and is about to wind up, bequeathing its possessions now to history, now to psychology'. But so far as Marx's approach was concerned, he presented it much as Marx himself had done in his unpublished notes for the *Contribution to the Critique of Political Economy*. In Sombart's words:

It never occurred to him to look for the individual motives of the persons exchanging, or even to proceed from the cost-of-production calculation. No, his train of thought was this: prices are formed by competition ... But competition itself is regulated by the rate of profit, the profit rate by the rate of surplus-value, and this by value, which is itself the expression of a socially determined fact, of the social productivity. [This succession] now presents itself in Marx's system in reverse order: value – surplus-value – profit – competition – prices, etc. If we wanted a catchphrase, we could say: the question for Marx is never the motivation, but always the limitation of the individual caprice of economic agents.

Marx spoke of the relation between value and price in terms of a 'constant negation of the negation': market prices negate value, yet value in turn is the law of 'motion' that governs the movement of prices, so that the immediacy of market prices is conceptually negated in what Marx called the 'price of production', which reflects an average rate of profit that would prevail if capitalism were to accomplish the impossible, namely, a crisis-free state of equilibrium. Marx saw value as the axis about which market prices move in response to changing conditions of supply and demand.[3] In Hegel's *Logic*, the contradiction between 'essence' and 'existence' was finally transcended in the Absolute Idea, or in thought absorbing into itself the alienated world of objects. In Marx's reinterpretation of Hegel, it is *labour* that must ultimately find the world of alienated 'things' to be its own creation. Marx's analogue for Hegel's Absolute Idea was a scientific plan, embracing the whole of economic life directly in terms of labour accounting – in other words, the rational self-determination of the associated producers. The 'extreme objectivism' to which Sombart referred ultimately pointed to the associated producers becoming the self-determining subjects and the conscious 'actors and authors' of their own history.[4]

∴

---

3   Marx 1973, pp. 137–8.
4   Marx 1977, p. 109.

Friedrich Engels's Comments on the Review by Werner Sombart

In Braun's *Archiv für soziale Gesetzgebung*, VII, no. 4, Werner Sombart gives an outline presentation of Marx's system which is quite excellent on the whole. This is the first time that a German university professor has managed to see by and large in Marx's writings what Marx actually said, and he further declares that criticism of the Marxian system should consist not in a refutation ('that can be left to someone with political ambition'), but rather in a further development. Sombart, too, is understandably preoccupied with our present subject. He discusses the significance of value in Marx's system and arrives at the following result. Value is not present at the phenomenal level, in the exchange relationship of capitalistically produced commodities; it does not dwell in the consciousness of the agents of capitalist production; it is not an empirical fact but an ideal or logical one; Marx's concept of value, in its material specificity, is nothing more than the economic expression of the fact that the social productivity of labour is the basis of economic existence; the law of value is what ultimately governs economic processes in a capitalist economic order, and its general content for such an economic order is that the value of commodities is the specific historical form in which the productivity of labour, which ultimately governs all economic processes, has its determining effect. This is what Sombart says. Now it cannot be said that this conception of the significance of the law of value for the capitalist form of production is incorrect. Yet to me it does seem too generalised, and capable of a closer and more precise formulation; in my view, it in no way exhausts the whole significance that the law of value has for those stages of society's economic development that are governed by this law.[5]

With both Sombart and Schmidt ... insufficient regard is paid to the fact that what is involved is not just a logical process but a historical one, and its explanatory reflection in thought, the logical following-up of its internal connections.[6]

Marx's law of value applies universally, as much as any economic laws do apply, for the entire period of simple commodity production, i.e. up to the time at which this undergoes a modification by the onset of the capitalist form of production. Up till then, prices gravitate to the values determined by Marx's law and oscillate around these values, so that the more completely simple commodity production develops, the more do average prices coincide with values

---

5 Engels, in Marx 1992, pp. 1031–2.
6 Engels, in Marx 1992, p. 1033.

for longer periods when not interrupted by external violent disturbances, and with the insignificant variations we mentioned earlier. Thus the Marxian law of value has a universal economic validity for an era lasting from the beginning of the exchange that transforms products into commodities down to the fifteenth century of our epoch. But commodity exchange dates from a time before any written history, going back to at least 3500 B.C. in Egypt, and 4000 B.C. or maybe even 6000 B.C. in Babylon; thus the law of value prevailed for a period of some five to seven millennia.[7]

∴

Werner Sombart's Review of Karl Marx, *Das Kapital. Kritik der politischen Oekonomie*. Dritter Band, erster Teil, 8°, XXVIII. und 448 s.; zweiter Teil, 422 S. Hamburg: Meissner 1894.

This journal's area of interest is limited to the discussion of social-policy and social-statistical issues, and it does not cover, among other things, economic theory. If, nevertheless, we use the appearance of the third volume of Marx's *Capital* as an opportunity for a purely theoretical study, this happens because the basic, systematic treatment of the whole field of economic science cannot be ignored, even in a socio-political magazine. But since a fruitful discussion of socio-political problems depends, in the last instance, on the reliability of the general theoretical foundation, every practical issue inevitably leads us back to the ultimate questions of economic theory. For that reason, this journal has also always taken an interest, despite the fundamental limitation of its area of interest, in a thorough examination of the basic theoretical works of political economy – it is enough to recall the reviews of Adolph Wagner and Julius Wolf.[8]

If I thus agreed with the editor to publish in this journal my criticism of the third volume of *Capital*, and of some fundamental discussions tied up with it, I did so in the conviction that, in the face of a work of *Capital*'s scope, the task of criticism cannot possibly be to have the final say a few months after its publication, or to 'settle' the debate on the book. Although we have had plenty of time to go into Marx's train of thought, and although the newly published third volume frequently only confirmed the results to which our own thinking

---

7   Engels, in Marx 1992, p. 1037.
8   Sombart 1892.

had led us on the basis of the earlier volumes, a system like Marxism,[9] whose criticism almost entirely lacks any preparatory work, obviously requires a kind of assessment, both intensive and extensive, that differs from what a critical review was in a position to offer. I therefore consider my principal role at this point to consist only of the following: to describe the overall impression made on me by the third volume of *Capital*, to offer primarily a formal assessment of the work; then to report on its contents as concisely as possible, making constant reference to those problems whose discussion basically dominates the debate on Marx; and, finally, to attempt to outline for the future criticism of Marx some leading basic principles. This latter task requires an outline of the economic foundations of the Marxian system, which I believe are still misunderstood in their essence.

I

In the preface to the first part of the third volume of *Capital*, Engels recounts the story of the passion of his editorial work, to the benefit and advantage of the reader, because from his description of Marx's manuscript and the way in which it was edited we gain very useful clues for assessing the individual parts of the work. In general, the third volume was a still more imperfect manuscript than the one Marx left for the second volume. In Engels's words: 'There was only one draft, and even this contained very major gaps'.[10] Nevertheless, Engels apparently did not change his editorial principle; he was inspired primarily by considerations of piety, not by the state of the material itself.

This time, too, Engels took care to use as many as possible of his friend's remarks in their original form. He tells us with particular satisfaction that, even in the most difficult and least completed part (the fifth), he 'finally managed

---

9   Despite the objections that my esteemed teacher Adolph Wagner (Wagner 1893, p. 281) raised against this expression that I used in the controversy with Julius Wolf, I am not ready to relinquish it. I am amazed that Wagner was irked at all by the expression that the doctrine of Marx 'claims on principle a position completely different from the rest of the socialist systems'. First, Wagner concedes this himself by saying that, even if in his opinion 'only partially and only to some extent', the 'anti-ethical' character of Marx's system claimed by me differentiates it, for example, from Rodbertus, among others. But even apart from this, I know of no theory of economic development in any of the major socialist systems, especially that of Rodbertus – and that's the point in Marx, because the 'metaphysical' theory of history about the succession of organic and critical periods [of Saint-Simon and his followers] cannot be inferred from his system. And that Rodbertus and Marx differed as fire and water in their whole conception of the world has been often attested by one of Wagner's assistants – Heinrich Dietzel.

10 Marx 1992, p. 92.

to introduce into the text all of the author's statements that were in any way pertinent to the matter in hand'.[11]

I do not know whether this method of editing has been the right one or, indeed, whether it was necessary even from considerations of piety. It has certainly hurt the general character of the work. Was it not Marx's intention rather to withhold from the world his unfinished work? Would it not have been better to single out the main features of the system and, after the corresponding editing, to present it to us in a more perfect form? Engels was capable of doing this like no other editor. As far as I am concerned, all the digressions, all the preliminary work found in Marx's manuscripts, could have been printed without abridgement in *Die Neue Zeit*. Now, everything is packaged in *Capital*: the finished passages next to the semi-finished ones, incidental arguments next to decisively important ones, details along with basic features. If Marx made pages-long extracts from parliamentary reports, he surely did that only to process them, not to publish them, as now has been done. If Part Five (on credit and banking) was the most imperfect part of the manuscript, it could have been quietly summarised in a few sentences, without doing any harm to the system, rather than publishing it without abridgement. But, in his editing of Marx's presentation, Engels also behaved, in my view, too carefully. He should have cut the eternal repetitions, which now occupy even more space in the third than in the second volume, and which often give the impression of hearing the colleague of a German professor. Everyone will agree that chapters devoted to mere calculations – such as 41, 42 and 43, whose results are not even readily utilisable (Engels himself felt compelled to set up another series of numbers)[12] – also do not add to the book. But these statements come *post festum* [after the fact] and do not alter the accomplished facts.[13] They are just meant to describe the general character of the work, particularly in its formal aspects.

---

11   Marx 1992, p. 96.
12   [Sombart refers to Chapter 41: Differential Rent II – First Case: Price of Production Constant; Chapter 42: Differential Rent II – Second Case: Price of Production Falling; and Chapter 43: Differential Rent II – Third Case: Rising Price of Production. Results].
13   On some points, however, it should probably not be ruled out that Engels could make some modifications to the text in later editions. For example, it is almost incomprehensible why we are expected to torment ourselves, in simple numerical examples, with the old-fashioned *English* currency system and its impossible divisions in pounds, shillings and pence, when we have the convenient decimal currency in Germany, or with acres and quarters, instead of hectolitres and hectares? It is also likely that Engels will convince himself, on closer examination, that entire pages from old reports of the 1840s and 1850s

It is obvious that enjoyment of the third volume is significantly affected by the inconveniences highlighted above. The irregularities make themselves felt often enough; the reading is frequently tedious and sometimes downright unpleasant. Despite all this, the third volume of *Capital* is a standard work, which stands incomparably higher than the previous volume and compares favourably with the first. Admittedly, the fresh, wild originality of the first volume does not often appear in the third; it is permeated by a quieter spirit. Instead of the dramatic *élan*, the epic peace has come, but certainly not to the detriment of science. The third volume will yield only scant material for socialist agitation, but this proves advantageous for theory. What made the first volume of *Capital* such a rich treasure trove of slogans and catchphrases for agitating 'comrades', and what also made it seem palatable and worth reading to the average economist, spiteful of theory and seized by the '*rage des faits*' [madness for facts] – the frequent descriptive and historical digressions, the presentation of English working conditions, the critical history of British labour legislation and the like – only interfered with the pleasure resulting from development of the system's ideas. From the standpoint of theory, the third volume does not have that useless ballast. Therefore, the joy experienced by the theorist in reading the third volume, despite all the irregularities I previously mentioned, will be more pure and unsullied. For me, the new book was as endearing, in its own way, as the first volume. I can therefore only draw the conclusion that economic science should welcome the appearance of the third volume as a joyous event that made the literary autumn of 1894 an exceptionally fertile one for our profession. Whatever one's position on the results of Marx's studies, no one with the slightest theoretical interest will be able to contemplate the culmination of Marx's system in the third volume of *Capital* without intellectual satisfaction.

Let us now try to acquaint ourselves with the contents of the third volume. I shall first sum up the author's reasoning without further critique. If I do this in more detail than usual in scientific practice, it is with the knowledge that the top priority for such a systematically misunderstood author as Marx is a clear rendering of his ideas.

---

are not consistent with the facts, as he often notices himself. Thus, for example, in my opinion the material of the fifth chapter is more or less dated. It is now very common, given the natural tendency of development of capitalism, to improve the spatial conditions of work, e.g. to build cleaner machine halls, better illuminated sheds, etc. simply from enlightened business interest. To this should be added the fact that capitalism takes advantage of the technical inventions, and now can, as cheaply as before, create better conditions of work, such as the illumination of working spaces with electric lighting, without hurting its business interests.

II

The overall task for the third volume was predetermined: if the first volume described the production process, and the second the circulation process of capital, the remaining task was to describe *the process of capitalist production as a whole*; in other words, the configuration of economic life organised in capitalist terms.

> In their actual movement, capitals confront one another in certain concrete forms, and, in relation to these, both the shape capital assumes in the immediate production process and its shape in the process of circulation appear merely as particular moments. The configurations of capital, as developed in this volume, thus approach step by step the form in which they appear on the surface of society, in the action of different capitals on one another, i.e. in competition, and in the everyday consciousness of the agents of production themselves.[14]

It goes without saying that they '*approach*' that form without ever reaching it. Also, the third book does not deal with the phenomena of real economic activity. The doctrine of competition was explicitly excluded from the exposition.

The third volume is divided into seven 'parts' with a total of 52 chapters.

Part one (chapters 1–7, pp. 117–238) deals with '*the transformation of surplus-value into profit, and of the rate of surplus-value into the rate of profit*'.

This first part has to solve the essentially formal task of portraying value and surplus value in their empirical forms as cost-price and profit respectively. From the capitalist point of view, *the commodity does not cost labour, but rather capital*: the outlay that the capitalist has to make, in order to produce a given commodity, is for him an expenditure of capital and appears to him as 'the cost' of that commodity; and the amount of capital expenditure determines the *cost-price*. But what the capitalist reaps as surplus value appears to him under the name of profit, as a result of his entire capital investment, not only of the amount of capital spent or, for instance, of the variable capital component alone. Next to cost-prices, therefore, appears the new category belonging to the capitalists' perception of the world, the economic category of profit. Thus $c = c + v + s$ is transformed first into $k + s$ and then into $k + p$: i.e. the value of commodities is transformed into cost-price plus profit.

Profit, as we are originally faced with it, is thus the same thing as surplus value, save in a mystified form, though one that necessarily arises from the

---

14   Marx 1992, p. 117.

capitalist mode of production. Because no distinction between constant and variable capital can be recognised in the apparent formation of the cost-price, the origin of the change in value, which occurs in the course of the production process, is shifted from variable capital to the capital as a whole. Because the price of labour power appears at one pole in the transformed form of wages, surplus value appears at the other pole in the transformed form of profit.[15]

Since surplus value appears here in the form of profit, as an excess over the total capital (c), then the rate of profit is = s/c (as opposed to the rate of surplus value, s/v). That is to say:

> In surplus-value, the relationship between capital and labour is laid bare. In the relationship between capital and profit, i.e. between capital and surplus-value as it appears on the one hand as an excess over the cost price of the commodity realized in the circulation process and on the other hand as an excess determined more precisely by its relationship to the total capital, *capital appears as a relationship to itself*, a relationship in which it is distinguished, as an original sum of value, from another new value that it posits.[16]

If we denote the rate of profit by p' and the rate of surplus value by s', we obtain the equation:

$$p' = s'v / (c + v) \text{ or } p' : s' = v : c^{[17]}$$

The rate of profit is thus a function of several variables. It is determined by two main factors: the rate of surplus value and the value composition of capital. A separate chapter (3) is devoted to the purely mathematical analysis of how the changes in these variables affect the rate of profit, while another chapter (4) investigates the effect of the turnover on the rate of profit. Chapter 5, of the first part, describes 'economy in the use of constant capital' and its importance for the level of the rate of profit. Given that the rate of profit, assuming a given surplus value, can only be increased by reducing the constant capital required for commodity production, the investigation of the factors that bring about such a reduction in the value of c is important: in addition to perpetual

---

15 Marx 1992, p. 127.
16 Marx 1992, p. 139.
17 [See Marx 1992, pp. 141–2].

improvement of machinery and diminution of the value (and thus of the cost) of the means of production, it is economy in the use of constant capital that chiefly comes into consideration here. It includes: savings in the conditions of work at the workers' expense, economy in generating and transmitting power and in buildings (the speeding-up of machinery, etc.), utilisation of the leftovers of production, and economy through inventions.

Finally, in the sixth chapter of this preparatory part, the effect of changes in price on the rate of profit is examined, with particular regard to the cotton crisis in 1861–5, while the last chapter of the first part is a collection of fragments brought together under the title 'supplementary remarks'.

The *second part* (chapters 8–12, pp. 241–313) deals with the *'transformation of profit into average profit'*. It is well known that this 'transformation' has been considered the great mystery that the third volume of *Capital* was supposed to elucidate above all. The so-called 'riddle' of the average rate of profit prompted a number of writers to search for solutions after Engels posited this as a 'task' in the preface to the second volume. The resulting 'prize essays', none of which will be granted the full prize, have now been subjected to thorough criticism by Engels in the preface to the third volume.[18] The familiar problem is again clarified in chapter 8 of this volume: how does it happen that equal capitals yield identical profits, despite having unequal organic compositions, if the surplus value is created only in proportion to the variable capital?

The (self-evident) 'solution' is this: unequal rates of profit would emerge if the commodities were sold at their values, but this is not the case: while a part of the commodities, those produced by capitals with a higher than average composition, are sold above their values, another part, produced by capitals with a below-average composition, will be sold below their values in the same proportion. From this arises an average rate of profit, as the hypothetical table on the following page shows ($s\,/\,v = 100$ percent).

According to Marx:

> The prices that arise when the average of the different rates of profit is drawn from the different spheres of production, and this average is added to the cost prices of these different spheres of production, are the *prices of production*.[19]

---

18 [For an assessment of the so-called 'prize essay competition' from the standpoint of bourgeois economics, see Howard and King 1989, pp. 21–41].

19 Marx 1992, p. 257.

Capital	Surplus value	Consumed c	Value of the commodities	Cost-price of the commodities	Price of the commodities	Profit rate	Deviation of price from value
I. 80 c + 20 v	20	50	90	70	92	22%	+ 2
II. 70 c + 30 v	30	51	111	81	103	22%	− 8
III. 60 c + 40 v	40	51	131	91	113	22%	− 18
IV. 85 c + 15 v	15	40	40	55	77	22%	+ 7
V. 95 c + 5 v	5	10	20	15	37	22%	+ 17

The price of production includes the average profit. And what we call price of production is in fact the same thing that Adam Smith calls 'natural price', Ricardo 'price of production' or 'cost of production' and the Physiocrats 'prix necessaire', though none of these people explained the difference between price of production and value.[20]

Thus although the capitalists in the different spheres of production get back on the sale of their commodities the capital values consumed to produce them, they do not secure the surplus-value and hence profit that is produced in their own sphere in connection with the production of these commodities. What they secure is only the surplus-value and hence profit that falls to the share of each aliquot part of the total social capital, when evenly distributed, from the total social surplus-value or profit produced in a given time by the social capital in all spheres of production ... The various different capitals here are in the position of shareholders in a joint-stock company, in which the dividends are evenly distributed for each 100 units, and hence are distinguished, as far as the individual capitalists are concerned, only according to the size of the capital that each of them has put into the common enterprise, according to his relative participation in this common enterprise, according to the number of his shares.[21]

Total profit and total surplus value are thus identical, and therefore 'the average profit can be nothing other than the total mass of surplus value, distributed

---

20   Marx 1992, p. 300.
21   Marx 1992, p. 257.

between the masses of capital in each sphere of production in proportion to their size'.[22]

The 'difficult question' – 'How does this equalisation lead to a general rate of profit?'[23] – is answered in chapter 10.

Here Marx takes as his starting point a condition of commodity exchange in which there is no capitalist production. In this situation, the goods would, under certain conditions,[24] be exchanged in proportion to their values, and moreover in the normal case, in which supply and demand coincide, according to their market values, i.e. according to the individual values of the commodities produced under the average conditions of a particular sphere of production.[25] But the discussion on the formation of the market values, which in the capitalist economic order correspond to the market prices of production, and of the market prices that deviate from them as a result of a change in the relationship between supply and demand, contains little of interest for the solution to the question of the formation of a general rate of profit; they merely prepare the ground for it.

The solution is rather to be found in pages 296–9, particularly in this paragraph:

> If commodities were sold at their values, however, this would mean very different rates of profit in the different spheres of production, as we have already explained, according to the differing organic composition of the masses of capital applied. Capital withdraws from a sphere with

---

22   Marx 1992, p. 274.
23   Ibid.
24   ['Apart from the way in which the law of value governs prices and their movement, it is also quite apposite to view the values of commodities not only as theoretically prior to the prices of production, but also as historically prior to them. This applies to those conditions in which the means of production belong to the worker, and this condition is to be found, in both the ancient and the modern world, among peasant proprietors and handicraftsmen who work for themselves. This agrees, moreover, with the opinion we expressed previously, that the development of products into commodities arises from exchange between different communities, and not between the members of one and the same community. This is true not only for the original condition, but also for later social conditions based on slavery and serfdom, and for the guild organization of handicraft production, as long as the means of production involved in each branch of production can be transferred from one sphere to another only with difficulty, and the different spheres of production therefore relate to one another, within certain limits, like foreign countries or communistic communities' (Marx 1992, pp. 277–8)].
25   Marx 1992, pp. 275 ff.

a low rate of profit and wends its way to others that yield higher profit. This constant migration, the distribution of capital between the different spheres according to where the profit rate is rising and where it is falling, is what produces a relationship between supply and demand such that the average profit is the same in the various different spheres; and values are therefore transformed into prices of production.[26]

These observations contain ambiguities, about which I shall speak in my criticism.

Part Three (chapters 13–15, pp. 317–48) develops in the most brilliant way the 'law of the tendential fall in the rate of profit', which follows from the value and surplus value theory as a natural consequence. 'The progressive tendency for the general rate of profit to fall is thus simply the expression, peculiar to the capitalist mode of production, of the progressive development of the social productivity of labour',[27] because this development presents itself under capitalism as a 'progressive decline in the variable capital in relation to the constant capital, and hence in relation to the total capital as well'.[28] The same rate of surplus value must thus be expressed in a falling rate of profit.

It is obvious that an increase in the mass of profit *can* be connected with a falling rate of profit. Marx undertakes to prove that they *have* to be connected in the capitalist economic system because, since its whole development leads to accumulation and therefore also to an increase in the number of workers, the mass of applied, and accordingly of unpaid, labour must also grow:[29]

> The same development of the productivity of social labour, the same laws that are evident in the relative fall in variable capital as a proportion of the total capital, and the accelerated accumulation that follows from this – while on the other hand this accumulation also reacts back to become the starting-point for a further development of productivity and a further relative decline in the variable capital – this same development is expressed, leaving aside temporary fluctuations, in the progressive increase in the total labour-power applied and in the progressive growth in the absolute mass of surplus-value and therefore in profit.[30]

---

26 Marx 1992, p. 297; see also p. 310.
27 Marx 1992, p. 319.
28 Marx 1992, p. 318.
29 Marx 1992, pp. 324–5.
30 Marx 1992, p. 326.

If, says Marx, one considers the enormous development of the productive forces of social labour only in the last 30 years, one can only wonder that the fall in the rate of profit was not much greater and faster. In order to explain this phenomenon, he is forced to assume that opposing influences are at play, which thwart and abolish the effect of the general law. Marx enumerates a series of such 'counteracting factors' in chapter 14.

But the vital conclusions for the theory of economic development are drawn from the law of the rate of profit, for the first time, in the significant chapter 15, dealing with the 'development of the internal contradictions of the law'. Here we come across, alongside old acquaintances from *Anti-Dühring*, in which Engels anticipated some of the ideas developed here, some totally new ways of thinking that have a decisive influence on the theory of development. The rate of profit, through whose action the capitalist mode of production will be driven to its end, is now placed at the centre of the theory as the driving force.[31] Thus, even if the basic ideas of the evolutionary theory have remained the same,[32]

---

31 ['It is the rate of profit that is the driving force in capitalist production, and nothing is produced save what can be produced at a profit. Hence the concern of the English economists over the decline in the profit rate. If Ricardo is disquieted even by the very possibility of this, that precisely shows his deep understanding of the conditions of capitalist production ... What disturbs Ricardo is the way that the rate of profit, which is the stimulus of capitalist production and both the condition for and the driving force in accumulation, is endangered by the development of production itself ... What is visible here in a purely economic manner, i.e. from the bourgeois standpoint, within the limits of capitalist understanding, from the standpoint of capitalist production itself, are its barriers, its relativity, the fact that it is not an absolute but only a historical mode of production, corresponding to a specific and limited epoch in the development of the material conditions of production' (Marx 1992, p. 368)].

32 ['The true barrier to capitalist production is capital itself. It is that capital and its self-valorization appear as the starting and finishing point, as the motive and purpose of production; production is production only for capital, and not the reverse, i.e. the means of production are not simply means for a steadily expanding pattern of life for the society of the producers. The barriers within which the maintenance and valorization of the capital-value has necessarily to move – and this in turn depends on the dispossession and impoverishment of the great mass of the producers – therefore come constantly into contradiction with the methods of production that capital must apply to its purpose and which set its course towards an unlimited expansion of production, to production as an end in itself, to an unrestricted development of the social productive powers of labour. The means – the unrestricted development of the forces of social production – comes into persistent conflict with the restricted end, the valorization of the existing capital. If the capitalist mode of production is therefore a historical means for developing the material powers of production and for creating a corresponding world market, it is at the same

the partially new details, in order to be understood, require a more detailed explanation and assessment than can be offered here.

Of outstanding importance for the understanding of Marx's economic system are the whole of part four and the first chapter of the fifth part [on interest-bearing capital].

Part Four (pp. 379–457) shows *the transformation of commodity capital and money capital into commercial capital and money-dealing capital*. 'Commercial capital, then, is nothing but the transformed form of a portion of this circulation capital which is always to be found on the market, in the course of its metamorphosis, and perpetually confined to the circulation sphere'.[33] Commodity capital becomes commercial or merchant's capital through the fact that the function of the capital located in the circulation process generally assumes an independent existence and becomes fixed as a special function of a specific capital, as a function assigned by the division of labour to a special class of capitalists.[34] We know from the second volume what the pure functions of capital are in the sphere of circulation. These 'pure functions' are 'the operations which the industrial capitalist has to undertake firstly to realize the value of his commodities, and secondly to transform this value back into the commodities' elements of production, the operations for effecting the metamorphoses of

---

time the constant contradiction between this historical task and the social relations of production corresponding to it' (Marx 1992, p. 359).

'In short, all the objections raised against the obvious phenomena of overproduction (phenomena that remain quite impervious to these objections) amount to saying that the barriers to capitalist production are not barriers to production in general and are therefore also not barriers to this specific, capitalist mode of production. But the contradiction in this capitalist mode of production consists precisely in its tendency towards the absolute development of productive forces that come into continuous conflict with the specific conditions of production in which capital moves, and can alone move' (Marx 1992, p. 367)].

33 Marx 1992, p. 380.
34 ['The movement of commodity capital has been analysed in Volume 2 [Chapter 3]. Taking the social capital as a whole, one part of this is always on the market as a commodity, waiting to pass over into money, even though this part is always composed of different elements, as well as changing in magnitude; another part is on the market as money, waiting to pass over into commodities. Capital is always involved in this movement of transition, this metamorphosis of form. In as much as this function acquires independent life as a special function of a special capital and is fixed by the division of labour as a function that falls to a particular species of capitalists, commodity capital becomes commodity-dealing capital or commercial capital' (Marx 1992, p. 379)].

commodity capital, C′–M–C, i.e. the acts of sale and purchase'.[35] The reason for the independence of these functions is the economy in intermediary trade.[36]

It is important to remind ourselves of the results of the investigations in the second volume of *Capital*, which are now elaborated upon.

> The pure functions of capital in the circulation sphere create neither value nor surplus-value ... What applies to the metamorphosis of commodity capital as such is naturally not changed in any way when a part of this capital assumes the form of commercial, commodity-dealing capital, and the operations which effect the metamorphosis of commodity capital come to appear as the special business of a special section of capitalists, or as the exclusive function of one portion of the money capital ... Commercial capital, therefore, stripped of all the heterogeneous functions that may be linked to it, such as storage, dispatch, transport, distribution and retailing, and confined to its true function of buying in order to sell, creates neither value nor surplus-value, but simply facilitates their realization, and with this also the actual exchange of the commodities, their transfer from one hand to another, society's metabolic process.[37]

However, since commercial capital, in order to operate, asserts a claim to the average profit, the surplus value allotted to it in the form of profit can only be a part of the surplus value created by so-called productive capital. Merchant's capital appropriates this value by entering *pro rata* [at the same rate] into the formation of the average rate of profit with the rest of the capital.[38] This means

---

35   Marx 1992, p. 395.
36   ['Given that commercial capital does not overstep its necessary proportions, we can assume the following.

'(1) As a result of the division of labour, the capital that is exclusively concerned with buying and selling is smaller than it would be if the industrial capitalist had to conduct the entire commercial part of his business himself. (And besides the money that has to be laid out on the purchase of commodities, this capital also includes the money laid out for the labour needed to pursue the merchant's business, as well as for the merchant's constant capital, warehouses, transport, etc.)

'(2) Because the merchant is exclusively concerned with this business, not only is the producer's commodity converted into money sooner, but the commodity capital itself goes through its metamorphosis more quickly than it would in the hands of the producer' (Marx 1992, pp. 387–8)].
37   Marx 1992, pp. 394–5.
38   ['Commercial capital thus contributes to the formation of the general rate of profit according to the proportion it forms in the total capital' (Marx 1992, p. 398)].

that the prices at which the commodities are sold by the industrial capitalist class, when we consider the totality of the commodities, are smaller than their values, so that now the real value or price of production can be denoted as $k + p + h$ (where h is the commercial profit). 'The merchant's sale price is higher than his purchase price not because it is above the total value, but rather because his purchase price is below this total value'.[39]

Now, it is interesting to note the consequence that must be drawn from this view of commercial profit for *the wages of the commercial employees* – namely, that these wages can, in fact, be nothing other than a part of the surplus value produced by industrial capital; because no matter how much money the merchant may make out of their labour, these clerks do not produce surplus value for him but only help him to appropriate a portion of the surplus value that the 'productive' workers created.[40] I believe, therefore, that it is misleading for Marx to speak about 'variable' capital and 'unpaid' labour when referring to the commercial wage-workers.[41] These terms must necessarily have a completely different meaning here than when they are applied to the industrial wage-workers, who directly produce values and surplus value.

Money-dealing capital (chapter 19) – which arises from the fact that the purely technical movements made by money in the circulation processes assume an independent existence as the function of a specific capital – is then described in a form totally analogous to the commercial capital.

Part Four closes with an economic-historical overview of the development of merchant's capital – to be sure a mere sketch, which in many respects has been superseded by newer research, but one that is still rich enough in brilliant ideas to be read with interest and to be of benefit to anyone.

In the following Part Five, which deals with *the division of profit into interest and profit of enterprise*, and with *interest-bearing capital*, the first chapters (21, 22, and 23) must, above all, claim our liveliest interest. Here the theory of interest and profit of enterprise are discussed in principle.

The theory of interest naturally follows from the theory of surplus value and profit. Interest is a portion of the profit that is paid by the functioning capital

---

39 Marx 1992, p. 400.
40 ['Since the merchant, being simply an agent of circulation, produces neither value nor surplus-value (for the additional value that he adds to commodities by his expenses is reducible to the addition of previously existing value, even though the question still arises here as to how he maintains and conserves the value of this constant capital), the commercial workers whom he employs in these same functions cannot possibly create surplus-value for him directly' (Marx 1992, p. 406)].
41 Marx 1992, pp. 407–8.

to the owners of [money] capital as compensation for relinquishing the use-value of capital, whose useful property consists of the fact that it can be used for the production of surplus value.[42] The 'natural' rate of interest is regulated by the supply and demand between the two kinds of capitalists, and its level is not determined by any law.[43]

What is left to profit, after the payment of interest, appears in qualitative determination as net profit or profit of enterprise, which now seems to be the result of capital as function vis-à-vis the interest rate as a product of capital as property.[44] If the capitalist himself manages his company, the profit can include the *wages of supervision and management*,[45] an amount that appears, completely separated from profits, as administrative wages, both in the workers' cooperative factories and in the capitalist joint-stock companies. It is self-

---

42   ['On the basis of capitalist production, money – taken here as the independent expression of a sum of value, whether this actually exists in money or in commodities – can be transformed into capital, and through this transformation it is turned from a given, fixed value into a self-valorizing value capable of increasing itself. It produces profit, i.e. it enables the capitalist to extract and appropriate for himself a certain quantity of unpaid labour, surplus product and surplus-value. In this way the money receives, besides the use-value which it possesses as money, an additional use-value, namely the ability to function as capital. Its use-value here consists precisely in the profit that it produces when transformed into capital. In this capacity of potential capital, as a means to the production of profit, it becomes a commodity, but a commodity of a special kind. Or what comes to the same thing, capital becomes a commodity' (Marx 1992, pp. 459–460)].

43   ['Capital further appears as a commodity in so far as the division of profit into interest and profit proper is governed by supply and demand, i.e. by competition, just like the market prices of commodities' (Marx 1992, p. 477). 'It is in fact only the division of capitalists into money capitalists and industrial capitalists that transforms a part of the profit into interest and creates the category of interest at all; and it is only the competition between these two kinds of capitalist that creates the rate of interest' (Marx 1992, p. 493). 'The prevailing average rate of interest in a country, as distinct from the constantly fluctuating market rate, cannot be determined by any law. There is no natural rate of interest, therefore, in the sense that economists speak of a natural rate of profit and a natural rate of wages' (Marx 1992, p. 484)].

44   ['Interest-bearing capital is capital *as property* as against capital *as function*' (Marx 1992, p. 503)].

45   ['The idea of profit of enterprise as a wage for supervising labour, an idea arising from the antithesis between this profit and interest, finds further support in that one part of the profit actually can be separated off as wages, and really does separate off; or rather, a part of wages, conversely, on the basis of the capitalist mode of production, appears as an integral component of profit' (Marx 1992, p. 507)].

evident that this work of supervision and management can be considered productive labour only to the extent that it must be performed in every combined mode of production, and insofar as it is determined by the historical form of the capitalist production process as a valorisation process.[46]

The stately remainder of Part Five (except for a very informative final chapter [chapter 36 on pre-capitalist relations] dealing with economic history) is dedicated to presenting the theory of *banking* and *credit*. We already pointed out at the beginning that this section was the child of sorrow in every respect. I doubt that it will make many friends in its present clumsy form. Those interested in the theory of economic systems will probably find Marx's views on economic crises interesting. Those views are quite rich, but they are buried under a mass of raw material – pages-long extracts from English banking inquiries of the 1840s. The rest should be reviewed by a specialist in the theory of money and credit. For our purpose, which essentially consists of properly identifying and organising the converging threads of the Marxian system in the third volume, we can dispense with a rendition of this part and limit ourselves to remarking that it includes no fewer than 11 chapters extending over 212 pages.[47]

Part Six brings us the *doctrine of ground rent* ('transformation of surplus profit into ground-rent').[48] It is self-evident that here, too, the prerequisite for the analysis is a purely capitalist organisation: it is necessary 'to consider all the specific relationships of production and exchange that arise from the investment of capital on the land'.[49] Ground rent is simply referred to as 'the autonomous, specific economic form of landed property on the basis of the capitalist mode of production'.[50]

> Thus it is not peculiar to ground-rent that agricultural products develop into values and as values, i.e. that they confront other commodities as commodities themselves and that the non-agricultural products confront them as commodities, nor that they develop as particular expressions of social labour. What is peculiar is that with the conditions in which the agricultural products develop as values (commodities), and with the conditions of realization of their values, landed property also develops

---

46   Marx 1992, pp. 507–14.
47   Marx 1992, Chapters 24–35, pp. 515–727.
48   Marx 1992, Chapters 37–47, pp. 751–951.
49   Marx 1992, p. 752.
50   Marx 1992, p. 762.

the power to appropriate a growing part of these values created without its assistance, and a growing part of the surplus-value is transformed into ground-rent.[51]

Marx distinguishes between differential ground rent and absolute ground rent. Differential rent is a surplus profit resulting from the excess of the general price of production of commodities over their individual price of production,[52] but it is different from other surplus profits because it does not spring from capital as such, but from the disposal over a natural force separate from capital that is limited in its scope and can be monopolised.[53] Differential rent appears in a twofold form: as rent from capital investments in more fertile soils vis-à-vis less fertile ones, and as rent from more productively invested capitals on soils of a given fertility (Differential rent I and II).

Although Marx, in his theory of differential rent, takes over a large stock of ideas from the classics, more so than in other parts of his system, his own theory is by no means a mere paraphrase of the classical theory of ground rent. Apart from the fact that its particulars are illuminated by the central sun of his system, it seems to me that Marx has also performed a considerable service in further developing the traditional ideas. If I had to point out where I see a significant advance over Ricardo and his successors, it would be in his attempt to offer a quantitative assessment and determination of the mass of rent, of the '*total rental*', and in the derivation from it of a rate of rent and the like;[54] but

---

51   Marx 1992, pp. 777–8.
52   ['This surplus profit is thus similarly equal to the difference between the individual price of production of these favoured producers and the general social price of production in the sphere of production as a whole, which is what governs the market. This difference is equal to the excess of the general production price of the commodity over its individual production price' (Marx 1992, p. 780)].
53   ['Capital cannot create a waterfall from its own resources. The surplus profit that arises from this use of the waterfall thus arises not from the capital but rather from the use by capital of a monopolizable and monopolized natural force. Under these conditions, the surplus profit is transformed into ground-rent, i.e. it accrues to the owner of the waterfall' (Marx 1992, p. 875)].
54   ['The proportion of the total rental, either to the total area of land cultivated or to the total capital invested in the soil ... is not determined only by the rent per acre or by the rate of rent on capital but just as much by the relative proportion of each soil type in the total acreage tilled; or, what comes to the same thing, by the distribution of the total capital applied among the various types of soil ... the relative level of average rents per acre, and the average rate of rent or the ratio of the total rental to the total capital invested in the soil, may rise or fall even though prices, the difference in fertility of the lands under cultivation

above all in the detailed proof of the mutual dependence and conditionality of differential rent I and II upon each other.[55] To go into details about this is not the task of this review.

That Marx, on the basis of his general economic theory, would arrive (as does Rodbertus, whose 'important text on rent'[56] he mentions approvingly) at the existence of an *'absolute ground rent'*, i.e. of a rent yielded by the worst class of soil, was to be expected from the outset: his basing of the configuration of economic life on historically established social-power relations necessarily leads to this conclusion.

> Legal ownership of land, by itself, does not give the proprietor any ground-rent. It certainly does give him the power, however, to withdraw his land from cultivation until economic conditions permit a valorization of it that yields him a surplus, whether the land is used for agriculture proper or for other productive purposes such as building, etc. He can neither increase nor reduce the absolute quantity of this field of occupation, but he can affect the quantity of it on the market.[57]

Landed property presents itself as a 'barrier that does not permit any new capital investment on formerly uncultivated or unleased land without levying a toll'.[58]

Finally, in order to integrate ground rent into Marx's system, let us recall that every normal ground rent can only be a component part of the surplus value produced by agricultural capital. Where it does not arise (as differential rent does) from the difference between the market price of production and the individual value of the commodity, it can be explained (as in the case of absolute ground rent) only on the basis of the difference between the higher rate of profit prevalent in the sphere of agricultural production in general and the [lower] general rate of profit.[59]

---

and the rent per acre or rate of rent for the capital invested per acre in each actual rent-bearing soil category, or for all actually rent-bearing capital, all remain the same, simply by an expansion of the cultivated area' (Marx 1992, p. 806)].

55 See, for instance, Marx 1992, p. 819.
56 Marx 1992, p. 913, note 41.
57 Marx 1992, p. 891.
58 Marx 1992, p. 896.
59 ['Absolute rent, arising from the excess value over and above the price of production, is simply a part of the agricultural surplus-value, the transformation of this surplus-value into rent, its seizure by the landowner; just as differential rent arises from the

Part Seven, *the final section of the work*, called *'The revenues and their sources'*[60] corresponds to the 'doctrine of distribution' in Say's system. In accordance with the whole arrangement of *Capital*, it can only be of a polemical character: the 'distribution' of the social product is described by Marx in connection with the doctrine of production and circulation.

Marx first turns, in chapter 48, against the absurdity of what he calls the 'trinity formula', i.e. the standard distribution scheme: capital-interest, land-rent, labour-wages. It would make some sense, he says, to regard capital, land and labour as claims entitling their owners to a share of the national income; but if they are treated, as often happens, as *sources* of the annually disposable wealth, one commits first the error of equating quite disparate things, because the alleged sources are related to each other as notary fees are to red turnips and music. And furthermore, one commits the second error of addressing certain things or social relations as sources of wealth, instead of the living productive power [of labour].[61] Thus chapter 49 criticises the mistake, which has never totally disappeared since Adam Smith, of resolving the prices of commodities into ground rent, profit and wages, as their component parts. Chapter 50 seeks to disprove the theory of the price-forming property of ground rent, profit and wages, while chapter 51 contains an *aperçu* of the historically conditioned character of the capitalist mode of production and distribution. Finally, chapter 52, entitled 'Classes', includes only two pages, followed by the concluding words from Engels: 'At this point the manuscript breaks off'.

How much more we could have learned! As it stands, *Capital* is only a powerful torso, and not just because the manuscript breaks off, but also because the previous paragraphs are not, as we know, the last word that Marx had to say. The final part, which seems once more to draw in broad strokes the main features of the system, makes an especially tired impression; it reflects all too well a decrease in the tremendous force of the author. For all the admirers of this genius, there is something melancholic to be able to feel, in such a palpable way, how a great spirit slowly advances towards his end.

---

       transformation of surplus profit into rent, its seizure by landed property, at the general governing price of production. These two forms of rent are the only normal ones. Apart from this, rent can derive only from a genuine monopoly price, which is determined neither by the price of production of the commodities nor by their value, but rather by the demand of the purchasers and their ability to pay, consideration of which therefore belongs to the theory of competition, where the actual movement of market prices is investigated' (Marx 1992, p. 898)].

60   Marx 1992, pp. 953–1025.
61   Marx 1992, pp. 953 ff.

III

We have thus gained an overview of the contents of the third volume. The next question that presents itself to us is this: what does this new part mean, what does it accomplish for the *Marxian system*? As our summary has already shown, entire aspects of this system are affected by the third volume. However, what captures our attention quite naturally is the key question for Karl Marx's economic system: the *value-* and *surplus value-*, hence *capital-theory*. This theory was supposed to find its completion in the third volume; all those who could not suppress their reservations about Marx's statements, especially those contained in the first volume, were referred to the analyses here.

Among many other objections to Marx's theory of capital, we know that the most significant one claimed that this theory left the fact of an equal [rate of] profit unexplained, because it saw variable capital – a part that is of relatively unequal size in different capitals – as the only value-creating component of capital. Does the third volume solve this so-called mystery? And will the principal objection to the Marxian theory of capital thus be swept away?

I believe that, for the majority of readers, the third volume will have the same effect as the responses of job candidates usually have on the board of examiners: a general shaking of the head!

What do we find in the first two parts of volume three? To put it in one word: an entire *production-cost-* and *profit-theory*, with slightly different words from those we are accustomed to hear, but otherwise in the framework a conceptual construction that is not entirely different from the traditional one.

What does that mean for the theory of value? Does it mean a retreat by the author? Does it mean an inconsistency in the system, or what? Those Marx-interpreters who thought they already saw, in the value and surplus value theory of the first volume, merely a disguised cost of production theory (!), a 'variant of the cost theory', will not be overly surprised by those strange first two parts of the third volume. The majority, however, will not be inclined to consider the 'solution' to the 'average rate of profit puzzle', as it is now given, as a 'solution' at all; they will think that the Gordian knot has been cut but by no means unloosed. For if now an 'ordinary' cost of production theory has suddenly emerged from obscurity, that means that the famous theory of value has fallen by the wayside; if I must ultimately have recourse to production costs in order to account for the profit, then why the whole cumbersome apparatus of value and surplus value theory?

Still others will judge differently. They will see in the comments of the third volume something completely self-evident that could not have been otherwise once the previous two volumes were written. For them, of course, no 'mystery' of any kind has ever existed.

Whence this striking difference of judgement? To me it seems to be due to the different views on value and surplus value in Marx. The whole 'mystery' has its origin in the confusion that exists almost universally today regarding the Marxian concept of value and surplus value.[62]

We shall only be able to gain a proper appreciation of the investigations of capital now contained in the third volume, therefore, if we are certain beforehand concerning *the significance of value in Marx's economic system*.

First, this is clear: what in the first volume was indicated only occasionally has now been often and explicitly expressed in the third volume: *value does not appear in the exchange ratio of the capitalistically-produced commodities*. It does not indicate, for example, the point around which market prices fluctuate, towards which they gravitate; and 'average prices' do not by any means correspond to values. Rather, it is precisely the characteristic feature of the capitalist mode of production that the commodities are not generally exchanged at their values, i.e. in proportion to the amounts of labour contained in them, and that it is instead pure coincidence if prices are equivalent to values.[63] The

---

62   Böhm-Bawerk recently remarked ('Wert', *Handwörterbuch der Staatswissenschaften*, VI, 1894, p. 688) that, as the result of the previous critique of Marx, the Marxian theory of value 'has definitively been proven to be inadequate by the learned world'. I cannot agree with the highly esteemed scholar in this. Böhm-Bawerk's claim cannot be correct if only because of the fact that, as far as I know, the Marxian theory of value *has not at all been the subject of discussion*, but only a phantom imagined by the critics in question. It would give me special satisfaction if Böhm-Bawerk were to modify the opinion quoted above after reading this review. Marx's theory may be *refutable*, but *refuted it has not been*.

63   [The Hegelian influence on this matter was evident in *Grundrisse* when Marx referred to the relation between value and price in terms of a 'constant negation of the negation':

'The value of commodities as determined by labour time is only their average value. The average appears as an external abstraction if it is calculated out as the average figure of an epoch, e.g. 1 lb. of coffee = 1s. if the average price of coffee is taken over 25 years; but it is very real if it is at the same time recognized as the driving force and the moving principle of the oscillations which commodity prices run through during a given epoch ... The market value is always different, is always below or above this average price of a commodity. Market value equates itself with real value by means of its constant oscillations, never by means of an equation with real value as if the latter were a third party, but rather by means of constant non-equation of itself (as Hegel would say, not by way of abstract identity, but by constant negation of the negation, i.e. of itself as negation of real value) ... Price therefore is distinguished from value ... because the latter appears as the law of the motions which the former runs through. But the two are constantly different and never balance out, or balance only coincidentally and exceptionally. The price of a commodity constantly stands above or below the value of a commodity, and the value of the commodity itself exists only in this up-and-down movement of commodity prices.

'normal' prices, or the amounts of money given for a commodity, thus represent an amount of value (labour) consistently different from the amount contained in the commodity. It is therefore possible, and it occurs often enough, that a price, and thus an amount of value expressed in money, is given to things that have absolutely no value, that is, those things that have cost no labour, such as land, or that cannot be reproduced through labour, such as antiques, art works of certain masters, etc.[64]

Further: value *does not live in the consciousness of capitalist agents of production*: it by no means governs the calculations of the capitalist. But it plays just as little a role, for instance, as a distribution factor in the allocation of society's annual product. It is, therefore, by no means a *fact of consciousness of the buyers and sellers of commodities*. Thus it is, in a word, not a 'condition of economic activity', to use Gerlach's well-chosen expression. Indeed, if 'value' does not exist in the phenomenal world of the capitalistically-moulded economic life, does it have no existence at all? This conclusion would be premature. There is obviously still a refuge for the value that has thus been done away with – *in the thoughts of the economic theorist*. In fact, if we want to characterise Marx's economic system with a catchword, it would be that *its value is not an empirical but a conceptual fact*.[65]

But, having said that, we are still far from finishing our investigation. For the time being we have completely abstracted from the question: what is the value of this value? A more precise determination of that formal characterisation is still necessary.

Supply and demand constantly determine the prices of commodities; never balance, or only coincidentally; but the cost of production, for its part, determines the oscillations of supply and demand' (Marx 1993, pp. 137–8).

In the same context Marx added:

'Because price is not equal to value, therefore the value-determining element – labour time – cannot be the element in which prices are expressed, because labour time would then have to express itself simultaneously as the determining and the non-determining element, as the equivalent and non-equivalent of itself. Because labour time as the measure of value exists only as an ideal, it cannot serve as the matter of price-comparisons ... Price as distinct from value is necessarily money price' (Marx 1993, p. 140)].

64   Marx 1992, pp. 772, 782, 786–7.
65   [Cf. Engels's comments: 'In Sombart's otherwise very good article on Volume III I also find this tendency to dilute the theory of value: he had also obviously expected a somewhat different solution?' Engels to Conrad Schmidt in Zurich, Ryde, Isle of Wight, 12 March 1895, in *MECW*, Vol. 50, p. 466].

First, then, the value-concept is a tool of our thinking, which we use to comprehend the phenomena of economic life; it is a logical[66] fact. What the value-notion does here is to make the commodities, which are qualitatively different as useful goods, appear for us in quantitative determination. It is clear that I am fulfilling this postulate by considering cheese, silk and shoe polish as mere products of abstract human labour, and by correlating them only quantitatively as amounts of labour, whose magnitudes are determined by an equal third [factor] contained in them, measurable in periods of time.[67] Conrad Schmidt has already commented similarly on the role of Marx's value: 'This concept of value is essential to our thinking if we want to understand the qualitatively different commodities as commensurable magnitudes, i.e. as they operate in exchange processes'. When he continues, however, Schmidt seems to me to want to place the value-notion in the consciousness of the exchanging agents: 'Only as a gelatinous mass of homogeneous abstract human labour do the commodities themselves appear to be comparable; only in that way is it understandable *that they can be equated in the exchange process* in certain proportions to each other'.[68]

Does this mean that the value-notion must be assumed to exist in the consciousness of the exchanging agents in order to explain the implementation of the act of exchange? But then value would be a 'condition of economic activity', while it previously appeared as if Schmidt had conceived the concept of value only as a 'condition of economic thought' (I choose this somewhat incorrect turn of phrase in order to bring out more clearly the antithetical character of Gerlach's expression).

In its day, however, this meritorious if not yet entirely clear allusion of Schmidt to the meaning of value in Marx was enough to elicit a very readable reply from the pen of Hugo Landé, in which he rejected with indignation Schmidt's interpretation of value with these words: 'The law of value is not, as Schmidt seems to think, a law of thought, indispensable to make the qualitatively different commodities appear to us as commensurable quantities. Rather, the law of value has a very real nature; it is a natural law of human action; it is

---

66 I use this term for brevity's sake, though I am well aware of its ambiguity in philosophical language.

67 Marx himself never says loudly and clearly that he wanted value to be understood in this way. Many places, however, where he refers to value as a necessary requisite of economic science and lets the quantities of commodities be 'measured' by means of value, etc., indicate that he wanted value to be understood in the above sense. I refer to the new volume of *Capital*, pp. 447–8, 917, 979 ff., 998 ff.

68 Schmidt 1893.

nothing more than an aspect of the law of competition'.[69] Despite the disputable character of Landé's subsequent comments, and despite the fact that the ideas now developed in the third volume of *Capital* are closer to Schmidt's than to his own conception, Landé is decidedly right against Schmidt when he says that the 'law of value' in Marx's system definitely plays the role of a 'natural law' (in the famous Marxian sense[70]), if not exactly of a natural law of human action. Compare the following places (I quote only from the third volume on purpose):

> Whatever may be the ways in which the *prices* of different commodities are first established or fixed in relation to one another, *the law of value governs their movement*.[71]

> What competition does *not* show, however, is the determination of values that governs the movement of production; that it is *values that stand behind the prices of production and ultimately determine them*.[72]

> *It is only as an inner law, a blind natural force vis-à-vis the individual agents, that the law of value operates here* and that the social balance of production is asserted in the midst of accidental fluctuations.[73]

Now, is there not an irreconcilable contradiction between these two assertions: that 'value' in Marx is only a 'tool of thought' and that the 'law of value', as a 'natural law', ultimately determines the entire economic life of humankind? I think not.

Let us look at the 'value-concept' more closely.[74] It consists of the fact that we represent to ourselves the commodities in their quantitative determination and in their mutual relationship – not as hard and heavy bodies, but as *products of labour*. But it is by no means indifferent that we give our concept of values

---

69 Landé 1893, p. 591.
70 ['Even when a society has begun to track down the natural laws of its movement – and it is the ultimate aim of this work to reveal the economic law of motion of modern society – it can neither leap over the natural phases of its development nor remove them by decree. But it can shorten and lessen the birth-pangs' (Marx 1976, p. 92)].
71 Marx 1992, p. 277.
72 Marx 1992, p. 311.
73 Marx 1992, p. 1020; see also pp. 428, 967–8, 998 ff., 1007–8.
74 [For Engels's comments on the following four paragraphs, see the Appendix to this document].

precisely that content, because by doing so we are saying that we regard the commodities as products of social labour, [and that this is] *the objectively most relevant economic fact* in them. Clearly, the economic life of people, their material culture, is determined by the quantity of economic goods that they are able to dispose of in a given period; but again, apart from all the accompanying circumstances and assuming equal natural conditions,[75] this depends mainly on the development of the social productivity of labour. Now, this is first of all only a *technical* fact, and thus both qualitatively and quantitatively determined: it expresses the fact that a particular kind of labour, i.e. concrete, individual labour, is able to produce an amount of qualitatively determined goods in a given interval of time. By means of the value notion, I now obliterate the qualitative differences in productive labour. By conceiving the goods as the embodiment of undifferentiated, abstract social labour, I do nothing else but give to the technical concept of productivity, or productive power, an adequate economic form, thus making it suitable for economic thinking.[76] *In Marx, the concept of value in its material determination is nothing but the economic expression for the fact of the social productivity of labour as the basis of economic existence.*

What about the 'law of value'? In its formal determination, this law reads as follows: the value of the commodities 'ultimately' governs the economic processes – in a capitalist economic system, of course.

If we apply this new definition to value, then the law of value, as a law of the capitalist economic system in the most general sense, has this content: *the value of the commodities is the specific historical form in which the social productivity of labour, determining all the economic processes, ultimately asserts itself.* It is the degree of social productivity of labour, its changes, etc., which, without the agents of production or any economically active individual being aware of it,

---

75   Marx distinguishes between the 'natural' productivity and the social productivity. Only the latter comes into consideration as the content of value. ['Assume that labour-saving machinery, chemical ancillaries, etc. take up a greater share, so that the constant capital grows in relation to the labour-power applied – not just in value but in quantity too. In agriculture, however (as also in mining), we not only have the social productivity of labour to consider but also its natural productivity, which depends on the natural conditions within which labour is carried on. It is possible for the increase in the social productivity of agriculture to simply compensate for the decline in natural productivity, or not even to do this much and this compensation can only be effective for a certain period – so that despite the technical development, the product does not become cheaper but is simply prevented from becoming dearer' (Marx 1992, p. 901)].

76   'When we have labour as value-forming in mind (!), we are not considering it in its concrete form as a condition of production, but rather in a social characteristic that is different from that of wage-labour' (Marx 1992, p. 962).

ultimately 'decides' about prices and the rate of surplus value – in short, the overall structure of economic life, setting strict limits to individual caprice. One can only correctly understand Marx's system if one realises that at its centre stands the concept of productivity, which finds its economic expression in the value-concept.[77]

Thus, a balance seems to have been struck between the opposite views embodied in Schmidt and Landé. The 'value-concept' is, indeed, an auxiliary agent of thought, but by making the subject of value an objective fact, crucial for economic life – the productivity of labour in its social determination – the 'law of value' actually becomes a 'law' governing the entire economic life, or perhaps it would be more correct to call it a 'regulating principle'. The significance of Marx's theory of value should, therefore, be sought in the fact that it has found the adequate economic expression for a technological fact, objectively governing the economic existence of human society.

Thus, the apparent contradiction in Marx's system, according to which the 'value of commodities' neither appears nor is present in the consciousness of the economically active individuals, and yet ultimately regulates and governs the economic processes, also solves itself. We 'experience' nothing from value; it fulfils its role in a 'secret' way; it is the 'hidden basis' [of economic phenomena];[78] the 'law of value' is 'an inner law',[79] etc.

---

[77] It should follow from our discussion that the 'labour theory of value' has a completely different meaning from the one conventionally attributed to it, for instance in Dietzel 1890, where labour is considered to be the content of the value notion only because the expenditure of human labour makes the good 'valuable' for us and because we valuate it in proportion to the amount of labour expended. It is to this *subjectivist labour theory of value*, leading back to Adam Smith but by no means to Ricardo, that Dietzel appeals, in my opinion mistakenly.

[78] ['In some spheres of production, therefore, experience shows that the average commodity price rises because wages have risen and falls because they have fallen. What is not "experienced" is the secret regulation of these changes by a commodity value independent of wages. If the rise in wages is local, on the other hand, taking place only in particular spheres of production as a result of specific circumstances, there may then be a corresponding nominal rise in the price of these commodities. This rise in the relative value of one kind of commodity, in relation to others for which wages remain unchanged, is then simply a reaction to the local disturbance of the uniform distribution of surplus-value over the various spheres of production, a means of adjusting the particular rates of profit to the general rate. "Experience" here again shows the determination of the price by wages. What is experienced in both of these cases is how wages have determined commodity prices. What is not experienced is the hidden basis of this relationship' (Marx 1992, p. 1008)].

[79] ['It is only as an inner law, a blind natural force vis-à-vis the individual agents, that the law

If we grasp in this way the concept of value and the law of value in Marx, we will be able to understand the nature of surplus value easily. In order to understand that, it is only necessary for us to adopt the standpoint of an economically active society. The starting point [in the determination of value] is the overall social labour-time, 'the total amount of labour which society has at its disposal'.[80] This social labour-time is expressed in a given amount of product, which represents a certain value.[81] Surplus-value is now, in its formal determination, the value of that amount of product constituting an excess over the other part of the social product, which is somehow set aside (left over); it is an objectification of the 'surplus-labour' of society. 'Surplus-labour' would also have to be performed, for example, in a socialist society, 'as labour beyond the extent of given needs'; it would be 'required as insurance against accidents and for the progressive extension of the reproduction process that is needed to keep pace with the development of needs and the progress of population'.[82]

But the peculiarity of the capitalist economic system consists precisely of the fact that a certain amount of social labour is appropriated by capital. This quantity of social labour, appropriated by capital, is the total surplus-labour (surplus value) in the capitalist sense.[83] The only question is: is this amount

---

of value operates here and that the social balance of production is asserted in the midst of accidental fluctuations' (ibid.)].

80   Marx 1992, p. 1022.

81   That the annual value of the product [*Produktenwert*] is actually greater than the annual value product [*Wertprodukt*], because it includes past labour, can be left out of consideration here. To develop the distinction between necessary labour and surplus labour, which is the only issue under consideration here, the value product can be identified with the value of the product (cf. Lexis 1885).

82   Marx 1992, p. 958. [It is worth noting that Marx spoke of surplus labour in Ancient Greece, Rome and similar communities:

'The survival of the commune is the reproduction of all its members as self-sustaining peasants, whose surplus time belongs precisely to the commune, the work of war, etc. The property in one's own labour is mediated by property in the condition of labour – the hide of land, guaranteed in turn by the existence of the commune, and that in turn by surplus labour in the form of military service etc. by the commune members. It is not cooperation in wealth-producing labour by means of which the commune member reproduces himself, but rather cooperation in the communal interests (imaginary and real), for the upholding of the association inwardly and outwardly' (Marx 1992, p. 476)].

83   See, for example, this passage: 'The average profit of the individual capitalist, or of any particular capital, is determined not by the surplus labour that this capital appropriates first-hand, but rather by the total surplus labour that the total capital appropriates, from which each particular capital simply draws its dividends as a proportional part of the total capital' (Marx 1992, p. 742).

of social labour appropriated by the capitalists quantitatively determinable? Marx replies: yes; it is all the labour in excess of the necessary labour required for the maintenance and reproduction of labour power.[84] The value of the total social product therefore splits into two parts: one part presents itself in that amount of products that is necessary for the maintenance, etc. of the productive workers, the other in the rest of the products, which are appropriated by the capitalist class.[85] The surplus value is therefore to be understood only as a 'social fact'.

Now comes the further question: how can the amount of *'necessary'* labour in the above sense be defined more closely? Obviously, a twofold determination is required here: first, the concept of necessary worker, of the 'productive' part of the population, must be determined; and then it is necessary to determine the amount of labour that must necessarily be expended for these productive workers.

Who are 'productive' in Marx's sense? *Those who create (add) value*. But this merely raises the further question: who adds values?

An embryonic criticism of Marx says: the manual workers. This is, of course, wrong. Already, in the first volume of *Capital*, it is specifically stated that not only manual labour but also the work of supervision and management is productive.[86] In the third volume we learn more precisely that, while the

---

[84] For instance: 'Capital directly pumps from the workers the surplus labour that is expressed in surplus-value and surplus product. It can be considered in this sense as the producer of surplus-value. Landed property has nothing to do with the actual production process. Its role is limited to transferring a part of the surplus-value produced from capital's pocket into its own' (Marx 1992, p. 960).

[85] This can be expressed in another way: 'The total labour of the working class can be divided in such a way that the part that produces the entire means of subsistence needed by the working class (including the means of production these require) performs the necessary labour for the entire society. The labour performed by the whole remaining part of the working class can be considered as surplus labour' (Marx 1992, p. 771).

[86] See, for example, this passage: 'In so far as the labour process is purely individual, the same worker unites in himself all the functions that later on become separated. When an individual appropriates natural objects for his own livelihood, he alone supervises his own activity. Later on he is supervised by others. The solitary man cannot operate upon nature without calling his own muscles into play under the control of his own brain. Just as head and hand belong together in the system of nature, so in the labour process mental and physical labour are united. Later on they become separate; and this separation develops into a hostile antagonism. The product is transformed from the direct product of the individual producer into a social product, the joint product of a collective labourer, i.e. a combination of workers, each of whom stands at a different distance from

'poor' hard-working bookkeepers and clerks do not create values, and therefore are not 'productive' workers, the perhaps royally paid directors, the industrial managers (whom Marx calls 'the soul of our industrial system'[87] [as opposed to the industrial capitalists]) can be productive workers.

The answer to our question, which we could have given with the help of the second volume (see, for example, chapter 6: the costs of circulation), is therefore this: productive = value-creating labour is that labour that is socially necessary *for the production of use-values in the amounts corresponding to the respective social needs*, labour that is thus not simply contingent on the peculiar historical character of the capitalist mode of production.

All the persons employed in the actual labour process, from the last worker to the manager of the enterprise (whose labour now appears as the 'collective worker'[88]), all the individuals active in the storage, transportation, forwarding and retail sale of the products constitute the 'productive' value-creating workforce. The value of the part of the social product made by them represents the

---

the actual manipulation of the object of labour. With the progressive accentuation of the co-operative character of the labour process, there necessarily occurs a progressive extension of the concept of productive labour, and of the concept of the bearer of that labour, the productive worker. In order to work productively, it is no longer necessary for the individual himself to put his hand to the object; it is sufficient for him to be an organ of the collective labourer, and to perform any one of its subordinate functions. The definition of productive labour given above, the original definition, is derived from the nature of material production itself, and it remains correct for the collective labourer, considered as a whole. But it no longer holds good for each member taken individually.

'Yet the concept of productive labour also becomes narrower. Capitalist production is not merely the production of commodities, it is, by its very essence, the production of surplus-value. The worker produces not for himself, but for capital. It is no longer sufficient, therefore, for him simply to produce. He must produce surplus-value. The only worker who is productive is one who produces surplus-value for the capitalist, or in other words contributes towards the self-valorization of capital. If we may take an example from outside the sphere of material production, a school-master is a productive worker when, in addition to belabouring the heads of his pupils, he works himself into the ground to enrich the owner of the school. That the latter has laid out his capital in a teaching factory, instead of a sausage factory, makes no difference to the relation. The concept of a productive worker therefore implies not merely a relation between the activity of work and its useful effect, between the worker and the product of his work, but also a specifically social relation of production, a relation with a historical origin which stamps the worker as capital's direct means of valorization' (Marx 1976, pp. 643–4). [Marx's most extensive treatment of productive and unproductive labour occurs in Addendum 12 in Marx 1963, pp. 389–413].

87 (Marx 1992, p. 510) [Marx quotes Ure's *Philosophy of Manufactures*].
88 Marx 1976, p. 458.

'necessary' labour-time. The part falling to the other persons represents the surplus value; in it, therefore, participate first of all the 'workers' contingent upon the *historical* character of the mode of production – thus the executives and managers of the production process, in its form as a valorisation process; further, all those persons performing purely circulation functions that only realise values; then the generally non-working recipients of rent- and interest-payments; and finally, of course, the social functionaries, such as clerks, physicians, preachers, etc.

The question now arises: how is the 'necessary' labour required for the maintenance and reproduction of the productive workers determined? If we consider the totality of the productive workers as the collective labour power of society (and this notion, in its social form, is necessary throughout to understand Marx), this question overlaps with another one: *what is the value-magnitude of the labour power?* Out of place as the theory of a minimum subsistence level is in Marx, it arises [as a necessary result] when we consider the problem in relation to the social collective worker – which is, in my opinion, the only way of posing the question in Marx's sense.

To be sure, in Marx's system there is no need to presuppose a fixed minimum magnitude of 'necessary' labour [i.e. the amount of labour destined to the maintenance and reproduction of productive workers]. That there is a tendency in the capitalist system of production to limit the majority of the workers to a certain minimum of means of subsistence is a separate question, which is extraneous to the structure of the economic system of Marx. That, as I understand it, requires only that the value of the labour power, *at a given period* and *in a given country*, can be assumed to be of a certain *magnitude*.

Marx now says again, explicitly in the third volume of *Capital*, that this value, i.e. the average wage (imagine, for example, the total sum of wages and managers' salaries paid annually in Germany divided by the number of recipients) is higher or lower than the 'minimum subsistence level' (incidentally, a term rarely used by Marx himself). See, for example, this passage:

> The worker, finally, as owner and seller of his personal labour-power, receives under the name of wages a part of the product; in this there is expressed the portion of his labour that we call necessary labour, i.e. labour necessary for the maintenance and reproduction of this labour-power, *whether the conditions of this maintenance and reproduction are poorer or richer, more favourable or less.*[89]

---

89   Marx 1992, p. 960.

And further:

> The actual value of his labour-power diverges from this physical minimum [the daily necessary means of subsistence]; it differs according to climate and the level of social development; it depends not only on physical needs but also on historically developed social needs, which become second nature. In each country, however, this governing average wage is a given quantity at a given time.[90]

That is the point.

Let us now remember our starting point: we started from the problematic relationship *of value and surplus value theory to the production-cost and profit theory*, and we said that relations between the two would be divested of their enigmatic character as soon as the essence of value and surplus value, as Marx intended them to be understood, was clarified. The question is whether we have accomplished the task we set ourselves and thus reached the correct standpoint to appreciate the statements contained in the third volume of *Capital*. It seems to me that we have.

The first objection that can be raised is probably this: that *formally* production costs have nothing to do with values, and profit has nothing to do with surplus value. Value and surplus value establish and make accessible to our understanding, to borrow a common expression in Marx, 'social facts' (the social productivity of labour – the relationship between social surplus value and necessary labour). Production costs and profit, on the other hand, are intrinsically empirical facts of individual, private gainful activity, calculations of the actual agents of production.

Since the prevailing economic order is characterised by its capitalist character, i.e. by the fact that production is managed at the instigation of private capitalists, it is obvious that, in the calculation of the expenditure required to produce a given commodity, and of the profits that can be made thereby, the capital spent – or more accurately, advanced – is the only magnitude taken into account. The expenditure of labour is as indifferent to the capitalists as the concrete form of their commodities as use-values. Their only interest is the valorisation of their capital; what concerns them is value and surplus value, obtaining lucrative prices and profit.

---

90   Marx 1992, p. 999.

> What the commodity costs the capitalist, and what it actually does cost to produce it, are two completely different quantities ... The capitalist cost of the commodity is measured by the expenditure of capital, [whereas the actual cost of the commodity is measured by the expenditure of labour].[91]

The purely empirical character of profit, living in the consciousness of the agents of production as the purpose and goal of all production, is excellently expressed in Malthus's sentence, quoted by Marx: 'The capitalist ... expects an equal profit upon all the parts of the capital which he advances'.[92]

It is obvious, therefore, that the surplus value generated by individual capitalists stands in no formal relationship to their profit. I was never able to understand how a reasonably sane man (which Marx was, despite everything) could be capable of such an absurdity as connecting the individually generated surplus value with profits. It would not be just a false theory, but pure and simple nonsense, to postulate some kind of relationship between individual surplus value and profit and to want artificially, for instance, to relate the huge capital invested in a blast furnace or an electric lighting system with the paltry chunks of surplus value that only the handful of employed workers supply, according to the Marxian theory ...

However, despite all this, the value and surplus value theory has more than a decorative character in Marx's system, as our previous presentation has made abundantly clear. It renders, as we have seen, a double service to this system:

1. It is a necessary condition to make the phenomena of the economic world accessible to our understanding.
2. It is the regulatory and determining instance of the economic processes; by means of it Marx introduces, if I am right, conformity to law in economic life.

There is, therefore, certainly a very important link between production prices and values, profits and surplus value *materially*.

Prices are ultimately determined by the expenditure that is socially necessary to produce the commodities,[93] their 'value', which appears *directly* in the influence of the changing productivity of labour on the rise and fall of prices, on their movement.

---

91 Marx 1992, p. 118.
92 Malthus 1836, p. 268, quoted in Marx 1992, p. 126.
93 Variant 'Scylla'! [Richtung 'Scylla']. See Böhm-Bawerk 1892, p. 330. [Sombart refers to the subtitle of section III. 'The two variants of the cost theory: its Scylla and Charybdis'].

Profits are regulated by the ratio of surplus-labour to necessary labour: the total surplus value equals total profit. Why, therefore, the rate of profit at a given moment is 20 percent and not 200 percent or 2,000 percent, necessarily depends on the total surplus value of society, which is divided between the capitalists, etc. It cannot be the object of this sketch to describe in detail the *conditionality*[94] of economic phenomena following from the law of value and surplus value, for that would mean reproducing the Marxian system, whose content consists of nothing more than showing this conditionality.

If one clearly realises the position of the law of value in Marx's system, as I have tried to show it, one will understand what he meant by the often-repeated but seldom-understood statement that he did not want to offer a theory of economic phenomena, but to uncover the 'inner' conformity to law of the capitalist economic order.

Marx also posited for political economy the proposition that science begins where common sense stops. He recalled the words of Hegel: 'What the common human understanding finds irrational is in fact rational, and what it finds rational is irrational'.[95] According to Marx, 'all science would be superfluous if the form of appearance of things directly coincided with their essence';[96] and therefore 'it is one of the tasks of science to reduce the visible and merely apparent movement to the actual inner movement'.[97] The goal of *Capital* is, accordingly, not to present 'the actual movement of competition' but rather 'the internal organization of the capitalist mode of production, its ideal average, as it were'.[98] All these (in part not completely clear) expressions boil down to the same basic idea, which I have previously tried to sift out of his economic system.

It is in this sense, lately, that I have always developed the economic theory of Marx, whenever there was a chance. The third volume of *Capital* gave me, in general, a loud and clear confirmation that my interpretation has been the correct one. Only the reading of particular passages has raised certain concerns for me. I do not know whether it is my poor understanding or the presence of certain ambiguities in Marx that brought about these concerns. Sometimes I got the impression that Marx had done away with the strict distinction between surplus value and profit, and wanted to establish a close relation between the two. This occurs, for example, in some remarks on the theory of ground

---

94   [*Bedingtheit*: conditionality, contingency, dependence, determination].
95   Marx 1992, p. 956.
96   Ibid.
97   Marx 1992, p. 428.
98   Marx 1992, p. 970.

rent, which I do not discuss here in detail, but above all in the doctrine of *the equalisation of the general rate of profit by competition*.⁹⁹ Here one can get the impression that Marx believed not only in theory, i.e. in the construction of the scientific system – where it is, of course, totally warranted – but also empirically (or, as Marx says, 'historically') that the surplus value in an individual sphere of production was the point from which capitalist production originates; as if actually, as a result of the unequal organic composition of the capitals, at first unequal profit rates had appeared according to the law of value, and then the unequal profits gradually balanced out through the outflow and inflow of capital, until they became an average profit as a result of the correspondingly reduced or increased prices. If this was Marx's opinion, it would be based, in my view, on a big mistake. It would be equally wrong, both logically and empirically: logically, because it would be a genuine break from all the leading ideas of *Capital* to throw together the social fact of the production of surplus value with the individual fact of costs.¹⁰⁰ But it would also be empirically false, because development has never taken place in the manner described, nor does it take place in that way today. If it did, it would certainly be seen in operation in the case of at least every new branch of business. If this idea were true, in considering historically the advance of capitalism, one would have to think of it as first occupying those spheres in which living labour preponderated and where, therefore, the composition of capital was below the average (with little constant and much variable), and then as passing slowly into other spheres, according to the degree to which prices had fallen in those first spheres in consequence of overproduction. In a sphere having a preponderance of means of production over living labour, capitalism would naturally, at the beginning, have realised so small a profit – being limited to the surplus value created by the individual – that it would have had no inducement to enter into that sphere. But capitalist production, at the beginning of its historical development, occurs even to some extent in branches of production of the latter kind, mining, etc. Capital would have had no reason to leave the sphere of circulation, in which it was prospering, and to go into the sphere of production, without the prospect of a 'customary profit', which, be it observed, existed in commercial profit prior to any capitalistic production. But we can also show the error of the assumption from the other side. If extremely high profits were obtained, at the beginning of capitalist production, in the spheres having a preponderance of living labour, it would imply that all at once capital had made use of the class of producers

---

99 [For Engels's comments on the preceding paragraphs, see the Appendix to this document].
100 [*Kostengestaltung*: cost structuring, structure of costs, budgeting].

concerned (who had up to that time been independent), as wage-earners; that is, let us say, at half the compensation they had hitherto procured, and had put the difference in the prices of the commodities, corresponding directly to the values, in its own pocket. Furthermore, it presupposes an altogether unrealistic idea: that capitalist production began with declassed individuals in some branches of production, which were totally new creations, and was therefore able to fix prices immediately according to the amounts of capital invested.

But if the assumption of an empirical connection between rates of profit and rates of surplus value is false historically, that is, false as regards the beginning of capitalism, it is even more so as regards conditions in which the capitalistic system of production is fully developed. Whether the composition of a capital, by means of which trade is carried on today, is ever so high or ever so low, the prices of its products and the calculation (and realisation) of the profits are based solely on the outlay of capital.

If at all times, earlier as well as today, capitals did, as a matter of fact, pass continually from one sphere of production into another, the main cause of this would certainly lie in the inequality of their profit rates. But this inequality most surely proceeds not from the organic composition of the capitals, but from some cause connected with competition. Those branches of production that today flourish more than any others are precisely those with capitals of very high composition, such as mining, chemical factories, breweries, steam mills, etc. Are these the spheres from which capitals have withdrawn and migrated until production has been proportionately limited and prices have risen?

No matter how one approaches this question, the assumption that profit rates have been formed in connection with the rates of surplus value, that they are somehow empirically connected, is against the actual development of things.

I repeat: such a hypothesis, which Marx *seems* to make in chapter 10 of the third volume of *Capital*[101] – as I said, his language is not free from ambiguity – is not only unnecessary and useless for Marx's economic system: it would really mean a flaw in the system if we were to retain it. Theoretically, of course, we need to proceed from the rate of surplus value in order to reach the profit rate, but empirically we certainly do not have to do that. Those 'equalisations' of high and low rates of profit, among capitals of different organic composition,

---

101 [Marx 1992, Chapter 10: The Equalization of the General Rate of Profit through Competition. Market Prices and Market Values. Surplus Profit, pp. 273–301].

into an average rate of profit are mental operations, but no events of real life. I shall therefore assume that this was also Marx's opinion, as long as Engels does not affirm the contrary.[102] But, even in that case, I would see in this point an imperfection, an inconsistency in Marx's train of thought, which he would probably have overcome had he been given the opportunity to complete his work.

IV

At the beginning of this study, I already said that to offer right now a somehow exhaustive *critique of the Marxian system* would be an almost impossible task. At any rate, I do not consider myself at all appointed to do that at the moment.

Not that I believe that Marxism is not open to criticism in general. Certainly it lays itself open to attack on several fronts. But, in my opinion, this criticism should consist of a further development, not a 'rebuttal'. That can be left to someone with political ambition; for the scholar, the question is surely not to 'refute' any well-grounded system. Have Quesnay, Smith, Ricardo and all the other leading thinkers been perhaps 'refuted'? They have accomplished their task; they made a contribution to the development of science; their mistakes have been forgotten and their truths have been turned to account. The same will happen with Marx. Yes, we can look forward to the battle that will break out around Marxism, which is one of the most imposing systems of political economy. There will be a happy race; the spirits of the marginal utility theorists will finally awake from their slumber, they will even clash violently. But it is just excellent that there should be disputes *in majorem scientiae gloriam* ['to the greater glory of science'].

There are some colleagues, especially among the elderly, who will be unable to suppress a smile at these words. They will ask whether it is really serious to bring back from the dead a long-buried ghost like Karl Marx, and to make his ten times 'refuted' system the object of criticism; indeed, to want to place it at the centre of scientific discussion. Well, we younger ones will see to it that their laughter passes away gradually. We believe that we are not at the end but precisely at the beginning of the Marx-critique. And we are not quite able to suppress our wonderment at the fact that people have already wanted to talk about a 'criticism' at all – before the system was completed!

---

102 [For Engels's comments on the following four paragraphs, see the Appendix to this document].

Of course, if the incipient new critique of Marx is to acquire the positive character that every major dispute of scientific opinions has, a prior condition must necessarily be fulfilled: one should first correctly understand Marx and argue only over what he meant, not about what he might have meant. It is a very unpleasant and thankless task to have to establish, in every criticism, only the *quid pro quos* [misunderstandings] that the critic in question is guilty of in his representation of Marx's thought. I consider, therefore, a brief outline of the basic ideas of the economic system of Marx not to be superfluous.

If people take the trouble, before offering a criticism of Marx, of first going into the spirit of Marxism, we must hopefully expect that, to begin with, all the mostly false traditional objections raised against Marx, which for almost thirty years now have been adorning our textbooks, will recede into the realm of shadows. Now I shall review briefly a certain 'well-known throng',[103] hoping for its imminent downfall, and I sincerely urge the respective fathers or adoptive fathers of these wayward spiritual offspring not to miss any suitable opportunity to bury them as deeply as possible. For ease of reference, I quote several passages from the third volume of *Capital*, in which the necessary information about these 'issues' can be obtained. I limit myself, as elsewhere in this study, to the economic system of Marx, leaving out of consideration both the philosophical foundations of Marxism and its peculiar theory of economic and social development.

1. At the head [of the objections against Marx] marches a proposition that has almost become a dogma and has achieved vested rights in all the traditional histories of political economy: that Marx, like all the 'scientific socialists', is indeed significant for the 'criticism' of political economy but not for the 'positive development' of science.[104] I could never quite understand this. In my view, in addition to the Austrian school, it is above all 'scientific socialism' that comes precisely into consideration for the 'positive development of economic theory'. At any rate, it has left behind a firmly established system ...

This is obviously an issue that cannot be settled with a couple of quotations: I go into it here only because I consider it the πρωτον φευδος [first fallacy] of

---

103 [A reference to Goethe's *Faust*, Vol. I (II. Before the city gate): 'Invoke not thus the well-known throng / which through the firmament diffused is faring, / and danger thousand-fold, our race to wrong / in every quarter is preparing'].

104 This objection cropped up again in the very readable inaugural lecture of a representative of the young Italian school influenced by Achille Loria, which otherwise glorifies Marx, the now Modena professor Ugo Rabbeno (Rabenno 1894).

the traditional critique of Marx, from whose erroneous nature many misunderstandings have followed.

2. The assertion that Marx had no understanding of the benefits of capitalism, of the historical contingency and historical justification of the capitalist economic order and, therefore, of the personal 'accomplishments' of the capitalists, can be even more briefly rejected. Have people never read the dithyrambic glorification of the historical mission of capitalism even in the *Communist Manifesto*? In the meantime, however, I just want to pick up a few passages from the third volume of *Capital*. Compare, for instance,[105] page 736, where credit is referred to as the means to absorb the best (!) people of the dominated classes into the dominant class (the bourgeoisie);[106]

> It is *one of the great results of the capitalist mode of production* that on the one hand it transforms agriculture from a merely empirical set of procedures, mechanically handed down and practised by the most undeveloped portion of society, into a conscious scientific application of agronomy, in so far as this is at all possible within the conditions of private property.[107]
>
> *The justification for landed property*, as that for all other forms of property, of a particular mode of production, *is that the mode of production itself*

---

105 [The function of the capitalist is discussed in the following passage: 'Given the surplus-value that accrues to a certain variable capital, it still depends very much on the business acumen of the individual, either the capitalist himself or his managers and salespeople, whether this same surplus-value is expressed in a higher or lower rate of profit and therefore whether it delivers a greater or lesser amount of profit' (Marx 1992, p. 235). See also chapter 23 on Interest and Profit of Enterprise, particularly this passage: 'Profit of enterprise arises from the function of capital in the reproduction process, i.e. as a result of the operations and activity by which the functioning capitalist mediates these functions of industrial and commercial capital. But it is no sinecure to be a representative of functioning capital, unlike the case with interest-bearing capital. On the basis of capitalist production the capitalist directs both the production process and the circulation process. The exploitation of productive labour takes effort, whether he does this himself or has it done in his name by others. In opposition to interest, therefore, his profit on enterprise presents itself to him as independent of his property in capital and rather as the result of his functions as non-owner, as a worker' (Marx 1992, p. 503)].
106 ['The more a dominant class is able to absorb the best people from the dominated classes, the more solid and dangerous is its rule' (Marx 1992, p. 736)].
107 Marx 1992, p. 752, Sombart's emphasis.

> *possesses a transitory historical necessity*, and so too therefore do the relations of production and exchange that arise from it.[108]
>
> [The title] was entirely created by the relations of production. Once these have reached the point where they have to be sloughed off, then the material source, *the economically and historically justified source of the title that arises from the process of life's social production*, disappears, and with it all transactions based on it.[109]
>
> It is *one of the civilizing aspects of capital* that it extorts this surplus labour in a manner and in conditions that are more advantageous to social relations and to the creation of elements for a new and higher formation than was the case under the earlier forms of slavery; serfdom, etc.[110]

3. In dealing with technical development, Marx overlooked the great influence exerted by the '*conformation of the market*' on modern economic life. If that is meant historically, it is based on an inaccurate knowledge of Marx. One need only think about the places in the *Communist Manifesto* where the influence on production of the enlargement of the market is discussed. Besides, one can now read, for instance, Chapter 20 of the third volume of *Capital*, entitled 'Historical Material on Merchant's Capital'. Certainly Marx has – I think quite correctly – pointed out with equal force that capitalist production itself, for the most part, creates the market. He literally describes the 'establishment of the world market' as one of the 'three cardinal facts about capitalist production'.[111] If, however, people with that objection want to refer to the peculiar conformation of the economic system, they are only saying that Marx intentionally left competition out of consideration. The question then arises: by what right did he do that? This question can only be answered in terms of the epistemological value of the method he followed.

We must now mention, among the traditional 'objections', those concerning the theory of value.

4. The theory of value is wrong because the commodities *cannot*, as has been proved, be exchanged in proportion to the amounts of labour contained in

---

108 Marx 1992, p. 760, Sombart's emphasis.
109 Marx 1992, p. 911, Sombart's emphasis.
110 Marx 1992, p. 958, Sombart's emphasis.
111 Marx 1992, p. 375.

them; in a word, value is not empirical. On this issue see the remarks contained in this study.

5. Qualitatively different labours cannot be reduced to abstract labour. This problem sorts itself out as soon as people regard 'value' as a social fact, that is, as an economic expression of social productivity.

6. Marx asserts that only manual labour is 'productive'. On this see the passages quoted above on manual labour.

7. The theory of value 'abstracts' from the use-value of the commodities. On this see now, among other passages:

> *This is in fact the law of value* as it makes itself felt, not in relation to the individual commodities or articles, but rather to the total products at a given time of particular spheres of social production autonomized by the division of labour; so that not only is no more labour-time devoted to each individual commodity than necessary, but out of the total social labour-time only the proportionate quantity needed is devoted to the various types of commodity. *Use-value still remains a condition.*[112]
>
> The social need, i.e. the use-value on the social scale, here appears decisive for the quota of total social labour-time that falls to the share of the various particular spheres of production. But this is simply the same law that is already exhibited by the individual commodity, i.e. that *its use-value is the precondition of its exchange-value and hence of its value.*[113]

Use-value is altogether the bearer of exchange-value but not its cause.[114] Most hard-pressed of all, I am afraid, will be those who want to refute the theory of value and capital for 'moral' reasons, because this objection is based on a seemingly ineradicable error: that the concepts of value, surplus value, exploitation, etc. have in Marx an ethical and not a purely economic content. Many blows will still have to be struck before this misunderstanding is definitely buried.

Perhaps the reading of the third volume of *Capital* will contribute significantly to a correct understanding of the nature of those categories. In order to

---

112   Marx 1992, p. 774, Sombart's emphasis.
113   Ibid.
114   Marx 1992, p. 786.

illustrate the 'ethical' character of Marx's theory of surplus value, I shall content myself in the meantime by presenting to the reader a passage from the third volume, which indicates that it is not just the wage-workers who are shamefully 'exploited' and vilely deprived of a part of what they 'deserve' but also – listen carefully – the *capitalists*!

> Just as the functioning capitalist pumps out surplus labour from the worker, and thus surplus-value and surplus product in the form of profit, so the landowner pumps out a part of this surplus-value or surplus profit in turn from the capitalist in the form of rent, according to the laws developed earlier.[115]

But enough of that. It was not my intention to give here an exhaustive review of the previous criticism of Marx, any more than I can, or want to, offer my own criticism.

I simply intended to postulate, in connection with the review of the third volume of *Capital*, some perhaps not entirely superfluous principles for the future critique of Marx. In conclusion, therefore, I would like to make the following remarks.

We shall have to understand Marx *methodologically* better than before, not just 'dogmatically'; i.e. we must be more clearly aware than before of the *sharp contrast* between Marx's form of apprehension [*Auffassungsweise*], his 'formulation of the problems', and the dominant way of thinking.

What, then, did Marx have in mind when he constructed his economic system? He described the 'ultimate aim' of *Capital* as 'to reveal the economic law of motion of modern society'.[116] For this purpose, he sought to uncover in his economic system the social relationships in which the individual economic existence is embedded – to reveal economically, as it were, the *relations of dependency*. For him, the question was to find the 'economic conditions which are *independent*'[117] of the individual's will, in order to determine what 'goes on behind his back, by virtue of relations *independent* of him'.[118] In order to illustrate this with an example, let us take Marx's explanation of the formation of prices. It never occurred to him to look for the individual motives of the persons exchanging, or even to proceed from the cost-of-production calculation. No, his train of thought was this: prices are formed by competition; as to how,

---

115   Marx 1992, p. 959.
116   Marx 1976, p. 92.
117   Marx 1992, p. 753.
118   Marx 1976, p. 1013.

that remains to be seen. *But* competition itself is regulated by the rate of profit, the profit rate by the rate of surplus value, and this by value, which is itself the expression of a socially determined fact, of the social productivity. [This succession] now presents itself in Marx's system in reverse order: value – surplus value – profit – competition – prices, etc. If we wanted a catchphrase, we could say: the question for Marx is never the motivation, but always the limitation of the individual caprice of economic agents.

This can be summarised in one word: Marx's economic system is characterised by an *extreme objectivism*. Here, into the Marxian system, emptied the stream that emanated from Quesnay and continued to flow via Ricardo to Rodbertus: the strictly objectivist view of the economy, which has its starting point in the economically active society and (formally) returns to it, seeking to uncover the social connections that in the last (material) instance are decisive for the individual economic sectors[119] and the economic processes.

The *subjectivist* tendency is the opposite: it ultimately attempts to explain the processes of economic life from the psyche of economic subjects, and it looks to psychological motivation for the conformity of economic life to law. Its natural starting point is the needy, or exchanging, single man – Hasbach has nicely revealed to us the historical origins of this way of thinking in the natural-law doctrine of the society based on exchange – and its leading concept, if it is reasonably consistent, is *utility*. It is a stream that sprang up early, but whose most powerful flows ran through the systems of Turgot and Adam Smith; a current that incorporated almost the entire dominant political economy, even if it has experienced in the Austrians its most consistent development. The current state of economic theory seems to be essentially determined by the prevailing subjectivism, which naturally empties into psychologism.[120] Everywhere, the 'motivation' of the (individual) economic action occupies centre stage in their system. The question here is not to decide whether subjectivist economics (described as historical, ethical, organic, abstract, traditional or otherwise) has a bright future, or whether it stands at the end of its development and is about to wind up, bequeathing its possessions now to history, now to psycho-

---

119 [*Einzelwirtschaft*].
120 It seemed likely that, among the moderns, Heinrich Dietzel would pursue an objectivist path in economic theory (see his review of *Der natürliche Wert* by Friedrich von Wieser in Dietzel 1885). However, in his writings he has become increasingly subjectivist, and Böhm-Bawerk was in my view absolutely right (see Böhm-Bawerk 1892, pp. 325, 336 ff.) when he addressed Dietzel as a halfway converted marginal utility theorist, just as he is right in finding no principled opposition between the methodological views of Carl Menger and Adolph Wagner.

logy. It is only necessary to point out that two worlds of economic thought exist side by side, almost independently of each other; two kinds of scientific observation, which have nothing more than the name in common. And it cannot be ruled out, I think, that all the partial and complete, more or less justified, more or less clear, more or less hackneyed contradictions in our schools, which have come up for discussion so often lately, will ultimately resolve themselves in this methodologically paramount opposition of objectivism and subjectivism.

Only full awareness of this contradiction will make a fruitful critique of Marx possible. Is it a coincidence that people have overlooked for so long this peculiarity of Marx's system – namely, the fact that he is a typical representative of objectivist political economy? For the most part, I think that the layout of Marx's *Capital* itself is to blame for that. People have overlooked its strictly objectivist core because it is presented in an extremely subjective *dress*! Let us recall the boisterous manner in which Marx lets the capitalist behave in the first volume as a 'character',[121] and we will find it understandable that his contemporaries, accustomed to subjectivist thinking, could see in his system nothing more than what the other presentations of political economy offered: an economic order developed out of the feelings, impulses, judgements, etc. of the subject.

It is obvious that people could not thus reach their goal, either in their assessment or in their criticism of Marx's system, because the problems, on whose solution the decisions on further questions depended, were not posed. I think that one should try to offer an evaluation and critique of Marx's system in the following way: is the objectivist tendency in economic science entitled to be exclusive or complementary? If we choose the former answer,[122] we should

---

121 ['The characters who appear on the economic stage are merely personifications of economic relations; it is as the bearers of these economic relations that they come into contact with each other' (Marx 1976, p. 179). The word *'Charaktermasken'* comes from Greek theatre, where the actors wore masks corresponding to the characters they were representing].

122 If this question is answered in the negative, the remaining ones are irrelevant. I just think the problem cannot be disposed of as short-handedly as Böhm-Bawerk has occasionally tried to do (see Böhm-Bawerk 1886, pp. 77 ff.). He takes for granted what is precisely the *thema probandi*: namely, that 'the social laws, whose research is the task of political economy, are based on concurrent [*übereinstimmenden*] actions of individuals' etc., and that 'only the permanence of this motif (to win as much "value" as possible) results in the conformity to law of our economic actions'. Certainly, if this regularity in the economy were only a psychological fact, and if its determination were the task of political economy, then there would be no doubt about the exclusive right of the psychological method. Both, however, must first be precisely proved.

further ask: is the Marxist method of quantitative determination of economic facts, through the intellectual tool of the concept of value, imperative? If so, is labour the correctly chosen content of the concept of value? In other words: is the social productivity, consequently analysed, just as much the principle of objectivist political economy as the utility of the subjectivists? If so, are Marx's reasoning, the structure of his system, his inferences, etc. contestable? Only then can the individual parts of the theory be tested in the corresponding order.

If these lines contribute even a little to turn the critique of Marx into more orderly channels, their purpose will be fulfilled.

Appendix: Engels to Werner Sombart in Breslau, London, 11 March 1895

Source: Karl Marx and Frederick Engels, *Selected Correspondence* (Moscow: Progress Publishers, 1965, pp. 479–81).

Dear Sir,

Replying to your note of the 14th of last month may I thank you for your kindness in sending me your work on Marx; I had already read it with great interest in the issue of the *Archiv*[123] which Dr. H. Braun was good enough to send me, and was pleased for once to find such understanding of *Capital* at a German University. Naturally I can't altogether agree with the wording in which you render Marx's exposition. Especially the definitions of the concept of value which you give on pages 576 and 577 seem to me to be rather all-embracing: I would first limit them historically by explicitly restricting them to the economic phase in which alone value has up to now been known, and could only have been known, namely, the forms of society in which commodity exchange, or commodity production, exists; in primitive communism value was unknown. And secondly it seems to me that the concept could also be defined in a narrower sense. But this would lead too far, in the main you are quite right.

Then, however, on page 586, you appeal directly to me, and the jovial manner with which you hold a pistol to my head made me laugh. But you need not worry, I shall 'not assure you of the contrary'. The logical sequence by which

---

123 *Archiv für soziale Gesetzgebung und Statistik*, Herausgegeben von Dr. Heinrich Braun, Bd. VII, Berlin, 1894, S. 555–94.

Marx deduces the general and equal rate of profit from the different values of $s / c = s / (c + v)$ produced in various capitalist enterprises is completely foreign to the mind of the individual capitalist. Inasmuch as it has a historical parallel, that is to say, as far as it exists in reality outside our heads, it manifests itself for instance in the fact that certain parts of the surplus value produced by capitalist A over and above the rate of profit, or above his share of the total surplus value, are transferred to the pocket of capitalist B whose output of surplus value remains as a rule below the customary dividend. But this process takes place objectively, in the things, unconsciously, and we can only now estimate how much work was required in order to achieve a proper understanding of these matters. If the *conscious* co-operation of the individual capitalists had been necessary to establish the average rate of profit, if the individual capitalist had *known* that he produces surplus value and how much of it, and that frequently he has to hand over part of his surplus value, then the relationship between surplus value and profit would have been fairly obvious from the outset and would presumably have already been described by Adam Smith, if not Petty.

According to Marx's views all history up to now, in the case of big events, has come about unconsciously, that is, the events and their further consequences have not been intended; the ordinary actors in history have either wanted to achieve something different, or else what they achieved has led to quite different unforeseeable consequences. Applied to the economic sphere: the individual capitalists, each on his own, chase after the *biggest* profit. Bourgeois economy discovers that this race in which every *one* chases after the *bigger* profit results in the general and *equal* rate of profit, the approximately *equal* ratio of profit for each one. Neither the capitalists nor the bourgeois economists, however, realise that the goal of this race is the uniform proportional distribution of the total surplus value calculated on the total capital.

But how has the equalisation been brought about in reality? This is a very interesting point, about which Marx himself does not say much. But his way of viewing things is not a doctrine but a method. It does not provide ready-made dogmas, but criteria for further research and the method for this research. Here therefore a certain amount of work has to be carried out, since Marx did not elaborate it himself in his first draft. First of all we have here the statements on pages 153–6, III, 1,[124] which are also important for your rendering of the concept of value and which prove that the concept has or had more reality than you ascribe to it. When commodity exchange began, when products gradually turned into commodities, they were exchanged approximately *according* to

---

124 Marx 1992, pp. 273–9.

their value. It was the amount of labour expended on two objects which provided the only standard for their quantitative comparison. Thus value had a *direct and real existence* at that time. We know that this direct realisation of value in exchange ceased and that now it no longer happens. And I believe that it won't be particularly difficult for you to trace the intermediate links, at least in general outline, that lead from directly real value to the value of the capitalist mode of production, which is so thoroughly hidden that our economists can calmly deny its existence. A genuinely historical exposition of these processes, which does indeed require thorough research but in return promises amply rewarding results, would be a very valuable supplement to *Capital*.[125]

Finally, I must also thank you for the high opinion which you have formed of me if you consider that I could have made something better of volume III. I cannot share your opinion, and believe I have done my duty by presenting Marx in Marx's words, even at the risk of requiring the reader to do a bit more thinking for himself.

Yours very respectfully,

F. Engels

---

125 [Engels himself dealt with the subject in 'Ergänzung und Nachtrag zum III. Buche des 'Kapital' I. Wertgezetz und Profitrate' ('Supplement to *Capital*, Volume Three, I. Law of Value and Rate of Profit'), which he wrote in the spring of 1895 (see Marx 1992, pp. 1028–45)].

DOCUMENT 5

Theories of Surplus Value (1905)

Heinrich Cunow

Source: Heinrich Cunow, '*Theorien über den Mehrwert*', Die Neue Zeit, 23. 1904–5, 1. Bd. (1905), 16, 17, 19, pp. 497–506, 547–55, 617–24.

A review of Karl Marx, *Theorien über den Mehrwert: aus dem nachgelassenen Manuskript 'Zur Kritik der politischen Ökonomie'*, Hrsg. von Karl Kautsky, Stuttgart: J.H.W. Dietz Nachf., 3 vols. in 4: 1 Die Anfänge der Theorie vom Mehrwert bis Adam Smith, 1905, XX, 430 s. (Internationale Bibliothek, 35).

Introduction by the Editors

With this article by Heinrich Cunow, we turn from the three volumes of *Capital* to reviews of the three volumes of *Theories of Surplus-Value*. Although the first part of this work appeared more than a decade after Volume III of *Capital*, Marx's analysis of previous theories of political economy was always an integral part of his research. The *Contribution to the Critique of Political Economy* (1859) already contained an historical survey of earlier analyses both of commodities and of theories of money, and Marx originally planned to include a similar survey concerning the production process of capital. But Marx changed his plans over time, and by 1865 he was instead contemplating using his notes on earlier economists for a fourth volume of *Capital*. After Marx died in 1883, Engels hoped to publish *Theories of Surplus-Value*, but his own death intervened in 1895. It was ultimately Karl Kautsky who accomplished this task in the years 1905–10. Curnow recounts the difficulties that Kautsky's work involved and praises him for not putting his own stamp on Marx's manuscripts.[1]

---

1 For a detailed account of the origins of this work, see the preface from the Institute of Marxism-Leninism in Marx 1963, pp. 13–34. According to this preface, the Kautsky edition has 'radical defects' (p. 20), beginning with the arrangement of the material and including 'distortions and revisions of Marx's text' (p. 23) that obscure 'questions of the class struggle' (p. 22). The editors at the Institute of Marxism-Leninism summarised Kautsky's editorial work this way: 'Finally, characteristic of the entire Kautsky edition are the numerous and sometimes extremely crude mistakes in deciphering the text of the manuscript, inaccurate and in

The logic that led Marx to investigate the work of previous economists was the same as led him to focus his 1844 manuscripts on a critical analysis of Feuerbach and of Hegelian philosophy. In that case, Marx concluded that Hegel's dialectic, albeit in mystified form, had actually grasped 'the self-creation of man as a process, objectification as loss of the object, as alienation and transcendence of this alienation, and ... he therefore grasps the nature of labor, and conceives objective man ... as the result of his own labor'.[2] Marx concluded that the history of industry must be regarded as 'the exoteric manifestation of human *faculties*'.

The next obvious step was to re-read the history of industry as the '*open book of human faculties*', or of man's own self-creation through labour.[3] In *The German Ideology*, written in 1845–6, Marx and Engels undertook to do precisely that; to initiate a reinterpretation of economic history in terms of historical materialism, beginning with the proposition that 'men must be in a position to live in order to "make history". But life involves before everything else eating and drinking, a habitation, clothing and many other things. The first historical act is thus the production of means to satisfy these ends, the production of material life itself'.[4]

If economic history opened one book, the history of economic thought must open another. That conclusion can be seen in the famous remark in the preface to the *Critique of Political Economy*: 'The mode of production of material life conditions the general process of social, political and intellectual life. It is not the consciousness of men that determines their existence, but the social existence that determines their consciousness'.[5] That being the case, the writings of earlier economists must themselves be a repository of insights into the emergence of capitalism and its implications, much as Hegel's philosophy provided an insight, albeit confused, into the meaning of history. Marx's investigation of his predecessors was not an exercise in intellectual history; rather, by critically analysing earlier economic literature, separating class interests from scientific advances, he was looking for the historical emergence of economic categor-

---

a number of cases obviously incorrect translations of English and French expressions occurring in the text, arbitrary editorial interpolations inconsistent with the movement of Marx's thought, the absolutely impermissible substitution of some of Marx's terms by others, and so on' (p. 24). Nevertheless, the same authors comment that 'Lenin had an extremely high regard for the theoretical analyses contained in the manuscript *Theories of Surplus-Value*' (p. 20).

2 Marx, cited by Fromm 1961, pp. 175–6.
3 Marx, cited by Fromm 1961, p. 134.
4 Marx and Engels 1964, p. 39.
5 Marx 1970, pp. 20–1.

ies with which he would concretely reconstruct capitalist society in terms of thought. As Heinrich Cunow remarked, 'many parts of the first volume of *Theories of Surplus-Value* actually appear as an application of the Marxist theory of history to political economy'.

Among the numerous writers mentioned in Part I of *Theories of Surplus-Value*, François Quesnay and Adam Smith were of decisive importance: Quesnay for his attempt to trace the social surplus to agricultural production, and Smith for attributing all economic growth to productive labour. The Physiocrats and Smith redirected economic thought away from the mercantilist preoccupation with net revenue as 'money', and instead studied the 'real' process of material production. Smith's accomplishment was to premise economic growth upon three fundamental conditions: 1) the expansion of 'productive' labour, creating vendible commodities that could be stocked and stored up as capital; 2) a high rate of social investment (capital accumulation); and 3) extensive division of labour to promote specialised skills and labour productivity[6] – all ideas that became central to Marx's account of capitalism's laws of motion.

Heinrich Cunow's review of *Theories of Surplus-Value* argues that the prominence Marx attributed to the Physiocrats and Adam Smith had the unfortunate implication of underestimating the contribution of Sir James Steuart. He claims that Steuart's concept of 'positive profit', as a 'surplus product' resulting from production rather than exchange, was an important step towards a scientific concept of surplus value. Cunow's thoughtful argument reflects his own background as editor and scholar. From 1898 he served as one of the editors of the SPD theoretical journal *Die Neue Zeit*, and from 1902 onwards he also worked as editor of the SPD central organ *Vorwärts*, where, together with Heinrich Ströbel, he was considered an anti-revisionist spokesman for the Left. In 1907, Cunow became a lecturer at the SPD party school in Berlin, teaching alongside Rudolf Hilferding, Rosa Luxemburg and Franz Mehring, who also wrote a review of the first volume of *Theories of Surplus-Value*.[7] His theoretical works included several studies in anthropology and a history of the revolutionary press during the French Revolution. He also pioneered the study of imperialism, being one of the first to emphasise the central role of banks and finance-capital in imperialist expansionism.[8]

---

6 Smith 2007, pp. 212–24. Smith's occasional contradictions in defining 'productive' labour are mentioned in this review by Cunow.
7 Mehring 1905 and Rosa Luxemburg, 'Aus dem literarischen Nachlaß von Karl Marx', Vorwärts, Nr. 7, 8. Januar 1905. Reprinted in Rosa Luxemburg, Gesammelte Werke, Bd. 1, 2. Hbd., pp. 462–476. Available online at the Marxists Internet Archive.
8 [(See his essay 'American Expansionist Policy in East Asia', originally published in *Die Neue Zeit* in June–July 1902, in Day and Gaido 2011, pp. 195–210)].

Heinrich Cunow's Review of Karl Marx, *Theories of Surplus-Value*, Part 1

1   *The Beginnings of the Theory of Surplus Value up to Adam Smith*[9]
For more than two decades the earth in the silent Highgate Cemetery has been covering the mortal remains of the brilliant thinker and fighter Karl Marx, but from the mind of that man a vibrant, active force still emanates. His thoughts not only guide the working class in its struggle; they are also the inexhaustible source from which economic science – however much this may be denied for political reasons – draws its deepest insights. Just as *Capital*, Marx's life-work, has been the most important economic and literary event of the second half of the nineteenth century, so it is also an economic standard at the entrance gate to the twentieth century, and its influence is expected to endure as long as the capitalist economic system that it describes and analyses.

How often guild economists have critically 'destroyed' this work in the nearly fifty years since publication of its first volume, and how many times this 'destruction' has been exultantly proclaimed by bourgeois newspapers! Yet while the writings of petty critics have mostly disappeared without a trace, and their names are forgotten, *Capital* still stands as a defiant rock in the surging seas. Entire economic schools have come and gone in the meantime. Where do we find today the liberal economic school, which, as an offshoot of Adam Smith's doctrines, dominated German liberal daily journalism in the 60s and 70s of the last century? Where is the historical school, [which in its time] was hailed by the peal of bells? It has outlived itself and become obsolete. It has accomplished some useful minor work that illuminated selected areas of capitalism's operation – small-scale hard labour – but not a single fundamental work. Even in the field of economic history, it has nothing of importance to show – naturally, since it does not have its own conception of history and was therefore unable to reach a viewpoint from which it could overlook the entire historical terrain to be explored, and from which it could recognise, in the maze of intersecting paths, the grand lines of the process of social development. This is why, even in the more intelligent circles of bourgeois economics, the

---

9   From the unpublished manuscript *Zur Kritik der politischen Ökonomie* [*On the Critique of Political Economy*] by Karl Marx, edited by Karl Kautsky, Stuttgart: J.H.W. Dietz Nachf., 1905. [We have been informed that a Russian translation, edited by Lawroff and Nikolai Petrovich, will soon be published by *Obrasowanje* in St. Petersburg. The editors. (Note by Karl Kautsky)].

historical school is today deemed to be only a makeshift; and the need for theoretical deepening, as it was once offered by the classical school of English political economy, increasingly manifests itself.

The first volume of Marx's *Theories of Surplus-Value* – edited by Kautsky from the manuscript left by Marx – which is nothing but a continuation of *A Contribution to the Critique of Political Economy*, meets this need to a degree unparalleled by any other economic work of the recent past. When Marx published this work in 1859, he regarded it as the beginning of a long series of monographs, in which he intended to deal systematically, from a critical-historical point of view, with all the most important problems of bourgeois economy, such as the structure of capital, landed property, wage-labour, public finance, trade and the world market. From 1844, when he concluded in Paris that the political and legal life of every historical epoch is determined by its material conditions of existence, by its economic character, Marx immediately threw himself into the study of political economy, as his reply to Proudhon's *Système des contradictions économiques ou Philosophie de la misère* proves. He eagerly continued those studies after his expulsion from Paris to Brussels, and then to London in 1850. The fruit of those studies was a series of short sketches, initially written to clarify his own ideas and to gain a thorough overview of the previous course of development of economic theory, in which Marx dealt with various issues of political economy in more or less detail and from a critical-historical point of view.

Marx prepared some of these works for the press in the winter of 1858–9. He combined them with the previously mentioned *Contribution to the Critique of Political Economy*, which deals, in an initial book, with simple commodity circulation and monetary circulation. They were to be followed, in a second book, by a further section on the general structure of capital; and this, in turn, was to be followed by a book on landed property and by another on wage-labour.

That was Marx's original plan, which he seems to have maintained until 1863. Then he dropped it and decided not to discuss the problems of political economy in direct connection with a critique of his predecessors, as he had first intended, but first to develop his own theories systematically, in their logical connection, and only later to follow this exposition with a history of economic theory in a special volume. Pursuing this new plan, in 1867 Marx published the first volume of *Capital*. He announced in the preface that this first book, analysing capital's process of production, would be followed by a second book on 'the process of circulation of capital' and the 'total process of capitalist production' (the conversion of surplus value into the various forms of profit), to which then would be added, as a third and final volume, a critical history of economic theories.

As we know, Marx's plan was not carried out even in this form. Following Marx's death in 1883, Friedrich Engels decided – if he did not want to abbreviate greatly Marx's posthumous manuscripts for the second volume, and to rework large parts of them completely – that instead of adding one additional book to the first one he had to add two more volumes on the process of capital's circulation and on the metamorphoses of surplus value, thus raising the total to three books.[10]

Because of his own sudden death, it was not given to Engels to edit the fourth volume. His place was taken by Karl Kautsky, at the request of Marx's heirs, because Engels had still not appointed a successor before his death. According to Engels's plans for the edition, Marx's posthumous manuscripts should have been turned, after eliminating the remarks already contained in the second and third volumes of *Capital*, into a *Critical History of the Theory of Surplus-Value*. In filial respect for Engels's wishes, Kautsky at first tried to follow these intentions, but in vain. In Marx's manuscript, the controversies and criticisms are bound up with historical digressions and with his own follow-up of the train of thought begun by the authors he criticises. Those elements are too closely interwoven – mutually complementing and determining each other – for them to be removed from their context without mutilating and injuring Marx's work. Most parts of the manuscript had to be completely rewritten, expanded and cast in a different form, or else Engels's plans had to be abandoned and Marx's draft had to be published while preserving its inner connection. What to do? A revision of the manuscript would have corresponded more to the intentions of Marx and Engels; eliminating some passages, which were similar to others appearing in the first three volumes of *Capital*, would have limited the extent of the new work, giving a better structure to the material and filling existing gaps – but a 'fourth volume of *Capital*', composed in this way, would not have been Marx's history of the theory of value and surplus value but rather a history of those theories, written by Kautsky on the basis of Marx's conception.

However tempting it must have been for Kautsky to write the fourth volume of *Capital*, and thus to link his name forever with the standard work of economic science, he decided to publish the manuscript in Marx's version. And for this modesty, for this voluntary demurral, he deserves our most heartfelt thanks. Although some things appear incomplete in the present work – upon reading it, one would often wish for some interrupted thoughts to be followed

---

10 [The subtitles of the three volumes of Marx's *Capital* read: Book I: The Process of Production of Capital; Book II: The Process of Circulation of Capital; and Book III: The Process of Capitalist Production as a Whole].

through and for the logical conclusion to be drawn from them – the first volume of *Theories of Surplus-Value*, as edited by Kautsky, appears as a great achievement and is fascinating in its overall impression. It is an unfinished intellectual structure, yet that of a brilliant architect; its subtle and yet massive lines, its boldly emerging pillars and columns, betray in their proud simplicity the hand of the Master, contemptuous of all petty flourishes and of all modern showmanship. In a way, the study of this structure – indeed, precisely of its unfinished parts – gives even greater pleasure than the study of *Capital*, for in the latter we find readily elaborated and polished forms, while the work that has recently appeared allows us an intimate look into Marx's intellectual workshop; it shows us Marx at work, the young Marx, whose impetuous urge to know and create had not yet been affected by later persistent and exhausting illnesses.

If the impression that the book made upon me is indicative of the impact it will have upon other socialist readers, then its success will be considerable despite some passages that are difficult to understand. I did not set out to read it with particular interest. If I have to be honest, at first I did so only because I had to, because I assumed that it would be merely a repetition, in different form, of remarks contained in individual chapters of the first three volumes of *Capital*. But the more I continued to read it, the more it fascinated me. A part of youth returned to life within me, a time when I first knew only a few socialist economic writings and yet, as befits a young businessman, was caught up in bourgeois economic doctrines and read for the first time the first volume of *Capital* – which, though I only half-understood much of it, opened up a new and different world for me.

But next to Marx we owe to the editor of the work, to Karl Kautsky, the fact that *Theories of Surplus-Value* appears today in this form. Kautsky assembled the book from an illegible, continuous manuscript, one lacking divisions into chapters or sections and containing countless digressions, repetitions and references to things already said. This was by no means an easy and minor task, because he had to string together remarks, scattered over 1,472 closely-written quarto pages, according to their conceptual connection, so that not only was the historical succession of the theories respected, but the whole thing was assembled into a logical structure, progressing from the simple to the complex – and yet giving to Marx what is Marx's. Kautsky managed to accomplish this task so that the reader, if he does not pay attention to the footnotes, hardly notices the composition of the text from all sorts of fragments.

2   The English Mercantilists

The first volume of *Theories of Surplus-Value*, assembled by Kautsky from the manuscript, deals with the beginnings of the theory of value and surplus value up to Adam Smith. Kautsky promises to publish in the second volume Marx's critique of Ricardo's *Principles of Political Economy*, while the third volume will critically follow the wanderings of Thomas Robert Malthus and describe the dissolution of the Ricardian School. Most of the first volume deals with Smith's conception of the theory of labour value and surplus value; with the transformation of surplus value into business profit, ground rent and [the interest on loan] capital; and with Smith's definition of productive labour. It is preceded by a brief characterisation of Physiocracy and of the English mercantilists' original views on surplus value, which constitutes, as it were, a kind of historical introduction to Smith's ideas and makes their connection with Physiocratic conceptions stand out more sharply.

The first 33 pages of the book, developing the concepts of value on the part of English mercantilism, are not found in Marx's manuscript in the context in which Kautsky presents them to us.[11] Kautsky pieced them together from fragments that Marx interposed in his criticism of the theories of Smith and Ricardo, in order to show how far back the first attempts in that direction go in the history of English political economy. Marx takes into consideration Sir William Petty, Charles d'Avenant, Dudley North, John Locke, David Hume, and Joseph Massie. The most detailed assessment is afforded to William Petty, the 'founder of modern political economy' as Marx calls him. With a certain reverence, which clearly shows how highly he values Petty as an economic theorist, Marx describes his determination of the value of commodities by the socially necessary labour required for their production; his distinction between natural prices (exchange-value) and the respective market price (*true price currant*); his conception of ground rent as the surplus that labourers working the land produce beyond their cost of maintenance; and his calculation of the value of land according to the magnitude of rent, taking as a basis John Graunt's work on the Bills of Mortality, which were generally considered correct in England at that time. As the basis for his criticism, Marx takes Petty's *Treatise on Taxes* and his *Political Arithmetick*. Marx seems to have been unacquainted, in the preparation of this manuscript, with Petty's *Quantulumcunque concerning Money*, published in 1682 and mentioned in Engels's *Anti-Dühring*, which in a way constitutes the culmination of Petty's development because it summarily deals with the relation between the value of commodities and the value of money (coin).

---

11 [In the English edition of *Theories of Surplus-Value* issued by Progress Publishers those remarks appear as Addenda at the end of the first volume. On Mercantilism see further Rudolf Hilferding, 'The Early Days of English Political Economy' (*Die Neue Zeit*, 29. Jg. 1. Bd., 1911, H. 26, S. 908–921), in *History of Political Economy*, Vol. 48, No. 3, September 2016, pp. 471–487].

The continuous presentation of the theories of surplus value first appears in Marx's manuscript with the criticism of Sir James Steuart, which, in my opinion, is the weakest part of the book. As in his 1859 *Contribution to the Critique of Political Economy*, so also in this document Marx sees Steuart – in my view exaggeratedly – as the scientific interpreter of a refined mercantilism, who closed the pre-classical period of English political economy and, as the last in a series, synthesised mercantilist principles into a carefully thought out system and employed a more precise formulation. This view is certainly true throughout. But Steuart's major work, *An Inquiry into the Principles of Political Economy*, demonstrates that he was already strongly influenced by French Physiocracy, which he encountered during the years of his stay in France. And this influence consists of the fact that Steuart's 'system' not only incorporates some physiocratic views as ornaments, but that he also, while trying to integrate them logically into English mercantilist views, actually came up with many new concepts and insights. His conclusions, however, are on the whole genuinely mercantilistic. This is partly explained by the fact that he repeatedly fails to find the synthesis between differing mercantilistic and physiocratic views, but still more by the postulates from which Steuart proceeds in his investigations and by the purposes that he pursues with them. We can only understand the tendencies of English political economy in the seventeenth and eighteenth centuries if we realise that its main representatives were not scholars, who sought to achieve a scientific reputation through their investigations, but mostly traders or civil servants working in public administration, the commercial service, the customs administration, or the colonial and financial offices, where it was considered axiomatic that Britain was ideally suited by its location, nature and historical development to be a manufacturing and commercial country like no other. The main purpose of their investigations was to show the vigorously developing English commercial bourgeoisie how to achieve this goal. Even in Petty we find this trade-policy and commercial character sharply defined. In his character, if not by profession, Petty was quite the English merchant; as private secretary of Henry Cromwell (son of the famous Oliver), he was largely responsible for the latter's financial and economic matters, especially when [Cromwell] took over the government of Ireland. D'Avenant was a financier and Inspector General of British foreign trade; Dudley North was first a wholesaler, then Commissioner-General of Customs and administrator of the English crown lands; Richard Cantillon was a merchant and later a banker; and even John Locke wrote his works on political economy as a well-appointed official of the British Colonial Office.

This character of English mercantilism also explains its deep understanding of the labour theory of value as well as of international trade issues. In its tendency, so to speak, it was only a theoretical reflection of the replacement of the rule of British feudalism by that of the urban trading and manufacturing bourgeoisie, [a transformation] brought about by the great English Revolution of the seventeenth century, which led to the victory of the bourgeoisie of the commercial cities, especially London, over the regime of the Stuarts, which was supported by the 'cavaliers' and the feudal-Catholic clergy. And its theoretical definitions were not mere word play but rather polemical weapons, sharpened by a consciousness of class antagonisms in the struggle against feudal landownership and its outdated conception of the state. Although he was a Scottish landlord, even James Steuart considered England to be the predestined commercial state, and his work specifically pursued the goal of providing England with a scientific guide for its economic policies – a fact already proclaimed in the subtitle of his work: *An Essay on the Science of Domestic Policy in Free Nations* (he particularly considered England to be such a 'free' nation). From this point of view, however, some of the French Physiocratic views naturally appear to Steuart to have been derived from other economic conditions, inappropriate for Britain's commercial purposes and unworthy of attention. But secondly, Steuart wants to obtain practical results for English economic policy. He therefore often abandons his theoretical discussions as soon as he thinks he has attained such a result. Investigations for their own sake do not interest him.

Despite this undeniable incompleteness and one-sidedness, one finds in Steuart really brilliant insights into the economic conditions of his time, insights that Marx definitely underestimates. Marx says, for example, on page 220 of his book:

> Steuart does not share the illusion that the surplus-value which accrues to the individual capitalist from selling the commodity above its value is a creation of new wealth. He distinguishes therefore between *positive* profit and *relative* profit.
>
> *Positive profit*, implies no loss to any body; it results from an *augmentation* of labour, industry, or ingenuity, and has the effect of swelling or augmenting the *public good* ... *Relative profit*, is what implies a loss to some body; it marks a vibration of the balance of wealth between parties, but implies *no addition to the general stock* ... The *compound* is easily understood; it is that species of profit ..., which is partly *relative*, and partly *positive* ... both kinds may subsist inseparably in the same transaction. (*Principles of Political Economy*, Vol. I, *The Works of Sir James Steuart*, etc., ed. by General Sir James Steuart, his son, etc., in 6 vols., London, 1805, pp. 275–76.)

Positive profit arises from '*augmentation* of labour, industry and ingenuity'. *How* it arises from this Steuart makes no attempt to explain. The further statement that the effect of this profit is to augment and swell '*the public good*' seems to indicate that Steuart means by it nothing but the greater mass of use-values produced in consequence of the development of the productive powers of labour, and that he thinks of this positive profit as quite distinct from capitalists' profit – which always presupposes an increase of exchange-value.[12]

This definition of 'positive profit' shows that Marx only half understood Steuart's conception of surplus value. Referring to primitive land cultivation, Steuart proceeds from the basic view that only the labour providing a surplus product [*Mehrertrag*: additional yield, increase in yield] can be considered to promote culture – i.e. only the labour creating a greater quantity of use-values than the ones consumed in production for the maintenance of the tiller of the soil and for amortisation of the wear and tear of the work tools. If labour does not produce this surplus product, if the product covers only the amount of use-values consumed in production, then population cannot increase and production cannot expand, because the fund necessary for this is lacking. As Steuart explains, 'the produce, therefore, of agriculture must be estimated, not according to the quantity of fruits only, but also according to the labour employed to produce them'; and he goes on to say that the most advantageous agriculture is the one supplying the largest product in proportion to the labour employed in production.[13]

But where does this surplus product come from? According to Steuart, it comes from the fact that the labourer works longer than he would have had to in order to produce his means of subsistence; that he performs *supplementary labour* – Steuart calls it 'additional labour'.[14] The production surplus is small at lower stages of agriculture, but it increases with the increase in the skill of the workers and the appropriateness of the tools, or with general productivity. If this surplus product of labour is immediately consumed individually by the worker, it produces no profit in Steuart's view. Only the part that is somehow converted into capital or, as Steuart put it, in a genuinely mercantilist form, into money, produces a profit, thereby increasing 'the good of society'.

---

12   Marx 1963, p. 41.
13   Steuart 1767, Vol. I, p. 127.
14   Steuart 1767, Vol. I, p. 467.

Admittedly, Steuart never goes beyond that insight; and it may be the fact that he became stranded in this ingenious formulation that led Marx to underestimate him. Steuart never drew the conclusion that, if the worker performs additional labour, the surplus product actually represents surplus labour. Instead, he conceives that 'surplus' in naive Physiocratic terms, as a product obtained by labour but actually springing from the 'fertility of the soil'. And still less did he draw the conclusion that the 'additional labour' is unpaid labour. When reading his work with the benefit of hindsight, it often seems as though he failed, beyond a certain point, to draw the necessary consequences from his inferences. Nevertheless, it is clear from Marx's remarks that he underrates the significance of Steuart's 'positive profit' when he says that it 'appears' as though Steuart had understood by it only the 'larger mass of use-values' resulting from the growth in productivity. Steuart actually understands it to mean the surplus product obtained in production, which, as an excess of production returns over production costs, is again partly applied to the social process of production and leads to its expansion.

In addition to this 'positive' (real) profit obtained in production, according to Steuart, there is also a 'relative', commercially obtained 'profit', the *profit upon alienation* (sales-profit), arising from the fact that goods are 'sold' above their value in trade. This profit is not positive; it does not spring from a growth in commodity values, but from their being over-priced. What one party wins, the other must lose. Accordingly, the total wealth of a country only changes if this profit is not made on the home market but in foreign trade.

> *Relative profit*, is what implies a loss to somebody; it marks a vibration of the balance of wealth between parties, but implies *no addition to the general stock*. Relative loss is what, on the contrary, implies a profit to somebody; it also marks a vibration of the balance, but takes nothing from the general stock.[15]

This misunderstanding of the nature of Steuart's 'profit' led Marx to another misconception.

> Profit, that is, surplus-value, is relative and resolves itself into 'a vibration of the balance of wealth between parties'. Steuart himself rejects the idea that surplus-value can be explained in this way. His theory of 'vibration of the balance of wealth between parties', however little it touches the

---

15   Steuart 1767, Vol. I, p. 206.

nature and origin of surplus-value itself, remains important in considering the distribution of surplus-value among different classes and among different categories such as profit, interest and rent.

That Steuart limits all profit of the individual capitalist to this 'relative profit', profit upon alienation, is shown by the following:

> The 'real value', he says, is determined by the 'quantity' of labour, which 'upon an average, a workman of the country in general may perform ... in a day, a week, a month'. Secondly: 'the value of the workman's subsistence and necessary expense, both for supplying his personal wants, and ... the instruments belonging to his profession, which must [...] taken upon [...] average as above ...' Thirdly: '... the values of the materials ...' (Steuart 1767, Vol. I, pp. 182–183). 'These three articles being known, the price of manufacture is determined. It cannot be lower than the amount of all the three, that is, than *the real value; whatever is higher, is the manufacturer's profit*. This will [...] be in proportion to *demand*, and therefore will fluctuate *according to circumstances*' (Steuart 1767, Vol. I, p. 183).[16]

In fact, this co-determination of the 'real' value by wages and raw materials is *not*, as Marx argues, confused, but is based upon an insight into the production process that can be called almost brilliant in light of the state of economic science at that time. Steuart wants to show in that chapter, which bears the title 'How the Prices of Goods are determined by Trade', what value components go into the 'price' regulated by supply and demand.[17] His train of thought is this: first to be considered is maintenance of the worker and of the tools he uses, as well as the price of the raw materials used – more precisely, replacement of the variable and constant capital spent. But, with this determination, the constituent elements of value are still incomplete; to them should be added the value of the surplus labour that the worker imparts to the product beyond the value of the means of subsistence he has received. How can we determine this addition of value? Steuart offers the following cumbersome definition:

> The first thing to be known of any manufacture when it comes to be sold, is, how much of it a person can perform in a day, a week, a month, according to the nature of the work, which may require more or less time

---

16   Marx 1963, p. 42.
17   Steuart 1767, Book II, Chapter IV.

to bring it to perfection. In making such estimates, regard is to be had to what, upon an average only, a workman of the country in general may perform, without supposing him the best or the worst in his profession; or having any peculiar advantage or disadvantage as to the place where he works.[18]

Next to wages, the value of raw material and the wear and tear of tools, Steuart therefore also wants to take into account the rate of average labour performance, or the productivity of labour. Though certainly naive and mistaken, this definition is rooted in a correct awareness that the 'real' value (i.e. the exchange-value) of a commodity not only refunds the production costs, but that to those costs is also added, in the course of production, a further increase in value (surplus value). If a commodity is sold below the sum of these value components, then its price, as Steuart says, falls short of its value; if it is sold more expensively, the price will be above its value and the manufacturer who obtained such a price will make a special sales-profit (*profit upon alienation*). The 'real' value of a commodity thus includes the 'additional' value created in production, but not the profit upon alienation, as Steuart says at the beginning of the chapter under consideration: 'In the price of goods, I consider two things as really existing, and quite different from one another; to wit; the real value of the commodity, and the profit upon alienation'.[19]

But if Marx perhaps underestimated Steuart's theoretical achievement in this respect, he would not have been Marx, the founder of the materialist conception of history, if he had not, on the other hand, also identified and recognised Steuart's historical understanding of the capital-formation process and of the bourgeois character of commodity production in England in the eighteenth century. Even in his *Introduction to a Contribution to the Critique of Political Economy* (Kautsky edition),[20] Marx notes that Steuart progressed beyond his predecessors.[21]

---

18 Steuart 1767, Vol. I, p. 181.
19 Steuart 1805, p. 244.
20 Marx 1903, p. 41.
21 [In the *Grundrisse*, which was not available to Cunow, Marx says something different: 'Smith and Ricardo still stand with both feet on the shoulders of the eighteenth-century prophets, in whose imaginations this eighteenth-century individual – the product on one side of the dissolution of the feudal forms of society, on the other side of the new forces of production developed since the sixteenth century – appears as an ideal, whose existence they project into the past. Not as a historic result but as history's point of departure. As the Natural Individual appropriate to their notion of human nature, not arising historically,

3   The Character of Physiocracy

Marx's voice resonates with full force for the first time in his characterisation of Physiocracy: a section that, in its concise and accurate presentation, far surpasses all the existing monographs dealing with Physiocracy and its place in the development of political economy. Marx gives no overall picture of Physiocratic theories; he limits himself to an outline of their main principles and the conclusions drawn from them. But just as a gifted illustrator is often able to represent the characteristic features of a personality more vividly in a few strokes than another might do in a fully executed portrait, so Marx also knew how to sketch with the utmost clarity the connection of ideas characterising the Physiocratic worldview. The basic conceptions constituting the foundations of the Physiocratic intellectual structure emerge, as it were, plastically and tangibly. Marx has a great advantage over all the bourgeois economists who have dealt critically with Physiocracy, an advantage that elevates his standpoint from the outset and gives him a much larger perspective for assessing the Physiocratic system. That advantage lies in his historical sense, which reveals to him the development of Physiocratic doctrines in their connection with the particular development of the French economy in the eighteenth century. Moreover, this standpoint enables him to show that the conceptions of Physiocratic theorists, despite the semi-feudal conclusions they drew from them, already contained the basic elements of English classical political economy. Compared with Marx, for instance, how insignificant appears Professor August Oncken, Berne's economic luminary and the special researcher in the field of Physiocratic theory, officially recognised as such by the scientific guild. In a painstaking and tormented work, which contrasts with Marx's brilliant conceptual sketch as some pedantically completed, ordinary little genre picture would with the brilliantly powerful strokes of Rembrandt, Oncken digs up Physiocratic formulations and calls their juxtaposition a 'History of Physiocracy'.[22] But this 'history' lacks every historical perspective, every historical standard, and Oncken gets so lost in his search for Physiocratic wisdom that a few years ago he famously undertook to prove the legitimacy of the agricultural demand for taxes on grain imports in present-day Germany with the help of Sir Josiah Child, Thomas Mun's reflections on the impact of British foreign trade on agricultural products, and Quesnay's plea for high corn prices.

---

but posited by nature. This illusion has been common to each new epoch to this day. Steuart avoided this simple-mindedness because as an aristocrat, and in antithesis to the eighteenth century, he had in some respects a more historical footing' (Marx 1993, p. 84)].

22 [A reference to Oncken 1893. Oncken was the editor of Quesnay 1888].

According to Marx, the difference between the views of Physiocracy and mercantilism lies in the fact that the Physiocrats shifted the investigation of the origin of surplus value away from the sphere of circulation and into the sphere of immediate production:

> In the Mercantile system, surplus-value is only relative – what one wins, the other loses: profit upon alienation or oscillation of wealth between different parties. So that within a country, if we consider the total capital, no creation of surplus-value in fact takes place. It can only arise in the relations between one nation and other nations. And the surplus realised by one nation as against the other takes the form of money (the balance of trade), because it is precisely money that is the direct and independent form of exchange-value. In opposition to this – for the Mercantile system in fact denies the creation of absolute surplus-value – the Physiocrats seek to explain absolute surplus-value: the net product. And since the net product is fixed in their minds as use-value, agriculture [is for them] the sole creator of it ...[23]

> Thus the Physiocrats saw the production of surplus-value as the essence of capitalist production. It was this phenomenon that they had to explain. And it remained the problem, after they had eliminated the profit upon alienation of the Mercantile system.[24]

In fact, the progress of Physiocracy lies in this shift of the research focus, in the transfer of the investigation to the sphere of production. However, in the previously mentioned English mercantilists, we already partially find the idea that, in addition to the commercially obtained relative profit, there is also a profit or 'surplus' in agriculture that consists of an excess of the production yield over the use-values that went into production. In this respect, we have also just seen how far James Steuart was able to go beyond the original mercantilist views; but even in Petty we already encounter the insight that the labour applied to cultivation of the soil provides a surplus, and that wherever the tiller of the soil is not simultaneously its owner, this surplus product devolves on the landowner as ground rent; [an insight] which Petty postulated in the totally physiocratic-looking sentence: 'Labour is the Father and active principle of Wealth, as Lands are the Mother'.[25]

---

23   Marx 1963, p. 66.
24   Marx 1963, p. 62.
25   [William Petty, *A Treatise of Taxes and Contributions* (1662); see Petty 1899, Vol. I, p. 68].

All such findings, however, never went beyond their initial stages. They did not lead to a closer examination of the surplus product obtained in agriculture, or more accurately, of profit – not because the English economists of the pre-classical period did not have the necessary acumen, but because England's economic development directed their investigations into other channels. Since the days of Cromwell, and especially the accession of William of Orange, England had developed into the first commercial country in the world. The former predominance of Spain and the Netherlands as commercial states was destroyed, and French naval power was broken. The English flag ruled the seas. England's foreign trade, her manufacturing industry, and her colonial possessions experienced a huge boom. Treasures flowed from all parts of the world into its port cities, and from there travelled on to the continental countries. The abundant profit that those commercial and colonial enterprises yielded was almost palpable in the constantly swelling number of those who participated in such undertakings and obtained enormous wealth. In the face of such obvious success, which soon found expression in the dogma that England was destined by its geographic position to be the world's commanding commercial state, a doctrine [such as Physiocracy], which put forward the claim that trade and a flourishing industry were of secondary importance for the increase of national wealth, necessarily seemed absurd. The task of the English economists (who, moreover, as already indicated, were directly interested in the commercial status of England, mainly as merchants and bankers or as officials of the British Trade and Colonial Office) rather appeared to be to investigate the principles according to which English trade had to be pursued in order to promote the country's wealth as much as possible.

Their investigations, therefore, followed that direction; and it is most interesting to see how the English economists, influenced by the views then prevailing in England, came to very different conclusions even when they proceeded from basic principles similar to those of the earlier French Physiocrats. For example, while French Physiocracy concluded that trade and industry were 'sterile', based upon the idea that only agriculture supplies a production surplus, James Steuart, raising the question of what happens to the agricultural surplus product if it does not find employment in trade and a market among the industrial population, came to the conclusion that agriculture can only spread and bring about an increase in population if it develops 'in line with industry'. Whereas in the theories of French Physiocrats the industrial middle class appears as a kind of parasite on rural landownership, in Steuart's view the extension of this middle class appears as a condition for the development of agricultural production.

The situation of France's foreign trade and manufacture in the middle of the eighteenth century was totally different. Both had increasingly lost their previous international importance. Completely pushed into the background by England, ruined by war and economic mismanagement, and loaded with enormous debt, the country appeared to have no other way to achieve a better economic position than to increase the cultivation of the soil and its yields. But this also raised the question of how best to increase this yield and its surplus over the costs [of production]. And that question led the Physiocrats to investigate further the nature of the surplus product and its distribution.

Marx critically follows the path of development that this investigation took among the various representatives of Physiocracy. He offers a short outline of the general nature of the Physiocratic system, dealing successively with the views of Turgot, Ferdinando Paoletti, Pietro Verri, Theodor Schmalz, the Count du Buat [Louis-Gabriel, Comte du Buat-Nançay], Necker, etc. He shows in detail how the surplus product, the so-called *produit net*, is initially deemed by the older Physiocrats to be only a surplus of use-values and is not conceived as surplus labour (i.e. as the product of unpaid labour) but rather as mere gift of beneficent nature. Thus the surplus product appears in the Physiocratic system as a gift from mother earth that is simply identified with ground rent, so that industrial profit and the interest on money only appear as different headings into which ground rent is distributed among landowners, industrialists and moneylenders in the circulation process – [i.e. those two categories of income, industrial profit and the interest on money, are regarded as] a tribute of agriculture to industry. But Marx was too much an historian, as well as an economist, to be satisfied with such critical references. In brief historical digressions, interspersed in the main text, he explains how the Physiocratic system – by regarding rural landowners as capitalists buying labour power on the one hand, and, on the other hand, by drawing from the alleged sterility of industrial production the implication that industrial enterprises should not be burdened either by taxes or by state intervention in their competition with each other – resulted, despite its feudal trappings, in the promotion of capitalist production:

> In the conclusions which the Physiocrats themselves draw, the ostensible veneration of landed property becomes transformed into the economic negation of it and the affirmation of capitalist production. On the one hand, all taxes are put on rent, or in other words, landed property is in part confiscated, which is what the legislation of the French Revolution sought to carry through and which is the final conclusion of the fully developed Ricardian modern political economy. By placing the burden of

tax entirely on rent, because it alone is surplus-value – and consequently any taxation of other forms of income ultimately falls on landed property, but in a roundabout way, and therefore in an economically harmful way, that hinders production – taxation and along with it all forms of State intervention, are removed from industry itself, and the latter is thus freed from all intervention by the State. This is ostensibly done for the benefit of landed property, not in the interests of industry but in the interests of landed property.

Connected with this is *laissez faire, laissez aller*; unhampered free competition, the removal from industry of all interference by the State, monopolies, etc. Since industry [as the Physiocrats see it] creates nothing, but only transforms values given it by agriculture into another form; since it adds no new value to them, but returns the values supplied to it, though in altered form, as an equivalent; it is naturally desirable that this process of transformation should proceed without interruptions and in the cheapest way; and this is only realised through free competition, by leaving capitalist production to its own devices. The emancipation of bourgeois society from the absolute monarchy set up on the ruins of feudal society thus takes place only in the interests of the feudal landowner transformed into a capitalist and bent solely on enrichment. The capitalists are only capitalists in the interests of the landowner, just as political economy in its later development would have them be capitalists only in the interests of the working class.[26]

The conclusion of the chapter on the Physiocrats is taken up by an explanation of Quesnay's *Tableau économique*. Marx simplifies it considerably. He summarises the fourteen mutual acts of circulation, postulated by Quesnay in the original *Tableau*, into five, but, on the other hand, he makes an interesting addition to it by not letting circulation start only in the act with which Quesnay initiates it (the payment of the annual rent by the tenants to the landowner), but also by assuming several other starting points for the circulation process and then investigating how, from these starting points, circulation appears to the tenant, to industrial capitalists and to the workers – an investigation providing an interesting complement to Marx's remarks on the metamorphosis of commodities contained in the first volume of *Capital* (Part One, Chapter 3.2.a).

---

26   Marx 1963, pp. 52–3. [On Physiocracy see further Исаак Ильич Рубин, Физиократы: Очерк из истории зкономической мысли. – Л.; М.: Книга, 1926. (Isaak Illich Rubin, Physiocrats: Essay on the History of Economic Thought, Leningrad and Moscow: Kniga, 1926. 151 pp.)]

4 Adam Smith

Adam Smith's famous book, *An Inquiry into the Nature and Causes of the Wealth of Nations*, whose concepts of value and surplus value Marx criticises in detail in the second chapter[27] of this book, represents, so to speak, a synthesis of the Physiocratic views on surplus value and the English mercantilists' theory of labour value and prices. The notion of surplus value, or rather of the profit identified with it, as 'profit upon alienation', naturally drove the English mercantilists to study exchange, i.e. the transformation of commodities into money and the merchants' re-conversion of their money into commodities. And the study of that process again led them to recognition of a continuous fluctuation of commodity prices in trade, without the properties [of commodities], their usefulness, having changed. As a result, the mercantilists soon began to distinguish between two values: a market value, determined by market conditions (*price, extrinsic value, contingent value, current price*, etc.), and an intrinsic value, inherent in the commodity as such (*intrinsic value, real value, natural value*, etc.).

The 'inner', 'real' value was initially conceived as a kind of use-value due to utility, but very early on it was recognised (in unrefined form, for example, already by Rice Vaughan) that even if every commodity must have a use-value in order to find a buyer in the market, the extent [*Grad*] of this use-value is not decisive for the price level. Vaughan already presented the wages of ordinary workers (*the price of labourers*) as the real factor determining the price of goods. With his followers, especially Petty, the place of wages, as measure of the exchange-value of goods, is taken more and more by the amount of labour measured in labour time, without, however, properly distinguishing between the amount of labour (the necessary labour time) and the value of labour [power]. On the contrary, time and again we find – most notably with William Harris – the desire to calculate the value of commodities on the basis of the 'price of labour' (wages).

The constant reappearance of this confusion – often in the same author who had previously determined the value of goods by the labour time required for their production – is explained very simply by English industry's stage of development. During the seventeenth and first half of the eighteenth century, we find only the first imperfect approaches to actual large-scale machine production in England. Even manufacturing industry had achieved some importance only in a few regions. Craft-like small-scale production outweighed them all by far. In this type of operation, in which the producer usually acts as the

---

27   [Chapter III in Marx 1963].

factory owner, worker, landowner and seller of his product, the value of the commodities actually is mostly equal to the value of the labour to be realised in the commodity price [*gleich dem sich im 'Arbeitspreis' realisierenden Werte der Arbeit*]. If he sold the product at its value, the craftsman, who devoted to the manufacture of a product ten hours of work, had to get exactly the amount of money required to buy the product of another ten hours of labour performed under the same circumstances. Because money served only as a medium of exchange, equal amounts of labour were thereby actually exchanged against each other. Each commodity simply materialised in another; and with the product that each of the small-scale producers received in exchange, they could again purchase – provided that exchange always took place at the commodities' values – other commodities containing ten hours of labour; or (if, for example, the desired product was not ready, but had first to be manufactured by craftsmen) they could purchase ten hours of living labour yet to be objectified [*noch nicht vergegenständlichter Arbeit*]. In the latter case, the 'value of labour' (the ten working hours) was exchanged directly against the ten-hour labour product. Value of labour and value of the commodities thus appear here as the same thing, as a mutual measure of exchange. The basic difference between those two values could first be clearly grasped only at that stage of development of capitalist economy in which the worker was no longer the owner of the means of production and of the product he created, and where the seller of that product was no longer the worker but the owner of the means of production who bought his labour power, the manufacturer. Indeed, that situation already existed in England in the eighteenth century, but small-craft individual production was still dominant.

To this should be added a second factor. To the extent that an historical view can be found in the English mercantilists, it consists of the fact that they look at the economic stage of their own time only as a continuation and a mere complication of an economic system existing, in its general outlines, in an unchanged form since the beginning of all culture; and from this they drew the conclusion that, in order to recognise those general outlines, they had to go back to those original pure conditions. This view was advanced most pronouncedly by James Steuart. Just as liberal vulgar economy was later to derive its naive concepts gladly from Robinson Crusoe, so Steuart, to exemplify his statements, fell back on the primitive agricultural forms of medieval England or even of the biblical patriarchs.

The French Physiocrats paid no heed to the labour theory of value, although they were sometimes quite familiar with English mercantilist doctrines. The shift in the analysis of surplus value, from the sphere of commodity circulation to the production process, made them look at exchange with different eyes. From the Physiocrats' standpoint, only agricultural production (but not industry and trade) supplies a net product, a surplus product, and industrial and commercial profit was simply that part of the ground rent flowing, in the process of circulation, to the classes with non-agricultural occupations. From this standpoint, it appeared completely futile to find in goods an inner real value that was not identical with the market price. It was enough to know that prices were determined by supply and demand. It was more important to find out how, in the circulation process, the surplus product generated in agriculture was distributed among the various occupational classes [*Erwerbsklassen*], and the Physiocratic investigations moved in this direction. Quesnay's table also serves this purpose. The question of how the price of a commodity is related to exchange-value, and of which factors determine the latter, was thus virtually disregarded by the Physiocrats.

The importance of Adam Smith lies in the fact that he recognised Physiocracy's neglect of the theory of value as a failure of this system; that he added to the English mercantilist theory of labour value the Physiocratic views on surplus value; and that, by trying to combine them both logically, he adapted them to the contemporary economic conditions of England, which were the most advanced in the world. This combination explains both the fact that Smith often suddenly goes backwards and forwards between mercantilist and Physiocratic views, and that he offers directly contradictory definitions of the same economic phenomena and relationships – often without being conscious of the contradiction. His overcoming of Physiocracy is far more practical than theoretical. He recognises that the theoretical conclusions of the Physiocratic economists do not agree with the phenomena of British economic life in his time; and when he confronts Physiocratic abstractions with actual conditions, he often makes the proper corrections and additions. But his insights into the inadequacy of Physiocratic doctrines are not solid or clear enough to enable him to overcome those doctrines theoretically, i.e. to prove the falsity of their individual premises and conclusions. He recognises that in many Physiocratic inferences there is a mistake, and sometimes he even sees where it lies, but for the most part his insight is not sufficient to recognise it as such in the deductions of the Physiocratic theoreticians and to replace it by another mediating moment [*Mittelglied*: mediating link, middle term].

Adam Smith's theoretical helplessness clearly appears in his critique of Physiocracy (Book IV, Chapter 9: 'Of the Agricultural Systems, or of those Systems of Political Economy, which Represent the Produce of Land, as either the Sole or the Principal, Source of the Revenue and Wealth of Every Country'). For instance, he did not confront the Physiocrats' assertion that only agricultural labour is productive, i.e. that it alone yields a surplus, by positing general human labour, regardless of the form in which it was applied and in what products it appears, as value-creating, and then by demonstrating how the profits of industrialists spring from precisely the same source of surplus value as ground rent because the industrial worker also does not receive in his wages the full equivalent of his labour output. Instead, Smith has recourse to a feeble excuse by arguing that after all, even according to the Physiocratic view, the artists, manufacturers and merchants produce yearly as much as they consume, and thus at least preserve the national wealth. But such people can no more be called unproductive than a couple who have produced only two children:

> We should not call a marriage barren or unproductive though it produced only a son and a daughter, to replace the father and mother, and though it did not increase the number of the human species, but only continued it as it was before. Farmers and country labourers, indeed, over and above the stock which maintains and employs them, reproduce annually a net produce, a free rent to the landlord. As a marriage which affords three children is certainly more productive than one which affords only two; so the labour of farmers and country labourers is certainly more productive than that of merchants, artificers, and manufacturers. The superior produce of the one class, however, does not render the other barren or unproductive.[28]

Smith's partiality for the views of the Physiocratic system, and his helplessness vis-à-vis their argumentation, can hardly be identified more clearly than in this passage from his major work. Yet this is the same Smith who, in other places, defines surplus value as unpaid labour, as the part of labour that the owners of the means of production, both in industry and in agriculture, appropriate in their exchange with living labour – the same Smith who regards ground rent and profit as equivalent forms of surplus value: a strange contradiction whose explanation, however, is very simple. His keen observation of the economic conditions of his time, and his pronounced Anglo-bourgeois instincts, lifted Smith above the Physiocratic system; but to dismantle that system critically, to draw a clear theoretical dividing line between it and his own system – that he could not do.

In his critique, Marx brings out sharply this theoretical dependence of the founder of classical political economy on French Physiocracy, without in any way underestimating the enormous progress represented by Adam Smith's

---

28   Adam Smith 1937, p. 639.

work. In his work *A Contribution to the Critique of Political Economy*, published in 1859, Marx already proves how Smith, in his determination of the value of commodities, mistakes the labour time required to produce commodities for the value of labour [power]; an equation that, as mentioned before, always shows up in English political economy of the eighteenth century. In the first volume of *Theories of Surplus-Value*, Marx continues the earlier criticism. He first examines under which conditions the amount of labour employed in the production of commodities actually corresponds to the value of labour, and then he goes on to show how Smith, recognising that the two no longer coincide in capitalist commodity production, does not come to the conclusion that they have shifted in their relationship to each other, but rather [mistakenly] infers (implying a whole series of other errors) that in capitalist economy labour also no longer determines exchange-value as an immanent measure of value, and that determination of the value of the commodities by the amount of labour contained in them thus actually applies only in the pre-capitalist economic period. And after Marx has analysed Smith's concept of value in this way, he deals with the sixth chapter of the first book of Smith's *The Wealth of Nations*, entitled 'On the Component Parts of the Price of Commodities', and shows how Smith admittedly conceives surplus value as unpaid labour but, on the other hand, does not distinguish surplus value, as a separate category, from its particular manifestations as ground rent and profit; and how, by defining capital and landed property as sources of exchange-value alongside labour, in contradiction with his previous reasoning, he finally goes astray and sees not only wages but also ground rent and profit as constitutive elements of the commodity's price.

Needless to say, Marx's critique of the relevant chapters of Smith's work is in the highest degree positive. Marx never limits himself to a mere defensive position such as the one adopted by Adam Smith vis-à-vis the Physiocratic theorists. While following Smith's faulty reasoning, Marx seeks to prove the falsity of his assumptions and inferences and, at the same time, to develop his own opposing views. Often those views even occupy a much larger space than the criticism. This is especially true of his treatment of Adam Smith's views on how prices can be resolved into wages, profit and ground rent. The contradictions in which Smith becomes entangled here give Marx the opportunity to investigate from all directions, in an appendix over 70 pages long, the question of the turnover and reproduction of constant capital (capital invested in means of production) in its relation to variable capital (capital invested in wages). Some of these explanations, worked out, completed and placed in a different context, later passed into the second volume of *Capital*, where they fill several chapters of Part Two on the turnover of capital, as well as in the nineteenth and twentieth chapter of Part Three on the reproduction and circulation of the total social capital. Despite the fact that this part of the first volume of *Theories of Surplus-Value* in a way offers expositions that parallel those contained in the second volume of *Capital*, it is very interesting for those who wish to know Marx as an intellectual worker. If the relevant sections of *Capital* appear as carefully thought out and constructed, the newly published earlier treatment of the problem has the advantage of greater freshness and a certain rough intellectual robustness; and the fact that Marx sometimes draws on one, sometimes on another of his predecessors, makes the presentation superior in immediacy and liveliness. Moreover, in the Annex [to the section on Adam Smith], individual aspects of the problem are dealt with far more extensively than in *Capital*: especially the various phases of the turnover of constant capital, as well as the relation between industrial consumption (consumption of means of production) and individual consumption (the consumption of foodstuffs [and articles for personal use]), and the various reverse effects of these two types of consumption on the process of industrial reproduction.

It appears here, much more clearly than in *Capital*, that even if Marx did not have the opportunity to formulate his own theory of crises, all the basic elements of such a theory are still to be found in his works; and he must have known very well himself how a shift in the relative magnitudes of industrial and individual consumption, induced by the development of capitalism, also had to change the nature of crises.

5 *Productive and Unproductive Labour*

As in most of his definitions, Adam Smith did not reach any single view in the determination of productive labour and its antithesis, unproductive labour. In the third chapter of the second book of his work, called 'On the Accumulation of Capital, or of Productive and Unproductive Labour', two mutually contradictory views instead run side by side. And if we look for the causes of this contradiction, it is again evident here that Smith succeeded neither in emancipating himself from the ideas of the English mercantilists nor in consistently developing the Physiocratic definition [of productive labour] in a direction corresponding to the character of capitalist production.

What is productive labour? The earliest English mercantilists initially derived the exchange-value of commodities from their usefulness to society and therefore saw in general use-value the real component of 'inner' value – until their observation of the price movement of goods in trade revealed to them the amount of labour contained in the commodities as the factor [determining] value. Thus the question: 'What is productive labour?' at first found with them a simple answer: productive labour is labour serving to satisfy the needs of society. But what kind of labour serves this purpose? According to the mercantilists' definition, productive labour was labour objectified in saleable use-values (commodities) that could therefore be turned into money, but especially in the activity of the merchants and sailors who sold those products in foreign countries at a profit, for they brought back to the country more money than the exported goods were worth on the domestic market and thus increased the national wealth. Therefore, says Petty, 'Husbandmen, Seamen, Soldiers, Artizans and Merchants, are the very Pillars of any Common-Wealth'.[29] Lowest among the productive occupational classes stood the peasants, the craftsmen were higher, and the merchants still higher insofar as they truly serve the sale of goods and are not just some 'sort of gamblers'. Highest of all stood the seamen who sold the goods abroad, because, as Petty says, 'There is much more to be gained by Manufacture than Husbandry, and by Merchandize than Manufacture'.[30] But a seaman, according to Petty, 'is in effect three Husbandmen' because he fulfils three functions: he is the carrier of the goods, their defender against attacks (i.e. at the same time a soldier), and thirdly, as a merchant, he brings foreign money into the country. 'The Labour of Seamen, and Freight of Ships, is always of the nature of an Exported Commodity, the overplus whereof, above what is Imported, brings home mony, &c'.[31]

By contrast, doctors, lawyers, civil servants, etc., and especially the clergy, are unproductive. Petty therefore recommends that celibacy be reintroduced for them and that their livings should be reduced by half. Even David Hume said: 'Lawyers and physicians beget no industry; and it is even at the expense of others they acquire their riches; so that they are sure to diminish the possessions of some of their fellow-citizens, as fast as they increase their own'.[32]

This concept of productive labour followed just as logically from the economic conditions of England at that time and from their ideological reflection in mercantilism as the opposite view – that only labour applied to the cultivation of the soil is productive – followed from the preconditions of Physiocracy. If the view that a country's wealth stems from the benefits obtained from foreign trade is abandoned, then the increase of that wealth can only be looked for in growth of the production surplus in agriculture, the *produit net*; and consequently the labour employed in industry and trade, even if it is essential for the total production process and useful, cannot be considered as a cause of an increase in national wealth, i.e. cannot be regarded as productive.

---

29 Petty 1899, p. 259.
30 Petty 1899, p. 256.
31 Petty 1899, p. 260.
32 Hume 1865, Vol. 3, p. 331.

Had Smith held onto this view consistently in his economic system, he would have come to the following conclusion: 'In the Physiocratic doctrine only agricultural labour is productive, because it alone supplies a surplus product that increases the wealth of society and makes possible a constant reproduction of durable goods [*Gebrauchsgüter*] on a wider basis. But, as I will now demonstrate, not only labour employed in agriculture but also labour applied in industry yields such a surplus product, and consequently industrial labour is also productive – particularly the labour that produces surplus value and through it an increase in the social capital'.

This is a very simple inference, and Smith actually reaches these conclusions; but, on the other hand, he is unable to cast off the views of the English economists of his time, according to which the only productive labour is that which creates marketable social use-values ([physical] commodities) and thus enriches the nation's circulation of goods. For example, he says at the beginning of the above-mentioned chapter on productive and unproductive labour:

> There is one sort of labour which adds to the value of the subject upon which it is bestowed: there is another which has no such effect. The former, as it produces a value, may be called productive; the latter, unproductive labour. Thus the labour of a manufacturer adds, generally, to the value of the materials which he works upon, that of his own maintenance, and of his master's profit. The labour of a menial servant, on the contrary, adds to the value of nothing. Though the manufacturer has his wages advanced to him by his master, he, in reality, costs him no expense, the value of those wages being generally restored, together with a profit, in the improved value of the subject upon which his labour is bestowed. But the maintenance of a menial servant never is restored. A man grows rich by employing a multitude of manufacturers: he grows poor, by maintaining a multitude of menial servants.[33]

The contradiction of Smith's conception already appears clearly in the first few sentences. He distinguishes between labour that adds new value to the product in which it is objectified, that produces surplus value, and labour that does not have such a result. Accordingly, his brief definition [of productive labour] should have read: productive labour is that labour which produces a surplus value; unproductive labour, that which does not generate any surplus value. Instead of this definition, however, Smith defines the first kind of labour

---

33 Adam Smith 1937, p. 314.

as 'productive' not because it creates surplus value but because it 'creates a value' in general. And furthermore, he contrasts not the labour that yields a profit (or, more correctly, surplus value) with that whose employment brings no profit to the capitalists, but rather the labour of the industrial worker with that of servants, and he finds the real difference between the activities of both in the fact that the former reimburses his wages in the value of the objects he produces while the latter does not.

Clearly, *two different* kinds of labour are defined here as 'productive': first, the labour that yields a profit for the 'master' (the industrial capitalist), and secondly, any labour in general that is materialised in a commodity and reproduces wages. The fact that this is no mere inaccuracy of expression is proved by the statement in a footnote to the last chapter of the fourth book, in which Smith, in his polemic against the Physiocrats, also defines as productive the labour that creates no surplus value but only replaces its own costs – and further by a subsequent utterance in the above quotation:

> The labour of the latter [i.e. menial servants], however, has its value, and deserves its reward as well as that of the former. But the labour of the manufacturer fixes and realizes itself in some particular subject or vendible commodity, which lasts for some time at least after that labour is past. It is, as it were, a certain quantity of labour stocked and stored up to be employed, if necessary, upon some other occasion. That subject, or what is the same thing, the price of that subject, can afterwards, if necessary, put into motion a quantity of labour equal to that which had originally produced it. The labour of the menial servant, on the contrary, does not fix or realize itself in any particular subject or vendible commodity ... The labour of some of the most respectable orders in the society is, like that of menial servants, unproductive of any value, and does not fix or realize itself in any permanent subject, or vendible commodity, which endures after that labour is past and for which an equal quantity of labour could afterwards be procured.[34]

By contrast, Smith elsewhere fittingly stresses that the essence of capitalist production consists of the creation of surplus value or – as Smith says, because he does not regard surplus value as a special category – in the generation of profit. And he further emphasises in the same chapter that the industrial capitalist only employs and regards as productive that labour which not only

---

34   Adam Smith 1937, pp. 314–15.

replaces for him the capital invested in the production process but additionally yields him a profit:

> Whatever part of his stock a man employs as a capital, he always expects it to be replaced to him with a profit. He employs it, therefore, in maintaining productive hands only; and after having served in the function of a capital to him, it constitutes a revenue to them. Whenever he employs any part of it in maintaining unproductive hands of any kind, that part is, from that moment, withdrawn from his capital, and placed in his stock reserved for immediate consumption.[35]

Marx demonstrates these contradictions in detail from an historical and dialectical point of view, by comparing and analysing Smith's most important observations in that chapter of *The Wealth of Nations* and by showing the reasoning underlying them. For him the concept of productive labour, as it appears in the different earlier economic schools, is not something accidental, a mere question of abstraction and definition, but the conceptual reflection of different economic stages: an historical category. At each [historical] stage, that labour is considered 'productive' that best corresponds to the conditions of existence of the prevailing economic system and its apparently appropriate direction. Thus, Smith's view is also to some extent historical. His definition of productive labour as 'surplus value-producing' labour – as labour that, in the exchange against the variable part of the industrial capital (invested in wages), not only reproduces that part but also provides the capitalist with a surplus product – is closely associated with his conception of the origin of surplus value. And since Smith's views on surplus value were, so to speak, just an extension of the Physiocratic conception of surplus value to capitalist industrial production, in his definition of productive labour he simply follows the course set by the Physiocrats, 'freeing it from misconceptions and thus developing its inner core'. Marx penetratingly exposes this connection and, drawing the consequences following from this view, he defines productive labour as that labour, exchanged directly against capital, which turns the means of production into capital in the first place. Unproductive labour, on the other hand, is labour not exchanged against capital but directly against revenue, i.e. labour exchanged for wages, industrial profit, ground rent or interest. Or in other words: *productive labour is labour purchased by a capitalist with a portion of his capital and employed in production in order to extract from it surplus value, while unpro-*

---

35   Adam Smith 1937, p. 316.

ductive labour, on the other hand, is labour that supplies someone with services or use-values for the satisfaction of his needs and is paid for from his income.

> Where all labour in part still pays itself (like for example the agricultural labour of the serfs) and in part is directly exchanged for revenue (like the manufacturing labour in the cities of Asia), no capital and no wage-labour exists in the sense of bourgeois political economy. These definitions are therefore not derived from the material characteristics of labour (neither from the nature of its product nor from the particular character of the labour as concrete labour), but from the definite social form, the social relations of production, within which the labour is realised.[36]

But [in Adam Smith] this view stands in sharp contradiction with another, which regards all commodity-producing labour, without distinction, as productive. This second view not only fails to take into account the production of surplus value, the foundation of the capitalist economy; it also includes the aspect of social usefulness, or rather of usability – for instance, when Adam Smith finds the unproductiveness of the servants' labour in the fact that this labour is not fixed in a durable object or saleable product, and that it disappears immediately at the moment of its execution.

By contrast, the first definition [of productive labour] disregards whether and to what extent the surplus value-creating labour is realised in some useful or useless, more or less easily marketable product. The capitalists do not care about the usefulness of the labour employed by them or about the usefulness of its product. From their point of view, as well as from that of the capitalist economy in general, it all depends upon whether the labour provides a surplus value. Therefore, the labour of a clown, who pulls off bad jokes in the service of his director but yields his employer a profit, is quite productive, although this labour is certainly not fixed in durable goods but disappears immediately after its execution. In contrast, the labour of a village tailor, whom the farmer takes into his house in order to help him make a pair of trousers, is unproductive because this tailor produces no surplus value for the farmer but only a use-value for the satisfaction of his needs.

> Labour which is to produce *commodities* must be useful labour; it must produce a *use-value*, it must manifest itself in a *use-value*. And consequently only labour which manifests itself in *commodities*, that is, in use-

---

36   Marx 1963, p. 157.

values, is labour for which capital is exchanged. This is a self-evident premise. But it is not this concrete character of labour, its use-value as such – that it is for example tailoring labour, cobbling, spinning, weaving, etc. – which forms its specific use-value for capital and consequently stamps it as *productive labour* in the system of capitalist production. What forms its *specific use-value* for capital is not its specific useful character, any more than it is the particular useful properties of the product in which it is materialised. But what forms its specific use-value for capital is its character as the element which creates exchange-value, abstract labour; and in fact not that it represents some particular quantity of this general labour, but that it represents a *greater* quantity than is *contained* in its price, that is to say, in *the value of the labour-power*.[37]

The productiveness or unproductiveness of labour is therefore not decided by its material result, but by whether it yields surplus value; a property that arises not from its content or from the usefulness of its result, but from the particular social form in which it was applied. The distinction [between productive and unproductive labour] expresses, as Marx says, a particular historical and social relation of production, and for that reason the concept of productivity also naturally changes in different economic systems.

But the capitalist economy is based upon the production of surplus value, without which it would be unable either to exist or to fulfil its social functions. If production of surplus value were to end, the whole contemporary economic regime would immediately cease to exist. Accordingly, under the present economic system, only that labour can be considered productive which makes possible the continuation and further development of that system.

In a special annex, Marx develops this view in compelling ways by elaborating on the conditions of the productivity of capital and investigating the various forms of exchange of labour against capital and revenue.

But if the concept of productive labour is determined by the character of every form of production, then it is folly to abstract from this character and to convert the question of what is productive labour from the standpoint of capital, of the contemporary economic system, into what is productive labour in general (productive labour in itself, regardless of its form of application and of the production process). [If the latter standpoint is adopted,] the answer always necessarily boils down to the truism that productive labour is any labour having utility, thus letting everyone determine at his pleasure just what is to

---

37 Marx 1963, Addenda, p. 400.

be understood by that 'utility'. Nevertheless, this is how the question was usually posed by Adam Smith's successors, especially by the liberal German vulgar economists. Unable to reason historically – to regard the capitalist economic system as a particular, historically determined stage in the process of economic development, with its own principles and laws – and usually mired in pseudo-professional snobbery, those economists turned the question of what is productive in today's economic system into the question of what is 'productive' in general, i.e. regardless of the historically given production and economic conditions – which is about as clever as asking what the stomach is 'in itself', unrelated to the other human body parts and regardless of its digestive function.

Of course, the answer to such a vague and indistinct question can only be: any labour that generates something is productive – a mere tautology, which is not made more palatable by the fact that superimposed upon it, usually by a detour through all sorts of philosophical musings about the 'ethics of work', is the qualification that labour should, of course, be useful. Nevertheless, further consideration of the word 'useful' immediately reveals that, while some people understand it as individual usefulness, or the 'good of the individual', others take it to mean so-called general or social utility (its benefits for a country or state), and by this social utility they usually mean the interests of their own social stratum.

Marx offers a delicious satire of these strange explanations of the concept of 'productive labour' by showing what comic proverbs some followers of Adam Smith came up with in their search for a definition. Monsieur Germain Garnier, the French translator of Smith's *Wealth of Nations*, grasped the word 'useful' in a purely individual sense and understood it to mean those results of labour that provide a benefit or convenience. Consequently, an adjunct perfumer is a highly productive worker – not because he yields a profit for his employer but because he makes people, à la Garnier, have a good odour, and this gives them aesthetic pleasure. Of course, from this standpoint the work of a prostitute is highly 'productive'. By contrast, according to 'servant of the Lord' Thomas Robert Malthus, who is more inclined to material possessions than to aesthetic pleasures, the only productive labour is that which produces wealth. Even more curious is the statement of Mr. Charles Ganilh. According to him, any worker who is paid, and who promotes production by turning his wages into means of consumption, is productive. Therefore, 'the work that produces pleasure' is highly productive, since all the workers in this field – the actors, musicians, etc. – usually consume a great deal. Destutt de Tracy regards idle landowners as the least productive and the industrial capitalists as the most productive kind of men; while, for instance, Say arrived at the profound wisdom that all labour is productive that has a result, but that the most productive is that labour whose products are durable or, as he puts it, not consumed immediately as soon as they are produced.

∴

Marx's *Capital* is not just a work of economic theory; it is also a work of economic history. His notion that economic laws do not apply uniformly to all stages of economic development, that each economic epoch has its own particular tendencies and conditions of existence, leads Marx, in his analysis of the capitalist economic system, to go back again and again to its original forms and, at the same time, to pursue its further development beyond the stage already reached. As a consequence, many parts of *Capital*, especially where he deals with the development of modern industry, contain the most interesting historical digressions. But this historical character stands out much more sharply in this first draft of Marx's work. It was natural that the critical follow-up of theoretical directions taken by earlier economic schools offered a far better opportunity to explain and prove how economic views are conditioned by the economic character of different times than did the systematic-theoretical presentation that Marx later chose for *Capital*. Thus, many parts of the first volume of *Theories of Surplus-Value* actually appear as an application of the Marxist theory of history to political economy.

By analysing the beginnings of our present economic system in such a way, Marx not only shows us its historical foundations but also sharpens our understanding of the economic conditions of our socialist movement as a class struggle. And this is particularly useful today, when all kinds of general cultural and humanitarian tendencies threaten everywhere – though in other countries even more so than in Germany – to blunt the sharpness of the socialist movement's class struggle. Marx's critique of England's economic theories clearly shows how bourgeois class consciousness rebelled in these theories against dying feudalism; how, indeed, in the most capable minds of eighteenth-century English political economy, the marked bourgeois instincts of their conceptions ran far ahead of their theoretical knowledge. Our contemporary movement can also avoid being diverted and temporarily misled into byways, and can only retain its unity and capacity for action, by remaining conscious of its specific, historically determined class character. In my opinion, the significance of Marx's new book lies especially (though by no means exclusively) in the fact that it forcefully draws our attention to this conditionality of our movement, inducing us to follow the principles of economic development that are hidden below the surface of daily events. I therefore strongly recommend its study to all comrades for whom the watchwords of the day are not the *ne plus ultra* [the last word] of all wisdom, and who want to grasp the driving forces behind the struggle. The study [of the first volume of *Theories of Surplus-Value*] is worth the effort it demands from the reader.

DOCUMENT 6

Marx's Critique of Ricardo (1906)

Gustav Eckstein

Source: Gustav Eckstein, 'Marx' Kritik Ricardos', *Die Neue Zeit*, 24. 1905–6, 2. Bd. (1906), H. 34, H. 36, pp. 245–52, 321–32.

A review of Karl Marx, *Theorien über den Mehrwert: Aus dem nachgelassenen Manuskript 'Zur Kritik der politischen Ökonomie' von Karl Marx*, hrsg. von Karl Kautsky, Stuttgart: J.H.W. Dietz Nachf., 3 vols. in 4 vols. 2,1: *David Ricardo*, 1905, XII, 344 S. (Internationale Bibliothek, 36), and 2,2: *David Ricardo*, 1905, IV, 384 S. (Internationale Bibliothek, 37).

Introduction by the Editors

In the second volume of *Theories of Surplus-Value*, Marx turned to a detailed examination of theories of land rent. The Physiocrats had seen agriculture as the source of the social surplus, and Thomas Malthus had claimed that luxurious consumption by landlords was essential to ensure an adequate market for industry. Adam Smith and David Ricardo cast landlords in a different role, seeing rent as a diversion of social revenue from productive purposes. Smith wrote that 'As soon as the land of any country has all become private property, the landlords, like all other men, love to reap where they never sowed, and demand a rent even for its natural produce'.[1]

David Ricardo's treatment of rent had both economic and political significance. In Ricardo's system, rent derived from diminishing returns on successive parcels of land brought under cultivation. If the most fertile land was cultivated first, followed by a second parcel of less fertility, the owner of the first parcel acquired the power to extract rent. A tenant who resisted could go elsewhere and cultivate less fertile land. The owner of any subsequent parcel, so long as it was more productive than the least fertile land currently in use, would likewise collect *differential rent*. If the total social income consisted of wages, profits and rents, and if the rent share steadily grew while real wages remained con-

---
1 Smith 1937, p. 49.

stant at the subsistence level, the result must be to reduce the remaining share going to profits and capital accumulation. In money terms, the price of foodstuffs would rise due to rising costs on less fertile land, money wages would rise in order to keep real wages constant, and the rate of profit would correspondingly decline. The prospect of a declining rate of profit became the principal argument against Britain's Corn Laws, or the taxation of grain imports, which were repealed in 1846.

The main problem with Ricardo's discussion of rent, as Gustav Eckstein points out in this document, was that it omitted what Marx called *absolute rent* and its role in the determination of prices and the average rate of profit. Eckstein explains that the question of absolute rent necessarily arises when the equalisation of profit rates is examined. With free competition, capitals will typically move from branches with a higher organic composition of capital than the average into those with a lower organic composition in the hope of capturing a larger return of surplus value. Eckstein observes that industries 'with low organic composition cannot, as a rule, avoid the influx of new capital and realise for themselves the surplus value exceeding the rate of profit'. However, since the owners of land control a non-renewable means of production, the movement of capital into agriculture, with its typically low organic composition, will not occur without a 'special compensation' being paid to landowners in the form of absolute rent; that is, an element of the total rent payment that can no longer be explained in terms of differing productivity of the land. In his book on *The Agrarian Question* (1899), Karl Kautsky briefly summarised this distinction between differential and absolute rent:

> ... the former is not an element in the determination of the prices of agricultural products, whilst the latter most certainly is. Differential rent is the product of prices of production, absolute ground-rent of the excess of market-prices over prices of production. The former is constituted out of the surplus, the extra-profit, obtained via the greater productivity of labour on better land, or in a more advantageous location. The latter, in contrast, owes nothing to any *additional yield* by certain sections of agricultural labour, and as a consequence can only come about via a *deduction*, which the landowner makes from the values available, a deduction from the mass of surplus-value implying either a *diminution* of profit or a *deduction* from wages. If food prices and wages rise, the profit of capital will fall. If prices rise without a proportional increase in wages, then it is the workers who will suffer.[2]

---

2   Kautsky 1988, Vol. 1, p. 82. See also Lenin's discussion of ground rent in his essay 'Karl Marx'

Since land rent, either differential or absolute, results from landlords' power to prevent agricultural surplus value from entering into the general process of profit equalisation, the appropriate capitalist response, as Ricardo saw, is to rempove barriers to imports. Ricardo helped to repeal Britain's agricultural tariffs, and Marx anticipated ultimate formation of a world market regulated by a world law of value. In Volume III of *Capital*, Marx devoted the whole of Part 6, including eleven chapters, to analysis of both differential and absolute rent.[3] In an earlier chapter on factors that offset the tendential fall in the rate of profit, Marx also noted that foreign trade can reduce the costs of both constant and variable capital, tending to sustain the rate of profit. He added, however, that foreign trade, in the long-run, can also contribute to a falling rate of profit: by cheapening the cost of variable capital relative to constant, it raises the organic composition of capital and also tends to increase overproduction relative to the absorptive capacity of foreign markets, 'so that it again has the opposite effect in the further course of development'.[4]

To explain commodity prices more generally, Ricardo adopted a labour theory of value. He divided capital into fixed and circulating components, including wage expenditures in the latter category and expenditures on machinery in the former, but he had no knowledge of unpaid labour or surplus value because his concept of circulating capital lacked the more exact concept of variable capital. Nor did his concept of fixed capital include a clear distinction between the fixed and circulating components of what Marx called constant capital. The result was that Ricardo had no comprehensive theory to explain the equalisa-

---

(1915a, pp. 67–8) and Lenin's note in 'The Agrarian Question and the "Critics of Marx"', in *Collected Works*, Vol. 5 (Moscow: Foreign Languages Publishing House, 1961), pp. 126–7.

3 Marx actually distinguished between three types of rent: 1) differential, 2) absolute (which contains an element of monopoly but depends on the lower technological development of agriculture vis-a-vis industry), and 3) purely monopoly rents: '... this absolute rent, arising from the excess value over and above the price of production, is simply a part of the agricultural surplus-value, the transformation of this surplus-value into rent, its seizure by the landowner; just as differential rent arises from the transformation of surplus profit into rent, its seizure by landed property, at the general governing price of production. These two forms of rent are the only normal ones. Apart from this, rent can derive only from a genuine monopoly price, which is determined neither by the price of production of the commodities nor by their value, but rather by the demand of the purchasers and their ability to pay, consideration of which therefore belongs to the theory of competition, where the actual movement of market prices is investigated' (Marx 1992, p. 898).

4 Marx 1992, p. 346.

tion of the profit rate on competing capitals. As Eckstein notes, 'he naively took it to be a given fact' that required no further theoretical analysis.[5]

Eckstein shows that Ricardo's lapses in explaining both rent and price formation were essentially the result of methodological failure. Ricardo advanced beyond Adam Smith when 'he conceived the law of value as the basic truth of his science', but he was unable to develop the entire system of political economy out of this basic principle. Marx's derivation of economic categories resulted from his conceptual reconstruction of capitalism by tracing all of its phenomena back to their common root, 'just as the reconstruction of the world in thought by Laplace was possible only when all celestial phenomena were shown to result from the activity of the law of gravity'. Eckstein concludes that the second volume of *Theories of Surplus-Value* is methodologically superior even to Volume III of *Capital*:

> Especially as regards methodological clarity, the presentation of ground rent, and particularly of absolute rent, is superior in this work compared to the third volume of *Capital*. There Marx posed the question of whether the existence of absolute ground rent is compatible with the law of value, thus proceeding according to the method of Ricardo. But in *Theories of Surplus-Value* he develops absolute rent directly from the law of value, and whoever compares the two presentations will realise how much more fertile the method is in the latter work.

∴

Gustav Eckstein's Review of the Second Volume of Marx's *Theories of Surplus-Value*

1   The Method

Ricardo says in the preface to *On the Principles of Political Economy and Taxation*: 'If the principles which he [the writer] deems correct, should be found to be so, it will be for others, more able than himself, to trace them to all their important consequences'. The person most able to cope with this task was

---

5   Ricardo recognised that prices of commodities produced with equal amounts of labour but with different amounts of fixed capital – or with different turnover periods for fixed capital – could not sell at the same price. But he considered such differences to be of secondary importance and took the labour theory of value to be generally valid as an approximate explanation of prices.

Karl Marx, and what enabled him to do so was, first and foremost, his superior method.

Adam Smith first had to define the field of the new science and describe its phenomena. He grouped and systematised them and tried to trace them back to more basic principles. It was only natural that in this way he could not reach a strict convergence of views, that his principles had to contradict each other, [an outcome] only veiled by the fact that he offered no precise formulation [of those principles]. Ricardo made an important step beyond the method of his teacher when he conceived the law of value as the basic truth of his science and then proceeded to show that all its phenomena not only did not contradict that law, but could also be traced back to this explanatory principle. One can, therefore, trace a parallel between the great advances of Ricardo over Adam Smith and the achievement that the reduction of Kepler's laws to the principle of gravity meant for astronomy. But just as this science only celebrated its greatest triumphs when it did not confine itself to describing the known phenomena of the skies, as determined by the force of gravity, but rather set out to reconstruct the structure of the universe according to this principle – thus proving, for example, the necessary existence of the planet Neptune before it was discovered – so also political economy first found its highest expression to date when Marx developed the totality of its phenomena out of its basic principle, the law of value.

Marx's method has often been misunderstood. It has been regarded as an arbitrary construction because people confused the nature of his presentation with his research. It was only after he traced the various phenomena of the economy back to their common root, in the law of value, that he set about to develop those phenomena out of that law, just as the reconstruction of the world in thought by Laplace was possible only when all celestial phenomena were shown to result from the activity of the law of gravity.

The essence of Marx's method had to reveal itself with particular precision as soon as Marx dealt comprehensively with the most important of his predecessors [Ricardo], with whom he has a common starting point but from whom he differs substantially in subsequent developments. For that reason alone, one had to be curious about the second volume of *Theories of Surplus-Value*, which includes the criticism of the Ricardian system, and the expectations placed upon it have not been disappointed.[6]

---

6 Marx 1905.

2   *Value Determined by Labour Time. Price of Production.*

The foundation of the Ricardian system, as is generally known, is the law of value, which states that the value of a commodity is determined by the amount of labour required for its production. But in the very formulation of this law Ricardo did not quite clearly enunciate what he meant by value. He speaks of value and exchange-value, of relative and absolute or real value, without, however, consistently maintaining these distinctions. His original view – that the labour value contained in commodities only has to reveal itself in exchange-value – fades in the later course of his presentation behind the shallower view that the essence of value amounts to nothing more than exchange.

In general, Ricardo's concepts still lack much in the way of precision even though he went far beyond Adam Smith in this respect. This [advance] is less evident in his method. But for the entire system of political economy to be developed organically from the law of value, a completely accurate terminology is necessary, such as the one provided Marx.

Now, it is immediately obvious that the value of a commodity is not determined only by the amount of labour directly used in its production. Rather, the value of raw materials, auxiliary materials, tools, etc. will also be reproduced; in short, everything that Marx referred to collectively as constant capital. But Ricardo uncritically threw together this distinction between variable capital, invested in wages, and the remaining constant capital, which is really essential for production, with the distinction between fixed and circulating capital taken from the sphere of circulation. As a result, he could not apprehend these two sets of categories in a precise manner. Marx has already shown elsewhere the errors that resulted from this confusion when analysing the processes of circulation.[7] However, it naturally had to be even more disastrous for the analysis of value formation. In particular, it led Ricardo to disregard completely raw and auxiliary materials, which he did not fit correctly into either of the two categories. But it also made it impossible for him to understand the nature of surplus value. Since he paid attention only to the differences in the circulation of capital, he missed the importance of the relationship between paid and unpaid labour, between variable capital and surplus value. He overlooked, therefore, the importance of the length of labour time for the rate and amount of surplus value and regarded the working day as a given and fixed magnitude.

In Ricardo, therefore, the nature of surplus value, as unpaid labour performed by the workers but appropriated by the capitalist, does not stand out

---

7   Vergl. *Kapital*, Band II, 2. Aufl., s. 185 ff. [Marx 1978, pp. 293 ff.].

clearly. This fountainhead of profit and rent was first developed by Ricardo's socialist disciples.

The fact that Ricardo did not have a precise definition of the organic composition of capital, and that he threw together circulating and variable capital, explains why he did not notice that the surplus value generated by a single capital does indeed stand in a certain ratio to its variable element, but not to [capital's] total magnitude, and therefore that the formation of surplus value out of unpaid labour contradicts at first glance the equality of the rate of profit, which he also recognised. For him, this levelling of profits was not a problem; he never investigated the extent to which it is compatible with the law of value; he naively took it to be a given fact. Marx showed, for the first time, that an apparent contradiction exists here, a contradiction that cannot be overcome as long as individual capitals are considered in isolation. It is competition that drives capital into those applications yielding a higher [rate of] surplus value than the average and pulls it out of those where the opposite is the case, and which brings about a deviation of the individual profit from surplus value and thus creates a distinction in principle between the individual values of a class of goods and their market value.[8]

Admittedly, Ricardo was aware that not all the phenomena of price formation can automatically be traced back to the law of value that he formulated. Smith had claimed, on the basis of his second definition [of value][9] – according

---

8   Strangely enough, people have often declared this development of the profit rate and the deviation of market values from individual values by Marx to be in contradiction with the formulations of the first volume of *Capital*. They argue that Marx gave up his own law of value by admitting that it is not valid in the capitalist world. For example, Bernstein quotes with great applause the following nonsense by Tugan-Baranovsky: 'Either the prices of commodities are determined by value – and in this case the values of goods do not coincide with the labour costs; or the prices of commodities are not determined by value – and in this case the concept of exchange value loses any specific sense, because exchange value cannot be considered otherwise than as the basis of price. In the first case, the Marxian theory of value collapses in ruins; in the second, it loses any relationship to the real facts of exchange, it is empty of content' (see *Dokumente des Sozialismus*, Volume v, p. 558, note). The falsehood and redundancy of the law of the mathematical pendulum, which is admittedly not directly followed by any single physical pendulum, could easily be 'proved' with exactly the same arguments.

9   ['Adam Smith, who so accurately defined the original source of exchangeable value, and who was bound in consistency to maintain, that all things became more or less valuable in proportion as more or less labour was bestowed on their production, has himself erected another standard measure of value, and speaks of things being more or less valuable, in proportion as they will exchange for more or less of this standard measure. Sometimes he

to which the value of a commodity is the sum of the wages, profits and rents required for its production – that a rise in wages always results in an increase in the price of the product. Ricardo refuted this proposition by showing that a rise in wages can, under certain circumstances, even bring about a reduction in the market value. On that occasion he came very close to the truth, but without being conscious of the importance and the fundamental significance of his discovery. He noted, for example:

> Since goods which sell for £5,000 may be the produce of a capital equal in amount to that from which are produced other goods which sell for £10,000, the profits on their manufacture will be the same; but those profits would be unequal, if the prices of the goods did not vary with a rise or fall in the rate of profits.[10]

With this proposition Ricardo admits the dependence of commodity prices on the rise or fall of the profit rate, but he does so in an unclear and vague manner, so that he himself overlooks the fact that in this way he breaks with the view he always held; namely, that the market prices of products are only the expression of their labour values.

Failure to recognise the importance of such a limitation of the law of value was predetermined by the starting point of the analysis. As mentioned above, Ricardo did not proceed from the question of how the equality of the profit rate asserts itself on the basis of the law of value, or of how it is consistent with that law, as would actually have corresponded to his method of analysis; for him it was first and foremost a question of investigating the influence of an increase in wages on the market value of products. Thus, he made any solution of the question difficult for himself from the outset by dealing with it in a completely incorrect context.

We have seen that Ricardo was unaware of the distinction between constant and variable capital; he only knew that between fixed and circulating capital, and he often confused circulating with variable capital. He had to face the question of whether the [organic] composition of capital exerted any influence

---

speaks of corn, at other times of labour, as a standard measure; not the quantity of labour bestowed on the production of any object, but the quantity which it can command in the market: as if these were two equivalent expressions, and as if because a man's labour had become doubly efficient, and he could therefore produce twice the quantity of a commodity, he would necessarily receive twice the former quantity in exchange for it' (Ricardo 1821, p. 5)].

10 Ricardo 1821, p. 41.

on the value of the product. Caught up, however, in his deficient terminology and conceptualisation, he lumped this issue together with the significance of different rates of the turnover of capital for value formation;[11] moreover, as he had anticipated the main point in the solution of the question, the transformation of surplus value into profit and the equalisation of the rate of profit, his attempt to solve the problem could only lead to confusion, which indeed prevails in the fourth section of the first chapter.[12]

Ricardo says there that the historically developed differentiation of capitals, between those in which the fixed element predominates and those in which wages play the dominant role, has brought about a modification of the law of value. The value of a product resolves itself, according to Ricardo (and in this respect he uncritically followed Adam Smith) into the three revenue forms: wages, profits and eventually ground rent. Constant capital, whose value reappears in the value of the product, is again totally forgotten here. Now, since according to Ricardo the working day is a fixed magnitude, a certain number of workers always supply the same mass of value. If the share of value falling to the workers grows – that is, if wages rise – this can only happen at the expense of profit (here again the part falling to rent is forgotten). A rise in wages thus always results in a decline in the rate of profit. Here, Ricardo again overlooks the fact that the rate of profit is not given by the ratio of surplus value to wages, but by its ratio to the total capital, i.e. that the rate of profit also decreases when this total capital grows more quickly than the surplus value produced by it. Given a general rise in wages, capitals of different [organic] composition thus yield very different profits. Those capitals that include less than the average wages would see their profits relatively little reduced, while those containing more than the average wages could see their profits disappear completely. Competition, however, would then cause an abundant inflow of capital, mainly in the form of credit, into the most profitable applications and an outflow from the profitless or loss-making ones. A new, lower rate of profit

---

11 [Ricardo saw that if two commodities were produced with the same amounts of labour and fixed capital, but in the one case the fixed capital was reproduced in one year while in the other it took two years, the result would be an 'interest' charge on fixed capital in the latter case, meaning the two commodities would not sell at exactly the same price. Nevertheless, he ignored this complication on the grounds that labour costs would provide a reliable measure of value for the 'average period of production'].

12 [A reference to David Ricardo 1821, *On the Principles of Political Economy and Taxation*, Chapter 1: On Value, Section IV: The principle that the quantity of labour bestowed on the production of commodities regulates their relative value, considerably modified by the employment of machinery and other fixed and durable capital].

would then be established; some values would have been increased, while the others would have fallen.

Ricardo did not deem it necessary to investigate whether this deviation of 'relative values' from labour values was a general phenomenon, and whether the equalisation of profits does not in principle presuppose such a deviation. He rather declared this striking phenomenon to be so insignificant that it could very well be ignored in the subsequent exposition.

Since Ricardo did not distinguish between surplus value and profit, he could not develop either of these two categories correctly; in particular, he had to form a completely false idea about the nature of the rate of profit. The extent of his confusion in this respect is apparent, among other things, in the fact that at one point he explicitly speaks of 'trades where profits are in proportion to the capital, and not in proportion to the quantity of labour employed'.[13] Thus, the validity of the general rate of profit, which is precisely the uniform relationship between profit and total capital, would be limited to some lines of business.

As we have seen, this deficient analysis of profit led Ricardo to regard the sum of wages and profits as constant, so that an increase in wages always resulted in a reduction of profit and thus of the rate of profit. He overlooked the fact that the rate of profit can rise or fall as a result of the rise or fall in ground rent; that the mass of profit depends not only upon the rate of surplus value but also upon the number of workers employed; that even at a given rate of surplus value the rate of profit depends upon the organic composition of capital and the value ratio of its different parts; and that, finally, the differences in circulation do not influence the rate of surplus value but rather the rate of profit.

3   Absolute Ground Rent. Rodbertus.

The equalisation of profit [rates], and thus the transformation of values into prices of production, presupposes a developed capitalist economic organisation and the prevalence of free competition. From time to time this enables capital to leave those areas of application where the values of goods are below their prices of production – i.e. where the organic composition of capital is above the average – for those where the opposite is the case. These industries with low organic composition of capital cannot, as a rule, avoid the influx of new capital and realise for themselves the surplus value exceeding the rate of profit. They must share it with the other capitalists unless [their monopoly control of] a means of production that is indispensable for this branch

---

13   Ricardo 1821, p. 418.

of industry enables them to avoid the impact of free competition. But this is the case throughout primary production as a result of private ownership of land. This land is only relinquished if capital pays a special compensation for its exploitation. But since the [organic] composition of invested capital is low in agriculture, as well as in mining – that is to say, relatively much living labour is used – here values always stand above the prices of production; and this difference, which is the source of absolute rent, can be offered to the landowner in return for him releasing it for exploitation. Because Ricardo did not recognise any basic difference between values and prices of production, absolute ground rent was absolutely incomprehensible for him. Thus, he contented himself with a theory of differential rent – that is, with trying to explain the differences in rent between soils with different fertility – while he neglected entirely to discuss the nature of rent itself. With him, the worst soil under cultivation bears no rent, although this conclusion does not follow even from his own assumptions. In the third volume of *Capital*, Marx has already proven that even the worst soil brought under cultivation can yield a differential rent as a result of successive applications of capital to this least fertile soil or to better ones.[14]

Ricardo and his school, as we have seen, ignored absolute rent, and they had to ignore it. Rodbertus, on the other hand, attempted to explain absolute ground rent on the basis of the law of value and thus to establish a new theory of rent. Marx, therefore, before he proceeds to criticise the Ricardian theory of rent, interpolates a discussion of Rodbertus's theory.

Analysing the law of value, Rodbertus noticed that the surplus value, which he calls 'rent', does not grow in proportion to all the invested capital but only to its variable part – by which, however, he understands not only wages, or the payment of living labour power, but also the wear and tear of fixed capital, the tools and machinery, etc. There remains, therefore, the value of the raw and auxiliary materials (called by him 'material value'), which does not go into the valorisation process as an element creating surplus value. On the other hand, in calculating the rate of profit, Rodbertus did not take into consideration the [organic] composition of capital but only the ratio between the created 'rent' and the total capital. Thus, if the rate of profit is given, there will be, wherever only variable capital goes into production, a difference between the total 'rent' (surplus value) generated in that branch of production and the profit allotted

---

14   It may be recalled here that earlier economists, such as Malthus, had already assumed [the existence of] a differential rent on the worst land under cultivation, because undeveloped land can also yield a return as pasture ground for sheep, etc.

to it according to the general rate [of profit]. This also applies to primary production, because, according to Rodbertus,

> Agriculture does not require any material which is the product of a previous production, in fact it actually begins the production, and in agriculture, that part of the property which is analogous with the material [i.e. with raw and auxiliary materials], would be the land itself, which is however assumed to be without cost.[15]

A part of the product, therefore, remains in agriculture and falls to the landowner as rent.

The first thing that stands out in this development is the erroneous inclusion of the wear and tear of fixed capital in its variable element. But, even on that basis, if Rodbertus had been consistent, he should have concluded that the dependence of surplus value on a part of capital that is not at all uniformly represented in the various areas of application utterly contradicts the equality of the rate of profit, as long as we accept that commodities are exchanged at their values. However, this escaped Rodbertus because, just as Ricardo did, he regarded the profit rate as given and did not see in it a problem; for him, it was just a question of a particular issue, the elucidation of absolute rent.

But that part of the value allotted to the replacement of tools, etc., does not belong to variable but to constant capital; therefore, even according to Rodbertus's remaining argument, there would be only a quantitative difference between the constant parts of agricultural and industrial capital – but constant capital would still exist in both cases. Rodbertus's assumptions, however, are also wrong because he assumes that agriculture has to purchase no raw materials. The fact that he was locked into the views of Pomeranian aristocratic estate owners, who were then still strongly steeped in natural economy, explains why he could ignore the importance of raw and auxiliary materials in agriculture. In fact, this value element is missing in primary production only in extractive industry (mining); but it is also lacking in the transportation industry, which, despite that fact, yields no special rent. A semblance of authority was given to Rodbertus's analysis only by the fact that he was setting agriculture as a whole against industry, which receives raw products from agriculture, while agriculture produces its own raw and auxiliary materials, whose value therefore does not have to be reimbursed to anyone. But, in order to be consistent, he should

---

15 [Rodbertus-Jagetzow 1851, pp. 97–8. Quoted in Marx 1963, Vol. II, p. 59].

also have taken into account the fact that agriculture owes its means of production to industry.

Thus, with his discovery that the surplus value generated by individual capitals is not proportional to those capitals themselves but only to their variable part, Rodbertus came close to the truth; but he missed it because he did not proceed consistently [on the basis of this assumption] and because he was only interested in explaining one specific phenomenon, ground rent, instead of developing the law of value from its foundations.

Marx's theory of absolute ground rent not only elucidates ground rent on the basis of the law of value but also shows its historical relativity – the conditions under which it appears and the influences to which it is subjected.

Above all, absolute ground rent can only appear – apart from the exceptional case in which the land is concentrated in a few hands and available in insufficient quantities, so that the agricultural products yield a monopoly price – if, and as long as, the organic composition of agricultural capital is lower than that of industrial capital, so that agriculture generates an excess value (*Überwert*) beyond the [average] rate of profit. Before the introduction of machinery into industry, the role of living labour was even greater in industry than in primary production. Since then, however, this relation has changed completely: with the blossoming of agricultural chemistry and the penetration of machinery [into agriculture], a change of tendency has recently occurred also in this field; the difference between values and prices of production has been reduced in agriculture, and with it also absolute ground rent. This [form of rent] is also determined by the level of the general rate of profit; yet it enters as a contributing factor into the prices of production of agricultural products.[16] The rise of absolute rent, therefore, goes hand in hand with a decline in the rate of profit. All the factors working towards reduction of the rate of profit therefore increase the [absolute] ground rent, if they do not simultaneously reduce the overall surplus value created in primary production to an even greater extent.

But for absolute ground rent to materialise, fulfilment of a second condition is still necessary. Landed property must stand in opposition to the ownership

---

16   [To be more precise, Eckstein should have referred here to 'the prices of agricultural products', not to 'the prices of production'. For Marx, absolute rent is the surplus that accrues to the landlord following the deduction of the price of production from the market price. In other words, absolute rent raises the market prices of agricultural products beyond their prices of production. The confusion may stem from the fact that Marx, when he wrote *Theories of Surplus-Value*, still did not employ the term 'price of production' (*Produktionspreis*) consistently, sometimes using instead *Kostenpreis* (cost price) or *Durchschnittspreis* (average price)].

of capital; it must constitute a barrier to its application. Where that is not the case, as in a peasant economy, where the owner cultivates his own plot of land, or in the colonies, where land is not yet appropriated, or is only minimally appropriated, or where capitalist plantations are managed as any other capitalist enterprise, an absolute rent in the capitalist sense is out of the question.

Nevertheless, this rent cannot be explained by a monopoly that actually does not exist in countries with a capitalist economy. It is only necessary that private ownership of land and its capitalist exploitation should be a barrier to the influx of capital. Whether that barrier comes into full effect and is fully utilised, i.e. whether the full difference [between agricultural values and prices] is appropriated by the landowners, depends upon the circumstances.

As we have seen, this disincentive to the application of capital in agriculture is not without influence on the formation of prices. It brings about a rise in the prices of raw materials and a reduction in the prices of industrial products, because the fact that the high [amounts of] surplus value produced in agriculture stay there and are not shared with the remaining total capital depresses the rate of profit, and with it the production prices.

4   *Value Determined by the Average Labour Time. Differential Rent.*
From the foregoing analysis it would follow that, just as the capitalists would be interested in increasing the rate of profit and therefore in an organic composition of capital as low as possible, the landowners would be interested in a low rate of profit, but still more in the difference between the production prices and values of primary products being as large as possible. In other words, landowners would be interested in capitals in the sphere of primary production having as low an organic composition as possible; that is to say, in having living labour in that sphere play the largest possible role and constant capital play the least possible role.

However, that tendency is thwarted and cancelled by another, stronger one. Thus far, we have spoken only of the value or, more precisely, the price of production of a certain type of goods. But that price is itself only a product of competition, which distributes the total capital of society among the various branches of production in accordance with the social need for the good in question. The total value of a certain type of goods is, therefore, determined by the total labour time applied to their production, while the price of production is determined by the total capital invested in that branch of production. The individual value, or rather the production price, of a given commodity is therefore the aliquot part of that total sum and will be regulated by the average production conditions.

Therefore, those capitalists who work less efficiently than the average in their industry obtain only part of the normal profit, while those who work with the most productive capitals obtain an excess profit. Each individual capitalist thus tries to increase the productive power of his own capital, i.e. to use as many labour-saving methods as possible, and to replace as much variable capital as possible by constant capital. To the agents of production, entangled in the appearances of competition, wages therefore appear as *faux frais* (incidental expenses), as a useless burden on production; likewise, the phenomenon that more productive capitals supply a greater quantity of commodities – so that the price of individual commodities sinks – metamorphoses in their minds into the belief that by arbitrarily reducing prices they can increase sales and thereby their profits. But wherever competition reigns freely, it strives to level out profits by driving capitals away from branches of production with low levels of profits and into the more profitable ones, thus forcing the capitalists to ensure that variable capital is always pushed back by constant capital. Thus, the effort to increase individual profits leads to a reduction of the rate of profit as a whole. The capitals invested in primary production cannot escape this tendency. The landowners, however, at first gain in two ways from this tendency, even if it also brings about a reduction in absolute ground rent. First, they often pocket part of the surplus profit obtained by the tenants, and secondly, the capitals invested in agriculture increase the value of the land, which after the expiry of the lease devolves on the landowner free of charge.

However, where the impact of free competition is limited by the fact that certain elements of production cannot be procured at any desired quantity or quality, the equalisation of profits cannot take place; some profits will remain below the average, while others will exceed it. By far the most important area in which this occurs is primary production, and Ricardo analysed this whole phenomenon [of rent] from that starting point. He therefore regarded it one-sidedly, from the wrong angle, without recognising its general meaning. The surplus profits resulting from this restriction of free competition in agriculture are the only form of rent that Ricardo knows.

In his development of ground rent, he assumes the existence a fictitious country in which soils of different fertility are present and waiting for their first appropriation. He actually had American conditions in mind. Of course, Carey[17] has already demonstrated that precisely there the actual development

---

17   [A reference to the American economist Henry Charles Carey (1793–1879). According to Marx: 'Most characteristic is the argument of Carey's school against the English economists. It attacks *Ricardo*, classical champion of the bourgeoisie and most stoic opponent

proceeded in a completely different way. Ricardo said that in such a country the most fertile lands would be appropriated first and that, as long as these lands abounded, there would be no ground rent (in fact, under those circumstances there would also have been no capitalist production). The growth of population would then, he argued, gradually have made necessary the cultivation of less fertile land, but that would only occur if the heightened demand increased the prices of agricultural products so much that they not only refunded the capital costs incurred, but also supplied the customary profit. [Agricultural] prices would therefore be determined by the individual value of those products produced under the most adverse conditions. Those produced under more favourable conditions would yield a surplus – ground rent. 'For rent is always the difference between the produce obtained by the employment of two equal quantities of capital and labour'.[18]

Ricardo arrived at this result because he was under the spell of the Malthusian theory, which says that population always presses on its means of subsistence; because his theory is based on the false assumption that cultivation always proceeds from more fertile to less fertile soils; because he did not deal with the problem of the equalisation of the prices of goods produced under different conditions in general terms but made a single question his starting point; and, finally, because he regarded commodities and values in isolation and not as products of the social production process.

Development can follow the path assumed by Ricardo, but this is by no means necessary, indeed it would be an exception. Agriculture, in its progress, turns now to more fertile, now to less fertile soils; those properties themselves change with the method of production and the mass of capital invested. Similarly, the amount of agricultural products produced can correspond to demand, exceed it or fall behind it. But, even under the conditions assumed by Ricardo, the effect expected by him would not happen. As we have seen, when the corn produced under the worst conditions regulates price, even the worst soil, or, more correctly, even the capital yielding the lowest return, still yields a rent.

---

of the proletariat, describing him as a man whose works provide an arsenal for anarchists, socialists, in brief for all "enemies of the bourgeois order." With fanaticism it attacks not only Ricardo but all other leading economists of modern bourgeois Europe, and reproaches these economic heralds of the bourgeoisie with having split society and with forging weapons for civil war by cynically providing the proof that the economic foundations of the various classes are bound to give rise to an inevitable and constantly growing antagonism between them' (Marx, 'Apropos Carey', *Die Reform*, No. 49, 17 September 1853, in *MECW*, Vol. 12, pp. 626–7)].

18   Ricardo 1821, p. 59.

The laws developed by Ricardo apply only to the case, which he especially denies, in which prices are dictated by the costs of production under particularly favourable conditions – i.e. when a relative overproduction of agricultural products has taken place. In that case, a significant portion of those products will be sold below their individual values; prices may go down to their prices of production, so that all absolute rent on the worst soils disappears and is only partly realised on many of the better soils. In general, a complete disappearance of absolute rent can hardly occur under the capitalist conditions of production assumed by Ricardo, because the landlords do not allow their lands to be worked without compensation. But it is possible, indeed, for rent to be paid when a rent no longer exists; for example, by settling wage-labourers on small plots, where rent swallows up both the eventual profit and a portion of wages. Where the landowner himself cultivates the soil, particularly in a peasant economy, there can be no question of ground rent – or of capitalist production in general.

For differential rent, on the other hand, Ricardo's development is on the whole correct, though not completely. In particular, the assumption that production must always turn to poorer soils is not only historically false but also irrelevant for his own theory of rent, whose laws apply both with a rising and with a falling productivity of the land taken into cultivation.

But as Ricardo saw in differential rent the only possible form of rent, he had to come to false conclusions once he turned to consider the laws of ground rent in general. Thus Ricardo found, for example, that improvements in agriculture always reduce monetary rents, both if those improvements involve a better use of land through more rational crop rotation and the like, and if they are caused by a cheapening or improvement of constant capital. This is indeed true for differential rent. But the cheapening or improvement of constant capital also changes the organic composition of capital; the percentage allotted to variable capital grows, so that more living labour (more value) is added to the raw materials, while production costs remain the same. As a consequence, the difference between those two magnitudes [values and production prices (production costs + the average rate of profit)], i.e. absolute rent, grows. Thus, even under these assumptions, the overall rent can remain the same or even increase.

Ricardo only dealt with that case – in which only constant capital decreases in value – but not with the general question of how the various changes in the [organic] composition of capital, as a result of fluctuations in the price of its constituent parts, affect the level of ground rent. In this case, too, he failed to solve the problem because he was interested only in one special case rather than in addressing the question as a matter of principle.

This deficiency makes itself felt even in the analysis of that case, of particular importance to Ricardo, in which agriculture progresses towards ever poorer soils. He traces the otherwise inexplicable and steady decline in the rate of profit back to this process. Since Ricardo identified surplus value with profit, he concluded that the fall in the profit [rate] was only possible due to an increase in wages brought about by a rise in the price of food. But this is a natural consequence of the increasing inefficiency of agriculture. Thus, [according to Ricardo,] the rate of profit decreases with the progress of society, while money wages, and particularly ground rent, steadily rise. Ricardo overlooked the fact that here, under his assumptions, the growth of differential rent, given also a decreasing productivity of agriculture on the better soil types, is constantly accompanied by a decreasing mass of total product in proportion to advanced capital of a given magnitude. As a result of the increase in the cost of food, wages in particular rise. As a consequence, out of an invested capital of, say, 100, a larger portion will be allotted to the variable capital, with which at the same time only fewer workers will be employed and less raw material will be processed. If the value of the elements of constant capital now simultaneously grows – and this can be assumed both in agriculture and in mining, because in those cases the products often go back into production as raw or auxiliary materials or in the form of fixed capital – the number of labourers employed will decrease in two respects. On the one hand, wages have increased; on the other hand, the constant capital, thus reduced in percentage terms, replaces only a part of the previously applied raw material and auxiliary material or, more precisely, machinery. Not only the mass of products decreases in proportion to the capital applied, but also rent compared to the result in the first case, whereas Ricardo assumed that a price increase in the elements of constant capital would bring about, on the contrary, precisely a further increase in rent.

But even apart from this, Ricardo developed and explained the fall in the profit rate incorrectly – not only in historical terms, since this fall is not prevented by the cheapening of agricultural products, but also theoretically, as we have seen. The rate of profit is not the same as the rate of surplus value; profit is not calculated on the variable capital but on the total capital. Rather, this fall in the rate of profit is due to the fact that, under the pressure of competition, the share of constant capital continuously grows at the expense of variable capital, i.e. to the fact that industry, as well as agriculture, is continually more productive. The surplus value increases in proportion to the wages disbursed, but it falls in relation to the total capital employed.

5   Value Determined by Socially Necessary Labour. Crises.

Ricardo says at one point: 'The labour of a million of men in manufactures, will always produce the same value, but will not always produce the same riches'.[19] This claim is absolutely incorrect, as Ricardo again forgets here the constant capital, which creates no new value but whose value always reappears in the product. Therefore, the larger the constant capital entering into the labour process, the greater – even if the working day remains unchanged – will be not only the mass of use-values produced, which Ricardo referred to as riches, but also the value produced. Thus, even if the working population remains stationary and only the organic composition of capital changes, the mass of value annually produced by industry will constantly increase. In actual fact, however, there is also a continual growth of the capital employed. Ricardo understood this process totally incorrectly, assuming that the accumulation of capital takes place in such a way that revenue will be 'consumed by productive instead of unproductive labourers',[20] or, in other words, that the surplus value will be converted into variable capital. Ricardo once again overlooks here the constant capital, which normally grows with accumulation even more quickly than the variable capital. Accumulation, therefore, presupposes not only a growth of the working population or the possibility of extending the working day, but also the presence of elements of the newly forming constant capital. Accumulation in some branches of industry thus presupposes the same phenomenon in many other branches. But even if there is no transformation of revenue into capital, which is certainly required by the nature of capitalist production, a fund would be available for accumulation – of which, however, Ricardo knows nothing. In particular, fixed capital (machinery, buildings, etc.) certainly goes wholly into the production process, but its value is not as a rule reproduced in a year; the replacement of its value is spread over a number of years, only at the end of which must the elements of the fixed capital in question be replaced in kind. In the meantime, a value accumulates from year to year that can be used to expand production and may be invested in circulating capital, whose value always returns to the capitalists.

Thus, the production of goods and values grows continuously, and now the question arises as to whether this process will also find its limit, [i.e.] whether an overproduction of goods and capitals can take place.

Ricardo denied the possibility of general overproduction, arguing that products are always exchanged against other products, that each purchase simul-

---

19   Ricardo 1821, p. 320.
20   Ricardo 1821, p. 163.

taneously requires a sale and vice versa, and that demand and supply always coincide. Overproduction can occur only in certain branches of production, such that the correct proportion in the supplies of goods would be disturbed. But this proportion will again be restored by the beneficial effects of free competition, which withdraws capitals from those applications and redirects them to those whose products are scarce. The needs of society are virtually unlimited: if, for example, 'the demand for corn is limited by the mouths which are to eat it',[21] the demand for personal possessions and all sorts of luxury goods is in fact unlimited.

This whole view reveals an astonishing naïveté. Ricardo poses the problem as if it were a question of the actual needs of people in general, as if the purpose of capitalist production were the satisfaction of needs, as if the means for satisfaction of those needs were simply exchanged between their producers. The capitalist world is transformed into a pastoral idyll. For Ricardo, this illusion was still possible because, in the youthful days of capitalism, not all its contradictions had yet emerged clearly and acutely. However, it is difficult to see how people can often adopt that standpoint even today.

The labour time invested in goods by the individual producers does not yet give them any value if it does not prove to be socially necessary, i.e. if it is not employed to satisfy a social need. But the magnitude of this need again depends on the amount of value; in the harsh reality of the capitalist world, for example, the demand for food is determined by not the size of the stomach, as Smith and Ricardo naively believed, but by that of the purse [i.e. of solvent demand]. Needs are not at all decisive, only the ability to pay. We thus have here a vicious circle: value depends on social needs, but these depend on the amount of value. People have often argued that this is an internal contradiction of Marx's theory of value, whereas, on the contrary, here lies precisely Marx's discovery of the fundamental contradiction of the capitalist economy. In fact, no capitalist knows whether the goods he produces will realise their price, whether production costs will be reimbursed and a profit generated. He can only guess with greater or lesser probability. He takes his goods to the market with a certain price dictated by the costs of production, i.e. indirectly by their value, and he must now wait and see if they will find buyers. If not, perhaps he will have to dispense with a portion of the profit, eventually with the whole of it; indeed, if he has to settle payments, for instance, he may have to write off his own costs, and the actual market value of the goods will amount to only a part of their individual value.

---

21   Ricardo 1821, p. 342.

> But the different kinds of individual labour represented in these particular use-values, in fact, become labour in general, and in this way social labour, only by actually being exchanged for one another in quantities which are proportional to the labour-time contained in them. Social labour-time exists in these commodities in a latent state, so to speak, and becomes evident only in the course of their exchange. The point of departure is not the labour of individuals considered as social labour, but on the contrary the particular kinds of labour of private individuals, i.e., labour which proves that it is universal social labour only by the supersession of its original character in the exchange process. Universal social labour is consequently not a ready-made prerequisite but an emerging result.[22]

This glaring contradiction is overridden on the basis of the capitalist economy by the fact that a commodity appears as the embodiment of social labour in itself, as money, against which every individual commodity must be exchanged in order to prove its social character. Money therefore does not act, as Ricardo assumed, simply as a means of circulation, to make the exchange of goods more comfortable. It is the yardstick applied to each commodity to find out to what extent it contains socially necessary labour. Money thus first makes possible the exchange of goods on a capitalist basis, but it cannot eliminate the enormous contradiction represented by the fact that the individual labour of producers, initially independent of each other, is at the same time social labour.[23]

---

22 Marx, *A Contribution to the Critique of Political Economy*, in MECW, Vol. 29, p. 286.
23 It is only natural that economists operating on the basis of the bourgeois standpoint, for whom it is therefore an axiom that the bourgeois, capitalist economy is free from internal contradictions, should not understand a theory that exhibits those contradictions, and should instead look for those contradictions in the theory itself. For them, a theory is good if it puts aside any determination of the economic relations and, of course, all the contrasts and contradictions. For them, capitalism and any other form of economy answers the purpose of satisfying needs in the most efficient way possible. The only difference between the different economic systems is their ability to achieve that purpose. Of course, according to this standpoint, with the huge increase in productivity that capitalism brings about, this ability has reached the highest level of perfection. Crises are just random blemishes that can be eliminated. As I said, it is understandable that such a theory should satisfy those who only want to see what suits the bourgeois consciousness. But it is difficult to understand how socialists can also turn to this watery soup of a theory and see in Marx's discovery of the internal contradictions of capitalism only contradictions in his own theory. See Bernstein 1905.

The case, therefore, is by no means as pleasant as Ricardo presented it; namely, that products are exchanged against each other and money plays only a mediating role. The difficulty for the commodity lies precisely in the conversion into money. *Hic Rhodus, hic salta*. Only by the ability to become money does the commodity prove to be a value; until then it is so only virtually. Its situation is not much better than that of the countless feature articles written every year, which remain for the most part virtual ones. Only a fraction of them become real by their actual inclusion in a newspaper.

If the anticipation of the capitalists proves to be wrong, and this gambling is always tricky, or if the conditions of demand have changed during production, a large number of commodities cannot manage to make that jump into the money form, and a devaluation of commodities and capital on a large scale takes place. The crisis breaks out.

To be sure, Ricardo did not deny that a partial overproduction can occur. But he failed to recognise the importance of this phenomenon. For with the extremely artificial and sensitive organism of the capitalist economic system, any major disturbance of the equilibrium entails a whole revolution. If, for example, the market is saturated in the textile industry, the spinner can no longer sell his product to the weaver. As a result, his consumption of wool, linen or silk, of coal and other auxiliary materials, of machinery and buildings, is hampered. In all those industries stagnation sets in, and with it dismissals of workers and reductions of wages. This restricts the consumption of capitalists and workers; the market also becomes overcrowded in the area of consumer goods production; the crisis becomes no longer partial, but general. The argument that only a partial overproduction can take place is, therefore, a very poor consolation, since a partial crisis must necessarily transform itself into a general one.

Ricardo explained the impossibility of general overproduction by the fact that human needs are unlimited, and that anyone can create the means to satisfy them by increasing his own production.

Here, then, not only are buyers and sellers equated, but also producers and consumers. But besides the fact that a large number of consumers do not produce at all, the mere relation between wage-worker and capitalist already implies that the workers – that is, the largest part of the consumers – are not consumers of a very large part of their products, namely of the means of production and work materials, but also, in particular, that workers are only consumers, or buyers, as long as they are overproducers, i.e. as long as they generate surplus value. To speak of an identity of producer and consumer is therefore absurd. Ricardo believed it was enough to produce values in order for others to be able to acquire them. But in this way he abstracted from all the formal determinations [*Formbestimmungen*][24] of capitalism. He confuses product and value, overlooking the fact that the worker is simply not in possession of the means of production and does not produce for himself but for the profit of his employer. This becomes obvious if we reduce his argument to its simplest form and ask ourselves: why do the workers themselves not produce the goods they need? In fact, the shoemaker usually suffers the worst lack of shoes if the shops are inundated with that product, etc. The limits of capitalist production are determined only by capital itself, while on the other hand most producers remain restricted to the average level of needs, and the system of capitalist production must be limited accordingly – hence the tendency of capitalism to expand the market by all means and at any price. Ricardo consequently denies the logical necessity of this expansion, but today it is no longer necessary to discuss it.[25]

All of these internal contradictions of the capitalist system first become visible in the field of circulation. Even on the basis of simple commodity circulation, the possibility of crises is given by the fact that sale and purchase do not at all necessarily coincide, and that money can therefore be withheld, for instance, to be stored up as treasure. If this phenomenon is here [under simple commodity production] still mostly accidental, on a capitalist basis it takes place regularly. All the contradictions of this system come to light in the form that the two phases of trade, purchase and sale, fall apart. If money is used just as medium of circulation, it may be withheld if the reproduction process encounters difficulties – because, for some reason, the market prices of goods have fallen far below their prices of production, so that the reproduction of capital is restricted as far as possible, or because, for instance, the elements of constant capital are not present in the necessary amounts. In this case, reproduction encounters not only technical but also economic difficulties, since the value and price of those elements [of constant capital] have increased. This

---

24 [Marx gave, as an example of the new *Formbestimmungen* arising from the circulation process, the distinction between fixed and circulating capital. Cf. also this passage from the *Grundrisse*: 'Necessary labour time is determined by the movement of capital itself ... This is the fundamental law of competition. Demand, supply, price (production cost) are further specific forms (*Formbestimmungen*: formal determinations); price as market price; or general price' (Marx 1993, p. 657)].

25 Only the understanding of the inherent contradictions of the law of value, which reach their full development in the capitalist world, allows one to understand not only economic crises but also all the desperate attempts of the capitalist world to get rid of these contradictions – our whole trade, customs and colonial policy – based on the artificial expansion of the market, [and] the cartels, which amount to its artificial regulation.

can occur as a result of poor harvests, or of an excessive investment of capital in machinery, etc.; it can be due to an intended enlargement of the scale of reproduction that is too rapid and for which the necessary preconditions were lacking.

But money can also serve as means of payment, as credit money, when it acts in two different moments, as a measure of value and as a realisation of value. But from this function of money further potential reasons for crisis independently arise if, in the meantime, there have been changes in the values or prices of the relevant goods, or if there is a delay in their realisation. Then a stoppage in the return flow of money occurs; the whole series of previous transactions that retrogressively depend upon this one cannot be settled.

The whole process of accumulation in the first place resolves itself into *production on an expanding scale*, which on the one hand corresponds to the natural growth of the population, and on the other hand, forms an inherent basis for the phenomena which appear during *crises*. The criterion of this expansion of production is *capital* itself, the existing level of the conditions of production and the unlimited desire of the capitalists to enrich themselves and to enlarge their capital, but by no means *consumption*, which from the outset is inhibited, since the majority of the population, the working people, can only expand their consumption within very narrow limits, whereas the demand for labour, although it grows *absolutely*, decreases *relatively*, to the same extent as capitalism develops. Moreover, all equalisations are *accidental*, and although the proportion of capital employed in individual spheres is equalised by a continuous process, the continuity of this process itself equally presupposes the constant disproportion which it has continuously, often violently, to even out.[26]

What Marx offers in this context is not a fully developed theory of crises; the controversy with Ricardo offered no chance for it. He merely had the opportunity of showing the possibility and the form of crises. Their actuality can only be shown on the basis of the developed laws of competition and credit, and by taking into consideration the actual constitution of society, which does not at all consist merely of the classes of workers and industrial capitalists.[27]

---

26   Marx 1968, p. 492.
27   A most interesting attempt to develop Marx's theory of economic crises on the basis of the law of value has been made by Otto Bauer (Bauer 1904).

6 Conclusion

In the present review I have tried to outline Marx's ideas in his critique of Ricardo. No more than a sketchy outline could be offered in the framework of an article, but it would give me the greatest satisfaction to know that I have succeeded in prompting my readers to acquaint themselves with this latest work from Marx's legacy [the second volume of *Theories of Surplus-Value*]. No one with any interest in theoretical study will go through this book without experiencing great pleasure. The peculiarity of Marx's research and method of presentation probably nowhere stands out so sharply and vividly as it does here, where he polemicises with the related but different views of Ricardo, and where he shows in so many examples how a precise conception of the law of value also leads to quantitative analyses of economic phenomena.[28] Especially as regards methodological clarity, the presentation of ground rent, and particularly of absolute rent, is superior in this work compared to the third volume of *Capital*. There Marx posed the question of whether the existence of absolute ground rent is compatible with the law of value, thus proceeding according to the method of Ricardo. But in *Theories of Surplus-Value* he develops absolute rent directly from the law of value, and whoever compares the two presentations will realise how much more fertile the method is in the latter work. Moreover, the presentation is particularly vivid here because of the controversy with Rodbertus. Similarly, the development of differential rent is here more detailed, more profound and in many cases even more significant than in *Capital*, not only because of the confrontation with Ricardo, but especially because here this form of rent is treated in conjunction with and on the basis of absolute rent. However, missing here is the whole development of differential rent II, which arises from the application of various more productive additional capitals to primary production.[29] Ricardo dealt with this form only in passing, and therefore there was no reason for controversy here. On the other hand, this form of rent is not so [very] necessary for understanding the other forms, so that its treatment was not as imperative as that of absolute rent to

---

28 After this, one can judge the validity of Bernstein's scornful remark (Bernstein 1905, p. 569): 'Today we research the laws of price formation more directly than by way of the intricacies of that metaphysical thing called "value"'. Bernstein wants to demonstrate the superfluity of the analysis of the law of value, after having demonstrated in his previous statements, to his own satisfaction, their barrenness. But the superiority of Marx's theory manifests itself precisely in the fact that it explains the phenomena of our economic life, while the marginal utility theory, for example, is merely a theoretical finery, about whose aesthetic value different views can, of course, be held.

29 [For Marx's discussion of differential rent II, see Marx 1992, pp. 812–71].

establish the [causal] connection. Moreover, not only in the field of the theory of rent but also in various other matters, the new work is a most welcome addition to Marx's main theoretical work, particularly in the treatment of the problem of crises. Of course, one can also notice in this work that the master was not destined to put the finishing touches to his work; we find some repetitions, while other matters are dealt with only relatively briefly and aphoristically.

Besides the critique of the foundations of the Ricardian system, the volume also includes a number of digressions concerning individual questions and the historical position of Ricardo's theories. Thus, the positions of [James] Anderson and [Adam] Smith on the theory of rent are discussed in detail, as is the question of the influence of machines on the production and valorisation process in Ricardo and [John] Barton, together with many other questions. However, as interesting as the discussion of all these questions is, the details essentially take second place vis-à-vis the major thrust running through the entire work – its methodological significance.

But it is not the method alone that explains Marx's superiority over Ricardo, apart from the individual circumstances of the two researchers, which we pass over here. A second factor of the utmost importance is the altered point of view.

Every age presents its own problems, i.e. exhibits phenomena that do not fit into the framework of the generally accepted explanations and cannot be reconciled with the complex of related and already known facts in the traditional manner. But natural mental inertia drives people for as long as possible to attempt to squeeze the new phenomena into the old categories, doing them more or less violence, until a researcher appears whose sight is sufficiently unprejudiced to see the inadequacy of the current explanations and to begin the development of science on a new basis. Until that happens, however, the mass and number of new phenomena is always already swollen, and the question arises as to what phenomena the researcher's attention should be turned to in the first place. In doing that, he is not quite free. The formulation of the problem is already a task of science, but posing it antedates that science; here its laws and rules do not apply, and the researcher is greatly influenced by his personal perceptions, his individual fate, his upbringing and occupation, his class membership.

Ricardo was a banker and lived during the youth of capitalism, under the intoxicating influence of the enormous increase in the productivity of social labour. For him, just as for Adam Smith, the goal of the economy was to create the greatest possible wealth, and the goal of his investigation was therefore [to analyse] what conditions must be met in order to further this purpose of producing as much wealth as possible. He saw that capitalism offered means for the achievement of this goal like no other economic system before it, and he therefore considered it to be the consummation of humankind's economic aspirations. And since, in his own time, the internal contradictions of this economic system had not emerged as sharply as they do today, he could overlook them, because his own [theoretical] presuppositions did not predispose him to look for those contradictions. He could always explain the crises that he witnessed as a result of accidents, which did not appear to be essential to capitalism – the major world crises arose only later. Likewise, the class antagonisms of capitalism had not yet entered into the consciousness of society. It was for those reasons that Ricardo could deny the possibility of crises by simply overlooking the fact that the aim of capitalist production is not the satisfaction of needs, but surplus value; and he could blur the class character of capital by regarding it merely as accumulated labour as distinct from actual [living] labour, not as an independent power facing the worker.

Although Ricardo was still so caught up in the bourgeois point of view, he was by no means an apologist for the bourgeoisie. As a true man of science, he drew the conclusions from his theoretical analyses, unconcerned about what class or clique benefitted from them. In this respect, he was very different from his contemporary Malthus, a sycophant of the landlord class. Marx has the highest regard and admiration for the honesty and theoretical impartiality of Ricardo, as opposed to the meanness and vulgarity of Malthus's deferential attitude towards the parasitic classes.

Before he approached the study of economic problems, Marx had been a philosopher and historian, educated in the Hegelian school, but also simultaneously a radical democrat, whose eye was not blinded to the ever more prominent class antagonism between capital and labour. He did not pose the problem as if it were a question of the goal of the economy in general; he inquired into the developmental trends of the historically given economic system, of capitalism. In this way, he adopted an independent, disinterested position. He recognised, as no one before him, the historical justification, the necessity of capitalism, but also its contradictions and its inherent tendencies towards dissolution.

Thus, he could fully appreciate, as no other researcher, the great merit of Ricardo's scientific achievements and, at the same time, account for his historical conditioning and his mistakes.

DOCUMENT 7

The Prehistory of Marxian Economics (1911–12)

Rudolf Hilferding

Source: Rudolf Hilferding, 'Aus der Vorgeschichte der Marxschen Ökonomie', *Die Neue Zeit*, 29. 1910–11, 2. Bd. (1911), H. 43, H. 44, H. 51, pp. 572–81, 620–8, 885–94, and 30. 1911–12, 1. Bd. (1912), H. 10, pp. 343–54.

Introduction by the Editors

Rudolf Hilferding's review of the third volume of *Theories of Surplus-Value* is an outstanding work of scholarship and certainly deserves to be brought to the attention of present-day readers. His account of the logical coherence of Marx's system, and of its relation to alternative views of philosophy and political economy, is so cogently argued that one wonders how it could possibly have escaped the attention of subsequent Marxist scholars. Hilferding wrote his review with two clear intentions in mind: first, to demonstrate the systemic integrity of Marx's work; second, to finally put to rest the long-disputed question of how Marx conceived the relation between science and philosophy.

In the first document of this collection, Marx's Russian reviewer, Illarion Kaufman, already struggled with the relation between science and philosophy. Kaufman thought Marx imposed Hegelian terminology on a work that in fact adopted the scientific approach of the biological sciences. Almost a century later, during the 1960s, this issue reappeared in a new round of debate sparked by the French Marxist Louis Althusser. Whereas Kaufman read Marx in terms of empiricism and an affinity with the natural sciences, Althusser claimed that Marx made an 'epistemological break' with Hegelian philosophy but simultaneously repudiated 'rationalist empiricism'.[1] The contrast between Kaufman and Althusser provides a helpful context in which to situate Hilferding's contribution.

Althusser thought Marx established a firm distinction between 'real' objects – which exist 'outside the head' of the investigator – and the true 'object

---

1 For Althusser's summary of the 'epistemological break', see Althusser 1969, p. 33.

of knowledge', which is 'a thought-object'.² It was this distinction that led Marx to an entirely new approach to science, which Althusser called 'theoretical practice of a scientific character'. Marx began his research not with 'facts' but with the particular 'abstractions' of Generality I (e.g. 'production', 'labour', 'exchange'). Marx then *critically* applied to this 'raw material' concepts from the existing 'theory' of political economy (Generality II), and the outcome was Generality III, a true grasp of the capitalist world as the 'concrete-in-thought'.³

Thought reconstructing itself through thought was Althusser's explanation of dialectical materialism.⁴ Since Althusser believed theoretical practice has its own 'protocols with which to *validate* the quality of its product',⁵ the 'proof' of science depended neither on social class nor on political struggle. Just as Marx thought Hegel misunderstood the true meaning of his own work, so Althusser claimed the identical conclusion applied to Marx, whose writings could only be fully understood through a 'symptomatic' reading aimed at disclosing hidden 'texts' that Marx himself either neglected or was unable to articulate.⁶

Althusser's understanding of Marx would have appeared bizarre to Hilferding, who began his review with two clear convictions: first, that Marx knew perfectly well what he was doing – his manuscript on 'The Method of Political Economy' had finally been published by Kautsky in 1903 – and second, that Marx's work must be seen as a coherent whole, issuing not from any 'epistemological break' with Hegel but rather from a critical reassessment.

Besides drawing upon Marx's own discussion of method, however, Hilferding also relied upon a more recent philosophy of science coming from the Austrian physicist Ernst Mach. Mach's positivism contradicted the influence on Marx coming from Hegel, but Hilferding thought it offered an instructive

---

2 Althusser and Balibar 1970, p. 41. Althusser affirmed this distinction by adding that it involved two entirely different 'production processes': 'While the production process of a given real object, a given real-concrete totality (e.g., a given historical nation) takes place entirely in the real and is carried out according to the real order of *real* genesis (the order of succession of the moments of *historical* genesis), the production process of the object of knowledge takes place entirely in knowledge and is carried out according to *a different order*, in which the thought categories which "reproduce" the real categories do *not* occupy *the same* place as they do in the order of real historical genesis, but quite different places assigned them by their function in the production process of the object of knowledge' (ibid.).

3 Althusser 1969, pp. 183–6.

4 For Althusser's discussion of the self-verifying movement of thought from what he calls Generality I to Generality III, see Althusser 1969, pp. 184–6.

5 Althusser and Balibar 1970, pp. 59–60.

6 Althusser and Balibar 1970, p. 28 and pp. 74–5.

way of conceiving the manner in which science confronts new problems. He summarised Mach's contribution this way:

> Ernst Mach described the development of science as an adaptation of thought to facts and of thoughts to one another. The adaptation of thought to facts is a biological necessity, a condition of the human vital process, in which science is also one of the weapons in the struggle for existence. Starting from this basic biological conception, in which Mach discusses the emergence and beginnings of mechanics or mathematics, he reaches conclusions similar to those of the materialist conception of history. But the adjustment of ideas to each other is a logical function of our thought, arising from its nature; it is simultaneously consequence and cause of the 'economy of thought' that seeks to classify all phenomena, as it were, in the most economical way possible, under the smallest possible number of concepts, and to grasp the fullness of reality under the smallest possible number of laws.

Borrowing Mach's ideas on how and why science progresses, Hilferding attributed the disintegration of the Ricardian system – the subject of the third volume of *Theories of Surplus-Value* – to its inability to accommodate a fundamentally new fact of the industrial revolution: namely, that machinery was increasingly displacing living labour. Gustav Eckstein's review of the second volume of *Theories of Surplus-Value* had already pointed out that Ricardo knew different combinations of labour and machinery must yield different rates of profit. Nevertheless, he treated such cases as exceptions to the general rule that profit derived solely from employment of living labour. Hilferding explains that Ricardo could not accommodate the rising organic composition of capital because he lacked a coherent concept of value that might also explain surplus value and its redistribution between competing capitals. It was precisely this issue that required Marx to begin Volume I of *Capital* with a fundamental reinterpretation of the theory of value.[7]

---

7 It is worth recalling that in the previous document of this collection Gustav Eckstein also dealt with the issue of how thoughts adjust to thoughts until new facts make fundamental reassessments necessary. Here is what Eckstein wrote on that topic: 'Every age presents its own problems, i.e. exhibits phenomena that do not fit into the framework of the generally accepted explanations and cannot be reconciled with the complex of related, already known facts in the traditional manner. But natural mental inertia drives people for as long as possible to attempt to squeeze the new phenomena into the old categories, doing them more or less violence, until a researcher appears whose sight is sufficiently unprejudiced to see the

Since existence determines consciousness, Marx, in his account of the Ricardian school's disintegration, also had to specify the class interests expressed in previous theories of political economy. Thomas Malthus, for example, proved to be a reactionary proponent of landlord interests. Ricardo's confusion over the rate of profit led Malthus back to earlier mercantilist ideas: profit was simply the capitalist's mark-up on production costs. Since profits were accumulated and not matched by any corresponding income going to workers, Malthus decided that crises must follow unless total demand could be supported by the luxurious consumption of landlords, a class that consumed without producing and thereby took goods out of the market rather than contributing to a possible over-supply.

Among the many thinkers whom Marx discussed in portraying the breakdown of the Ricardian system, the most prominent were James Mill, John Ramsay McCulloch and Richard Jones. Hilferding surveys Marx's account of how Mill sought to restore logical consistency to Ricardo's system by explaining away new realities; how McCulloch confused the 'actions' of machinery with living labour and ended with the fetishism of capital; and finally, how Jones criticised Ricardo's method from an historicist point of view. The first three, in Mach's terms, adjusted thought to thoughts, whereas Jones was more concerned with the relation between thoughts and real historical facts.

Hilferding had the highest regard for Jones, who, as a scholar of Indian affairs, clearly saw that Ricardo's theory of rent could not possibly apply in pre-capitalist circumstances. Whereas Ricardo conceived the method of political economy in terms of deductive reasoning issuing in 'purely abstract principles', Jones recognised that patterns of social organisation differ profoundly according to historically conditioned forms of labour and property ownership. Emphasising Jones's pioneering work, Hilferding concluded that while Marx obviously learned much from both Hegel and Ricardo, he also drew upon Jones's *inductive* approach to create an entirely new point of view for interpreting both history and political economy. At the close of his review, Hilferding offered his own reappraisal of the formative influences on Marx coming from these three major predecessors:

> inadequacy of the current explanations and to begin the development of science on a new basis. Until that happens, however, the mass and number of new phenomena is always already swollen, and the question arises as to what phenomena the researcher's attention should be turned to in the first place. In doing that, he is not quite free. The formulation of the problem is already a task of science, but posing it antedates that science; here its laws and rules do not apply, and the researcher is greatly influenced by his personal perceptions, his individual fate, his upbringing and occupation, his class membership'.

By breathing historical life into Ricardo's 'abstract principles', by turning economics into history and history into economics, Marx overcame the unhistorical rationalism of the classics and the irrational conservatism of the historians, along with the utopianism of previous socialism. Economics was now no longer seen as a science of dead things, of the largest possible production or the best possible distribution. It was the understanding of social conditions, of the relations between the classes, of the necessity of the class struggle and its outcome. The conformity to law of the self-development of [Hegel's] Idea became the conformity to law of the will of classes, as determined by their social relationships, which we learned to recognise through economic science. The idea of evolution, stripped of its idealistic form, seized the social sciences.

∴

Rudolf Hilferding's Review of Part 3 of *Theories of Surplus-Value*

The development of the science [of political economy] is of interest in showing how *thought* extracts from the endless multitude of details with which it is initially confronted the simple principles of the thing [*Sache*], the understanding which works within it and controls it (see Smith, Say, and Ricardo).[8]

The economic work of Karl Marx, which began to appear in 1859 with publication of *A Contribution to the Critique of Political Economy*, has taken 51 years to be made public – a process that now, 27 years after the author's death, has concluded with publication of the final volume of *Theories of Surplus-Value*. With painful accuracy, loving care and pious caution, Karl Kautsky, appointed guardian of Marx's estate after Engels's death, has sought to edit from a posthumous manuscript the four books[9] that show us Marx as an historian of economics. Anyone who has had the occasion of looking even fleetingly at Marx's manuscripts in their original version knows what great and laborious work was involved in this editing, and how much the scientific world is indebted to Kautsky. We would not emphasise here this editorial work – which

---

8   Hegel 1996, § 189, p. 227.
9   [The second book of *Theories of Surplus-Value*, dealing with David Ricardo, was issued in two separate volumes in the original German edition: *Theorien über den Mehrwert. Aus dem nachgelassenen Manuskript 'Zur Kritik der politischen Ökonomie'*, hrsg. von Karl Kautsky].

is beyond all praise and whose successful conclusion entailed as necessary conditions not only scientific knowledge but also full devotion to the master's work – were such emphasis not required in order to dispel any suspicion of its omission being dictated by even the slightest personal objection against the editor of Marx's legacy, or of springing from anything but purely scientific interests. In the preface to the second and third volumes of *Capital*, Engels already pointed out to what great lengths he had to go in order to let Marx speak for himself, withdrawing completely behind the work of his friend, and Kautsky has remained faithful to this programme. And yet, we cannot suppress the desire for scientific research to have access to Marx's economic manuscripts in their original form and completeness. However much the editors have been concerned with avoiding subjective judgements, they cannot be completely eliminated in such [editorial] work. The inevitable omissions and additions necessarily appear in the arrangement of the material, giving us a work that does not exclusively spring from Marx's pen. But it would be of the utmost importance to have the Marxian train of thought in all its completeness, for it is the sign of genius, and especially of the genius of Marx's logical energy and incredible power of abstraction, [to develop] series of ideas whose ultimate consequences were first illuminated by phenomena taking place much later, ideas that at the time of their formation hardly revealed their significance to their creator let alone to anyone else. For instance, the significance of Marx's theory of money first becomes completely clear if we try to apply it to the monetary phenomena of recent times, and it leads in many points to conclusions that Marx himself had not yet drawn because his ideas were lacking the impressions that the future would produce; conclusions that we can draw later with very little intellectual exertion.

Thus, many of the statements concerning capitalist credit in the second and third volumes of *Capital* have only become clear, in all their momentous significance, after being illustrated by the modern development of finance capital. And it is precisely the fifth section of the third volume of *Capital* – which contains the brilliant study on interest-bearing capital – that, according to Engels's testimony, has been most revised and is therefore most likely to contain subjective additions by the editor. At the same time, abridgements also had to be made here, mainly of illustrative material going beyond the scope of a readable book.

To this list should be added yet another reason for making the manuscripts accessible to a wider circle of readers. The *Theories of Surplus-Value* offer to their readers, particularly in those parts containing the theoretical digressions, a deep insight into the nature of Marx's thought, which overcame the most difficult problems of scientific research. It is a veritable university of thought that is opened up here, and there is no doubt that such a schooling in logic (*Denklehre*), which would be of incomparable educational value, could still win much from publication of the manuscripts. People would see Marx's thought at its wonderful work; they could make the attempt to follow it and learn what would be impossible to learn anywhere else. If we had academies of sciences deserving of their name, here would be an urgent task for them. As it is, we believe it remains a *nobile officium*, a noble obligation of the German party, the heir to Marx's and Engels's legacy, regardless of financial concerns, to do what, as things stand today, it alone is capable of doing and therefore bound to do. A truly scientific and complete edition of the works of Marx and Engels, for which the need is already asserting itself, would be hardy imaginable without publication of the manuscripts as well. In the meantime, however, provisions should be made to ensure that, as long as this publication has not taken place, at least a number of copies of the manuscripts are made and kept in the archives of the party and perhaps also in a few good libraries.

1   *The Method of Writing the History of Science*

I

> For the objects under consideration must already be known fairly completely before it can be possible to prescribe the rules according to which a science of them is to be obtained.[10]

The *Theories of Surplus-Value* are of great importance not only for the history of the development of economic thought. They are also most interesting from the standpoint of the materialist conception of history, for they show us Marx not only as an economist but also as an actor in the history of science. At the same time, these volumes are the only attempt made thus far to fathom science from the standpoint of the Marxist conception.

If we now examine the presentation of all three volumes in terms of their method, to start with we get a big surprise: this is Hegel! What Marx brings to the presentation is the self-development of economic science, as it starts with the first correct insights of Petty and Franklin (who recognised labour as the common denominator of commodities and money) and ends up in the Marxian system. And the comparison with Hegel suggests itself: for him, the history of philosophy is the self-development of the Idea, which in his

---

10   Kant 1929, p. 94.

own system reaches self-consciousness so that previous history is only the prehistory of Hegelian philosophy in both temporal and logical sequence.

We know that this presentation follows directly from Hegel's conception of history, for which reality is nothing other than the manifestation of the absolute Idea, which develops out of itself in the dialectical process of thesis and antithesis into ever higher forms. We have now become foreign to Hegelian idealism; the conception of reality as a materialisation of the Idea seems to us something completely mystical and incomprehensible. To our reasoning, which springs from totally different presuppositions, his system is comprehensible only historically, as the extreme logical consequence of idealism, as a completion of the thought structure whose basic principles were laid down by Kant, Fichte and Schelling. Let us remember, however, how great was the historical influence of this doctrine, how a whole historical era, with the most prodigious spiritual energy and effort, [confronted] all the problems of the human sciences under its inescapable spell; let us recall the fact that the spiritual revolution associated with the names of Feuerbach and Marx had its starting point in this system, and we will then understand the question that was so overwhelming for Marx's contemporaries that they fell under the influence of this philosophy without resistance and with long-lasting effects.

We know that it was the idea of development, here consistently applied for the first time to all the fields of nature and society, albeit in an idealistic form, that led to the triumph of Hegel's philosophy. The idea that everything that happens is not just a succession of events, but a succession of events necessarily following each other, that this succession takes place according to immanent laws underlying the development, and that only now these laws make themselves understandable for the first time; this idea of development's intrinsic conformity to law was what the Hegelian system begat as the inalienable property of the spiritual treasure of humanity. Even if it was also an idealistic misunderstanding, it was an understanding that suddenly illuminated the hitherto inexplicable course of [historical] events.

And recognition of the self-development of the Idea, as the self-development of socialised humanity or of human society, could appear as confirmation of the mechanism of Hegel's mind, of the dialectic always negating itself again and again, as a Copernican revolution resulting from the most extreme idealism. [Marx] found the driving force of this development in the interaction between people and the real world that surrounds them, expressing itself decisively in the economic activities of humankind. In place of the dialectical self-movement of ideas he set the socially determined human being in all his reality, acting and being acted upon, changing and being changed, as the engine of his own history. And instead of the conformity to law of the absolute [Spirit], he recognised in the conformity to law that underlies [historical] development the conformity of social life to real economic laws.[11]

But the idea of development, however far-reaching the significance of its application to history and thus to the perception of social events, did not by itself turn Hegelian philosophy into the forerunner that prepared the way for social theory.

If reality were nothing but the objectification of the Idea, the Idea could only reach consciousness, and thus the task of philosophy could only be fulfilled, in the conceptual grasp of reality. 'Everywhere in his works', says Lassalle in his preface to the *System of Acquired Rights*, 'Hegel always emphasised tirelessly that philosophy is identical with the *totality of the empirical*, that nothing is more necessary for philosophy than the immersion in the empirical sciences'.[12] And Max Adler says the same:

> If one tries to understand Hegel's philosophy from its motives, clearly developed by Hegel himself, one by no means gets the impression that it is nothing but a mere aberration of fantastic speculation. Rather, the enormous impact that Hegel's philosophy exerted on his contemporaries, and the lasting effects that it has even today, seem to lie in the fact that, despite the form in which it is constructed and its metaphysics of the absolute Spirit, in a sense it represents, vis-à-vis Fichte and Schelling's idealistic philosophy, a *return to reality*, a *tendency* to understand the laws governing *experience* itself, rather than a mere speculation about reality.[13]

Precisely that which contemporary epistemological thought considers a step backwards, was a tremendous step forward *historically*: while Kant focused on the problem of the *forms* of knowledge, and by that very fact drove investigation away from all *content* of cognition, Hegel saw his task precisely in proving the necessity of the content of all experience, a proof he found in the identity of the becoming of experience with the self-development of the concept. Thus reality became again the subject matter of philosophy, and only in that way was it possible for Hegelian philosophy itself to be negated by science, freed from all metaphysics. In contrast to Kantianism, it is the rich content of reality

---

11   [Here Hilferding paraphrases Max Adler: 'The transformation of the Hegelian autonomy of the absolute spirit into the only possible autonomy of the human mind under certain circumstances was nothing but the gradual formation of the materialistic conception of history' (Adler 1908, p. 54)].

12   Lasalle 1861, p. xiii.

13   Adler 1908, p. 12.

in Hegel's thought that gave it such great historical effectiveness. While Kant's thought was lost to his contemporaries precisely in its most fertile kernel of truth – while in general it had a limited effect on the epistemological problem and, according to Otto Bauer's expression, played, from the standpoint of general scientific methodology, a role not to be underestimated as the frontier guard against all metaphysical errors and false formulations of problems – it was from Hegel's philosophy that the tremendous progress of the humanities in our own times sprang forth.

Therefore, by making the Idea the demiurge of reality, Hegel also created a particular method of research. And this method, once stripped of its metaphysical appearances, proved to be extremely fruitful, for it actually corresponded to the nature of intellectual research. We know from Marx himself how he deliberately transferred Hegel's method to economics. In fact, this transference is not primarily to be found where it is usually sought: in the presentation of real antagonisms between classes and in discovery of the contradiction between the socio-historical limitations of the capitalist mode of production and the social need, whose bearer is the proletariat, to control the productive forces that sprang from capitalist organisation but are more and more outgrowing it. Instead, it fulfilled its specific logical role in the way in which economic concepts were developed and presented [by Marx].[14] Marx explained this aspect very clearly in the Introduction to *A Contribution to the Critique of Political Economy*:

---

14 In his excellent essay, 'Marx and the Dialectic', printed as an appendix to his pamphlet *Marx as Thinker*, Max Adler has uncovered the causes of the confusion about the concept of dialectics, which consists of the fact that in Hegel two very different things appear under the same name of dialectics, sometimes a way of thinking, i.e. a method, and sometimes a way of being, that is an essential condition. 'If we call these two meanings, which indeed had to come together as a result of the identity standpoint of Hegel's philosophy, with special names, if we call the method, i.e. the demonstration of the contradictory character of *thought* in the flow of its contents *dialectics*, as Hegel himself did, and the contradictory character of *being* in the course of its real processes *antagonism*, it becomes at once clear what completely disparate things the Hegelian dialectic could unite, above all because it was not just merely a method.

'The criticism and overcoming of Hegel consisted for Marx now in the tearing apart of that mystical appearance in which *dialectics* are constituted at the same time as *antagonism*, and this was done by that luminous insight which dissolved the metaphysical character of Hegelian dialectic while at the same time preserved its method, showing that the self-movement of the logical categories was only the movement of individual thought, through which the latter went from one determination of thought to another. In this way the mystification of the thought process as a creative power was eliminated, thought [was no longer considered] as a movement creating the world out of itself, while at the

It would seem to be the proper thing seems to start with the real and concrete elements, with the actual pre-conditions, e.g., to start in the sphere of economy with population, which forms the basis and the subject of the whole social process of production. Closer consideration shows, however, that this is wrong. Population is an abstraction if, for instance, one disregards the classes of which it is composed. These classes in turn remain empty terms if one does not know the factors on which they depend, e.g., wage-labour, capital, and so on. These presuppose exchange, division of labour, prices, etc. For example, capital is nothing without wage-labour, without value, money, price, etc. If one were to take population as the point of departure, it would be a very vague notion of a complex whole and through closer definition one would arrive analytically at increasingly simple concepts; from imaginary concrete terms one would move to more and more tenuous abstractions until one reached the most simple definitions. From there it would be necessary to make the journey again in the opposite direction until one arrived once more at the concept of population, which is this time not a vague definition of a whole, but a totality comprising many determinations and relations. The first course is the historical one taken by political economy at its inception. The seventeenth-century economists, for example, always took as their starting point the living organism, the population, the nation, the State, several States, etc., but analysis led them always in the end to the discovery of a few decisive, abstract, general relations such as division of labour, money, and value. When these separate factors were more or less clearly deduced and established, economic systems were evolved from which simple concepts, such as labour, division of labour, demand, exchange-value, advanced to categories like State, international exchange and world market. The latter is obviously the correct scientific method. The concrete is concrete because it is a synthesis of many determinations, thus representing the unity of diverse aspects. It appears therefore in reasoning as a summing-up, a result, and not as the starting point, although it is the real point of origin and thus also the point of origin of perception [*Anschauung*] and imagination. The first procedure attenuates meaningful images to abstract definitions, the second leads from abstract definitions by way of

same time Hegel's deep insight into thought itself, as a peculiar movement, was retained. Thought was no longer conceived of as the external connection of rigid concepts, but as the passing over and emerging from one another of all its determinations, as an *internal conformity to law* – that was the core of the dialectic, which Marx and Engels did not allow to get lost again' (Adler 1908, p. 86).

reasoning thought to the reproduction of the concrete situation.[15] Hegel accordingly conceived the illusory idea that the real world is the result of thinking which causes its own synthesis, its own deepening and its own movement; whereas the method of advancing from the abstract to the concrete is simply the way in which thinking assimilates the concrete and reproduces it as a concrete mental category. This is, however, by no means the process of evolution of the concrete world itself. For example, the simplest economic category, e.g., exchange-value, presupposes population, a population moreover which produces under definite conditions, as well as a distinct kind of family, or community, or State, etc. Exchange-value cannot exist except as an abstract, *unilateral* relation of an already existing concrete organic whole. But exchange-value as a category leads an antediluvian existence. Thus to consciousness – and this comprises philosophical consciousness – which regards the comprehending mind as the real man, and hence the comprehended world as such as the only real world; to consciousness, therefore, the evolution of categories appears as the actual process of production – which unfortunately is given an impulse from outside – whose result is the world; and this (which is, however, again a tautological expression) is true in so far as the concrete totality regarded as a conceptual, as a mental phenomenon fact, is indeed a product of thinking, of comprehension; but it is by no means a product of the Idea which evolves spontaneously and whose thinking proceeds outside and above perception and imagination, but is the result of the assimilation and transformation of perceptions and images into concepts. The totality, as a conceptual entity seen by the intellect is a product of the thinking intellect which assimilates the world in the only

---

15   We know that in thought we go from composite concretes to simple universals by way of abstraction. 'The decisive role of abstraction in enquiry is obvious. We can neither keep track of all the details of a phenomenon nor would it be sensible to do so. We take notice of those features that are of interest to us, and of those that depend on them. The enquirer's first task is thus to compare different cases in order to emphasize the mutually dependent features and to set aside as incidental or irrelevant for the purpose in hand all the rest that have no bearing on the situation examined. This process of abstraction can yield highly important discoveries; as Apelt [Apelt 1854, p. 59] points out, in consciousness the compound and special always precedes the simple and general: the latter is secured only by abstraction which is thus the method for seeking principles' (Mach 1975, pp. 99–100). This alone shows how wrong it is to equate deduction and induction as equivalent sources of knowledge. Rather, deduction alone is a scientific rendition (*Darstellungsart*: modality of representation), which must however be intellectually preceded by induction, in order for deduction to be able finally to go from the universal to representation of the particular.

way open to it, a way which differs from the artistic, religious and practically intelligent assimilation of this world. The concrete subject remains outside the intellect and independent of it – that is, so long as the intellect adopts a purely speculative, purely theoretical attitude. The subject, society, must always be envisaged therefore as the pre-condition of comprehension even when the theoretical method is employed.[16]

Furthermore – and this reinforces the appearance of Hegel's construction – the (logically) simple categories can also have really existed historically before the more concrete ones, so that historical development at the same time appears as logical.

Money may exist, and did exist historically, before capital existed, before banks existed, before wage labour existed, etc. Thus in this respect it may be said that the simpler category can express the dominant relations of a less developed whole, or else those subordinate relations of a more developed whole which already had a historic existence before this whole developed in the direction expressed by a more concrete category. To that extent the path of abstract thought, rising from the simple to the combined, would correspond to the real historical process.[17]

We can see that what Hegel teaches as ontology[18] is also, or rather is in reality, the method, the course [of development] of scientific thought. Once the metaphysical garb is cast off, the idea of development underlying the Hegelian

---

16   Marx 1970, pp. 205–7.
17   Marx 1993, p. 102.
18   Cf., for example, the following passage: 'The determinations in the development of the concept are on the one hand themselves concepts, but on the other hand, since the concept is essentially Idea, they have the form of existence [*Dasein*], and the series of concepts which results is therefore at the same time a series of *shapes*; this is how science should regard them.
    'In the more speculative sense, the *mode of existence* of a concept and its *determinacy* are one and the same thing. But it should be noted that the moments, whose result is a further determined form [of the concept], precede it as determinations of the concept in the scientific development of the Idea, but do not come before it as shapes in its temporal development. Thus the Idea, in its determination as the family, presupposes those determinations of the concept from which, in a later section of this work, it [i.e. the Idea] will be shown to result. But the other side of this development is that these inner presuppositions should also be present for themselves as *shapes*, such as the right of property, contract, morality, etc., and it is only at a more advanced stage of culture

conception must lead to very fruitful results, and nowhere are they more fertile than in the field of history, which, in the opinion of bourgeois rationalism of the eighteenth century, was a jumble of nonsense and fortuitous events, into which Enlightenment, for the first time, would be able artificially to introduce reason from outside, because then enlightened people would begin to 'make history', replacing the lack of discernment [that had prevailed] in all previous eras. By looking for reason in history, Hegel first formulated – if still in a metaphysical way – the problem of its necessary course [of development] in accordance with laws. Everything that is, and everything that was, is rational[19] – this proposition, as Engels showed in *Ludwig Feuerbach and the End of Classical German Philosophy*, was not only revolutionary because it agrees with rationalism, the ideology of the revolutionary bourgeoisie, in bringing everything that exists before the tribunal of reason and discarding as irrational everything that exists in the eternally renewed progress of its self-development; it also opened up the bourgeois world in general to historical understanding for the first time. Until then historical insight was much more the inheritance of classes that were threatened in their rule and invoked history in order to justify that rule,

---

[*Bildung*] that the moments of development attain this distinctive shape of existence' (Hegel 1996, § 32, pp. 60–1).

Cf. also the addition to this paragraph: 'The Idea must continually determine itself further within itself, for it is initially no more than an abstract concept. But this initial abstract concept is never abandoned. On the contrary, it merely becomes continually richer in itself, so that the last determination is also the richest ... We merely wish to observe how the concept determines itself, and we force ourselves not to add anything of our own thoughts and opinions. What we obtain in this way, however, is a series of thoughts and another series of existent shapes, in which it may happen that the temporal sequence of their actual appearance is to some extent different from the conceptual sequence. Thus, we cannot say, for example, that property existed before the family, although property is nevertheless dealt with first. One might accordingly ask at this point why we do not begin with the highest instance, that is, with the concretely true. The answer will be that we wish to see the truth precisely in the form of a result, and it is essential for this purpose that we should first comprehend the abstract concept itself. What is actual, the shape which the concept assumes, is therefore from our point of view only the subsequent and further stage, even if it should itself come first in actuality. The course we follow is that whereby the abstract forms reveal themselves not as existing for themselves, but as untrue' (Hegel 1996, § 32, pp. 61–2).

Cf. also the famous statement on his method that Marx gave in the second preface to *Capital*.

19 ['Was vernünftig ist, das ist wirklich; und was wirklich ist, das ist vernünftig' (Hegel 1972, *Grundlinien der Philosophie des Rechts*, Frankfurt am Main, s. 11), translated as 'What is rational is actual; and what is actual is rational' (Hegel 1996, p. 20, Preface)].

while the revolutionary bourgeoisie, starting from natural law, rejected previous history as irrational. It was generally the conservative writers who, vis-à-vis revolutionary-liberal ones, had the deeper understanding of history. Indeed rationalism, precisely because of the greater simplicity and straightforwardness in the thought of revolutionary classes focused on their struggle, was also originally the way of thinking of the working class awakening to its emancipatory strivings, which again and again, despite the very different approach of Marxism, strove to see socialist solutions not in their historical conditionality and relativity but as absolute postulates of rational thought. The insight into the historical conditionality of all social events, and therefore also into the relative necessity and the eventual demise of capitalism, as it stands in magnificent simplicity in the *Communist Manifesto* for instance, was handed down as a direct heritage from Hegel to Marxism,[20] and only the knowledge of economic phenomena as historical ones made possible the fruitful work of *Capital*.

If, however, according to Hegel, reality is the gradual realisation of the Idea, the grasping of this reality, that is science, must reflect those gradations, so that between the history of science and the real development there is a thoroughgoing parallelism. Just as in reality the Idea came to ever higher completion in objectivity, so it came, at the same time, to progressive self-consciousness in the minds of men. The writing of the history of science should therefore describe this progressive realisation, which corresponds precisely to the real development. Thus, the historical presentation of science must be able to show how the completed system arose from the first beginnings in a sequence that corresponds throughout to logical deduction.

Hegel's philosophy, therefore, naturally meant a revolution in previous historiography. In place of a pragmatic representation in chronological sequence, the self-development of the Idea had to be demonstrated in all areas of physical and spiritual events. Hegel himself tried his hand at the history of philosophy.

---

20 But it reads as a direct rejection of any utopianism when Hegel says: 'It is *this very relation of philosophy to actuality* which is the subject of misunderstandings, and I accordingly come back to my earlier observation that, since philosophy is *exploration of the rational*, it is for that very reason *the comprehension of the present and the actual*, not the setting up of a *world beyond* which exists God knows where – or rather, of which we can very well say that we know where it exists, namely in the errors of a one-sided and empty ratiocination' (Hegel 1996, Preface, p. xix). 'Like empiricism, philosophy, too (§ 7), knows only what *is*; it does not know [*weiss*] what only *ought* to be and thus *is not there*' (Hegel 2010a, § 38, p. 79). It is in general a legacy of Hegel's idea – that nothing is more hateful than the manufacture of ready recipes about what *ought to be* – that protected Marx from the start against all temptations of utopian socialism.

The attempt failed and was bound to fail, because the ontological assumption that reality is only a product of the Idea, and that the succession of philosophical systems therefore had to be the same as the sequence of logical concepts in the deduction of the Hegelian system, proved to be inappropriate, and instead of historical writing led to arbitrary constructions. As Eduard Zeller says, 'any survey of the past will show us how impossible it is to recognise, even approximately, the order of the Hegelian or any other speculative logic in the order of philosophic systems, unless we make out of them something quite different from what they really are. This attempt is, therefore, a failure both in principle and practice, and the truth that it contains is only the universal conviction that the development of history is internally governed by regular laws'.[21]

But the question again posed itself: What is that legitimate kernel that misled Hegel in his historical writing; what is the real content underlying his illusion? And the answer to this question is all the more urgent, because it was precisely Marx's presentation that led us back to Hegel's historical writing. Perhaps we may come closer to the answer if we inquire into the specific conditions that the history of science imposes upon its researcher.

II

Ernst Mach described the development of science as an adaptation of thought to facts and of thoughts to one another. The adaptation of thought to facts is a biological necessity, a condition of the human vital process, in which science is also one of the weapons in the struggle for existence. Starting from this basic biological conception, in which Mach discusses the emergence and beginnings of mechanics or mathematics, he reaches conclusions similar to those of the materialist conception of history. But the adjustment of ideas to each other is a logical function of our thought, arising from its nature; it is simultaneously consequence and cause of the 'economy of thought' that seeks to classify all phenomena, as it were, in the most economical way possible, under the smallest possible number of concepts, and to grasp the fullness of reality under the smallest possible number of laws.[22]

Starting from completely different premises, Kant described the accordance of judgements with the unity of cognition as the criterion of scientific experience. What Mach describes as a process, as the ever-renewing course of adapt-

---

21   Zeller 1881, Vol. I, p. 14.
22   To think 'economically', that is, to subsume the elements common in different phenomena, thought operates with abstraction. '*Production in general* is an abstraction, but a sensible abstraction in so far as it actually emphasises and defines the common aspects and thus avoids repetition' (Marx 1970, p. 190).

ations, is posited [by Kant] from the beginning as a result, as a logical condition of truth. But since the unity of cognition is again made problematic by any new knowledge, truth is also given as process, and the truth achieved every time is only a temporary moment in the eternal search for truth. But the unity of cognition, the agreement of ideas with each other, is at any given moment a requirement of our thinking.

The adaptation of thoughts to each other thus appears as a vehicle of scientific progress, resulting from the nature of thought itself and following from pursuit of the unity of cognition. What in Hegel is the self-development of the Idea, appears here as a biological-natural property of thought that constitutes a condition for scientific progress.

In reality, however, the adaptation of ideas to facts and the adaptation of thoughts to one another are quite different processes, and have a completely different significance for the development of science. The adaptation of thoughts to one another is the common condition of scientific thought in general; it is a logical prerequisite for scientific thought to be possible at all. The logical power of individual thinkers is certainly different, and therefore one researcher may discover in the complex of thoughts logical inconsistencies that another had overlooked. And thus within a scientific system, by purely logical work, there develops a tighter systematisation and an adjustment of the individual elements of thought, a progress towards greater consolidation. An example: Adam Smith determined the value of commodities by the amount of labour required for their production. This determination is mixed up and replaced by him with another, according to which the value of commodities is determined by the amount of commodities (e.g. corn), with which a definite amount of living labour can be purchased. He even lets the value of a pair of shoes be determined by the 10 hours of labour that their production required; then again, he determines the value of these hours of labour by a bushel of corn, the wage of a worker for a 10-hour working day. The second determination is logically mistaken, because it lets value be determined by value, and therefore includes a circular argument. It is also, at the same time, mistaken in reality, because the worker in *capitalist* society (although not in simple commodity production, from whose conditions Smith's illusion arose)[23] does not receive for 10 hours of labour the value of 10 hours. Ricardo demonstrated this logical fallacy and thus eliminated the erroneous equation of the determination of value by labour time with its determination by the 'price of labour'. He retained, however, the category 'value of labour', and with it the

---

23   Marx 1859, p. 42, and Marx 1905–10, pp. 126 ff.

logical inconsistency according to which the value, for example, of 10 hours of labour is precisely 10 hours, but the worker receives for them less value, otherwise no surplus value would be possible. This logical contradiction was then removed by Marx, who showed that the 'value of labour' has no economic reality at all, and that it is only the expression for the value of labour power, which is determined by the labour time required for its production. The capitalist buys the labour power, whose production costs, for instance, the 5 hours of labour required to produce the necessities consumed by the worker, while the worker works, for example, 10 hours, during which he produces a value of 10 hours, for whose appropriation the capitalist must pay wages worth only 5 hours.

By disclosing this appearance, Marx also discovered the foundations on which he could build his theory of surplus value, which is much more developed vis-à-vis Ricardo's. From the outset, Marx's economic thought began with the adjustment of economic thought, as formulated in classical theory, to facts with which it evidently no longer agreed. And here again, his cardinal problem was the question of how the equality of the profit [rate] of capital is compatible with the validity of the law of value. Ricardo himself had already seen the problem, but he referred to the deviation of prices from values, resulting from the equalisation of profits, as an occasional deviation from the law of value, as an exception to the rule. What was intellectually still tolerable in Ricardo's time, when differences in the organic composition of capitals were relatively unimportant – even though the contradiction arose immediately – had already become unbearable in Marx's time and led to abandonment of the foundations of the theory. The new facts, which economic development had brought into being, called for the adaptation of thought, and this again made that which previously still seemed logically possible now appear inadequate or irrelevant. To solve the problem of [the equalisation of] the rate of profit, the deeply penetrating analysis and renewal of the theory of value, contained in the first volume of *Capital*, became necessary. That this was in fact the psychological course of development of Marx's thought is already evident, apart from methodological considerations, in the formulation of the problem in the *Critique of Political Economy* (2nd edition, p. 44ff.). But it also follows from the way in which all these problems appear as logical problems, as tasks of adaptation.

But, at the same time, from this also follows the insight that the decisive thing for scientific progress is new *facts*. If, in the field of natural sciences, these facts are above all the new problems posed by technology, in the social sciences they are the new social facts created by economic development. The adaptation of thoughts to one another is only the *condition* of scientific progress; the adaptation of thought to facts, however, is progress itself. At the same time, in the fulfilment of this condition [i.e. in the adaptation of thoughts to one another], appear the personal, individual barriers represented by the thinking power of the individual researchers, so that in the same objective conditions, i.e. in presence of the same complexes of facts, advances in knowledge are made possible by the fact that the greater thinker still carries out adjustments of thought processes to one another, whereas the weaker thinker considers the problems already solved. This distinction between subjective and objective thought conditions is an important problem for Marxist historical writing, a warning against simplifying too much in deriving ideological phenomena [from material conditions], thus running the risk of overlooking the independent part played by conscious processes in scientific progress.

This adjustment, however, can also be of a different kind. It is possible for the scientific acquisition of new facts to make the previous views completely impossible, either causing the scientific system to break down completely or else removing, extending, modifying and restricting only parts of it, while leaving the foundations untouched. Now, economic theory – to the extent that Marx considers it in the *Theories of Surplus-Value* – is the explanation of capitalist society, whose basic fact is commodity production. This basic organisation of economic life, which remains constant despite all the colossal and tempestuous development, explains why economic theory also reflects this development, why it retains the basic laws already discovered very early on, just developing them further without ever completely giving them up. The actual development of capitalism thus corresponds to the logical development of the theory. From the first formulation of the law of labour value, in Petty and Franklin, to the subtlest remarks of the second and third volume of *Capital*, a logical development thus arises. And this is, on the one hand, really so and cannot be otherwise, since science is only the conceptual grasp of reality (which can only be understood as a development from simple commodity production to the capitalist world market), whose foundations were thus already revealed in its simplest and most general connections by the first thinkers. On the other hand, however, it is also mere appearance.

As Marx looked in economics for the internal law of motion of society, so also in presentation of the theory he also looked for the internal course of development, which alone offers the correct understanding. This internal path is, however, the unfolding of the labour theory of value; everything that leads away from this is irrelevant for development of the theory and does not come into consideration for its real history. As history in Hegel only begins with the building of the state, and stateless nations have no history, so for Marx economic theory begins with the first discovery of labour as a measure of value. Except that this position is just as arbitrary as, for instance, that of modern chemists, who date the history of modern chemistry from the discovery of oxygen and recognition of its importance for the combustion process. Of course, in this case too there is a difference between the history of the social sciences and that of the natural sciences. A history of mechanics, for example, showing us the development of knowledge from its beginnings to the present, would essentially contain the presentation of real scientific progress, and in this way it would satisfy our historical interest. The listing of all the countless mistakes that unscientific speculation brought to this area lacks scientific-historical interest, even if they possess antique charm or if, from a very different standpoint, some of their assumptions may interest the cultural historians. It is different with the history of economics; here the opposition to scientific ideas, the holding of opinions unscientific in the strict sense, if only they were widely held, is historically important – though certainly not for the development of pure economic theory – because particular political opinions were hiding within them. Thus, the opinions of Malthus against the labour theory of value are, at the same time, a defence of aristocratic and high-church interests against liberal-bourgeois industrial demands. But the inclusion of all these doctrines, leading away from development of the labour theory of value, would immediately have destroyed the image of logical development, as it now unfolds for us in the *Theories of Surplus-Value*. Marx, however, did not omit them for constructive purposes, but because in fact they have no interest for writing the history of *political economy*, only for a history of sociological opinions foreign to pure economics. The opinions at variance with the development of the labour theory of value are explained by economic-political interests; they are therefore at odds with scientific impartiality, in contradiction with the inner necessity of scientific development, and thus fall outside the framework of an account that wants to show only that inner necessity.

What Marx offers us, then, is not a history of economic theory in its historical and sociological significance – that is, above all, in its significance for practical economic policy – but rather the discovery of its inner development, which presents itself naturally as a logical sequence. He thus made possible, for the first time, a real understanding of the course of development of the theory, which now appears not as a random sequence of hypotheses and doctrines but as a natural system of thoughts that [not only] follow each other but also emerge from each other. The disturbing accessories of elements foreign to this development, even if they had very great appeal in their time, are removed [by Marx]. Of course, such historical writing, which does not proceed pragmatically-chronologically but only reveals the hidden layout of the structure, is only possible from a specific standpoint.[24] The history of economics, as Marx writes it, is at the same time the phylogenetic and partly also the ontogenetic developmental history of the Marxian system. But it is a silly claim that it should be otherwise. Such a demand would mean nothing less than that economic theorists should relinquish what constitutes precisely the criterion of any scientific insight, the universal validity of its results. If they are asked to do that, they should consider the results of their research only as a subjective, more or less probable conviction, rather than as an objective, that is generally valid, scientific statement – an unreasonable demand that can only be made by someone who denies the possibility of social science in general.

This is the case because, in writing the history of economics, as with any other science, what Zeller said about writing the history of philosophy applies:

> Whether in regard to the history of Philosophy it is necessary or even advantageous for the writer to possess any philosophic conviction of his own, is a question that would scarcely have been raised had not the dread of a philosophic construction of history caused some minds to overlook the most simple and obvious truths. Few would maintain that the history of law, for instance, would find its best exponent in a person who had no opinions on the subject of jurisprudence; or political history, in one who embraced no theory of politics. It is hard to see why it should be otherwise with the history of Philosophy. How can the historian even understand the doctrines of the philosophers; by what standard is he to judge of their importance; how can he discern the internal connection of the systems, or form any opinion respecting their reciprocal relations, unless he is guided in his labours by fixed philosophic principles? But the more developed and mutually consistent these principles are, the more must we ascribe to him a definite system; and since clearly developed and consistent principles are undoubtedly to be desired in a writer of history, we cannot avoid the conclusion that it is necessary and good that he should bring with him to the study of the earlier Philosophy a philosophic system of his own. It is possible, indeed, that his system may be too contracted to interpret for him the meaning of his predecessors; it is also possible that he may apply it to history in a perverse manner, by introducing his own opinions into the doctrines of previous philosophers, and constructing out of his

---

24 Hence the absolute discrepancy between Böhm-Bawerk's history of the theories of interest and Marx's exposition. Böhm-Bawerk considers important precisely what Marx rejects as unscientific [Cf. Böhm-Bawerk 1890].

own system that which he should have tried to understand by its help. But we must not make the general principle answerable for these faults of individuals; and still less can we hope to escape them by entering on the history of Philosophy devoid of any philosophic conviction. The human mind is not like a *tabula rasa*, the facts of history are not simply reflected in it like a picture on a photographic plate, but every view of a given occurrence is arrived at by independent observation, combination, and judgment of the facts. Philosophic impartiality, therefore, does not consist in the absence of all presuppositions, but in bringing to the study of past events presuppositions that are true. The man who is without any philosophic standpoint is not on that account without any standpoint whatever; he who has formed no scientific opinion on philosophic questions has an unscientific opinion about them. To say that we should bring to the history of Philosophy no philosophy of our own, really means that in dealing with it we should give the preference to unscientific notions as compared with scientific ideas. And the same reasoning would apply to the assertion that the historian ought to form his system in the course of writing his history, from history itself; that by means of history he is to emancipate himself from any preconceived system, in order thus to attain the universal and the true. From what point of view then is he to regard history, that it may do him this service? From the false and narrow point of view which he must quit that he may rightly comprehend history? Or from the universal point of view which history itself must first enable him to attain? The one is manifestly as impracticable as the other, and we are ultimately confined within this circle: that he alone completely understands the history of Philosophy who possesses true and complete philosophy; and that he only arrives at true philosophy who is led to it by understanding history. Nor can this circle ever be entirely escaped: the history of Philosophy is the test of the truth of systems; and to have a philosophic system is the condition of a man's understanding history. The truer and the more comprehensive a philosophy is, the better will it teach us the importance of previous philosophies; and the more unintelligible we find the history of Philosophy, the greater reason have we to doubt the truth of our own philosophic conceptions. But the only conclusion to be drawn from this is that we ought never to regard the work of science as finished in the historic any more than in the philosophic domain. As in a general manner, Philosophy and Experimental Science mutually require and condition one another, so it is here. Each forward movement of philosophic knowledge offers new points of view to historic reflection, facilitates the comprehension of the earlier systems, of their interconnection and relations; while, on the other hand, each newly attained perception of the manner in which the problems of Philosophy have been solved or regarded by others, and of the internal connection and consequences of their theories, instructs us afresh concerning the questions which Philosophy has to answer, the different courses it may pursue in answering them, and the consequences which may be anticipated from the adoption of each course.[25]

We must therefore also consider the new light that the *Theories of Surplus-Value* has cast upon previous economic research as an indirect proof of the truth of Marx's economic concepts.

However, the logical presentation hides, on the other hand, the contrast between Marx and his predecessors arising from their sociological positions and, what is more important, from the fundamental dissimilarity of their social-theoretical views. What distinguishes Marx from all his predecessors is the social theory underlying his system, the *materialist conception of history*. Not just because it implies the realisation that economic categories are also historical – this insight alone is not the essential thing – but rather because only discovery of the contradictory character of social life made possible discovery of the development mechanism and the description of how economic categories arise, change and cease to exist, and how all this takes place according to certain laws. This was possible only through the discovery of socialised man and the type of social relations [in which he is embedded] as the reality behind the material appearance of economic relations, so that in economics the general ideas underlying the materialist conception of history about social man, as the motive force of history, were demonstrated in particular, thus destroying the material appearance, the economic fetishism, and revealing the actions of living men behind the price movements, the turnover of commodities and so on.

Precisely this peculiarity of Marxism remains in the dark in the logical presentation of *Theories of Surplus-Value*, so that Marx himself appears only as someone who rounds off rather than revolutionises his science. But the underlying causes in the development of previous economics also do not at first appear in Marx's historical writing. The reason is as follows.

Often what appears as a logical adaptation of thoughts to each other is in fact first triggered by the emergence of new facts and the need to explain them. But if this new fact is not particularly emphasised as the cause of the specific

---

25 Zeller 1881, Vol. I, pp. 22–5.

formulation of the problem, because in the intellectual context it is not the fact but the solution of the problem that appears as the essential thing, the appearance can easily arise that a new logical conclusion has simply emerged from the existing ideas because the logically perfect and consistent thought has only now come into (logical) contradiction with the other thoughts, causing a new adaptation of thoughts to one another. Thus arises, once again, the appearance of a purely logical development of systems of ideas in a science.

Now, that is the way Marx proceeds in the main in *Theories of Surplus-Value*. Materialist historical writing should proceed historically-genetically; it should show, on the basis of the presentation of the stage of economic and historical development already reached, what problems were actually posed to economic thinking; how, for instance, to single out one case very generally, due to the devaluation caused by the influx of precious metals following the discovery of America, and as a result of the debasement of coin by the princes, the problem of the relationship between commodity and money arose; how this issue gained new urgency and demanded a more accurate formulation due to the state experiments with paper currency and its devaluation (which, for example, induced Ricardo to undertake his investigations [of the currency issue]); [or] how the introduction of machinery led to a distinction between the material and personal components of capital and brought to the centre of economic research the problem of the equalisation of the rate of profit, which seemed inconsistent with the labour theory of value. And next to this objective emergence of the problems, a historical-genetic exposition must also show how the attempted explanations of the economists were conditioned by the subjective opinions of the authors as representatives of certain economic-class interests, and how economic-policy motives and interests influenced economical-theoretical views. The rule of the mercantilists, the Physiocrats, the theories of Adam Smith and Ricardo, and the break-up of these theories in the conservative reaction of Malthus, on the one hand, and the ethical-socialist opposition of the Socialists, on the other hand, are indeed only the expression of the economic rule first of commercial and then of industrial capital, and of their being challenged by the conservative-agrarian strata, on the one hand, and by the emerging proletariat, on the other.

The presentation of all these moments, which would prove the history of political economy to be only an ideological reflection of real economic development – since the retroactive effect of ideology [on the economy] would again be particularly posed – does not appear in the *Theories of Surplus-Value*. This can be explained only partly due to the plan of work, as we know it from *A Contribution to the Critique of Political Economy*. There, Marx first gave the theoretical development of economic categories, for instance, commodity or money.

The theoretical presentation was then followed by an historical account of the development of the concept in previous economics. From the beginning, all the emphasis was placed on proving the logical (scientific) development of the concept, while the psychological explanation as to why the authors arrived at their conceptualisation due to concrete economic conditions faded into the background, although it was often masterfully sketched with some strokes. In *Theories of Surplus-Value*, the logical interest comes to the fore even more strongly than in *A Contribution to the Critique of Political Economy*. But that is totally correct; in the history of any science, real understanding first requires the presentation of what Marx calls its internal course of development. Only in this way can the essential [phenomena], which are really relevant for the development [of that science], be separated from the inessential and irrelevant. Presentation of the logical development is thus the preparatory work that must be performed in order to proceed to the historical-genetic explanation.

Precisely the *Theories of Surplus-Value* are a proof of how fruitful this preparatory work is, indeed, how it is the really essential thing to be accomplished. The chaos of innumerable economic doctrines is organised for the first time. And the ordering principle is nothing arbitrary, brought into the course [of development] of the science from outside. Rather, the inner link, binding all the thoughts essential for the progress of knowledge, is made visible. In this case, too, Marx proves to be the great realist who spotted, behind the bewildering variety of phenomena, the law of their becoming.

But from the nature of the represented object also follows another [thing], which at least partially annuls what we have just come to know as a defect. We know that economic theories are based on recognition of the conformity of social life to law, but this conformity to law must be researched in order to regulate social life on the basis of this knowledge; theory is in the service of policy, just as science in general is in the service of practice, which does not change the fact that the ideal of every scientific worker must be to pursue science for science's sake, as long as he just pursues scientific research. But since economics serves economic policy, the economists are motivated or determined in their scientific statements by economic-policy ideals and interests. These are expressed consciously or unconsciously in their scientific opinions. But what in the historical-genetic study, through which the researchers have arrived at their results, would be a prerequisite, appears in the economic system itself as a result, as a postulation of the economic policy of the researcher. By analysing the economists, often pursuing the economic-policy consequences of their systems to the last detail, Marx lays bare in a most surprising way the class influences from which the system grew and the practical impulses behind the theoretical opinions. This task is indisputably carried out most masterfully in the examination of the Physiocrats, where the presentation of practical policy reveals all the mysteries in the theory that so often led previous researchers astray.

But the fact that such historical-genetic knowledge can be gained directly from the logical examination of the system is accounted for by the nature of social science. Social thought is determined by social being, which again includes within itself the thinking people. What determines man appears to him as a goal of his will, because will can only be determined by awakening certain goals in the willing subject. Only by his pursuit of those goals, by acting in a purposeful way, can necessity come into being. That man has a *goal*, and that therefore the act can only be realised by him as an agent, gives man consciousness of his free will; but that he *must* have that goal accounts, for the outside observer, for the necessity of human history and the possibility of its knowledge. But in his economic policy the economic researcher sets for himself those goals, whose knowledge at the same time betrays his motives to the outside observer. By upholding in their policies the goals of industrial capital, the Physiocrats, who seemed in theory to appear as representatives of landed property, revealed themselves to us as spokesmen of the capitalist class, and the knowledge of their motives explains also the peculiarity of their theoretical position.

2   *From Ricardo to Jones*

The appearance of the third volume of *Theories of Surplus-Value* also definitely documents and puts an end to an old legend. When the third volume of *Capital* appeared, bourgeois economists argued that the explanation of the equalisation of the profit rate stands in contradiction with the labour theory of value in the first volume. [They argued that] Marx had actually been unable to explain the problem on the basis of his theory of value – something that he, the strong logician, must have been conscious of. But since he had announced the solution, whose impossibility he must surely have felt in the course of his investigation, he pretended to offer a sham solution with the help of the dialectical art of the third volume. The discoverer's glory for this profound view belongs to the Italian University Professor [Achille] Loria. Mr. Böhm-Bawerk freely translated it into German, and for a while it was the *communis opinio*, the common opinion of many professors of economics. Certainly the study of the three volumes [of *Capital*], which together revealed Marx's economics for the first time – whereas on the basis of the first volume alone, ideas had to arise that were necessarily incomplete and even mistaken – had to make every unbiased student realise that the entire work, in all its individual investigations, in the exact analysis of surplus value and its rate, in the distinction between constant and variable and between fixed and circulating capital, in the observation of the conditions of circulation, was precisely aimed at the solution of the problem, which had already been posed by Ricardo and around which the whole post-Ricardian economics turned to a large extent. But the allegation that Marx himself had refuted the first volume by means of the third was too cosy; because of its sociological consequences, the labour theory of value was too much hated by bourgeois economics for logical proof alone to be able finally to put an end to the legend. And even the passing remark by Engels in the preface to the third volume of *Capital*, indicating that already between 1863 and 1867 Marx not only had the first volume ready for printing but had also completed the two last books of *Capital* in outline, attracted no attention. Now, however, Kautsky is able to provide irrefutable detailed evidence, from the manuscript of *Theories of Surplus-Value*, that the leading ideas of the second and third volumes of *Capital* were developed in manuscript by Marx before the publication of the first volume. Specifically, Kautsky has published in the preface [to the third volume of *Theories of Surplus-Value*], from a manuscript found in a notebook of the year 1862, the plan that Marx outlined for those analyses that today make up the third volume of *Capital*. And this puts an end, once and for all, to the chatter according to which Marx's most brilliant accomplishment, the explanation of the equalisation of the profit rate on the basis of the labour theory of value, which freed the theory of a contradiction that had repeatedly put it into question, was only a kind of subterfuge and a white lie. Kautsky summarises in this way what has now been irrefutably established on the basis of the sources, even for the most finicky critics:

> In any case, the layout of the first and third volume is already enough to show that at the time of its drafting the plan of *Capital* had already been settled upon by Marx in all its principles ... At that time (1862), five years before the appearance of the first volume, the whole of *Capital* was thought out to the end, not only as regards its general train of thought, but also as regards the planned structure with which it was finally published.[26]

Useful as this evidence is, because its cogency does not require any insight – which unfortunately is rare – into the course of development of economic theory in general and of Marx's economic theory in particular, the study of the

---

26   Kautsky, 'Preface' to Marx 1905–10, p. ix.

volume that we will now discuss in more detail[27] would be more than enough to demonstrate how much the problem of the profit rate has occupied economic thought since Ricardo.

The third volume of *Theories of Surplus-Value* covers the period from Ricardo to Marx. The historical account is much more cohesive than in earlier volumes, because there are no detailed theoretical deductions. And the writers dealt with are particularly interesting, because they mark the transition to economic Marxism on the one hand, and to vulgar economics on the other. This intermediate period in the history of economics is all the more interesting because it has almost completely fallen into oblivion, so that is presentation partly sheds an entirely new light on the development since Ricardo.

Marx's formulation of the problem is directly linked to Ricardo, and here the focus of the question is: how can we explain, on the basis of the theory of value, the equality of the profit rate, which completely contradicts the proposition that labour determines value? The volume under consideration provides detailed proof that this was precisely the problem whose solution Marx himself posed as a task in his critique of previous economics. The problem itself was already present in Ricardo, but he again pushed it aside unresolved. What was it?

We know that, in the various branches of production, the composition of the capital that Marx called organic is very different. In one branch of production, an enterprise of one million marks may spend 800,000 marks in buildings, machinery, raw materials, etc. and 200,000 marks on wages for 2,000 workers; in another branch of production, alternatively, only 200,000 marks may be required for the physical capital, whereas 8,000 workers are employed, who earn 800,000 marks in wages. It is now an immediate conclusion from the theory of value that, with the same degree of exploitation of labour (i.e. if, for example, in both branches of production each worker works an equal length of time to reproduce the value of his wages and to produce surplus value for the capitalist), the surplus value generated by 8,000 workers will also be four times as large as that produced by 2,000 workers. But then the [rate of] profit, that is, the surplus value calculated on [i.e. divided by] the total capital of one million, will be different in the same proportion, which contradicts the proposition that capitals of the same size must yield the same profit. Marx solved this problem by showing, in the third volume of *Capital*, how the competition of

---

27 Compare the discussion of the previous two volumes [of *Theories of Surplus-Value*] by Heinrich Cunow 1905, 'Theorien über den Mehrwert', *Die Neue Zeit*, 23. 1. Bd. 17, 19, S. 497–506, 547–55, 617–24, and by Gustav Eckstein 1906, 'Marx' Kritik Ricardos', *Die Neue Zeit*, 24. 2. Bd. H. 34, S. 245–52, H. 36, S. 321–32. [See this volume, Documents 5 and 6].

capitals for their spheres of investment brings about such a distribution of capital among the various branches of industry that the commodities are sold not at their value but at their prices of production. At the end of the period of production, capitalist I in our example would have a value of 1,200,000 marks, while capitalist II would have 1,800,000 marks; the first would realise a profit of 20 percent, the other of 80 percent. But that would only have the effect of a number of capitalists I transferring their capitals to the second sphere of production; thus, in the first sphere of production a reduced supply would arise and in the second an increased supply; and this would go on until both capitalists have the same valorisation (exploitation) conditions for their capital. That would be the case if the total surplus value of one million marks produced by them were spread equally over the total capital of two million; and this happens if both sell their commodities at 1,500,000 marks; then they would both obtain from their equal capitals of one million the same profit [rate] of 50 percent.

Ricardo paused at the fact of the equal [rate of] profit. He explained the deviations of prices [from labour values] as mere exceptions to the rule of the law of value. Hence, he totally failed to explain how such an exception, which logically was the very opposite of the rule, could come into being. For that very reason, the exception had to appear as a contradiction, as an abolition of the rule; and all the more so because, with the unfolding industrial revolution, the organic composition of capital was steadily rising, and the difference between the organic composition in the different branches of production was becoming increasingly large, so that the deviation from the law of value, not its validity, appeared to be the rule. The law of value simply did not regulate prices and was therefore generally wrong. Thus profits could not, or not solely, originate in labour; they had no direct relation to it, but somehow came evenly from capital, whether from its material components or from labour.

If a thinker poses himself his task only incompletely, if he is not totally conscious of the problem to be solved, the premises remain incomplete and imperfect; because the process of actual thought is different from what it appears to be in the scientific presentation. In the latter, the inferences arise out of a series of premises in a deductive process. Actual thought proceeds from the consequences given in reality, in order to find from there the conditions of their occurrence. In the thought *process* premises and consequences, which are separated in the presentation, are united, and only if the thinker is aware of all the consequences – and these are precisely the phenomena to be explained, and therefore the problem – does thought arrive at the totality of the premises. In thought, the formulation of the problem and its solution are therefore interdependent, and if the problem is recognised only incompletely, the premises also remain incomplete and faulty. And this, again, in a double sense: since the statement of the premises and their splitting into the separate logical links is incomplete, not all the conclusions implicitly contained in them are drawn. This is the case with Ricardo: by leaving the problem of the transformation of values into prices of production unresolved, his theory of value and surplus value also remained incomplete and therefore still contradictory. Only when Marx formulated the problem of the explanation of real prices, not as exceptions to the theory of value but as something to be explained on its basis, was it possible to eliminate the contradictions in the theory of value, develop it fully and discover all the intermediate links explaining the transformation of values into production prices. The problem itself, however, was posed by the development of technology and by the resulting enormous expansion of the constant, and especially the fixed, capital in relation to the variable. It is to this new fact that economics had to be adapted.

But it was precisely Ricardo who formulated the problem for his successors by postulating, in his unwavering love of truth, actual price formation as an exception to his theory of value, thus showing it to be contradictory. Opponents and students built upon it. With *Malthus* began the reaction. But scientific reaction consists in not really overcoming the logical contradictions of a scientific system, whether it is a contradiction of thoughts among themselves or a contradiction between thoughts and facts (which, as known facts, are likewise thoughts), but in concealing them. The difficulties are only apparently removed by shifting them into a different chain of thoughts in which they disappear – only in order to give way, to be sure, to larger contradictions, which, however, are still not recognised as such or appear habitual and natural to unscientific thinkers. Malthus is typical of such a scientific reactionary. He proceeds correctly from Ricardo's inconsistencies – not, however, in order to eliminate those inconsistencies, but to do away with Ricardo's correct premises.

Ricardo's theory of surplus value suffered from the contradiction of letting capital, that is, accumulated labour, be directly exchanged with living labour. The capitalist pays to the worker the 'value of labour'. The value of a 10-hour work is obviously the value of 10 hours. But if the capitalist pays to the worker the value of his labour, there is no room for surplus value. Marx proved that the worker does not sell his labour but his labour power, whose value is equal to the value of the labour contained in the worker's means of subsistence. If the worker needs for his upkeep means of subsistence worth 5 hours of labour, but works in the service of the capitalist for 10 hours, he produces a value of 10 hours, from which the capitalist receives 5 hours as unpaid surplus value.

Ricardo had already construed the 'value of labour' as the value of the means of subsistence of the worker, but without eliminating the contradiction of his formulation. Here Malthus appeared.

> The points of departure for Malthus' attack are, on the one hand, the origin of surplus-value and [on the other] the way in which Ricardo conceives the equalisation of cost-prices in different spheres of the employment of capital as a modification of the law of value itself [as well as] his continual confusion of profit with surplus-value (direct identification of one with the other). Malthus does not unravel these contradictions and *quid pro quos* but accepts them from Ricardo in order to be able to overthrow the Ricardian law of value, etc., by using this confusion and to draw conclusions acceptable to his protectors [namely, the landowners and their appendages – R.H.].[28]

Thus Malthus arrives at denial of the [labour] theory of value and reverts to the mercantilist notion that profit comes only from the price addition that the capitalists make to the production costs. The workers can therefore buy with their wages only a part of the commodities from the capitalists, because the capitalist adds his profit to the wages. If the wages are worth 100, the capitalist sells the commodities at 110, and 10 remain in his hands unsold. It would not help him if he were to sell them to other capitalists. For if capitalist A sells to capitalist B a commodity worth 100 at 110, B will also sell his commodity with the same surcharge to A. Malthus solves the difficulty by introducing a class of buyers who pay for the commodities at their nominal values without, in turn, selling goods. The profit is realised by selling as little as possible of the total product back to the workers and as much as possible to this class that pays in cash without itself selling, and that buys in order to consume. The landowners, receiving rents and buying with them commodities from the capitalists, are therefore unproductive consumers. But those landlords are not enough; recourse must also be had to artificial means. These consist of high taxes, a mass of state- and church-sinecure holders, a significant national debt and, from time to time, costly wars. These are Malthus's 'remedies' [to the problem of underconsumption].

Marx describes the economic motives that determined Malthus's theory as follows:

---

28 Marx 1971, p. 14.

Malthus correctly draws the conclusions from his basic theory of value. But this theory, for its part, suits his purpose remarkably well – an apologia for the existing state of affairs in England, for landlordism, 'State and Church', pensioners, tax-gatherers, tenths [tithes], national debt, stock-jobbers, beadles, parsons and menial servants ('national expenditure') assailed by the Ricardians as so many useless and superannuated drawbacks of bourgeois production and as nuisances. For all that, Ricardo championed bourgeois production insofar as it [signified] the most unrestricted development of the social productive forces, unconcerned for the fate of those who participate in production, be they capitalists or workers. He insisted upon the historical justification and necessity of this stage of development. His very lack of a historical sense of the past meant that he regarded everything from the historical standpoint of his time. Malthus also wishes to see the freest possible development of capitalist production, however only insofar as the condition of this development is the poverty of its main basis, the working classes, but at the same time he wants it to adapt itself to the 'consumption needs' of the aristocracy and its branches in State and Church, to serve as the material basis for the antiquated claims of the representatives of interests inherited from feudalism and the absolute monarchy. Malthus wants bourgeois production as long as it is not revolutionary, constitutes no historical factor of development but merely creates a broader and more comfortable material basis for the 'old' society.[29]

Malthus's own teachings were easily dismissed by the followers of Ricardo. His theory of profit is dispatched by one of them as follows:

> We are continually puzzled, in his (Malthus's) speculations, between the object of increasing production and that of checking it. When a man is in want of a demand, does Mr. Malthus recommend him to pay some other person to take off his goods?[30]

But the inconsistencies in Ricardo's theory, which Malthus inveighed against, were more difficult to eliminate. And on this attempt the Ricardian school finally foundered, but not without having made in the process a number of

---

29 Marx 1971, p. 52.
30 Bailey 1821, p. 55, cited in Marx 1971, p. 60.

findings that allowed the eventual solution of the problem. Marx describes the procedures of these Ricardians in the example of James Mill.

> Mill was the first to present Ricardo's theory in systematic form, even though he did it only in rather abstract outlines. What he tries to achieve is formal, logical consistency. The *disintegration* of the Ricardian school 'therefore' begins with him. With the master what is new and significant develops vigorously amid the 'manure' of contradictions out of the contradictory phenomena. The underlying contradictions themselves testify to the richness of the living foundation from which the theory itself developed. It is different with the disciple. His raw material is no longer reality, but the new theoretical form in which the master had sublimated it. It is in part the *theoretical disagreement of opponents of the new theory and in part the often paradoxical relationship of this theory to reality* which drive him to seek *to refute* his opponents and explain away reality. In doing so, he entangles himself in contradictions and with his attempt to solve these he demonstrates the incipient *disintegration of the theory* which he dogmatically espouses.[31]

These comments are also an excellent characterisation of the doctrinal dogmatism to which the vulgarisers of any groundbreaking theory so easily succumb.

The main difficulties faced by Ricardo's school were these: first, to explain how the exchange of capital and labour takes place in conformity with the law of value, a difficulty that neither the bourgeois nor the socialist Ricardians were able to overcome. The problem was first solved by Marx, who showed that not capital and labour but rather capital and labour power are exchanged. The second difficulty was that *capitals of equal size*, whatever their organic composition, always yielded the *same* profit. This problem of the general [or equal] rate of profit is also the problem of how values turn into prices of production.

> The difficulty arose because *capitals of equal magnitude*, but of unequal composition – it is immaterial whether the unequal composition is due to the capitals containing unequal proportions of constant and variable capital, or of fixed and circulating capital, or to the unequal period of circulation of the capitals – set in motion unequal quantities of imme-

---

31   Marx 1971, p. 85.

diate labour, and therefore unequal quantities of unpaid labour; consequently they cannot appropriate equal quantities of surplus-value or surplus product in the process of production. Hence they cannot yield equal profit if profit is nothing but the surplus-value calculated on the value of the whole capital advanced. *If, however, the surplus-value were something different from (unpaid) labour, then labour could after all not be the 'foundation and measure' of the value of commodities.*

The difficulties arising in this context were discovered by Ricardo himself (although not in their general form) and set forth by him as exceptions to the law of value. Malthus used these exceptions to throw the whole law overboard on the grounds that the exceptions constituted the rule. Torrens, who also criticised Ricardo, indicated the problem at any rate when he said that *capitals of equal size set unequal quantities of labour in motion, and nevertheless produce commodities of equal 'values', hence value cannot be determined by labour.* Ditto Bailey, etc. Mill for his part accepted the exceptions noted by Ricardo as exceptions, and he had no scruples about them except with regard to one single form. One particular *cause of the equalisation* of the profits of the capitalists he found incompatible with the law. It was the following. Certain commodities remain in the process of production (for example, wine in the cellar) without any labour being applied to them; there is a period during which they are subject to certain natural processes (for example, prolonged breaks in labour occur in agriculture and in tanning before certain new chemicals are applied – these cases are not mentioned by Mill). These periods are nevertheless considered as profit-yielding. The period of time during which the commodity is not being worked on by labour [is regarded] as labour-time (the same thing in general applies where a *longer period of circulation time is involved*). *Mill 'lied' his way – so to speak – out of the difficulty by saying that one can consider the time in which the wine,* for example, is in the cellar as a period when it is soaking up labour, although according to the assumption this is, in point of fact, not the case. Otherwise one would have to say that 'time' creates profit and [according to Mill] time as such is 'sound and fury'. McCulloch uses this balderdash of Mill as a starting-point, or rather he reproduces it in his customary affected, plagiarist manner in a general form in which the latent nonsense becomes apparent and the last vestiges of the Ricardian system, as of all economic thinking whatsoever, are happily discarded.[32]

---

32 Marx 1971, p. 178.

McCulloch tried to solve the contradiction by calling the 'actions' of the means of production *labour*, and making them produce value just like human labour. He therefore identified the natural properties of use-values, such as the mechanical labour performed by a machine, with the social relations between men, as they appear in their activities in the production process.

> Like all economists worth naming, [including] Adam Smith (although in a fit of humour he once called the ox a productive labourer), [says Marx, perhaps projecting a bit too much his own more developed and more clear insight into the consciousness of his predecessors – R.H.] Ricardo emphasises that labour as *human activity*, even more, as socially determined *human activity*, is the sole source of value. It is precisely through the consistency with which he treats the value of commodities as merely 'representing' socially determined labour, that Ricardo differs from the other economists. All these economists understand more or less clearly, but Ricardo more clearly than the others, that the exchange-value of *things* is a mere expression, a specific social form, of the productive activity of men, something entirely different from things and their use as things, whether in industrial or in non-industrial consumption. For them, value is, in fact, simply an objectively expressed relation of the productive activity of men, of the different types of labour to one another.[33]

McCulloch, by regarding 'labour in general' – regardless of whether it is mechanical, animal or human – and therefore all the actions of the means of production, as equally value-creating, mixed up the natural properties of things with the social determination of commodities, confusing use-value and value, and thus fell into the fetishism that underlies the pseudo-science of vulgar economics.

Marx mentions John Stuart Mill as the last Ricardian. He, too, failed because of the confusion between surplus value and profit. His attempt to prove Ricardo's doctrine – that the level of profit stands directly in inverse proportion to the level of wages – led Marx to investigations that belong to the theory of combination, which we shall discuss in another context.[34]

Simultaneously with the development of bourgeois economics arose its negation in the *socialist and communist systems*. The plan of Marx's work, however, includes only that group of socialists who, remaining on the grounds

---

33   Marx 1971, p. 181.
34   [Cf. Hilferding 1912a].

of Ricardo's teachings, sought to develop from their results socialist, or at least proletarian, consequences. Marx mentions three of them: the writer of an anonymous pamphlet, published under the title *The Source and Remedy of the National Difficulties* in London 1821 [Charles Wentworth Dilke], Ravenstone and Hodgskin. Marx outlines the following characteristics of this group:

> The opposition evoked by the Ricardian theory – on the basis of its own assumptions – has the following characteristic feature.
>
> To the same extent as political economy developed – and this development finds its most trenchant expression in Ricardo, as far as fundamental principles are concerned – it presented labour as the sole element of value and the only creator of use-values, and the development of the productive forces as the only real means for increasing wealth; the greatest possible development of the productive power of labour as the economic basis of society. This is, in fact, the foundation of *capitalist production*. Ricardo's work, in particular, which demonstrates that the law of value is not invalidated either by landed property or by capitalist accumulation, etc., is, in reality, only concerned with eliminating all contradictions or phenomena which appear to run counter to this conception. But in the same measure as it is understood that labour is the *sole* source of exchange-value and the active source of use-value, '*capital*' is likewise conceived by the same economists, in particular by Ricardo (and even more by Torrens, Malthus, Bailey, and others after him), as the regulator of production, the source of wealth and the aim of production, whereas labour is regarded as wage-labour, whose representative and real instrument is inevitably a pauper (to which Malthus's theory of population contributed), a mere production cost and instrument of production dependent on a minimum wage and forced to drop even below this minimum as soon as the existing quantity of labour is 'superfluous' for capital. In this contradiction, political economy merely expressed the essence of capitalist production or, if you like, of wage-labour, of labour alienated from itself, which stands confronted by the wealth it has created as alien wealth, by its own productive power as the productive power of its product, by its enrichment as its own impoverishment and by its social power as the power of society. But this definite, *specific*, historical form of social labour, which is exemplified in capitalist production, is proclaimed by these economists as the general, eternal form, as a natural phenomenon, and these relations of production as the absolutely (not historically) necessary, natural and reasonable relations of social labour. Their thoughts being entirely confined within the

bounds of capitalist production, they assert that the *contradictory* form in which social labour manifests itself there, is just as necessary as labour itself freed from this contradiction. Since in the self-same breath they proclaim on the one hand, *labour* as such (for them, labour is synonymous with wage-labour) and on the other, *capital* as such – that is the poverty of the workers and the wealth of the idlers – to be the sole source of wealth, they are perpetually involved in absolute contradictions without being in the slightest degree aware of them. (Sismondi was epoch-making in political economy because he had an inkling of this contradiction.) Ricardo's phrase 'labour *or* capital' reveals in a most striking fashion both the contradiction inherent in the terms and the naïvety with which they are stated to be identical.

Since the same real development which provided bourgeois political economy with this striking theoretical expression, unfolded the real contradictions contained in it, especially the contradiction between the growing wealth of the English 'nation' and the growing misery of the workers, and since moreover these contradictions are given a *theoretically* compelling if unconscious expression in the Ricardian theory, etc., it was natural for those thinkers who rallied to the side of the proletariat to seize on this contradiction, for which they found the theoretical ground already prepared. Labour is the sole source of exchange-value and the only active creator of use-value. This is what you say. On the other hand, you say that *capital* is everything, and the worker is nothing or a mere production cost of capital. You have refuted yourselves. Capital is *nothing* but defrauding of the worker. *Labour* is *everything*.

This, in fact, is the ultimate meaning of all the writings which defend the interests of the proletariat from the Ricardian standpoint basing themselves on his assumptions. Just as little as he [Ricardo] understands the identity of *capital* and *labour* in his own system, do they *understand* the contradiction they describe. That is why the most important among them – Hodgskin, for example – accept all the economic pre-conditions of capitalist production as eternal forms and only desire to eliminate capital, which is both the basis and necessary consequence [of these preconditions].[35]

---

35   Marx 1971, pp. 259–60.

At the same time, these writings also meant a step forward for economic theory. The pamphleteer [Charles Wentworth Dilke] consequently resolved surplus value into surplus *labour*, in contrast to the opponents and successors of Ricardo, who clung to his confusion of surplus value and profit. He drew the conclusion that capital is superfluous and surplus labour must be eliminated. 'The next consequence therefore would be, that where men heretofore laboured twelve hours they would now labour six, and this is national wealth, this is national prosperity'.[36]

Ravenstone further identified relative surplus value, which depends on the degree of development of the productive force of labour. He drew from it the conclusion that growth in the productivity of labour only increases the alien wealth that controls labour, namely capital.

Hodgskin, finally, upheld the proposition that capital is unproductive. [According to him,] the productivity of labour does not depend on the available mass of capital. He sought to prove that the effects attributed to circulating capital, a stock of goods, are actually the result of 'coexisting labour'. Albeit in unclear form, he already anticipated, in embryo, an understanding of the fetishism that attributes to *things* the effects that correspond to social *relations*.

Among the socialists, Marx includes a group of three authors – George Ramsay, [Antoine-Elisée] Cherbuliez and Richard Jones – whose common denominator is that, unlike the classics, they do not take the capitalist mode of production, and therefore capital, for an *absolute* form of production, but merely as a 'fortuitous' *historical* condition. Ramsay has the merit of having drawn a clear distinction between constant and variable capital, a distinction of fundamental importance for recognition of the origin of surplus value. But he still assigned to these capital components the name of fixed and circulating capital, a difference arising in circulation. He remained in the dark concerning the creation of surplus value and did not succeed in developing the transformation of surplus value into profit or, consequently, that of values into production prices. Ramsay declared the means of production and the raw materials (which he called fixed capital), on the one hand, and living labour, on the other hand, to be necessary conditions of production. By contrast, it was merely due to the 'deplorable poverty of the mass of the people' that the worker's means of subsistence should in general assume the form of 'circulating capital'. Labour is a condition of production, but not wage-labour.

---

36   Dilke 1821, p. 5.

Ramsay attempts in earnest, and not merely in words as the other economists do, to reduce capital to 'a portion of the national wealth, employed, or meant to be employed, in favouring reproduction' (op. cit., p. 21); he therefore declares wage-labour and consequently capital – that is *the social form which the means of reproduction assume on the basis of wage-labour* – to be unimportant and due merely to the poverty of the mass of the people.[37]

Similar in his critical performance is *Cherbuliez*, who, influenced by Sismondi, makes a series of excellent observations, particularly on the tendency towards concentration and on the equalisation of profit rates. The most important of this group, and one of the most interesting post-Ricardian economists in general, is *Richard Jones*. He is also the immediate precursor of Marx in his conception of history. We must therefore speak in more detail about him and his relationship to Marx.

3   Richard Jones

Richard Jones was born in 1790. In 1816 he left the University of Cambridge [where he studied law at Caius College until ill health intervened. He then took orders and for several years held curacies in Sussex and Kent.] His main work, *An Essay on the Distribution of Wealth and on the Sources of Taxation, Part I: Rent*, was published in 1831 in London. Soon after [in 1833], he became professor of political economy at the newly founded King's College, where he delivered his inaugural lecture, the *Introductory Lecture on Political Economy*, on 27 February 1833. In 1835 he was appointed successor of Malthus [in the chair of political economy and history] at the East India College of Haileybury. He died on 20 January 1855. His writings, with the exception of the first book, have been collected under the title *Literary Remains: Consisting of Lectures and Tracts on Political Economy of the late Rev. Richard Jones*, ed. by William Whewell.[38] The editor of the volume was John Cazenove.

Marx praised Jones's first book because it was characterised by what is lacking in all English economists since Sir James Steuart, namely, a sense of the historical difference in modes of production. Whereas Ricardo gave the finishing touches to deductive political economy, Jones himself celebrated his friend Whewell, the famous author of the *History of the Inductive Sciences* (1837), as the founder of the inductive system of political economy. Considering

---

37   Marx 1971, p. 257.
38   Jones 1859.

the further fact that Jones showed little interest in specifically theoretical problems, he can be rightly regarded as the father of the historical school.[39]

Jones was a member of the established Church of England and had close relationships with the Archbishop of Canterbury and the Bishop of London. As their agent, and as representative of the ecclesiastical (and conservative) interests, he was a member of the commission set up to oversee the redemption of tithes. Representing the Archbishop, he was one of three commissioners who supervised the substitution [of monetary payments for tithes in kind, stipulated by the Tithe Commutation Act of 1836].

If this shows his political stance, it is also relevant for his scientific views that he was bound by personal friendship with Malthus. All his writings show a great respect for the scientific importance and the personality of Malthus. There is no doubt that Jones placed Malthus above Ricardo, as in fact did many of his contemporaries. Even more important, however, was the close relationship that united him with such distinguished naturalists as John Herschel and Whewell. Jones sought with full awareness to transfer the inductive method of the natural sciences, which he considered the only legitimate one, to economics. He anticipated, for the most part, the whole subsequent dispute on method,[40] which the German historical school waged with so much

---

39 As did John Kells Ingram in his *A History of Political Economy* (Ingram 1887, pp. 142–5). It is characteristic that Böhm-Bawerk, in his *Capital and Interest: A Critical History of Economical Theory*, can only say about Jones that he 'contributes nothing of great consequence to our subject' (Böhm-Bawerk 1890, p. 102).

40 [*Methodenstreit* ('strife over methods') is a term referring to a controversy over the method and epistemological character of economics carried on in the late 1880s and early 1890s between the supporters of the Austrian school of Economics, led by Carl Menger, and the proponents of the (German) Historical school, led by Gustav von Schmoller. The Historical school contended that economists could develop new and better social laws from the collection and study of statistics and historical materials, and they distrusted theories not derived from historical experience. The Austrian school, by contrast, believed that economics was the work of philosophical logic and could only develop rules from first principles, taking their theories of human action to be universally valid. Menger concentrated upon subjective factors, emphasising the atomistic nature of economics. He said the grounds for economics were built upon self-interest, utility maximisation, and complete knowledge. He said aggregative, collective ideas could not have an adequate foundation unless they rested upon individual components. The term 'Austrian school of economics' came into existence as a result of the *Methodenstreit*, when Schmoller used it in an unfavourable review of one of Menger's later books, intending to convey an impression of the backwardness and obscurantism of Habsburg Austria compared to the more modern Prussians].

pleasure and so few results. Already in his book on rents, he printed in the appendix, as an illustration of his method, a passage from Herschel's *Study of Natural Philosophy*.[41] The main and ultimate source of our knowledge is experience, which people acquire through observation and experiment. In the introduction to *Text Book of Lectures on the Political Economy of Nations*, etc., he sharply counterposed his method, which proceeded from history and observation, to the dominant method (i.e. Ricardo's), which sought to derive economic laws from purely abstract principles, and he did likewise in many other places.

If Jones adopted his method from the then mightily developing natural sciences, his historical-critical attitude towards absolutising the capitalist mode of production in Ricardo's system was apparently elicited by his study of India's social conditions, especially its landed property system, which was particularly familiar to him as lecturer at the East India College. In India he discovered both the shortcomings of Ricardo's 'abstract principles' and generalisations and the historical contingency of capitalist laws of distribution, as they appear in Ricardo's theory of rent and profit. There was, however, yet another immediate practical-political reason that made him take a stand against Ricardo. Jones, like Malthus, was a conservative. However, there is no trace in him of that coarse material interestedness, which again and again shines through Malthus's sanctimonious and good-natured phraseology. His friendship for Malthus certainly did not hinder him from criticising the disastrous 'consequences and excesses' resulting from Malthusian population theory, thereby actually criticising Malthus's theory itself. In particular, Jones's short treatise on the theory of population[42] showed very well the superiority of his historical method vis-à-vis the alleged 'conformity to natural law' of the Malthusian theorems. Even if, unlike Marx, he did not reach the conclusion that every particular social order has its own population law, and that social causes are therefore decisive for the actual course of population growth (given unchanging natural-biological foundations), he sharply emphasised the social factors vis-à-vis Malthus's allegedly natural law. And he took the sting out of the anti-labour consequences of Malthus's doctrine, which legal practice followed at the time in the Poor Law, by emphatically refuting Malthus's observation that the misery of the workers was the main factor preventing their too rapid proliferation, and by arguing that it was precisely an improved standard of living of the working masses that would bring about a 'moral check', i.e. would create

---

41   Herschel 1831.
42   [Jones, *Lectures on Population*, in Jones 1859, pp. 93–140].

social factors that would prevent a harmfully excessive demographic increase. In contrast to Malthus's theory and to the doctrine of the 'iron' law of wages, it follows directly from Jones's view that he sees improvement of the workers' living conditions as both possible and desirable.[43]

But if Jones was a stranger to any anti-labour tendency, he still felt hurt in his conservative disposition by the unbiased ruthlessness of Ricardo's teachings, because they clearly showed the antagonism between the major classes of bourgeois society. According to Ricardo, profit and wages were inversely proportional; one could only rise at the expense of the other. Ground rent was just a surplus profit and, as such, a tribute that the landowners levied upon the productive classes, upon industrialists and capitalists, by virtue of their monopoly of the land. With the progress of society, increasingly less fertile soils must be brought into cultivation in order to satisfy the [growing] demand for food, thus raising ground rent. With the rise in food prices, however, wages must also increase and, as a result, profits must fall. But the falling rate of profit hinders or slows down further accumulation, which is the precondition of any social progress. Thus the landowners' interests are totally opposed to social progress. And these theoretical teachings had already condensed into practical demands. Radical Ricardians called for the abolition of landed property as an unnecessary barrier to capitalist development, while the socialists, based on the antagonistic relationship between profit and wages, demanded the elimination of capitalist relations. Jones defended the harmony of interests of all classes vis-à-vis this proclamation of class antagonisms. If he rejected the anti-labour consequences of Malthus's [theory], he was no less opposed to the socialist claims of Godwin, that *'ingenious, but incautious, speculator'*,[44] and to the Ricardians' hostility towards landed property. Against the Ricardians' pessimism concerning the fall in the rate of profit, he proclaimed the optimistic theory that a rise in labour productivity would increase the share of all classes in the social product – a view, however, which implies a confusion of use-value and value. Jones was everywhere motivated by these political considerations of the conservatives against Ricardo and his radical followers. These polemical-conservative considerations also limited Jones's historical understanding, occasionally misleading him into making the opposite mistakes from the ones the

---

43 In this regard compare the passages in the *Literary Remains etc.*, the *Lectures on Population* [in Jones 1859, pp. 93–140] and *A Short Tract of Political Economy* etc. [in Jones 1859, pp. 185–290] especially pp. 248 ff.

44 [Jones, *A Short Tract on Political Economy, including some Account of the Anglo-Indian Revenue Systems*, in Jones 1859, p. 243].

classics had made. If the latter transferred capitalist ideas to pre-capitalist conditions, Jones sometimes sought, on the contrary, to draw material from pre-capitalist conditions for his polemics against Ricardo's laws.

If Jones here again proved correct against Ricardo on many points, it was because the relationships between the classes in capitalist society are in fact more complicated than they appear in the almost mathematically simplified form that Ricardo gave them. Insofar as Jones, apart from the historical qualifications he made to Ricardo's laws, was correct against Ricardo, he owed that to his emphasis on the social cohesion of the capitalist classes [i.e. the landlords and capitalists] as against the factors separating and opposing them.

Of all the economists before Marx, Jones was the one who most clearly recognised and enunciated the historical character of capitalism. In his book on rents, he showed that capitalist rents, to which alone Ricardo's laws apply to a certain extent, presuppose capitalist landed property, and that this in turn presupposes capitalist industry, the transformation of the labourer into a wage-worker, the appearance of an independent capitalist class, and equalisation of the rates of profit. Following rents in all their transformations, from their crudest form as forced labour to modern monetary rent (*farmers' rent*), he set earlier forms of society against capitalist social relations and everywhere found that a *specific form of labour* and its conditions corresponded to a certain form of rent, i.e. to a certain form of landed property. In all previous forms, the landlord was the direct appropriator of the surplus labour; only in capitalist society does the capitalist take his place.

Marx discussed in detail the corrections that Jones made to Ricardo's theory of rent. Important and interesting as these observations are for rent theory (for example, Jones's polemic against the 'law' of diminishing returns in agriculture), we omit them here in order to proceed to Jones's historical standpoint. Jones is serious about the conception of capital as an historical category. Capital is no longer a sum of means of production and foodstuffs, but rather a particular form of the labour fund, a certain way in which the means of labour and the articles of personal consumption are provided to the workers, a social relationship emerging late in history. The whole economic structure of society revolves around the form of labour, i.e. the form in which the worker acquires his means of subsistence, or the portion of his product that sustains his livelihood. In the *Introductory Lectures* he states:

> ... by economical structure of nations, I mean those relations between the different classes which are established in the first instance by the institution of property in the soil, and by the distribution of its surplus produce; afterwards modified and changed (to a greater or less extent)

by the introduction of capitalists as agents in producing and exchanging wealth, and in feeding and employing the labouring population.[45]

With great clarity Jones highlighted the different forms of labour as the distinguishing characteristic of societies. In the *Text Book of Lectures on the Political Economy of Nations*, for example, he said wage-labour is 'the great distinctive phenomenon of our actual economical condition'.[46] Jones also suggested, at least, the origin of capital, the separation of workers from their means of production, when describing the appropriation of common lands by the landowners. He not only saw in that [process] a social cause of the intensification of religious disputes; in the workers set 'free' he also saw the proletarians, who filled the streets as beggars and tramps until they were gradually absorbed by the emerging manufacturers. Our presentation, Jones concludes in this section, has thus reached the point from which we date the emergence in England of a class of capitalists, as represented by our modern tenants.[47]

But what gives Jones's historical observations their importance is the fact that they flow from an insight into the relationship between economics and history that makes him one of the most important *precursors of the materialist conception of history*. Marx quoted the following paragraphs from his *Text Book of Lectures on the Political Economy of Nations*:

---

45   Jones 1833, pp. 21–2, cited in Marx 1971, p. 413.
46   Jones 1859, p. 16.
47   ['The hired laborers, the farming servants, the journeymen mechanics, – the manufacturing operatives, as they desire to be called, – form the bulk of the working classes, in the village as in the town; – the great distinctive phenomenon of our actual economical condition. The threefold division of laborers which I have presented to you is founded, you will observe, entirely on the difference in the nature and formation of the funds which supply their wages. This division is new, and it may be thought, perhaps, at first sight, that the novelty is, at best, uncalled for; that a difference in the sources of their wages hardly justifies our viewing laborers as forming distinct classes for the purposes of economical reasoning. [But] we shall find very great differences in the productive power of nations occasioned by the prevalence of one or the other of the classes I have described. Is this doubted? Then imagine the farming capitalist, as distinct from the laborer, to vanish from England, and let the land be parcelled out amongst the agricultural laborers as peasant occupiers. Empty her manufactories and workshops, and let her non-agricultural population ply in her streets, as in the East, with such implements and resources as a mere workman could command, soliciting employment from the chance customers they may find; would not the nation be at once transformed? would not its productive power have undergone a mighty change? and would not all the elements which now bind together her social system be changed too?' (Jones 1859, pp. 16–17)].

As communities *change their powers of production*, they *necessarily change their habits too*.⁴⁸

During their progress in advance, all the different classes of the community find that they are connected with other classes *by new relations*, are assuming *new positions*, and are surrounded by new moral and social dangers, and *new conditions* of social and political excellence.⁴⁹

Great political, social, moral and intellectual changes, *accompany changes in the economical organization of communities*, and the agencies and the means, affluent or scanty, by which the tasks of industry are carried on. These changes necessarily exercise a commanding influence over the different political and social elements to be found in the populations where they take place; that influence extends to the intellectual character, to the habits, manners, morals, and happiness of nations.⁵⁰

These paragraphs could easily be multiplied. For instance, Jones believed that differences in race and temperament played only a small part in [influencing] the differences of accumulation among various peoples, because 'great bodies of men are very much the creatures of circumstances, and of the education which those circumstances give'.⁵¹ In this regard, he also shows that, with advancing accumulation, the legal obstacles opposing capitalism must fall, and bourgeois liberty and equality must take their place. 'It is the distribution of its wealth', he says in another place, 'which determines always the social, and most often the political, relations of human society; and until we analyzed it, we cannot understand their internal mechanism'.⁵² The subordination of labour to capital, he says in the *Lectures on Labour and Capital*, has 'social and political consequences [that] have been not less important than its economical ones, and they react upon each other'.⁵³ And elsewhere Jones ridicules the ideological view of Montesquieu, who ascribed the landed aristocracy's resistance to monarchical absolutism to its sense of honour, while much more obvious reasons (economic ones, of course) were available, especially considering that, despite its sense of honour, the aristocracy had failed to protect its peasants against oppressive taxation.

---

48   Jones 1859, p. 410.
49   Jones 1859, pp. 410–11.
50   Jones 1859, p. 405. The three paragraphs are cited in Marx 1971, pp. 430–1.
51   Jones 1859, p. 54.
52   Jones 1859, p. 75.
53   Ibid.

Jones expressed his views most extensively in the following passage of the *Text Book of Lectures on the Political Economy of Nations*:

> We have before us the wide scene of the nations of the earth earning, by the decree of heaven, their daily bread by labour, and man is connected with man by ties which grow and are formed by their fellowship in the task. Those ties and relations extend from the monarch on the throne, through all the varied division of the population of nations, to the labourer at his work.
>
> Out of these physical conditions and moral ties spring the most exalted virtues, public and private, which can adorn or protect society. We must not despise those ties, nor let the physical wants of men, and these their first social consequences, seem alien to the loftier parts of our nature. As well might we despise the precious brilliant [i.e. diamond] because it is elaborated in the mine from the lowest earthly elements.
>
> We shall speak hereafter, no doubt, and that without at all diverging from our proper path, of laws and legislators, – of the voice and arm of justice embodied in sacred institutions, – of the influence of self-imposed restraint on the lower appetites of our nature, and we shall see how the manners and the morals, and the most precious energies of nations, receive their polish and their strength from the struggle. We shall trace the history of opinions and see how the strength and the aberrations of human intellect have influenced, in their turn, the fate of generations and nations. Our subject will lead us necessarily into the region of such inquiries. But if we are to treat them as philosophers, we must be patient and learn their inner nature as we learn a language, by dwelling on and dissecting its humblest elements. Such primary elements in economical and political philosophy are the needs and wants of man, and the ties and duties which arise during his efforts to supply them. Let us but be content to track these things carefully and steadily among the varied people which are about to present themselves to our observation, and I venture to promise that you shall not be discontented with the loftiness or dignity of the views of men and communities, of the moral government of God, and the varied career of nations, at which we shall arrive before our course is over.[54]

---

54   Jones 1859, pp. 407–8.

Jones never tired of writing variations of those passages in his works, which, unfortunately, are almost all sketches or fragments. To be sure, alongside those passages are others in which Jones wants to trace the prosperity of England back to its liberal institutions, but those paragraphs remain isolated.[55] That he did not reach complete methodological clarity regarding the relation between economics and politics is also shown by his frequent appeals to the category of interaction. Thus he says, for example, in a characteristic way: 'There is a constant interaction between the political and economical condition of a people ..., the multiplication of orders, and the modification of aristocratic power by the introduction of the democratic element into the government of nations'.[56]

And Jones remains, despite his aversion to socialism, impartial enough to accept historical development not only in the past but also for the future, in contrast to those representatives of the historical school, to whom history only shows its *a posteriori*.

> The first capitalist employers – those who first advance the wages of labour from accumulated stock, and seek a revenue in the shape of profits from such advance – have been ordinarily a class distinct from the labourers themselves: a state of things may hereafter exist, and parts of the world may be approaching to it, under which the labourers and the owners of accumulated stock, may be identical; but in the progress of nations, which we are now observing, this has never yet been the case ... This [separation of the worker from the means of production] may not be as desirable a state of things as that in which labourers and capitalists are identified; but we must still accept it as constituting a stage in the march of industry, which has hitherto marked the progress of advancing nations. At that stage the people of Asia have not yet arrived.[57]

Marx comments on this passage:

---

55   'It is natural to inquire to what cause is to be ascribed the early and great efficiency of agricultural labour, the consequently large and enlarging size and number of non-agricultural classes, and that rapid career of prosperity which has substituted capital for the other two branches of the labour fund in England. These happy phenomena are to be attributed chiefly, though not exclusively, to our just and liberal political institutions, which have been as propitious to our national fortunes as those of other nations have frequently been adverse to theirs' (Jones 1859, p. 222).
56   Jones 1859, pp. 232–3.
57   Jones 1859, pp. 444–5.

> Here Jones states quite explicitly that capital and the capitalist mode of production are to be 'accepted' merely as a transitional phase in the development of social production, a phase which, if one considers the development of the productive forces of social labour, constitutes a gigantic advance on all preceding forms, but which is by no means the end result; on the contrary, the necessity of its destruction is contained in the antagonism between 'owners of accumulated wealth' and the 'actual labourers'.[58]

Before we proceed to the ultimate answer to the question of Jones's role in economics and his relationship to Marx, we want to reproduce Marx's opinion:

> The sentence: 'Capital, or accumulated stock, after performing various other functions in the production of wealth, only takes up late that of advancing to the labourer his wages' (p. 79) is the most complete expression of the contradiction; on the one hand, it expresses a correct historical conception of capital, but, on the other hand, a shadow is cast over it by the narrow-minded notion of the economist that 'stock' as such is capital. Hence 'the accumulated stock' becomes a person who 'performs the function of advancing wages' to men. Jones is still rooted in economic prejudice when he solves [the problem], a solution becomes necessary as soon as the capitalist mode of production is regarded as a determinate historical category and no longer as an eternal natural relation of production.
>
> One can see what a great leap forward there was from Ramsay to Jones. Ramsay regards precisely that function of capital which makes it capital – the advancing of wages – as accidental, due only to the poverty of the people, and irrelevant to the production process as such. In this narrow circumscribed manner, Ramsay *denies* the necessity for the capitalist mode of production. Jones, on the other hand, (strange that they were both priests of the Established Church. The ministers of the English Church seem to think more than their continental brethren) demonstrates that it is precisely this function that makes capital capital and gives rise to the most characteristic features of the capitalist mode of production. He shows how this form occurs only at a certain level of development of the productive forces and that it then creates an entirely new mater-

---

58 Marx 1971, p. 428.

ial basis. Consequently, however, his comprehension of the fact that this form 'can be superseded' and of the merely transitory historical necessity for this form, is quite different from that of Ramsay and more profound. [...]

One can see here how the real science of political economy ends by regarding the bourgeois production relations as merely *historical* ones, leading to higher relations in which the antagonism on which they are based is resolved. By analysing them political economy breaks down the apparently mutually independent forms in which wealth appears. This analysis (even in Ricardo's works) goes so far that:

1) *The independent, material form of wealth* disappears and wealth is shown to be simply the activity of men. Everything which is not the result of human activity, of labour, is nature and, as such, is not social wealth. The phantom of the world of goods fades away and it is seen to be simply a continually disappearing and continually reproduced objectivisation of human labour. All solid material wealth is only transitory materialisation of social labour, crystallisation of the production process whose measure is time, the measure of a movement itself.

2) The manifold forms in which the various component parts of wealth are distributed amongst different sections of society lose their apparent independence. Interest is merely a part of profit, rent is merely surplus profit. Both are consequently merged in profit, which itself can be reduced to surplus-value, that is, to unpaid labour. The value of the commodity itself, however, can only be reduced to labour-time. The Ricardian school reaches the point where it rejects one of the forms of appropriation of this surplus-value – landed property (rent) – as useless, insofar as it is pocketed by private individuals. It rejects the idea that the landowner can play a part in capitalist production. The antithesis is thus reduced to that between capitalist and wage-labourer. This relationship, however, is regarded by the Ricardian school as given, as a natural law, on which the production process itself is based. The later economists go one step further and, like Jones, admit only the historical justification for this relationship. But from the moment that the bourgeois mode of production and the conditions of production and distribution which correspond to it are recognised as historical, the delusion of regarding them as natural laws of production vanishes and the prospect

opens up of a new society, [a new] economic social formation, to which capitalism is only the transition.[59]

What is Jones's relation to Marx? There is no doubt that, of the precursors of Marx, he is the one who came closest to the materialist conception of history. To be sure, this conception is not yet systematically developed in Jones. He is not clearly aware of the materialist conception of history as the general law of motion of historical events; and recognition of class struggles, as the form of motion of social formations based upon private property, is completely lacking in him. Jones nowhere goes beyond a general formulation [of the materialist conception of history]; moreover, in the historical parts [of his works] a systematic application [of those concepts] to the various stages of development is missing. But Jones already distinguished himself from most other writers who came close to materialist historical formulations, because he arrived at his conception of history from *economics* and not, like the others, either from an indeterminate theory of environmental determinism or from the generalisation of obvious political or social antagonisms (such the contradiction between rich and poor, workers and idlers, urban and rural residents, landowners and manufacturers) as a cause of historical events. Jones starts directly from the form of labour that determined property relations, upon which the various relationships between the social classes then arose, in turn determining their legal relations, feelings and thoughts. But this recognition – important as it is in itself, and important as its economic-historical results are vis-à-vis the non-historical view of the classics – remains completely barren for economic theory. And if Kautsky rightly says in the preface [to the third volume of *Theories of Surplus-Value*] that Marx begins where Jones ends, to this should be added that Marx also begins where Ricardo stops.

And this is the *fundamentally* new element in Marx: that he attempts to *combine* the historical conception that Jones counterposes to Ricardo's 'abstract method' with the latter, and in that way to complete it and revolutionise it. Jones is the simple negation of Ricardo, the purely external contradiction. He does not care any further about Ricardo's theory, except where he corrects or completes individual results, especially in the theory of rent. Jones continues to operate silently with Ricardo's or even Malthus's theory of value, without worrying much about their differences, which seem to him irrelevant. He has no explanation for complicated phenomena such as crises. Nowhere did he try to go beyond *historical description* to *theoretical comprehension*. That is precisely

---

59 Marx 1971, pp. 428–9.

Marx's achievement: that he placed recognition of the historical and social character of economic categories at the service of transforming [economic] theory. The problem presents itself for Marx at the point where Jones either accepts or rejects the results of previous theories. The realisation that economic relations are social relations led him to discover the fetishism of the concepts of commodity, money and capital. Labour appeared to him in its [historical] determination as wage-labour in its socially necessary form; the economic production process [appeared to him] in its double form as the labour process and the valorisation (exploitation) process, the commodity as use-value and as value. Capital is no longer a material stock [of goods], but the social relationship in which wage-labour is in opposition to the monopoly of the means of production. The worker sells his labour power; the product belongs to the capitalists, on whom the surplus labour devolves. The magnitude of the surplus labour, i.e. the surplus value, is determined by the division of the newly created value between workers and capitalists, i.e. by the amount of wages or variable capital. The distinction between variable and constant capital is thereby given, and in the development of this ratio of the organic composition of capital Marx found capitalism's most important law of motion. The differences in form between fixed and circulating capital, originating in circulation, was recognised as secondary vis-à-vis the distinction between constant and variable capital, arising from the valorisation process. The competition between capitalists for spheres of investment brings about equalisation of the different rates of profit into the average profit rate, which determines the transformation of values into prices of production. The historical-social view of economic categories destroyed their fetish character and led to solution of the problems upon which Ricardo and his followers foundered. *The economic theory of scientific Marxism grew out of the specifically Marxist union of the 'inductive method' of Jones and the abstract method of Ricardo.*

And the economic categories, once discovered, *remained* historical; their operation did not suddenly stop after they were discovered, nor will it be suddenly terminated by force, as utopian socialism wanted, thinking that it could substitute categories concocted in its imagination for the real ones. The distinguishing feature of scientific socialism is precisely that socialism is nothing but the result of the full development of the capitalist economy. It is not discovery of the rules for establishment of socialist societies, but rather explanation of the laws of the *capitalist* world that turns socialism into a science, demonstrating its inevitability as a necessary stage in social development. By breathing historical life into Ricardo's 'abstract principles', by turning economics into history and history into economics, Marx overcame the unhistorical rationalism of the classics and the irrational conservatism of the historians, along with the utopianism of previous socialism.[60] Economics was now no longer seen as a science of dead things, of the largest possible production or the best possible distribution. It was the understanding of social conditions, of the relations between the classes, of the necessity of the class struggle and its outcome. The conformity to law of the self-development of [Hegel's] Idea became the conformity to law of the will of classes, as determined by their social relationships, which we learned to recognise through economic science. The idea of evolution, stripped of its idealistic form, seized the social sciences.

∴

We have reached the end. With Jones, political economy arrives at the point where its previous conscious or unconscious assumption – the necessity, or the implicitly assumed existence, of the bourgeois form of production – had to be dropped in order to make possible further progress of the science. It is the point from which economics goes backwards towards vulgar economy or forwards to scientific socialism. In the final chapter [of the third volume of *Theories of Surplus-Value*], Marx offers a brilliant description of vulgar economy's relapse into the worst fetishism.

It is a splendid irony. Since the first volume of *Capital* appeared, countless attempts have been made to discover the precursors of Marx's ideas. A whole literature has developed, and now all the pundits must see that they were on the wrong track, that only in his posthumous work did Marx point them in the

---

60 'We should also not fail to recognise how the detachment of Marx's own fundamental view from utopian socialism only was made possible by his conception of theory as actually known historical necessity, as the conformity to law of self-consciousness, as experienced and understood causality. This has not been sufficiently emphasised, and we therefore run the risk of blurring again the distinction, so lively felt and sharply worked out conceptually by Marx, between his socialism and any utopianism. For modern socialism is not separated from utopianism by what people usually stress as its distinguishing feature, namely, that its political action and therefore its social praxis are guided by scientific knowledge; because the utopians also wanted to change the world through science, *and that was precisely the utopia*. The really essential difference is that this theoretical guidance of social praxis is only the systematisation of the tendencies existing in the social development process itself; that the science that illuminates modern socialism is nothing but *the real mass movement itself, only conceptually expressed*. The science of utopianism was the system of the rational exertions of the will of great individual minds; the science of modern socialism, by contrast, is nothing but the system of social volitions itself, only conceptually expressed' (Adler 1908, p. 86).

right direction. They were on the wrong track because the history of scientific socialism's development is much more the development of science than the development of socialism. German philosophy, French historiography, English political economy – consolidated in their aggregate results and united in the irresistible drive to find a scientific solution to the great problems posed by the revolutionary era – *tantae molis erat* [so great was the effort][61] to establish the foundations of scientific socialism. Is it any wonder that it has remained so steadfast, that the task of science continues to be not the laying of new foundations, but only the continued building [on the foundations of Marxism]?

Like no other thinker before him, Marx wrote the history of his predecessors with care and accuracy. If the work remained a torso, still all the essential moments in the development of science are emphasised. Equally true for this historical work is what Ernst Mach, another great researcher and historian of his science, mentioned in his introduction to *The Science of Mechanics* as the reason of his enterprise:

> We now propose to enter more minutely into the proposed subject of our inquiries, and, at the same time, without making the history of mechanics the chief topic of discussion, to consider its historical development so far as this is requisite to an understanding of the present state of mechanical science, and so far as it does not conflict with the unity of treatment of our main subject. Apart from the consideration that we cannot afford to neglect the great incentives that it is in our power to derive from the foremost intellects of all epochs, incentives which taken as a whole are more fruitful than the greatest men of the present day are able to offer, there is no grander, no more intellectually elevating spectacle than that of the utterances of the fundamental investigators in their gigantic power. Possessed as yet of no methods, for these were first created by their labours, and are only rendered comprehensible to us by their performances, they grapple with and subjugate the object of their inquiry, and imprint upon it the forms of conceptual thought. They who

---

61 ['*Tantae molis erat romanam condere gentem imperiumque*' ('So great was the effort required to found the Roman race') – Virgil, *Aeneid*, 1.33. A reference to *Capital*'s chapter on 'The Genesis of the Industrial Capitalist': '*Tantae molis erat* to establish the "eternal natural laws" of the capitalist mode of production, to complete the process of separation between the workers and the conditions of their labour, to transform, at one pole, the social means of production and subsistence into capital, and at the opposite pole, the mass of the population into wage-labourers, into the free "labouring poor", that artificial product of modern history' (Marx 1976, p. 925)].

know the entire course of the development of science, will, as a matter of course, judge more freely and more correctly of the significance of any present scientific movement than they who, limited in their views to the age in which their own lives have been spent, contemplate merely the momentary trend that the course of intellectual events takes at the present moment.[62]

But the history of the development of science is not always the simultaneous history of the rising awareness of the individual thinker. A detailed study of the theories certainly indicates that Marx first discovered many elements of his thought in his predecessors only after his system as a whole had been completed. But those details are at most of psychological or philological interest, for what a colossal work has Marx accomplished! Very few achievements in the history of science can be placed on the same level with it, even if he placed all the accumulated labour of previous thinkers at the service of his work. Speaking of Adam Smith, Jones offers these beautiful words:

> None but those ignorant of the ordinary march of knowledge will think it derogatory to the great Economist that he did not create all the light he used; that he seized the trembling and imperfect beams which, in the general progress of thought, many other intellects had begun to emit, and knit them with a strong hand into a perfect ray; which sheds a light upon the path of nations that can only disappear with the disappearance of the accumulated knowledge of our race. Such is the appointed task of all great leaders, in both moral and physical science; and such are the achievements which leave the human race their everlasting debtors.[63]

But about Marx we must say – now that we have learned from him personally how his economic system has become the dazzling conclusion of a brilliant development – that he accomplished something even greater. He not only collected and knit, but infinitely increased the intensity and fire of the light. He has accomplished the work that Hegel demands from a great man: 'He who expresses the will of his age, tells it what its will is, and accomplishes this will is the great man of the age. What he does is the essence and inner content of the age, and he gives the latter *actuality*'.[64]

---

62 Mach 1893, p. 7.
63 Jones 1859, pp. 407–8.
64 Hegel 1996, §318, p. 355.

Thus Marx has fulfilled the promise he made in *Rheinische Zeitung*: to subject to a thorough critique the communist ideas that, in the form they took in those days, could not even be granted theoretical objectivity.[65] He fulfilled the promise, driven by the desire for spiritual power and imbued with the firm conviction that

> the real *danger* lies not in *practical attempts*, but in the *theoretical elaboration* of communist ideas, for practical attempts, even *mass attempts*, can be answered by *cannon* as soon as they become dangerous, whereas *ideas*, which have conquered our intellect and taken possession of our minds, ideas to which reason has fettered our conscience, are chains from which one cannot free oneself without a broken heart; they are demons which human beings can vanquish only by submitting to them.[66]

---

65 ['The *Rheinische Zeitung*, which does not admit that communist ideas in their present form possess even *theoretical reality*, and therefore can still less desire their *practical realisation*, or even consider it possible, will subject these ideas to thoroughgoing criticism' Marx 1842, 'Communism and the Augsburg *Allgemeine Zeitung*', *Rheinische Zeitung*, 289, 16 October, in *MECW*, Vol. 1, p. 220].

66 Marx 1842, 'Communism and the Augsburg *Allgemeine Zeitung*', *Rheinische Zeitung*, 289, 16 October, in *MECW*, Vol. 1, pp. 220–1.

DOCUMENT 8

Theories of Surplus Value (1910)

Otto Bauer

Source: Otto Bauer, 'Theorien über den Mehrwert', *Der Kampf*, Band 3 (1910), s. 344 ff., reprinted in *Werkausgabe*, Band 8, pp. 365–76.

Introduction by the Editors

Readers who have worked their way through the previous seven documents in this collection will find that this article by Otto Bauer provides a convenient summary of what has gone before. Bauer wrote the article for a general educated reader, not for specialists who had already studied Marx closely and were familiar with both Volume III of *Capital* and the three Parts of *Theories of Surplus-Value*. But even for the more specialised reader, Bauer occasionally makes important connections and comparisons, based upon his own close understanding, that will fill in lacunae that may otherwise have gone unnoticed or been lost among details. Whereas previous documents investigated particular works of Marx with a microscope, Bauer makes a different sort of contribution, portraying the whole of Marx's economic writing with a focus not on method but directly upon the key issues of theory. Bauer looks not at the separate pieces of the puzzle, but rather at the finished system finally made available by the editorial work of Karl Kautsky.

∴

Otto Bauer's Review of Marx's *Contribution to Political Economy*

The appearance of the last volume of *Theories of Surplus-Value* is an important event in the realm of science. Marx's economic work now stands complete before us. Only now do we get to know the final part of the work – the part that Friedrich Engels intended to publish as a fourth volume of *Capital* – whose first part Karl Marx published in 1859.

Science owes heartfelt thanks to Kautsky, who edited the four-volume work. Kautsky has carried out his task admirably. He has retained the character of

Marx's work: the character of notes for self-understanding, which makes it an invaluable contribution to knowledge of the master's personality and enables us to see Marx's working method much more clearly than in *Capital*. But he [Kautsky] has arranged and articulated the notes so well that the fundamental ideas are not lost in the wealth of details that illustrate and complement many parts of *Capital*.

In this part of his work, Marx has given us a history of political economy. The characteristics of his historical narrative, trained in Hegel's [method], stand out vividly. Just as Hegel arranges all the older philosophical systems as integral parts of his own, as phases of its development, identifying this development with the self-development of Spirit in general, so Marx looks not only for the basic ideas of his theory, but also for each one of its component parts in the economists of the two preceding centuries, and he shows the internal development of those elements until their systematic organisation in his own doctrine reflects the development of bourgeois society. Marx traces his value and surplus value theory back to Petty; his price and profit theory back to Turgot; his theory of accumulation, of the reserve army and the rate of profit back to Adam Smith. The teachings of these men thus appear in a context that had to remain hidden to the authors themselves, and this link raises the collection of literary-historical notes to the level of historical science. This method separates Marx from bourgeois historiography and establishes his superiority. The bourgeois historiography of half a century has produced no work on the history of political economy that could measure up to it.

Theories of Surplus-Value is a difficult work that requires wide knowledge. It must find its readers in the circle of scholars, not in the mass of the people. However, the completion of its publication is an important event for us, because it contains a wealth of most fruitful suggestions for the popularisation of those parts of Marx's theory that are the foundations of modern socialism. For that reason, an overview of the contents of the work will probably be welcome by many readers of *Der Kampf*. We cannot go here into the many valuable details it includes, but we will attempt to outline in a few broad strokes the layout of the work.

The oldest view of surplus value is that of the capitalist entrepreneur; surplus value seems to him a mere addition to the acquisition or cost price. This is the capital gain, the *profit upon alienation* of Steuart,[1] the *profit d'expropriation* [profit on alienation] of the French mercantilists. The buyer loses what the

---

[1] Sir James Denham Steuart (1712–80) lived in France from 1746 to 1763 and was a theorist of value and population [note by Bauer].

seller wins. Therefore, surplus value remains unexplained within a single economic area and in the world economy as a whole. However the nation, the state will be enriched by them [the merchants] making such profit in foreign trade; this view thus led to the demand for an economic policy that guaranteed an active [positive] balance of trade [i.e. to mercantilism].

The surplus value that is realised in the circulation of goods within an economic region can only be explained if, as a result of the social production of commodities, the fund is discovered from which all the revenues mediated by circulation are defrayed. This fund can be represented most clearly as the surplus product of agricultural production. The soil produces so much revenue that, after setting apart the seed and those amounts [of grain] required to feed the workers, a surplus will still be left. The attempt to trace all forms of surplus value back to the agricultural net income led the Physiocrats to the first systematic presentation of the social reproduction process. Thus the Physiocrats already formulated the most important problems of political economy. If we place the presentation of this system in *Theories of Surplus-Value* alongside that of *Capital* and *Anti-Dühring*, we now have a deeply penetrating analysis of the Physiocratic doctrines, surpassing everything that bourgeois historiography has been able to say down to the present date on this first attempt at a systematic presentation of the production and distribution of values.

While surplus value was first regarded in France, then still largely agrarian, as the net product of agriculture, the English economists, living in the era between the English and the French Revolution, then recognised as value-creating not only agricultural labour but labour per se, and surplus labour not only as the agricultural net product, but as the net product of social labour in general. The landlord class wanted to portray ground rent as a legitimate source of income and the rate of interest as sinful usury. The theoreticians of the bourgeoisie answered that rent and interest are essentially the same, since the surplus of the produce of labour over the wages of the workers was the source of both. Thus was surplus value discovered, but although the starting point of those English economists was correct, it was also more developed and complicated than that of the Physiocrats, and they were therefore much less able than the Physiocrats to explain the whole of the capitalist economy on its foundations. But in dealing with the economic issues of their time they made a series of valuable partial discoveries, which were taken over by the classics.

Like his English predecessors, Adam Smith determined the value of commodities by the labour necessary for their production. He not only traced rent (like the Physiocrats) and the rate of interest (like Petty, Locke and Hume), but also entrepreneurial profit back to the difference between the values of the goods and the wages of the workers who produced them. Now it was necessary to explain from this basic insight all the phenomena of capitalist economy. In trying to do this, Smith became entangled in contradictions. But that is precisely the significant thing. By contradicting himself, by abruptly juxtaposing incompatible propositions, he set the tasks of his successors.

Here Ricardo stepped in and removed the contradictions in Smith's theory. Smith still confused the labour necessary for the production of goods with the labour that these goods *commanded*, that they could buy, while Ricardo sharply distinguished between those two concepts and determined the value of the goods consistently by the former criterion. Smith thought that the law, according to which the values of goods are determined by labour, applies only to simple commodity production and is modified by the development of property in land and capital ownership. Ricardo wants to retain the law also for developed capitalist production; the theory of rent and the investigation of whether changes in wages affect value are the focus of his system, because he wants to show that value is also determined by labour when developed landed property and capitalist relations are given. If all branches of social income are derived from labour, then the development of the work process, of the productive forces, appears as the goal of all the economic endeavours. By being ready, with the same ruthlessness, to sacrifice the interests of all classes to this objective, Ricardo represents the truly great side of capitalism, the development of the productive forces. His teaching is the weapon of the bourgeoisie: on the one hand against the landlord class, because ground rent is merely a deduction from profit and the idle landlord is a parasite who does not increase the wealth of society; and on the other hand against the workers, because profit is necessary, since only a class living off surplus value and driven by the profit motive can develop the productive forces. The greater the profit, the more rapidly capital grows and the more workers it can employ. These claims were challenged by the representatives of both the landlord class and the workers.

Malthus appeared as the spokesman of landlords, bureaucrats and priests. If Ricardo only had in mind the positive side of capitalism, the development of the productive forces, Malthus, following Sismondi, portrayed the negative side, the contradictions of the capitalist mode of production and the antagonisms it developed. But he portrays them as a representative of the classes of the past. The misery of the workers is a natural law for him. Since the workers' wages are less than the value of the commodities, the working class cannot buy [all] the goods it has produced. But the capitalist class must sell those goods in order to realise the profits. Since the working class cannot buy them, the capitalist class could not realise its profits if there were no classes that consume without producing, buying without selling: landlords, officials and priests. The same man who said that the workers must go hungry because too little food is produced also said that society could not exist were it not for classes that consume without producing. The Ricardians scoffed at this theory: 'Are the capitalists' profits made possible by them giving away their goods to idle consumers? Because that is what they do when they pay the rent to the landlord, the salaries to the civil servants, and the sinecures to the priests, with which those classes then buy the goods'. But the representatives of the workers replied: 'You ridicule Malthus's apologetics for the unproductive classes, but you teach us the same: you tell us to be content with our meagre wages and that the fruit of our labour must be given away to the capitalists, who will then use it to employ us'.

The socialists spoke as representatives of the workers. Marx mentions the author of an anonymous pamphlet of 1821 [Charles Wentworth Dilke, author of *The Source and Remedy of the National Difficulties, deduced from Principles of Political Economy*], Ravenstone and Hodgskin. Leaning on Ricardo's theory, they said: labour is the source of value, capital is unproductive, and all income of the propertied classes flows from the exploitation of the working class. We do not need capital; we want to abolish surplus labour. The author of the pamphlet declared: 'A nation is really rich only if no interest is paid for the use of capital; when only six hours instead of twelve hours are worked ... "Wealth [...] is *disposable time*, and nothing more" '.[2]

Pressed on the one hand by the Malthusians and on the other by the socialists, Ricardo's disciples strove to develop the doctrines of their master, but they ran into contradictions. With the development of the productive forces grows the misery of the workers made redundant by the machines, but the rate of profit also sinks; how is that possible, since, according to Ricardo's doctrine, the profit rate is higher, the lower the wages? The same capital yields the same profit whether it employs much or little labour; how is that possible if, according to Ricardo, only labour creates value? Unable to resolve these contradictions, Ricardo's disciples abandoned the foundations of their master's doctrines. Capital and land were turned into sources of value next to labour.

---

2 [Quoted in Marx 1971, p. 256. A footnote reads: 'The following sentence is Marx's paraphrase (written in German) of the ideas the author sets forth in the pamphlet'. The original reads: 'When, however, it shall have arrived at this maximum (of wealth), it would be ridiculous to suppose that society would still continue to exert its utmost productive power. The next consequence therefore would be, that where men heretofore laboured twelve hours they would now labour six, and *this* is national wealth, this is national prosperity. After all their idle sophistry, there is, thank God! no means of adding to *the wealth of a nation* but by adding to the facilities of living: so that wealth is liberty – liberty to seek recreation – liberty to enjoy life – liberty to improve the mind: it is disposable time, and nothing more' (Dilke 1821, p. 5)].

The dissolution of the Ricardian school gave birth to *vulgar* economics. Now capital had the mysterious property of breeding interest, just as the soil itself produced ground rent and labour wages. Economic life no longer appeared as the totality of the relations among people; lifeless things now dominated people and assigned to them their income. [According to the new apologetics,] the rule of capital is necessary because we cannot produce without means of production and without accumulated stocks of raw materials, and landed property is necessary because the soil is the basis of all labour. Exploitation is a natural law; profits are the wages of supervision by the managers of production; and capitalist production is production in general, the only possible production. The louder the criticism of capitalism, the more economics turned into capitalist apologetics, bent on the defence and glorification of capitalism.

Political economy was substantiated with the deduction of ground rent, interest and profit of enterprise from production [i.e. from labour]. By tracing surplus profit back from circulation to production, economists no longer explained it as a surcharge, as *profit upon alienation*, but instead looked for its origin in the net product. Yet they still envisaged the production of goods only as capitalist commodity production. Capitalism seemed to them the *absolute* [mode of] production. The technical and natural conditions of production in general were mixed up with the special social conditions under which a particular, historically determined and historically transient mode of production, the capitalist mode of production, takes place. Capital was for them nothing but the totality of the means of production and hoards. The wages of the workers are determined by the amount of means of consumption that can be produced and are low because no more can be produced. The accumulation of capital was equated with expansion of the undertakings and the means of production required by society, and is therefore just as necessary as the latter. But the more acutely class antagonisms developed, the more rapidly matured the recognition that capitalism is not the law of production in general, but only a transient form of production determined by certain social relations between men. Ricardo had already resolved profit, interest and ground rent into labour; Hodgskin went beyond him by tracing circulating capital, which the older economists regarded as a stock of goods, back to the juxtaposition of labours of different kinds.[3] By showing that the effects that had been attributed to a stock of goods were in fact attributable to the coexistence of different labours, a rela-

---

3 [Bauer refers to the fact that, according to Marx, circulating capital (a category arising from circulation) includes both variable capital and a section of the constant capital].

tion between working people took the place of a thing. Here is a root of Marx's resolution of the fetish character of the commodity and capital. Ramsay went even further: he said that capital is not necessary but is due only to the poverty of the masses, thus already indicating that capital is an historical category. Capital is not a condition of all production but only a relation of the producers to each other, given certain historical conditions. Comparing it with the many pre-capitalist modes of production, Jones finally regarded the capitalist mode of production as a transient phase in the development of humankind, a stage of development that can be followed by another in which the workers themselves will be the owners of the means of production and of the stocks necessary for labour. As he surveyed the changes in the productive forces and in the relations of production, he also recognised that the *ideological superstructure* changed with them. Thus Jones already enunciated the fundamental ideas of the materialist conception of history:

> 'As communities *change their powers of production*, they *necessarily change their habits too*' (Richard Jones, *Text-book of Lectures on the Political Economy of Nations*, Hertford, 1852, p. 48). 'During their progress in advance, all the different classes of the community find that they are connected with other classes *by new relations*, are assuming *new positions*, and are surrounded by new moral and social dangers, and *new conditions* of social and political excellence' (loc. cit.). 'Great political, social, moral and intellectual changes, *accompany changes in the economical organization of communities*, and the agencies and the means, affluent or scanty, by which the tasks of industry are carried on. These changes necessarily exercise a commanding influence over the different political and social elements to be found in the populations where they take place; that influence extends to the intellectual character, to the habits, manners, morals, and happiness of nations'.[4]

Kautsky says, quite rightly, that Karl Marx starts where Richard Jones stopped. Marx took the foundations of his theory of surplus value from the classics. His first task was to unfold what was already contained as a germ in his predecessors. Value was already determined by labour. Ricardo had already occasionally further defined labour as socially determined, saying that social labour is the common measure of goods, because all goods are products of social labour. Marx elaborated this idea by tracing concrete individual labours back to aver-

---

4 Jones 1852, p. 45, cited in Marx 1971, p. 430.

age social labour as the value-creating substance. The classics regarded wages as the monetary expression of the *value of labour*. But if stored up labour is exchanged against actual labour, how can it happen that unequal amounts of labour are exchanged? How then is surplus value possible? Ricardo's disciples were incapable of solving this problem. James Mill relinquished the theory of value, for he knew how to determine the *value of labour* only by supply and demand; Bailey pointed out the problem, and McCulloch helped himself out of the difficulty with mere phrases. Marx solved the problem by substituting the value of labour *power* for the *value of labour*.

Thus the theory of surplus value has been completed. The classics had already traced profit and ground rent back to labour. The author of the pamphlet of 1821 had already grouped them together under the concept of interest. Marx regarded them as forms of surplus value. But now the most important and difficult task had to be accomplished: Marx had to show how the concrete empirical forms of profit and ground rent can be deduced from surplus value.

The tendency to the *equalisation of the rates of profit* was already known to Turgot. Adam Smith abruptly juxtaposed it with the law of value. Ricardo first raised the question of how the equality of profit rates of capitals, which set in motion different amounts of labour, was compatible with the law that only value-creating labour generates surplus value. But Ricardo did not formulate the problem in general terms; he examined only two special cases, in which he had already pointed to the deviation of prices from values. He argued that changes in wages and differences in turnover periods brought about *exceptions* to the law of value. James Mill then added other exceptions. The exceptions soon appeared to be the rule. Malthus pitted that difficulty against Ricardo's theory of value. Bailey was misled by it into relinquishing the concept of *absolute* value. Torrens tried to find a way out of it by assuming that not only direct [i.e. living] labour but also accumulated labour had value-creating power. McCulloch equated the *actions* of the means of production with those of human labour. By doing so, however, he completely relinquished the theory of value, which regards value as a relation between the productive activities of people expressed through things. The problem on which the classics foundered first found its solution in Marx. He solved it by distinguishing prices of production from values, and by conceiving social surplus value, determined by the difference between the value product of social labour and the value of the total labour power, as the fund that is distributed among individual capitals according to the law of the average rate of profit, which controls price formation. Marx considered his new independent achievement to be not the discovery of surplus value, but the proof that the phenomena of profit, which apparently contradict the law of value, can only be understood as quotas of the surplus value; and with this the problem, already formulated by the Physiocrats, was really solved for the first time: the problem of tracing all the incomes mediated by circulation back to the net product of social labour. This historical background has to be remembered in order to recognise the absurdity of the ordinary criticism of Marx. Where Marx's real contribution lies – in the distinction between prices of production and values, between profit and surplus value – his critics saw a way out of an awkward situation. And because they are unable to find the solution to the problem of surplus value in production, with marginal utility theory they went back to circulation, proclaiming the *old profit upon alienation*, under a new name, to be a new discovery.

With the deviation of production prices from values, however, new paths were also opened up for the theory of *ground rent*. The Physiocrats had conceived rent as the surplus of the crop yields beyond the food requirements of the tillers of the soil. But already Petty and Locke no longer derived rent from the land, but from labour. Ground rent now appeared as a surplus of the prices of agricultural products over their values. Developed by Anderson, the theory of ground rent was taken over by West and Malthus, who turned it into a population theory. Ricardo, in turn, related it systematically to the labour theory of value. Ricardo's theoretical interest in the theory of rent lay in proving that ground rent does not contradict the law of value. Since in Ricardo price and value coincide, he could only introduce ground rent as differential rent, as the surplus of the market value over the individual value. By distinguishing between prices of production and values, Marx could factor in the absolute rent, as the difference between value and price of production, which appears wherever agricultural products are sold at their value. The differential rents are only different magnitudes of the absolute rent.[5] Marx's theoretical interest in absolute rent must be understood in this historical context. Nevertheless, I have the impression that this is the ephemeral part in Marx's theory. The cumbersome presentation in *Theories of Surplus-Value* of the question whether the price of corn can rise over its value or fall below it – a question raised by Marx himself[6] – no more offers a completely satisfactory answer than the shorter presentation in *Capital*. It seems to me that Marx relapses here into the error he

---

5 ['*Die Differentialrenten sind nur noch verschiedene Größen der absoluten Rente*'. Readers will notice that this statement is confusing, due to either a typographical error or a lack of Bauer's usual care in writing. Whatever the case, Marx saw absolute rent as a surplus in addition to differential rent, the latter being determined by the price of production of agricultural products (see Document 6 in this volume)].

6 See Marx 1968, p. 316.

had himself overcome; namely, directly linking price and value rather than postulating a mediated relationship between them. If the criticism of Marx were about theoretical ideas rather than about politics, then it would be directed here, at the weakest point of the Marxian system.

Marx's theory of prices of production is based on recognition of the diversities in the organic composition of capital. Marx confronts the distinction between fixed and circulating capital, originating in the sphere of circulation, which the Physiocrats bequeathed to the classics, with the distinction between constant and variable capital, originating in the value-forming process itself. The development of the productive forces finds its specific economic expression in the progress to a higher organic composition of capital. Thus theory passes over from the old static problem of value distribution to the problem of exploring the laws of motion of the capitalist economy. The problems of accumulation and the rate of profit, already posed by the older economists, now took on new shape.

Smith believed that value resolves itself completely into the revenues of workers, capitalists and landowners. He therefore equated the accumulation of capital with the employment of a growing number of productive workers, assuming that the demand for labour power grows in the same proportion as capital. But despite the rapid accumulation, development of the factory system now produced the industrial reserve army. Malthus believed he could explain this by the fact that the accumulation of capital does not proceed as quickly as the growth of population. Barton first pointed out that the demand for labour power grows not with the accumulation of capital in general, but only with the growth of circulating capital. In this way the importance of the composition of capital was already discovered, and Smith's theories (and with them Malthus's) theories were overcome. Ricardo adopted Barton's theory. Finally, Ramsay restricted the concept of circulating capital to wage capital, thus already discovering the correct determination of the organic composition of capital. But a misunderstanding still remained with Barton-Ricardo-Ramsay. They believed that circulating capital constitutes an ever smaller part of total capital, because the labour employed in the production of necessary foodstuffs constitutes an ever smaller proportion of total labour – as if foodstuffs, provided only that they were produced in sufficient quantities, must find their way to the workers made redundant by the machines. They saw the actual effect of changes in the organic composition of capital as the cause. This was a retrogression to the crudely material conception of the Physiocrats, a confusion of the special laws of capitalist production with the laws of production in general, a remnant of Malthus's view that the misery of the working class is due to the fact that production is unable to provide the growing population with foodstuffs. The same error appeared in Cherbuliez.[7] On the other hand, the pamphlet of 1821 already pointed out that foreign trade always allows conversion of necessary food into luxury goods and elements of constant capital. The income of the working class does not depend on the mass of food that can be turned into variable capital, but on that mass which is actually transformed into variable capital. The error was systematically overcome by Marx's presentation of the social reproduction process. He began by rebutting Smith's mistake that value can be resolved into revenues. In that way, the equation of accumulation with growth in the employment of productive workers was repealed. Capital can be exchanged not only against revenues, but also against capital. The revenue of the workers does not grow with the accumulation of capital in general, but only with the accumulation of variable capital. The distribution of labour among the different productive sectors adjusts to the ratio of constant to variable capital and of the latter to the surplus value; the adjustment is completed when the constant capital and the accumulated part of the surplus value of the consumption goods industries are exchanged against the variable capital and the consumed part of the surplus value of the means of production industries. This adaptation can, however, only take place as a result of disruptions and crises. The problem thus finds its solution in a new *Tableau Économique*.[8]

The theory of the *profit rate* is closely linked to this analysis. Smith had already observed that the rate of profit falls; he was glad about it and considered it a driving force of economic progress. To his followers, however, the fall in the rate of profit looked like a disaster that threatens capitalist society. Since Ricardo equated profit with surplus value, he could only explain the fall in the rate of profit as a result of the fall in the rate of surplus value; he argued that the rate of surplus value must fall because the growing difficulty in supplying food increases the value of labour power. In that way his doctrine again touches on the theory of population. John Stuart Mill laboriously tried to prove Ricardo's views. The more clearly it appeared that the rate of profit falls precisely with the development of the productive forces, the closer subsequent economists came to the correct solution. The pamphlet of 1821 and Hodgskin already derived the fall in the rate of profit from changes in the organic composition of capital, though still not universally but only in one specific case: when capital grows more quickly than the working population, so that equal amounts of living labour are confronted with growing masses of capital. For the rate of profit to

---

7   Antoine-Elisée Cherbuliez (1797–1869), Swiss political scientist, occasionally also active in Paris and an opponent of socialism (ed.).

8   [Bauer is referring to the arithmetic reproduction schemes that Marx provided in Volume II of *Capital* and Karl Kautsky discussed in Document 3 of this volume].

remain unchanged, surplus labour had to be expanded more and more at the expense of necessary labour; as soon as that was no longer possible, the rate began to decline. Ramsay came even closer to a general solution by determining the rate of profit not only by the rate of surplus value but also by the extent of constant capital, and by deriving its fall from the growth of that part of the value of the product 'which must be put aside to replace the fixed capital'. Marx concluded the series. The realisation, contrary to Adam Smith's opinion, that capital is exchanged not only against revenue but also against capital, explains why revenues can grow more slowly than capital, so that, with the same rate of surplus value and with the same distribution of revenues, the profit rate decreases when the constant capital grows more quickly than the variable.

Thus, the problems raised by classical economics found their solution in the system developed by Marx. The tool that Marx used in this accomplishment was recognition of the dichotomy between constant and variable capital, whose mathematically expressed ratio reflects the development of the productive forces in economic terms. Thus economics discovered, as contradictions and antagonisms developed together with the productive forces under the rule of the capitalist relations of production, that the capitalist relations abolish themselves [*sich aufheben*: sublate, negate and transcend themselves] and must be replaced by other relations of production. The analysis of the capitalist mode of production turned into its criticism. By finding the solution to its problems in Marx's system, bourgeois economics ceased to be bourgeois economics and became socialist economics.

DOCUMENT 9

A Contribution to the Understanding of Marx's Research Method (1910)

Heinrich Cunow*

Source: Heinrich Cunow, 'Zum Verständnis der Marxschen Forschungsmethode', *Die Neue Zeit*, 28. 1909–10, 2. Bd. (1910), H. 53, S. 1001–10.

Introduction by the Editors

Heinrich Cunow's essay on Marx's research method is a response to Revisionism in the Social-Democratic parties and empiricism in the social sciences. Revisionists were rejecting Marx's conclusions because capitalism appeared

---

* Heinrich Cunow (1862–1936) was a German Social-Democratic Party journalist and historian. From 1898, he served as one of the editors of the SPD theoretical journal *Die Neue Zeit*, and, from 1902 onwards, he also worked as editor of the SPD central organ *Vorwärts*, where, together with Heinrich Ströbel, he was considered an anti-revisionist spokesman for the Left. In his articles for *Die Neue Zeit*, Cunow pioneered the study of American imperialism, but also, and more importantly, he emphasised the central role of banks and finance-capital in imperialist expansionism (Cf. Day and Gaido (eds.) 2011, pp. 177–210). In 1907, Cunow became a lecturer at the SPD party school in Berlin, teaching alongside Franz Mehring, Rudolf Hilferding and Rosa Luxemburg. His theoretical works include several studies in anthropology and a history of the revolutionary press during the French Revolution. In August 1914, Cunow and his editorial colleagues at *Vorwärts* opposed the Reichstag's approval for war-loans, but, in mid-October 1914, he shifted to the chauvinist position of the SPD-majority led by Friedrich Ebert. In 1915, he attempted a theoretical justification for war-loans, arguing that Marxists should not oppose imperialism because it represented a step forward compared to competitive capitalism, and neither Europe nor the rest of the world was yet prepared for socialism. During the War, Cunow worked for the Hamburger *Echo* and Parvus's newspaper *Die Glocke*. After the split between the Independent Socialist Party of Germany (USPD) and the SPD in October 1917, he remained in the latter and succeeded Kautsky as editor of *Die Neue Zeit* from 1917 to 1923. In 1919, he was elected to the National Assembly; in the same year, he was appointed Extraordinary Professor of Ethnology at the Humboldt University of Berlin. From 1919 to 1925, he was a member of the Prussian State-Parliament. For further biographical details, see Florath 1987.

not to conform to the essential laws that Marx discussed in *Capital*. Empirical political economy proposed to study a world of facts without considering their necessary and essential *logical* connections. For 'vulgar' economists, the 'facts' are the 'facts'; if they follow one another in some order, then it must be the facts that constitute the order. The problem, of course, is that the facts may just as well appear in some different order at different times and in different places. In that case, the world of phenomena would be 'meaningless' – unless the facts can be shown to conceal what is 'real', namely, a logical pattern that governs appearances. Cunow explains that in the determination of economic laws, Marx was influenced by Hegel's logical distinction between the 'real' and the appearances that merely 'exist'.

The distinction between reality and appearance is as old as Plato, who reasoned that all sensations presuppose concepts. A concept is a class, or a universal; and if existent things can only be known through universals, then the universals themselves must be objective. Objective universals are Ideas that are beyond all specifics of time and place. For Plato, 'things' are imperfect copies of universal Ideas. For Aristotle, 'things' are a combination of 'matter' and 'form'. Since form implies the purpose of a thing, or the end towards which the thing moves, Aristotle says ends are logically prior to beginnings.

Hegel's *Logic* addresses these same issues. The doctrine of Being traces the movement from indeterminacy through the categories of Quality and Quantity to Measure. Next comes the doctrine of Essence, demonstrating that essence has its 'being' in appearances. The union of essence and appearance is 'Actuality'. Beyond the doctrine of Essence is that of the Notion, or self-determining thought that culminates in the thought of thought. The Absolute Idea, the end of Hegel's *Logic*, is the identical 'subject-object' and the dialectical 'unity of the concept and reality'.[1] The Absolute Idea is also the form of logic, which is the dialectical method. The end, therefore, is the beginning, for the contradiction of indeterminate Being, which is unformed and therefore nothing (i.e. no-thing), is what initially sets the entire *Logic* in motion.

Marx, says Cunow, speaks of 'absolute' laws in a similar sense, that is, as dialectical principles of movement. Economic laws are the *real* logic behind the facts of economic *history*. Like Hegel's laws of logic, they are also dialectical and must entail contradictions. Cunow points out that the same holds in any physical science. The law of gravity is not an illusion because it is contradicted by centrifugal forces. Similarly, the law of the falling rate of profit is not an illusion because profits rise temporarily during a business cycle.

---

1 Hegel 2010b, pp. 672–3.

The laws of capitalist development, rather than being contradicted by transitory phenomena, are the real explanation of such contradictions. To account for contradictions, says Cunow, is the purpose of all science, which would *'be superfluous if the form of appearance of things directly coincided with their essence'.*

∴

Heinrich Cunow on Marx's Research Method

Two or three decades ago, especially among the academic youth, it was, so to speak, *de rigueur* in the socialist world to avow oneself a Marxist. The older utopian-socialist doctrines had hopelessly collapsed. Their beautiful dreams too clearly contrasted with the capitalist economic development taking place for the entire world to see, with its increasingly intensifying class struggle between workers and entrepreneurs. On the other hand, that development provided almost daily new evidence of the accuracy of Marx's theories. In the vortex of the sinking, old and sentimental socialist ideas, only Marx's own doctrine appeared as a massive solid structure. Only there was to be found, according to all appearances, the sought-for agreement between socialist theory and the new phenomena of social life, resting on a solid scientific foundation; and thus many socialist politicians and writers, who had never penetrated deeply into the universe of Marx's ideas and had never understood his method of work, called themselves Marxists.

Today the situation is *reversed*, at least for the socialist movement in Central and Western Europe. Many, who once called themselves Marxists, have returned to their earlier circle of ideas, to a bourgeois radicalism permeated by sentimental socialism, and they advocate some kind of 'turning back' whether to the teachings of Proudhon, Kant, Hume, or even Rousseau.[2] To be sure, Marx

---

2 [The reference is to Eduard Bernstein's call during the 'Revisionist Controversy' for a return to the critical attitude of Immanuel Kant in revising Marxist theory: 'Social Democracy needs a Kant to judge the received judgment and subject it to the most trenchant criticism, to show where its apparent materialism is the highest and therefore most easily misleading ideology, and to show that contempt for the ideal and the magnifying of material factors until they become omnipotent forces of evolution is a self-deception which has been, and will be, exposed as such by the very actions of those who proclaim it' (Bernstein 1993, p. 209). In response, G.V. Plekhanov wrote: '... we have not the least desire to follow this "critic's advice"

is granted a place of honour in the history of socialism, but – so proclaim these reactionaries – most of his theories have been rendered obsolete by the recent facts of economic development, and Marxism finds itself in a state of mental paralysis. Its once-living theses have become numb, dead formulas, and for that reason a thorough review of the theoretical legacy of Karl Marx is urgently needed.

What explains this change? In part, to be sure, disappointed hopes and a realisation that the bourgeois world has much greater vitality than was once thought: a realisation that makes the revolutionising of the present social system appear to be far away; but also, to a very considerable extent, as we already said, the fact that those who call for a revision of Marx's doctrines never penetrated into the very essence of Marx's method of investigation. As they once decided to call themselves Marxists only by observing that Marx's teachings outwardly corresponded to the phenomena of economic development, now they think they have recognised that this agreement no longer exists, and they have decided to turn away from Marxism and return to the earlier stages of their development. The fundamental difference between Marx's and today's economic working methodology [*volkswirtschaftlichen Arbeitsmethodik*: method of work in economics] has never been clear to them, and thus they also do not see that this outward correspondence [between Marx's theory and the facts of contemporary economic development], required by them and sorely lacking, does not at all constitute an immediate criterion of [the correctness of] Marx's theory, because that theory by no means attempts to explain individual phenomena emerging to the surface of the capitalist machine in their configuration at any particular time. Marx rather wants to determine the laws or tendencies underlying the capitalist economic formation and its evolution, which he describes as 'natural laws' of the economy, and wherever possible their 'pure' effect, unmodified by various counter-influences.

That is a very different goal from the one that contemporary political economy, as taught at the universities and applied in the bourgeois press to elucidate economic problems, for the most part sets itself today. Contemporary bourgeois economics does not want to (and usually does not claim to) discover the laws of capitalist economy, as the classics of English political economy once did. It merely seeks to provide explanations for the economic processes taking place before our eyes, and often only for the outward form of those processes. Its method, therefore, is not the analytical-abstract one, which seeks

---

when he calls us "*back to Kant*". On the contrary, we call him *back ... to a study of philosophy*' (Plekhanov 1898a, p. 331)].

to understand the laws at play by eliminating the accompanying phenomena and grasping the processes under investigation in their purest possible form. Rather, it proceeds in a purely empirical-combinatorial way, often even in what Marx mocked in *Capital* as a *crudely empirical way*.[3] It thinks that economic phenomena are just as they present themselves to the observer, i.e. they are regarded as given facts, without the more or less random concomitant circumstances [*Nebenumstände*] having been separated out by a penetrating analysis, and then a causal nexus is assumed to exist between them because of their apparent outward connection, and often even only because of their temporal succession. Thus, to illustrate this method with some examples from recent times, there are contemporary economists who, finding that, at the beginning of the economic crises, the warehouses are filled with goods, mainly with items of personal consumption, immediately draw the conclusion that too few of such goods had been consumed during the preceding period of prosperity, and that crises therefore arise from *general under-consumption*. Other economists have observed that before the crisis, as a rule, a so-called cash shortage occurs and the bank discount rate on bills, as well as the private discount, increases significantly; they conclude from this that the crisis is a mere consequence of the shortage of money, that the latter arises from the fact that, during the preceding period of economic upswing, not enough new capital was accumulated for the expansion of the production process and too large a share of production went into means of subsistence, and that crises do not therefore result from under-consumption but from *relative over-consumption*. Again, a third group of economists finds that, before the crisis, the shares listed on the stock exchange experienced a tremendous rise, until then suddenly a rapid fall in share prices occurred on a certain day; they conclude from this that crises are the result of unhealthy stock market speculation and its effect on production activity.

Such examples of a totally crude empirical approach, which concludes from the temporal succession of two or more economic phenomena that the latter phenomenon must simply be the result of the former, can be multiplied indefinitely. Let us recall here only the nice theories about the organisation of production and the future prevention of economic crises by the trusts – theories that have been thoroughly refuted by the latest crises in Germany and America, but which vulgar economics could easily have discovered to be erroneous before this refutation, if only it had studied analytically the question of how contemporary capitalist economy balances supply and demand by com-

---

3 [A reference to this passage in the second volume of *Capital*: 'The crudely empirical way in which Smith opens his investigation ...' (Marx 1978, p. 269)].

modity production constantly outstripping demand and falling behind it, and by the over- and undervaluation of products resulting from these fluctuations. Thus, the adjustment of supply and demand likewise cannot lead to a [crisis-free] regulation of economic activity, because the market demand is something constantly fluctuating, *and when demand becomes abnormal, the supply that adapts to it also becomes abnormal.*

But not only do these kinds of economists simply conclude, without further ado and from the temporal succession of two phenomena, that a causal link must exist between the two; they often go a few giant steps beyond that and immediately construct, when they encounter apparent analogies in the previous course of economic development, all sorts of beautiful laws, often the kind of 'eternal' or 'general' laws that apply, in their opinion, not only to capitalist economy, but to the economy '*in itself*', even to Caesar's Germans or the Iroquois of James Fenimore Cooper's time.

Marx's method stands in the sharpest contrast to this practice. To draw such causal inferences, or even to derive economic laws, from some arbitrarily chosen events from ancient and modern times, because of their apparent outward conformity, appeared to Marx totally unscientific. In his view, such laws can be discovered only by way of a logical deduction from proven general basic facts. Also, Marx was, in a sense, an empiricist; he also proceeded from the phenomena of economic life at different times; but he did not use those phenomena in the way in which they present themselves outwardly to the observer in order to build his system. Everyday experience, he says, grasps only the *deceptive appearance of things*; any such phenomenon must therefore first be investigated in its real essence, *it must be scientifically analysed*: an activity which he compares in the preface to the first edition of the first volume of *Capital* to 'microscopic anatomy'.[4] The final shape of economic relations, as they outwardly manifest themselves to our observation, is in fact quite different from their essence, their often veiled real character and the concept corresponding to it. Thus, it is also completely wrong to accept those external appearances as the given, actual facts and to draw conclusions from them. The task of science is rather to penetrate through the outward appearance to the inner nature of economic processes.

From this standpoint, in *Capital* Marx hurls at vulgar economy the accusation that, in its crude empiricism, it only sees the outward manifestations, and usually only seeks to clarify conceptually and to systematise those ideas that force themselves onto the merchant and the manufacturer in their economic

---

4 Marx 1976, p. 90.

activity, without penetrating more deeply into their internal connections. Thus he says, for instance, in the first volume of *Capital*, that vulgar ('crudely empirical') political economy 'relies here as elsewhere *on the mere semblance as opposed to the law which regulates and determines the phenomena*'.[5] 'That in their appearance things are often presented in an inverted way is something fairly familiar in every science, apart from political economy'.[6]

And even more characteristic of Marx's methodology is perhaps the following passage in *Capital*:

> Vulgar economics actually does nothing more than interpret, systematize and turn into apologetics the notions of agents trapped within bourgeois relations of production. So it should not surprise us that precisely in the estranged form of appearance of economic relations that involves these prima facie absurd and complete contradictions – *and all science would be superfluous if the form of appearance of things directly coincided with their essence* – that precisely here vulgar economics feels completely at home, these relationships appearing all the more self-evident to it, the more their inner connections remain hidden, even though they are comprehensible to the popular mind.[7]

Marx insists that the economist should approach the study of economic laws just as the physicist approaches the determination of physical laws. As the physicist tries to discover 'pure' laws and, to this end, abstracts from particular concomitant circumstances and disturbing influences, which in reality are always present, so Marx seeks to derive analytically, as far as possible, the economic laws in their 'pure' form from their basic conditions, thrusting aside the disturbances that always appear. He says himself, comparing his method with that of the physicist:

> The physicist either observes natural processes where they occur in their most significant form, and are least affected by disturbing influences, or, wherever possible, he makes experiments under conditions which ensure that the process will occur in its pure state.[8]

---

5 Marx 1976, pp. 419–20.
6 Marx 1976, p. 677.
7 Marx 1992, p. 956.
8 Marx 1976, p. 90.

So the economic theorist should also proceed in his field, in the field of political economy. And since economic processes are often linked to all kinds of accidental circumstances, since they are therefore not only the effect of a law but also the result of many laws or tendencies, more or less criss-crossing, mutually abrogating, weakening or complementing each other, the researcher must distinguish between the main phenomena and the accidental circumstances, abstracting from the randomly or regularly occurring disturbing influences, and separating out, as far as possible, the individual causes and their special effects in the consideration of the original [causal] nexuses. He must know how to separate out and isolate.

Of course, this method too does not always provide a correct result, because accuracy depends not only on the method but also on how the researcher follows it in practice, how deeply his analysis penetrates, how far he recognises the accidental circumstances as such, and how much he separates the essential from the inessential. But in any case, according to the opinion of Karl Marx, only in this way is it possible to recognise the underlying laws of economic phenomena. For example, Marx does not derive his law of value from price phenomena emerging to the surface of the economy, but by way of logical deduction from the nature of commodity exchange. And he does not obtain his law of capitalist accumulation by starting from phenomena of concentration, but rather through a penetrating analysis of the capitalist reproduction process, of the transformation of surplus value into capital and of the changes taking place during this process in the mutual proportions of the individual components of capital. And only after he has deductively derived the tendencies of accumulation from certain basic facts of the process of capital formation and expansion, or, as he himself says, '*the absolute general law of capitalist accumulation*',[9] does he proceed to offer 'illustrations' of this law, that is to say, to prove from English economic history how the conditions of individual strata of the English working classes developed under the effect of this law.

A cursory glance at the method used here by Marx is enough to see immediately how much this process differs from the crude empirical-historical method of that practical economics that we find in the columns of the financial and commercial press. The methodologists among these people proceed the other way round and, on the basis of mere outward similarities, want to combine different kinds of phenomena of concentration of capital and then, by drawing a diagonal through this pile, to derive a so-called average law. It is quite natural that this empirical economics, which merely takes the superficial phe-

---

9 Marx 1976, p. 798.

nomena of economic life to be its basic elements, should find the method of Karl Marx totally incomprehensible. Thus, for example, Mr. Böhm-Bawerk, the much-admired Austrian professor and former Finance Minister, says of Marx's theory of value:

> Now Marx, instead of proving his thesis from experience or from its operant motives – that is, empirically or psychologically – prefers another, and for such a subject somewhat singular line of evidence – the method of a purely logical proof, *a dialectic[al] deduction from the very nature of exchange*.[10]

Such laws of motion (tendencies), inferred by way of deduction from certain basic facts, Marx calls '*pure*' or '*absolute*' laws – 'absolute' in the sense of the philosopher Hegel, whose student Marx was. That is, the term 'absolute law' is not to be understood, according to contemporary parlance, as an '*unrestricted*' or always applicable law, but as an ultimate principle of movement underlying the manifold changing phenomena of a certain type, as a basic trend of development, more or less hidden under the outward forms of appearance. For that reason, it is by no means a contradiction – as claimed by those theorists who never understood Marx – when Marx, after explaining in the first volume of *Capital* the law of capitalist accumulation and characterising it as 'an absolute and general law', immediately afterwards says: '*Like all other laws, it is modified in its working by many circumstances, the analysis of which does not concern us here*'.[11]

Thus, although the law of accumulation is an 'absolute' and 'general' law of the capitalist economy, it is not 'unrestrictedly' valid, nor will it always show its effects in the same way. Its effects are rather – as with other economic laws – modified (that is, altered, diverted or restricted) by 'many circumstances'.

Is that not a contradiction?

---

10   Böhm-Bawerk 1896, p. 68.
11   Marx 1976, p. 798. In Chapter 14 of Volume III of *Capital* Marx discusses several factors that counteract the 'law' of the falling rate of profit and comments: 'We have shown in general, therefore, how the same causes that bring about a fall in the general rate of profit provoke countereffects that inhibit this fall, delay it and in part even paralyse it. These do not annul the law, but they weaken its effect. If this were not the case, it would not be the fall in the general rate of profit that was incomprehensible, but rather the relative slowness of this fall. The law operates therefore simply as a tendency, whose effect is decisive only under certain particular circumstances and over long periods' (Marx 1992, p. 346).

Only for those who do not understand Marx's method. Because, just as the laws of physics do not always manifest themselves in a pure form but are thwarted by the counter-effects of other laws, so also in the economy the 'absolute' laws, which are the *basic tendencies of movement*, do not always manifest themselves in the same way. There is not one, but many economic laws, and none has its own particular self-contained scope or sphere of action in which it rules unchallenged. Economic life is rather a resultant of many laws that mutually limit, weaken and abrogate each other in their effects: *a product of many forces and counter-forces crisscrossing in many ways*.

If that is so, why was it necessary to research the so-called 'absolute' or 'pure' economic laws? Marx replies: because only by not sticking to the outward appearance, by analytically penetrating into the basic laws of economic life, is the social movement understandable! Appearances, says Marx, are deceptive. Just as the human body is not understandable as long as we only look at its overall appearance and its external functions, and just as we are first able to understand its vital mechanism when we dissect it, researching the functions of its individual parts, both in themselves and in their interconnection, penetrating down to its basic element, to the cell, so it is also necessary for us in the economic field to identify first, through careful analysis, the basic economic laws in their purity, unaffected by any side effect, and only then to get to know the deviations (modifications) that they suffer under the influence of other laws.

But if Marx conceives economic development, so to speak, as a 'natural historical process', he does not claim that economic laws are 'natural laws' in the same sense as the laws of physics. While theorists of the classical school of English political economy, on whose shoulders Marx stands, regarded the laws they discovered in the economic conditions surrounding them as the laws of economic activity in general, which, ever since man produced and exchanged, always determined his economic life – although their effects naturally did not emerge so clearly during the earlier, simpler stages of development – according to Marx, every economic period has *its own special laws*. Whenever such an economic phase has outlived itself and another begins, more or less new economic laws also appear in place of the old ones. Economic laws are in fact, according to Marx, nothing but the laws of social relations between people, and because society is not something unchanging and rigid, but is always reshaped anew in the course of development, every new social formation has its new special laws.

All economic laws must therefore be regarded as *historically determined*. As a consequence, the object of economic research cannot be to construct laws suitable for all economic stages, 'eternally' valid laws. Each economic era must be seen in its historical contingency, in its dependence on special laws. Besides, as Marx stated in the preface to the second edition of the first volume of *Capital*, in reference to a criticism of his work in the *European Messenger* (*Vyestnik Evropy*)[12] of St. Petersburg, for him the most important thing is to find the law of change of economic phenomena, 'the law of their variation, of their development, i.e. of their transition from one form into another, from one series of connections into a different one'.[13]

Such an analytic-deductive method of research must necessarily come into conflict with the approach prevailing today in almost all historical and social sciences, which, despite all their occasional flirting with the theory of knowledge, usually accept social phenomena as they outwardly manifest themselves to our senses, without deeper analysis; and is it quite natural not only that the method used by Marx in *Capital* should be found by 'scientists' of this kind to be a 'hair-splitting play with concepts', but also that some of the smartest of these 'scholars', among them particularly the Italian Professor Achille Loria, should have discovered that Marx, in his diabolical malice, merely wanted to lead his readers and followers by the nose. Is it not folly, so these gentlemen argue, to use a complicated, painstaking analysis to work out 'absolute' economic laws and then afterwards state that those laws are not at all 'absolute'; that is, that they do not have absolute validity, but that their action is rather always affected or even abolished by other laws? – i.e. to construct laws that actually are, according to his own admission, not at all effective in practical economic life! Is that not a ridiculous analytical gimmick? Thus, for example, Marx investigates, in the first 100 pages of *Capital*, exchange-value and the metamorphoses of the commodity, and after he has found, in his opinion, this value, he says that it expresses itself in the commodity price and that the price is therefore the monetary expression for the amount of labour materialised in the commodities. But, then again, he afterwards denies that average prices correspond to the magnitudes of exchange-values; and finally, in the third volume of *Capital* (Part 1, Section 2), he states that the market prices of commodities are, indeed, determined on the whole by the socially necessary labour time required for their production, but that not just the law of value must be taken into consideration as a factor in [the determination of] the magnitudes of prices, and that alongside the law of value also operates the law of the equal average rate of profit, that is, the equalisation of the different profit rates through competition.

---

12 [See Document 1 in this volume].
13 Marx 1976, p. 100.

Is that not a contradiction, a self-refutation of Marx's law of value? Absolutely not! Because the economy and its various manifestations, as mentioned earlier, are not the result of one, but of different laws criss-crossing in their effects, and the impairment of the effect of a law by the effect of another law can never be regarded as a refutation of the first law, especially not when, as in this case, the so-called 'disturbance' can be accurately traced and, in a sense, even foreseen. For example, does the law of adhesion not apply in the field of physics because it is often modified or cancelled in its effects by the opposite law of cohesion? Is gravity just an illusion because centrifugal force often more or less paralyses it? Is the law of gravity just a silly construction because it only applies in a vacuum, while the atmosphere is filled with air and, because of the resistance of that air, the effects of the law are in many ways affected and appear to have been altered? Whoever says that all those laws do not exist, because their effect is not always the same and is often modified or abolished by other laws, thereby *negates the whole of modern science*.

It is therefore quite funny when people, among them many of the so-called revisionists, learnedly argue that many of Marx's laws, such as the law of accumulation and concentration, cannot be right, because their effects were not always felt, or not in all branches of production or in all capitalist countries. This is every bit as scientific as if someone announced, full of wisdom, that there is no law of gravity, because gravity sometimes cannot be recognised. Certainly, Marx's method is not correct because of the fact that Marx applied it; and even assuming that it is correct, that would not mean that each individual research result that Marx reached is true, for even a correct method can, of course, be used incorrectly, even by those who created it. Thus, one can surely raise no objection when opponents take up Marx's method and try to prove that it is faulty, inaccurate, or contradictory, or when they try to demonstrate that the basic facts from which Marx proceeds and the various elements of his argumentation are erroneous. But to claim that this or that economic law does not exist because of the fact that its effect cannot temporarily be seen, only shows that the 'Marx-critics' in question have never understood the difference between Marx's method and the crudely empirical method of ordinary financial-press economics.

It usually turns out that those critics understand nothing concerning the methodological questions raised. So we can often hear, for example, that yes, Marx's law of accumulation and concentration is not *entirely* wrong, because it is valid for industry, although not for agriculture – or rather, that it is actually not valid only for German, Belgian and English agriculture, because one finds in agriculture in North America, Russia or some other country a remarkable concentration of capital and enterprises, just as so and so many decades earlier

Germany had its agricultural concentration. This reasoning betrays immediately that the speaker did not understand even the most basic elements of Marx's method, because in that case he would have known that the idea that the laws of capitalist production could be valid only occasionally and at some places is absurd. A capitalist law applies to the whole area of the capitalist mode of production, not only for individual countries and not from time to time. To be sure, its effect in particular countries can be thwarted or paralysed by various other opposing forces, for example, by economic, commercial and tariff policies, settlement and mortgage legislation, competition from neighbouring countries on domestic and international food markets, artificial maintenance of certain agricultural operations and settlement forms through tax, land, export premiums, etc.

The fact that these and other counter-effects are present and may temporarily or permanently weaken or prevent in any given country the concentration of capital or enterprises does not at all mean that there is absolutely no law of concentration in the capitalist economy. That law merely operates, as does any other economic law, in different ways and to varying degrees under different circumstances.

Therefore, whoever wants to understand Marx's [economic] theory correctly and comprehensively must first familiarise himself with the method used by Karl Marx. That knowledge is the first precondition for understanding the great economic life-work of this mighty thinker. Whoever does not understand Marx's methodology cannot understand his argumentation and appreciate the importance of his research results. For them, *Capital* remains an accumulation of sharp-witted but mostly useless analyses and constructions.

DOCUMENT 10

On the History of the Theory of Value (1903)

Rudolf Hilferding

Source: Rudolf Hilferding, 'Zur Geschichte der Werttheorie', *Die Neue Zeit*, 21. 1902–3, 1. Bd. (1903), H. 7, S. 213–17.

A review of Wilhelm Liebknecht, *Zur Geschichte der Werttheorie in England* [*The History of the Theory of Value in England*], Jena: Fischer, 1902.

Introduction by the Editors

In this essay Rudolf Hilferding addresses a twofold meaning of labour: as a physiological *fact*, and as a social-economic *category* of capitalist society. In the first sense, as Wilhelm Liebknecht[1] pointed out, labour is an expenditure of human energy. In that regard he cited Marx's comment in *Capital* that all human labour is 'essentially the expenditure of human brain, nerves, muscles and sense organs'. As Hilferding notes, the conclusion would appear to be that 'the value of a product depends solely upon the amount of energy spent upon its production, which in turn is evidently determined by two factors: the duration and the intensity of labour. Skilled labour is more value-creating than simple labour only if it is also more intensive, which tends to be correct in general terms'.

But Hilferding adds that Marx's theory of labour value must also be understood 'on methodological grounds', which in turn leads to the treatment of labour as a social-economic category. In his notes on 'The Method of Political Economy', Marx spoke of labour as one of the 'most simple definitions', reached through analysis of an initially given abstraction, a pre-given whole such as the economy or population. After arriving analytically at the most 'simple concepts', it is then necessary to reconstruct society in thought, ending with 'a totality comprising many determinations and relations'.[2] From the perspective

---

1 The Wilhelm Liebknecht who authored the book reviewed by Hilferding was a brother of Karl Liebknecht and the fourth son of Wilhelm Liebknecht (senior), one of the initial leaders of the German Social-Democratic Party.
2 Marx 1970, pp. 205–6.

of political economy, the social significance of any simple concept is determined by the whole in which it is situated.[3] Labour, as a physiological fact, has a very different meaning from labour as an economic category in the social system of capitalism.

It is true, Marx notes, that simple categories, including labour, may have an independent 'historical or natural existence' that precedes their more concrete forms.[4] Physical 'possession', for example, precedes the legal form of 'property'; and 'Money may exist and has existed in historical time before capital, banks, wage-labour, etc. came into being'.[5] Nevertheless, the simple category only reaches 'its complete intensive and extensive development ... in a complex social formation ...'.[6]

In the context of emerging capitalism, Adam Smith was able to treat 'labour as such', whether in manufacturing, commerce or agriculture, as the universal activity that produces wealth. 'It might seem', wrote Marx, 'that ... merely an abstract expression was found for the simplest and most ancient relation in which human beings act as producers – irrespective of the type of society they live in. This is true in one respect, but not in another'.[7] It was true in the sense that labour obviously occurred in primitive communities, but the universal abstraction of *labour as value* logically presupposed generalised commodity exchange. The social form of *wage-labour*, in turn, presupposes private ownership of the means of production. As Hilferding comments, wage-labour is 'an *historical form*, through which the proportional distribution of the total labour of society, required for production [*Herstellung*] of the social product, asserts itself in a society characterised by the fact that the connection of social labour takes place through the private exchange of individual labour products'.

In the notes on method, Marx gave the following account of the universal role of wage-labour as a social category of capitalist society:

---

[3] In his notes on 'The Method of Political Economy' Marx wrote: 'Just as in general when examining any historical or social science, so also in the case of the development of economic categories is it always necessary to remember that the subject, in this context contemporary bourgeois society, is presupposed both in reality and in the mind, and that therefore categories express forms of existence and conditions of existence – and sometimes merely separate aspects – of this particular society, the subject; thus the category, *even from the scientific standpoint*, by no means begins at the moment when it is discussed *as such*' (Marx 1970, p. 212).

[4] Marx 1970, p. 207.
[5] Marx 1970, p. 208.
[6] Marx 1970, p. 209.
[7] Ibid.

The fact that the specific kind of labour is irrelevant presupposes a highly developed complex of actually existing kinds of labour, none of which is any more the all-important one [as, for instance, agricultural labour was in feudal society]. The most general abstractions [e.g. wage-labour creating value] arise on the whole when concrete development is most profuse, so that a specific quality is seen to be common to many phenomena, or common to them all. Then it is no longer perceived solely in a particular form ... The simplest abstraction [labour *sans phrase*] ... which expresses an ancient relation existing in all social formations, nevertheless appears to be actually true in this abstract form only as a category of the most modern society ... The example of labour strikingly demonstrates how even the most abstract categories, despite their validity in all epochs – precisely because they are abstractions – are equally a product of historical conditions even in the specific form of abstractions, and they retain their full validity only for and within the framework of these conditions.[8]

The labour that concerns Marx is the social category of *wage-labour*, whose value is the objective cost of reproducing labour power – including both means of subsistence and, as Hilferding points out, the educational costs involved in the reproduction of skilled and complex labour – which in turn determines the value of commodities, the rate of surplus value, the tendency towards the social average rate of profit, and thus ultimately the distribution of all the productive forces of capitalist society.

As an '*economic* category', says Hilferding, labour must be regarded 'in its specific social *form*, in its social function. This happens when the total labour of society is regarded as a unit, of which each individual labour represents only the aliquot part. Only as part of a unit, of the total labour, are the individual labours mutually comparable; and their common measure is simple average labour – an historically, not a physiologically, determined magnitude, which changes with alterations of the historical circumstances'. Whereas Liebknecht understood 'the concept of labour, as the value-principle, in physiological terms', Hilferding explains why that view is fundamentally mistaken: 'Production and the labour spent upon it must be regarded not as a natural but as a social fact'.

∴

---

8   Marx 1970, p. 210.

Rudolf Hilferding's Review of Wilhelm Liebknecht, *Zur Geschichte der Werttheorie in England* [*The History of the Theory of Value in England*]

In economic literature there is still no history of economic doctrines that can meet even modest standards. The circumstances have not been conducive to fulfilment of this task. The speed of social development, whose inner laws economics attempts to discover, has quickly made every system of political economy appear obsolete; a new one, better adapted to new phenomena and interests, soon appeared inevitable; and pressing problems left no room for detailed historical consideration. But our own times are likewise not favourable for the start [of such an enterprise]. The development of social contradictions more and more deprives bourgeois democracy of its innocence. Its representatives have abandoned too long ago the reckless disinterestedness of the great economists not to dread its reappearance. Finally, as the break-up continued and the [German] historical school negated the very possibility of a theoretical economics,[9] it has seemed a totally idle enterprise to write a history of political economy that would be a mere catalogue of fruitless errors.

We must, therefore, content ourselves for the time being with some preliminary monographs dealing with individual doctrines or particular periods. But most of these presentations suffer from the drawback that the subjective views of the author constitute an obstacle to objective assessment of the economists. If a judgement of the significance of individual doctrines can only be understood contextually, in connection with an entire system, and if severance of this connection by any particular monograph [*Einzeldarstellung*: individual presentation] already provides an opportunity in advance for arbitrary or unjustified objections, then a merely historical study of economic theories [*dogmengeschichtliche Studie*] offers no objective standard whatever for appraising an economic doctrine. It will only be possible to offer an objective judgement of an economic doctrine, freed as much as possible from subjective opinions – to show its significance and relative correctness, its lasting contributions and its errors – when the nature of the presentation itself is different, when a materialist historiography reveals the reasons for emergence of individual doctrines, accounting for their origin in economic conditions and laying bare their connection with the positions the author adopted towards the social struggles of his time. But this task has hardly been undertaken thus far for the

---

9 [On the German historical school, see Documents 12 and 13 in this volume].

major schools of political economy, let alone being attempted for individual economists and their doctrines.¹⁰

Wilhelm Liebknecht most likely thought something similar when he published his work on the history of the theory of value in England.¹¹ By choosing, however, to describe the theory of value as the basis of any great economic system [i.e. system of economic thought], he preserves the unity of the presentation as he portrays the characteristic traits and essential elements of each doctrine. And since he traces the historical development of criticism, he [also] secures his subjective point of view – which, in the absence of a genetic derivation,¹² must guide him in the arrangement and assessment of the authors – against eventual attacks and thus avoids any charge of arbitrariness.

Liebknecht is a supporter of the labour theory of value. He sees in Ricardo the leading exponent of that theory prior to Marx, and, while describing Ricardo's predecessors in chronological sequence, he arranges the economists who came after Ricardo according to the position they adopted towards that theory. But if, in his criticism, he wanted to secure the labour theory of value, and in that way his own standpoint, against its enemies, he also had to include in his presentation that theory's most developed form, i.e. he had to include Karl Marx's system in his survey. Thus, his historical presentation offers a successful overview, based on a thorough knowledge of the subject at hand, of the development of the theory of value in England, which basically consisted of the ever more detailed elaboration of the theory of labour value.

---

10   [The earliest systematic history of political economy from a Marxist point of view was Rubin 1979, a translation by Donald Filtzer of the second, revised Russian-language edition of 1929].

11   Liebknecht 1902.

12   [Cf. Marx on the 'genetic presentation' (*genetischen Darstellung*): 'Classical political economy occasionally contradicts itself in this analysis. It often attempts directly, leaving out the intermediate links, to carry through the reduction and to prove that the various forms are derived from one and the same source. This is however a necessary consequence of its analytical method, with which criticism and understanding must begin. Classical economy is not interested in elaborating how the various forms come into being, but seeks to reduce them to their unity by means of analysis (*Sie hat nicht das Interesse, die verschiedenen Formen genetisch zu entwickeln, sondern sie durch Analyse auf ihre Einheit zurückzuführen*), because it starts from them as given premises. But analysis is the necessary prerequisite of genetical presentation, and of the understanding of the real, formative process in its different phases (*Die Analyse aber die notwendige Voraussetzung der genetischen Darstellung, des Begreifens des wirklichen Gestaltungsprozesses in seinen verschiednen Phasen*)' (Marx 1969, Vol. III, p. 500)].

With the author's guidance, it is pleasing to follow how the original subjective conception – which looked for the *cause of valorisation* and regarded value as something only relative – was increasingly displaced by objectivist tendencies that strove to find an absolute standard of value, and how this [effort] was simultaneously accompanied by the separation of use-value, as a natural category, from exchange-value as a social category, until finally the labour theory of value was developed by Marx as the strictest objectivism. Marx regards the social category of exchange-value only as an *historical form*, through which the proportional distribution of the total labour of society, required for production [*Herstellung*] of the social product, asserts itself in a society characterised by the fact that the connection of social labour takes place through the private exchange of individual labour products. By doing so, Marx substituted the objective standpoint of social production and distribution for the subjective starting point, viewed as the motivation for individuals engaged in economic activities.

In the second part of the work, in his criticism of the theories [of value], Liebknecht first briefly shows the groundlessness of the theory of supply and demand as well as of the theory of production costs, in order to discuss in more detail the labour theory of value in its Marxist form. First of all, in an analysis that is all the more commendable given the many errors prevailing among both friends and opponents on the issue, he explains exactly what the progress from Ricardo to Marx involved. We would only have wished that the advance by Marx had been appreciated not only on purely economic but also on methodological grounds, which, of course, is impossible without probing more deeply into the connection between Marx's economics and his general social-theoretical views. But perhaps this task would have gone beyond the scope of Liebknecht's presentation.

In his criticism of objections to the labour theory of value, Liebknecht first dismisses the tedious misunderstanding of those who interpret the theory in ethical terms and foist upon Marx *judgements*, whereas what he offers are *explanations*. Then Liebknecht considers in more detail two objections, one of which concerns the role of use-value in Marx's system while the other deals with the problem of skilled labour. The question of the significance of use-value leads to a debate with *marginal utility psychology*, whose inadequacy on the crucial points Liebknecht successfully demonstrates.

It appears to us, however, that his remarks are less felicitous concerning the relation between simple and skilled labour. Liebknecht understands the concept of labour, as the value-principle, in physiological terms, referring to the well-known passage in *Capital* that says:

however varied the useful kinds of labour, or productive activities, it is a physiological fact that they are functions of the human organism, and that each such function, whatever may be its nature or its form, is essentially the expenditure of human brain, nerves, muscles and sense organs.[13]

But if one understands labour physiologically – and Liebknecht argues that one should regard this principle as underlying the whole system – one can only eliminate differences between various kinds of labour by reducing them to their physiological common measure; that is, to energy that is originally accumulated as potential energy in the human body through metabolism and then becomes fluid energy through labour. Accordingly, the value of a product depends solely upon the amount of energy spent upon its production, which in turn is evidently determined by two factors: the duration and the intensity of labour. Skilled labour is more value-creating than simple labour only if it is also more intensive, which tends to be correct in general terms.

[But] we believe that this view is based upon a fundamental mistake. If labour is to be postulated as the value-principle, the question under consideration is not physiological but economical. It is difficult to see how the physiological concept of labour – incidentally, a view of labour in terms of mechanics would have fit Liebknecht's presentation better – can explain any economic phenomenon at all. Physiologically, animal labour is just the same as human labour, which is why Adam Smith once declared the labour of domestic animals to be as value-creating as that of field workers, an opinion that one should not counter with the objection that for people only *their* labour comes into consideration, because with this appeal to human interest one immediately gives up the objective standpoint. Liebknecht's quotation from Marx, so often misunderstood, refers only to the content of the concept of value, i.e. it merely states the *natural* fact that goods must be produced, that they are the products of labour. But if I consider that labour from a mechanical, physiological, technical or some other point of view, it will never be an *economic* category, and only as such can labour be the starting point of economic analysis – i.e. become the value-principle. Production and the labour spent upon it must be regarded not as a natural but as a social fact. But labour is a social and especially an economic category only when individual labour is regarded in its specific social *form*, in its social function. This happens when the total labour of society is regarded as a unit, of which each individual labour represents only the aliquot part. Only as part of a unit, of the total labour, are the individual labours

---

13 Marx 1976, p. 164.

mutually comparable; and their common measure is simple average labour – an historically, not a physiologically, determined magnitude, which changes with alterations of the historical circumstances. The introduction of public elementary school reduces the level of many previously skilled labours to simple average labour. On the other hand, capitalist development, when accompanied by physical degeneration of the population, brings previously simple labour, requiring great physical strength and dexterity, back to the level of skilled labour. And skilled or complicated labour is many times simple labour in a proportion determined not physiologically but economically; that is, in proportion to how much simple labour must be applied to generate complex labour through an educational process, which again must be regarded only from an economic and not from a physiological or psychological point of view. This is so because simple average labour, in its historical determination, is at the disposal of society for its production, but skilled labour is itself first a product of society. Its production involves the expenditure of a series of labours that produce complex labour; labours whose value-creating force exists in a latent form in complex labour and first becomes available through its expenditure.[14]

But it is an unsupported claim to say that the value of complex labour power and its products stands in a certain proportion to physiological performance. A hard-working agricultural labourer certainly does not consume less energy than a Lancashire frame tenter [who looks after spinning frames], despite the great difference in both their wages and the value of their products. But we cannot refer to education, higher living standards and the like without returning to social factors, thus departing from the physiological point of view. That standpoint, however, is not only methodologically flawed; it is also entirely inappropriate for explaining economic phenomena in general. Instead of looking for the equality of qualitatively different labours in their character as parts

---

14   The problem of skilled labour and skilled labour power will be treated in more detail in a different context, which we hope will soon be available to our readers. Here these indications must suffice. (We likewise hope soon to be able to publish this rather extensive work, which we accepted many months ago but have thus far been unable to print due to reasons of space). (The editors [Karl Kautsky]). [Hilferding refers here to his famous work, *Böhm-Bawerk's Criticism of Marx*, usually issued in English together with Eugen Böhm von Bawerk's *Karl Marx and the Close of His System*. Hilferding's work was published the following year, not however in *Die Neue Zeit* but in the book series launched by the Austro-Marxists: *Marx-Studien: Blätter zur Theorie und Politik des wissenschaftlichen Sozialismus*, hrsg. von Dr. Max Adler und Dr. Rudolf Hilferding, Wien, 1904, Band 1, pp. 1–61. Cf. Hilferding 1904, pp. 123–48, Chapter I: 'Value as an Economic Category'. On this topic, see Bauer 1906, a review of Deutsch 1904].

of total social labour, it seeks to resolve their differences into mere differences of intensity, an attempt that must fail if only because an accurate measure for intensity exists only with qualitatively equal labours and consists of the amount of products they produce.

But this objection to Liebknecht's attempt to solve a problem, which is one of the most controversial issues in economic theory, does not affect the value of his study. Its historical part successfully fills a gap in the literature, and its criticisms are highly stimulating even where one cannot always agree with him on particulars.

DOCUMENT 11

Karl Marx's Formulation of the Problem of Theoretical Economics (1905)

Rudolf Hilferding

Source: Rudolf Hilferding, 'Zur Problemstellung der theoretischen Ökonomie bei Karl Marx', *Die Neue Zeit*, 23. 1904–5, 1. Bd. (1905), H. 4, S. 101–12. [A review of Isaiah Rosenberg, *Ricardo und Marx als Werttheoretiker. Eine Kritische Studie* (*Ricardo and Marx as Value Theorists. A Critical Study*), Wien: Ignaz Brand, 1904].

Introduction by the Editors

In his review of Isaiah Rosenberg's book comparing Ricardo and Marx, Rudolf Hilferding provides a concise account of Marx's view of the subject matter of theoretical economics, an issue that will later reappear in much greater detail in the works of Isaak Rubin.[1] The focus of Marx's concern, Hilferding points out, was not economic history, and still less the technical development of forces of production, but rather the *social form* of commodity production and its consequences for capitalist society.

For Marx's predecessors, particularly Ricardo, the commodity was a pre-given fact and not subject to further inquiry. Since he presupposed the capitalist *form* of production and exchange as 'natural and unchanging', Ricardo concentrated on the *content* of economic goods and thereby arrived at his labour theory of value. But Ricardo assumed what Marx took to be problematic; that is, how a society of self-interested and mutually indifferent individuals exists and reproduces itself. Prior to capitalism, no social organisation had ever existed in which production of use-values occurred mainly for sale into an unknown market. All previous communities were connected, to one degree or another, by 'a common will to joint action'. Marx's concern, Hilferding explains, was to discover what motivates self-seeking individuals 'who work for each other without

---

1 See in particular Rubin's 'The Dialectical Development of Categories in Marx's Economic System' (Document 20).

knowing each other'. 'What constitutes this circle of people as a society; and what is the law of motion for this society that makes it intrinsically different from previous ones?'

The 'epistemological peculiarity' of capitalist society involved spontaneous economic regulation that was independent of any conscious will. According to marginalist theory, there is no mystery here: each individual subjectively determines value for himself, and production is explained by the profile of total demand. But this *illusion* of autonomy actually presupposed the *reality* of commodity fetishism and an objective law of value that operates with 'social-natural necessity'.

Whereas Ricardo assumed economic categories to be empirical, quantitative and immutable, Marx's awareness of capitalism's historical character led him to see individual labours as parts of the total labour of a society objectively regulated by unconscious forces. The 'good', Hilferding writes, became a 'commodity' because of relations of production that preclude any other form of social-economic mediation. Only by resolving the mystery of commodity production 'could Marx arrive at the basic distinction between concrete labour, creating use-value, and abstract, social, value-creating labour' – that is, labour in the form of exchange-value – and thus show 'the starting-point of political economy'. With the labour theory of value, Ricardo 'had found the key, but not the door that the key unlocked ... Karl Marx first opened it up for us. He was the discoverer of socialist society because ... he was "the discoverer of the capitalist mode of production"'.

∴

Rudolf Hilferding on Karl Marx's Formulation of the Problem of Theoretical Economics

Marx's standing in political economy and his relation to his predecessors, the classics, has not so far been satisfactorily investigated. That is hardly surprising, given the lack of interest on the part of official economics in theoretical problems. But socialist literature also lacks an exhaustive presentation. Here people usually follow the sketch of Marx's relation to Smith and Ricardo and their socialist interpreters, given by Friedrich Engels in his preface to the second volume of *Capital*, which was classic in its brevity and rigour. This sketch was written before publication of the third volume and is incomplete if only for that reason. Despite that fact, it stresses precisely the crucial issue for research – the fundamental standpoint adopted by Marx on the problem of theoretical economics – for it was this radically different standpoint that made possible all the progress on individual issues. People cannot possibly grasp this fact if they limit themselves to comparing individual issues, regardless of the difference in standpoints.

And yet that is the path taken most often; for instance, in the recently published study on Ricardo and Marx as value theorists, written by Dr. Rosenberg (Rosenberg 1904).[2] For that reason, it is more of a preliminary work than a solution of the problem, which, indeed, is not even posed in its entirety, for it does not examine the entire systems of Marx and Ricardo but only their value theories. We think that is an undue restriction of the subject, because the theory of value is the foundation of the entire economic doctrine. How much it is so, determines the unity of the latter. The extent to which the theory of value is the foundation of an economic doctrine determines precisely the internal cohesion of that system. The understanding of the theory of value can only be gained and its significance assessed from the whole [economic] system. It is therefore a merit and not a drawback of the book that Rosenberg does not adhere too closely to his restriction of the subject matter, but rather always goes into the overall system. This should have made it even more imperative, therefore, to point out the fundamental divergence between the two systems; yet this task, as a brief overview of the contents of the book will show, was never undertaken.

Rosenberg begins with an account of Ricardo's doctrines, which is all the more necessary because those doctrines are now often presented in a very strange way. The more official economics turns away from the labour theory of value, the greater is the effort to prove that the theory's most important representative suffered from inconsistencies in his starting points, and thus to deny his significance as a theorist of labour value. Rosenberg counters those attempts in detail. That polemic is on the whole very well conducted, though the details sometimes appear a little overdone. In particular, in his observations on the role of absolute value[3] and on the solution of the problem of the equal rate of profit, Rosenberg now and then seems to attribute to Ricardo insights that, with such clarity, are only the result of Marx's thought.

After a criticism of the Ricardian theory of value, whose main faults, according to Rosenberg, are the modest attention paid to 'absolute value' and the lack of a solution to the problem of equalisation of the rate of profit on the basis of the labour theory of value, we get a description of Marx's system that is, on the

---

2   Rosenberg 1904.
3   Rosenberg 1904, p. 55.

whole, successful. In a final section, Rosenberg then compares the doctrines of the two economists, reaching the conclusion that 'Marx is a direct successor to Ricardo in the elaboration and development of the labour theory of value' even if his system was 'a completely independent and original creation of a great, independent, brilliant mind'.[4]

It would be very interesting to follow the details of Rosenberg's analysis, especially since we by no means always agree with his remarks on what Ricardo and Marx had in common and what separated them. To mention a minor point, for instance, we think that Rosenberg is wrong when he ascribes to Marx the theory that labour in transportation does not create value and surplus value but rather belongs to circulation costs.[5] A look at the second volume of *Capital* shows that Marx taught the exact opposite:

> The quantity of products is not increased by their transport. The change in their natural properties that may be effected by transport is also, certain exceptions apart, not an intended useful effect, but rather an unavoidable evil. But the use-value of things is realized only in their consumption, and their consumption may make a change of location necessary, and thus also the additional production process of the transport industry. The productive capital invested in this industry thus adds value to the products transported, partly through the value carried over from the means of transport, partly through the value added by the work of transport. This latter addition of value can be divided, as with all capitalist production, into replacement of wages and surplus-value.[6]

Rosenberg seems to be in the dark about the criteria [determining] value-creating labour. Labour creates value only in a commodity-producing society. In that kind of society, any productive labour is value-creating; and any labour that is necessary for *society*, for the purpose of social production, is productive even apart from the specific historical form that production assumes in a given society. It is only under certain circumstances that this [social] form makes goods appear as values, and therefore makes productive labour appear as value-creating labour. But the distinguishing mark of productivity, which in a commodity-producing society is at the same time the distinguishing mark of value creation, is the same in all social formations. However, the production

---

4 Rosenberg 1904, p. 127.
5 Rosenberg 1904, p. 112.
6 Marx 1978, pp. 226–7.

process only ends with the creation of goods that are ready for use – which may include, under certain circumstances, their transportation to the consumers' location. Conversely, labour spent only for the purpose of capitalist circulation, which arises *only* from a definite historical organisation of the production process, is not value-creating.[7]

But to continue following all the details would not carry us very far, nor would it be very fruitful. These are errors that knowledgeable people will correct easily by themselves.

More important, it seems to us, is to attempt to indicate the differences between Marx and Ricardo insofar as they deal with matters of principle. Rosenberg thinks that 'These differences lie only to a very small extent within the sphere of value theory. On the whole, they are only consequences of the differences in the historical, sociological and philosophical views of both men'.[8] But this in no way relieves us of the need to offer an analysis, for these differences, if they are to have any meaning, must also manifest themselves in the economic field and especially in the foundation of the economic system, in the theory of value – all the more so since Marx applied himself to the study of economics precisely in consequence of his overall historical and sociological views. Indeed, it is precisely the essentially different position that economics occupy in Marx's overall conception that gave his economic doctrines their fundamental importance.

∴

The history of political economy is a piece of self-knowledge of bourgeois society. But knowledge stands in the service of the will. And the content of the will of the new society was profit. Wealth and the acquisition of wealth was the goal that drove its collective action, its policy. *How does the nation get rich?* That was the issue raised by the politicians and taken over by the theorists, who posed the question: *What is the wealth of nations?* One remembers the response that the monetary and mercantile system tried to give. Adam Smith posed the same problem, but he expanded it by including the question of the distribution of wealth in his field of investigation – or 'the order according to which its [labour's] produce is naturally distributed among the different

---

7   'The general law is that *all circulation costs that arise simply from a change in form of the commodity cannot add any value to it*' (Marx 1978, pp. 225–6).
8   Rosenberg 1904, p. 51.

ranks of the people'.[9] For Ricardo, however, the problem of 'What is wealth' is solved; for him, the main issue of economics is discovery of the laws governing distribution. And he was followed in that respect not only by his bourgeois supporters and opponents but also by socialists, who likewise pushed to the foreground the distribution problem as *the* major problem of economics, and who, since they remained caught up in Ricardo's economic solution, fled from economics into ethics in order to condemn economics as unjust and to develop, with [William] Thompson, the principles best leading to the happiness of humankind.

It is different with Marx. For him, the question concerning the nature of wealth is not at all a question of political economy. Wealth is a sum of use-values, and these are a product of the activities of man and nature; their increase is the natural consequence of growth in labour's productivity, as depicted by the history of technology. For Marx, the question is: What is the *form* of wealth? This question had not been posed at all by classical economics. Indeed – and this constitutes the peculiarity of classical economics' historical position vis-à-vis its predecessors – it had shifted the production process to the centre of its investigation in order to fight against the doctrine of the creation of wealth by circulation, as developed in the monetary and mercantile system. But in its search after wealth, which for it was indiscriminately both use- and exchange-value, it held fast to the content. The form adopted by wealth was self-evident for classical economics, which held on to bourgeois society as the unconscious precondition of its thinking. That is why it was so difficult for it to distinguish between the technical and economic aspects [of wealth] – economically speaking, between use-value and value – and why this distinction remained so incomplete not only in the Physiocrats but also in Adam Smith. Ricardo was the first who consistently maintained this separation, but without substantiating it clearly enough – which from his point of view was also impossible, as we shall see.

What is wealth, how is it produced, how is it distributed? Those had also been the problems of bourgeois economics. What then is the advance in Marx? Precisely the fact that for him there is a problem, where for others there had been a self-evident precondition. Marx asked: what form does wealth adopt according to the historically changing circumstances under which people produce? How does wealth appear? And he gave his famous answer: 'The wealth

---

9 [The title of Book I of Adam Smith's *Wealth of Nations* reads: 'On the Causes of Improvement in the productive Powers of Labour, and of the Order according to which its Produce is naturally distributed among the different Ranks of the People'].

of societies in which the capitalist mode of production prevails appears as an "immense collection of commodities"; the individual commodity appears as its elementary form. Our investigation therefore begins with the analysis of the commodity'.[10] In that way, the problem of *theoretical* economics was for the first time completely and exhaustively formulated. This, however, requires a more detailed explanation.

[Marx's definition] excluded in advance any mixing up technical and economic analysis, because the question of the production *process*, which is the subject matter of technology, does not interest us here at all, and neither does the finished product itself, with its various natural properties. What interests us now is only a single, but particularly important, property adopted by the object; namely, that of being a commodity – an object which has no use for its owner but only for others, for someone else in *society*. The object was in that way recognised as a mere symbol, as a mediator of a social relation, a relation that could only arise in a specific form of society and, of course, could not be a relationship between objects but only between people, the members of this society. If we therefore succeed in finding the law that regulates the relations of these objects to each other, would this not also mean finding the 'law of motion of society' itself, the law that connects its individual members, shows the *mutual* dependence of their economic activities, and thus solves the problem of theoretical economics?

Further consideration will give us the answer to this question and, at the same time, will show us more clearly where the problem of theoretical economics lies and what answer that problem requires.

We have seen how Marx did not look at the production *process*, how his analysis rather focused on the social form assumed by the products resulting from production. But the product, in its social-formal determination [*gesellschaftlichen Formbestimmtheit*], is no longer a product of the production process that simply owes its natural properties to the changes made to it for the purpose of its intended use; instead, it is an expression of the production *relations* in which its producers stand. Now the question is no longer the natural side of production, the influence of humans on nature, but the *mutual relations of people in production*. However, the question concerning the relations of production can be answered in two ways, and the kind of answer separates *economic history* from *theoretical economics*. The former investigates the formation of the production relations; it may show us how, under certain natural conditions and at a given stage of development of the productive forces, certain relations of

---

10   Marx 1976, p. 125.

production emerge, and how the production relations in turn react upon the productive forces, further developing and transforming them.

Can this historic-genetic approach [of economic history] lead us to a full understanding of these production relations?

We would be satisfied with knowledge of the origin of the production relations if these relations were transparent; a scientific approach would require going no further. But when is that the case? The complexity, enormity and difficulty of the production *process* do not concern us here. The production relations themselves must contain the criterion for deciding whether, besides their genetic explanation, a *theoretical* understanding is also necessary. But this criterion must be contained in the nature of the production relations themselves, i.e. in the way in which they are constituted, and this constitution can evidently be only twofold.

People can relate to each other *consciously* in their production as parts of a production *community*; [in that case,] their behaviour in production and their mutual relations are uniformly regulated. Their labour organisation and the distribution of their products are placed under central control. The relations of production appear directly as social relations; the relations between individuals, to the extent that they are related to the economy, appear determined by the social order, and their private desires appear embedded in social relations. The production relations themselves are *immediately* understood to be *consciously* organised and desired by the community. With the explanation of the origin of this organisation and its description, the task is exhausted. Economic analysis here dissolves itself into *economic history*. In this kind of society there is no room for theoretical economics.[11]

The case is quite different, however, when the regulation of production relations is not a conscious one. The social relations now appear unintended or, more accurately, not consciously wanted, and therefore as the blind and random result of countless individual actions independent of each other. The

---

11   Similarly, but without further explanation, Konrad Schmidt says in an excellent article: 'I have called modern economic life a mechanism regulated by law (of course economic, not legal), and the knowledge of these objectively tangible laws the essential task of political economy. But must each economic order be subject to such covertly working laws? This [necessity] does not lie in the concept of economic order itself. As long as people consume the products of their labour themselves or must cede part of them to the ruling class for direct consumption, the economic order remains transparent, simple and clear. To understand such an economic order means to describe it and to demonstrate the historical causes of its formation and development' (Schmidt 1892, pp. 421ff.). [See Document 14 in this volume].

social context itself, and its regulation, now become problematic, and the question arises: What motivates this group of people who work for each other without knowing each other, who *share* [the products of their labour] between each other without *knowing* each other? What is the labour organisation that determines the distribution of their products, which must be distributed in order for them to be useful at all? What constitutes this circle of people as a society; and what is the law of motion for this society that makes it intrinsically different from previous ones? Earlier they were connected by a common will to joint action. Now they are isolated from each other as private individuals, acting according to one's own free will at one's own risk.[12] Only necessity forces them to relate to each other; not, however, as people united by a common goal, but by [the fact that they] exchange things with each other, because only as property owners do they have any interest in other property owners. Their *social* relationship appears reduced to the *private* relationship of exchange. But exchange, as such, is first of all only a private relationship. For two people to exchange, nothing more is needed than for each of them to have an object and to be willing to give it up for another. As such, exchange is a phenomenon belonging to all social formations, because all social formations know property.[13]

---

12 We cannot fail to quote here the words with which Ferdinand Tönnies characterises society: 'The theory of *Gesellschaft* takes as its starting point a group of people who, as in *Gemeinschaft*, live peacefully alongside one another, but in this case without being essentially united – indeed, on the contrary, they are here essentially detached. In *Gemeinschaft* they stay together in spite of everything that separates them; in *Gesellschaft* they remain separate in spite of everything that unites them. As a result, there are no activities taking place which are derived from an *a priori* and pre-determined unity and which therefore express the will and spirit of this unity through any individual who performs them. Nothing happens in *Gesellschaft* that is more important for the individual's wider group than it is for himself. On the contrary, everyone is out for himself alone and living in a state of tension against everyone else. The various spheres of power and activity are sharply demarcated, so that everyone resists contact with others and excludes them from his own spheres, regarding any such overtures as hostile. Such a *negative* attitude is the normal and basic way in which these power-conscious people relate to one another, and it is characteristic of *Gesellschaft* at any given moment in time. Nobody wants to do anything for anyone else, nobody wants to yield or give anything unless he gets something in return that he regards as at least an *equal* trade-off. Indeed it is essential that it should be more desirable to him than whatever he has already, for only by getting something that seems better can he be persuaded to give up something good' (Tönnies 2001, p. 52).

13 'All production is appropriation of nature on the part of an individual within and through a specific form of society. In this sense it is a tautology to say that property (appropriation)

In fact, the exchange of pen-holders and stamps in school, or the exchange of riding horses and automobiles between two members of a socialist society is a private event of no concern to theoretical economics. The fundamental illusion of marginal utility theory is that it wants to understand the laws of capitalist *society* through the analysis of exchange as a purely *private* act.

For us, the first question that arises is this: What turns exchange into a social phenomenon? Obviously, that the social relation is first expressed, and can only be expressed through the act of exchange. [In capitalist society] people enter into economic relations (we are not talking about political, literary or religious relations) in no other way than through the act of exchange. The law that shows how the exchange [*Tauschverkehr*] is regulated is therefore, at the same time, the law of motion of society. Finding that law of motion was the task that Marx posited as the problem of theoretical economics. And with that task the field of theoretical economics was at the same time clearly formulated and its method determined.[14] Theoretical economics was separated from economic history. While the field of economic history includes all social formations, the problem for theoretical economics only arises at all in a specific historical-social organisation; societies whose relations of production are consciously regulated – i.e. communist societies, wherein society has the right to dispose of all the means of production – are not the subjects of theoretical economics. All members of such society are immediately conscious of its regulation; it is as much understood as, for instance, *legal propositions*, which people describe and arrange according to their origin, because their economic organisation is only a part of the conscious organisation of their social life in general. They are

---

is a precondition of production. But it is altogether ridiculous to leap from that to a specific form of property, e.g. private property' (Marx 1993, p. 87).

14 Insofar as the confusion between economic history and theoretical economics underlies the *Methodenstreit*, Karl Menger has already revealed the monstrous *quid pro quo* of that view. Here we shall just say a word about the status of economic policy, which is usually seen as the third component part of political economy. It is – and on this we agree with Menger – applied science, but it does not always have to be an application of the doctrines of theoretical economics. It is such only when theoretical economics must first demonstrate the principles of economic policy. A principle of economic policy is, however, always a certain interest. Policy is based on theoretical economics only where that interest can first be clearly recognised by economic-theoretical analysis. That is only the case where it is a matter of the interests of *economic classes*, which can be clearly recognised when theory has demonstrated the function of those classes in social production. In a socialist society, the principle of economic policy is the general interest and is based on the most rational use of technology, not on theoretical economics. [For further detail on this issue, see Document 6 in this volume].

entitled to grasp the content of the economy, not just its form. Their 'external regulation' [*äußere Regelung*], to use Stammler's expression, is at the same time an internal regulation, because the 'matter of social life', the economy, is also consciously regulated.

This is quite different from that other kind of social formation, which manifests itself only in the act of exchange, which, in turn, presupposes the individual's right to dispose of his objects, i.e. private property. Here the question under consideration is the law that dominates the economy of this society. What is it here that determines the organisation of labour that secures the production and reproduction of needs [*Bedarf*: demand, requirements] in the necessary quantity and the required proportion? And finally, how are the production *relations* themselves reproduced, automatically remaining constant, without the intervention of a purposeful consciousness? Who created the relations of dominance and subordination between the members of that society and their interaction, which, for all that, must secure the social purpose, the self-preservation of society, in an unplanned way?

In short, it is necessary to find the inner lawfulness of a society that has only become conscious of external regulation [*äußere Regelung*], which amounts to nothing more than the principle of private property.[15]

All the standards [*gesetzten Normen*] that come into consideration for economics are therefore nothing but consequences of this uppermost, purely formal principle [of private property], which purposefully ignores the content of economic events because it answers only to the wills of individuals. Marx is concerned with internal regulation, in other words, with the law that turns this society of commodity-producers, dissolved into its constituent elements formally by private property and materially by development of the division of labour, into a community of production, transforming the individual actions [of its members] into actions necessarily determined by society.

This is, therefore, the 'epistemological peculiarity' of these production relations, to which Marx did justice with the peculiarity of his formulation of the

---

15   From the unconsciousness of the economic and the consciousness of the politico-legal regulation arises, within commodity-producing society, the specific problem of how the latter, consciously apprehended, is related to the former, whose changes are detected only *post factum* by theoretical knowledge. This is the problem that underlies Karner's [Karl Renner's] study (Renner 1949, the German subtitle was left out in the English version: *Ein Beitrag zur Kritik des bürgerlichen Rechts: A Contribution to the Critique of Bourgeois/Civil Law*). [The contrast is between the inner regulation imposed by the laws of commodity production and the external regulation imposed by legal norms (a society of commodity producers is bound by law to the exchange of equivalents in the form of a free contract)].

problem [of theoretical economics]. However, this peculiarity does not consist, as Dietzel believes, in the *great number* of theoretical mysteries offered by the competitive system and in the difficulty of solving them.[16]

Rather, there is only *one* riddle that we must solve: namely, to discover in the exchange act, as the basic process in which the social relations manifest themselves, the law that prevails in this society and must assert itself in order to make possible in the long run the social production process, that is the satisfaction of social needs by the total labour of society.

It is a 'mystery' that is not at all posited by other social formations, so that, for instance, commodity-producing society simply presents an additional problem for theoretical solution. Rather, these production relations, due to the unconscious way in which individual members are related to each other within them, are the only ones positing a problem for theoretical economics. It is necessary to investigate the *social order*. But this social order, as Sombart already noted, is for this society by no means identical with the external regulation [*äußere Regelung*].[17] It is first recognised when, next to the external regulation, economic theory, for which this social order is the logical precondition, has discovered the internal conformity to law [*Gesetzlichkeit*], the law of the economy.

The production relations are thus a unity of internal conformity to law and external regulation, and both are only an expression of 'definite, necessary relations, independent of their will', which people enter into 'in the social production of their existence' and which are 'appropriate to a given stage in the development of their material forces of production'.[18]

External regulation appears only in commodity-producing society, because it is the only consciously determined, independent [regulation], separated from the internal conformity to law, while this separation [between regulation and internal conformity to law] does not exist in communal production, where both are included in an undifferentiated way in the consciously regulated social order.

However, the character of this law – that is, the claim of its validity – is likewise clear from the preceding [remarks]. It is a law that determines the behaviour of production agents *within the relations of production* with natural necessity, because the character of the necessity can be none other if it has to act through the wills of individuals, themselves determined by the nature of the production relations. In this law, the social relationship – which here is

---

16   Dietzel 1895, p. 90.
17   Sombart 1899, p. 311.
18   Marx 1970, p. 20.

not directly intended and produced by conscious, collective action but is only identified after the event by theoreticians [of political economy] – asserts itself with natural necessity vis-à-vis the individuals. It differs from natural law only by the fact that it operates within a historically specific form of organisation of human society. To denote this fact, it has very well been said that it operates with social-natural necessity.[19]

The method, however, with which this law could be found, was the *analysis* of this social relationship as it appears in the simplest social act, exchange, and its material substrate, the commodity (not the 'good'). By identifying the 'social substance' of the commodity,[20] by demonstrating that the question under consideration, behind the seemingly material relations of the commodities, is actually human relationships, moreover, human relationships within very specific relations of production in commodity-producing society – i.e. through the discovery of the fetish character of the commodity – the 'mystery' of society was then resolved.

It is, however, a different way of positing the problem [of theoretical economics], which must not be overlooked if we want to analyse the relationship of Marx to Ricardo, because it is only from here that one can clearly distinguish the very different meaning of both systems. Ricardo presupposes the production relations as something given, natural and unchanging.[21]

What interests Ricardo is distribution, which he also conceives only in the narrow sense of distribution of products, whereas it also means, at the same time, the distribution of people among the various spheres of production and

---

19   See Karner 1904, p. 108 [Renner 1949].

20   'As the *exchange values* of commodities are only *social functions* of those things, and have nothing at all to do with the *natural* qualities, we must first ask: What is the common *social substance* of all commodities? It is *labour*' (Marx 2006, p. 30).

21   'It is one of the chief failings of classical political economy that it has never succeeded, by means of its analysis of commodities, and in particular of their value, in discovering the form of value which in fact turns value into exchange-value. Even its best representatives, Adam Smith and Ricardo, treat the form of value as something of indifference, something external to the nature of the commodity itself. The explanation for this is not simply that their attention is entirely absorbed by the analysis of the magnitude of value. It lies deeper. The value-form of the product of labour is the most abstract, but also the most universal form of the bourgeois mode of production; by that fact it stamps the bourgeois mode of production as a particular kind of social production of a historical and transitory character. If then we make the mistake of treating it as the eternal natural form of social production, we necessarily overlook the specificity of the value-form, and consequently of the commodity-form, together with its further developments, the money form, the capital form, etc.' (Marx 1976, p. 174, note 34).

the determination of their relative positions as workers, capitalists, etc. in production. His categories, therefore, remain natural categories; for him, value is still a property of the goods, namely, that of being a product of labour, just as with another category of goods their property is that of being scarce. Thus capital [for Ricardo] is nothing but 'accumulated labour', a mere 'economic name', as Marx once said, for the means of production. Ricardo, therefore, offers no sufficient justification for the law of value, which to him appears to be more of a happily discovered, empirically intrusive fact than the result of a rigorous analysis.

And since, for him, value is primarily the criterion for distribution, and it is a requirement for any criterion that it be as accurate as possible, Ricardo also always has the tendency to determine economic categories – which with him are immutable natural categories anyway – quantitatively as far as possible. Thus he arrives, to highlight just one point, at the equation of wages with the sum of the natural subsistence minimum of the worker, and at his doctrine of the iron law of wages, which blocked his insight into the mechanism of accumulation and into capitalism's historical law of population. Thus, he takes the 'law of diminishing returns' in agriculture in a narrow sense, turning the rise of ground rent into the actual law of motion of capitalist society and thus overlooking the dominant role of capital, whose historical barrier appears in the fall of the rate of profit, which he explained in a totally incorrect way.

By contrast, for Marx the question is first of all to analyse the [social] form that turns each good into a commodity. The good is a commodity because its producers stand in a particular social relationship, in which they have to confront each other as independent commodity producers. In this way the good, instead of being a natural, entirely unproblematic thing, is the expression of a social relationship, thus also acquiring a social dimension.[22] The fact that

---

22 It is therefore the formal determination of wealth, rather than wealth itself, that constitutes the problem for theoretical economics. In this, their formal determination, however, the goods, use-values, become commodities, and therefore become exchange-values and have a value. As use-values, by contrast, 'they constitute the material content of wealth, whatever its social form may be' (Marx 1976, p. 126).

Sapienti sat [*est*] (a word to the wise is sufficient). For Eduard Bernstein's sake the following should also be noted. Amidst the comic excitement that the publication of the *Marx-Studien* threw him into (see his criticism in *Dokumenten des Sozialismus*, Vol. IV, p. 153), he discovered that behind use-value lies the whole of political economy. This is not exactly precise, but on the other hand it is correct if we think that theoretical economics begins as soon as it finds out about use-value and discovers there the people in their relations of production. But this is certainly not the opinion of Bernstein, who

the good is a labour product ceases to be its natural property and now becomes a social fact. Now it is necessary to find the law of that society as a community of production and therefore of *labour*. The individual labour thus appears, from a completely new perspective, as part of the total labour at the disposal of that production community, and only from this point of view is it value-creating. Only then could Marx arrive at the basic distinction between concrete labour, creating use-value, and abstract, social, value-creating labour, and thus show the starting point of political economy.

Through analysis of the *commodity form* – in other words, through discovery that the question under consideration was the historically transitory way in which the members of a community of labour [*Arbeitsgemeinschaft*], lacking conscious regulation, relate to each other by means of their power of disposition [*Verfügungsgewalt*] over the things necessary for the social metabolism – Marx also came to realise the *content* of the value notion. Ricardo, by contrast, headed directly to the content, remained stuck at the very beginning of the analysis of value, and had to do without a more accurate insight into the character of value. Finally, he had only exchange-value in mind, the reason for the mutual changes in the exchange of goods, which may have appeared sufficient to him given his narrow formulation of the problem [of theoretical economics]. But realisation that the question under consideration here is nothing but historically specific relations between the producers is also a prerequisite for recognising the laws of distribution in capitalist society, which cannot be understood without recognising the capital nature of the relation of exploitation underlying them. That capital gains power, and that this power in turn alters the

---

rather – in opposition to the view of the author (which is incidentally self-evident, not only undisputed but always emphasised also by the psychological school) that the use-value is an individual relationship between a thing and a man – sees in 'use value, with which economics is concerned, a thoroughly social category'. We will ignore the fact that *social* is said here rather than *economic*. Worse, however, is the fact that Bernstein here wants to turn a thing into a social category, because, given the fact that things cannot form a society, they can only be described as social categories if they become the expression of human and indeed human *social* relations. Use-value can be described as a social category if, and only if, it becomes the conscious purpose of society, the object of its conscious social action. This can only happen in a socialist society, which sets for itself the goal of conscious management of production of use-values; but that is by no means the case in capitalist society. An absolute or objective use-value, set without reference to a consciousness requiring the good, is a contradiction in terms. But if use-value can be referred to as a *social* category in a socialist society, in this case it is not an *economic* category, not the object of an economic-*theoretical* analysis, because consciously regulated production relations do not require this analysis.

social distribution in a modification of the law of value, could not be seen by Ricardo. For him, the problem of the equal rate of profit remained a mystery upon which his theory foundered, while Marx's theory celebrated its greatest triumph precisely there. But the shortcoming in the formulation of the problem [of theoretical economics], which Ricardo limited to distribution, also made him overlook completely the actual task, which to him appeared self-evident, because for him the production relation was unalterably given: namely, to find the law of the conservation and development of these relations of production.

Ricardo had found the key, but not the door that the key unlocked. And like him, his successors also did not find that door that led out of bourgeois society – even if, like the Socialists, they searched for it. Karl Marx first opened it up for us. He was the discoverer of socialist society because, according to Tönnies's expression, he was 'the discoverer of the capitalist mode of production'.[23]

---

23 [In the English version of Tönnies's book this sentence is mistranslated as 'the "detective" who unmasked the capitalist method of production' (Tönnies 2001, p. 13)].

DOCUMENT 12

Back to Adam Smith! (1900)

Rosa Luxemburg

Source: Rosa Luxemburg, 'Zurück auf Adam Smith!', *Die Neue Zeit*, 8. 1899–1900, 2. Bd. (1900), H. 33, S. 180–6. [A review of Richard Schüller, *Die Wirthschaftspolitik der historischen Schule*, Berlin: Carl Heymann Verlag, 1899].

Introduction by the Editors

Rosa Luxemburg deals in this essay with an issue that will be familiar to every reader with an interest in economic theory and method. The question is whether economics should be regarded as a 'science' of universal validity, as suggested by the classics, especially by the deductive method of Ricardo; whether it is better conceived as the study of one aspect of a culturally delimited sphere of interaction, as Hegel's treatment of 'civil society' would suggest; or whether, as Marx believed, theoretical economics has universality validity but only with respect to the specific stage of capitalist commodity exchange (the argument made by Hilferding in the previous article).

While Adam Smith was certainly conscious of history, he also regarded capitalism as the natural order of mature societies. The *Wealth of Nations* abounds with references to 'natural liberty'. In one of the more famous such passages, Smith comments: 'All systems, either of preference or of restraint ... being ... completely taken away, the obvious and simple system of natural liberty establishes itself of its own accord. Every man, as long as he does not violate the laws of justice, is left perfectly free to pursue his own interest his own way, and to bring both his industry and capital into competition with those of any other man, or order of men'.[1] Remove the *visible* hand of the state (privileged mercantilist monopolies), and the 'invisible hand' of the market will naturally replace it. In our own day it remains a common assumption of neoliberalism that 'rational' economic decisions can be abstracted from the ethics, social norms and historical circumstances of particular societies.[2]

---

1 Smith 1937, p. 651.
2 Ibid.

The reaction to this type of thinking has always been that culture trumps markets. One of the most persuasive such arguments came in the twentieth-century economic anthropology of Karl Polanyi, who argued in *The Great Transformation* that the normal pattern of human history is for all 'economic' activity – understood substantively as the appropriation of nature – to be culturally 'embedded' in social norms and institutions. Polanyi regarded the liberal market ideal as a radical departure from the normal order of human community, in which a self-regulating economic 'system', resulting from the 'commodity fiction', threatens the survival of both man and nature.[3]

The nineteenth-century German historical school likewise regarded economic activity as bounded by culture and tradition, with the implication that there could be no such thing as a universal economic 'science'. If economic behaviour is dependent upon cultural expectations, which are specific to time and place, then the very concept of 'economy' becomes inseparable from a discrete community conceived as an organic whole. The founders of the school, Wilhelm Roscher, Bruno Hildebrand, and Karl Knies, repudiated the deductive method in favour of an historical-inductive approach that would treat economic phenomena merely as a single element of an integral social order. Subsequent proponents of the historical approach also often linked history and culture to protectionist economic policies for the purpose of nation-building. In both theory and policy they circumscribed economic thought within culture and institutions.

Rosa Luxemburg's essay was sparked by Richard Schüller's call for repudiation of this approach and a return to the deductive methodology of the classics. She argues that the issue was not one of inductive versus deductive method, but rather of the state of capitalist development. The historical school was essentially reactionary. Just as its romantic predecessors articulated the fears of Prussian feudalists and the members of threatened craft-guilds in face of early capitalist development, so the historical school expressed the fears of the newly emerging German bourgeoisie, opposing liberalism in recognition of the fact that the classical doctrines ultimately gave birth to Ricardian-inspired socialism and eventually Marxism.

---

3 Polanyi denied that either labour, land or money can properly be regarded as 'commodities': 'Labor is only another name for a human activity which goes with life itself, which in its turn is not produced for sale but for entirely different reasons ...; land is only another name for nature, which is not produced by man; actual money, finally, is merely a token of purchasing power ... None of them is produced for sale. The commodity description of labour, land, and money is entirely fictitious' (Polanyi 2001, p. 72).

Luxemburg concluded that the only real accomplishment of the historical school, in its resistance first to capitalism and later to socialism, was 'the spontaneous decomposition and abdication of economics as a science'. The only true science of economics was Marxism, which paid due respect both to history and to capitalism's universalising tendencies. Richard Schüller thought the recovery of economic theory from romantic illusions required a reversion to the deductive method. Luxemburg replied that method was indeed the issue, but the correct response came from Marx, who converted 'the *metaphysical deduction* of the classics into its opposite, into *dialectical deduction*'. The choice before political economy was not between an inductive or deductive approach, or between classical liberalism and reaction, but between moving forward along the path opened up by Marx and declaring the final bankruptcy of theoretical economics 'as a science'.

∴

Rosa Luxemburg on the German Historical School

In the pages of this journal [*Die Neue Zeit*] Eduard Bernstein has already reviewed an earlier work by Dr. Schüller called *Classical Political Economy and its Opponents*.[4] What currently lies before us is a continuation of these studies under the title *The Economic Policy of the Historical School*.[5]

The subject is intrinsically one of the most interesting ones, for several reasons. In the first place, because the historical school basically represents the only real national product of the German bourgeoisie in the field of economic theory. The classical-liberal period in Germany, as elsewhere, was only an offshoot of English classicism; and the romantic tendency of Haller-Müller,[6] influential as it was in practice, hardly deserves the name of a school of political economy. It never made any attempt to postulate a positive economic theory, and pretty much its only literary follower was, as far as we know, the famous Jarcke, who, according to Börne, was sent off from the Austrian to the Prussian council for the purpose of advocating Metternich's policy.[7] In the same way,

---

4   Bernstein 1895b, a review of Schüller 1895.
5   Schüller 1899.
6   [A reference to Adam Heinrich Müller (1779–1829) and Karl Ludwig von Haller (1768–1854)].
7   [Karl Ernst Jarcke (1801–52) was a German publisher and professor of criminal law. He took up the study of jurisprudence and at an early age became professor of criminal law at Bonn and later in Berlin. After the outbreak of the July Revolution in Paris, he wrote an

Friedrich List's 'national system' of political economy must be viewed more as an amateurish essay than as a theoretical doctrine. Only the historical school has postulated a whole system of economic doctrine and gained a very large number of supporters among both specialised scholars and men of practice.

There is also the fact that in its internal history the historical school is a true reflection of the history of the German bourgeoisie. An investigation of the doctrines, methods, and developmental phases of this school would at the same time provide a sketch of the modern development of the German bourgeoisie itself – that is to say, if it is dealt with in connection with the facts of economic and social life.

It cannot be said that Dr. Schüller has conceived his task as we have formulated it here. What he offers instead is a very sketchily worked out series of economic-political portraits of significant classical-liberal, reactionary-romantic and historical theorists, to which he attaches a bunch of general observations, just as easily jotted down, about the different methods of the above-mentioned tendencies.

Dr. Schüller justly calls the *deductive method* of research the most outstanding characteristic of classical-liberal political economy and the basis of its progressive effect in practice. Equally correct is the observation that abandonment of the deductive method of research has resulted in the lack of any fixed principles, and consequently in the theoretical barrenness and backwardness of the historical school in terms of economic policy. With Schüller, the whole issue is a vehement case for the method of classical economics and a warning for contemporary economists to return to that method. But why did the historical school abandon the method of research of the classics, and how can one explain, given its shallowness and backwardness, its extensive and long-lasting influence on German political economy? That is a question for which we find no answer in Dr. Schüller's work. And yet only a clear explanation of this question can turn Schüller's warning to contemporary economists, with which his whole analysis ends, into something meaningful.

---

anonymous political brochure, *Die französische Revolution von 1830*, which met the approval of the anti-revolutionary circle of friends of then Crown Prince (later King Frederick William IV of Prussia), who were influenced by Romanticism and by Karl Ludwig von Haller. Jarcke assumed the editorship of the periodical *Politische Wochenblatt*, founded by these men in 1831 to promote their ideas. In 1832 Metternich called him to the State Chancery in Vienna to succeed the late Friedrich von Gentz. In 1838 he founded, with George Phillips, the *Historisch-politische Blätter* to support Catholic interests in Germany. When Metternich was overthrown in 1848, Jarcke left Vienna but returned after the triumph of the counterrevolution and died shortly thereafter].

The undivided rule of classical economic doctrine at the beginning of the nineteenth century in Germany is well known. It was not such a great exaggeration for [Alexander von der] Marwitz to write in 1810 to Rahel [Levin] that, next to Napoleon, Adam Smith was the most powerful monarch in Europe. In Prussia, all the statesmen of the Stein-Hardenberg period were students of Adam Smith.[8] Most official declarations of the government at that time bear the clear stamp of the classical doctrine. Indeed, even the high military – [Count Neidhardt von] Gneisenau, [Gerhard von] Scharnhorst, Job von Witzleben – were enthusiastic supporters of classical liberalism. The theories of Smith were the Bible of the whole renovation period in Germany, which for a short period after the defeat at Jena [on 14 October 1806] threatened the position of the consequent reaction.

But that was precisely the reason why these theories soon had to lead to an opposition. The progressive reforms of Stein-Hardenberg did not arise from a strong bourgeois movement or from society itself. They were rather elicited from the ruling circles by the French military blows and were simply imposed by these circles on society. They soon brought forth an opposition from two camps: on the one hand, from the feudal Junker class, who wanted the preservation of serfdom, and on the other hand from those elements of the middle classes who first saw their interests threatened by the new reforms – mainly the artisan class, then still strong, which was severely damaged both

---

8 [The Stein-Hardenberg Reforms were bourgeois reforms implemented in Prussia from 1807 to 1814, under the impact of the military defeats in the hands of Napoleon, by governments headed by Baron vom Stein and Karl August von Hardenberg. The Edict of 1807 freed the peasants from hereditary servitude and permitted landowners to dispose of their property as they saw fit, making it possible for burghers and peasants to acquire land; the edict did not affect, however, the peasants' obligations deriving from the tenure of land. The Edict of 1811, designed to regulate the freeing of the peasants, made it extremely difficult for the peasants to redeem their obligations; in order to become a freeholder, the peasant had to cede one-third to one-half of the land he occupied or pay 25 times the amount of the yearly lease. In 1810 and 1811 legislation was enacted to remove restrictions on productive activity, thereby abolishing the guild system, which had slowed the development of industry. Under the military reform of 1807–14 members of the nobility were no longer guaranteed officers' posts, and the use of corporal punishment was sharply curtailed. The implementation of army reforms on the bourgeois model was completed when *de facto* universal military service was introduced (subsequently enacted into law in 1814), and a national militia – the *Landwehr* – was established. For an analysis of the way in which the agrarian reforms fostered the development of capitalism in agriculture along 'the Prussian path', by which many vestiges of feudalism were retained, see Droz 1974].

by the abolition of guild laws and by English imports favoured by the liberal commercial policy.

In the first case, the opposition expressed itself in the reactionary-romantic tendency of Haller-Müller,[9] in the second, in the older historical school of [Friedrich Julius von] Soden, [Heinrich] Luden, [Friedrich von] Cölln, etc. If we take into consideration the nature of the social foundations from which those two economic tendencies rebelling against the classical school emerged, their dissimilar theoretical character is easily explained.

The rebellious Junkers, whose protest against the inauguration of bourgeois development was expressed in the romantic school of Haller, set against the reforms criticised by them a definite, consistent opposite 'ideal': medieval feudalism. Just as clear, consistent and strong as the Metternichean reaction and the era of the Holy Alliance was the theoretical expression of that policy: the economic theory of the romantic school. It proceeded from certain fixed 'principles'; namely, the principles of feudal natural economy, which it applied consistently to all questions of economic policy.

It was different with the second opposition camp. If the social layer of the traditional (*zünftig*: belonging to a guild) middle class – the master artisans and shopkeepers – was threatened in its very existence by the reforms, on the other hand they could not long to return to the era of the undivided rule of feudalism, whose iron pressure had also left bloody scars on them. Those elements were unable to put forward a definite, positive economic program because they did not constitute a united social whole. Wavering between contemporary bourgeois development and feudal traditions, fearing harm from one and the other, they merely managed to fight at one time against liberal political economy from the feudal point of view, then against the romantic theories from the liberal point of view, always rejecting the consequences following from the starting point and stopping halfway.

---

9 [Karl Ludwig von Haller (1768–1854) was a Swiss constitutional lawyer, politician, journalist and economist in Zurich. He was known for his work *Restauration der Staatswissenschaften* (1816–34), in which he called, in the aftermath of the Congress of Vienna of 1815, for the revival of royal power and its legitimacy, thus becoming the representative of extreme conservatism. Adam Heinrich Müller (1779–1829) was a German publicist, theorist of the state and forerunner of economic romanticism. In 1826, at the instance of Prince von Metternich, he was ennobled as Ritter von Nittersdorf. He was recalled to Vienna (1827), appointed imperial counsellor, and employed in the service of the chancellery. His ideal was medieval feudalism, on which the reorganisation of political institutions had to be modelled. His position in political economy was defined by his strong opposition to Adam Smith's system of political economy. He was also opposed to free trade].

Entirely different is the character of the later historical school, founded by Hildebrand and Roscher.[10] While [in the older historical school] we see a protest of the guild-belonging petty bourgeoisie in the name of the medieval mode of production against the advancing bourgeois order, here it is the modern bourgeoisie itself which raises objections against the consequences of its own class rule.

Classical political economy had everywhere, with invincible logic, turned into self-criticism, into criticism of the bourgeois order. In England, Ricardo constituted the immediate starting point of an entire school of English Socialists (Thompson, Gray, Bray, and others); in France, the first trivialisation of classical economics by Say follows hard on the heels of Sismondi; in Germany, we find socialist echoes already in Rau, who was followed by Thünen and Rodbertus;[11] in Marx, the transformation of classical economics into its opposite, into the socialist analysis of capitalism, is completed.

The socialist critique, i.e. the consequence, could only be denied if the starting point, classical economics, was overcome. The results of the investigation of bourgeois commodity economy, as offered by classical economics in a coherent system, could not simply be negated or corrected. There was no other way but to fight the investigation itself, the method [of classical political economy]. If the purpose of classical economics was to understand the principles and basic laws of bourgeois economy, the historical school, by contrast, set itself the task of mystifying the inner workings of this economy. In the old historical school, the aversion to the 'levelling' tendencies and 'categorical' assertions of classical liberalism was merely a protest [on behalf] of medieval diversity and specialisation of conditions, in accordance with the social nature of the pre-capitalist mode of production. Here, in Roscher, Knies and Hildebrand [i.e. in the new historical school], the 'historical' criticism of the 'absolute' theories of classicism is a protest of bourgeois society against the knowledge of its own internal laws. But since concealment of these laws was the purpose, the 'historical' occupation and reason for existence of the new historical school, the *failure to recognise (Verkennung)* the laws of social economy was raised to the level of a scientific dogma, of an economic method.

Suum cuique [to each according to his own merits]: the rise of the English bourgeoisie resulted in construction of the magnificent doctrinal edifice of

---

10 [A reference to Wilhelm Roscher (1817–94) and Bruno Hildebrand (1812–78)].
11 [Karl Heinrich Rau (1792–1871), Johann Heinrich von Thünen (1783–1850), Johann Karl Rodbertus (1805–75)].

the classical school, in the creation of political economy, while the emergence of the German bourgeoisie found its spiritual expression in the spontaneous decomposition and abdication of economics as a science.

The lack of principle of the historical school – of which Schüller rightly accuses it but without giving any plausible explanation – thus finds sufficient reason in the actual historical conditions of Germany, in the history of the bourgeoisie, in the ever more sharply emerging class antagonisms. And similarly, the fact that Roscher's school, for all its scientific wretchedness and practical barrenness, could gain such an influence, can be explained much better by the same actual conditions than by the circumstance that [through it] 'the main tendencies corresponding to the economic and social questions of the present are first grasped in their development'.

Just the opposite! The historical school did not arise because the socialist doctrine of political economy – obviously the main tendency corresponding to the economic and social questions of the present – had not yet emerged, but because it had already reached a high level of development, i.e. [it arose] as a reaction against this doctrine.

Because he treats the question without relating it to the social foundation, Dr. Schüller commits the double error of conflating the old historical tendency of the first decades of the nineteenth century with Roscher's doctrine, which is essentially different from it, as if they were one and the same school, and also of regarding the new historical school as a result of the absence of a socialist tendency – rather than seeing it, on the contrary, as a reaction against the socialist critique.

Dr. Schüller's study wants to be more than a scientific monograph. It ends, as we have mentioned, with an exhortation to the current generation of German economists to go back to the methods of classical economics if they want to face the problems of contemporary social life with the same understanding as the classics brought to the problems of their time.

This well-intentioned appeal: Back to classical method! – which is evidently the leading thought of Schüller's two economic works – is undoubtedly very attractive as a wish to breathe fresh air into the stifling atmosphere of contemporary German economics. But through his advice Dr. Schüller once again shows that, by regarding academic economic questions as if they were unconnected with the social foundations of each particular period, he is unable to understand both the nature of the classical school he admires and the contemporary tasks of political economy.

Dr. Schüller traces the greatness of classical economy back to its deductive method, to its principled handling of economic problems. But the deductive method, taken abstractly, is a purely formal academic concept that tells us nothing about the nature of the research method practiced by Adam Smith's school. If it were just a question of 'applying commonly accepted principles to research', then, in addition to those of the classical economists, many other principles should be brought in. If the deductive principles of Smith and Ricardo, as Dr. Schüller formulated them, were called freedom of economic activity, freedom of movement, and freedom of trade, those of Adam Müller and Haller were called patrimonial jurisdiction, servitude, patriarchal state, etc. As deductions, they are methodologically of equal value. In its day, nobody had dealt such heavy blows against the lack of principles of the historical school, nobody had preached with such pathos the necessity of 'eternal laws' as the starting point of economic analysis, as precisely the romantic school.

If, therefore, the deductive method of classical economics led to a deep knowledge of bourgeois economy, while the romantic deductions of Haller and Müller merely led to a greater reputation of their supporters among the Crown Prince Friedrich Wilhelm IV and Metternich, this was obviously due to the fact that only the classical-liberal deductions corresponded to [the needs of] social development at that time and corresponded to the essence of the bourgeois economy.

But the fact that the general principles of bourgeois economy became, in Adam Smith and Ricardo, the absolute 'principles' of their research expresses yet another fact – namely, that the classics considered modern commodity economy to be the absolute, the *normal human* economy. And this was the real principle from which they proceeded; this was the real secret of their wonder-working deductive method.

It was this unlimited and completely untroubled faith in the normal human economy – that is to say, in the natural right of the capitalist commodity economy – that gave the classics of political economy that impartiality of research, that lack of consideration for the consequences, that ability to rise above their immediate surroundings and to grasp the inner workings of the bourgeois mode of production with piercing eyes.

Later, the growing doubts about the bourgeois order gave rise, on the one hand, to the apologetics of vulgar economy, which turned attention away from the investigation of general laws and towards the justification of individual phenomena, and, on the other hand, to the resignation of the historical school, which renounced in advance any research into the foundations of the economy and declared the task of science to be mere description of the past and of that which exists. The bourgeois mode of production constitutes the basis and the starting point of all these economic schools. But the belief in the absolute and normal character of the bourgeois order was peculiar only of the classical school, and that is precisely what made it *classical*.

This circumstance explains not only the general scientific achievements of Adam Smith's school but also the specific characteristics of its research method. Cosmopolitanism, the levelling treatment of man, individualism, the view of economic self-interest as the sole basis of all actions, etc. – all the elements for which the historical critics reproach them – flow from the same concept of the universal human normality of capitalist commodity economy, of the commodity producer as the normal human type in general.

But this same view also set in advance certain objective limits to the subjectively dauntless, completely unbiased research of Adam Smith's school. The innermost essence of the bourgeois mode of production, its true secret, can be deciphered only if it is regarded in movement, in its historical conditionality. And precisely this is precluded from the outset by the view of commodity economy as the normal, absolute form of social production.

Let us take an example. Unconcerned about the social consequences of its teachings, classical economy recognised human labour as the only value-creating factor, and it elaborated that theory until it reached the crystalline clarity we find in the Ricardian system.

But the fundamental difference between Ricardo's and Marx's labour theory of value – a difference that is not only overlooked by bourgeois economists but also often unnoticed in the popularisation of Marx's theory – is that Ricardo, in accordance with his general natural-law conception of bourgeois economy, considered value creation as a *natural* property of human labour, of the individual, concrete labour of single men.[12]

Marx, on the other hand, recognised in value an *abstraction* made by society under certain conditions, which enabled him to distinguish the two sides of commodity-producing labour: the concrete individual labour and the undifferentiated social labour. This distinction first made possible the solution of the *mystery of money*, which suddenly revealed itself as if under the glow of a spotlight.

---

12   This view appears even more pronouncedly in Adam Smith, who, for instance, simply declared the 'disposition to truck' to be a peculiarity of human nature, after previously looking for it, to no avail, in animals, dogs, etc. [*Wealth of Nations*, Book 1, Chapter 2, Of the Principle which gives occasion to the Division of Labour]. This, like many other places [in Smith's book] has, as is well-known, given occasion to many smug smiles and shrugs among later economists. These smart aleck disciples of Smith have no idea that it is precisely in the naïve assertions of the old master that his 'classical deduction' is most classically expressed, and that they, the bourgeois economists, have irretrievably lost, together with that naïveté, also the hair of Samson, the primary source of their research strength.

But in order to distinguish in this way, within the womb of bourgeois economy, *statically*, the double-sided character of labour – the working people and the value-creating commodity producers – Marx initially had to distinguish *dynamically*, in historical sequence, the commodity producers from the working people in general; that is, he had to recognise commodity production merely as a specific historical form of social production. In a word, Marx had to decipher the hieroglyph of capitalist economy and approach the investigation [of capitalist society] with a deduction that was the *opposite* of the deduction of the classics. Rather than proceeding from the belief in the normal human character of the bourgeois mode of production, he had to do so with insight into its historical transience – he had to turn the *metaphysical deduction* of the classics into its opposite, into *dialectical deduction*.

The progress of political economy beyond Smith and Ricardo, its further development, was therefore determined precisely by the *overcoming* of the deductive method of that school to which Schüller today wants us to return; not only because that method, as already stated, sets fixed limits to knowledge, but also because those limits had already been reached by the classics themselves. In Ricardo's teaching the classical method of economics had yielded the maximum of which it was capable, and it had been thrown into the junk room, not only as a dangerous tool that turned against the society that was undertaking that research, but also as one that had scientifically had its day. A return to the method of the classical school would not lead to a revival in economics, as Dr. Schüller argues, but would, on the contrary, bring about a huge regression. That this return is *scientifically* impossible is proven precisely by Marx's work, which represents a direct continuation of the classical theory on new foundations.

But this return is also *socially* impossible. And that is proven, on the other hand, by the fact that classical economics was followed by the decay of that science into vulgar economics and the historical school. Since the emergence of these tendencies, the social conditions, which had to undermine that classically serene faith in the absolute character of capitalist commodity economy, have only developed further in the same direction. Not only do class antagonisms manifest themselves incomparably more harshly, but the self-negation of the capitalist mode of production has become manifest. It is impossible to take the starting point of bourgeois economic policy, as before, to be the freedom of trade, while a general reversion to protective tariffs is taking place; and it is equally impossible to proceed from the dogma of free competition while production is monopolised more and more by cartels. The 'principles' of Adam Smith and Ricardo now belong both scientifically and socially to the past.

Schüller's admonition to return to the method of classical economics, which is not being made for the first time, is by the way interesting as a fragment of that general [movement] 'Back', which today seems to be the slogan of bourgeois social science. Back to Kant in philosophy,[13] back to Adam Smith in economics! A convulsive falling back to standpoints already overcome is a sure sign of the hopelessness that afflicts the bourgeoisie both spiritually and socially. But a return is just as little possible in science as it is in the actual development of society.

There is a way forward only along the path of the *dialectical method* already followed by Marx. This should become clear to all those young economists who, like Dr. Schüller, are sincere enough not to find any satisfaction in the confusion, lack of system, banality and stupidity of contemporary bourgeois economics, and brave enough to sacrifice class prejudice for scientific knowledge. Even nowadays, bourgeois theorists have unavoidably been living off Marx's theory for decades, and any halfway clever idea that occurs to them is directly or indirectly borrowed from that doctrine.[14]

Just as bourgeois society has only two alternatives – to evolve and become socialist or to perish – so also political economy has only one choice: to move forward along the path opened up by Marx or to declare its bankruptcy as a science.

---

13   [A call made by Eduard Bernstein during the revisionist controversy (see Bernstein 1898, p. 226)].

14   It appears particularly tragicomic that recently, in our own ranks, attempts have earnestly been made [by Eduard Bernstein] to borrow from young bourgeois economists – and moreover from those discreetly living off the Marxian treasures to bolster their professorial careers – in order to renovate the Marxist doctrine and 'develop it further'. The process reminds one vividly of a drunken man trying to fetch a pinch of snuff from his own shadow.

DOCUMENT 13

Werner Sombart's *Modern Capitalism* (1903)

Rudolf Hilferding

Source: Rudolf Hilferding, 'Werner Sombart, *Der moderne Kapitalismus*', in *Zeitschrift für Volkswirtschaft, Sozialpolitik und Verwaltung*, 12 (1903), pp. 446–53.

A review of Werner Sombart, *Der moderne Kapitalismus*, Leipzig: Duncker & Humblot, 1902. Bd. I. *Die Genesis des Kapitalismus*. Bd. II. *Die Theorie der kapitalistischen Entwicklung*.

Introduction by the Editors

Of the many Marx-critiques at the turn of the twentieth century, two stand out in terms of originality and insight. One, which is widely influential to this day, is Max Weber's *The Protestant Ethic and the Spirit of Capitalism*;[1] the second, which nowadays is largely forgotten, is Werner Sombart's *Modern Capitalism*.[2] Sombart and Weber were contemporaries, who independently concluded that historical materialism, in the works of Engels and some leading Social Democrats such as Kautsky, had become much too one-sided in emphasising the

---

1 In 1998 the International Sociological Association declared Weber's book to be the fourth most influential text in sociology during the entire twentieth century. While Weber was critical of economic determinism, he never intended to replace it with an alternative, purely idealistic theory. He believed that there are no 'laws' to history, only particular conjunctions of material and spiritual conditions that may or may not have lasting economic effects. At the close of *The Protestant Ethic* he wrote: 'But it is, of course, not my aim to substitute for a one-sided materialistic an equally one-sided spiritualistic causal interpretation of culture and of history. Each is equally possible, but each, if it does not serve as the preparation, but as the conclusion of an investigation, accomplishes equally little in the interest of historical truth'. Marx, of course, also mentioned the role of Puritanism in accelerating capital accumulation: 'Incidentally, in so far as the hoarder of money combines asceticism with assiduous diligence he is intrinsically a Protestant by religion and still more a Puritan' (see Marx 1970, p. 130, and Marx 1976, p. 231).
2 One of the reasons for Sombart's eclipse was certainly his later support of Nazism (on this issue, see Grundmann and Sterr 2001).

dependence of culture upon economics. In 1905 Weber famously argued that the Protestant Reformation, most notably Calvinism, created the spiritual conditions for the 'rationalisation' of thought that attended accelerated capital accumulation from the sixteenth century onwards. Werner Sombart's *Modern Capitalism*, published in two volumes in 1902, pursued a related theme in arguing that Marxism systematically discounted the importance of 'spirit' in economic history.

Sombart's work was inspired partly by Marx's *Capital* and partly by Sombart's own early association with the German Historical school (his teacher, Gustav von Schmoller, was the leading representative of the school from the 1870s onward and had a particular interest in identifying cultural trends through historical inquiry). Whereas authors of the historical school never attempted a comprehensive theory of causality, Sombart believed forms of economic organisation must ultimately be explained in terms of the cultural primacy of a particular view of the world. Although he reversed Marx's conviction that economic life determines culture, he still described his research as 'nothing other than a continuation and in a certain sense a completion of that of Marx'.[3]

Readers will recall that in the 1890s Sombart sympathised with Marxism, writing the review of Volume III of *Capital* that we have included in this volume and that Engels described as 'excellent'. But Sombart became increasingly sceptical, as did Social-Democratic revisionists, of the proletariat's capacity to develop a unifying class consciousness. Regarding the capitalist spirit of calculating entrepreneurship as the dominant cultural fact of modern times, Sombart took this particular attitude of mind to be the defining principle of recent economic history. Differentiating between handicraft production for use, and capitalist production for exchange, he explained the rise of modern capitalism in terms of the pursuit of profit and the spirit of enterprise (limitless acquisition and competition). Capitalism instrumentalises both nature and workers, culminating in an objectified 'system' that operates independently of human will and is indifferent to the destruction inflicted upon earlier, more organic forms of civilisation.[4]

Sombart's ethical-cultural critique of capitalism obviously drew upon not merely the reactionary illusions of the German historical school but also Marx's own commentaries on fetishism and dehumanisation in *Capital* and elsewhere.

---

3 Sombart, cited in Parsons 1928, p. 661. This classical essay by Parsons, which continues in *The Journal of Political Economy*, Vol. 37, No. 1 (February 1929), pp. 31–51, remains an informative account of the relation between Sombart, Weber and Marx.
4 See Parsons 1928, pp. 650–1.

Where he differed fundamentally, however, was in denying Marx's dialectical method and with it any explanation of how successive, thoroughly different stages of economic history might be logically connected. Historical periods were defined in terms of their specific ordering 'principle' – which led Sombart to claim a theory of causality – but, as Rudolf Hilferding writes, there is in fact no explanation in Sombart's work of any causal connection *between successive principles*, which appear, therefore, as matters of pure contingency.[5]

For Marx, the craftsman's concern with stability of social status reflected the fact that he produces for a known buyer in circumstances of simple commodity exchange. The capitalist, in contrast, produces for an unknown market that compels him to accumulate in order to survive. By ignoring the primacy of economic activity in determining these contrasting attitudes, and by regarding consciousness instead as the autonomous determinant of forms of organisation, Sombart ends by resurrecting a pervasive dualism rather than a coherent theory of historical causality. Like his predecessors in the Historical school, says Hilferding, he 'confuses theory and history', with the result that his economic historiography, the one redeeming feature of *Modern Capitalism*, vindicates his work only because he 'tends not to apply his method too strictly'. Hilferding concludes that 'The economic historian Sombart has proved more fortunate than the social theorist'.[6]

∵

Rudolf Hilferding on Werner Sombart's *Modern Capitalism*

In his large, two-volume work, *Modern Capitalism*, Professor Werner Sombart attempts 'to trace the capitalist system from its beginnings to the present day'. His book therefore sets out to be, first of all, an historical description of capitalism, a commendable task if only because it fills a notable gap in our literature on economic history. The wish has already been voiced long ago, in

---

5 Parsons also comments that this discontinuity of economic systems in Sombart's work 'is radically opposed to the hypothesis of continuous evolution as held by most Western sociologists ... [T]he process of social change is certainly neither so radically discontinuous nor so radically determined by any "principles" as Sombart would have us believe' (Parsons 1928, p. 653).
6 For further socialist criticisms of Sombart, see Bax 1900, Luxemburg 1900b, Adler 1903, and Luxemburg 1903.

face of the growing number of monographs and detailed investigations in the field of economic history, for a synoptic presentation of the large amount of accumulated material. A field particularly neglected by research involved the origins of capitalism, as Marx described them for England in the chapters [of *Capital*] dealing with primitive accumulation, up to the triumph of the modern economic system in the last half century. It is really a peculiar phenomenon, often painfully felt, that we are frequently more familiar with the economic life of the Middle Ages than with that of our own time.

Sombart's *Modern Capitalism* has thoroughly changed this situation. With particular reference to German conditions, we now have a presentation of economic life as it was shaped by the craft system. It describes in detail how the basic idea of the craftsman, to secure a traditional livelihood, befitting his social status [*standesgemäße Nahrung*], by his own work, [which was] initially only artisanal work for others [*zunächst nur gewerbliche Arbeit für andere*], pervaded the entire economic system. Before us arises a vivid picture of the craftsman, of how he produced and how he brought his goods to market as a retailer. Where it was practised professionally, the trade of the Middle Ages also bore a thoroughly artisan character, while the lucrative business of large-scale 'opportunity trade'[7] was reserved for non-traders, such as councillors and mayors, wealthy families or monasteries and religious orders.

The book then moves on to show us the rise of the capitalist economy. Here vast new material, in part unique, is elaborated in a clear and concise presentation. Sombart places particular emphasis on the role played by the transfer of assets in the development of capitalism. He describes in detail the participation of the emerging merchant and usurer in the public revenues of the state and in the rents of feudal lords through the acquisition of landownership entitlements; the growth and accumulation especially of urban land rent; the urbanisation of the country gentry; and the colonial economy and its significance for the accumulation of money.

These were the objective conditions of capitalism. In the resulting social milieu, the subjective conditions of the capitalist economy now became effective. The acquisitive instinct awakened: the pursuit of profit, the prevalent motive of capitalist economic subjects, replaced the motive of the craftsman, his striving to gain a livelihood befitting his social status. Economic rationalism and 'calculation' [*Rechenhaftigkeit*: the capacity for calculating and accounting in business] developed.

---

7 [*Gelegenheitshandel*: trade carried out by someone who is not a full-time professional merchant].

This is followed by a comparison between German economic life in the mid-nineteenth century, the period of early capitalism, and that of the end of the nineteenth century, which shows the victory of capitalism first in the field of industrial production. In this way we get an interesting description of the most recent economic history. Based on the large amount of material brought to light by the investigations of the *Verein für Socialpolitik* (Social Policy Association),[8] the volume concludes with a thorough presentation of the current position of crafts and craftsmen.

The second volume then shows us the re-foundation and reorganisation of economic life [by capitalism]. In new legislation it creates the form appropriate to its new content; and the development of new technology, which is here assessed from an economic point of view, brings about the ever richer development of that content. The stormy flow of the stream of modern life is vividly illustrated in the brilliantly written chapter on 'The New Style of Economic Life', which shows the permeation of all action by the pursuit of profit. That is followed by a description of the development of modern agriculture and the dissolution of its old economic conditions. In the following section, Sombart then describes urban development: the origin and nature of the modern city. The ensuing chapters deal with the restructuring of demand and the reorganisation of commodity sales, which now have to satisfy the changing needs of consumption.

The second volume concludes with a 'theory of commercial competition'. Sombart had already described how capitalism overcame the old crafts on all fronts; here, he gives us a systematic presentation of the reason why that victory was necessary. He begins by placing the discussion on a new, rational basis. The question under discussion is no longer the superiority of small or large-scale enterprise, but rather the adaptability of two different economic systems, that of crafts and that of capitalism.

Sombart attaches great importance to the distinction between a business [*Betrieb*] and the economy [*Wirtschaft*], and he precedes his work with an introduction elaborating upon it. A business is an institution for the purpose of performing continued work, i.e. merely a means to produce commodit-

---

8 [The *Verein für Socialpolitik* (Social Policy Association) was the professional association of German economists, founded in 1873. The activities of the association focused on opposing both laissez-faire in social policy and the revolutionary social ideas of emerging socialism. According to Gustav von Schmoller, chairman of the *Verein* from 1890 to 1917, the founders of the association wanted 'to raise, educate and reconcile the lower classes on the basis of the existing order'].

ies. By economy, he (Sombart) understands an organisation of economic life, created by an economic subject [a particular spirit] to achieve the efficiency [*Nutzeffekt*] corresponding to its economic principle.[9] This distinction is fruitful because it allows us to go beyond the one-sided treatment of the question of competition merely from the standpoint of the technical superiority of small versus large-scale businesses, as it is usually formulated, to a standpoint comprising all the factors at work. Sombart then examines in detail how the superiority of the capitalist economic organisation manifests itself. It appears in the quality of the performance – capital supplies goods more quickly and in massive quantity – as well as in the quality of the goods offered, particularly through the disposal of highly skilled labour, which today is monopolised by capital. The arts and crafts today, as Sombart shows in the interesting chapter on artistic craft, are almost exclusively organised by large-scale capital. And just as in the battle for the best performance, capital also wins in the price war, which is described at length. The crafts have been crippled more and more, and it is a dream to believe that their destruction can be prevented through compulsory enrolment in cooperatives and the like. Abusive employment of juvenile labour power can likewise change nothing. The delivery of apprentices

---

9 [Talcott Parsons summarises Sombart's understanding of 'the economy' as follows:

'In conformity with [his] general view of economics stands the leading concept of his work, that of the economic system. He defines it as follows: "Under this term I understand a peculiarly ordered form of economic activity, a particular organization of economic life within which a particular mental attitude predominates and a particular technique is applied." This economic system is to be constructed in the purity of an "ideal type" to be used for the analysis of concrete reality, and will be found to correspond more or less closely to the historical facts. The empirical equivalent of the economic system is for Sombart the economic epoch, a period of time in history within which a particular economic system or form of economic life has predominated.

'Every economic system has, he maintains, three aspects: a form of organization, a technique, and a mental attitude or spirit. Of these three, the side which he most strongly emphasizes is that of the spirit. In Sombart's own words: "It is a fundamental contention of this work that at different times different attitudes toward economic life have prevailed, and that it is the spirit which has created a suitable form for itself and has thus created economic organization." Each spirit is for him a thoroughly unique phenomenon, occurring only once in history. There is no line of development leading from spirit to spirit, and thus from system to system, and each is, therefore, to be considered by and for itself.

'He uses the conception of the spirit as the means to bring order and unity into the historical material ... It gives a unity to his presentation which marks a great advance over the entirely disconnected studies of historical facts presented by the historical school proper' (Parsons 1928, p. 644)].

to the crafts is a danger for our industrial future, whose increasingly urgent task is to provide the necessary number of well-trained, qualified workers, who can no longer be trained by the degenerating crafts.

These are precisely the chapters that offer the greatest interest for us here in Austria, the promised land of middle-class politics for guild members. What Waentig's excellent book[10] describes in detail – the complete uselessness of middle-class politics and its deleterious effect on general industrial development – is proved here to be a necessity in the context of a causal derivation. Sombart's compelling arguments, summarising everything that can be said against middle-class politics from a scientific and economic standpoint, can hardly be refuted. Middle-class politics will henceforth no longer be conducted with scientific arguments. Austrian economists have every reason to give their full attention to this section of the book.

But with this synopsis, which is naturally brief, given the large scope of the work, our task has hardly begun, for Sombart wants to offer more than economic history. His book also claims to be a theory; moreover, when he proceeds to define it more closely, it is to be an historical-social theory. Thus Sombart hopes, as he explains in his preface, to reconcile the contradiction between empiricism and theory and to point out new pathways for economic research.

So what is the essence of this historical-social theory? Sombart sees the 'specificity of theory in ordering [historical events] from the point of view of a single explanatory principle'.[11] Between the two explanations possible here [teleological and casual], he chooses the causal. This is because causal consideration of the nature of the modern economy, with its dependence on the dominant market laws, (which, like the laws of nature, do not care for determination of aims by individuals), is more adequate than the teleological treatment. It is, therefore, the particular historical structure of capitalist society that decides the choice of causal explanation, whereas, for instance, explanation of the historical nature of an economy [*Wirtschaft*], consciously directed by the institutions of society, requires a teleological consideration.

At the beginning of the causal series, Sombart places human motives [*die menschlichen Motive*] in their particular historical configuration. He sees the world of crafts causally shaped by the desire of the artisans for a standard of living befitting their social status [*standesgemäß*], while the world of capitalism is dominated by acquisitiveness, by the quest for profit, whose bearers –

---

10   Waentig 1898.
11   Sombart 1902, Vol. I, p. xiii.

the capitalist economic subjects, traders and businessmen – now remodel the craftsman's world according to their wishes. Of course, those [ideal] motives cannot come into being at will. They are tied to a particular configuration of external conditions within which they occur. These objective conditions must be given in order to understand the effectiveness of the motives, the subjective conditions. Only in a peculiar world, such as the declining Middle Ages, could the emerging capitalist spirit produce our present peculiar economic system. There are thus, at any one time, various theories only for distinct social conditions, i.e. there are only historical theories and no general social theory. [In Sombart's book] there is a theory of modern capitalism, but not a theory of capitalism itself. The choice of the ordering principle is therefore not subjective: rather, history decides on the ordering principle at any one time. Mercantilism, in which the economy had to appear consciously regulated by social institutions, naturally sprang from purposeful ideas [*Zweckgedanken*]. In the classics, the casual and teleological points of view went side by side, but then Karl Marx undertook to explain the economic system from a strictly causal point of view.

Strict distinction between economic principles also underlies Sombart's classification of economic systems, of which he distinguishes two according to their prevailing principles: the provision of goods and services to satisfy the needs and wants of the population [*Bedarfsdeckungswirtschaft*],[12] and production for profit [*Erwerbswirtschaft*]. This looks like the adoption of an idea on which Karl Marx lays great stress; namely, that the purpose of simple commodity production (as it developed historically, for instance, in the medieval economy) is use-value, while the purpose of capitalism is exchange-value, and therefore capitalist society can only be understood if one recognises the search for surplus value as its driving motive. But while in Marx this motivation, as we shall see later, grows out of the prevailing production conditions, Sombart postulates it as a precondition for the formation of these relations of production. Is the scientific purpose pursued by Sombart promoted in this way? His work is supposed to give a theory of economic development.[13] He sees his chief task in the causal explanation of the objective facts of economic life; research therefore 'necessarily always leads back in time from a phenomenon of the present to one of the past' – a conclusion, says Sombart, which results in the 'first attempt at a theoretical justification of the historical perspective in the

---

12   [Sombart mentions state-operated railways and postal services as examples of this type of enterprise].

13   Sombart 1902, Vol. I, p. xxviii.

field of economics'. However, it is difficult to suppress the sceptical question: Why on earth should an historical perspective for the presentation of economic history first be theoretically justified?

But does Sombart's approach really fulfil the task he set for it? If historical development is really presented in its continuous course, then the question naturally arises as to how one economy develops from another that preceded it. Here, Sombart's theory lets us down completely. His two economic principles confront each other abruptly, without any attempt being made to establish a connection [between them]. And Sombart has to admit this himself when he suddenly declares that only when the economic principle shapes the economic order according to its needs do we posit it from the viewpoint of necessity, while the genesis of the economic principle itself we posit from the point of view of contingency.[14] This looks like an admission that Sombart's 'historical-social theory' is actually not a theory of development. That is proven especially by the chapter dealing with the emergence of the 'new spirit', i.e. with the subjective condition of capitalism. The 'new spirit', to our surprise, appears as an old spirit, as the *auri sacra fames*[15] with which humanity is constitutionally afflicted, and about which the tales of Midas and the Argonauts already tell us. But this spirit, the search for gold, for more and more of the glittering metal, only seizes mankind suddenly 'in the fullness of time' (Gal 4:4),[16] as the Biblical expression goes, not quite exactly from an historical standpoint. Robber barony and sale of indulgences, gold rushes and alchemy, all tried to satisfy the craving for gold, and now arises the idea of putting economic activity also at the service of that purpose. The leitmotiv of economic activity ceased to be to achieve a standard of living befitting one's social status, becoming instead money-making. 'When, where, and how that thought first came into the world, will probably always be shrouded in impenetrable darkness'.[17] And in this darkness the cruel author suddenly abandons the anxious reader, while he himself, under the protective cover of darkness, makes the *salto mortale* (somersault) across the chasm separating the world of the craftsmen from that of the capitalists. One cannot blame the reader if he refuses to follow Sombart in this death-leap of 'historical social theory'. Painfully groping alone in the dark, the reader looks for means to illuminate the darkness and find a

---

14   Sombart 1902, Vol. I, p. 398.
15   ['accursed hunger for gold' (Virgil, *Aenead*, 3, 57)].
16   ['But when the fullness of the time had come, God sent forth His Son, born of a woman, born under the law, to redeem those who were under the law, that we might receive the adoption as sons' (Galatians 4:4–5)].
17   Sombart 1902, Vol. I, p. 338.

bridge over the gap. And it is not too difficult. He finds the means to do that in the chapters describing the objective conditions under which the 'new spirit' developed its effectiveness. To be sure, the bold jumper Sombart would look at this enterprise contemptuously. But it no longer frightens the destitute[18] to clash with Sombart here.

In his preface, Sombart claims that the motivations of living people are the ultimate, primary active causes we can go back to.[19] In order not to fall into an extremely idealistic conception that does violence to the facts, Sombart tries to understand those motives historically. But since he sees them as the primary factors, he is forced to leave them just to follow one another, while the task of a theory of development should be to derive them from one another. The unity of human practice, from which the various maxims could have been identified as the consequences of determining factors at any one time, is thereby destroyed. There is suddenly a gap in the explanation in which one motive replaces the other; here the causal derivation stops, as Sombart himself must admit.

And Sombart's standpoint necessarily had to lead to this result. We must, he says in the preface,[20] go no further back than to human motives, because otherwise we are forced into an infinite regression, 'which can find its end only in the understanding of the movement of the smallest parts and the laws regulating them'. Here we run into 'the not yet bridged gap of psychological causation, which is different from mechanical causality'. Sombart seems to confuse here the ontological (metaphysical) question of the relationship between mind and matter with the question of the determination of human will by the configuration of the outside world. But while critical philosophy has proven the unsolvable metaphysical character of the first question and its false formulation of the problem,[21] the second question is one whose correct answer is the fundamental condition of all social science. By confusing the two problems, Sombart not only does not align himself with Karl Marx, but rather stands methodologically in sharpest contrast to the founder of the materialist conception of history.

The materialist conception of history – and we should not still have to explain today that this scientific view of history has nothing in common with any materialistic metaphysics – explains the social life and activity of people,

---

18   [*den Verlassenen*: Another Biblical reference: 'He will regard the prayer of the destitute, and not despise their prayer' (Psalm 102:17)].
19   Sombart 1902, Vol. I, p. xviii.
20   Sombart 1902, Vol. I, p. xix.
21   [Note the Kantian standpoint assumed by Hilferding here, common to all the Austro-Marxists].

i.e. of people engaged in activities relevant to historical development, from their relations of production, as the basic associative relationship.[22] The question of whether motives or objective conditions are 'primary', a formulation of the problem that is really a repetition of the question of dogmatic metaphysics concerning the primacy of 'spirit' or 'matter', does not exist for the materialist conception of history. Rather, just as critical philosophy first made comprehensible our ability to understand nature by accounting for the world as our representation, and therefore as adequate for our thinking and accessible to the unity of thought, so the materialist conception of history also represents nothing more than the substantiation of the possibility of social monism. This is done by proving that the whole human environment, as [made up of] purely historical behaviour, first becomes operative when it is incorporated into the unity of human action, that is, once it has become part of social life.

But the foundations of the social existence of man – who is naturally associated as *zoon politikon* (ζῷον πολιτικόν: political animal) – which drive him forward in this associative relationship and therefore in his [historical] development, are the relations of production, [i.e.] human 'subjective' relations and not 'objective' conditions, which from this standpoint [of the materialist conception of history] ultimately exist just as little as, from the standpoint of critical philosophy, do objective variables [*Größen*: quantities], which arise only from the subjective forms of intuition.[23] By taking nature, the 'milieu', the 'objective conditions' as a mere substrate for the fundamental social relations between people, which they must enter into in order to earn a living, the unity of the process between man and nature, whose dialectical unfolding accounts for the changing content of history, appears in the production process.

But Sombart, who allegedly wants to develop further the 'revolutionary' concepts of Marx and reformulate them in evolutionary terms, is in reality far

---

22   [*Produktionsverhältnissen als dem grundlegenden Verhältnis aller Vergesellschaftung*: literally: 'the relations of production as the fundamental relationship of all socialisation'. However, Hilferding is not employing here the term *Vergesellschaftung* in its usual sense of 'socialisation', but in Max Weber's meaning of 'association' or 'associative relationship'].

23   ['*Wie etwa vom Standpunkt der kritischen Philosophie objektive Größen, die nur aus den subjektiven Anschauungsformen entspringen*'. A reference to Kant's *Critique of Pure Reason*: 'The form of mathematical cognition is the cause of its pertaining solely to quanta. For only the concept of magnitudes [*Größen*] can be constructed, i.e., exhibited a priori in intuition, while qualities cannot be exhibited in anything but empirical intuition' (Kant 1998, p. 631)].

behind him when, instead of [upholding] monism, he separates out objective and subjective conditions in the manner of dualism, which are then to celebrate their union in the concrete course of history, while no one knows how and when and why.

But Sombart is driven even further. [He argues that] dualism pervades the whole of history. But this dualism occurs on one side, on the side of subjective conditions: a multiplicity of motives, depending on the historical eras, which face each other abruptly. The unity of the human psyche is thus lost, and we get a different psyche for every historical epoch. People's behaviour is not regarded, for instance, as determined in a particular way in a specific historical period, but, on the contrary, human behaviour is seen as essentially different in different eras, and each time a different history develops according to the respective prevailing purposes. The causal analysis thus necessarily becomes teleological. That cannot be otherwise if it is assumed that psychological factors are the primary 'causes'. As a matter of fact, [according to Sombart] it is the different purpose pursued by the economic subjects at different times that takes hold of the economy and makes it subservient to that purpose. From this basically teleological point of view it does not matter that the *telos* [the ultimate end of a goal-directed process] is every time historically different and is not Sombart's *telos* but that of simple artisans or driven capitalists. The causal analysis would only be possible if the motives had been presented as an historical result, while in Sombart they are rather taken as a prerequisite. Since the diversity of motives is in reality the product of a long historical development, it is plainly wrong to take them as preconditions for a theory of historical development, while – once seen as products of history – they can constitute a starting point for a systematic ordering of economic systems. But since Sombart presents the motives – which to him necessarily appear as purposes that cannot be further derived [from other causes] – in diametrical opposition to each other, instead of seeing them only as different determined moments in the unity of the human will, he completely disrupts the continuity of historical development and is forced to become truly 'revolutionary', to use Sombart's word. The emergence of motivation, which should be historically determined, remains unexplained. The motives appear to him as the *deus ex machina* [a god introduced into a play to resolve the entanglements of the plot], or rather the *dei ex machina*, because the worldly-wise Sombart is a polytheist. And against the charge of arbitrariness, which could so easily be made against the selection of motives, there is really no defence other than the one employed by Sombart: let someone else try something different – the typical excuse of bad poets against the objections of their critics, which they do not know how to rebut.

This abrupt juxtaposition [of motives] seems to originate in Sombart's aversion to 'discursive political economy', whose findings, however, in our opinion, are able to make this mediation [*Vermittlung*]. The operating profit of the artisan is fixed in advance because a continuous change in technology, i.e. the qualitative change in production that characterises the modern economy, is impossible [in handicraft production]. Also, the quantitative expansion of production is confined to very narrow limits, both as regards the number of assistants and the prolongation of the working time. The personal intervention of the master [in the labour process] acts as a barrier, excluding in advance the possibility of an unlimited increase in revenues from a business. This makes competition in the modern sense impossible. As a result, the craftsman knows the outcome beforehand as more or less invariable; it can only be a question of relatively small differences in his conventional standards of living. It is different with the capitalist. The separation of ownership of the means of production and labour – and the relation between the means of production and the workers, is for Marx the objective criterion for distinguishing between economic systems, from whose diversity must be derived the diversity of precepts of the economic subjects – this separation makes possible the unlimited increase of revenue. The qualitative and quantitative changes in the production process provide the basis for capitalist competition, whose law necessarily forces upon the capitalist the continuous improvement and expansion of his business as an imperative for his preservation. From an economic point of view, he can only behave as if increasing his profits were his only motive, whatever may stir a beautiful capitalist spirit in particular cases. In purely economic terms: the conservative economic principle of the craftsman and the revolutionary economic principle of the capitalist follow necessarily from the fact that, generally speaking, simple reproduction is the law of motion of the craft economy, while reproduction on an expanded scale is the law of the capitalist economy.

The transformation of mental behaviour, however, occurred gradually and was not too difficult, probably often involving the same people, or at least people belonging to the same class. And in the beginning was the economic deed.[24] At first the economy, particularly trade, was profitable; it was then continued and expanded because it was lucrative and initially allowed for a better living. The striving for better living standards gradually became the pursuit of profit – originally essentially the same striving for the customary livelihood, just intensified. Only the further development of capitalism turned

---

24 [A paraphrase of Goethe: 'In the beginning was the deed!' (*Faust* I, 1237)].

the means, profit, into the purpose, through the laws of economic life itself, which turned the desire to make profit into a necessity on penalty of ruin in capitalist competition.

Thus, it is essential precisely for the historical presentation, which must be at the same time a history of development, to recognise the intrinsic connection of an economic system. This means, however, that theoretical or, as Sombart says, discursive political economy is necessary precisely for the completeness of historical comprehension. Even Sombart cannot entirely disavow this. Still, he is methodologically trained to reproduce blindly the heavy-handed dogma of the historical school, which confuses theory and history and declares political economy to be only possible as history. But Sombart wants to reduce 'discursive' economics to a propaedeutic that takes care of the necessary conceptualisation, and he describes it as clumsiness on the part of the author to allow readers to know how he arrived at those concepts. But can there be anything more telling than the fact that here Sombart declares theoretical economy to be a private matter, giving an account of which is something superfluous?

We have seen how this standpoint fails in the historical presentation. Its starting point, the prevailing motives, is too narrow to encompass the entire area of historical development. If it does not stand out in Sombart's account, it is because in his historical presentation in the first volume he essentially confines himself to describing the objective conditions of the origin of capitalism, making no reference to motives at all, and only then follows the sphere of industrial life in its development. Here the pursuit of profit is an appropriate organising principle for the presentation, because it unfolds also in reality. Theory does not need to take anything else into consideration for the derivation of its laws, but it is otherwise with the history of development. In the latter, proceeding from those single motives results in a one-sided view that actually does violence to the fullness of life. History is in reality a result of struggles, in which the combatants mass together in large groups – organised in the final analysis according to their economic interests – whose actions are guided by different, often opposing interests, all of which have a furthering or inhibiting impact on historical development.

With his prevalent motives (which become for him the only active ones), Sombart assumed the sole and absolute domination of a single class, and he neglected the impact of all others. If that already means a deficiency in the narrow circle of economic history – and we ascribe it to the fact that Sombart glides almost carelessly over the origins of the modern proletariat, which was often created out of formerly independent social strata by the most violent methods – it makes the establishment of a connection between economic history and general historical development even more impossible. To be sure, Sombart was misled into doing this by his stand on economic policy, by his tendency also to regard future development as a peaceful one resulting from the social policies of the capitalist class, and by his efforts to eliminate theoretically the contradiction between bourgeois and socialist society.

But where Sombart proceeds to a systematic presentation – particularly in the section called the 'Theory of Industrial Competition' – he leaves his method completely aside and takes as the basis of his whole presentation and argumentation a theory of production costs. It is obvious that this whole section would not have been possible without the work of theoretical economics, on whose results it is based. Sombart can, in fact, so little dispense with theoretical economics that he rather presupposes its existence, thus unwillingly paying it homage.

So why does Sombart's work still bring much enlightenment and provide many insights into economic relationships? In our opinion, this is because the founder of 'historical social theory' has tended in fact not to apply his method too strictly. It is not 'history' that made the choice of the organising principles for Sombart. Rather, under the pseudonym 'history' hides the name of Karl Marx.

The very fact that Sombart sees the driving force for the development of economic life solely in the economic sphere is a Marxian principle. The formulation of his economic principles is nothing but a re-application of Marx's teachings; except that Sombart splits the unity of the Marxist conception of history dualistically and thus arrives at the contrast between objective and subjective conditions, although often the practice of his presentation, but not his theory, knows how to overcome this dualism. It would be wrong to try to counterpose Sombart's theory, as idealistic or psychological, to the materialist conception of history. It is none of the above because it is ultimately not deterministic, for the motives are posited one after the other as autonomous powers, independent of each other, instead of being derived from each other. But still: once their existence is admitted – and that they exist and must exist has been proved, in our opinion, by Marxism – they turn out to be felicitous organising principles of historical presentation.

But in those many chapters where the specific nature of his theory did not come to bear – and they constitute most of the book (which, therefore, despite Sombart's pursuit of uniformity, also has a dualistic character) – the reader is given the clues that allow him to establish the continuity of historical development. The economic historian Sombart has proved more fortunate than the social theorist.

DOCUMENT 14

The Psychological Tendency in Recent Political Economy (1892)

*Conrad Schmidt**

Source: Conrad Schmidt, 'Die psychologische Richtung in der neueren National-Oekonomie', *Die Neue Zeit*, 10. 1891–2, 2. Bd. (1892), H. 41, S. 421–9, 459–64.

Introduction by the Editors

There is much irony in the fact that just as Marx was working to complete *Capital*, and then Engels to make Volumes II and III of *Capital* available, a new approach to economic theory, beginning from a viewpoint exactly the opposite of Marx's, was emerging in Britain and continental Europe. The so-called 'marginalist revolution', a response to the disintegration of the Ricardian

---

* Conrad Schmidt (1863–1932) was a German economist and journalist. In the mid-1880s he studied in Berlin and received his doctorate in 1887 in Leipzig with the thesis *Der natürliche Arbeitslohn* (*The Natural Wage*), in which he compared the wages and exploitation theories of Johann Karl Rodbertus and Karl Marx. Schmidt rejected Marx's theory as an unproven hypothesis in favour of Rodbertus's views, which were based on the assumption of natural rights. After further study, Schmidt revised this judgement and became a follower of Marxism. In 1889 he published a book for the so-called 'prize-essay competition', in which Engels challenged the economists to explain how the formation of an average rate of profit could be made compatible with law of labour value – a solution finally revealed with the publication of the third volume of *Capital* in 1894. Schmidt's book was called *The Average Rate of Profit on the Basis of Marx's Law of Value* (Schmidt 1889), and gave rise to a lively correspondence between him and Engels. Volumes 48 to 50 of Marx and Engels's *Collected Works* include 16 letters addressed by Engels to Conrad Schmidt, ranging from 26 November 1887 to 6 April 1895. In 1890 Schmidt became, at Engels's advice, editor of the journal *Züricher Post*, and published a brochure on *The Social Question and Land Nationalisation* (Schmidt 1890). With the outbreak of the revisionist controversy in 1896, he became an outspoken supporter of Eduard Bernstein and a frequent contributor to his journal *Sozialistische Monatshefte* (Schmidt 1898). After Schmidt's conversion to revisionism, Plekhanov crossed swords with him on the pages of *Die Neue Zeit*, particularly because of calls from Schmidt and Bernstein to go 'back to Kant' (see Plekhanov 1898b). For a book-length biography, see Owetschkinm 2003.

school, began in the early 1870s in the works of William Stanley Jevons in Britain, Léon Walras in Switzerland, and Carl Menger in Austria. Its effect was to do to political economy what Marx had done to Hegel: the principle of 'marginal utility' would turn political economy on its head.

The traditional approach, beginning with Adam Smith and extending through the works of Ricardo and Marx, was principally concerned with the dynamic of capital accumulation and other conditions for economic growth. Smith and Marx were profoundly aware of stages of *history*, and both measured material progress in terms of expanding the social product in physical terms. But as capitalism in Europe and America entered the 'long depression' of the late nineteenth century, the marginalists replaced the focus on growth with the question of how capitalism tends towards equilibrium by efficiently allocating given resources among competing wants. Jevons famously defined the 'economic problem' as one of maximising the utility of the social product, given 'a certain population, with various needs and powers of production, in possession of certain lands and other sources of material'.[1]

Whereas political economy previously emphasised the conditions for increasing *supply*, the marginalists concentrated instead on *demand*. The centrality of the 'consumer' replaced that of worker and capitalist; personal saving replaced capitalist accumulation; and individual judgements of 'utility', or what Marx called use-value, replaced objectively determined exchange-values. The grand panorama of capitalist expansion collapsed into a new narrative of abstract individuals, each making purely subjective appraisals of the value of separate commodities and thereby ultimately determining price as an aggregate expression of their individual preferences.

Instead of social existence determining consciousness, exactly the opposite chain of causality was now said to prevail. The exploited worker was replaced by the self-determining individual. The poor were to be regarded as 'sovereign' consumers in the same sense as princes, aristocrats, landlords or employers. A neo-Kantian world of individual responsibility was to replace a world of class struggle. Value, surplus value and exploitation would vanish simply by looking at things from a different 'point of view'. Marx's laws of history would be replaced by universal principles of individual, utility-maximising choice.

---

1   Jevons 1871, p. 255. In *Economic Theory in Retrospect* Mark Blaug wrote: 'If we are going to describe the last quarter of the 19th century as a period when economists developed a new "paradigm", the only defensible definition of that paradigm is the proposition that pricing and resource allocation with fixed supplies of the factors of production is *the* economic problem ...' (Blaug 1985, p. 306).

Carl Menger, founder of the Austrian school of subjective economic theory, thought that 'exact' economic laws could be discovered, to which exceptions were inconceivable due to the logical force of the 'laws of thinking'.[2]

Menger believed that even the value of means of production is determined by consumers. How much are machines or raw materials worth? That depends on the – utility of the goods they might be used to produce.[3] What is the value of a unit of constant capital? That depends on the expected satisfaction from consuming additional units of the commodity in whose production the capital might be employed. The value of any 'factor' of production 'is merely the importance we attribute to those satisfactions'.[4] Whereas Marx saw demand being determined by production, which a) distributes income in a predictable pattern between social classes, and b) objectively determines prices on the basis of labour costs, prices were now to be explained entirely in terms of subjective judgements of consumer satisfaction.

Conrad Schmidt, in the article that follows, responded to this new 'psychological tendency' in economic theory by first hypothetically adopting the perspective of an individual consumer. He agreed that if a single individual *already has* determinate quantities of two goods at his disposal, he will surely judge the utility of acquiring an additional (or marginal) unit of one or the other on the basis of his subjective expectation of relative satisfaction. It was clear that 'under certain circumstances, value estimation is actually regulated in this manner, by the stock of goods alone'.

But the obvious problem is that *costs* of production have not been considered. If the same individual must also *produce* the goods in question, then 'The greater or lesser difficulty in replacing the goods manifests itself in the larger or smaller quantity of labour which the individual would have to expend in reproducing those goods'. If the argument is carried one step further, the isol-

---

[2] According to Samuel Bostaph, Menger 'sought the "simplest" elements of everything real; and then, in the search for economic laws, he sought to isolate them and to use the "simple elements" so obtained to deduce "how more complicated phenomena develop from the simplest, in part even unempirical elements of the real world ...". He believed that ... general connections between economic phenomena could be discovered in an "exact" sense as "exact" laws. An "exact" or causal law was an absolute statement of necessity to which ... exceptions were inconceivable because of the "laws of thinking"' (Bostaph 1994, p. 463).

[3] Menger differentiated between commodities for consumption (lower-order goods) and those used for production (higher-order goods), claiming that 'the value of goods of higher order is always and without exception determined by the prospective value of the goods of lower order in whose production they serve' (Menger 2007, p. 150).

[4] Menger 2007, p. 152.

ated individual gives way to individual commodity producers, in which case their own self-interest will lead each to produce and exchange according to his labour expenditures. Add capitalist production, and the result will be Marx's account of the objective determination of exchange-value according to direct and indirect expenditures of labour.

The second part of Schmidt's argument elaborates some of the implications. In social terms – as distinct from the perspective of an abstract individual – the cheapest goods are not generally the ones least required, or those yielding the least subjective satisfaction; they are the only ones that most people can afford. If a harvest failure makes bread scarce, it would be absurd to say that the ensuing price rise occurs because one of the *least* necessary needs is no longer satisfied, or, to put in another way, that bread has become more expensive because the marginal unit is now satisfying *more* necessary needs, namely, those of the wealthy.

Conrad Schmidt's contribution clearly exposed the one-sidedness of a theory that began and ended with abstract individuals, whose preferences as consumers were supposed to explain the entire system of market prices. After reading the article, Engels wrote to Schmidt that 'Your essay in the *Neue Zeit* gave me great pleasure. It's as if cut out for this country [Britain], since the *Fabian Society* positively pullulates with Jevons-Mengerians who look down with infinite contempt on a Marx they have long since outdistanced'.[5] In terms of the history of economic thought, however, the marginalist approach had an impact that went far beyond Fabian socialism or the Revisionist tendency on the European continent.

Schmidt himself inadvertently raised the problem. He recognised that 'If people were only consumers, and goods fell down upon them from the sky, then in fact everybody would value his property according to the marginal utility theory alone'. Yet even if goods did not fall from the sky, it was also obvious that every individual, when spending his income, would purchase

> a specific type of goods only as long as the satisfaction of needs (marginal utility), achieved by the last monetary unit, is greater than the utility effect to be obtained through an alternative expenditure of that unit. This law, formulated in the jargon of marginal utility theory, is simply the precise expression of the self-evident truth that everybody, in spending his money, seeks to satisfy his system of needs as perfectly as possible.

---

5 Engels to Conrad Schmidt, 12 September 1892, in *MECW*, Vol. 49, p. 526.

This meant two principles were involved. Individuals with purchasing power at their disposal would make decisions on the basis of marginal utility, yet there was also an objective determination of price on the basis of labour expended. How, then, did the two principles *interact*? Schmidt concluded that they did not. The way in which an individual spent his money *presupposed* that prices were already determined. On the road from speculation to the real world, the second principle must prevail: 'The more regular and better organised the functioning of the economy, and the more cautious the provision for the accumulation of stocks of goods becomes, the more will this second principle of value estimation supersede the first principle of marginal utility'.

In terms of the subsequent development of economic theory, it was Alfred Marshall, professor of political economy at Cambridge University, who addressed this issue most directly in an effort to reconcile marginalism with the traditions of earlier thinkers. Marshall had no interest in Marx, but he was equally unimpressed by the one-sidedness of a demand-centred determination of prices.[6] In his *Principles of Economics*, first published in 1890, Marshall combined the theory of diminishing marginal utility with the principle of diminishing marginal productivity – anticipated by Ricardo with reference to agriculture – and reconceived the question of price determination in terms of the point of intersection between the schedules of demand and supply. Individuals made purchase decisions on the basis of marginal utility; and any change in the pattern of demand would affect prices due to a change in marginal production costs.[7]

Schmidt's achievement was to specify the logical circularity in Menger's scheme: it proposed 'to deduce the price of goods, given by the marginal utility consideration [*Grenznutzüberlegung*], from the marginal utility considera-

---

6 On the question of whether utility or 'real' costs determine price, Marshall wrote: 'We might as reasonably dispute whether it is the upper or the under blade of a pair of scissors that cuts a piece of paper, as whether value is governed by utility [demand] or cost of production [supply]. It is true that when one blade is held still, and the cutting is effected by moving the other, we may say with careless brevity that the cutting is done by the second; but the statement is not strictly accurate, and is to be excused only so long as it claims to be merely a popular and not a strictly scientific account of what happens' (Marshall 1895, Vol. I, p. 427).

7 In terms of the Austrian school, in 1886 Eugen Böhm-Bawerk applied the concept of marginal product in subjective terms that amplified but also remained consistent with Menger's original account: the value of any means of production is determined by the least valuable (or marginal) commodity in whose production they might be economically employed, which in turn depends upon consumers' judgements of marginal utility (Böhm-Bawerk 2005, pp. 161–7).

tion itself'. In a footnote, Schmidt mentioned that 'the changing relationship between supply and demand, given *constant commodity values*, continually produces *price fluctuations*', but he did not see how that same change would affect *values* themselves. Among Marxists, the question of how demand affects the *value* of commodities was more effectively explored by Isaak I. Rubin in the 1920s.

In his *Essays on Marx's Theory of Value*, Rubin derived his own supply curve directly from Marx. He saw that demand influences price through a change in costs due to the changing technical conditions of production. Increased demand draws less efficient firms into production, thereby raising the market value of the commodities produced: 'the extension of production to worse enterprises changes the average magnitude of socially-necessary labor per unit of output, i.e., changes the value (or price of production). These changes are explained by the technical conditions of a given branch'.[8]

The result of Rubin's study was a positively sloped supply curve, demonstrating that 'even if price is determined by supply and demand, the law of value in turn regulates supply. Supply changes in relation to the development of productive forces and to changes in the quantity of socially-necessary labor', all of which would be reflected in the prices of production that would prevail with an equalised rate of profit. The theory of marginal utility had produced a debate that moved in a 'vicious circle'. What determines what? Does demand determine supply, or supply demand? Rubin replied that the solution had already been provided by Marx: it is 'the labor theory of value [that] emerges from this vicious circle'.[9]

∴

The Psychological Tendency in Recent Political Economy (Conrad Schmidt)

I

A huge, bewildering mechanism, guided by hidden powerful laws, in eternal motion and held in check by no limits, mountains or seas – thus the economic life of modern times appears to us. Just as astronomy proves that the earth,

---

8   Rubin 1990, p. 211.

9   Rubin 1990, p. 213. These issues are discussed in more detail in Rubin's critical commentary on the Austrian school, the next Document in this volume.

which the naïve observer considers fixed and independent, is a tiny planet obeying the general laws of the universe, so the social point of view regards the single individual, who likewise considers himself so very free and independent, as a true microcosm, a vanishing atom in the movement of the economic mechanism, which is entirely free from any individual caprice.

To penetrate into the inner workings of this mechanism, to try to understand the conformity to law behind the infinite diversity of external appearances, objectively and from a unifying perspective – that is surely one of the most challenging tasks the scientific mind can conceive. This task is all the more compelling because this economic order, which today rules over the people, emerged historically from the work of the people themselves, even if it was not a purposeful work; and just as it came into being through an historical process, so it is also bound, given the restless developmental needs of humanity, to experience its own historical downfall. Economic research, by subjecting that economic order to the deepest analysis, is directly connected with the great problem of the social development of contemporary humanity.

I have called modern economic life a mechanism, regulated by laws (of course economic, not legal), and knowledge of these objectively understandable laws is the essential task of political economy. But must each economic order be subject to such covertly working laws? This [necessity] does not inhere in the concept of economic order itself. As long as people consume the products of their labour themselves, or must cede part of them to the ruling class for direct consumption, the economic order remains transparent, simple and clear. To understand such an economic order means to describe it and to demonstrate the historical causes of its formation and development. No economic laws are necessary in order to understand that. The reason driving modern economists to investigate such laws must not, therefore, be the fact that we have an economic order in general, but that we have this particular [capitalist] economic order. The distinctive factor, which makes the modern economic order different from all previous, less complicated organisms, is that, in the whole area under its sphere of influence, it rests on commodity production, i.e. on purchase and sale of the goods produced. The omnipresence and omnipotence of money, which mediates both the distribution and production of goods – that is the hallmark of its nature, the wellspring of its strength and of its weaknesses. The mystery, which must be solved in order to gain real knowledge of the modern economic order – as well as to explain the monetary income of the different social classes (the workers as much as the capitalists), and thus their conditions of existence and their [political] tendencies – lies in the fact that all goods, including the labour power of the people themselves, are exchanged for money at a price and, moreover, at *specific* prices.

And this mystery does not disappear if we describe the external form of modern economic life with even the most exhaustive statistics, or if we research ever so accurately the origin of this new social order, its struggles and its fate. This riddle can only be solved if we understand the universal, objective and comprehensible law that rules the exchange of commodities for money. All the laws to which we are subject in economic life today lead back to this first, great and universal law, without which all the rest remain in darkness. It is the riddle of prices that forces modern economists to look for a hidden, objective economic law.

If all goods are exchanged against one and the same good, namely, against money, they thereby equate themselves with each other. Despite all their differences, despite their incommensurability, a common factor must therefore exist that makes this equalisation, this commensurability of the seemingly incommensurable units, possible. And this common factor in all commodities can be nothing other than the fact that they are labour products, products of human labour *per se*, expended in any form. As crystallisations of abstract, equal labour, the commodities are values. As soon as commodity exchange has developed into a monetary economy, they express their value in a single commodity, which, as a result, receives general social validity [*Gültigkeit*] within the circulation of commodities – i.e. receives a monetary character. In its essence, then, price is the monetary expression of value. In the amount of money represented by the price of a commodity, the same amount of abstract labour is contained as in the commodity itself. If, however, the price can express the value of a commodity, and if the price must be understood, by its very nature, as value expression, it by no means follows, as Marx himself explicitly pointed out, that in each price relation the value of the commodity must come to an exact expression. Economics does not deal with random and individual deviations, but with general [laws].[10] The cause and extent of those deviations must be

---

10   Above all, the question under consideration here is how, on the basis of the law of value, the existence of ground rent is possible. Likewise, the fact that capitals of equal size, no matter how much or how little living labour they employ, receive on average the same profit indicates that the prices of commodities do not coincide absolutely with the quantities of labour stored up in them. According to Engels's introduction to Volume II of *Capital*, the solution to this problem is available in Marx's manuscripts and will appear in the third volume, which must also give Marx's position on the problem of ground rent. Among the many 'refutations' of Marx's theory, this issue has recently come insistently to fore. People argue – to be sure, without a shred of evidence – that there is here an insoluble contradiction to the law of value, a contradiction that must lead to its downfall! As if apparently no less striking and incontrovertible contradictions were not already

developed from the law of value itself. Whether or not such deviations exist, it is necessary in any case to find a general objective law regulating the exchange-value and the price of commodities; and such a law must be founded upon the general nature common to all commodities, that of being the product of abstract, equal average labour.

We cannot describe here, even in outline, how Karl Marx continued with wonderful energy, after a long interruption, the value analysis begun by Smith and Ricardo, how far he followed the law of value regulating price formation in the complications of reality, what phenomena can be considered as solved by the already published first two volumes of *Capital*, and which ones still wait for their solution, for that would be impossible within the limits set for this essay. However, it is probably worthwhile to clarify a preliminary question that in recent times often confronts the 'deductive' tendency in political economy; namely, the question of *whether such an objective and covertly working law of value can exist at all*. Most economic writers make things extremely simple for themselves. They explain prices at one time by the costs of production, then from supply and demand, and then from wages, profits and rents, etc., without thinking that what is to be explained, in all those cases, is presupposed.[11] In the name of *psychology*, an opposition has recently arisen against this unprincipled

---

raised by the theory – for instance, the contradiction that labour, which is the measure of all values, is itself sold, and so receives a special value. The simple Marxian definition according to which not labour, but labour *power*, is sold, removed that contradiction at one stroke. One should therefore, in all fairness, wait with such claims until Marx's train of thought itself becomes available for examination, and thus the basis for a criticism is created. Mr. Böhm-Bawerk, in an essay to which we shall return later, pleads in favour of psychological economics as the last choice, because Marx's theory, the dogma of pious Socialists, comes into insoluble contradiction with experience. Proof: the phenomenon of the average profit rate and the tendency of the prices of the products to rise when wages rise. A convenient way of reckoning! By the way, as regards the second objection, it falls apart in the easiest way. Both wage increases and the increases in product prices are consequences of a favourable market conjuncture, which is expressed in an increased demand for goods, i.e. in increased production, and therefore in an increased demand for labour power. Marx never dreamed of denying, but rather stressed most emphatically, that the changing relationship between supply and demand, given *constant commodity values*, continually produces *price fluctuations* (Cf. e.g. Volume I of *Capital*, third chapter, the section on money as a 'measure of value').

11   Production costs are the outlays in capital equipment and workers necessary for the production of a certain quantity of commodities. The price of the means of production and of labour is thereby assumed to exist. The relation between supply and demand can be, and often is, the same with the most expensive as well as with the cheapest commodities, and yet the huge differences in commodity prices continue to exist quietly.

eclectic style, as well as against scientific research based upon analysis of an objective law of value. This psychological tendency was inaugurated by the Englishman [William Stanley] Jevons, though it has followers in different countries and its main camp is in the Austrian universities. Its best-known spokesmen there are Menger, Böhm-Bawerk and Wieser.[12]

The argumentation of that school runs something like this: Each commodity exchange is always conditioned by the mutual consent of two contracting parties. But the will, as a rule, is guided only by psychological motives and, in the economic sphere, by selfish motives. The conclusion of each act of exchange thus depends solely on whether the contracting parties, according to their subjective estimates of value, regard the particular exchange as beneficial. Assuming this is the case, the deal *must* materialise; otherwise it *cannot* come into being. The factors on which everything depends in exchange are therefore the subjective value estimates; if one wants to know how the exchange-value of goods is determined, it is necessary to find the *principle of subjective value estimation through psychological analysis*. From this standpoint, the existence of an objective law of value, directly or indirectly determining exchange-value according to the real amount of labour embodied in the products, and without regard for such subjective factors, appears from the outset to be impossible. It is not this or that result of the objective theory of value, but rather the theory itself that is called into question. Psychology, investigating subjective factors, should take its place. That is the fundamental significance of the new school.

This much is obvious: the discovery of an objective law of value, no matter how it may be formulated, can never be consciously intended [by this school], because the individual will only follows the impulses of individual interest. The only question is *whether, by the individual will doing this, by all the individual wills doing this, an objective law still can (and indeed must) unconsciously and unintentionally arise*, a law of value as envisaged by the classics of political economy, to whose rule all the individual acts of exchange are subject. We shall now consider the remarks of the value psychologists from that point of view. A *double* question is under discussion here: first, whether their analysis

---

What can be explained from the relation of supply and demand are therefore not prices, but only their variations. Prices have to be assumed as determined elsewhere. Wages are ultimately the price of labour power; profit is a part of the price of the capitalistically produced commodities; ground rent is the capitalistically produced product of the soil. To explain prices from wages, profits and rents therefore means, once again, to explain prices from prices.

12 [Carl Menger (1840–1921), Eugen von Böhm-Bawerk (1851–1914) and Friedrich von Wieser (1851–1926). Cf. Horwitz 2003].

takes into consideration the psychological factors that are really crucial in the determination of exchange-value; and then, whether these really operative psychological factors preclude the existence of an objective law of value or whether, on the contrary, they permit its existence or even presuppose it as a necessary consequence. The examination will therefore be somewhat tedious, because we must begin with abstract isolated persons, as postulated by the barren arbitrariness of this school of psychologists, who believe that in this way they are able to recognise most clearly the general principle of value-judgements and the valuation of goods.

The psychological condition of any production, and moreover of exchange, is that the goods under consideration should be the object of a value estimation. But their value is estimated because these goods are means for the satisfaction of needs – provided that they are not, as with air, sunlight, water, etc. available in unlimited and never-decreasing quantities. In general, the question arises: how is the measure [*Maß*] of our value estimation determined? The Mengerians claim that it is determined not according to the abstract but according to the *concrete, or rather subjective use-value* that the things have for the individual. Abstract use-value depends upon the satisfaction of needs by a good; thus bread satisfies hunger, clothes satisfy the need for clothing, stucco satisfies vanity, etc. Therefore, a value estimation, based upon abstract use-value, would appraise the value of goods according to the importance of the satisfaction of needs. It would, for instance, declare a certain amount of bread more valuable than an equivalent quantity of clothes or even of stucco.[13] It is clear that in this way one cannot solve the problem of exchange-value, because that value is obviously determined in a way totally independent of the abstract importance of the goods. What happens now with concrete, or subjective, use-value? Can it be independent from abstract use-value, from the social significance of goods? The Mengerians claim so, and they exemplify their view with the isolated subject in possession of a stock of goods; in a sense, the economic Adam. In this case, the subjective value estimation is, in fact, essentially independent of the abstract use-value of goods. Let us assume, for example, that the isolated individual has a lot of bread and relatively little wine. Bread is certainly a more necessary and more important good than wine. However, despite this difference in abstract use-value, the loss of a certain amount of bread will, under those circumstances, probably feel less painful for the isolated indi-

---

13 What is actually an 'equivalent quantity'? Does that mean an equal weight or an equal number of units, or what? A single standard to measure the amounts of qualitatively different goods does not exist.

vidual than that of a corresponding amount of wine; he will value wine more than bread. The *subjective estimation of value* of the goods therefore depends not on the quality of those goods, or rather on the satisfaction of needs they provide, but on *the amount of a specific sort of goods available for the needs of the subject*, because on that amount depends the extent to which a certain kind of need on the part of the subject will be satisfied.

Herewith we have arrived at the much-vaunted theory of *marginal utility*. The marginal utility means the last, weakest, relatively most unnecessary satisfaction of needs that I can expect from a given quantity of goods. The value that I attach to goods of a certain kind should be based on marginal utility thus defined. Marginal utility seems to the psychological school to be the general and only principle of value estimation, from which the exchange-value and the price of goods are derived.

We shall explain value estimation, based on marginal utility, by means of a brief example that is freely modelled on a similar one given by Böhm-Bawerk. Our isolated individual has, according to our assumptions, a lot of bread available, let us say, 5 pounds per day, of which 2½ he consumes himself, and 2½ he uses to feed animals that he keeps for pleasure. If he loses half a pound per day, the loss will be little felt, because the continuing fall in the satisfaction of needs will be of minor importance; the feeding of animals will be somewhat limited. The loss of a further half pound will be felt more sharply, since now the animals have to suffer hunger, and possibly their maintenance will be called into question. Therefore, the value estimation of half a pound of bread, which was low when the individual disposed of 5 pounds, will be greater if he disposes of only 4½ pounds, because the marginal utility, i.e. the last, relatively most unnecessary satisfaction of needs, which was to be expected from the half-pound, has changed. It has become more important, its marginal utility has increased, and that change in the amount of marginal utility is expressed in the new value estimation. The further the amount of bread decreases, the more important is the relatively most unnecessary satisfaction of needs, the marginal utility, which is to be expected by the subject from half a pound. If he only possesses the 2½ pounds of bread required for his own consumption, the loss of half a pound means that his habitual food wants will not be satisfied; the loss of a further half pound means that his appetite will not be satisfied; and the loss of a further half pound will mean hunger.

We can see that the marginal utility of goods, at the disposal of the individual for consumption, varies with their quantity. The quantity of goods is compared with the quantity of needs; the last, only just covered ranking of needs [*Bedürfnißstaffel*] regulates the marginal utility that goods of this kind have for the individual, and thus the individual value estimation of such goods in general.

It is obvious that, under certain circumstances, value estimation is actually regulated in this manner, by the stock of goods alone – for example, when students mutually exchange their stamps and other treasures, or to take an example very popular in the Mengerian school, in desert travel, where no replacement for the existing provisions is to be expected. But the question is whether – if one selects circumstances a little less arbitrarily and fancifully and more in accordance with economic reality – marginal utility can remain as the only defining principle of individual value estimations.

Now, the isolated man, regarded as the economic nucleus, is inconceivable without an isolated economy. In Conrad's *Jahrbücher für Nationalökonomie und Statistik* (1890), Professor [Heinrich] Dietzel has already strikingly demonstrated to the Mengerians that this not quite unimportant fact throws their entire analysis into disarray.[14] If people were only consumers, and goods fell down upon them from the sky, then in fact everybody would value his property according to the marginal utility theory alone. But since people are themselves producers of their goods, and as a rule can always replace them by labour, they have absolutely no reason to value their products solely according to the ranking of needs covered by those products. The value estimation may just as well depend on the greater or lesser difficulty with which those goods can be replaced. In an isolated economy, moreover, they can only be replaced in one way: by the labour of the economic subjects themselves. The greater or

---

14 [Dietzel 1890]. In this year's March issue of the *Jahrbücher* Mr. Böhm-Bawerk published a reply to Dietzel's essay, in which he exploited very cleverly all the weak points of his opponents [Böhm-Bawerk 1892]. Dietzel in fact argued against the marginal utility doctrine from the standpoint of the theory that derives value from the cost of production. Böhm-Bawerk therefore had an easy game revealing the fundamental internal contradiction of his opponent (see above, note 2). The marginal utility theoreticians do not deny that in a commodity-producing society the value of the products stands in a necessary ratio to the costs incurred. But, according to their doctrine, the amount of the costs itself, the value spent in the form of means of production and labour, is determined by the value of the finished products, i.e. by their utility, especially their marginal utility. Inadequate as this value determination is, it is still better than a doctrine that remains stuck in a circular argument, deducing value from value, and the price of the products from the price of labour (and besides, possibly without mediation, also from the prices of the means of production). This inadequacy of the cost [of production] theory does not mean, however, that Dietzel's counter-argument is incorrect as far as the *isolated* economy of the marginal utility theoreticians is concerned. Böhm-Bawerk can bring forward nothing against the fact that the relative value of reproducible goods (and these are, Dietzel argues, *by far* the most important types of good) is estimated by the economic subject according to the expenditure of human labour necessary for their reproduction.

lesser difficulty in replacing the goods manifests itself in the larger or smaller quantity of labour which the individual would have to expend in reproducing those goods. Already in the isolated economy, therefore, the value estimation can be totally independent of the existing stock of goods and the marginal utility of the commodities determined by it: they can be evaluated according to the amount of labour that their replacement costs. The more regular and better organised the functioning of the economy, and the more cautious the provision for the accumulation of stocks of goods becomes, the more will this second principle of value estimation supersede the first principle of marginal utility.

What this Mengerian school wants to prove by psychological analysis, namely, that the subjective value estimation of goods can only be determined by the marginal utility they provide, is contradicted precisely by psychological analysis even for the isolated economy – if only one does not forget the economy in economic analysis, and in the analysis of goods, therefore, their reproducibility. The objection that value estimation, according to the costs of reproduction, does not represent a new standard of valuation but only another application of the marginal utility principle, is likewise unwarranted, because from the last ranking of needs satisfied by a given stock of goods, i.e. from their marginal utility, absolutely nothing can be inferred about the quantity of labour required for reproducing one of those goods. The valuation from the first standpoint can thus come into conflict with the valuation from the second standpoint.[15]

We see that, even in an isolated economy, economic value judgements will be more or less dominated by an objective factor – the amount of labour necessary to replace the goods. Only the wonderful one-sidedness of value psychologists could deny that. The question now is whether – if we substitute for isolated economic subjects people who are associated by exchange (furthermore, through purchase and sale), in short, a *commodity-producing society* – such an objective factor is not equally possible, or rather necessary, as the regulating principle of social value judgements, and thus of the exchange-value of goods,

---

15 [In fact, the developed marginal theory explains the supply of wage-labour in terms of an individual weighing the rising disutility of labour-effort against the expected gain in utility from added income. The point is that the judgement remains a purely *subjective* one for each individual to make, the total result being a positively sloped social supply curve for labour. In the discussion that follows, Schmidt undertakes to refute this view by reference to self-employed commodity producers rather than wage-labourers, in which case the exchange of one producer's embodied labour for that of another appears more transparently].

despite all the marginal utility psychology. This lengthy detour, through the isolated economy of the marginal utility theoreticians, was necessary in order to explain their views. Those views first become significant when marginal utility theoreticians turn from the economy of isolated subjects to the economy of exchanging subjects, from fantasy to reality, and then claim to understand the latter.

Commodity production, with free competition, has fully developed only in the capitalist form [of the economy], whose existence rests upon the antagonistic and opposing classes of industrial capitalists, landowners and wage-workers. The production and circulation of commodities ultimately takes place through those classes. Political economy has to prove how the law of value, that is, the objective determination of the value of commodities by the amount of abstract labour necessary for the production of those commodities, comes into being in *this* historically given world. The psychological school, which denies the possibility of an objective law regulating exchange, does not regard commodity-producing society in its historically developed form, but in a completely general form. The psychological school boils down to the argument that the exchanging parties (buyers and sellers) do not want to realise some objective law of value but only to look after their own individual benefit in the individual transaction; and that the labour time necessary for the production of commodities, since it is not the reason determining exchange-value in the consciousness of the exchanging subjects, therefore cannot be the factor determining exchange-value at all. This objection, which only bears in mind the most general features of commodity exchange, will be refuted most clearly if we disregard all the complications arising from the historical class character of commodity-producing society and regard commodity production in its most general undeveloped form, i.e. if we assume that the actual commodity producers exchange their products against each other directly, without the intervention of capitalists and landlords. If we are able to show that labour is the determining factor of exchange-value here, even if the parties to the transactions, looking after their own benefit, are unaware of it, then the psychological argument, which wants to infer the impossibility of an objective law of value from the [exchanging subjects'] lack of awareness of it, will be generally – that is, also for capitalist commodity production – refuted. Of course, the form in which the law of value is realised in capitalist commodity production cannot be the same as in the simple social order assumed by us. But if that form is developed by economic science in all its details, it will also appear as the psychologically necessary result of the competing individual wills, as the form in which an objective law of value is realised in simple commodity production, as a psychologically necessary result.

In such a society of independent commodity producers, everybody brings his entire labour product into the market and seeks to exchange it for the goods he needs. Everybody is concerned only about his own benefit. Everybody will, therefore, in exchanging his own products against other goods, always seek to exchange the smallest possible quantity of his own products for the largest possible amount of someone else's goods. He is compelled to do that by the endeavour to obtain the greatest possible satisfaction of his needs.

But his products, like everybody else's, embody the quantity of labour spent in their production. Each aliquot part of a product represents a corresponding fraction of the amount of labour crystallised in the entire product. The striving to exchange the smallest possible quantity of one's own product for the largest possible amount of someone else's product therefore implies, even if the individual exchanging parties are unaware of it, the quest to get the largest possible amount of someone else's labour for the smallest possible quantity of one's own labour. The advantageousness of exchange is measured, in a sense, by the extent to which this endeavour is successful. This much is also clear from the outset: the competition between producers, belonging to one and the same industry, makes certain that the exchange-value of their products is uniform [*einheitlich*: standardised]. A cannot sell more dearly than its competitor B, and B cannot sell more dearly than A. If competition guarantees this uniformity of exchange-values within an industry, a limit is set to the competitors' aspirations to increase as much as possible the exchange-value of their own commodities vis-à-vis those of all others, a limit that is independent of their arbitrary wills. Meanwhile, however, the law that regulates this limit, the norm that governs this uniform exchange-value, is, of course, not yet determined by the fact that we know that this value must be uniform.

Such a norm exists, however, and it presents itself as a necessary result of the psychologically necessary competition of all individuals for their greatest possible advantage. Competition, which makes it impossible for members of an industry to sell their own commodities more profitably than their competitors – this same competition also makes it impossible, at least in the long run, for the producers of an industry to exchange their products more advantageously than the producers of other industries. They would exchange more profitably if the product of their labour had a higher exchange-value than products manufactured with the same amount of labour in other industries. In that case, however, the privileged industry would experience an influx of new producers until the pressure of the increasing supply of this type of commodities again led to the loss of that specific advantage. Competition thus ensures that, in the long run, the products of an industry cannot be exchanged on the market more profitably than the rest, i.e. it ensures that products containing the same amount of labour, no matter in which industry it was spent, have the same exchange-value. The fact that one commodity is the common medium of exchange, i.e. that it possesses a money character, cannot of course alter this tendency to equalisation. *Thus we see that, even if the realisation of this objective law of value is not consciously desired by the individual contracting parties, it is still guaranteed, in a society of independent commodity producers, by the free play of economic self-interests whose only goal is their own benefit.* The analysis of the decisive psychological factors in a commodity-producing society, far from making the appearance of an objective law of value impossible, actually *directly demonstrates* its necessity, assuming the existence of simple commodity production.

Thus the fundamental conclusion that the representatives of this school wanted to deduce from the psychological determination of the act of exchange is disproved; namely, that the concept of an objective law of value, regulating by and large all acts of exchange, is contradictory and absurd in itself. The preliminary question formulated by us above, by means of which they hoped to cut the ground from under any objective theory of value, is finally settled. For if the existence of an objective law of value has just been proved to be necessary in simple commodity production, precisely on the basis of psychologically motivated individual wills – how could the struggle of these psychologically motivated individual wills, in developed capitalist commodity production, make impossible the realisation of such a law (albeit in different form)?

II

We have already seen that the psychological school of economics errs in its analysis because it disregards the psychological factors that are really relevant for commodity exchange. If that were not the case, they would immediately have convinced themselves, by the argument we have just developed, that the psychological motivation of exchange reveals the existence of an objective law of value rather than refutes it, as they argue. However, that would only be an indirect refutation of the marginal utility theory. Given the epochal meaning that its supporters attribute to this theory, the contempt with which they treat all the achievements of classical economics – a contempt that only finds its counterpart in their respect and admiration for their own achievements – and the relatively great popularity of the school, it may perhaps appear immodest to settle accounts indirectly with the marginal utility concept in this summary manner.

We have left the marginal utility concept completely aside in our psychological derivation of exchange-value, even though it should be, according to the assurances of the whole school, the only principle of all value judgements and hence of the exchange-value of goods. Let us now see *whether a derivation of exchange-value from the marginal utility principle in a commodity-producing society* is, I will not say correct, but only *imaginable*. If not, what *appearances* could its apostles invoke?

The *first question* is whether, in a commodity-producing society, a derivation of the exchange-value of goods from the marginal utility principle is even possible. The marginal utility of goods should be calculated, as we have seen, according to the last satisfaction of needs provided by it. A subject who wants to valuate his goods according to the marginal utility principle must therefore – this is the presupposition – be in possession of a stock of goods serving for the satisfaction of needs. But the precondition for a valuation [of goods], on the basis of marginal utility, does not at all exist in a commodity-producing society. The goods that the producer exchanges are produced for the market; he does not (and usually cannot) consume them himself. His goods, produced for the market, thus offer him, as such, no satisfaction of needs and consequently no marginal utility. Therefore, there is no possibility of him valuating them according to their marginal utility, which should thus determine their exchange-value. In a commodity-producing society, marginal utility, so conceived, is, as a value principle, nothing more than a mere contradiction in terms.

If we assume, instead of a direct exchange of goods, an exchange mediated by money, in which the contracting parties face each other not as two commodity-owners but as money- and commodity-owners, as buyers and sellers, this changes absolutely nothing in favour of marginal utility theory. The seller's stock of commodities is just as little meant to satisfy the immediate wants of its owner as is the buyer's supply of money. Therefore, the commodity unit of the seller can just as little be valuated according to the marginal utility theory as can the monetary unit of the buyer.

But if money does not directly provide any satisfaction of needs, the means of subsistence bought with it do. Thus a subterfuge appears to present itself: even if the buyer cannot valuate money according to the theory of marginal utility, yet the goods bought with that money can be so valuated, and more or less can accordingly be paid for them. But for goods to be valuated by a subject according to the theory of marginal utility, we must assume – I repeat – that the person under consideration already possesses a stock of those goods.[16] He can

---

16 [The marginal theorist would reply that if the individual had consumed such goods in the past, he would remember his previous judgement of their relative utility. If the goods had not been consumed in the past, the individual would subjectively estimate their expected utility. In a modern capitalist economy, the whole point of consumer propaganda (the advertising industry) is to predetermine such judgements].

only have a stock, however, if he bought it, and he could only buy those goods at a fixed price. The possession of a stock of goods, from which the marginal utility theoreticians must start in order to explain the exchange-value and price of goods, presupposes what must be explained, namely the price of goods.

They want to avoid these impossibilities by replacing the individuals with the masses. The goods, which are accumulated in the hands of the sellers, confront the mass of consumers. Each one of these consumers needs goods, and the multiplicity of those needs will be at least partially satisfied if these goods pass into the hands of the consumers through purchase. Just as individuals have different rankings of needs, so do the masses. The psychological school starts from here. Among all of those rankings of needs finally satisfied by the goods, one must be the lowest. *The lowest ranking of needs is the marginal utility that goods of this kind have for society, and it is the one ultimately determining the exchange-value of commodities.* Proof: as a rule, the price of the products is lower, the greater their number, and higher, the fewer of these products are available. 'The more individual goods are available of any class, the more completely can the wants to which they relate be satisfied, and the less important are the wants which are last satisfied – those whose satisfaction is imperilled by the failure of one of the goods. In other words, the more individual goods there are available in any class, the smaller is the marginal utility which determines the value'.[17] Thus the psychological school explains the, at first sight, striking phenomenon that relatively useless things can have a very high value, while very useful ones can have a very small value.

This evidence only proves that the imagination of the marginal utility theoreticians does to economic facts what some famous fantasies did with world history. The facts have to give birth to an order as if they were in front of a Prussian corporal, and turn upside down by word of command. Of course, cheap products are not cheap because they are available in bulk, but they are rather available in bulk because they are cheap.[18] Most people in modern society are poor devils, who can buy only the cheapest means of consumption. The cheapest commodities are thus, precisely because they are cheap, the ones most in demand, and therefore also the ones most mass-produced. To deduce their cheapness from their quantity is to confuse cause and effect.

But quite apart from the unfortunate conclusion, the argument is untenable in itself. The marginal utility was determined as the last ranking of needs

---

17   Böhm-Bawerk 1891, p. 152.
18   I disregard, as everywhere, the so-called monopoly goods that are of secondary importance for political economy.

satisfied by a stock of goods at the disposal of a subject. But even if we replace the individuals by the masses, we must not forget that these people (the totality of the consumers) in reality have no stock of goods available, and that the precondition for a *direct* marginal utility valuation [of goods] is therefore missing for the masses as well as for the individuals in a commodity-producing society. The stock of goods must first be acquired by *purchase*. If the prices paid for this purchase were governed by the marginal utility principle, one would necessarily have to assume that the price level is determined by the last ranking of needs satisfied by those goods *after they came into the hands of consumers* – or, to give it another name, by *the estimated social marginal utility*. But that is again absurd.

Let us assume that the grain harvest was bad and that the amount of bread offered for sale in society was correspondingly reduced by a certain percentage. According to the law of supply and demand, the price of bread will go up.[19] Why? The marginal utility theoreticians say: because the estimated social marginal utility of bread has increased. Since the amount of bread was reduced, only a smaller quantity of needs than normal can be satisfied. According to marginal utility theory, the relatively most unnecessary satisfaction of needs would therefore be discontinued, therewith increasing the estimated social marginal utility [of bread], and this rise [in its marginal utility] would be the cause of the price increase. But what actually is discontinued [in this example], is not the *relatively most unnecessary satisfaction of needs*, but part of the most urgently felt *satisfaction of needs of the poorest*, who can no longer buy [bread] to the former extent due to the increase in prices. The bread consumption and, if you will, the bread waste of the property owners, on the other hand, will not be modified in the least. The relatively most unnecessary needs will be satisfied as before; the estimated social *marginal utility* remains therefore *unchanged*, while *prices vary*. The assumption that the estimated social marginal utility [of goods] can be the cause of price variations and, moreover, of the determination of prices is therefore untenable.

It turns out that the psychologists, who transferred the marginal utility concept from the individual who owns a stock of goods to the class of buyers who first buy a stock by purchase, have achieved absolutely nothing. The problem of exchange-value defies all of those efforts. They believe, incidentally, that in this way their doctrine can be harmonised with the theory that explains

---

19 That the *abnormal reduction* of the price of one kind of commodities will *increase* their price is, of course, no contradiction to the above rule. That would be the case if the quantity in which commodities are *normally* brought to the market *determined* their price.

exchange-value by the relation between supply and demand and, indeed, that they can prove this theory to be a consequence of their wider general principle. Apart from the fact that supply and demand explain only the fluctuations in prices and not the prices themselves, and that therefore even a happily accomplished marriage between both theories would only prove that two different errors get along well together, it is clear that this marriage has also failed. For whatever one might accuse the supply and demand doctrinaires of, at least they do not usually forget that not demand *per se*, but only *effective* demand can have an influence on the determination of prices. But whether a demand is solvent or not depends, as the above-mentioned example clearly illustrates, by no means on the intensity of the subjective needs, but first of all on the monetary income of the buyers. The needs, as such, are absolutely indifferent to price formation. Only when they can legitimise themselves through money do they count. Therefore, subjective need, in the form of marginal utility, cannot possibly be the regulating principle of prices. The marginal utility doctrine, which gives itself the airs of being a philosophical deepening of the theory of supply and demand, has not even come close to the latter in the explanation of price phenomena.

But how was it possible – and this brings us to our *final question* – for a theory so obviously in contradiction with all the facts of economic life to have such an impact? It rests on a dazzling, bewildering *quid pro quo*. It seems to me to draw its strength from the fact that *marginal utility* is, if not the principle regulating prices, then the norm according to which the buyer of the commodities *categorises* [*einteilt*: arranges, divides into classes] *his monetary income*. Although money has no direct use-value for its owner, it does have use-value for him as a medium of exchange, because it gives him the goods he wants in order to satisfy his needs. The utility of money, as a medium of exchange, is generally determined according to the volume of goods that can be bought with it. Besides, it is clear that even this application of the Mengerian school's utility concept can be of no use, because the level of commodity prices, which is to be explained, is assumed here as given. If the utility of money therefore depends on the goods that can be bought with it, the [amount of] goods that can be bought again depends on their prices.

Now, if money has a utility in accordance with the satisfaction of needs achieved by it, it follows that the concept of marginal utility must be applicable to it. If one spends money for the purchase of certain goods, the ranking of needs satisfied by the last commodity unit will steadily decrease with the increasing stock of goods, and finally a point will come when more money spent on goods of this kind will no longer seem worthwhile to the subject, and the remaining money will therefore be used to satisfy other needs. The last, relatively most unnecessary satisfaction of needs achieved by spending a monetary unit in the purchase of certain kinds of goods is the relatively weakest satisfaction of needs, the marginal utility that the monetary unit spent for this purpose has. Generally speaking, the following law holds: Everybody will successively invest monetary units in the purchase of a specific type of goods only as long as the satisfaction of needs (marginal utility), achieved by the last monetary unit, is greater than the utility effect to be obtained through an alternative expenditure of that unit. This law, formulated in the jargon of marginal utility theory, is simply the precise expression of the self-evident truth that everybody, in spending his money, seeks to satisfy his system of needs as perfectly as possible. It applies everywhere and determines everybody, no matter what kind of goods he buys or how many of them. The thrifty as well as the spendthrift are subject to it.

That is the reason why the marginal utility theory appears so natural and clear. And it would indeed be so, had it set itself the admittedly most modest goal of finding the formula according to which, at given commodity prices, the individual categorises his monetary income. Because – and this should not be forgotten – the *precondition* for the utility and the marginal utility of money, about which the individual thinks when he spends it, is that *the monetary price of goods should have a well-known given magnitude*. The error and the insolvable contradiction [of the marginal utility theory] begin as soon as one wants to deduce the price of goods, given by the marginal utility consideration [*Grenznutzüberlegung*], from the marginal utility consideration itself.

One can ultimately speak about the marginal utility of a monetary unit in a *double* sense. One meaning refers to a *specific* type of need that is to be satisfied by the monetary expenditure. The last, relatively most unnecessary satisfaction of this need, provided by the expenditure of a monetary unit, indicates the marginal utility of this unit, i.e. of the monetary unit spent in the satisfaction of this specific need. The marginal utility of a monetary unit has hitherto always been mentioned in this specific sense. On the other hand, one can ignore differences between the specific kinds of needs on which money was spent, and designate the marginal utility that a monetary unit, as such, has for the subject, as the *absolutely* unnecessary and most dispensable satisfaction of needs that the subject obtains through the expenditure of a monetary unit. The concept of the marginal utility of money is, in this case, taken in the most general sense, regardless of any specific, given type of need. It can be said from this standpoint that the marginal utility of a monetary unit must be different, depending on the size of the income someone has; moreover, [it will be] all the higher, the smaller is the income, and the lower, the larger is the income. Of course! A fifty-cent piece in the hands of the worker has a different meaning from [the same coin] in the hands of a rentier. The reason is obvious: because the income of the worker only suffices very imperfectly to satisfy his needs, while that of the rentier satisfies his own needs comparatively perfectly. The last, relatively most unnecessary satisfaction of needs that the worker obtains with 50 pennies is far more important to him than the most unnecessary satisfaction of needs that the rentier obtains with the same expenditure of money. That has not been disputed by anyone. But it only follows from this that the worker buys for himself other means of consumption than the rentier, because, as a result of the inequality of monetary income, the division and use of money will be different. The worker will limit his needs and therefore buy cheap commodities, while the rentier, who can afford them, will buy more expensive commodities. But this most self-evident statement of fact is totally irrelevant for the explanation of the exchange-value of commodities and the formation of prices. For it is surely obvious, that the commodities demanded by the workers are not cheap because the workers buy them, but, conversely, the workers demand commodities of a certain kind because they are cheap. Their lower exchange-value, or their cheapness, is not at all determined by the personal circumstances of the purchasing consumers, but by the relatively small quantity of labour with which they can be manufactured. The great discovery that a given monetary unit, depending upon the monetary income of the owner, represents a greater or lesser marginal utility is therefore just as correct as it is immaterial, because it is self-evident and a matter of indifference for explaining the exchange-value phenomenon.[20]

In estimating the value of his money as [he does] in its distribution, the subject therefore really always employs marginal utility considerations. All the semblance of naturalness, which the explanation of the magnitude of exchange-value from the marginal utility principle superficially has, flows from this simple but, for the determination of exchange-value, actually entirely irrelevant fact; this is the popular *quid pro quo* operating in the background, which has made the fortune of the marginal utility theory, whose whole psychology never goes beyond the one-sided consumer standpoint. It exerts its power of abstraction by abstracting from all the essential psychological factors lying beyond this one-sided position, which must in reality determine the exchange-value of goods. Once those factors are taken into account, the existence of an

---

20 [This observation often came to be used, however, as a utilitarian argument by liberal social reformers in favour of income redistribution through taxation and public expenditure. This argument ultimately failed on the grounds that individual utilities are incomparable: the utility of an additional unit of money might, for example, actually mean more to the pathological miser than to the impoverished but ascetic poet].

objective law of value appears not only possible but necessary. But the basic belief that had been challenged in order to conjure up the philosophical truths of psychology emerges from the court of appeal all the more firmly. It remains the first and most important task of economic science to investigate [economic phenomena] according to an objective law of value controlling price formation, not only in simple but also in capitalist commodity production. The fact that only one person has furthered that great work since Ricardo's death, and that this person is Marx, whose theoretic-economic critique unfolded into the most profound social criticism, surely does not make the counter-arguments of the psychological school more valid. But it is, according to the psychological valuation principle, perhaps a factor explaining why the marginal utility of those arguments, and with it their subjective and market value, has increased considerably.

DOCUMENT 15

The Austrian School (1926)

Isaak Il'ich Rubin

Source: I.I. Rubin, 'Avstriiskaya Shkola', in *Bol'shaya Sovetskaya Entsiklopediya* (First edition), Vol. 1, Moscow, 1926, pp. 244–54.

Introduction by the Editors

The central theme of all of Isaak Rubin's writings, as will become evident in the next section of this book, is that historically formed social relations between people are the proper subject matter of political economy. Accordingly, Marxism concentrates on the dialectical emergence of economic *forms*, with economic history and development of the means of production serving to inform that analysis. The Austrian theory of marginalism, with its ontological individualism and purely subjective theory of value, is therefore the antithesis of Rubin's own convictions as a Marxist. In this essay, written for the first edition of the *Great Soviet Encyclopaedia*, Rubin provides a scientific critique of marginalism, concentrating upon logical contradictions inherent in the Austrian theory of subjective value as the conceptual basis of price determination.

Whereas Marxism starts with the social whole, analyses it and then reconstructs it concretely in thought, the psychological theory of value looks for the 'final causes' of price changes in judgements of marginal utility by singular individuals. The result, in Rubin's account, is a series of problems involving: a) how to determine the summary value of a series of units, each of diminishing marginal utility; b) how to price means of production when their value is regarded as a derivative of the *differing* values of things they may be used to produce; c) how to impute discrete values to two or more means of production that may be used to produce a particular commodity; and d) how to explain exchange-value and profit.

Like Conrad Schmidt in the previous article, Rubin emphasises the individualistic ontology and methodological subjectivism that distinguished the Austrian school. Reducing the whole of capitalist society to an aggregation of self-determining Robinson Crusoes, the Austrians, in Rubin's judgement, displaced the German Historical school principally because they provided a *theory* that 'corresponds with the ideology of the bourgeoisie in the epoch of capitalism's decline'. Whereas the Historical school limited itself to history, and history objectively pointed to the replacement of capitalism by socialism, the ideological mystification of Austrian theory appeared to be a more 'acute theoretical weapon for the struggle against Marxism'.

∴

Isaak I. Rubin on the Austrian School of Economic Theory

1   *History*

The theory that the exchange-values[1] and prices of commodities are determined in the final analysis by their use-value, or subjective utility, is known as the Austrian or psychological school of political economy. The rudiments of such a theory are found in certain eighteenth-century economists, particularly Condillac. But up to the end of the nineteenth century these views had not spread. In science the objective theory of value continued to prevail as set out by the classics (Smith and Ricardo). The mid-nineteenth century work of Gossen, who was a predecessor of the Austrian school, went unnoticed. It was in the 1870s that works appeared almost simultaneously by Carl Menger, [William Stanley] Jevons and Léon Walras, the founders of the new school, among whom Menger developed most thoroughly the psychological foundation of the theory and Walras the mathematical. During the 1880s [Friedrich von] Wieser and [Eugen von] Böhm-Bawerk, students of Menger (all three of them lived in Austria), worked out in detail the psychological theory that is also frequently called the Austrian theory. By the end of the nineteenth century it became widespread in bourgeois university science in almost all countries of the world. A critical attitude towards this theory has only recently grown up, and even among bourgeois scholars an effort can now be seen to return to the theory of the classics, although usually in a half-hearted and compromising manner.

The mathematical theory was also developed at the same time as the psychological one, especially in England, America and Italy (with the result that it has come to be known as the Anglo-American theory). The focus of research

---

1   Since the Austrian school begins with the concept of subjective utility, for the sake of clarity in this presentation we use the term *ценность* [referring to something that is valuable] as distinct from *стоимость* [the 'value' of a commodity in terms of its economic cost of production or, more specifically, its labour cost in Marxist terms. Unless indicated otherwise, this translation will follow Rubin's usage and render *ценность* in the former sense].

for both of these theories is the influence of changes in the quantity of goods upon their price and value. But there are also important methodological differences between them. The psychological theory begins with the motivation of a separate individual living in conditions of a natural economy; it sees the ultimate cause of changes in the price and value of a good in the individual's subjective evaluations, which vary in response to the quantity of goods that he has at his disposal. The mathematical theory, on the other hand, begins with the phenomena of developed exchange and studies the correlation between the quantity of goods and their objective market price. Ignoring the question of the final cause of changes in prices (i.e. the problem of value), this theory restricts itself to investigating the functional dependence between the level of market prices and the quantity of goods (the laws of supply and demand). The resulting mathematical 'formulae of exchange' are then also applied to the phenomena of production and distribution, thereby restricting the entire purview of economic science to a study of the quantitative changes of market prices.

2   *The Subjective Theory and Marginal Utility*
In a modern exchange society, commodities have a determinate price in which their objective exchange-value is expressed. The Austrian school claims that we can only understand the origin of exchange-value and the laws that govern its changes after a preliminary investigation of the subjective value that items possess in the conditions of a natural economy. By *subjective value* is meant the importance that the subject assigns to a particular item as a necessary condition for satisfying his needs. The classical economists observed long ago that items with a very high use-value – bread, for instance – are given a much lower evaluation in the market than items that have less use-value, e.g. diamonds; and thus they concluded that while only items with use-value also have exchange-value, the magnitude of the latter does not depend upon the magnitude of the former. In order to surmount this discrepancy between use-value and exchange-value, the Austrian economists worked out a new concept of need and of use-value. In their opinion the economic subject, in his calculations and activities, is led not by need in general, e.g. for bread, but by his concrete need for a specific quantity of bread. For instance, he needs one pound of bread per day in order to sustain life. Once he has this pound of bread, he feels the need for a second pound for the sake of a more bountiful diet. He needs a third pound to feed the household chicken, a fourth pound for making vodka, and a fifth for feeding the parrot. Each of these concrete needs is weaker than the preceding one and stronger than the one that follows. If the first need is felt with an intensity that we can denote by the number 10, the next needs, let us

say, are represented by 8, 6, 4 and 1. The intensity of a need diminishes as it is satisfied, and each successive degree of need is less intensive than the previous one, which has already been satisfied ('Gossen's law', or the 'law of the satiation of need'). With the gradual satisfaction of a given need, its intensity diminishes and ultimately declines to nil. If a man has all of his daily five pounds of bread, even including enough to please the parrot, his need for bread will be weaker than his need for items of adornment. Let the scale of need for items of adornment be expressed by the figures 3 and 1. This means that the need for the first item of adornment is equal to 3, while the need for another item of adornment is equal to 1. The scale of need for bread, as we have seen, is 10, 8, 6, 4, and 1. If we divide all of a person's needs into several basic groups (the first being for bread, the second for clothing, the third for housing, the fourth for adornments, etc.), and if we provide for each group a numerical scale for the decline of needs as they are satisfied, then we find that although the generic need for bread is typically greater than the generic need for adornments, the concrete need for adornments (diamonds, for instance) can still be more intensive than the concrete need for the bread that is used, for example, to feed the parrot (Menger's *'scale of needs'*).

If the intensity of a given need declines as the need is satisfied, the question then is: What determines the degree of satisfaction? Clearly, that depends on the quantity of goods at the individual's disposal. If the available supply of a particular good exceeds the quantity needed to satisfy all of the needs for it, then that good – even though it has use-value, or the ability to satisfy human need – will not have subjective value since the loss of a unit of this good will have no effect on the individual's well-being. Such goods (air, for example) are said to be 'free', as distinct from 'economic' goods, which are distinguished not only by their usefulness but also by their relative scarcity; that is, they are available in such limited quantity that losing a unit of such a good will compel the individual to forgo satisfaction of some other need. If the supply of bread is only one pound, the subjective value of the latter is equal to 10. If the supply of bread is 3 pounds, then losing one pound of bread will compel the individual to forgo his third need (feeding the household chicken), which is measured by the figure 6. This means that if the supply is 1 pound, the value of one unit of the good is 10; if the supply increases to 3 pounds, the value is 6; and if the supply is 5 pounds, the value of a pound of bread is 1. In the eyes of the person possessing them, all units of the particular good's supply have the identical subjective value, since loss of any one of these units causes him to forgo satisfaction of the least urgent need (e.g. feeding the parrot) among those that can be satisfied with the existing supply of the good. This means that the subjective value of a given good is determined by the utility of the last unit of the existing supply, which enables satisfaction of the least intensive need (the theory of marginal utility). The greater is the supply, the weaker will be the last need it serves to satisfy, the lower will be the marginal utility, and thus the lower will be the subjective value that the individual assigns to a unit of the particular good. Conversely, with a reduction of the supply of a good, the value of a unit rises. The subjective value of the given good depends upon the magnitude of its supply, and it changes in inverse proportion to changes in the magnitude of the latter (the 'law of supply', to use Wieser's expression). The value of a good for different people, or for a single individual at different times, will vary and will have a different individual-psychological or subjective character.

If, with a supply of bread amounting to 5 pounds, the value of each pound is 1, then we may ask: What is the value of the entire supply? The Austrian economists give different answers to this question. Wieser says that once the value of each pound of bread equals 1, the value of all five pounds is $1 \times 5 = 5$; that is, the marginal utility is multiplied by the number of units of the particular good. But Böhm-Bawerk says that even though the value of each pound of bread is 1, loss of the entire supply would mean forgoing satisfaction of the five needs that are expressed by the figures $10 + 8 + 6 + 4 + 1 = 29$. This means that the value of the entire supply is 29. Wieser's view contradicts the foundations of the Austrian theory, while Böhm-Bawerk's contradicts the facts.

3 The Value of Means of Production

Marginal utility determines the value of 'consumer goods' or 'first-order goods', i.e. items of consumption. The value of the latter, in turn, determines the value of the means of production required in order to make them, the so-called 'producer goods' or 'higher-order goods'.[2] If bread is the consumer good, then the flour and labour needed in baking the bread are goods of the second order, while grain, millstones and the labour of grinding the grain are goods of the third order, and so on. The producer goods are regarded as material things, as are labour expenditures. For the sake of simplification, let us suppose that for production of consumer good A it is enough to have only a single producer good of the second order, A_2 (it makes no difference whether this is a thing, labour, or some combination of the two); and for production of the latter we require the third-order good A_3, etc. It is clear that each of these producer goods (A_2, A_3, A_4 and so forth) makes it possible to acquire product A, following one

---

2 [The term that Böhm-Bawerk uses is '*Güter entfernterer Ordnung*', which Rubin might have better translated as 'goods of higher rank'].

or several stages of production, so that each has a value equal to the value of the latter. Accordingly, the value of the producer good, with the help of which consumer good A can be produced – either directly or through a number of intermediate stages of production – is determined by the marginal utility of the latter. The value of items of consumption and the value of the means of production required in order to make them are equal – not, however, because the former is determined by the latter, as classical theory thought, but rather because the latter is determined by the former.

If, as is generally the case, different units of a given producer good (iron, for example) are used for making various consumer goods with different marginal utilities (such as a stove with a marginal utility of 20, a spade of 17, and a bucket of 15), then it is understandable that the loss of one unit of iron means having to forgo production of the bucket. This means that the value of the means of production depends on the value of the 'marginal product', that is, the product with the least marginal utility among those that are made with the help of the given supply of means of production. In the present case the value of each unit of iron, including that expended in producing the stove, is equal only to 15, in which case the value of the stove itself also falls to 15, since loss of the stove does not entail forgoing the marginal utility of 20 that it provides, but only the expenditure of a unit of iron in making a new stove, and that is valued at 15. It follows that the various consumer goods (the stove, the spade and the bucket), regardless of their individual marginal utilities, have an identical value if they are produced with the help of an identical quantity of the same means of production (or labour). The value of the products being reproduced is determined by the value of the means of production expended in making them; but the value of the latter is determined, in turn, by the utility of the 'marginal product'. The bucket imparts its value (of 15) to the iron, and the latter imparts the same value to the stove and the spade. In the final analysis, the value of both consumer and producer goods is determined by the marginal utility of the 'marginal product' (the bucket). Thus the Austrian school, although it recognises the action of the 'law of costs of production', regards it merely as a particular instance of applying the 'law of marginal utility' to the goods being reproduced.

4   The Theory of Imputation (or of Distribution)

We have looked at a case in which one producer good (iron) is used in making several consumer goods. But the reverse condition also generally prevails: to make a given consumer good A (the bucket) requires an aggregate or combination of several producer goods, for example, B and C, or labour and the material means of production that the Austrian economists call 'capital' (we are leaving aside land, the third factor of production). The given labour and the given means of production are 'complementary' goods (they complement one another), since it is only possible to make the bucket by taking them together. The aggregate value of the two of them is determined by the marginal utility of the bucket; that is, it is equal to 15. But which part of this value must be assigned or 'imputed' to the labour and which to the iron? In short, how is the value of the final product distributed between the different means of production that are needed to make it (for example, 'labour' and 'capital')? The Austrian school has not managed to provide a satisfactory answer to this problem of 'imputation' or 'distribution'. Wieser suggests comparing the value of the given product (the bucket) with the value of some other product made with the help of the same producer goods B and C, but taken in different proportions. With the help of such method we can find, in his opinion, the comparative value of B and C.

Böhm-Bawerk constructs a very complex theory of 'complementary goods'. He suggests finding first the value of one of the complementary producer goods, B for example. This is possible only in a case where B can be used separately from other means of production and where it thus acquires a separate and 'isolated' value, or alternatively in the case where B can be replaced by some other good having a determinate value of 5 for instance. In that case, B also acquires a value equal to 5. Subtracting the value of the 'replaced member' B, that is, 5, from the value of the product (the bucket), which is equal to 15, we are left with the balance of 10, which represents the value of C. The invalidity of the theory of 'imputation' given by Wieser and Böhm-Bawerck is acknowledged even by certain supporters of the same school.

This teaching, according to which: 1) the value of consumer goods is determined by their marginal utility, 2) the value of producer goods is determined by the marginal utility of the products they are used in making, and specifically by the value of the 'marginal product', while 3) this value is divided in a determinate proportion between all the producer goods involved in making the product – constitutes the theory of 'subjective value'.

5   *Objective (Exchange-) Value*

By this term the Austrian economists understand the possibility of acquiring, in exchange for any given good, a certain quantity of another good, so that the latter represents the price of the first good. The exchange-value of any item is expressed in its price. To understand objective exchange-value is possible only on the basis of subjective use-value, since the market price of a commodity is the result of an encounter between different subjective appraisals on the part of participants in the exchange. First of all, it is obvious that two people can enter into mutual exchange only given the condition that each of them appraises the value of the good to be received in the exchange as higher than the good they will give up in order to acquire it; that is, if the subjective appraisal by each of the two contracting parties is the opposite of the other's appraisal. Let us now take the case of developed exchange, where a multitude of buyers encounter a multitude of sellers, each of whom competes with the others. For this purpose Böhm-Bawerk provides the following scheme (in which the exchange occurs through money):

Buyers			Sellers		
A_1 evaluates a horse at the price of		300	B_1 evaluates his horse at the price of		100
A_2	"	280	B_2	"	110
A_3	"	260	B_3	"	150
A_4	"	240	B_4	"	170
A_5	"	220	B_5	"	200
A_6 evaluates a horse at the price of		210	B_6	"	215
A_7	"	200	B_7	"	250
A_8	"	180	B_8	"	260
A_9	"	170			
A_{10}	"	150			

The buyers are arranged in a series, beginning with those having the highest evaluations: they are willing to pay a high price and thus enter into exchange sooner and are more 'exchange-ready'. The series of sellers also begins with the more 'exchange-ready', that is, those whose subjective evaluations are lower. It is obvious that only 5 pairs of buyers and sellers will enter into exchange, since the evaluations of the remaining buyers are below those of the remaining sellers, thus excluding the possibility of exchange. This means that all the buyers and sellers below the dotted line are excluded from exchange. The seller A_5 and the buyer B_5 are the final pair participating in exchange, while A_6 and B_6 are the first pair excluded from exchange. Both of these are called 'marginal pairs'. They play the decisive role in exchange since the objective market price that is established for all other exchange participants depends upon their subjective evaluations. That price cannot be higher than the evaluation of buyer A_5, that is, 220 roubles, for otherwise A_5 will withdraw from the exchange and the demand will turn out to be less than the supply, which will cause a decline in price. Yet the price also cannot be higher than 215, or the evaluation of seller B_6, for otherwise B_6 will also want to sell his horse, and the supply will again exceed the demand. Contrariwise, supply will fall below demand if the price is lower than the evaluation of B_5, that is, 200 roubles, or below the evaluation of A_6, namely, 210 roubles. This means that the market price cannot exceed the subjective evaluation of the last actual buyer or of the first excluded seller, and it cannot be lower than the subjective evaluation of the last actual seller or of the first excluded buyer. In the present case the price will be established between 210 and 215 roubles, since only with such a price will the number of those who wish to buy be equal to the number of those who wish to sell; that is to say, equilibrium will be established between demand and supply. Thus the price of the commodity is determined by the subjective evaluations of the two marginal pairs.

At first sight it may appear that the Austrian school has actually demonstrated that objective exchange-value is determined by subjective use-value. It must be remembered, however, that as soon as the market price of different items is established, the parties to exchange cease to evaluate them according to their marginal utility or use-value. If they wish to determine the subjective value of one or another item for themselves, they start out with its determined price or its objective exchange-value.

Consider first a buyer or consumer. Is he really inclined to assign a very high evaluation to his coat, which protects him from the cold? Not at all. The Austrian economists themselves recognise that if the market price of a coat is 100 roubles, then its owner, in the event that he loses it, will buy another coat and will then evaluate it not according to its own marginal utility, which is very high, but according to the 'substitution utility' of those items that he could buy for the 100 roubles if he did not have to use that money to buy a coat. But in order to determine this 'substitution utility' it is first necessary to know the precise quantity of other items that can be purchased for the 100 roubles; that is to say, a determinate price for those other items is presupposed.

Now consider the seller or producer. For him, the marginal utility of his commodities is nil because he personally has no demand for them. He evaluates them not according to their use-value but according to the magnitude of their production costs. If the price of the commodity does not cover the costs of production (plus the average profit), the producer will either cease or curtail production. If cotton or textile machinery becomes less expensive, the cloth producer, in order to expand his sales, will lower the price for cloth even when its marginal utility remains unchanged in the eyes of the purchaser. The producer always has to deal with objective exchange-value. Even if, for some reason, he wants to determine for himself the subjective value of a given lot of cloth, which can be sold for 1,000 roubles, he will evaluate it not according to its marginal utility but in terms of the utility of those items he could purchase with the 1,000 roubles acquired by selling the cloth. He will evaluate the cloth (as Böhm-Bawerk recognises) according to its 'subjective exchange-value', which will be higher, the higher is its objective value or price. Consequently, in a commodity economy it is not prices that are determined by subjective evaluations, but rather the latter emerge on the basis of prices that are determined beforehand. Even if the Austrian theory had correctly explained the laws governing the subjective evaluation of goods in a natural economy, and of the formation of prices in the transition from natural economy to one of exchange – which is also doubtful for a whole number of reasons, particularly since the general possibility of comparing and measuring utilities has not been established – [the theory] would still not apply to the phenomena of an exchange economy. The position of the Austrian school is especially problematic when it attempts to explain the phenomena of a capitalist economy, and this is clearly evident in its theory of profit.

6   The Theory of Profit

If product A, having a value of 110, is produced with the help of producer goods B and C (for example, labour and the material means of production that the Austrian economists call 'capital'), then the value of B and C, taken together, is also equal to 110. The Austrian school considers this to be beyond dispute, even though it cannot resolve the problem of 'imputation' or 'distribution' of the value of 110 between B and C. However, capitalist reality demonstrates that B and C, taken together, in fact have a value not of 110 but of something less, say 100. The capitalist pays 100 roubles altogether for the labour of workers (B) and the means of production C, and after a year he receives product A with a price of 110 roubles. The surplus of ten roubles represents his profit. Does not the fact of the existence of profit contradict the position of the Austrian school, which says that the value of producer goods is equal to the value of the consumer goods made with their help? In order to resolve this contradiction, Böhm-Bawerk constructed his theory of profit.

It is enormously important for an economic subject to know not only the marginal utility of goods but also when the goods are acquired. A pound of bread that is acquired today and a pound of bread subject to a year's wait have different subjective values for the individual. The future good has a lower value than the same good acquired today. The higher evaluation of today's goods is explained by the fact that: 1) the subject calculates that in future he will have a more abundant supply of goods, which therefore have a lower marginal utility for him than today's goods; 2) as a result of insufficient consciousness or lack of will, he cares too little about satisfying his future needs and mistakenly evaluates them as less than current needs; 3) or finally, the third and most important cause of a high appraisal of current needs involves higher technical productivity.

Suppose that a fisherman, having virtually no means of production, acquires with some difficulty the two poods of fish required to sustain himself weekly, or 100 poods in the course of a year. If he had an inventory of 100 poods, he could devote part of the year to making means of production or 'capital' – for example, he could collect wood and iron ore for 3 months, spend 3 months working them up, and 3 months using them to make a boat and instruments – in order to devote the final 3 months of the year directly to fishing. As a result of this 'capitalist' or 'roundabout' production, which is technically more advanced, he would acquire 110 poods of fish by the end of the year, whereas if he occupies himself throughout the year with fishing, but not having the benefit of these means of production, he will have difficulty in acquiring 2 poods weekly or 100 poods in the course of the entire year. Since the current availability of 100 units of the given good makes it possible to acquire, by means of 'roundabout' production, 110 such units in the course of a year, it is clear that the 100 current units have the same value as the 110 future units expected after a year has transpired.

The labour of a worker (B) and means of production (C), purchased by the capitalist, actually represent 'future goods', for only after completion of the production process, which may continue perhaps for an entire year, do they turn into consumer good A, which has a value of 110 roubles. B and C currently have a value that does not exceed 100 roubles, but after a year they 'mature' into consumer good A, whose value is 110 roubles. The capitalist acquires the profit of 10 roubles not from exploiting the labour of workers, but because he has 'waited out' the time required for the 'maturation' process whereby future goods become current goods.

Böhm-Bawerk's theory of profit has been criticised on several grounds. It has been pointed out to him that in capitalist society the work of acquiring the iron, making the boats and nets, catching the fish, etc., is divided up between separate enterprises. Each of them works throughout the year and continuously sends its product to market; the iron, the nets, the fish etc. Since the sequential phases of production are completed simultaneously by different capitalists, not one of them has to 'wait out' the time between first acquiring the raw material and then making the final item for consumption. The bankruptcy of Böhm-Bawerk's theory is recognised even by some Austrian economists: Wieser offers a theory of the 'productivity' of capital; Schumpeter denies the possibility of profit as a continuous income and acknowledges only the possibility of profits being temporarily received by owners of enterprises that surpass the average in terms of their level of technical perfection (differential profit, or super-profit).[3]

7 Method

A summary appraisal of works by the Austrian school comes to this: it has worked out a more or less complete theory of subjective value in terms of logic (although it is psychologically contentious and sociologically barren); in its efforts to deduce the laws of objective exchange-value from subjective value it encounters a number of contradictions; and it has been unable to resolve more or less satisfactorily the problems of distribution in general or of the profit of capital in particular. The failure by the Austrian school to explain the basic phenomena of a commodity economy, and especially of a capitalist economy (exchange-value and money, capital and profit), is the inevitable consequence of the method it adopts. Political economy does not study the technical side of the economy but rather its determinate social form, namely, commodity-capitalist economy. It begins with the existence of objective-social and historically changing relations between people, which correspond to a given state of the productive forces. The Austrian school begins not with the objective-social relations between people but with the psychology and motives of separate individuals (the subjective-psychological method); it studies 'economic activity' in general, independently of the historical form of the economy; it looks for the economy's motive force not in the sphere of people's productive activity but rather in the sphere of consumption.

The Austrian school takes a single individual, isolated from the entire social environment and confronting nature alone, and asks how this person will satisfy his needs with the aid of the material goods on hand and depending upon their greater or lesser scarcity. Insofar as it studies the psychology and 'appraisals' of such an isolated subject, it cannot possibly construct a bridge from him to a person whose economic activity occurs in a determinate social environment and who occupies a determinate social position in the social production process. Even in its own special sphere, which deals with the motivation and psychology of economic subjects, the Austrian school has been unable to provide fruitful results, since it studies the psychology of 'natural' man, which has nothing in common with the psychology of members of a commodity-capitalist society. In the representations of the Austrian school, the latter appear as Robinson Crusoes, and all social-economic phenomena are converted into natural-technical elements of consumption and production that are subject to

---

3 This was the theme of Schumpeter 1934, originally published in German in 1911.

psychological 'appraisal'; value is the significance of the item for consumption, capital is the means for its production, and so forth. Depriving the production process of its given social – namely, capitalist – form, the Austrian economists thereby dismiss the question of the latter's historically transitory character. They are willing to introduce into capitalist economy modest improvements that alleviate the class struggle, but they respond negatively to any idea of the possibility of eliminating capitalism and the capitalists, in whose initiative and energy they see the sole impetus for powerfully developing the productive forces (Schumpeter).

Certain doctrines of the Austrians have the character not so much of theoretical explanation as of justification for capitalist society (the theory of imputation and especially of profit). These explicit social sympathies on the part of Austrian economists, together with the fundamental peculiarities of their theoretical position – replacement of the capitalist form of economy with 'pure economic activity' in general; transformation of a society consisting of specific classes into an aggregation of individual Robinson Crusoes; the idea that the moving forces of the economy are the psychological experiences and motivations of separate individuals as consumers; transfer of the research focus from the sphere of production to the sphere of consumption; ignoring the dynamic of the economy and its tendencies of development – all of these attributes characterise their doctrine as a theoretical tendency that corresponds with the ideology of the bourgeoisie in the epoch of capitalism's decline, a time when any objective study of the tendencies of social development leads to the conclusion of capitalist economy's inevitable destruction.

In this epoch the objective, social and historical method (the nucleus of which was established by the classics, as the leading ideologists of a young and progressive bourgeoisie) becomes the exclusive property of Marxist economic theory, while bourgeois science appeals to the subjective, psychological and anti-historical method. The allegedly unchanging psychological 'nature' of man comes to serve as the starting point for theoretical research and as an argument for the impossibility of a socialist economy. It is not surprising that the Austrian school has come out with a zealous polemic against Marxism and has enjoyed rapid and clamorous success amongst bourgeois scholars, who have seen in it – following the long period during which the historical school predominated, with its narrow empiricism and abandonment of theory – an acute theoretical weapon for the struggle against Marxism and socialism.

Literature: The most important works by the Austrian economists are: Menger, *Grundsätze der Volkswirtschaftslehre* (Russian translation: *Osnovaniya politicheskoi ekonomii*, 1903); Böhm-Bawerk, *Grundzüge der Theorie des wirtschaft-*

lichen Güterwerts (Russian translation: *Osnovye teorii tsennosti khozyaistvennykh blag*, 1904); Böhm-Bawerk, *Capital und Capitalzins*, 2 volumes (Russian translation of the first volume: *Kapital i pribyl'*, 1909); Böhm-Bawerk, *Karl Marx and the Close of his system* (Russian translation: *Teoriya Marksa i ee kritika*, 1897); Wieser, *Der natürliche Wert* (1889); Wieser, *Theorie der gesellschaftlichen Wirtschaft* (in Volume I of *Grundrisse der Socialoekonomie*, 1914); Criticism of the Austrian School; Bukharin, N., *Politicheskaya ekonimya rant'e*, 1923 (English translation: *The Economic Theory of the Leisure Class*); the collection *Osnovnye problemy politicheskoi ekonomii*, 1924 (edited by Sh. Dvolaitsky and I.I. Rubin); Hilferding, *Böhm-Baverk kak kritika Marksa*, 1923 (English translation: *Böhm-Bawerk's Criticism of Marx*).

I. Rubin

Appendix

In his *Essays on Marx's Theory of Value*, Isaak Rubin includes a chapter on 'Value and Social Need' that elaborates several of the issues posed in his entry on the Austrian school for the *Great Soviet Encyclopaedia*. Since Marx treats value as the essence of price phenomena, the issue that concerns Rubin is how value relates to social need and demand: 'the value of commodities does not only depend on the *productivity of labor* (which expresses that quantity of labor necessary for the production of commodities under given, average technical conditions), but also on the volume of *social needs* or demand'.[4]

Marx frequently pointed out that demand is determined both by effective demand and by changing commodity prices, with the volume of demand being more or less elastic (i.e. more or less responsive to price changes), depending upon the commodity's position on the scale of subsistence needs.[5] The result, Rubin said, is the familiar demand 'schedule', or curve of social demand. In Volume III of *Capital*, Marx wrote that demand 'moves in the opposite direction to price, expanding when it falls and vice versa'.[6] 'It is evident ... that the expansion or contraction of the market depends on the price of the individual commodity and stands in an inverse relationship to the rise or fall in this price'.[7]

---

4   Rubin 1990, p. 184.
5   Rubin 1990, p. 186.
6   Rubin 1990, p. 292.
7   Marx 1992, p. 203.

But if we assume constant technology, together with 'a given structure of needs and given purchasing power',[8] then Rubin said the conclusion of marginal utility theorists is refuted: value is what determines the volume of demand, not the reverse.[9] 'The real volume of demand is determined by the magnitude of the *productivity of labor*';[10] and equilibrium entails all commodities selling at their values (or prices of production), which in turn presupposes equilibrium between the various branches of production (i.e. all commodities selling at a price that yields the social average rate of profit).

Rubin acknowledges that an upward shift in demand 'can take place because of an increase of purchasing power of the population, or because of increased requirements for a given product'.[11] If the production technique is still assumed not to have changed, a higher market price will give producers a 'superprofit', causing an expansion of production and possibly a movement of capital from other industries. Production will then expand until equilibrium between the various branches of production is restored.[12] The value of the commodity, and thus its price of production will remain constant, but a larger volume of the commodity will be produced due to the increased capacity of producers.

The question changes, however, if technology and labour productivity no longer remain constant. Ricardo saw, for example, that an increase of output in agriculture brings diminishing returns and raises the value of agricultural products. If the total output of a manufactured commodity likewise comes from enterprises with differing levels of productivity, then the market value of commodities is 'determined by the value of commodities produced in average or less favorable conditions', which are now the ones that define 'socially necessary' labour.[13] When the price rises, 'production will attract enterprises with

---

8   Rubin 1990, p. 186; cf. pp. 195–6.
9   Rubin 1990, p. 190. In Volume III of *Capital* Marx writes: 'If the market value changes, the conditions at which the whole mass of commodities can be sold will also change. If the market value falls, the social need is on average expanded (this always means here the need which has money to back it up), and within certain limits the society can absorb larger quantities of commodities. If the market value rises, the social need for the commodities contracts and smaller quantities are absorbed. Thus if supply and demand regulate market price, or rather the departures of market price from market value, the market value in turn regulates the relationship between demand and supply, or the centre around which fluctuations of demand and supply make the market price oscillate' (Marx 1992, p. 282).
10 Rubin 1990, p. 188.
11 Rubin 1990, p. 192.
12 Rubin 1990, pp. 192–3.
13 Rubin 1990, pp. 206–7.

average or low productivity'.[14] As a result, value will increase at the same time as supply. This means demand will influence value, but only indirectly, 'namely by changing the volume of production and thus its technical conditions':[15] Rubin writes that 'the extension of production to worse enterprises changes the average magnitude of socially-necessary labor per unit of output, i.e. changes the value (or price of production). These changes are explained by the technical conditions of a given branch'.[16]

The difference between Rubin's interpretation and that of the 'Anglo-American and mathematical schools in political economy, including Marshall',[17] is that the latter do not ask '*why* prices change' but only show '*how* simultaneous changes in price and demand (or supply) take place'.[18] This relation between demand and supply, which Rubin calls 'functional', is illustrated in the following diagram.

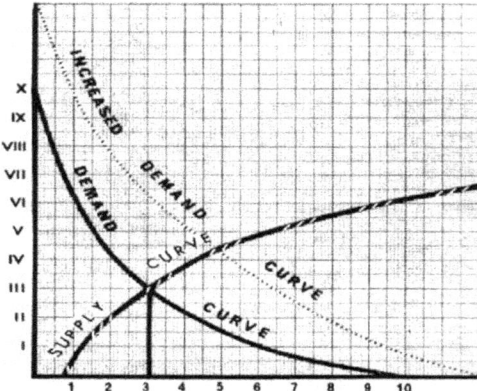

DIAGRAM 1

The diagram appears to show that price is determined 'exclusively by the demand and supply curves'. In the present case, the change of demand causes a rise in price (measured on the horizontal axis) from 3 roubles to 5 roubles and an increase of output from 300,000 units (III) to 450,000 units. Alternatively, a

---

14   Rubin 1990, p. 207.
15   Rubin 1990, p. 209.
16   Rubin 1990, p. 211.
17   Rubin 1990, p. 208.
18   Rubin 1990, p. 213. Marshall saw the short-run supply curve as dependent upon rising marginal costs, but he did not develop a long-run average-cost curve as the 'envelope' for short-run average cost curves (see Blaug 1985, pp. 376–80).

fall in demand might cause production to contract, say, to 150,000 units selling at 1.5 roubles per unit. The diagram implies that *any* level of supply is conceivable, depending upon changes in demand. 'It seems', says Rubin, 'as if the price is not determined by the conditions of production, but exclusively by the demand and supply curves'.[19] However, Rubin objects that 'Such a supply curve is possible [only] if we are dealing with a market situation at a *given moment*'.[20] In extraordinary conditions, and for brief periods, an unusual increase in prices may force some producers to sell at 'catastrophically' low prices or 'to deliver to the market all stocks and inventories and to expand production immediately, if this is possible'.[21]

But such a state of affairs cannot long continue. The problem with the diagram is that it 'only gives us a picture of a *momentary state of the market* but does not show us a *long-range, stable equilibrium between demand and supply*, which may be theoretically understood only as the result of *equilibrium between the various branches of production*'.[22] Thus, 'from the accidental price of one day we [must] pass to the permanent, stable, *average price* which determines the *constant, average, normal volume of demand and supply*'.[23] Over a longer period of time, catastrophically low prices would drive capital elsewhere in search of the normal average rate of profit, or extraordinarily high prices would attract new capital to the industry in question.[24]

The result is that, given no significant technological change, and with 'an average, long-range volume of supply and demand', the long-run supply 'curve' would simply be a vertical line, which Rubin represents in a second diagram. Now, 'The magnitude of the value (3 roubles) determines the volume of effective demand for a given commodity and the corresponding volume of supply (300,000 units of output)'.[25] A permanent increase in demand may result in increased supply – for instance, from 300,000 to 600,000 – as new capitals are attracted from other sectors, but the price of production, with no change of labour productivity, would remain constant. 'This price is determined exclusively by the productivity of labour or by the technical conditions of production'.[26]

---

19   Rubin 1990, p. 215.
20   Ibid.
21   Rubin 1990, pp. 215–16.
22   Rubin 1990, p. 216.
23   Ibid.
24   Ibid.
25   Rubin 1990, p. 217.
26   Rubin 1990, p. 218.

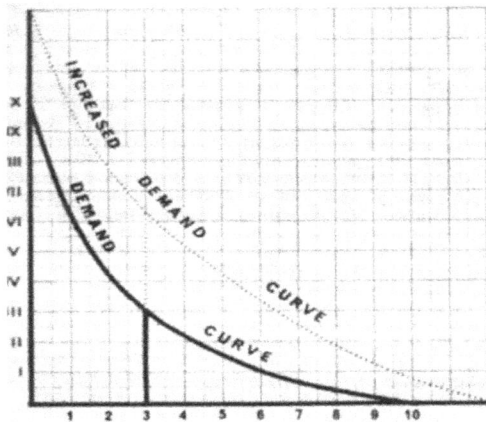

DIAGRAM 2

Finally, Rubin reintroduces the additional fact that enterprises within a particular sector will normally have differences in their levels of productivity, a condition represented in a third diagram.

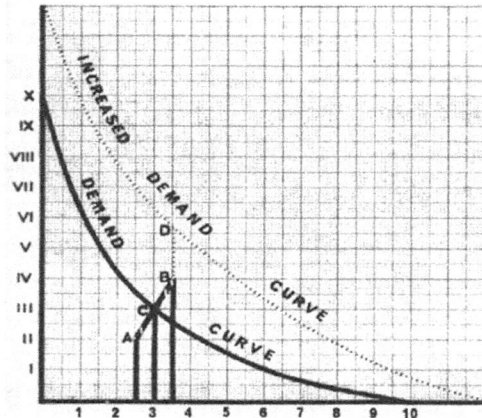

DIAGRAM 3

In this case, the *most efficient* enterprises can produce 200,000 units at a price of 2.5 roubles; if the pressure of demand causes *average enterprises* to add to total output, raising it to 300,000, the price will rise to 3 roubles per unit; and if *least efficient* enterprises then also become involved, supply will rise to 400,000 units at a price of 3.5 roubles. 'Curve ACB is the supply curve. The point of intersection of this supply curve with the demand curve (at point C) determines the actual volume of supply and the corresponding value or center of price fluctuations'.[27] If the new schedule of demand were to become permanent, then, once again, the supply would permanently increase, in this case through a vertical movement upward of the schedule ACB, and the new level of C would be the point of intersection with the new demand curve.

The salient point of Rubin's analysis is that there is, indeed, a demand curve, reflecting an inverse relation between quantity and price. Marx understood this, and so, for that matter, did Adam Smith. The demand curve was no unique discovery by marginal utility theory. Secondly, Rubin concluded that there is also a supply curve, albeit limited within a predetermined range by the existing state of labour productivity and the corresponding price of production.[28] Rubin's argument upheld the view that Marx first stated in the *Grundrisse* and ultimately repeated in Volume III of *Capital*: that is, that price is 'nominal' but value is 'real', and the law of the latter 'appears as the law of motions which the former runs through'.[29]

---

27   Rubin 1990, p. 219.
28   In Rubin's third diagram, a permanent increase in demand, represented by the dotted line, would have the effect of attracting more capital investment, but price variation would remain confined, other conditions remaining the same, within the range of 2.5 to 3.5 roubles. The difference between Rubin's conclusion and that of conventional liberal theory is that the latter sees the costs of production varying not merely with technology but also with the *scale of output*, in which case the long-run supply curve resembles more closely the one in Rubin's first diagram. An extensive discussion of this and related issues can be found in Blaug 1985, pp. 373–5 et seq.
29   Marx 1993, pp. 137–8. Readers will note that by the time Marx wrote Volume III of *Capital*, the term 'cost of production' was replaced by the 'price of production', which includes the social average rate of profit.

DOCUMENT 16

Marx's Teaching on Production and Consumption (1930)

Isaak Il'ich Rubin

Source: I.I. Rubin, '*Uchenie Marksa o proizvodstve I potreblenii*', in *Arkhiv K. Marksa i F. Engel'sa*, Moscow: Gosudarstvennoe Izdael'stvo, 1930, pp. 58–131.

Introduction by the Editors

In this essay, Isaak Rubin writes that the relation between production and consumption, although Marx did not treat it systematically in any single text, is nevertheless essential 'for a proper understanding of the methodological foundations of Marx's entire economic theory'. Rubin adds, however, that Marx's views on the topic have 'hitherto attracted attention not so much from Marxists as from Marx's critics, who, with considerable monotony, have one after the other repeated the favourite argument that Marx ignores the process of consuming products and forgets the existence of use-value'. Rubin dismisses this argument and attributes it to the marginalist preoccupation with individual judgements of utility, which are said to determine a commodity's value.

Marx, in contrast, always regarded exchange-value in objective terms and treated consumption as one moment in the reproduction process as a whole. In his critique of the Austrian school, written in 1926 for the Great Soviet Encyclopaedia, Rubin had already objected that the Austrians excluded social classes; replaced capitalism with 'pure economic activity'; transformed society into 'an aggregation of individual Robinson Crusoes'; explained economic decisions in terms of 'psychological experiences'; transferred the focus of research from the sphere of production to consumption; and thus ignored capitalism's dynamic tendencies of development.

To this day, undergraduate textbooks explain a consumer's purchase decisions by reference to the point of tangency between a 'budget line' and an 'indifference curve' (which maps equal utilities); producers, in similar manner, determine purchases of 'factors of production' at the point of tangency between an 'equal-cost line' and an 'equal-product curve'. All such decisions are 'rationally' explained without any reference to historical or cultural context. Human beings are replaced by a consistent set of preferences; capitalist enterprises are replaced by a marginal cost curve and a social demand curve. One of Rubin's objectives in this essay is to repudiate this abstract indifference to context. He emphasises that human 'needs' cannot be understood merely as the subjective whims of consumers; like means of production and the changing forms of production relations, they are always a product of history.

The immediate incentive for Rubin's study came from publication of sections of Marx's *1844 Manuscripts*, which appeared in 1927 at the initiative of David B. Ryazanov, Rubin's close friend and Director of the Marx-Engels Institute. These notebooks, which Marx wrote for personal use as background for *The Holy Family* (1845), demonstrated more clearly than any other source Marx's debt to Hegel and also to Ludwig Feuerbach's anthropological reinterpretation of the Hegelian dialectic of objectification and alienation.

Rubin begins by noting that Feuerbach replaced Hegel's idealistic understanding of 'need' with the natural needs of man. But Marx went beyond Feuerbach, as Ryazanov commented, by 'further developing all the revolutionary elements of the Hegelian dialectic'. Marx asked how the *active* nature of man manifests itself in work – in 'the concrete activity of self-objectification'[1] – and how the things created to satisfy needs act in turn upon the producer, enriching his senses and his needs as an *historically* changing *social* being. Marx saw needs developing with the social division of labour in the historical process of social production: 'The history of *industry* and industry as it *objectively* exists is an open book of the *human faculties*, and a human *psychology* which can be sensuously apprehended'.[2]

From general laws of the development of needs, Marx turned to needs and consumption in commodity-producing society. The division of labour entails satisfaction of needs through exchange, with the result that every individual endeavours to awaken new needs in the other. Marx wrote that 'Everyone tries to establish over others an *alien* power in order to find there the satisfaction of his own egoistic need'.[3] Rubin points to the 'artificial awakening of refined, unnatural and even imaginary lusts, fantasies, caprices and whims'. The refinement of needs, which has the potential of advancing culture and human sensitivity, turns out instead to be dehumanising when the lavish consumption of the rich is accompanied by the degradation of human needs among workers. As Marx commented,

---

1   Marx, cited in Fromm 1961, p. 189.
2   Marx, cited in Fromm 1961, p. 134.
3   Marx, cited in Fromm 1961, pp. 139–40.

> For the worker even the need for fresh air ceases to be a need ... Light, air, and the simplest *animal* cleanliness cease to be human needs. Filth, this corruption and putrefaction which runs in the *sewers* of civilization (this is to be taken literally), becomes the element in which man lives. None of his senses exist any longer, either in a human form, or even in a non-human form.[4]

In the *1844 Manuscripts*, Marx already interpreted consumption and the development of needs with reference to social class, but he had yet to provide an historical account of the relation between needs and production. At this point Rubin turns to *The German Ideology*,[5] in which Marx described production of new needs as 'the first historical act'.[6] Whereas bourgeois economists assume a totality of needs to be given in advance and completely independent of the means to satisfy them, Marx linked production of needs with the developing means of production. Rubin observes that now 'the mediating link between man and nature is the instrument of labour; and the enormous importance of the instrument of labour is emphasised both in the process of development of man's productive activity and in the process of development of human needs'.

The next major text that Rubin considers is *A Contribution to the Critique of Political Economy* (1859). With the historical connection between needs and production established, the next question concerned exchange and distribution. In a commodity-producing society, the immediate purpose of production becomes exchange-value rather than use-value. Production and consumption begin to separate at the same time as they remain connected. Here the commodity appears as an immediate unity of use-value and exchange-value, yet the two remain contradictory: the commodity *is* a use-value, but it is also *not* directly a use-value. Marx explained that 'A commodity can only therefore become

---

4 Marx, cited in Fromm 1961, pp. 141–2.
5 A section of *The German Ideology* was first published by Ryazanov in 1924. See 'K. Marks i F. Engel's o Feierbakhe. Tezisy o Feierbakhe. Proekt predisloviya k "Nemetskoi ideologii". Feierbakh (Idealisticheskaya i materialistichjeskaya tochka preniya)', in *Arkhiv K. Marksa i F. Engel'sa*, Volume I (Moscow, 1924), pp. 191–256; the German original of this section was published in 1926: *Marx und Engels über Feuerbach. Der erste Teil der 'Deutschen Ideologie'*, in *Marx-Engels-Archiv. Zeitschrift des Marx-Engels-Instituts in Moskau*. Hrsg. von D. Rjazanov, Band 1, 1926, s. 205–306.
6 Marx and Engels 1964, p. 39. The complete text of *The German Ideology* was first published in Russian and in German in 1932.

a use-value if it is realised as an exchange-value, while it can only be realised as an exchange-value if it is alienated and functions as a use-value'.[7] Showing how the commodity-form necessarily entails mediation through the 'absolute form' of exchange-value, or money as the universal commodity, Rubin follows Marx in distinguishing the circuit C–M–C from M–C–M. In an important footnote he points out that Marx's account of the dual nature of the commodity was directly reminiscent of Hegel's dialectic of Being and Nothingness:

> While Hegel considers first 'being' and then 'nothingness', in order subsequently to reconcile them in 'becoming', Marx follows the same scheme: first he considers both use-value and exchange-value as being; then comes the contradiction of their being, followed by exploration of their becoming, i.e. the process of the actual movement of commodities in exchange. The similarity with Hegel's schemes can also be noted at another point: use-value and exchange-value are initially regarded as isolated determinations; then they enter into an external connection, and each is regarded as the external means for realisation of the other. Next comes the interpenetration of these opposites when they adopt the form of the commodity and of money.[8]

In the remainder of the document Rubin follows, through several levels of complexity, the relation between production and consumption in capitalist society. Here the primacy of exchange-value over use-value becomes all the more evident with production for an unknown market. In simple commodity production, the ultimate aim of the handicraftsman was still to satisfy his needs. Now the

---

7 Marx 1970, p. 43.
8 Viewing Marx's work as a whole, it would probably be better to regard Marx's analogue of Hegel's 'Being' as the essential human capacity for 'free, conscious activity' in the *1844 Manuscripts* (Marx, cited in Fromm, 1961, p. 100) and subsequently as the creative capacity for labour, which in Hegelian terms is also 'Nothing' until labour concretely determines itself in Quality (use-value), followed by Quantity (exchange-value) and Measure (money-price as the expression of abstract social labour and thus the medium of circulation). Quality, Quantity and Measure are the three divisions of the Doctrine of Being in Hegel's *Logic*. Just as the *Logic* ultimately transcends the contradiction between Essence and Existence in the Doctrine of the Notion, culminating in the Absolute Idea or infinite dialectical cognition, in Marx's *Grundrisse* the analogue of the Absolute Idea may be regarded as the 'human being who has become' – the one 'in whose head exists the accumulated knowledge of society' (p. 712), for 'the absolute working out of [human] creative potentialities ... makes ... the development of all human powers as such the end in itself' (Marx 1993, p. 488).

two moments of the reproduction process are further separated at the same time as they remain necessarily connected through market demand. Demand, in turn, assumes a determinate character depending upon the class distribution of incomes. The development of production creates growing needs for both items of consumption and means of production, yet there is a 'law inherent in capitalist economy that keeps the workers' consumption at a low level despite the gigantic growth of labour productivity'. Consumption remains determined by production and the social forms within which it occurs, not 'by the needs and arbitrary will of separate individuals'.

Marx was concerned neither with the subjective usefulness of labour nor with the objective utility of the product, but rather with the production relations between people. Having set out that methodological principle, Rubin then recounts the various ways in which use-value figures in 'the determinations of economic form', moving from the commodity's initial change of form, through exchange, to the constant and variable forms of capital, which Marx distinguishes in terms of their respective *social functions* rather than any material-technical differences. In the reproduction schemes of Volume II of *Capital*, the natural form of products had to be considered when examining macroeconomic relations between the two departments of industry, but again Rubin emphasises that Marx was concerned principally with the *social structure* of the reproduction process, not with concrete use-values. Marx also attached unique importance to the 'formal use-value' of money, as well as to the peculiar use-value of money-capital and of labour power to the capitalist (its capacity, as abstract labour, to create surplus value), but he did so in order to explain capitalism as a social form of production relations.

Rubin's theme throughout this essay is that use-value, while never absent from Marx's work, must always be considered in historical context and cannot be regarded as 'an independent object for research in theoretical economics':

> The capitalist production process is a unity of the labour process (i.e. the process of producing use-values) and the process of the production and expansion of value. Political economy takes the latter aspect of the production process, i.e. the process of the production and expansion of value, to be the special subject matter of its investigation. But the process of the expansion of value represents the form in which the process of the production of products, or of use-values, occurs. Thus, the latter process is always a part of our investigation, although not as an independent object for analysis by this science but rather as another side of the single process of reproduction, which we study as the 'social structure of production' (Lenin). It follows that use-value is included within the ambit of our

investigation only insofar as this is necessary in order to understand the process of the production and expansion of value.

∴

Isaak Rubin on Marx's Theory of Production and Consumption

Until now, Marxist literature has lacked a systematic presentation and analysis of Marx's teaching on the link between production and consumption. Meanwhile, this teaching is of great importance for a proper understanding of the methodological foundations of Marx's entire economic theory. This teaching has hitherto attracted attention not so much from Marxists as from Marx's critics, who, with considerable monotony, have one after the other repeated the favourite argument that Marx ignores the process of consuming products and forgets the existence of use-value. The absurdities that critics reach on this point can be seen in the case of [Emil] Hammacher. The latter attributes to Marx 'the false background idea that under capitalism the natural properties of the commodity are not valued at all'. And with the learned air of a connoisseur, Hammacher instructs Marx that 'in the capitalist system, too, the material property of the commodity remains decisive'.[9]

Such absurd reproaches are explained by the completely different approaches taken by Marx and his critics to the problem of use-value. The critics, being close to the Austrian school, or 'reconciling' exchange-value with use-value, regard the latter as the factor that determines the commodity's value. Finding that Marx acknowledges no such role for use-value, they conclude that Marx 'ignores' the process of consumption. Further elucidation will convince us of the falsity of this conclusion. In numerous observations by Marx and Engels – which, it is true, are scattered throughout their various works and nowhere treated systematically – we do find considerable material for a proper understanding of the process of consumption, as one of the moments of the reproduction process as a whole. In this article, we intend to give a systematic presentation and analysis of this material, without attempting an exhaustive treatment of the question.

The question of the connection between production and consumption is a borderline question that is equally interesting both to the theory of historical

---

9   Hammacher 1909, p. 545. [For further comments on Hammacher, see also Rubin 1990, pp. 53–9].

materialism and to economic theory. We therefore find in Marx and Engels: 1) a general teaching on production and consumption, insofar as they represent necessary moments of reproduction in any economic formation; 2) a special teaching on production and consumption in capitalist society. We shall set out the first teaching in chapter I and the second in chapter II. Finally, chapter III is devoted to the question of the extent to which the consumption process falls within political economy's sphere of research; in particular, we shall devote considerable attention in the last chapter to 'formal use-value', which plays a prominent role in Marxist theory but has not attracted the attention of investigators.

I The General Teaching on Production and Consumption

In this chapter we present Marx's general teaching on the connection between production and consumption as it occurs in various economic formations, not merely in capitalist society. We shall arrange the presentation in chronological order, beginning with the early preparatory works by Marx for *The Holy Family* (1844), which were published by D.B. Ryazanov in the third volume of *The Archive of K. Marx and F. Engels*.[10] Following analysis of this work, we shall turn to *The German Ideology* (in the winter of 1845–6) and then conclude this chapter with the *Contribution to the Critique of Political Economy* (1858), in which Marx's general teaching on the connection between production and consumption finds it most complete formulation.

1) Preparatory Work for *The Holy Family*

In the third volume of the *Archive*, D.B. Ryazanov published the early preparatory notes for *The Holy Family*, which were written by Marx in 1844.[11] During this period, Marx was still interested primarily in problems of philosophy, law and the state. But questions relating to theoretical economics – in the form of separate observations or longer commentaries – were already closely intertwined with these issues. It is precisely because economic material, in these early works by Marx, was still not segregated from the philosophical and historical-sociological material, that analysis of it presents significant difficulties but is also of enormous interest. Together with very interesting observations on the division of labour, the connection of the division of labour with private property, etc., we find in this work the germ of the teaching on the connec-

---

10 [See Ryazanov 1927, pp. 191–256].
11 They are reproduced in the third volume of *Collected Works* by K. Marx and F. Engels, which was published in 1929.

tion between production and consumption that Marx subsequently developed more fully in his *Contribution to the Critique of Political economy* and in other works.

During 1843–4 Marx was considerably influenced by the philosophical works of Feuerbach. As D.B. Ryazanov justifiably noted, however, 'Marx, having adopted the anthropology of Feuerbach, differs from the latter by preserving and further developing all the revolutionary elements of the Hegelian dialectic'.[12] The correctness of this observation is confirmed in Marx's discussions of human needs, which we assemble below. They could only be formulated by Marx on the basis of an organic reworking of the ideas that he found in both Hegel and Feuerbach.

The idea of the unity of human needs and the objects required to satisfy them was clearly expressed by Hegel.[13] But with him it assumes an idealistic character, since man is regarded purely as spiritual 'self-consciousness', and the object is something created by spirit itself in its own 'otherness' [*Anderssein*], having only the appearance, therefore, of independence in relation to the subject. The latter is conscious that the external thing is only the product of the otherness of self-consciousness, that it 'belongs to its own essential nature and yet is lacking in it'. The subject sees in the external thing its own 'one-sidedness' and, at the same time, it knows that the object 'contains the *possibility* of the satisfying its appetite [or desire], that the object is, therefore, *conformable* to the appetite and that just for this reason the latter is excited by the object'. Hence, there emerges in the subject the need to satisfy its desire through elimination (consumption) of the external thing, and thus to prove the imaginary character of the latter's independence and its real identity with the subject itself. 'By the satisfaction of appetite, the implicit identity of the subject and the object is made explicit [*gesetzt*], the one-sidedness of subjectivity and the apparent indifference of the object are superseded [*aufgehoben*]'.

Bolland, the well-known commentator on Hegel's works, expressed the basic idea of these arguments from Hegel with the following brief note: 'The satisfaction of desires in fact shows the essential unity of opposites', i.e. of the subject and the object. For Hegel, this unity has an idealistic character: the object is merely the otherness of the subject, and the latter represents the pure spiritual essence of self-consciousness. Despite this idealistic character of Hegel's conception, we see within it a number of interesting moments that Feuerbach

---

12   Ryazanov 1927, p. 133.
13   See Hegel 1921, pp. 120–2. For more detail, see Hegel 1906, pp. 911–15. The following quotations are taken from the latter publication, pp. 912–13. [Hegel 1971, § 426–7 and *Zusatz* to § 427, pp. 167–9].

and Marx subsequently developed further. These include: the subject's feeling of one-sidedness and 'need' for the external object; the role of the latter as a necessary complement to the being of the subject itself; the correspondence of the external thing to the desires being satisfied through its assistance; and, finally, as a general philosophical foundation for all of these moments, the doctrine of the unity of subject and object – interpreted, it is true, in an idealistic spirit.

Feuerbach reworked the teaching on needs in a materialistic spirit. We shall cite two typical quotations from him, taken from exactly those works that made the greatest impression on Marx during this period. In his 'Preliminary Theses on the Reform of Philosophy' (1843), Feuerbach wrote: 'Only the *needy* entity is a *necessary* entity. Existence without need is unnecessary existence ... Only the entity rich in pain is a divine entity. An essence without suffering is an essence without an essence, an entity devoid of sensibility, devoid of matter'.[14]

Whereas man, for Hegel, experiences need for an external thing because the latter originates in the creative act of 'other-being' by the purely spiritual essence of man himself, of his 'self-consciousness', with Feuerbach the need for an external thing arises precisely from the sensuous, material nature of man. A non-material, purely spiritual man – despite Hegel's opinion – would have no need whatever for external things.

Feuerbach's thoughts [directed] against Hegel were even more pointed in his next work, *Principles of the Philosophy of the Future* (1843): 'Only a *sensuous* being needs other, external objects for its being. I do need air in order to breathe, water to drink, light to see, vegetable and animal materials to eat; but nothing, at least directly, in order to think ... That being that breathes *necessarily* relates itself to a being external to itself and has its *essential* object through which it is what it is *outside itself*'.[15]

In 1844, when Marx wrote his preliminary work for *The Holy Family*, he relied upon Feuerbach's philosophy and waged a decisive struggle against Hegel's idealistic views. It is understandable, therefore, that in this early work, when discussing needs and consumption, he follows Feuerbach's example of strongly emphasising the sensuous nature of man. He writes:

> *Man* is directly a *natural being*. As a natural being and as a living natural being he is, on the one hand, endowed with *natural powers* and *faculties*,

---

14   Feuerbach 1983, p. 163, the translator notes that 'essence' and 'entity' in this paragraph are both translations of *Wesen*.
15   Feuerbach 1983, p. 8.

which exist in him as tendencies and abilities, as *drives*. On the other hand, as a natural, embodied, sentient, objective being he is a *suffering*, conditioned and limited being, like animals and plants. The *objects* of his drives exist outside himself as *objects* independent of him, yet they are *objects* of his *needs*, essential *objects* which are indispensable to the exercise and confirmation of his faculties ... *To be* objective, natural, sentient and at the same time to have object, nature and sense outside oneself, or to be oneself object, nature and sense for a third person, is the same thing. *Hunger* is a natural *need*; it requires therefore a *nature* outside itself, an *object* outside itself, in order to be satisfied and stilled. Hunger is the objective need of a body for an *object* which exists outside itself and which is essential for its integration and the expression of its nature. A being which does not have its nature outside itself is not a *natural* being and does not share in the being of nature. A being which has no object outside itself is not an objective being.[16]

The reader will easily notice the similarity between these words from Marx and the quotations provided above from the works of Feuerbach. As with Feuerbach, Marx takes the sensuous character of man as the starting point for his discussion, explaining man's inseparable connection with nature. Marx writes that 'Sense experience (see Feuerbach) must be the basis of all science',[17] and on this foundation he erects his doctrine of needs. It is precisely from the sensuous nature of man that Marx, following Feuerbach's example, draws the closest possible connection between human needs and the objects that serve for their satisfaction. As a natural being, man requires natural objects found outside himself; but these objects, on the other hand, serve precisely to satisfy man's needs, to complement the manifestation of his life.

If Marx had confined himself to clarifying the sensuous-passive nature of man, he would not have moved beyond the circle of ideas sketched by Feuerbach. But, as D.B. Ryazanov noted concerning the passage cited above, Marx, even in the period of his enthusiasm for Feuerbach, 'preserves and further develops all the revolutionary elements of the Hegelian dialectic'. And we shall also find confirmation of this fact in Marx's teaching on needs and consumption. In this early work by Marx that we have been discussing, man already appears not merely as a passive being, experiencing the need for external objects, but also as an *active, historically* changing and *social* being.

---

16 Marx, in Fromm 1961, p. 138.
17 Marx, in Fromm 1961, p. 136.

In the passage cited above, Marx already characterises the nature of man from the very outset in terms of his active-passive duality. Man is not merely a passive being, suffering from unsatisfied needs, but also an active being, who is endowed with 'natural forces' that become manifest in his activity. Whereas Hegel treated the active side of man in terms of the abstract and purely spiritual activity of 'self-consciousness', Marx replaces it with 'the replete, living, sensuous, concrete activity of self-objectification',[18] that is, with the activity of labour. But man, with his labour activity, already appears not just as a natural but also as a social being: 'The activity of labour and spirit, both in their content *and in their mode of appearance*, are *social* activity and *social* spirit'.[19] Man's historically changing nature follows from his social nature: 'The whole of what is called world history is nothing but the creation of man by human labour'.[20]

As we see, even though Marx took Feuerbach's 'natural' man as the starting point for his discussion, he did not stop there. From natural man he turned to social man, to the active and historically changing man. And it was precisely with regard to social man that he further developed his essential thoughts on the connection between production and consumption.

It is in society that the connection already noted, between human needs and the objects that serve to satisfy them, appears with the greatest force. In society, all objects appear not in the form directly given by nature; they are no longer natural objects but are created by man himself. They represent the manifestation of his vital powers, a social manifestation of man's own nature.

> It is only when objective reality everywhere becomes for man in society the reality of human faculties, human reality, and thus the reality of his own faculties, that all *objects* become for him the *objectification of himself*. The objects then confirm and realize his individuality.[21]

The objects themselves appear as humanised, i.e. as the result of human activity and the manifestation of human powers.

---

18   Marx, in Fromm 1961, p. 189.
19   Marx, in Fromm 1961, p. 128. Note that Rubin's translation uses the word 'spirit', which is not in the standard English translation: 'Activity and mind are social in their content as well as in their *origin*; they are *social* activity and *social* mind'.
20   Marx, in Fromm 1961, p. 138.
21   Marx, in Fromm 1961, p. 132.

However, man's activity changes not merely the external objects to which it is immediately directed but also the very sensitivities of man himself, his needs. 'Man's musical sense is only awakened by music'.[22]

> The *senses* of social man are different from those of non-social man. It is only through the objectively deployed wealth of the human being that the wealth of subjective *human* sensibility (a musical ear, an eye which is sensitive to the beauty of form, in short, senses which are capable of *human* satisfaction and which confirm themselves as *human* faculties) is cultivated or created.[23]

It is only in the presence of the objectively developed wealth of the human essence, i.e. the diverse world of objects, created through human activity, that the development and refinement of human needs, of human sensitivities, becomes possible. In this manner, a simultaneous process occurs of the humanisation of the world of things surrounding man, and also of the sensitivities (needs) of man himself; and this process results from the activity of man, which serves, in turn, to manifest the vital forces inherent in human nature.

Marx's thinking, evidently, takes the following course. The active nature of man manifests itself in active work, and thus also in the things it helps to create. These things, created for the satisfaction of human needs, act in turn upon man, enriching his senses and his needs. It is precisely because this vigorous activity of man simultaneously transforms both the objects of the external world and the needs of man himself, that complete correspondence emerges between human needs and the objects that serve to satisfy them. The needs and the objects needed are not two different series of phenomena, alien to one another and interacting externally. What we see is mutual interpenetration of these series of phenomena, for the objects are created by human activity precisely for the satisfaction of needs, and the latter, in turn, become developed and enriched only under the influence of the surrounding, humanly created world of objects. Here Marx already sets out quite clearly the idea of the dialectical connection and interpenetration of man's needs and the objects that serve to satisfy them. In this early work, he already overcame the widespread view that needs and objects are only externally connected. He already overcame here the fallacy of bourgeois economists, who begin their discourses with the existence of human needs – which they regard as given in advance and not

---

22 Marx, in Fromm 1961, p. 132.
23 Marx, in Fromm 1961, p. 133.

connected to the production process and the world of things it creates – and then treat objects as external means for the satisfaction of these given needs. It is enough just to point out that the Austrian school's entire doctrine concerning needs is founded precisely upon such a purely mechanical representation of the connection between needs and objects. There is no need to add that such representation lay at the basis of Bentham's utilitarian theory and of all those economists of the Ricardian school who followed him on this question. In the work that we are examining, Marx already scornfully rejected this utilitarian and hedonistic psychology, which considers phenomena 'from the viewpoint of an external relation of utility', and for which the 'great wealth' of human creativity is expressed only in such terms as 'need, common need'.[24] Marx provided a further and more detailed critique of this utilitarian psychology in his work aimed at [Max] Stirner, which was first published by D.B. Ryazanov in the fourth volume of the *Archive of K. Marx and F. Engels*.[25]

His understanding of the dialectical connection between needs and external objects opened up for Marx wide possibilities for a proper interpretation of the laws of the development of human needs. In fact, in the work already cited we find the germ of the idea that the entire process of the development of human senses and needs results from the development of human activity itself.

> The *cultivation* of the five senses is the work of all previous history. *Sense* which is subservient to crude needs has only a *restricted* meaning. For a starving man the human form of food does not exist, but only its abstract character as food. It could just as well exist in the most crude form, and it is impossible to say in what way this feeding-activity would differ from that of animals.[26]

Here Marx sets out the idea that even when we speak of the need for food, which is rooted in the physical nature of man, this need itself changes and assumes different forms in the course of historical development, i.e. it is a product of history. (A further development of this same idea, again with reference to hunger, is given by Marx in his *Contribution to the Critique of Political Economy*, of which we shall have more to say later).

Marx then gives a still more precise formula of the development of needs. Since needs develop and are enriched together with enrichment of the world of

---

24   Marx, in Fromm 1961, p. 135.
25   [See K. Marks i F. Engels 1929, 'Iz "Nemetskoi ideologii"', in *Arkhiv K. Marksa i F. Engel'sa*, Volume IV (Moscow-Leningrad), pp. 215–91].
26   Marx, in Fromm 1961, p. 133.

objects that surrounds man, and since the world of objects is created by human labour, or by industry, it follows that we must look for a final explanation of the process of the change of human needs in the process of industry's development. In the history of industry, we must find the explanation for the process of development and the growing complexity of human sensitivities and needs. 'The history of *industry* and industry as it *objectively* exists is an *open book* of the *human faculties*, and a human *psychology* which can be sensuously apprehended'.[27] Industry is 'the *exoteric* manifestation of the essential human *faculties*'.[28]

The discussions by Marx that we have been presenting, which were in his preliminary work for *The Holy Family*, already contain the nucleus of fruitful thoughts concerning the connection between production and consumption. Needs do not stand mechanically in opposition to external objects but are instead regarded as inseparably connected with the latter. The very process of the development of human needs is considered as an historical process, whose course depends upon the development of industry, i.e. of vital human activity, of human labour. Nevertheless, in the discussions by Marx that we have been considering there remain certain inadequacies that are possibly explained by the influence of Feuerbachian philosophy. Marx begins his discussions with reference to the essential powers of man, which are manifested in the activity that gives birth to the diverse world of objects. The process of simultaneous and parallel enrichment of the world of objects and of human needs is considered as the manifestation of man's essential powers, as the discovery of his inclinations, which exist – even if in undeveloped form – in the nature of man. Moreover, although Marx already emphasises the importance of vital, practical activity – in the sense of causes that bring about the change of human needs – what stands out is not so much the vital activity of man in the production process as the perception of things that this activity generates.

To this point we have outlined Marx's thinking on the general laws of the development of needs. We can presuppose that the conditions for the enrichment of human sensitivities and needs that Marx describes can only fully exist, in his opinion, in a socialist society. The picture that is given, of the 'natural' development of human sensitivities and needs under the influence of the growing diversity and enrichment of the world of objects, is treated by Marx as an ideal that comes to full realisation in socialist society.[29] As the antithesis of this

---

27   Marx, in Fromm 1961, p. 134.
28   Marx, in Fromm 1961, p. 135.
29   We find direct reference to this point in Marx, in Fromm 1961, pp. 130–3.

picture of the growth of human needs, Marx portrayed for us the state of affairs that prevails in the bourgeois economy.

Let us now turn to the analysis of needs and consumption in a bourgeois economy. Marx does not yet distinguish between simple commodity economy and capitalist economy, but we shall try to separate those features in his comments that are typical of any commodity economy from those specific to capitalist economy. Marx characterises bourgeois society as follows:

> *Society*, as it appears to the political economist, is *civil society*, in which each individual is a totality of needs and only exists for another person, as another exists for him, in so far as each becomes a means for the other.[30]

This characterisation of bourgeois society, which is frequently encountered in Marx, is developed by him in more detail in *The Holy Family*:

> Since the need of one individual has no self-understood sense for the other egotistic individual capable of satisfying that need and therefore no direct connection with its satisfaction, each individual has to create that connection; it thus becomes the intermediary between the need of another and the object of that need.[31]

It is easy to see here that Marx has in mind a peculiarity that characterises any commodity economy: every individual satisfies his needs only by means of satisfying the needs of others. This particular aspect of the process of satisfying human needs in commodity economy was observed even by Adam Smith, who wrote in the second chapter of his *Wealth of Nations*:

> ... man has almost constant occasion for the help of his brethren, and it is in vain for him to expect it from their benevolence only. He will be more likely to prevail if he can interest their self-love in his favour, and show them that it is for their own advantage to do for him what he requires of them.[32]

It is probably due to Smith's influence that Hegel also noted the interdependence of members of 'civil society' in the satisfaction of their needs.[33]

---

30   Marx, in Fromm 1961, p. 153.
31   Marx and Engels 1956, pp. 162–3.
32   Smith 1937, p. 14.
33   Hegel 1967, p. 127. [In paragraph 189 Hegel writes: 'Political economy is the science which

Marx expressed the identical thought in the passage that we cited above, characterising the fundamental peculiarity of the process of satisfying needs in commodity economy. Subsequently, in the *Critique of Political Economy*, Marx developed this idea that satisfaction of the producer's needs in commodity economy is possible only by means of exchange. From this idea he derived a whole series of extremely important and interesting conclusions regarding the contradiction between use-value and exchange-value. But, in the early work that we are examining, Marx had yet to undertake the analysis of simple commodity economy. He noted the interdependence of commodity producers in satisfying their needs only in order to turn directly to capitalist economy and to reveal all of its essential and irremediable flaws. He did this in the excerpt from the early works that was published by D.B. Ryazanov under the heading 'Need, Production and Division of Labour'.[34]

Marx begins this passage with the following considerations. Once the commodity producer can satisfy his needs only after first satisfying the needs of another individual, his interest is in artificially awakening in the latter a new kind of need.

> Every man speculates upon creating a *new* need in another in order to force him to a new sacrifice, to place him in a new dependence, and to entice him into a new kind of pleasure and thereby into economic ruin. Everyone tries to establish over others an *alien* power in order to find there the satisfaction of his own egoistic need.[35]

The result is artificial awakening of refined, unnatural and even imaginary lusts, fantasies, caprices and whims.

---

starts from this view of needs and labour but then has the task of explaining mass-relationships and mass-movements in their complexity and their qualitative and quantitative character. This is one of the sciences which have arisen out of the conditions of the modern world. Its development affords the interesting spectacle (as in Smith, Say, and Ricardo), of thought working upon the endless mass of details which confront it at the outset and extracting therefrom the simple principles of the thing, the Understanding effective in the thing and directing it' (Hegel 1967, pp. 126–7). Hegel adds in Addition 120, that political economy is 'a science which is a credit to thought because it finds laws for a mass of accidents' (Hegel 1967, p. 268)].

34   See Marx, in Fromm 1961, pp. 139–95. [The source that Rubin has in mind is 'K. Marks i F. Engel's o Feierbakhe', in *Arkhiv K. Marks i F. Engel'sa*, Vol. I (Moscow, 1924), pp. 191–256].

35   Marx, in Fromm 1961, pp. 139–40.

> No eunuch flatters his tyrant more shamefully or seeks by more infamous means to stimulate his jaded appetite, in order to gain some favor, than does the eunuch of industry, the entrepreneur, in order to acquire a few silver coins or to charm the gold from the purse of his dearly beloved neighbor ... The entrepreneur accedes to the most depraved fancies of his neighbor, plays the role of pander between him and his needs, awakens unhealthy appetites in him, and watches for every weakness in order, later, to claim the remuneration for this labor of love.[36]

Hence the growing refinement of needs, the whims of the rich, the quest for luxuries and profligate consumption.

It is easy to show here that Marx is gradually making the transition from simple commodity economy to capitalist economy. He moves from the fact that every commodity producer can satisfy his needs only by means of exchange to the conclusion that sellers need to awaken the artificial need of the buyer for items of luxury. But it is perfectly obvious that the latter can only occur in class society, where the possessing classes acquire for themselves a greater mass of surplus value. The possibility of profligate luxury is created precisely through the exploitation of one class by another; it is not the result of sellers awakening artificial needs on the part of buyers, as Marx still suggests in this early work.

The great interest that Marx and Engels, in their early works, take in the problem of luxury and wastefulness is to be explained mainly by the way in which they were influenced by the works of utopian socialists, who saw in the luxuries and profligacy of the idle rich one of the foremost evils of capitalist society. Marx's interest in the problem of luxury is also partly explained by the fact that this question was a topic of heated debates between two groups of economists in the classical school. Those economists who represented the landowning aristocracy (Malthus, Lauderdale and others) argued that the landowners' wasteful way of life, involving consumption of significant luxuries, creates the market for capitalist industry. Economists who represented the industrial bourgeoisie (Ricardo, Say and others) demonstrated, in opposition to the first group, the great damage resulting from non-productive consumption on the part of idle landowners, and they recommended the thrift that contributes to accumulation of new capitals and to the expansion of production. In the early work that we are examining, Marx treats in detail this quarrel between the supporters of luxury and those of thrift, demonstrating the fallacies in the positions

---

36 Marx, in Fromm 1961, pp. 140–1.

of both sides. The former economists were in error when they proposed wastefulness as a direct means of enrichment, but the other side was

> hypocritical in not admitting that it is caprice and fancy which determine production. They forget the 'refined needs', and that without consumption there would be no production. They forget that through competition production must become ever more universal and luxurious; that consumption determines the value of a thing, and that consumption is determined by fashion.[37]

We can see that Marx was still influenced here by arguments developed in the quarrels over luxury by the utopian socialists on the one hand, and by Malthus and his supporters on the other. Marx still attaches decisive importance to the refined needs of the rich, to their whims and caprice, overestimating their significance for the process of capitalist production as a whole. He even refers to the opinion of economists that a thing's 'value is determined by use', probably having in mind a similar doctrine from Say. The same thought, concerning the influence of the whims of the rich on the value of products, was expressed by Engels in his early article 'Outlines of a Critique of Political Economy', in which he wrote that 'utility depends on chance, on fashion, on the whim of the rich'.[38]

If we leave aside the exaggerated importance that Marx attributes to non-productive consumption by the rich, we can note one very valuable feature of these early reflections. From the very outset he poses the entire problem of consumption in terms of a class point of view: he characterises the consumption of the separate classes that constitute capitalist society and meticulously notes the features typical of each of them. Marx describes the profligate way of life that he regards as typical of the landlord class; the industrial bourgeoisie, to the contrary, displays a sober and prosaic way of thinking. It is true that the industrialist, as we have already seen, artificially awakens a need in buyers and thus promotes the consumption of items of luxury. But, in the further course of its development, the industrial bourgeoisie actively comes out against the luxury and wastefulness of landowners.

> Of course, the industrial capitalist also has his pleasures. He does not by any means return to an unnatural simplicity in his needs, but his enjoyment is only a secondary matter; it is recreation subordinated to

---

37 Marx, in Fromm 1961, p. 144.
38 *MECW*, Vol. 3, pp. 426–7.

production and thus a *calculated, economic* enjoyment, for he charges his pleasures as an expense of capital and what he squanders must not be more than can be replaced with profit by the reproduction of capital. Thus enjoyment is subordinated to capital and the pleasure-loving individual is subordinated to the capital-accumulating individual, whereas formerly the contrary was the case.[39]

Here Marx again clearly notes the class character of consumption, the various specific features that characterise consumption by the industrial capitalists, and how it differs from the consumption of landowners.[40]

However, while the different character of consumption on the part of different classes already emerges clearly when speaking of landowners and industrial capitalists, the class character of consumption appears still more strikingly with regard to the opposition between the possessing classes and the workers. Capitalist society simultaneously creates, on the one hand, 'refinement of needs and of the means to satisfy them' while, on the other hand, it produces 'a bestial savagery, a complete, primitive and abstract simplicity of needs'.[41] As in the case of other socialists, Marx paints in vivid colours the low level and the simplicity of needs to which the worker is brought in capitalist society. For the worker, not only does the process of gradual enrichment of human needs – which Marx previously described in a society devoid of class differences – cease to operate; in a capitalist economy, not even the purely physical or natural needs, which the worker experiences due to his physical nature, are satisfied.

> For the worker even the need for fresh air ceases to be a need ... Light, air, and the simplest *animal* cleanliness cease to be human needs. *Filth*, this corruption and putrefaction which runs in the *sewers* of civilization (this is to be taken literally) becomes the *element in which man lives*. Total and *unnatural* neglect, putrefied nature, becomes the *element in which he lives*. None of his senses exist any longer, either in a human form, or even in a *non-human*, animal form.[42]

---

39   Marx, in Fromm 1961, p. 152.
40   In *Capital* Marx repeats this distinction between the consumption of industrial capitalists and landowners. [See Marx 1976, pp. 742–3]. See also the article cited previously by D.B. Ryazanov, p. 141.
41   Marx, in Fromm 1961, p. 141.
42   Marx, in Fromm 1961, pp. 141–2.

Whereas we previously traced the gradual enrichment and humanisation of sensitivities and needs, now we observe the reverse process of the degradation of human needs to the level of animal needs and even beyond. Marx illustrates this process again by taking the example of food.

> It is not enough that man should lose his human needs; even *animal* needs disappear. The Irish no longer have any need but that of *eating – eating potatoes*, and then only the worst kind, *mouldy potatoes*.⁴³

But Marx regards the workers' consumption not just as the striking antithesis of consumption by the profligate rich; he emphasises not only their sharp opposition but also the inseparable connection between them. And here we see the fruitfulness of the dialectical method with which Marx operates throughout all of his works. The wasteful consumption of the rich and the meagre consumption of workers are two sides of one and the same capitalist society; they complement and mutually condition each other. 'The growth of needs and of the means to satisfy them results in a lack of needs and of means'.⁴⁴ The industrial bourgeoisie draws profit both from the debauchery of the landlords and from the crude needs of the workers.

> The *crude* need of the worker is a much greater source of profit than the *refined* need of the wealthy. The cellar dwellings in London bring their landlords more than do the palaces; i.e., they constitute *greater wealth* as far as the landlord is concerned and thus, in economic terms, greater *social* wealth. Just as industry speculates upon the refinement of needs so also it speculates upon their *crudeness*, and upon their artificially produced crudeness.⁴⁵

Marx already notes here the enormous importance for capitalist production not only of luxurious consumption by the propertied classes but also of the mass consumption of simple products by the workers. As we have already seen, however, the young Marx still exaggerates the role of luxuries, as did other early socialists. Subsequently, in *The Poverty of Philosophy*, Marx assigns primary importance to items of mass consumption.

---

43   Marx, in Fromm 1961, p. 142.
44   Ibid.
45   Marx, in Fromm 1961, p. 146.

We can see that the preliminary notes for *The Holy Family* contain several interesting commentaries by Marx regarding both the laws of development of human needs in general and, in particular, the character of consumption in capitalist society. As for the first part, there Marx emphasises the historically variable character of man's needs and the inseparable connection between the process of development of needs and the process of development of human activity, expressed in the process of production. In the second part, in his consideration of capitalist economy, Marx dramatically portrays the class character of consumption and notes the specific features of consumption by landlords, industrial capitalists and workers. In this respect, even in his early notes, Marx surpasses many of his contemporary bourgeois economists, who contrived to discuss 'consumers' without first of all drawing a clear distinction between worker-consumers and capitalist-consumers. However, Marx's treatment of consumption by the different classes is not yet connected with an analysis of the capitalist production process as a whole; instead, it involves separate observations that have more of a sociological and journalistic character rather than an economic one. A second shortcoming of these discussions of capitalist economy is the fact that they are not connected with the preceding commentaries on the laws of development of human needs in general. The second excerpt, in which Marx paints consumption in capitalist society, is more of an antithesis to the thinking in the first excerpt than a continuation and development. The first excerpt deals with the enrichment of human needs, the second with their coarsening. In the first manuscript, the issue is humanisation of the senses and of needs, whereas in the second they are deprived of their human character (and this applies not just to the starving worker but also to the profligate rich, as Marx notes).[46] The first manuscript deals with the 'natural' process of enrichment of human needs in a society without class differences, while the second describes the 'anti-natural' character of consumption by the workers, as well as by the rich, in capitalist society.

2)   The German Ideology

Marx's subsequent thinking moved in the same two directions that we have already noted in the preliminary work for *The Holy Family*. On the one hand, Marx had to formulate in more detail and more precisely his views on the general laws of the development of human needs; on the other hand, he had to connect the problem of consumption in capitalist economy with an analysis of the process of capitalist production as a whole. Marx completed

---

46   Marx, in Fromm 1961, pp. 143, 150–1.

the first task in *The German Ideology* and in his *Contribution to the Critique of Political Economy*. He worked on completing the second task in *The Poverty of Philosophy* and in *Capital*. For the sake of clarity of presentation, in what follows we shall separate these two problems and deal, first of all, with Marx's doctrine concerning the law of development of human needs insofar as this pattern holds for any social formation. Marx dedicated several interesting observations to exactly this question in *The German Ideology*, written in the winter of 1845–6 and published by D.B. Ryazanov in the first volume of the *Archive of K. Marx and F. Engels*.[47] On this question, as on others, Marx took an important step forward in *The German Ideology* compared with the preparatory work for *The Holy Family*. This is perfectly understandable, for it was precisely in *The German Ideology* that Marx and Engels gave the first broad outline of their theory of historical materialism. The question of the development of human needs constitutes a part of the theory of historical materialism, and for that reason it is perfectly natural that Marx and Engels, in *The German Ideology*, gave a more precise formulation of their ideas regarding the development of needs and of consumption.

Whereas Marx began the notes for *The Holy Family* with man as a natural being, his starting point in *The German Ideology* is the existence of individuals who are distinguished in terms of a definite physical nature. 'Thus the first fact to be established is the physical organisation of these individuals and their consequent relation to the rest of nature'.[48] Due to their physical nature, people have definite needs for food, a habitation, etc.

> Men must be in a position to live in order to be able to 'make history'.[49] But life involves before everything else eating and drinking, a habitation, clothing and many other things. The first historical act is thus the production of the means to satisfy these needs, the production of material life itself.[50]

Here Marx clearly emphasises the decisive role of production for the whole of human life, while in the preliminary work for *The Holy Family* he more fre-

---

47 ['K. Marks i F. Engel's o Feierbakhe', in *Arkhiv K. Marks i F. Engel'sa*, Vol. I (Moscow, 1924), pp. 191–256].
48 Marx and Engels 1964, p. 31.
49 Marx added a note at this point: 'Hegel. Geological, hydrographical, etc. conditions. Human bodies. Needs, labour'. Here, too, we see remnants of the influence upon Marx of Hegel's doctrine of needs.
50 Marx and Engels 1964, p. 38.

quently uses the vague term 'human activity'. This emphasis upon the role of the production process immediately gave Marx the possibility of correctly posing the question of the law-governed development of needs. Marx portrayed the connection between the development of production and the growth of needs in the following manner, which has great significance for our theme. Marx initially wrote these words: 'The facility acquired in satisfying original needs now gives birth to new needs'.[51] But these words were crossed out by Marx and replaced with the following: 'The satisfaction of the first need (the action of satisfying, and the instrument of satisfaction which has been acquired) leads to new needs; and this production of new needs is the first historical act'.[52]

It may seem, at first, that there is no great difference between the original version of the sentence, which was crossed out, and the final version; in fact, the difference between them is significant. In the first version of the sentence, Marx (or Engels) had not yet finally broken with the notion, widespread at the time, of so-called unlimited human needs. According to this notion, which is widespread to this day in bourgeois political economy, the needs of man are by nature infinite, and precisely which portion of these needs will in fact be satisfied depends on the availability of external resources. The totality of needs is taken as something given in advance and completely independent of the means for satisfying them. External things appear only in the role of means for the satisfaction of needs that are given in advance. In view of the unlimited character of needs, the satisfaction of one portion of them quickly calls forth other needs, which follow in terms of their degree of intensity. The mechanical opposition between unlimited needs and the limited world of external means for satisfying them, and the detachment of needs from the production process – these are the distinguishing features of this conception.[53] Marx's discussion of the dialectical connection between needs and external objects,

---

51   It is possible that the words we are quoting were written by Engels. We shall leave that question aside.
52   Marx and Engels 1964, p. 39.
53   The extent to which this conception is still shared by bourgeois economists can be shown by many examples. Let us cite the words of Gottl-Ottlilienfeld: 'In the final analysis, our *will* (Wollen) is manifest in our needs; the will, in principle, has no limits. Will is opposed to our *ability* (Können), which is measured in turn by the degree of our power over the means of satisfying (needs); but every ability is, in principle limited, since otherwise it would be all-powerful. Limited ability and unlimited will. This inevitably leads to conflict' (Gottl-Ottlilienfeld 1914, p. 208). Gottl's words dramatically illustrate that the basis for the doctrine of unlimited human needs is an idealistic conception of an unlimited human

which he outlines in the early manuscripts for *The Holy Family*, precludes for him any possibility of believing in the fiction of an unlimited world of needs that exists independently of the development of the production process itself. Indeed, in the new version of the sentence, Marx provides a completely different conception of the development of needs: already the issue is no longer one of the appearance of needs that exist in themselves (even though they cannot, in fact, be satisfied), without any dependence upon the given process of production; now it is the very process of production that brings forth new needs. A process occurs of giving 'birth to new needs', and this process results from development of the process of man's productive activity. Marx particularly notes here the enormous role played by the appearance of new means of production. Development of the means of production plays a revolutionising role not only in the process of man's productive activity but also in the development of human needs themselves.

In *The German Ideology*, the dialectical connection between production and needs is already clarified much more appropriately than in the preliminary work for *The Holy Family*. Whereas in the earlier work Marx already emphasised the importance of man's vital activity, in the subsequent work this idea is replaced by a more precise concept of the production of material life. While Marx already spoke in the previous work of the effect of man upon nature, now the mediating link between man and nature is the instrument of labour; and the enormous importance of the instrument of labour is emphasised both in the process of development of man's productive activity and in the process of development of human needs. Finally, whereas in Marx's earlier work one encounters, alongside a proper understanding of the historical character of the process of change in human needs, references to man's natural endowments, now the problem of the change of human nature itself is posed with greater force and specificity.

Despite the proper framing of the problem of the connection between production and consumption in *The German Ideology*, this problem still required further elaboration. Only in his final formulation of the theory of historical materialism – and particularly in his economic theory, which is set out in the three volumes of *Capital* – did Marx provide a number of more concrete references to the laws of the development of needs. In *The German Ideology*, the question was still not sufficiently worked out; it is quite understandable, therefore, that along with a generally correct formulation of the dependence

---

spirit. [Today's typical textbook definition of the 'economic problem' is that it involves 'the allocation of scarce resources between competing wants'].

of the development of needs upon development of man's productive activity, we also encounter repetition of the current and widespread views concerning the dependence of change in needs on the growth of population. Marx says in one place that 'increased needs create new social relations and the increased population new needs'.[54] Elsewhere, we read that at the basis of the increase of labour productivity and the growth of needs is the increase of population.[55] To explain the flourishing of weaving during the epoch of early capitalism, Marx refers to the demand for cloth for clothing that comes with the increase of population.[56] Together with population growth, as a factor determining the level of needs, Marx also refers to the state of culture. He speaks of more coarse or developed needs being conditioned by the existing level of culture.[57]

The German Ideology is simultaneously a sociological and an historical study; on the one hand, Marx and Engels set out here the general foundations for the theory of historical materialism, while on the other hand – based upon this theory – they attempt to outline a picture of the economic and social-political development of Europe from the Middle Ages up to the epoch of capitalism. It is understandable, therefore, that together with general discussions of the connection between production and consumption, we find a number of separate and brief observations regarding the peculiarities of the process of consumption in capitalist economy. We find the interesting comment that in capitalist society, based upon the division of labour, there is already the possibility that 'enjoyment and labour, production and consumption – devolve upon different individuals'. Subsequently, as we shall see, Marx often returns to this idea of the detachment of consumption from production in commodity economy, and especially in capitalist economy. Marx further notes that the emergence and growth of towns signifies the 'concentration' of needs,[58] a fact that actually does characterise the process of consumption in capitalist society. We also find the point that the need for items of luxury grows under the influence of an increasing accumulation of capital and the expansion of commerce.[59] Here we already have a more realistic and historically correct explanation of the growing need for items of luxury than we find in the notes for *The Holy Family*.

---

54   Marx and Engels 1964, p. 40.
55   Marx and Engels 1964, p. 42.
56   Marx and Engels 1964, p. 70.
57   Marx and Engels 1964, p. 69.
58   Marx and Engels 1964, p. 64.
59   Marx and Engels 1964, p. 70.

3) A Contribution to the Critique of Political Economy

In the *Contribution to the Critique of Political Economy*, Marx presents in a much more complete manner his doctrine regarding the relation between production and consumption. Here Marx specifically discusses the question of the relation between the various moments of the reproduction process as a whole, i.e. between production, in the narrow sense of the word, consumption, and distribution and exchange. Marx devotes a small section of the work, including several very interesting pages, to the specific question of the mutual relation between production and consumption.[60] We shall see that the issue in this section is not only the particular features of the consumption process in capitalist economy but also the broader question of the connection between production and consumption in general. Marx shows that this connection is threefold. We can briefly designate these three forms of connection between production and consumption as 1) their direct identity, 2) their external opposition, and 3) their mutual interpenetration.

First of all, we notice the immediate identity between production and consumption. Every act of production is also directly an act of consumption, both of labour power itself and of means of production (materials, machines, etc.). On the other hand, every act of consumption represents reproduction of human labour power, i.e. is an act of producing labour power. We can regard both acts (production and consumption) as production. The first act involves production of things; the second, production of human labour power. But we are equally justified in regarding both acts as consumption. In the first act, labour power and means of production are consumed; in the second, the means of consumption that are required for the reproduction of labour power. 'Production is thus at the same time consumption, and consumption is at the same time production. Each is simultaneously its opposite'.[61]

However, this direct identity of production and consumption does not in the slightest degree exclude their opposition; we must not close our eyes to the fact that in the one case we have the production of objects that are needed to satisfy human needs, whereas in the other case we have the production of labour power, i.e. the consumption of those same objects that were previously produced. In the first stage, human labour power creates objects in the course of productive activity, whereas in the second stage the objects are consumed by man and reproduce his labour power. Each of these acts excludes the other act. The act of production does not include the consumption of means of subsist-

---

60   Marx 1970, pp. 195–9.
61   Marx 1970, p. 196.

ence, which is necessary for restoration of the expended labour power; on the other hand, in the act of consumption, things are by no means produced but are expended and eliminated. Therefore, together with the immediate identity of production and consumption there is also their immediate opposition, the opposition between production, in the narrow sense of the word, and consumption in the narrow sense, as between two mutually exclusive acts. 'The direct unity, in which production is concurrent with consumption and consumption with production, does not affect their simultaneous duality'.[62]

The opposition between the acts of production and consumption does not mean the absence of any connection between them. They are connected, but only as two external acts that are foreign to one another. An 'intermediary' movement occurs between them; each of these acts mediates the other, i.e. serves as its external means. Indeed, consumption cannot exist without production, for in that case there would be no thing or object that could be consumed. But without consumption, on the other hand, the very act of production would be pointless. True, the object might be produced, but, if it does not enter into consumption, it remains simply a natural thing and not a product; it is only a product when it serves the goals of consumption.

We have established, therefore, the link between production and consumption: 'each appears as a means of the other, as being induced by it', which is the expression of their mutual dependence.[63] This dependence, however, has an external character; it connects two phenomena that are foreign and external to each other. It is a movement in which they are 'brought into mutual relation and appear to be indispensable to each other, but nevertheless remain external to each other'.[64]

Thus far we have considered first the direct identity of production and consumption and then their direct opposition. But, if we look more closely at the connection between them, we discover that they are essentially two acts of one and the same process of reproduction. Each act necessarily passes over into the other and, at the same time, includes the latter within itself (although this inclusion is not direct, as in the first case, but rather occurs as the moment of opposition). If we look at the act of production not as an isolated act but rather as a regular and recurring process, we shall see that its first moment – production in the narrow sense – must necessarily pass into the second moment – consumption in the narrow sense. Production cannot

---

62   Ibid.
63   Marx 1970, p. 198.
64   Ibid.

resume afresh while the product has not been consumed or the labour power, which was expended in the production process, has not been restored. It is only consumption, by restoring labour power, that creates the *possibility* of the production process being repeated; at the same time, it creates the *necessity* for such consumption because disappearance of the product makes further consumption impossible and requires a new production process. Production necessarily causes consumption, which in turn requires the ensuing act of production. Consumption, which necessitates the ensuing act of production, simultaneously guarantees repetition of the act of production. 'Each of them by being carried through creates the other, it creates itself as the other' (Kautsky inserted a question mark here, but there is no doubt that Marx intended to use precisely this terminology).[65] The necessity of this recurrence expresses the fact that production and consumption, each in the narrow sense, represent merely two subordinate moments of the single process of reproduction.

The necessary passage of one moment into the other is complemented by their interpenetration. Each of these moments includes the other within itself, but here the issue is not their direct identity, as in the first case, but rather their mediated identity. Each of the two moments, without ceasing to differ from the other, at the same time contains it within itself. Consumption penetrates production, and production penetrates consumption.

Consumption's penetration of production consists of the fact that in the very act of production the ensuing act of consumption is already anticipated, and the object is produced specifically for the act of consumption. Even before the object is produced, it already exists ideally in the mind of the producer 'as an internal image, a need, a motive, a purpose'.

> Consumption creates the need for *new* production, and therefore provides the conceptual, intrinsically actuating reason for production, which is the pre-condition for production. Consumption furnishes the impulse to produce, and also provides the object which acts as the determining purpose of production.[66]

Production is directed in advance to a determinate end, to creation of a determinate object that serves consumption. Marx comments upon this peculiarity of human labour in *Capital*:

---

65   Ibid.
66   Marx 1970, pp. 196–7.

> A spider conducts operations which resemble those of the weaver, and a bee would put many a human architect to shame by the construction of its honeycomb cells. But what distinguishes the worst architect from the best of bees is that the architect builds the cell in his mind before he constructs it in wax. At the end of every labour process, a result emerges which had already been conceived by the worker at the beginning, hence already existed ideally.[67]

If consumption penetrates and influences production, the reverse is also true – production penetrates consumption and determines its character. The very mode of consumption is determined by the mode of production. 'Production provides not only the object of consumption, it also gives consumption a distinct form, a character, a finish'.[68] The very character of consumption changes in accordance with a change of the production process and of the character of products that result from it.

> The object is not simply an object in general, but a particular object which must be consumed in a particular way, a way determined by production. Hunger is hunger; but the hunger that is satisfied by cooked meat, eaten with knife and fork, differs from hunger that devours raw meat with the help of hands, nails and teeth. Production thus produces not only the object of consumption but also the mode of consumption, not only objectively but also subjectively. Production therefore creates the consumer.[69]

We encounter here the same example of hunger that Marx already referred to in his preliminary works for *The Holy Family*. There, too, he distinguished the human form of hunger from the animal way of satisfying the need for food. But here he emphasises even more clearly the historically variable character even of those needs that are grounded directly in the physical nature of man. Under the influence of change in the production process, the character of the need for food and the mode of satisfying it also change. Insofar as the issue is not consumption in general but a *determinate* mode of consumption (for example, of cooked meat with the aid of a knife and fork), this determinate mode of

---

67   Marx 1976, p. 284.
68   Marx 1970, p. 197.
69   Ibid.

consumption is already the result of a determinate condition of production and, consequently, it includes the latter within itself as its own condition.

Production calls forth not only a determinate character of need and consumption, but also completely new needs. Economists customarily operate with a broad and indeterminate conception of the need for food, clothing, etc. What is actually involved is not only the need for food in general but also the need for concrete items with which the members of a given society and a given class customarily satisfy their need for food. But the need for determinate items is not something given in advance; it results from the adoption of these very same items. In the preliminary notes for *The Holy Family*, Marx already said that the very development of human activity summons forth the development of human senses, that only music awakens man's musical sensitivities. He develops these thoughts further in the work that we are presently analysing. Need itself arises from the object:

> The need felt for the object is induced by the perception of the object. An *objet d'art* creates a public that has artistic taste and is able to enjoy beauty – and the same can be said of any other product. Production accordingly produces not only an object for the subject, but also a subject for the object. Hence, production produces consumption: 1) by providing the material of consumption; 2) by determining the mode of consumption; 3) by creating in the consumer a need for the objects which it first presents as products. It therefore produces the object of consumption, the mode of consumption and the urge to consume.[70]

One can easily see that these commentaries by Marx on production and consumption are arranged in a scheme that reminds us of the dialectical triad. At first, Marx considers the direct unity or identity of production and consumption; then he turns to their opposition in order, at the third stage of the discussion, to show the unity of these opposites, or the interpenetration of production and consumption. At the second stage of the discussion, production and consumption are regarded as phenomena that are external to one another, each serving as external means for the other. At the third stage, production and consumption are already being considered from the viewpoint of the law of the unity and interpenetration of opposites.

It would be a mistake to think that Marx adopts this scheme here out of love for Hegelian schemes. Marx uses the Hegelian schemes only when they

---

70   Marx 1970, p. 197.

reflect actual reality. And there is no denying that the link between production and consumption is actually encountered in all three of the forms that Marx discusses: as a direct identity of production and consumption, as an external interaction, and as an internal unity and interpenetration.

Even more interesting is the fact that, in the triad we have been considering, Marx endeavoured not only to reflect actual reality but also to show that the thinking of economists, which was submerged in the analysis of capitalist reality, dwelt first on the one and then on the other member of this triad. He shows that the direct identity of production and consumption attracted the attention of economists, who considered it in their investigations of productive labour and productive consumption.[71] The external interaction also, in Marx words, attracted economists' attention: 'There is no consumption without production, and no production without consumption. This proposition appears in various forms in political economy'.[72] Finally, Marx observes that the third type of connection between production and consumption, namely, their interpenetration, likewise did not escape the view of economists: 'The last kind of identity, which is defined in point 3, has been variously interpreted by economists when discussing the relation of demand and supply, of objects and needs, of needs created by society and natural needs'.[73] But, whereas economists before Marx restricted themselves to separate remarks concerning the connection between production and consumption and usually saw it in a one-sided manner, with Marx we see in several pages of the *Contribution to the Critique of Political Economy* a synthetic understanding of how production and consumption are connected as moments of the single process of reproduction.

Starting from these considerations, Marx investigates not only the unity of production and consumption but also their differences and opposition.

> The conclusion which follows from this is not that production, distribution, exchange and consumption are identical, but that they are links of a single whole, different aspects of one unit. Production is the decisive phase, both with regard to the contradictory aspects of production and with regard to the other phases. The process always starts afresh with production.[74]

---

71   Marx 1970, p. 195.
72   Marx 1970, p. 198.
73   Marx 1970, p. 190.
74   Marx 1970, pp. 204–5.

The unity of production and consumption does not exclude the fact that the driving moment of the entire process of reproduction is precisely production, not consumption. 'That exchange and consumption cannot be the decisive elements is obvious'.[75] Production is the 'actual point of departure' and thus the decisive moment.

> Consumption, as a necessity and as a need, is itself an intrinsic aspect of productive activity; the latter, however, is the point where realisation begins and is therefore also the decisive phase in which the entire process repeats itself from the beginning. An individual produces an object and, by consuming it, returns again to the point of departure: he returns, however, as a productive individual and as an individual who reproduces himself. Consumption is thus a moment of production.[76]

This doctrine of the primacy of production over consumption is the conclusion that must follow from the entire preceding exposition of Marx's teaching on consumption. Consumption is the passive reception of things that are created by human labour; the latter is the active creative moment and, precisely because of its active character, the driving moment of the whole of social life. It is not only the satisfaction of needs that is dependent upon production; need itself, as we have already seen above, expresses a determinate active manifestation of human power and a perception of the external things that result from this creative activity. Thus, the whole of social life is regarded by Marx as a single process of vital human activity, as the process of reproduction of human life, in which consumption is one of the intermediary moments.

We have presented a detailed exposition of Marx's reasoning in the *Contribution to the Critique of Political Economy*. In this work, Marx summarised his teaching on the connection between production and consumption as it occurs in any kind of economic formation. Most of the reasoning that Marx presents here is equally applicable both to a capitalist and to a feudal economy, and even to the economy of a single subject. 'Production and consumption, if considered as activities of one subject or of single individuals, appear in any case as moments of one process whose actual point of departure is production, which is accordingly the decisive factor'.[77] Marx shows here that the stated laws of the

---

75 Marx 1970, p. 205.
76 Marx 1970, p. 199.
77 Ibid.

connection between production and consumption become much more complex when it is a case not of a separate individual but of an entire society.

> But in society, the relation of the producer to the product after its completion is purely extrinsic, and the return of the product to the subject depends on his relations to other individuals. The product does not immediately come into his possession. Its immediate appropriation, moreover, is not his aim, if he produces within society. *Distribution*, which on the basis of social laws determines the individual's share in the world of products, intervenes between the producer and the products, i.e., between production and consumption.[78]

If, in any social formation, the connection between production and consumption is complicated by the fact that distribution stands between them, it acquires an especially complex form in capitalist society. Here any understanding of this connection becomes impossible apart from an analysis of exchange and distribution, and an analysis of the entire class structure of capitalist society.

II *Production and Consumption in a Commodity-Capitalist Economy*

In commodity-capitalist society, the connection between production and consumption becomes considerably more complex. With commodity economy in general, the intermediate position between production and consumption is taken by *exchange*: the commodity must pass through the sphere of exchange in order to reach the sphere of consumption. Insofar as capitalist economy is involved, rather than just commodity economy, the decisive influence on the process of consumption becomes the specific class structure of capitalist society, with its corresponding *distribution* of incomes between the different social classes. We shall consider these complex forms of the connection between production and consumption in the second and third sections of this chapter. In the first section, we provide a summary of Marx's observations concerning the transition from natural economy to commodity-capitalist economy, with its gradual increase of the role of exchange-value as the motivating purpose of the production process.

---

78 Ibid.

1)   Use-Value and Exchange-Value as the Motivating Purpose of the Production Process

In commodity economy, the product becomes a use-value for its owner only through its alienation. This means that the commodity producer is directly interested not in his product's qualities as a use-value, but rather in the magnitude of its exchange-value. This is the basis for the general distinction between two types of economy: in certain social formations the use-value of the product is of primary significance, while in others it is the exchange-value. The most vivid example of the former economy is the purely natural economy of primitive peoples, which has no exchange at all; the clearest example of the second sort of economy is developed capitalist production. We often encounter in Marx the distinction between these two types of economy, but we also find him pointing to a whole series of intermediate types of economy that represent the gradual transition from a purely natural to a capitalist economy.

In a purely natural economy, use-value prevails exclusively; for instance, the entire production process of the patriarchal family has nothing to do with exchange and aims directly at satisfying the needs of its members. The first breach in this natural economy comes with the appearance of some product or other in a quantity that surpasses the immediate needs of the given economy.[79] On the basis of a geographic division of labour, various products are produced by different communities in quantities that exceed the needs of members of a particular community. On this basis arises the first exchange between different communities; and a given product, being a direct use-value for members of the community, is also partially transformed into a commodity for external exchange. But, since the given product is produced mainly for their own consumption, it is not yet a commodity prior to the act of exchange and only becomes such in the act of exchange itself.[80] We can characterise this stage of exchange as the exchange of surplus production, in which the product only begins to be transformed into a commodity and becomes such only in the actual exchange act.

The next stage of exchange starts from the moment when some of the products begin to be produced especially for exchange.

> The need for others' objects of utility gradually establishes itself. The constant repetition of exchange makes it a normal social process. In the course of time, therefore, at least some part of the products of labour

---

79   Marx 1976, p. 182.
80   Marx 1976, p. 181.

must be produced intentionally for the purpose of exchange. From that moment the distinction between the usefulness of things for direct consumption and their usefulness in exchange becomes firmly established. Their use-value becomes distinguished from their exchange-value.[81]

So long as exchange still has the character of natural exchange, i.e. the direct exchange of products, the separation of exchange-value from use-value is still concealed; the product, in its natural form, serves simultaneously as both use-value and exchange-value. 'The articles exchanged do not acquire a value-form independent of their own use-value, or of the individual needs of the exchangers'.[82] The character of the commodity, as exchange-value, does not become fully developed since the commodity still does not possess the ability to be exchanged for any other product of social labour. The exchange-value of the commodity acquires an independent form only with the appearance of money and its separation from the entire world of other commodities.

While the production of a surplus product brought the appearance of exchange, the further development of exchange, in turn, 'promotes the generation of a surplus product designed to go into exchange, so as to increase the consumption or the hoards of the producers (which we take here to mean the owners of the products). It thus gives production a character oriented more and more towards exchange-value'.[83]

> Trade naturally reacts back to a greater or lesser extent on the communities between which it is pursued; it subjects production more and more to exchange-value, by making consumption and satisfaction more dependent on sale than on the direct use of the product. In this way it dissolves the old relationships. It increases monetary circulation. It no longer just takes hold of surplus production, but gradually gobbles up production itself and makes entire branches of production dependent on it. This solvent effect, however, depends very much on the nature of the community of producers.[84]

In societies where conditions did not exist for the development of capitalism, a significantly developed monetary exchange existed side by side with various forms of natural economy (the patriarchal family, slave-owning economy,

---

81 Marx 1976, p. 182.
82 Ibid.
83 Marx 1992, p. 443.
84 Marx 1992, p. 448.

the feudal manor). Thus the development of trade, on the one hand, increasingly imparted to the economy the character of production whose purpose was exchange-value, yet the primary goal of the economy still remained the production of use-value. 'The circulation of money and commodities can serve spheres of production with the most diverse organisation, which in their internal structure are still oriented principally to the production of use-values'.[85]

We have outlined several stages in the development of production and exchange, with the gradual strengthening of the role of exchange-value: a purely natural economy, the occasional exchange of surpluses, production of a part of the output especially for exchange, and the gradual increase of that part at the expense of the part intended for direct consumption. It can be said that a struggle occurs in these stages of development between use-value and exchange-value for the role of driving purpose or impelling motive of the production process. They fulfil this role simultaneously, with gradual displacement of the role of use-value and gradual strengthening of the role of exchange-value. This process is only finally completed in capitalist economy.

> The extent to which production goes into trade and passes through the hands of merchants depends on the mode of production, reaching a maximum with the full development of capitalist production, where the product is produced simply as a commodity and not at all as a direct means of subsistence.[86]

It is only with fully developed capitalist production that we have the complete dominance of exchange-value. However, we can theoretically imagine this dominance of exchange-value also in the conditions of simple commodity economy, assuming that the latter is the prevalent type of economy and has squeezed out the remnants of natural production. If we imagine a society of simple commodity producers (handicraftsmen, for instance), who produce their entire product for sale, we find that the direct purpose of production is already exchange-value, not use-value. The immediate objective of the simple commodity producers consists of acquiring, through sale of their products, the greatest possible sum of exchange-value. However, even if use-value has already lost the role of motivating purpose for production, it still continues to fulfil this role indirectly by means of exchange-value (money). Indeed, in the society that we are assuming, the handicraftsman spends the sum of money

---

85   Marx 1992, p. 445.
86   Marx 1992, pp. 442–3.

received from sale of the product on the purchase of items that serve to satisfy his needs (together, of course, with necessary means of production). Here there is commodity circulation according to the formula C–M–C; the money, in this case, serves the handicraftsman only as a means to acquire the sum of items of consumption that he requires. Hence, the dual position that a simple commodity economy occupies. It is distinguished from natural economy by the dominance of exchange-value, which is the motivating purpose of the production process itself. But, by comparison with capitalist economy, it is still characterised by production to satisfy the personal needs of the producers themselves (not directly, it is true, but rather indirectly through the medium of money). It is precisely from this point of view that Marx clearly counterposes two forms of circulation, C–M–C and M–C–M:

> The path C–M–C proceeds from the extreme constituted by one commodity, and ends with the extreme constituted by another, which falls out of circulation and into consumption. Consumption, the satisfaction of needs, in short use-value, is therefore its final goal. The path M–C–M, however, proceeds from the extreme of money and finally returns to that same extreme. Its driving and motivating force, its determining purpose, is therefore exchange-value.[87]

> The repetition or renewal of the act of selling in order to buy finds its measure and its goal (as does the process itself) in a final purpose which lies outside it, namely consumption, the satisfaction of definite needs.[88]

> The simple circulation of commodities – selling in order to buy – is a means to a final goal which lies outside circulation, namely the appropriation of use-values, the satisfaction of needs. As against this, the circulation of money as capital is an end in itself, for the valorisation of value takes place only within this constantly renewed movement ... Use-values must therefore never be treated as the immediate aim of the capitalist.[89]

It may appear, at first sight, that Marx contradicts himself here. He previously said that the development of commerce increasingly gives production the character of production with the goal of exchange-value. It would seem

---

87   Marx 1976, p. 250.
88   Marx 1976, p. 252.
89   Marx 1976, pp. 253–4.

that, with the complete prevalence of simple commodity economy, the sole purpose of production is already exchange-value, not consumption, yet Marx declares that the final goal of the circuit C–M–C is use-value. The seeming contradiction vanishes if we recall that a long process of historical development is involved, which begins with purely natural economy and ends with developed capitalism. This protracted process of historical development is characterised by exchange-value gradually squeezing out use-value as the motive and purpose of production. It is completely understandable, therefore, that any given stage, by comparison with the previous one, reveals the increasing prevalence of exchange-value while at the same time, when compared to the subsequent stage of development, it reveals an insufficient ascendancy of exchange-value. That is particularly the case with the intermediate place occupied by simple commodity economy. In the latter, the goal of production is *immediately* exchange-value alone, although *ultimately*, or in the final analysis, the goal of production is to satisfy the personal needs of the producer himself. Thus, in all three of the excerpts that we have just cited, Marx says that use-value is the '*final*' (but not the immediate) goal of the circuit C–M–C.

Marx draws a sharp distinction between the two types of circulation, C–M–C and M–C–M. The difference between simple commodity economy and capitalist economy is expressed by the difference between these two forms of circulation. Faithful to the dialectical method, which enjoins us to look for gradual transitions between opposing forms of phenomena, in this case too Marx endeavours to follow exactly the transitional forms between the two circuits. Marx specifies these transitional forms when investigating the functions of money as a hoard and as means of payment. Within the limits of commodity circulation C–M–C itself, forms emerge that prepare the transition to the circuit M–C–M. In the circuit C–M–C, sale occurs in order that the money received may be used to acquire necessary means of consumption. However, if the commodity producer retains the money acquired through sale in the form of a hoard, in that case commodities are sold 'not in order to buy commodities, but in order to replace their commodity-form by their money-form. Instead of being merely a way of mediating the metabolic process [*Stoffwechsel*], this change of form becomes an end in itself'.[90] Or, as Marx says in the *Critique of Political Economy*, 'Exchange-value, which was merely a form, is turned into the content of the movement'; that is to say, it fulfils, in rudimentary form, the role that it fulfils in a more developed manner in the circuit M–C–M. Whereas the final goal of the circuit C–M–C is to satisfy the personal needs

---

90   Marx 1976, pp. 227–8.

of the producer, the withholding of money in the form of a hoard already requires that the commodity producer refrain from satisfying his personal needs.[91]

When investigating the function of money as means of payment, Marx notes another transitional form between the two circuits of commodity circulation. If the commodity producer sells his product in order, with the money acquired, to retire a monetary obligation entered into previously, then use-value has already ceased to be the final purpose of his sale.

> The money no longer mediates the process. It brings it to an end by emerging independently, as the absolute form of existence of exchange-value, in other words the universal commodity. The seller turned his commodity into money in order to satisfy some need; the hoarder in order to preserve the monetary form of his commodity, and the indebted purchaser in order to be able to pay. If he does not pay, his goods will be sold compulsorily. The value-form of the commodity, money, has now become the self-sufficient purpose of the sale, owing to a social necessity springing from the conditions of the process of circulation itself.[92]

In this case, sale of the commodity no longer has the satisfaction of needs and of the producer's personal inclinations as its final goal.

In analysing the functions of money as a hoard and as means of payment, we have seen the further marginalisation of use-value as the final goal of commodity production and exchange, a process that finally reaches completion, as we noted earlier, in the circuit M–C–M.

> The circuit of money capital is thus the most one-sided, hence most striking and characteristic form of appearance of the circuit of industrial capital, in which its aim and driving motive – the valorisation of value, money-making and accumulation – appears in a form that leaps to the eye ...[93]

This circuit expresses the fact that exchange-value, not use-value, is the end in itself that determines the movement; and it 'expresses money-making, the driving motive of capitalist production, most palpably. The production process

---

91 Marx 1976, p. 231.
92 Marx 1976, p. 234.
93 Marx 1978, p. 140.

appears simply as an unavoidable middle term, a necessary evil for the purpose of money-making'.[94]

Whereas in simple commodity economy the producer endeavoured, by selling his product, to receive a determinate sum only in order to use it to satisfy his personal needs, the opposite occurs in capitalist economy; the production of use-value serves merely as a means to extract profit for the expansion of capital.

> Use-value is certainly not *la chose qu'on aime pour lui-même* in the production of commodities. Use-values are produced by capitalists only because and in so far as they form the material substratum of exchange-value, are the bearers of exchange-value.[95]

The striving for unlimited enrichment also characterised the accumulator of a hoard, but in the case of the simple commodity producer, who does not exploit another person's labour, this could only occur to a limited extent. This pursuit could only find a broad sphere of operation in a society founded upon class antagonism and exploitation of the surplus-labour of a significant number of people.[96]

---

94   Marx 1978, p. 137.
95   Marx 1976, p. 293.
96   As we know, capital did not invent surplus-value; the exploitation of surplus-value also existed earlier, but it is only with the dominance of commodity production that it assumed the specific character of the quest for unlimited expansion of exchange-value. Marx shows how the character of the exploitation of surplus-value changed as the transition occurred from natural to commodity economy. 'It is however clear that in any economic formation of society where the use-value rather than the exchange-value of the product predominates, surplus-labour will be restricted by a more or less confined set of needs, and that no boundless thirst for surplus-labour will arise from the character of production itself' [Marx 1976, p. 345]. The development of money economy and of exchange alters the character of the exploitation of surplus-labour. In the conditions of a slave economy, it leads to 'the transformation of a patriarchal slave system oriented towards the production of the direct means of subsistence into one oriented towards the production of surplus-value' [Marx 1992, pp. 449–50]. The exploitation of slave labour takes on especially cruel forms when it involves the extraction of exchange-value in its autonomous, money form, namely, in the production of gold and silver [Marx 1976, p. 345]. In conditions of feudal economy, the possibility of selling a commodity on the market caused the feudal lord to seek more corvée labour from the peasants under his control [Marx 1976, p. 346]. Finally, in capitalist economy the thirst for surplus-labour appears in the attempt to extend the working day indefinitely.

Thus capitalist economy differs markedly from that 'commodity production, whose purpose is the existence of the producers'.[97] That is why Marx always vehemently protests against vulgar political economy, which conceives the capitalist production process as

> the simple production of commodities, use-values destined for consumption of some kind or other, which the capitalist produced only in order to replace them with commodities of a different use-value, or to exchange them with these, as vulgar economics incorrectly puts it.[98]

In capitalist society, use-value no longer plays the role of indirect purpose of production as it did in simple commodity economy.

In capitalist economy, exchange-value has overwhelming significance, not use-value. However, even within the limits of capitalist economy itself, in order to mark all the dialectical transitions between different stages of the process, Marx notes the gradually strengthening role of exchange-value at the expense of use-value. In this connection, Marx draws a distinction between the simple reproduction of capital and expanded reproduction. With simple reproduction, the entire mass of surplus value is spent to satisfy the personal needs of the class of capitalists. Although the purpose of the production process is expansion of surplus value, i.e. conversion of the sum M into (M+m), the whole of the extracted sum of surplus value (m) is expended only on satisfying the personal needs of the capitalists. This is explained by the following statement from Marx:

> Simple reproduction is oriented by nature to consumption as its aim. Even though the squeezing out of surplus-value appears as the driving motive of the individual capitalist, this surplus-value – no matter what its proportionate size – can be used here, in the last analysis, only for his individual consumption.[99]

With the will to do so, a captious critic might see a contradiction in Marx's remark even here. Previously Marx argued that the aim of capitalist economy, as distinct from simple commodity economy, is the expansion of exchange-value, yet now he says that the aim of simple reproduction of capital is con-

---

97 Marx 1978, p. 155.
98 Marx 1978, p. 149.
99 Marx 1978, p. 487.

sumption. But, in this case too, the apparent contradiction vanishes with a proper understanding of the dialectical movement of Marx's thought. By comparison with simple commodity economy, the simple reproduction of capital signifies an increase in the role of exchange-value at the expense of use-value. With the transition from simple to expanded reproduction, we observe a further increase in the role of exchange-value.

The remarks that we have cited from Marx show that, for capitalists, the motive of personal consumption, while it does not play the predominant role in capitalist production, still retains a certain importance. 'In so far as simple reproduction is also part of any annual reproduction on an expanded scale, and the major part at that, this motive remains alongside the motive of enrichment as such and in opposition to it'.[100] While the motive of personal consumption persists for the capitalists, however, it still gives way gradually to the motive of enrichment. In other words, simple reproduction, as such, contradicts the very essence of capitalist economy and necessarily passes over into expanded reproduction; and it is only with the latter that the scale of personal consumption by the capitalists steadily diminishes relative to the accumulated part of surplus value. Only expanded reproduction represents the type of economy in which the predominance of exchange-value acquires full force.

As we see, Marx describes a complex picture of the gradually increasing role of exchange-value at the expense of use-value. We can note the following stages in this lengthy historical process:

1) *Purely natural* economy, characterised by the complete rule of use-value.
2) The incidental exchange of *surplus* products. The motivating purpose of production is still use-value, and exchange-value is only beginning to emerge.
3) *Part* of the product is produced *intentionally for exchange*; the goal of production is simultaneously use-value and exchange-value. The relative force of each depends upon the relative volume of production that is intended for personal use and production that is intended for the market.
4) *Simple commodity economy*, in which all products are produced for sale. The immediate motive for production is exchange-value, but indirectly its purpose is to satisfy the personal needs of the commodity producers.
5) *Transitional* forms from simple commodity economy to capitalist economy (the hoard and means of payment). Sale of the product no longer has the goal of satisfying the personal needs of the commodity producers.

---

100   Ibid.

6) *Capitalist* economy, in the form of *simple* reproduction. The goal of production is the increase of exchange-value, or the extraction of surplus value, but the resulting sum of surplus value is spent entirely on satisfying the personal needs of the capitalist.
7) *Capitalist* economy, in the form of *expanded* reproduction, where the resulting surplus value is accumulated as capital while only a small and steadily diminishing part of it is spent on satisfying the personal needs of the capitalist.

2)   The Contradiction between Use-Value and Exchange-Value[101]

In the first chapter, we examined the link between production and consumption in the general form that it assumes in any economic formation. Now we turn to investigate the connection between production and consumption in commodity economy, and we begin the analysis with the particular features of simple commodity economy, or a society of simple commodity producers. Its characteristic feature is the separation of production from consumption – a separation that develops together with the development of commodity economy itself. In natural economy, the product is a use-value for the producer himself; at a further stage of development, the products that are produced in excess, and therefore are not required for satisfying the needs of their owner, enter into exchange. The nucleus of the value form appears; the process of transforming use-values into commodities begins. If exchange still has a natural character, the exchanging products are still directly use-values, although neither of them is a use-value for its owner. Ultimately, when the products are produced specifically for sale in an unknown market, the final separation of exchange-value from use-value occurs. All the products being produced are now commodities for sale, not for satisfying the needs of the producers themselves. On the other hand, the producer now acquires all the products that he needs with the help of exchange. The product becomes a commodity, which has a dual nature – as use-value and as exchange-value.

Marx analyses this dual nature of the commodity in the opening pages of the *Critique of Political Economy* and of *Capital*. By way of analysis, Marx dissects the single commodity into its two sides, each of which he considers separately. On the first two pages, he briefly considers the commodity's use-value, in order subsequently to undertake a detailed analysis of the commodity's other

---

[101] Here and in what follows we use the term 'exchange-value' to mean the same as the term 'value'. [Readers will note that in this section Rubin briefly repeats parts of the argument that have gone before. He gives no reason, but presumably he resumed writing at a later date].

side, its value. Through an *analytical* approach, Marx here examines the *difference* between the two aspects of the commodity. But following this analytical dissection of the commodity, Marx turns to a synthetic investigation of the actual exchange process, wherein commodities appear simultaneously as both use-values and exchange-values. Marx emphasises, in both the *Critique* and in *Capital*, the need to move from an isolated examination of the commodity's separate aspects to a synthetic examination of the commodity's movement as a whole. 'So far two aspects of the commodity – use-value and exchange-value – have been examined, but each one separately. The commodity, however, is the direct *unity* of use-value and exchange-value'.[102] Once we move from an isolated examination of use-value and exchange-value to the conditions of their joint existence within a single commodity, we come to the question of the contradiction between value and use-value.

> The commodity is *immediate unity of use-value and exchange-value*, i.e., of two opposite moments. It is, therefore, an immediate *contradiction*. This contradiction must develop as soon as the commodity is not, as it has been so far, analytically considered once under the angle of use-value, once under the angle of exchange-value, but as soon as it is placed as a whole into an actual relation with other commodities. The *actual* relation of commodities with each other, however, is their *exchange process*.[103]

From the difference between use-value and exchange-value, Marx turns to their contradiction (within unity, i.e. the commodity). To understand Marx's teaching on the contradiction between use-value and exchange-value presents major difficulties, and this has caused particularly sharp attacks from his critics, who claim that Marx becomes involved here in metaphysical discussions that have no connection with reality. In fact, this teaching from Marx reflects the real processes of commodity economy. The problem that Marx faced here can be expressed as follows: To what extent is there a change in the nature of use-value and exchange-value when they exist jointly within a single commodity? Whereas to this point the isolated study of these two aspects of the commodity has revealed to us the nature of each of them, now the question arises as to the possibility of simultaneous co-existence, within the commodity, of both of these aspects in the form that we found when we considered them in isolation. And Marx comes to the conclusion that the joint existence of these two aspects

---

102   Marx 1970, p. 41.
103   Marx 1867, p. 44.

within the commodity makes a specific impression upon each of them, such that the presence of each of these aspects limits the other, as it were, and prevents it from appearing directly with the whole range of determinations that we saw when we considered each of them in isolation.

Marx begins his discussion with use-value. We know that every commodity is, first of all, a use-value. But if we recall that the commodity is also an exchange-value, we will see that this latter aspect limits its character as a use-value and does not allow it to appear directly in the role of use-value. Actually, once the product has been produced for sale it is no longer directly a use-value for its owner. At the same time, however, it is also not yet a direct use-value for others because they do not yet possess it. It is only by moving from one hand to another, i.e. by means of exchange, that the commodity can become a use-value for other people and thus also for its owner, for it is only by way of exchanging his product that the latter can acquire other products that he requires in order to satisfy his needs.

> The commodity *is* a use-value, wheat, linen, a diamond, machinery, etc., but as a commodity it is simultaneously *not* a use-value. It would not be a commodity if it were a use-value for its owner, that is, a direct means for the satisfaction of his own needs ... The commodity therefore *has* still to *become* [*werden*] a use-value, in the first place a use-value for others ... Thus the use-values of commodities *become* [*werden*] use-values by a mutual exchange of places: they pass from the hands of those for whom they were means of exchange into the hands of those for whom they serve as consumer goods ... Hence, only by being realised as exchange-values can they be realised as use-values.[104]

This brings us to the following conclusion. The fact that the commodity is an exchange-value precludes it from being a direct use-value either for its owner or for other people. We have two contradictory claims: 1) the commodity *is* a use-value, and 2) the commodity *is not* directly a use-value. There is only one way out of this contradiction: the commodity must become a use-value. It is a use-value, but not directly, only in a roundabout way through exchange, in which it realises its use-value. Exchange-value appears here as the external means enabling the commodity to become a use-value.

If realisation of the commodity's exchange-value is the condition for realising its use-value, there is also a reverse relation between these two sides of the

---

104 Marx 1970, pp. 42–3.

commodity: in order to realise its exchange-value, the commodity must display and prove its use-value. Whereas we previously concluded that the commodity's character as exchange-value prevents it from appearing directly in the role of use-value, now we are persuaded that the reverse also holds true: the commodity's character as use-value does not allow it to appear directly in the role of exchange-value. As exchange-value, the commodity is an embodiment of directly social labour-time in the sense that 'it can freely take the place of a definite quantity of any other commodity, irrespective of whether or not it constitutes a use-value for the owner of the other commodity'.[105] This characteristic is what distinguishes the exchange-value of the commodity so long as we regard it in isolation. But if we remember that the commodity is also a use-value, this latter fact already prevents the commodity from directly manifesting its inherent character as exchange-value. The commodity cannot yet freely replace any other product of social labour, for 'alienation of a commodity as a use-value is only possible to the person for whom it is a use-value, i.e., an object satisfying particular needs'.[106] Before it can be replaced with any other product, at the commodity owner's discretion, the given commodity must be brought 'into contact with the particular need of which it is the object'.[107] In other words, prior to its alienation as use-value, the commodity is *'not* immediately exchange-value, but has still to *become* [*werden*] exchange-value'.[108] Here we again have two contradictory assertions: 1) the commodity *is* exchange-value; 2) the commodity *is not* directly exchange-value. With this contradiction, too, there can be only one way out: the commodity must still *become* exchange-value precisely through the roundabout way in which it discloses its use-value to a particular person, i.e. through the roundabout route of exchange. The realisation of use-value appears here as an external means for realising its exchange-value. 'A commodity can only therefore become a use-value if it is realised as an exchange-value, while it can only be realised as an exchange-value if it is alienated and functions as a use-value'.[109]

---

105   Marx 1970, p. 44.
106   Marx 1970, p. 43.
107   Ibid.
108   Ibid.
109   Ibid. It is easy to see here an external resemblance between Marx's discussion and Hegel's schemes at the beginning of his *Logic*. While Hegel considers first 'being' and then 'nothingness', in order subsequently to reconcile them in 'becoming', Marx follows the same scheme: first he considers both use-value and exchange-value as being; then comes the contradiction of their being, followed by exploration of their becoming, i.e. the process of the actual movement of commodities in exchange. The similarity with Hegel's schemes

It is only through the exchange process that the actual realisation of the commodity's dual nature occurs, i.e. its exchange-value and its use-value. Prior to the exchange process, the joint existence within the commodity of these two contradictory sides makes impossible the direct manifestation of either of them in all the richness of its determinations; each side, as it were, is limited by the presence of the other and, for that reason, acquires a different character, which we could not have revealed by taking them in isolation but which we must now study. Let us consider the novelty that appears in the nature of each of these aspects of the commodity thanks to the presence within it of the other aspect.

First, let us briefly examine the changes that exchange-value undergoes due to being connected with the concrete use-value of the commodity. As use-value, the commodity must pass to precisely the person who requires it in order to satisfy his needs, and this means that it still does not possess a directly social character and cannot yet be exchanged for any other product at the discretion of its owner. The social nature of value is still limited and constrained, as it were, by the fact that it is connected with the concrete natural form of the commodity. The value still has a potential character and will only be fully realised when the commodity casts off its given concrete and natural form, i.e. when it is converted into money. Hence the need for division of the commodity into the commodity and money, or, as Marx sometimes puts it, the division of value into the commodity form and the money form of value. It is only in the latter that the directly social nature of value finds full realisation. In the former, this social nature of value is still confined due to the presence within the commodity of its other side, i.e. concrete use-value. The presence of use-value has an effect upon the character of exchange-value, converting the latter into a potential, or a commodity whose value still needs to be realised.

On the other hand, the presence of exchange-value leaves its mark on the character of the commodity's use-value. In the first pages of the *Critique* and of *Capital*, use-value is considered in isolation from exchange-value, i.e. as the ability to satisfy a human need, which inheres in the product completely apart from one or another form of economy. Use-value is considered in terms of its indifference to the social form of the product. 'Whatever its social form may be, wealth always consists of use-values, which in the first instance are not

---

can also be noted at another point: use-value and exchange-value are initially regarded as isolated determinations; then they enter into an external connection, and each is regarded as the external means for realisation of the other. Next comes the interpenetration of these opposites when they adopt the form of the commodity and of money.

affected by this form'.[110] But use-value retains this indifference only so long as we regard it in isolation from exchange-value. When we turn to examine the use-value of a *commodity*, we see that the presence of exchange-value also leaves its mark upon use-value. Insofar as we are speaking of a commodity, its use-value has a special character by comparison, for example, with a product of feudal society. Here the issue is not one of change in the natural form of the product but rather of change in the social nature of use-value itself. The relation of the product as use-value to the producer and consumer becomes a different one in commodity economy by comparison with other forms of economy. Here the product is no longer a use-value for the producer; rather it is produced as a use-value in order to satisfy the needs of other persons, i.e. it is produced for sale. Now the producer 'must not only produce-use-values, but use-values for others, social use-values'.[111] This 'social use-value' is also the modified form that use-value only acquires in commodity economy under the influence of exchange-value. The joint existence within the commodity of exchange-value and use-value alters the very character of the latter.

These words from Marx concerning 'social use-value' are not always correctly understood. Often this term is used in the sense of any use-value that is produced for the needs of members of a social group. From this point of view, the term social use-value can be applied both to a product that the medieval peasant produced for the needs of the manor and to the product that will be produced in a socialist commune. But with this expansive understanding of the term its whole specificity is eliminated. Marx had in mind not any use-value that is produced for a society with any social form of economy, but rather the use-value of the *commodity*. This is why Engels considered it necessary to add the following observation to the words that we have cited from Marx:

> The medieval peasant produced a corn-rent for the feudal lord and a corn-tithe for the priest; but neither the corn-rent nor the corn-tithe became commodities simply by being produced for others. In order to become a commodity, the product must be transferred to the other person, for whom it serves as a use-value, *through the medium of exchange*.[112]

Engels explains that when Marx speaks of social use-value he has in mind *the use-value of a commodity*, which passes from producer to consumer by way

---

110 Marx 1970, pp. 27–8.
111 Marx 1976, p. 131.
112 Ibid.

of exchange. This necessary passage through the sphere of exchange leaves a certain mark upon the commodity not merely in the sense that the latter appears as exchange-value; it also leaves a certain mark upon the other aspect of the commodity, upon its use-value. The product's use-value, because of its connection with its exchange-value, acquires a special social character or 'social distinction'. 'As a useful thing the commodity has social determinacy insofar as it is a use-value for others but not for its owner, i.e., insofar as it satisfies social needs'.[113]

3) Production and Consumption in Capitalist Society

Marx has traced economic development, which was accompanied by gradual marginalisation of use-value as the motivating goal of production and by gradual increase of the role of exchange-value. At the same time, this change also meant an altered relation between production and consumption. In natural economy, for instance in the patriarchal family, production was aimed directly at satisfying members' needs. Such an immediate connection between production and consumption exists in every organised economy, for example, in a socialist commune. Marx and Engels frequently pointed out that the distinguishing feature of a socialist commune is the adjustment of production to the volume of social needs that have to be satisfied and, in one manner or another, are calculated in advance.[114]

With the emergence and development of exchange, as we know, the product is not produced directly for satisfaction of needs but for sale. So long, however, as it is a matter of simple commodity economy, for instance handicrafts, production occurs to fulfil a specific order or for a very local market. In such case the volume of demand, or of the social needs to be satisfied, is approximately known in advance and has a determining effect on the volume of production. At the same time, the volume of production is determined by the volume of the craftsman's own customary needs, which have to be met after he has sold the articles he makes. It is only in developed capitalist production that use-value finally ceases to be the motivating goal of the production process. The capitalist strives to acquire profit, and the entire production process is subordinate to this purpose. Production of the product, as a use-value, is not the capitalist's objective, and the same also applies to the worker: 'The product of his activity, therefore, is not the aim of his activity. What he produces for himself is not the silk that he weaves, not the gold that he draws up the mining shaft, not

---

113   Marx 1867, p. 22.
114   Marx 1992, p. 370; see also Marx 1977, pp. 70–1.

the palace that he builds'.¹¹⁵ In capitalist society, there is further separation of production from consumption, of the producer from the consumer.

Along with the separation of production from consumption, a certain necessary connection is preserved between them. As we already clarified in the first chapter, production and consumption are mutually connected and mutually determined. How does this connection occur in capitalist society? This connection occurs through *demand*. Since the needs of society's members are not calculated in advance and cannot themselves govern production, social needs exert an influence upon the production process only indirectly, through effective demand. If the producer himself does not adopt the goal of satisfying social needs, he must still take them into account because the commodity must be sold to the consumer. Social need, in the form of effective demand, has an effect upon the direction of the production process: the producer must fabricate only those products for which there is a demand. But we must remember, on the other hand, that social need can only have such effect provided that it takes the form of effective demand, i.e. if the consumer is able to pay the necessary (money) equivalent, whose value is equal to the value of the product he is purchasing. Marx points out more than once that when we speak of correspondence between production and needs in capitalist society, the issue is not one of 'absolute' needs or of 'genuine' social needs, but only of solvent social need represented in the market, i.e., the sum of social demand.¹¹⁶

This solvent social need, or social demand, has a determinate character. Production of the given product must not only satisfy social need in general but also correspond to the specific volume of this social need, i.e. to the determinate sum of social demand for the given product. The use-value of a certain volume of particular products 'depends on its adequacy to the quantitatively specific social need for each particular kind of product and therefore on the proportional division of the labour between these various spheres of production in accordance with these social needs, which are quantitatively circumscribed'.¹¹⁷ Social need, or social demand, has a definite magnitude, and it is precisely through this quantitative specificity that it has an influence upon the direction of the production process.

Are we not introducing a dualism into our economic theory by recognising this effect of demand upon the character of the production process? Are we not abandoning the monistic principle of the primacy of production over con-

---

115 Marx 2006, p. 19.
116 Marx 1992, pp. 289–90.
117 Marx 1992, p. 774.

sumption? It is true that in an organised community we also saw an immediate and direct influence of the character of consumption upon the character of production, but in that case production and consumption were the actions of a single production process: consumption was merely a moment of the production process as a whole, and it is perfectly understandable that there was interaction between the individual moments of the latter. In capitalist economy, production has separated off from consumption, and social needs have taken the form of effective demand, which, operating from the side as it were, as a kind of external force, affect the production process. Let us remember, however, that while production is externally separated from consumption this fact does not, even in capitalist economy, eliminate their necessary internal connection. Social needs, having assumed the form of social demand, change and develop according to change in the production process itself. And in capitalist society, production in the narrow sense and consumption are only particular elements of the single process of production. In the first place, the necessary connection between them is preserved, even if only through a long series of intermediate links, through social demand. We must, accordingly, examine this social demand and demonstrate that in its movement it is conditioned by the movement of the production process.

It appears at first sight that demand is determined by the needs and arbitrary will of separate individuals, appearing in the role of consumers. But as early as *The Poverty of Philosophy* Marx noted the incorrectness of such a view of demand:

> The consumer is no freer than the producer. His estimation depends on his means and his needs. Both of these are determined by his social position, which itself depends on the whole social organization. True, the worker who buys potatoes and the kept woman who buys lace both follow their respective estimations. But the difference in their estimations is explained by the difference in the positions which they occupy in society, and which themselves are the products of social organization.[118]

If we consider the demand not of one or another separate individual but rather of a significant mass of purchasers, we will find a certain regular pattern in its movement. Either directly or in the final analysis, demand is determined by the condition of the production process, and specifically by the development of the productive forces and the character of the production relations that prevail in

---

118   Marx 1977, p. 36.

the given society. In chapter ten of the third volume of *Capital*, Marx examines in detail the dependence of social demand upon social production.

First of all, it is important to point out that the dimensions of social demand are themselves not given and fixed in advance. We took the magnitude of social demand as given when we said earlier that production of each product must correspond to the social need for it (or the demand), but this same magnitude, in turn, requires explanation.

> It would seem ... that there is on the side of demand a certain magnitude of definite social wants which require for their satisfaction a definite quantity of an article on the market. In fact, however, the quantitative determination of this need is completely elastic and fluctuating. Its fixed character is mere illusion. If means of subsistence were *cheaper* or money wages *higher*, the workers would buy more of them, and a greater 'social need' for these kinds of commodity would appear.[119]

Thus, the volume of social demand for a given product depends first of all upon the *price* of the product, and secondly upon the size of the consumers' *incomes*. But the price of the product is determined by its value, which depends, in turn, upon the quantity of labour required for its production, i.e. upon the development of labour productivity. On the other hand, the size of the income of a particular group of people depends upon the class position that they occupy in society, i.e. upon the character of the production relations inherent in the given mode of production. Consequently, insofar as demand depends upon prices and incomes, it is determined by the character of the production process. It is true that with a given level of prices and incomes, demand for a specific product may change depending upon the changing need for it, but this need itself varies according to changes in the society's living conditions, which in the final analysis depend upon changes in the production process. Let us now examine in more detail the dependence of the volume of demand upon each of the conditions that we have listed.

We shall deal, first of all, with the influence of the product's *price* upon the volume of demand. Marx often points out that the volume of demand for a particular product depends upon that product's price, which is determined, in turn, by its value. 'The expansion or contraction of the market depends on the price of the individual commodity and stands in an inverse relationship to the

---

119 Marx 1992, pp. 289–90.

rise or fall in this price'.[120] Demand 'moves in the opposite direction to prices, expanding when they fall and vice versa'.[121]

> If the market value falls, the social need is on average expanded (this always means here the need which has money to back it up), and within certain limits the society can absorb larger quantities of commodities. If the market value rises, the social need for the commodities contracts and smaller quantities are absorbed.[122]

At this point the reader might raise the following question: If the price of the commodity determines the demand for it, is there not also a reverse dependence here of the price of the commodity upon the demand for it? Actually the price of commodities does fluctuate, as everyone knows, under the influence of fluctuations in the demand for them; but demand can have an influence only upon the commodity's market price, not upon its average price, which depends upon its value.[123] There is a regulator in the very mechanism of commodity economy that, by means of the expansion and contraction of production, tends to eliminate any deviation of the market prices of commodities from their value (or their price of production). Whatever may be the magnitude of social need for the given product – whether, for example, we are speaking of a product of mass consumption, for which there is a demand from millions of buyers, or of a refined luxury product that is accessible only to a narrow circle of buyers – production of the given product has a tendency to be established at exactly the level where its market prices have their value (or their price of production in capitalist society) as their centre of gravity. It is precisely because the capitalist is completely indifferent as to which product to produce that the use-value of the product cannot play the role of a factor determining its value. It is not demand that has the determining effect upon the value of the product but rather the opposite; the magnitude of the product's value determines the average volume of demand that exists for this product. 'If supply and demand regulate market price, or rather the departures of market price from market value, the market value in turn regulates the relationship between demand and supply'.[124]

---

120   Marx 1992, p. 203.
121   Marx 1992, p. 292.
122   Marx 1992, p. 282.
123   [For elaboration of this point, see the appendix to Rubin's essay in this volume on 'The Austrian School'].
124   Marx 1992, p. 282.

Let us turn now to the question of demand's dependence upon the distribution of *incomes* between different social classes. In *The Poverty of Philosophy* Marx already indicated that 'The use of products is determined by the social conditions in which the consumers find themselves placed, and these conditions themselves are based on class antagonism'.[125] It is only the class division of a capitalist society, built upon an antagonistic foundation, that can explain to us the character of the supply and demand that prevails within it. Marx emphasised this idea even more decisively in *Capital*:

> Let us note here, but merely in passing, that the 'social need' which governs the principle of demand is basically conditioned by the relationship of the different classes and their respective economic positions; in the first place, therefore, particularly by the proportion between the total surplus-value and wages, and secondly, by the proportion between the various parts into which surplus-value itself is divided (profit, interest, ground-rent, taxes, etc.). Here again we can see how absolutely nothing can be explained by the relationship of demand and supply, before explaining the basis on which this relationship functions.[126]

It follows that the social need for products is determined first and foremost by the relation of surplus value to wages, i.e. by the relations of distribution, which are only the other side of the production relations within capitalist society. The dual class character of *incomes* (i.e. the division of newly created value into wages and surplus value) has its necessary consequence in the dual class character of *demand and consumption*.

Let us begin by characterising the consumption of *workers* and the demand that they bring to the market. The fact that the class of workers in capitalist society is deprived of the means of production, and that it receives income only in the form of wages, has a determining effect upon the character of the demand represented by workers. In the first place, the workers represent demand only for items of consumption, not for means of production;[127] and secondly, they represent demand only for the means of subsistence that are necessary for reproduction of their labour power. The workers' consumption, together with the demand that they represent in the market, is limited to the necessary means of subsistence.

---

125 Marx 1977, p. 57.
126 Marx 1992, p. 282.
127 Marx 1992, pp. 289–90.

At first sight, it may seem that precisely here we find a vivid example of the dependence of demand upon purely natural conditions that are rooted in the physical nature of man. One may think that the volume of workers' demand is determined by their 'natural' needs, satisfaction of which is absolutely necessary in order to support human life. But this frontier of the so-called physiological minimum means of subsistence is only the lower boundary for the average volume of workers' demand. In his teaching on the value of labour power, Marx assumes that the average wage is determined by the level of the workers' 'necessary' requirements, which exceed the sum of 'natural' needs.[128] As examples of natural needs, Marx lists food, clothing, fuel and housing but, as mentioned previously, the very mode of satisfying these natural needs changes in different historical epochs and, accordingly, has a socially conditioned character. This is all the more true of 'intellectual and social requirements', the extent and number of which are determined by 'the general level of civilisation'.[129]

> The number and extent of his so-called necessary requirements, as also the manner in which they are satisfied, are themselves products of history, and depend therefore to a great extent on the level of civilization attained by a country; in particular they depend on the conditions in which, and consequently on the habits and expectations with which, the class of free workers has been formed.[130]

Not only is the character of working-class needs determined by development of the society's living conditions and, in the final analysis, by its productive forces, but even the level of satisfaction that the worker experiences from consuming one or another product depends upon his surrounding social conditions. Marx speaks of this at one place in *Wage Labour and Capital*:

> Although the pleasures of the labourer have increased, the social gratification which they afford has fallen in comparison with the increased pleasures of the capitalist, which are inaccessible to the worker, in comparison with the stage of development of society in general. Our wants and pleasures have their origin in society; we therefore measure them

---

128 Marx 1976, p. 275.
129 Marx 1976, p. 341.
130 Marx 1976, p. 275.

in relation to society; we do not measure them in relation to the objects which serve for their gratification. Since they are of a social nature, they are of a relative nature.[131]

Thus the incomes of workers in capitalist society are so limited that they can only represent demand for necessary means of subsistence. On the other hand, let us recall what was previously said concerning the influence of the price of a given product on the volume of demand for it. This means that workers represent a demand almost exclusively for the least costly and thus the poorest means of consumption. In *The Poverty of Philosophy*, Marx was most emphatic regarding this condition. 'Why are cotton, potatoes and spirits the pivots of bourgeois society? Because the least amount of labour is needed to produce them, and, consequently, they have the lowest price'.[132] The character of consumption depends entirely upon production conditions for the products. 'Economics prevailed, and dictated its orders to consumption'.[133]

It is obvious, therefore, just how mistaken it is to say – without any further explanation – that capitalist production, as with any production in general, satisfies social needs. This formula is only true if we understand the latter to mean only those needs that are acknowledged by capitalist society, i.e. that are represented by effective demand. The capitalists are not concerned with the fact that the needs of broad masses of people are only minimally satisfied and that, consequently, an enormous mass of needs remains completely unsatisfied. Capitalist production satisfies only those needs that appear in the form of effective demand. This is precisely why Marx frequently emphasised

---

131 Marx 2006, p. 33. As can be seen from Marx's notes on workers' wages, which were first published by D.B. Ryazanov, Marx adopted the idea that we have quoted from Cherbuliez. In his notes that we have cited, we find the following quotation from the work of Cherbuliez: 'It is not so much the *absolute* consumption of the worker as his *relative* consumption which makes his position either happy or unhappy. Beyond the necessary consumption ... the *value* of what we enjoy is *essentially relative*' (Marx, in MECW, Vol. 6, p. 421). Marx cites Cherbuliez at greater length in *Theories of Surplus-Value*, Part III (Marx 1971, pp. 362–98). It is interesting that Marx thought it necessary to express his disagreement with Chernyshevsky, who took the opposing view and wrote: 'A man suffers or does not suffer a need, is either prosperous or not prosperous, not by comparison with others but with himself. The measure here is given by the nature of man'. Opposite these words from Chernyshevsky, Marx placed a question mark on the margin of his book (See *Arkhiv K. Marksa i F. Engel'sa*, Moscow-Leningrad, Vol. IV, 1929, p. 386).
132 Marx 1977, p. 57.
133 Ibid.

the entirely different character of the link between production and consumption in capitalist and socialist society.

> In a future society, in which class antagonism will have ceased, in which there will no longer be any classes, use will no longer be determined by the *minimum* time of production; but the time of production devoted to different articles will be determined by the degree of their social utility.[134]

Since the character of the incomes received by workers determines the character of their consumption and the demand that they bring to the market, it is perfectly understandable that the consumption of workers changes with a change in the wage. We are familiar with Marx's teaching regarding the influence of the rising organic composition of capital and of the reserve army [of labour] upon the magnitude of the wage. We know Marx's teaching involving the tendency that exists within capitalist society towards impoverishment of the working class. It is quite evident that this general pattern for the development of wages necessarily brings forth a corresponding change in the workers' consumption.

Such changes, although only of a temporary character, are also caused by passing changes in the level of wages. As we know, the wage fluctuates in the course of the industrial cycle: it rises in years of prosperity and falls in years of depression. Marx carefully noted the influence that movement of the conjuncture has upon the workers' consumption: he pointed out that in years of prosperity 'It is ... not only the consumption of necessary means of subsistence that rises; the working class ... also takes a temporary share in the consumption of luxury articles'.[135] On the contrary, during years of depression the wage falls and the result is to reduce the consumption of workers and the demand that they represent in the market.

We can see that the character of the workers' demand and consumption is determined entirely by their position in the production process, i.e. by the character of production relations in capitalist society. In the first place, the level of imperative needs on the part of the workers is determined by the general conditions of social life; secondly, the class position of the workers entirely determines the general structure of demand that they represent in the market – they represent demand only for the necessary means of subsistence; thirdly, the workers' consumption depends upon the level of prices for products in

---

134   Marx 1977, p. 58.
135   Marx 1978, p. 486.

the sense that workers represent a high demand only for the most inexpensive commodities; fourthly, the general tendency towards reduction of the relative share of the working class in the social product has a definite influence upon the volume of demand and consumption by the workers; fifthly, and finally, temporary fluctuations in the volume of consumption and demand by the workers are determined by the temporary fluctuations of wages in the course of the conjuncture.

Let us turn from workers' consumption to that of the capitalists. For now, we shall speak only of their personal consumption. The capitalists' personal consumption has a completely different character from the personal consumption of the workers, and this difference in consumption directly reflects the different character and level of their incomes. The capitalists demand products that are different from those consumed by workers. First of all, insofar as they consume necessary means of subsistence (bread, meat and so forth), these products are usually different in terms of their quality and value from the workers' means of consumption.[136] Moreover, the capitalists consume luxury items, which Marx understands to mean those products that enter into consumption only by the capitalist class.[137] Thus Marx distinguishes between three groups of items of consumption: 1) the workers' necessary means of subsistence, 2) the capitalists' necessary means of subsistence, and 3) items of luxury.[138] It is interesting to note that Marx takes the basis for this classification of consumer items to be the class principle of including one product or another in the consumer budget of one or another social class.

Thus the character of the incomes received by capitalists makes its impression upon the character of their consumption. True, in the present case this dependence does not have so direct a character as in the consumption of workers. There is a very close connection between the magnitude of the worker's wage and the extent of his consumption, since the worker usually spends almost the entire wage in buying means of subsistence. The capitalist only spends a small part of his profit on his personal consumption and accumulates the remainder in the form of capital, i.e. he spends it to purchase means of production and labour power. Hence the personal consumption of the capitalist depends not only upon the general sum of profit that he acquires, but also upon the proportion in which he divides this profit between the fund for personal consumption and the fund for accumulation. However, in this case too

---

136   Marx 1978, p. 479.
137   Ibid.
138   Marx 1978, pp. 479, 482–3.

we can observe a certain regular pattern in the capitalists' behaviour, which varies according to changes in the general conditions of capitalist production. In different epochs of capitalism's development, the personal consumption of the capitalists assumes a different character.

> At the historical dawn of the capitalist mode of production ... avarice, and the drive for self-enrichment, are the passions which are entirely predominant. But the progress of capitalist production not only creates a world of delights; it lays open, in the form of speculation and the credit system, a thousand sources of sudden enrichment. When a certain stage of development has been reached, a conventional degree of prodigality, which is also an exhibition of wealth, and consequently a guarantee of creditworthiness, becomes a business necessity to the 'unfortunate' capitalist. Luxury enters into capital's expenses of representation ... Thus although the expenditure of the capitalist never possesses the *bona fide* character of the dashing feudal lord's prodigality, but, on the contrary, is always restrained by the sordid avarice and anxious calculation lurking in the background, this expenditure nevertheless grows with his accumulation, without the one necessarily restricting the other.[139]

As capitalism develops, the consumption of the capitalist class enormously increases. But, since the volume of profits that they receive grows even more quickly, expenditures on personal consumption take an ever-diminishing share of the capitalists' profits. Thus, the development of consumption by the capitalists shows a certain regular pattern, which is determined by the general tendencies of the development of capitalist production.

If the sum of consumer items and luxuries obtained by the capitalist class has a general tendency to grow enormously, at the same time it fluctuates from time to time according to the movement of the conjuncture. In periods of industrial prosperity, the consumption of capitalists grows together with the demand that they represent in the market for consumer items, and especially for luxuries.[140] Marx anticipated the most recent research into the influence of the conjuncture's movement on the extent of consumption by both workers and capitalists. He meticulously noted the periodic expansion and contraction of the consumption process, which in turn only reflects the movement of the production process.

---

139   Marx 1976, p. 741.
140   Marx 1978, pp. 414, 486; Marx 1992, p. 344.

Demand from the capitalists for consumer items constitutes only an insignificant part of the general demand that they represent in the market. The capitalists spend an enormous and ever-increasing portion of their profits not on personal consumption but in the form of capital that is being accumulated. They enter the market as purchasers of means of production and of labour power. Insofar as the capitalist buys labour power, 'the capitalist's demand for labour-power is indirectly also a demand for the means of consumption that enter into the consumption of the working class'.[141] But, together with the growth of the organic composition of capital, an ever larger part of the sum they are accumulating is spent not on the purchase of labour power but on the purchase of means of production, i.e. on materials and on the instruments of labour. The sole purchasers of means of production in capitalist society are the capitalists; their demand for means of production constitutes an enormous portion of the total demand in the market.

This fact is imperative for an understanding of the entire character of capitalist production. In *The Poverty of Philosophy* Marx already wrote: 'Most often, needs arise directly from production or from a state of affairs based on production. World trade turns almost entirely round the needs, not of individual consumption, but of production'.[142] In capitalist society, we must note two completely different sorts of consumers: 'individual consumers', representing demand for items of consumption, and 'productive consumers', who represent demand for means of production.[143] If the volume of demand for means of consumption, as we have seen above, depends upon the general conditions of the production process, this applies all the more to productive demand, i.e. to demand for the means of production. If the capitalist buys cotton to work up into cotton fabric, his demand for the cotton already has an entirely different character from the consumer's need for the product in satisfying his personal requirements. The capitalist only buys cotton insofar as processing it promises to bring him a profit. 'His need for cotton is modified fundamentally by the fact that all it really clothes is his need to make a profit'.[144] The demand for means of production depends most directly upon conditions in the production process, not just indirectly as in the case of demand for items of personal consumption.

Since demand by capitalists for means of production is determined by the capitalists' pursuit of profit, it has already ceased to be a direct reflection of the social need for items of consumption. And since, on the other hand, the volume

---

141   Marx 1978, p. 197.
142   Marx 1977, p. 36.
143   Marx 1978, p. 512.
144   Marx 1992, p. 290.

of demand for means of production has an enormous influence upon the entire production process, the latter becomes, to a certain extent, independent of the consumption process. Hence the typical capitalist tendency towards expansion of production beyond the limits of effective demand, or beyond the social need supported by effective demand.

> Since capital's purpose is not the satisfaction of needs but the production of profit, and since it attains this purpose only by methods that determine the mass of production by reference exclusively to the yardstick of production, and not the reverse, there must be a constant tension between the restricted dimensions of consumption on the capitalist basis, and a production that is constantly striving to overcome these immanent barriers.[145]

'Production takes place without regard to the existing limits to consumption, but is limited only by capital itself'.[146] This endeavour to expand production can only be realised in practice due to the fact that a larger share of the profit is accumulated and, as a result, a new demand for means of production appears in the market. In others words, production in capitalist economy creates, within limits, its own market because the expansion of production represents demand for means of production, and this type of demand is enormously important in capitalist society.

The enormous and ever-growing significance of productive demand makes the scale of production extremely elastic and, within certain limits, independent of social needs in the narrow sense of the word, i.e. of the current condition of effective demand for items of consumption. However, this is only true within certain limits, for in the final analysis the means of production are intended precisely for creating means of consumption. In the first instance, the extent of productive demand is independent of consumption, but in the final analysis it is still limited by personal consumption because the production of constant capital never occurs for its own sake but ultimately results in production of means of consumption.[147] It is true that the reproduction process, within certain limits, may be conducted on the previous or even on an expanded scale, even if the commodities being turned out actually have not entered into the sphere of personal or productive consumption.[148] But the possibility of a fur-

---

145 Marx 1992, p. 365.
146 Marx 1968, p. 520.
147 Marx 1992, p. 420.
148 Marx 1978, p. 156.

ther expansion of production ultimately encounters the limits imposed by the low level of consumption on the part of the popular masses. In capitalist society, the antagonistic relations of distribution 'reduce the consumption of the vast majority of society to a minimum level, only capable of varying within more or less narrow limits'.[149] Consequently, 'the more productivity develops, the more it comes into conflict with the narrow basis on which consumption rests'.[150] Production's relative independence of consumption, conditioned by the capitalists' drive for unlimited expansion of production and by the steadily increasing role of productive demand, nevertheless occurs within certain limits; when these limits are exceeded, the necessary inner connection between production and consumption becomes evident and a crisis breaks out.

We can now summarise our discussion of the link between production and consumption in capitalist economy. In the first chapters, we clarified Marx's general doctrine on the link between production and consumption. We saw that these two moments of the process of reproduction penetrate one another: production is directed to the preparation of products that serve consumption; and the latter, in turn, change in a manner that depends upon the production process itself.

In simple commodity economy, the connection between production and consumption already becomes more extended and complex. The goal of production is not direct satisfaction of the producer's needs. The latter produces the product not for the sake of use-value but rather for exchange-value. Nevertheless, a close link between production and consumption is preserved. On the one hand, the producer is very familiar with the traditional and slowly changing volume of demand that exists for the products that he produces. Consequently, the needs of the purchasers, expressed in the demand that they pose, are considered and taken into account in advance by the producer. On the other hand, in simple commodity economy, where there is no division of classes and class exploitation, the benefits from rising labour productivity accrue to the producer himself. The rise in labour productivity and the growth in the volume of products that serve to satisfy human needs cause an increase of needs and of consumption on the part of the members of society. The development of production is accompanied by a growth of consumption.

A further separation of production from consumption occurs in capitalist economy, where the capitalists' goal is the acquisition of profits. The capit-

---

149 Marx 1992, p. 352.
150 Marx 1992, p. 353.

alist produces not to satisfy the needs of members of society but rather to satisfy effective demand. The demand in the market for means of consumption has a clearly expressed class character and is conditioned by the distribution of social income between society's different classes. The incomes of the working class remain at a very low level, and the demand from workers for means of consumption remains at that same level. The needs of the broad popular masses are not the motivating purpose that directs production. On the other hand, a colossal increase of labour productivity and of the dimensions of social wealth is not accompanied by a corresponding growth of working-class consumption. Whereas in the economy of a patriarchal family, or of a socialist commune, there is a directly acting law, as a result of which the needs of society develop 'together with the means of their satisfaction and in direct dependence upon development of the latter', in capitalist society this law appears in modified form. The growth of labour productivity and the colossal increase of social wealth do not cause – or at best cause only to an insignificant degree – an increase of the extent of consumption by the working class.

> We cannot imagine capitalism without a contradiction between production and consumption, without the tremendous growth of production being accompanied by an extremely slow growth (or even stagnation and worsening) of consumption by the people.[151]

This peculiarity of the capitalist economy was already noted by Marx, as we have seen, in his early preparatory works for *The Holy Family*. But there Marx, being still influenced by the ideas of utopian socialism, sharply contrasted the 'natural' law of the growth of human needs with the 'unnatural' law of the degradation of the working class in the conditions of capitalist economy. But now Marx reveals the dialectical contradiction between the two laws: between the general law of the growth of needs, accompanying the development of production, and the law inherent in capitalist economy that keeps the workers' consumption at a low level despite a gigantic growth of labour productivity. Marx reveals the entire mechanism of capitalist economy, in which the increase of social labour productivity, accompanied by growth of the organic composition of capital and of the reserve army [of labour], does not bring with it a rise of the consumption and well-being of the working class. 'Marx's theory showed how the contradiction, inherent in capitalism, comes about, how the tremend-

---

151 Lenin 1899e, p. 162.

ous growth of production is definitely not accompanied by a corresponding growth in people's consumption'.[152]

The general law, according to which the growth of production is accompanied by the growth of needs, becomes significantly complicated and modified in capitalist economy, yet in the final analysis it still continues to operate. The growth of labour productivity causes a decline in the value of various items of consumption, thereby making them accessible to the working masses. It is true, even in this best of cases, that only an insignificant part of the benefits resulting from the growth in social labour productivity accrues to the working class; even in this, the most beneficial of all cases for the workers, the volume of products obtained by the worker in natural form increases, but not the sum of the values that he acquires. Accordingly, the increase of labour productivity has an effect upon the volume of the workers' consumption only to a very limited extent and indirectly (through a reduction of the value of products).

If the increasing scale of production and of social wealth has only an indirect influence upon the workers' *consumption*, it has a much more significant influence upon development of the workers' *needs*. The very fact of a colossal growth of social wealth, accompanied by an enormous rise of well-being and of the level of personal consumption by capitalists and those groups of the population close to them, cannot but cause an increase of the workers' needs, as Marx already noted in his work *Wage Labour and Capital*. The discrepancy between workers' needs and the means for their satisfaction assumes an ever more acute character.

In conditions of capitalist economy, the growth of production also has, in addition to its indirect and restricted influence upon the extent of consumption by the workers, an indirect influence, namely: 1) it is accompanied by enormous growth of personal consumption on the part of the class of capitalists and those groups of the population close to them; and 2) it causes an enormous expansion of demand by the capitalists for means of production. An important part of the profits is accumulated in the form of capital and is used – after deducting the sum required for the purchase of labour power – for purchasing means of production. Production itself partially creates its own market, and its expansion causes an enormous increase of demand for means of production even with a stationary, declining, or slowly rising level of personal consumption by the working masses. Growth of this demand for means of production makes capitalist production relatively independent of the narrow basis of personal consumption on the part of the working masses. However,

---

152 Lenin 1899c, p. 87.

this independence has only a temporary and relative character. An increase of the demand for means of production is equivalent to further expansion of the process of production itself. Consequently, the growth of productive demand, making production for a time independent of the scale of personal consumption, in the final analysis merely intensifies the contradiction between the colossal development of the productive forces and the 'conditions of distribution and consumption' in which it occurs; this contradiction periodically finds expression in acute crises and ultimately leads to the necessity of social revolution.

As we see, in capitalist society the link between production and consumption has a very complex and tangled character. Consumption affects production only by way of effective demand. For an understanding of the character of demand in capitalist society we must focus attention more upon: 1) the distribution of *incomes* between different social classes, which conditions the extent of their demand for commodities, and 2) the enormous importance of demand for *means of production*. In his commentaries, Marx strongly emphasised precisely these two conditions, which have an essential influence upon the entire structure of demand in capitalist society.

> For simply buying and selling, it is enough that commodity producers confront one another. Demand and supply, on further analysis, imply the existence of various different classes and segments of classes which distribute the total social revenue among themselves and consume it as such, thus making up a demand created out of revenue; while it is also necessary to understand the overall configuration of the capitalist production process if one is to comprehend the demand and supply generated among the producers as such.[153]

Together with these two extremely important factors, which determine the structure of demand in capitalist society, in the latter there is a whole series of other conditions that further complicate and confuse the link between production and consumption. One need only mention the role of consumption on the part of non-productive groups of the population, or the enormous expansion of the commercial apparatus, which lengthens the path from the producer to the consumer.

It may appear, at first sight, that production and consumption in capitalist society are completely detached from, and independent of, one another.

---

153   Marx 1992, p. 296.

Production is conducted not to satisfy the needs of society's members but to acquire profit; to a significant extent it is independent of the volume of personal consumption and directed in large part to the satisfaction of productive demand, i.e. to expansion of the production process itself. On the other hand, consumption by the popular masses also does not change directly under the influence of growth of the production process and of social wealth. However, the separation of production from consumption does not eliminate their internal connection. On the one hand, production is ultimately restricted within the narrow limits imposed upon it by the 'conditions of distribution and consumption'; on the other hand, consumption constitutes a moment of the entire process of reproduction, either flowing directly from the needs of the production process (the demand for means of production) or else being conditioned by the relations of distribution and, in the first place, by the level of wages (the workers' demand for items of personal consumption).

III *Use-Value and the Subject Matter of Political Economy*
1) Is Use-Value Part of the Subject Matter of Political Economy?
We must now address the question of the extent to which use-value is studied by political economy. As we already know, Marx's critics often accuse him of ignoring use-value. Scrutiny of Marx's works has already convinced us that Marx by no means ignored the process of consumption; he considered it to be one of the moments of the process of reproduction as a whole. Now we must answer the question as to how far the economist takes use-value into account when analysing the production process.

The capitalist production process is a unity of the labour process (i.e. the process of producing use-values) and the process of the production and expansion of value. Political economy takes the latter aspect of the production process, i.e. the process of the production and expansion of value, to be the special subject matter of its investigation. But the process of the expansion of value represents the form in which the process of the production of products, or of use-values, occurs. Thus, the latter process is always a part of our investigation, although not as an independent object for analysis by this science but rather as another side of the single process of reproduction, which we study as the 'social structure of production' (Lenin). It follows that use-value is included within the ambit of our investigation only insofar as this is necessary in order to understand the process of the production and expansion of value.

Marx often emphasised that use-value does not represent an independent subject matter for investigation in theoretical economics. In the first pages of the *Critique* he pointed out that use-value as such, i.e. in its indifference to the determination of economic form, lies beyond political economy's sphere of study.[154] Marx spoke of this in his letter to Engels, dated 2 April 1858, in which he explained to him the content of the *Critique*. In this letter we read:

> Use-value – whether regarded subjectively as the *usefulness* of labour, or objectively as the *utility* of the product – is shown here simply as the material prerequisite of value, and one which for the present is entirely irrelevant to the formal economic definition.[155]

These words from Marx indicate, in the first place, that use-value is not an independent object for research in theoretical economics, and secondly, that it must be taken into account insofar as this is necessary for an investigation of the 'determinations of economic form', i.e. of the production relations between people. Let us now consider, with a number of examples, the degree to which Marx does pay attention to the use-value of commodities in the course of his investigation.

As we have already seen in Chapter II (section 2), at the beginning of his study Marx considers exchange-value apart from and completely independently of use-value, in order subsequently to study the conditions of their coexistence in the commodity. Here, in his teaching on the contradiction between use-value and exchange-value, the presence of the latter is always presupposed by Marx and taken into account. We shall not understand the laws of the movement of value (for instance, the doctrine of the forms of value, or of the division of the commodity into commodity and money), if we leave aside the fact that exchange-value is only one side of the commodity, which appears on the other side as use-value. But it by no means follows that Marx is engaged here in a study of use-value. Marx limits himself here to the presupposition that the commodity is not only exchange-value but also use-value. This presupposition is quite sufficient for the purpose of his research.

From an analysis of the individual commodity, as a unity of value and use-value, Marx turns to the actual process of the exchange of commodities, i.e. to commodity circulation in the form C–M–C. Marx emphasises that he is studying this circuit of commodities as a process of the 'change of form' (*Formwechsel*) of commodities, not as a process of the social 'exchange of things' (*Stoffwechsel*). According to Marx, economists were not able to understand correctly the circuit C–M–C precisely because they directed their attention to its material side and overlooked the process involving the form itself of the commodity.[156]

---

154 Marx 1970, p. 2.
155 *MECW*, Vol. 40, p. 298.
156 Marx 1976, p. 199.

Does this mean that in his research Marx ignored the 'exchange of things', which occurs through the 'change of form' C–M–C? Such an assumption would, of course, be incorrect. If we ignored the social exchange of things, we would also be unable to understand the change of form that it serves. To be sure, in order to understand the movement of commodities in the circuit C–M–C, we must take into account the fact that what is involved is a product that is made by the commodity producer for sale and must serve indirectly as an item of consumption not for the commodity producer himself but for another person, i.e. for the purchaser. We shall not understand the first metamorphosis of the commodity, C–M, if we forget that the product follows a certain path from producer to consumer. In a word, in order to understand the circuit C–M–C in terms of its social form, we must always remember the other side of this same circuit, i.e. the process of the movement of products, or of use-values, from the producer to the consumer. But the latter process has a place in our investigation not as an independent topic for analysis but only as the other side of a single process of commodity production and circulation.

To this point, Marx has presupposed that the commodity – considered either as a separate commodity or in the movement of the circuit C–M–C – possesses use-value. But if we turn to investigation of the entire mass of commodities produced in a given branch of production, then it will already not suffice to presuppose that the separate exemplars of this commodity mass represent use-values. We must also assume that this entire commodity mass, taken as a whole and in quantitative terms, corresponds to social need, i.e. to the effective demand for commodities of this particular type. Here we already presuppose not only the existence of use-value but also the presence of 'use-value on the social scale', i.e. of a quantitatively determined social need. 'The social need, i.e. the use-value on the social scale, here appears decisive for the quota of total social labour-time that falls to the share of the various particular spheres of production'.[157] It would be a mistake, however, to think that Marx takes the subject matter of his special investigation here to be the determinate, concrete character of this social need. Marx limits himself to the general presupposition that the social need for each type of product has a quantitatively determined character. This assumption is quite sufficient for understanding the conditions of the process of reproduction as a whole, and Marx provides no further study of the concrete structure of social needs. Here, as elsewhere, the process of the consumption of products is taken into account only as a moment of the process of social reproduction, i.e. insofar as the structure of social needs is determined

---

157   Marx 1992, p. 774.

by the conditions of the production process (see above, Chapter II, section 3) and, on the other hand, exerts its own influence on the latter.

In the examples that we have cited, Marx took use-value into consideration insofar as he had to begin with certain general assumptions concerning the process of consumption. But the determinate use-value of products is also very significant for the direct process of production itself. Consequently, Marx also takes it into account when studying the latter, insofar as he has to elucidate the technical side of the production process. Let us consider a few examples.

We shall not understand the division of capital into two distinct forms (constant and variable capital) if we ignore the fact that the former is spent on the purchase of dead means of production while the latter is spent on living labour power. Accordingly, at the basis of these two distinct forms of capital lies a material difference between elements required for the technical process of production. Thus, in an examination of constant and variable capital, the specific material form that distinguishes the different elements of production from one another is always taken into account. But, at the same time, it would be the greatest error to identify the difference between constant and variable capital with a material or technical difference between means of production and labour power. Marx spoke out decisively against vulgar economists who saw the difference between the separate parts of capital only in the fact that they serve 'to pay for materially different elements of production'. Marx sees this difference in the social function of constant and variable capital, in their different functional role in the process of expanding value.[158] The technical difference between elements of production is subject to no special analysis by Marx and is only considered insofar as this is necessary in order to understand the division of capital into constant and variable.

We find the same relation between value and use-value in Marx's doctrine concerning fixed and circulating capital. This division is also based upon a difference in the technical functioning of the different elements of production. The textile machine wears out slowly and serves for many years, whereas the cotton is processed during a single production period. These technical differences serve as the basis on which the economic difference between fixed and circulating capital arises. But on this point, once again, Marx decisively objects to those economists who attribute a technical rather than an economic character to the difference between fixed and circulating capital. From Marx's point of view, the difference between fixed and circulating capital consists of

---

158 Marx 1992, p. 122.

the different manner in which their *value* is transferred to the product.[159] As for the technical differences that result from the specific nature of the use-value of cotton and of the machine, and from the different conditions of their functioning in the process of labour, Marx subjects them to no special analysis.

On the basis of his teaching with regard to constant and variable capital, Marx constructed his doctrine concerning the organic composition of capital. Here, too, we can clearly follow the precise way in which Marx associates value with use-value. The organic composition of capital is the composition of capital *according to value*; but the value composition of capital is regarded as the organic composition of capital only when it reflects the technical composition of capital, i.e. the relation between quantities of living labour and dead means of production. The organic composition of capital grows on the basis of its technical composition, but it does not correspond to the latter. Marx takes precisely the organic composition of capital and the laws of its changes as the subject matter for special investigation. Of course, we are not able to disclose this pattern (for instance, the law of the rising organic composition of capital) unless we turn our attention to processes that are occurring in the technical process of production and that are causing the rise of the technical composition of capital (i.e. growth of the quantity of dead means of production at the expense of living labour). It is extremely interesting to follow the precise manner in which Marx brings into his investigation the fact of a rise in the technical composition of capital. He briefly points out that, as a result of the increase of labour productivity, there is a steady increase of the quantity of material and machines at the disposal of a single worker. Without examining this process in detail, Marx only briefly mentions it insofar as this is necessary for understanding the very important economic changes that result; for example, the rise in the organic composition of capital, the displacement of workers by machines, the formation of the reserve army, etc. If Marx had made the rise of the technical composition of capital a topic of special investigation, he would have had to provide us with enormous technological material, illustrating the process whereby living labour is displaced by dead labour in the different branches of production. He did not do so because he includes the rise of the technical composition of capital in his research only insofar as this is necessary for understanding the law-governed development of the organic composition of capital.

Thus, Marx does not make use-value a special subject matter of his investigation, although he does take it into account both in his comments on the process of consumption and in his examination of the process of production.

---

159 Marx 1978, pp. 243–4.

Marx must pay all the more attention to use-value in his teaching on the process of reproduction, which is outlined in Volume II of *Capital*. 'The overall process of reproduction here includes the consumption process mediated by circulation, just as much as the reproduction of capital itself'.[160] When investigating this process of reproduction as a whole, it is not enough to presuppose that the commodity has use-value; in order that the process of social reproduction might be completed without hindrance, it is necessary that the social product include within itself several subdivisions between products that are differentiated in terms of their natural form, or their use-values. In terms of natural form, the social product is divided, first and foremost, between the two great subdivisions: 1) means of production, and 2) means of consumption. The latter group of products, in turn, can be divided into two sub-groups that are distinguished by their natural form: 1) means of consumption by the workers, and 2) means of consumption by the capitalists. Thus, in studying social reproduction as a whole, it is necessary to consider not just the reproduction process of *value* and *capital*, but also reproduction of the *product in natural form*.

> The product of an individual capital ... may have any natural form whatsoever. The only condition is that it really should have a use form, a use-value, that stamps it as a member of the commodity world capable of circulation ... It is different with the product of the total social capital. All material elements of the reproduction must be parts of this product in their natural form.[161]

This is explained by the fact that, in Volume II of *Capital*, Marx is not only investigating the process of reproduction of the component parts of capital and surplus value (c, v, s) but also taking into account the reproduction of the product in natural form (means of production, means of consumption by workers, and means of consumption by capitalists).

Of course, in Volume II of *Capital* Marx is also examining the direct process of reproduction of *capital*, not the reproduction process of *products*, but since the reproduction of capital requires the availability of definite products in natural form (for example, means of production, means of consumption for workers, etc.), we must take into account the production process of the latter. And Marx does in fact include this process in his investigation to the extent that it is necessary for understanding the process of capital's reproduction. We

---

160 Marx 1978, p. 469.
161 Marx 1978, p. 508.

know, for example, that the value of variable capital must be reproduced in the value of the social product. But the variable capital is spent in the form of wages for the purchase of labour power, and the wages are spent by workers to purchase means of consumption. Accordingly, the social nature of variable capital requires inclusion in the social product of quantitatively determined components that take the natural form of means of consumption for the workers. And the presence of such components is presupposed by Marx. In this context, Marx limits himself to this presupposition, considering it unnecessary to conduct a special analysis of the concrete natural form of the group of means of consumption for the workers.

Thus, in his schemes of reproduction, Marx is not at all concerned with a detailed analysis of the social product in terms of its natural form or use-value. Marx borrows from the sphere of the production process of use-values only a few general conditions that are connected with the process of capital's reproduction; he includes these conditions in the investigation to the extent required for understanding the social structure of the reproduction process. And this is precisely the sort of formulation that we find in Marx in connection with his theory of reproduction. It is exactly with regard to the latter that Marx says: 'This is yet another example of how important is the analysis of *use-value for the determinations of economic form*'.[162] Marx uses almost the same words to express this idea in another place:

> In considering surplus-value as such, the original form of the product, hence of the surplus product, is of no consequence. It becomes important when considering the actual process of reproduction, partly in order to understand its forms, and partly in order to grasp the influence of luxury production, etc., on reproduction. Here is another example of how *use-value* as such acquires economic significance.[163]

It is clearly evident from these formulations by Marx that use-value is taken into account insofar as it is important for investigating 'the determinations of economic form', i.e. the production relations between people.

This is what explains the fact that Marx and Engels did not include the conditions of consumption in the subject matter studied by political economy, although, as we have already been persuaded more than once, they by no means ignored the process of consumption. In his *Contribution to the Critique*

---

162   Marx 1968, p. 489. This translation speaks of 'the determination of economic phenomena'.
163   Marx 1971, pp. 251–2.

of Political Economy, Marx pursues the idea that the process of reproduction includes within itself production, exchange, distribution and consumption as its subordinate moments. The reader might think that the process of consumption must be included in the subject matter of the study of political economy on an equal footing with the processes of exchange and distribution. It is not possible to agree with this opinion. We find direct references on this point in both Marx and Engels. In the preface to Volume I of *Capital* Marx wrote: 'What I have to examine in this work is the capitalist mode of production, and the relations of *production and forms of intercourse* [*Verkehrsverhältnisse*] that correspond to it'.[164] There is no mention of the process of consumption. It is true that Marx also neglects to mention the relations of distribution, but, if we understand that distributive relations are only the other side of production relations, then the need to include them in the subject matter studied by political economy becomes obvious. Indeed, we find direct references to this fact in Engels's *Anti-Dühring*. Political economy, in the broad sense of the term, is defined by Engels as 'the science of the laws, conditions, and forms of *production and exchange* of products in different human societies and of the corresponding modes of *distribution* of these products'.[165] In this formula, too, which lists in detail the various aspects of the subject matter of political economy, the latter does not include the process of consumption.[166] The process of consumption is not a topic for direct analysis in Marxist political economy, and it is taken into account only insofar as this is necessary for understanding the capitalist process of reproduction as a whole, with its corresponding relations of production, exchange and distribution.

2) Formal Use-Value

Along with use-value in the narrow sense of the term, we do encounter in Marx's teaching the use of this concept in a different sense. While Marx points out at the beginning of *Capital* that use-value in capitalist society acquires the special social form of exchange-value and thus becomes the commodity, he has something completely different in view when he speaks, for example, of the use-value of money (meaning precisely money, not metal). In this case, it is not use-value that acquires a special social form (such would apply only to the use-value of the metal from which money is made, not to money itself);

---

164 [Rubin did not cite the source for this excerpt. It can be found in Marx 1976, p. 90].
165 Engels 1954, p. 203.
166 It might be objected that in this formulation Engels is speaking of political economy in the broad, rather than in the narrow, sense of the word. But with regard to this point, once again, he draws no distinction between the two.

rather, it is the *social form* itself of a given item that acquires for the commodity producer a special *use-value* thanks to the fact that it gives him the possibility of exchanging that item for any other. In this case, the use-value depends not on the natural features of the item but instead represents a social feature entirely generated by the social form of the economy, i.e. by the character of its prevailing production relations between people.

On the second page of the *Critique of Political Economy*, we encounter the following vague remark: 'Use-value, in its indifference to the determination of economic form, i.e., use-value as use-value, lies outside the sphere of investigation of political economy. Use-value belongs in the latter sphere only when it is itself a determination of form'.[167] At first sight this comment seems so vague and incomprehensible that P. Rumyantsev, the original translator of the *Critique*, thought it necessary to render it as follows: 'It [use-value] belongs to this sphere only insofar as it *determines* itself the economic forms'. Taken on its own, the idea expressed by Rumyantsev is not subject to any particular objections. Indeed, in those cases where use-value has a determining influence on the economic forms, we must investigate it in order to understand these economic forms correctly. But the fact is that in this case Marx is speaking of something completely different. As can be seen from the literal text of his sentence, he is speaking not of use-value that *determines* economic forms, but of use-value that '*is itself* a determination of form'.

At first sight this sentence seems very obscure, but it is fully explicable if we turn to the pages of the *Critique* where Marx speaks of the use-value of money: 'This latter use-value [the use-value of the universal equivalent] is itself *a determination of form*, i.e., it arises from the specific role which this commodity plays as a result of the universal action exerted on it by the other commodities in the exchange process'.[168] It is obvious that even on the second page of the *Critique* Marx understood the use-value that 'is itself a determination of form' to mean the use-value of money, which is conditioned not by the natural attributes of the metal from which money is made but rather by the social functions of the latter. Since *this* use-value is not use-value in the narrow sense of the term, i.e. as conditioned by the natural features of a product, but is rather the social form a thing, expressing the production relations between people, it is directly a topic for study by political economy.

The concept of use-value in the expanded and purely social sense is used by Marx not only with regard to money; he speaks in the same sense of the

---

167   Marx 1970, p. 2.
168   Marx 1970, p. 47 [Rubin's emphasis].

use-value of labour power and of the use-value of money-capital that is lent. In all of these cases, the concept of use-value has a purely social character and is used by Marx in a special sense that is completely absent from the works of bourgeois economists. We must, therefore, clarify this concept and take note of the important occasions when it is used by Marx.

a)   *The Use-Value of Money*

We have already seen that the making of products for exchange itself causes a 'distinction between the usefulness of things for direct consumption and their usefulness in exchange'.[169] The thing, in addition to its direct usefulness as an item of consumption, acquires for its possessor a special usefulness, consisting of its ability to exchange for other products that he requires. If the producer makes a product exclusively for sale, then, essentially speaking, it is the exchange-value alone of this product that represents usefulness for him. For him, 'its only direct use-value is as a bearer of exchange-value, and consequently, a means of exchange'.[170] In this sentence, the dialectical movement of Marx's thought is clearly evident. If use-value, in the conditions of commodity economy, acquires the character of exchange-value, the converse also holds: the exchange-value of the product assumes for its possessor a special usefulness or use-value, giving him the possibility of acquiring, in exchange for the given product, the means of consumption that he needs.

With the detachment of the universal equivalent from the sphere of all other commodities, its specific use-value is reinforced, consisting of its ability to exchange directly for any other commodity. The specific *use-value of money* emerges:

> The commodity which has been set apart as universal equivalent acquires a dual use-value. In addition to its *particular* use-value as an individual commodity it acquires a *universal* use-value. This latter use-value is itself a *determination of form*, i.e., it arises from the specific role which this commodity plays as a result of the universal action exerted on it by the other commodities in the exchange process.[171]

The money commodity acquires a dual use-value. Alongside its *special* use-value as a given commodity (gold, for instance, serves to fill teeth, it

---

169   Marx 1976, p. 182.
170   Marx 1976, p. 179.
171   Marx 1970, p. 47 [Rubin's emphasis].

forms the raw material for luxury articles, etc.) it acquires a *formal* use-value, arising out of its specific social functions.[172]

Elsewhere Marx calls the use-value of money '*functional*'.[173] This designation of the use-value of money as 'formal' or 'functional' is perfectly understandable. The specific use-value of money follows from the special social form or function that the given item fulfils in the capacity of universal equivalent. Only in commodity economy, with its inherent system of production relations between people, does a universal equivalent appear with its inherent formal use-value.

It is perfectly understandable that the use-value of money differs fundamentally from use-value in the narrow sense, as possessed by other commodities.

> The use-value of each commodity, as an object which satisfies particular needs, has a different value in different hands, e.g., it has one value for the person who alienates the commodity, and it has a different value for the person who purchases it. The commodity which has been set apart as the universal equivalent is now an object which satisfies a universal need arising from the exchange process itself, and it has the identical use-value for everybody, consisting of its ability to be the bearer of exchange-value, or a universal means of exchange.[174]

The universal need for money is something completely different from the need that an individual experiences for one or another item of consumption. Items of consumption are necessary to the commodity producer as an individual; the need for money characterises precisely his nature as a commodity producer. Thus, the need for money is a purely social need in the sense that it arises only in a determinate form of economy, namely, the commodity form. Thus Marx wrote in the preliminary work for *The Holy Family*: 'The need for money is therefore the real need created by the modern economy, and the only need which it creates'.[175]

Accordingly, money has a dual use-value. However, neither of them serves directly to satisfy any concrete need of the possessor of money. The concrete use-value of the money material, gold for example, can be made use of only in

---

172   Marx 1976, p. 184 [Rubin's emphasis].
173   Marx 1971, p. 460.
174   Marx 1970, pp. 47–8.
175   Marx, in Fromm 1961, p. 54.

the case when gold does not yet serve in the capacity of money: when gold fulfils the function of money, its concrete use-value cannot be utilised. But the possessor of money, at the same time, still does not acquire any direct usefulness from the specific use-value of money, which consists of its suitability for exchange. This use-value of money still has an 'ideal' character, since it is yet to be realised by way of exchange for those concrete use-values that the commodity producer requires for satisfaction of his needs. Thus Marx characterises money as 'real exchange-value and only nominal use-value'.[176] This ideal use-value has yet to be realised: 'The use-value of this commodity, though real, seems in the exchange process to have merely a *formal* existence, which has still to be realised by conversion into actual use-values'.[177] The formal, functional, or ideal use-value of money has yet to be realised and to find its embodiment in the concrete use-value for which the money exchanges. In the exchange of money for linen, the latter represents concrete embodiment of the use-value of money.[178]

As we see, Marx speaks of the use-value of money in different senses. First of all, the material from which money is made possesses concrete use-value, for instance, gold for the filling of teeth, the making of jewellery, etc.; second, money has a formal or functional use-value that satisfies 'universal need' and results from the social function that money performs in commodity society; third, the use-value of money can be understood as the use-value of the commodities that are purchased with the help of money.

b)   *The Hoard*

In simple commodity economy, the commodity producer endeavours to gain from the sale of his product the largest possible sum of money, but the latter serves him in the purchase of necessary items of consumption. Accordingly, the formal use-value of money here plays a role merely as representative of the concrete use-values of those products that will be purchased by the commodity producer. Exchange-value is the representative of use-value. But already, within the limits of simple commodity economy, the commodity producer is compelled to undertake a number of activities whose direct goal is the formal use-value of money itself (i.e. exchange-value), and not the concrete use-value of those products that can be purchased with the help of money. In such case, the money already ceases to be a means of circulation that is spent on the pur-

---

176   Marx 1970, p. 139.
177   Marx 1970, p. 48 [Rubin's emphasis].
178   Marx 1976, p. 203.

chase of necessary items of consumption. This change of character on money's part is revealed in its functions as a hoard and as means of payment. Marx initially shows that the commodity producer's need to retain the money, which is gained from sale of the product, is dictated by the requirement of satisfying his personal needs. The commodity producer's needs continuously recur and impel him to purchase other people's commodities, while the production and sale of his own commodity involves specific periods of time and is subject to various contingencies.[179] For this reason, the commodity producer temporarily withholds a part of the money acquired in order gradually to spend it, as required, for the satisfaction of his needs. In this case, money fulfils the role only of 'detained coin' (i.e. of temporarily immobilised means of circulation), not the role of a hoard.

Money begins to play the latter role only from the moment when it is withdrawn from circulation precisely in order to preserve exchange-value in its directly social form. Marx shows that the very fact of the appearance and spread of commodity circulation already brings to life a 'need and passionate desire' to hold on to money in the form of a hoard.[180] The mere fact that it is possible to retain in one's own hands exchange-value, in its money form, evokes the passionate desire and need to retain money: 'With the possibility of keeping hold of the commodity as exchange-value, or exchange-value as a commodity, the lust for gold awakens'.[181] Money represents an enormous social power, and this 'social power becomes the private power of private persons'.[182] The passion to accumulate money itself results from the fact that money exists, i.e. it results from the determinate social form of the economy. 'Money is not just *an* object of the passion for enrichment; it is *the* object of it'.[183]

As we see, an objective social fact – the emergence and spread of commodity production and of monetary circulation – is the source for the appearance and spread of new human passions, new needs, and new motives for behaviour. The activity of the commodity producer, selling his product with the goal of accumulating a hoard, is already fundamentally different in terms of character and motive from the activity of a commodity producer who sells his product in order to use the money acquired to purchase necessary items of consumption. The behaviour of the latter commodity producer is directed by his endeavour to satisfy personal needs; the activity of the former commodity producer is

---

179   Marx 1976, p. 228.
180   Marx 1976, p. 227.
181   Marx 1976, p. 229.
182   Marx 1976, p. 230.
183   Marx 1970, p. 132.

directed to the satisfaction of his need for money, i.e. a need that appeared and grew only together with a determinate social form of economy.

> The simple fact that the commodity-owner is able to retain his commodities in the form of exchange-value, or to retain the exchange-value as commodities, makes the exchange of commodities, in order to recover them transformed into gold, the specific motive of circulation. The metamorphosis of commodities C–M takes place for the sake of their metamorphosis, for the purpose of transforming particular physical wealth into general social wealth. Change of form – instead of exchange of matter – becomes an end in itself. Exchange-value, which was merely a form, is turned into the content of the movement.[184]

The newly emerged need, the need for money, not only acts alongside of the personal needs of the commodity producer; it endeavours to drive them out and take their place. In order to accumulate money, the commodity producer must sell as much as possible and purchase as little as possible; he must restrict the satisfaction of his personal needs. 'The hoarder therefore sacrifices the lusts of his flesh to the fetish of gold. He takes the gospel of abstinence very seriously'.[185] The 'natural' needs of the individual are relegated to the background by his new and purely social need to have in his hands the enormous social power that money represents. 'Because he desires to satisfy all social requirements, he scarcely satisfies the most urgent physical wants'.[186]

By its very nature, the need for accumulation of a hoard is unlimited, as distinct from an individual's personal needs, which always have a concrete character and require concrete products for their satisfaction.

> The formation of hoards therefore has no intrinsic limits, no bounds in itself, but is an unending process, each particular result of which provides an impulse for a new beginning. Although the hoard can only be increased by being preserved, on the other hand it can only be preserved by being increased.[187]

The more the need to accumulate a hoard is satisfied, the stronger it becomes in demanding further accumulation of the hoard. The accumulation of hoards,

---

184 Marx 1970, pp. 127–8.
185 Marx 1976, p. 231.
186 Marx 1970, p. 134.
187 Marx 1970, p. 132.

therefore, is an activity that tends perpetually to be repeated, and the need for money is the sort of need that is never satisfied by the result achieved. The continuously repeated activity of accumulating a hoard makes a definite impression upon the individual, transforms him into the specific social type of a 'professional hoarder' and imparts to him, as Marx says, a specific 'economic character'. This hoarder is also distinguished by a specific psychological way of life that has often been clearly described in world literature. *Miserliness* not only becomes the life's work of the hoarder, but it is also sanctioned and sanctified by religion and encouraged by the Fathers of the Church in their exhortations as well as by the Mercantilists in their works.[188] The puritan creed, with its severe preaching of frugality and asceticism, reflected the need of early capitalist economy for a more extensive accumulation of hoards.

The spread and strengthening of the function of money as a hoard signifies a new stage in the history of human needs. It indicates the extension and intensification of the specific, formal use-value of money. If the need for money, as means of circulation, reflected only the commodity producer's need for items of consumption, the need for money as a hoard already lacks any 'natural' character and is itself generated by the social form of the economy, namely, by the spread of commodity production and circulation. The functioning of money, in the role of a hoard, is accompanied by the appearance of completely new and 'formal' needs that are inherent only in the commodity producer, not in the individual in general. The need for money is already an end in itself in the activity of the commodity producer, no longer involving merely his quest to satisfy personal needs. Moreover, the need for money aims to marginalise the 'natural' needs of the individual for items of consumption. Exchange-value already becomes an end in itself and is no longer the representative of use-value. This marginalisation of use-value into the background is revealed not only in the activities of separate commodity producers but also in the character of the entire production process. Whereas previously the simple commodity producer's scale of production was determined by the extent of his personal needs, which await satisfaction, now these limits upon production already fall away. The commodity producer, withholding and accumulating money as a hoard, must expand production as much as he can with his still backward and imperfect means of production. 'The accumulation of money for the sake of money is in fact the barbaric form of production for the sake of production, i.e.,

---

188 Marx 1978, p. 139.

the development of the productive powers of social labour *beyond the limits of customary requirements*'.[189]

c) *Means of Payment*

We see a further increase of the need for money, as such, with the appearance of money's new function, namely, as means of payment. The commodity producer, who bought a commodity on credit, must now sell his own product not in order to use the money acquired for the purchase of necessary items of consumption but rather to retire his debt with the money he has received. For him, the money no longer represents use-value or consumer items but rather an end in itself. Now the commodity producer no longer needs concrete use-values but instead the specific, formal use-value that money possesses.

By comparison with a hoard, the function of money as means of payment demonstrates further intensification of the importance that the formal use-value of money has for the commodity producer. For the accumulator of a hoard, the issue of whether to retain the money himself or to spend it on the purchase of consumer items depended upon his arbitrary judgement. If the money must fulfil the role of means of payment, the commodity producer is already compelled to use the money for this purpose and cannot spend it upon his own personal consumption. He must convert the product into money; and he needs the money, in turn, to pay the debt, i.e. it must serve as formal use-value.

> The conversion of products into money in the sphere of circulation appears originally simply as an individual necessity for the commodity-owner when his own product does not constitute use-value for himself, but has still to become a use-value through alienation. In order to make payment on the contractual settlement day, however, he must already have sold commodities. The evolution of the circulation process thus turns selling into a *social necessity* for him, quite irrespective of his *individual needs* ... The conversion of commodities into money as a final act, or the first metamorphosis of commodities as the ultimate goal, which in hoarding appeared to be the whim of the commodity-owner, has now become an economic function. The motive and the content of selling for the sake of payment constitutes the content of the circulation process, a content arising from its very form.[190]

---

189 Marx 1970, p. 134.
190 Marx 1970, pp. 141–2 [Rubin's emphasis].

The development of commodity circulation itself causes the appearance of a new need, the need for money for payment; this need for money presupposes the extension of commodity production and circulation, and the intensification of the formal use-value that inheres in money. The need for money, as means of payment, is independent of the personal needs of the commodity producer; it represents a purely social need that arises only in the given system of production relations between people, and it entirely subordinates the commodity producer to itself.

The activities of the commodity producer are subordinated to the laws of social necessity; and this necessity has an economic character, since the need for payment of debt is imposed by the entire system of relations among people as commodity producers. But this economic necessity is also sanctioned by juridical necessity; the commodity producer knows that, if he refuses to pay the debt, his property will be subject to forced sale according to the law.[191] As the activity of the hoarder is sanctified by religion, so the relation between the commodity producer-creditor and the commodity producer-debtor is regulated by the law.[192]

We have seen that money, as a hoard, already ceased to be the representative of concrete use-values for the commodity producer; and conversely, concrete use-values were significant to him only insofar as they represented universal wealth – money. It is exactly the same with the commodity producer who sells his product with the purpose of retiring a previous debt; concrete use-values only play the role of representatives of abstract wealth – money. For this reason, any inability to sell the product in periods of crisis is the equivalent for him of the complete loss of use-value. In moments of monetary crisis, use-values become something completely useless by comparison with cash.[193]

Thus, the spread of money in the role of means of payment signifies a strengthening and expansion of the need for money for the sake of its specific, formal use-value. This need is independent of the personal needs of individual commodity producers. The satisfaction of this universal need for money is dictated to each individual commodity producer by the force of laws of social necessity; it is imposed upon him by the entire network of social production relations in which he is included.

---

191 Marx 1976, p. 234.
192 Marx 1970, p. 140.
193 Marx 1970, p. 146.

d)   *The Use-Value of Labour Power*

The development of commodity economy brings the appearance of a new use-value, the 'formal' use-value of money. As we know, however, the development of commodity economy does not stop there. As a result of the expropriation of small producers, the simple commodity economy is transformed into a capitalist one. In the latter, money already serves not simply as means of circulation, i.e. as the mediating link in exchange of one product for another, but also as capital. The emergence and development of capitalist relations causes the appearance of new types of 'functional', or 'formal', use-value. Insofar as the process of producing capital is concerned, the self-expansion of the latter has its source in the exploitation of wage-labour or labour power. For the capitalist, labour power is the means for extraction of surplus value or profit. In that capacity, labour power acquires for the capitalist a special use-value that is formal, or functional, in the sense that labour power possesses it only in the conditions of capitalist economy.

The use-value of labour power consists, above all, in its active manifestations, i.e. in labour.[194] The use-value of labour power is expressed 'only in the actual utilization, in the process of the consumption of the labour-power'.[195]

The capitalist buys labour power, which, in the process of production, appears as activity, as labour. But since labour in capitalist society has a dual character, the following question arises: Does the use-value of labour power lie in its ability to be the source of concrete labour or of abstract labour? Marx provides an unequivocal response to this question:

> The value of labour-power, and the value which that labour-power valorizes [*verwertet*] in the labour-process, are two entirely different magnitudes; and this difference was what the capitalist had in mind when he was purchasing the labour-power. The useful quality of labour-power, by virtue of which it makes yarn or boots, was to the capitalist merely the necessary condition for his activity; for in order to create value labour must be expended in a useful manner. What was really decisive for him was *the specific use-value* which this commodity possesses of being *the source of value*, even of more value than it has itself. This is the specific service the capitalist expects from labour-power.[196]

---

194   Marx 1976, pp. 277–8.
195   Marx 1976, p. 279.
196   Marx 1976, pp. 300–1 [Rubin's emphasis].

Thus, the specific use-value of labour power is its property of being the source of abstract labour, or of value. It is true that we encounter expressions at certain places in Marx that appear to suggest, at first sight, that the use-value of labour power appears in concrete acts of labour, or in concrete labour. But Marx always emphasises that concrete labour appears here only as the necessary condition for appropriation by the capitalist of abstract labour, or of value.

> It is not this concrete character of labour, its use-value as such – that it is for example tailoring labour, cobbling, spinning, weaving, etc. – which forms its specific use-value for capital ... what forms its specific use-value for capital is its character as the element which creates exchange-value, abstract labour.[197]

If we considered the use-value of labour power to be its ability to serve as the source of concrete labour, we would have no way of showing the difference between the purchase of labour power and the purchase of a service. Yet Marx thought it necessary to make a clear distinction between these two types of purchase and sale, regarding only the first type as the characteristic accompaniment of capitalist economy.

> Labour-power is not purchased under this system for the purpose of satisfying the personal needs of the buyer, either by its service or through its product. The aim of the buyer is to increase the value of his capital, the production of commodities which contain more labour than he paid for, and therefore contain a portion of value which costs him nothing and is nevertheless realized [*realisiert*] through the sale of those commodities.[198]

Thus the purchase of labour power must be strictly distinguished from the purchase of so-called 'services', i.e. from purchase of the worker's capacity for concrete labour that serves to satisfy the personal needs of the buyer. The hiring of a gardener by the capitalist owner of a great horticultural establishment is an act of purchasing labour power, but if the same capitalist hires a gardener to care for the garden of his own estate, this involves not the purchase of labour power but rather the purchase of a service. Marx always condemned the representatives of vulgar political economy for confusing these two types of purchase.

---

197 Marx 1963, p. 400.
198 Marx 1976, p. 769.

Instead of speaking of wage-labour, the term 'services' is used. This word again omits the specific characteristic of wage-labour and of its use – namely, that it increases the value of the commodities against which it is exchanged, that it creates surplus-value – and in doing so, it disregards the specific relationship through which money and commodities are transformed into capital. '*Service*' is labour seen only as *use-value* (which is a side issue in capitalist production) just as the term 'product' fails to express the essence of *commodity* and its inherent contradiction.[199]

Thus, the use-value of labour power is its ability to create value. This is why labour power is defined by Marx as a commodity, whose use-value possesses the specific property of being the source of value.[200] But labour power is purchased by the capitalist only because it is the source of a greater sum of values than the value of this labour power itself. Labour power is the source not only of value but also of surplus value, and it is precisely acquisition of the latter that constitutes the purpose for which the capitalist buys labour power. For this reason, Marx often defines the use-value of labour power as its ability to create a surplus of value, or surplus value. 'The use-value of labour power for the industrial capitalist is that of producing more value (profit) in its use than it possesses and costs itself. This excess value is its use-value for the industrial capitalist'.[201]

Following this exposition, it is easy to understand that the use-value of labour power also has a formal, or functional, character, just as the use-value of money does. Labour power only has the ability to be a source of value and surplus value within a determinate social-economic formation and in the presence of a determinate system of production relations between people. When Marx speaks of the specific use-value of labour power, he has in mind not its technical ability to be the source of concrete labour but rather its social ability to be the source of abstract labour, or of value. This use-value has a formal character because it results from the specific form of wage-labour that is inherent in the capitalist economy.

e) *The Use-Value of Loanable Money-Capital*

It is only due to the exploitation of labour power in the production process that the capitalist class as a whole can extract surplus value. But with the division of

---

199   Marx 1968, p. 501.
200   Marx 1976, p. 270.
201   Marx 1992, p. 473.

this class into industrial and money capitalists, the latter acquire the possibility of extracting surplus value in the form of interest without participating directly in the organisation of the production process. The money capitalist lends his money-capital to the industrialist from whom he receives, in the form of interest, a portion of the surplus value extracted by the latter. The sum of money that the industrial capitalist receives on loan has for him a special use-value, consisting of its ability to be a source of surplus value.

> What then is the use-value that the money capitalist alienates for the duration of the loan and makes over to the productive capitalist, the borrower? It is the use-value that money receives through the fact that it can be transformed into capital, that it can function as capital so as to produce in its movement a definite surplus-value, the average profit ... besides conserving its original value. With other commodities, the use-value is ultimately consumed, and in this way the substance of the commodity disappears, and with it its value. The commodity of capital, on the other hand, has the peculiar property that the consumption of its use-value not only maintains its value and use-value but in fact increases it. It is this use-value that money has as capital – the capacity to produce the average profit – that the money capitalist alienates to the industrial capitalist for the period during which he gives him control of the capital loaned.[202]

It is quite obvious that this use-value of the loan of money-capital has a formal or functional character, i.e. it results from the capitalist system of production relations. 'As distinct from an ordinary commodity, however, this use-value is itself a value, i.e., the excess of the value that results from the use of the money as capital over its original magnitude. *The profit is this use-value*'.[203] 'Value as such (interest) comes to be *the use-value* of capital'.[204]

This use-value is possessed by capital that is provided as a loan, i.e. capital as a commodity. But in a developed capitalist economy, every more or less important sum of money can function in the role of capital. Consequently, the aforementioned specific use-value inheres not only in capital as a commodity but also in money as capital. In a developed capitalist economy, every significant sum of money can be regarded as a specific form of capital and, in turn,

---

202 Marx 1992, pp. 472–3.
203 Marx 1992, p. 473.
204 Marx 1992, p. 476, note.

has the ability to be transformed into capital. Thus money, together with the formal use-value that it possesses in any commodity economy (namely, the ability to serve as means of circulation, as a hoard and as means of payment), also acquires in capitalist economy a second, formal use-value, consisting of its ability to serve as a source of surplus value.

It goes without saying that the use-value of capital as a commodity, and of money as capital, is itself inextricably connected with the use-value of labour power that we considered previously. If labour power did not possess the property of being a source of value and surplus value, neither money-capital nor money could be a source of the latter. Money-capital has the capacity to be a source of the average profit precisely because it can be spent on the purchase of labour power, which has the capacity to be a source of value and surplus value.

> Since, on the basis of capitalist production, a certain sum of values represented in money or commodities – actually in money, the converted form of the commodity – makes it possible to extract a certain amount of labour gratis from the workers and to appropriate a certain amount of surplus-value, surplus-labour, surplus product, it is obvious that money itself can be sold as a commodity, that is, as a commodity *sui generis*.[205]

Accordingly, *the use-value* of capital as a commodity has its source in *the use-value of labour power*. On the surface of the market, however, this internal connection between phenomena is obscured and hidden due to the separation of the class of money capitalists from industrial capitalists. Since the money capitalist is not directly involved in the production process and does not purchase labour power, the illusion arises that money capital, by itself, has the capacity to create interest, completely apart from its use to purchase labour power, which is employed in the process of production.

Since the use-value of loanable money-capital has its source in labour power, it is not surprising that a certain analogy can be drawn between them.

> The money loaned in this way is to a certain extent analogous in this respect to labour-power, in its position vis-à-vis the industrial capitalist ... The use-value of labour-power for the industrial capitalist is that of producing more value (profit) in its use than it possesses and costs itself. This excess value is its use-value for the industrial capitalist. And the use-

---

205 Marx 1971, p. 455.

value of the loaned money capital similarly appears as a capacity to annex and increase value.[206]

Marx makes the same point in another place: 'Just as in the case of labour-power, *the use-value of money here becomes that* of creating exchange-value, *more exchange-value than it itself contains*'.[207]

We began with the use-value of money, and we have ended with the same issue. But if money appeared originally as money, now it plays the role of capital. If the use-value of money, as money, resulted from the particular features of commodity economy, the use-value of money as capital results from the particular features of capitalist economy. In both cases, the social form of the commodity itself (i.e. money) acquires a particular and specific use-value. As distinct from the use-value that inheres in a concrete product, independently of any determinate social form of the production process, the present case involves use-value as the result of a specific social form of economy. This use-value has a functional, or formal, character.

---

206   Marx 1992, p. 473.
207   Marx 1971, p. 458.

DOCUMENT 17

Fundamental Features of Marx's Theory of Value and How It Differs from Ricardo's Theory (1924)

Isaak Il'ich Rubin

Source: Introduction to I[saiah] Rosenberg, *Teoriya stoimosti u Ricardo i u Marksa: kriticheskii etyud* (Moscow: Moskovskii rabochii, 1924), pp. 6–62.[1]

Introduction by the Editors

In his essay on Marx's teaching regarding production and consumption, Isaak Rubin analysed the relation between use-value and exchange-value, emphasising that the concrete use-value of particular commodities was not a primary concern for Marx as distinct from the economists of the Austrian school. Marx was interested in the social process of the production and expansion of value, not in use-value as such. In this essay Rubin addresses a related duality, that between *concrete* and *abstract* labour, in order to draw a similar distinction between Marx and Ricardo in terms of their respective theories of value. 'It is', he explains, 'precisely in the "dual character of labour" that Marx saw the central element of his theory of value ... [T]he dual character of labour reflects the difference between the *material-technical* process of production and its *social form*. This difference ... is the basis of the whole of Marxist economic theory, including the theory of value'.

Just as marginal utility theory emphasises concrete use-values rather than the value 'form', so Ricardo studied the material-technical process of production, and particularly the result of changes in labour productivity, without reference to the particular 'social form' of capitalist production relations. Both essays express Rubin's recurring theme that the fundamental distinction of Marxist political economy, deriving from awareness of the specificity of the capitalist mode of production, is Marx's elaboration of historically formed *pro*-

---

1 The German edition of the book is Rosenberg 1904. Some sections of this essay by Rubin have also appeared in Chapters 1, 2, 4 and 8 of Rubin 1990. We have retranslated them for this volume.

duction relations between people. While Adam Smith was aware of historical stages, moving from the Age of Hunters to that of Shepherds, then to Agriculture and eventually to Commerce[2] – which he regarded as most appropriate for the flourishing of human nature – Ricardo turned the study of political economy in a different direction by taking capitalist relations to be fixed and beyond the scope of inquiry. With few exceptions, such as Richard Jones and later the German historical school, Ricardo's lack of interest in history became a common characteristic of bourgeois economic theory,[3] culminating in the marginalists' preoccupation with a universal logic of price determination through subjective, individual judgements.

Throughout all the works by Rubin that we have translated for this volume, he assesses economic theory with reference to 'determinations of form' in their historical context. The dialectical logic of Marx's work apprehends in theory the logical succession of production relations arising from the fundamental contradictions of commodity production and exchange. In terms of philosophical sophistication, Rubin's work is reminiscent of the pioneering essays by Georg Lukács in *History and Class Consciousness*. Lukács declared that the bourgeoisie is at home with its non-historical and formal-mathematical way of thinking – which he described as 'false consciousness' in a world of 'reification' – because an historical awareness, and particularly an attempt to theorise the periodic crises that generate historical change, would require a dialectical approach, demonstrating that capitalism points beyond itself to socialism.[4] In

---

2 Smith 1982, p. 27.

3 Today, economic theory is treated as applied mathematics, leaving 'history' and the history of economic thought on the margins of the discipline or even completely absent from undergraduate education.

4 Lukács 1971, p. 105. Lukács associates the word 'reification' with 'false consciousness' because 'reification' means 'the treatment of something abstract as a material or concrete thing' (*Encyclopædia Britannica Ultimate Reference Suite*, Chicago: Encyclopædia Britannica, 2011). The *Oxford International Dictionary of the English Language* (1958) gives this entry for 'Reify': 'To convert mentally into a thing; to materialize'. In this essay Rubin uses the words 'вещный' and 'овеществленный', which may be translated as 'thing-like' and 'thingified', respectively. Both words are better translated as 'reified'. Rubin also speaks of 'овеществление' ('reification'). Notations will be provided where these words occur in the text.

In *History and Class Consciousness* Lukács says the following of bourgeois economy theory:

'The limits of the abstract and formal method are revealed in the fact that its chosen goal is an abstract system of "laws" ... But the formal abstraction of these "laws" transform[s] economics into a closed partial system. And this in turn is unable to penetrate its own material substratum, nor can it advance from there to an understanding of society in its entirety and so it is compelled to view that substratum as an immutable, eternal "datum". Science

their consciousness of Marx's methodological debt to Hegel, Rubin and Lukács far surpassed most of their Marxist contemporaries.

Following Hegel's principle that the whole is logically prior to the parts, Marx emphasised in the *Contribution to the Critique of Political Economy* that political economy presupposes capitalist society as its subject, and that the resulting economic categories are exclusively those of the capitalist social formation. Labour and means of production certainly predate capitalism, but when Marx writes of labour and means of production his concern is *wage-labour* and means of production that are owned by *capital*. The categories of political economy are 'abstractions' that 'retain their full validity only for and within' a specific historical context.[5]

> Just as in general when examining any historical or social science, so also in the development of economic categories it is always necessary to remember that the subject, in this context contemporary bourgeois society, is presupposed both in reality and in the mind, and that therefore categories express forms of existence and conditions of existence – and sometimes merely separate aspects – of this particular society, the subject; thus the category, *even from the scientific standpoint*, by no means begins at the moment when it is discussed *as such*.[6]

In terms of logic, Hegel also believed that the whole is implicit in the parts and can therefore be deduced from them. Marx translated this to mean that all the contradictions of capitalism are implicit in the fundamental contra-

---

is thereby debarred from comprehending the development and the demise, the social character of its own material base, no less than the range of possible attitudes towards it and the nature of its own formal system' (Lukács 1971, p. 105).

In *Capital*, Vol. III, Marx wrote:

'[The] irrational forms in which certain economic relationships appear and are grasped in practice do not bother the practical bearers of these relationships in their everyday dealings; since they are accustomed to operating within these forms, it does not strike them as anything worth thinking about. A complete contradiction holds nothing at all mysterious for them. In forms of appearance that are estranged from their inner connection and, taken in isolation, are absurd, they feel as much at home as a fish in water. What Hegel says about certain mathematical formulae applies here too, namely that what the common human understanding finds irrational is in fact rational, and what it finds rational is irrational' (Marx 1992, p. 914).

5 Marx 1970, p. 212.
6 Ibid.

diction of the commodity.⁷ Rubin follows Marx in emphasising that concrete individual labour, in a commodity-producing society, can only become social labour through a process of abstraction that generates the dialectic of reification. 'Value' is a social form, whose content is concrete labour that has been abstracted.

> The equalisation of all types of labour through market equalisation of all the products of labour as values – this is what Marx means by the concept of abstract labour. And since the equalisation of labour through the equalisation of things results from the social form of commodity economy, in which there is no direct social organisation and equalisation of labour, it follows that abstract labour is a social and historical concept. *Abstract labour does not express a physiological equality of the various types of labour, but rather the social equalisation of various types of labour that occurs in the specific form of market equalisation of the products of labour as values.*⁸

Value, money, capital, and the various other categories of political economy are, on the one hand, relations between people; but they are simultaneously 'things' that have acquired a social-functional existence. Exchange-value is not the inherent property of a useful product of human labour, nor is wage-labour the natural form of human productive activity. Nevertheless, the requirement that labour become abstract in order to appear as social labour also entails the consequence that the resulting social forms appear to be real and concrete. 'This "reification"⁹ consists of the fact that the thing, with respect to which

---

7 Lukács remarked that 'the essence of the dialectical method lies in the fact that in every aspect correctly grasped by the dialectic the whole totality is comprehended ... [T]he chapter [in *Capital*] dealing with the fetish character of the commodity contains within itself the whole of historical materialism ...' (Lukács 1971, p. 170). Lenin added in his *Philosophical Notebooks*: 'In his *Capital*, Marx first analyses the simplest, most ordinary and fundamental, most common and everyday *relation* of bourgeois (commodity) society, a relation encountered billions of times, viz., the exchange of commodities. In this very simple phenomenon (in this "cell" of bourgeois society) analysis reveals *all* the contradictions (or the germs of *all* contradictions) of modern society. The subsequent exposition shows us the development (*both* growth *and* movement) of these contradictions and of this society in the Σ [the sum] of its individual parts. From its beginning to its end' (Lenin 1915b, pp. 358–9).
8 Compare this comment with Hilferding's criticism of Wilhelm Liebknecht in Document 10 of this volume.
9 Here Rubin speaks of 'овеществление'.

people enter into a certain relation between themselves, fulfils a special *social function* of linking people together, the function of mediator or "bearer" of the particular production relation between people'.

It was perfectly understandable, therefore, for classical political economy to treat earlier social formations as 'obsolete' or 'artificial'. Capitalism appeared to be 'rational' and 'natural' precisely because it answered, at least for a time, the need of the productive forces to develop. But, in that sense, the social forms of reification also became objectively necessary. Previous human communities mediated diverse human labour activities through culture, consensus, or some recognised social authority. Capitalism, in contrast, depends upon the regulating role of the law of value. Marx saw that reification will only end when the associated producers socialise the means of production and consciously plan their own labour activities. All the elements of social labour will then become concrete and truly rational through the exercise of conscious foresight.

In this essay, Rubin emphasises the integrity of Marx's work at the same time as he explains its originality. He shows the logical connections between the three volumes of *Capital*, refutes the allegation of a contradiction between the labour theory of value and the average rate of profit, and concludes that Marx, while he was Ricardo's successor in terms of seeing labour as the *content* of value, also advanced far beyond Ricardo in his differentiation between concrete and abstract labour, and the resulting treatment of value as a specific historical *form*. With his elaboration of the 'dual character' of both labour and value, Marx, rather than completing the theory of the classics, became the originator of an entirely new economic theory.

∴

Isaak Rubin on Marx's Theory of Value and How It Differs from Ricardo's Theory

1   *Introduction*

The question of the relationship of Marx's economic theory to the theories of his classical predecessors, and especially to Ricardo's theory, is one of great scientific interest. We can confidently say that without a clear grasp of Marx's relationship to Ricardo we cannot achieve a proper understanding of the novelty that Marx brought to theoretical economics or of the place he occupies in the history of economic thought. At first sight, it would appear that this question must have been resolved long ago and cannot be open to any particular doubts in our time. A century has already passed since Ricardo's great work appeared, and more than half a century since the day when Volume I of *Capital* first saw the light. Is it really possible that even up to the present day the question of Marx's relationship to classical political economy is still not finally resolved? One has to say that, unfortunately, that is exactly how matters stand. It is difficult to find any two economists who are in complete agreement on this question, and the reader will find quite a few contradictory judgements on the matter in the book by Rosenberg that we are bringing to his attention. In our day this question still provokes lively debates, and economic science is less able than ever before to consider it resolved.

Strange though this phenomenon may first appear, there is a twofold reason for it. On the one hand, since the end of the nineteenth century bourgeois economic science has been intensively reconsidering its formerly prevalent views concerning the theory of value in Smith and Ricardo. Until that time the economic theory of the classics, with one or another modification, represented the generally accepted basis upon which newer theoretical constructs arose. The historical school's attacks on the abstract, deductive method of the classics failed because the historical school quickly revealed its own complete theoretical inadequacy. Things changed dramatically at the end of the nineteenth century. The theory of marginal utility appeared on the scene of official science and speedily prevailed. This theory could not ignore the objective theory of value that the classics set out in their day and that served as the starting point for Marx's theory of value. The most uncompromising representatives of the subjective school launched a decisive frontal attack on the classics, attempting to show how incorrect, contradictory and unsubstantiated their theories were. Other representatives of official science preferred to encircle the classics from the rear and to show that, in essence, they never supported the theory of labour value and that it was simply an error to regard them in such terms over the course of a century. Adam Smith now began to be described as a theorist of subjective labour value or even of use-value (a view with some foundation), and as a precursor of the theory of marginal utility (for which there is no foundation). In Ricardo's doctrine there was now discerned a theory of costs of production but with no connection to labour value. Insofar as Smith is concerned, the critical 'revision' of previously accepted views of his theory of value provided some positive results in our opinion and underlined the variety of ideological influences and theoretical motives that were intertwined in his theory. But even these positive results were presented by critics in an extremely one-sided and exaggerated form, and this applies all the more to Ricardo. Attempts to deny the importance that the theory of labour value had for Ricardo are fundamentally false and do not so much correct as distort perspectives in the development of economic thought.

If bourgeois economic science has recently busied itself with 'reappraising what was valuable' in the classical school, Marxist thought, on the other hand, has acquired in the three volumes of *Theories of Surplus-Value* new and extensive material that permits us to look more deeply into the relationship between Marx's theory and the theories of his predecessors. This question awaits detailed study. In our day it not only continues to cause disagreements between supporters and opponents of Marxism, but even within each of these two camps it fails to find a unanimous response. The complexity and debateable character of the question of Marx's relationship to the classics fully justifies translation into Russian of Rosenberg's book on theories of value in Marx and Ricardo. The author – a supporter of Marx's theory of value – clearly and systematically presents the teachings of Ricardo and Marx and compares their merits. On a whole series of points, he attentively traces both the similarities and the differences between the two thinkers. However, this systematic and detailed analysis of separate points in the two theories, which is the great achievement of Rosenberg's book, is also the source of its weaknesses.[10] The author does not elucidate the general, methodological foundations of the two theories and, as a result, is inclined to treat them as similar without sufficiently clarifying the difference of principle between them. Rosenberg is also led in this direction by his heated and completely successful polemic against the critics who claim that Ricardo's theory has no connection with the theory of labour value. His forceful emphasis upon Ricardo's importance as a theorist of labour value on the one hand, and the absence of any characterisation of the general methodological principles of Marx's theory of value on the other, lead Rosenberg to an extreme convergence of the two theories. The author notes several disagreements between them on individual questions, but he is unable to show just what is new in principle in Marx's contribution to economic science and what distinguishes him from Ricardo. The author himself senses this fact, and he even asserts that the disagreements between Ricardo and Marx are 'only very slightly' a result of differences between their theories of value and are explained, for the most part, by the differences between their 'historical, sociological and philosophical views' (p. 112). It is not possible to agree with this opinion. There is a fundamental difference between the economic theories of Ricardo and Marx in general terms, and particularly between their theories of value. Our intention in this article will be to clarify this aspect of the question and thus to correct the perspective that one gets from reading Rosenberg's book. In conformity with this objective, our article cannot undertake a detailed

---

10   See Hilferding 1922, pp. 63–78. [See Document 11 in this volume].

analysis of individual questions but instead provides a general outline of the methodological foundations of Marxist economic theory and a general characterisation of his theory of value. We then turn to a comparison of the theories of Ricardo and Marx in which we touch upon our points of disagreement with Rosenberg's presentation.

2 Methodological Foundations of Marx's Economic Theory

In conceptual terms, Marx's economic theory is closely related to his sociological theory, the theory of historical materialism. Years ago Hilferding noted that the theory of historical materialism and the theory of labour value have a common starting point, namely, labour 'in its importance as the element that constitutes human society and whose development determines, in the last instance, social development'.[11] We can study the labour activity of people, joined together in a society, from two different perspectives: either as the aggregate of means of production and technical devices, with whose assistance man overcomes nature and produces the products he requires, or as the sum total of social relations that connect people in the process of production. Hence the difference between the technical and the economic – between the material-technical process of production and its social form, between the productive forces and the social relations of production among people. Both the theory of historical materialism and Marx's economic theory revolve around one and the same basic question of the relationship between the productive forces and the production relations among people. The subject of investigation is the same in both cases: *the change of production relations among people in accordance with development of the productive forces*. The adjustment of people's production relations to development of the productive forces – a process that occurs in the form of a gradually increasing contradiction between them, which in turn brings cataclysms – represents the basic theme of the theory of historical materialism. Taking the same general methodological approach to commodity-capitalist society, we come to Marx's economic theory. It investigates *the production relations among people in capitalist society*, the process of their adaptation to the given level of development of the productive forces, and growth of the contradiction between them, which is expressed, among other things, in crises.

Thus political economy does not study the labour process as such, in terms of its material-technical aspect, but rather *the social forms of labour organisation*

---

11 Hilferding, *Böhm-Bawerk, kak kritik Marksa* (Moscow: Moskovskii rabochii, 1923), p. 16. [Hilferding 1904].

in capitalist society. Marx's economic theory includes the technique of production, or the productive forces, in the investigation – and the same holds for the theory of historical materialism – only as the precondition or starting point, and they are invoked only insofar as they are needed in order to explain the actual subject being studied, namely, the production relations between people. Marx's consistent distinction between the production process as such and its social form provides him with the key for understanding the entire economic system. It immediately determines the method of political economy as a *social and historical* science. In the diverse and multifaceted chaos of economic life, which involves 'socially combined and scientifically arranged' processes of production,[12] it immediately directs our attention precisely to the 'social combinations' of people in the process of production, to their production relations, for which the technique of production serves as the precondition or the basis. Political economy is a science not of the relations of *things to things*, as vulgar economists have supposed, or of the relations of *people to things*, as the theory of marginal utility claims, but of the relations of *people to people* in the process of production.

Investigating the production relations among people in commodity-capitalist society, political economy presupposes a specific social form of economy and a specific type of society. We cannot properly understand a single comment in Marx's *Capital* unless we keep in mind that it concerns phenomena occurring within a specific society. 'Just as in any *historical social science*, so with regard to economic categories it is always necessary to remember that both in reality and in the mind there is a given subject, in this case *contemporary bourgeois society*, and that the categories therefore express forms of being, conditions of existence – and often only separate aspects – of this specific society, of this subject'.[13] 'In the theoretical method of political economy the subject, that is, society, must always be envisaged as the presupposition'.[14] Beginning with a specific sociological presupposition, namely, with a definite social structure of the economy, political economy must above all provide us with a characterisation of this form of economy and its attendant production relations between people. Marx gives us such a general characterisation in his 'theory of commodity fetishism', which is best understood as a general theory of the production relations of commodity-capitalist society. Once we have familiarised ourselves in this chapter with the general character of these production

---

12   Marx 1976, p. 780.
13   Marx 1970, p. 212 [Rubin's emphasis].
14   Marx 1970, p. 207.

relations, we shall deal in the following chapter with one of these relations, namely, the relation between commodity producers, which is investigated by the theory of value.

Turning to analysis of commodity-capitalist society, we must regard it first of all as a commodity economy consisting of a multitude of separate private undertakings, organised and directed by separate commodity producers on the basis of private property right. The general structure of commodity economy displays the following basic attributes: 1) the individual cells of the economy, that is, the separate private enterprises, are *formally independent* of each other; 2) they are *materially connected* with each other as a result of the social division of labour, in terms of which they are complementary; and 3) a direct link between individual commodity producers is established only through *exchange*, which also indirectly influences their *productive* activity. Within his own enterprise, each commodity producer can freely decide to produce any product with the use of any suitable means of production. But when he takes the finished product of his labour to market for the purpose of exchange, he is not free to establish the exchange proportions but must comply with conditions in the market (the conjuncture) that are the same for all producers of the given product. The producer's dependence upon the market means dependence of his productive activity upon the productive activity of all other members of society. If cloth makers have sent too much cloth to market, then Ivanov, a cloth maker who has not increased his production, nonetheless suffers from a fall in cloth prices and is compelled to curtail his production. If other cloth makers have adopted improved means of production (machines, for example), our cloth maker must likewise improve his production technology. In terms of the pattern, scale and methods of production, an individual commodity producer, who is formally independent from the others, is in fact closely tied up with them through the market, through exchange. Individual commodity producers, who are not linked with one another through social relations in the actual production process, are connected through exchange, through the production relation of buying and selling, through the movement of things. The labour activities of people are connected through the products of labour, and people are connected by things. The exchange of things affects the labour activities of people, and without exchange the very process of capitalist production is impossible. '[T]he capitalist production process, taken as a whole, is a unity of the production and circulation processes'.[15]

---

15   Marx 1992, p. 117.

This role of exchange, as a necessary moment of the production process itself, results from the unorganised character or so-called 'anarchy' of capitalist production. In a socialist society, exchange in its contemporary form would be redundant. Social organs would determine in advance the specific production relations between people that are needed for a proper and steady course of the material-technical production process. Consumer goods and means of production would move from one person to another not on the basis of exchange, or through buying and selling, but in a pattern that is predetermined by society and meets the requirements of the technical production process.

In capitalist society we have an example of organised production relations in the organisation of labour within the enterprise (the technical division of labour), compared with the unorganised distribution of labour between the separate private enterprises (the social division of labour). Suppose that one employer owns a large textile factory that includes divisions for spinning, weaving and dyeing. The engineers, workers and employees are assigned in advance between these divisions according to a definite plan. They are linked together beforehand by definite and permanent production relations that correspond to requirements of the technical process of production. And that is precisely why, within the process of production, things move from one person to another according to the position of these people in production and the production relations between them. Having received yarn from the mill and worked it up into cloth, the director of the cloth division does not send the fabric back to the director of the spinning mill as an equivalent (replacement) for the yarn he previously received. He sends it on to the dyeing department, because the permanent production relations that are established between workers of the weaving mill and those of the dyeing department predetermine the movement of things, the product of labour, from the people employed in the previous phase of production (weaving) to those employed at the next stage (dyeing). The production relations between people are organised in advance for the *purpose* of the material production of things, but not *by way of* the things. On the other hand, the thing moves in the production process from some people to others *on the basis* of the production relations that exist between them, but its movement *does not create* the production relations. The production relations between *people* have an exclusively *social* character, while the movement of *things* has a purely *technical* character. Both of these aspects are consciously adjusted to each other beforehand but retain a different character.

The case is quite different if spinning, weaving and dyeing belong to three different entrepreneurs, A, B and C. Here A does not transfer the yarn he has produced to B solely on the basis that B can rework it into cloth, that is, give it a form useful to society. That is not his business; generally speaking, he has no desire simply to deliver his yarn but rather to sell it, that is, to transfer it to the sort of person who will give him a corresponding sum of money in exchange, or else some other thing of equal value, an equivalent. Who this person might be is a matter of indifference to him. Not being connected with anyone else by permanent social production relations, A enters into the production relation of buying and selling with anyone who has a definite thing, an equivalent sum of money, and who is willing to give it to him in exchange for the yarn. This production relation is confined to the movement of things, namely, by the yarn going from A to the buyer and by the money going from the buyer to A. Thus, the production relations between commodity owners do not exist in advance but are established in the act of purchase and sale, by means of the transfer of things from one person to another; they have, therefore, not only a *social* character but also one of *things*. On the other hand, the thing moves from one person to another not on the basis of production relations previously existing between them but through purchase and sale, which is limited to the transfer of this thing. The transfer of things establishes the production relations between people and has not only *technical* but also *social* significance.

As we see, the basic production relation between people in a commodity society, namely, purchase and sale, is distinguished from production relations of an organised type by the following peculiarities: 1) it is established voluntarily, depending upon how advantageous it is to the participants, so that the *social* connection takes the form of a *private* transaction; 2) it links the participants for a brief interval without creating any permanent production relations between them, yet these *brief* and *interrupted* deals of purchase and sale, taken together, must secure the *permanence* and *continuity* of the social process of production; 3) it links people at the moment when transfer of a thing occurs between them and is limited to this transfer, so that the relation between *people* takes the form of an equalisation of *things*. The establishment of production relations between people does not precede the transfer of things but rather coincides with it. 'The exchange of commodities is the process in which the social exchange of things, i.e., the exchange of particular products of private individuals, involves simultaneous establishment (*Erzeugung*) of definite social production relations, into which individuals enter through this exchange of things'.[16] To put it differently, exchange, or the act of purchase and sale, combines within itself social-economic moments (relations between people) and material-objective moments (the movement of things in the pro-

---

16 Marx 1970, pp. 51–2.

cess of production) that are inseparable. In commodity-capitalist society these two moments are not organised and coordinated in advance, and that is precisely why each separate act of exchange can be accomplished only as a result of the joint and simultaneous occurrence of both of these moments, each of which entails the other. The transfer of things is not possible without the special production relation of purchase and sale being established between their owners. And conversely, people enter into relations with each other not as members of a society, in which they occupy a definite place in the social process of production, but merely as the owners of things.

If any given person enters into production relations with other people merely as the owner of a certain thing, it follows that the thing in question, no matter to whom it belongs, gives its owner the possibility of assuming a definite place in the system of production relations. Insofar as possession of the thing is the *condition* for establishing production relations between people, it appears that the thing itself possesses the ability, the *property*, of establishing production relations. If owners of commodities associate through the exchange of things, and if the given thing enables its owner to enter into an exchange relation with other commodity owners, then the thing itself acquires the special property of being exchangeable – it has 'value'. If the given thing links together two commodity owners, one of whom is a capitalist and the other a worker, then it is not merely a 'value' but also a 'capital'. If the capitalist enters into a production relation with a landowner, then the value or the money that he transfers to the landowner, and through which he enters into a production relation with him, represents 'rent'. The money paid by an industrial capitalist to a financial capitalist for the use of capital borrowed from him is termed 'interest'. *Every type of production relation between people attributes to the things, through which people enter into a production link, a special 'social property', a 'social (economic) form'.* A particular thing, besides being a use-value, or a material thing with definite properties that qualify it to be an item of consumption or a means of production – that is, to fulfil a *technical function* in the process of material production – also fulfils the *social function* of linking people together. People establish their mutual production relations through the medium of things. The things, therefore, become the 'mediators', the 'bearers' of social relations between people. The relations between people are expressed in these social properties acquired by things; they become 'reified'.[17]

Thus, people in commodity-capitalist society enter into social production relations exclusively as commodity owners, as owners of things, while the

---

17   'они "овеществляются"'.

things, conversely, thereby acquire special social properties, a special social form. In place of 'direct social relations between persons and their work', which are established in societies with an organised economy, here we find 'material [*dinglich*] relations between persons and social relations between things'.[18] These two particular characteristics of commodity society – 'personification of things and reification of the relations of production'[19] – are essentially but two sides of one and the same phenomenon that we have described above: the intimate connection and 'direct coalescence' between the process of establishing production relations between people and the movement of things in the process of material production. This 'coalescence' of the technical and social moments of production is regarded by everyday thought, and also by 'vulgar economists', as their identity, and thus the errors arise that Marx disclosed in his theory of commodity fetishism. The errors of bourgeois economists are twofold: 1) either they derive *social* from *technical* phenomena, attributing definite social properties (value, money, capital etc.) to things as such, as elements of technical production (for instance, by deriving the property of capital from the technical functions of means of production); or else 2) they derive *technical* from *social* phenomena (for instance, they assign to capital – i.e. to the social form that capitalist society imposes upon the instruments of labour – the capacity of means of production to raise labour productivity, which is their technical function). Both of these errors, which at first sight appear to be opposite in character, involve one and the same basic methodological defect: identification of the material process of production with its social form, of technique with economics, and of the technical with the social functions of things. This defect was eliminated by Marx's new sociological method.

As we have seen, Marx's method involves consistently distinguishing between productive forces and production relations, between the material process of production and its social form. Political economy investigates the labour activity of people not in terms of its technical devices and instruments of labour but with regard to its social form. It studies the *production relations* established between people in the process of production. But since people in commodity-capitalist society are connected by production relations through the transfer of things, it follows that the production relations among people

---

18 Marx 1976, p. 166.
19 Marx 1992, p. 969. [In this case Fernbach translates as 'reification' the German word '*Versachlichung*' from '*Sache*' (thing, object). Elsewhere he employs the same English rendering for the German word '*Verdinglichung*', from the word '*Ding*' ('thing'), which is legitimate since they are synonymous].

take on a *reified*[20] character. This 'reification'[21] consists of the fact that the thing, with respect to which people enter into a certain relation between themselves, fulfils a special *social function* of linking people together, the function of mediator or 'bearer' of the particular production relation between people. In addition to its material or technical existence as a concrete item of consumption or means of production, the thing acquires, as it were, a *social* or *functional existence*, that is, a special social property (value, money, capital, etc.) that expresses the given production relation between people and gives to the thing a special *social form*, a 'determination of form' (*Formbestimmtheit*). Thus the basic concepts or *categories* of political economy express fundamental *social-economic forms* that characterise the different types of production relations between people and are communicated by the things through which, or involving which, these relations between people are established.

Turning to investigation of the 'economic structure of society', or the 'totality of these relations of production' between people (see the preface to *A Contribution to the Critique of Political Economy*[22]), Marx distinguishes the specific forms or *types of production relations*[23] between people in capitalist society. The order in which Marx studies them is established as follows. Certain of these relations between people presuppose the presence of other types of production relations between members of the given society, while the latter relations do not presuppose the necessary existence of the former and are thus their precondition. For instance, the relation between the money capitalist C and the industrial capitalist B, expressed in the latter receiving a sum of money from the former, already presupposes production relations between the industrial capitalist B and the worker A (or, to be more accurate, many workers). On the other hand, the relation between the industrial capitalist and the worker does not entail the need for the former to receive money on loan from capitalist C. Hence, it is understandable that the economic categories 'capital' and 'surplus value' precede the categories of 'loan capital' and 'interest'. Furthermore, the relation between the industrial capitalist and the worker has the form of purchase and sale of labour power, and it additionally presupposes that the [capitalist] produces a commodity for sale, i.e. is linked to other members of

---

20 [The term that Rubin uses is 'вещный'].
21 [Here Rubin speaks of 'овеществление'].
22 Marx 1970, p. 20.
23 We have in mind not the different types or forms of economy (feudal, capitalist, and so forth) but the different types or forms of production relations between people within the context of a capitalist economy.

society by production relations of commodity owner to commodity owner. The relation between commodity owners, i.e. of purchase and sale, does not presuppose a necessary production link between industrial capitalist and worker. It is understandable, therefore, that the category of 'commodity' or 'value' precedes the category of 'capital'. The logical order of economic categories issues from the character of the production relations they express. Marx's economic system investigates *a series of increasingly complex types of production relations* between people, expressed in a series of increasingly complex *social forms* that are assumed by things. Through all the economic categories, we can follow this link between a given type of production relations among people and the corresponding social function or social form of things.

The fundamental production relation between people, as commodity owners exchanging the products of their labour, gives to [their products] the unique property of being exchangeable in the special 'form of value', as if it were inherent in their nature. Regular exchange relations between people, as a result of which the social activity of commodity owners singles out one commodity (gold, for instance) as a universal equivalent that can be exchanged directly for any other commodity, give to this particular commodity the special function of money, or the 'money form'. This money form, in turn, represents several different functions or forms depending on the character of the production relations between buyers and sellers. If transfer of the commodity from seller to buyer and the reverse transfer of money occur simultaneously, then money fulfils the function or takes the form of 'means of circulation'. If transfer of the commodity precedes the transfer of money, and the relation between seller and buyer turns into the relation between creditor and borrower, then money acquires the function or form of 'means of payment'. If the seller holds on to the money that he receives through sale, postponing the moment of his entry into a new production relation as buyer, then money acquires the function or form of a 'hoard'. Each social function or form of money expresses a different character or type of production relations between the exchanging parties.

With the appearance of a new type of production relations, namely capitalist ones, that link the commodity-owning capitalist with the commodity-owning worker, the money, whose transfer between them establishes the production relation, acquires the new social function or form of 'capital'. More precisely, the money, which directly links the capitalist with the worker, fulfils the function or has the form of 'variable capital'. But, to establish production relations with workers, the capitalist must also possess means of production, or money that indirectly serves the establishment of production relations between capitalist and workers and has the function or form of 'constant capital'. Insofar as we are considering production relations between the class of capitalists and the class of workers in the process of production, we are dealing with 'productive capital' or 'capital in the phase of production'. But before production can begin, the capitalist has entered the market as buyer of means of production and labour power. To this production relation, between the capitalist as buyer and the other commodity owners, corresponds the function or form of 'money capital'. At the conclusion of production the capitalist emerges as seller of his commodity, which finds expression in the function or form of 'commodity capital'. Thus the metamorphosis, or 'transformation' of capital's form, reflects the different forms of production relations between people.

But we have still not exhausted the production relations linking the industrial capitalist with other members of society. In the first place, through competition between capitals and their transfer from one branch to another, the industrial capitalists of one branch are linked to all other industrial capitalists, and this link is expressed in the formation of a 'general average rate of profit' and the sale of commodities at 'prices of production'. Moreover, the class of capitalists is itself divided into several social groups or sub-classes: industrial, merchant and money (or financial) capitalists. Together with these groups, representing the aggregate class of capitalists, there is also the class of landowners. The production relations between these various social groups create new social-economic 'forms': merchant capital and commercial profit, loan capital and interest, along with rent. Capital 'steps as it were from its internal organic life into its external relations, relations where it is not *capital and labour* that confront one another, but on the one hand *capital and capital*, and on the other hand individuals as simple *buyers and sellers*'.[24] Here the issue concerns different types of production relations: 1) between capitalists and workers; 2) between capitalists and other members of society, who appear in the role of buyers and sellers; 3) between separate groups of industrial capitalists and also between the industrial capitalists as a whole and other capitalist groups, i.e. merchant and money capitalists (including the relation between capitalists and landowners). The first type of production relations, representing the basis of capitalist society, is studied by Marx in Volume I of *Capital*, the second type in Volume II, and the third type in Volume III. As for the fundamental production relation of commodity society, the relation between people as commodity producers, Marx provides this analysis in the *Critique of Political Economy* and repeats it in the first section of Volume I of *Capital* under the heading 'Commodities and Money', which represents, as it were, the introduc-

---

24   Marx 1992, p. 135 [Rubin's emphasis].

tion to *Capital*.[25] Marx's system investigates a series of increasingly complex types of production relations between people, to which corresponds a series of increasingly complex economic forms.

Thus the basic categories of political economy express different types of production relations that take on the form of things. Values are only 'relations of men in their productive activity'[26] that are expressed in things. Capital is a social relation expressed 'between things and as things'.[27] Since production relations connect people in commodity society only through things, the latter fulfil a special social function. If economic categories express the production relations between people, we can say with equal justification that they express different *social functions* that are fulfilled by things as the 'bearers' of different production relations. From this point of view, value, money, capital, constant and variable capital, fixed and circulating, etc. represent different social functions. 'What is at issue here is not a set of definitions (of fixed and circulating capital – I.R.), under which *things* are to be subsumed. It is rather definite *functions* that are expressed in specific *categories*'.[28] 'The property of being capital cannot be attributed to things as such ... but is rather a function with which they are or are not endowed according to the given conditions'.[29]

We can see that the categories of political economy express different social functions of things that correspond to the different production relations of people. But, as Marx says, the social function performed by a thing gives it a particular social character, a definite *social form* or 'determination of form' (*Formbestimmtheit*). In the preface to the first edition of Volume I of *Capital*, Marx speaks of the difficulties 'in the analysis of economic forms' in general, and particularly of the 'value-form' and the 'money-form'.[30] The formation of money represents a new 'determinate form'.[31] The different functions of money are at the same time various 'determinate forms'.[32] Capital is 'the *social form which the means of reproduction assume on the basis of wage-labour*',[33] a specific

---

25 In the first draft Marx proposed calling this section: 'Introduction. Commodity. Money'. See Marx 1963, p. 414.
26 Marx 1971, p. 129.
27 Marx 1971, p. 137.
28 Marx 1978, p. 303.
29 Marx 1978, p. 281.
30 Marx 1978, p. 90.
31 Marx 1970, p. 47.
32 Marx 1970, pp. 64, 68.
33 Marx 1971, p. 328.

'social determination'.³⁴ *Marx's system analyses a series of increasingly complex economic forms or 'determinations of form' (Formbestimmtheiten) that correspond to a series of increasingly complex production relations between people.* These forms or functions have a social character since they inhere not in things as such, but in things that are part of a definite social context, things through which, or relative to which, people enter into certain production relations between themselves. These forms do not reflect the properties of things but the properties of the social context.

Sometimes Marx speaks simply of 'form', or 'determinate form', but he frequently uses the following expressions: social form, economic form, historical-social form, social determination of form, economic determination of form, or historical-social determination. Sometimes Marx speaks of things acquiring 'social existence', 'functional existence', 'formal existence' or 'ideal existence', all of which contrast with their 'material', 'objective', 'immediate' or 'actual' existence. In the same sense, the social form or function contrasts with 'material content', 'material substance', 'content', 'substance', 'elements of production', material and objective elements and conditions of production. All of these expressions, which convey the difference between the technical and social functions of things, between the technical role of instruments and conditions of labour and their social form, essentially point to the fundamental difference that we established previously.

At issue is the fundamental distinction between the process of material production and its social form, or the two aspects, technical and social, of one and the same labour activity on the part of people. Political economy studies the production relations between people, i.e. the social forms of the production process as distinct from its material-technical 'content' or 'substance'. Of course, the production relations between people emerge on the basis of a certain condition of the productive forces, and the economic categories presuppose definite technical conditions. But the latter appear in political economy not as conditions for the process of production, viewed in technical terms, but rather as preconditions of the determinate social-economic forms that the production process assumes. The subject of investigation for political economy involves these 'economic forms', or types of production relations between people that have taken on the form of social functions and the social forms of things.

---

34 Marx 1971, p. 492.

3   Marx's Theory of Value

We can see that all the basic concepts of political economy express reified[35] production relations between *people*. If we come to the theory of value from this perspective, we face the task of showing that value expresses 1) a social relation between *people* that 2) has taken the form of *things* and 3) is connected with the process of *production*.

At first sight value, as with the other categories of political economy, appears to us as the attribute of a thing. Observing the phenomena of value, we see that every thing in the market exchanges for a certain quantity of every other thing or – in conditions of developed exchange – for a certain sum of money (gold) with which one can purchase any other thing in the market (of course, within the limits of the given sum of money). That sum of money, or the price, changes almost daily, depending upon the conjuncture in the market. Today there is a shortage of cloth in the market and its price rises to 3 roubles 20 kopeks per yard. A week later the cloth offered in the market exceeds the normal supply, and the price falls to 2 roubles 75 kopeks per yard. These daily changes and fluctuations of price, taken over a more or less prolonged period, move about a certain average level, an average price that is equal, for example, to 3 roubles per yard. In capitalist society this average price is proportional not to the labour-value of the product, that is, to the quantity of labour needed for its production, but to the so-called 'price of production', which equals the sum of the costs of production for a given product plus the average profit on the capital invested.

To simplify the analysis, however, we shall now abstract from the fact that the cloth is produced by a capitalist with the use of hired labour. Indeed, Marx's entire method, as we have seen, consists of singling out for investigation particular types of production relations that provide a picture of capitalist economy only in the aggregate. For now we shall analyse only a single fundamental type of production relations between people in commodity society, namely, the relation between them as *individual commodity producers who are formally independent of each other*. All we know is that the cloth is produced by commodity producers and brought to market for exchange or sale to other commodity producers. We have before us a society of commodity producers, or a so-called 'simple commodity economy' as distinct from a more complex capitalist one. In the conditions of a simple commodity economy, the average prices for the products of labour, which are proportional to their labour-value, represent the average level about which market prices fluctuate and with which they

---

35   [The text speaks of 'овеществленные производственные отношения'].

would correspond in the event that social labour was proportionally distributed between the different branches of production and, as a result, a condition of equilibrium was established between them.

Every society that is based upon division of labour necessarily presupposes a certain distribution of social labour among the different branches of production. *Every system of division of labour is, at the same time, a system of labour distribution.* In primitive communist society, in the patriarchal peasant family or in socialist society, the labour of all members of a given economic unit is consciously allocated in advance between particular kinds of tasks, depending upon the character of the needs of members of the group and upon the level of labour productivity. In commodity economy there is no one to regulate the distribution of labour between individual branches of production and the separate enterprises. Not a single cloth-maker knows in advance how much cloth society requires at a particular moment or how much is being produced at the same time in all the cloth-producing enterprises. Consequently, cloth production at one time outpaces demand (overproduction) and at another time lags behind it (underproduction). In other words, the quantity of social labour expended on cloth production turns out first to be excessive and then to be insufficient. The equilibrium between the cloth industry and other branches of production is gradually disrupted. A commodity economy is a system of continuously disrupted equilibrium.

But if that is the case, how does it continue to exist as an aggregate of different branches of production that complement each other? Commodity economy can only exist because every disruption of equilibrium calls forth a tendency towards its restoration. This tendency to restore equilibrium is inherent in the very mechanism of the market and market prices. In commodity society not a single commodity producer directs another either to expand or to curtail production. But, through their activity in relation to things, people influence the labour activity of others – without knowing that they are doing so – and motivate them to expand or curtail production. Overproduction of cloth and the resulting fall in prices below value induce cloth-makers to curtail production, and the reverse occurs in the case of underproduction. The deviation of market prices from value represents the mechanism through which overproduction and underproduction are overcome, creating a tendency towards re-establishment of equilibrium between a given branch of production and the other branches of the economy.

Thus, the exchange of two different commodities according to their value corresponds to a condition of equilibrium between these two branches of production, in which case all movement of labour from one branch into the other ceases. But it is obvious, in that event, that the exchange of two commodities according to their value equalises the benefits that commodity producers derive from production in the two branches and eliminates any motive for moving from one branch to the other. In simple commodity economy such equalisation of the conditions of production in the various branches signifies that some definite quantity of labour, expended by producers in the different spheres of the economy, furnishes a product of equal value. *The values of commodities on the market are directly proportional to the quantities of labour required for production.* If, given the current state of technique, production of a yard of cloth requires on average 3 hours of labour (including also the labour expended on material, means of production, and so forth), while production of a pair of shoes requires 9 hours of labour – assuming that the labour of cloth-makers and shoe-makers is equally skilled – then the exchange of three yards of cloth for one pair of shoes corresponds to a condition of equilibrium between cloth and shoe production.

But if value is determined by the quantity of labour that is socially necessary to produce one unit of the commodity, this *quantity of labour depends in turn on labour productivity.* The development of labour productivity reduces the socially necessary labour-time and lowers the value of a unit of the commodity. Introduction of machines, for example, makes it possible to produce a pair of shoes in 6 hours instead of the former 9 and thus lowers their value from 9 roubles to 6 roubles (an hour of labour in shoe-making being understood to create, on average, 1 rouble's worth of value). The cheaper shoes begin to penetrate into the countryside, squeezing out bast sandals and homemade footwear. The demand for shoes grows, and shoe production expands. A certain reallocation of productive forces occurs in the economy. Thus development of labour productivity brings about a change in value of the products of labour; and the change of value, in turn, affects the distribution of social labour between the various branches of production. From labour productivity, to labour value, to the distribution of social labour: such is the scheme of a commodity economy in which value plays the role of regulator, establishing equilibrium – amongst all the constant deviations and fluctuations – in the distribution of social labour between the various branches of the economy. *The law of value is the law of equilibrium in commodity society.*

The theory of value investigates the laws of exchange, equating things in the market only insofar as they are connected with the laws of production and labour distribution in a commodity economy. Every exchange proportion involving two commodities – meaning average proportions, not fortuitous market prices – corresponds to a certain state of productivity and labour distribution between the branches that produce those commodities. Through the equalisation of things, as products of labour, the market equalises different concrete types of labour as components of the aggregate social labour that is distributed between various branches. The common understanding of the theory of value, as a theory limited to investigation of the exchange *relations between things*, is therefore mistaken. Through the law-governed equalisation of things, it endeavours to disclose the laws of labour equilibrium. However, the view that Marx's theory studies the *relation of labour to the thing*, as the product of labour, is also incorrect. The relation of labour to the thing involves a particular concrete type of labour and a particular concrete thing; this is a technical relation, which, in itself, is of no interest to the theory of value. The subject matter of the latter is *the relation between various types of labour* in the process of its distribution, which is established through the exchange *relations between things* as the products of labour. Thus the Marxist theory of value fully satisfies the previously mentioned general methodological demands of Marxist economic theory, which studies neither the relation between things nor the relation of people to things, but rather the relation between people who are connected by way of things.

We have now set out the general movement of ideas leading to Marx's theory of value. According to the critics, on the very first pages of *Capital* Marx begins his discussion with the fact of equality between two commodities in exchange and asserts that equalisation of things on the market is impossible without equality of the labour expenditures required for their production. This view of Marxist theory is fundamentally incorrect. Marx takes commodity society as his starting point, with all of its characteristic production relations between individual commodity producers. Due to the anarchy of production, changes in the productivity and distribution of various types of labour cannot become manifest in any other way except as changes of the exchange proportions of commodities on the market. Changes in the labour activity of people necessarily take the form of changes in the value of commodities. This law of 'labour-value' represents the distinguishing feature of a commodity economy.

Let us imagine a society with a regulated equalisation and distribution of labour, in which individual members have the right to exchange products and, for one reason or another, do practise such exchange. This exchange represents a social phenomenon of a completely different order from the exchange that occurs in commodity economy. In the latter, the exchange is part of the very process of reproduction, whereas exchange in the former takes place alongside of production and is not part of it. It neither regulates the distribution of labour nor is it regulated in turn by the law of 'labour value'. If it happens that some regular pattern of exchange also occurs in this society, it will nevertheless not be a pattern connected with law-governed distribution of social labour. As we see, *the law of labour value does not result from the exchange and equalisation of things as such, but rather from the peculiar social function of this exchange in commodity production*, from the peculiar social form of the economy.

This brings us to *the social form of value*. In commodity economy value fulfils the role of regulator in the distribution of social labour. Does this role of value result from the *technical* or the *social* specificities of commodity economy, i.e. from the condition of its productive forces or from its intrinsic production relations between people? It is enough simply to pose the question in order to answer it in the latter sense. It is not every distribution of social labour that imparts to the product of labour the value form, but only such labour distribution that, instead of being directly controlled by society, is regulated indirectly through the market and the exchange of things. In a primitive communist community or a feudal village, the product of labour is 'valuable' in the sense of usefulness, or use-value,[36] but it does not have 'value'. It acquires the latter only in conditions where it is produced especially for sale and acquires in the market an objective and precisely determined 'valuation'[37] that equalises it, through money, with all other commodities and gives it the ability to be exchanged for any other commodity. In other words, a definite form of economy (commodity economy) is presupposed along with a definite form of labour organisation in the form of separate, privately owned enterprises. It is not labour as such, but only *labour organised in a particular social form* (the form of commodity economy) that imparts 'value' to the product of labour. If the relation between the producers is one of mutual independence as autonomous *commodity producers*, then the products of their labour confront each other in the market as 'values'. The formal equality of commodity producers, as economic subjects and counterparts in the production relation of purchase and sale, finds its expression in equality of the products of labour as values. The value of things reflects a determinate type of production relations between people.

If the product of labour acquires value only within a particular social form of labour organisation, it follows that value is not a 'property' of the product of labour but a determinate '*social form*' or '*social function*', *which the product of labour fulfils as a connecting link between scattered commodity producers*, as an 'intermediary' or 'bearer' of the production relations between them. At first sight, of course, value does appear simply to be one of the properties of the thing. When we say that 'a table is made of oak, that it is round, finished, and costs or has a value of 25 roubles', it may appear that this sentence imparts

---

36   [The text says: '... продукт труда имеет «ценность» в смысле полезности, потребительной стоимости'].

37   [The term used in the text is 'расценка'].

information concerning four properties of the table. But if we think further, we realise that the first three properties of the table are quite different from the fourth. They characterise the table as a material thing. Insofar as the table is a product of human labour, these properties represent the result of concrete labour by the wood-worker; they give us certain information about the technical aspect of wood-working labour. A person familiar with these properties of the table creates a picture of the technical aspect of production and acquires an idea of the material, the auxiliary items, the technical devices and even the technical skill of the wood-worker. But, however long he contemplates the table, he knows nothing of the social relations of production between the person who produced the table and other people. He does not know whether the producer is an independent artisan, a handicraftsman, a wage-worker, perhaps a member of a socialist commune or simply a person fond of tables who made it for himself.

The properties of a product of labour, when expressed by saying 'the table has a value of 25 roubles', are of a completely different order. This expression indicates that the table is a commodity, that it is produced for the market, that the person who produced it is connected with other members of society through the production relations of commodity owners, and that the economy has a specific social form, namely, the form of commodity economy. We learn nothing about the technical side of production or the thing itself, only about the social form of production and the people participating in it. This means that 'value' characterises not the thing but the human society in which it is produced. This is not a property of the thing but a 'social form' that the thing acquires due to the fact that through it people enter into definite production relations with one another. Value is 'a social relation regarded as a thing', a production relation between people that has assumed the form of a property belonging to the thing. The labour relations of commodity producers, or social labour, is 'reified'[38] or 'crystallised' in the value of the products of labour. This means that *a determinate social form of labour organisation imparts a special social form to the products of labour*. The Marxist theory of value does not study the relation between labour as a technical activity and the product of labour as a material thing, but rather the relation between the social form of labour and the social form of the products of labour. 'The labour that creates (or more accurately, determines, *setzende*) exchange-value is a specific *social form of labour*'.[39] It creates a 'specific *social form* of wealth, exchange-value'.[40]

---

38 'осуществляется'.
39 Marx 1970, p. 36 [Rubin's emphasis].
40 Marx 1970, p. 37, note.

Marx's teaching on the *'form of value'* (i.e. the social form taken by the product of labour) is the result of a particular social form of labour itself and represents Marx's new and unique contribution to the theory of labour value. The proposition that labour creates value was known long before Marx, but in Marx's theory it acquires a completely different meaning. Marx drew a precise distinction between the material-technical process of production and its social form, between labour as an aggregation of *technical functions* (*concrete labour*) and labour viewed in terms of its *social form* in commodity-capitalist society (*abstract labour or universal labour*). The specificity of commodity economy consists of the fact that the material-technical process of production is not organised by society and is undertaken by separate commodity producers. Concrete labour is simultaneously the private labour of separate individuals. The *private* labour of the individual commodity producer is connected with the labour of all other commodity produces and becomes *social* labour only insofar as its product is equated with all other commodities in the market. As we have seen, this market equalisation of all commodities, expressed through the valuation of them all in terms of one and the same commodity, gold (or money), simultaneously signifies the equalisation of all the concrete types of labour expended in the different spheres of the economy. This means that the private labour of a separate individual assumes the character of social labour not in the process of production itself but in the act of exchange, which represents an abstraction from the concrete specificities of particular things and particular types of labour. The equalisation of all types of labour through market equalisation of all the products of labour as values – this is what Marx means by the concept of abstract labour. And since the equalisation of labour through the equalisation of things results from the social form of commodity economy, in which there is no direct social organisation and equalisation of labour, it follows that abstract labour is a social and historical concept. *Abstract labour does not express a physiological equality of the various types of labour, but rather the social equalisation of various types of labour that occurs in the specific form of market equalisation of the products of labour as values.*

The uniqueness of the Marxist theory of value resides in the fact that it clarified precisely *what* labour creates value. 'Marx ... investigated labour from the point of view of its value-creating quality, and established for the first time *what* labour, why, how it formed value, and that value in general is nothing more than congealed labour of *this* kind'.[41] It is precisely in the 'dual character of labour' that Marx saw the central element of his theory of value.[42]

---

41   Marx 1978, p. 99, Engels's emphasis.
42   Marx 1976, p. 131; letter from Marx to Engels, 8 January 1868, in *MECW*, Vol. 42, p. 514.

Thus, the dual character of labour reflects the difference between the *material-technical* process of production and its *social form*. This difference, which we explained in the previous chapter, is the basis of the whole of Marxist economic theory, including the theory of value. From this fundamental distinction follows the difference between *concrete* and *abstract* labour, which in turn is reflected in the contradiction between *use-value and exchange-value*. In the first chapter of *Capital*, Marx's exposition moves in the reverse direction. He begins his analysis with market phenomena that are susceptible to observation, with the contradiction between use-value and exchange-value. From this contradiction, which can be discerned on the surface of phenomena, he probes more deeply into the dual character of labour as concrete and abstract – in order at the end of the first chapter, in the section on 'commodity fetishism', to reveal the social forms assumed by the material-technical process of production. Marx moves from things, through labour, to human society; from phenomena that are visibly obvious to phenomena that must yet be revealed by scientific analysis. But the structure of Marx's argument is the reverse of his exposition in the first chapter of *Capital*. From the difference between the process of production and its social form – from the social structure of commodity economy – he turns to the dual character of labour, viewed in its technical and social aspects, and to the dual nature of the commodity as use-value and exchange-value. From a superficial reading of *Capital* it may appear that, in the contradiction between use-value and exchange-value, Marx sees different properties of the thing as such (that is how Böhm-Bawerk and a number of other critics have understood Marx). What is actually involved is the distinction between the 'material' and 'functional' existence of the thing, between the product of labour and its social form, between the thing and the production relations of people that have 'coalesced' with the thing, that is to say, that appear by way of the thing.

Thus we have a deep and inseparable connection between the Marxist theory of value and the general methodological foundations set out in his theory of commodity fetishism. Value is the production relation between autonomous commodity producers that has taken the form of a property of the thing and is connected with the distribution of social labour. Or, to regard the same phenomenon from the other perspective, value is the ability of every product of the labour of every commodity producer to exchange for products of the labour of any other commodity producer in a certain proportion that corresponds to the level of productivity and the proportional distribution of social labour. What is involved is a relation between *people* that has taken on the form of a property of *things* and is associated with the process of the distribution of labour *in production* – or, in other words, *a reified production relation between people*.⁴³ The reification⁴⁴ of labour in value represents the most important conclusion from the theory of commodity fetishism, which explains the inevitable 'reification'⁴⁵ of production relations between people in commodity economy. The theory of value does not affirm the material condensation of labour, as a factor of production, in things, as the products of labour – a phenomenon that occurs in all historical formations and represents the technical precondition of value but is not its source – rather, it concerns the fetishised and reified expression⁴⁶ of the labour relations of people in the value of things. Labour is 'crystallised' or takes form in value in the sense that by taking on the social 'form of value' it thereby finds expression or 'presents itself' (*sich darstellt*). Marx uses the latter expression most frequently to characterise the relations between abstract labour and value. One cannot help but be surprised by the fact that Marx's critics have failed to notice this inseparable connection between his theory of value and his teaching with regard to the reification⁴⁷ or fetishisation of production relations between people, and that they have understood the Marxist theory of value in a mechanistic-naturalistic rather than a sociological sense.

Thus the Marxist theory of value is built upon two essential foundations: 1) on the doctrine of the *form of value* as a reified expression⁴⁸ of social production relations between autonomous commodity producers; and 2) on the doctrine concerning *the distribution of social labour* and the dependence of the magnitude of value upon the development of *labour productivity*. These are two sides of one and the same process: the theory of value studies the social form of value that is assumed by the process of the distribution of labour in commodity-capitalist economy. 'The *form* in which this *proportional distribution of labour* asserts itself in a state of society in which the interconnection of social labour expresses itself as the *private exchange* of the individual products of labour, is precisely the *exchange value* of these products'.⁴⁹ Value, therefore, is connected simultaneously both with the social *form* of the social production process and with its material-technical labour *content*. And this is understandable if we recall that value, as in the case of all other economic categories, expresses not the *relations between people* in general but precisely

---

43   ['овеществленное производственное отношение людей'].
44   ['овществление'].
45   ['овществление'].
46   ['овеществленное выражение'].
47   ['овеществлении'].
48   ['вещное выражение'].
49   Letter from Marx to Kugelmann, 11 July 1868, in *MECW*, Vol. 43, p. 68 [Rubin's emphasis].

the *production* relations between people. Labour is the 'content' or 'substance' of value – these expressions by Marx mean that the process of labour distribution and the development of labour productivity in commodity society assume the social form of value. The mysterious 'substance' of value, which has provoked such attacks upon Marx by his critics, means nothing more nor less than the material-technical labour process that occurs within the given social form.[50] Labour, as the 'substance' of value abstracted from its form, is simply the expenditure of labour with no regard to the social form of labour organisation; and labour in that sense is only the presupposition of the theory of value. The subject matter of the latter is labour expenditure expressed not directly in units of social labour but in the quantity of products received in exchange for the given commodity, i.e. labour expenditure that has taken the form of the value of the commodity. But, on the other hand, the social 'form of value' must be substantiated with a determinate material-technical labour content; the form of value, like all other 'economic forms' or 'determinations of form' (*Formbestimmtheiten*), is investigated by political economy precisely as the organising social form of the material-technical process of production.

Insofar as Marx studies value as a social form of the product of labour, which is conditioned by a determinate social form of labour organisation, it is the *qualitative*, *sociological* aspect of value – abstract labour – that comes to the forefront. Insofar as the process of labour distribution and the development of labour productivity occur within the given social form, and the movement of the 'quantitatively determined amounts of society's aggregate labour'[51] is subordinate to the 'iron law of strictly defined proportions and relations',[52] it is the *quantitative* aspect of the phenomena of value or, if one may put it this way, the *mathematical* aspect (socially necessary labour) that takes on enormous significance. The fundamental error of the majority of Marx's critics consists of the fact that 1) they have completely misunderstood the qualitative, sociological aspect of the Marxist theory of value, and 2) they have restricted themselves to the quantitative aspect, to the investigation of exchange proportions – that is, to quantitative relations between the values of things – while ignoring the quantitative relations of the masses of the social labour that is distributed between the separate branches of production and individual enterprises and is the basis [for quantitative relations of value].

---

50   For the contradiction between substance and form, see the preceding chapter.
51   Letter from Marx to Kugelmann, 11 July 1868, in *MECW*, Vol. 43, p. 68.
52   Marx 1976, p. 476.

4   Marx and Ricardo

Turning now to the question of the relation of the Marxist theory of value to Ricardo's theory of value, we propose the following thesis: Marx was Ricardo's successor in terms of his teaching on the *content* of value but not on the *form* of value. Marx found in Ricardo the teaching that *changes in the magnitude of the value of commodities depend on changes in the productivity of labour*, but he did not find there any understanding of the *social form of value as the reified expression*[53] *of social production relations between people*. Marx's unique sociological *method* entailed a change in the *object* of the investigation itself: from being a property of things, value becomes the social production relation between people that has taken the form of things.

We have seen that the basis of Marx's doctrine concerning the form of value was the clearly defined difference between the material-technical process of production and its social form. Ricardo was unaware of this difference, with the result that the social form of value lay beyond his field of vision. Ricardo's theory of value differed from Marx's in that: 1) the *material-technical* process of production is not distinguished from its capitalist *social* form; 2) the result is lack of any clear understanding of *the dual character of labour*, regarded in terms of its technical aspect (concrete labour) or its social aspect (abstract labour); and 3) there is no understanding of the social *form of value* as the result of a definite social form of labour organisation. Let us consider each of these logically interconnected points in turn.

a)   The Production Process and Its Social Form

Classical political economy, which pioneered freedom for industrial development, opposed the obsolete restrictions of feudal, guild and mercantilist origin – on the grounds that they were irrational and artificial – in favour of the new capitalist form of industry as the rational and 'natural order'. The capitalist system, which answered the need of the productive forces to develop, appeared to classical economists to be 'as much a self-evident and nature-imposed necessity as productive labour itself'.[54] They regarded the capitalist form of economy as 'the eternal natural form of social production'.[55] The social forms characterising a given social formation were transformed into 'absolute forms'[56] and 'natural laws' of production forms.[57] Economic categories were transformed

---

53   'вещное выражение'.
54   Marx 1976, p. 175.
55   Marx 1976, p. 174.
56   Marx 1971, p. 239.
57   Marx 1971, p. 429.

from being *historical* into being *eternal*, from being *social* into being *natural*. The economic laws resulting from a given social form of production were taken to be inherent in the material-technical process of production as such.

Once the material process of production is inextricably merged and identified with its social form, then, of course, any contradiction between them is impossible. 'Ricardo regards bourgeois, or more precisely, capitalist production as the *absolute form* of production, whose specific forms of production relations can therefore never enter into contradiction with or enfetter'[58] production as such. These words from Marx affirm, in the best way possible, that the difference between the process of production and its social form represents the common starting point both for the theory of historical materialism and for Marx's economic theory. With Ricardo, the productive forces move *together with* the production relations, and thus contradiction between them is excluded.[59] With Marx, the productive forces move *within* the given production relations, constantly running into their limitations and straining to break free of them.

b)   The Dual Character of Labour

Identifying the process of production with its social form makes it impossible to draw any clear distinction between the technical and social aspects of production, or between concrete and abstract labour. Ricardo consistently put forth the idea that value is determined by labour. But precisely what labour or, more precisely, which aspect of labour – to this question he provides no answer. Ricardo never says that the thing becomes value not because it is a product of labour but because it is a product of labour organised in the social form of commodity economy. He lacks any clear understanding of the dual character of labour. 'Classical political economy ... nowhere distinguishes explicitly and with a clear awareness between labour as it appears in the value of the product, and the same labour as it appears in the product's use-value'.[60] Ricardo 'confuses'[61] these two aspects of labour. The result of this confusion of the technical and social aspects of labour is that the first aspect comes strikingly to the forefront, and it is precisely the social form of labour organisation that is ignored. Ricardo 'did not understand the specific form in which labour is an element of

58   Marx 1971, p. 55.
59   [This statement is not entirely correct, since Ricardo saw that ground rent tends to swallow up profits due to diminishing fertility of the soil. His most radical disciples (and even Lenin, much later) came to the conclusion that the land must be nationalised].
60   Marx 1976, p. 173, footnote.
61   Marx 1971, p. 139.

value, and failed in particular to grasp that the labour of the individual must present itself as abstract general labour and, in this form, as *social* labour'.[62]

Rosenberg does not once mention the absence in Ricardo of any clear concept of abstract labour – a point that Marx considered of paramount importance. After posing the question of 'precisely what labour creates value', Rosenberg looks at the difference between Ricardo and Marx in their teachings on socially necessary labour and productive labour.[63] But this difference, despite its obvious importance, recedes into the background by comparison with the fundamental difference between concrete and abstract labour. Rosenberg's only possible justification is the fact that the Marxist concept of abstract labour has generally been understood in a physiological sense. From this point of view, it really is difficult to discern a difference in principle between Ricardo's understanding of labour and Marx's. After all, Ricardo also examined the labour that creates value from the quantitative side, and there is no doubt that he understood the general physiological unity of different types of labour. The concept of abstract labour in the physiological sense was known not only to Ricardo but also to [Benjamin] Franklin.[64] But the concept of abstract labour as a special social form of labour organisation, in which the 'qualitative unity or equality'[65] of different types of labour is established through market equalisation of the products of labour, is unique to Marx's theory of value and distinguishes it from the classics' theory of value and especially from Ricardo's.

c) The Form of Value

The consistent distinction that Marx draws between the process of production and its social form, between concrete and abstract labour, allowed him to develop the doctrine of the social 'form of value' that is assumed by the products of labour and expresses a definite type of social production relations between people as autonomous commodity producers. Marx's new and original contribution to the theory of labour value, when compared to Ricardo, is his teaching on the form of value. 'It is one of the chief failings of classical political economy that it has never succeeded, by means of its analysis of commodities, and in particular of their value, in discovering the *form of value* which in fact turns value into exchange-value'.[66] An understanding of the value form

---

62 Marx 1971, p. 137.
63 For Rosenberg's mistakes in the section dealing with productive labour, see Hilferding 1922, pp. 107–8. [See Document 11 in this volume].
64 Marx 1976, p. 173 and Marx 1970, pp. 56–7.
65 Marx 1976, p. 173, footnote.
66 Marx 1976, p. 174, footnote.

is decisively important, for it is 'the most universal form of the bourgeois mode of production' and stamps it as 'a particular kind of social production of a historical and transitory character'.[67] Without understanding the value form it is impossible to grasp the given social – namely, capitalist – form of economy and all of its characteristic economic forms: the money form, the form of capital, and so forth. The 'value form' means that in commodity society the labour expenditures of people take the form of value, as a property of the products of labour, and quantitative changes in labour expenditures take the form of quantitative changes in the value of things. The production relations between people are 'reified'.[68] The teaching on the 'form of value' reveals the true social nature of value, which is not a property of the thing but rather a reified expression[69] of the production-labour relations between people.

If labour expenditures take the form of the value of things, then the 'form of value' represents the mediating link that connects the development of labour productivity with a change in the magnitude of value on the part of the products of labour. Ignoring this mediating link, Ricardo directly connected the two antipodes, seeing in the alteration of exchange proportions between commodities a direct and natural consequence of the fact of the development of labour productivity, regarded in technical terms and independently of the social form of production. For this reason labour appears as a technical factor of production, and value appears as a property of the thing. From a social form that expresses the social connection between people, which is established through the medium of things, value was transformed into a property of the thing, which results from the technical connection between the product of labour and labour as a factor of production. Ricardo disclosed the technical fact of the development of labour productivity, which is the basis for changes in the magnitude of value, but he was not interested in the question of why this technical fact assumes precisely the given social form of value. He reduced value to labour, as its technical 'content' or 'substance', but he did not clarify why labour takes on the social 'form of value'.

The conclusion that we have come to appears paradoxical at first glance. In any event, it is sharply at odds with the opinion of most of Marx's critics, who claim that the fundamental difference between Ricardo and Marx is to be found precisely in the latter's teaching on labour as the 'substance' of value. In their opinion, Ricardo established the causal dependence between changes in the

---

67   Ibid.
68   ['овеществляются'].
69   ['вещное выражение'].

magnitude of value on the part of commodities and changes in the quantity of labour required for their production, leaving aside the question of the nature or essence of value itself. Not being satisfied with a study of causal connections of the phenomena of value, Marx taught that labour not only determines but also *is* value, that it is the *substance* or *essence* of value. This metaphysical teaching by Marx on the substance of value represents, in [the critics'] view, Marx's original contribution to the theory of value – and this novelty detracts from rather than improving upon Ricardo's theory. This view on the part of Marx's critics is explained by their mistaken impression that Marx sees in labour some sort of metaphysical essence of value, its material substratum so to speak. As we already know, such a naturalistic view of the relation between labour and value is foreign to Marx. The expression that labour represents the 'content' or 'substance' of value simply means that at the basis of changes of value lie changes occurring in the material-technical process of production, in the development of labour productivity. This aspect of phenomena was especially emphasised precisely by Ricardo, with the consequence that the fundamental difference between him and Marx is found not in the teaching on the 'substance' of value but rather in the doctrine concerning the 'form of value'.

This is exactly how Marx posed the question for himself. As he said in his own words, Ricardo directly emphasised in various places that 'labour is the factor the different commodities have in *common*, which constitutes their uniformity, their *substance*, the intrinsic foundation of their value. The thing he failed to investigate, however, is the specific *form* in which labour plays that role'.[70] Ricardo 'does not even examine the form of value – the particular form which labour assumes as the substance of value. He only examines the magnitudes of value ...'.[71] Marx expresses essentially the same idea in his chapter on commodity fetishism, only he replaces the term 'substance' with the term 'content': 'Political economy has indeed analysed value and its magnitude, however incompletely, and has uncovered the *content* concealed within these forms. But it has never once asked the question why this content has assumed that particular *form*, that is to say, why labour is expressed in value, and why the measurement of labour by its duration is expressed in the magnitude of the value of the product'.[72] In other words, the classics demonstrated that labour is the content of value, whereas Marx wanted to clarify why labour takes the form

---

70 Marx 1971, p. 138 [Rubin's emphasis].
71 Marx 1971, p. 172.
72 Marx 1976, pp. 173–4.

of value. The attention of the classics was directed to revealing the material-technical basis of the given social forms, which they simply took as given and not subject to further analysis. Marx, for his part, took up the goal of discovering the laws of the emergence and development of the social forms assumed by the material-technical process of production at a given stage of development of the productive forces.

This is the most profound difference between the method of the classics and that of Marx, and it reflects different necessary stages in the development of economic thought. Scientific analysis begins 'with the results of the process of development ready to hand',[73] with the multitude of social-economic forms that it finds already established and fixed in the surrounding reality (value, money, capital, wages, etc.). These forms 'already possess the fixed quality of natural forms of social life before man seeks to give an account not of their *historical* character, for in his eyes they are immutable, but [only] of their *content* and meaning'.[74] Not analysing the given social-economic forms, the classics wanted only to disclose their content, their material-technical basis. In value they found labour; in capital, the means of production; in wages, the means of the workers' subsistence; and in profits, the abundance of products provided by growth of labour productivity. Starting from pre-given social forms, and taking them to be the eternal and natural forms of the production process, they did not raise the question of their origin. 'Classical economy is not interested in elaborating how the various forms come into being, but seeks to reduce them to their unity by means of analysis, because it starts from them as given premises'.[75] Once the given social-economic forms were reduced to their material-technical content, the classics considered their work to be finished. But at precisely the point where they conclude their analysis, Marx goes further. Not being confined within the horizon of a capitalist economy, and seeing it merely as one of many possible forms of economy that have existed, Marx poses the question: Why is it that a given material-technical content, at a certain stage in development of the productive forces, takes exactly the given social form? Marx's methodological formulation of the problem runs approximately as follows: Why does labour take the form of value; the means of production, the form of capital; the means of workers' subsistence, the form of wages; and growth of labour productivity, the form of an increase of surplus value? He directs his attention to analysis of the social forms of the economy and to the laws of their origin

---

73 Marx 1976, p. 168.
74 Ibid [Rubin's emphasis].
75 Marx 1971, p. 500.

and development, to the 'real, formative process (*Gestaltungsprozess*) in its different phases'.[76] This *genetic* method of Marx is the opposite of the *analytic* method of the classics.[77] The specific feature of Marx's genetic method is found, as we see, not only in its historical but also in its sociological character, in its close attention to investigation of the social forms of economy. The classics, starting from the social forms as given, endeavoured mainly to disclose their material-technical basis. Beginning with the existing condition of the material production process, and with the given level of productive forces, Marx endeavours to explain the origin and character of the social forms assumed by the material process of production. This is what accounts for Marx's predominant interest, as we have already mentioned, in economic forms in general and the value form in particular.

d) Value and Labour Productivity

If his teaching on the form of value is the most original part of Marx's value theory and distinguishes it from Ricardo's theory, Marx is also heir to Ricardo in his doctrine of the dependence of changes in value on the development of labour productivity. Whereas Ricardo did not investigate the connection between the phenomena of value and the social form of production, the link between these phenomena and the material-technical process of production attracted closer attention and constituted the central theme of his theory. If Marx's theory of value could be called one of social production, Ricardo's would have to be termed one of production. Ricardo's theory of value is a doctrine of the *causal* dependence of changes in the magnitude of the value of commodities in *capitalist* society on the development of *labour productivity*. We have deliberately accentuated the specific words that distinguish the particular characteristics

---

76   Ibid.

77   Cf. Marx on the 'genetic presentation' (*genetischen Darstellung*): 'Classical political economy occasionally contradicts itself in this analysis. It often attempts directly, leaving out the intermediate links, to carry through the reduction and to prove that the various forms are derived from one and the same source. This is however a necessary consequence of its analytical method, with which criticism and understanding must begin. Classical economy is not interested in elaborating how the various forms come into being, but seeks to reduce them to their unity by means of analysis (*Sie hat nicht das Interesse, die verschiedenen Formen genetisch zu entwickeln, sondern sie durch Analyse auf ihre Einheit zurückzuführen*), because it starts from them as given premises. But analysis is the necessary prerequisite of genetical presentation, and of the understanding of the real, formative process in its different phases (*Die Analyse aber die notwendige Voraussetzung der genetischen Darstellung, des Begreifens des wirklichen Gestaltungsprozesses in seinen verschiednen Phasen*)' (Marx 1971, p. 500).

of Ricardo's work from that of his predecessors, Adam Smith in particular. 1) With Smith, study of the causal dependence of changes in the value of commodities is confused with the search for a measure that accurately defines the degree of these changes. The confusion of these two methodologically different approaches did enormous harm to political economy as a science, [and that harm] continues to be felt right up to the present day. To Ricardo belongs the great service of consistently adopting a *scientific-causal* point of view in the theory of value. 2) As a result of confusing the cause of value changes with the measure of value, Smith also confused the labour expended on production of the commodity with the labour that might be acquired in exchange for the given commodity. Hence, the entanglement of objective labour value in his theory with subjective labour value. Ricardo, having posed the question of the cause of value changes, located this cause in changes of the quantity of labour expended on production of the commodity. He consistently adopted the viewpoint of *objective* labour value. 3) Smith saw the law of labour value (in its objective formulation) holding only for pre-capitalist forms of economy. Ricardo regarded it as a law that also operates (with certain deviations) in a *capitalist* economy, without contradicting the phenomena of profit and rent. 4) In the development of *labour productivity* Ricardo saw the final cause of the economic phenomena he was investigating. The development of labour productivity determines the value of commodities in general and of workers' means of subsistence in particular, thereby determining both wages and the profit that depends upon them. Differences of labour productivity on various land parcels create differential rent, the sole type of rent known to Ricardo. On the one hand, we see a strict mathematical formulation of the laws of change of the magnitude of value (and also of wages, profit, rent and so forth), depending upon quantitative changes in the mass of labour in production; on the other hand, there is indifference to the social forms of production. These are the two basic features of Ricardo's theory. The first feature makes him the precursor of Marx; the second reveals to us what was missing from Ricardo's theory and what Marx contributed to science.

If Ricardo had no interest in the social nature or form of value, or in the given social form of labour, he nevertheless fully understood that changes in the magnitude of value, like the underlying changes in labour productivity, are essentially social phenomena. He studied these changes as law-governed phenomena that are both objective (not depending on the will of separate individuals) and far-reaching – or, as N. Sieber puts it, typical and average.[78]

---

78   N[ikolai] Sieber, *David Ricardo and Karl Marx* (St. Petersburg, 1897), p. 82 et seq [For

He saw the ultimate cause of changes in the magnitude of value in changes occurring in social production, although he regarded the latter not in terms of its social form but in terms of its material-technical content – not as the totality of production relations but as a sum of technical, concrete labour activities. But his consistent discernment of value in the social process of production was, in itself, Ricardo's great service that prepared the way for Marx.[79] We are totally unable, therefore, to agree with Rosenberg, who sees one of the fundamental differences between Marx and Ricardo in the fact that the latter allegedly studied the phenomena of value from a private perspective and not from the point of view of political economy. If that were really the case, one could only be amazed as to how Ricardo, beginning from a private-economic point of view, managed to give a theory of capitalist economy so elaborate that 'In his theory of value', according to Rosenberg's exaggerated expression, 'Marx stands upon the shoulders of Ricardo' (p. 186). In reality, it was only the point of view of political economy that allowed Ricardo to construct his theory. He took the national economy as the subject of his investigation, although he did not examine its social form.

e)   Relative and Absolute Value

Similarly, we cannot agree with Rosenberg's view that the second fundamental difference between Ricardo and Marx involves neglect by the former of 'abso-

---

commentary on Sieber, see articles by James D. White and David Smith, together with a brief translation of Sieber's work, in Part I of Paul Zarembka (ed.), *Marx's Capital and Capitalism; Markets in a Socialist Alternative* (Research in Political Economy, Volume 19, 2001)].

[79] On occasion this even causes Marx to attribute to Ricardo views that, in our opinion, were only later developed by Marx himself. One can still agree with Marx that, as a result of studying the classics, and especially Ricardo, 'The phantom of the world of goods fades away and it is seen to be simply a continually disappearing and continually reproduced objectivisation of human labour' (Marx 1971, p. 429). However, we cannot agree [with Marx's comment] that for Ricardo 'the exchange-value of *things* is a mere expression, a specific social form, of the productive activity of men' (Marx 1971, p. 181). In other places Marx gives a more careful appraisal of the classics, noting both sides of their system – the social-productive and the material-technical, the first of which was developed by Marx and the latter by the so-called vulgar economists (see the Addenda to *Surplus-Value* III, 'Revenue and its Sources. Vulgar Political Economy'). In general and on the whole, one can say that Marx was more inclined to exaggerate than to understate the great services of the classics. Among many Marxists, and particularly in Rosenberg's book, the inclination to find similarity between the classics' teaching on value and Marx's own theory is even more pronounced.

lute value' (pp. 188, 185, 116, 118). This opinion is widespread in both the Marxist and the anti-Marxist literature. However, we find it impossible to see any difference in principle between Marx and Ricardo on precisely this point. In one place Marx notes that '*Relative value* means first of all *magnitude of value* in contradistinction to the quality of having *value* at all ... and secondly, the value of one commodity expressed in the use-value of another commodity'.[80] In other words, we are dealing here with three different concepts: 1) the value of the commodity expressed in the use-value of another commodity, for instance, the value of one pair of boots equals three yards of cloth; 2) the magnitude of the commodity's value as determined by the amount of labour expended on its production, for instance, the magnitude of value of a pair of boots is defined as nine hours of labour, or the magnitude of value of a pair of boots relates to that of a yard of cloth as nine hours of labour to three hours of labour; 3) the quality of value in general, without specifying its magnitude, for instance, a pair of boots has the form of value in general. The first concept is called relative value; the second, as Marx indicates, is also sometimes called relative but more often absolute value.[81] The third is always called absolute. It would be more correct to dispose of this unclear terminology and to characterise these three concepts as 1) the exchange proportion between two commodities, 2) the quantitatively determined labour value of the commodity, or its magnitude of value, and 3) the quality or form of value in general terms, without any determination of its magnitude.

Can one say that Ricardo studies only relative value, in the sense of the first concept, i.e. the exchange proportions of commodities apart from any dependence upon labour expenditures in their production? It is enough just to read the first chapter of Ricardo's work in order to convince oneself that, in studying any exchange proportions between commodities and the changes that occur, Ricardo invariably poses the question of whether there was any change in the quantity of labour expended on production of the given commodity.[82] Ricardo investigates the second sort of phenomena that we mentioned – that is, labour value from the quantitative side – and ignores only the third problem: the quality of value in general or, more accurately, the social form of value. To call this

---

80   Marx 1971, p. 132.
81   Marx 1968, pp. 19–22.
82   See Ricardo 1821. [The first chapter of Ricardo's *The Principles of Political Economy and Taxation*, 'On Value', frequently makes the point mentioned by Rubin. On p. 7 Ricardo says: 'If the quantity of labour realised in commodities regulates their exchangeable value, every increase of the quantity of labour must augment the value of that commodity on which it is exercised, as every diminution must lower it' (Ricardo, 1821, p. 4)].

'form of value' absolute value would involve a misuse of terminology. In his frequent observations that Ricardo is interested only in the magnitude of value, Marx intended primarily to emphasise the absence in Ricardo of any teaching on the social form of labour or the form of value.[83] It is here, and not in the teaching on absolute value, that the fundamental difference between Ricardo and Marx is to be found.

It is from this fundamental difference that the difference in formulating the theory of money also arises. It was only his teaching on the form of value that allowed Marx to develop his theory of money. Ricardo was not able to explain the need for the formation of money, which for him remained something external and circumstantial that did not necessarily follow from the character of a commodity economy. It is thus impossible to agree with Rosenberg, who, drawing an extremely close affinity between the theories of value on the part of Ricardo and Marx, finds one of the fundamental disagreements between them in their different views concerning the theory of money (pp. 179, 188). The difference between Ricardo and Marx on the theory of money is not fundamental but derivative, resulting from their differences in posing the theory of value.

f)   Capital and Surplus Value

If Ricardo, already in the theory of value, had to encounter insurmountable difficulties because the social nature of value, as a production relation between people, was not clear to him, the same must be said all the more with regard to the theory of capital and surplus value.

Marx's method, as we have seen, consists of singling out and consistently investigating the different types of production relations between people in a capitalist economy, beginning with the simplest. After considering the relations between people as autonomous commodity producers (the theory of value and money), he analyses the relation between capitalists and workers (the theory of capital and surplus value) in order to turn then to relations between industrial capitalists in various spheres of production (the theory of the equal rate of profit and the price of production). The manufacturer sells the cloth produced in his factory. Would it seem that there could be anything simpler than this transaction? Yet for Marx this transaction represents a very complex social phenomenon in which several relations are intertwined: the relation of the manufacturer 1) to the buyers, 2) to his workers, and 3) to other industrial capitalists. By force of logical analysis Marx highlights these different types of production relations between people, studying them consistently in

---

83   Marx 1971, p. 131.

the order of their complexity. Ricardo, whose attention is fixed not on production relations between people but on the movement of prices for things, sees here only a single transaction in the sale of cloth, in which it is presupposed, from the very outset, that the seller is a capitalist who, because of competition with other capitalists, receives from the sale an average profit on his capital. Ricardo assumes beforehand the simultaneous existence of all the types of production relations between people. From the very first pages of his book, which investigate value, he already presupposes the existence of capital and the average norm of profit. 'It is precisely Ricardo's mistake that in his first chapter, on value, all sorts of categories that still have to be arrived at are assumed *as given*'.[84] Marx arranges these categories in terms of a certain scientific perspective, whereas Ricardo has them all on a single plane where they clash and contradict one another.

In Marx's system, the theory of capital is set out after the theory of value and precedes the theory of prices of production and the equal norm of profit. Since Ricardo assumes all these categories to be in existence from the very beginning, the results are that 1) the category of capital is frequently confused, on the one hand, with the simpler category of value, and 2) surplus value, on the other hand, is confused with the more complex category of profit.

Consequently, Ricardo is unable to understand 'the specific distinction between *commodity and capital*',[85] that is, he cannot understand that conversion of the commodity (value) into capital presupposes that, apart from the production relations between people as commodity producers, there also exists a new type of production relations between people as capitalists and workers.

1) Whereas for Marx, capital is a reified expression[86] of the production relations between capitalists and workers, Ricardo gives a material or technical definition of capital as means of production in the broad sense of the word, including also the workers' means of consumption.[87] Rosenberg completely ignores this decisive point (p. 177).

2) Ricardo's capital is simply 'accumulated labour', as opposed to living, or 'immediate, labour'.[88] The social distinction between capital and labour is transformed into a technical distinction between accumulated and

---

84   Letter from Marx to Kugelmann, 11 July 1868, in *MECW*, Vol. 43, p. 69.
85   Marx 1968, p. 403.
86   ['вещное выражение'].
87   Ricardo 1821, pp. 25–6.
88   Marx 1968, pp. 398–9.

immediate labour. Both of the basic categories of capitalist economy, capital and labour power (hired labour) are dissolved into 'labour', a category of simple commodity economy.

3) If, for Ricardo, the exchange of capital for labour power – the fundamental production relation of capitalist society – has the character of a simple exchange between accumulated and immediate labour, then the formation of surplus value becomes incomprehensible. From the viewpoint of the formation of *value*, immediate labour and accumulated labour play completely different roles;[89] and exchange between them in accordance with the law of value, i.e. the exchange of equivalents, evidently leaves no place for surplus value.

4) Resolution of this problem of the formation of surplus value requires that accumulated labour and immediate labour acquire a specific social character. 'Accumulated labour', in the hands of a small part of the population (the capitalist class), serves as the means for social domination and exploitation of the labour of workers, i.e. as 'capital'. 'Immediate labour', as distinct from the means of production monopolised by the capitalists, is transformed into a special commodity, 'labour power' (hired labour), which is sold by workers to the capitalist. Only the social relation between capitalists and workers, between 'capital' and 'labour power', can explain how the formal exchange of equivalents is in fact an exchange of nonequivalents.

In his preface to Volume II of *Capital*, Engels pointed out that Marx, with his teaching that capital exchanges not for labour but for labour power, solved 'one of the difficulties which had caused the Ricardian school to founder'.[90] Rosenberg disputes Engels's view on the grounds that 'Ricardo, in his theory, did in fact always distinguish the two concepts of labour and labour power' (p. 119).[91] But the whole question, really, is whether Ricardo sees a technical or a social difference between them.

> Instead of *labour*, Ricardo should have discussed labour power. But had he done so, *capital* would also have been revealed as the material conditions of labour, confronting the labourer as power that had acquired an independent existence, and capital would at once have been revealed

---

89   Marx 1968, p. 399.
90   Engels, in Marx 1978, p. 99.
91   Rosenberg's claim that Marx differed from Engels (pp. 118–19) in his appraisal of this aspect of Ricardo's theory is entirely incorrect.

as a *definite social relationship*. Ricardo thus only distinguishes capital as 'accumulated labour' from 'immediate labour'. And it is something purely physical, only an element in the labour-process, from which the relation between labour and capital, wages and profits, could never be developed.[92]

These words from Marx explain his thinking excellently: when Ricardo says that capital exchanges for labour, of course he understands this to mean that the exchange involves living, immediate labour (labour power in the technical sense), but he loses sight of the special social-class form of this 'immediate labour', which is deprived of means of production and thus sold to the capitalist as a commodity – labour power (hired labour or labour power in the social sense). The difference between 'labour' and 'labour power' has a social, not a technical, character.[93]

If, on the one hand, Ricardo confused capital and labour power (the fundamental concepts of capitalist economy) with labour as the creator of value (the fundamental concept of a simple commodity economy), he also confused, on the other hand, surplus value with the more complex category of profit. Nowhere did Ricardo investigate 'surplus-value as such, i.e. independently of its particular forms, such as profit, ground rent, etc.'.[94] This means that he never singled out for special study the production relation between the class of capitalists and the class of wage-workers, viewed apart from the production relations that exist between separate groups of capitalists or between capitalists and landowners. Ricardo mistakenly 'identifies surplus-value with profit' and confuses the laws of surplus value with the laws of profit.[95]

If the weakness of Ricardo's theory of surplus value lies in ignoring social forms and the production relations between people, its strength comes in the study of the magnitudes and quantitative changes of surplus value (which he confuses, as we have shown, with profit). The law, according to which wages and surplus value change in opposite directions (although formulated in too absolute a form), and the influence of changes in labour productivity on the magnitude of wages and thereby on the magnitude of surplus value – these are the basic phenomena investigated by Ricardo. And here, as in the theory of

---

92   Marx 1968, p. 400.
93   For more detail on this point, see my *Essays on Marx's Theory of Value* [Rubin 1990].
94   Marx 1976, p. 660. [See also Marx 1968, p. 373: 'Nowhere does Ricardo consider *surplus-value* separately and independently from its particular forms – profit (interest) and rent'].
95   Marx 1968, p. 376. [See also Marx 1976, p. 660: 'He therefore fails to differentiate between the laws governing the rate of surplus-value and those governing the rate of profit'].

value, we find Ricardo's predominant interest in changes of labour productivity as the fundamental cause of changes in the magnitude of surplus value; in other words, he is predominantly interested in relative and not in absolute surplus value.[96] As for factors of a social character that influence the magnitude of surplus value – such as the length of the working day, the intensity of labour or the number of workers – they are left unexplored by Ricardo.[97] 'He recognises no change either in the length of the working day or in the intensity of labour, so that with him the productivity of labour becomes the only variable factor'.[98]

g) Prices of Production

After completing his investigation of the production relations between commodity owners (the theory of value) and between capitalists and workers (the theory of capital), in Volume III of *Capital* Marx turns to study the production relations between industrial capitalists in different spheres of production (the theory of prices of production).[99] The competition of capitals in different spheres of production leads to formation of a general average rate of profit and to the sale of commodities at prices of production, which are equal to costs of production plus the average profit and do not correspond quantitatively with the labour value of commodities. But since the magnitudes of production costs and of the average profit, as well as their changes, are explained by changes in labour productivity and in the labour value of commodities, this means that the laws governing changes in the prices of production can only be understood by starting with the law of value. On the other hand, the average rate of profit and the prices of production, being regulators of the distribution of capitals between the separate spheres of production, also indirectly – through the distribution of capitals – regulate the distribution of social labour between them. The capitalist economy is a system of dispersed capitals within a moving equilibrium of capitals, but at the same time it never ceases – as with any economy built upon division of labour – to be a system of labour that is also dispersed and in equilibrium. All that is required is the ability to discern, beneath the visible process of distribution of capitals, the invisible process of the distribution of social labour. Marx succeeded in clearly showing the connection between these two processes because he clarified the concept that serves as the connect-

---

96 Marx 1968, p. 406.
97 Ibid.
98 Marx 1976, p. 660.
99 Here we mention only these three basic types of production relations of capitalist society, leaving aside the other production relations that Marx investigated (between industrial, merchant and money capitalists, and also between capitalists and landowners).

ing link between them, namely, the organic composition of capital. Knowing the division of capital into constant and variable, together with the norm of surplus value, we can easily move from the distribution of capitals to the distribution of labour. Let equal capitals of 100 be invested in two spheres of the national economy. The organic composition of capital in the first sphere is 80c + 20v, and in the second sphere 70c + 30v ('c' stands for constant capital and 'v' for variable). If the rate of surplus value is equal to 100%, then we know that the general sum of both dead and living labour that is involved in production consists in the first sphere of 120, and in the second of 130. The corresponding magnitude of living labour is 40 in the first sphere and 60 in the second.[100] From the distribution of capitals we come to the distribution of labour.

Thus, while Marx gives in Volume III of *Capital* the theory of *prices of production* as regulator in the *distribution of capitals*, this theory, in both of its aspects, is connected with the theory of value; on the one hand, prices of production are derived from labour value, while on the other hand, the distribution of capitals leads us to the distribution of social labour. In place of the scheme of a simple commodity economy (labour productivity – labour value – the distribution of social labour), we get a more complex scheme for a capitalist economy (labour productivity – labour value – prices of production – the distribution of capitals – the distribution of social labour). The Marxist theory of prices of production does not contradict the theory of labour value; it is built upon and includes it as one of its component parts. And this is understandable if we recall that the theory of labour value studies only one type of production relations between people (those between commodity owners), whereas the theory of prices of production presupposes existence of all three basic types of production relations between people in capitalist society (the relation between commodity owners, between capitalists and workers, and between separate groups of industrial capitalists). If we confine ourselves, as we are doing here, only to these three types of production relations, then a capitalist economy can be likened to a three-dimensional space in which orientation is possible only with the aid of three measurements or three planes. Just as a three-dimensional space cannot be reduced to a single plane, so the theory of capitalist economy cannot be reduced solely to the theory of value. But just as orientation in space requires determination of the distance of a given point from each of the three initial planes, so the theory of capitalist economy already presupposes a teaching concerning the production relations between

---

100 [The sums of 40 and 60 include expenditures of living labour plus the corresponding surplus value in the respective spheres].

commodity owners, i.e. the theory of labour value. Marx's opponents, who see a contradiction between the theory of labour value and the theory of prices of production, do not understand Marx's method, which entails consistent investigation of the various types of production relations or, so to speak, of different social measurements.[101]

Whereas Marx locates these three types of production relations on different but coordinated scientific planes, thereby eliminating the seeming contradiction between them, Ricardo, as we have seen, locates all these phenomena on a single plane, compelling them, so to speak, to meet head-to-head. In the very first chapter of his work, which is devoted to value, he already presupposes both a capitalist economy in general and the average norm of profit. Ricardo was the first to understand and formulate the contradiction between the theory of labour value and the tendency, peculiar to a capitalist economy, towards equalisation of the profit rate. (Adam Smith circumvented this contradiction by locating the operation of the law of labour value in the period before capitalism). But due to the very method of his investigation, which included immediate juxtaposition of various economic categories while ignoring the intermediate links between them, he was unable to pose the problem in all its breadth. Since Ricardo presupposed an average rate of profit from the very outset, i.e. the sale of commodities at prices proportional not to their labour value but to prices of production, he could thereby avoid the fundamental problem of formation of the average rate of profit and the conversion of value into the price of production. His attention was focused, therefore, on a partial question: Does an increase or decrease of wages, independently of changes of labour value, influence the relative prices of commodities produced by capitals of different organic composition? (Ricardo has in mind different relations between fixed and circulating capitals, with the consequence of different periods of time during which capital must be advanced by the capitalists). With Ricardo, this partial question occludes the fundamental problem of conversion of surplus value into the average profit, and of value into the price of production. Whereas for Marx the price of production, as compared with value, represents a new 'determination of form' corresponding to a more complex type of production relations between people, Ricardo sees it as an 'exception' to the law of labour value. Wishing, however, to preserve the latter, he calms his own doubts by concluding that these 'exceptions' play a secondary role, and that the result-

---

101 A detailed presentation of the Marxist theory of prices of production will be found in the second edition of our book *Essays on the Marxist Theory of Value*, which is currently being prepared for publication [Rubin 1990].

ing deviations of prices from value are insignificant compared to the influence that the quantity of labour required for the production of commodities has upon their value.

Summarising the conclusions of this chapter, we think it necessary to recall that it has no intention of providing a detailed analysis of the complex question of Marx's relation to Ricardo; its purpose is merely to note the general standpoint from which, in our opinion, the question must be approached. Examination of the specific partial theories of Ricardo and Marx, and comparative analysis of their points of similarity and difference, can only be fruitful if they are illuminated by a clear understanding of the basic methodological specificities of the two theories. We see the difference in principle, which separates Marx's theory from Ricardo's, in the distinction Marx draws between the material-technical process of production and its social form[102] – a difference that excludes neither their interaction nor the causal dependence of changes in people's production relations upon development of the productive forces. Political economy studies the social form of the economy; and Marx's position in this regard threw new and unexpected light upon all economic phenomena, including those that had already been studied by the classics. Marx showed us all the economic categories in a new perspective and from a new standpoint that fundamentally changes our view of the nature of economic phenomena. From being the properties of things, economic categories are transformed into production relations between people that assume reified form.[103] Marx consistently follows this general methodological approach in his doctrine of value, money, capital and so forth. In terms of the theory of value, this general methodological approach brings to the forefront the doctrine of the social 'form of value'. The teaching on value, as a social form of the product of labour that follows from a determinate social form of labour organisation, is Marx's new and original contribution to the theory of value. Rather than completing the theory of the classics, it makes him the originator of a new economic theory.

---

102 [This distinction is clear in *Capital*, Vol. I, Chapter 7: 'The Labour Process and the Valorization Process', where Marx makes the distinction between the technical *Arbeitsprozeß* (labour process) and its social forms: *Wertbildungsprozeß* (the process of value-creation, in simple commodity production) and *Verwertungsprozeß* (the valorisation process, or extraction of unpaid surplus labour, in capitalist commodity production)].

103 ['вещную форму'].

DOCUMENT 18

Towards a History of the Text of the First Chapter of Marx's *Capital* (1929)

Isaak Il'ich Rubin

Source: *Arkhiv K. Marksa i F. Engel'sa*, Volume 4, 1929, pp. 63–91.

Introduction by the Editors

Most readers of this volume will agree with Isaak Rubin's opening remark that 'the first chapter of *Capital* is enormously difficult to understand ... Even people who have spent many years studying Marx's *Capital* find, each time they re-read the first chapter of the work, new shades of meaning that previously escaped their attention'. After cautioning his readers to anticipate a complex piece of work, Rubin then fulfils that expectation with a detailed textual analysis of the theory of value in Marx's *Contribution to the Critique of Political Economy* and in *Capital*, with *Theories of Surplus-Value* providing important connecting links between the two.

It is generally understood that the *Critique* was the precursor to Marx's *Capital*. That being the case, the problem that Rubin poses is how and why the two works *differ* so substantially when comparing Marx's expositions of the theory of value. That Marx was not satisfied with his preliminary account in the *Critique* is demonstrated by the fact that he rewrote the work in the first three chapters of *Capital*, to which he also added numerous revisions of the first chapter in the second edition. The reason, explains Rubin, is that 'in the *Critique* Marx did not yet draw a sharp distinction between value and exchange-value ... [T]he *Critique* still lacks any teaching on the development of the poles of value (i.e. the relative and equivalent forms of value) and on development of the forms of value (i.e., the simple, expanded, general and monetary forms of value)'.

In the *Critique* Marx did not yet strictly distinguish the *content* of value from the *form*; he treated exchange-value *quantitatively*, whereas in *Capital* he added a *qualitative* dimension. Rubin demonstrates this point by reference to the distinction between the 'value relation' – relating the quantity of materialised labour in one commodity to that in another – and the 'value expression', in which one commodity is expressed in terms of the use-value of another commodity. In the latter case, the first commodity takes the 'relative form' and the second the 'equivalent form', a qualitative difference that points to exchange-value itself as a distinct value 'form'. Both sides of the equation still contain the same quantity of materialised labour, their 'common denominator', but Rubin emphasises that the change of form in the 'value expression' sets in motion 'the dialectical (logical and historical) transformation of one form of value into the other'. It is the 'polar' distinction in *Capital* between the 'relative' and 'equivalent' forms of value that points to the emergence of money, as the universal equivalent, and to Marx's distinction between concrete and abstract labour.

The need for such distinction arose from the fact that Ricardo did not differentiate between value and exchange-value. As Rubin comments, 'the conversion of commodities into money seemed to him to be a purely formal and external act'. The result, however, was to create an 'impassable abyss' between value and exchange-value, leading Samuel Bailey, a critic of Ricardo, to argue that the labour theory of value makes no sense. Bailey thought the value of any commodity is measured in terms of how much of any other commodity it exchanges for. There are as many types of value as there are commodities, and all values are purely relative: 'A thing cannot be valuable within itself any more than a thing can be distant in itself without reference to another thing'. The result, as Marx objected, would be that exchange-value is something 'accidental and purely relative'.[1] In that case, Rubin notes, there would remain 'no objective lawfulness at the basis of exchange phenomena'. 'If our goal is to reveal the lawfulness of exchange phenomena, we cannot regard the value of the commodity as something fortuitous and arbitrary, established anew with each act of exchange of a given commodity for another concrete commodity'.

In this scholarly and elegantly constructed argument, Rubin traces the development of Marx's thinking, both terminologically and conceptually, from the *Critique* to *Capital*. He explains that the structure of Marx's argument in *Capital*, as distinct from the *Critique*, resulted from the need to address two challenges simultaneously. First, Marx had to respond to Bailey's criticism of Ricardo; second, he had to clear up the confusion left by Ricardo in the first place. The difference between Ricardo and Bailey was that 'the former ignored the form of value, while the latter thought it possible to manage without the concept of value'.

In his concluding paragraph, Rubin provides a concise summary of the logical arrangement of his own thoughts. Since this document involves a level

---

[1] Marx 1976, p. 126.

of complexity that rivals the first chapter of *Capital* itself, readers will find it helpful to begin with Rubin's concluding comments in mind:

> While the classics concentrated their attention on value and regarded the form of value as something external and inconsequential, Bailey fell into the opposite error. He turned his attention mainly to the *multiplicity* of value expressions and imagined that 'by pointing to the multiplicity of the relative expressions of the same commodity-value he had obliterated any possibility of a conceptual determination of value'.[2] In order to deflect Bailey's attacks, which threatened the entire theory of labour value, Marx had to draw a sharp distinction between 'value' and 'value expressions', from which logically followed the need to provide separate analyses of value and exchange-value. But it was only possible finally to overcome Bailey's criticism by filling the gap left by Ricardo ... As distinct from the classics, [Marx] supplements the doctrine of value with the [separate] doctrine of 'the form of value, or exchange-value' ... The need to arrange the investigation in these two opposing directions is what explains the unique structure of the first chapter of *Capital*.

∴

Isaak Rubin on the First Chapter of Marx's *Capital*

Marx's supporters and opponents both recognise that the first chapter of Volume I of *Capital* is the cornerstone of the whole immense structure of Marx's economic theory. It is just as widely acknowledged that the first chapter of *Capital* is enormously difficult to understand due to the complexity of its content and the elaborate form that Marx gives here to his thoughts. It is not simply a question of the difficulties that this chapter presents to novices who have only recently begun to study *Capital*. Even people who have spent many years studying Marx's *Capital* find, each time they re-read the first chapter of the work, new shades of meaning that previously escaped their attention. In order to penetrate more deeply into the incomparable wealth of ideas that Marx brought together in the first volume of his work, it is necessary to subject this chapter to detailed theoretical and historical analysis. It is particularly necessary to trace the way in which Marx developed his theory of value over

---

2   Marx 1976, p. 155, footnote 25.

many years and even decades, giving his ideas a newer and more complex formulation. One of the most essential tasks for those studying the Marxist theory of value is to determine how and why Marx arrived at the complex categories and unique terms that he employs in the first chapter of *Capital*. Completing that task will not only be of great historical interest – since it will help us to reveal the historical development of Marx's views – but will also be of considerable help to us in theoretically elucidating the complex categories and terms that occur so frequently in the Marxist theory of value.

We know that Marx left us with three versions of the first chapter of Volume I of *Capital*: the version in the first edition of 1867; the version in the second edition of 1872; and finally the version in the French edition that appeared in parts from 1873–5.

We should also recall that Marx's *Contribution to the Critique of Political Economy*, published in 1859, represents nothing less than the first published version of the thoughts that later became the contents of chapters 1–3 of the first volume of *Capital*. Thus, we essentially have at our disposal four versions of the first chapter of *Capital*, written over a period of no less than 16 years. Of all the chapters of the first volume of *Capital*, it was precisely the first chapter that Marx reworked most radically. As he proceeded, the interval of time between successive versions shortened; and parallel with this, the number and significance of the innovations and changes that Marx thought it necessary to make in each new version also diminished. By comparison with the second edition of 1872, in the French edition of 1873 Marx introduced only individual corrections of a stylistic and editorial character. Much more numerous and essential were the changes that Marx included in the second edition of 1872, compared to the first edition of 1867. However, even those changes affected mainly the character of argumentation, the forms of exposition and the arrangement of material (in the first edition, in particular, the influence of Hegelian terminology and Hegelian schemes was much more apparent). The fundamental concepts and terms were retained by Marx as they had appeared previously.

As one might expect, we find the most obvious difference when comparing the first chapter of *Capital* with the first chapter of *A Contribution to the Critique of Political Economy*. More is involved here than a different sort of argumentation or a different form of exposition. In the first chapter of *Capital* we find a whole series of the most important concepts and terms that were either still missing from the *Critique* or else were encountered there only in embryonic form. Thus, leaving aside for the moment the variations that we encounter in the different editions of *Capital*, in this article we shall limit ourselves to comparing the exposition of the theory of value in the *Critique* and in *Capital*. In the first chapter of our article we shall find that in the *Critique*

Marx did not yet draw a sharp distinction between value and exchange-value or give a detailed account of exchange-value. In particular, the *Critique* still lacks any teaching on the development of the poles of value (i.e. the relative and equivalent form of value) and on development of the forms of value (i.e. the simple, expanded, general and monetary forms of value). In the second chapter we shall attempt to trace the causes that convinced Marx, in *Capital* as distinct from the *Critique*, to draw a sharp distinction between value and exchange-value. In this respect we shall find that Marx apparently decided upon the need to make this clear distinction during his polemic against Bailey, a critic of Ricardo and a decisive opponent of the theory of labour value.

1   *Value and Exchange-Value in the* Critique *and in* Capital

Marx's *Contribution to the Critique of Political Economy* consists of two chapters: the first is devoted to 'the commodity' and the second to 'money'. Each of these chapters, in addition to a theoretical exposition of the question, also includes special historical digressions in which Marx critically sets out doctrines on the particular question from economists who preceded him in the seventeenth to nineteenth centuries. The first chapter includes 'Historical Notes on the Analysis of Commodities', and the second has two similar historical digressions: 'Theories of the Standard of Money' and 'Theories of the Medium of Circulation and of Money'. As we know, Marx originally intended to provide each section of *Capital* – each being devoted to presenting a particular problem – with a special historical digression describing the development of economic ideas pertaining to the given problem. But Marx subsequently gave up on combining theory and history, the ponderous mode of presentation he had used in the *Critique*. Marx omitted most of his historical digressions from the text of *Capital*. The relevant notes by Marx were subsequently edited by K. Kautsky and published with the title *Theories of Surplus-Value*.

The change of plan for the presentation of *Capital* explains the absence from the first volume of *Capital* of the kind of historical digressions included in the *Critique*. Marx used the remaining material, representing the content of the *Critique*, as the basis for the first section of Volume I of *Capital*.[3] The first chapter of the *Critique*, dealing with the theory of value, corresponds to the first two chapters of *Capital*; the second chapter of the *Critique*, devoted to the theory of money, corresponds to the third chapter of *Capital*. The part

---

3   In the preface to the first edition of Volume I of *Capital* Marx wrote: 'The substance of that earlier work is summarised in the first chapter of this volume' [Marx 1976, p. 89]. It must be added that in the first edition (1867), the first chapter of *Capital* included the doctrine of the commodity and of money, that is, it corresponded to chapters 1–3 of later editions of *Capital*.

referring to the theory of money was subject to the fewest changes, mainly in the form of abbreviation. In contrast, the part devoted to the theory of value was significantly expanded by Marx (by more than 2½ times if the historical digressions are excluded) and was also fundamentally reworked. It is precisely in the theory of value that Marx continued to seek new and more accurate formulations for his ideas.

As we have already noted, the first short chapter of the *Critique* contains the material that entered later, in expanded and reworked form, into the first and second chapters of *Capital*. Let us now attempt a more precise comparison between these chapters of the *Critique* and of *Capital*. In the second edition of *Capital*, the first chapter is divided into four sections, but from the point of view of internal content it can be divided into three parts: the first and second sections contain the teaching on value (and the labour that creates value); the third, the teaching on the form of value or exchange-value; and the fourth section, the doctrine of commodity fetishism. The second chapter, entitled 'The Process of Exchange', shows the genesis of money from the process of exchange and, in particular, from the contradiction hidden in the commodity between value and exchange-value. Accordingly, the entire content of the first two chapters of *Capital* can be divided into four parts dealing with:

1. Value (the first and second sections of the first chapter),
2. The form of value or exchange-value (the third section of the first chapter),
3. Commodity fetishism (the fourth section of the first chapter),
4. The origin of money (the second chapter).

It is more difficult to specify the content of the first chapter in the *Critique*. The method of presentation that Marx used in the *Critique* makes it very complicated to separate the individual parts analytically and to isolate them strictly one from the other. Nevertheless, equipped with the conclusions to which we are led by the rigorous analysis that Marx gives in *Capital*, it is easy for us also to distinguish three different parts in the first chapter of the *Critique*. The first part (pages 1–15 of the German edition [Marx 1970, pp. 27–38], excluding the last paragraph on page 15),[4] includes the doctrine of value and runs parallel – notwithstanding all the differences in mode of exposition – to

---

4   [In the text, Rubin provides page numbers from the 1907 (or 1924) German edition of the *Critique*. Here we give corresponding references to the first German edition (Marx 1859). We provide the corresponding page numbers in the English translation (Marx 1970)].

the first two sections of the first chapter of *Capital*. In the second part, including just four short pages (from the last paragraph of page 15 to the last paragraph of page 19 [Marx 1970, pp. 38–41]), we can discern, as we shall see below, a weak embryo of those ideas on exchange-value that later acquired from Marx a completely new development in the third section of the first chapter of *Capital*. Finally, the last part of the first chapter of the *Critique* (from the final paragraph on page 19 to page 32 [Marx 1970, pp. 42–52]) investigates the emergence of money from development of the contradiction between value and use-value and, in general terms, corresponds to the second chapter of *Capital*. As for the teaching on commodity fetishism (set out in detail in the fourth section of the first chapter of *Capital*), in the first chapter of the *Critique* it is given only a couple of pages (9–11 [Marx 1970, pp. 34–5]) in the first part, which is devoted to an analysis of value and the labour that creates value.

We can see that of the four points mentioned above, which Marx developed in detail in *Capital*, only the first and last points (i.e. the doctrine of value and the doctrine of the origin of money) were also more or less fully set out in the *Critique*. The teaching on commodity fetishism was only superficially and very briefly touched upon in the *Critique* even though its main ideas were set out quite clearly and correctly. Finally, as we shall see below, the greatest difference between the *Critique* and *Capital* is found in the teaching concerning the form of value and exchange-value. One can say that, in the treatment of the theory of value, the basic difference between the *Critique* and *Capital* is precisely the absence from the *Critique* of any clearly established difference between value and exchange-value, or, what amounts to the same thing, any clearly developed teaching on exchange-value. We must consider in more detail this essential difference between the first chapter of the *Critique* and the first chapter of *Capital*.

Marx strictly distinguishes in *Capital* between the *value* of the commodity, representing a certain quantity of 'materialised' labour or labour time, and its *exchange-value*, i.e. value expressed in the use-value of another commodity. The first concept is denoted by the term *Wert* (value), the second by the term *Tauschwert* (exchange-value).

To denote the concept of value in the *Critique of Political Economy*, Marx still uses both terms, *Tauschwert* and *Wert*, without any distinction. Most often he uses the term *Tauschwert*, particularly in the first chapter, which is devoted especially to the theory of value. The term *Wert* is usually found when speaking of the *magnitude* of value. Both terms are often encountered side by side, replacing each other arbitrarily.[5]

---

5 See Marx 1859, pp. 17–18, or pp. 16–17 of the English translation, where *Wert des Kaffees* is

Thus the terms *Wert* and *Tauschwert* still signify one and the same concept in the *Critique*. But precisely which concept is it that they denote, value or exchange-value? There is no doubt that in the *Critique* both of these terms denote value – a concept for which Marx subsequently, in *Capital*, used the term *Wert*. This is proven not only by the fact that in *Capital* Marx uses the term *Wert* in many places, while in the corresponding places in the *Critique* he still used the term *Tauschwert*. On every page of the *Critique* we find the term *Tauschwert*, in the sense of the value of a commodity, expressed as a certain quantity of labour. To cite only the clearest of examples, let us point out that on page 52 the *Tauschwert* of a quarter of wheat is expressed as 30 labour days at the same time as its price (*Preis*) is expressed as 1 ounce of gold.[6] On page 14 we read: 'The amount of labour-time contained in the commodity, i.e. its *Tauschwert*',[7] and so on.

If the term *Tauschwert*, like *Wert*, denotes the concept of value in the *Critique* (i.e. corresponds to the term *Wert* that is used in *Capital*), then we can legitimately suppose that the concept of exchange-value, developed by Marx in *Capital* under the heading of *Tauschwert*, had not yet been sufficiently clarified in the *Critique*. Actually, a comparison of Marx's two works leads us to the following conclusion, which at first sight is paradoxical: although on the terminological side *Tauschwert* figures most prominently in the *Critique*, not *Wert*, Marx concentrated his attention here essentially on the analysis of value and did not give us a clearly developed concept of exchange-value. On the other hand, although the terminological novelty of *Capital* consists of the frequent usage of the term *Wert* in place of *Tauschwert*, the essential innovation that Marx gives us here consists of a clearly developed doctrine of exchange-value as distinct from value.

What we have said should not be understood to mean that in the *Critique* Marx ignored the fact that in a commodity economy the labour expenditures that determine the magnitude of a commodity's value are not expressed directly but only indirectly in the form of equating one commodity with another. In the *Critique* Marx understands by value not labour expenditure as such, but the equating of commodities with each other that is expressed in a specific social form. And that is not all. In the *Critique*, as distinct from *Capital*, he has in view from the very outset one specific form of value, namely, the most

---

mentioned and the following sentence speaks of *Tauschwert einer Ware* in the same sense. On page 50 (67 in the English translation) there is mention of *Tauschwert des Goldes*, and the following sentence refers to *Wert einer Unze Gold*, etc.

6 [Marx 1970, p. 69].
7 [Marx 1970, p. 37].

developed or monetary form of value.[8] But precisely because value appears from the outset in the *Critique* in this developed form, which is adequate for the content of value, Marx does not see any need for a special analysis of the form of value as distinct from the content. It is only in *Capital*, where Marx's goal is to trace the development of forms of value from the simplest up to the money form – a development whose moving force is the contradiction between value and use-value – that the need to provide a separate analysis of the content of value and the form of value becomes apparent. On this point, as with many others, a characteristic distinction appears between Marx's exposition in *Capital* and his exposition in the *Critique*. In the *Critique*, the individual elements of the problem appear in a seamless or, more correctly, a cohesive manner. In *Capital* they are distinguished from each other and subject to separate analysis. Thanks to this fact, the analysis becomes more forceful, and the characteristic features of each element, taken separately, emerge more clearly. But for the unprepared reader there also emerges, on the other hand, a danger of detaching the individual elements of the problem from each other and of forgetting the inseparable bond that unites them. In particular, the reader must never forget that in the first and second sections of the first chapter of *Capital*, although Marx gives an analysis of the content of value separate from its form, he constantly presupposes the latter.

We have reached the conclusion that in the *Critique*, for all intents and purposes, Marx understands *Tauschwert* as value. We find no clearly developed doctrine of exchange-value in the *Critique*. But does this mean that in the *Critique* we find no indications of the concept of exchange-value that Marx subsequently developed in more detail in *Capital*? This supposition would be all the more improbable since in the *Critique*, as we have already seen, Marx considers value from the very beginning in a specific form, namely, in the money form. It would be passing strange if we found in the *Critique* no reference to exchange-value even in its most external and obvious form, namely, in the form of a quantitative relation between the commodities being exchanged.

The fact is that we do encounter exchange-value, viewed in this most external and purely quantitative way, on the very first pages of the *Critique*. It even represents the starting point for Marx's discussion: 'Exchange-value

---

8 See Marx's letter to Engels of 22 June 1867: 'In my first presentation (Duncker), I avoided the difficulty of the development by not actually analysing the *way value is expressed* until it appears as its developed form, as expressed in money' (*MECW*, Vol. 42, pp. 384–5, emphasis in the original).

seems at first to be a *quantitative relation*, the proportion in which use-values are exchanged for one another'.⁹ Marx also retains this famous sentence in *Capital*.¹⁰ However, Marx quickly adds in *Capital* that, insofar as we limit our investigation to the purely quantitative side of exchange-value, we can easily get the false impression that exchange-value is something 'accidental and purely relative'. It is precisely in order to show the falsity of this idea, which was defended by Bailey,¹¹ that Marx thought it necessary in *Capital*, after the sentence we have cited, to direct the course of the investigation abruptly from exchange-value to the value concealed by it and to give a special analysis of the latter. In the *Critique* we do not find Marx clearly emphasising this same turning point in the investigation. It is as if Marx did not yet see or consider it necessary to underline all of the dangers concealed in a purely quantitative investigation of exchange-value. In *Capital* Marx underlines the lack of correspondence between exchange-value and the content it expresses; in the *Critique* he frequently notes a correspondence between them. Thus in *Capital*, after the sentence we have cited concerning exchange-value as a 'quantitative relation', Marx foresees the possibility that the reader might suppose exchange-value to be something 'accidental and purely relative'. In the *Critique*, following the same sentence, he comes directly to the conclusion that the commodities being exchanged 'take one another's place in the exchange process, are regarded as equivalents, and despite their motley appearance have a common denominator'.¹² In the *Critique* the unity of the substance of value, which is contained

---

9   Marx 1970, p. 28.
10 Marx 1976, p. 126.
11 See below the second chapter entitled 'Marx and Bailey'.
12 Marx 1970, p. 28. Here (page 3 of the 1859 German edition), as in many other places, Marx's use of '*Einheit*' – [translated above as 'common denominator'] – means '*единство*', not '*единица*'. It is unfortunate that translators often mistakenly use the word '*единица*'. [In Russian, '*единство*' implies a wide-reaching 'unity' or 'common denominator' of many things, whereas '*единица*' implies a 'unit']. For instance, on page 14 of the German edition of Volume I of *Capital* Marx writes: 'Man mag daher eine einzelne Ware drehen und wenden, wie man will, sie bleibt unfaßbar als Wertding. Erinnern wir uns jedoch, daß die Waren nur Wertgegenständlichkeit besitzen, sofern sie Ausdrücke derselben gesellschaftlichen Einheit, menschlicher Arbeit, sind, daß ihre Wertgegenständlichkeit also rein gesellschaftlich ist, so versteht sich auch von selbst, daß sie nur im gesellschaftlichen Verhältnis von Ware zu Ware erscheinen kann' (Marx-Engels *Werke*, Band 23, 'Das Kapital', Bd. I, erster Abschnitt, Berlin/DDR: Dietz Verlag, 1968, p. 62). On p. 11 of the 1928 Russian edition the relevant passage is translated as '*выражения одной и той же единица челевеческого труда*' ['expressions of one and the same unit of human labour']. [The standard English-language version of *Capital* translates this as: 'We may twist and turn a single com-

in all commodities, stands in the forefront, and it overshadows both the difference in forms of value and the different roles of the two commodities that comprise the poles of the value expression. Thanks to this fact, the exposition in the *Critique* leads us smoothly and even imperceptibly, without any sharp dialectical transitions, from exchange-value, in the sense of a quantitative relation between the commodities being exchanged, to their value. This transition is further facilitated by the fact, as we have already seen above, that the latter concept, i.e. the concept of value, is also denoted in the *Critique* by the term *Tauschwert*.

If we encounter the concept of exchange-value in the *Critique* in the sense of a quantitative relation between commodities being exchanged, it is more difficult to answer the question of whether we also encounter there the concept of exchange-value viewed qualitatively. In order to answer this question more precisely, we must clarify exactly what exchange-value means in *Capital*, as distinct from value on the one hand and from the quantitative relation between commodities being exchanged on the other.

Insofar as we regard commodities as values, we ascertain the unity or identity of their social nature. As *values* all commodities are completely *equal* one to the other. The external character of this equality is expressed in the 'value equation' (*Wertgleichung*): for example, 20 yards of linen = 1 coat. From this equation we learn the 'quantitative relation' or 'value relation' (*Wertverhältnis*) of the two commodities. We see that the value of one yard of linen is twenty times *less* than the value of one coat, but we do not know precisely what the value of linen (or of a coat) is *equal to*.

Let us now suppose that we face the task of determining the value of linen on the basis of the same equation. For this purpose we must resort to the following example: we have to take the value of one commodity (the coat, for example) as a given magnitude and determine the value of the second commodity (linen) as a certain number of units of the first commodity. In this case we say that the value of 20 yards of linen = 1 coat, and we then have a special 'value expression' (*Wertausdruck*) for linen. It may appear at first glance that this 'value expression' differs in no way from the 'value relation' that we spoke of

---

modity as we wish; it remains impossible to grasp it as a thing possessing value. However, let us remember that commodities possess an objective character as values only in so far as they are all expressions of an identical social substance, human labour, that their objective character as values is therefore purely social. From this it follows self-evidently that it can only appear in the social relation between commodity and commodity' (Marx 1976, p. 138)].

previously. But in fact there is an essential difference between them. Previously we noted that the *value* of 20 yards of linen is equal to the *value* of one coat, that is, the *value* of commodities figured on both sides of the equation. Now we are asserting that the *value* of 20 yards of linen is equal to *1 coat*, i.e. to a given concrete item or use-value of another commodity. We now have a special 'value expression' of one commodity (linen) in the *use-value* of another commodity (the coat). Whereas in the 'value relation' both commodities played a completely identical role – and this equation expressed their equality as values – in the 'value expression' each commodity plays a qualitatively different role.[13] Using the terminology that Marx employed in *Capital*, we must say that linen here has the 'relative' form of value and the coat the 'equivalent' form of value.

It may seem at first that the different roles fulfilled by the two commodities in the 'value expression' eliminate their equality as 'values'. In fact this is not the case. In a commodity economy the equality of products of labour is not established in advance by any social organ but is expressed by means of a complex process of movement in which product A appears without yet being equated with product B and is, therefore, in fact still not equated with it. In the doctrine of value we abstract from this intervening process and regard commodities in terms of their equality as values. But in the doctrine of exchange-value we study precisely this intervening process of equalisation in which the commodities necessarily fulfil different roles.

Let us now return to the *Critique* and pose the question of whether we can find there the doctrine of 'value expression', 'exchange-value' or the 'form of value'. As for the latter term, it is not found anywhere in the *Critique*. The term 'exchange-value' (*Tauschwert*) occurs quite frequently in the *Critique*, but we already know that this is to designate value, not exchange-value. It remains, therefore, to search in the *Critique* for some indication of the 'value expression'.

---

13   This exposition explains why Marx differentiated between '*Wertverhältnis*' ('value relation') and '*Wertausdruck*' ('value expression'). In Russian translation these concepts are sometimes mistakenly identified. For example, on p. 12 of the Russian edition of *Capital*, Volume I (1928) we read: '*проследить развитие того выражение стоимости* ('*Wertausdruck*'), *каким* является *отношение стоимостей* ("*Wertverhältnis*") *товаров*'. In the original [as re-translated by Rubin into Russian] Marx wrote: '*развитие того выражение стоимости, которое* содержится *в отношение стоимостей товаров*'. [In German: '*Um herauszufinden, wie der einfache Wertausdruck einer Ware im Wertverhältnis zweier Waren steckt*'] Marx frequently says that 'the value relation' ('*отношение стоимостей*' or '*Wertverhältnis*') includes the '*выражение стоимости*' ('value expression' or '*Wertausdruck*').

And the fact is that in the previously mentioned second part of the first chapter of the *Critique*, which involves no more than four pages (15–19),[14] we do find the embryo of a doctrine of the 'value expression' or exchange-value.

After Marx considered commodities in the first part of the first chapter of the *Critique* in terms of their equality as values, he begins the second part with the following words:

> The exchange-value (*Tauschwert*, which is understood in fact as value – I.R.) of a commodity is not expressed in its own use-value ... The exchange-value of one commodity thus manifests itself in the use-values of other commodities. In fact the exchange-value of one commodity, expressed in the use-value of another commodity, represents equivalence.[15] If I say, for example, that one yard of linen is worth two pounds of coffee, then the exchange-value of linen is expressed in the use-value of coffee and is, moreover, expressed in a definite quantity of this use-value. Once this proportion is given, the value of any quantity of linen can be expressed in terms of coffee.[16]

In the passage just cited we have a direct indication that the value of a commodity is expressed in the use-value of another commodity, i.e. it takes the form of exchange-value. It was also clear to Marx already in the *Critique* that a change in the exchange-value of a commodity does not correspond quantitatively with a change of its value:

> We have seen that the *exchange-value* of a commodity varies with the quantity of labour time directly contained in it. Its *realised* exchange-value, that is, its exchange-value *expressed in the use-values* of other commodities, must also depend on the degree to which the labour time expended on the production of all other commodities varies.[17]

The 'exchange-value' of commodity A depends solely on the quantity of labour expended on its production. But its 'realised exchange-value' can also change in accordance with a change of the quantity of labour expended on the production of commodity B, which is exchanged for commodity A. The 'exchange-

14 [Marx 1970, pp. 38–41].
15 We shall return below to this definition of an equivalent.
16 Marx 1970, p. 38.
17 Marx 1970, p. 40 [Rubin's emphasis].

value' of commodity A may remain unchanged regardless of a change of its 'realised exchange-value'. Evidently Marx here too understands the first term, as he does elsewhere, to mean essentially the *value* of the commodity, while the latter term signifies its *exchange-value*.

In these quotations we can see the embryo of the idea that the value of a commodity must be 'realised' (*realisiert*) or 'expressed' (*ausgedrückt*) in 'the use-values of other commodities'. These expressions are frequently used in the same sense in the *Critique*.[18] Elsewhere in the *Critique* Marx uses other terms to express the same idea. The exchange-value of the commodity finds its 'real expression' (*realer Ausdruck*) or 'representation' (*Darstellung*) in the use-values of other commodities and 'manifests itself' (*manifestiert sich*) in them.[19]

In the expressions that we have quoted we can see an embryonic doctrine of the distinction between exchange-value and value. In the *Critique*, however, this doctrine is still embryonic. Both value and exchange-value are still designated here by one and the same term, by *Tauschwert*. Here the whole qualitative originality associated with the fact that the value of one commodity is expressed in the use-value of another commodity has not yet come to Marx's attention. The qualitatively different roles fulfilled by the two commodities in the expression of value are not yet clarified. Here the 'value expression' is yet to be distinguished with sufficient clarity from the quantitative 'value relation', which is expressed in the equality of commodities as values. The particular qualitative features of the category of exchange-value – as distinct from value on the one hand and from the 'value relation' on the other – have yet to be clearly developed. Marx's thinking is oriented above all on the quantitative features of the 'value expression'. 'Once the proportion is given, the value of any quantity of linen can be expressed in terms of coffee'[20] – this sort of purely quantitative conclusion is what interests Marx above all. Later, in the first edition of Volume I of *Capital*,[21] Marx himself realised that a predominant interest in the quantitative side of the question cannot lead to a correct understanding

---

18 See for example: 'the exchange-value' is 'expressed' in a series of equations (Marx 1970, p. 39); 'the exchange-value of linen is expressed in the use-value of coffee' (Marx 1970, p. 38); 'the exchange-value of a bushel of wheat' is expressed in 'its equivalents' (Marx 1970, p. 40); 'The exchange-value of any commodity ... is measured successively [or expressed] in terms of definite quantities of the use-values of all other commodities' (Marx 1970, p. 39).

19 In this footnote Rubin cites pp. 15, 19, 24 and 50 of the 1907 (or 1924) edition of *Zur Kritik der Politischen Oekonomie*.

20 Marx 1970, p. 38.

21 Marx 1867, pp. 20–1.

of exchange-value and of the need for a polar division of the different functions between the two commodities – a division that contains the nucleus of the need for the emergence of money.

We have arrived at the conclusion that the concept of exchange-value is not yet clearly developed in the *Critique*. It is perfectly natural, for this reason, that in the *Critique* we still do not find any doctrine of the different forms of value, the teaching to which Marx devoted so much attention in *Capital*. In *Capital*, as we know, Marx investigates the different forms of value on the one hand (simple, expanded, general and monetary); and on the other hand, for each expression of value Marx in turn differentiates the two poles of relative value and equivalent value. In the *Critique* we still find neither a doctrine of the forms of value nor a doctrine of the poles of value. All we can point to are the weak embryos of ideas from which Marx later built his doctrine of the forms of value. As for the doctrine of the development of opposition between the poles of value, in the *Critique* we do not find even a suggestion of this idea.

Since value appears in the *Critique* from the very outset in its most developed form, in its universal or monetary form, it is understandable that there would be no point in looking here for a doctrine of the different forms of value. It is true that in the *Critique*, too, for purposes of illustration, Marx willingly takes examples of the exchange of one commodity for another commodity, but from the very beginning he regards this exchange as one moment of a multilateral exchange of a given commodity for all other commodities. To convince ourselves of this fact, let us follow the development of Marx's thinking in the second of the three parts to which we have referred.

Turning in the second part to an investigation of exchange-value, Marx takes for example the exchange of one commodity for another commodity: 'If one says, for instance, that one yard of linen is worth two pounds of coffee, then the exchange-value of linen (which, as we know, is understood to mean value – I.R.) is expressed in the use-value of coffee, and it is moreover expressed in a definite quantity of this use-value'.[22] We know that in *Capital* Marx sets out this case of the exchange of one commodity for another commodity for detailed analysis under the heading of the simple form of value. In the *Critique*, without subjecting this equation to any special analysis, he quickly includes it in a whole system of equations that express the value of the same yard of linen in terms of an endless series of other commodities. 'It is evident that the exchange-value of a commodity, e.g., linen, is not exhaustively expressed by the proportion in which a particular commodity, e.g., coffee, forms its equivalent

---

22   Marx 1970, p. 38.

... The exchange-value of this particular commodity (linen – I.R.) can therefore be exhaustively expressed only by an infinite number of equations',[23] namely in the following series:

   1 yard of linen = ½ pound of tea,
   1 yard of linen = 2 pounds of coffee,
   1 yard of linen = 8 pounds of bread,
   1 yard of linen = 6 yards of calico, etc.

Speaking in terms of *Capital*, we could say that Marx has passed from the simple to the developed form of value. But whereas what is really involved in *Capital* is the dialectical (logical and historical) transformation of one form of value into another, in the *Critique* Marx limits himself to observing that the equation of two commodities (linen and coffee) involves nothing more than one instance of an entire system of equations expressing the value of linen. Whereas the equation of two commodities in *Capital* represents a particular form of value, having at least a very relative autonomy, in the *Critique* [the equation] appears from the very outset in the modest role of a subordinate member of a whole system of equations.

But Marx soon passes beyond this system of equations. 'If the exchange-value of one yard of linen is expressed in ½ pound of tea, or 2 pounds of coffee, or 8 pounds of bread, or 6 yards of calico etc., it follows that coffee, tea, calico, bread etc. must be equal to one another in the proportion in which they are equal to a third magnitude, namely linen; and therefore linen serves as the common measure of their exchange-value'.[24] To use the terms of *Capital* once again, Marx has passed here from the developed form of value to the universal. But, in this case too, one cannot speak of the dialectical transformation of one form of value into another. Whereas in *Capital* the developed form of value *becomes* (logically and historically) the universal form, in the *Critique* Marx limits himself to observing that the system of equations in question *is* nothing but the same system of equations inverted (i.e. in which the items on the left are moved to the right, and those on the right to the left). Here Marx does not show us the dialectical development of the different forms of value but provides only a logical analysis of exchange-value, which appears from the very beginning in its most advanced, universal form. In *Capital* the transition from developed to universal form of value is accompanied by a clear change in the social character

---

23   Marx 1970, p. 39.
24   Ibid.

of the commodity selected (linen), which remains on the right hand side of the equation in the role of universal equivalent. In the *Critique*, every commodity is regarded simultaneously as 'the exclusive commodity, which serves as the common measure of the exchange-values of all other commodities', and as 'one of the many commodities in the series in which any other commodity directly expresses its exchange-value'.[25]

Thus in the *Critique* we have found only weak rudiments of the doctrine of forms of value. Marx here emphasises most forcefully the unity of the substance of value and occludes the difference of forms of value. This is precisely what explains the absence from the *Critique* of any doctrine concerning the development of the forms and the poles of value.

In *Capital*, as we know, Marx draws a sharp distinction between the two poles of value. Commodity A, whose value is expressed in commodity B, has the relative form of value. Commodity B, in terms of which the value of commodity A is expressed, has the equivalent form of value or functions as the equivalent.[26] In A and B, the two commodities that are being equated with each other, the substance of value (labour) is qualitatively identical and quantitatively of the same magnitude. But the two commodities play different roles in the expression of value and have different forms of value.

In the *Critique* this difference of form does not yet attract Marx's attention. It is true that just as Marx regards value in the *Critique* in its most developed universal or monetary form, so he knows perfectly well the difference of the two poles of value in their more developed form, namely, in the form of the polar opposition between the commodity and money. But insofar as Marx remains within the limits of the theory of value (as distinct from the theory of money), the different roles fulfilled by the two commodities being equated is not yet clear to him. Here he still underlines the unity that characterises the two commodities being equated in the 'expression of their equivalence'. Both of the commodities A and B, which figure in the given expression, are considered 'equivalent'.[27] Here equivalence is understood in most cases in the sense of being 'equal in value' – a feature that applies identically to both of the commodities being equated. This is what explains the unusual definition of equivalence that we find in the *Critique*: 'In fact the exchange-value of one commodity expressed in the use-value of another commodity represents equivalence'.[28] Let us recall that in *Capital* Marx uses almost exactly the same

25 Marx 1970, p. 40.
26 Marx 1976, pp. 139–40.
27 Marx 1970, p. 40.
28 Marx 1970, p. 38.

words to characterise precisely the relative, not the equivalent, form of value: 'The value of commodity A, thus expressed in the use-value of commodity B, has the form of relative value'.[29] At first sight the reader may suppose that what is called equivalent in the *Critique* is the same form of value as is called relative in *Capital*. But that would be a mistake. In the *Critique* Marx simply does not distinguish the two poles of value from each other and speaks identically of the commodity on the left side of the exchange equation and of the commodity on the right side as equivalent. On one and the same page we encounter the term 'equivalent' in both of these senses. On page 15 Marx gives a series of equations in which one and the same commodity, namely, one yard of linen, is equated with a whole series of other commodities. On this occasion Marx tells us that the use-values of all the other commodities form the equivalent of linen. Here the term 'equivalent' is used in the same sense as in *Capital*. But in the very next sentence we learn that in this series of equations linen is the 'exhaustive expression for a universal equivalent', i.e. a commodity equivalent to all other commodities.[30] Both the linen and the commodities in which its value is expressed are, therefore, called 'equivalent'.[31]

The evolution of the term 'equivalent' in Marx's works is highly indicative. When Marx was mainly concerned with the equality of all commodities as values, the term 'equivalent' (or 'equivalence' in the sense of equal values) emphasised the *equality* of the commodities being exchanged. When Marx was concerned with the different roles played by two commodities in the value expression, the term 'equivalent' *distinguished* the role of one commodity from

---

29   Marx 1976, p. 144.
30   Marx 1970, p. 39.
31   Failure to understand Marx's unique terminology in the *Critique* often leads to a mistaken interpretation of this text. For example, on page 26 of the German edition of the *Critique* we read: '2 pounds of coffee = 1 yard of linen is now a comprehensive expression for the exchange-value of coffee, for in this expression it appears as the direct equivalent to a definite quantity of any other commodity' (see the English version, p. 47). In *Capital* Marx would say that coffee has the relative form of value, while linen fulfils the role of universal equivalent. But in the *Critique* Marx also calls the coffee 'equivalent' because, by way of the linen (as universal equivalent) it is equated with any other commodity. It was apparently incomprehensible to the Russian translator why coffee should be called equivalent, and he thought it necessary to rephrase the sentence this way: 'The equation 2 pounds of coffee = 1 yard of cloth is now a comprehensive expression of the exchange-value of coffee, for in this expression the *yard of cloth* is the direct equivalent for a certain quantity of any other commodity' (See the Russian edition published by Leningrad Communist University, 1922, p. 50). In Marx's usage, the gender of the pronoun 'it' ('*er*') indicates that the reference could only be to the coffee, not to the linen ('*Leinwand*'), which is feminine.

the other commodity, which assumed the relative form of value. In the first edition of *Capital* (1867) Marx still considered it necessary to recall this dual meaning of the term 'equivalent'. Marx wrote:

> We can also express the formula 20 yards of linen = 1 coat, or 20 yards of linen are worth 1 coat, in the following way: 20 yards of linen and 1 coat *are equivalents*, or *both are values of equal magnitude*. Here we do not express *the value* of either of the two commodities *in the use-value* of the other. Neither of the two commodities is hence set up in *equivalent-form*. *Equivalent* here means only *something equal in magnitude*, both things having been silently reduced in our heads to the abstraction *value*.[32]

In the *Critique* Marx applies the term 'equivalent' equally to both poles of the value expression, i.e. both to the pole that in *Capital* is denoted as equivalent and to the pole that in *Capital* is specifically called relative value. It is perfectly understandable, therefore, that in the *Critique* the term '*relative value*' can still not be found in the sense in which it is used in *Capital*. Indeed, while in *Capital* the relative value of commodity A is called its value, expressed in the use-value of another commodity (for example, commodity B), in the *Critique* it is a matter of the 'relative value' (*relativer Wert*) of two or *several* commodities (for example, commodities A and B), i.e. of *the comparative magnitude of their values*. While in *Capital* the term 'relative value' is applied only to *one* pole of the 'value *expression*' (*Wertausdruck*), in the *Critique* it is used to characterise the 'value *relation*' (*Wertverhältnis*) of *both* commodities. In order to explain this difference more clearly to the reader, let us recall what we said above concerning the distinction between the 'value expression' and the 'value relation'. Suppose the relative value (i.e. the value relation) of tea and coffee is 4:1, that is, one pound of tea has four times more value than a pound of coffee. Here, by the 'relative values' of tea and coffee we understand the comparative magnitudes of their value; but in this case neither the value of tea nor the value of coffee has any special designation. It is a different matter when we say that the value of 1 pound of tea is equal to 4 pounds of coffee; here tea has the 'relative form of value' in the sense that its value receives specific expression in the use-value of coffee (and the latter commodity for this reason fulfils the role of equivalent). In this case the two commodities play different roles, whereas in the first case they were exactly the same.

---

32 Marx 1867, p. 769.

The concept of relative value, as opposed to the equivalent form of value, is found only in *Capital*. The *Critique* speaks of relative values only in the first sense, i.e. in the same sense in which the concept of relative value is generally used by Ricardo. Thus in the *Critique* there is talk of the 'relative value' of an endless variety of use-values and of the 'relative value of the two metals' (gold and silver).[33]

As we see, the evolution of the term 'relative value' runs perfectly parallel to the evolution of the term 'equivalent'. At the beginning both terms emphasised the *equality* of two commodities exchanging for each other. Later they served to characterise the *different* and *opposing* roles that these commodities play in the act of exchange. It is true that in *Capital* Marx sometimes uses these terms in the former sense, but their new significance becomes ever more apparent as terms that signify the different and opposite poles of the value expression.

2   Marx and Bailey

As we explained in the first chapter, in the *Critique of Political Economy* Marx still does not make a clear distinction between value and exchange-value. Marx draws this distinction in clear and precise form in the first chapter of Volume I of *Capital*. What is it that convinced Marx to take a closer look at this question? Apparently he was persuaded to do so by the need to defend the theory of labour value against fierce attacks upon it by [Samuel] Bailey.

Bailey appeared as a decisive and zealous opponent of Ricardo's doctrine, which he subjected to sharp criticism in his work *A Critical Dissertation on the Nature, Measure and Causes of Value* (1825). This work provoked a great row and a heated polemic between its author and the supporters of Ricardo. Despite the fact that Bailey criticised Ricardo's theory from the viewpoint of superficial and vulgar [political] economy, he did succeed, as Marx noted,[34] in disclosing its real weak points.

Ricardo claimed that the value of the commodity is determined by labour. But he was completely uninterested in the form of value, regarding it as secondary and of no consequence. He did not distinguish value from exchange-value, and the conversion of commodities into money seemed to him to be a purely formal and external act.[35] But in reality the value of the commodity appears in the form of exchange-value: it takes the form of the sum of money or a certain quantity of other commodities received in exchange for the given commod-

---

33   Marx 1970, pp. 75, 149.
34   Marx 1976, p. 155, footnote 25.
35   Marx 1971, pp. 131, 138.

ity. In Ricardo's theory an impassable abyss opened between the value of the commodity, expressed in a certain quantity of labour, and its exchange-value, expressed in a certain quantity of other things; there was no bridge from the former to the latter, and Bailey directed his blows at this weak point.

If Ricardo, having concentrated his attention on value, ignored the form of value, Bailey took the opposite route. He considers phenomena in the form they take in the acts of market exchange. In exchange, however, the value of the commodity does not express itself apart from other commodities. It appears only in an external form, in a certain amount of other commodities (or a certain sum of money). Therefore, says Bailey, we can only speak of the relative value of a given commodity A in terms of another commodity B, C, D, E, etc. But it is foolish to speak of the value of commodity A in general without accurately specifying the concrete commodity for which commodity A is being exchanged and with which it is being compared. It is not possible to speak of the *absolute* value of commodity A, only of its *relative* value compared with commodity B (or C, D, E, etc.). 'There are a thousand different types of value – as many types of value as there are commodities'.[36]

But relative value always presupposes a relation of two commodities and therefore must have a two-sided character. The relative value of commodity A in terms of commodity B, for instance 4:1 (i.e. a formula showing that one unit of commodity A has four times more value than a unit of commodity B), simultaneously expresses the relative value of commodity B in terms of commodity A, namely, 1:4. Thus any change of this formula of exchange, for instance its conversion into the formula 3:1, means not only a change of the relative value of commodity A but also a simultaneous change (in the opposite direction) of the relative value of B. On this basis Bailey denies the view of Ricardo's supporters concerning the possibility of a change in the relative value of commodity A and commodity B in the absence of any change in the value of commodity B itself. Since Bailey rejects the concept of a given commodity's absolute value, and since it is possible to speak only of the relative value of a commodity, Bailey's conclusion is perfectly understandable – that any change in the value of commodity A (expressed in terms of B) means a simultaneous change in the value of commodity B (expressed in terms of A): 'The value of commodity A cannot increase in relation to B without the value of B decreasing in relation to A'.[37]

---

36   Bailey 1825, p. 39.
37   Bailey 1825, p. 12.

Rejection of the concept of absolute value leads Bailey to a whole series of errors of which we will note the most important. In the first place, we could not say that the value of a given commodity has changed while the value of the commodities for which it is exchanged remains constant. Second, the approach taken by economists in adding the values of different commodities to achieve a sum of values must be rejected. Third, we could not compare the value of a given commodity in different periods of time.

In order to defend the theory of labour value against Bailey's attacks, it was necessary to draw a clear distinction between value and exchange-value. It was precisely by ignoring this distinction that Ricardo created the opening for Bailey's attacks. Thus it is quite understandable that the main purpose of Marx's polemic against Bailey, in the third volume of *Theories of Surplus-Value*, is to show the distinction between the value of the commodity and the form of its appearance as exchange-value.

Above all Marx shows that consistently following Bailey's point of view must lead to complete denial of any law governing exchange. If we cannot speak of the value of commodity A in itself, then we are in no position to say whether the exchange of A for B corresponds with their values or not. We may note that in the given case a certain quantity of linen was in fact exchanged for a certain quantity of coffee. But we cannot say whether this exchange relation is legitimate and normal: 'Then one could not speak of a relation in which it exchanges but only of a relation in which it is or *has been exchanged*'.[38]

If we do not wish to abandon knowledge of lawfulness at the basis of exchange phenomena, then we must recognise that 'objects are not exchanged in arbitrary proportions but as commodities, that is, as objects each of which has a value and which exchange with one another *in proportion to their equivalence*'.[39] In other words, if our goal is to reveal the lawfulness of exchange phenomena, we cannot regard the value of the commodity as something fortuitous and arbitrary, established anew with each act of exchange of a given commodity for another concrete commodity.

Starting from this viewpoint, Marx comes to the conclusion that the value of the commodity must be distinguished from its exchange-value. His discussion proceeds as follows. A given commodity, linen for example, exchanges for many other commodities such as bread, coffee, a coat, etc. To assume that in each of these acts of exchange our linen assumes a different value would mean to deny any lawfulness in exchange phenomena. It is obvious that linen

---

38   Marx 1971, p. 142.
39   Marx 1971, p. 140.

has a completely determined value that in one instance finds itself expressed in exchange for bread, in another in the exchange for coffee, etc. We must, therefore, distinguish the value of the linen, which remains identical in all these exchange acts, from the different forms of its manifestation in bread, coffee and so forth, that is, from its exchange-value.

This discussion is outlined in the first pages of *Theories* that Marx devotes to Bailey:

> The *value* of the same commodity can, without changing, be expressed in infinitely *different* quantities of use-values, always according to whether I express it in the use-value of this or that commodity. This does not alter the value, although it does alter the way it is expressed. In the same way, all the various quantities of different use-values in which the value of the commodity A can be expressed, are equivalents and are related to one another not only as values, but as equal values, so that when these very unequal quantities of use-value replace one another, the value remains completely unchanged, as if it had not found expression in quite different use-values.[40]

In another place Marx briefly summarises these considerations in the following words:

> Although the commodity has a thousand different kinds of value [expressions], or a thousand different prices, all these thousand expressions always express *the same value.* [This is] the best proof that all these different expressions are *equivalents* which not only can replace one another in this expression, but do replace one another in exchange itself.[41]

In these quotations from Marx we find a difference more precisely drawn between value and its mode of expression: *one and the same value has a multitude of different kinds of expression,* or is expressed in the most diverse use-values. From this we can draw the reverse conclusion: if a particular quantity of one use-value is equated in exchange with a particular quantity of another

---

40   Marx 1971, p. 127.
41   In *Capital* Marx understands price (*Preis*) only as value expressed in Money. In *Theories of Surplus-Value* he calls price the exchange-value of the commodity, which may be expressed either in another commodity or in money. Marx calls the latter price, as distinct from price in general, the 'money price' (*Geldpreis*). See Marx 1971, p. 147.

use-value, then they must both be equal to a third quantity, namely, the value that inheres in each of them. The equality of two use-values in exchange presupposes that they are both equal in a third sense, or that there is within them both something that is common, namely, value of a certain magnitude. This reverse conclusion is already indicated by Marx in both of the excerpts that we have quoted, and it is expressed even more clearly in another place:

> He (Bailey) even forgets the simple consideration that if y yards of linen = x pounds of straw, this [implies] a parity between the two unequal things – linen and straw – making them equal magnitudes. This existence of theirs as things that are equal must surely be different from their existence as straw and linen. It is not as straw and linen that they are equated, but as equivalents. The one side of the equation must, therefore, express the same value as the other. The value of the straw and linen must, therefore, be neither straw nor linen, but something common to both and different from both commodities considered as straw and linen.[42]

In other words, the equation of commodity A with commodity B is possible only on condition that 'there exists a common element for A and B, or if A and B are different representations of the same element'.[43]

Marx illustrates these arguments with a geometric example. In order to make a comparison of different geometric figures, for example a triangle and a parallelogram, they must be reduced to something common, namely, the product of the base and the height.[44]

A reader who is quite familiar with Marx's *Capital* will probably have noticed already that the excerpts we have cited correspond perfectly with certain arguments by Marx on the first pages of the first volume of *Capital*. In order to leave the reader without a shadow of doubt on this account, we think it necessary to quote here in full the corresponding three paragraphs from the first volume

---

42 Marx 1971, pp. 139–40.
43 Marx 1971, p. 160. It is interesting to note certain peculiarities in the terminology that Marx employs in *Theories*. Here, as in the *Critique*, he does not yet use the term 'form of value' (he only sometimes reproaches the classics for not investigating value 'in terms of form'); the terms *Tauschwert* and *Wert* are used synonymously for value (the latter term being used more frequently than in the *Critique*). Usually in *Theories* Marx opposes exchange-value (i.e. value) to its various 'expressions'.
44 Marx uses this geometric example (which also occurs in Hegel) twice. See Marx 1971, pp. 143–4, footnote, and also pp. 160–1.

of *Capital*. We shall cite the text from the first edition of *Capital* (1867), where the similarity is most obvious between Marx's comments and his arguments against Bailey in the third volume of *Theories of Surplus-Value*:

> Any commodity, for instance a quarter of wheat, is exchanged *in different proportions* with other commodities. Nevertheless, its exchange-value remains *constant*, whether it is expressed in x cotton, y silk, z gold, etc. It must, therefore, be something different from its various *kinds of expression*.[45]

> Let us take the example of two commodities, e.g., wheat and iron. The proportions in which they are exchangeable, whatever those proportions may be, can always be represented by an equation in which a given quantity of wheat is equated to some quantity of iron: *e.g.*, 1 quarter of wheat = x cwt. of iron. What does this equation tell us? It tells us that *one and the same value exists in two different things*, in 1 quarter of wheat and in x cwt. of iron. The two things must therefore be equal to a *third*, which in itself is neither the one nor the other. Thus, each of them, insofar as it is an exchange-value, must be reducible apart from the other to this third.

> A simple geometrical illustration will make this clear. In order to calculate and compare the areas of rectilinear figures, we decompose them into triangles. But the area of the triangle itself is expressed by something totally different from its visible figure, namely, by half the product of the base and the height. In the same way the exchange-values of commodities must be capable of being expressed in terms of something common to them all, of which they represent a greater or lesser quantity.[46]

---

45   It is interesting to note that in the first edition of *Capital*, as in the *Critique*, Marx still opposes 'exchange-value' to the different 'kinds of expression'. In the second edition of *Capital* Marx completely changed this paragraph: 'Any commodity, let us suppose a quarter of wheat ... exchanges in various proportions for other commodities. Therefore wheat, instead of one *exchange-value has many* ... It follows ... that exchange-value can in general be only a *kind of expression*, a "form of manifestation" of any commodity as distinguished from its content'. Here exchange-value is already no longer opposed to its mode of expression but is itself merely the 'mode of expression' of value. But the French edition of *Capital* (and also the German edition edited by K. Kautsky, as well as the Russian translation by V. Bazarov and I. Stepanov) cites the paragraph given in the first edition.

46   [This paragraph and the two that precede it come from] Marx 1867, p. 3, Marx's italics.

The similarity between these three paragraphs from the first volume of *Capital* with the excerpts above from *Theories of Surplus-Value* is striking. The first paragraph repeats the position that Marx develops in detail in his polemic against Bailey: the value of a given commodity can be expressed in the most diverse use-values. Beginning with this basic position, in the second paragraph Marx draws the opposite conclusion, also seen in *Theories of Surplus-Value*: two use-values that are equal to each other are equal to some third thing.[47] Finally, in the third paragraph Marx uses the geometric example with which we are already familiar.

Our comparison of these two texts by Marx throws clear light upon the origin and meaning of the arguments developed by Marx in the three paragraphs from the first volume of *Capital* – arguments that have been subject to every conceivable misinterpretation and to this day provoke sharp objections from Marx's critics. The direct purpose of these arguments was to defend the theory of labour value against attacks from Bailey, and that meant it was necessary to draw a clear distinction between the value of the commodity and its exchange-value, expressed in terms of other commodities. That this is precisely the goal that Marx was pursuing in the initial pages of *Capital* could be assumed even without comparing this text with the section of the third volume of *Theories of Surplus-Value* devoted to Bailey. To convince oneself, it is enough just to read in *Capital* the paragraph that precedes the three paragraphs we have quoted:

> Exchange-value appears first of all as the quantitative relation, the proportion in which use-values of one kind exchange for use-values of another kind. This relation changes constantly with time and place. Hence exchange-value appears to be something accidental and purely relative, and consequently an intrinsic value, i.e. an exchange-value that is inseparably connected with the commodity, inherent in it, seems a contradiction in terms. Let us consider the matter more closely.[48]

After this come the three paragraphs that we quoted from Marx. Obviously, Marx's objective was to reveal the error of regarding exchange-value as something 'accidental and purely relative', and the clearest representative of that sort of view was precisely Bailey. Now that we have compared Marx's two texts, we

---

47   The commentators and critics of *Capital* usually concentrate all their attention on the second of these three paragraphs of the first volume of *Capital* without noticing that it is nothing but the reverse of the conclusion reached in the first paragraph.

48   Marx 1976, p. 126.

may say with even greater conviction and precision not only that posing the problem of value in the first pages of *Capital* was dictated by the need to deflect Bailey's attacks, but also that Marx's corresponding argument was first set out in the section of *Theories of Surplus-Value* devoted to Bailey. If we compare the text of the *Critique of Political Economy* with the text of the first volume of *Capital*, we see that in the first couple of pages of both works Marx's expositions approximately correspond. Beginning, however, with the paragraphs quoted above, the text of *Capital* gives us something new in principle when compared to the text of the *Critique of Political Economy*, namely, a sharper distinction between value and exchange-value.[49]

In order to disclose more clearly the difference between the 'value itself' of the commodity and the 'expression' of this value in the use-values of other commodities, in the same section of *Theories* that Marx devoted to Bailey he shows that a change in the 'expression' of value frequently does not correspond with a change of the value itself. For instance, suppose that the quantity of commodities received in exchange for commodity A is reduced, i.e. the exchange-value of commodity A declines 'insofar as it is realised in other commodities, that is, its exchange-value expressed in the use-values of all other commodities'.[50] But this reduction in the 'realised exchange-value' of commodity A may have been the result of two different and opposing causes: either a reduction of the quantity of labour time required for production of commodity A or an increase of the labour time necessary for production of the other commodities. 'The same phenomenon occurs in both cases although from completely opposite causes'. Accordingly, the changed 'expression' of commodity A's value still does not show that the value 'itself' has changed.

Essentially, these considerations by Marx just repeat ideas that he had already developed in *The Critique of Political Economy*.[51] But in the polemic against Bailey Marx focuses his thinking in a specific direction. In *The Critique of Political Economy* he simply wanted to show that changes of 'realised exchange-value, i.e. expressed in the use-values of other commodities',[52] can be caused not only by changes of the labour time required to produce the given commodity but also by changes of the labour time required to produce the other commodities. Although in the *Critique* Marx did not essentially confuse this 'realised exchange-value' of commodity A with its 'exchange-value' (by which

---

49   See the first chapter of this essay.
50   Marx 1971, p. 126.
51   Marx 1970, pp. 38–40.
52   Marx 1970, p. 40. See the first chapter of this essay.

he meant its value), he did not consider it necessary to emphasise their distinction, still less to present them as opposites. In the polemic against Bailey, Marx focuses the same thoughts in precisely this direction and summarises this way: 'From this it obviously follows that the rate at which commodities exchange with one another as use-values, although it is an *expression* of their value, their *realised* value, is not their value itself, since the same proportion of value can be represented by quite different quantities of use-values'.[53]

It is interesting to note that the focus of Marx's thought in this direction continues and becomes even more emphatic in *Capital*. The reasoning that we have been considering, which is encountered both in *The Critique of Political Economy* and in *Theories of Surplus-Value*, is carried over by Marx to the first volume of *Capital*, where it is developed in even greater detail in the third section of the first chapter in the paragraph on 'Quantitative Determination of the Relative Form of Value'. Marx summarises this point as follows:

> Thus real changes in the magnitude of value are neither unequivocally nor exhaustively reflected in their relative expression, or, in other words, in the magnitude of the relative value. The relative value of a commodity may vary, although its value remains constant. Its relative value may remain constant, although its value varies; and finally, simultaneous variations in the magnitude of its value and in the relative expression of that magnitude do not by any means have to correspond at all points.[54]

The content of this summation by Marx allows us to conclude quite convincingly that it is aimed precisely at Bailey, who continuously confused value with exchange-value. In a footnote to the summation,[55] Marx polemicises with the economist [John] Broadhurst, whose arguments correspond with those of Bailey.[56]

Finally, we also find included at the end of the first chapter of *Capital* signs of the arguments that Marx developed against Bailey in the third volume of *Theories*.

---

53 Marx 1971, p. 127, Marx's emphasis. Let me again draw the reader's attention to the similarity between Marx's terminology in *Theories* and in the *Critique*. In *Theories*, too, he speaks of 'realised' value and of the 'expression' of value in places where *Capital* would refer to 'exchange-value'. (See the previous chapter of this essay).
54 Marx 1976, p. 146.
55 Marx 1976, pp. 146–7.
56 [See Broadhurst 1842].

Bailey accused Ricardo of transforming value from a relation between things into something absolute:

> As we cannot speak of the distance of any object without implying some other object, in relation to which the first stands at some distance, so we cannot speak of the value of a commodity but in reference to another commodity with which it is compared. A thing cannot be valuable in itself without reference to another thing, any more than a thing can be distant in itself without reference to another thing.[57]

Marx appropriately makes the following notation to these words by Bailey: 'Is social labour, to which the value of a commodity is related, not another thing?'.[58] Marx means to say that by recognising value as an expression of social labour we do not in the slightest transform it, as Bailey thinks, from something relative into something absolute. We only relate it to social labour rather than to other commodities.

Marx returns more than once to Bailey's objections against 'absolute' labour value, not only elsewhere in the third volume of *Theories of Surplus-Value* but also in the second volume of that work, in an analysis of Ricardo's theory, where Marx again has to take into account Bailey's criticism.[59]

Marx comes to the conclusion, as a result of his reasoning, that Bailey's denunciation of the imaginary absolute character of the concept of labour value is completely unfounded:

> It is quite incorrect to say that the value of a commodity is thereby transformed from something *relative* into something *absolute*. On the contrary, as a use-value the commodity appears as something independent. On the other hand, as value it appears as something merely *relative* (*gesetztes*), something determined by its relation to socially necessary, equal, simple labour time.[60]

It is Bailey himself, thanks to his denial of value as an expression of social labour, who falls into a fetishistic representation of value as a property of the things themselves – although, it is true, not of things viewed in isolation from

---

57 Bailey 1825, p. 5.
58 Marx 1971, p. 143.
59 Marx 1971, pp. 129–30 et seq., and Marx 1968, pp. 170–2.
60 Marx 1971, p. 129, Marx's emphasis.

one another but rather in their relation to one another.⁶¹ In order to prove this, Marx quotes the following words by Bailey: 'Riches are the attribute of men; value is the attribute of commodities. A man or a community is rich; a pearl or a diamond is valuable'.⁶²

The polemic that we have set out by Marx against Bailey on the question of the 'absolute' character of value is also reflected in *Capital*. If the three paragraphs that we quoted earlier from the initial pages of *Capital* contain a veiled polemic against Bailey, in the middle and at the end of the first chapter of *Capital* Marx comes out openly against him.⁶³ He mercilessly discloses the fetishistic character of Bailey's ideas, which is revealed with utmost clarity in the sentence just quoted,⁶⁴ and in a corresponding footnote Marx briefly summarises his thoughts on the absolute character of value:

> Both the author of *Observations etc.*, and S. Bailey accuse Ricardo of converting exchange-value from something relative into something absolute. The reverse is true. He has reduced the apparent relativity which these things (diamonds, pearls, etc.) possess to the true relation hidden behind the appearance, namely their relativity as mere expressions of human labour. If the followers of Ricardo answer Bailey somewhat rudely, but by no means convincingly, this is because they are unable to find in Ricardo's own works any elucidation of the inner connection between value and the form of value, or exchange-value.⁶⁵

We have traced in the first chapter of *Capital* the direct or hidden echoes of Marx's polemic against Bailey. It can be said, more or less certainly, that it was precisely Bailey's critical arguments, aimed at Ricardo, that encouraged Marx to become more closely concerned with the question of the difference between value and exchange-value. It is most probable that it was precisely in his objections to Bailey, which occurred in the third volume of *Theories of Surplus-Value*, that Marx first outlined the course of thought that was later famously formulated in the three paragraphs from the first pages of Capital. Apparently it was against Bailey that Marx honed the conclusions at the end

---

61 Marx 1971, p. 161.
62 Bailey 1825, p. 165.
63 In Marx 1976, see the footnotes on pages 141, 155, 177. See also the footnote on pp. 146–7 dealing with [John] Broadhurst.
64 Marx also quotes this passage from Bailey at the end of the first chapter of Volume I of *Capital* (Marx 1976), in footnote 37 on p. 177.
65 Marx 1976, p. 177, footnote 38.

of his paragraph on 'Quantitative Determination of Relative Value'. And finally, Marx's polemic against Bailey, who claimed that supporters of the theory of labour value converted the concept of value into something 'absolute', was also reflected in the first chapter of *Capital*.

Bailey's critical argumentation, despite all the superficiality of the author's initial point of view, did partly stumble upon genuine weaknesses in Ricardo's theory. Consequently, it was impossible to overcome Bailey's critical objections to Ricardo without overcoming Ricardo's own theory, i.e. without a new and more profound basis for the theory of labour value. Indeed, the two antipodes, Ricardo and Bailey, suffered from the same error: confusing value with exchange-value. Marx pointed out that Ricardo confused value with 'the exchange-value of the commodity, as it *manifests itself, appears* in the process of commodity exchange'.[66] On the other hand, he accused Bailey of confusing 'the form of value with value itself'.[67] The difference between Ricardo and Bailey lay in the fact that the former ignored the form of value, while the latter thought it possible to manage without the concept of value. With the aid of a clearly stated distinction between value and exchange-value, Marx simultaneously eliminated the errors – which at first appeared to be opposites but had a single foundation – of these two economists.

Although, as we have seen, Marx's construction simultaneously overcame the one-sidedness of both Bailey and Ricardo, it was necessary for him to arrange his presentation in two opposing directions. Insofar as Marx responded to Bailey's blows, he had to demonstrate that in order to explain various 'expressions of value', i.e. exchange-value, we must turn to 'value itself'.[68] Conversely, insofar as his goal was to deepen and transform Ricardo's theory, he had to uncover the 'various aspects' of the development of the concept of value,[69] 'the different instances of definitions of value, which are not explained by Ricardo but only occur de facto and are confused with one another'.[70] In the first chapter of *Capital* Marx also arranged his presentation in these two directions. In the first section of this chapter (to which the second is added as a supplement), he shows that the analysis of exchange-value necessarily leads us to formation of the concept of value; thus Marx cuts the ground out from under Bailey. In the third section he shows that value necessarily takes on determin-

---

66   Marx 1971, p. 125.
67   Marx 1976, p. 141, footnote 17.
68   Marx 1971, p. 127.
69   Marx 1971, p. 125.
70   Marx 1971, p. 172.

ate form, and he gives a detailed analysis of these forms, thereby filling the gap in Ricardo's teaching. Marx emphasises that both of the stages that we have noted are inseparably connected. In the first section he indicates to the reader that 'The progress of the investigation will lead us back to exchange-value as the necessary mode of expression, or form of appearance, of value'.[71] On the other hand, when Marx turns to the second half of his investigation at the beginning of the third section, he again reminds the reader of its inseparable tie with the first half of the study: 'In fact we started from exchange-value, or the exchange relation of commodities, in order to track down the value that lay hidden within it. We must now return to this form of appearance of value'.[72]

It is understandable that it is precisely in the first part of Marx's investigation that we find more obvious signs of the argumentation that he developed against Bailey in the third volume of *Theories*. Indeed, it is precisely in the first part that Marx showed the necessity of forming a concept of value, against which idea Bailey aimed all of his blows. In the second part we find Marx's teaching on the forms of value – the doctrine representing the most original part of the Marxist theory of value, which is completely missing in Ricardo and Bailey but cannot be regarded as a direct refutation of Bailey's ideas. This is explained by the interesting fact that in Marx's notes against Bailey, in the third volume of *Theories of Surplus-Value*, we find the argumentation that he developed later in the first section of the first chapter of *Capital*, but we do not yet find the ideas that lie at the basis of the third section, namely, the doctrine of the different forms of value and of the poles of value.[73] In the section of *Theories* that he devotes to Bailey, Marx still has in view only the most developed, universal or monetary form of value and has yet to clarify the development of the poles of value.

But if the polemic against Bailey did not yet lead Marx directly to analysis of the different forms and poles of value, it did, in any event, prepare the way. The basic defect of Bailey's conception was, first, that he confused value with exchange-value, and second, that he directed his attention exclusively to a quantitative definition of exchange-value.[74] Bailey's first error was already revealed by Marx in *Theories*, where he drew a sharp distinction between 'value' and the various 'value expressions'. This clear distinction necessarily led Marx to give a separate analysis of value on the one hand, and of exchange-value on

---

71 Marx 1976, p. 128.
72 Marx 1976, p. 139.
73 See the first chapter of this essay.
74 Marx 1976, p. 141, footnote 17.

the other. It is true that in *Theories* Marx devoted his attention mainly to the first task, which he subsequently developed further in sections 1–2 of the first chapter of *Capital*. In *Theories* Marx did not yet give a special analysis of the different forms of value or 'value expressions'. But the need for that analysis flowed directly from the general way in which Marx posed the problem in the polemic against Bailey. A special analysis of value had to be supplemented by a special analysis of exchange-value, which Marx provided later in the third section of the first chapter of *Capital*. We may suppose that when Marx turned to a special analysis of exchange-value, he focused his attention mainly on getting beyond the second mistake that he saw in Bailey, who limited the investigation to the quantitative aspect of exchange-value. As opposed to Bailey, Marx put the qualitative aspect of exchange-value in the forefront and thus came to his teaching on the poles of value and the different forms of value.

At one essential point in Marx's notes against Bailey we can see the clear embryo of ideas that Marx later developed in his teaching on the forms of value.

The main objective of the analysis of different forms of value that Marx gives in the third section of the first chapter of *Capital* was to prove that 'The simple commodity form is therefore the germ of the money-form'.[75] In a letter to Engels on 22 June 1867, underlining the great importance of the section on forms of value, Marx added: 'The economists have hitherto overlooked the very simple fact that the equation *20 yards of linen = 1 coat* is but the primitive form of *20 yards of linen = £2*'.[76] Here Marx points out that in *Capital*, for the first time, he provided an analysis of the simple form of value that was missing from *The Critique of Political Economy*.[77]

If we acknowledge that Marx's goal in the third section of the first chapter of *Capital* was to reduce the money form of value, in which the commodity is equated with the universal equivalent, to the simple form of value, in which one commodity is equated with another, then we can find a faint suggestion of this thought in Marx's notes against Bailey. Bailey asserted that it is only the daily habit of expressing the value of all commodities in terms of money that can give rise to the impression that commodities have absolute value. If we compared linen not with a certain sum of money but with another concrete commodity, for instance, a coat, bread, coffee, etc., then, according to Bailey, we would easily convince ourselves of the purely relative character of value. This reasoning by Bailey evokes the following rebuff from Marx:

---

75   Marx 1976, p. 163.
76   Letter from Marx to Engels, 22 June 1867, in *MECW*, Vol. 42, p. 384.
77   See the first chapter of this essay.

> Mr. Bailey is of the opinion that if one were to consider *only two commodities* – in exchange with one another – one would automatically discover the mere relativity of *value* in his sense. The fool. As if it were not just as necessary to say in connection with two commodities that exchange with one another – two products that are related to one another as *commodities* – as it would be in the case of a thousand commodities, *why* they are identical.[78]

As we see, the polemic against Bailey pushed Marx towards *posing* the problem of the exchange of *two* commodities for each other, i.e. towards analysis of the 'simple form of value'. However, Marx was reluctant in his thinking to move in this direction. Marx did not yet consider it necessary to single out for special analysis the case of exchange of two commodities for each other (or the simple form of value). Such a special analysis, apparently, still seemed redundant to him from both an historical and a logical point of view. From the historical point of view, Marx could not help but understand that the random exchange of two products for each other preceded the development of commodity economy and of exchange-value. Immediately following the words that we have quoted, Marx adds: 'For that matter, if only two products existed, the products would never become commodities, and consequently the exchange-value of commodities would never evolve either'.[79] Insofar as Marx's goal was to understand the laws of a developed commodity economy and of developed exchange-value, he obviously still considered it necessary to begin his research with the comprehensive exchange of commodities and not with the exchange of two products for each other.

Thus, at the time of his polemic against Bailey, Marx still viewed a special analysis of the exchange of two commodities for each other as redundant from the historical point of view. As for the logical worth of such an analysis, in this period Marx apparently still thought such analysis could provide us with little that was new by comparison with analysis of the exchange of one commodity for 'a thousand' other commodities (or for a certain sum of money). In both cases we have to answer the same question as to 'why they (the commodities) are identical', i.e. we must reveal the identity of their social character, their unity as *values*. The identical social content of all the listed acts of exchange still obscured from Marx's vision their difference of form. Fully absorbed in looking

---

78 Marx 1971, p. 144, Marx's emphasis.
79 Marx 1971, p. 144.

for the single substance of commodities, i.e. value, Marx did not pay sufficient attention to the difference in forms of value:

> ... how can one express x cotton in y money? The question resolves itself into this – how is it at all possible to express one commodity in another, or how to present commodities as equivalents? Only the elaboration of value, *independent of the representation* of one commodity in another, provides the answer.[80]

Here Marx comes very close to formulating the question of the link between money and the simple forms of value. True, even here he is still inclined to focus on the unity of their content by comparison with their differences of form, but nevertheless the question of the difference of these forms was already posed, and its solution required a special analysis of 'the form of value, or exchange-value'[81] that Marx later worked out in *Capital*.

We can now summarise our conclusions. The unique structure of the first chapter of *Capital* consists of the fact that Marx analysed value and exchange-value separately. Marx evidently came to this strict demarcation of concepts in the course of his polemic against Bailey. Marx counted Bailey among those 'few economists who have concerned themselves with the analysis of the form of value'.[82] While the classics concentrated their attention on value and regarded the form of value as something external and inconsequential, Bailey fell into the opposite error. He turned his attention mainly to the *multiplicity* of value expressions and imagined that 'by pointing to the multiplicity of the relative expressions of the same commodity-value he had obliterated any possibility of a conceptual determination of value'.[83] In order to deflect Bailey's attacks, which threatened to overturn the entire theory of labour value, Marx had to draw a sharp distinction between 'value' and 'value expressions', from which logically followed the need to provide separate analyses of value and exchange-value. But it was only possible finally to overcome Bailey's criticism by filling the gap left by Ricardo. Marx therefore faced a dual task. First, behind the *multiplicity* of value expressions he had to uncover the *unity* at their base, i.e. value (and ultimately labour), and secondly he had to show how one and the same *value* can be expressed in the most diverse *forms of value*. In contrast

---

80   Marx 1971, p. 162 [Rubin's emphasis].
81   [The heading of Section 3, Chapter 1, of *Capital*, Vol. I].
82   Marx 1976, p. 141, footnote 17.
83   Marx 1976, p. 155, footnote 25.

with Bailey, in sections 1–2 of the first chapter of *Capital* Marx moves in his investigation from exchange-value to value. As distinct from the classics, he supplements the doctrine of value with the doctrine of 'the form of value, or exchange-value', which is set out in the third section of the same chapter. The need to arrange the investigation in these two opposing directions is what explains the unique structure of the first chapter of *Capital*.

    I. Rubin

DOCUMENT 19

Essays on Marx's Theory of Money (1926–8)

Isaak Il'ich Rubin

Source: First published in Ya.A. Kuz'minov et al. (eds.), *Istoki: Sotsiokul'turnaya sreda ekonomicheskoi deyatel'nosti i ekonomicheskovo poznaniya* (Moscow: Izdatel'skii dom Vysshei shkoly ekonomiki, 2011), pp. 501–617.[1]

Introduction by the Editors

In the previous document of this volume, Isaak Rubin offered guidance to the first chapter of Marx's *Capital*, which he described as 'enormously difficult to understand'. The present document, written during the same period, pursues a similar theme but goes much further to examine the whole of Part One of the

---

[1] This manuscript, handwritten with a pencil, was never published in Rubin's lifetime and appeared in print for the first time in 2011 thanks to his family, who preserved the work, and to Lyudmila L. Vasina, Candidate of Economic Science at the Russian State Archive of Social-political History, who prepared it for publication and shared it with the editors of this volume. Vasina suggests that Rubin conceived the project in 1923, during his incarceration in Moscow's Butyrsky prison, where he also worked on a new Russian translation of Marx's *Contribution to the Critique of Political Economy* (*Istoki*, p. 492). In the original manuscript, Rubin frequently used abbreviations, which are filled in by use of square brackets in the published Russian text. The meaning of the abbreviations is always clear, leaving no room for misinterpretation, but that aspect of the text cannot be reproduced in our translation. Rubin also added numerous marginal comments. The published Russian version uses square brackets to indicate those comments, including section headings. To minimise distraction, in most cases we leave out the square brackets and instead use footnotes to indicate marginal additions to the manuscript. Readers who are familiar with Rubin's *Essays on Marx's Theory of Value* (Rubin 1990) will recognise in this work a continuation of the earlier study as Rubin followed Marx's path from the theory of value to the theory of money. Vasina noted that Rubin did not complete this project, probably because the mounting political attacks on his earlier *Essays* convinced him that there was no chance of having his work on the theory of money published (*Istoki*, pp. 498–9). In the biographical appendix to this volume, written by L.L. Vasina and Ya.G. Rokityanskii, readers will find a summary of Rubin's continuous struggle with Soviet officialdom, beginning with his first arrest in 1921 and ending with his execution by the NKVD in November 1937 for allegedly forming a Trotskyist counter-revolutionary organisation.

first volume of *Capital*, including 'The Commodity'; 'The Process of Exchange'; and 'Money, or the Circulation of Commodities'. The logic of Rubin's approach is made clear at the outset: he will presuppose, together with Marx, that the whole is logically prior to the parts. To begin with the 'value' of a 'commodity' is to presuppose the whole of a commodity-producing society – a particular stage of history, a particular form of property, a particular distribution of social classes, etc. – whose cell-form is determined by analysis, and whose contradictions must then be reconstructed categorically. In his notes on 'The Method of Political Economy', Marx wrote:

> Just as in general when examining any historical or social science, so also in the case of economic categories it is always necessary to remember that the subject, in this case contemporary bourgeois society, is presupposed both in reality and in the mind, and that therefore categories express forms of existence and conditions of existence – and sometimes merely separate aspects – of this particular society, the subject; thus the category, *even from the scientific standpoint*, by no means begins at the moment when it is discussed *as such*.[2]

Adopting Hegel's method, Marx saw that discussion of an initial category *begins* with the presupposition of its developed form. Yet eight years after publication of the *Critique*, Marx was still struggling with the implications of his method in writing the first edition of *Capital*. The problem was how to begin at the beginning – the value-form – when the beginning presupposes the end. How does one *begin* with the *end*? Writing his introduction to the first edition of *Capital*, even Marx expressed sympathy for his readers:

> Beginnings are always difficult in all sciences. The understanding of the first chapter, especially the section that contains the analysis of commodities, will therefore present the greatest difficulty. I have popularized the passages concerning the substance of value and the magnitude of value as much as possible. The value-form, whose fully developed shape is the money-form, is very simple and slight in content. Nevertheless, the human mind has sought in vain for more than 2,000 years to get to the bottom of it, while on the other hand there has been at least an approximation to a successful analysis of forms which are much richer in content and more complex. Why? Because the complete body is easier to study

---

2 Marx 1970, p. 212.

than its cells. Moreover, in the analysis of economic forms neither microscopes nor chemical reagents are of assistance. The power of abstraction must replace both.

These two excerpts from Marx also tell us much about Rubin's approach in the following essays. The theory of money begins with the theory of value, and Rubin introduces his commentary on the latter by specifying what Marx was abstracting from but also presupposing, namely, the fully developed circulation of commodities. On his opening page Rubin tells us that 'The theory of money only results from the theory of value but, conversely, the theory of value cannot be constructed without the theory of money ...'. Why is this important? Rubin answers that if Marx had not presupposed money as the medium of developed commodity circulation, he would have had to begin with the exchange of two items *in natura* – that is, with two *non-commodities* – in which case it might very well make sense to say, together with the marginal utility school, that 'such exchange may be regulated by the individual requirements of the participants and by their subjective appraisal of the relative usefulness of products'. Only by explicitly beginning with commodity production – the production of *useful* things *for sale* – was it possible for Marx 'to eliminate in advance the individual-psychological way of posing the question (i.e. use-value) and *from the very beginning to define the subject matter of his investigation, exchange-value, as an object belonging to the social world*, as a social function or form of the product of labour.'[3]

The commodity, being an attribute of a particular 'social world', is also necessarily one of the latter's forms: it is a 'social form' of production relations between people, the theme that runs through all of Rubin's work. Marx's marginalist critics, Rubin writes, displayed 'complete helplessness' by trying to combine 'subjective psychologism' with 'objective naturalism', whereas Marx saw that commodity production can only be understood by adopting the dialectical method, which, since it examines the structure of commodity-producing society, is simultaneously a 'sociological method'. Political economy analytically determines its fundamental category and then synthetically reconstructs its subject matter in theory, moving, in this case, from social labour

---

3 Rubin subsequently points out that to begin with the 'commodity' is to also presuppose preceding periods of production and the movement of labour between various branches of industry, i.e. processes that have already created determinate production costs and an anticipated average rate of profit, in which case it would be all the more pointless to initiate a theory of price determination with individual judgements of marginal utility.

to the developed theory of money. When he first introduces the question of money directly, Rubin gives provides a map of his essays that will be helpful to keep in mind:

> Examination of *the mechanism of social dependence between the equation of labour and the equation of commodities ... constitutes the theme of the Marxist theory of value*, or the first stage of our investigation. After showing how the equation of labour takes the form of the generalised equation of commodities, Marx turns to analysis of the latter process, showing that the *generalised equation of commodities is only possible in the form of them all being equated with one and the same designated commodity*, which acquires the character of money. This is the theory of *the origin and social function of money*, or the second stage of the study. Only after that is it possible to turn to consideration of the *individual properties of money as finished results of the process of circulation*, which at first appear to be independent of the latter and to inhere in money itself. This is the theory of the *separate functions of money*, or the third stage of the investigation. In other words, these three stages of the investigation can be characterised as the doctrine 1) of value, or of the commodity; 2) of the transformation of the commodity into money; and 3) of money itself.[4]

Marx begins by setting aside the subjective intentions of exchange participants. All commodities are qualitatively equal in terms of the unity of their social function as products of labour, but for exchange to occur they must overcome their quantitative inequality as use-values: they must be equalised in terms of the abstract, socially necessary labour that they represent, or their common property as exchange-value. But since exchange is always, as Rubin emphasises, a production relation between people, how do the participants themselves relate to one another in the exchange process? If they are not making judgements on the basis of marginal utility, how is the exchange act structured?

---

4   A few paragraphs later, Rubin offers further guidance when he summarises the order of Marx's reasoning:
   'From the concrete phenomenon of money it is necessary to descend to the equation of commodities or the value-form, and from the latter still further to the doctrine of the content of value or social labour. The first level of the investigation leads from social labour (or the content of value) to the form of value; the second, from the form of value to money; and the third treats money as the finished result. As we see, the separate levels of the study gradually pass from one to the other, for the final link of one is the first link of the next. The link that connects the theory of value with the theory of money is the doctrine of the value-form'.

When Rubin poses this question, it seems difficult to imagine that he does not have in the back of his mind another famous text by Hegel, *The Philosophy of Right*. Much as Marx's *Capital* begins with the abstraction of the commodity, Hegel's political philosophy began with the concept of the individual person's 'abstract right'. But where Marx spoke of a society of commodity producers connected through the movement of things, Hegel emphasised ties of consciousness. The absolutely free will has the abstract universality of a person, a form that acquires content in property, the 'first embodiment of freedom'.[5] But since existence as a determinate being is also existence for another, the relation of will to will emerges in the sphere of contract, whereby each holds and may exchange property through participation in a higher form of consciousness, a 'common will'.[6] The universal that mediates contractual relations, according to Hegel, is *value*:

> Since in real contract each party retains the same property with which he enters the contract and which at the same time he surrenders ... [w]hat remains identical is the value, in respect of which the subjects of the contract are equal ... Value is the universal in which the subjects of the contract participate.[7]

If the contract is violated, however, a 'wrong' is done that must be made right. Each must do what morality says 'ought' to be done, but since subjective moral judgements may differ, 'abstract right' turns out to presuppose 'ethical life', which ultimately involves the laws of the state as universal thoughts that simultaneously form and are formed by the consciousness of citizens.

Rubin's treatment of commodity owners runs parallel to Hegel's account of the parties to a contract. In the act of exchange, each makes a claim upon the other, but who is to adjudicate incompatible claims? Formally, the parties are equal participants, yet it appears to the individual commodity owner that his own will is passive and subordinate to that of the purchaser, who, as, the theory of marginal utility suggests, will actively make his own judgement of the commodity's value. The participants are equal but unequal. In this case, however, the question is irrelevant. It is not Hegel's laws of ethical life but rather Marx's objective law of value that dictates the rate at which one commodity exchanges for another.

---

5 Hegel 1967, p. 42.
6 Hegel 1967, p. 57.
7 Hegel 1967, p. 59.

In Marx's terms, the law of value means that the exchange process lays down its own law. Rubin comments that 'Within the [allegedly] "metaphysical" shell of the doctrine concerning the dual nature of the commodity, we find a sociological analysis of the production relations between commodity producers'. The general form of exchangeability entails money, as the universal measure of abstract labour and exchange-value. And money, in turn, now appears as the true *reified* 'carrier' of the economic relation: 'The commodity that *fulfils the function of active initiator of the production relations of exchange between commodity producers, i.e., that possesses the capacity for direct universal exchangeability for any other commodity, is money*'.

Hegel's juridical law is rightful and therefore also rightfully coercive. Rubin points out that the law of value, and commodity circulation mediated by money, are also 'means of coercion':

> Money is a 'social force', it 'measures the social wealth of its owner' his social power.[8] The 'free' exchange agreement, formally presupposing the absolute equality of both participants, in fact resides in the initiative of one of them, the owner of money. This is what overcomes the limitation and restriction of the exchange process founded upon the correspondence of will between two counterparties. The foundation of commodity society is 'the juridical relation, whose form is the contract'. However, 'The content of this juridical relation (or relation of two wills) is itself determined by the economic relation'.[9] The economic relation of exchange, being completed by the development of money, introduces lawfulness and constancy into a system of juridical relations based upon the correspondence of the individual wills of separate persons.

Money directly enters the analysis at precisely the point corresponding to Hegel's turn from 'abstract right' to ethical life (or the *institutionalisation* of a common will). With Marx, money settles who is passive and who is active. Commodity production involves a 'free agreement' and 'coincidence of will' that can be *initiated* by either party to an exchange – provided one is the possessor of money, or of a commodity that is freely exchangeable for money in accordance with the law of value. Rubin writes:

---

8 Marx 1976, p. 230.
9 Marx 1976, p. 178.

The seeming freedom of 'motivation' on the part of separate commodity producers necessarily presupposes an objective 'limitation' (restriction, constraint) of action on the part of all commodity producers taken together: the former, without the latter, would make the social process of production impossible by transforming society into a chaos of uncoordinated and intersecting activities by individual people.

In the *Philosophy of Right*, Hegel understood the contribution of political economy in discovering the immanent lawfulness of the market amongst a seeming chaos of accidents.[10] The salient weakness of Hegel's political philosophy, however, was that in his account of 'civil society' he moved from the shared consciousness of the family to class divisions – which then had to be reconciled in the laws of the state, which are thoughts and thus can be universally shared – with little more to offer in the way of economic insight. To fill this gap, and thus to shift the entire dialectical analysis from subjectivity to objectivity, was Marx's undertaking in the *Critique of Political Economy* and later in *Capital*. With a comprehensive analysis of the history and categories of money and exchange, Rubin guides his reader through the first three chapters of *Capital*, ending at the point where Marx turns from the accumulation of money – as a hoard – to the transition to the next higher category, *capital*. 'The ultimate product of commodity circulation', Marx wrote at the beginning of the fourth chapter, 'is the first form of the appearance of capital'.[11]

∴

Isaak I. Rubin on Marx's Theory of Money

1 *Marx's Theory of Value and the Theory of Money*

Marx's theory of money is closely, even inseparably, connected with his theory of value. The connection is even closer than between other parts of Marx's eco-

---

10 In *The Philosophy of Right*, Hegel commented that 'Political economy ... affords the interesting spectacle (as in Smith, Say, and Ricardo) of thought working upon the endless mass of details which confront it at the outset and extracting therefrom the simple principles of the thing, the Understanding effective in the thing and directing it' (para. 189). Political economy was 'a science which is a credit to thought because it finds laws for a mass of accidents ... The most remarkable thing here is this mutual interlocking of particulars, which is what one would least expect ... at first sight ...' (Hegel 1967, pp. 126–7).

11 Marx 1976, p. 247.

nomic theory. Of course, Marx's theory of capital is also built upon his theory of value, without which it could not be understood. Still, it investigates a different and more complex type of production relations between people as capitalists and wage-workers, whereas the theory of value examines a simpler type of production relations between people as independent commodity producers. The theory of money does not study a type of production relations different from those that Marx considers in his theory of value; rather it looks at the same type in more developed form. Money not only grows out of the commodity but always presupposes the commodity. The relation between the owner of a commodity and the owner of money is also a relation between independent commodity producers. The owner of money was yesterday the producer and owner of the commodity, which he sold for money. Insofar as exchange of the commodity for money is essentially the exchange of commodity for commodity (C–M–C), i.e. the equation of all commodities, this aspect of the exchange process is studied by the theory of value. Insofar as the exchange of commodity for commodity invariably occurs in the form of commodity for money, and money for commodity (C–M and M–C), this aspect of the exchange process is studied by the theory of money. Both theories examine different sides of one and the same process.

This is what explains the dual character of the link between these two theories. The theory of capital presupposes the theory of value, but Marx constructs the latter without the aid of presuppositions that underpin the former. The theory of money not only results from the theory of value but, conversely, the theory of value cannot be constructed without the theory of money and is only completed in the latter. At the basis of the Marxist theory of value lie the presuppositions of a money economy; more precisely, for the starting point of his analysis Marx takes the fact of the generalised equation of all commodities for one another, which characterises the money economy and is impossible without the mediation of money.

The ensuing chapters of this work are devoted to examining and substantiating Marx's theory of money, which he builds upon, and which results from, the theory of value. In the first chapter we shall examine the reverse side of this dependence between the two theories, which has not received due attention. We shall consider the question of the extent to which the Marxist theory of value is founded upon the presuppositions of a money economy.

The usual discussions of Marx's reasoning in his theory of value proceed as follows. First of all, Marx takes the fact of the exchange of two commodities, that is, the fact of the equation of the exchange-value of two goods that differ from one another in terms of their use-value. From the fact of their equivalence or commensurability, he draws the conclusion that there must be a specific measure whereby they are compared, and he finds that measure in labour. It appears, at first sight, that this reasoning correctly represents Marx's thinking in the first pages of *Capital*. However, a more attentive examination of Marx shows us how completely mistaken is the view that reduces his theory of value to 1) an analysis of the fact of exchange between two commodities, and 2) the attempt to find a measure for their comparison.

For the starting point of his analysis, Marx does not take *the equation of the commodity form alone, but rather the equation of each commodity with all others that are found on the market, i.e. the generalised equation of any commodity with any other*. The commodity is not produced at the order of particular individuals but for the market, for an undefined and extensive circle of purchasers. It is not produced for exchange with any other specific commodities but for sale in exchange for money, with which it is possible to purchase any other commodities. In the market, the commodity receives a certain valuation, a market price or objective exchange-value (here we leave aside any deviations of price from value), which is independent of and not bound by the will of separate individuals but is rather an objectively necessary result of the activities of the entire market, of the totality of buyers and sellers. Each commodity is equated with all others (which is only possible through the medium of money). Each commodity has the character of exchange-value, i.e. its owner has the ability to equate it with any other commodity and exchange it for any other (by means of money). Only in these conditions is it possible to speak of the existence of a commodity and exchange-value, or of the suitability of the commodity for exchange in general, i.e. regardless of the type of commodity for which it exchanges or which individuals are involved in the exchange. There is no exchange-value in conditions where exchange of the product is possible only for specific products or between specific individuals; [in those conditions] exchange-value does not yet exist, and the theory of value does not apply to this sort of exchange.

The fact that Marx takes analysis of the commodity's suitability for generalised equation as his starting point is established beyond any doubt by his reasoning in the *Critique of Political Economy* and in *Capital*. The fundamental fact, with which the *Critique* begins, is that commodities 'are able in definite proportions to take one another's place in the exchange process, i.e., they are equivalents'.[12] The entire reasoning of the *Critique* is based on the fact that the exchange-value of one product is expressed in terms of *all* other products. Speaking of the equation of linen with coffee, Marx adds that the exchange-value of the former 'is not exhaustively expressed' by this proportion but only

---

12   Marx 1970, p. 34.

by an 'infinite number of equations' with all other commodities.[13] Linen yarn and linen are equivalent to each other only insofar as they are 'equivalents of *any* use-value which contains the same amount of labour time'.[14]

Marx gives essentially the same reasoning in the first pages of *Capital*. Readers generally focus their attention on the famous example of comparing two commodities, wheat and iron, while the full course of Marx's reasoning is hidden from view. Before turning to the example of wheat and iron, Marx notes the fact that wheat can be exchanged with all other commodities: 'A given commodity, a quarter of wheat for example, *is exchanged for other commodities in the most diverse proportions*, for instance, for 20 pounds of boot polish, for two yards of silk, for ½ ounce of gold, etc.; however, the exchange-value of the quarter of wheat remains constant whether it is expressed in terms of boot polish, silk or gold'.[15] The equation of two commodities, wheat and iron, is only one of many that equate wheat with all other commodities.

Marx's thinking emerges all the more clearly in the same passage, corrected for the French edition, which Marx edited himself: 'A given commodity, a quarter of wheat for example, is exchanged for x boot polish, y silk or z gold, etc. In short, it is exchanged for other commodities in the most diverse proportions. Therefore the wheat has many exchange-values instead of one. But x boot polish, y silk or z gold, etc., each represent the exchange-value of one quarter of wheat. Therefore x boot polish, y silk or z gold, etc., must, as exchange-values, be *mutually replaceable* or of identical magnitude. It follows from this that, firstly, the valid exchange-values of a particular commodity express *something equal* ...'.[16] Once a given commodity equates with *all* other commodities, all of the latter equated with one another. This text, which reproduces the thinking in the *Critique*, emphasises the fact of the generalised equation of all commodities with one another, or what amounts to the same thing, of the given commodity with all the others, and this is the starting point for the analysis in the theory of value.

Marx's thinking continues as follows: *If a given commodity equates with two other commodities, then the latter must equate with one another*, expressing one and the same value in two different forms. The reverse conclusion then follows: *If any two commodities* (wheat and iron, for example) *are equal to one another, then they must both be equal to some third one*. This position, developed by Marx in the example of wheat and iron and illustrated in the famous comparison

---

13   Marx 1970, p. 38.
14   Marx 1970, p. 33.
15   Marx 1976, p. 127 [Rubin's emphasis].
16   Ibid. [Rubin's emphasis].

with a triangle[17] – which has given rise to many misinterpretations – is the conclusion that follows from the initial fact of the equation of each commodity with all the others. This is the second link in the chain of reasoning, which is usually interpreted mistakenly to be the first. The equation of two commodities gives Marx the right to infer their equality in value terms only because he deals not with some isolated equation but with one link in an endless series of equations, in which any two commodities equate with all the others. This way of thinking on Marx's part is perfectly evident not only in the *Critique*, where it is the basis for the whole exposition, but also in *Capital* and – perhaps even more clearly – in the brochure *Value, Price and Profit*.[18]

Marx also emphasises in *Theories of Surplus-Value* that exchange-value presupposes the generalised equation of all commodities with each other, not just of two of them: 'If only two products existed, the products would never become commodities, and consequently the exchange-value of commodities would never evolve either'.[19] As value, the product must be 'directly convertible from one use-value into all others'.[20]

From what has been said, we can draw the following conclusion. In his theory of value, Marx's starting point is not the analysis of some random equation of two commodities *in natura*, but rather the generalised equation of each product with all others, which occurs in the form of an objective market valuation of each commodity by way of money. Leaving the role of money temporarily aside, Marx investigates the general character and principal results of this social process that leads to the generalised equation of all the products of labour. Marx does not investigate exchange in general, but rather developed (essentially monetary) exchange as the fundamental social form of the social 'exchange of things', i.e. of social production. The Marxist theory of value is not a 'dialectical deduction from the essence of exchange', as [Eugen] Böhm-Bawerk claims, but an analysis of a determinate social form of production, namely, of a commodity economy.

---

17 Rubin has in mind the following passage in the first volume of *Capital*: 'In order to determine and compare the areas of all rectilinear figures we split them up into triangles. Then the triangle itself is reduced to an expression totally different from its visible shape: half the product of the base and the altitude. In the same way the exchange values of commodities must be reduced to a common element, of which they represent a greater or a lesser quantity' (ibid.).

18 Marx 2006.

19 Marx 1971, p. 144.

20 Marx 1971, p. 135.

It will now be easier for us to explain one point that has given rise to particular attacks from Böhm-Bawerk. On what basis does Marx assert, from the very outset, that the exchange-value of commodities is an 'abstraction from their use-vales',[21] which he will set aside in the analysis of value? If it were a case of the random exchange of two products *in natura*, then Böhm-Bawerk would be correct in saying that such exchange may be regulated by the individual requirements of the participants and by their subjective appraisal of the relative usefulness of the products. Insofar as the objective exchange-value of a given product is involved, being equated with all other products without regard to their distinctions or the personality of their producers, what we have is an objective, law-governed social process of the equation of *all* use-values, i.e. 'abstraction from their use-values'. This does not mean that the usefulness of commodities plays no role, for example, in the motivation of the purchasers. (But the exchange-value of the product – i.e. its ability to be exchanged for any other use-value, belonging to any commodity owner, and to move in any direction in the market – cannot be explained by these motives). Marx is not interested in the individual motives of the purchasers but in the social process of exchange, which objectively consists of the equation of one [commodity] with the other within determinate law-governed proportions that are being established for all use-values without exception.

We have established, therefore, the error of the view that sees Marx taking for his starting point exchange as such, or the very fact of the comparability of two products. No less mistaken is the supposition that Marx concludes, from the fact of the comparability of the two products, that there must be some measure for the comparison, which he finds in labour. Following [David] Ricardo's example, Marx decisively rejected even posing the question of a measure of value, which for Adam Smith was inseparably intertwined with the question of the cause of regular changes in the value of products, thus confusing the question [of the measure of value] and preventing its correct resolution. Ricardo sharply criticised Smith's teaching on the measure of value and transferred the entire theory of value to the plane of a scientific-causal examination of exchange phenomena and of changes in the value of products. The view of certain writers – to the effect that Marx weakened this strictly causal posing of the theory of value, passed on to him by Ricardo, by introducing into it elements of evaluation – has no foundation.[22] Marx is sharply critical of rais-

---

21 Marx 1976, p. 127.
22 This is the opinion of [Franz] Petry (see Petry 1916, p. 2).

ing the question of an 'invariable measure of value',[23] and he even reproaches Ricardo for certain expressions that could be interpreted in that sense.[24] It is true that we encounter in Marx the doctrine of labour as the 'immanent measure of value'.[25] But Marx frequently emphasises that he understands 'immanent measure' in a completely different sense from the customary or 'external measure', which is not labour but money.[26] Labour is the 'immanent measure' of value only because it is the *'causa efficiens'* (the operative cause), or its substance.[27] Quantitative changes in the productivity of labour are the cause of changes in the value of commodities. This position, translated into the language of Hegelian philosophy, says that labour is the 'immanent measure' of value.[28]

Those writers who interpret Marx's theory of value in the sense of searching for a measure of value have not clearly considered whether the question involves a measure that helps the parties in an exchange to equate the products they are exchanging, or whether it involves instead a measure that makes it possible for a theoretical investigator to assert equality between the exchanging products. Breaking down the question in this way clarifies it and leaves no doubt that Marx resisted posing the question in both of these senses. Marx had no intention of asserting that two products exchange for one another because the persons making the exchange regard their products as containing equal quantities of labour, as such: 1) Marx is interested in the objective result of the exchange process, not in the subjective motives of parties to the exchange; and 2) insofar as subjective motives are concerned, it is impossible to assume that the buyers know the comparative labour expenditures required for the produc-

---

23   Marx 1971, pp. 133, 134–5, 145–6, 155.
24   See this passage: 'Ricardo often gives the impression, and sometimes indeed writes, as if the quantity of labour is the solution to the false, or falsely conceived problem of an "invariable measure of value" in the same way as corn, money, wages, etc., were previously considered and advanced as panaceas of this kind, In Ricardo's work this false impression arises because for him the decisive task is the definition of the magnitude of value. Because of this he does not understand the specific form in which labour is an element of value, and fails in particular to grasp that the labour of the individual must present itself as abstract general labour and, in this form, as *social* labour. Therefore he has not understood that the development of money is connected with the nature of value and with the determination of this value by labour-time' (Marx 1971, p. 137).
25   Marx 1971, p. 128.
26   Marx 1971, pp. 128, 133, 137–8, 155.
27   Marx says: 'The "cause" of value is the substance of value and hence also its immanent measure' (Marx 1971, p. 163).
28   Regarding the concept of 'measure' in Hegel, see Fischer 1902, pp. 490–5.

tion of various products and that they consciously take these expenditures as the basis for determining the exchange-value of the latter.

To pose the question in the second sense that we mentioned would mean that since two commodities are equated with one another we must, as theoretical investigators, disclose the moment of their equality and indicate what property is common to both of them and makes them equal to one another. The theorist is obliged to reveal the moment of equality between two phenomena only if he is himself comparing these phenomena and asserting that they are identical in nature. But the fact that wheat equates with iron on the market does not mean that the theorist must demonstrate where their equality lies, or what makes them equal. The theorist encounters a definite fact and is obliged to explain it. This means that, upon observing the fact of equalisation between wheat and iron, he asks himself: is this phenomenon distinguished by having the character of being constant and law-governed, and if so, what is its cause, i.e. what are the phenomena that condition the existence and changes of the given phenomenon? The aim is not to show what makes wheat and iron equal, but rather to disclose the law-governed and objective social fact of market equalisation between wheat and iron – that is the task of the theoretical economist. Marx poses the question in exactly this manner, and it is an inadequate understanding of this way of posing the question that has prevented critics, and sometimes even commentators on Marx, from correctly grasping his theory of value.

To understand properly the basis of Marx's theory of value, one must firmly grasp, as indicated above, that the starting point for Marx's analysis is the fact of developed exchange and the generalised equation of all commodities with each other. Once every commodity, upon receiving a certain valuation in the market, is thereby equated with all other commodities and can be exchanged for any of them in some definite proportion – completely apart from the fact of whether the owner of the second commodity has any need for the first one – this exchangeability, or exchange-value of the commodity, is its social property. In the process of developed market exchange, every commodity is fully equal, as exchange-value, to any other commodity and can replace it in some definite proportion. This means that in the real process of market exchange all commodities are really equal to one another, equal not in terms of their material properties but in terms of their social function. Since the social function of commodities in the market consists of being counterposed to other commodities; and since, in this process of the mutual counterposing of commodities, every commodity can replace any other commodity in some definite proportion, it follows that the generalised equation of commodities in the market means the *unity of their social function*, or of their social nature.

Marx's argumentation is usually presented this way: *since* commodities can equate with one another, we must find in them something that is common and unifying. It is more correct to express Marx's thinking approximately as follows: *the fact* that commodities really equate with one another on the market is the unity of their social function. Now the task is to explain the social character of this fact of the generalised equation of commodities and, specifically, to indicate its necessary connection with the given social structure of the economy, its role or social function in the economy and the lawfulness involved in the equation of commodities, i.e. the causes that explain an increase or decrease of their exchange-value. In other words, the task that emerges is that of investigating the qualitative and quantitative aspects of exchange-value. And since the latter represents the social function acquired by products of labour within a specific social context, our task then becomes one of analysing this social environment of the commodity economy. This analysis discloses: 1) the need for a generalised equation of commodities as the sole form of social connection between formally dissociated yet materially connected commodity producers; 2) the role of commodity equalisation as regulator of the ebbs and flows of labour in different branches of production, i.e. the social function of exchange-value as regulator of the distribution of social labour; and finally, 3) the laws of changes in the exchange-value of commodities, depending upon changes in the productivity of social labour. We see how a determinate social structure of the economy, or a determinate type of production-labour relations between people, creates a definite social function or social form of the products of labour, namely, their exchange-value. And this is what constitutes Marx's theory of value.

Accordingly, we regard as incorrect the view that Marx – taking the equation of two commodities as the starting point for his analysis, i.e. the fact of exchange as such, apart from its social form – is searching for a measure for comparing these commodities. From the very outset Marx has in view a developed commodity economy with the generalised equation of commodities, characterised by the ability of each commodity to exchange in some definite proportion for any other commodity. It is only this starting point that made it possible for Marx to eliminate in advance the individual-psychological way of posing the question (i.e. use-value) and *from the very beginning to define the subject matter of his investigation, exchange-value, as an object belonging to the social world,* as a social function or form of the product of labour. This is what determined the entire method of the investigation. In order to explain the social form of products of labour, it was necessary to turn to analysis of the social form of the organisation of labour, which is 'expressed' or 'materialised' in the former.

This way of thinking on Marx's part emerges very clearly in his brochure *Value, Price and Profit*. After characterising the fact of the generalised equation of commodities, Marx turns from the commodity to labour in the following way:

> What is the common *social substance* of all commodities? It is *labour* ... And I say not only *labour*, but *social labour* ... [T]o produce a *commodity*, a man must not only produce an article satisfying some *social* want, but his labour itself must form part and parcel of the total sum of labour expended by society. It must be subordinate to the *division of labour within society*. It is nothing without the other divisions of labour, and on its part is required to *be integrated* with them.[29]

Marx forcefully emphasises that he is speaking of labour not in its natural but in its social form, and of the process of the social division of labour, of which exchange-value is the expression. The latter is right away defined by Marx as a 'social function' or form of the products of labour, which must correspond to a definite 'social substance', i.e. to a certain distribution of social labour.

This is essentially the same course that Marx's thinking follows in *Capital*. After noting the qualitative equality of all commodities as values, Marx sees in them a 'materialised', 'crystallised' (i.e. fixed in the form of the social properties of products of labour[30]) expression of 'their common social substance',[31] and expressions of 'an identical social substance, human labour'.[32] The equation of commodities on the market expresses the equation of social labour in the process of its distribution between different branches of production. This process equates all the different kinds of separate labour expenditures – which originally appeared in the form of private, concrete, qualitatively diverse and individual labour expenditures – and it is only as a result of the exchange process that they are transformed into social, abstract, simple and socially necessary labour. To the qualitative equality of commodities in the market corresponds the qualitative equality of labour in the social process of its distribution. Therefore, after beginning with the equality of commodities as things in exchange, on the third page of *Capital* Marx already passes directly to its corol-

---

29 Marx 2006, pp. 30–1.
30 Compare this with the comment in *Value, Price and Profit*: 'If we consider commodities as values, we consider them exclusively under the single aspect of realised, fixed, or, if you like, crystallised social labour' (Marx 2006, p. 31).
31 Marx 1976, p. 128.
32 Marx 1976, p. 138.

lary in the process of social production – to the equality of labour, analysing this labour as uniform and homogeneous, corresponding to the uniformity and homogeneity of all commodities as exchange-values. The abstract character of labour emerges here as the correlative of the generalised equation of commodities, which finds its full expression through the medium of money. From the developed form of exchange, Marx turns directly (in the first two sections of the first chapter of *Capital*) to developed abstract labour, temporarily setting aside the entire protracted and complex social process that converts private and unequal labour into social and equalised labour. Marx turns to review this social process only in the third section (The Value-Form, or Exchange-Value) in order finally, in the fourth section (The Fetishism of the Commodity and its Secret), to come to the more profound basis of this process, the social structure of commodity economy. Marx begins with the finished result of the social process in order then to show us the development of the latter and to reveal its basis. The first chapter of the *Critique* follows approximately the same construction. After giving a detailed analysis of exchange-value and abstract labour, Marx says:

> So far two aspects of the commodity – use-value and exchange-value – have been examined, but each time one-sidedly. The commodity, however, is the direct *unity* of use-value and exchange-value, and at the same time it is a commodity only in relation to other commodities. The *exchange process* of commodities is the *real* relation that exists between them.[33]

Following the 'one-sided' analysis of exchange-value and abstract labour, as the completed final results of the social process, Marx turns to examine the actual process that converts use-value into exchange-value, private labour into social labour. In the postface[34] to the second edition of *Capital*, Marx himself mentioned this particular aspect of his study:

> Of course, the method of presentation must differ in form from that of inquiry. The latter has to appropriate the material in detail, to analyse its different forms of development and to track down their inner connection. Only after this work has been done can the real movement be appropriately presented. If this is done successfully, if the life of the subject-matter

---

33 Marx 1970, p. 41.
34 [The manuscript mistakenly refers to the preface].

is now reflected back in the ideas, then it may appear as if we have before us an *a priori* construction.[35]

This method of Marx's investigation, beginning with analysis of finished results and ending with the social process of development, actually did prevent his critics from seeing his method of investigation and became the source of numerous charges that the Marxist theory of value is an *a priori* construction. It also prompted many of Marx's supporters to find the basis for his theory of value in the first pages of *Capital*, which deal with the content of value or abstract labour. This view, as we have seen, is mistaken. The opening pages of *Capital* only give an analysis of the complete and finished result, which is the object of the investigation: value and its correlative in abstract labour. We only find the investigation of the actual process of development of the phenomena of value in the sections devoted to the 'value-form' and 'commodity fetishism'. This process of the development of value is simultaneously the process of the development of money.

Now we can see clearly the close connection between the theory of value and the theory of money in Marx's economic system. This connection consists not only of the generally recognised fact that the theory of money is built upon the theory of value, but also of the fact that the latter only finds its completion in the theory of money. The presentation of the theory of value in the first chapter of *Capital*, as in the *Critique of Political Economy*, consists of two parts: an analysis of the concepts of exchange-value and abstract labour (the substance of value), and an explanation of the process of development of exchange-value (the form of value). The first part, as we have seen, presupposes generalised equation of all commodities with one another and thus of all types of labour – a process that corresponds to monetary exchange. The second part, describing the development of exchange-value as the capacity of the commodity to enter into generalised exchange, simultaneously shows the development of the money-form. It is true that the 'money-form' is only the final and most developed of the 'forms of value' (simple, expanded, general and monetary) that Marx considers. It may seem, therefore, that there are forms of value whose existence precedes the money-form, and that consequently exchange-value may exist at a stage of social development that precedes the appearance of money. We consider such a presupposition, which relies upon the terminology that Marx has used with regard to all the preceding phases of exchange as expressions of the 'value-form', to be mistaken. The forms of

---

35   Marx 1976, p. 102.

value that precede its general form are not only the embryo of the money-form but also merely the embryonic form of value. The development of exchange-value appears only with the 'general form', which essentially coincides with the appearance of money.

The close connection between the theories of value and money is clearly revealed in the very organisation of Marx's work. The first chapter of the *Critique of Political Economy*, entitled 'The Commodity', also essentially contains the foundations of the theory of money. Immediately following analysis of the concepts of value and abstract labour, Marx turns to an exposition of the actual exchange process – which converts use-value into exchange-value, and concrete labour into abstract labour – and simultaneously shows us also the development of money as the necessary correlative of exchange-value and abstract labour (beginning on page 19 of the manuscript).[36] The second chapter, on 'money', traces the separate functions of money but still does not provide a general theory of money. *Capital* is pretty much the same. In the first chapter on 'The Commodity', the part dealing with forms of value essentially contains the theory of money that Marx develops systematically and in more detail in the second chapter on 'The Process of Exchange'. Here, too, the general theory of money is provided in close connection with the theory of value, while the third chapter, entitled 'Money', is concerned only with the separate functions of money.

The theory of value and the theory of money together characterise one and the same fundamental type of production relations between commodity producers, who complement one another through their labour activity in the production process but remain formally independent and only come into contact with one another in the process of exchange. Insofar as we are concerned with the social unity of the process of production and the distribution of social labour, which occurs through the mediation of exchange, we have the theory of value. Insofar as our attention is directed to the exchange process, with its private acts of purchase and sale as the necessary form of realising the unity of the social production process, we have the theory of money. Only the two theories, taken together, give us a general picture of commodity economy with all of its structural duality: the unity of the social process of production and its fragmentation between individual private undertakings.

---

36 Marx 1970, p. 48. [Marx writes that money, which 'represents the exchange-value of all commodities', is 'a crystallisation of the exchange-value of commodities and is formed in the exchange process'].

2 The Need for Money

It is often thought that in the theory of value Marx describes exchange that occurs without the mediation of money, while in the theory of money he shows the emergence, development and role of money. We have already seen that such a view must be recognised as mistaken. From the very start of his investigation, Marx presupposes the generalised exchange of all commodities, which is only possible through the mediation of money. However, in analysing this complex phenomenon of money economy, Marx adheres, as always, to the method of consecutively separating and explaining different aspects. It would be incorrect to regard each of them as a separate object of investigation: each characterises one abstract aspect of the phenomenon as a whole, studied at a particular level of examination, and only altogether do they provide a complete picture of the phenomenon being studied.

In the concrete reality of money economy, we observe the facts of purchases and sales, of the exchange of commodities for money and the reverse. Regarding these concrete facts, Marx says in effect: let us begin by abstracting from the impossibility of each commodity exchanging for others except through the mediation of money. Let us regard the entire exchange process as a process of the generalised, mutual equation of all the products of labour in the market – a process through which the equation and distribution of all types of labour in social production is completed. In other words, let us see how, in commodity economy, the entire process of distribution and equation of social labour occurs in the form of the equation of the products of labour as values. Examination of *the mechanism of social dependence between the equation of labour and the equation of commodities also constitutes the theme of the Marxist theory of value*, or the first stage of our investigation. After showing how the equation of labour takes the form of the generalised equation of commodities, Marx turns to analysis of the latter process, showing that the *generalised equation of commodities is only possible in the form of them all being equated with one and the same designated commodity*, which acquires the character of money. This is the theory of *the origin and social function of money*, or the second stage of the study. Only after that is it possible to turn to consideration of the *individual properties of money as finished results of the process of circulation*, which at first appear to be independent of the latter and to inhere in money itself. This is the theory of the *separate functions of money*, or the third stage of the investigation. In other words, these three stages of the investigation can be characterised as the doctrine 1) of value, or of the commodity; 2) of the transformation of the commodity into money; and 3) of money itself. The second stage is integrally connected with the first, and this is explained by the fact, as we noted above, that the theory of money is set out by Marx in two places: first, in close connection with the theory of value (in the first chapter of the *Critique*, and in the section on the value-form in *Capital* and also in the second chapter), and secondly, independently (in chapter two of the *Critique* and chapter three of *Capital*). The second, transitional stage involves special difficulties for the study, since 'The movement through which this process has been mediated vanishes in its own result, leaving no trace behind'.[37] The third stage of the study deals with the functions of money, which stand out and are immediately apparent to everyone. The first stage, or the theory of value, is more abstract and difficult but, given a certain familiarity with abstract thought, it is still easy to grasp the entire process of exchange as the equation of things, which is closely associated with the equation of labour. However, the greatest difficulties in the way of understanding come at the second stage, which traces the social process whose result is the coalescence of the function of money with a determinate natural product that appears to have a natural rather than a social character.[38]

Marx himself more than once notes the different levels of abstraction through which his investigation moves:

> The fact that commodity owners *treat one another's labour* as universal social labour appears in the form of their *treating their own commodities* as exchange-values; and *the interrelation of commodities* as exchange-values in the exchange process appears as their universal *relation to a particular commodity* as the adequate expression of their exchange-value; this in turn appears as *the specific relation of this particular commodity to all other commodities* and hence as the distinctive, as it were naturally evolved, social character of a thing.[39]

Here we see clearly laid out, in synthetic order, the whole path of the study's ascent from social labour through value to money. Sometimes Marx draws attention to the same path in the reverse, analytical order: 'But how can one express x cotton in y money? This question resolves itself into this – how is it at all possible to express one commodity in another, or to present commodities as equivalents? Only the elaboration of value, independent of the representation of one commodity in another, provides the answer'.[40] From the concrete

---

37 Marx 1976, p. 187.
38 [The sentence is double-underlined in pencil].
39 Marx 1970, p. 48 [Rubin's emphasis. Rubin comments that the Russian translation he was using was incorrect].
40 Marx 1971, p. 162.

phenomenon of money it is necessary to descend to the equation of commodities or the value-form, and from the latter still further to the doctrine of the content of value or social labour. The first level of the investigation leads from social labour (or the content of value) to the form of value; the second, from the form of value to money; and the third treats money as the finished result. As we see, the separate levels of the study gradually pass from one to the other, for the final link of one is the first link of the next. The link that connects the theory of value with the theory of money is the doctrine of the value-form.

Now we can specify more clearly which task Marx pursues in the second stage of his study, in the general theory of money. He does not simply provide a scheme of the gradual historical development of money parallel with the development of exchange itself. His fundamental task has a theoretical, not an historical, character. It is not enough to trace the origin and development of money. It is still necessary to disclose the lawfulness that makes money the necessary consequence and accompaniment of a developed commodity economy. The internal connection between them must be demonstrated. *The analysis of commodity economy must show us that the generalised exchange of commodities is impossible without the mediation of money.* That is the theme that Marx works out in the general theory of money.

To pose the question of *the necessity of money*, which can explain for us the powerful, universal and unstoppable expansion of money in accordance with the development of commodity exchange – this is the characteristic specificity of Marxist theory that differentiates it from many others. Followers of the classical school, for the most part, explained the origin of money in terms of its conveniences for exchange and the greater ease of monetary as opposed to natural exchange. But can conveniences alone explain the spontaneous and universal spread of money? Enormous difficulties are involved in the explanation of money for any theories that are built not on analysis of the objective structure of commodity economy but rather on a description of the subjective motives of economic actors, abstracted from the concrete social and historical context. In the theory of money, the Austrian school demonstrates its complete helplessness. As one author has commented, the leading representatives of the subjective theory of price, [E.] Fillippovich and C[arl] Menger, derive the value of money from the objective, natural properties of gold.[41] Subjective pyschologism is supplemented with objective naturalism. Other authors are clearly aware of the incompatibility of a subjective theory of price with the

---

41   Kaulla 1920, pp. 15, 18.

fact of objective valuation of commodities in terms of money: 'The subjective worth of goods, as a subjective-psychological fact, cannot be reconciled with [their] objective-quantitative expression' in terms of money; the emergence of such monetary expression constitutes 'a problem that is not accessible to human understanding'(!).[42] This acknowledgement is equivalent to the complete bankruptcy of the psychological method in the explanation of money as one of the fundamental phenomena of a modern economy. This phenomenon can only be understood on the basis of the sociological method, beginning with analysis of the social structure of commodity economy.

3 Money as the Result of Contradiction between the Use-Value and Exchange-Value of the Commodity

As we know, Marx derived the need for money from the contradiction between the use-value and exchange-value of the commodity. This part of Marx's teaching has often provoked the charge of 'metaphysics' and of being a dialectical game of abstract concepts. It is regarded as abstract and scholastic speculation, having nothing in common with real life.

Actually, this part of the theory, in which Marx 'flirts with Hegelianism' most directly, can create such an impression at first sight. The exposition is always conducted on the basis of his analysis of abstract concepts, their opposition, the enunciation of contradictions and their dialectical reconciliation. This character of the presentation is most striking in the *Critique of Political Economy*. However, our appraisal of the general doctrine of money, as it is set out in the *Critique* and in *Capital*, changes if we recall that beneath each external category in the Marxist economic system is concealed a specific type of production relations between people. Within the abstract metaphysical shell we find a profound sociological nucleus. The general Marxist teaching on money turns out to be a continuation of the analysis of production relations of the commodity economy, which Marx initiates in his theory of value.

[A] *Division of labour*.[43] The basic contradiction of commodity economy consists, on the one hand, of the fact that it comprises a multitude of formally independent private undertakings that are separate from one another, while on the other hand the latter are materially bound together and mutually complementary. Due to the division of labour and exchange,

---

42 Elster 1920, p. 53.
43 [A heading written into the margin].

the labour of the individual producer acquires a twofold social character. On the one hand, it must, as a definite useful kind of labour, satisfy a definite social need, and thus maintain its position as an element of the total labour, which originally sprang up spontaneously. On the other hand, it can satisfy the manifold needs of the individual producer himself only in so far as every particular kind of useful private labour can be exchanged with, i.e. counts as the equal of, every other kind of useful private labour.[44]

In a commodity economy, the system of social division of labour can itself be considered from two sides: the technical and the social. On the one hand, it represents the sum total of mutually complementary and diversified types of concrete labour, expressing the 'qualitative difference between the useful forms of labour' that are conducted independently;[45] while on the other hand it represents the sum total of different types of labour that have been equated and have found their equilibrium one with the other, or – as the result of this process of the equalisation of labour – the sum total of homogeneous social labour, which is distributed between the different branches of production.[46] Thus, as we mentioned above, the private labour of each separate commodity producer must acquire a social character in a double sense: the material-technical and the formal-social. On the one hand, it must satisfy a definite social need, while on the other it must be interchangeable with any other sort of commodity.

The only condition in which the labour of a separate person could directly acquire a social character is if it were organised on a social scale and by a social organ that would take into account beforehand the specific technical content of each person's labour and include it in a social plan of the economy, i.e. by the establishment of production relations between a given individual and the other members of society that would certify its social character. This labour of society's individual members would be given a guarantee of its material usefulness and a simultaneous sanction of its social equivalence with any other type of labour. But, in that case, we would have before us not a commodity economy

---

44 Marx 1976, p. 166. [Here Rubin offers a critical comment on the grammatical structure of Marx's original sentence in German. The passage cited here from the Mandel and Fowkes edition rephrases the sentence in the manner that Rubin suggests would be logically more correct].

45 Marx 1976, p. 133.

46 Marx points out that Petty and Adam Smith understood only the first aspect of the division of labour. See the note in Marx 1970, pp. 52–3.

but a socialist one, and directly social rather than private labour. Commodity economy is characterised by anarchy of production and by the absence of any direct, social organisation of labour. The private labour of a separate commodity producer, within the production process, does not yet possess a social character in this double sense: it has neither a guarantee of being materially useful (since the given product may turn out to be unnecessary in general, or be produced in too great a quantity), nor a sanction of social equivalence (since, as a result of over-production or use by the given producer of backward means of production, the product of his labour may be equated on the market with the product of a smaller quantity of other labour). Even at the conclusion of the production process there is no single social organ that checks and sanctions *post factum* the labour expended by the individual commodity producer. Such a check and sanction, or 'follow-up control' so to speak, is not realised by any consciously active social organ but occurs unconsciously through the activity of the market mechanism, i.e. through the collision of the activities of separate commodity producers, each of whom consciously pursues only the goal of exchanging the product of his labour most profitably, and whose interaction has the unconscious, objective social result, as it were, of checking and sanctioning the labour expenditures incurred by the separate commodity producers. We say 'as it were' because, with reference to the heterogeneous and unconscious result of the interaction of a multitude of people, we can only speak of a 'check' and 'sanction' in a conditional and figurative sense. It would be more accurate to say that the following process occurs here. Either the given product of labour finds a consumer and simultaneously provides its producer with the possibility of acquiring for himself, in exchange, the product of the same quantity of labour by other producers – and in that case the objective result of exchange is a tendency to maintain and continue the given labour in the further process of reproduction. In other words, the given labour expenditure turns out to be included within the system of social division of labour both in the material-technical and in the social sense, i.e. as a useful expenditure of concrete labour and as a share of the aggregate social labour that is equivalent to (equated with) others. Or else, in the case of over-production or the use of backward instruments of labour, the exchange occurs unprofitably for the given producer, and its objective result is a tendency to squeeze out the given labour expenditures and replace them with others capable of being fully included within the mechanism of social production. The objective result of market exchange is, therefore, a social selection of various types and modes of labour, their inclusion within the social mechanism of production or their exclusion from it, which is something of a check and sanction of the labour of separate commodity producers that is only in this manner transformed from private into social labour.

[B] *Duality of exchange and of things?*[47] However, such selection of different types of labour occurs in commodity economy not directly but indirectly, through the selection of products of labour that are either rejected or accepted by the market. Inclusion of a given labour expenditure within the social mechanism of production occurs as a result of, and by means of, inclusion of its product within the general mass of commodities being sold on the market. A given product of labour receives a 'valuation' on the market, exchange-value, equating it in one proportion or another with every other commodity on the market. Through this equation of the products of different types of labour, and through the equation of the latter, there also occurs a tendency to establish a moving equilibrium between the various branches of production. The social process of equating various types of labour, which are distributed between the separate branches of production, takes the form of a special social property of the products of labour, or their 'exchange-value'. The social properties of labour assume the form of properties of a thing; they become 'reified' or 'fetishised'. The exchange of products reflects the socially useful character of private labours in the form that the product of labour must be useful, not to the producer himself but to others, and 'the social character of the equality of the various kinds of labour is reflected in the form of the common character, as values, possessed by these materially different things, the products of labour'.[48] The product of labour becomes a commodity or a value. Besides its direct, material-technical existence, as a concrete item of consumption or means of production, it acquires a special social 'function' or 'form'; it becomes the 'carrier' of the production relations between people.

The result is that the process of the exchange of products acquires a dual character: on the one hand, it involves the movement of material things from producers to consumers (through a number of intermediaries), and on the other hand, the movement of those same things as carriers of the production relations between people, i.e. the process of establishing production relations between the commodity producers who are participating in exchange. 'The exchange of commodities is a process in which the social exchange of things, i.e., exchange of the particular products of private individuals, simultaneously means establishment of definite social production relations into which people enter during this exchange of things'.[49] The first side of exchange we will call the material-technical, and the second, the formal-social. It is social because

---

47   [A heading written into the margin].
48   Marx 1976, p. 166. [Here a note is written in pencil in the margin: 'From labour to the thing.'].
49   Marx 1970, pp. 51–2.

the commodity producers, who are independent of each other, enter into a social connection through exchanging the products of their labour; it is formal because the specific type or character of this connection between commodity producers imparts a special social form to the products of their labour.[50] As we know, the basic peculiarity of commodity economy is the fact that individual private commodity producers enter into mutual production relations exclusively as the owners of specific material things, with the result, conversely, that it is possession of the thing that gives its owner the possibility of entering into production relations with other people. The social relations become 'reified', and the things acquire social features. The result is creation of a close link between the material and social sides of the production process. The products of labour move about from one commodity owner to another on the basis of a particular agreement that they enter into, or a production relation of exchange; and the latter, in turn, is established between these persons only with reference to, and for the purpose of, the movement of material things from one to the other. This coalescence – of the material movement of the products of labour with the process of establishing production relations between people – finds expression in the dual character of the individual commodity, which represents a fusion of the production relations of <u>exchange</u>[51]-value with the material thing (use-value). As use-value, every commodity is one element of the social exchange of things, of the movement of material things. As exchange-value, it enables its producer to enter into a production relation with other producers. From this dual nature of the commodity, Marx also derived the need for money. We already know, however, that this dual character of the commodity represents nothing more than the expression of the dual character of exchange itself, in which the production relations between people are established through the movement of things. The type of production relations between people is what characterises commodity economy and creates the need for money.[52] The production relations between commodity producers – on the one hand connecting all members of society, i.e. being distinguished by a generalised character while, on the other hand, being conditioned and limited by their possession of certain concrete useful things – can only be established through the mediation of money. This condition is what we must now elaborate.

---

50   [Beginning here, the text has a vertical pencil line in the margin].
51   ['Exchange' is underlined in ink and there is a question mark in the margin].
52   [The line in the margin ends here].

[c] *The Movement of Use-Value*.[53] The dual character of exchange, as the simultaneous process of material movement of things from one member of society to another and of establishing production relations between them, imparts a dual character to the position of the commodity producer in exchange, i.e. to his relation with the other commodity producers participating in exchange. On the one hand, he owns property in *things*, which must follow a certain path in the social exchange of things. On the other hand, he is a *property-owner* of things, and in exactly that sense he is a full participant in the given system of social production relations. Let us consider his position in terms of these two perspectives.

Insofar as the product is a material thing with useful properties, a use-value, it is not needed by the commodity producer himself. 'For the owner, his commodity possesses no direct use-value. Otherwise, he would not bring it to market. It has use-value for others'.[54] The commodity must move, therefore, from the producer's establishment to those of users, i.e. to undertakings where there is need for the given commodity as a concrete useful thing, as an item of consumption or as means of production. The commodity moves to the establishments of those commodity producers who represent an effective demand for it, in other words, who wish to purchase the given commodity and also are in a position to provide a corresponding equivalent (of the same value), i.e. who are able to compensate its value with an equal value of the commodities they produce. Although the demand comes from individual commodity producers, who are led at first glance by their own subjective needs and wishes, it is still not arbitrary. Its general magnitude and direction are disclosed in the midst of constant deviations and disruptions of a definite law-governed pattern, which results from the lawfulness of the social production process. Each establishment represents a demand for the items of consumption and means of production that it requires for the production process, i.e. for further continuation of its production activity. The character of the means of production, demanded by individual undertakings, is directly determined by the character of the production process. And this is what determines – although by a more direct route, through the process of distribution – both the quantity and character of the items of consumption for which individual commodity producers represent a demand.[55]

---

53   [A heading written into the margin].
54   Marx 1976, p. 179.
55   [This statement is marked off in the margin in pencil].

Thus, the lawfulness of the movement of products of labour from one undertaking to another is determined, in the final analysis, by the lawfulness of the social production process in a broad sense, which here includes the process of distribution. However, since production is organised in a commodity society by individual private commodity producers – each of whom independently decides, although he takes into account the market conjuncture, whether he can, at any given moment, expand his production and personal consumption or whether he must curtail them – it follows that the law-governed pattern of the social exchange of things cannot be manifested except through the demand and supply of separate commodity producers. 'To *become* a use-value, the commodity must encounter the particular need which it can satisfy. Thus the use-values of commodities *become* use-values by a mutual exchange of places: they pass from the hands of those for whom they were means of exchange into the hands of those for whom they serve as consumer goods'.[56] The direction of this movement of the commodity, as use-value, is determined not by the producer but by the consumer. 'The alienation of a commodity as a use-value is only possible to the person for whom it is a use-value, i.e., an object satisfying particular needs'.[57]

Thus, insofar as the given commodity producer is the owner of a material thing, the latter, in the social exchange of things, must follow a completely determined path that is independent of the will of its producer. On a social scale this path is determined, in general and on the whole, by a law-governed pattern of the social exchange of things, which appears to the given commodity producer to depend upon the will of the consumer, upon his demand. The passage of the commodity from the producer's establishment to that of the consumer is, for the former, a process independent of his will and externally predetermined. In this process, he is compelled to play a passive role. And since passage of the commodity from one establishment to the other is not possible except by establishing between them the production relation of exchange, our commodity producer figures on the passive side of the given production relation as being virtually without a will of his own, as the silent custodian of a material thing.[58]

[D] *Exchange-value*.[59] However, there is more than this to the commodity producer's role in the market. As we know, he is not simply the custodian of a

---

56   Marx 1970, p. 42.
57   Marx 1970, p. 43.
58   [In the margin Rubin marks this sentence in pencil and adds: 'and price?'].
59   [A heading written into the margin].

material thing; precisely because he possesses the latter he is also a fully qualified subject of social production relations. In exchange for his commodity, he must receive other commodities of equal value. He is not merely a producer, awaiting a demand from the side of the consumer, but is simultaneously a consumer, presenting a demand for the commodities he requires. The scope and magnitude of the latter are determined by the needs of his establishment and by the character of his personal consumption, which depends in turn upon the volume of his revenues – that is, in the final analysis, once again upon the position he occupies in the system of social production and distribution. But our commodity producer, as autonomous manager of his own private establishment, makes his own specific decisions concerning what commodities he requires in exchange for his own.[60] Casting his own commodity into the market, he can demand, to the sum of its value, whatever other commodities are in the market, i.e. that are being produced in the given society. It is precisely this generalised character of exchange that characterises commodity economy with its generalised equation of all types of labour and the constant flows of labour from one branch of production to another. The commodity producer can exchange his commodity for any other commodity; this means that he can enter into a production relation with any other commodity producer. Only in these circumstances can it be said that the product of his labour has become a commodity and has exchange-value. Hitherto, for as long as the product of a given type of labour only exchanges between certain specific people or for other specified products, the commodity and exchange-value are only present in incipient forms.

Thus 'exchange-value', as an objective social property of the product of labour, or as its social function, consists of the possibility of exchanging the given product in a determinate proportion with any other product, or in its equation with all the other products of labour. 'The product as value must be the embodiment of social labour and, as such, be directly convertible from one use-value into all others'.[61] Marx considers the characteristic feature of exchange-value to be precisely its capacity for 'direct convertibility': the given commodity equates with all others and can be exchanged for any of them;[62] it has, if one may put it this way, the ability to move in any direction in the market. 'A commodity functions as an exchange-value if it can freely take the place of a definite quantity of any other commodity, irrespective of whether or not

---

60 [The foregoing statement is marked in pencil in the margin].
61 Marx 1971, p. 135.
62 [From this point the passage is marked with pencil in the margin].

it constitutes a use-value for the owner of the other commodity'.⁶³ Of course, it is not really the commodity itself but rather the commodity producer who possesses this ability to move in any direction in the market: the existence of the commodity, which possesses exchange-value, permits him to enter into a production relation of exchange with any other commodity producer, regardless of whether he requires his⁶⁴ commodity or not. Formally, of course, this act of exchange cannot be completed without the agreement or against the will of the second commodity producer, but such agreement almost always exists in fact and is assured in a developed commodity economy: the producers, as we have seen, are willing to deliver the product of their labour to anyone who gives them equal value in exchange. The 'exchange-value' of the product of labour consists of the fact that possession of the latter gives the commodity producer the ability *to enter into a production relation of exchange with any other commodity producer*. The product of labour acquires a special social function as the mediator or 'carrier of production relations' between people; it becomes the 'active carrier of exchange-value'.⁶⁵ The commodity producer becomes an active initiator of production relations with other members of society.

[E] *The dual position of the commodity owner.*⁶⁶ As we see, the unique production relations that prevail in commodity economy, connecting people through the mediation of things, create a dual position for the commodity producer in the market process of exchange: insofar as the product of labour is a use-value, whose movement is externally predetermined for a given commodity producer, the latter plays the role of a passive participant in the production relation; insofar as the product of his labour represents an exchange-value, the commodity producer plays the role of active initiator of the production relation. *This dual, passive-active character of the production relations between commodity producers is formulated by Marx in his well-known*⁶⁷ *teaching regarding the dual nature of the commodity as use-value and exchange-value*:

> One and the same relation must therefore be simultaneously a relation of essentially equal commodities which differ only in magnitude, i.e., a

---

63 Marx 1970, pp. 43–4. [Here the marginal marking ends].
64 [The manuscript is corrected here in pencil, with '*его*' (his) replacing '*этом*' (this); this passage is marked in pencil in the margin].
65 Marx 1970, p. 42.
66 [A heading written into the margin].
67 [Here the word 'famous' (*знаменитом*) was crossed out in pencil and replaced with 'well-known' (*известном*)].

relation which expresses their equality as materialisations of universal labour-time, and at the same time it must be their relation as qualitatively different things, as distinct use-values for distinct needs, in short a relation which differentiates them as actual use-values. But equality and inequality thus posited are mutually exclusive.[68]

This 'equality' of commodities, as exchange-values, enables the producer to equate the product of his labour with any other product, i.e. to emerge as active participant in the production relation of exchange. An 'inequality' of commodities, as use-values, signifies the need to connect the given product of labour with some other person's effective demand, or the need for the given commodity producer to wait while other commodity producers equate the products of their own labour with the given product, i.e. the need to be a passive participant in the production relation of exchange. Within the 'metaphysical' shell of the doctrine concerning the dual nature of the commodity, we find a sociological analysis of the production relations between commodity producers.

We have noted that each commodity producer must appear, in his relation to the others, in the dual role of active initiator and passive godfather of the production relation of exchange. The exchange participant's simultaneous fulfilment of both of these roles, passive and active, is possible only in the case of natural exchange, which is determined simultaneously by the demand from a given exchange participant for the product of another's labour and by the demand from the latter for the product of the first participant's labour. But such simultaneous union in a single person of the passive and active role in fact eliminates his active capacity, i.e. deprives him of the possibility of exchanging the product of his labour for any other according to his own discretion. Here there is no generalised exchange and equation of the products of labour, and thus there is still no developed exchange-value. Exchange still has an occasional and limited character and is determined by the individual needs of particular people. Generalised exchange presupposes the possibility of exchanging each product of labour for any other product; accordingly, the active role of the given commodity producer, as initiator of the production relation of exchange, must not be paralysed by his simultaneous role as the passive godfather. And this means that every commodity producer must appear consecutively in both of these roles, being alternately first in one and then in the other.

Thus, at any particular moment in every process of exchange, the given commodity producer plays either the active or the passive role. It is readily under-

---

68   Marx 1970, p. 44.

stood that the second participant in the exchange must always play the role opposite to that of the first. If given commodity producer A actively establishes, at his own discretion, a production relation with any one of the other commodity producers, this means that the latter, at this particular moment, is deprived of the ability to choose, at his own discretion, the counterparty to the exchange transaction. The polar division between active and passive roles on the part of the two participants in the exchange finds expression in the polar division between the products of their labour in the simultaneous roles of exchange-value and use-value.[69] If the product of labour A, at any given moment, may be exchanged for any one of the other commodities, then the latter [are] obviously deprived at that moment of a similar opportunity. If commodity A is able to move freely in any direction in the market, and thus play the role of exchange-value, which is capable of generalised equalisation, then other commodities are simultaneously restricted in their movement, playing the passive role of use-value. In *Capital* Marx emphasises that it is impossible for both participants in an act of exchange to emerge simultaneously in the active role:

> The owner of a commodity is prepared to part with it only in return for other commodities whose use-value satisfies his own need. So far, exchange is merely an individual process for him. On the other hand, he desires to realise his commodity, as a value, in any other suitable commodity of the same value. It does not matter to him whether his own commodity has any use-value for the owner of the other commodity or not. From this point of view, exchange is for him a general social process. *But the same process cannot be simultaneously for all owners of commodities both exclusively individual and exclusively social and general.*

> Let us look at the matter a little more closely. To the owner of a commodity, every other commodity counts as the particular equivalent of his own commodity. Hence his own commodity is the universal equivalent for all the others. *But since this applies to every owner, there is in fact no commodity acting as universal equivalent*, and the commodities possess no general relative form of value under which they can be equated as values and have the magnitude of their values compared.[70]

---

69 [In the margin Rubin inserts a question mark: '?'].
70 Marx 1976, p. 180 [Rubin's emphasis].

The simultaneous appearance of all commodity owners in the active role, as initiator of the production relations of exchange, leads to mutual paralysis of their activity. The simultaneous appearance of both of the products of labour, which are being exchanged, in the role of exchange-value, which can be exchanged for any other product of labour (i.e. in the role of universal equivalent for all other commodities), results in none of them being able to play this role. If one of the exchanging commodities has the capacity to be directly exchanged for any other commodity, then the second commodity, which is involved in the given act of exchange, does not have this capacity: it cannot be exchanged directly for any other product but only through the mediation of its exchange with the first commodity:

> It is by no means self-evident that the form of direct and universal exchangeability is an antagonistic form, as inseparable from its opposite, the form of non-direct exchangeability, as the positivity of one pole of a magnet is from the negativity of the other pole. This has allowed the illusion to arise that all commodities can simultaneously be imprinted with the stamp of direct exchangeability, in the same way that it might be imagined that all Catholics can be popes.[71]

This brings us to the following conclusions. On the one hand, every commodity producer in the process of exchange must alternately play the active role of initiator of production relations and the passive role of godfather of productive relations established by others. On the other hand, it is not possible for both participants in the exchange to appear simultaneously in the active role: the active role of one simultaneously means the passive role of the other.[72] The production link between the two commodity producers in the act of exchange not only creates a certain coordination between them but also contains a certain element of subordination, i.e. a dissimilar allocation of the active and passive role. As we know, however, in commodity society there is no organ that consciously establishes in advance a specific relation between the independent producers. The commodity owners oppose each other in exchange as fully equal economic subjects, whose social position in the act of exchange depends exclusively upon the character of the things in their possession: the production relations between them have the character of 'things'. Consequently, the active

---

71 Marx 1976, p. 161, footnote. [There is a line in the margin marking the quotation].
72 The first aspect is emphasised more by Marx in his *Critique of Political Economy*; the second, in chapter 2 of *Capital* and the doctrine of forms of value.

role of a given commodity producer in the act of exchange is also directly determined not by his social function in the production process but by the fact of his possessing a certain thing, i.e. by the social function of the thing.[73] Once it happens that in every exchange act one of the commodity owners must play the active role of initiator and creator of the given production relation, and once he can play such role exclusively as the owner of determinate things or commodities, then the conclusion that inevitably follows is this: the possession of some determinate commodity gives their owner the possibility of entering into the production relation of exchange with any other commodity owner, in other words, makes it possible to exchange the given commodity for any other that he chooses. The commodity *that fulfils the social function of active initiator of the production relations of exchange between commodity producers, i.e. that possesses the capacity for direct universal exchangeability for any other commodity*, is *money*.

In *Capital* Marx defines money as the 'universal equivalent', or the commodity in 'the form of universal equivalent'.[74] In general terms, Marx always considers the characteristic feature of an equivalent to be its capacity for 'direct exchangeability'.[75] A universal equivalent is a commodity that appears in the 'form of direct and universal exchangeability',[76] i.e. having the capacity to be directly exchanged for any other commodity. In this ability to play the role of active initiator of the production relation of exchange, of being the 'active carrier of exchange-value' and 'the carrier of the economic relation',[77] we also find the fundamental character of money – its social function or social form. Although he expresses it differently, Marx gives essentially the same definition of money in the *Critique of Political Economy*: 'The particular commodity which thus represents the exchange-value of all commodities, that is to say, the exchange-value of commodities regarded as a particular, exclusive commodity, constitutes *money*. It is a crystallisation of the exchange-value of commodities and is formed in the exchange process by the commodities themselves'.[78] (As we previously discussed in detail, Marx always emphasises, particularly in the *Critique*, that the characteristic feature of the commodity as exchange-value is the ability to be exchanged for any other commodity, or to replace it

---

73   [This statement and part of the suggestion that follows, up to the colon, are marked off in the margin in pencil with the comment: 'мало', ('inadequate' or 'add more')].
74   Marx 1976, p. 160.
75   Marx 1976, pp. 149, 152, 154, 161.
76   Marx 1976, p. 161, footnote.
77   Marx 1970, p. 42.
78   Marx 1970, p. 48.

in some definite proportion). Money, as the 'crystallisation of exchange-value', also means fixation of this capacity for generalised equalisation, or for direct universal exchangeability, in a definite concrete commodity (gold). The definition of money that Marx gives in the *Critique* corresponds fully with his definition in *Capital*.

[F] *Money as means of coercion*.[79] Summarising what we have set out, we can say that the development and universal spread of money is the necessary result of the structure of commodity society itself, which combines the social unity of the material process of production with the formal independence of private undertakings. Movement of the products of labour, in the process of production and consumption, is left to the discretion of separate private commodity producers, but each of the latter is also bound by the will of his counterparty. The act of direct exchange of the products of labour of two commodity producers can only be established on the principles of 'free' agreement, or a coincidence of will, on the part of the two counterparties. The act of exchange, conditioned by the need of each participant to acquire the product of the labour of the other participant, inevitably has an individual and random character. A social process of exchange, distinguished by law-governed constancy, is only possible if the movement of products can occur at the initiative *of any*[80] of the commodity producers. And this occurs when a commodity historically emerges in the exchange process whose possession gives its owner the ability to appear as initiator and active establisher of the production relation of exchange, i.e. money.[81] In the system of private establishments, which are formally equal and permit mutual coordination of activities only on the principles of agreement, money introduces the first differentiation in the active and passive roles fulfilled alternately by each commodity producer; it introduces the germ of a form of subjugation (coercion) and subordination. Money is a 'social force', it 'measures the social wealth of its owner', his social power.[82] The 'free' exchange agreement, formally presupposing the absolute equality of both participants, in fact resides in the initiative of one of them, the owner of money. This is what overcomes the limitation and restriction of the exchange process founded upon the correspondence of will between two counterparties. The foundation of commodity society is 'the juridical relation, whose form is the contract'. However, 'The content of this juridical relation (or relation of

---

79   [A heading written into the margin].
80   [Rubin originally wrote *one* but corrected it in pencil].
81   [A section of the document, beginning here, is marked in pencil as 'inadequate'].
82   Marx 1976, p. 230.

two wills) is itself determined by the economic relation'.[83] The economic relation of exchange, being completed by the development of money, introduces lawfulness and constancy into a system of juridical relations based upon the correspondence of the individual wills of separate persons.

[G] *The teaching of Rykachev*.[84] In the book by A[ndrei M.] Rykachev, *Money and the Power of Money*, we find a perfectly clear understanding that modern exchange, as 'a normal process, in which each participant of the process makes calculations in advance and does so with no regard to the calculations and wishes of all the others',[85] cannot be based upon the sort of free agreement that presupposes 'the necessity of waiting upon or obtaining a correspondence of two or more wills'.[86] 'Agreement is a very elementary form of the exchange of services, so elementary that on its own it is not able to satisfy the demands of any developed human society and is necessarily supplemented by other forms – by direct compulsion or by monetary assessment'.[87] 'Money is essentially the means of securing freedom of choice of economic goods',[88] freeing the participants in exchange from dependence upon the will of other commodity owners. But A. Rykachev forgets what is most essential and important: that the possibility for free choice of economic goods by one participant in the exchange act means the simultaneous lack of such freedom, i.e. coercion, for the other participant in the same act. The active role of *one participant*[89] in exchange presupposes a passive role on the other side. If modern exchange is 'a normal process, in which each participant of the process makes calculations in advance and does so with no regard to the calculations and wishes of all the others', this is only possible under one condition: if 'the calculations and wishes of all the other' commodity producers are regularly determined by the objective social processes of production and exchange. The seeming freedom of 'motivation' on the part of separate commodity producers necessarily presupposes an objective 'limitation' (restriction, constraint) of action on the part of all commodity producers taken together: the former, without the latter, would make the social process of production impossible by transforming society into a chaos of uncoordinated and intersecting activities by individual

---

83   Marx 1976, p. 178. [The section marked off in pencil in the margin ends here].
84   [A heading written into the margin].
85   Rykachev 1910, p. 81.
86   Rykachev 1910, p. 61.
87   Rykachev 1910, p. 163.
88   Rykachev 1910, p. 77.
89   [Inserted in pencil].

people. The basic social function of money in commodity economy consists not so much of its role as instrument for free motivation as of its role as instrument of 'limitation', or suppression of the motives of commodity producers. The tokens, which in socialist society will give individual members the right to acquire from social stocks any products in some determinate quantity, will do no worse than today's money in fulfilling the role of 'securing freedom of choice of economic goods'. But they will not directly determine the motives and actions of the producers, and for that reason they will not be 'money' in today's sense of the word. Losing sight of the role of money as instrument of coercion, A. Rykachev concludes that 'purchase and sale cease to be a bilateral transaction and become a series of unilateral acts by buyers and sellers, independently pursuing their own interests'.[90] Commodity society, as portrayed by A. Rykachev, is transformed into a fantastic kingdom of universal and unrestricted freedom: each unilaterally does whatever he pleases, yet exchange still retains the character of a 'normal process'. The real fact is that, even with monetary exchange, the system of production relations between people is based not upon unilateral acts but upon bilateral deals – with the distinction, however, that the active and passive roles are differentiated in the persons of the different parties to the transaction.

Of course, there is no reason to be surprised by the fact that A. Rykachev – although he believes that his definition of money, as a means to free choice of economic goods, essentially corresponds with the Marxist definition of money as universal equivalent[91] – in reality has completely misunderstood the most essential aspect of Marx's teaching on the limiting and socially constraining role of money. For him, Marx's doctrine remains a 'philosophical speculation', the functioning 'result of a logical development of internal contradictions allegedly contained within the concept of the commodity'.[92]

The definition of money that we have given differs from the definition given by [Rudolf] Hilferding: 'The object which is thus authorised by the common action of commodities to express the value of all other commodities is – money'.[93] In our definition, money is a thing that, through the collective activities of commodities, has acquired the authority actively to establish the production relation of exchange, i.e. it has acquired the capacity of direct exchangeability. The result of this fundamental character of money is that it fulfils the function of measure of value, which Hilferding takes as the basis of

---

90   Rykachev 1910, p. 66.
91   Rykachev 1910, p. 104.
92   Rykachev 1910, p. 102.
93   Hilferding 1981, p. 32.

his definition. We have not accepted Hilferding's definition for the following two reasons. First, our goal has been to clarify the meaning of the definition that Marx himself gives. For Marx, the universal equivalent is a commodity that possesses the capacity for direct and universal exchangeability, whereas Hilferding defines the equivalent as 'the commodity in which all other commodities express their value'.[94] And here, as we see, Hilferding begins with the function of measure of value. For Marx, the measure of value is only 'one of the functions of money, or money in a particular, determinate form'.[95] Second, we consider it proper to give a definition of money that characterises the production relations between people, the expression of which is this given external category, i.e. the money-form of the commodity. Our definition emphasises that what is involved is the active establishment of exchange, i.e. the production relation of exchange between two commodity producers, with a polar differentiation between them of the active and passive roles. This is a determinate type of relations between people – a type that assigns a special material property to the 'money' commodity that is found in the hands of the active participant in exchange. Of course, Hilferding's formula also speaks implicitly of the same type of production relations between people, but it does not characterise them directly.

4 The Emergence of Money

We have seen that a developed commodity economy, with a generalised exchange of commodities, necessarily presupposes the detachment, from the sphere of all commodities, of a single commodity that possesses the property of direct exchangeability, i.e. that fulfils the function of money. But at this point we have still not answered the question of how this detachment of money occurred in fact, or what is the historical process of the emergence and development of money.

Of course Marx, whose basic task was the explanation of phenomena in capitalist society, could not become involved in specialised historical research concerning the origin of money – research that involves the pre-historical and very earliest historical epochs. Yet, on the other hand, while regarding all aspects of the contemporary economic system as historically transitional, and considering them in terms of their historical development, Marx could not but pay attention to the question of the historical origin of money. His observations on this account, despite their brevity, are very interesting and valuable.

---

94   Hilferding 1981, p. 34.
95   Marx 1971, p. 133.

Besides these comments of a purely historical character, we encounter in Marx, and especially in his teaching on money, a unique interlacing of the historical and theoretical points of view. 'Flirting' with Hegelianism, as he put it, Marx frequently represents earlier phases of historical development as separate 'moments' or aspects of the subsequently more developed form of the same phenomenon. Or conversely, stages in the logical analysis of a complex phenomenon are presented in the form of consecutive stages or phases of historical development. Such a splicing together of theoretical and historical research is especially evident in Marx's doctrine on the 'forms of value', and this makes it extremely difficult to understand.

In the first half of the nineteenth century a rationalistic answer was most frequently given to the question of the origins of money as well as to all the other forms of social life. Scholars noted the utility or expediency of a given social institution, money for example, and then considered their task to be completed. It was assumed that the usefulness of any given institution served as a directly persuasive motive for people consciously to introduce it. Analysing the difficulties of natural exchange and its facilitation through use of money, scholars suggested that people agreed, by way of some special understanding or social contract, to consider some commodity or other as money in order to facilitate exchange. Other scholars saw the source of money's lineage in the invention of individual peoples (the theory of the archaeologist [August] Böckh)[96] or in the conscious activity of a state authority.

At a time when [today's] most recent archaeological, ethnographic and historical findings – showing the social-spontaneity of the development of money – were still unknown, Marx's service lay in the fact that he staunchly defended such a view, starting from his general historical and economic conception. Money was the result of a gradual expansion and growing complexity of exchange, [emerging] through countless repetition of a mass of uncon-

---

96   [Rubin has in mind the German philologist and student of antiquity, August Böckh, who in his work *Metrologische Untersuchungen über Gewichte, Münzfüsse und Masse des Alterthums in ihrem Zusammenhange*, published in Berlin in 1838, argued that the first monetary units of weight were defined theoretically and introduced as a result of administrative commands. In the view of Vladimir V. Svyatlovsky, whose work *Proiskhozhdenie deneg i denezhnykh znakov* (*The Origin of Money and Monetary Tokens*) (Moscow: Gos. Izd., 1923) served as Rubin's source for this information, Böckh's theory lacked any real historical basis and was 'inspired by recollection of the activity of the Great French Revolution, which, in exactly that manner, resolved the question of the new metric system'. See V.V. Svyatlovsky, *Ukaz. Soch.* p. 4].

scious[97] actions on the part of exchange participants and without any decisive, conscious influence on the part of a state authority. In other words, the origin of money had a social-economic and not a governmental – a spontaneous and not a conscious – character. 'Money is not the result of deliberation or of agreement, but has come into being spontaneously in the course of exchange'.[98] 'The natural instinct of the owners of commodities'[99] persuaded them to do the deed before thinking about it. These activities on the part of exchange participants were determined by the character and requirements of the exchange process.

Exchange originally emerged not between members of a community, who lived in conditions of a natural and occasionally a communist economy, but between different communities or their members.[100] From there exchange gradually penetrates into the community itself, promoting its dissolution.[101] The products of labour, becoming commodities in inter-communal exchange, also acquire exchange-value within the community.[102] Exchange initially involves a small number of products and has an exceptional and fortuitous character. It occurs in the form of natural exchange, in which both of the exchanging products are use-values for the parties to the exchange. On the other hand, the product is still not produced especially for exchange, and only the surplus that is left over, after satisfying their own needs, enters into exchange. Thus, in both the objective production process and in the consciousness of the participants, exchange-value has still not separated from use-values.[103] Each of the two exchanging products determines the movement of the other product and, in its movement, is determined by the latter, i.e. fulfils simultaneously the passive role of use-value and the active role of exchange-value, or equivalent.[104] The random character of exchange also entails random and fluctuating quantitative proportions between the things being exchanged. In general this stage of natural exchange 'signifies the beginning of the transformation of use-values into commodities rather than the transformation of

---

97   Not 'unconscious' in an absolute sense, but insofar as the goal of exchange participants was not the creation of money, which emerged as an unintended 'heterogeneous' result of their numerous activities.
98   Marx 1970, p. 49.
99   Marx 1976, p. 180.
100 Marx 1976, p. 182.
101 Marx 1970, p. 50.
102 Ibid.
103 Ibid.
104 [There is a question mark '?' in the margin beside this statement].

commodities into money'.¹⁰⁵ The product of labour acquires the nuclear form of exchange-value, corresponding generally (but not completely) with what Marx, in his scheme of development of the value-form, called 'the simple, isolated or accidental form of value'.¹⁰⁶

Having appeared on the basis of a primitive-rudimentary division of labour between separate communities, elicited partly by the difference of environmental and natural conditions, exchange in turn provides a powerful stimulus to the division of labour. Growth of the division of labour leads to the expansion and deepening of exchange, both in the sense of the quantitative increase of portions of the given product entering into exchange and in terms of drawing into exchange new kinds of products that hitherto were consumed within the original community. In this process of gradual attraction of new types of products into exchange, those products of labour that are already widely used as items of exchange usually separate out and acquire particular importance. Each person who brings his product to market endeavours to exchange it for one of these most widely used items of exchange, either because he requires these products more frequently in view of their wider use or because they give him the ability to use them in the next exchange for the concrete product that he does require. One or several products are most frequently exchanged for all the others and are most frequently equated with them. Usually such a role is played not by one but by several commodities, between which a certain proportion of exchange is established in turn. A system of evaluation of one commodity in terms of several others is established. With the Bondu tribe of western Sudan, one slave = one rifle and two bottles of powder, or = 5 bottles of powder = one hundred pieces of cloth.

For the Darfurs of Central Africa, one slave equalled 30 pieces of cotton cloth of a particular length, or six bulls, or ten Spanish dollars of a particular coinage.¹⁰⁷ M[ikhail I.] Tugan-Baranovsky correctly observes that such a system of evaluation, which is widespread in the early stages of exchange, corresponds to Marx's 'expanded form of value'.¹⁰⁸

The development of exchange does not stop here. The process of differentiation continues in the direction of distinguishing from the entire group of commodities the one that figures most often in exchange. 'Commercial intercourse, in which the owners of commodities exchange and compare their own articles with various other articles, never takes place unless different kinds of

---

105   Ibid.
106   Marx 1976, pp. 139–54.
107   Helfferich 1923, pp. 13–14.
108   Tugan-Baronovsky 1917, p. 242. [See Marx 1976, pp. 154–7].

commodities belonging to different owners are exchanged for, and equated as values with, one single further kind of commodity'.[109] In place of the evaluation of one commodity in terms of several others comes the evaluation of several commodities in terms of one and the same commodity as their equivalent. At the outset, 'The universal equivalent form comes and goes with the momentary social contacts which call it into existence. It is transiently attached to this or that commodity in alternation. But with the development of exchange it fixes itself firmly and exclusively onto particular kinds of commodity, i.e., it crystallises out into the money-form'.[110] A long process of historical development was required before this monetary function was affixed to precious metals. With different tribes and peoples, the role of money was fulfilled by various commodities, and with each people the money material changed in the course of time. If one were to list all of the commodities that have served in their day and in different localities as money, the result would be an extremely long and diverse list of the most dissimilar items. The selection of one or another item was determined by a whole series of objective conditions: the type of economy practised by a given tribe, the extent of its wealth, its relations with other tribes, etc. In the *Critique* Marx says that the role of money is usually fulfilled by 'the most common use-value', which constitutes 'the most substantial physical element' in the wealth of the given tribe.[111] In *Capital* Marx makes this observation in more detail. The role of money was fulfilled either by the most important items that are acquired abroad, through external exchange, and which thus represented a kind of natural form for the manifestation of the exchange-value of indigenous products; or else by the item of consumption that represented the main element of indigenous alienable wealth, for example, cattle, slaves, etc.[112] Generally speaking, these observations by Marx are fully confirmed by the most recent ethnography and archaeology. [Karl] Helfferich summarises these findings with the following words: 'Among hunting peoples weapons serve above all as the medium of exchange; among pastoral people, cattle; among tribes trading with foreign merchants, the commodities that are acquired from the latter or given to them in exchange'.[113] Together with these groups of items, which serve most frequently as primitive money, Helfferich also includes a group of items of adornment, among which are the

---

109 Marx 1976, pp. 182–3.
110 Marx 1976, p. 183.
111 Marx 1970, p. 49.
112 Marx 1976, p. 183.
113 Helfferich 1923, p. 16. The role of items acquired through external exchange as the first kind of money was noted by Wagner. See Wagner 1909, p. 130.

precious metals. However, one must not overlook the fact that items of adornment are often included in the first of the groups mentioned by Marx (i.e. items of import), and furthermore that the metals in general, and partly also the precious metals, were among the most important means of production for primitive peoples.

Metals originally fulfilled the role of money alongside other commodities. Occasionally, one and the same tribe evaluated commodities simultaneously in terms of metal, cattle and so forth. But gradually the metals displaced other commodities that had fulfilled the function of money. The cause for this must be found in the well-known natural properties of metals – their uniformity and divisibility – thanks to which they are best suited to express quantitative differences. To this must be added their high degree of durability and, for precious metals, their high specific value, as a result of which they gradually displaced the more common metals and relegated them to the sphere of small change.[114] 'Gold and silver are not by nature money, but money consists by its nature of gold and silver'.[115] The conversion of precious metals into money presupposes a certain social structure, founded upon commodity economy and developed exchange. But existence of the latter inevitably causes the appearance of money and the fixation upon one commodity or another of the social function of money, the best carriers of which, in the final analysis, are the precious metals. Imagine that the world had no items distinguished by their uniformity and divisibility to such an ideal extent as the precious metals. In that case, the development of exchange would affix the function of money to some other product of labour, although, no doubt, exchange would then encounter a number of technical inconveniences that are overcome with the use of precious metals in the role of money.[116] The appearance of money is exclusively a consequence of the social structure of the economy, and the fixation of this function precisely upon the precious metals is explained above all by the natural properties of the latter.

Metals were originally used in the form of pieces, bars, rings etc. To make payment, the metal was weighed, which in many languages resulted in the verbs 'to pay' and 'to weigh' emerging from a common root. With the passage of time and for ease of payment, metals begin to be produced in the form of pieces, bars and so forth, having a certain purity and a specific weight. In

---

114   Marx 1970, pp. 153–4.
115   Marx 1970, p. 155; see also Marx 1976, p. 183.
116   See the article by E. Preobrazhensky concerning the Russian rouble in *Vestnik Sotsialisticheskoi Akademii* for 1923 [Preobrazhensky 1923].

Babylon, where precious metals first took the role of money, a special system of weights was worked out: a specific weight, called a 'talent', was divided into 60 'mina', each of which was subdivided into 60 'shekels'. This system, based upon the 'talent', became very widespread and, in modified form, passed into Egypt, the Near East and Greece. The Levant, as the centre of vital trade relations at the crossroads between Greece, Egypt and Assyria-Babylonia, naturally also became the centre for further development of precious metals in the role of money. Wealthy Phoenician merchants put a stamp upon metal bars, testifying to their purity and weight. From there it was just one step to coins, which represent nothing but a piece of metal with a certain purity and weight and stamped by the local state authority. The first coins also appeared in the Levant in the eighth and seventh centuries B.C. according to some scholars, in Lydia according to others, and in the Greek colonies of Asia Minor. They rapidly spread to other countries.

The appearance of coins was of colossal importance in the history of the circulation of money. Subsequently metal, in its function as money or carrier of exchange-value in an external and visible manner, became distinguished from the same metal as a use-value. Within the limits of a given state, only that state's coins are legal and obligatory as the means of exchange and payment. When he accepts coins, an exchange participant has no interest in the actual weight and purity of the metal they contain. On the other hand, metal bars do not function as money within the country. Nevertheless, the significance of coins as legal means of payment and exchange can be seen even today in their close link, even if it is not always direct, with the value of precious metal. Numerous attempts by state authorities to use their monetary regalia (the monopolistic right to coin money), or the right to issue paper money, in order finally to sever the country's monetary system from its metallic base, have usually ended in failure and provoked a very strong reaction on the part of commodity circulation. A graphic confirmation of the latter is the current return by Russia, Germany and other states to a monetary system that, although not directly involving gold circulation, is all the same 'based upon'[117] gold. Insofar as the subject-matter of our study is not the degree and forms of influence by a state power over the monetary circulation, but instead the laws of the latter, as determined by the development of commodity exchange, we do not see any great difference

---

117 [The phrase used in the text is 'прислонненой к золоту', with the literal meaning of 'leaning upon gold', which suggests a more indirect connection than convertibility. At the time when Rubin wrote, the Soviet Union was using the nominally convertible *chervonets* rouble, which had been introduced in 1925].

between a pre-minted and a minted circulation, or to use [Georg F.] Knapp's expression, between 'pensatory' and 'chartal' means of payment.[118]

Nevertheless, such a difference can be asserted from an evolutionary-historical point of view. Coinage was one of the stages of an evolution that began long before the appearance of coins, and one must not consider the first money, as Knapp does, to be only the first coins. In minting the first coins, the state authority confirmed and legalised the status of a money circulation that had existed before it intervened – on the basis of countless unconscious activities by commodity owners and due to the requirements of commodity exchange. The state authority used the same metal for coinage as previously functioned as money. It could not alter the value of this metal, i.e. the proportions of its exchange with other commodities. Even the weight of coin, for the most part, was not established by the arbitrary act of state power but rather conformed to the weight of metal bars that circulated before the appearance of coins. The most recent findings have shed clear light upon the close connections between various stages of monetary circulation. For example, the famous scholar [William] Ridgeway believes that the golden talent was originally a nugget of gold exactly equal to the price of a bull. When metal squeezed cattle out of the role of money, the monetary unit of metallic circulation was determined on the basis of a hereditary connection with the former monetary unit, which was the bull. In this way, Ridgeway intends to explain the striking similarity between the weight of ancient gold coins and the golden items that served as money amongst the most varied peoples. Ridgeway hypothesises that throughout Europe and the Levant the price of cattle was approximately identical, explaining the almost identical weight of gold items and coins (a weight of about 130–135 grains) that represented the original price of a bull.[119] This is why the image of a bull, and of cattle in general, is found so frequently on ancient coins, and why the very designation of money in many languages originates from the appellation of cattle.

The original designation of money also pointed to a connection with a certain weight of metal. The coin's designation corresponded to the weight of a piece of metal – a talent, pound, etc. 'The names given to the standards of money or of price were originally taken from the pre-existing names of the standards of weight'.[120] It is only in the process of a long historical development

---

118   [The reference is to the ideas developed by Georg Friedrich Knapp in the first two chapters of his work *Staatliche Theorie des Geldes* (Knapp 1921). Knapp referred to payments involving metal that had to be weighed as 'pensatory'; 'chartal' means of payment involved 'nominal' or 'fiat' money].
119   Svyatlovsky 1923, p. 45. [The reference by Svyatlovsky is to Ridgeway 1892].
120   Marx 1976, p. 192.

that the monetary standard became detached from the standard of weight and was independently established by the state authority. The latter may arbitrarily establish the weight and appellation of each coin, but it is constrained both in the choice of metal and with regard to its value, which directly or indirectly is reflected in the purchasing power of the coin.

5   *Money and Abstract-Social Labour*

In the previous chapters we have considered the process of the emergence of money and the need for the latter in commodity society, where people are connected by production relations through generalised equation of the products of their labour as values. Now let us consider how the equation of commodities, occurring through the medium of money, leads to the equation of labour and makes money the expression of social and abstract labour.

[A] *The First Characteristic*.[121] The process of money's development leads to fixation of the functions of money upon some concrete commodity, ultimately upon gold. Gold is the commodity that can be exchanged directly for any other commodity, and thus every commodity owner must exchange the product of his labour – he must sell it – first of all for gold as the universal equivalent. Gold, as exchange-value, is able to replace any commodity in some given proportion; it is distinct from all other commodities, which lack this capacity for direct exchangeability. 'A single commodity, the linen, therefore has the form of direct exchangeability with all other commodities, in other words it has a directly social form because, and insofar as, no other commodity is in this situation'.[122] There occurs an external and visible separation of use-value from exchange-value; the former is represented by all the concrete commodities; the latter by gold as money. The exchange of commodities for money converts use-value into exchange-value because gold, a concrete product of labour, or a specific use-value, fulfils the role of money. It would seem that the exchange of commodity A for so many ounces of gold still does not provide us with an exact determination of the value of A, for we do not know the value of the given sum of gold. But this value can also be determined in commodity economy, not directly in labour units but indirectly in terms of the quantity of another commodity given in exchange for the gold.[123] But after the equation of gold with some other commodity B, the question arises as to the value of

---

121   [A heading written into the margin].
122   Marx 1976, p. 161. [Rubin notes that in this example Marx has linen functioning hypothetically as the universal equivalent].
123   [The statement is marked off in the margin in pencil].

the latter, and so forth. In reality, however, the commodity producers, equating their commodities with gold and thus determining their value, have no further question regarding the value of gold. They obviously have a vital interest in the question of the purchasing power of the gold they are acquiring, but this is a question as to how many concrete use-values can be acquired for the abstract money unit (i.e. the unit of exchange-value), not one that concerns the exchange-value of given use-values or of concrete commodities.[124] The latter question is resolved by the equation of commodities with gold, which therefore, in its concrete form as a known item, assumes a definite value. 'In the equation of value the equivalent always has the form of a simple quantity of some article, of a use-value.' This 'use-value becomes the form of appearance of its opposite, value'.[125] This is how Marx states the first peculiarity of the equivalent form.[126]

But how can the natural form of gold express the exchange-value of commodity *A*? This is only possible because gold possesses the property of direct and universal exchangeability, because not only commodity A equates with it but also all other commodities. Thus commodity *A*, being equated with gold, equates with all other commodities. This is how it expresses its exchange-value, i.e. its capacity for generalised exchange with any other commodity. The universal form of value 'expresses the values of the world of commodities through one single kind of commodity set apart from the rest, through linen for example, and thus represents the values of all commodities by means of their equality with linen'.[127] In other words, the generalised equation of all commodities with each other occurs in commodity economy through the equation of each of them with a single, select and concrete commodity (gold).[128] *Equation of a given commodity with gold, which is equated in turn with all other commodities, simultaneously means equation of the given commodity with all others*. Through equation with *one* concrete commodity, equation with all commodities occurs. This is the real phenomenon, occurring daily in the market, that Marx had in mind with his abstract formula of use-value as the form of manifestation of exchange[129]-value, or to say the same thing differently, of the concrete commodity as mediator of the generalised equation of all commodities. In this

---

124 [The last part of this statement is marked off in pencil in the margin].
125 Marx 1976, p. 148.
126 [The foregoing two sentences are marked off in pencil in the margin].
127 Marx 1976, p. 158.
128 [The following three sentences, ending with 'equation of all commodities', are marked off in pencil in the margin].
129 [The word 'exchange' is inserted in pencil].

phenomenon we see not the result of some mysterious capacity of use-value to serve as the form of manifestation of its opposite, but the result of countless activities by commodity producers, equating their commodities with one and the same select commodity. 'A commodity only acquires a general expression of its value if, at the same time, all other commodities express their values in the same equivalent; and every newly emergent commodity must follow suit'.[130]

[B] *The Second Characteristic*.[131] Thus, in commodity economy the generalised equation of commodities with one another occurs in the form of their equation with one and the same select commodity, gold. As we know, however, it is through the market process of the equation of commodities that the social process of distributing and equating labour between different branches of production occurs. This does not involve some mental act of abstracting from the concrete specificities of separate types of labour and equating them with identical, abstract human labour in general – a mental act that might occur in the mind of the exchange participant or of a theoretical investigator. Marx is not interested in 'the subjective equality of the labours of individuals' but rather in 'the objective equalisation that the social process forcibly establishes between unequal kinds of labour',[132] which is expressed in the equilibrium between different kinds of labour or between separate branches of production. In commodity economy, which is consciously regulated by no one, such equilibrium between separate spheres of production (being constantly disrupted and appearing only in the form of a tendency), is established only through the market equation of their products as values and in a certain proportion. 'It is only the expression of *equivalence between different sorts of commodities* which brings to view the specific character of value-creating labour, by *actually reducing* the different kinds of labour embedded in the different kinds of commodity to their common quality of being human labour in general'.[133] Let us now consider how this equation of different kinds of labour occurs.

'By equating, for example, the coat as a thing of value to the linen, we equate the labour embedded in the coat with the labour embedded in the linen'.[134] If the coat were equated with all other commodities, this would mean the equation of sartorial labour with all other kinds of concrete labour. In other words, given a specific ratio of exchange between the coat and every other

---

130   Marx 1976, p. 159.
131   [A heading written into the margin].
132   Marx 1970, p. 59.
133   Marx 1976, p. 142 [Rubin's emphasis].
134   Ibid.

commodity, an equilibrium would be established between sartorial labour and the other corresponding spheres of production. The concrete labour of the tailor would be equated with any other concrete type of labour or with abstract labour in general. As we have seen, though, commodities are generally equated with one another not directly but only through the equation of each with a particular commodity, with gold. Consequently, the generalised equation of all concrete kinds of labour also occurs only through the equation of each of them with the concrete kind of labour that is being expended on the production of gold. Concrete labour A, being equated with the concrete labour producing gold, turns out thereby to be equated with every concrete kind of labour and, as a result, is a part of the aggregate of abstract social labour that is distributed between various branches of production. 'The body of the commodity, which serves as the equivalent, always figures as the embodiment of abstract human labour, and is always the product of some specific useful and concrete labour. This concrete labour therefore becomes the expression of abstract human labour'.[135] 'The equivalent form therefore possesses a second peculiarity: in it, concrete labour becomes the form of manifestation of its opposite, abstract human labour'.[136] We likewise have to regard this peculiarity not as some mysterious property of the labour expended on production of the equivalent (gold), but exclusively as the result of the social process of all other concrete kinds of labour being equated with it. The second peculiarity of the equivalent form means that *the equation of every concrete kind of labour with all other kinds occurs only through its equation with the concrete labour expended on production of the equivalent.*

In the theory of value, we said that in the distribution of labour between branches of production – A (for example, tailoring) and B (for example, weaving) – a condition of equilibrium is theoretically established when the exchange of a coat for cloth occurs on the market in a certain proportion that is determined by the labour expenditures on these two products; any deviation of prices from this exchange proportion initiates the ebb and flow of labour, i.e. a redistribution of labour between these two spheres of production. In other words, we presupposed that in the equation of products of the two branches in question, and in the equation of labour expended in them, there occurs a process of direct interaction between them. Now we can describe that same process in more detail and in a manner that is closer to reality. Both products are equated on the market with gold and not directly with one another. The

---

135   Marx 1976, p. 150.
136   Ibid.

equilibrium between these two spheres of production emerges in the condition of definite market prices for their products, i.e. in their proportionate exchange for gold. A deviation of these prices from the specific level that corresponds to the conditions of labour productivity in the two spheres, and thus to the labour value of their products, causes a redistribution of labour between these spheres. And since sphere A, through the price of its products (i.e. the rate at which they exchange for gold), is equated not just with sphere B but also with all the other spheres of the economy, it follows in this case that the redistribution of labour between spheres A and B will be determined not by their relative profitability alone, in relation to each other, but by their profitability in relation to all the other spheres. Assume that, with the given market prices, production in sphere A is more profitable than in sphere B, but production in both of these spheres is less profitable than in all other spheres of the economy, C, D, E, etc. In that case, there will not be a redistribution of labour from sphere B to sphere A, as may be expected from the direct interaction of these two spheres; instead, there will be an outflow of labour from both of them into other branches of production. Through market prices, each type of labour is equated with all others, i.e. concrete labour is converted into abstract labour.

[C] *Third*.[137] Thus, in the process of exchange the equivalent is equated with all other commodities, and the concrete labour that is expended in its production, being equated with all other concrete kinds of labour, thereby acquires the character of abstract labour. But once the labour expended in production of the equivalent is equated with any other type of labour, this means that it appears in directly social form. Although the gold industry is organised in the form of private capitalist enterprises, and thus labour in gold mining, as with all other commodity-producing labour, is the labour of private individuals, it is nevertheless 'labour in its directly social[138] form'.[139] The owner of gold appears as representative of the 'social power of money', of the socially acknowledged and socially significant kind of labour; he can enter into any act of exchange as the active participant, and in that way he reveals his equality with any other commodity producer. To the contrary, the owner of a concrete commodity – a coat, for instance – in order to become socially equal and to have the same significance as any other commodity owner, must first exchange his commodity for money, i.e. equate his private[140] labour with the private labour of the gold

---

137   [A heading written into the margin].
138   [Underlined in pencil].
139   Marx 1976, p. 150.
140   [In Russian, 'частный' (private) sometimes means the same as 'конкретный' (concrete)

producer,[141] which appears in the form of directly social labour. In the same way, the labour of the tailor acquires the character of directly social labour. 'Thus the equivalent form has a third peculiarity: private labour takes the form of its opposite, namely labour in its directly social form'.[142]

[D] *'Forms' of Exchange?*[143] Now we can summarise Marx's teaching on the 'peculiarities of the equivalent form'. Although Marx illustrates his thoughts in the various forms of the equivalent, beginning with an 'accidental' initial selection[144] and ending with the developed 'universal equivalent', nevertheless the totality of his thinking refers precisely to the universal equivalent, or to money.[145] The universal equivalent, or money, separates out of the commodity environment in the course of a gradual, slow evolution. The appearance of money imparted to the entire process of exchange a completely new character. Exchange is not only the movement of material things from one commodity producer to another, 'the social exchange of things', but also involves a change of the social 'form' of things and of the commodity producers. Circulation is a 'social process which products must pass through and in which they assume specific social characters'.[146] It is precisely this social form of exchange, and not its material content, that Marx investigates in his theory of money. 'We therefore have to consider the whole process in its formal aspect, that is to say, the change in form or the metamorphosis of commodities through which the social metabolism is mediated'.[147] Just as Marx, in the theory of value, places in the forefront the study of the social 'form of value', so also in the theory of money he is concerned with the 'change of forms'. And just as he holds economists at fault, in the theory of value, for seeing only the material content of the process and overlooking its social form, so he also makes analogous reproaches in the theory of money:

---

or 'особенный' (special, particular). Marx here uses the term 'Privatarbeit', that is, labour organised in the form of a private capitalist (or, generally speaking, a private commodity-producing) enterprise].

141 [There is a question mark '?' here in the margin].
142 Marx 1976, p. 151.
143 [A heading written into the margin].
144 Marx 1976, pp. 139–54.
145 Marx 1976, pp. 198–9. [A note by Rubin refers the reader the reader to an appendix, but the appendix is missing from his document.]
146 Marx 1992, p. 1020. [This sentence is marked in pencil in the margin].
147 Marx 1976, pp. 198–9.

This change of form has been very imperfectly grasped as yet, owing to the circumstance that, quite apart from the lack of clarity in the concept of value itself, every change of form in a commodity results from the exchange of two commodities, namely an ordinary commodity and the money commodity. If we keep in mind only the material aspect, that is, the exchange of the commodity for gold, we overlook the very thing we ought to observe, namely what has happened to the form of the commodity.[148]

[E] *Threefold equalisation.*[149] What does this 'change of form', which takes place in the process of exchange, consist of? In the exchange process, what occurs is *a change of the social form or social character of the commodity producers, of things, and of labour*. We have previously considered in detail the necessity of a change in the social role of commodity producers in the exchange process. The latter enter exchange as representatives of a private establishment or of private labour, as passive godfathers of the production relations, and they exit from the exchange process as representatives of the social power of money or of social labour, as active initiators of production relations. Since, in commodity economy, the change in the social role of commodity producers depends upon their possession of certain things and imparts to the latter a definite social form, a change also occurs in the social form of the thing, or of the product of labour, in parallel with the change of the commodity producers' social role: from a concrete use-value, capable of moving only in the direction of the consumer, it is transformed into exchange-value or the universal equivalent, possessing universal direct exchangeability, i.e. it is capable of moving in any direction in the market. The change in the social character of the commodity producer, which is closely connected with change in the social form of the product of labour,[150] leads also to a change of the social character of the labour of the commodity producer: through exchange of the product of his labour for the universal equivalent, his labour is included in the system of social division of labour; and through being equated with all other kinds of labour, it is converted from concrete into abstract [labour]. In the theory of value, we came to the conclusion that value is 'the production relation between autonomous commodity producers, expressed in the material form of equalisation of commodities and closely

---

148   Marx 1976, p. 199.
149   [A heading written into the margin].
150   Compare this with the apt observation by F. Petry: 'The metamorphosis of the commodity is a change in the social position of its producer, the private labour of the latter acquires the form of socially significant labour' (Petry 1916, pp. 64–5).

connected in its movement with the equilibrium and distribution of labour in the material process of production'.[151] In other words, there exists in commodity economy an equality of commodity producers, which is expressed in the equality of commodities and which, through this mediation, leads to the equalisation of labour. But how is such equalisation of commodity producers, commodities and labour possible in commodity economy, where such equalisation is not consciously produced, and where separate private commodity producers (the inequality of commodity producers), applying their labour at their own discretion in different branches of production (the inequality of concrete types of labour), produce items that are necessary to satisfy the most varied needs (the inequality of use-values)? The theory of money gives us the answer to this question. In the direct process of production, it is true that the separate private commodity producers, with the help of concrete labour expenditures, create the most varied use-values. But in the process of exchange a transformation occurs of the social character of the commodity owners, of the commodities and of labour. The detachment of one commodity, gold for example, in the form of universal equivalent, means that this commodity is equated with all others, its owner is socially equal to all other commodity owners, and the labour expended in gold mining is equated with all other types of commodities. Thus any commodity, through its exchange for gold, becomes equated with all other commodities (the conversion of use-value into exchange-value), and at the same time a change occurs both in the social character of its owner (the conversion of private into social labour) and of the labour expended upon it (the conversion of concrete into abstract labour). The result of the exchange process is the equality of commodity producers, the equation of commodities, and the equation of labour. This threefold equation, occurring in the real process of market exchange, is what Marx described in his teaching on the three peculiarities of the equivalent form.

The close connection between the three sides of the exchange process – the equality of commodity producers, the equation of commodities and the equation of labour – explains, in the final analysis, the fundamental specificity of commodity economy, which involves the 'reification' of people's production relations or 'commodity fetishism'. The commodity producers enter into a production relation between themselves only through exchanging the products of labour, and for each modification of the type of relations between people there is a corresponding modification of the social function or social form of things

---

151 [This excerpt comes from p. 60 of the first edition of Rubin's *Ocherki po teorii stoimosti Marksa*, Moscow: Gosizdat, 1923. For an English version see Rubin 1990].

through which these relations are established. Hence the close ties between the processes of equalisation of people, things and labour. In the chapter on money, Marx notes the dependence of these processes on the reification of people's production relations:

> There is an antithesis, immanent in the commodity, between *use-value and value*, between *private* labour which must simultaneously manifest itself as directly *social* labour, and a particular *concrete* kind of labour which simultaneously counts as *abstract* universal labour, between the *conversion of things into persons and the conversion of persons into things*; the antithetical phases of the metamorphosis of the commodity are the developed forms of motion of this immanent contradiction.[152]

The threefold characterisation of the process of equalisation, being the result of exchange, is sometimes replaced by Marx with a twofold characterisation of this process, leading to the equalisation of commodities and of labour. In the *Critique of Political Economy* Marx sees in the appearance of money a resolution of two of the fundamental difficulties of exchange: the first lies in the antithesis of use-value and exchange-value, and the second in the antithesis 'of the particular kinds of labour of private individuals' and 'universal social labour'.[153] The process of exchange, through the mediation of money, equalises things and equalises labour.[154] A more detailed development of this twofold formula is found in *Theories of Surplus-Value*:

> The fact that the *exchange-value* of the commodity *assumes an independent existence* in money is itself the result of the process of exchange, the development of the contradiction of *use-value and exchange-value* embodied in the commodity, and of another no less important contradiction embodied in it, namely, that the *definite, particular labour of the private individual* must manifest itself as its opposite, as *equal, necessary, general labour* and, in this form, *social labour*.[155]

This formulation is especially valuable because here Marx describes the process of the equalisation of labour as removing all the differences between the labours of separate commodity producers. One commodity producer stands

---

152 Marx 1976, p. 209.
153 Marx 1970, p. 45.
154 [The previous sentence is marked off in pencil in the margin].
155 Marx 1971, p. 130.

opposed to the other as a private person; he works in a particular sphere of production; the labour with which he busies himself has a certain degree of skill (which in some cases may be nil or even less than nil, i.e. may rank, in terms of skill, even below simple average labour); and finally, his labour expenditures are individual, differing qualitatively and quantitatively from the labour expenditures of other producers making the same product. This means that the labour of the commodity producer is private, concrete and skilled (i.e. having one or another degree of skill and individuality). In the process of exchange, through the equalisation of all products, a real connection is established between the separate spheres of production – the possibility of the ebb and flow of labour between them, a tendency towards a certain equilibrium between them. As a result of exchange, not only are all the private establishments equated (the conversion of private into social labour) as well as all the spheres of production or types of labour (the conversion of concrete into abstract labour), but additionally there is equalisation between types of labour that are distinguished by various degrees of skill (the conversion of skilled labour into simple) and of labour expenditures occurring in different enterprises of one and the same production sphere, involving different levels of productivity (the conversion of individual labour into socially necessary [labour]). Through the single act of exchange there is a simultaneous conversion of labour that is private, concrete, skilled and individual into labour that is social, abstract, simple and socially necessary. This is what Marx had in view in the formulation that we have given.[156] Hilferding gives the same kind of formula: 'The concerted action of commodities in exchange transforms private, individual and concrete labour time into the general, socially necessary and abstract labour time which is the essence of value'.[157] Hilferding omits here only the reduction of skilled labour to simple labour, which occurs simultaneously in the same process.

6   Measure of Value

Measure of value and medium of circulation. Economic science continues up to the present day the debate over whether the fundamental and original function of money is its role as measure of value or as medium of exchange. Some scholars point out that gold only becomes the measure of value for all other commodities if all those commodities exchange for it. Accordingly, the function as medium of circulation is primary (C[arl] Menger, K[arl] Helfferich).

---

156   By 'equal' Marx understands precisely simple, average, untrained labour, and by 'necessary' he understands socially necessary labour (see Marx 1971, p. 130). By 'universal' he means, as in the *Critique*, labour that is abstract.

157   Hilferding 1981, p. 33.

Other scholars object that gold is the universal medium of exchange only in those circumstances where, on the one hand, all commodities are evaluated in abstract units of account and, on the other hand, where a certain quantity of gold is equated with the same accounting unit (the rouble, for instance).[158] This means that the function as measure of value must be recognised as primary ([Gustav] Cassel, [Alfred] Amonn). Thus [each] function is, as it were, the logical presupposition of the other, and consequently the question that we have raised cannot be resolved by way of logical analysis.

Likewise, the question cannot be resolved through historical research. On the one hand, there is no doubt that long before all commodities began to be evaluated in gold, the latter already served as the mediator of exchange transactions, or as the medium of exchange. Yet, on the other hand, we know that in the most ancient times there were instances of the use of gold in the role of measure of value, although gold did not actually figure at the time in the act of exchange:

> In the third millennium B.C., for example, ancient Egyptians already used copper and gold (but not silver) as a money commodity and general measure of value, although the commodities appraised with the help of money exchanged directly for the most part. If a bull were involved in one such transaction, its price might be fixed at 119 copper utnu (14.4 kilograms of copper). It might be exchanged for a reed mat, appraised at 35 utnu, 5 measures of honey at 4 utnu, 8 measures of oil at 10 utnu, and seven other articles for the remainder. In this case, copper functions as the measure of value [although not as the medium of exchange – I.R.].[159]

The impossibility of resolving the question of the logical or historical priority of one or the other of these two functions of money has compelled many scholars to recognise both functions as fundamental, primary and of equal significance. Thus A[dolf] Wagner defines money as follows: 'Money, in the economic sense, is an object joining within itself two economic functions in the exchange transaction: as medium of circulation and as measure of value'.[160]

In Marxist literature, the most widespread view assigns decisive importance to money's function as measure of value. 'This function of money is also

---

158   [The sentence is marked off in pencil in the margin].
159   Kautsky 1923, p. 146. [Kautsky's essay was published originally in German in 1918. Although Rubin's text referred to the third *century* B.C., Kautsky was speaking of Egypt in the third *millennium* B.C. We have made the correction to Rubin's text.]
160   Wagner 1909, p. 119.

necessary and important for the development of commodity production, as important as circulation itself. Even in its capacity of medium of circulation, the money commodity is less important than in its role as measure of value'.[161] Still more decisive in this sense is Hilferding, who takes money's role as measure of value to be the fundamental feature in its definition: 'The object which is thus authorised by the common action of commodities to express the value of all other commodities is – money'.[162] Yet looking more closely at this definition convinces us that Hilferding did not succeed entirely in <u>eliminating from his definition the reference</u>[163] to money's role as medium of circulation. What does it mean to refer to the 'common action of commodities'? It means that a determinate thing has acquired the capacity to express the value of all commodities due to the fact that all commodities exchange for it, thus also giving it the character of medium of circulation.

In Marx we likewise do not find any direct answer to the question that interests us. A superficial reading of Marx might suggest that in various places he expresses contradictory opinions. In one place he says: 'It [gold – I.R.] thus acts as a universal measure of value, and only through performing this function does gold, the specific equivalent commodity, become money'.[164] It would appear that the function as measure of value is fundamental. But, 'On the other hand, gold serves as an ideal measure of value only because it has already established itself as the money commodity in the process of exchange'.[165] Evidently, Marx did not derive the function of medium of circulation from the function of measure of value.

In order to understand Marx's thinking properly, we must turn our attention to the specific feature of his doctrine concerning the functions of money. The separate 'functions' or 'determinate forms' of money are what Marx calls the properties of money, which, being acquired by a particular commodity as the result of long historical development, fuse with the natural form of this commodity and become, as it were, 'a social property inherent in its nature'.[166] Gold already appears in the circuit of exchange with the specific inherent functions of measure of value and medium of exchange, which thereby appear to be emerging not from the nature of the exchange circuit, i.e. from the social production relations of commodity owners, but from the nature of gold

---

161 Kautsky 1923, p. 146.
162 Hilferding 1981, p. 32.
163 [Underlined in pencil].
164 Marx 1976, p. 188.
165 Marx 1976, p. 198.
166 Marx 1976, p. 187.

itself.¹⁶⁷ Marx assumes the task of showing that these 'thing-like' properties of gold are only 'reified' or 'crystallised', i.e. they are fastened to gold as the results of production relations between people, more specifically, due to the continuously repeated social actions of commodity owners in the process of mutual and generalised exchange of the products of different kinds of labour through the mediation of gold. Marx wants to disclose this 'mediating movement' (the social activities of commodity owners – I.R.), which is visible¹⁶⁸ in the reified functions of money yet 'vanishes in its own result, leaving no trace behind'.¹⁶⁹

What we have been saying explains the specificity of Marx's method that distinguishes his teaching concerning the functions of money: *instead of deriving one reified function of money from the other, his goal is to derive both of these functions from the continuously repeated social activities and relations of the commodity owners*. Marx describes this process as follows. 'Commercial intercourse, in which the owners of commodities exchange and compare their own articles with various other articles, never takes place unless different kinds of commodities belonging to different owners are exchanged for, and equated as values with, one single further kind of commodity'.¹⁷⁰ That commodity plays the role of money, but only within the limits of the exchange relation in which it figures as the equivalent. It rapidly loses this transient equivalent form upon completion of this exchange relation between people, i.e. of 'the momentary social contacts which call it into existence'.¹⁷¹ In its rudimentary form of money, the commodity in question already simultaneously fulfils, in an elementary way, the function both of measure of value and of medium of circulation. As Marx shows, the other commodities 'are exchanged for'¹⁷² this third commodity and 'equated¹⁷³ as values' with it. In reality, however, this commodity fulfils the role of equivalent only momentarily, within the limits of the given exchange relation. Countless repetition of such acts of exchange, in which commodities exchange for one and the same third commodity and are equated with it as values, separate this commodity from the others and attach to it the permanent character of equivalent, or of money. Thereafter this commodity, gold for example, 'appears to have the equivalent form independently of this rela-

---

167 ['Itself' is underlined in pencil].
168 [Underlined in pencil].
169 Marx 1976, p. 187.
170 Marx 1976, pp. 182–3.
171 Marx 1976, p. 183.
172 [Underlined in pencil].
173 [Underlined in pencil].

tion',[174] i.e. independently of one act of exchange or another. In each exchange act gold appears with its character as money already 'crystallised' and fastened to it. It is only from this moment that the reified category of money appears, with its permanent[175] inherent functions: as measure of value and medium of exchange.

Thus the development of both functions of money occurs in parallel during one and the same social process. For a long time gold, not yet being the permanent bearer of these functions, fulfilled them in a series of separate exchange acts. With the gradual entry of gold into circulation, the products of labour increasingly begin to be evaluated in terms of gold, and conversely, the gradual spread of valuations in terms of gold reinforces the position of the latter as medium of circulation. Both sides of this process of the genesis and development of money are closely tied together and mutually support one another. The final result of this protracted process is the 'fixation' or 'crystallisation' in gold of both of the fundamental functions of money, since gold up to this time frequently – although sporadically and with lapses – already fulfilled both the role of the commodity for which other [commodities] 'exchanged' (i.e. medium of circulation) and also the role of the commodity with which they were equated (i.e. measure of value). It is precisely in this preparatory social process that one must look for the roots of both functions of money rather than deriving one function from the other. This is precisely why Marx, when analysing both of these functions, endeavours first of all to show how both of them, appearing at first sight to be inherent in gold itself, actually serve to reflect the overall social process of the exchange of commodities.

One-sided theories, which endeavour to derive one function of gold from the other, can only be explained in terms of ignoring the preparatory process of the development of money. But is it really possible to suggest that gold had already become the universal medium of circulation and only subsequently acquired the property of measure of value? The point is that before assuming its permanently fixed property as universal medium of circulation, gold already figured in countless exchange transactions while simultaneously serving as the material in which the exchanging commodities were evaluated. And conversely, can one suppose that it was only after gold became the generally recognised measure of value that it actually entered into circulation? Indeed, this would amount to thinking that someone produced in advance a general evaluation of all the

---

174   Marx 1976, p. 187.
175   [Underlined in pencil].

products of labour in terms of gold, including even the property of the commodity owners, and only then actually put gold into circulation.

The circumstance that both of these functions become affixed to gold as the result of a long process of development does not exclude the possibility that, in the course of further development, circumstances appear that cause a separation of the function of medium of circulation, which begins to be fulfilled by other kinds of metallic money (silver, copper) or by paper money alongside of or in place of gold.

What is a Measure of Value?

What, precisely, is the function of money as measure of value – economists give the most diverse, and sometimes totally unclear, answers to this question. In most cases, these answers suffer from an individualistic-rationalistic approach to the question. The economist asks why the individual, when participating in commodity exchange, requires a measure of value for commodities. Finding one or another answer, i.e. having indicated the benefit or convenience that the individual might derive in exchange by using a universal measure of value, the economist considers that the social nature of the latter has already been clarified, although by this point he has sometimes not even begun to consider real economic phenomena, confining his attention entirely to an analysis of rationalistic arguments showing the benefit of using a measure of value.

[A] *The subjective theory*.[176] Among supporters of the theory of subjective value one often finds, either directly or implicitly, the notion that a measure of value is required for measuring (or comparing) the marginal utility of different products. In their opinion, the exchange act is the result of a psychic[177] act of measurement (or comparison) of the marginal utility of the products being exchanged. In order for the exchange participant more easily to determine the subjective marginal utility of different products, he needs to have a definite unit of measurement. The marginal utility of a unit of gold is used, as an item of luxury that serves to satisfy certain needs and thus possesses a known utility.

This notion differs so radically from reality that even a majority of the supporters of the theory of subjective value do not consider it possible to

---

176   [A heading written into the margin].
177   [In the original version of Rubin's text, the Russian word used here is 'психологический' (psychological), but a note in the margin said this should be replaced by 'психический' (psychic)].

apply it so directly to the phenomena of exchanging the commodity for money. Leaving aside the general question of whether the objective act of the equation of commodities can be explained by the subjective appraisals of parties to the exchange, there is no doubt that in the exchange of the commodity for money a subjective appraisal of the marginal utility of the money material (gold) generally does not occur in reality. 'If he (a party to the exchange – I.R.) wishes to use means of payment in a circular manner (i.e. for exchange – I.R.), then he is interested only in their significance, which is a juridical property; the type and quantity of the thing is a matter of indifference to him'.[178] Knapp is mistaken, of course, when he substitutes the juridical significance of money for its 'economic' significance, i.e. for its objective purchasing power. But he and his supporters are absolutely correct in denying the fact of any subjective appraisal of the money material's utility on the part of the participants in the exchange. But it is pointless when economists who share Knapp's view in this regard accuse all of their opponents – indiscriminately lumping them together under the tag of 'metallists' – of locating the fundamental value of money in the value of the money material as 'a means of satisfying some need and as an item for subjective appraisals'.[179] In Marxist theory, the money material plays a role (insofar as it is a matter of developed commodity society, not of the primitive forms of money) not as an item for subjective appraisals but rather as the product of a determinate quantity of labour.

[B] *Subjective labour value*.[180] However, this generally accepted position in Marxist theory is not understood by everyone in the same way. Often Marx's theory of value is understood to mean that commodity owners, in the act of exchange, equate two different products with one another on the basis of recognising them as products of different quantities of abstract labour. Such a subjective-individualistic understanding of the theory of labour [underlined in pencil] value leads to the following sort of theory of money. Money serves commodity owners as an instrument for stating and measuring the amounts of abstract labour contained in commodities. In a weakened form we encounter this sort of view in I[osif] A. Trakhtenberg:

> Each act of exchange requires a qualitative comparison of the products and a quantitative comparison. To compare them quantitatively means

---

178 Knapp 1921, p. 36.
179 Schumpeter 1917, p. 640.
180 [A heading written into the margin].

to determine the amount of socially necessary labour embodied in each commodity, taken in abstraction from all their concrete properties. In order to determine this quantity, it is necessary to have something that can serve as a *pure embodiment of abstract labour*, by means of which commodities can be equated with each other and the abstract human labour embodied in each commodity may be quantitatively compared.[181]

Evidently I.A. Trakhtenberg is interested in the objective and not the subjective side of this process, but his manner of presentation leads to understanding it in a subjective-individualistic sense. In reality, commodities are not equated with each other because the commodity owners subjectively equate their labour; rather, the objective process of equating different kinds of labour occurs as a result of, and by means of, the equation of commodities as values in the market. The commodity owners are not subjectively concerned with ascertaining the amount of abstract labour in commodities. Commodities do not equate with gold because the latter is a 'pure embodiment of abstract labour'; to the contrary, gold is the embodiment of abstract labour because all commodities equate with it.

[c] *Equilibrium through price*.[182] As in the theory of value, so also in the theory of money we must exclude from the concept of 'measure of value' any subjective-individualistic elements and envision the entire process objectively. In commodity economy, the distribution of social labour between different branches of production occurs spontaneously by means of the expansion of production in the more profitable ones and contraction in the less profitable ones. Equilibrium between separate branches of production can be established in the conditions of a simple commodity economy only when their products exchange in proportion to the labour that is socially necessary for their production. To the condition of equilibrium between two given branches of production corresponds a determinate, normal ratio of exchange between their products, which corresponds to the labour values of the latter. Any deviation of the actual proportions of the market exchange of these products, either upwards or downwards from this normal proportion, evokes a redistribution of labour between the two branches, an outflow of labour from the one into the other.

---

181 Trakhtenberg 1922, pp. 17–18.
182 [A heading written into the margin].

Such is the general scheme of equilibrium in commodity economy insofar as we have in view the process of direct equation in the market of the products of two different production branches, between which is directly established, in this way, a certain condition of equilibrium. But to the extent that, in the process of exchange, one specific commodity (gold) is singled out, for which all other commodities most frequently exchange and with which they are equated, the scheme of equilibrium that we developed above takes on a different and more complex form. The direct exchange of two commodities gives way to indirect monetary exchange through the mediation of a third commodity, gold. Now the products of the two different branches of production are equated with one another indirectly, through the equation of each with one and the same third commodity, gold. And since, in commodity economy, the process of market equation of the products of labour as values is closely connected with the process of distribution of labour between the corresponding branches of production, it follows that evolution of the first process from direct to monetary exchange is also inevitably accompanied by fundamental changes in the process of the distribution of social labour.

We are leaving aside here changes of a material character that result from the development of money economy, i.e. the transition of separate establishments, under the influence of steadily growing monetary exchange, into another type of occupation or a different kind of labour (for instance, the movement from one agricultural crop to another, the squeezing out of household industrial production with the expansion of commercial agriculture, the curtailment of agriculture in favour of industry, etc.). Here we are interested only in change of a formal character, i.e. *change of the social form of the process itself, which establishes equilibrium in the distribution of social labour between the different branches of production.* From this point forward, with the development of monetary exchange, the flow of labour from one branch into another is regulated by the movement of monetary prices for their products, i.e. by the sum of money that can be acquired from their sale in the market. The distribution of social labour between branches A and B now depends directly not upon a change of the proportions in which their products exchange for one another, but rather upon a change of the proportions in which each of them exchanges for gold, i.e. upon their price. Equilibrium in the distribution of labour between branch A on the one hand, and all the other branches of production on the other, is established by a determinate price for products of A that corresponds to their labour value. If their market price falls below this normal price, production in branch A contracts, i.e. a redistribution of productive forces occurs from branch A into more profitable branches. The opposite occurs if the market price rises above this normal price. In other words, even before their products are sold in the market, the producers already have a mental appraisal of them in terms of gold, i.e. they count upon receiving a definite selling price with which they will continue production of the given products in the same volume as before. Any deviation of market prices, either upwards or downwards from this anticipated price, will cause a contraction or expansion of production in the given branch. Thus, the anticipated normal price, or the normal valuation of the product, is the regulator of the distribution of labour between a given branch of production and the others. It corresponds to a condition of equilibrium between them, and since the latter occurs with the exchange of the products of different kinds of labour according to their values, it follows that the preliminary appraisal of the products is an expression of their value and that money, in this act of appraisal, fulfils the function of measure of value.

[D] *Isolated evaluation*.[183] Let us now consider this act of evaluating a commodity prior to its sale in more detail, in the form it takes in reality. The cloth producer appraises a yard of cloth in advance as being worth 3 roubles, i.e. he equates it with a certain sum of gold. This act can be regarded either from the side of the object of exchange (a thing), or from the side of its subject (a person). In the first case, we have before us a definite rate of exchange between things, their equality with one another, which initially appears to follow from their properties. It seems to us that the yard of cloth possesses the unique ability to exchange for 3 roubles: 'It is the private task, so to speak, of the individual commodity to give itself a form of value, and it accomplishes this task without the aid of the others'.[184] We have a unique act of equality between two things. From the side of the subject of the exchange, the same act appears to us as a certain subjective appraisal of the cloth, arising from one or another motive and equating one product with the other according to the significance attached to them by the subject. We have a single act with a subjective-psychological[185] character. In both instances, the appraisal appears as a separate, isolated act, involving only the particular individual and two particular commodities. This seemingly isolated character of the evaluation of commodities is explained by the fact that the latter initially appears in a 'simple form of value', as an act of equality between only two commodities. But if one of these commodities (gold) is already the universal equivalent, with which all other commodities are

---

183   [A heading written into the margin].
184   Marx 1976, pp. 158–9.
185   [In the margin, 'subjective-psychological' is replaced by 'subjective-psychic'. See above, footnote 177].

equated and also exchange, then what we actually have is not a singular but a universal form of value, not an individual act of appraisal but an act having a social character.

The social character of the act of evaluation[186] appears first of all in the fact that it presupposes certain definite social conditions as being given. The latter refer to the *social form* of the process of production and exchange and also to its *technical aspect*. The given act of appraising a yard of cloth as being worth 3 roubles presupposes: 1) that all commodity producers evaluate their products in terms of gold, i.e. assign the form of price to their exchange-values; and 2) that labour productivity in the cloth industry is at such a level that sale of the cloth at the price of 3 roubles per yard corresponds to a condition of equilibrium between the cloth industry and the other branches of production. The first condition, expressing a determinate social form of the process of reproduction (including both production and exchange), makes the act of evaluation possible in qualitative terms. The second condition, expressing a determinate condition of the technique of production, makes the same act of evaluation possible in quantitative terms.

[E] *The qualitative aspect.*[187] In the act of appraisal 'one has to distinguish a qualitative and a quantitative aspect'.[188] Let us first consider the former. From the qualitative side, the act of appraisal means the equation of one concrete commodity (cloth) with another concrete commodity (gold), which in turn is already equated with all other commodities and has thus acquired the character of an abstract commodity, i.e. a commodity that can take the shape of any use-value. In being equated with gold, the cloth is equated with all other commodities and acquires the ability to exchange for any other commodity. The concrete labour of the cloth producer is thereby also equated with all other kinds of labour. Use-value becomes exchange-value, while private and concrete labour becomes social and abstract labour. The act of evaluation means a qualitative change (for the time being expected and ideal) of the social nature of both the product of labour and of the labour itself.

However, such a change in the social nature of the cloth, through its equation with gold, already presupposes a difference between their social natures, i.e. it already presupposes the collective activities of all commodity producers, consisting of the fact that they exchange all of their products for gold and thus

---

186   ['Its social character' is written in the margin].
187   [A heading written into the margin].
188   Marx 1970, p. 66.

impart to the latter the character of universal equivalent or money. By means of its equation with gold, the cloth can be evaluated, i.e. can acquire a price, which expresses its exchange-value, only provided that all other commodities are evaluated in terms of gold. 'Gold becomes the measure of value only because the exchange-value of all commodities is estimated in terms of gold'.[189] 'If the values of all commodities were measured in silver or wheat or copper, and accordingly expressed in terms of silver, wheat or copper prices, then silver, wheat or copper would become the measure of value and consequently universal equivalents'.[190] Apart from such 'universal action of all other commodities',[191] i.e. apart from the collective actions of all commodity producers, the particular act of evaluating the cloth would be impossible since by this act the cloth, through the mediation of gold, is equated with all other commodities, i.e. gold in this case fulfils the role of money.

> The general form of value can only arise as the joint contribution of the whole world of commodities. A commodity only acquires a general expression of its value if, at the same time, all other commodities express their values in the same equivalent; and every newly emergent commodity must follow suit.[192]

These words from Marx emphasise all the more strongly the dependence of the act of evaluation by the given producer on the activities of all the other commodity producers. The given producer can evaluate his product in terms of gold as money (and not gold as a concrete product) only provided that all other commodity producers do the same thing simultaneously. And conversely, in the latter circumstance our commodity producer is also compelled to evaluate his product in gold and, in response to the fluctuations of market prices for this product in terms of gold, to expand or curtail his production.

[F] *The quantitative aspect.*[193] We now turn from the qualitative aspect of the act of evaluation to its quantitative aspect. It is not only cloth in general that equates with gold as the universal equivalent but a specific quantity of cloth, 1 yard, which equates with a specific quantity of gold, 3 roubles. Gold

---

189   Ibid.
190   Ibid.
191   Marx 1970, p. 46.
192   Marx 1976, p. 159.
193   [A heading written into the margin].

is already not just the universal equivalent but also the measure of value.[194] The evaluation of a yard of cloth as 3 roubles does not mean that its producer will never, in any circumstances, agree to sell the particular yard of cloth more cheaply; in a bad market conjuncture he will be forced to do so. On the other hand, this does not mean that the cloth producer would not like to receive more for it; in a favourable conjuncture he will attempt to raise his price. Finally, the evaluation of the cloth also does not mean that in this way the producer summarises his subjective appraisals of the usefulness of a yard of cloth on the one hand and of a certain quantity of gold on the other. The evaluation of a yard of cloth as 3 roubles represents a preliminary mental statement of the proportion of exchange with which the producer wishes to and is able to continue the reproduction of cloth on the former scale.[195] This preliminary evaluation or normal estimate of the commodity is a mental anticipation of the conditions of the market conjuncture that correspond to a state of equilibrium in the economy. It serves as regulator for the individual commodity producer, to which he adjusts his economic activity. A deviation of market prices above or below this normal calculation leads him to expand or curtail production.

[G] *The continuity of price formation.*[196] The ability of the commodity producer, through his calculation, to anticipate the condition of equilibrium in the social economy is explained by the fact that this calculation is itself the result and reflection of a long and spontaneous process of interaction and mutual adjustment of all the branches of the economy, between which a relative condition of equilibrium is ultimately established through numerous frictions and disruptions. This equilibrium corresponds to a specific condition of the productive forces in the various branches of production and is sustained (with constant deviations) by the mechanism of fluctuations in market prices around an average level that corresponds to the labour value of individual products in the conditions of a simple commodity economy. The result of this process of mutual adjustment between all the branches of production is a certain average evaluation of their products, which in the calculation of the producer becomes a mental anticipation (expectation) of the future condition of equilibrium between these branches of production.

---

194 [The statement is marked off in pencil in the margin].
195 In the analysis of the theory of money we abstract from the phenomena of expanded reproduction.
196 [A heading written into the margin].

With the given state of labour productivity in the cloth industry, specifically, with a price of 3 roubles per yard, which corresponds to the labour value of the cloth, equilibrium is established (in the form of a tendency) between this branch of production and all the others. The average price of 3 roubles – a result and sedimentation of a long process of competition – is already fixed as the normal evaluation for a yard of cloth. This precisely fixed price of 3 roubles also serves as starting point for the producer in the process of calculating his commodity. In the event of a change in the conditions of production – for example, an increase in the price of material, a cheapening of production due to technical improvements etc. – this figure will be subject, of course, to correction and change. But the producer, in any case, has a starting point for his calculation, in which the social process of competition has already been summarised and the condition of the productive forces in the given branch has been objectively taken into account. The producer has no need, with each new production process, to begin all of his calculations anew or to involve himself with a subjective accounting of labour productivity and of the labour value of the product (failure to understand this point is where the error lies in the theory of subjective labour value). He begins with prices that are already determined, namely, with the given prices for material, machines and so forth (i.e. the costs of production) on the one hand, and with an assumed and anticipated price for his product on the other. Marx never thought to deny that each given state of prices arises on the basis of the previous state of prices, nor did he ever assert that with each new production process the evaluation is derived[197] [-underlined in pencil] anew on the basis of the labour values of the products.[198] However, one must not of course – as happens with the cost-of-production theory – take this observation of a fact, that is, of the incessancy of price changes and of the connection between separate phases of price formation, as a causal explanation. It is still necessary to disclose the causes that regulate both the relative magnitudes of average prices for different commodities and also, particularly, their movement, i.e. the process of their changes. The task of the theory of value is to find these causes.

Thus, the quantitative aspect of the act of evaluation also turns out to be dependent upon social conditions. This dependence is manifested in the fact that: 1) evaluation is not an expression of subjective appraisals by the producer but rather of the objective condition of the productive forces; 2) this condition

---

197 [The word used in the text is 'выводится'].
198 Marx was accused of this by A. Graziadei (see Graziadei 1923, pp. 17, 38–9, 67, 104, 106 et seq.).

of the productive forces is summarised in the form of evaluation or the calculation of commodities not by the efforts of a single commodity producer, but by the collective activities of all commodity producers, the result of which serves as the starting point for the act of evaluation by the given producer. In other words, a change in the productive forces is not registered directly in the consciousness of the commodity producer <u>in the form of a corresponding change in subjective value</u> [underlined in pencil], but rather evokes a series of collective actions on the part of commodity producers (the curtailment and expansion of production, the move from one branch of industry to another, etc.), whose result is objectified or 'crystallised' in the social properties of things, for example, as certain average prices, which in turn are already noted and taken into account in the consciousness of the individual commodity producer and serve as the point of departure for his calculations. Thus, the dependence of the act of evaluation of the commodity upon the preceding state of prices expresses nothing other than the dependence of the individual producer's activities upon social conditions.

[H] *The continuity of reproduction.*[199] The uninterrupted process of price formation, which we have been describing, reflects the uninterrupted process of reproduction. It does not begin with a clean slate but already presupposes the results of past production that are fixed in the form of determinate prices. Although social relations only connect the commodity producers indirectly through the act of market exchange and are interrupted thereafter, their result is to affix to the products of labour a determinate social character, for example, determinate average prices. Once the commodity producer has purchased material, machines and other things on the market and put them into operation in the process of production, they have ceased to be commodities and become elements of production, but this does not mean that the social form that these commodities acquired in the exchange process (their determinate exchange-value or price) vanishes without a trace when the latter is completed. On the contrary, it becomes fixed and crystallised in these things as a social property that appears to inhere in them and is preserved by them upon completion of the production relation of purchase and sale in which they have been involved in the market. The cotton, having left the market for the spinner's workshop, does not cease to be regarded by him as a thing with a determinate price. In his technical operations with the cotton, he must not for a moment forget the price of this kind of material. Thus the prices that are established

---

199 [A heading written into the margin].

in the process of exchange continue their activity in the ensuing process of production. On the other hand, since the given process of production must be followed once more by the process of exchange, the prospects for the product's future realisation are already considered, calculated and taken into account in the process of production itself. The product, while it is still in the production process and has yet to become a commodity, already has an anticipated price that is expressed, as we discussed in detail above, in its evaluation or normal accounting.

Thus, if we said in the theory of value that in the direct production process the given commodity producer acts independently of other commodity producers – the anarchy of commodity production – with whom he is connected only in the process of exchange, this statement would be correct insofar as we spoke of the processes of production and exchange while considering each separately, from an abstract point of view. In actual reality, however, the given process of production is only one of the repeating phases of an uninterrupted social process of reproduction, a phase that precedes and is followed by the act of exchange. For this reason, the dense network of social connections, which tightly ties the producer to the process of exchange in the market, is not interrupted during the intervening period of production but rather continues its activity as the result of the preceding process of exchange and as anticipation of the one to come. This network of social connections, through its offshoots of the past and filaments of the future, embraces the production process, thereby establishing the continuity of social connections between people, and of the social form of things, throughout the entire process of reproduction. The commodity producer, whose activity in his workshop is formally autonomous and independent of other commodity producers, in reality does not escape for a moment from this dense network of social ties that unite him with them and determine his economic activity. In exactly the same way, the means of production located in his workshop, as well as the finished product gradually maturing from them, cannot for a moment be considered as purely technical elements of production, deprived of social form. Removed to the quiet of the workshop, and absorbed by the technical process of production, they are momentarily not active carriers of the production relations between people, but this does not cause them to lose their character as carriers of past and future production relations. They preserve the imprint of their social origin and destiny. Herein lies the fundamental sociological meaning of Marx's teaching concerning the measure of value, which represents nothing other than a doctrine of the *evaluation of the product of labour in the process of production, which precedes the act of exchange.*

[1] *Evaluation prior to exchange.*[200] Marx strongly emphasises that the act of evaluating the commodity in terms of money occurs even prior to the latter's entry into the exchange process – not in the sense that in the act of exchange itself, before paying his money, the buyer must establish a price for the commodity through mutual agreement with the seller,[201] but in the sense described above of the normal calculation or evaluation of the product that occurs during the actual process of production. The fixation of exchange proportions, with a formal mutual agreement between seller and buyer (in fact it may be determined unilaterally by the seller or by the buyer), occurs not only in regular but also in the casual exchange of two commodities, and not only in monetary but also in natural exchange. It is another matter with the evaluation of the product that precedes the exchange act itself, occurring in the production process and anticipating the conditions in which normal reproduction can continue, and which can preserve the equilibrium between the given branch of production and the others. It is precisely this act of preliminary evaluation of the product that is an indispensable attribute of commodity production. The latter is characterised not by the fact that products of labour are sold, but by the fact that they are already produced for the purpose of sale. With occasional exchange, the product of labour acquires a passing form as an object of exchange (a commodity) only at the very moment of the exchange, without being a commodity or exchange-value either before or after the exchange act. 'The articles A and B in this case are not as yet commodities, but become so only through the act of exchange'.[202] This means that we still do not have commodity production as a determinate and stable system of production relations between people, with the corresponding reified category of value as a stable social form of the thing. Commodity production develops only to the extent that the products of labour begin to be produced '*intentionally for the purpose of exchange*'.[203] Once products are produced especially 'for the purpose of being exchanged', 'their character as values has already to be taken into consideration *during production*'.[204] And this becomes evident precisely in the fact that in the production process itself the product is assigned a definite evaluation based upon the previous exchange process, with its inherent phenomena of price formation, and in anticipation of price formation in the future process of exchange.

---

200   [A heading written into the margin].
201   This is how I.A. Trakhtenberg sees the function of money as measure of value (Trakhtenberg 1922, pp. 30–1).
202   Marx 1976, p. 181.
203   Marx 1976, p. 182 [Rubin's emphasis].
204   Marx 1976, p. 166 [Rubin's emphasis].

Once the product already acquires a preliminary evaluation in the production process itself, the consequence is that it enters the exchange process possessing an exchange-value already determined and corresponding to its price. Marx is forceful in emphasising this condition. 'Commodities enter into the process of exchange with a *determinate price*'[205] and as 'use-values with determinate prices'.[206] Marx refers to the absurd hypothesis that 'commodities enter into the process of circulation without a price'.[207] These persistent comments by Marx have usually been understood in the sense that during the working up of the product, in the course of production, a certain quantity of socially necessary labour is already expended so that the value of the product is consequently determined not by the conditions of market exchange but by the technical conditions that characterise the production process and by the act of exchange that precedes it. However, such an understanding has the effect of narrowing Marx's meaning. Marx claimed that in the production process itself we already have in finished form not only certain technical conditions but also a determinate social form of production (production for the purpose of sale, or a commodity economy). For that reason, the product of labour is already, in the production process itself, not only the result of a determinate labour expenditure but also a thing with a determinate social form, namely, a commodity that has acquired a certain evaluation in terms of money. Marx's teaching on the function of a measure of value, which is fulfilled by money even prior to the process of circulation, will only become fully understandable to us in connection with his teaching that the character of things 'as values has already to be taken into consideration during production', and that the product of labour therefore acquires a certain evaluation already in the production process itself and enters into the process of circulation with a determinate price. But in order to understand this possibility of an evaluation of the product of labour even prior to the act of exchange, we must remember that before the given process of production there was already a process of exchange, the results of which, in the form of the determinate social properties of things and the system of prices for different commodities, serve in turn as the presuppositions of the given process of production.

[J] *The ideal character of evaluation.*[208] Once the act of evaluation of the commodity takes place even before the latter enters into exchange, it follows that

---

205   Marx 1970, p. 87.
206   Marx 1970, p. 88.
207   Marx 1976, p. 220.
208   [A heading written into the margin].

this act has an ideal character, and 'in its function as measure of value, money therefore serves only in an imaginary or ideal capacity'.[209] The preliminary evaluation of the product establishes, so to speak, an 'equilibrium price' of the commodity, i.e. the level of price that corresponds to the condition of equilibrium between the given branch of production and the others. And since in commodity society, with its anarchy of production, such an equilibrium condition is possible only as an ideal average, from which the actual distribution of social labour constantly deviates in one direction or another, this preliminary evaluation of the commodity is only an anticipation of its ideal average price, from which prices also constantly deviate upwards or downwards. 'The establishment of their price is merely their ideal conversion into the universal equivalent, an equation with gold which still has to be put into practice'.[210] The possibility of realising this preliminary and ideal evaluation of the commodity on the market 'depends on whether or not the [commodity] turns out to be a use-value, whether or not the quantity of labour time contained in it proves to be the quantity of labour time necessarily required by society for [its] production'.[211]

Here we encounter a very essential difference between price, i.e. the exchange value of the commodity, expressed in money, and the exchange-value that we investigated in the theory of value. In the theory of value, we presupposed equilibrium between the separate branches of production so that the products of different types of labour equate with each other as values, and the same holds for different types of labour. But, in commodity economy, such an equation of labour is not a conscious presupposition of the social process of production, only the result of a spontaneous process of competition, with inequalities and disproportions that inevitably arise in the distribution of labour. This peculiarity of commodity economy is also reflected in evaluation of the commodity in terms of money, demonstrating that the equation of a given commodity with all other commodities, and thus of a given type of labour with all others, is not an accomplished fact but is only subject to future realisation.[212] Equation of a given commodity with all others is only possible through its equation with gold. But gold, precisely because all other commodities are equated through its mediation (i.e. all commodity producers exchange their products for gold), possesses the special social form of money, which does not characterise all other commodities. This specific feature of the detached

---

209   Marx 1976, p. 190.
210   Marx 1970, p. 68.
211   Marx 1970, p. 69.
212   [The end of this sentence is set off in the margin with a question mark '?'].

commodity, or money, consists of the fact that it can always be exchanged for any concrete commodity, whereas the latter cannot always be exchanged for gold. The evaluation of the yard of cloth as 3 roubles means that it is possible at any moment to acquire a yard of cloth for 3 roubles; it does not mean that, conversely, the yard of cloth can at any moment exchange for 3 roubles.[213] This means that evaluation of the commodity in terms of gold involves both the moment of their equality (equation of the commodity with gold) and also the moment of inequality (the difference between the social form of money and the social form of the commodity). In other words, equation of the given commodity with all others has not yet occurred and depends upon whether it is actually equated in the market with gold, with which it is unequal in terms of social form. Evaluation of the commodity, therefore,

> entails the necessity for alienation of commodities in exchange for glittering gold and thus the possibility of their non-alienation. In short, there is here contained in latent form the whole contradiction which arises because the product is a commodity, or because the particular labour of an isolated individual can become socially effective only if it is expressed as its direct opposite, i.e., abstract universal labour.[214]

The act of evaluating the commodity reveals its ideal character not only because, as an ideal act, it precedes the process of exchange, but also because its realisation by way of the latter is always completed more or less approximately, with deviations of the market price upwards or downwards compared with the evaluation. 'The possibility, therefore, of a quantitative incongruity between price and the magnitude of value, i.e., the possibility that the price may diverge from the magnitude of value, is inherent in the price-form itself'.[215]

7 *Medium of Circulation*

From the ideal act of evaluating the commodity, which precedes the process of circulation, Marx then turns to the latter. Only in the actual process of circulation is it discovered how far the commodity can be realised in accordance with its preliminary evaluation, in other words, the degree to which the market price approaches the commodity's value. The greater is the factual deviation of labour distribution between individual branches of production from a propor-

---

213 Marx 1976, p. 196.
214 Marx 1970, pp. 69–70.
215 Marx 1976, p. 196.

tional distribution of social labour, the greater will be the deviation of market price from value. A ten-hour expenditure of labour by a given producer may, on the market, be reduced to five hours of socially necessary labour, i.e. the product of his ten hours of private and concrete labour may be sold on the market at a price corresponding only to five hours of social and abstract labour. This can occur because, at the current moment, there is a lack of social demand (expressed as effective demand) for the given product; because the volume of production of the given product quantitatively exceeded the current demand for it; or because the given producer works in backward technical conditions and his individual labour expenditure exceeds the average, socially necessary labour.[216]

Investigating the function of money as medium of circulation, Marx uses the same method as when studying the function of money as measure of value. At first sight, it seemed to us that money, in itself, has the property of measuring the value of the commodity. Marx showed that it acquires such a property as the result of a long process of the generalised equation of all commodities with one another through the mediation of money, i.e. as the result of the 'generalised activity of all commodities', which in fact represents the generalised activity of all commodity producers. Marx takes the same approach in analysing the medium of circulation. At first sight it seems that money, on its own, possesses the property of medium of circulation: it buys every sort of commodity, as if setting them in motion with its own force. Marx derives this 'reified' property of money, however, from the movement of the commodities themselves, which reflects, in turn, certain activities and interconnections between the commodity producers themselves. Accordingly, Marx first of all analyses the movement, or the 'metamorphosis of commodities', and only subsequently turns to the 'circulation of money'.

Turning to analysis of the process of commodity circulation, Marx distinguishes within it two aspects: *Stoffwechsel* and *Formwechsel* – the 'metabolism' of things and the 'change of forms'. 'Insofar as the process of exchange transfers commodities from hands in which they are non use-values into hands in which they are use-values', this process is a social exchange of things, i.e. a movement of material things.[217] The 'material moment' of this process consists of the fact that: 1) there first of all occurs a real 'exchange of the commodity for gold', of 'an ordinary commodity and the money commodity',[218] both of which move,

---

216 Marx 1976, p. 202.
217 Marx 1976, p. 198.
218 Marx 1976, p. 199.

in the form of determinate material things, in opposing directions: the commodity from the hands of the seller into those of the buyer, and the gold from the hands of the buyer into those of the seller; and 2) after this happens, the same opposing movement of commodity and gold is repeated once more: the former seller now parts with his gold and receives in exchange the products that he requires. As a result of this entire process, 'the product of one kind of useful labour replaces that of another'.[219] 'As far as concerns its material content, the movement is C–C, the exchange of one commodity for another, the exchange of quantities of social labour, in whose result the process itself becomes extinguished'[220] (i.e. the social aspect of the process).

As we can see from the foregoing, the material-technical side of the circulation process, consisting of the movement of things (commodities and gold) from hand to hand, conceals from us its social form, which is the real subject matter of Marx's investigation. Things interest Marx only as the 'carriers' of production relations between people, i.e. not in terms of their material-technical properties but in terms of their social form or social properties, which they acquire only in the presence of determinate production relations between people. The things, which appear in the circulation process and at first sight are distinguished only by their material properties (gold and the other commodities), are in fact distinguished from one another by their social forms. Gold enters the exchange process as a product of labour that is already equated with all other commodities, able to exchange directly for any other commodity, and for that reason fulfilling the special social function of universal equivalent or the expression of abstract-social labour. The commodity opposes gold as a product of labour yet to be equated with other commodities, in other words, as the product of private and concrete labour. Once the commodity and gold are distinguished by their different social forms, the exchange of the commodity for gold means not just the replacement of one material thing by another but also a change in the very social form of the thing (*Formwechsel*). Marx is interested in precisely this 'change in form or the metamorphosis of commodities',[221] which serves the social exchange of things. His goal is to investigate 'the whole process in its formal aspect',[222] that is, the social form rather than the material properties of the products of labour.

But Marx cannot stop there. The point is that the entire social form of things is a reflection of a determinate social form of labour organisation, i.e.

---

219 Marx 1976, p. 198.
220 Marx 1976, p. 200.
221 Marx 1976, p. 199.
222 Marx 1976, p. 198.

of determinate production relations between people. The circulation process is not only *the material movement of things* (the exchange of things) and *the change of their social forms* (the metamorphosis of commodities), but also the movement of *production relations* between individual commodity producers who are the participants in exchange. The contrast between the social form of the commodity and money reflects the contrast between the different social activities fulfilled by the seller and the buyer.

> These two antithetical transmutations of the commodity are accomplished through two antithetical social processes in which the commodity-owner takes part, and are reflected in the antithetical economic characteristics of the two processes. By taking part in the act of sale, the commodity-owner becomes a seller; in the act of purchase, he becomes a buyer.[223]

As we know from the theory of commodity fetishism, the differentiation of production relations between commodity owners, consisting of the fact that in the act of exchange they fulfil opposing roles (as buyer and seller), finds 'reified' expression in the differentiation of the social form of the things being exchanged (the commodity and money). Differentiation of the products of labour into the commodity and money results from a change of production relations between commodity owners and the squeezing out of natural exchange. But once the altered exchange relation has congealed or become 'reified' in the form of the money function of a detached commodity (gold), possession of the latter by a given commodity owner also determines his role in the act of exchange as buyer; and conversely, the commodity owner's possession of other commodities (i.e. ordinary commodities), apart from the one that has become detached, predetermines his role in the given exchange act as seller. Thus, if the social forms of the commodity and money result from a determinate structure of the economy and of the production relations between people, so, on the other hand, the position of the individual in a given concrete act of exchange is determined by the social form of the things belonging to him. In the exchange process 'they confront one another in the antithetical roles of buyer and seller, one personifying a sugar-loaf, the other gold. Just as the sugar-loaf becomes gold, so the seller becomes a buyer'.[224] The change in the 'social character' of the commodity owners occurs in parallel with the change in the

---

223 Marx 1976, p. 206.
224 Marx 1970, pp. 94–5.

social form of things. To understand the latter process, it is necessary to clarify the particular characteristics of the former.

It is not surprising, therefore, that in this case, as in other parts of his system, Marx concentrates his attention on an investigation of the type of production relations between people that assigns a special form to money circulation. We find such an analysis of the production relations between people in Marx's well-known teaching on the circuit C–M–C.

A researcher who begins his analysis with the external phenomena of money circulation will see in the latter nothing more than 'a mass of random purchases and sales taking place simultaneously'.[225] Each of these acts is absolutely no different from the others, [all of them] representing exchange of a commodity for money. The very same act that, from the seller's side represents sale or C–M, from the buyer's side is the purchase M–C. In each of these acts, money plays the role of means of purchase and successively realises the prices of various commodities that on their own appear to be immobile.[226] Once commodity c_1 has been purchased with a particular rouble, the former seller, with the same rouble, purchases another commodity c_2, while the former owner of the [second commodity] uses the same rouble to purchase c_3 and so on. All of these acts of exchange are uncoordinated and not in any way connected. A new commodity figures in each of them and has nothing in common with the previous one. Each commodity is sold only once, i.e. it exchanges only one time for money and then immediately enters into the buyer's sphere of consumption. The entire process of exchange has the appearance of a chaotic mass of purchases and sales, randomly coinciding or occurring successively with nothing to link them together.

In order to find a lawful pattern in this seeming chaos, we must refocus our attention away from money and commodities as such and onto the commodity producers. 'The two moments of this metamorphosis are at once distinct transactions [by the commodity owner] – selling, or the exchange of commodity for money, and buying, or the exchange of the money for a commodity – and the unity of the two acts: selling in order to buy'.[227] As soon as we take the commodity producer as the starting point for our investigation, the acts of exchange quickly arrange themselves in a definite, lawful and necessary sequence. The actions of each commodity producer must follow in definite order: first the sale C–M and then the purchase M–C, with the sale being completed precisely

---

225   Marx 1970, p. 98.
226   Marx 1970, p. 100.
227   Marx 1976, p. 200.

for the purpose of becoming able to make a purchase, in other words, a regular sequence of one act after another resulting from the internal connection between them. And this internal connection, in turn, is determined by the fundamental character of commodity economy.

Once the commodity producers are connected with each other by the social division of labour and are producing commodities for the market, the process of production must be followed by the process of circulation. Only the latter enables the commodity producer to acquire 'his other means of subsistence and of production'[228] in place of the commodities he has worked up and does not need himself. Until he acquires the latter, he cannot renew the production process without having the means of production that it requires and that he has expended in the previous period of production, or the means of subsistence for feeding himself and his family during the next period of production. But, in order that he might appropriate the necessary means of production and subsistence for himself, according to his own choices, he must first convert the commodities he has prepared into money, i.e. sell them on the market.

> The social division of labour makes the nature of his labour as one-sided as his needs are many-sided. This is precisely the reason why the product of his labour serves him solely as an exchange-value. But it cannot acquire universal social validity as an equivalent form except by being converted into money. That money, however, is in someone else's pocket.[229]

'A man who has produced, does not have the choice of selling or not selling. He *must* sell'.[230] This means that the necessary completion of the production process is the act of selling the commodity and, in order to be able to begin a new process of production, the commodity producer, having sold his commodity, must necessarily appear in the role of buyer of the corresponding means of production and subsistence. The circulation process, in the form of a lawful repetition of the two acts (C–M and M–C), is the necessary mediating link between two processes of production, completing the first and preparing for the second. The circulation process appears as part of the general process of reproduction, and the lawful course of the latter presupposes the lawful flow of the former. Independently of the will of particular individuals, the very mechanism of commodity economy necessarily imparts the following form to the

---

228   Ibid.
229   Marx 1976, p. 201.
230   Marx 1968, p. 503.

entire process of reproduction: 1) the production process; 2) the circulation process (sale, or C–M, and purchase, M–C); 3) the production process – and so forth. The periodic pulse of the reproduction process includes the pulse of the circulation process in a proper sequence of its two acts, C–M and M–C, which oppose and 'complement each other'.[231]

At first glance, the internal connection of the two acts of circulation (C–M and M–C), which enter into one and the same process of reproduction and complement each other, is concealed because they each appear in a distinct and separate form. Indeed, what constitutes the specificity of monetary exchange is that the direct identity between alienation of the product of his labour and the acquisition of someone else's labour is divided into 'the two antithetical segments of sale and purchase'.[232] This division of the two acts is manifest in the fact that: 1) in the act of purchase our commodity producer, having previously sold his commodity to person A, now enters into a production relation with another person B; 2) the act of purchase can proceed in some other place and not where the act of sale occurred; and 3) the act of purchase can be postponed for a certain time and need not follow immediately after the act of sale. There is a personal, spatial and temporal separation between the two acts of the circulation process.

> Each individual sale or purchase stands as an independent isolated transaction, whose complementary transaction ... may be separated from it temporally and spatially ... Any M–C may follow any particular C–M, i.e., the second section of the life cycle of any commodity may follow the first section of the life cycle of any other commodity.[233]

This separation of the two acts in the process of circulation gives the latter the appearance of 'an exceedingly haphazard coincidence and succession of motley phases of various complete metamorphoses'.[234] 'The actual process of circulation *appears*, therefore, not as a complete metamorphosis of the commodity, i.e., not as its movement through opposite phases, but as a mere accumulation of numerous purchases and sales which chance to occur simultaneously or successively'.[235]

---

231 Marx 1976, p. 209.
232 Ibid.
233 Marx 1970, pp. 93–4.
234 Marx 1970, p. 94. Marx calls both acts of circulation, taken as the whole, or C–M–C, the 'complete metamorphosis'.
235 Ibid.

This chaotic picture of the circulation process does not, however, give us a proper representation of the latter, for the process appears to lose 'its distinct form',[236] i.e. its law-governed social character. In order to disclose the latter, Marx, in his usual manner, tried to find behind this movement of things the determinate production relations between people. Having begun with the investigation of an economy of commodity producers, with its inherent proper and rhythmic sequence of the production process and of both acts of the circulation process (C–M–C), Marx found in the market the pivot around which the disorderly dance of commodities revolves. This pivot must be sought not in the things themselves but in the production relations between people, more precisely, in the activities of the commodity producers and their mutual relations with the world of other commodity producers. Beneath the personal, spatial and temporal separation between the two acts of circulation, Marx found within them both a single stable centre: the figure of the commodity producer, who participates in both acts of exchange (C–M and M–C)[237] and includes them both in the single process of reproduction that is fulfilled at his establishment. Without denying the enormous importance of the separation of exchange into the two opposing acts of purchase and sale, and sharply criticising those economists who underestimated this moment,[238] Marx at the same time also revealed a certain 'internal unity' of the two 'independent' acts of the circulation process.[239] This unity consists of the fact that both acts, C–M and M–C, are complementary yet distinct links in the single circulation process of C–M–C. From this point of view, any transaction of purchase and sale is revealed not as an isolated act, but instead it has its place in the general system of commodity circulation. Insofar as this transaction is considered from the side of the buyer, as M–C, it completes a previous act of sale into which the current buyer entered as seller, and it prepares for him the possibility of renewing the production process. Regarding it from the side of the seller, as C–M, it completes the just concluded process of production and, in turn, must invariably find its complement in the ensuing act M–C, even if the latter is postponed for a time and completed elsewhere. Separated spatially and temporally, the two opposing acts of C–M and M–C are tied together as necessary links of the single process of reproduction. They are connected not only with one another but

---

236 Ibid.
237 Thus 'The complete metamorphosis of a commodity, in its simplest form, implies four *dénouements* and three *dramatis personae*' since one of them participates in both acts of circulation (Marx 1976, p. 206).
238 Marx 1970, p. 97.
239 Marx 1976, p. 209.

also with other acts of circulation.[240] Since each of these acts arises from the interaction (exchange) between two establishments, it enters simultaneously into the reproduction process both of the given establishment and of its counterpart:

> At the same time as this commodity begins the first phase of its circuit and undergoes the first metamorphosis, another commodity commences the second phase of the circuit, passes through its second metamorphosis and drops out of circulation; the first commodity, on the other hand, enters the second phase of the circuit, passes through its second metamorphosis and drops out of circulation, while a third commodity enters the sphere of circulation, passes through the first phase of its cycle and accomplishes the first metamorphosis. Thus the total circuit C–M–C representing the complete metamorphosis of a commodity is simultaneously the end of a complete metamorphosis of the second commodity and the beginning of a complete metamorphosis of a third commodity.[241]

The metamorphoses of the individual commodities are entwined with each other. 'The circuit made by one commodity in the course of its metamorphoses is inextricably entwined with the circuits of other commodities. This whole process constitutes *the circulation of commodities*'.[242]

We must remember well that not every exchange of products for money is included in the concept of commodity circulation. Exchange becomes commodity circulation only provided that 1) it is repeated periodically and 2) in the specific social form of C–M–C, which presupposes that the production of a given establishment is alienated with the aim of using the money acquired to purchase the means of production and subsistence required for further production. Where this is not the case, there may be monetary trade, but there is no circulation of commodities in the form that characterises commodity economy. Consider an example from the economy of the late Middle Ages. The peasant sold a portion of his grain in the city for money and paid the latter as quitrent to the feudal landlord. The latter used it to buy luxury items from the merchant, which the latter imported from the East. Here we have a series

---

240 [In the margin there is a question mark '?' beside this statement].
241 Marx 1970, pp. 92–3. Most indicative for the development of Marx's ideas is the dual process of circulation, which he frequently mentions. As an object of the production relations between people, the commodity begins 'the first phase of its circuit'. As a thing with a determinate social form, it completes the 'first metamorphosis'.
242 Marx 1976, p. 207 [Rubin's emphasis].

of transactions of purchase and sale, or monetary trade, but there is no circulation of commodities in the form C–M–C. The peasant sells his grain, but the money that he receives is handed over to the feudal lord. For the peasant household, the act C–M is not followed by the act M–C. Conversely, the feudal lord completes the act M–C, but the latter is not the completion of the act C–M since the feudal lord acquired the money not from sale of his products but rather as quitrent from the peasant, i.e. he received it in his capacity as feudalist and not as a commodity producer. The feudal form of production relations between people creates a special form of exchange[243] that is distinguished from the form C–M–C, which characterises commodity economy with its inherent production relations between people as commodity owners. It is only in this social form of C–M–C that exchange becomes the circulation of commodities, and it is only 'as mediator in the process of commodity circulation that money fulfils the function of medium of circulation'.[244] People usually understand the function of medium of circulation simply as the role of money as instrument of exchange. That, as we now see, is incorrect. It is only in a determinate social form of economy (namely, the commodity economy), with its associated form of exchange (namely, C–M–C), that money fulfils the function of medium of circulation. 'Money emerges thus as a mere medium of *exchange of commodities*, not however as a medium of exchange in general, but a medium of exchange adapted to the process of circulation, i.e., *a medium of circulation*'.[245] In a different social context, distinguished by a different character of the production relations between people, money can serve as the instrument of exchange without functioning, however, as medium of circulation in the sense indicated.

Thus, from a determinate type of production relations between people as commodity owners, Marx derives a determinate form of commodity circulation (C–M–C) – which in turn stipulates the specific function of money as medium of circulation – and a determinate form of the movement of money. The uninterrupted and periodically repeated process of reproduction, organised on the principles of commodity economy, presupposes that the commodity producer periodically produces the commodity, periodically puts it into circulation, i.e. sells it for money, and, with the money acquired, periodically

---

243 The result of this character of medieval exchange was the outflow of money (precious metals) from Europe to the East, which continued, at times weakening or intensifying, throughout the entire Middle Ages. See: W[erner] Sombart, *Der moderne Kapitalismus*, 4. Aufl., München, Leipzig: Duncker und Humblot, 1921, Bd. I., Hlbd. 1., pp. 418, 420, 423.
244 Marx 1976, pp. 210–12.
245 Marx 1970, p. 96 [Rubin's emphasis].

purchases the products that he requires in order to resume production. The commodity producer's expenditure of the money in this form already presupposes that the production process will be repeated and that the newly worked up commodities will again be sold, and thus that the money resulting from the act C–M will return to the commodity producer in order to depart from him again in the act M–C. In other words, a periodic pulse beat of money occurs, periodically flowing into a given establishment and then flowing out of it.

> But since there are new use-values produced continuously in the form of commodities, which must therefore be thrown continuously afresh into the sphere of circulation, the circuit C–M–C is renewed and repeated by the same commodity owners. The money they have spent as buyers returns to them when they once more become sellers of commodities. The perpetual renewal of commodity circulation is reflected in the fact that over the entire surface of bourgeois society money not only circulates from one person to another but that at the same time it describes a number of distinct small circuits, starting from an infinite variety of points and returning to the same points, in order to repeat the movement afresh.[246]

Insofar as simple reproduction is involved, i.e. reproduction on the previous scale rather than expanded reproduction, one and the same sum of money periodically flows into a given establishment and periodically exits from it (assuming that the value of commodities and of money does not change).

Since every sale is simultaneously a purchase and vice versa, this means that every inflow of money into a given establishment (in the act C–M) signals a simultaneous outflow of the same sum of money from other establishments (in the act M–C). Conversely, every outflow of money from one establishment means its inflow into other establishments. In other words, money continually flows from one establishment to others, pausing in each for an interval of time (now shorter, now longer) between the moment of the act of sale C–M and the moment of the ensuing act of purchase M–C. Money, accordingly, is continually

---

246 Marx 1970, pp. 99–100. The 'return of money to its starting point' is often noted by Marx, moreover, in Volume II of *Capital* with the famous schemes of the reproduction of the total social capital and its component parts. It is true that elsewhere Marx seems to weaken this claim, showing that this tendency for money to return to its starting point does not happen in every single case of circulation in simple commodity economy (Marx 1970, pp. 97–8), but in our opinion he has no intention of denying the general importance of this tendency for commodity economy.

moving in the circulation process, and this is precisely its function as medium of circulation. If we take a so-called 'national economy', consisting of a determinate number of interconnected private undertakings, then in the condition of simple reproduction and the absence of foreign trade, a determinate sum of money circulates in the given economy, constantly flowing from one establishment to the others and remaining (with the exception of worn-out coins) in the given sphere of circulation. It is only in the form of commodity circulation (C–M–C) that the sum of circulating money represents, for the given sphere of circulation, a determinate and constant magnitude (other conditions remaining the same), analysis of which involves the question of the quantity of money.

The character of commodity circulation in the form C–M–C is determined by the fundamental specificities of money's circulation: its constant movement in circulation, its periodic inflow into each establishment and, finally, the function that money fulfils in each separate act of purchase and sale. Here we come to a unique aspect of Marx's teaching on money that has not been given sufficient attention. *The process of replacing a given commodity (linen) with gold (money), and the latter with another commodity (Bibles), is described by Marx as a process involving a change of form of the first commodity (the linen).* This is the central idea of Marx's theory of the 'metamorphosis of the commodity', and for a better explanation of this we shall cite a few excerpts from Marx.

What is it that we observe directly in the act of purchase and sale? 'The striking phenomenon here is that a commodity and gold, 20 yards of linen and £2, have changed hands and places, in other words that they have been exchanged'.[247] But behind this external appearance of one thing being replaced by another, Marx discerns a process involving a change of form on the part of the first thing.

> At the outset the commodity appears as a particular use-value, then sheds this form of existence and assumes that of exchange-value or universal equivalent – which is entirely distinct from its natural form – finally it sheds this as well and emerges as a real use-value which can serve particular needs. In this last form it drops out of the sphere of circulation and enters that of consumption.[248]

In the circuit C–M–C (linen-gold-Bible), the gold and the Bible are no more than forms that the linen assumes. With the sale of the linen, what occurs is a leap

---

247   Marx 1976, p. 203.
248   Marx 1970, p. 88.

of value 'from the body of the commodity into the body of the gold'.[249] The bodies of commodities, their use-values, change over to the money side, 'while their soul, the exchange-value, is turned into gold'.[250] The linen 'changes its commodity-form into its money-form', which becomes 'the first term of its final metamorphosis M–C, its transformation back into the shape of the Bible'.[251] In the second act M–C (purchase of the Bible), it is still the movement of the linen itself that continues, only now transformed into the money-form; the commodity 'passes through the second phase of its circulation, no longer in its natural shape, but in its [golden] state'.[252] The entire process C–M–C represents the conversion of form, or the metamorphosis of the first commodity, the linen.

At first sight, this teaching on the metamorphosis of the commodity cannot help but seem strange and even to contradict reality. It seems to us that in the act C–M gold has replaced the linen, and there is no change of form on the part of the linen. We are confident that simultaneously with the act C–M, i.e. with sale of the linen, the latter leaves the sphere of circulation and enters the sphere of consumption. Marx claims that although 'the commodity, in its shape as an object of utility, falls out of circulation into consumption',[253] the linen, as a commodity or exchange-value, still continues its movement within circulation in the form of gold. It is only when the gold, acquired for the linen, is given in return for the Bible, that the linen actually moves from the sphere of circulation into the sphere of consumption.

These claims by Marx concerning the 'reincarnation' of the linen in gold and the Bible, while initially appearing somewhat incomprehensible, take on a completely real meaning from the point of view of his theory of commodity fetishism. The entire process described by Marx, *the process of the metamorphosis of the commodity, must be regarded as a movement of the production relations between people, which does not correspond with the movement of things although it is closely connected with it*. From the 'material' point of view (i.e. from the point of view of the movement of things), there is obviously no incarnation of linen in the gold or the Bible; the linen is simply replaced by gold, and the latter by the Bible. But we come to a different conclusion from the point of view of the production relations of which these things are the carriers. Our commodity owner made the linen as a commodity with a determinate exchange-value that already, in the production process itself, acquires a certain evaluation in

---

249 Marx 1976, p. 200.
250 Marx 1970, p. 92.
251 Marx 1976, p. 212.
252 Marx 1976, p. 211.
253 Ibid.

terms of gold.[254] By the very fact of producing the linen, the commodity owner already enters into a certain production link with other commodity owners: he is a claimant upon other use-values that are equal in value to his linen. The exchange-value of the linen is an expression of this ability, on the part of its producer, to enter into such a production relation of exchange. But thus far we are speaking only of a possibility, or of a potential production relation of exchange. From the moment of the linen's sale, i.e. its exchange for gold, the potential production relation between the given commodity owner and the others is actively manifested; his product is swallowed up by the market and he, as the owner of gold, becomes an active participant in the production relation of exchange. In purchasing the Bible, he realises this production relation. One and the same production link between the given commodity owner and the others, founded upon the fact that he produces a product (linen) as a commodity,[255] extends through the ensuing phases: from being a potential it becomes active in order then to be realised. The unity of this production link, in all its phases, is shown by the fact that each previous phase necessarily presupposes the one that follows, and the latter is impossible without the former. *The continuity of the different phases of the production relation of commodity owners is reflected in the continuity of things as the carriers of these consecutive phases.*[256] Since people in commodity society are connected through things, each phase of the production relation between people corresponds to a special social form of things: the 'commodity form' (linen), the 'stripping off of the commodity form' (gold) and the 'return to the commodity form' (the Bible).[257] On the other hand, insofar as the different phases of the production relation between people constitute a certain unity, the materially different carriers of these phases (linen, gold, Bible) are merely forms of one and the same value.

Now we can understand why the linen, following its sale, continues its existence as value in the form of money and still remains within the sphere of circulation. Of course, the material body of the linen, following its sale, leaves the sphere of circulation for the sphere of consumption. But is there an end to the production relation, of which the linen was the carrier, namely, the production tie between the producer of the linen and the other commodity owners, a connection founded on the fact that the first among them produced the linen as a commodity for the market? With the sale of the linen, this

---

254   See our earlier chapter [6] in this work on money as 'Measure of Value'.
255   Here we presuppose, as in the theory of money in general, a condition of equilibrium in social production and thus of commodities being sold according to their value.
256   More accurately: the continuity of this social form of the things.
257   Marx 1976, p. 207.

production relation not only has not come to an end; rather, it is only now that it actively appears, so to speak, and has acquired a socially significant form. This means that the exchange-value of the linen, as the expression of this production relation, still continues to exist, being 'attached' to or 'reified' in the gold. It is only through purchase of the Bible that the producer of the linen realises and simultaneously terminates his production relation with all commodity owners, which is tied to the fact of the linen's production. Thus, it is only with purchase of the Bible that the linen, as exchange-value, departs from the sphere of circulation for the sphere of consumption.

If the linen, through sale, assumes the form of gold, it follows that the gold is a converted form of the linen. *In circulation the gold is always the converted or money-form of the commodities.* Marx strongly emphasises this idea. Of course, at its point of production the gold enters into circulation as a simple commodity, opposed to others and exchanging for them in the act of direct barter.[258] The gold and the linen enter into such an act in identical social form, and the value of each of them is expressed in the other. But if we abstract from these points of entry of new gold into circulation and take the latter as a continuing and endlessly repeating process, then the gold enters not with the quality of a simple commodity but with the quality of money, i.e. a commodity already equated with all other commodities. Here the value of the linen is expressed one-sidedly, namely, only in the gold, whereas the value of the gold is expressed not in some quantity of linen, for which it is purchased, but instead can only be expressed in the totality of all commodities, i.e. in the general level of prices. In each particular act of exchange, the gold enters as the converted form of any commodity whatsoever. Every commodity owner (apart from the gold producer) can enter the act M–C in the role of purchaser only provided that he has already previously sold his commodity and, consequently, the gold in his hands already represents the incarnation of his commodity's 'alienated form'.[259] Our commodity owner can sell his linen to another commodity owner only on condition that the latter has already sold his commodity, for example, wheat. This means that, in the given act C–M (sale of the linen), the gold already enters with the quality of the converted or money-form of the wheat. Upon completion of this act of selling the linen, the same gold becomes the converted form of the linen until it is exchanged for the Bible, etc. The movement of gold is the 'movement of the metamorphosed commodity'.[260]

---

258   Marx 1970, p. 90.
259   Marx 1976, p. 212.
260   Marx 1970, p. 99.

At first sight, Marx's assertion regarding the character of gold as the transformed commodity appears to us to be just as strange and incomprehensible as the claim we have just scrutinised: that after its sale the commodity continues to exist in the form of gold. The former claim is the conclusion drawn from the latter, and it likewise reveals its meaning to us only when translated from the language of reified relations into the language of production relations between people. From the reified point of view, a gold rouble is a gold rouble, completely apart from whether it is acquired through the sale of wheat or iron; it is impossible to know 'whether it represents transformed iron or transformed wheat'.[261] But the character of the production relations of exchange, into which the owner of the gold rouble now enters in the market, depends in no small measure precisely upon whether he acquired this rouble from the sale of wheat or of iron. *The action by the owner of gold, who is entering into the act M–C in the role of buyer, depends upon the preceding act C–M, in which the same individual was seller, meaning that in the act M–C the gold appears as the converted form of a particular commodity.* This position helps us to understand the mechanism of market exchange.

Let us suppose that we are taking a snapshot of the state of the market at any given moment. On one side we find the sellers, the commodity owners, and[262] on the other side the buyers, the owners of money. The latter appear as the active participants in exchange; according to their own choice and, as it appears at first sight, their own will, they select the commodities they want. Demand, represented by the sum of money in the hands of all buyers (for instance, a million gold roubles), seems to us to be the primary and determining force of market exchange. Being the determining sum, the demand, for its own part, appears to be completely undetermined in both qualitative and quantitative terms: in qualitative terms, because it represents a certain sum of homogeneous and abstract monetary units (roubles) – each of which can be directed to the purchase of any commodities – which therefore contain within themselves no evidence of a definite concrete demand; in quantitative terms, because the sum of a million roubles enters into market circulation as a final sum, given in advance, whose origin is unknown to us.

This portrayal of the mechanism of market exchange is extremely one-sided and erroneous, singling out one link (demand) and declining to analyse those factors by which it, in turn, is determined. Such an analysis will show us first that the sum of money, which represents demand from the side of buyers at this

---

261   Marx 1970, p. 94.
262   [Underlined in pencil].

particular moment, is acquired by the latter through the preceding sale of the commodities they produced. This sum of *money, therefore, is the converted or money-form of the production by commodity owners who are presently appearing in the role of buyers*.[263] The current acts of purchase M–C are the complements of previous acts of sale C–M, and the current demand is determined, both quantitatively and qualitatively, by the preceding process of production. Above all, it is obvious that the volume of demand from the side of the buyers depends on the quantity of commodities or exchange-values that they first produced and realised in the market in the preceding acts of sale C–M. Furthermore, the character and volume of the production of each commodity owner also influences the qualitative side of the demand that they represent in the market. This is self-evident insofar as we are speaking of demand for means of production, material, machines, supplementary materials and so forth. Depending upon whether the given commodity owner acquired his money from the sale of iron or wheat, he will necessarily spend a part of the money received on the purchase of one or another means of production required in order to resume the labour process. He will spend the remainder of the proceeds on means of consumption. The quality and quantity of the means of consumption he acquires depend primarily upon the magnitude of the remaining sum, and that magnitude, in turn, is determined by the scale and method of his production.

Thus, the volume and character of demand depend upon the volume and character of production; the acts of purchase M–C are really complementary to the preceding acts of sale C–M; and the gold that figures in the acts M–C is the converted or money-form of the production realised in the acts C–M. It is not discernible whether a gold rouble is transformed iron or transformed wheat, but its further fate largely depends upon which it is. The same gold rouble represents transformed wheat for the peasant and, after it passes to the weaver, transformed linen, next a transformed Bible, etc. Imprinted upon the glistening, solid and constant gold rouble are the social production relations of which, in this case, it is the 'carrier'. And here, as in other parts of his theory, Marx's analysis discloses from behind congealed things the flexible, dynamic and fluid production relations between people. The reified economic categories acquire a magnified flexibility, reflecting all the diversity in the changing rainbow of social relations between people.

As in his teaching on the measure of value, Marx's doctrine on the function of money in the role of medium of circulation reveals a deep sociological character in the fact that it takes as given a determinate type of production rela-

---

263 This assumes, of course, that only commodity producers face one another in the market.

tions between people as commodity owners. The commonly accepted notion that, prior to the exchange act, gold fulfils the function of measure of value wherever it is conceivable to equate the product with a certain quantity of gold, and the function of medium of circulation wherever they are actually exchanged, does not apply to Marx's theory. That view suggests that gold fulfils both of these functions in every random exchange, provided only that it is the commonly used means for comparing and exchanging different products (for example, in the monetary exchange between tribes with a predominantly natural economy, or in occasional exchange on the periphery of a society with a commodity economy, etc.). From Marx's point of view, it is only possible here to speak of money's process of emergence and development, not of the functions that are inherent in it with a regular process of commodity production. Here there is no function as measure of value, for there is no value itself as the regulator of production. Here there is no medium of circulation, for there is no commodity circulation as a necessary constituent element in the process of reproduction. It is only where the product is produced in advance as a commodity, and where it acquires even in the production process a preliminary evaluation in terms of gold – which expresses the level of prices with which equilibrium is maintained between the given production branch and all the others – that gold fulfils the function of measure of value. Only where the production process is invariably followed by the exchange process in both of its phases (C–M and M–C), as the necessary condition for resuming production, does gold fulfil the function of medium of circulation. It is easy to see that both of these functions presuppose a developed commodity economy, in which production is intended in advance for exchange (hence the preliminary evaluation of the commodity and the function of gold as measure of value), and on the other hand, exchange is only an intermediate stage of the entire reproduction process (hence the metamorphosis of the commodity and the function of gold as medium of circulation).

8 Money as a Hoard

If the circulation of commodities in the form C–M–C occurs more or less uninterruptedly, and each act of sale C–M is quickly followed by its complementary act of purchase M–C, money will quickly pass from hand to hand and fulfil the function of medium of circulation. 'But as soon as the series of metamorphoses (of the commodity – I.R.) is interrupted, as soon as sales are not supplemented by subsequent purchases',[264] the money remains for a long period in the hands of the seller, fulfilling the function of a hoard.

---

264 Marx 1976, p. 227.

In historical terms, the collection of treasure began very early. Even before precious metals became money, they were readily accumulated as a concrete item of consumption (i.e. as a luxury item) that was most suitable, because of its durability, for the preservation of wealth. As exchange and money develop, accumulation of precious metals already concentrates in the hands of the owners not merely stable and highly prized items of consumption but also the 'absolutely social form of wealth which is always ready to be used'.[265] Only from this moment is it possible to speak of a hoard not in the sense of a sum of concrete and useful items but rather in the sense of a 'social force' that is concentrated in the hands of 'private persons'.[266] So long as the slave or feudal economy prevails, money, of course, is not the only 'social force' because the members of society are not 'private persons' who relate to each other as independent and equal commodity owners. The members of society are still connected by relations of feudal domination, serfdom, etc. But, if the owner of money is compelled to reckon with a prince or feudal landlord, he possesses all the more advantage because of that same backwardness of social relations, by comparison with the owner of use-values when both parties occupy an equal social position. It is precisely the prevalence of natural economy and the inadequate development of exchange that makes it impossible, or in the best of cases problematic, to transform any use-value into money.[267] This means that the seller endeavours all the more to retain the money received as a hoard, as a social force that – while it does not yet replace all other social ties – already successfully supplements, modifies and to some extent dissolves them. Describing the widespread custom in the East (especially in India) of collecting a hoard, Adolf Wagner says: 'For many "little" people a hoard plays the role of a savings bank in the event of need or of high prices, with which to guarantee survival ... For the wealthy, for the aristocracy and the princes, a hoard serves as a means of social and political domination, specifically for gift-giving,[268]

---

265 Marx 1976, p. 229.
266 Marx 1976, p. 230.
267 Marx 1992, p. 448.
268 These 'gifts' often served the giver as a means of strengthening his social position, purchasing the assistance or neutrality of a powerful neighbour, etc. In the mid-eighteenth century, one of the Indian princes, occupying his throne with the aid of English troops, gave to the commander of the latter, the famous Clive, a 'gift' of 2–3 million gold roubles. See Th.B. Macauly, 'Lord Clive', in *Critical and Historical Essays*, London: J.M. Dent and Sons Ltd., 1907, Vol. I, p. 518. The history of India abounds with such examples. 'According to the lists laid before Parliament, between 1757 and 1766 the company (the reference is to the East-India Company, which employed the illustrious Clive – I.R.) and its officials

paying for services, retaining servants, waging war, paying taxes, etc.'.[269] In ancient and feudal society, the 'professional hoarder' frequently became a moneylender and, through his activity, contributed all the more to dissolution of the economic forms inherent in such societies.[270]

In developed commodity society, the formation of a hoard is one of the normal, continuous and necessary functions of commodity circulation. If, on the one hand, the latter presupposes the uninterrupted circuit C–M–C, on the other hand it ruptures this circuit into two acts, C–M and M–C, creating the possibility and occasionally even the necessity of a prolonged postponement of the second act. Every commodity owner must alternately assume the roles of seller and buyer, but at the same time he must retain for a time a portion of the money received from selling rather than put it into circulation. As we have seen above, the commodity producer spends the money received from sales on the purchase of means of consumption and means of production. For both of these purposes he must now and again withhold money in the form of a reserve fund or a hoard.

The commodity producer completes the sale of his products periodically, at the end of each production process. The periods when sales occur, therefore, are conditioned by the periods of production. The peasant, for example, sells most of his products every autumn. The production periods are shorter in industry, but for every commodity producer these periods are fixed. Expenditures by the latter on means of consumption depend on the character of the various needs and their periodic recurrence.[271] For certain requirements (sustenance, for example), periodic expenditures frequently occur before the production process ends, whereas for other needs (for example, clothing and housing) they occur less frequently. This means that after the production process and the sale of finished lots of commodities are completed, the commodity producer must retain out of the money received: 1) a sum needed for regular expenditures upon means of consumption (food) over the duration of the next period of production, and 2) a corresponding sum for gradual accumulation of the fund for one-time expenditures that occur over several periods of production. If the production process lasts three months, and the producer replaces his wearing apparel once a year at a cost of 200 roubles, then from the sum

---

obtained £6,000,000 between 1757 and 1766 from the Indians in the form of gifts' (Marx 1976, p. 917).

269 Wagner 1909, p. 377.
270 Marx 1992, pp. 729–34.
271 Marx 1970, pp. 125–6.

received from selling the products of each production period a sum of 50 roubles must be set aside for this purpose.

The same forms of reserves must be set aside from the sums intended for purchasing means of production in the broad sense of the word. If wages are paid weekly to workers, and fixed capital (machines) is replaced every five years, then after each production period, lasting three months, the capitalist must allocate to the reserve fund: 1) a sum equal to 12 times the total of wages paid out weekly, and 2) a sum equal to 1/20 of the value of the machines that are wearing out. In a capitalist economy, where the fixed capital takes on enormous dimensions, such sums being set aside for its 'amortisation' or retirement are extremely significant. In simple commodity economy, the difference in the periods of expenditure of various sums on means of production also occurs, but it is not so great. Thus, in simple commodity economy it is also necessary to accumulate certain reserve funds – although not so extensive – for the purpose of both consumption and production. Still more profound is the difference between simple commodity economy and capitalist economy in terms of how the reserve funds are accumulated. With a developed credit system, and especially with a banking system, it is possible to speak of the 'accumulation' of a hoard only in a figurative, not in a literal, sense of the word.[272] The commodity producer does not 'accumulate' reserve funds on his own but instead deposits them in the bank, which uses their temporary inactivity to lend them to other commodity producers who need cash at any given moment. But in the theory of money, Marx abstracts from the presence of a credit system and assumes real accumulation, i.e. retention by each commodity producer of a certain sum of money that serves as a reserve fund.

Thus, even if we assume that the commodity producer intends to spend the entire sum of money received from sale of the commodities on means of consumption and means of production, a portion of this money will still be retained temporarily in his own hands as the reserve fund. A certain portion of this money will be spent gradually in the near future and thus constitutes his 'cash balance'. This is his 'reserve fund of coin',[273] or temporarily 'suspended coin', which may not be spent at the moment but still does not essentially leave the sphere of circulation. This 'cash reserve fund' can be regarded as 'a constituent element of the total amount of money always in circulation';[274] as distinct from coin, therefore, it is not a hoard in the sense of 'money' that is

---

272 Marx 1970, p. 133.
273 Marx 1970, p. 126.
274 Marx 1970, p. 137.

withdrawn from the sphere of circulation.[275] This role of 'money', withdrawn from circulation, is fulfilled by sums of money that are to be spent on means of consumption and means of production only after a more or less lengthy interval of time (for example, after the wearing out of fixed capital), and thus they temporarily leave the 'stream of circulation', settling or 'congealing' in the form of a hoard. This is a 'reserve fund of purchasing power', formation of which is a necessary consequence of money's function as means of payment, i.e. as medium of circulation. With the expansion of credit transactions and of the payment function of money, the commodity producer must also gradually accumulate sums needed to pay his debts at the appointed time. A 'reserve fund of means of payment' emerges, based upon money's function as means of payment. Both reserve funds (for purchasing and for payment) constitute a hoard or 'monetary reserve fund', as distinct from the previously mentioned 'reserve fund of coin'.[276]

Until now we have assumed that the money temporarily withdrawn from circulation as a reserve fund must at some definite time be returned to circulation. In other words, we have assumed that ultimately all money received by commodity producers from the sale of products is spent on the purchase of other products. It is possible, however, that the commodity producer will keep a part of this money with the intention of not returning it to circulation. In that case we are dealing not with a temporary interruption (very brief in the case of a reserve fund of coin and somewhat longer in the case of a reserve fund of money) between the acts C–M and M–C; instead, the whole circulation ends with the act C–M, which is not followed by the second act of purchase, M–C. The money received from sale C–M is transformed into a hoard, which we can distinguish from a reserve fund of money by designating it as an 'accumulating hoard'. And this is the accumulation of a hoard in the precise[277] sense of the word.

Now let us consider which technical and social conditions of production permit such accumulation of hoards as a more or less continuous phenomenon. In order for the commodity producer to retain part of the money received from sale of products as an accumulating hoard, it is necessary that the receipts leave him with a certain surplus beyond the sums required for the purchase of means of consumption and means of production. The commodity producer cannot curtail purchase of means of production, since the inevitable con-

---

275 [The last part of the statement is marked off in pencil in the margin].
276 Marx 1970, p. 126. Here Marx is distinguishing 'money' from 'small change'.
277 [Here the text is corrected in pencil to say first 'precise', then 'narrow', and then 'restricted'].

sequence will be reduction of the scale of future production and consequently a decline of future receipts, or revenues. True, the commodity producer may curtail his personal requirements and reduce expenditure on the purchase of means of consumption. Such curtailment of personal consumption is, in fact, widely practised in a peasant and handicraft economy, although it is confined, of course, within narrow limits. Most often 'economy' in personal consumption, which characterises the first stage of accumulating a hoard in the pre-capitalist epoch, consists not so much of curtailing personal consumption as of avoiding its expansion, which may be possible with the given level of development of the productive forces. The commodity producer's labour productivity has already reached such a level of development that the selling price of his products leaves a surplus to cover expenditures on the purchase of customary consumer items and of the necessary means of production. The technical conditions of production admit, therefore, of the possibility of expanding personal consumption, but the social form of the production process, namely, development of monetary exchange and of the 'social power' of money, persuade the commodity producer to retain this money in the form of a hoard. Accordingly, the supportive conditions for accumulation of a hoard in the primitive form that we have been describing are: a certain level of development of labour productivity and the development of money as the 'absolutely social form of wealth which is always ready to be used'[278] and which, for that reason, is always attractive to the commodity owner. Thanks to the first condition, the commodity producer acquires a certain monetary surplus after selling his products and covering the necessary expenses, while the second condition persuades him to avoid spending this surplus on increasing his personal consumption; the result is that the monetary surplus is retained in the form of an 'accumulating hoard'. The accumulation of a hoard, becoming a permanent feature, indicates that the economy of the given commodity producer has already outgrown the limits dictated by the need to satisfy his personal requirements and those of his family. 'The accumulation of money for the sake of money is in fact the barbaric form of production for the sake of production, i.e., the development of the productive powers of social labour beyond the limits of customary requirements'.[279]

In capitalist society, the accumulation of hoards is transformed into the accumulation of capital, and its character completely changes. As in the case of the person accumulating a hoard, the capitalist does not spend the surplus

---

278 Marx 1976, p. 229.
279 Marx 1970, p. 134.

revenue (or spends very little of it) on expanding personal consumption, but instead he 'accumulates' (this is the so-called 'accumulating part of surplus value', as distinct from the part being 'consumed'). But unlike the accumulator of a hoard, he puts this additional money to work rather than withdrawing it from circulation: he either expands his own production, i.e. purchases new means of production and more labour power, or else he lends the money, usually through the mediation of a bank, to other capitalists for expansion of their production. Even for the brief interval of time during which this money is not at work, he does not keep it to himself but places it in a current account at the bank, receiving a corresponding payment of interest. A modern banking system makes it possible for the capitalist to retain the 'social power' that money represents (namely, the possibility of entering at any moment, as an active participant, into the production relation of exchange) without keeping his money to himself. The capitalist concentrates in his own hands the social 'power of money' without retaining in his own possession the things that in themselves have the properties of money. But, at primitive stages of development, concentration of the social 'power of money' in the hands of individual commodity producers – as with the 'reification' of production relations between people that is inherent in commodity economy – is possible only in the form of a real concentration of things, of money (as gold). 'To the simple owner of commodities among the barbarians, and even to the peasant of Western Europe, value is inseparable from the value-form, hence an increase in his hoard of gold and silver is an increase in value'.[280] The item being accumulated is, so to speak, 'money in kind', in the form of gold and silver coins or bars that can be transformed into coins. The habit of burying money in the ground is widespread in the East,[281] while in Europe money was hidden in 'cash-boxes', 'stockings', etc. This primitive form of accumulating a hoard was widespread during the pre-capitalist period and the early stages of the capitalist period, and it is still encountered in petty-bourgeois circles, particularly among the peasantry.

Along with the accumulation of a hoard in the form of coins and bars, there is also the accumulation of 'a hoard in aesthetic form', in the form of gold and silver commodities as concrete items of consumption and luxury (vessels, adornments, etc.). The fact that these items are made from the same material that serves as money distinguishes them from other items of consumption. Although in their direct form they are concrete items of consumption, in the first place they can at any moment be converted into money, and secondly,

---

280   Marx 1976, p. 229.
281   Marx 1970, p. 130.

their utilisation as use-values serves as the most flamboyant and demonstrative indicator of the social power of money that is concentrated in the hands of their owner. 'Although at certain stages of production the commodity owner hides his treasures, he is impelled to show to other commodity owners that he is a *rico hombre*, whenever he can safely do so. He bedecks himself and his house with gold'.[282] Whereas in peasant and petty-bourgeois contexts one often encounters 'avaricious' types, who gather their hoards brick by brick at the cost of denying their own necessities, at further stages of the bourgeoisie's development there are expenditures on items of luxury. In tranquil times, their own norms of luxury emerge among circles of the middle bourgeoisie: it is shameful to have fewer gold items than is customary in the given social circle, but it is also shameful to flaunt an excess of luxury items that clearly does not correspond to the material status of the particular family. To exceed the norm dramatically converts use of precious things from a form of collecting a hoard into an indicator of the misappropriation of cash, into 'prodigality' and 'extravagance'. Such excessive use of luxury items is usually widespread among circles of the bourgeoisie who are rapidly becoming rich, among the upstarts of the 'nouveaux riches'. If the small and middle bourgeoisie, at the turning point from feudalism to capitalism, lead a 'puritan'[283] way of life and sharply condemn the feudal nobility for prodigality and extravagance, the upper bourgeoisie, who are rapidly becoming wealthy, endeavour to eclipse them [the nobles] with the splendour of their own way of life.[284]

The gold that is withdrawn from circulation in one form or another (a reserve fund of coin, a reserve fund of money, an accumulating hoard or a hoard in aesthetic form), is not separated by an insurmountable boundary from the gold that circulates. Gold routinely moves from the sphere of circulation into the form of a hoard and back again. If the two processes balance each other, the quantitative relation between circulating gold and the hoards remains con-

---

282   Marx 1970, p. 134.
283   'Incidentally, in so far as the hoarder of money combines asceticism with assiduous diligence he is intrinsically a Protestant by religion and still more a Puritan' (Marx 1970, p. 130). These words from Marx were brilliantly confirmed in the famous work by Max Weber concerning the link between Puritanism and 'the spirit of capitalism'. Sombart, in his book *Der Bourgeois* [translated into English as *The Quintessence of Capitalism*] quite correctly imposed some limit on Weber's conclusions, which clearly exaggerated the role of Puritanism in the emergence and development of capitalism.
284   Concerning the luxuries of the 'newly rich', who emerged from the ranks of the bourgeoisie in the seventeenth to eighteenth century, see: Werner Sombart, *Der moderne Kapitalismus*, 4. Aufl., Bd. I., Hldb. 2., München, Leipzig: Duncker und Humblot, 1921, p. 727 et seq.

stant. If the circulation sphere requires more gold – due, for example, to an increase in the commodity turnover or a rise in commodity prices – then a portion of the gold flows from the form of a hoard into the sphere of circulation. Conversely, i.e. when the opposite conditions prevail, there is an increase of the hoard. Thus, the hoard fulfils the role of a reservoir from which the sphere of circulation acquires any additional quantity of money it needs and into which it discards any excessive quantity of money. The quantity of money in circulation thereby adjusts to the needs of commodity circulation, and money circulation 'never overflows' its banks.[285] With a metallic circulation, the quantity of money in circulation is automatically regulated by the spontaneous mechanism of money circulation.

The link between hoards and the sphere of circulation differs, however, for different portions of the gold that is withdrawn from circulation. The reserve fund of coin flows continuously into circulation and, properly speaking, can be regarded as being constantly in the sphere of circulation. The money reserve fund flows into circulation at times determined by its character and purpose (for example, when a machine wears out or a payment falls due). An accumulating hoard (in a capitalist society, bank reserves) partially flows into the sphere of circulation, usually at moments when the latter has an increased need for money, for example, at moments when the conjuncture reaches its peak, when the quantity of circulating commodities increases at the same time as their prices rise. And finally, the most remote and weakest link connects the sphere of circulation with a hoard in aesthetic form, i.e. with gold and silver commodities. It is only in periods of social storms, wars, revolutions and so forth that such items of luxury are transformed into money in significant amounts.[286]

The passage of gold from the form of a hoard into the sphere of circulation and back signifies an alteration of its social function or form, even though in most cases its natural form remains constant. The same gold coins can serve today as medium of circulation, tomorrow as a reserve fund, and subsequently as an accumulating hoard. Insofar as the latter consists not of coin but of gold and silver bars, they can enter, in the same form of bars, into the sphere of international circulation, or they can just as easily be minted again into coin to meet the needs of domestic circulation. Likewise, gold and silver commodities can easily be minted, if necessary, into coin. This ability of the precious metals to pass from the form of coin into the form of bars, and from the latter into the

---

285 Marx 1976, p. 232.
286 Marx 1976, p. 231; also Marx 1970, p. 135.

form of luxury items and back again – makes them the material most highly suited to fulfil the function of 'money, which must constantly change from one form into another'.[287]

Marx's conclusions regarding the function of money as a hoard refer mainly to the primitive form of accumulating a hoard, which corresponds to the conditions of simple commodity economy. For that reason they provide us with comparatively little material for understanding the economic functions and character of a hoard in conditions of a capitalist economy, with its highly developed and extremely complex credit system. But, on the other hand, these conclusions from Marx do provide us with extremely interesting sociological material that often escapes attention and, for that reason, requires that we consider it in more detail.

Earlier, in the chapter on the medium of circulation, we saw that money fulfils a determinate function (medium of circulation) only in the presence of certain production relations between commodity owners (who are alternately fulfilling the roles of seller and buyer) and a certain form of commodity circulation (the circuit C–M–C). Now we must show the same link between various social phenomena (the production relations between people, the forms of commodity circulation, and the functions or forms of money) in the case of money's function as a hoard. We have already noted above that money is transformed into a hoard 'because the metamorphosis of the commodity was interrupted' and 'a sale is not immediately turned into a purchase'.[288] A disruption occurs between C–M and M–C, and the very character of commodity circulation changes as a consequence. 'The *money* is petrified into a *hoard*, and the *seller of commodities* becomes *a hoarder of money*'.[289] What we see is the process of a simultaneous and parallel change in the social character of *people*, *commodities* and *money*. Let us consider what this change in the production relations between people entails, i.e. what it is that distinguishes the position of the accumulator of a hoard in the social production process from the position of the commodity owner who is not accumulating a hoard.

Money's function as medium of circulation, in an uninterrupted circuit of C–M–C, assumed that each private establishment buys products with the full sum of money for which it previously sold its own products, i.e. equilibrium was assumed between the production and consumption of each private undertaking. Accumulation of a hoard by a given commodity owner begins precisely

---

287   Marx 1970, p. 155.
288   Marx 1970, p. 125.
289   Marx 1976, p. 228.

when the equilibrium between his production and consumption is disrupted, when the former exceeds the latter, when more commodities are thrown into circulation (i.e. for a greater sum of exchange-value or money) than are drawn from it in the form of commodities, and the entire difference is removed from circulation in the form of money and preserved as a hoard. 'The owner of commodities who has now become a hoarder of money must sell as much as possible and buy as little as possible'.[290] The surplus of production over consumption means a change in the position occupied by the given private establishment in the total social production process; a change of the quantitative relationship between sellers and buyers means a qualitative change of the production relations that connect the given commodity owner with the others.

Thus, when the collector of a hoard sells his commodity,[291] this act of sale, C–M, appears externally to be no different from similar acts of sale being completed by the commodity owners who are not accumulating a hoard. But there is an essential and profound difference between them. The commodity owner, as participant in the circuit C–M–C, sells his production, which later he consumes in changed form[292] (i.e. after selling it and buying means of consumption and means of production with the money received), and thus after the social role of seller he fulfils the role of buyer. The collector of a hoard sells the commodity for a sum that creates an excess of his production over consumption; he acts one-sidedly in the social role of seller and simultaneously as the collector of a hoard.[293] The act of sale C–M, occurring in isolation, differs from the act of sale C–M as part of the uninterrupted circuit C–M–C, not only in terms of its origin and objective result but also in terms of its subjective motive. In the circuit C–M–C, sale occurs precisely for the sake of the ensuing purchase, and thus its goal is to replace one use-value c_1, by means of the money M, with another use-value c_2. The final goal of the circuit C–M–C lies in consumption. With the accumulation of a hoard, sale C–M occurs not with the goal of acquiring money for purchasing, but exclusively in order to convert C into M, to acquire its money equivalent in place of the commodity. 'Commodities are sold not in order to buy commodities, but in order to replace their commodity-form

---

290   Marx 1970, p. 128.
291   Here, of course, we are speaking only of that commodity whose value, after the sale, he will retain (turn into a hoard). Insofar as he sells a portion of his commodities with the aim of using the money to buy others, he appears not as a hoarder but as an ordinary participant in the circuit M–C–M.
292   We refer here to both personal and productive consumption.
293   Insofar as he is a buyer, he is not a hoarder.

by their money-form. Instead of being merely a way of mediating the metabolic process [*Stoffwechsel*], this change of form becomes an end in itself'.[294] As we see, the transformation of money from medium of circulation into a hoard presupposes an entire complex of social phenomena involving a simultaneous and parallel change of the relation between production and consumption, of the production relations between commodity owners, of the driving motives behind exchange, of the forms of commodity circulation, and of the functions or forms of money.

At first sight, it may appear that the final cause of the move from circuit C–M–C to the accumulation of a hoard is a change in the driving motives of the commodity producer who is participating in the exchange. Such an understanding, which searches for the final cause of a change of economic phenomena in the psyche of an individual economic actor, could not be more foreign to Marx. True to the method of historical materialism, Marx strongly emphasises in this case that the very fact of appearance among the actors in exchange of a new type of economic motivation is the result of a change that has occurred in the production relations between people. The endeavour to convert the commodity into money can become an autonomous motive of exchange only provided that there has already been a detachment of the money-form of the product from its commodity-form; that is, if commodity owners, through their activities, have already assigned to one commodity the character of money, which has the capacity for universal and direct exchangeability.

> The passion for enrichment by contrast with the urge to acquire particular material wealth, i.e., use-values, such as clothes, jewellery, herds of cattle, etc., becomes possible only when general wealth as such is represented by a specific thing and can thus be retained as a particular commodity. Money therefore appears both as the object and the *source* of the desire for riches.[295]

If the passion for enrichment is already the result of money's appearance, then conversely the latter necessarily gives birth to a new driving motive for exchange, the endeavour to exchange the commodity for money with the aim of accumulating a hoard. 'When the circulation of commodities first develops, there also develops *the necessity and the passionate endeavour* to hold fast to the product of the first metamorphosis. This product is the transformed shape

---

294 Marx 1976, pp. 227–8.
295 Marx 1970, p. 132.

of the commodity, or its gold chrysalis'.[296] 'With the possibility of keeping hold of the commodity as exchange-value, or exchange-value as a commodity, the lust for gold awakens'.[297] 'The simple fact that the commodity-owner is able to retain his commodities in the form of exchange-value, or to retain the exchange-value as commodities, makes the exchange of commodities, in order to recover them transformed into gold, the specific *motive* of circulation'.[298] New economic 'facts' give birth to new economic 'motives', and the social *activity* of commodity producers, which results in the appearance of money, also calls to life a new type of economic *motivation*.

This new type of economic motivation consists of the fact that the commodity owner already enters into exchange not with the goal of acquiring 'subsistence', or replacing one use-value with another as in the circuit C–M–C, but with the goal of acquiring and retaining the money-form of his commodity. His only wish is to complete the 'change of form', more precisely, to give his product a different social form (the money-form) and himself a different social character, the character of subject of 'the social power of money', with the ability to appear at any moment as the active participant in the production relations of exchange. The accumulation of a hoard effects the first breach in simple commodity (handicraft and peasant) economy, which is based upon 'the idea of subsistence'. The goal of economic activity becomes exchange-value in itself, not as a means for acquiring use-value. 'The underlying reason is the fact that exchange-value as such becomes the goal, and consequently also an expansion of exchange-value'.[299] This drive to multiply exchange-value is common both to the collector of a hoard and to the capitalist.[300] But there is a profound difference between them. The latter, in the presence of a developed capitalist economy, and particularly of a class of wage-workers, has the ability to increase his value, throwing it into circulation. The formula for the movement of capital is M-C-S-(M+m), i.e. the 'self-expansion' of value in the process of circulation (which includes the process of production). In the pre-capitalist epoch, the collector of a hoard has only one, quite different way to multiply exchange-value: to repeat the act of sale C_1–M_1, C_2–M_2, C_3–M_3 etc., retaining sums of money in his own hands and gradually adding one to another. In place of the 'self-expansion' of value, here only its 'accumulation' is possible in the literal sense of the word, i.e. the accumulation or addition of one sum to another: $M_1+M_2+M_3$ and so

---

296 Marx 1976, p. 227.
297 Marx 1976, p. 229. [Rubin's note in the margin pertaining to this passage says: 'discard'].
298 Marx 1970, p. 127.
299 Marx 1970, p. 132.
300 Marx 1976, p. 254.

forth. Whereas the capitalist throws money into circulation, the collector of a hoard 'rescues' it from circulation, keeping it to himself and preventing it from fulfilling the function of medium of circulation.

Does this not mean that the money, as a hoard, fulfils no social function at all, that the hoarding of money, especially in the form of burying it in the ground, tears it from the network of social ties and represents the complete, even if temporary, cessation of its social functions? There are some economists who suggest that a hoard fulfils a special 'economic function' only from the moment when it is put out by its owner as a loan to another person,[301] but not during the time when it is withdrawn from circulation. Marx foresaw this doubt and responded to it. His attention, as always, was focused not on the gold buried in the ground but on the social production relation of which it is the carrier. 'If the hoard were not constantly in tension with circulation, it would now simply be a heap of useless metal, its monetary soul would have disappeared and nothing but burnt-out ashes of circulation, its *caput mortuum*, would remain'.[302] Marx's idea, expressed in a metaphorical way, only becomes understandable in light of his teaching on the social production relations between people. These social relations constitute the 'soul' of things, without which they become 'burnt-out ashes', a 'body' without 'a social *nervus rerum*'.[303] In commodity economy a 'social power', consisting of the ability to establish production relations of exchange, belongs to the individual as owner of 'an external object capable of becoming the private property of an individual. Thus the social power becomes the private power of private persons'.[304] It is precisely in order to concentrate in his own hands this social power of commodity owners that he wrests gold from its social ties in the process of circulation. Social wealth 'is turned into an imperishable subterranean hoard with an entirely furtive private relationship to the commodity-owner'.[305] 'The social connection, in its compact (compacted) form – for the commodity owner this connection consists of the commodity, and the adequate form of the commodity is money – is withheld from the social movement'.[306] By burying a hoard in the ground, however, its possessor does not tear himself from the network of social ties that connect him with the entire society of commodity producers. Denying essentials to himself,

---

301 See, for example, Steinberg 1922, p. 7.
302 Marx 1970, p. 131. [*Caput mortuum*, freely translated, means *lifeless remains*].
303 Ibid. [*Nervus rerum* refers to the moving spirit of things].
304 Marx 1976, pp. 229–30.
305 Marx 1970, p. 130.
306 Marx 1970, p. 131.

and following an anchorite's[307] way of life, he is by no means an anchorite who has fled into the desert to avoid people. Gold's possessor, even when it is buried in the ground, does not cease to be possessor of the social power of which it is the carrier. This power remains a potential, and with the onset of favourable conditions it actively appears: the collector of the hoard then turns into the moneylender, the merchant or the industrial capitalist. But even before that happens – and despite all his seemingly asocial character – he in fact represents a certain definite social type. He acquires his hoard by means of certain social activities, namely, through a series of repeated acts of sale that are not complemented by acts of purchase.[308] He endlessly strives to repeat these activities. The words we have quoted from Marx – saying that the hoard is 'constantly in tension with circulation' – refer, of course, to the collector of the hoard. The hoard itself can be buried in the ground, but 'its monetary soul' and constant 'tension with circulation'[309] continue to live in its possessor as the striving constantly to repeat the acts of sale and accumulation.

Marx also derives this tendency of accumulation, its repetitiousness or 'unlimited character', from the social nature of money as the object of accumulation.

> Qualitatively or formally considered, money is independent of all limits, that is, it is the universal representative of material wealth because it is directly convertible into any other commodity. But at the same time every actual sum of money is limited in amount, and therefore has only a limited efficacy as a means of purchase. This contradiction between the quantitative limitation and the qualitative lack of limitation of money keeps driving the hoarder back to his Sisyphean task: accumulation.[310]

'The formation of hoards, therefore, has no intrinsic limits, no bounds in itself, but is an unending process, each particular result of which provides an *impulse for a new beginning*'.[311] The social nature of money, as the universal equivalent, not only calls to life the accumulation of money as a new compelling motive of exchange but also continuously sustains the activity resulting from this

---

307 [The word 'anchorite' comes from ancient Greek and refers to the ascetic who has withdrawn from society for a life of prayer].
308 Recall that here Marx has in mind the commodity producer who is converting the selling price of his commodities into a hoard.
309 Ibid.
310 Marx 1976, pp. 230–1.
311 Marx 1970, p. 132 [Rubin's emphasis].

motive. It creates *the tendency towards repeated acts of accumulation and the intensification of its motives*. Repetition and intensification of a particular type of economic motivation leaves its imprint on the entire *psyche* of the hoarder. Repeated acts of accumulation make their subject into a definite social type or *economic character*.

Marx devotes a few lines to portraying the psychology of the hoarder, which is replete with contradictions and has often been described in literature. The collector of a hoard 'cares for wealth only in its social form, and accordingly he hides it away from society. He wants commodities in a form in which they can always circulate, and he therefore withdraws them from circulation. He adores exchange-value, and he consequently refrains from exchange'.[312] At the basis of this contradiction lies the contradiction between the 'functional' and the 'material' existence of money, between the social production relation and the thing that is their carrier: the need to retain the thing in his 'private' possession, in order to have the ability to act as the subject of 'social' relations, is what gives the accumulation of hoards its character founded upon contradictions.

The repetitiveness of the acts of accumulation and their inherent driving motives make their subject into a definite social-economic type. In this respect, the social role of the hoarder differs from the social role of the ordinary commodity owner who participates in the circuit C–M–C. The buyer or seller in the circuit C–M–C completes a definite 'social act' or fulfils an 'economic function'.[313] But fulfilling this sort of function (for example, that of the seller) already presupposes the need for the same person to fulfil the opposing function (i.e. of the buyer). Each person alternately fulfils different functions. 'Consequently, buying and selling are not functions that are fixed, but functions that are constantly changing in the process of commodity circulation in terms of the people who fulfil them'.[314] As distinct from 'transient' roles that 'are played alternately by the same actors' in circulation, there are economic roles that are 'capable of a more rigid crystallisation',[315] i.e. they become affixed to separate individuals, as their special economic function, and they make a permanent impression upon them. In one of our opening chapters, we showed that the opposition between buyer and seller represents the first, rudimentary form of social differentiation between commodity producers. But that was only a differentiation of economic functions, without any differentiation of individuals,

---

312   Marx 1970, p. 134.
313   Marx 1976, p. 213. [See also Marx 1970, p. 164].
314   Marx 1976, pp. 222–3.
315   Marx 1976, p. 233.

since every commodity owner briefly and alternately fulfilled both functions. But insofar as an economic function creates a tendency towards repetition of a specific kind of actions and the exclusion of opposing ones, it makes the given subject into a definite social-economic type. And precisely such capacity for crystallisation is especially marked in the accumulation of a hoard, with its tendency to affix a definite type of economic motivation and to involve repetition of particular activities. Thus, accumulation of a hoard creates the 'professional hoarder', and the *differentiation of economic functions becomes fixed as the differentiation of individuals*. A given production relation of commodity owners – or what is the same thing, their social activity – in creating the conditions for its continuous reproduction and repetition by one and the same individuals, makes a certain imprint both on the individual engaging in the activity and on the things that figure as the links connecting the individuals. Accumulation of a hoard, as a series of repeated actions, becomes 'fixed' or 'crystallised': 1) in the function of money as a hoard and 2) in the social type of the hoarder, with his characteristic mental disposition. The social character of people's activities determines the social type of the people involved and of their mentality, on the one hand, and the social form of things on the other. The differentiation of economic functions (i.e. of production relations) leads to differentiation of the economic characters of people on the one hand, and of material economic categories on the other. The transformation of the simple commodity producer into the collector of a hoard represents the first step on the road from a society of equal commodity producers towards a capitalist society, with its profound differentiation of individuals expressed in the class division of society.

The passage from the 'transitory role' of buyer or seller to the 'crystallised' role of collector of a hoard has an interesting parallel in the passage from the 'transitory' function of money, as medium of circulation, to its 'congealed' or 'crystallised' function as a hoard. Marx makes a precise distinction between 'money in its fluid form' and money 'as a crystalline product of circulation'.[316] To the first belongs the medium of circulation; to the latter, a hoard as well as means of payment. To clarify the difference between them, Marx often reverts to figuratively comparing them with the process of crystallisation and with the general processes of a substance's transition from a liquid to a solid state. The medium of circulation stands opposed to a hoard, as the 'liquid form of wealth' does to its 'petrification'.[317] 'In order for money to flow constantly in the form

---

316   Marx 1970, p. 159.
317   Marx 1970, p. 134.

of coin, coin must constantly congeal[318] in the form of money'.[319] 'The medium of circulation solidified (*erstarrt*) as money'.[320] The passage of the medium of circulation into a hoard is characterised as 'solidification' (*Erstarrung*); the hoard, in the return passage into circulation, 'streams' (*ergiessen*).[321] Of course, in this case all of these comparisons occur to Marx because of a single fact – that gold, as medium of circulation, really does move or 'flow', while as a hoard, as the primitive form of accumulation, it actually lies idle and 'solidifies'. But we must not fail to notice that Marx uses the same comparisons in cases where there can be no talk of any real immobilisation of one or another real thing. For him, 'crystallisation' most often means the enduring affixation to a thing of a determinate social form, or to an individual, of a determinate social character. Consequently, we must conclude that Marx designates the medium of circulation as the 'fluid' form of money not only because the thing that fulfils this function really does move, but also because the corresponding economic functions of sale or purchase have a 'transitory' character, being fulfilled briefly and alternately by different individuals.[322] A hoard is designated as one of the 'frozen' and 'crystallised' forms of money not simply because it lies immobile in the ground or in a cash-box, but also because the corresponding economic function of collecting a hoard has a tendency to 'become crystallised', or affixed over a long period, to a particular individual. And here, as elsewhere in the Marxist system, a difference in the social form of things reflects a difference in the social production relations between people.

318 Or 'settle' (*gerinnen*). It is interesting to recall that in value Marx sees 'congealed labour time' (*festgeronnene Arbeitszeit*) or the 'crystallisation' of labour (Marx 1970, p. 29). (For more on the concept of 'crystallisation' in Marx see [at this point, the lower part of the manuscript has been torn off and it is not possible to restore the lost text]).
319 Marx 1970, p. 126.
320 Marx 1970, p. 136.
321 Ibid.
322 For this reason, the medium of circulation is likewise only a 'transient' monetary form of the commodity itself. See the chapter on medium of circulation.

DOCUMENT 20

The Dialectical Development of Categories in Marx's Economic System (1929)

Isaak Il'ich Rubin

Source: I. Rubin, 'Dialekticheskoe razvitie kategorii v ekonomicheskoi sisteme Marksa: Ispravlennaya i dopolnennaya stenogramma doklada, prochitannovo 30 marta 1929 g. na dispute v Institute Krasnoi Professury', in *Pod znamenem Marksizma*, No. 4, April 1929, pp. 82–108, No. 5, May 1929, pp. 51–82. For a summary of Rubin's report, the co-report by S.A. Bessonov, and the ensuing debate, see *Problemy Ekonomiki*, No. 4, April 1929, pp. 203–38.

Introduction by the Editors

In the first document translated for this book, Illarion Kaufman questioned whether Marx was seriously indebted to Hegel or merely used Hegelian language to present conclusions drawn by analogy with the biological sciences. Since Marx was 'more realistic than all of his predecessors', Kaufman had difficulty understanding why the 'external form of his presentation' should be so suggestive of German idealist philosophy in 'the bad sense of the word'. The issue of methodology has reappeared throughout the documents that we have translated, but nowhere is it more central than in this essay by Isaak Rubin, which specifically addresses the 'dialectical development of categories' in the three volumes of Marx's *Capital*. There is no question that this essay represents a theoretical triumph on Rubin's part that far surpassed the insight of almost all of his predecessors and contemporaries.

In his commentaries on Hegel's *Science of Logic*, Lenin made the famous notation that 'It is impossible completely to understand Marx's *Capital*, and especially its first chapter, without having thoroughly studied and understood the *whole* of Hegel's *Logic*. Consequently, half a century later none of the Marxists understood Marx!!'.[1] Lenin added in his *Philosophical Notebooks* that

---

1   Lenin 1912, p. 180.

In his *Capital*, Marx first analyses the simplest, most ordinary and fundamental, most common and everyday *relation* of bourgeois (commodity) society, a relation encountered billions of times, viz., the exchange of commodities. In this very simple phenomenon (in this 'cell' of bourgeois society) analysis reveals *all* the contradictions (or the germs of *all* contradictions) of modern society. The subsequent exposition shows us the development (*both* growth *and* movement) of these contradictions and of this society in the Σ [the sum] of its individual parts. From its beginning to its end.[2]

We quote these comments from Lenin because they also summarise Isaak Rubin's theme in this essay, which is devoted entirely to Marx's dialectical method. Here Rubin completed the undertaking that Lenin projected: he began with the initial 'cell' of bourgeois society and then followed Marx in dialectically (that is, logically and historically) revealing all the fundamental contradictions of capitalist society. Like Lenin, Rubin understood that Marx's *Capital* was conceived in his critical appropriation of Hegel's *Logic*. Rubin's work is all the more remarkable since it was published in 1929, at a time when Stalin's suppression of creative thought was already well under way in the Soviet Union – a fact reflected in Rubin's need, at the beginning of his paper, to refute spurious criticisms of his earlier *Essays on Marx's Theory of Value*. These opening pages only emphasise all the more the elegance of Rubin's insight and his remarkable clarity of presentation. Rubin provides a methodological roadmap of Marx's work that remains unsurpassed.

As in Hegel's *Logic*, Rubin's analysis moves within a dialectical circle of necessity – from the immediacy of a simple category (the commodity, for example) through its internal differentiation (the poles of value) to a new self-identity in a higher category (in this case money serving as universal equivalent for the circulation of commodities) – which again proves contradictory (money as a private hoard or means of settling private credit obligations, each with the capacity to disrupt circulation) and thereby necessitates further movement. Rubin shows that in the entire dialectical movement of *Capital*, there is a sequential process of immediacy dissolving into contradiction and then returning in the immediacy of a more complex, but also transitory, self-identity – all of which expresses continuously changing production relations between people. Each group of phenomena, which constitutes a unity, gives way to polarisation and difference; and each group, which appears to be contradictory, constitutes

---

2 Lenin 1915b, pp. 360–1.

a unity within whose limits the phenomena are antitheses. In the first volume of *Capital* Marx wrote: 'To say that ... mutually independent and antithetical processes form an internal unity is to say also that their internal unity moves forward through external antitheses'.[3] 'Such', adds Rubin, 'is the dual character of the law of the unity of opposites ...'. Rubin emphasises that, throughout this dialectical movement, nothing is ever lost. It is the self-movement of the commodity that results in wage-labour and capital; but conversely, capital is inconceivable without commodity production. The higher categories always contain the lower, just as the lower give rise to the higher.

Marx discovered this logical-historical movement when he combined the *analytical* with the *synthetic* method. Through analysis he deconstructed capitalism to arrive at the fundamental concepts of labour and the commodity; through synthesis he categorically reconstructed the contradictory (but still law-governed) unity of capitalism as a whole. This uniqueness of method was what enabled him to resolve the dilemmas left by his predecessors, particularly David Ricardo with his incomplete labour theory of value. Rubin points out that earlier political economy suffered from an essential deficiency:

> ... the classics attempted, with the help of analysis, to reduce the detachment and alienation of forms of wealth from one another to their internal unity – in the final analysis, to labour. But the classical school was limited by this analytical reduction and did not take the reverse synthetic route; it did not show how different forms arise from unity, gradually separating and becoming externally independent of one another; it did not show us the process of the gradual development and formation of forms, the process of the 'genesis' of forms.

Marx, in contrast, looked beyond the 'appearance' of phenomena to discover their internal connections as parts of the single process of social production. In Marx's analysis, phenomena that have 'become detached' are revealed as 'alienated' production relations between people, or social forms of human relations that have, as Rubin says, 'coalesced' with things. The reified 'determinations of form', at each level of analysis, are shown confronting one another in a condition of contradiction and struggle, yet ultimately the entire system points beyond itself to the restoration of human community. Marx's understanding of history begins with the patriarchal family and primitive community; it ends with the projection of a restored community that transcends class divisions but

---

3   Marx 1976, p. 209.

also retains the wealth of history. As Rubin writes, a history of class struggle, culminating in the conflict between those who own and those who create the means of production, prepares the ground

> for a real 'removal' of the alienated and detached forms of social life and for a genuine revelation of the unity that lies at their basis. The more the power of 'alienated' labour (capital) grows over living labour, the more the conditions are created for the elimination of this alienation. It is precisely because capital develops the powerful productive forces of labour, which can no longer operate within the limits of capitalist production relations, that it also prepares its own end.

In his 1924 essay on the differences between Marx's and Ricardo's theory of value, Rubin had already incorporated the *1844 Manuscripts* to explain the 'dual character' of labour and value, which, through commodity fetishism, transformed 'things' into the 'mediators' and 'bearers' of production relations between people. This essay completes the argument of that earlier essay by analysing still more comprehensively the way in which Marx appropriated Hegel's dialectical methodology. In Hegel's system, the end is implicit in the beginning: philosophy is the highest form of labour, but thought reflecting upon thought is also logic, and the *Logic* is where Hegel's *Encyclopaedia of the Philosophical Sciences* begins. For Marx, *concrete labour* is the beginning of the story; and rational, self-determining social labour – labour reflecting upon itself, projecting its own future and thereby transcending *abstraction* and reification – is the end. Marx, as Kaufman said, was 'more realistic than all of his predecessors'. However, as Lenin and Rubin understood, he was also able to achieve that realism precisely because of his ability to draw upon Hegel in a *philosophically* inspired *science* of political economy.

∴

Isaak Rubin on Marx's Dialectical Development of Categories

1 *The Subject Matter of Political Economy*
My objective will not be to give either an exhaustive or even a complete statement of the theme I have selected. A complete elaboration of the question of the dialectical development of categories in Marx would require the joint efforts of several comrades, including both economists and philosophers. I shall limit my theme in two ways: first, I shall not be touching upon the philo-

sophical foundations of the dialectical method – that is a matter for philosophers. We economists adopt the basic positions of the dialectical method in the general form given by Marx and Engels, and our task is to show how Marx applied these basic positions of the dialectical method to the various economic categories in *Capital*. The second limitation will be the following: dialectical logic involves such a wealth of forms of thought that it would be impossible to exhaust them in a single report. My task, therefore, will be to trace the manner in which Marx applies the fundamental law of dialectics – the law of the unity of opposites, together with the law of negation – to economic categories in the three volumes of *Capital*.

Once we speak of the dialectical development of categories, we presuppose that the entire system of Marx's economic categories represents a single, orderly system that entails the internal unity and consistency of all its parts. In other words, we presuppose a single, orderly system of economic categories that reflects a system of production relations between people even though it is replete with the greatest contradictions.

At this point we encounter the following question: if we take the system of production relations as a whole, do we not thereby detach this system from the development of material productive forces? Are the critics, who say that we separate production relations from the productive forces, not correct? Are the critics not correct when they say that the subject matter of political economy involves, to the same extent and on an equal basis, both the production relations between people in capitalist society and the productive forces? In other words, we have to begin with the question of the subject matter of political economy. This question has provoked and continues to provoke lively debates in which two tendencies are evident: some economists maintain the long-standing Marxist doctrine, which sees political economy as the science of production relations between people in capitalist society; and other economists, who do not have the courage to reject this traditional Marxist definition, wish to blunt the precision of this clear and vivid definition. They demand direct inclusion of the productive forces in the subject matter investigated by political economy.

How do matters stand on this question that currently divides Marxist economists? S[ergei] Bessonov gave the following formulation in his article: political economy investigates 'the linkage and the contradictions between productive forces and production relations'.[4] He forgets that we can study the linkage

---

4   See the journal *Problemy Ekonomiki*, No. 1, 1929, p. 129. Our response to this article by Bessonov will appear in No. 3 of *Problemy Ekonomiki*. [Rubin's response to Bessonov was also included

and contradictions between productive forces and production relations from two sides – in terms of production relations and in terms of the productive forces.

In theoretical political economy, we take our direct subject matter to be study of the production relations between people in a capitalist economy, and our objective is to reveal all of the regular patterns involved in this sphere. But the production relations do, indeed, develop in a way that depends upon changes in the productive forces; in turn, they also have a reverse effect upon development of the productive forces. Thus, to explain the development of production relations, we must continuously make reference to development of the productive forces. Secondly, before beginning a study of the whole system of production relations in a capitalist economy, we must clarify just which development on the part of the productive forces has brought about the existing system of production relations. But that is not all. Throughout our entire study we must look to the sphere of development of the material productive forces for the causes of change in economic forms and in the production relations between people. In the movement from one form to another, in the transition from value to capital, and in the explanation of why capital divides into industrial, commercial and money capital – we must look to the sphere of material productive forces for the causes that evoke changes in the production relations between people. We cannot always specify these causes that issue from the sphere of material production, and Marx did not always show us precisely which changes in the productive forces brought forth one or another change in production relations. But it is our duty, in principle, to look to the sphere of development of the material productive forces for the causes of changes in production relations.

At the same time, we must also study the reverse influence of production relations upon the productive forces. However, this by no means implies that we take the productive forces to be the direct object of our study – and anyone who is familiar with the elementary principles of classification in the sciences will understand this without any difficulty. The various sciences study different aspects of a single reality. The various social sciences study different aspects of the life of society. Given the inseparable connection and interaction between the different aspects of social life, every science, which studies one aspect of life in society, must, in research intended to explain its own object, always include phenomena from the adjacent sphere; that is, phenomena that

---

in the 4th Russian edition of his *Essays on Marx's Theory of Value*. See I.I. Rubin, *Ocherki po teorii stoimosti Marksa* (Moscow: Gosudarstvennoe Izdatel'stvo, 1929), pp. 304–63].

are the direct object of study for other related sciences. For example, the science that studies law cannot understand the development of law without reference to development of the economy, and particularly to development of the material productive forces. Otherwise, such a science of law would not be a Marxist science. Nevertheless, the science of law does not take the economy to be the subject matter of its investigation. To explain the production relations between people and how they change, political economy must refer to development of the material productive forces; but, given this fact, we do not take our objective in political economy to be study of all the regular patterns occurring in the sphere of development of the material productive forces. We invoke them in our investigation only insofar as we must do so in order to explain the laws involved in changes of the production relations between people. And even in this case, while we refer to material from the sphere of the productive forces, we do not so much become involved in a special analysis and investigation of this material ourselves as simply make use of what is given and established in the adjacent sciences. Thus we have an interest in seeing the science of social technology become sufficiently developed to provide us with adequate material concerning development of the productive forces within capitalism so that we may use this material to explain the development of production relations between people. And this also means that, for those of us in political economy, the direct object of investigation is the production relations between people. The presupposition of our research is the material productive forces.

We frequently hear this sort of reproach: once you assign the role of presupposition to the productive forces, you attribute to them some kind of modest place in the development of society and deny their role as motive force for the whole of social development. This objection is based upon a crude misunderstanding. We do not counterpose the word 'presupposition' to the term 'motive force'. Every Marxist is obliged to recognise that the motive force for the whole of social development is precisely development of the material productive forces. But this motive force for the whole of social development is not what we study in theoretical political economy. We resort continuously to development of the productive forces in order to explain the production relations between people, and this means that the material productive forces are the presupposition of our research. The word 'presupposition' does not stand opposed to the term 'motive force'; it marks a distinction from the 'object' of the investigation. Every science has its own direct object of investigation. All related phenomena, which we invoke in a given science insofar as they are necessary in order to explain the direct object of our research, are referred to in science as a presupposition of the investigation. Anyone who does not understand this distinction does not understand either the ABC of the classification of sciences or the ABC of the division of labour between the different sciences.

Let us take an example to illustrate the idea. Everyone understands that there is an inseparable connection between the technical composition of capital and growth of the organic composition of capital. At the same time, though, everyone who studies *Capital* knows that Marx took for the direct subject matter of his research the growth of the organic composition of capital, that is, growth of the value relations between the parts of capital insofar as these value relations reflect the changing proportion between dead means of production and living labour; that is, insofar as they reflect changes occurring in the sphere of technique, in the sphere of the material productive forces. Does this mean that Marx made growth of the technical composition of capital the direct subject matter of his investigation? Anyone who has read *Capital* knows that Marx did not do that. Marx gave us the basic formula of growth of the technical composition of capital in order to explain growth of the organic composition of capital, and then he investigates in detail the influence of growth of the organic composition of capital on the concentration of production, on expansion of the reserve army [of labour], and so forth. In a word, he explores the production relations between people, as expressed in an entire series of economic phenomena; and meanwhile, growth of the technical composition of capital, for Marx, is the basis or presupposition of his research, not the direct object. If Marx had wanted to study directly the growth of the technical composition of capital, he would have had to collect an enormous volume of detail, portraying the increase of dead means of production relative to living labour. He would have had to provide a great volume of material describing the development and condition of technique in capitalist society. That is not what Marx did, because that sort of special research into changes in the sphere of technique between dead means of production and living labour – research that is completely necessary and can cast much light upon the development of economic phenomena – cannot enter directly into the economic system that Marx provides.

Bessonov objects to the existence of two sciences, one of which studies productive forces while the other deals with the production relations of capitalist society. Apparently he thinks that the existence of two sciences will create a rupture between the productive forces and the production relations. But it would surely be most naïve to think that, in order to preserve the connection between the two phenomena, one must directly study them within a single science. Would the link between the productive forces and the relations of production really be guaranteed by looking at them in terms of a single science? Such a joining together into a single science of different sides of economic life, which differ in terms of their character and the laws of their development, does not in the slightest degree ensure us against a rupture between these two sides; and, contrariwise, you can study these two sides in terms of two different sciences, while also studying each in advance as part of a single economic process, as a part that presupposes its other side and is inextricably connected with it. Only in this way can you ensure against a rupture, and not at all by joining together what cannot be joined, by doing violence to theoretical political economy, or by aiming to tear apart the entire structure of the economic system that Marx outlined in *Capital*.

Bessonov says that I am 'dreaming up' new sciences: a science of social technique and a science of the production relations between people. I could claim, with much greater justification, that Bessonov wants to invent a single science that studies both the production relations between people and the productive forces. You see, we Marxists always pride ourselves on the fact that, as soon as we begin to discuss production or the economy, we establish a precise distinction between the relation of man to nature and the relation of people to people. We have always considered this to be a superiority of Marxist compared to bourgeois science. We have always laughed at bourgeois scholars, who spend several volumes discussing production without taking the trouble to clarify whether the issue is the material-technical side of production or the production relations between people. As I will further demonstrate, all Marxists, including Lenin, have drawn a clear distinction, as soon as they began to speak about production, between the material-technical process of production and the production relations between people. Marx always said that political economy studies the production relations between people while the material-technical process of production relates to the sphere of technology. Marx emphasises the need to work out a special science, a 'critical history of technology' that would show 'the material basis of every particular organisation of society'.[5] That is why, in my *Essays*, I also pointed out that the material productive forces are studied by a special science of social technique, a science that must undergo extensive development.[6]

Of course, the material productive forces are essentially a social phenomenon. They change in the course of historical development and bring about changes in the production relations between people. This means that the material productive forces are also, essentially, an historical and social phenomenon, just as the production relations between people are. But the point is that we are not obliged to include all social phenomena in a single science.

---

5 Marx 1976, p. 493, footnote 4.
6 Rubin 1990, pp. 2–3.

The fact that the productive forces are a social phenomenon in no way requires us to include them directly in the subject matter of our investigation. Those economists who want to concoct a single new science of the economy are forgetting that every science is a product of long historical development, and that we Marxists are also obliged to approach science itself from an historical point of view. We cannot conceive our task in such manner that we can now sit at a table and begin anew the classification of sciences. Such a view would be non-historical and non-Marxist.

What is it that we are disputing? Is it a question as to which object we should choose for a science that we will invent and create in the future, or are we arguing over the issue of what, in fact, is the object of political economy, which has developed in the course of two centuries and found its completion in Marx's system? It is precisely the latter that we are presently disputing. Political economy, which received orderly and finished form in Marx's *Capital*, is the science of the production relations between people. We can even explain why, by force of historical necessity, it became the science of production relations between people. How did political economy emerge? It began with the discussions and disputes of seventeenth-century mercantilists concerning wages, profit and rent; that is, it began with questions relating to the distribution of aggregate value between the different social classes. It reflected the struggle of social classes for their position within the given system of production relations between people. Political economy originated as the result of a fierce struggle between different classes and groups. It developed as the science of wages, profit and rent; in short, as the science of the system of values, or of the production relations between people. The various bourgeois schools struggled to strengthen their positions within the limits of the given capitalist system of production relations between people. Marx raised the question to an unattained height when he spoke of change of the production relations between people as such, of destruction of the entire system of production relations in capitalist economy and their replacement by a new system, by a socialist economy. It was precisely this grandiose task, encountered by Marx as the ideologist of the working class, that convinced Marx to define political economy as the science of production relations between people.

And what was the substance of the harsh critique that Marx directed against bourgeois economics? It consisted of the following: bourgeois economists argued that the basic phenomena of capitalism – profit, wages, interest and rent – necessarily result from the very nature of the production process and cannot be altered as the social form of the economy changes. Marx said to the bourgeois economists: all of these phenomena, which you attribute to the production process as such, are a result of the capitalist form of the production process; all of these phenomena have an historical and transitory character that is connected with the given social system of production relations between people. Consequently – said Marx – when development of the productive forces creates the necessity for demolition of the old system of production relations between people, all economic laws will acquire new form and all economic phenomena will be different. This was the sharpest critical weapon with which Marx struggled against vulgar political economy. This sharp critical weapon was the doctrine that all economic phenomena express the production relations between people. Anyone who wishes to throw away this definition of political economy, as the science of production relations between people, is light-headedly relinquishing the sharpest weapon with the help of which Marxist science has achieved enormous successes. Our critics must take into account that they are rejecting the definition that all Marxists share, without any exception, and that has frequently been repeated in the works of Marx, Engels, Plekhanov, Lenin, Hilferding, R[osa] Luxemburg and others.

Plekhanov uses the following expressions to characterise the revolutionary upheaval in science produced by Marx: 'The economic categories themselves express nothing but mutual relations between people, or of entire classes of society, within the social process of production. Economic science only adopted the correct viewpoint when it understood this and became engaged in an investigation of these mutual relations that are hidden behind the imaginary qualities of things and behind the mysterious properties of economic categories' (Vol. VI, p. 170). Marx never ceased to repeat, at every step, that all economic categories are essentially an expression of the production relations between people. Value is an expression of the production relations between people, money is an expression of the production relations between people, and capital is an expression of the production relations between people. Marx produced a revolution in science, particularly in the teaching on capital, thanks to the fact that he saw in capital an expression of the production relations between people. And in *The Poverty of Philosophy* Marx says that 'economic categories are only the theoretical expressions, the abstractions of the social relations of production'.[7] Engels repeats the same idea: 'Political economy is not concerned with things but with relations between people, and in the final analysis between classes; these relations, however, are always *bound to things* and *appear as things*' (*Pod Znamenem Marksizma*, 1923, Nos. 2–3, p. 56).[8] This

---

7 Marx 1977, p. 102.
8 [See the review of *A Contribution to the Critique of Political Economy* by Engels in Marx 1970, p. 226].

very same definition was repeated more than once by Lenin in his most diverse works and in various ways of expression. He wrote that the subject matter of political economy 'is not by any means "the production of material values", as is often claimed – that is the subject of technology – but the social relations of people in production'.[9] Lenin was so fond of this traditional Marxist distinction between the two sides of the production process that he repeated it in practically all of his works. He mentioned it in his book on Sismondi,[10] in 'What are the "Friends of the People"',[11] and in his review of the book by [Alexander] Bogdanov;[12] everywhere you find the idea emphasised that political economy investigates the social relations between people. We demand from our critics a clear and direct answer – Do they agree with this long-standing Marxist definition of the subject matter of political economy or do they not?

... If they agree that the subject matter of political economy is the social relations between people, and if they are simply emphasising that when studying the production relations between people we must constantly refer to development of the productive forces, as the motive force that brings about change of the production relations between people – then a basis can be found for a mutual convergence of viewpoints concerning the subject matter of political economy. But if they persist in rejecting the established Marxist definition of political economy as the science of production relations between people, and if they say – as Bessonov writes today in his theses – that both the production relations and the productive forces are 'equally' the subject matter investigated by political economy, then the consequence is their rejection of the definition that all Marxists have shared without exception. They are thereby introducing the greatest confusion into the definition of political economy's subject matter. They are obscuring a question already resolved thanks to Marx's ingenious efforts. They are erasing a fundamental distinction between Marxist and bourgeois political economy.

I have no wish to burden you with quotations, but I can show you by reference to the example of [Gustav] Cassel, one of the potentates of thought in modern bourgeois political economy, that all of his efforts are aimed precisely at showing that the fundamental economic phenomena, particularly profit and interest, necessarily result from the material features of the production process. It is precisely in order to struggle against this basic direction of bourgeois thought that we must preserve the sharp weapon of criticism given to us by

---

9   Lenin 1897, p. 202.
10 Lenin 1897.
11 Lenin 1894a.
12 Lenin 1898.

Marx, which consists of the fact that we regard all economic phenomena as the expression of production relations between people. Moreover, I would even say that those comrades who so love the productive forces actually wish to confine all study of the productive forces to those few chapters and separate observations for which we can find room within the sphere of our science, the sphere of theoretical political economy. They are ignoring the fact that, in order to study the laws of development of the productive forces in capitalism, we have to collect extensive materials and subject them to thorough analysis and research, that we require a special science that is now partially being created. Essentially speaking, those comrades who demand inclusion of the productive forces in the subject matter of political economy can only inhibit the development of a science of the productive forces, including development of a science especially devoted to study of the productive forces of a capitalist economy.

In order to prevent a rupture between the productive forces and production relations, we certainly have no need to join both elements together within a single science; but we must define production relations in such manner as to connect them indissolubly with the productive forces, and at each stage of our investigation we must make reference to development of the material productive forces. In order to avoid any misunderstanding, I repeat that every Marxist must eagerly support the explanation of all changes of production relations in terms of changes of the material productive forces. If you were able to prove that the function of means of payment developed from the function of means of circulation, and did so directly under the influence of the material process of production, that would be a great achievement for Marxist political economy. But we have not yet done so. For the present, we still cannot always specify the causes, for example, of the appearance a given function of money – nor can we, at each stage of the investigation, specify exactly all of the causes of the change of economic forms – that are included in the development of the material productive forces. In general terms, we can and must do so, but without obscuring the differences between various sides of the production process, and by remaining entirely on the ground of the established Marxist definition of political economy as the science of production relations between people.

Many comrades say: why did Marx pay so much attention in *Capital* to questions of technology, to questions of the development of technique? But just read Marx, comrades, not by snatching individual pages but rather by taking him in the context of his ideas as a whole. Consider an example. Marx writes about the development of machines. In the lengthy chapter 15,[13] which

---

13 [The text refers to chapter 13].

includes more than 115 pages, Marx devotes the first 12 pages to the development of machines in order to provide a basis for his further research; and following this first point, concerning the development of machines, you see another nine sections that study the influence of the development of machines on the production relations between people. The second section speaks of value, of the transfer of the machine's value to the products; the third, of the effect of machines upon the workers; the fourth, of factories; the fifth, of the struggle between workers and machines; and the subsequent sections speak of the theory of compensation, of the repulsion and attraction of workers, of the effect of machines upon handicrafts, and finally, of factory legislation. Marx derives a whole series of economic phenomena from the fact of the development of machines. Moreover, if you read through these 12 pages that are devoted to the development of machines, you will see that Marx begins with the introduction of machines as a means for producing surplus value, and he ends once more with the study of machines as a specific mode of increasing surplus value. Sixty years have passed since *Capital* was written. During that time the history of technique, and particularly the history of machines, has seen great accomplishments. Today's economist, unlike Marx, has no need to acquire information on the history of machines from scattered individual observations. And so I ask: is it possible to include the tens and hundreds of works on the history of technique within the theoretical system given to us by Marx? It is enough just to pose concretely the question of the actual classification of the sciences, which has emerged as a result of their two-hundred year history; it is enough just to look, with eyes wide open, at the actual division of labour that has been established between the sciences – and then you will see that any mention of including the productive forces and relations of production within the sphere of political economy, on an equal footing, is simply empty talk with no possibility of disclosing any real content. In the question of the subject matter of political economy, we are obliged to stick with the old position of Marx; we are obliged to preserve the definition of political economy as the science of production relations between people. We must continually emphasise that the production relations are only one side of the production process, and that their entire development is conditioned by movement of the material productive forces. In order to explain changes in the production relations between people, we must look for a corresponding cause in the material process of production. But the direct subject matter of our research in theoretical political economy remains the production relations between people.

2 The Dialectical Unity of the System of Production Relations

I now turn to the second point of my report – to the question of the dialectical unity of the system of production relations between people. We have come to the conclusion that production relations change in a way that depends upon development of the material productive forces. But now we encounter the following question: if production relations change under the influence of changes in the material productive forces, is the unity of the whole system of production relations, which characterises a given economic formation, still preserved? It is true that certain critics deny the very existence of this single system of production relations between people. Bessonov writes in his theses: 'Political economy does not study a "system" of production relations, because a "system" is something frozen and completed, but rather "the relations of production in a given, historically defined society, in their inception, development, and decline"'. (The closing words are taken from the works of Lenin).[14] In a word, Bessonov does not recognise the system of production relations as the subject matter of political economy, but rather their *development*. But how can a 'system' be counterposed to its 'development'? Why can we not study a system of relations of production in their inception, development and decline? Suppose we take seriously Bessonov's thesis that political economy does not study a system of production relations. In that case, what do we do with Marx's position, which says that we are investigating an 'economic structure'? The point is that Marx's greatest service lies precisely in the fact that he found different economic structures, different social formations. In his early work on 'What the "Friends of the People" Are', Lenin points out frequently that this was Marx's greatest service. From a multitude of diverse and tangled social relations, Marx knew how to discern an economic structure as the unity of production relations of the given society. Can it be that an economic structure is not a system? Is an economic formation really not a system? In Lenin's 'What the "Friends of the People" Are', you find the following sentence: Marx takes 'one of the social-economic formations – the *system* of commodity production'.[15] 'The system of commodity production' and 'the system of capitalist economy' – evidently Bessonov believes we must not speak in such terms because a system, in his view, means something that is frozen.

Marx always considered that the production relations represent a certain single system whose parts are interconnected. In *The Poverty of Philosophy*

---

14 [Lenin 1915a, p. 59].
15 Lenin 1894a, p. 141.

Marx writes: 'The production relations of every society form a whole'.[16] What does this mean? It means that they constitute a system. True, Marx does not say that this system is frozen and unchanging, as Bessonov writes, for there are indeed systems – and we may mention to him in secret that this includes every system in the world – that emerge, develop and perish. At the end of his *Critique of Political Economy*, Marx writes about [Thomas] Tooke. He says that Tooke studied the various functions of money instead of looking at one or another function one-sidedly, yet Marx says that he did so 'without paying any attention to the organic relation of these aspects either with one another or with the system of economic categories as a whole'.[17] As you see, Marx speaks of a 'system of economic categories'. How is it possible to deny that the production relations represent a single system?

In his article on the *Critique*, Engels thought it necessary to emphasise that 'Hardly any attempt has been made since Hegel's death to set forth any branch of science in its specific inner coherence'.[18] He regarded Marx's *Critique* as an attempt to discern this internal coherence of all the elements of a given science, i.e. to consider, as a whole, the given system of economic categories and the economic relations between people that they express.

This is all the more clearly evident in Lenin's writings on Hegel's *Logic*, which have recently been published. There Lenin gives the following exact formulation: 'As the simple form of value, the individual act of exchange of one given commodity for another already includes in an underdeveloped form *all* the main contradictions of capitalism'.[19] If you do not have a system of economic categories, how can this form of value include within itself, in underdeveloped form, the main contradictions of capitalism?

Thus the production relations of a capitalist economy and its corresponding economic categories constitute a single, determinate system of interconnected parts, in which one form arises historically from another form and operates on the basis of that other form. But at the same time, as we have just mentioned, production relations change in a way dependent upon the material productive forces. How do we resolve this apparent contradiction? On the one hand, all production relations are interconnected and form a certain system; but on the other hand, production relations change in a way dependent upon a change of the material productive forces.

---

16   Marx 1977, p. 103.
17   Marx 1970, p. 186.
18   Engels, in Marx 1970, p. 222.
19   Lenin 1912, pp. 178–9.

The system of categories of political economy represents a developing and increasingly complex system of different production relations that are expressed in different social forms – in the social form of value, capital, etc. Does the social form of capital arise from the social form of value or from development of the material productive forces? I am deliberately posing the question in such a ridiculous form as 'either-or' in order to demonstrate for you the impossibility of framing the question in this non-dialectical form. We know how this social form of capital emerged. We know that a simple commodity economy previously existed, although it was not yet adequately developed, and that it represented a unity of productive forces and their social forms. In particular, there existed in the simple commodity economy, although not yet adequately developed, the social form of value. We know that, precisely due to pressure from development of material productive forces, the production relations between simple commodity producers grew over into production relations of the capitalist type. We know that this growing over was not merely quantitative but was also qualitative; it was an entire historical upheaval, a leap. Bessonov accuses me of making no allowance for a leap between different social formations. I wrote explicitly in my *Essays* (p. 102) that 'An enormous historical revolution (described by Marx in the chapter on primitive capitalist accumulation) was necessary for the transformation of money into capital'.[20] One social form arises from another simpler social form under the pressure of change on the part of the material productive forces. But it arises not in the empty vacuum of space, or directly as a passive reflex of the existing condition of the productive forces, nor in a manner disconnected from other social forms and other production relations between people.

Thus, in response to the question posed above, it will be correct to answer as follows: within the limits of a given system of economy, each complex form of production relations between people arises from a simpler form of production relations under pressure from a change in the productive forces. Translating this formulation from the language of production relations into the language of economic categories, or forms, we come to this conclusion: within the limits of the given economic system, each economic category or form arises from the development of a previous, simpler economic category or form under pressure from development of the productive forces.

Now you can see the total lack of any grounds for the charge hurled at me by certain critics. '*To deduce form from form – that is Rubin's closed circle of scholastic thought. To deduce a social form from content extraneous to it – that is the*

---

20 Rubin 1990, p. 91.

real course of Marx's thought' (S. Bessonov's review in *Izvestiya TsiK*, 30 November 1928). This is precisely the false, non-dialectical posing of an 'either-or' question that I mentioned above. A complex social form arises *either* from a simpler social form *or* from content extraneous to it – that is how the critic poses the question. A complex social form arises from a simpler social form under pressure from a determinate development of content, that is, from the material productive forces – that is our response, which is in full agreement with Marx. The critic attributes to us the idea of an immaculate conception of one social form from another, without any intervention from the profane matter of the productive forces. But this accusation is totally groundless. The critic forgets that behind every social form are concealed the production relations of many millions of people, which recur day in and day out and represent enormous diversity. This is the constant sea of motion in which the process of changing production relations, under pressure from development of the productive forces, endlessly occurs and new types of production relations between people appear. When you think in the language of categories or social forms, it appears strange that a new and more complex form is born from a preceding one that is simpler, since you regard a social form as something static and congealed. But if you recall that behind each social form are concealed the daily recurring relations of a multitude of people, then you will already find here the dynamic element, the presence of enormous diversity that makes continuous development possible – under the influence, to be sure, of development of the productive forces.

We must beware of two extremes. The first extreme can be encapsulated as follows. We take a determinate social form (value, for instance) and by way of a dialectical development of the given concept we try to deduce from it a whole series of other social forms (money, capital, etc.), without making any reference in explaining this development to the process of movement on the part of the material productive forces. This would mean replacing the dialectic of matter, or of real phenomena, with a dialectic of concepts. But I have always objected to precisely this [way of thinking]. In *Essays* (third edition, p. 102) I wrote that 'In Marx's work, one concept is transformed into another, not in terms of the power of immanent logical development, but through the presence of an entire series of accompanying social-economic conditions'.[21] It is not for nothing that certain critics, who do incline towards a dialectic of concepts, have accused me of replacing the 'abstract' method with a 'concrete-descriptive' one.

---

21   Ibid.

All of this demonstrates the complete lack of any grounds for the accusation, levelled against me by S. Bessonov, of an inclination towards 'the self-development of concepts'. But we must not, out of legitimate fear of the self-development of concepts, fall into the opposite extreme and sever the dialectical link between various social forms. If you are going to regard every economic form as the direct passive reflex of a change in the material process of production, then the entire scheme of social development appears incorrectly as follows. A given condition of the material production process exists, together with a corresponding production relation between people, or a social form. Then the material process of production changed, it assumed a new appearance; and we, having forgotten our previous social form – which already existed and was in effect – regard the new social form as a passive reflex of the new condition of the productive forces, which arises in empty space apart from any connection with the already existing social forms. This means severing the dialectical connection between all social forms. Your new and more complex social form arose not directly from the productive forces, but from the previous, simpler social form. A new production relation between people emerged from the former production relations under pressure from development of the material productive forces. Only with this understanding can you preserve the internal unity and dialectical coherence of Marx's entire economic theory, in which all social forms (value, money, capital, etc.) are inextricably interconnected both in their historical emergence and in their simultaneous operation.

If Bessonov followed his thinking through to the end, he would have this sort of picture. A definite condition of the productive forces exists; and corresponding to it are definite production relations. The condition of the productive forces changes (within the limits of the given economic formation), and then new production relations correspond to it, having nothing in common with the preceding ones. As with, say, two-storied houses, on the lower floor are the productive forces, on the upper are the production relations, and alongside the given house stands another house with no connection to the first one. Bessonov is willing to allow passage ways on the lower floors, but the upper levels must not communicate in any way. The more complex form of production relations between people has nothing in common with the preceding, simpler form of production relations, but is a direct passive reflex of the productive forces. In short, this is a genuine system of English, or if you do not like that appellation, Scottish cottages, which stand side by side and do not communicate. And I propose to my critics the following question: given your understanding of the dependence of production relations on the productive forces, how can you conceive the dialectical unity of all economic categories?

How can you explain Lenin's saying that all of the contradictions of capitalism are included, in undeveloped form, in the simple form of value? How can you preserve the unity of the entire system of production relations, and the unity of the entire system of economic categories, which for Marx make up the content of the three volumes of *Capital*? In his theses Bessonov quite consistently denies the existence of a 'system' of production relations between people. One might expect that he will be even more consistent and will deny the dialectical unity of the entire system of economic categories that constitute the content of the three volumes of Marx's *Capital*.

Knowing that on the question of the subject matter of political economy we take our stand on the orthodox Marxist point of view, our critics make an about-turn and hurl another accusation at us. They charge us with studying not the production relations between people, but only the reified form of their manifestation. They say that, for us, the production relations between people disappear behind the reified form of manifestation. Therefore, having previously charged that we study the production relations but not the productive forces, they now accuse us of examining not the production relations but rather the reified form of their appearance. Our critics then draw the following conclusion: once, in their opinion, the type of production relations between people is occluded in my *Essays* by the reified form of manifestation, all difference is then erased between social formations of the economy, including the difference between simple commodity production, a capitalist economy and the Soviet economy. The distinction between types of production relations between people is wiped out because they have the same external form of expression, for instance, in the form of value and money. Bessonov bases this accusation on the following three arguments.

The first argument:

> The categories of a capitalist economy are regarded by him (by Rubin) simply as a complication of the categories of commodity economy. It is redundant to point out how little such a viewpoint resembles the Marxist conception. Capitalist society, according to Marx, is not a mere 'complication' of commodity economy; it is a type of society that is *different* in principle, although it still has the same commodity basis, and it appears as the result of a cataclysm, a leap, never as the result of a simple 'complication'. There is no place for this 'leap', for this cataclysm, in Rubin's 'theory', which regards all societies, wherein relations between people are enveloped in reification, as merely being more or less complex but essentially no different one from the other (Review by Bessonov in *Izvestiya TsiK*, 30 November 1928).

The second argument: Rubin discards all questions having to do with the distribution of means of production between different classes and groups of the population, and from this point of view he once again obscures and erases the difference between the simple commodity economy, the capitalist economy and the Soviet economy.

The third argument: By assigning exaggerated importance to the reified form of manifestation – to value and money – Rubin thereby effaces the difference of production relations between people.

Even without examining these arguments, one can say in advance that on this particular point the critics attribute ideas to me that directly contradict everything that follows from the way the question is formulated in the *Essays*. Indeed, the whole formulation in the *Essays* is intended to take examination of a given system of production relations between people, a given social type of economy, and a given economic *structure* as the starting point. I explicitly claim that all of the economic phenomena investigated by our science are connected precisely with the given capitalist system of economy and can have no place in any other economic system. And after I draw such a sharp distinction between different systems of economy, I am accused of finding identical laws for different social forms, for different economic structures, for simple commodity economy, capitalist economy and the Soviet economy.

Let us analyse these arguments in detail. The first: Rubin regards capitalism as merely a complication of simple commodity economy and not a leap. In my *Essays* (p. 42) I wrote: 'Marx's economic system analyses a series of *production relations* of increasingly complex types. These production relations are expressed in a series of *social forms* of increasing complexity – these being the social forms acquired by things'.[22] But on the very same page 42 I wrote a footnote that Bessonov either did not read or does not include: 'We have in mind various forms or types of production relations among people in a *capitalist* society, and not various types of production relations that characterise *different* types of social formations'.[23] You can see how the question is formulated in the *Essays*. I take a given type of economy – a capitalist economy – and within the limits of that given system I study the relation of different and gradually more complex social forms, or production relations, in both their historical emergence and their simultaneous operation. I emphasise that the issue concerns the increasing complexity of types of production relations within the *limits* of a capitalist economy; yet here the critic attributes the idea to me that a simple

---

22 Rubin 1990, p. 32.
23 Rubin 1990, p. 31.

complication, without any qualitative leap, represents the transition from *one* system of production relations to another.

The second accusation: Rubin is interested in the reified form of social phenomena, in the external form of their manifestation, and this external form of manifestation occludes for him the various types of production relations between people. To make such a statement is to distort the central idea of the *Essays*. Indeed, their central idea is the following: behind each social form of things there is concealed a definite type of production relations between people. If it happens that behind one and the same form of external appearance there are concealed different types of production relations between people, we must not confuse these different types of production relations but rather differentiate between them and separate them out. I wrote that 'We classify economic phenomena into groups and build concepts on the basis of the identity of the production relations that the phenomena express, and not on the basis of the coincidence of their material expressions'.[24] Is it permissible to confuse the price form in a simple commodity economy with that in a capitalist economy and in the Soviet economy? Can the price form be confused when behind it are concealed completely different production relations between people, based upon a different distribution of means of production between different classes? I shall not even speak of the fact that even the external forms of manifestation are not identical here. Even an external, superficial observer knows that the price established by planning organs, or by co-operative organs – even in terms of external appearances – is fundamentally different from a price that is established on the basis of the law of value and the spontaneous activity of the market. Even the external form of manifestation of these economic phenomena is strikingly different. But aside from that, even if you do not sometimes discern a difference between external forms of manifestation, you are still obliged to look above all at the type of production relations concealed behind this external form of appearances. Only by completely distorting the fundamental idea – the foundation of the *Essays* – can one say that, for me, the external form of appearance conceals and obscures the difference of production relations between people. To the contrary, the methodological rule, which I repeat on every page of the *Essays*, is this: search everywhere for the specificity of production relations between people, and reveal the difference between them even when they are concealed behind identical external forms of manifestation. Always regard the social form of things merely as the expression of production relations between people. In political economy, we investigate the

---

24   Rubin 1990, p. 45.

social form of things (value, money, capital, profit and wages) because the production relations in a capitalist economy are reified; however, in studying each of these forms, we must constantly refer to the production relations between people that they conceal, and we must consider the role of given forms as an expression of the relations between people. That is the fundamental idea that I endeavoured to emphasise in my *Essays*, and [my purpose was] certainly not to direct your attention away from production relations to the social forms of things. I sought to reveal the role of the social forms of things as expressions of the production relations between people and as the regulator of the social process of production.

Bessonov's third argument: Rubin obscures the difference between various forms of economy because he has absolutely no interest in the question of the distribution of means of production between various classes of the population. To substantiate this assertion Bessonov cites one – as he calls it – 'astounding' comment in my *Essays*. Let us consider just who is amazed by this astounding comment. This shocking remark comes in a footnote on page 40 of the *Essays*.[25] I write in the note that we must distinguish two problems. One problem concerns the influence upon the character of production relations of the distribution of means of production between classes of the population. This problem exists for every society, just as much for a feudal one as for a capitalist one. The other problem concerns the 'coalescence' of production relations with the elements of material production; this is the problem of commodity fetishism in the narrow sense of the word. This problem exists only in capitalist society. Bessonov draws from this the following conclusion: since I write in the footnote that here, when we are investigating commodity fetishism, we are interested precisely in the latter problem, this means that Rubin completely disassociates himself from such a cardinal problem as the dependence of production relations upon the condition and distribution of the productive forces. And once that happens, Rubin mixes up the distribution of means of production between different classes in a simple commodity economy, a capitalist economy and the Soviet economy. For him [Rubin], this question of the distribution of means of production is non-existent.

The argument that I have cited demonstrates very clearly Bessonov's method of waging a polemic. Every one of us agrees that in order to understand a footnote it does no harm to read the text as well. A footnote customarily refers to

---

25 [There is an error in the text. The correct reference is to p. 30. See I.I. Rubin, *Ocherki po teorri stoimosti Marksa*, Izdanie chetvertovo (Moscow-Leningrad: Gosudarstvennoe Izdatel'stvo, 1929). See the English translation of the third edition: Rubin 1990, p. 30].

some text; and in the text (pp. 39–40) I write that the law of dependence of production relations upon the distribution of means of production between the various classes is 'a general sociological law that holds for all social formations', because even 'in feudal society production relations between people are established *on the basis* of the distribution of things among them and *for* things, but not *through* things'.[26] This means that there exists for feudal society the problem of the dependence of production relations upon the distribution of means of production between various classes, but not the problem of commodity fetishism. 'The specific nature of the commodity-capitalist economy resides in the fact that production relations among people are not established only *for* things, but *through* things'.[27] What is the consequence? The consequence is that for a commodity-capitalist economy, *two* problems exist: one problem is the dependence of production relations upon the distribution of means of production; the other problem, which is specifically new, is the problem of commodity fetishism. In my footnote on the same page 40 I explicitly wrote that the first problem exists 'in the economic sphere of various social formations'. The problem of commodity fetishism holds only for capitalist economy. You can see, therefore, just how critics have contrived to distort my thinking. I said that the problem of the dependence of production relations upon distribution of the means of production holds for all formations, including capitalism; I write that for capitalism there exists *not only* this problem of the dependence of production relations upon distribution of the means of production, *but also* the problem of commodity fetishism. Yet Bessonov writes: for Rubin there exists only the problem of commodity fetishism, and for him the problem of the dependence of production relations upon the distribution of means of production does not exist. Where I write '*not only, but also*', the critics inscribe the word '*only*' – a slight alteration but one that significantly alters the text. You can see that this method of polemicising is rather monotonous. The only variation is that one time the text is read without reading the footnote; the next time the footnote is read without reading the text.

Thus, the first device of the critics is the following: where the author writes 'not only, but also', the critics write 'only'. And the second device is this: where the author has included no such word, the critics write in 'only'. On page 139 of his article Bessonov writes: Rubin 'says that only "exchange inseparably includes within itself the social-economic and material-objective moments"'.

---

26 Rubin 1990, p. 29.
27 Ibid.

Take page 26 of the *Essays*, to which Bessonov refers, and you will see that a new paragraph begins with the word 'exchange'.[28] The word 'only' is added by Bessonov. Nowhere do I claim that 'only' exchange includes within itself the material-technical and social-economic moments. To the contrary, in tens of places I write that the process of production also has two sides: the material-technical and the social-economic. In the present case, evidently, Bessonov has no inkling of the fact that when I write that exchange contains within itself the social-economic and material moments, I am repeating a phrase that Marx used on tens of occasions. Marx says that exchange includes the 'exchange of things' and the 'change of forms'.

The third device of the polemic is to enclose words in quotation marks and then attribute them to me when I used no such words. On that same page 139 Bessonov says: 'Rubin, in a hundred different ways, explains to us that technology ... is something belonging to the "natural relations of things"'. I knew that such words as the 'natural relations of things' were not mine, and after a search I discovered in Bessonov's article a long quotation from a book by [Alfred] Ammon, in which it was obvious that these words belong to Ammon but were attributed to me. These examples are sufficient to characterise the polemical devices used by our critics.

In concluding this part of my report, I address to my critics the following two fundamental questions. On the first topic, the subject matter of political economy, my question is this: do they recognise the traditional Marxist definition of political economy's subject matter; do they acknowledge that political economy examines the production relations between people; or do they lack the courage to repudiate this definition explicitly? With regard to the second topic, I ask them: if they deny the existence of a 'system' of production relations between people; if they deny that some social forms arise from other social forms under pressure from development of the productive forces; and if they sever the connection between various social forms and economic categories – then how is the dialectical unity of Marx's entire system preserved?

Disclaiming the traditional definition of the subject matter of political economy, and repudiating the dialectical unity of Marx's entire system – such is the truly 'orthodox' doctrine that Bessonov and other critics are proposing to us.

---

28   [I.I. Rubin, *Ocherki po teorri stoimosti Marksa*, Izdanie chetvertovo (Moscow-Leningrad: Gosudarstvennoe Izdatel'stvo, 1929), p. 19. For the English translation, see Rubin 1990, p. 17. Here the sentence is translated as: 'Social-economic (relations among people) and material-objective (movement of things within the process of production) aspects are indissolubly united in the process of exchange'].

I now turn to the question of the dialectical development of categories in Marx's *Capital*. The first thing that will be of interest to us is how Marx applies the law of the unity of opposites in connection with the law of negation. In other words, not only do I not deny leaps in the transition from one system of production relations to another, but I consider that even within a given system of production relations, within the system of capitalism – as Marx shows us when moving from one category to another – each successive category is not merely a further development of the preceding one but also its negation. Here we have a qualitative change in production relations within a given system and within a given economic structure. From Marx's point of view, a given group of phenomena, by virtue of their internal contradictions, take on a new form, a more developed and complex form in opposition to the first form. Gradually becoming more complex, the phenomena take on a new form that is opposed to the first and original form. This idea constitutes the central position of Marx's dialectical method. Marx shows that within each group of phenomena, which constitute a certain unity, differentiation, polarisation, separation of different qualities and the appearance of opposing elements necessarily occur due to internal contradictions. In other words, there is a necessary appearance of opposition within a group of phenomena that constitute a known unity. This is the first aspect of the law of the unity of opposites.

This position also leads to the reverse position: if contradiction necessarily appears within every group of phenomena that constitute a certain unity, then we can say, conversely, that a group of phenomena, which are opposed to and distinct from one another, form a certain unity within whose limits they are antitheses. Such is the dual character of the law of the unity of opposites: the appearance of contradictions within a group of phenomena that constitute a unity, and the maintenance of unity within a group of phenomena that constitute opposition. These two sides of the law are emphasised by Marx in the first volume of *Capital* when he writes: 'To say that these mutually independent and antithetical processes form an internal unity is to say also that their internal unity moves forward through external antitheses'.[29] If processes that are apparently independent of each other form a unity, then from the other perspective this is a divided unity, a unity with internal contradictions that move within this unity and propel the movement of the entire process. If, from this point of view, you recall the method that Marx used in political economy, you will see that this method displays the characteristics of his dialectical method in general. We know that under all the reified categories Marx saw the production

---

29 Marx 1976, p. 209.

relations between people. Viewed externally, the whole economic life of capitalist society appears as the movement of things and changes in their character. We see the movement of prices, commodities, the value of money, the level of wages, etc. All of these phenomena are reified; from the outside they appear to be separate and opposed phenomena, dispersed alongside one another in the space of social life (understanding space, of course, in the allegorical sense). We see that these phenomena act upon one another, but they act from without, as if they are alien to one another, as if they are independent and separated, and that is why we cannot always reveal the true cause of their movement. For instance, we see that a change in the prices of commodities that are means of subsistence for workers changes the level of wages. The value of products has an influence upon the wage level. But, in capitalist society, we also see the reverse phenomenon – the level of wages, at least in part, causes a change in the prices of commodities. When we observe the external side of this series of reified phenomena, which are dispersed alongside one another, we may come to the most contradictory and mistaken conclusions. Adam Smith, for example, when he observes this external side of phenomena, arrives at two opposing conclusions concerning the inter-relation between value and incomes. Smith says that the value of products breaks down into incomes – wages, profit and rent – meaning that value is something primary and that the change of value determines the movement of incomes. But Smith also falls into the opposing view, saying that a change in the magnitude of incomes (wages, profit and rent) changes the magnitude of the value of the product. Until now this debate over what is primary, value or income – that is, whether value must be taken as primary and then be divided into incomes, or whether incomes must be taken as primary and then be used to constitute value – to this day the debate has yet to be resolved in bourgeois political economy. Marx followed Ricardo and took the view that value is primary. But modern bourgeois political economy occasionally attempts to take the magnitude of incomes as the starting point.[30]

I use this example merely to demonstrate that, in viewing phenomena from the outside, we are frequently confused when explaining their mutual connections. We notice that one phenomenon acts upon the other, while the second also acts upon the first, but we do not know where the motivating cause of the entire system of given phenomena originates. Marx succeeded in replacing this study of phenomena from the outside with an investigation of the internal laws concealed behind them; and he did so precisely because behind the external form he revealed the movement of production relations between people.

---

30   [In this volume, see Rubin's essay on 'The Austrian School', Document 15].

The specificity of the dialectical method is already expressed in this revolution accomplished by Marx, i.e. in the replacement of reified categories by the production relations between people. What the dialectical method demands of us is that we replace examination of congealed things, isolated from one another, with a study of fluid and dynamic processes that are connected with one another. This is the first methodological directive that Engels frequently reiterated. And Marx's method in political economy actually fulfils this directive, transforming all the congealed forms of things, differentiated from one another, dispersed and immobile as it were, into eternally changing, fluid and fully dynamic processes – into the change of production relations between people – a process that is evoked, in turn, by change of the material productive forces.

Moreover, Marx shows us how determinate production relations between people, in particular the relations between commodity producers, become more complex due to internal contradictions and give birth to new forms of relations between people that are opposed to the previous ones and differentiated from them. Marx shows us the gradually increasing complexity of production relations between people, the genesis of new and qualitatively different forms, and the appearance of antithetical forms within a group of phenomena that previously constituted a unity. Marx thereby discloses to us a system of production relations, becoming gradually more complex and assuming a new form that is antithetical to the former one and, at the same time, constituting a unity with it, a unity within which they interact. He likewise makes full use in political economy of the law of negation, i.e. the law of the appearance of new forms that are antithetical to the previous ones, and at the same time he shows the unity of all these forms, revealing to us the unity of opposites. In this way, Marx realises the fundamental demand of the dialectical method, the demand of the law of the unity of opposites, the demand that we recognise opposition within phenomena and at the same time apprehend their unity. I shall now attempt to show briefly how the law of the unity of opposites is deployed by Marx throughout the three volumes of *Capital*.

3   *Division of the Commodity into Commodity and Money*
Let us begin with the question of the division of the commodity into commodity and money, or the doctrine of the different forms of value. This teaching on the break-up of the commodity into commodity and money is, at the same time, a teaching on the dual character of the commodity. According to Marx, the dual character of the commodity is an expression of the dual character of labour as concrete and abstract. The dual character of labour, in turn, points to the contradiction concealed in the very structure of commodity economy,

which, on the one hand, is a sum of labour activities that complement one another and constitute a certain material unity, while on the other hand it has a spontaneous character and rests upon the dispersal of means of production between separate individuals who produce products as commodities and sell these commodities to each other. This contradiction in the structure of commodity economy is manifested in the dual character of labour. The dual character of labour is reflected in the dual character of the commodity. The dual character of the commodity finds expression in the appearance of the commodity and money.

Let us think further about Marx's teaching on the dual character of the commodity. This involves one of the most important and, at the same time, most difficult points of Marx's theory. Critics of Marx have often reproached him for his teaching on the dual theory of the commodity, claiming that he engages in metaphysical discourses that have no basis in real economic phenomena. In order to demonstrate that Marx was by no means involved here in a purely logical splitting of concepts, having no correspondence to real phenomena, I suggest that you first consider this question analytically, i.e. beginning not with the contradictory character of labour and the commodity but rather taking the reverse approach, beginning with the more complex and already developed forms that occur on the surface of economic life.

What is it that we see on the surface of economic life? We see the commodity and money, opposed to each other in the space of social life, replacing each other and moving about from one place to another. In the *Critique* Marx says that if you regard the phenomenon of exchange from without, it seems that what you have before you is a whole series of activities with no inter-connections. You see how a given rouble today buys item A and therefore changes places with item A. Subsequently, the very same rouble travels onward and takes the place of commodity B, then of C, etc. Here, says Marx, the process 'loses its distinct form'.[31] We do not know the social process because it is concealed behind this movement of money and commodities. However, Marx says, let us consider the process differently; more precisely, remember that the commodity and money, which at first sight appear to be opposed to each other in space, in reality represent two sequential phases in the movement of one and the same commodity. Instead of saying that linen stands opposed to a certain quantity of money, and instead of examining these two things that are changing places, focus upon the change of social form that is occurring here. Then you will see that, essentially speaking, when linen takes the place of money its

---

31   Marx 1970, p. 94.

conversion into a certain sum of money represents nothing but movement of the linen itself, and thus also of the linen's value, through two opposing phases. Conversion of the commodity into money is nothing but the movement of the commodity through two opposing phases.

Thus you see here the first example of Marx's method, which consists of the following: he regards two things, opposed to each other in space, as the expression of two phases of one and the same process, as the passage of one and the same commodity through two phases. The necessary result is that value must also pass through these two phases, at first being a value that is fastened to a restricted use-value, and then taking on another form of value, the money form.

Once Marx has reduced the commodity and money to two sequential phases in the movement of one and the same commodity, the question then arises: Why is it that the commodity must invariably pass through these two phases, through the commodity phase and the money phase? Marx's answer is: this occurs because the commodity has two antithetical aspects that must find their expression in movement and, for that reason, cannot be revealed otherwise than by the passage of the commodity through the two opposing phases of the process. In other words, it is precisely because Marx saw, in the exchange of the commodity for money, two phases in the movement of one and the same commodity, that he came to the idea that the commodity itself is necessarily distinguished by an internal contradiction. In turn, Marx traced this dual and contradictory character of the commodity to the dual and contradictory character of the labour that creates the commodity. Consider this one typical remark that Marx makes in the first edition of Volume I of *Capital*, [a remark] that takes us directly to the very essence of the teaching on the dual character of labour:

> Since [private labour] is not directly social labour, the *social* form [of labour] is first of all a form distinct from the natural forms of real useful labour, a form foreign to them and abstract, and secondly, all the different kinds of private labour get their *social* character only *antithetically (gegensätzlich)*, by all being equated to one exclusive kind of private labour ...[32]

What is Marx saying in this sentence about the dual character of labour? He is saying that since labour in its natural form is not directly social labour, the

---

32   Marx 1867, p. 33.

social form of this labour is an abstract form that is alien to it and contradicts the natural form of the given labour. There emerges a contradiction between the two forms of labour: the natural form of labour and the social form of labour. The social character of labour is separate and alienated from the labour itself, being opposed to it as the abstract form of labour. To put it differently, the labour of each commodity producer, in order to reveal its social character, must invariably assume this form of abstract generality – or the labour of the commodity producer must have a dual form – in order to reveal its social character. It must have the natural form, and simultaneously it must be equated with labour that is abstract and alien to it. This means that the labour of every commodity producer must pass through two antithetical phases of movement. From the natural form in which it now finds itself, it must pass over into the abstract form, into a form that is antithetical to this natural form. This does not mean that in its first phase of movement the labour is solely natural. On its own, the very fact that this labour must invariably pass over into the following phase imposes upon it from the very outset a dual character. Thus labour, in each of its phases of movement, has a dual character: in the first phase, labour is directly natural labour, yet ideally, or potentially, it is labour of an opposite type, abstract labour. Only in the second phase is this social character of labour finally disclosed and realised.

The commodity, which is the product of this same labour, must pass through the same two phases for the full disclosure of its social character. Here we come to the fundamental doctrine concerning the contradictory character of the commodity, namely, that the commodity contains within itself a contradiction that must be resolved by movement, by the passage of the commodity through the two antithetical phases. What does this contradiction involve? It involves the same contradiction as in the case of labour, and Marx has much to say about it in the *Critique*. On the one hand, the commodity is [a value in terms of labour],[33] a property that makes it possible for its owner to exchange it for any other commodity. It has an acknowledged social character. On the other hand, this same commodity is a use-value, a natural product in which value is fixed as a certain social property. So long as this property is naturally fixed in the given commodity, so long as value is fixed in the linen, this linen represents, as Marx says, a product of individual labour whose social character is not yet recognised and certified by society. As Marx comments in one place: 'on the one hand, commodities must enter the exchange process as reified universal labour-

---

33 [There is a typographical error in the text that appears to involve omission of one line of print].

time, on the other hand, the labour-time of individuals becomes materialised universal labour-time only as the result of the exchange process'.[34] The labour that creates the commodity must, on the one hand, be social labour even before the process of exchange, while on the other hand it is only through the process of exchange that its social character is revealed. And this means that the commodity, in order to reveal its social character, must invariably pass from the form in which its social character is still constrained, due to the limited use-value in which it is fixed, to the form of a directly social product, that is, to the form of such product as may be exchanged for any other product, [to a form] that represents the direct embodiment of social labour and gives its possessor the ability to acquire the same amount of social labour in the form of any other product. We therefore find ourselves at the next stage of our discussion. We can say that commodities exist. Every commodity is a unity of value and use-value. And in every commodity there is a contradiction: on the one hand, it has the social character of value, but on the other hand its social property, being fixed in a limited use-value, can still neither be revealed directly nor give the owner of the commodity the possibility of having at his disposal a certain quantity of social labour in the form of any other product in natural form.

Following this teaching on the dual character of the commodity, or the doctrine of value in general, Marx turns to his teaching on the simple form of value, or the doctrine of *exchange-value*. What is the essence of this doctrine of exchange-value? It consists of the following. If we take a group of commodities, which in terms of their character all resemble one another – since each of them represents a unity of value and use-value – if we take this group of commodities that are similar in terms of their social character but internally contradictory, then the moment these commodities enter into exchange for one another a differentiation of functions between them must necessarily appear, and the different characters of these commodities must be revealed. Here we come to Marx's teaching on the simple form of value, or the teaching that concerns their differentiation and the appearance of the polar-opposite functions of both commodities, with the resulting need for the appearance of two forms of value – the relative form of value and the equivalent form of value. In other words, what is involved is the break-up of the whole world of commodities into two groups, into the group of simple commodities and the universal equivalent – money. In this doctrine we have a strikingly clear example of the application of the law of the unity of opposites, according to which a group of items with a singular character splits, due to the contradiction

---

34 Marx 1970, p. 45.

that inheres within them, into two opposing parts. The social form of the commodity, which was previously identical but at the same time internally contradictory, divides into two opposing forms, into the form of the simple commodity and money. In the *Critique of Political Economy*, Marx does not show us the development of this process. In the *Critique of Political Economy* Marx shows us the dual character of labour; this dual character of labour corresponds to the dual character of the commodity, which finds expression in the division of the commodity into the commodity and money. In the *Critique*, this division of the commodity into the commodity and money is, so to speak, the correlate of the dual character of the commodity and the dual character of the labour creating the commodity. However, Marx does not show us how the commodity, as a unity of use-value and value, divides into these two opposing forms. He only completed this work in *Capital* with his doctrine of the forms of value, which is one of the most important parts of Marx's teaching.

How does Marx show us that two commodities, which enter into exchange for one another, must invariably perform different functions in this exchange? We can say that the teaching on the simple form of value is a doctrine of the appearance of initial differentiation in the relations of commodity producers, of the appearance of initial contradiction within a group of commodities that hitherto had a perfectly identical social character but were internally contradictory. And that is precisely why we have here the appearance of the initial differentiation of production relations between people and the social forms of things (within the limits of a commodity economy), and why the simple form of value is significant as the cell-form, which in Lenin's words already has concealed within itself all the contradictions of the capitalist economy.[35]

Why must a differentiation of functions invariably begin between commodity A and commodity B, which exchange for one another? In his article on the 'Critique of Political Economy' Engels explains briefly: once we have a relation of two commodities, we also have two sides of this relationship. Once we have two sides of a relationship, they differ from one another and are opposed to one another. If we apply this general guidance to the case at hand, then we must see Marx's doctrine of the simple commodity form approximately as follows. Two commodities, A and B, enter into exchange for one another in conditions where the character of both commodities is perfectly identical but each commodity is internally contradictory. In what sense is each commodity internally contradictory? In the sense that, on the one hand, it reveals its social character, its character as value, only through equalisation with the other product. Product

---

35 Lenin 1915b, pp. 360–1.

A reveals its social character through equalisation with product B. But product B, at the same time, reveals its social character only through the same exchange with product A. In this act of exchange, each product must perform two completely antithetical roles. Each commodity must disclose its social character through exchange for the other product, and at the same time it must serve as the material for disclosing the other product's social character. The impossibility of a single commodity fulfilling these two functions at one and the same time is self-evident. As Marx says, 'the form of direct and universal exchangeability is an antagonistic (*gegensätzliche*) form, as inseparable from its object, the form of non-direct exchangeability, as the positivity of one pole of a magnet is from the negativity of the other pole'.[36] The form of universal direct exchangeability, the directly social form characterising one product, excludes such directly exchangeable form for any other product that enters into exchange with it.

Indeed, let us suppose that product B has the direct social form, i.e. is the product of recognised social labour and can be exchanged for the product of any other social labour. But if commodity B has the significance of being a product of directly social labour and thus can take the place of any other product (for instance, product A), by the same token the other product, in this same act, cannot play such a role of a directly social product that has the form of direct universal exchangeability. In the given act of exchange, the two commodities perform different functions: commodity A appears as a product of private labour, commodity B as the product of directly social labour. But the point is that each commodity is contradictory in character, being the product of both private and social labour. Accordingly, the two commodities not only perform different functions in the given phase of exchange, but each of them must also, in another phase of exchange, fulfil a function opposite to the one being fulfilled by it in the given phase of exchange. And this also means that the dual character of the commodity cannot be expressed in any other way than by the fact that each commodity, in the exchange process, must pass through two phases. The first phase consists of the fact that commodity A, by means of exchange for the natural form of B, the other commodity, discloses its social character and acquires the form of direct universal exchangeability. It acquires this form only as a result of the given act of exchange. In the second phase, this commodity already enters into the exchange process as the directly social commodity, freed from its connection with the restricted natural form of the given product. In other words, no single commodity can express its

---

36 Marx 1976, p. 161, footnote 26.

social character in any other way than as means of exchange for the natural form of the other product. The result, therefore, is that the value of product A is equal to the use-value of product B in its natural form. Here we have the differentiation of functions, of the roles of the two commodities that enter into exchange. The one commodity expresses its value through the natural form of the other commodity; and the other commodity, in its natural form, serves as the expression of the first commodity's value. The appearance of this differentiation in the hitherto uniform world of commodities was developed by Marx in his doctrine of the simple form of value.

It would be a very protracted process to retrace all of the subtle dialectical transitions with whose help Marx shows us how two commodities, which are fully equal to each other, begin in the act of exchange to play an unequal, dissimilar and differentiated role. It is very interesting to trace how Marx comes to the idea, through the equality of the two commodities A and B, of the need for the polarisation of functions, the need for them to fulfil two contradictory functions. In the beginning, the term that Marx uses is the value relation of the two commodities, i.e. the relation in which they both fulfil the same role. Marx then goes one step further and says: if you have the value relation of two commodities, A and B, then from this 'value relation' (*Wertverhältniss*) of the two commodities we can also find the 'expression of value' (*Wertausdruck*) for one of these commodities. We can express the value of commodity A in commodity B. As Marx says, in the value relation of the two commodities is included the expression of value of one of these commodities in the other commodity, or '*Wertausdruck*' is included in '*Wertverhältniss*'. If you read the first chapter of Marx's *Capital* you will see that Marx draws a distinction between the 'value relation' of the two commodities and the 'expression of value' of the one commodity in the other commodity.[37]

What does this distinction involve? When you speak of the 'value relation' A to value B, what you mean is that the *value* of commodity A equals the *value* of commodity B, i.e. *value* figures on both sides of your equation. You have discovered the equivalence of two values, but you have not found the value of either product. All you have found is that the value of A equals the value of B, but you have not determined whether this value is 1, 10 or 100. If you wish to know the value even of one of these commodities, you have no alternative but to take the value of one commodity as given and express the value of the other in the use-value of the first. The value of commodity A equals product B

---

37   [See the previous essay in this volume for Rubin's discussion of the 'value relation' and the 'value expression' in the first chapter of *Capital*].

in its natural form. Now *value* will figure on the left side of your equation, and on the right side – an item in *natural* form, an item that you take as such – in its own skin, as Marx said – to be the embodiment of value. Compare these two expressions: 1) the *value* of A equals the *value* of B; 2) the *value* of A equals B. At first glance these two expressions do not appear to be different from one other, yet there is a fundamental difference between them. In the first formula you have value on both sides of the equation, yet value is not expressed; and in the second formula, the value of one product is expressed in the use-value of the other. The two commodities play completely different roles. This difference of roles consists of the fact that commodity A has value only insofar as it is equivalent to commodity B, i.e. commodity A represents value not directly but rather indirectly, by way commodity B, i.e. it appears indirectly as only as *use-value*. Commodity B, in its natural form, appears directly as the embodiment of *value*. 'The internal opposition (*Gegensatz*) between use-value and value, hidden within the commodity, is therefore represented on the surface by an external opposition, i.e., by a relation between the two commodities ...'.[38]

In this formula we already see an initial differentiation, although still weak, between the two commodities, an emergence of two different and antithetical forms of value. Commodity A has the form of value *apart* from its own natural form, and commodity B has value in its own natural form. Generalising, we may say that we have reached two forms of value: one form of value *apart* from the natural form of the product, and another form of value directly *fused* with the natural form of the product. We have found two forms of value directly opposed to each other: the relative and the equivalent.[39]

So long as we take only the two given commodities, A and B, these commodities possess their forms of value (relative and equivalent) only *within their given relation* to each other. It is only when we correlate commodity A with commodity B that the first acquires the relative and the other the equivalent form of value. The active role here belongs to A; it is A that expresses its value in commodity B. It is only because the producer of commodity A correlates his product with commodity B that the latter, within the limits of the given relation between the two commodity producers, fulfils the special function of equivalent. In the given relation of two commodities (for example, 20 yards of linen = 1 coat), value is focused and polarised on one side, in the coat; yet the issue is precisely the value of the linen itself, which has found expression in the nat-

---

38   Marx 1976, p. 153.
39   [See Rubin's discussion of the 'relative' and 'equivalent' forms of value in the previous document].

ural form of the coat. Here 'the linen's own existence as value comes into view or receives an independent expression'.[40]

We must turn our attention to the following terminology of Marx. Marx says that the value of the linen, because it is expressed in the coat, 'receives an *independent* expression'. In the first edition of *Capital*,[41] Marx wrote that the commodity 'receives *a value form distinct, separate and independent from its natural form*'. 'Exchange value is [therefore] in the first place *the independent form of appearance of the value of the commodity*'.[42] The value of the linen has received a separate form apart the item in which it finds itself, the form of another natural item that opposes it. Value has received an 'alienated' and separate form as exchange-value. A process of 'alienation' and isolation has occurred. The value of the linen, as it were, has separated from the linen itself, or as Marx often says, the internal contradiction, concealed within the commodity itself, has taken the form of an external contradiction.

When we are speaking of the exchange of two commodities, a polarisation of functions occurs and these commodities play a different role. But this difference, as Marx explains in the first edition of *Capital* (p. 29), is merely 'passing' and 'formal'. There is only a formal differentiation of the functions of A and B, which only prevails within the limits of their given relationship with each other. If B is taken out of its relationship with A, it will not play the role of equivalent. In a word, the separation of money from the sphere of all commodities has yet to occur, and equivalent B is the same kind of commodity as all the rest. You can reverse the given equation, and then B will no longer play the role of equivalent in relation to A. Thus, the given relationship between these two commodities has a passing and transitory character. Their difference of functions has not yet become fixed. In this simple form of value, therefore, 'it is still difficult to keep hold of the polar antagonism' in the functions of the two commodities.[43] True, this simple form of value already contains within itself 'this antithesis, but it does not fix it';[44] i.e. it does not fasten a specific function to one commodity or the other. As Marx says in the first edition of *Capital* (p. 23), the development still occurs 'uniformly' for both of the commodities, A and B, which are found on the two sides of the equation. This 'uniformity' of development of the two parts of the equation already disappears in the developed form of value, because product A reveals its social character only through its

---

40   Marx 1976, p. 141.
41   Marx 1867, p. 768.
42   Marx 1867, p. 775.
43   Marx 1976, p. 160.
44   Ibid.

equalisation with *an entire series* of other products playing the role of equivalents. The difference and antithesis between the two poles of the expression of value acquires here a more profound character. Finally, when the social division of labour and [commodity] exchange expand, all commodities begin to be compared with one commodity – gold – and the function of universal equivalent coalesces with the natural form of the latter as the antithesis between the two sides of the expression of value further 'develops and hardens'.[45] In the simple form of value, where commodity B fulfils the function of equivalent only within its given relationship with another commodity, the illusion arises that it has 'the equivalent form independently of this relation'.[46] In the money form this illusion 'becomes stronger' and finally 'ossifies' (*verknöchert*).[47] 'The form of universal equivalent *coalesces* with the natural form of a certain type of commodity, or *crystallises* in the money form'.[48] This process of the ossification or crystallisation of social forms is traced by Marx through all three volumes of *Capital*. In the present case, this term means the following: whereas previously commodity B assumed the property of equivalent only within its given relationship with commodity A, and whereas until now a thing acquired a social property only in the presence of a given relationship between two commodity producers, in the money form the universal equivalent possesses the property of being directly the embodiment of value and of abstract labour, independently of the concrete relationship into which it enters with some other particular commodity. Gold is the universal equivalent not only at the moment when linen is equated with it but even apart from this act. This social function becomes fastened to it as a thing with definite natural properties.

Whereas previously commodity B acquired the property of equivalent because commodity A exchanged for it, the matter is different when applied to gold. Every commodity must be directly exchangeable into gold because gold has the property of universal equivalent. 'Without any initiative on their part, the commodities find their own value-configuration *ready to hand*, in the form of a physical commodity existing *outside but also alongside them*'.[49] The inner contradiction of the commodity, requiring its necessary movement through the two sequential and antithetical phases of the exchange process, has taken the form of the external contradiction between the commodity and money, arranged, as it were, side by side in space. Every commodity now finds the

---

45 Marx 1867, p. 781.
46 Marx 1976, p. 187.
47 See Marx 1867, p. 33.
48 Marx 1976, p. 187.
49 Ibid.

form of money readily available and detached from the commodity itself. In Marx's words, the commodity finds the ready form of money, a fixed and crystallised money form; it finds the objective stability of a universal equivalent in an objectively fixed form. We saw previously that all commodities, through their own activity, create the social property of the commodity that separates out as the universal equivalent. But now that this separation is completed, it appears to us that it is the money that sets the commodities in motion. Whereas in reality 'the money form is merely the reflection thrown upon a single commodity by the relations between all other commodities',[50] it appears that the commodities, for their own part, are passive and are set in motion by this most detached commodity, by money. In this connection Marx uses a formulation to which he often returns later. He says that gold essentially became money only thanks to the movement of all the commodities that exchange for it, yet the '*movement through which this process has been mediated* vanishes in its own result, leaving no trace behind'.[51] The entire complex social process of the detachment of money from the commodity world has taken place behind the backs of commodity producers; it has vanished in its own result, and gold in itself, in its natural form, is money. We do not see the entire social process that has created this result, and enormous force of analysis is required in order to reconstruct the whole process whereby a complex form detaches from a homogeneous setting, a process involving the emergence of antithetical forms when previously they were uniform, i.e. a process subject to the action of the law of negation and the law of the unity of opposites.

In his teaching on the forms of value, Marx has traced the process of gradual intensification of the contradiction between the two poles of the value expression, ending with the bifurcation of the commodity into the simple commodity and money. In accordance with the law of the unity of opposites, however, Marx shows us not merely the necessary emergence of opposition in a previously homogeneous setting, but also the necessary preservation of unity between the phenomena that have been released from each other. Parallel with the intensifying *antithesis* between the two commodities participating in exchange, there is also intensification of the *unity* that binds them together – and this happens precisely because each of them takes on an increasingly one-sided character, which demands to be supplemented in the form of another commodity that is distinguished by the opposite properties. In the simple form of value, the difference between products A and B had a 'passing' and 'formal' character.

---

50   Marx 1976, p. 184.
51   Marx 1976, p. 187.

The unity that connects them was also transitory and contingent: product A can be just as easily exchanged for any other product – C, D, E etc. – as for the given product B. In the money form of value, when product B (gold) has finally become the universal equivalent, product A must be directly exchanged for B; it is correlated with B and has the money form in advance, even before the act of exchange. Along with the intensifying contradiction between A and B, the unity that binds them together also intensifies. What does this entail? In the first place, it entails the unity of their *genesis*, of their historical origin from a group of homogeneous commodities that subsequently divided into two groups. This unity is manifest, secondly, in the fact that every commodity must invariably pass through the two stages, through the *two phases* (of simple commodity and money), and only by passing through both of these phases does it reveal its social character. In the third place, this unity appears in the fact that the relative form of value is inconceivable without an equivalent, for the very concept of relative form presupposes a relation to some other commodity that is the material for the given commodity's expression of value; and conversely, the equivalent form is impossible without the relative form, or in a word, without the *interdependence* of these antithetical forms. Finally, we have not only the interdependence but also the *interpenetration* of these forms, since from the moment when the break-up of the commodity world into the simple commodity and money has occurred, every commodity must invariably pass through the two phases and be converted into money. This means that every commodity, without yet being really converted into money, still has the potential or the ideal form of money, which fulfils the role of measure of value. The commodity includes within itself the potential form of money, and money is essentially the 'metamorphosed commodity', that is, it bears the imprint of the previous exchange of the given commodity for a given sum of money. Thus we have a genetic unity of the origin of these two antithetical forms, an internal bond between them as two sequential phases in the movement of one and the same commodity, a mutual conditioning because neither of these forms can be conceived without the other, and finally, their interpenetration since each of them is not simply a single form but also potentially the other form. Therefore, in the doctrine of the bifurcation of the commodity into simple commodity and money, in this doctrine of their intensifying antithesis and at the same time their mutually complementary character, i.e. their unity, we have a striking illustration of *the law of the unity of opposites*.

This teaching from Marx concerning the genesis of money must, in the first place, explain the *historical* process of the emergence of money from the commodity (or more accurately, from products that find themselves in the process of conversion into commodities); and secondly, it must disclose the laws of the *simultaneous* and mutually conditioned movement of commodities and money in the developed capitalist economy. Correspondingly, the law of the unity of opposites, in the given case, must also demonstrate to us first the unity of historical roots and the process of gradual separation of the two antithetical forms of the commodity; and secondly, it must reveal the unity and difference between the movement of commodities and money in the capitalist economy. Marx's critics have asserted that in his teaching on the contradictory character of the commodity and its bifurcation into the simple commodity and money, Marx resorted to the 'self-development of concepts'. This is untrue. Marx's teaching reflects a real social process that, on the one hand, took place in a definite historical period (different for different peoples) and, on the other hand, has left its result in the capitalist economy by way of two opposing and interacting spheres: commodity circulation and money circulation. The separating out of money was the result of the increasingly frequent repetition of the movement of commodities in exchange; this movement of commodities reflected a determinate character of the production relations between members of society as commodity producers; finally, the spread of this particular type of production relations was brought about by the requirements of the material process of production. We can observe the connection between these phenomena approximately as follows.

Development of the social division of labour, both within a single community and between foreign communities, strengthened the demand for a social 'exchange of things', for acquiring the products of foreign labour. Arising on the basis of an already existing difference between spheres of production, exchange reinforced and further developed this difference. Within the community, separate parts and spheres of production, which previously had a directly social character, 'attain such a degree of independence that the sole bond still connecting the various kinds of work is the exchange of products as commodities'.[52] 'Independence' (*Verselbständigung*) of different types of labour, done by different individuals, develops. Within the community – partly under the pressure of exchange with foreign (*fremde*) communities – there arises a 'relation of mutual estrangement' (*Fremdheit*) between its individual members who turn into commodity producers. The labour of separate individuals becomes 'independent', while at the same time the material connection strengthens between individuals and different types of labour. This fundamental contradiction of commodity economy increasingly deepens, on the one hand, as the social division of labour develops, and on the other hand,

---

52   Marx 1976, p. 472.

due to the disorganisation and spontaneity of the economy. The activities and production relations of commodity producers become increasingly differentiated, 'segregated' and 'alienated', while at the same time a parallel 'reification' and 'coalescence' with things occurs. The differentiation of activities and of relations between commodity producers; the 'objectification' (*Versachlichung*) of production relations, their 'coalescence' with things, and their 'ossification' (*Verknöcherung*) as the social forms of things; the gradually growing 'independence' (*Verselbständigung*) and 'alienation' (*Entfremdung*) of production relations and the corresponding social forms of things; the genesis from simple forms to the more complex, which are antithetical to the former and at the same time constitute a unity with them – all of these are simply different aspects of the grandiose process of the development of a society of commodity producers that is becoming ever more complex. This process is the simultaneous realisation of the sociological law of the social division of labour and of the differentiation of functions between the individual members and groups of society; of the economic law of the reification of production relations and their coalescence with things; and of the general dialectical law of the unity of opposites. With these three dimensions, let us now briefly take a closer look at the process we have been describing – of the bifurcation of the commodity into the simple commodity and money.

Marx shows that the bifurcation of the commodity is a reflection of the bifurcation of the functions of commodity producers.

> The commodity-owners entered the sphere of circulation merely as guardians of commodities. Within this sphere they confront one another in the antithetical (*gegensätzliche*) roles of buyer and seller, one personifying a sugar-loaf, the other gold. Just as the sugar-loaf becomes gold, so the seller becomes a buyer. These distinctive social characters are, therefore, by no means due to human individuality as such, but to the exchange relations of persons who produce their goods in the specific form of commodities.[53]

In this passage Marx excellently conveys the link between the differentiation of activities and of the social characters of people, between the personification of things and the growing antithesis (and unity) between the activities of people and the social forms of things.

---

53 Marx 1970, pp. 94–5.

The process of the commodity's bifurcation means not only the original differentiation of the functions of commodity producers but also the original reification of production relations in things. The doctrine concerning the genesis of money is a teaching on the 'coalescence' of the production relations between people with the natural form of things. In this teaching, Marx showed us how social functions, which were initially acquired by things only within given determinate production relations between people, become congealed in the thing alongside of the given production relations. Marx emphasised many times the specificity of the equivalent, which consists of the fact that although it initially acquires its social form only within the given relations between commodities A and B, it appears to us that this social form belongs to it by nature. And when this social form, due to the development of exchange and of the activities of all commodity producers, coalesces with gold, we come directly to a social form, naturally inherent in the given product, which is independent of all those production relations in which it figures at any given moment. We reach a social form that is frozen, ossified, crystallised and has coalesced with a thing.

On the one hand, therefore, you have here a striking illustration of Marx's doctrine concerning the reification of production relations, their coalescence with the natural form of things, and the acquisition by the thing of social functions that it possesses independently of the concrete production relations within which it figures at a given moment. On the other hand, we also have in this doctrine concerning the forms of value a clear example of the gradual intensification of the antithesis between commodities and money that expresses the two sides of the commodity's character, the gradual strengthening of this contradiction that was originally only temporary and transitory. Marx's teaching concerning the break-up of the commodity into two opposing forms is a striking illustration of the dialectical laws of negation and of the unity of opposites.

In the process of the commodity's bifurcation, the differentiation of functions between people, the reification of production relations and the development of contradiction within unity still have an elementary character. Indeed, 'the opposition (*Gegensatz*) between buyer and seller' still has a 'superficial and formal' character,[54] since the person who at one given moment comes forth in the role of seller appears sometime later in the role of buyer. It is true that, corresponding to the difference between commodity and money, there are the different economic functions of commodity producers: 'Two antithetical trans-

---

54   Marx 1976, p. 95.

mutations of the commodity (C–M and M–C) are accomplished through two antithetical social processes in which the commodity owner takes part, and are reflected in the antithetical economic characteristics of the two processes'.[55] But 'the owner of the commodity successively changes his role from seller to buyer. Being a seller and being a buyer are therefore not fixed roles, but constantly attach themselves to different persons in the course of the circulation of commodities'.[56] The different economic functions have not yet 'crystallised' and permanently fastened themselves to specific persons.

Just as the differentiation of functions between buyer and seller still has a preliminary and undeveloped character, so the process of the reification of production relations between people in the commodity and money also has an elementary character by comparison with more complex forms (capital, interest, etc.).

Finally, the development of contradiction within unity still has an elementary character in the process of the bifurcation of the commodity. But since 'the contradiction (*Gegensatz*) of commodity and money is the abstract and general form of all contradictions inherent in the bourgeois mode of labour',[57] we shall many times encounter the further development and growing complexity of this contradiction in what follows.

4   *The Functions of Money*[58]

Marx regards the formation of *value* as a process in which the production relations between people, as commodity producers, find their expression in the form of value – a property inherent, as it were, in the product of labour. Marx regards the formation of *money* as a process in which the relation between commodities as values is expressed in the form of their relation to one particular commodity that plays the role of universal equivalent, or money. Marx expressed the inseparable link between these two processes in the following words:

> The fact that commodity owners treat one another's labour as universal social labour appears in the form of their treating their own commodities as exchange-values; and the interrelation of commodities as exchange-values in the exchange process appears as their universal relation to a par-

---

55   Marx 1976, p. 206.
56   Ibid.
57   Marx 1970, p. 96.
58   [The following pages of this document come from *Pod Znamenem Markiszma*, No. 5, 1929, pp. 51–82].

ticular commodity as the adequate expression of their exchange-value; this in turn appears as the specific relation of this particular commodity to all other commodities and hence as the distinctive, as it were naturally evolved, social character of a thing.[59]

These words from Marx clearly demonstrate the process of gradual fetishisation, or the reification of production relations between people. The production relations between people take on the form of the social properties of things. As production relations between people become more complex, the social forms of things likewise become more complex. The process of fetishisation of social relations between people involves, therefore, many stages. In the case that we are considering, the movement of production relations between people assumes the form of the movement of commodities, and the movement of commodities is reflected in the movement of prices. Value, being the expression of production relations between people, in turn represents the basis upon which money emerges as a more complex and fetishised social form of things.

The task of a dialectical examination consists of demonstrating the necessary emergence of the more complex forms of things from simpler ones. The investigator must reconstruct a picture of the development of production relations between people and of the corresponding social properties of things, moving from the simpler forms to the more complex. It is precisely this synthetic path of investigation, moving from the production relations between people to the commodity, and from the commodity to money, that Marx outlines in the excerpt quoted above.

Obviously, the synthetic path of investigation, from simpler forms to the more complex, does not exclude an analytical approach but rather presupposes it. Every investigation begins with analysis of a complex form for the purpose of discerning the simpler forms from which it has developed. With the help of analysis, we detect behind the movement of money the movement of commodities, and we examine the latter as the expression of production relations between people, which are determined, in turn, by the requirements of the material-technical process of production or by the 'exchange of things':

> The different determinations of form that *money* assumes in the process of circulation are essentially only crystallisations of the change of forms on the part of *commodities* themselves, which in turn are only the object-

---

59   Marx 1970, p. 48.

ive expressions of changing *social relations* in which commodity-owners conduct their *exchange of things*.[60]

Here Marx analytically sketches the path of investigation from more complex forms to the simpler ones: from money to the commodity, and from the commodity to the production relations between people.

In both types of study, the analytic and the synthetic, money appears before us as the reified expression of production relations between people. We cannot, however, reduce money directly to people's production relations (nor can we deduce it from the latter). Money is the product of a very complex process of the reification of production relations between people – a process that we must examine in terms of all the intermediate links. The mediating link between people's production relations and the money category is the category of the commodity, or value. Our investigation, therefore, divides into two stages. In the first stage, the theory of value, we study the process of the materialisation of people's production relations in the value of commodities. In the second stage, the theory of money, we must demonstrate how the movement of commodities is expressed in the movement of money. The link between the commodity and money represents the principal theme of Marx's theory of money. And in this regard, being true to his fundamental methodological principle, Marx indicates that our main task consists of examining the genesis of the complex form from the simpler one. 'The difficulty lies not in comprehending that money is a commodity, but in discovering how, why and by what means a commodity becomes money'.[61]

The teaching concerning the genesis of money from the commodity has already been set out above. We presuppose that the division of the commodity into the simple commodity and money has already been completed, and that two separate yet closely related spheres face one another: commodity circulation and the circulation of money. Now we must examine the movement of money, since on the one hand it has a special character that is distinct from the movement of commodities, while on the other hand it reflects the movement of the latter. We must indicate how the various forms of the movement of commodities are expressed in the different forms assumed by money. It is precisely this connection between the forms of movement on the part of commodities and the forms of money that Marx continuously emphasises: 'The moving relations of commodities to each other crystallise as different determ-

---

60 Marx 1970, p. 139 [Rubin's emphasis].
61 Marx 1976, p. 186.

inations of the universal equivalent, and thus the process of exchange is simultaneously the process of the circulation of money'.[62] 'The determinate form in which gold crystallises into money depends on how the commodities represent their own exchange-value to each other'.[63] 'The change of form on the part of commodities themselves simultaneously crystallises into determinate forms of money'.[64]

With regard to this process, Marx frequently uses the term 'crystallises'. Marx's critics have thought that when he speaks of the 'crystallisation' of labour in the value of the commodity, he has in view the material-technical process of the 'settling' or 'congealing' of labour in the product. As we see, the term 'crystallisation' is in fact used by Marx in another sense. Marx uses this term to characterise social, not technical processes. When Marx says that 'The change of form on the part of commodities themselves simultaneously crystallises into determinate forms of money,' he has in view the process of the gradually increasing complexity and 'congealment' of the social forms of things – a process in which the development of simpler forms leads to formation of more complex forms. This formation from a simpler form of more complex forms, which differ in character from the former, is what Marx calls the process of 'crystallisation', i.e. it is the process of *detachment* of more complex forms. It is readily understandable that Marx speaks so frequently of the process of 'crystallisation', because the fundamental task of a dialectical investigation consists of explaining the necessary formation of more and more complex forms of phenomena.

There is a *dual* task involved in studying the genesis of complex forms of phenomena from simple ones. On the one hand, the investigator must show how development of the simplest form leads to formation of a complex form. Here the investigator must emphasise the inseparable *connection* between the two forms – what they have in common and what makes the more complex form a further development or expression of the simpler form. On the other hand, however, the investigator must also show that the complex form, which has grown out of the simple one, simultaneously differs from it in character, i.e. that it represents not only further development but also *negation* of the properties characterising the first form. He must demonstrate that the complex form, although it has grown out of the simple one, is at the same time its antithesis.

---

62   Marx 1970, p. 52.
63   Marx 1970, p. 68.
64   Marx 1970, p. 86.

Applying this general principle to the theory of money, here too we charge the investigator with a dual task. He must show that money has its basis in the commodity and also that money, in the process of its development, detaches from the commodity and becomes opposed to it (so that the commodity is thereby also turned into a simple commodity, i.e. the opposite of money). While in the passages quoted above Marx showed the internal connection between the commodity and money, in other places he emphasises that they are opposed to one another. Marx often says that money is essentially a distinct and specific commodity that is 'detached' from the sphere of other commodities. Gold and silver 'oppose other commodities as the materialisation of general labour-time'.[65] 'Gold and silver, as the direct embodiment of social labour ... confront other profane commodities'.[66] Money, consequently, has not only developed from the commodity but is at the same time opposed to the commodity and 'alienated' from it. The process of the formation of money from the commodity is at the same time the process of the gradual 'alienation' of money from the world of commodities, a process of gradual polarisation between the character of commodities and the character of money. The different forms of money express different stages in this gradually intensifying 'alienation' of money from commodities. We shall demonstrate this fact using examples of the separate forms of money, which we shall consider in the same order as Marx examined them.

Insofar as money fulfils the function of the *measure of value*, the alienation of money from the commodity involves its elementary, insufficiently developed character. This close connection between money, as measure of value, and commodities becomes manifest in both the origin and the character of the measure of value.

As for the *origin* of the measure of value, Marx never tires of repeating that the measure of value is called to life by the movement and general activity of the commodities themselves. Commodities themselves 'initially create the form in which they ideally appear to each other as exchange-values'.[67] 'Because the commodities themselves assume the form of exchange-value for one another, they turn gold into the universal equivalent or into money',[68] that is, into the form of measure of value. Marx wants to demonstrate that the genesis of the measure of value finds its explanation in the movement of the commodities themselves.

---

65   Marx 1970, p. 91.
66   Marx 1970, p. 159.
67   Marx 1970, p. 65.
68   Ibid.

It is not only the genesis of the measure of value, but also its *character* that reveals the close connection between money and commodities. When we say that the value of a table equals ten roubles, the conversion of the commodity into money still has a theoretical and conceptual character, and the money itself is still 'ideal' money. Money does not yet exist as a real object, separated from the commodity, but rather appears here only as an ideal money-form, which inheres in the commodity itself and represents a property of the latter. We may even say that money represents here nothing more than a special property of the commodity itself, its money-existence or its money-form. The 'existence of commodities as money is indeed not yet separated from their real existence'.[69] It follows that here the value of the commodity, likewise, is actually not yet distinguished from the natural form of the latter and does not have the form of a real thing that is opposed to the commodity. 'The exchange-value of the commodity acquires only an ideal existence, as distinct from the commodity'.[70]

Of course, this does not mean that there is still no difference between commodities and money. If money fulfils the function of measure of value, this presupposes that the separation of money from the sphere of the commodity world has already occurred. But in its function as measure of value, money still retains a very close link with commodities and appears as one of the properties of the commodity opposed to its other properties. When we determine the value of the commodity as ten roubles, we oppose one property (i.e. its value, which equals ten roubles) to the other properties whereby it distinguishes itself as a determinate material object. Value appears as one of the properties of the commodity itself, [a property] that is ideally the antithesis of its use-value. The alienation of money from the commodity still has a preliminary and ideal character, and 'gold is the antithesis of the real commodity only as a conceived measure of value'.[71] When money is regarded only as the money-form of the commodity itself, the latter appears as a 'dual existence' – in reality as use-value, and ideally as value.[72] The value of the commodity has still not really separated from the natural form of the product itself, as the product of concrete labour, and thus abstract labour has still not become separated and found expression in the form of a particular real object.

Thus money, in its form as measure of value, still retains a very close link with commodities: money appears as the *money-form of the commodity* but not as

---

69 Marx 1970, p. 68.
70 Marx 1970, p. 114.
71 Marx 1970, p. 69.
72 Marx 1970, p. 68.

a real object that is opposed to the commodity. This is what Marx has in mind when he says that money, as measure of value, has a 'nebulous' and 'chimerical' form.[73] This form of money, as we shall see below, is the antithesis of the 'fluid' and 'firm' forms of money, in which the process of the alienation of money from commodities finds its further development.

With the goal of following the subtle dialectical transitions from one form of phenomena to the next, Marx, in the paragraph on the measure of value, already points to the need for conversion of money from the gaseous and ghostly form just described to a more stable and fixed form. Money already partially acquires a more fixed form in the transition from measure of value to a *standard of prices*. When we express the value of a table not as a certain quantity of gold in terms of units of weight (for example, ounces) but rather as a certain quantity of money units (roubles, for instance), we now have greater 'stability and exactitude of the proportions'.[74] Gold emerges here as the 'standard of prices'.[75]

However, in the form of standard of prices, the fixation of money still has an exclusively technical character. Ten roubles here fulfils the exact same role as does a certain quantity of gold in ounces, and accounting money does not cease to be ideal money. In order to disclose the need for further alienation of money from the commodity, we must reveal the need for the conversion of ideal into real money. This need follows from the very character of ideal money. Although ideal money appears only as the external form of the commodity itself, we must not forget that the commodity here is ideally equated with another commodity (gold) that is distinguished from it. Gold is a commodity distinct from wheat, and consequently the ideal equalisation of wheat with gold is 'an ideal equation with gold that still has to be realised'.[76] Thus, in the ideal form of money, as measure of value, is already hidden 'the necessity for alienation of commodities in exchange for glittering gold and thus the possibility of their non-alienation'.[77] From this follows the necessity of a transition from measure of value to means of circulation, from the less alienated form of money to the more alienated.

---

73 Marx 1970, pp. 70, 147.
74 Marx 1970, p. 71.
75 Marx 1970, pp. 70–1.
76 Marx 1970, p. 48.
77 Marx 1970, p. 69. [In this passage Marx does not use the usual German word for 'alienation' (*Entfremdung*) but rather *Entäußerung*, meaning both 'externalisation' and 'alienation'. Similarly, the English translation 'non-alienation' at the end of the quotation refers to the German word *Nichtveräußerung*, which can also be rendered as 'non-realisation' (Marx-Engels *Werke*, Band 13, p. 54)].

As *means of circulation*, money has a more alienated form than as measure of value. Here alienation of money from the commodity finds its further development. This is manifested in the conversion of ideal into real or actual money. 'Gold, which as measure of value was only ideal money and in fact figured only as the money-name for commodities themselves, is transformed into actual money'.[78] From the money-form of the commodity itself, money is transformed into a real object existing alongside the commodity and opposed to it. If, as measure of value, 'the money-existence of the commodity was still not separated in fact from its real existence', now the commodity, which exchanges for money as means of circulation, already 'acquires an existence free of any tie to its natural form of existence'.[79] Movement of the commodities themselves acquires the form of movement as a special thing, gold, which is external and foreign to them. 'The changes in the form of a commodity, its transformation into money and its retransformation from money, in other words the movement of the total metamorphosis of a commodity, accordingly appear as the external movement of a single coin'.[80] 'The movement of forms of the commodity – a movement occurring in the form of a process – appears as [money's] own movement'.[81] It appears to us that money sets in motion the commodities, which themselves appear to be motionless. Money is not only alien to the commodities and opposed to them, but movement of the commodities themselves also appears to us to be the result of the movement of money, which is external to them. But since the movement itself of commodities is nothing more than an expression of the commodity producers' own activities, it is not surprising that 'their own overall movement (that of the commodity producers), by means of which they complete the metabolism of their own labours, opposes them as the movement of a thing, as the circulation of gold'.[82]

However, this alienated form of money in relation to commodities must not obscure from the investigator the indissoluble internal *connection* between them. This close bond appears in this context both in the *origin* of money and in the *character* of its movement as means of circulation. If gold became the measure of value, it is only because all commodities measured their value in its terms, and now it becomes real money thanks only to the overall alienation of

---

78 Marx 1970, p. 89.
79 Marx 1970, pp. 87–8.
80 Marx 1970, p. 99.
81 Marx 1970, p. 101.
82 Ibid.

the commodities for gold.[83] Money, both as measure of value and as means of circulation, reveals in its genesis its dependence upon movement of the commodities themselves.

This dependence is also revealed in the character of money's movement as means of circulation. From the excerpts that we have already cited, we have seen that the movement of money, which seems as though it is alien and external to the movement of commodities, is actually only a reflection of the latter. 'The circulation of money is merely a manifestation of the metamorphosis of commodities, or a change of form through which the social exchange of things is completed'.[84] The means of circulation is simply the 'metamorphosed' commodity, and the movement of gold's metamorphosis is 'the movement of the metamorphosed commodity'.[85] 'The process of the circulation (of money) is the movement of the metamorphosis of the commodity world and must, for that reason, reflect the latter in its general movement'.[86] The movement of commodities is reflected or reverberates in the movement of money as means of circulation.[87] This is exactly why the quantity of means of circulation depends upon the sum of the prices of commodities in circulation; and thus money, in its function as means of circulation, which is only a passing expression of the value of the commodity itself, can be replaced with symbolic money.

While money, therefore, as means of circulation, acquires the form of a specific object, existing alongside commodities, in this function money only plays the role of *mediator* in the movement of commodities. As means of circulation, money serves simply 'as the intermediary link in the dynamic unity C–M–C or as the merely transitory form of exchange-value'.[88] Money serves as mediator for the conversion of one commodity into another commodity, and gold, in this function, is simply the commodity's own 'transitory money-form'.[89]

Up to this point we have been considering money in its function or form as means of circulation. In this form, money has been only a means for the circulation of commodities, and it has represented or 'reflected' in its own movement the movement of the commodities themselves. However, in this process of detachment, the 'alienation' of money from commodities does not come to a stop. In its subsequent development, money assumes a form that

---

83   Marx 1970, p. 89.
84   Marx 1970, p. 136.
85   Marx 1970, p. 99.
86   Marx 1970, p. 94.
87   Ibid.
88   Marx 1970, p. 150.
89   Marx 1970, p. 92.

is even more alienated and thus becomes more strikingly antithetical to the commodity. In this case, we have money in the proper sense of the word, 'money as such' (the hoard, means of payment and world money). Let us begin our analysis with *hoards*.

In this connection, as elsewhere, Marx endeavours first of all to show the *origin* of a new and more complex form from a simpler one and to reveal the most subtle dialectical transitions between them. For this purpose, he shows first that money, as means of circulation, already includes within itself the 'possibility' for the emergence of a more complex form of money in the form of a hoard. The function of money, as means of circulation, has presupposed that the circuit C–M–C represents a 'moving unity' in which purchase immediately follows sale. But the division of the process of exchange into two acts (of sale and purchase) already conceals within itself the 'possibility' of an interruption of the metamorphosis of the commodity following completion of the first act.[90] The possibility of such an interruption resides in the fact that the commodity, as a result of the act of sale, has assumed the form of money, 'the golden chrysalis', and in this form it 'possesses it own stable existence'.[91] 'The golden chrysalis state forms an independent phase in the life of the commodity, in which it can remain for a shorter or longer period'.[92]

In order for this possibility to become reality, it is necessary to indicate the causes that are at work within the sphere of commodity production and circulation itself that bring about a suspension or interruption of the commodity's metamorphosis. One such cause is the circumstance that the production process continues over a more or less long period of time, whereas the purchase of commodities, to satisfy the needs of the producer and his family, must occur more frequently. Thus the commodity producer, after selling the commodities he has produced, must retain a part of the money in order to spend it gradually on the purchase of items for personal consumption. This *'retained coin'* is the transitional form between coins, or means of circulation, and a hoard. While it remains in 'the hands of the seller, who receives it in return for a commodity, it is money, and not coin; but when it leaves his hands it becomes a coin once more'.[93] Or as Marx put it in *Capital*, money appears for a short time as a 'crystal of value' in order soon afterwards to dissolve into the transitory 'equivalent form of the commodity'.[94]

---

90   Marx 1970, p. 96.
91   Marx 1970, p. 125.
92   Marx 1970, p. 91.
93   Marx 1970, p. 125.
94   Marx 1976, p. 207.

In the form of retained coin, there are already indications of the conversion of money from flexible means of circulation, expressing the fluid unity of the two acts of sale and purchase, into the congealed 'crystal of value', which indicates a suspension or 'freezing' of the process of circulation on the part of commodities themselves. In that event, the producer withholds money for himself precisely in order to be able to spend it whenever necessary. 'So that money as coin may flow continuously, coin must continuously congeal into money'.[95] In this sentence, Marx clearly emphasises the contradiction between the two forms of money, as 'fluid' and 'congealed', together with the origin of the latter form in the former.

The form of retained coin, in which the first signs of the 'congealing' of money appear, is still not regarded by Marx as the form of a hoard. The retention of cash is only a necessary 'technical aspect of the circulation of money'; and thus the retained money is not considered to be a hoard but only a part of the general fund of means of circulation temporarily awaiting its turn to enter into actual circulation.[96]

Marx refuses to regard retained coin as a hoard because the temporary pause in the metamorphosis of the commodity, which we considered above, does not in the slightest degree alter the character of the commodity producer's activities. As before, the commodity producer sells his commodity in order to use the money earned in order to purchase necessary means of subsistence. It is precisely in order to have the possibility of buying these necessary means of subsistence that he temporarily keeps for himself the retained cash.

In order for money to acquire the new form of a hoard, the character of the commodity producer's activity must change. Such change has already been fully prepared by the preceding development of the circulation of commodities and money, and it necessarily arises from this source. The commodity, being transformed through sale into money, acquires thereby a form that is capable, at any given moment, of being converted into some use-value. It acquires a form of 'always being alienated', i.e. a form always capable of alienation. This circumstance alone – that the commodity producer can retain the commodity in its money-form, which is always suitable for alienation – has the capacity to evoke a change in the character of the commodity producer. The sale of commodities, in order to convert and retain them in the form of gold, becomes the motive for circulation itself. 'The metamorphosis of commodities, C–M, takes place for the sake of their metamorphosis, for the purpose of transforming particular phys-

---

95   Marx 1970, p. 126.
96   Ibid.

ical wealth into general social wealth. Change of form – instead of exchange of matter – becomes an end in itself. Exchange-value, which was merely a form, is turned into the content of the movement'.[97]

Now we can already see a *qualitative change* in the character of the commodity producer's activities and motives. He now sells his commodity not in order to purchase use-values, but instead to retain in his hands value itself, in its money-form, always ready for alienation. It is only from this moment that money acquires the new form of a hoard.

From various perspectives Marx illuminates the dialectical connection between the new form of money as a *hoard* and its previous form as *means of circulation*. On the one hand, he meticulously discloses their internal link. We have seen that this link already appeared in the origin of the new form of money as a hoard. The emergence of this form was prepared by development of the preceding form and necessarily resulted from it. This link is reflected in the entire character of money's functioning as a hoard. At first sight, the withdrawal of money from circulation, as a hoard, is the direct antithesis of money functioning as means of circulation. But this contradiction is only absolute so long as we limit our investigation to the sphere of money itself and leave out of account the sphere of commodity circulation, which is concealed behind it. When we also include the latter in the scope of our investigation, we shall see that the withdrawal of money from circulation occurs precisely in order to preserve the commodity in its money-form, always ready for circulation:

> Commodities remain wealth, that is, commodities, only while they keep within the sphere of circulation, and they remain in this *fluid* state only in so far as they *ossify* (*verknöchert*) into silver and gold. They remain within the *flow* of movement as *crystals* of the circulation process. But gold and silver are themselves confirmed in the role of money only insofar as they are not essentially means of circulation. *As non-means of circulation, they are essentially money*. Thus withdrawal of the commodity from circulation in the form of gold is the sole means of keeping it constantly within circulation.[98]

With these words Marx masterfully discloses the unity and connection between phenomena that have a different appearance externally due to their antithetical character. It is precisely because the movement of commodit-

---

97 Marx 1970, pp. 127–8.
98 Marx 1970, p. 128.

ies takes the form of alienating from itself the movement of money that the endeavour to retain the commodity in a form constantly suitable for circulation takes the form of the withdrawal of money from circulation as a hoard. The necessary internal connection between means of circulation and a hoard is also manifested in the fact that the commodity producer, who is accumulating a hoard, strives to multiply it continuously and, for that purpose, must throw into circulation newer and newer masses of commodities. The hoard, even if buried in the ground, is 'in constant tension with circulation'.[99] The hoard may be buried in the ground, but 'its money-soul, its constant endeavour to enter into circulation, moves to the person who has gathered the hoard'.[100]

Furthermore, the hoard maintains close contact with the sphere of circulation insofar as it represents the *reserve fund* from which money continuously flows into the sphere of circulation, and into which it continuously flows back from the latter. The need for these continuing inflows and outflows of money results from the character of money as means of circulation. As means of circulation, money functions in a quantity that is determined by the requirements of commodity circulation itself. And since the requirements of commodity circulation vary continuously in terms of money (depending upon changes in the volume of commodities, their prices, the velocity of the circulation of coin, etc.), there also emerges a continuous need to increase or decrease the quantity of money functioning as means of circulation. This increase or decrease is effected thanks to the continuous flows of money from the reserve fund of hoards into the sphere of circulation and back again. What occurs is '*solidification* of circulating money into hoards and the *flowing* of the hoards into circulation'.[101] This congealing and outflow, in turn, reflects the movement of the commodities themselves. The movement of money from the form of a hoard to the form of means of circulation occurs when there is a '*fluid* unity of purchase and sale' in the commodity world. And contrariwise, when the movement of commodities slows, 'the means of circulation *congeal* into money in unusually large measure, and the reserves of the hoards are replenished beyond their average level'.[102]

To this point we have been considering the connection of a hoard with the sphere of circulation. However, this connection did not at all prevent Marx

---

99   Marx 1970, p. 132.
100 Marx 1970, p. 131.
101 Marx 1970, p. 136 [Rubin's emphasis].
102 Marx 1970, pp. 136–7.

from emphasising the *antithetical* character of money as a hoard and money as means of circulation. Marx frequently characterises this change in the form of money as its conversion from a fluid into a congealed condition. 'The money is petrified into a hoard, and the seller of commodities becomes a hoarder of money'.[103] A contradiction emerges between 'the fluid form of wealth and its petrified form'.[104] The investigator must examine both of these forms of money, in their unity as well as in their contradiction. The mistake of various economic schools has consisted of the fact that they one-sidedly considered money only in one of these two antithetical forms. Thus the mercantilists considered money only as a hoard, and the classics, only as means of circulation. 'By contrast with the monetary and mercantile systems, which knew money only in its determinacy of form as a *crystalline* product of circulation, it was perfectly apposite that classical [political] economy regarded money, above all, in its *fluid* form'.[105] Ricardo examined 'the *fluid* form of money, in isolation', as means of circulation.[106]

Marx often calls the conversion of money from the fluid into the congealed form its conversion into a 'crystal of the process of circulation' or the crystalline product of circulation. This process of congealment or crystallisation of money indicates that the movement of money has gained greater independence and autonomy in relation to the movement of commodities than it possessed with the functioning of money as means of circulation. In the latter case, money was only the 'passing money-form of the commodity'. As a hoard, money is no longer the same passing form of the commodity.[107] Whereas money, as means of circulation, only expressed the value of the commodity itself, in its capacity as hoard of the commodity's value money has already assumed an independent external form and been distinguished from the commodity itself. As a hoard, money is the first 'independent existence (*Verselbständigung*) of exchange value';[108] it is 'money or exchange which has assumed an independent existence (*verselbständigter*)'.[109]

While Marx regarded the measure of value as a 'gaseous' form of money, and the means of circulation as 'fluid', the hoard already emerges as the 'congealed',

---

103   Marx 1976, p. 228.
104   Marx 1970, p. 134.
105   Marx 1970, p. 159 [Rubin's emphasis].
106   Marx 1970, p. 185 [Rubin's emphasis].
107   Marx 1970, p. 127.
108   Marx 1970, p. 134.
109   Marx 1970, p. 131.

'solid' and 'crystalline' form of money. This process of the gradual 'condensation' of money signifies that money's movement is more and more standing apart and acquiring an independent character in relation to the movement of commodities. As measure of value, money was only ideally the antithesis of the commodity. With the development of new forms of money, the antithesis between commodities and money intensifies. As means of circulation, money was already the real antithesis of commodities, but only in order to become the passing money-form of the commodity itself in the circuit C–M–C. As a hoard, money acquires a much more independent character. Just as Catholics recognise only the Pope as being infallible, so gold and silver now stand opposed to all simple commodities 'as the direct embodiment of social labour'.[110] If money, as means of circulation, only played the role of 'representative' of commodities, now, insofar as the hoard is concerned, all commodities emerge merely as the 'representatives of gold'.[111] Whereas previously the commodity producer viewed money as a means to acquire commodities, now he views commodities as means for the acquisition of money.

What this discloses is the process of gradual *isolation* and *alienation* of money from commodities. Despite the fact that money arose from the commodity and is subordinated in its movement to the movement of the world of commodities, it acquires ever-growing independence in relation to the latter. The transition of money from measure of value into means of circulation, and from the latter into a hoard, is presented to us by Marx as a process of the gradual alienation, congealment and crystallisation of money.

Since we have already looked in detail at the process of the congealment or alienation of money in the form of a hoard, we can only deal briefly with [money as] *means of payment*. Above all, Marx believes it necessary to prove that the appearance of a new and more complex form of money results from the development and requirements of commodity circulation itself and its underlying conditions of production. Since production of diverse commodities requires different periods of time, the moments of beginning and end for the production of different commodities do not correspond. The commodity producer frequently has to appear as a purchaser before he has sold his own commodity. Purchase, or M–C, must be completed before sale, or C–M, is completed. Since the producer has not yet sold his commodity and therefore does not yet have money, he can only complete a purchase on credit. The seller becomes the creditor, and the buyer the debtor. After the commodity produ-

---

110   Marx 1970, p. 159.
111   Marx 1970, p. 124.

cer has completed the act of purchase, or M–C, on credit, he must, according to the date specified in the agreement, retire his debt. For that purpose he now needs to complete his hitherto postponed act of the commodity's metamorphosis, i.e. the sale C–M. But since C–M is now completed only after the act of M–C, the character of the first act changes entirely. Now the commodity producer sells his commodity not in order to use the proceeds to purchase means of subsistence for himself, but instead he sells his commodity in order, with the help of the proceeds, to retire his debt. Now he wants to 'acquire money not as a means of purchase, but as a means of payment, as the absolute form of exchange-value'.[112] Money acquires the new form of means of payment.

Whereas money as a hoard was taken out of circulation, now money as means of circulation returns to circulation – no longer, however, as a 'passing means of circulation but rather as the universal equivalent in its settled existence, as the absolute commodity'.[113] 'Means of payment enter into circulation only after the commodity has already exited from it. Money no longer serves the process. It independently completes it as the absolute form of existence of exchange-value, in other words the universal commodity'.[114]

Because money turns from being a mediating moment of the circulation process into its final link, it appears in more striking form as the *antithesis* of commodities. Money 'enters into circulation as the only adequate equivalent of the commodity, as the absolute embodiment of exchange-value, as the last word of the exchange process'.[115] In money, as means of payment, we no longer have a passing money-form of the value of the commodity, but we have instead reached the 'independent (*verselbständigter*) existence of exchange-value'.[116]

Since sale of the commodity now serves the commodity producer only as a means for the acquisition of money, which he needs for repayment of a debt, all commodities now serve him only in the modest role of 'representatives' of money. From being a modest representative of commodities, money has become the absolute existence of value. The contradiction between commodities and money acquires here the most striking and acute form, especially in periods of monetary crises. It is true that the hoarder also regarded money as the sole wealth, and commodities in their natural form as things deprived of

---

112   Marx 1970, p. 141.
113   Marx 1970, p. 146.
114   Marx 1976, p. 234.
115   Marx 1970, p. 141.
116   Marx 1970, p. 148.

true value. But in that case it was a matter only of the imaginary annulment of the value of all commodities in face of gold as the sole embodiment of value and true wealth. So far as money as means of payment is concerned, at moments of crises we observe not just the conceivable but 'the actual devaluation and worthlessness of all physical wealth'.[117]

> Now money can no longer be replaced by profane commodities. The use-value of the commodity becomes valueless, and the value of the commodity vanishes in the face of its own form of value. Only yesterday the bourgeois, drunk with the flourishing of industry, considered money through the haze of enlightened philosophy and declared it to be an empty appearance: 'Only the commodity is money.' Today the cry of those same bourgeois, in all corners of the world market, is: 'Only money is a commodity!' As the hart thirsts for fresh water, so the bourgeois soul now thirsts for money, the only wealth. In time of crisis, the antithesis between the commodity and money – its embodiment as value – is raised to the level of an absolute contradiction.[118]

The alienation of money from the commodity has assumed here its most acute character by comparison with the forms of money that we have considered to this point.

We have followed the gradual intensification of the antithesis between the commodity and money. But we have become convinced, at the same time, that the different functions of money are inseparably linked with one another, and that the money-circulation reflects, as a whole, the movement in the world of commodities. Moreover, we can even say that parallel with the intensification of the antithesis between the commodity and money the unity that binds them together also intensifies. Money fulfils the function of measure of value for every particular commodity, and the function of means of circulation presupposes 'the circulation of commodities' in which the 'circuit, described by the series of metamorphoses of every given commodity, is inseparably interwoven with the circuit of other commodities'.[119] The extension of the function of a hoard indicates that the goal of the production process has become exchange-value, not use-value.[120] Finally, the 'degree to which money develops as the

---

117 Marx 1970, p. 146.
118 Marx 1976, p. 236.
119 Marx 1976, p. 212.
120 Marx 1970, p. 132.

exclusive means of payment indicates the degree to which exchange-value has taken possession of production in its entirety'.[121] The increasing complexity of the forms of money, which we have been describing, reflects the increasing complexity of production relations between commodity producers:

> The process of the metamorphosis of commodities, which gives birth to the various determinations of the form of money, also involves a metamorphosis of the commodity owners, or changes in the social character of their existence for each other. In the process of the commodity's metamorphosis, the commodity owner changes character as many times as the commodity changes character, or as many times as money assumes new forms. Thus, the original commodity owners opposed each other only as commodity owners; then one became a seller and the other a buyer; then each became buyer and seller in turn; subsequently they became the accumulators of hoards; and finally, they became rich people. Thus the commodity owners leave the process of circulation as different people than they were when they entered it.[122]

5 Capital

To this point we have considered the categories of a simple commodity economy. Given the breadth of the theme, we shall examine the following categories more briefly.

In the *transition* from simple commodity economy to capitalist economy, we already see a vivid example of applying the law of the unity of opposites. Viewed from the outside, the difference between them is seen in the distinction between the *two formulae of circulation*: C–M–C and M–C–M. The two formulae are antithetical to each other: in the second formula, the acts of purchase and sale are the reverse of what occurs in the first. In a simple commodity economy, circulation includes sale for the sake of purchase. In a capitalist economy, circulation includes purchase for the sake of sale. In the first formula, the commodity plays the role of extremes; in the second formula, it is money. In a simple commodity economy, circulation is completed in order to exchange one use-value for another. In a capitalist economy, the purpose of circulation is the expansion of value, i.e. the acquisition of surplus value.

Despite this *contradiction* between the two formulae of circulation, they constitute a *unity* that is evident both in their historical origin and in their sim-

---

121   Marx 1970, pp. 143–4.
122   Marx 1970, p. 138.

ultaneous operation. Historically the second formula, M–C–M, resulted from development of the first formula, C–M–C. It was only as a result of protracted development of the simple commodity economy that capitalist economy appeared with its inherent formula of circulation, M–C–M. However, once the latter formula of circulation appeared, being characteristic of a capitalist economy, the formula of simple commodity circulation, C–M–C, did not disappear; on the contrary, it reached its widest development precisely from this time onwards, since it is only in the capitalist period that commodity production and circulation embraced the entire economy. Thus circulation in the form of M–C–M, being antithetical by nature to circulation in the form of C–M–C, operated simultaneously with the latter and is based upon it. 'Insofar as the two phases, M–C and C^1–M^1, are acts of circulation, the circulation of capital constitutes part of commodity circulation in general. But insofar as they are functionally determined parts, or stages in the accumulation of capital, ... capital completes its own circuit within the general commodity circulation'.[123]

The unity of the two forms of circulation is revealed in their *interdependence*. The circulation of capital cannot be completed in the absence of commodity circulation in general. On the other hand, commodity circulation occurs in forms that are inherent in capitalism. The circulation of capital, M–C–M, can only be completed when there is a commodity in the market – labour power – completing its own circulation in the form C–M–C (the worker sells his labour power for money in order to use that money to purchase necessary means of consumption). On the other hand, the circulation of labour power, in the form C–M–C, is impossible in the absence of capital's circulation in the form M–C–M. Alongside this interdependence of the two forms of circulation, we also observe their *interpenetration*. The circulation of capital includes in itself the circulation of labour power, since the capitalist purchases labour power: and conversely, the sale of labour power by the worker, i.e. the act, from the worker's viewpoint, of entering the circulation C–M–C, simultaneously signifies the purchase of labour power by the capitalist, i.e. the act of entering the circulation M–C–M.

The unity and opposition of the two formulae of circulation, C–M–C and M–C–M, simply reflects the fact that the capitalist economy is simultaneously a further *development* and a *negation* of the simple commodity economy. It is a further development of the simple commodity economy because it arose historically from the simple commodity economy and at the same time operates on the basis of commodity and money circulation. On the other hand,

---

123   Marx 1978, p. 178.

however, the laws of commodity circulation, in the conditions of capitalist economy, acquire a form that is antithetical to the forms that distinguish them in a simple commodity economy. If simple commodity economy was based upon the exchange of equivalents, in capitalist economy we are dealing with the capitalist's appropriation of the workers' unpaid labour.

> The exchange of equivalents, the original operation with which we started, is now turned round in such a way that there is only an apparent exchange ... The relation of exchange between capitalist and worker becomes a mere semblance belonging only to the process of circulation, it becomes a mere form which is alien to the content of the transaction itself, and merely mystifies it.[124]

But this antithesis between the laws of simple commodity economy and the laws of capitalist economy does not eliminate their unity, for 'the original transformation of money into capital takes place in the most exact accordance with the economic laws of commodity production and with the rights of property derived from them'.[125] In other words, the capitalist economy represents simultaneously both a further development and the negation of the simple commodity economy. 'The laws of appropriation or of private property, laws based on the production and circulation of commodities, become changed into their direct opposite through their own internal and inexorable dialectic'.[126] The connection between simple commodity economy and capitalist economy has the character, therefore, of a *unity of opposites*.

Now let us turn to the characteristics of *capital* itself. In the formula M–C–M we already see two of the basic features of capital: first, capital is *self-expanding* value, i.e. value that acquires surplus value; and second, capital finds itself in continuous movement, alternately taking the form of *money* and then the form of the *commodity*. These two features of capital are connected precisely with the fact that capitalism is, on the one hand, the negation of simple commodity production and, on the other hand, its further development. Insofar as capital is self-expanding value, it is distinguished by specific features that are absent from a simple commodity economy. These specific features are essentially the class relations between capitalist and worker, including the appropriation by the former of the latter's unpaid labour. On the other

---

124 Marx 1976, pp. 729–30.
125 Marx 1976, p. 731.
126 Marx 1976, p. 729.

hand, capitalist relations do not eliminate commodity production but instead develop upon its basis. Just as in commodity production we have the constant movement of money and commodities, so capital must alternately take the form of commodity and money. In Volume II of *Capital* Marx emphasised the need to study both of these sides of capital: 'Capital, as self-expanding value, does not just comprise class relations, a definite social character that depends on the existence of labour as wage-labour. It is a movement, a circulatory process through different stages, which itself in turn includes three different forms of the circulatory process'.[127] In other words, we must study capital both in the sphere of *production* and in the sphere of *circulation*. Marx devotes the first volume of *Capital* to investigating the former and the second volume to the latter.

Let us consider capital in the sphere of direct *production*. From this point of view, we see that capital is the *class relation* between capitalists and workers. The emergence of these class relations signals the appearance of acute class contradictions in the society of commodity producers, which we have hitherto regarded as a homogeneous environment of completely identical commodity producers. We know that in this case the stratification of a society of identical commodity producers into two antithetical classes was a long historical process, accompanied by the violent seizure of land from the peasantry, the ruin of small commodity producers and the plundering of colonies. This was the process of primitive capitalist accumulation. The 'separation' of the means of production from the workers, and the appearance of capital, only occurred as a result of this long and violent historical process. We must not suppose, therefore, that Marx arrived at the category of capital by way of a simple logic inherent in development of the categories of simple commodity economy, i.e. the commodity and money. The category of capital, for Marx, is a reflection of actual reality, since real phenomena, corresponding to the categories of simple commodity economy, grew by way of a long historical process into other real phenomena corresponding to the category of capital. It is precisely because the new production relations between the class of capitalists and the class of workers became manifest in reality itself that Marx introduces into his system the new category of capital. But, on the other hand, since the new production relations between capitalists and workers operate on the basis and in the form of production relations between commodity producers, the category of capital does not eliminate the categories of commodity and money but is the further development of these same categories.

---

127   Marx 1978, p. 185.

The appearance of capital signified the appearance of *contradictions* within the previously homogeneous environment. In Marx's words, the 'polarisation of the commodity market' occurred together with the appearance of 'two kinds of commodity owners', namely, the owners of the means of production and the sellers of labour power.[128] There was a further development of the process of 'alienation' that we observed in simple commodity economy. But, whereas in simple commodity economy the commodity and money were 'alienated' from labour only after the labour process was completed, in capitalist economy the alienation of labour power from the means of production takes place even before the process of direct production. 'These means of production confront the possessor of labour-power as someone else's property. The buyer, conversely, is confronted by the seller of labour as another's labour-power'.[129] This process of 'alienation' and 'detachment' of the means of production from labour power is emphasised by Marx in several of his works. Marx says the means of production oppose the worker as 'alienated and independent', as 'the alienated, independent conditions' of labour.[130] The means of production assume an 'alien form', a 'detached' form and an 'antithetical' form; i.e. a form in which they are opposed to the worker and, for exactly that reason, acquire the social character of capital.[131] What occurs is the process of alienation (*Entfremdung*) of the means of production through their becoming independent (*Verselbständigung*) of the workers.

Thus the appearance of capital marked the appearance of contradiction within a previously homogeneous social environment. What occurred here was the appearance of the greatest *class* antitheses and contradictions in the history of the world. This appearance of contradictions between classes is decisively important because it prepares the subjective factor of class struggle, which creates, on the basis of all the antitheses and contradictions created by capitalist economy, the possibility of transition from this economy to a new and higher stage. Thus it is precisely here, in this sphere of class polarisation that we have been describing, that the central knot of contradictions of capitalist economy is tied, which must resolve all of the latter's inherent contradictions. The entire grandiose knot of diverse antitheses and contradictions in the capitalist economy can only be resolved thanks to the powerful class contradiction between capital and labour that occurs in the sphere of direct production.

---

128   Marx 1976, p. 874.
129   Marx 1978, p. 115.
130   Marx 1971, pp. 264, 293.
131   Marx 1971, pp. 259, 275–6.

The contradiction between capital and labour does not eliminate their interaction. The means of production, constituting capital, are created by human labour; and from this point of view they represent objectified labour as distinct from living labour. But in the conditions of capitalist economy, this objectified labour has come to dominate living labour: capital has subordinated labour to itself and absorbed it. This inclusion of labour in capital occurs when labour power exchanges itself for variable capital and is already part of capital in the process of direct production.

This *interaction* between capital and labour imposes special features upon both of them and evokes a certain 'bifurcation' of both capital and labour. Because capital must be exchanged for labour power, it separates into two parts. That part of capital spent directly on the purchase of labour power is called *variable* capital. The part of capital spent on acquiring material means of production is called *constant* capital. The need for this bifurcation of capital is explained by the dual character of labour as abstract and concrete. Insofar as the capitalist is interested in appropriating unpaid labour, he expends capital on the hiring of labour power. But insofar as the worker's labour is not merely abstract but also concrete labour, in order to be applied it requires the presence of determinate means of production. In order to set labour power in motion, the capitalist must buy not only this labour power but also certain means of production. Accordingly, part of the capital must be converted into constant capital.

We also see a 'bifurcation' in the sphere of labour. Due to the fact that labour is purchased by capital, it separates into two parts: *paid and unpaid labour*. The value created by the worker's labour is divided into two parts: *the value of labour power and surplus value*. In turn, the surplus value 'bifurcates' and assumes two forms: *absolute and relative* surplus value. And in this connection Marx notes not only the difference between these two forms of surplus value but also their interdependence and the passing of one form into the other.[132]

Thus far we have established two divisions. Capital separates into constant and variable; and the value created by the worker's labour separates into the value of labour power and surplus value. But we must not forget that the value of labour power is exactly the same as the variable capital. Indeed, it is precisely variable capital that pays the value of labour power. If we therefore include the value of labour power in capital itself, we reach a new antithesis of *capital and surplus value*. Thus we have three pairs of contradictions: 1) constant and variable capital; 2) the value of labour power and surplus value; and 3) capital and

---

132 Marx 1976, p. 1025.

surplus value. The relation between constant and variable capital determines the *organic composition* of capital (c/v); the relation between surplus value and the value of labour power determines the *rate of surplus value* (s/v); and finally, the relation between surplus value and capital determines the *rate of profit* (s/c+v). Each of these magnitudes is characterised by a certain tendency of movement that depends, in the final analysis, upon the development of labour productivity. As the productive power of labour grows and the successes of technique advance, the relative measure of constant capital increases by comparison with variable capital, and thus the organic composition of capital rises and creates the basis for a powerful concentration of capital. This development of labour productivity, which cheapens the means of consumption of the workers and thus the value of labour power, acts in the direction of raising the rate of surplus value. Finally, the rise in the organic composition of capital creates a tendency to reduce the rate of profit.

From capital in the sphere of production we turn to capital in the sphere of *circulation*. We have thus far considered capital as the class relation between capitalists and workers, i.e. we have considered the specific features of capital that distinguish it from simple commodity economy. As we already know, though, capitalist economy is the further development of the same commodity economy. With the appearance of capital, the commodity and money do not disappear; they become subordinate moments of capital's own movement. Capital alternately takes the form of *commodity* and *money* when passing through different stages. 'In the circulation M–C–M both the money and the commodity function only as different modes of existence of value itself ... [Value] is constantly changing from one form into the other'.[133] Whereas in simple commodity economy we observed the process of division of the commodity into the simple commodity and money (and thus the division of value into the commodity form and the money form), now it seems that we revert to value in general. Capital is self-expanding value. This value alternately takes first one form and then the other. 'Those who consider the autonomisation (*Verselbständigung*) of value as a mere abstraction forget that the movement of industrial capital is this abstraction *in actu*. Here value passes through different forms, different movements in which it is both preserved and increases'.[134] The process of the 'independent isolation' of value here reaches its highest development. 'In capital, the autonomisation of value (*Verselbständigung*) appears

---

133   Marx 1976, p. 255.
134   Marx 1978, p. 185.

much more powerfully than in money'.¹³⁵ Capital in circulation represents a unity of opposites – *of the commodity and money*.

We have seen that capital, in the sphere of direct production, is a unity of opposites – of materialised and personal factors of production that are 'alienated' and 'isolated' from each other – which takes a contradictory class form. In just the same way, capital in the sphere of circulation represents a unity of opposites – of the commodity and money, in other words, of commodity-capital and money-capital. Finally, capital as a whole also represents a unity of opposites, namely, a unity of capital in *production* and capital in *circulation*.

> The reproduction process of capital as a whole is the unity of its production phase and its circulation phase, so that it comprises both these processes or phases ... If they were only separate, without being a unity, then their unity could not be established by force and there could be no crisis. If they were only a unity without being separate, then no violent separation would be possible implying a crisis.¹³⁶

We can now summarise. We can consider the appearance of capital as a process in which are simultaneously realised: 1) the sociological law of the differentiation of social *groups and classes*; 2) the economic law of the *reification* of production relations between people; and 3) the general dialectical law of the *unity of opposites*. We already observed, in simple commodity economy, the process of the differentiation of functions between commodity producers. We saw the appearance of new 'social characters' on the part of the commodity producer: the accumulator of a hoard, the creditor and the debtor. But all of these were the sort of functions that were alternately fulfilled first by one commodity producer and then by another; these functions were not 'crystallised' in specific persons. True, Marx noted that the function of creditor already revealed the capacity for a 'more stable crystallisation',¹³⁷ i.e. the capacity to become fixed either permanently or for a long time in particular persons. But in simple commodity economy, as a general rule, the creditor and debtor are not members of different classes but only different functions that are alternately fulfilled by different commodity producers. It is only with the appearance of capitalists and workers that the division of commodity society into classes occurs; only from that time does there appear an acute class contradiction between persons

---

135 Marx 1971, p. 131.
136 Marx 1968, p. 513.
137 Marx 1976, p. 233.

who possess the means of production and persons who are condemned for an entire lifetime to sell their labour power. This appearance of class contradictions marked an entire historic upheaval, a leap from a society of homogeneous commodity producers to a society of commodity producers who are torn apart by class contradictions.

Parallel with this growing complexity of the *production relations* between people, the *economic forms of things* also became more complex; whereas previously the product of labour assumed the form of commodity or money, now came a new social form – capital. In capital, the *fetishisation* of production relations acquires a more concealed and obscure form than in the commodity and money. Already, in the process of direct production, 'capital becomes a very mystical being, since all the productive forces of social labour appear attributable to it, and not to labour as such, as a power springing forth from its own womb'.[138] In the process of direct production, the productive forces of labour already appear to be the productive forces of capital. Capital emerges as value that is capable of self-expansion. Further fetishisation of production relations between people occurs in the sphere of the circulation of capital. This sphere of circulation gives rise to new 'determinations of form',[139] to 'new forms arising from the process of circulation',[140] for instance, the forms of fixed and circulating capital and so forth. For this reason the illusion appears that value and surplus value emerge in the process of circulation.

The process that we have described, of the differentiation of social groups and the reification of production relations between people, takes place on the basis of the general dialectical law of the unity of opposites. The appearance of capital signifies the appearance of class contradictions in the formerly homogeneous social sphere of commodity producers. The unity of opposites between *capital and wage-labour* in the sphere of production; the unity of opposites between *the commodity and money* in the sphere of circulation; and the unity between capital *in production* and capital *in circulation* – in all of these phenomena we see the realisation of the general dialectical law of the unity of opposites.

6   *The Circulation of Capital*

Marx's doctrine concerning the *circulation* of capital results from his teaching on the unity of capital in production and capital in circulation. Actually, capital

---

138   Marx 1992, p. 966.
139   Marx 1992, pp. 966–7.
140   Marx 1978, p. 136.

in circulation must assume two different forms: money capital and commodity capital. Consequently, capital in circulation divides, and in place of the former two-sided division of capital we get a three-sided division: *money* capital, *productive* capital and *commodity* capital. This is the doctrine of the different functions or phases in the movement of capital.

In reality, these different phases of capital's movement stand apart from one another as three *detached* forms of capital that are opposed to one another. On the surface of phenomena we see: 1) industrial capital that is involved directly in the process of production; 2) commodity-commercial capital, or merchant capital, that is involved in servicing the sphere of circulation; and 3) money-commercial capital that is in the hands of money capitalists and lent by them to capitalists in production. We have here three completely separated forms of capital, belonging to three different groups of the capitalist class, moving as if on the basis of completely different laws and opposing each other as independent spheres of capital investment.

What is it that constituted the upheaval caused by Marx in his teaching on the circulation of capital? This upheaval is the same as the one caused by his teaching on money. The contradiction between the commodity and money, which oppose each other in space, was transformed by Marx into the sequence of the commodity's movement through two antithetical phases. Marx regarded objects that are distributed alongside one another *in space* as different phases of the movement of one and the same process *in time*. Marx also applied this approach in his teaching on the circuit of capital. He showed that all three spheres of capital, existing beside one another in space, must be considered as different *phases or stages of movement* of one and the same capital, i.e. as parts of a single integral process and not as independent and isolated phenomena. Money and commodity capital must be deprived of their separation and be regarded as detached parts of the single process of capital's movement.

> Money capital and commodity capital, in so far as they appear and function as bearers of their own peculiar branches of business alongside industrial capital, are now only modes of the independent existence (*verselbständigte*) of the various functional forms that industrial capital constantly assumes and discards within the circulation sphere.[141]

---

141   Marx 1978, p. 136.

Thus Marx reduces the *external* antithesis of three detached forms of capital to a *sequence* of phases in the movement of one and the same capital. Every capital must pass through three phases: the first is money capital, the second is productive capital, and the third is commodity capital. From the contradiction between phenomena in space we turn to the development of phenomena in time. We convert the external antithesis of the three detached forms of capital into an internal antithesis of capital as a single process that necessarily passes through three distinct stages of movement. The structure of Volumes II and III of Marx's *Capital* becomes clear to us from this point of view. In the third volume of *Capital*, commodity-commercial capital and money-commercial capital emerge as detached and independent spheres of the application of capital. But we cannot understand the laws of their movement as long as we consider them as detached and isolated forms of capital: the laws of their movement can only be disclosed if we consider these forms of capital as parts and moments of the process of capital's movement as a whole. And it is precisely in Volume II of *Capital* that Marx transforms commodity-commercial capital into the commodity form of industrial capital.

> Money capital, commodity capital and productive capital thus do not denote independent varieties of capital, whose functions constitute the content of branches of business that are independent and separate from one another. They are simply particular functional forms of industrial capital, which takes on all three forms in turn.[142]

Once we have reduced the three opposing forms of capital to three phases in the movement of one and the same capital, we consider these three phases as revealing the *internal contradictions* that are hidden in the nature of capital. The necessity of the differentiation within capital of three distinct phases or stages of movement follows from the very nature of capital, which represents self-expanding value alternately taking the forms of commodity and money. In this movement is revealed the internal antithesis hidden within capital: '... in this function as circulation capital, it is distinguished from its own existence as productive capital. These are two separate and distinct forms of existence of the same capital'.[143] We find 'the different forms with which capital clothes itself in its different stages'.[144]

---

142   Marx 1978, p. 133.
143   Marx 1992, p. 380.
144   Marx 1976, p. 109.

Once capital alternately passes through three different phases (money, productive and commercial capital), at any moment one part of capital is in one phase, a second part in another, and a third in a third phase. The *sequence* itself of the phases of capital's movement in time leads to the simultaneous existence of three different forms of capital in space. 'The sequence in space is itself only a result of the sequence in time'.[145] 'The forms are therefore fluid forms, and their simultaneity is mediated by their succession'.[146]

In order, therefore, to understand the laws of capital's movement, we must consider capital as a unity of opposites, or as a *unity of three different phases*. But that is not all. Suppose we do see capital as the unity of three phases (money, productive and commodity capital), i.e. in the form of circulation M–C ... P ... C–M. Although we have taken into account all three phases of capital, our investigation is still one-sided because we began with the money form capital and concluded with the money form. From this one-sided viewpoint, the circulation of capital appears to us as the circulation of *money* capital; the circulation of capital will appear differently to us if we begin and end our examination from a different viewpoint with the phase of industrial capital. In that case we have the circuit of *productive* capital (P ... C–M–C ... P). Finally, if we begin our examination by taking the phase of commodity capital, we have the circuit of commodity capital (C^1–M^1–C ... P ... C^1). The mercantilists considered the entire circulation of capital from the first point of view, the classics did so from the second point of view, and the physiocrats from the third point of view. As a result, the investigation of capital by the economists of all three of these schools had a one-sided character. We only reach a complete representation of the circulation of capital when we consider it from all three points of view, i.e. as the circulation of money capital, as the circulation of productive capital, and as the circulation of commodity capital.

> If we take all three forms together, then all the premises of the process appear as its result, as premises produced by the process itself. Each moment appears as a point of departure, of transit, and of return. The total process presents itself as the unity of the process of production and the process of circulation; the production process is the mediator of the circulation process, and vice versa.[147]

---

145   Marx 1978, p. 183.
146   Marx 1978, p. 184.
147   Marx 1976, p. 180.

We see just how necessary the application of the law of the unity of opposites is for understanding capital's movement. We must consider the process of capital's movement not simply as the unity of three antithetical *phases*, but also as the unity of three *circuits* of capital. 'The total process is in fact the unity of the three circuits, which are the different forms in which the continuity of the process is expressed'.[148]

Marx does not stop with reducing the opposing forms of capital to the unity of capital's movement through three different phases. Analytically reducing the entire process to its *unity*, he then shows us how the three independent and separate forms of capital become *detached* from a single capital. He follows the process of the 'separation' and 'alienation' of the different forms of capital from each other. This alienation consists of the fact that the different functions of capital, for instance the commercial operations, now become not the incidental operations of the industrial capitalist himself but instead separate out and become the special operations of a special group, the merchants; what occurs is the 'detachment' of a special group from the capitalist class, devoting itself to servicing the commercial or the money circulation.

Of course, this break up of the capitalist class into three separate groups is explained, in the final analysis, by development of the material process of production, by expansion of the market and the growing volume of production. These changes in the process of the production and exchange of commodities make it impossible for the industrial capitalist to combine in his own person the functions of director of production, of merchant, of banker and so forth. A 'separation' and 'alienation' of these functions from one another occurs; for example, special groups of merchants appear. From this moment, 'instead of being an incidental operation carried out by the producer himself, this function (trade) now appears as the exclusive operation of a particular species of capitalist, the merchant, and acquires independence (*verselbständigt*) as the business of a particular capital investment'.[149] The separation and detachment of money-commercial capital occurs in exactly the same way. 'A definite part of the total capital now separates off and becomes autonomous (*verselbständigt*) in the form of money capital, its capitalist function consisting exclusively in that it performs these operations ... for the entire class of industrial and commercial capitalists'.[150]

This separation of a special group of capitalists is a clear illustration of the further *differentiation of social groups* and of the further deepening of the *social*

---

148   Marx 1978, pp. 183–4.
149   Marx 1992, p. 382.
150   Marx 1992, p. 431.

division of labour. With regard to the separation of commercial capitalists, Marx writes that 'It is a particular form of the social division of labour'.[151]

As we see, commodity-commercial capital and money-commercial capital are only detached parts of the single process of the movement of capital. It follows, in the first place, that the laws of their movement can only be understood on the basis of the general movement of industrial capital as a whole; and secondly, that these detached forms of capital acquire a certain relative autonomy that appears in the specific laws of their movement; in other words, the movement of these detached parts of capital can be understood only on the basis of the law of the unity of opposites.

Marx frequently emphasises this *dual* character of the detached parts of capital. On the one hand, he emphasises their *connection* with the movement of capital as a whole: 'The movements of this money capital are thus again simply movements of a now independent (*verselbständigter*) part of the industrial capital in the course of its reproduction process'.[152] On the other hand, however, once this part of capital becomes detached it has already assumed a certain relative *autonomy* and becomes subordinate to particular laws.

> In commercial and money-dealing capital, the distinction between industrial capital as productive capital and the same capital in the sphere of circulation attain autonomy (*verslbständigt*) in the following way: the specific forms and functions that capital temporarily assumes in the latter case come to appear as independent forms and functions of a part of capital that has separated off and become completely confined to this sphere.[153]

Engels also emphasises this relative *autonomy* of the parts that have separated off. Engels considers this process of separation of the various forms against the broad background of the social division of labour.

> Where there is division of labour on a social scale, the various sections become mutually independent. Production is, in the final analysis, the decisive factor. But as soon as trade in products becomes independent of actual production, the former follows a trend of its own which is, by and large, undoubtedly dictated by production but, in specific cases and

---

151 Marx 1992, p. 384.
152 Marx 1992, p. 431.
153 Marx 1992, p. 440.

within the framework of that general dependence, does in turn obey laws of its own, laws inherent in the nature of this new factor; it is a trend having its own phases and reacting in turn on the trend of production.[154]

In the same way the trade in money develops 'in its own way subject to the special laws and distinctive phases determined by its own nature'.[155]

It is precisely this relative autonomy of commodity-commercial and money-commercial capital that *conceals* from our view their unity and connection with the process of industrial capital's movement as a whole. If commercial operations were not conducted by a special merchant, but instead by agents employed by the manufacturer himself, 'this connection would not be obscured for one moment'.[156] But once the detachment of a special group of merchants has occurred, commodity-commercial capital externally separates from industrial capital, and precisely this 'autonomous separation' 'conceals various moments of the movement'.[157] Money, productive and commodity capital, being in fact only moments of the single process of capital's movement, become detached and acquire a certain autonomy, acting – or so it seems from the outside – autonomously and independently of each other. This is exactly why economists, observing the outer surface of phenomena and considering commodity-commercial and money-commercial capital in their 'detached' form, were not able to understand the internal laws of capital's movement; they came to the most absurd conclusions concerning the emergence of commercial profit within the sphere of circulation itself. It was only Marx who succeeded in clarifying the problem of commercial profit because he shattered the external illusion of the independent movement of commodity-commercial capital and considered it as inextricably connected with the movement of industrial capital as a whole. Only application of the law of the unity of opposites enabled Marx to resolve this difficult problem.

As we see, in his teaching on the circulation of capital, Marx again showed us the realisation of the three laws mentioned above. On the one hand, we observe a picture of the gradually increasing complexity of the *class structure* of society. In the teaching on simple commodity economy, we had to deal only with simple commodity producers; in the doctrine of capital, we deal with the production relations of two classes of society, the capitalists and the workers; and finally, in the teaching on the circulation of capital, we see a further complication of the

---

154 Letter from Engels to Conrad Schmidt, 27 October 1890, in *MECW*, Vol. 49, p. 58.
155 Letter from Engels to Conrad Schmidt, 27 October 1890, in *MECW*, Vol. 49, p. 59.
156 Marx 1992, p. 382.
157 Marx 1978, p. 191.

social structure – the disintegration of the capitalist class into several special and independent groups (industrial, commercial and money capitalists).

As the complexity of the production relations between people and of the social *forms of things* grows, the process of reification and the fetishisation of people's production relations also develop. Commodity-commercial capital and money-commercial capital acquire an independent form, separated and detached from the direct process of production; and, thanks to this, the illusion arises of the formation of surplus value in the circulation process, and the production relations between members of society take on a more intricate and fetishised character.

The process of increasing complexity that we have been describing, along with the reification of production relations between people, occurs in conformity with the general dialectical law of the *unity of opposites*. The movement of capital, which we previously considered as a single process, falls apart into a series of detached and relatively autonomous spheres, in each of which we find specific forms of movement. Contradiction emerges within a group of phenomena that form a unity but, on the other hand, unity is preserved between these opposing phenomena. The detached parts of capital (commodity-commercial, money-commercial and productive capital), although they possess relative autonomy, are still altogether subordinated in their movement to the laws of industrial capital's movement as a whole. The movement of the production process continues to prevail over all the parts of capital that have become detached from it and acquired their own outwardly independent and alien form.

7   The Dissolution of Surplus-Value into Incomes

As we have seen above, the value of the annual product in capitalist society (including the value of the expended means of production) splits into *capital and surplus value*. We have already traced the process of the complication and detachment of the separate parts of capital. Now we must consider the process of the gradual complication and detachment of the different parts of *surplus value*; in other words, the process of the dissolution of surplus value into separate types of non-labour incomes (the profit of enterprise, interest, commercial profit and ground rent). Marx devoted the greater part of Volume III of *Capital* to this question. In a letter to Engels, Marx wrote: 'In Book III we then come to the conversion of surplus value into its different forms and separate component parts'.[158]

---

158   Letter from Marx to Engels, 30 April 1868, in *MECW*, Vol. 43, p. 21.

The disintegration of *surplus value* into different forms of revenue is a process that runs parallel to the process described above of the disintegration of industrial *capital* into separate and autonomous forms. Actually, once the dissolution of *capital* into commodity-commercial, money-commercial and industrial capital – belonging to different groups of capitalists and constituting separate branches – has occurred, it is perfectly understandable that surplus value has also divided into separate parts, acquired by different groups of capitalists and having different forms. On the surface of phenomena we already encounter these different types of non-labour income in finished and independent form or, as Marx says, in 'solid' form. We already encounter forms of income that are separate from one another (the profit of enterprise, commercial profit, interest), are externally distinct from one another, and appear to move independently of each other, each on the basis of its own inherent laws. And in this case the first task facing Marx was to uncover the unity lying at the basis of these different forms of non-labour revenues in order to deprive them of their seeming independence and present them as detached parts of a single mass of surplus value. In their theory of value the classics had already outlined a way to resolving this question, but they were still not familiar with surplus value in its general form. It was only Marx, with his doctrine of surplus value in Volume I of *Capital*, who really revealed the unity underlying all non-labour revenues. It was with good reason that Marx considered the very best part of *Capital* to be his doctrine of the dual character of labour along with that of surplus value; that is 'the treatment of *surplus-value regardless of its particular* forms as profit, interest, ground rent, etc.'.[159] In another letter Marx spoke even more clearly of the singularity of his doctrine of surplus value: 'in contrast to *all* previous political economy, which *from the outset* treated the particular fragments of surplus value with their fixed forms of rent, profit and interest as already given, I begin by dealing with the general form of surplus value, in which all these elements are still undifferentiated, in solution as it were'.[160] Here Marx expressed the central idea that guided him throughout his entire investigation, the idea of conversion of the frozen and detached social forms of things, which externally oppose and contradict one another, into parts of a single fluid process, parts of the single mass of social labour at the disposal of society.

As we have already seen, however, Marx never restricted himself to the *analytical* reduction of detached social forms to a single process of which they are

---

159 Letter from Marx to Engels, 24 August 1867, in *MECW*, Vol. 42, p. 243, original emphasis.
160 Letter from Marx to Engels, 8 January 1868, in *MECW*, Vol. 42, p. 315, original emphasis.

parts; in addition, he always takes the reverse *synthetic* route and shows us the process of gradual detachment and alienation of these different social forms, the process of the 'genesis of forms'. The causes of this detachment of the separate forms of surplus value were clarified in the doctrine of the circulation of capital. The detachment of separate spheres of capital investment occurred as the process of material production and exchange expanded; simultaneously, the class of capitalists dissolved into separate groups, and surplus value dissolved into separate types of non-labour revenues. Just as the separate forms of capital move as if independent of each other, so the different parts of surplus value become detached from one another and acquire the form of separate and independent revenues, moving as if on the basis of different laws. 'The different components of surplus-value appear in the form of mutually independent revenues'.[161] 'The division of profit into profit of enterprise and interest ... completes the autonomisation (*Verselbständigung*) of the form of surplus-value, the ossification (*Verknöcherung*) of its form as against its substance, its essence'.[162]

Together with profit, a special form of revenue appears, *interest*, which moves on the basis of distinct laws. The appearance of interest means the further detachment and alienation of surplus value from its source – social labour. Whereas profit still retains a memory of its origin in labour, with interest the connection between revenue and the surplus labour of the workers is completely torn apart.[163] Thus interest-bearing loan capital, as Marx often puts it, is the 'most alienated' form of capital. This 'self-acting fetish' is completely torn apart from the direct process of production, having acquired independent existence and appearing to be an independent source of non-labour revenue. The process of the fetishisation of social relations reaches the extreme.

In *ground rent* we find an equally extreme detachment and fetishisation of the social relations between people:

> Since in this case one part of the surplus-value seems directly bound up not with social relations but rather with a natural element, the earth, the form of mutual alienation and ossification (*Entfremdung und Verknöcherung*) of the various portions of surplus-value is complete, the inner connection definitively torn asunder and its source completely buried, precisely through the assertion of their autonomy (*Verselbständigung*) vis-à-

---

161 Marx 1992, pp. 983–4.
162 Marx 1992, p. 968.
163 Ibid.

vis each other by the various relations of production which are bound up with the different material elements of the production process.[164]

The various parts of surplus value, which in fact serve to express social relations between people, fasten onto separate material elements of production and seem to originate in the latter; the land appears to bring forth rent, capital begets interest, and labour creates wages. 'Capital, landed property and labour appear to those agents of production as three separate and independent sources, and it appears that from these three arise three different components of the annually produced value'.[165] Vulgar economists generalise these notions of the capitalists with the *Trinity Formula* that Marx critically scrutinised in chapter 48 of Volume III of *Capital*.[166] Instead of reducing the different types of non-labour revenues to their single source – surplus value and surplus labour – vulgar economists, with their formula, only reflect the external detachment and alienation of different forms of non-labour income that strike the eye on the surface of capitalist society.

The *detachment* of different forms of non-labour income explains to us the illusion that arises in capitalist society. The value of products (if we subtract the value of expended means of production) breaks down into 'three component parts, which take the shape of autonomous and mutually independent forms of revenue, namely wages, profit and ground rent'.[167] But these forms of revenue, being results of the production process, are simultaneously its presuppositions. The capitalist, upon entering into the production process, already anticipates the need to acquire a definite sum of profit, interest and ground rent as a result of this process. It seems to him that the *value* of the product consists of these revenues; and the *revenues* appear to him as something primary with the value of the product as something derivative, which is acquired as a result of adding up revenues. He perceives the entire process

> not as the dissolution of a value magnitude given in advance into three parts which assume the mutually independent forms of revenue, but conversely as the formation of this value magnitude from the sum of the component elements of wages, profit and ground-rent, taken as determined independently and separately. The reason why this illusion would necessarily arise is that in the real movement of individual capitals and their

---

164 Ibid.
165 Marx 1992, p. 961.
166 Marx 1992, pp. 953–70.
167 Marx 1992, pp. 1006–7.

commodity product it is not the value of commodities that appears [as] the premise of its own dissolution but, on the contrary, the components into which it can be dissolved function as the premises for a commodity's value.[168]

This illusion explains the debate that bourgeois political economy is waging up to the present day over which is the primary element, value or revenues. We already find two answers to this question in Adam Smith, who correctly claimed that the value of the product *dissolves* into revenues, but then he mistakenly thought the value of the product is *composed* of revenues. The first viewpoint was adopted and further developed by Ricardo; the second viewpoint became the basis for the schemes of vulgar economists. Marx carried forward the work of Ricardo. He began his investigations with the value of the product, defined as a quantity of [labour in] the commodity, and then disclosed the origin of surplus value and the process of its dissolution into the separate non-labour incomes. But Marx did not stop there: he pointed out that revenues, being the result of the production process, become simultaneously its presupposition. In particular the average profit, added to the costs of production, forms the commodity's price of production. Thus the revenue (namely, the average rate of profit), being secondary in relation to the value of the commodity, in turn determines the commodity's price of production.

The seeming independence of the separate types of non-labour income does not alter the fact that they are all components of a single mass of surplus value and move within limits determined by the magnitude of the latter. And since surplus value, together with the value of labour power, are only parts of a common sum of value, newly produced by the labour of workers, it is understandable that a close connection and interaction exist between the movement of non-labour revenues and the movement of wages. With his teaching on revenues, Marx created a scientific basis for the understanding of *class struggle*, and he underlined this fact in his letter to Engels where he sets out the contents of Volume III of *Capital*: 'since those 3 items (wages, rent, profit (interest)) constitute the sources of income of the 3 classes of landowners, capitalists and wage-labourers, we have the *class struggle*, as the conclusion in which the movement and disintegration of the whole shit resolves itself' [der *Klassenkampf* als Schluß, worin sich die Bewegung und Auflösung der ganzen Scheiße auflöst].[169]

---

168 Marx 1992, pp. 1009–10.
169 Letter from Marx to Engels, 30 April 1868, in *MECW*, Vol. 43, p. 25, original emphasis.

8 Crises

We have traced the grandiose process of the *detachment and alienation* from one another of the different production relations between people and the various parts of social labour, which take on distinctive and independent forms (the commodity, money, capital and surplus value, the different forms of capital, and the various non-labour incomes). This process of detachment and alienation of people's production relations, and the corresponding social forms of things, arises due to the disorganisation and anarchy of capitalist production. But, on the other hand, the development of capitalist economy is accompanied by enormous growth of the productive forces and ever-increasing integration of the process of material production, which embraces the most diverse parts of the globe and makes them all into elements of a single system of the social division of labour. This growth in the unity of the system of material production occurs parallel with a multiplication of the social forms of things, which have become frozen and alienated, are externally antithetical to one another, and act with relative autonomy. This detachment of the production relations between people, and of the social forms of things, is one of the main moments to which Marx points in his theory of *crises*. Marx considers a crisis as the moment when the external detachment of separate processes has reached it greatest force, when their relative autonomy and their movement according to their own relatively different laws leads to destruction of the unity of the social production process, a unity that lies at the foundation of all these detached forms. 'When the assertion of their external independence (*Verselbständigung*) proceeds to a certain critical point, their unity violently makes itself felt by producing – a crisis'.[170]

Our task does not include a presentation of Marx's theory of crises. Marx sees the fundamental cause of crises in the inevitable contradictions of a capitalist economy between the striving for unlimited growth of the *productive forces* and the limited basis of *the production relations between people*. 'It is the unconditional development of the productive forces, and therefore mass production on the basis of a mass of producers who are confined within the bounds of the necessary means of subsistence on the one hand and, on the other, the barrier set up by the capitalists' profit, which [forms] the basis of modern overproduction'.[171] Here Marx shows, in abbreviated form, the fundamental causes of crises. On the one hand, the mighty development of productive forces on the basis of cooperation, machines and other advances of technique lead to

---

170 Marx 1976, p. 209.
171 Marx 1968, p. 528.

colossal growth of production; but the limited 'conditions of distribution and consumption'[172] under capitalism – which are the other side of the production relations between people – do not correspond to this colossal growth of the productive forces. The constraint that development of the productive forces encounters in the conditions of distribution and consumption lies first in the fact that production can only be conducted so long as it provides the capitalist with the average *rate of profit*, and secondly in the fact that the *consumption* by an enormous mass of society, on the basis of antagonistic relations of distribution, is reduced to a minimum that varies only within narrow limits.[173] The contradiction between productive forces and production relations is expressed, therefore, in the contradiction between production and distribution and between production and consumption. The crisis is directly expressed in the impossibility of realising commodities at prices that deliver the average rate of profit, i.e. in the contradiction between the process of the direct production of capital and the process of capital's circulation. In crises, therefore, is manifested the contradiction between all the aspects of a single process of social production that have become detached from one another: between production and circulation, production and distribution, and production and consumption.

Crises are inherent only in the capitalist economy, not in a simple commodity economy. But since division of the commodity into commodity and money – and thus dissolution of the single act of exchange into two independent acts of purchase and sale – already occurs in simple commodity economy, here there is already a possibility (although not a necessity) of crises.[174] It is interesting to show that all the forms of detachment that we have been considering above – of people's production relations and of the social forms of things – are considered by Marx to be the conditions or moments of a crisis.

We began our presentation with dissolution of the commodity into *the commodity and money*; this metamorphosis of the commodity, in which the contradiction between value and use-value is already manifested, is 'the *most abstract form of crisis* (and therefore the formal possibility of crisis)'.[175]

> Since they (purchase and sale) are connected with one another, the detachment (*Verselbständigung*) of these two interconnected moments can only show itself forcibly, as a destructive process. It is precisely in a

---

172 Marx 1992, p. 352.
173 Ibid.
174 Marx 1971, p. 502.
175 Marx 1968, p. 509.

crisis that they show their unity, a unity in difference. The independence that these interconnected and complementary moments have assumed in relation to each other is forcibly destroyed. Thus the crisis manifests the unity of two moments that have become detached (*verselbständigten*) from each other.[176]

Therefore, the dissolution of the commodity into commodity and money creates the first and most abstract possibility of a crisis. In the doctrine concerning the functions of money, we traced the gradual alienation of money from the commodity; this alienation became very pronounced in the function of *means of payment*. Indeed, the appearance of this function of means of payment begets the second condition for the possibility of crises since, given the connection of a whole series of commodity producers through a chain of debt obligations, the impossibility of one of them selling his commodities immediately affects the entire series of others. 'It can therefore be said that the crisis in its first form is the metamorphosis of the commodity itself, the falling asunder of purchase and sale. The crisis in its second form is the function of money as a means of payment ... Both these forms are as yet quite abstract, although the second is more concrete than the first'.[177] In a capitalist economy, with its widespread branches connecting debt claims and the obligations of commodity producers, development of money's function as means of payment plays an especially important role as a condition making the appearance of crises possible.[178]

Thus far we have been dealing with the categories of a simple commodity economy that give rise to the possibility of a crisis but not the necessity. The necessity of crises lies not in the conditions of a simple commodity economy but in the conditions of a *capitalist* economy, to which we now turn: 'The contradictions inherent in the circulation of commodities, which are further developed in the circulation of money – and thus, also, the possibilities of crisis – reproduce themselves, automatically, in capital, since developed circulation of commodities and of money, in fact, only takes place on the basis of capital'.[179] Insofar as we are investigating the sphere of the direct production of capital, we will not find any new elements that would explain to us the possibility and necessity of crises. It is true that, insofar as the process of production

---

176 Marx 1968, p. 500.
177 Marx 1968, p. 510.
178 Marx 1968, p. 511.
179 Marx 1968, p. 512.

is the process of producing surplus value, it already contains those contradictions that find their expression in crises; but this possibility of crises can only show up due to dissolution of the process of production of capital into the process of *direct production* and the process of *circulation*.[180] In this dissolution we find reproduced, in a new form and on a new basis, the dissolution of the commodity into the commodity and money, which, as we have already seen above, represented the first and most abstract possibility of crises:

> The total process of the reproduction of capital is a unity of its phase of production and its phase of circulation; it is one process that passes through two processes as its phases. Therein lies a more developed possibility or abstract form of crisis ... Crisis is the forcible establishment of unity between moments that have become detached and the forcible detachment of moments that are essentially one.[181]

A crisis arises on the basis of detachment of the sphere of capital's circulation from the sphere of direct production. We have seen, however, that even within the sphere of circulation capital takes the different and detached forms of commodity-commercial and money-commercial capital; each of these has relative independence from the process of production and moves on the basis of specific and particular laws. This detachment of the different parts of *capital* also constitutes one of the important conditions for a crisis. Detachment of the sphere of trade from the sphere of production; the dissolution of trade into wholesale, retail, etc.; and the independent and unique movement of loan capital and interest – all of these phenomena, as we know, play a significant role in explaining the course of crises.

Following the detachment of different forms of capital, we considered the detachment of different parts of *surplus value* in the form of specific non-labour revenues (profit, interest, commercial profit, and rent). We entered the sphere of distribution, in which the production relations between people emerge simultaneously as those of distribution. For Marx, the relative autonomy of movement that separate revenues acquire is also one of the most essential moments affecting the crisis. We know that the separate types of revenue are not simply the result but also the presupposition of the production process, and above all that is the role played by the *average rate of profit*, which is the regulator of the expansion and contraction of production. The

---

180 Marx 1968, p. 509.
181 Marx 1968, p. 513.

capitalist anticipates in advance the average rate of profit and, depending upon the possibility of receiving a higher or lower rate of profit, he either expands or contracts production. This autonomous role of the average rate of profit, which is anticipated in advance by the capitalist, has enormous significance for understanding crises. Essentially speaking, the crisis comes exactly when the conditions for the capitalist to receive the average rate of profit disappear. 'Periodically too much is produced in the way of means of labour and means of subsistence, too much to function as means for exploiting the workers at a given rate of profit'.[182] In this connection Marx attaches enormous importance in his teaching on crises to the law of the tendency for the rate of profit to fall.

However, the presuppositions of the production process include not only the norm of profit but also the other non-labour revenues. Their magnitude is taken as pre-given, and participants in production expect in advance to acquire these non-labour revenues in a certain amount. 'One part of the average profit, in the form of interest, confronts the functioning capitalist from an independent position as an element already presupposed in the production of commodities and their value ... The same can be said of ground-rent'.[183] So long as production continues under the previous conditions, these revenues are actually received in the customary measure, and the expectations of production participants are in fact justified. But with the change of production conditions that accompanies the onset of a crisis, the possibility of acquiring these revenues in the customary sums disappears. With the onset of a crisis, we clearly see the inadaptability of these detached social forms of things, and particularly of the different forms of non-labour revenues, to the conditions of the production process. In the conditions of a crisis, 'The fixed charges – interest, rent – which were based on the anticipation of a *constant* rate of profit and exploitation of labour, remain the same and in part *cannot be paid*'.[184] The crisis puts an end to the seeming autonomy of different forms of non-labour revenues. So long as the production process moves in unchanging conditions that are continuously repeated, it can appear that the separate revenues really are independent of each other and that their sum constitutes the value of the commodity. As we know however, these different and antithetical forms of revenue are in fact connected through the unity of the entire mass of social labour and the mass of value that it creates. In normal conditions, the connection of different revenues with the value of commodities, and their limitation as a result of this value,

---

182 Marx 1992, p. 366.
183 Marx 1992, p. 1011.
184 Marx 1968, p. 516.

is not detectable on the surface of phenomena.[185] But a crisis, which changes the general conditions of production and thus the conditions for the formation of value and surplus value, reveals the interconnectedness of all incomes and their subordination to the law of value. 'It is *crises* that put an end to this apparent *independence* of the various elements into which the price of production dissolves and which it continually reproduces'.[186]

The distributive relations of capitalist society, which, in Marx's words, are merely the other side of the production relations, form the basis for the appearance of a contradiction between *production and consumption*. The antagonistic relations of distribution 'reduce the consumption of the vast majority of society to a minimum level, only capable of varying within more or less narrow limits'. Consequently, 'the more labour productivity develops, the more it comes into conflict with the narrow basis upon which consumption rests'.[187] On the one hand, a characteristic feature of capitalist society is precisely the separation of production from consumption and the antithesis between them: on the other hand, the unity of these two moments is forcibly restored in a crisis.[188]

Crises reveal with particular clarity the character of capitalist society as a *unity of opposites*. If capitalist society did not constitute a system of detached and relatively autonomous production relations between people and social forms of things – a system replete with the greatest contradictions – crises could not occur. On the other hand, however, these same crises reveal the character of this system as a unity and display the subordination of all the detached elements to its single regulating law of value. Crises temporarily re-establish equilibrium, but only in order to create the basis for a wider development and intensification of capitalism's inherent contradictions. The conditions are increasingly created, therefore, for the onset of a grandiose crisis that destroys the very system of production relations in capitalist society and makes necessary the transition from the capitalist form of economy to the socialist one.

9   Conclusion

The development of Marx's theory through the three volumes of *Capital* can be seen as a clear example of the application to political economy of the dialectical law of the *unity of opposites*. Crossing from one form of production relations to another, Marx shows the process of their gradually increasing

---

[185] Marx 1992, p. 1007.
[186] Marx 1971, p. 518.
[187] Marx 1992, pp. 352–3.
[188] Marx 1968, p. 500.

complexity, of the gradual appearance of qualitatively new forms that are antithetical to the previous forms, and the process of their gradual detachment and alienation. Parallel with the appearance of contradictions within a group of phenomena that constitute a unity, these detached forms are all the more closely bound together due to the material unity of the entire production process. Forms that are antithetical and detached from each other preserve their unity. The fundamental concept, upon which Marx builds his entire system, is the concept of a determinate mass of social labour and the value it creates; this mass of value constitutes the general frame within whose limits the entire system of capitalist economy moves. Within this mass of value, a mass of surplus value becomes detached and in turn constitutes the framework within whose limits all the forms of non-labour revenues move. Considering all the social forms of things as variations of the form of a single mass of value, or a single mass of social labour, Marx discloses the internal law that unites them; he destroys the external independence and isolation of separate economic phenomena, considering them as subordinate parts and forms of a single process of the movement of social labour.

The external *autonomy* and '*alienation*' of all economic phenomena in capitalist society has its basic cause in the anarchic and unorganised character of the latter, in the dissolution of society into a number of partial and 'independent' undertakings that find themselves in a relation of 'reciprocal alienation' from one another.[189] This relation of mutual alienation between people finds its expression in the whole of economic life, in which the 'appearance of strangeness' prevails.[190] The production relations between people are reified and fastened to the material elements of production, being alienated from human labour itself and from one another and taking on an irrational and estranged form. It is precisely in this external form that they are understood by the capitalists themselves and by vulgar economists.

The *classical school* had already cleared a path for revealing a single dynamic and fluid process of the development of people's production relations behind the social forms of things.

> It is the great merit of classical economics to have dissolved this false appearance and deception, this autonomization and ossification (*Verselbständigung und Verknöcherung*) of the different social elements of wealth

---

189 Marx 1976, p. 182.
190 Marx, 1976, p. 186 (In the Russian translation, these words appear as an 'incomprehensible character').

vis-à-vis one another, this personification of things and reification of the relations of production, this religion of everyday life, by reducing interest to a part of profit and rent to the surplus above the average profit, so that they both coincide in surplus-value; by presenting the circulation process as simply a metamorphosis of forms, and finally in the immediate process of production reducing the value and surplus-value of commodities to labour.[191]

According to Marx, the classics destroyed the detachment of the different forms both of non-labour income and of capital and revealed in labour the source of value and surplus value. However, apart from the fact that the classics did not fully resolve this problem, only outlining the way to a solution, their method suffered from the following essential deficiency: the classics attempted, with the help of analysis, to reduce the detachment and alienation of forms of wealth from one another to their internal unity – in the final analysis, to labour. But the classical school was limited by this analytical reduction and did not take the reverse synthetic route; it did not show how different forms arise from unity, gradually separating and becoming externally independent of one another; it did not show us the process of the gradual development and formation of forms, the process of the 'genesis' of forms.[192] Since the classics could not move from unity to the variation of forms on the surface of phenomena, when explaining the latter they often fell themselves into vulgar, fetishistic notions, resulting in the mixing up of the labour point of view and the vulgar point of view in the system of the classics.

Marx managed not only to uncover the *unity* lying at the basis of contradictory phenomena but also to trace the entire process of the *genesis of forms*, which leads to differentiation within unity and the appearance within it of antithetical forms. Marx considered the social forms of things, which appear externally to be autonomous and alien to one another, to be 'the estranged form of appearance of economic relations'.[193] Marx traces the process of the gradually increasing complexity of the reification of production relations between people: 'The relations of production become objectified and acquire an independent existence (*Verselbständigung*) in relation to the agents of production'.[194] There occurs a mutual detachment of production relations, which are

---

191   Marx 1992, p. 969.
192   Marx 1971I, p. 491.
193   Marx 1992, p. 956.
194   Marx 1992, p. 969. [Here Rubin is partly paraphrasing and partly quoting. In the original

now bound up with the various material elements of the process of production.[195] The further the differentiation of society proceeds, with its stratification into different classes and groups, the more complex become the production relations between them, the more detached from one another are the different spheres of the process of social production, the more fetishised are social relations, and the more concealed is the internal law on the basis of which they move:

> The actual production process, as the unity of the immediate production process and the process of circulation, produces new configurations in which the threads of the inner connection get more and more lost, the relations of production becoming independent of one another (*sich gegeneinander verselbständigen*) and the components of value ossifying (*sich gegeneinander verknöchern*) into independent forms.[196]

The vulgar economists confined themselves to consideration of economic phenomena in their reified, detached and isolated form; this means that they also confined themselves to considering the surface of phenomena, to investigation of the 'appearance' of phenomena. In contrast to them, Marx wants to uncover the 'internal' law of the phenomena. For that purpose he deprives economic phenomena of their seeming external autonomy, considering them in their internal connection with one another as parts of the single process of social production. From this point of view, the interaction between them already has the character not of an interaction between detached phenomena that are alien to one another; it is already a case of their interaction within the limits of a single process, in relation to which they are only externally detached parts and forms. They already emerge not as '*detached*' from one another, but as the parts of a single production process that have '*become detached*'; not as 'alien' to one another, but as the '*alienated*' production relations between people and the social forms of things. And this is precisely why they already emerge not as indifferent to one another, but instead as simultaneously connected with one another by a relation of unity and a relation of antithesis. In Marx's words, the vulgar economists consider 'the different forms of surplus value and the forms of capitalist production not as alienated [*entfremdet*], but

---

text, Marx speaks of presenting 'the reification of the relations of production and their autonomisation vis-à-vis the agents of production' ['*der Versachlichung der Produktionsverhältnisse und ihrer Verselbständigung gegenüber den Produktionsagenten*'].

195   Marx 1992, p. 968.
196   Marx 1992, p. 967.

as alien [*fremd*] and indifferent forms, merely different from one another but not *antagonistic* to one another'.[197] This is precisely why economic phenomena appear as the detached and alienated parts of a *single* process; they are not indifferent to one another but find themselves in a condition of contradiction and struggle with one another. This struggle of the different opposing and contradictory elements of capitalist economy, finding their highest expression in the struggle between the classes of capitalists and workers, prepares the ground for a real 'removal' of the alienated and detached forms of social life and for a genuine revelation of the unity that lies at their basis. The more the power of 'alienated' labour (capital) over living labour grows, the more the conditions are created for the elimination of this alienation. It is precisely because capital develops the powerful productive forces of labour, which can no longer operate within the limits of capitalist production relations, that it also prepares its own end:

> Capital shows itself more and more to be a social power, with the capitalist as its functionary – a power that no longer stands in any possible kind of relationship to what the work of one particular individual can create, but an alienated social power which has gained an autonomous position (*entfremdete, verselbständigte gesellschaftliche Macht*) and confronts society as a thing, and as the power that the capitalist has through this thing. The contradiction between the general social power into which capital has developed and the private power of the individual capitalists over these social conditions of production develops ever more blatantly while this development also contains the solution to this situation, in that it simultaneously raises the conditions of production into general, communal, social conditions of production.[198]

Marx thinks of the social revolution as the destruction of the 'alienated' and 'detached' forms of production relations between people.

---

197 Marx 1967l, p. 503. It is interesting that this thought concerning the difference between 'foreign' and 'alienated' can be found even in Marx's earliest works. For instance, in one of the early works from 1844 Marx wrote about 'supersession of objectivity in the condition of *alienation* (which has to develop from indifferent otherness to real antagonistic alienation)' (Marx, in Fromm 1961, p. 183).

198 Marx 1992, p. 372.

APPENDIX

Pages from the Life and Creative Work of Economist I.I. Rubin (1992)*

Lyudmila L. Vasina and Yakov G. Rokityansky

Source: L.L. Vasina and Ya.G. Rokityansky, 'Stranitsy zhizni i tvorchestva ekonomista I.I. Rubina', in *Vestnik Rossiiskoi akademii nauk*, No. 8, 1992, pp. 129–44.

Introduction by the Editors

We conclude this volume with a biographical essay, written in 1992 by Lyudmila L. Vasina and Yakov G. Rokityansky (1940–2013), the two Russian scholars who led the effort to restore Isaak I. Rubin to his proper place in the history of Marxist scholarship. In addition to the document that follows, Lyudmila L. Vasina was responsible for the original Russian-language publication of Rubin's *Essays on Marx's Theory of Money* (which we have translated as Document 19 in this volume). Two years after the biographical essay, Yakov G. Rokityansky also published the NKVD transcript of Isaak Rubin's final interrogation in Aktyubinsk (Kazakhstan) in November 1937. The most remarkable revelation in Rokityansky's later article was an inventory of scholarly materials that the NKVD took from Rubin at the time of his arrest.[1] The list included the following:

1) The History of Economic Thought in the second half of the nineteenth century, written on foolscap and apparently intended as a continuation of Rubin's book *A History of Economic Thought*, which ended at the mid-nineteenth century with John Stuart Mill;
2) a 380-page work on Johann Karl Rodbertus;
3) a 429-page work on the Anglo-American school (Rokityansky speculated that this probably included Alfred Marshall in the UK and J.B. Clark in the US);
4) a 110-page work on Adam Smith and his teaching on capital;
5) 8 notebooks on the theory of economic crises;

---

* For permission to translate and publish this document, the editors wish to express their gratitude to Lyudmila L. Vasina of the Russian State Archive of Social-Political History.
1 Ya.G. Rokityanskii, 'Poslednie dni Professora I.I. Rubina', in *Vestnik Rossiiskoi Akademii Nauk*, Vol. 64, No. 9 (1994), p. 830.

6) 3 notebooks on the distinctions of Marxist socialism;
7) 3 notebooks on Henri de Saint-Simon and other economists;
8) 148 pages on the Mathematical school (Rokityansky thought this would probably have included such writers as Léon Walras, Vilfredo Pareto, William Stanley Jevons, Francis Edgeworth, Gustav Casell and Knut Wicksell);
9) 148 pages on Walras (Rokityansky had difficulty deciphering the handwriting on the NKVD list, but 'Walras' was his best guess);
10) 20 pages on Wicksell (the name of 'Wicksell' was also Rokityansky's best guess); and
11) Several other notes and drafts by Rubin.

Discussing the scholarly materials seized by the NKVD, Rokityansky added:

> There are reasons to think that the list of scientific works, confiscated at the time of the arrest, was compiled at the request of the professor himself. Apparently, he hoped to have these manuscripts returned after he was released. Perhaps he also had his family in mind. It is most probable, however, that the scientific works written by Rubin in Aktyubinsk were destroyed after he was shot.[2]

Isaak Rubin was interrogated on 23 November. On 25 November he was charged with leading an 'anti-Soviet, Trotskyist organisation', whose purpose was to agitate against the leadership of the Communist Party and the Soviet government, to spread rumours that would aid the Fascist states, and ultimately to restore capitalism in the USSR. On 25 November a tribunal sentenced Rubin to be shot. The sentence was carried out on 27 November 1937.

∴

Lyudmila L. Vasina and Yakov G. Rokityansky on the Life and Work of Isaak Il'ich Rubin

The name of professor Isaak Il'ich Rubin (1886–1937), author of several extremely interesting works on theoretical problems of political economy and the history of economic thought, frequently appeared on the pages of various publications both before and after the revolution. Towards the end of the 1920s he emerged as one of

---

2 Ya.G. Rokityanskii, 'Poslednie dni Professora I.I. Rubina' in *Vestnik Rossiiskoi Akademii Nauk*, Vol. 64, No. 9 (1994), p. 829.

the leading economic scholars in the country. Rubin's articles provoked sharp debates, and his lectures were very popular. But it was precisely during the 1920s that Isaak Il'ich was subject to a series of arrests. His fate as a 'permanent prisoner' was unique even for those years. His scientific accomplishment was amazing: while a captive, he continued to think and work intensively in prisons, concentration camps and exile, as well as during the brief intervals between arrests. In November 1937 this scholar was executed, his books were relegated to special depositories, and for half a century his name was struck from his country's scientific life. One of the goals of this article is the restoration of historical justice. The authors have drawn upon a wide range of archival materials, including those held by the former KGB, as well as upon previously unknown works by the scholar and manuscripts and documents that were kindly provided by Doctor of biological science M.V. Zheltenkova and engineer V.V. Zheltenkov, niece and nephew of Professor Rubin.

Two of Professor Rubin's most important works were long ago translated, published and positively received in the West.[3] In our own country, the books and works by this scholar remained until very recently in the special depositories of libraries, while his scientific views were either ignored or not assessed in an objective manner. A brief biographical note in the encyclopaedia of 'Political Economy' provided just about the only mention of Rubin, and even that reference repeated the customary interpretation: 'Rubin led the so-called idealistic tendency in political economy (sometimes called the "Rubin school" in the literature). Rubin's position was subjected to sharp criticism in the works of Soviet economists'.[4]

Is it not time to recall the dramatic fate and scientific achievement of this talented researcher?

∴

Isaak Il'ich Rubin was born on 12 June 1886 to a well-to-do Jewish family in Dvinsk. His father was a homeowner and hereditary honorary citizen of the city. From the age of five, the young boy attended a *kheder*;[5] he then completed the classical gymnasium in Vitebsk; and from 1906–10 he studied in the law faculty of Petersburg University, where the economic disciplines were taught by then famous professors I.I. Kaufman and M.I. Tugan-Baranovsky. Upon completing university, I.I. Rubin became a specialist in the areas of economic science and civil law. In his 'Biography' he later recalled: 'Since

---

3   Rubin 1979 and 1990.
4   V.E. Manevich, 'Rubin, Issak Il'ich', in *Ekonomicheskaya Entsiklopediya: Politicheskaya ekonomiya*, Vol. 3 (Moscow: Sovetskaya entsiklopediya, 1979), p. 510.
5   A *kheder* was a religious elementary school.

an academic career was closed to me, after completing university I busied myself for several years with practising law (mainly labour law) and at the same time, in 1913–14, published several scientific works on civil law'.[6] We have managed to find the works on legal issues mentioned in this autobiography, which involved commentary on a number of articles of civil law[7] and on the law concerning soldiers' pensions.[8]

In 1912 Rubin moved to Moscow, where he first worked as a barrister; and from 1915 to August 1917 he was secretary of the Union of Cities and of the Zemstvo Union. From May until the beginning of November 1917, he worked at the newspaper *Izvestiya Moskovskovo Rabochevo Soveta*. There he published ten articles: on the mechanism of settling labour disputes with the help of conciliation boards, on ways to combat unemployment, on the III All-Russian Congress of Trade Unions, on the creation and functioning of municipal and trade-union labour exchanges, on national service, etc.[9] Rubin's brochures on *Conciliation Chambers and the Arbitration Court*[10] and on *Unemployment Insurance*,[11] published in 1917–18, were also devoted to social issues, as were more than 15 articles in the journals *Rabochii mir* and *Prodovol'sytvennoe delo*. Here are the titles of just a few of them: 'Unemployment and the Struggle Against it in the Moscow Region', 'Trade Unions and the Regulation of Industry', 'The Nationalisation of Factories', 'Revolution and the Economy of Germany', 'Social Classes in Hungary', and 'The Proletariat in Austria'. These materials are not simply of historical interest. Today it is still possible to learn much from them that is useful concerning our own pressing economic problems.

In 1919 Isaak Il'ich's scientific and teaching activity commences. Here is another excerpt from his *Autobiography*:

> *In 1919 I was invited* by D.B. Ryazanov to translate the works of Marx. At that *time I began, together with* Sh.M. Dvolaitsky, to assemble the collection *Osnovnye problemy politicheskoi ekonomii* (which appeared in 1922). From mid-1919 until

---

6   I.I. Rubin, *Zhizneopisanie* in TsGAOR [Central State Archive of the October Revolution], F. 5144, Op. 20, D. 4, S. 126.
7   I.I. Rubin, *Kommentarii k zakonam: o vyzove naslednikov (st. 1249–53), prinyatie nasledstva i posledstviya onavo (st. 1257–8, 1260–4), otrechenie ot nasledtsva i posledstviya onavo (st. 1265–78), o vvode vo vladenie po nasledstvu (st. 1297–9)*, in A.E. Varms and V.B. El'yashevich (eds.), *Zakony grazhdanskie* (Sv. Zak. T. x, ch. 1) *Prakticheskii i teoretichekii komentarii*, 3rd ed. (Moscow, 1914), pp. 112–14, 158–62, 195–215, 278–81.
8   I.I. Rubin, *Komentarii k zakonu o pensiyakh dlya soldat* (M.: Izd. Yurid. Otdela Soyuza gorodov, 1915).
9   *Izvestiya Moskovskovo Rabochevo Soveta*. 1917. Nos. 72, 75, 87, 97, 103, 106, 122, 145, 180, 191.
10   I.I. Rubin, *Primiritel'nye kamery i treteiskii sud* (M-: Mosk. Sovet rab. dep., 1917).
11   I.I. Rubin, *Strakhovanie ot bezrabotitsy*. (Sergiev Posad: Mosk. Sovet rab. dep., 1918).

1921 I taught social sciences for the Moscow Military-Technical courses, and in the summer of 1920 I taught a course in political economy for teachers under the People's Commissariat of Education. From February 1920 until 1922 I worked at the Commissariat of Education on a commission to create programmes for schools, on a commission to draft curriculum plans for universities, and as head of the department of social science at the Humanitarian-Pedagogical Institute. In February 1921 I was appointed professor of First Moscow University, and subsequently I taught political economy at First Moscow University, at the Institute of Red Professors, at the Institute of National Economy, and at Sverdlovsk University.

By the early 1920s Rubin emerged as one of the country's leading scholars. He became an historian of economic thought, a translator and commentator on works by West-European economists, and a brilliant lecturer. And it was at precisely this time of Rubin's rapid scientific rise that he found himself, in February 1921, behind bars. In terms of his political convictions, he was a social democrat. He joined the 'Bund' in 1904 and did active propaganda work amongst Jewish workers in the Pale of Settlement. In 1905 he was arrested, but he was amnestied after the tsar's Manifesto of 17 October.

Rubin had no enthusiasm for the October Revolution, fearing that counter-revolutionary forces would come to power if it were defeated. Following October he continued his activities in the Bund's Moscow organisation. When a split occurred at the Moscow conference in 1920, he remained with those who refused to merge with the RCP(B). Together with this group, which declared itself successor to the Bund, Rubin left the meeting hall. In his address to like-minded thinkers on the tasks of the trade-union movement, he defended the need for 'trade unions that are independent of the state, as organs of proletarian class spontaneity that are constructed from top to bottom on the electoral principle, preserving a constant and close bond with the working masses and accountable to those masses'.[12] Rubin was elected to the Central Committee of the Bund and became its Secretary. It was precisely on account of his being part of the Bund's leadership that he was arrested on 20 February 1921 and committed to the Butyrsky prison.

> Citizen Rubin – his trial concluded – was arrested on 20.11 of this year, in the *Vpered* club, at a plenary meeting of the C[entral] C[ommittee]. of the Bund (S-D), of which he is Secretary. Among the party literature that was gathered, nothing was found that would indicate any illegal character of his party work ... Taking into account that the investigation did not establish any concrete grounds

---

12 *K raskolu 'Bunda' (Materialy i dokumenty)*. (Vitebsk: 1920), pp. 20–2.

for prosecuting citizen Rubin, I would consider it possible to end the case against citizen Rubin and to return the correspondence and documents seized from him.[13]

This recommendation was implemented, and the arrestee was freed 'on bail and with the obligation to appear immediately upon summons from the VChK [the Cheka]'.[14]

The next time Rubin was seized was on the night of 5–6 November of the same year, 1921. He was a deputy of the Moscow Soviet, and the Menshevik fraction of the Soviet protested: 'We believe that this latest raid by the VChK can only be regarded as a continuation of the policy of short-sighted terrorism on the part of leading circles of the Communist party against the RSDRP [the Russian Social-Democratic Workers' Party], whose economic programme, in its essentials, the RKP [the Russian Communist Party] is currently attempting to implement'.[15]

But his fellow scholars saved him. The investigation file includes a letter to the VChK from then Rector of MGU [Moscow State University], the famous historian V.P. Volgin. It is dated 6 November 1921 (i.e. it was sent on the day of the arrest), and it gives an account of Rubin's teaching activity at MGU. Here is the text:

> On the night of 5–6 November Isaak Il'ich Rubin, professor of the Faculty of Social Sciences and the Department of Political Economy, was arrested in his apartment. His arrest causes significant damage to the Faculty's teaching as he gives classes there in the theory of Marxism, of which he is himself an adherent, and this course is an essential component of the basic programme of the Faculty's teaching. In view of this fact it is vitally important to the Presidium of the University – in the interest of properly conducting the University's educational work – that Professor I.I. Rubin return as quickly as possible to his teaching duties, and for that reason the Presidium submits to the All-Russian Extraordinary Commission its urgent appeal for a most expeditious review of Prof. Rubin's case and, as soon as possible, for a change in the measures of personal custody to which he is subject. Convinced of Professor Rubin's loyalty to the governing authorities, the Presidium asks that the All-Russian Extraordinary Commission release him on bail to the members of the University's Presidium, and takes upon itself full responsibility for ensuring that, in the event of his being released, Professor Rubin will be on call to the appropriate government organs and will not in any manner abuse the trust placed in him upon being released from arrest.[16]

---

13   *Tsentral'nyi arkhiv* MBRF, *No. R-28327, L. 9.*
14   *Tsentral'nyi arkhiv* MBRF, *No. R-28327, L. 11.*
15   *Tsentral'nyi arkhiv* MBRF, *No. R-28327, L. 31.*
16   *Tsentral'nyi arkhiv* MBRF, *No. R-28327, L. 29.*

The case also involved a letter from A.V. Lunacharsky to V.P. Menzhinsky, the vice-chairman of the VChK (dated 14 November 1921). Rubin, it says, 'works intensively at Narkompros [the Commissariat of Education]', and it asks that 'the review of his case be accelerated and, if circumstances permit, that he be returned as soon as possible to fulfilling his duties'. On 19 November the dean of the faculty of social sciences at MGU [Moscow State University], N.M. Dukin, also sent a letter to the VChK:

> For this reason, and taking into account the fact that Professor Rubin is entrusted, as a valuable teacher and steadfast Marxist, with conducting a special seminar on 'Marx's theory of value', which is attended by a large audience, the faculty office of the dean hereby requests the earliest possible release of Prof. Rubin from arrest so that he might continue to conduct classes, since a major interruption of them in mid-semester is extremely undesirable.[17]

The petitions from his academic colleagues were effective. On 22 November 1921, a resolution of the Presidium of VChK declared: 'Citizen Rubin is released from custody on bail in the charge of the President of Moscow State University, comrade Volgin. The investigation of the case continues.'[18] During his two brief stays in prison in 1921, I.I. Rubin continued his academic work. In letters addressed to the prison authorities, he asks permission to receive the books and notebooks etc. required for his work.

Following November 1921, I.I. Rubin was free for one year and three months. He taught again at MGU, IKP [the Institute of Red Professors] and other educational institutions, published a number of reviews and articles, and prepared the first edition of his major work, *Essays on Marx's Theory of Value*.[19] On 27 February 1923 the professor was arrested anew. This time he spent more than three and a half years in prison and exile. On 13 April 1923, the NKVD commission on administrative exile resolved to intern Rubin in the Archangel concentration camp for three years.[20] The resolution was justified as follows by Ivanov, the assistant head of the second department of the OGPU [the Unified State Political Directorate]:

> Taking into account that the investigation does not have sufficient evidence to bring I.I. Rubin to trial under article 62, but that his anti-Soviet activity has been fully demonstrated, I propose: that this case and its conclusion be submitted to the NKVD commission on administrative exile with the recommendation that

---

17 *Tsentral'nyi arkhiv MBRF*, No. R-28327, L. 32.
18 *Tsentral'nyi arkhiv MBRF*, No. R-28327, L. 40–3.
19 I.I. Rubin, *Ocherki po teorii stoimosti Marksa* (Moscow: Gosizdat, 1923).
20 *Tsentral'nyi arkhiv MBRF*, No. P-40156, L. 32.

citizen Rubin Isaak Il'ich be held in the Archangel concentration camp for a term of 3 years. The case is concluded and to be deposited in the SOGPU archive.[21]

For Rubin, this sort of decision was the equivalent of a death sentence. A very sick man, he could hardly endure three years in a northern concentration camp. For a month there was a struggle for the scientist's life. His colleagues did everything to prevent him from being sent away. His wife, Polina Petrovna Rubina (1884–1958) made many efforts. On 19 April she sent a letter to the USSR ambassador to Germany, N.N. Krestinsky, asking that he help to secure a 'review of the sentence and its immediate suspension'. She recalled that 'For the past three years Isaak Il'ich has been involved in his work of studying Marx's theory of value, the result of which was the book by Isaak Il'ich, *Essays on Marx's Theory of Value*, which appeared a month ago and was published by Gosizdat [the State Publishing House] in Moscow'.[22] N.N. Krestinsky responded quickly to the letter: 'I believe – he wrote to deputy chairman of OGPU, I.S. Unshlikht – that in his case it would be more proper to let him go abroad. When he is abroad, he can do no harm to us … For this reason I raise the question of reviewing the decision and of exiling Rubin from the country'.[23] On 23 April, Polina Petrovna requested OGPU 'to review the sentence and replace it with exile abroad or to some provincial city'. She added: 'If such resolution is not possible, I ask that he be left in one of the Moscow prisons'.[24]

On 10 May 1923, the OGPU commandant of Butyrsky prison received the order 'to hold up until further notice, in view of his illness, the dispatch of citizen Rubin Isaak Il'ich, who has been sentenced to Archangel concentration camp'.[25] True, the leadership of OGPU still sent him away in the autumn of 1923, but to the Suzdal concentration camp rather than Archangel. The file of the investigation includes a letter from there, written by I.I. Rubin on 28 October 1923: 'Eight months of imprisonment have severely undermined my already poor health (cardiac neurosis, pulmonary tuberculosis, chronic stomach disease); in Suzdal I have been kept in a basement cell, with huge damp areas on the walls'. Rubin noted that his confinement in Suzdal was even more agonising and damaging to his nerves than the 'very harsh regime' to which he had been subjected in Butyrka.[26] Soon afterward Rubin was returned to Butyrsky prison.

---

21 *Tsentral'nyi arkhiv* MBRF, No. P-40156, L. 36–7 [The SOCPU was the secret department of the GPU, the State Political Administration, under the People's Commissariat of Internal Affairs (NKVD)].

22 *Tsentral'nyi arkhiv* MBRF, No. P-40156, L. 14–17.

23 *Tsentral'nyi arkhiv* MBRF, No. P-40156, L. 19–20.

24 *Tsentral'nyi arkhiv* MBRF, No. P-40156, L. 21–2.

25 *Tsentral'nyi arkhiv* MBRF, No. P-40156, L. 40.

26 *Tsentral'nyi arkhiv* MBRF, No. P-40156, L. 68. ['Butyrka' is a colloquial way of referring to Moscow's Butyrsky Prison].

The OGPU's severity towards the scholar was primarily due to the fact that he did not change his political views. He spoke of himself as a 'political prisoner' and ventured dangerous *démarches*: 'I hereby declare that today, 1 May 1924, the holiday of the international working class, I am undertaking a one-day hunger strike in mourning for the comrade-socialists who have perished in prison and exile and as a sign of protest against the unprecedented brutal regime (...) used by the Bolsheviks against socialists'.[27] In such circumstances it was very difficult for those who wanted to make things easier for Rubin to secure any positive results. The director of the Institute of K. Marx and F. Engels, academician D.B. Ryazanov, was even prepared to take responsibility for his bail. Later he recalled:

> Despite all my attempts at persuasion, Rubin remained steadfast. He refused to be freed under my warranty, giving me his word that he disclaims any practical work and is prepared to devote himself entirely to scientific work. 'And if one of the old comrades calls on me in Kashin – it was assumed that he would not be living in Moscow – I will not inform on him and will only let you down.'

Rubin's sister, B.I. Zheltenkova, also pleaded for him. In the summer of 1924 she submitted a request to A.I. Rykov, the chairman of Sovnarkom [the Council of Ministers], for her brother's early release. 'If it is not possible for him to be released', she wrote, 'I ask that he be exiled for the remainder of his sentence to one of the cities near Moscow'.[28]

In November 1924 Rubin's fate took a definite turn. The intercessors finally managed to agree with the leadership of OGPU on a solution to the problem. On their advice, apparently, I.I. Rubin appealed to Menzhinsky on 4 September 1924, to replace his remaining sentence to the concentration camp with 'exile to one of the provincial cities of European Russia ... or to somewhere in Crimea'.[29] On 19 December 1924, a special meeting of the OGPU collegiate ordered that Rubin be released from prison and sent, for the remainder of his term, to the city of Karasubazar on the Crimean peninsula.[30]

In Karasubazar (renamed Belogorsk since 1944) the scholar and his wife had two rooms in a single-storey cabin. Their life was not serene. Moreover, during the winter Rubin's health deteriorated. The leadership of OGPU decisively refused a request to move him to some other locale in Crimea that would be better for his health. In April of 1926 the scholar wrote: 'Due to the impossibility of a timely change of residence, I spent the winter of 1925–6 in a condition of permanent illness. I was bed-ridden for

---

27   *Tsentral'nyi arkhiv* MBRF, No. P-40156, L. 91.
28   *Tsentral'nyi arkhiv* MBRF, No. P-40156, L. 110.
29   *Tsentral'nyi arkhiv* MBRF, No. P-40156, 120–1.
30   *Tsentral'nyi arkhiv* MBRF, No. P-40156, 126–7.

three months and suffered acute articular rheumatism, with the result that my health (especially my heart condition) seriously worsened and now requires long-term special treatment'.[31]

On 13 April 1926 the term of exile ended. Rubin's colleagues did everything they could to secure his return to Moscow. This is how, on 29 March, Sh.M. Dvolaitsky justified the need for the scholar's return to his work of teaching at the Institute of Red Professors:

> Rubin is presently the leading expert (...) on Marxism (apart from Bukharin). His principal work, in my view, is a brilliant interpretation of Marx's theory of value. In any event, I cannot think of a single other work in this field that is on the level of Rubin's book. He is also involved with the history of economic thought ... He has been able to do an excellent study not only of Marx's predecessors and contemporaries but also of current bourgeois literature on economic theory. Of course, it would be impossible for us to find a second such teacher for the Institute ... My opinion of Rubin, so far as I am aware, is the common view of our comrade-economists. Bukharin also holds him in very high regard.[32]

On 9 April 1926, the rector of the IKP [Institute of Red Professors], academician and historian M.N. Pokrovsky, called for Rubin's return to work at the Institute:

> Since Professor Rubin is an outstanding expert in the area of Marx's economic theory and in the history of economic thought, and since the IKP is lacking in precisely such leaders, it considers it permissible to request that he be allowed to reside in Moscow in order that he may be employed, as previously, to conduct seminars in the basic courses ... Professor Rubin's political position will have no influence on such highly qualified Party members as the students at the Institute of Red Professors.[33]

But these petitions were ignored. The conclusion of the case reads: 'During his time in exile Rubin remained, as before, a Menshevik, adopting an implacable position towards the Soviet authority and maintaining contact with exiles in other cities, with the consequence that his residence in any of the central industrial areas, upon completing his exile, constitutes a social threat'.[34] The scholar was forbidden, for a period of three

---

31 *Tsentral'nyi arkhiv* MBRF, No. P-40156, L. 171.
32 *Tsentral'nyi arkhiv* MBRF, No. P-40156, L. 169.
33 *Tsentral'nyi arkhiv* MBRF, No. P-40156, L. 168.
34 *Tsentral'nyi arkhiv* MBRF, No. P-40156, L. 173.

years, to live in Moscow, Leningrad, Tula, Nizhny Novgorod or Ivanovo-Voznesensk. At the end of August he received permission to settle in Saratov. However, the OGPU received still more petitions. At this stage, in addition to academician D.B. Ryazanov, A.I. Rykov and N.I. Bukharin also pleaded on Rubin's behalf. In October their intercession had an effect. Rubin was allowed to visit Moscow for three weeks, and on 26 November 1926, a special meeting of the OGPU collegiate resolved: 'to grant Rubin Isaak Il'ich early release from punishment and to allow him to reside freely anywhere in the USSR'.[35]

In Rubin's 'Autobiography' we find these words: 'From 1923 until 1926 I was busy with literary-scientific work and wrote a number of scientific works'.[36] At first sight, this may appear curious. Indeed, throughout this time Rubin was in a cell at Butyrsky prison, in the Suzdal concentration camp, then again in Butyrka, and then in exile at Karasubazar. But when paging through the investigation of his case, one becomes convinced that during his confinement Isaak Il'ich really did work intensively. There is a record of all the books, journals and other materials that arrived for Rubin from 1923–6, and also of all the times when he was permitted to send out manuscripts that he had completed in prison. In addition, the case file includes voluminous correspondence that is indicative of his intensive scientific work. The prison authorities did not suppress the professor's scientific studies. Up to the time of his arrest he had completed a number of tasks and secured publications with various publishers, including the Institute of K. Marx and F. Engels. At that time, the heads of these institutions could still exercise influence upon the leadership of the OGPU.

The case file includes numerous letters from individual scholars and institutions (above all, from the Institute of K. Marx and F. Engels) to the OGPU requesting the dispatch to Rubin of one or another publication. Here, for example, is a letter from Sh.M. Dvolaitsky dated 4 September, 1923:

> Please send the enclosed book [*Ricardo und Marx als Werttheoretiker* by I. Rosenberg] to I.I. Rubin in Butyrsky prison and advise him that the book is being sent so that he might write his introductory chapter. The book, together with Rubin's introduction, will be published by the 'Moskovskii rabochii' press and will be included in the 'Economic Series' that I am editing. I ask you not to delay, so as not to postpone the appearance of the book.[37]

---

35 *Tsentral'nyi arkhiv* MBRF, No. P-40156, L. 200.
36 I.I. Rubin, *Zhizneopisanie* in TsGAOR [Central State Archive of the October Revolution], F. 5144, Op. 20, D. 4, S. 126.
37 *Tsentral'nyi arkhiv* MBRF, No. P-40156, L. 58.

And here is a letter from IME [the Institute of K. Marx and F. Engels] to the OGPU on 21 June 1924:

> The Institute is entrusting comrade A.D. Markov with: 1) delivering for Rubin the translation of Marx's *Contribution to the Critique of Political Economy* in two copies (the manuscript of the translation and its typed version); and 2) with acquiring material for the Institute that we learned of from your Secretariat.[38]

During his captivity (from the spring of 1923 to the autumn of 1926) the scholar completed a total of approximately twenty scientific works, including monographs, translations of books and articles involving economics, forewords, articles in journals and in the BSE [Great Soviet Encyclopaedia], and commentary on texts. This work included the second edition of *Essays on Marx's Theory of Value* (1924), expanded to twice the original length; the translation and foreword to I. Rosenberg's *Teoriya stoimosti u Ricardo i u Marksa* [*The Theory of Value in Marx and in Ricardo*]; the second edition of the book (with R.M. Kabo) *Narodnoe khozyaistvo v ocherkakh i kartinkakh* (1924) [*The National Economy in Essays and Pictures*]; an introductory article for the book by W. Liebknecht, *Istoria teorii stoimosti v Anglii* (1924) [*History of the Theory of Value in England*] (Rubin was also scientific editor for the translation of this book); the translation of a book by G. Levy [with the Russian title] *Osnovy mirovovo khozyaistvo* [*Foundations of the World Economy*]; as well as the books *Istoriya ekonomicheskoi mysly* (1926) [*A History of Economic Thought*], *Fiziokraty* (1925) [*The Physiocrats*] and *Sovremennye ekonomisty na Zapade* (1927) [*Contemporary Economists in the West*]. During this same period I.I. Rubin prepared a new translation of Marx's *Contribution to the Critique of Political Economy* and a series of articles and reviews for the journal '*Arkhiv K. Marksa i F. Engel'sa*' ['Archive of K. Marx and F. Engels']; he also compiled the anthology *Klassiki politicheskoi ekonomii ot XVII do XIX v.* [*Classics of Political Economy from the Seventeenth to the Nineteenth Century*], providing each section with his own thoughtful introductory remarks. For the first edition of the *Great Soviet Encyclopaedia* he wrote, while in prison, the articles on 'The Austrian school', 'Amortisation', and

---

38   *Tsentral'nyi arkhiv* MBRF, *No. P-40156, L. 102.* [The reference is to Rubin's work on translating into Russian Marx's *Contribution to the Critique of Political Economy*, which he was commissioned to do in 1924, while in Butyrsky prison, by D.B. Ryazanov, head of the Institute of K. Marx and F. Engels. See: Lyudmila L. Vasina, 'I.I. Rubin i evo rukopis' 'Ocherki po teorii deneg Marksa', in Ya.I. Kuz'minov et al. (eds.), *Istoki: sotsiokul'turnaya sreda ekonomicheskoi deyatel'nosti i ekonomicheskovo poznaniya* (Moscow: Izdatel'skii dom Vysshei shkoli ekonomiki, 2011), p. 482. The translation was eventually completed in the years 1927–30, when Rubin worked at the Institute with Ryazanov.]

'Vulgar Political Economy'. In Butyrsky prison Professor Rubin began the manuscript on *Ocherki po teorii deneg Marksa* [*Essays on Marx's Theory of Money*]. There he developed further the ideas in his *Essays on Marx's Theory of Value*. This work continued in 1927-8, when the manuscript was completely rewritten and prepared for publication. In the scientific work of our country, this was the first special investigation of Marx's theory of money. However, the professor did not manage to publish the work, and it remains unknown to this day.[39] Fortunately, the manuscript has been preserved by I.I. Rubin's relatives.

Doing scientific work in the conditions of detention was a great feat for the scholar. In Suzdal concentration camp he had to write and read with the light of a kerosene lamp. A quite indicative episode occurred following 19 December, 1924, in Butyrsky prison. The order came to release him from prison and send him on to Karasubazar. But the prisoner requested ... a postponement of his release. His motive:

> I have in hand two large works, one of which is of an educational nature (*Khrestomatiya po istorii politicheskoi ekonomii* [*A Reader on the History of Political Economy*], some 450 pages long), which must be sent quickly to Gosizdat, and the final editing will take no more than 6–7 days. In case of a speedy departure, I will be deprived of the opportunity to send the only manuscript, the fruit of half a year's work, and at the least it will be delayed by 2–3 months.[40]

This unusual request from the detainee was granted, and his stay in the prison was extended by several days. By 27 December 1924, I.I. Rubin completed the entire work, and only then was he sent into exile.

In Karasubazar the professor worked no less intensively. In the director's archives of the Institute of K. Marx and F. Engels there are five Crimean letters by I.I. Rubin. They speak of receiving books from the IME [Institute of World Economy] library and of returning them, of the translation into Russian of K. Marx's *Marginal Notes on A. Wagner's 'Lehrbuch der Politischen Ökonomie'* (second edition Volume I, 1879), and of the translation into German of Rubin's article 'Shtol'tsman kak kritik Marksa' ['Stolzmann as a Critic of Marx'].[41] Concerning this article, he wrote on 14 August:

> I hope that you will act expeditiously in order that all my corrections will quickly be made. In view of the difficulty and crucial character of the theme, appearance of the work without my corrections would be most undesirable and would

---

39 [The manuscript was published in 2011 and is translated for this volume as Document 19].
40 *Tsentral'nyi arkhiv* MBRF, *No. P-40156, L. 128.*
41 [For Rubin's work on Stolzmann, see I.I. Rubin, *Sovremennye ekonomisty na Zapade* (Moscow and Leningrad: Gosudatstvennoe Izdatel'stvo, 1927), pp. 97–172].

inevitably provoke unfavourable criticism of carelessness in the work (technical terms, quotations, the title, etc). Hence, if the manuscript has already been sent to the press, I request that you urgently notify the editors, without waiting for the manuscripts, that corrections have been made to the article and that they absolutely must be included.[42]

The self-sacrificing scientific work of I.I. Rubin from 1923–6 certainly deserves recognition in the history of science. Of course, without the solidarity and assistance of his professor-colleagues he would not have been able to work, nor would he have managed to get out of his prison cell and then from exile to Moscow at the end of 1926. Had it not been for their assistance, not a single one of the numerous scientific works that he wrote from 1923–6 would have seen the light. In the foreword to the third edition of *Essays on Marx's Theory of Value*, Rubin wrote: 'In the appearance of the first two editions of this work, I received significant assistance from D.B. Ryazanov and Sh.M. Dvolaitsky, to whom I extend my sincere appreciation'.[43]

At the end of 1926 I.I. Rubin was given a position at the Institute of K. Marx and F. Engels. Here he enjoyed significant opportunities for fruitful scientific activity. He soon headed the office of political economy, which in those years was the centre for preparing K. Marx's economic writings for publication and possessed a unique collection of approximately 14,000 books on problems of political economy and the history of economic thought.[44] At the Institute from 1927–30, Rubin prepared for publication Marx's *Contribution to the Critique of Political Economy*,[45] translated several other writings by Marx, began work on a new edition of *Capital*, and collaborated in compiling several thematically focused collective works. He translated the classics of political economy, in particular Adam Smith's *Inquiry into the Nature and Causes of the Wealth of Nations*. He also continued his own research in the areas of economic theory and the history of economic thought, publishing several new articles.[46] Each

---

42 *Rossiiskii tsentr khraneniya i izucheniya dokumentov noveishei istorii* (RTsKhIDNI), F. 71.
43 I.I. Rubin, *Ocherki po teorii stoimosti Marksa*, 4th edn. (Moscow-Leningrad: Gosizdat, 1930), p. 4. [The authors refer in the text to the third edition, but their footnote refers to the fourth edition].
44 *Institut K. Marksa i F. Engel'sa pri TsIK SSSR* (Moscow-Leningrad: Gosizdat, 1930), pp. 33–5.
45 K. Marks, *K kritike politicheskoi ekonomii* (Moscow-Leningrad: Gosizdat, 1929; 2nd edition, 1930).
46 See I.I. Rubin, 'Dialekticheskoe razvitie kategorii v ekonomicheskoi sisteme Marksa' ('The Dialectical Development of Categories in Marx's Economic System'), in 'Pod znamenem Marksizma', No. 4, 1929, pp. 81–108; I.I. Rubin, 'Uchenie Marksa o proizvodstve i potreblenii' ('Marx's Teaching on Production and Consumption'), in *Arkhiv K. Marksa i F. Engel'sa*, Volume 5 (Moscow-Leningrad: 1930), pp. 58–131; I.I. Rubin, 'Abstraktnyi trud i stoimost''

year saw republication of his *History of Economic Thought*, the most famous textbook used for this course.[47] He regularly produced detailed scholarly critiques of foreign and soviet literature on problems of political economy and the theory of Marxism.[48] He also resumed his teaching activity at IKP [the Institute of Red Professors] as well as at the Institute of National Economy, MGU [Moscow State University], the Institute of Economics and RANION [the Russian Association of Scientific-Research Institutes for the Social Sciences], giving lectures on political economy, *Capital* and the history of economic doctrines. His lectures always drew large audiences and attracted lively interest in scientific circles.

I.I. Rubin stood out among economists in the 1920s with his attempt to approach Marx's economic theory in a more scientific manner. He did not, of course, overcome the one-sided and apologetic interpretation of Marxism that had become the only permissible social theory after 1917. However, as distinct from the overwhelming majority among the first generation of soviet economists, Rubin tried to see Marx's views within the context of the nineteenth-century system of economic science. This could not go unpunished.

In 1928 a discussion began concerning I.I. Rubin's book *Essays on Marx's Theory of Value*. The discussion initially took the character of a scientific dispute, but then the critical commentary on the book's ideas and positions passed over into political accusations. The author was condemned for falsification of the economic theory of Marxism, for an idealistic approach to economic categories, for detaching form from content, etc. His ideas were branded with the term 'Rubinshchina',[49] and he was personally declared to be the leader of an idealistic tendency in political economy.[50]

---

v sisteme Marksa' ('Abstract Labour and Value in Marx's System') (Moscow: Proletarskoe slovo, 1928).

47   I.I. Rubin, *Istoriya ekonomicheskoi mysly*. 2nd edn. (Moscow-Leningrad: Gosizdat, 1928); 3rd edn. (Moscow-Leningrad: 1929); 4th edn. (Moscow-Leningrad: 1930).

48   See I.I. Rubin, 'Iz istorii literatury o marksovoi teorii deneg', in *Arkhiv K. Marksa i F. Engel'sa*, Volume 3 (Moscow-Leningrad: 1927), pp. 491–8; I.I. Rubin, 'Politicheskaya ekonomiya' in *Arkhiv K. Marksa i F. Engel'sa*, Volume 4 (Moscow-Leningrad: 1929), pp. 485–95; I.I. Rubin, 'Novyi "anti-Marx"' (a review of the book by Karl Muhs, *Anti-Marx*)', in *Arkhiv K. Marksa i F. Engel'sa*, Volume 4 (Moscow-Leningrad: 1929), pp. 454–63.

49   Roughly translated, this term means 'the terrible time of Rubin'.

50   See S. Shabs, 'Eshche raz o probleme obshchestvennovo truda v ekonomicheskoi sisteme Marksa (otvet na antikritiku I. Rubina)', in *Pod znamenem Marksizma*, Nos. 7–8, 1928, pp. 112–49; S.A. Bessonov, 'Protiv vykholashchivaniya marksizma' in *Problemy ekonomiki*, No. 1, 1929, pp. 123–44 and No. 2, pp. 78–117; S.A. Bessonov and A.F. Kon (eds.), *Rubinshchina ili marksizma: Protiv idealizma i metafiziki v politicheskoi ekonomii. Sbornik ctatei* (Moscow-Leningrad: Gosizdat, 1930); G. Abezgauz and G. Dukor, *Ocherki metodologii politicheskoi ekonomii. S predisloviem S.L. Rodina* (Moscow-Leningrad: Gosizdat, 1931).

The discussion came to an end at the beginning of 1930 with an article by V. Milyutin and B. Borilin, 'On the Disagreements in Political Economy', published in the journal 'Bol'shevik',[51] the theoretical organ of the TsK VKP(B) [the Central Committee of the Communist Party].

Soon Rubin began to be hounded in the national press. In a *Pravda* article of 19 November he was labelled 'a participant in a recently exposed Menshevik-kulak group of wreckers'.[52] At the beginning of 1930 the scholar was compelled to end his teaching at IKP and other educational institutions. On 22 November he sent a letter to the editors of *Pravda* in which he denied participating in the activities of any groups of wreckers, but on 1 December he submitted his resignation from the Institute of K. Marx and F. Engels.[53]

By the beginning of the 1930s it was difficult for any independently-minded social scientist to continue working. After securing victory over his political opponents in the leadership of the VKP(B), Stalin set the repressive machine in motion against dissidents both within the party and beyond. In these conditions the fate of a former political prisoner, an original scholar whose work had created a stir in economic science, was a foregone conclusion. The denouement was accelerated by two factors: first, by the organisation at the end of 1930 and the beginning of 1931 of a show trial, according to Stalin's script, against former Mensheviks; and second, Stalin's desire to do away with academician D.B. Ryazanov, whom he hated. Rubin's arrest did not take long, coming on the eve of 23–24 December 1930.

For nearly a month the officers of the OGPU failed to secure the evidence they needed. Rubin's sister, B.I. Zheltenkova, speaks of this in her recollections.[54] Her information is confirmed by the investigation, which includes Rubin's original response to the arrest order: 'I acknowledge no guilt; I have had absolutely no relation whatsoever with the Menshevik party since 1923 and have not even had any contact with persons who might be assumed to be members of the Menshevik party'.[55]

During trial preparations, savage methods were applied to extract the necessary depositions.[56] Stalin himself defined them as early as October 1930 in a letter to V.P. Menzhinsky: first, acquaint those accused with the 'assigned' testimonies, then 'interrogate most severely' and put those who refuse to cooperate 'through the sys-

---

51   V. Milyutin and B. Borilin, 'K raznoglasiyam v politicheskoi ekonomii', in *Bol'shevik*, No. 2, 1930, pp. 48–63.
52   Ya. Mushpert, 'Za deistvitel'nuyu bor'bu protiv levakov', in *Pravda*, 19 November 1930.
53   *Tsentral'nyi arkhiv MBRF. № N-7824, T. 11, L. 8,9*.
54   Medvedev 1989, pp. 280–4.
55   Medvedev 1989, pp. 276–7.
56   Ibid.

tem'.⁵⁷ Stalin was especially interested in the 'depositions' of Rubin, who was subjected to the harshest methods of pressure – endless interrogation, beatings, solitary confinement in a stone cell the size of a man, humiliation and torture, sleep deprivation, and so forth.⁵⁸

Finally the scholar, seriously ill and exhausted by endless humiliations, could endure no more. B.I. Zheltenkova recalls:

> My brother agreed to confess that he was a member of the programme commission of the Union Bureau, and that he, Rubin, had kept documents of the Menshevik Centre in his office at the Institute, and when he resigned from the Institute, he had handed them over in a sealed envelope to Ryazanov, as materials on the history of the Social-Democratic movement. Rubin had supposedly asked Ryazanov to keep these documents for a short time ... He decided to make it look as if he had deceived Ryazanov, who trusted him totally. My brother stubbornly kept to this position in all his depositions: Ryazanov had trusted him personally, and he, Rubin, had betrayed that trust. No one could shake him from this position.⁵⁹

On 8 February 1931, the OGPU investigators forced Rubin to write a letter to Ryazanov, in which he requested the latter to return the non-existing documents since they were supposedly needed for the investigation.⁶⁰ On the evening of 12 February Stalin summoned academician Ryazanov and, with V.M. Molotov present, presented him with the fabricated letter from Rubin. On the eve of 15–16 February Ryazanov was arrested. On 20 February a confrontation occurred. After the first three questions, Ryazanov broke it off. He saw the intimidated and trembling Isaak Il'ich Rubin, barely able to squeeze out a word, and apparently understood it all: 'My brother right then was taken to his cell; in his cell he began to beat his head against the wall. Anyone who knew how calm and self-controlled Rubin was can understand what a state he had been brought to'.⁶¹

Of course, one can accuse Professor Rubin of betraying the man who, in 1923–6, saved him from certain ruin, returned him to science and helped him right up to the time of his arrest. But one must also take into account the circumstances in which this

---

57 The term used is 'провести сквозь строй'. See the letter from Stalin to Molotov, in *Kommunist*, No. 11, 1990, pp. 99–100. The letter to Menzinsky is cited in Stalin's correspondence with Molotov.
58 Medvedev 1989, pp. 281–2.
59 Medvedev 1989, p. 282.
60 *Tsentral'nyi arkhiv* MBRF. № N-7824, T. 11, L. 160.
61 Medvedev 1989, p. 283.

drama occurred. What could a scholar do to oppose the deadly grip of the General Secretary and his henchmen? Even at the price of his own life he could not have saved Ryazanov.

At the trial of the 'Union Bureau of the Tsk RSDRP (Mensheviks)' from 1–9 March 1931, I.I. Rubin was sentenced to five years of imprisonment. On 22 September 1933, the collegium of the OGPU decided 'to amend the previous sentence of Rubin Isaak Il'ich and send him to Tugai for the remainder of his term'.[62] Then he found himself in Aktyubinsk [Kazakhstan]. Having visited him there, B.I. Zheltenkova recalls:

> In Aktyubinsk my brother got work in a consumer co-operative, as a plan economist. In addition he continued to do his scholarly work ... My brother told me that he had no wish to return to Moscow; he did not want to meet his former circle of acquaintances. That showed how deeply he was shaken by all that he had been through. Only his great optimism, which was characteristic of him, and his deep scholarly interests, gave him the strength to live.[63]

... On 19 November 1937, Professor I.I. Rubin was again arrested. On this occasion he was charged with creating a counter-revolutionary organisation. On 25 November a 'troika' sentenced him to be shot, and he was executed within a day. We are publishing for the first time the exact date of the scholar's death: 27 November 1937. We have managed to determine this date after studying the corresponding archival materials of the KGB, which are now declassified. Until now the dates for I.I. Rubin's life were given as: (1886 – year of death unknown). That is what is found in the 'Political Economy' encyclopaedia to which we referred at the beginning of this article.[64]

In the years 1989–91 I.I. Rubin was unconditionally rehabilitated with respect to all the trials of the 1920s and 1930s.

---

62   *Tsentral'nyi arkhiv MBRF, No. P-40156, L. 217.*
63   Medvedev 1989, p. 284.
64   See footnote 4 above. [The ellipsis at the beginning of this paragraph is to indicate that we have omitted one paragraph from this biographical essay, which referred briefly to an article by Rubin entitled 'Uchenie Ricardo o kapitale' ('Ricardo's Doctrine on Capital'). The article on Ricardo, now available online at the Marxists Internet Archive, accompanied the essay by Vasina and Rokityansky and appeared in *Vestnik Rossiiskoi akademii nauk*, No. 8, 1992, pp. 144–52].

References

Adler, Max 1903, 'Sombarts "historische Sozialtheorie"', *Die Neue Zeit*, 21, 1. Bd., H. 16, H. 18, 485–91, 550–60.
Adler, Max 1908, *Marx als Denker: Zum 25. Todesjahre von Karl Marx*, Berlin: Buchhandlung Vorwärts.
Althusser, Louis 1969, *For Marx*, London: Allen Lane, the Penguin Press.
Althusser, Louis and Étienne Balibar 1970, *Reading Capital*, London: NLB.
Aquinas, Thomas 1988, *St. Thomas Aquinas on Politics and Ethics*, translated and edited by Paul E. Sigmund, New York: Norton.
Aristotle 1952, *The Politics of Aristotle*, translated by Ernest Barker, New York and London: Oxford University Press.
Ashley, W.J. 1893, *An Introduction to English Economic History and Theory*, London: Longmans, Green and Co.
Bailey, Samuel 1821, *An Inquiry into Those Principles advocated by Mr. Malthus Relative to the Nature of Demand and the Necessity of Consumption*, London: R. Hunter.
Bailey, Samuel 1825, *A Critical Dissertation on the Nature, Measures, and Causes of Value; Chiefly in Reference to the Writing of Mr. Ricardo and his Followers*, London: R. Hunter, 1825.
Bauer, Otto 1904, 'Marx' Theorie der Wirtschaftskrisen', *Die Neue Zeit*, 23, 1. Bd., 133–48, 164–70.
Bauer, Otto 1906, 'Qualifizierte Arbeit und Kapitalismus', *Die Neue Zeit*, 24, 1. Bd., H. 20, 644–57.
Bauer, Otto 1907, 'Mathematische Formeln gegen Tugan-Baranowsky', *Die Neue Zeit*, 25, 1. Bd., H. 18, 822–3.
Bauer, Otto 1908, 'Die Geschichte eines Buches', *Die Neue Zeit*, 26, 1. Bd., H. 1, 23–33.
Bauer, Otto 1910a, 'Theorien über den Mehrwert', *Der Kampf*, Band 3, reprinted in *Werkausgabe*, Band 8, 365–76.
Bauer, Otto 1910b, 'Das Finanzkapital', *Der Kampf*, 3 (June): 391–7.
Bax, Ernest Belfort 1884, 'A French Economist on Collectivism', *To-day*, July–December, Vol. II, No. 3 (New Series), 295–303.
Bax, Ernest Belfort 1900, 'Die "Lehren" des Herrn Professor Sombart', *Die Neue Zeit*, 18, 2. Bd., H. 46, 591–6.
Beiser, Frederick C. (ed.) 1993, *The Cambridge Companion to Hegel*, Cambridge: Cambridge University Press.
Bernstein, Eduard 1895a, 'Der dritte Band des *"Kapital"*', *Die Neue Zeit*, 13, 1. Bd., H. 11, H. 12, H. 13, H. 14, H. 16, H. 17, H. 20, 333–8, 364–71, 388–98, 426–32, 485–92, 516–24, 624–32.
Bernstein, Eduard 1895b, Eduard Bernstein, 'Die klassische Nationalökonomie und ihre Gegner', *Die Neue Zeit*, 13, 2. Bd., H. 33, S. 211–14.

Bernstein, Eduard 1898, 'Das realistische und das ideologische Moment im Sozialismus: Probleme des Sozialismus, 2. Serie II.', *Die Neue Zeit*, 16, 2. Bd., H. 34, H. 39, S. 225–32, 388–95.

Bernstein, Eduard 1899, 'Arbeitswerth oder Nutzwerth?: Antwort an Karl Kautsky', *Die Neue Zeit*, 17, 2. Bd., H. 44, 548–54. Reprinted in *Zur Theorie und Geschichte des Sozialismus: Gesammelte Abhandlungen*, Teil III: *Sozialistische Controversen*, Berlin, 1904, 101–15.

Bernstein, Eduard 1900, 'Zur Theorie des Arbeitswerths', *Die Neue Zeit*, 18, 1. Bd., H. 12, 356–63.

Bernstein, Eduard 1905, 'Allerhand Werttheoretisches', *Dokumente des Sozialismus*, Berlin, Band V, 221–4, 270–4, 367–72, 436–8, 555–9.

Bernstein, Eduard 1993, *The Preconditions of Socialism*, edited and translated by Henry Tudor, Cambridge: Cambridge University Press.

Blaug, Mark 1985, *Economic Theory in Retrospect*, Cambridge: Cambridge University Press.

Block, Maurice 1884a, 'Le Capital de Karl Marx, à propos d'une anticritique', *Journal des Économistes*, XXVIII, No. 10 (Octobre), 130–6.

Block, Maurice 1884b, 'Le Capital de Karl Marx, dernières observations', *Journal des Économistes*, XXVII, No. 12 (Décembre), 464–6.

Böckh, August 1838, *Metrologische Untersuchungen über Gewichte, Münzfüsse und Masse des Alterthums in ihrem Zusammenhange*, Berlin: Verlag von Veit und Comp.

Bogdanov, A., Sh. Dvolaitskii and J. Fineberg 1927, *A Short Course of Economic Science*, London: Communist Party of Great Britain.

Böhm-Bawerk, Eugen von 1886, 'Grundzüge der Theorie des wirtschaftlichen Güterwerts', *Jahrbücher für Nationalökonomie und Statistik*, N. F., Band 13, 1–82, 477–541.

Böhm-Bawerk, Eugen von 1890, *Capital and Interest: A Critical History of Economical Theory*, London: Macmillan.

Böhm-Bawerk, Eugen von 1891, *The Positive Theory of Capital*, London: Macmillan.

Böhm-Bawerk, Eugen von 1892, 'Wert, Kosten und Grenznutzen', *Jahrbücher für Nationalökonomie und Statistik*, Jg. 58, Heft 3, 321–67. [English translation: 'Value, Cost, and Marginal Utility', *The Quarterly Journal of Austrian Economics*, Vol. 5, No. 3 (Fall 2002), 37–79].

Böhm-Bawerk, Eugen von 1894, 'Wert', *Handwörterbuch der Staatswissenschaften*, Jena, Bd. 6.

Böhm-Bawerk, Eugen von 1896, *Karl Marx and the Close of His System: A Criticism*, edited with an introduction by Paul M. Sweezy, Auburn, Alabama: Ludwig von Mises Institute.

Böhm-Bawerk, Eugen von 2005, *Basic Principles of Economic Value*, Grove City: Libertarian Press.

Bostaph, Samuel 1994, 'The Methodenstreit', in *The Elgar Companion to Austrian Economics*, edited by Peter J. Boettke, Cheltenham: Edgar Elgar Publishing.

Boudin, Louis 1907, 'Mathematische Formeln gegen Karl Mark', *Die Neue Zeit*, 25, 1. Bd., H. 16, H. 17, H. 18, 524–53, 557–67, 603–10.

Braunthal, Alfred 1924, 'Kautsky als Geldtheoretiker', in *Der lebendige Marxismus: Festgabe zum 70. Geburtstage von Karl Kautsky*, edited by Otto Jenssen, Jena: Thüringer Verlagsanstalt.

Broadhurst, John 1842, *Political Economy*, London: Hatchard and Son.

Bucharin, Nikolai 1914, 'Eine Ökonomie ohne Wert', *Die Neue Zeit*, 32, 1. Bd., H. 22, H. 23, 806–16, 850–8.

Bukharin, Nikolai 1927, *The Economic Theory of the Leisure Class*, New York: International Publishers.

Calvin, John 1844, *Institutes of the Christian Religion*, 2 vols, translated by John Allen, Philadelphia: Presbyterian Board of Publication.

Carver, Terrell (ed.) 1991, *The Cambridge Companion to Marx*, Cambridge: Cambridge University Press.

Cohen, Hermann 1885, *Kants Theorie der Erfahrung*, Berlin: Bruno Cassirer.

Cohen, Hermann 1904, *Ethik des reinen Willens*, Berlin: Bruno Cassirer.

Cornu, Auguste 1955–70, *Karl Marx et Friedrich Engels: Leur vie et leur oeuvre*, tome I: *Les années d'enfance et de jeunesse, la gauche hégélienne, 1818/1820–1844*, Paris: Presses Universitaires de France, 1955, tome II: *Du libéralisme démocratique au communisme, la 'Gazette rhénane', les 'Annales franco-allemandes', 1842–1844*, Paris: Presses Universitaires de France, 1958, tome III: *Marx à Paris*, Paris: Presses Universitaires de France, 1962, tome IV: *La formation du matérialisme historique (1845–1846)*, Paris: Presses Universitaires de France, 1970.

Cunow, Heinrich 1905, 'Theorien über den Mehrwert: I. Die Anfänge der Theorie vom Mehrwert bis Adam Smith', *Die Neue Zeit*, 23, 1. Bd., H. 16, H. 17, H. 19, 497–506, 547–55, 617–24.

Cunow, Heinrich 1910, 'Zum Verständnis der Marxschen Forschungsmethode', *Die Neue Zeit*, 28, 2. Bd., H. 53, 1001–10.

Day, Richard B. 1980, 'Rosa Luxemburg and the Accumulation of Capital', *Critique*, Vol. 12, No. 1 (Winter), 81–96.

Day, Richard B. 1987, 'Democratic Control and the Dignity of Politics – An Analysis of "The Revolution Betrayed"', *Comparative Economic Studies*, XXIX, No. 3 (Fall), 4–29.

Day, Richard B. 1988, 'Leon Trotsky on the Dialectics of Democratic Control', in *The Soviet Economy on the Brink of Reform*, edited by Peter Wiles, Boston: Unwin Hyman.

Day, Richard B. and Daniel Gaido (eds.) 2009, *Witnesses to Permanent Revolution: The Documentary Record*, Leiden: Brill.

Day, Richard B. and Daniel Gaido (eds.) 2011, *Discovering Imperialism: Social Democracy to World War I*, Leiden: Brill.

Deutsch, Hanns 1904, *Qualifizierte Arbeit und Kapitalismus. Werttheorie und Entwicklungstendenzen*, Wien: Stern.

Dietzel, Heinrich 1885, 'Friedrich von Wieser, Der natürliche Wert' [Rezension], *Jahrbücher für Nationalökonomie und Statistik*, N. F. 11, no. 45, vol. 11, 161–2.

Dietzel, Heinrich 1890, 'Die klassische Werttheorie und die Theorie vom Grenznutzen', *Jahrbücher für Nationalökonomie und Statistik*, N.F., Bd. 20, 561–606.

Dietzel, Heinrich 1895, *Theoretische Sozialökonomie*, Leipzig: C.F. Winter'sche Verlag.

Dilke, Charles Wentworth 1821, *The Source and Remedy of the National Difficulties deduced from Principles of Political Economy, in a Letter to Lord John Russell*, London: Rodwell and Martin.

Droz, Jacques 1974, *Histoire de l'Allemagne. 1. La formation de l'unité allemande: 1789–1871*, Paris: Hatier Université.

Duhem, Pierre 1906, *La théorie physique: Son objet, et sa structure*, Paris: Chevalier & Rivière.

Durant, Will 1980, *The Reformation*, New York: Simon and Schuster.

Eckstein, Gustav 1902, 'Die vierfache Wurzel des Satzes vom unzureichenden Grunde der Grenznutzentheorie: Eine Robinsonade', *Die Neue Zeit*, 20, 2. Bd., H. 26–52, 810–16.

Eckstein, Gustav 1906, 'Marx' Kritik Ricardos', *Die Neue Zeit*, 24, 2. Bd., H. 34, H. 36, 245–52, H. 36, 321–32.

Elster, Karl 1920, *Die Seele des Geldes*, Jena: Fischer.

Engels, Friedrich 1878, *Herrn Eugen Dührings Umwälzung der Wissenschaft*, Leipzig: Genossenschafts-Buchdruckerei.

Engels, Friedrich 1891, 'In the Case of Brentano vs. Marx: Regarding Alleged Falsifications of Quotation: The Story and Documents', in *Collected Works*, Vol. 27, by Karl Marx and Frederick Engels, Moscow: Progress Publishers.

Engels, Friedrich and Karl Kautsky 1887a, 'Juristen-Sozialismus', *Die Neue Zeit*, 5, H. 2, 49–62. Reprinted in *Marx-Engels-Gesamtausgabe*, Erste Abteilung, Band 31: Karl Marx/Friedrich Engels: *Werke, Artikel, Entwürfe. Oktober 1886 bis Februar 1891*, bearbeitet von Renate Merkel-Melis, Berlin: Akademie Verlag, 2002 (text: 397–413, apparat: 1147–57).

Engels, Friedrich and Karl Kautsky 1887b, 'Lawyers' Socialism', in *Collected Works*, Vol. 26, by Karl Marx and Frederick Engels, Moscow: Progress Publishers, 1990.

Engels, Friedrich 1954, *Anti-Dühring*, Moscow: Foreign Languages Publishing House.

Feuerbach, Ludwig 1855, *The Essence of Christianity*, translated by Marian Evans, New York: Calvin Blanchard.

Feuerbach, Ludwig 1983, 'Provisional Theses for the Reformation of Philosophy (1843)', in *The Young Hegelians: An Anthology*, edited by Lawrence S. Stepelevich, Cambridge: Cambridge University Press.

Feuerbach, Ludwig 1986, *Principles of the Philosophy of the Future*, translated by Manfred Vogel, Indianapolis: Hackett Publishing Company.

Fischer, Kuno 1902, *History of Modern Philosophy*, St. Petersburg: Zhukovsky, Vol. 8, part I.

Florath, Bernd 1987, 'Heinrich Cunow. Eine biographisch-historiographische Skizze', *Jahrbuch für Geschichte*, Vol. 34, 85–145.

Fromm, Erich 1961, *Marx's Concept of Man*, New York: Frederick Ungar.

Gaido, Daniel and Manuel Quiroga 2013, 'The Early Reception of Rosa Luxemburg's Theory of Imperialism,' *Capital & Class*, 37, No. 3, 437–55.

Goldmann, Lucien 1971, *Immanuel Kant*, London: NLB.

Gottl-Ottlilienfeld, Friedrich von 1914, *Wirtschaft und Technik. Aus: Grundriss der Sozialökonomik*, Abteilung 2, Tübingen: Mohr.

Gottschalch, Wilfried 1962, *Strukturveränderungen der Gesellschaft und politisches Handeln in der Lehre von Rudolf Hilferding*, Berlin: Duncker & Humbolt.

Graziadei, Antonio 1923, *Preis und Mehrpreis in der kapitalistischen Wirtschaft: Kritik der Marxschen Werttheorie*, übersetzt von Elisabeth Wiener, Berlin: Prager.

Grundmann, Reiner and Nico Sterr 2001, 'Why is Werner Sombart Not Part of the Core of Classical Sociology? From Fame to (Near) Oblivion', *Journal of Classical Sociology*, 1, No. 2, 257–87.

Hammacher, Emil 1909, *Das philosophisch-oekonomische System des Marxismus*, Leipzig: Duncker and Humblot.

Hanisch, Ernst 2011, *Der grosse Illusionist: Otto Bauer (1881–1938)*, Wien: Böhlau Verlag.

Hartnack, Justus 1968, *Kant's Theory of Knowledge*, translated by M. Holmes Hartshorne, London: Macmillan.

Hegel, Georg W.F. 1874, *The Logic of Hegel*, translated from the *Encyclopædia of the Philosophical Sciences*, Oxford: Clarendon Press.

Hegel, Georg W.F. 1900, *The Philosophy of History*, translated by J. Sibree, New York: Willey Book Co.

Hegel, Georg W.F. 1967, *Hegel's Philosophy of Right*, translated with notes by T.M. Knox, Oxford: Oxford University Press.

Hegel, Georg W.F. 1971, *Hegel's Philosophy of Mind: Being Part Three of the 'Encyclopaedia of the Philosophical Sciences (1830)'*, translated by William Wallace, together with the *Zusätze* in Boumann's text (1845), translated by A.V. Miller, with foreword by J.N. Findlay, Oxford: Clarendon Press.

Hegel, Georg W.F. 1975, *Hegel's Logic*, translated by William Wallace, Oxford: Clarendon Press.

Hegel, Georg W.F. 1979, *Hegel's 'System of Ethical Life' and 'First Philosophy of Spirit'*, edited and translated by H.S. Harris and T.M. Knox, Albany, NY: New York University Press.

Hegel, Georg W.F. 1988, *Introduction to the Philosophy of History*, translated by Leo Rauch, Indianapolis and Cambridge: Hackett.

Hegel, Georg W.F. 1996, *Elements of the Philosophy of Right*, translated by H.B. Nisbet, edited by Allen Wood, Cambridge: Cambridge University Press.

Hegel, Georg W.F. 2010a, *Encyclopaedia of the Philosophical Sciences in Basic Outline, Part I: Science of Logic*, translated and edited by Klaus Brinkmann and Daniel O. Dahlstrom, Cambridge: Cambridge University Press.

Hegel, Georg W.F. 2010b, *The Science of Logic*, translated and edited by George Di Giovanni, Cambridge: Cambridge University Press.

Heinrich, Michael 1996, 'Engels' Edition of the Third Volume of *Capital* and Marx's Original Manuscript', *Science and Society*, 60, No. 4 (Winter), 452–66.

Helfferich, Karl 1923, *Das Geld*, Leipzig: C.L. Hirschfeld.

Herschel, John F.W. 1831, *A Preliminary Discourse on the Study of Natural Philosophy*, London: Longman.

Hilferding, Rudolf 1903a, 'Zur Geschichte der Werttheorie', *Die Neue Zeit*, 21, 1. Bd., H. 7, 213–17.

Hilferding, Rudolf 1903b, 'Der Funktionswechsel des Schutzzolles: Tendenz der modernen Handelspolitik', *Die Neue Zeit*, 21, 2. Bd., H. 35, 274–81.

Hilferding, Rudolf 1903c, 'Werner Sombart, *Der moderne Kapitalismus*', in *Zeitschrift für Volkswirtschaft, Sozialpolitik und Verwaltung*, 12, S. 446–53. Reprinted in Bernhard vom Brocke (ed.), *Sombarts 'Moderner Kapitalismus': Materialien zur Kritik und Rezeption*, München: Deutscher Taschenbuch Verlag, 1987.

Hilferding, Rudolf 1904, *Böhm-Bawerk's Criticism of Marx*, in *Karl Marx and the Close of His System, together with an Appendix consisting of an article by Ladislaus von Bortkiewicz on the transformation of values into prices of production in the Marxian System*, edited by Paul M. Sweezy, New York: A.M. Kelley, 1949. Originally published in *Marx-Studien: Blätter für Theorie und Politik des wissenschaftlichen Sozialismus*, Band 1, 1–61.

Hilferding, Rudolf 1905, 'Zur Problemstellung der theoretischen Ökonomie bei Karl Marx', *Die Neue Zeit*, 23, 1. Bd., H. 4, 101–12.

Hilferding, Rudolf 1911, 'Aus der Frühzeit der englischen Nationalökonomie', *Die Neue Zeit*, 29, 1. Bd., H. 26, 908–21.

Hilferding, Rudolf 1911–12, 'Aus der Vorgeschichte der Marxschen Ökonomie', *Die Neue Zeit*, 29, 2. Bd., H. 43, H. 44, H. 51, 572–81, 620–8, 885–94, and 30, 1. Bd., H. 10, 343–54.

Hilferding, Rudolf 1912a, 'Zur Theorie der Kombination', *Die Neue Zeit*, 30, 1. Bd., H. 16, 550–7.

Hilferding, Rudolf 1912b, 'Geld und Ware', *Die Neue Zeit*, 30, 1. Bd., H. 22, 773–82.

Hilferding, Rudolf 1912c, 'Ludwig von Mises, *Theorie des Geldes und der Umlaufmittel*. Duncker & Humblot. 1912. V und 476 Seiten' [Rezension], *Die Neue Zeit*, 30, 2. Bd., H. 52, 1024–7.

Hilferding, Rudolf 1919, 'Franz Petry, *Der soziale Gehalt der Marxschen Werttheorie*, Jena,

1916, [Rezension]', *Archiv für die Geschichte des Sozialismus und der Arbeiterbewegung*, Jg. 8, s. 439–48.

Hilferding, Rudolf 1922, 'Postanovka problemy teoreticheskoi ekonomii u Marksa', in *Osnovnye problemy politicheskoi ekonomii*, edited by Sh. Dvolaitsky and I. Rubin, 63–78.

Hilferding, Rudolf 1981 [1910], *Finance Capital: A Study of the Latest Phase of Capitalist Development*, London: Routledge & Kegan Paul.

Horwitz, Steven 2003, 'The Austrian Marginalists: Menger, Böhm-Bawerk, and Wieser', in *A Companion to the History of Economic Thought*, edited by Warren J. Samuels, Jeff E. Biddle and John B. Davis, London: Blackwell, 262–77.

Howard, M.C. and J.E. King 1989, A *History of Marxian Economics*, Vol. 1: 1883–1929, Princeton, NJ: Princeton University Press.

Hume, David 1865, *The Philosophical Works of David Hume*, Boston: Little, Brown and Company.

Ingram, John Kells 1887, *A History of Political Economy*, New York: Macmillan Company.

Jevons, William Stanley 1871, *The Theory of Political Economy*, London, New York: Macmillan.

Jones, Richard 1831, *An Essay on the Distribution of Wealth and on the Sources of Taxation*, Part I: Rent, London: John Murray.

Jones, Richard 1833, *An Introductory Lecture on Political Economy: Delivered at King's College, London, 27th February, 1833; to which is added A Syllabus of a Course of Lectures on the Wages of Labor, to be Delivered at King's College, London, in the Month of April, 1833*, London: John Murray.

Jones, Richard 1852, *Text-Book of Lectures on the Political Economy of Nations: Delivered at the East India College, Haileybury*, Hertford: Stephen Austin.

Jones, Richard 1859, *Literary Remains: Consisting of Lectures and Tracts on Political Economy of the late Rev. Richard Jones*, edited, with a prefatory notice, by the Rev. William Whewell, London: John Murray.

Kant, Immanuel 1965, *The Metaphysical Elements of Justice*, translated by John Ladd, Indianapolis: Bobbs-Merrill.

Kant, Immanuel 1970, *Kant's Political Writings*, edited by Hans Reiss, Cambridge: Cambridge University Press.

Kant, Immanuel 1991, *The Metaphysics of Morals*, translated by Mary Gregor, Cambridge: Cambridge University Press.

Kant, Immanuel 1998a, *Critique of Pure Reason*, translated and edited by Paul Guyer and Allen W. Wood, Cambridge: Cambridge University Press.

Kant, Immanuel 1998b, *Religion within the Boundaries of Mere Reason*, translated and edited by Allen Wood and George di Giovanni, Cambridge: Cambridge University Press.

Kant, Immanuel 2002, *Critique of the Power of Judgement*, edited by Paul Guyer, translated by Paul Guyer and Eric Matthews, Cambridge: Cambridge University Press.

Kant, Immanuel 2008, *Fundamental Principles of the Metaphysic of Morals*, translated by Thomas Kingsmill Abbott, Rockville, MD: Arc Manor.

Karner, Josef 1904, *Die soziale Funktion der Rechtsinstitute, besonders des Eigentums*, Wien: Brand. *Marx-Studien*, Bd. I. [English version: Renner 1949].

Kaufman, Illarion Ignat'evich 1872, 'Kapital. Kritika politicheskoi ekonomii', *Vestnik Evropy*, No. 5, May, 427–37.

Kaulla, Rudolf 1920, *Die Grundlagen des Geldwerts*, Stuttgart, Berlin: Verlagsgenossenschaft 'Freiheit'.

Kautsky, Karl 1884, 'Das *"Kapital"* von Rodbertus', *Die Neue Zeit*, 2, H. 8, H. 9, 337–50, 385–402.

Kautsky, Karl 1886, '*"Das Elend der Philosophie"* und *"Das Kapital"*', *Die Neue Zeit*, 4, H. 1, H. 2, H. 3, H. 4, 7–19, 49–58, 117–29, 157–65.

Kautsky, Karl 1887, *Karl Marx' oekonomische Lehren: Gemeinverständlich dargestellt und erläutert*, Stuttgart: J.H.W. Dietz.

Kautsky, Karl 1888, 'Lujo Brentano, *Die klassische Nationalökonomie. Vortrag gehalten beim Antritt des Leramts an der Universität Wien am 17. April 1888*. Leipzig, Duncker & Humbolt. 32 s.: [Rezension]', *Die Neue Zeit*, 6, H. 9, S. 426–8.

Kautsky, Karl 1889, 'Die Bergarbeiter und der Bauernkrieg: vornehmlich in Thüringen', *Die Neue Zeit*, 7, H. 7, S. 289–97, H. 8, S. 337–50, H. 9, S. 410–17, H. 10, S. 443–53, H. 11, S. 507–15.

Kautsky, Karl 1891, 'Wie Brentano Marx vernichtete: I. Marx und Brentano', *Die Neue Zeit*, 9. 2. Bd., H. 32, S. 161–73.

Kautsky, Karl 1899, *Bernstein und das sozialdemokratische Programm. Eine Antikritik*, Stuttgart: Dietz.

Kautsky, Karl 1899a, *Die Agrarfrage*, Stuttgart: J.H.W. Dietz Nachf.

Kautsky, Karl 1899b, 'Bernstein über die Werththeorie und die Klassen', *Die Neue Zeit*, 17, 2. Bd., H. 29, 68–81.

Kautsky, Karl 1900, 'Schippel, Brentano und die Flottenvorlage', *Die Neue Zeit*, 18, 1. Bd., H. 24, H. 25, H. 26, S. 740–51, 772–82, 804–16.

Kautsky, Karl 1900b, 'Zwei Kritiker meiner *"Agrarfrage"*', *Die Neue Zeit*, 18, 1. Bd., H. 10, H. 11, H. 12, H. 14, H. 15, 292–300, 338–46, 363–8, 428–36, 470–7.

Kautsky, Karl 1902, 'Krisentheorien', *Die Neue Zeit*, 20, 2. Bd., H. 2–28, H. 3–29, H. 4–30, H. 5–31, 37–47, 76–81, 110–18, 133–43.

Kautsky, Karl 1905, 'Brentanos Preisrätsel für Marxisten', *Die Neue Zeit*, 23, 1. Bd., H. 22, 714–22.

Kautsky, Karl 1906, 'Der amerikanische Arbeiter', *Die Neue Zeit*, 24, 1. Bd., H. 21, H. 22, H. 23, H. 24, 676–83, 717–27, 740–52, 773–87. [English version: 'The American Worker', in Day and Gaido 2009, pp. 609–61].

Kautsky, Karl 1910, *The Class Struggle*, Chicago, IL: Charles H. Kerr.

Kautsky, Karl 1911, 'Finanzkapital und Krisen (Rudolf Hilferding, *Das Finanzkapital*)', *Die Neue Zeit*, 29, 1. Bd., H. 22, 23, 24, 25, 764–72, 797–804, 838–64, 874–83.

Kautsky, Karl 1921, *Are the Jews a Race?*, London: Jonathan Cape.

Kautsky, Karl 1923, 'Den'gi', *Den'gi i denezhnoe obrashchenie v osveshchenii marksizma*, Moscow: Finansovo-ekonomicheskoe byuro NKF. [Original German version: *Sozialdemokratische Bemerkungen zur Uebergangswirtschaft*, Leipzig: Verlag der Leipziger Buchdruckerei, 1918].

Kautsky, Karl 1988 [1899], *The Agrarian Question*, translated by Peter Burgess, London: Zwan Publications.

Knapp, Georg Friedrich 1921, *Staatliche Theorie des Geldes*, 3 Aufl., Munich, Leipzig: Dunker und Humblot.

Lafargue, Paul 1881, 'M. Paul Leroy-Beaulieu', *l'Egalité*, 25 Décembre.

Lafargue, Paul 1884a, 'La théorie de la plus-value de Karl Marx et la critique de M. Paul Leroy-Beaulieu', *Journal des Économistes*, XXVII, No. 9 (Septembre), 379–91.

Lafargue, Paul 1884b, 'Le Capital de Karl Marx et la critique de M. Block', *Journal des Économistes*, XXVIII, No. 10 (Octobre), 278–87.

Lafargue, Paul 1892, 'La théorie de la valeur et de la plus-value de Marx et les économistes bourgeois', *Revue Socialiste*, XVI, No. 93 (Septembre), 288–95.

Landé, Hugo 1893, 'Mehrwerth und Profit: Ein ökonomischer Versuch', *Die Neue Zeit*, 11, 1. Bd., H. 19, 588–94.

Lassalle, Ferdinand 1861, *Das System der erworbenen Rechte. Eine Versöhnung des positiven Rechts und der Rechtsphilosophie*, Leipzig: F.A. Brockhaus.

Lenin, V.I. 1893, 'On the So-Called Market Question', in *Collected Works*, Vol. 1, by V.I. Lenin, Moscow: Progress Publishers, 1964.

Lenin, V.I. 1894a, *What the 'Friends of the People' Are and How They Fight the Social-Democrats (A Reply to Articles in 'Russkoye Bogatstvo' Opposing the Marxists)*, in *Collected Works*, by V.I. Lenin, Moscow: Progress Publishers, 1972.

Lenin, V.I. 1894b, 'The Economic Content of Narodism and the Criticism of it in Mr. Struve's Book (The Reflection of Marxism in Bourgeois Literature)', in *Collected Works*, Vol. 1, by V.I. Lenin, Moscow: Progress Publishers, 1972.

Lenin, V.I. 1897, *A Characterisation of Economic Romanticism (Sismondi and Our Native Sismondists)*, in *Collected Works*, Vol. 2, by V.I. Lenin, Moscow: Progress Publishers, 1960.

Lenin, V.I. 1898, 'Book Review: A. Bogdanov. *A Short Course of Economic Science*', in *Collected Works*, Vol. 4, by V.I. Lenin, Moscow: Progress Publishers, 1964.

Lenin, V.I. 1899a, *The Development of Capitalism in Russia: The Process of the Formation of a Home Market for Large-Scale Industry*, in *Collected Works*, Vol. 3, by V.I. Lenin, Moscow: Progress Publishers, 1964.

Lenin, V.I. 1899b, 'Book Review: Parvus, *The World Market and the Agricultural Crisis*', *Nachalo*, No. 3, February, in *Collected Works*, Vol. 4, by V.I. Lenin, Moscow: Progress Publishers, 1964.

Lenin, V.I. 1899c, 'Once More on the Theory of Realisation', in *Collected Works*, Vol. 4, by V.I. Lenin, Moscow: Progress Publishers, 1964.

Lenin, V.I. 1899d, 'Book Review: Karl Kautsky. *Die Agrarfrage*', *Nachalo*, No. 4, April, in *Collected Works*, Vol. 4, by V.I. Lenin, Moscow: Progress Publishers, 1964.

Lenin, V.I. 1899e, 'Reply to Mr. P. Nezhdanov', in *Collected Works*, Vol. 4, by V.I. Lenin, Moscow: Progress Publishers, 1964.

Lenin, V.I. 1912, 'Conspectus of Hegel's Book *Science of Logic*', in *Collected Works*, Vol. 38, by V.I. Lenin, Moscow: Progress Publishers, 1972.

Lenin, V.I. 1915a, 'Karl Marx: A Brief Biographical Sketch With an Exposition of Marxism', first published in 1915 in the *Granat Encyclopaedia*, Seventh Edition, Vol. 28, in *Collected Works*, Vol. 21, by V.I. Lenin, Moscow: Progress Publishers, 1974.

Lenin, V.I. 1915b, 'On the Question of Dialectics', in *Collected Works*, Vol. 38, by V.I. Lenin, Moscow: Progress Publishers, 1972.

Lenin, V.I. 1916, *Imperialism, the Highest Stage of Capitalism: A Popular Outline*, in *Collected Works*, Vol. 22, by V.I. Lenin, Moscow: Progress Publishers, 1974.

Lenin, V.I. 1968, *Notebooks on Imperialism*, in *Collected Works*, Vol. 39, by V.I. Lenin, Moscow: Progress Publishers.

Lewis, Ewart 1954, *Medieval Political Ideas*, New York: Alfred A. Knopf.

Lexis, Wilhelm 1885, 'Die Marxsche Kapitaltheorie', *Jahrbücher Jahrbücher für Nationalökonomie und Statistik*, N. F., Band 11, 452–65.

Liebknecht, Wilhelm 1902, *Zur Geschichte der Werttheorie in England*, Jena: Fischer.

Lukács, Georg 1971, *History and Class Consciousness*, London: Merlin.

Luxemburg, Rosa 1900a, 'Zurück auf Adam Smith!', *Die Neue Zeit*, 18, 2. Bd., H. 33, 180–6.

Luxemburg, Rosa 1900b, 'Die "deutsche Wissenschaft" hinter den Arbeitern', *Die Neue Zeit*, 18, 2. Bd., H. 51, H. 52, 740–7, 773–82.

Luxemburg, Rosa 1903, 'Im Rate der Gelehrten', *Die Neue Zeit*, 22, 1. Bd., H. 1, 5–10.

Luxemburg, Rosa 1971, *Selected Political Writings of Rosa Luxemburg*, New York: Monthly Review Press.

Luxemburg, Rosa 1986, *The Mass Strike*, London: Bookmarks.

Luxemburg, Rosa 1989, *Reform and Revolution*, London: Bookmarks.

Luxemburg, Rosa 2003, *The Accumulation of Capital*, London: Routledge & Kegan Paul.

Mach, Ernst 1893, *The Science of Mechanics: A Critical and Historical Account of its Development*, LaSalle, IL: Open Court Publishing Company.

Mach, Ernst 1905, *Erkenntnis und Irrtum: Skizzen zur Psychologie der Forschung*, Leipzig: Johann Ambrosius Barth.

Mach, Ernst 1975, *Knowledge and Error: Sketches on the Psychology of Enquiry*, Dordrecht, Hollad: D. Reidel Publishing Company. [Translation of Mach, Ernst 1905, *Erkenntnis und Irrtum: Skizzen zur Psychologie der Forschung*, Leipzig: Johann Ambrosius Barth].

Maksakovsky, Pavel V. 2004, *The Capitalist Cycle*, edited and translated by Richard B. Day, Leiden and Boston: Brill.

Malthus, Thomas Robert 1836, *Principles of Political Economy*, 2nd edition, London: W. Pickering.

Marshall, Alfred, 1895, *Principles of Economics*, London, New York: Macmillan.
Marx, Karl 1859, *Zur Kritik der Politischen Oekonomie*, Berlin: Verlag von Franz Duncker.
Marx, Karl 1867, *Das Kapital*, Erstausgabe, Hamburg: Verlag von Otto Meissner.
Marx, Karl 1891, 'Zur Kritik des sozialdemokratischen Parteiprogramms: Aus dem Nachlaß von Karl Marx', *Die Neue Zeit*, 9, 1. Bd., H. 18, 561–75.
Marx, Karl 1903, 'Einleitung zu einer Kritik der politischen Ökonomie' (23 August 1857), *Die Neue Zeit*, 21, 1. Bd., H. 23, 24, 25, S. 710–18, 741–5, 772–81.
Marx, Karl 1905–10, *Theorien über den Mehrwert: Aus dem nachgelassenen Manuskript 'Zur Kritik der politischen Ökonomie'*, Hrsg. von Karl Kautsky, Stuttgart: J.H.W. Dietz Nachf., 3 vols. in 4: 1. *Die Anfänge der Theorie vom Mehrwert bis Adam Smith*, 1905, XX, 430 s. (Internationale Bibliothek, 35); 2,1. *David Ricardo*, 1905, XII, 344 s. (Internationale Bibliothek, 36); 2,2. *David Ricardo*, 1905, IV, 384 s. (Internationale Bibliothek, 37); 3. *Von Ricardo zur Vulgärökonomie*, 1910, XIV, 602 s. (Internationale Bibliothek, 37/a).
Marx, Karl 1963, *Theories of Surplus-Value (Volume IV of Capital)*, Volume I, Moscow: Progress Publishers.
Marx, Karl 1968, *Theories of Surplus-Value (Volume IV of Capital)*, Volume II, Moscow: Progress Publishers.
Marx, Karl 1970, *A Contribution to the Critique of Political Economy*, Moscow: Progress Publishers.
Marx, Karl 1971, *Theories of Surplus-Value (Volume IV of Capital)*, Volume III, Moscow: Progress Publishers.
Marx, Karl 1976, *Capital: A Critique of Political Economy*, Volume I, introduced by Ernest Mandel, translated David Fernbach, London: Penguin.
Marx, Karl 1977, *The Poverty of Philosophy*, Peking: Foreign Languages Press.
Marx, Karl 1978, *Capital: A Critique of Political Economy*, Volume II, introduced by Ernest Mandel, translated David Fernbach, London: Penguin.
Marx, Karl 1992, *Capital: A Critique of Political Economy*, Vol. III, introduced by Ernest Mandel, translated David Fernbach, London: Penguin.
Marx, Karl 1993, *Grundrisse: Foundations of the Critique of Political Economy (Rough Draft)*, translated with a foreword by Martin Nicolaus, London: Penguin.
Marx, Karl 2006, *Wage-Labour and Capital* and *Value, Price and Profit*, New York: International Publishers.
Marx, Karl 2009, *Critique of Hegel's Philosophy of Right*, translated by Annette Jolin and Joseph O'Malley, Cambridge: Cambridge University Press.
Marx, Karl and Friedrich Engels 1962, *Manifesto of the Communist Party*, in *Selected Works*, Volume 1, by Karl Marx and Frederick Engels, Moscow: Foreign Languages Publishing House.
Marx, Karl and Friedrich Engels 1964, *The German Ideology*, Moscow: Progress Publishers.

Marx-Aveling, Eleanor 1895, 'Wie Lujo Brentano zitirt', *Die Neue Zeit*, 13, 1. Bd., H. 9, S. 260–6.

Mead, G.H. 1934, *Mind, Self, and Society from the Standpoint of a Social Behaviorist*, edited by C.W. Morris, Chicago, IL: University of Chicago Press.

MECW: Marx, Karl, and Friedrich Engels 1975–2004, *Collected Works*, 50 Vols, New York: International Publishers.

Medvedev, Roy 1989, *Let History Judge*, New York: Columbia University Press.

Mehring, Franz 1905, 'Ein neues Werk von Karl Marx' (4. Februar 1905), in *Aufsätze zur Geschichte der Arbeiterbewegung*, Berlin: Dietz, 1980 (*Gesammelte Schriften*, Bd. 4).

Menger, Carl 1899, *The Right to the Whole Produce of Labour: The Origin and Development of the Theory of Labour's Claim to the Whole Product of Industry*, New York: The Macmillan Company.

Menger, Carl 2007, *Principles of Economics*, Auburn, AL: Ludwig von Mises Institute.

Merkel-Melis 2002, *Marx-Engels-Gesamtausgabe*, Erste Abteilung, Band 31: Karl Marx/ Friedrich Engels: *Werke, Artikel, Entwürfe. Oktober 1886 bis Februar 1891*, Bearbeitet von Renate Merkel-Melis, Berlin: Akademie Verlag.

Mun, Thomas 1664, *England's Treasure by Forraign Trade. or The Ballance of our Forraign Trade is The Rule of our Treasure*, Written by Thomas Mun, of Lond. Merchant, And now published for the Common good by his Son John Mun of Bearsted in the County of Kent, Esquire. London, Printed by J.O. for Thomas Clark.

Niebuhr, Reinhold 1944, *The Children of Light and the Children of Darkness*, Chicago, IL: University of Chicago Press.

Oncken, August 1893, *Zur Geschichte der Physiokratie*, Leipzig: Duncker & Humblot.

Owetschkin, Dimitrij 2003, *Conrad Schmidt, der Revisionismus und die sozialdemokratische Theorie: Zur theoretischen Entwicklung der Sozialdemokratie vor 1914*, Klartext.

Park, Thomas 1812, *Supplement to the Harleian Miscellany: Consisting of Miscellaneous Pieces not included in the former edition*, Vol. 1, selected and prepared by Thomas Park, London: Printed for White and Cochrane.

Parsons, Talcott 1928, '"Capitalism" in Recent German Literature: Sombart and Weber', *The Journal of Political Economy*, 36, No. 6 (December), 641–61.

Parsons, Talcott 1929, '"Capitalism" in Recent German Literature: Sombart and Weber', *The Journal of Political Economy*, 37, No. 1 (February), 31–51.

Parvus [J.H.], 1892, 'Ökonomische Taschenspielerei. Eine Böhm-Bawerkiade', *Die Neue Zeit*, 10, 1. Bd., H. 17, H. 18, H. 19, 524–31, 549–56, 590–6.

Parvus (Alexander Helphand) 1896, 'Der Weltmarkt und die Agrarkrisis', *Die Neue Zeit*, 14, 1. Bd., H. 7, H. 9, H. 11, H. 17, H. 18, H. 20, H. 21, H. 24, H. 25, H. 26, 197–202, 276–83, 335–42, 514–26, 621–31, 747–58, 781–8, 818–27.

Petry, Franz 1916, *Der soziale Gehalt der Marxschen Werttheorie*, Jena: Fischer.

Petty, William 1899, *Economic Writings of Sir William Petty; together with the Observa-*

tions Upon the Bills of Mortality, edited by Charles Henry Hull, Cambridge: Cambridge University Press.

Pirenne, Henri 1937, *Economic and Social History of Medieval Europe*, New York: Harcourt, Brace and World.

Plekhanov, Georgi 1898a, 'Bernstein and Materialism' (July 1898), in *Selected Philosophical Works*, Vol. 2, by Georgi Plekhanov, Moscow: Progress Publishers, 1976.

Plekhanov, Georgi 1898b, 'Conrad Schmidt versus Karl Marx and Frederick Engels', in *Selected Philosophical Works*, Vol. 2, by Georgi Plekhanov, Moscow: Progress Publishers, 1976.

Plekhanov, Georgi 1898c, 'Materialism or Kantianism', in *Selected Philosophical Works*, Vol. 2, by Georgi Plekhanov, Moscow: Progress Publishers, 1976.

Polanyi, Karl 2001, *The Great Transformation: The Political and Economic Origins of Our Time*, Boston: Beacon Press.

Preobrazhensky, E.A. 1923, 'Teoreticheskie spory o zolotom i tovarnom ruble', *Vestnik Sotsialisticheskoi Akademii*, Moscow and Petrograd, No. 3, 58–84.

Proudhon, Pierre-Joseph 1876, *What is Property? An Inquiry into the Principle of Right and of Government*, Princeton, Mass.: B.R. Tucker.

Pugh, G.T. 1983, *Economic Theory and Political Thought in German Social Democracy: An essay in the 'Rezeption' of Marx's Capital with particular reference to Kautsky, Parvus, Hilferding and Luxemburg*, Unpublished PhD thesis, Canterbury: University of Kent.

Quesnay, François 1888, *Œuvres économiques et philosophiques de F. Quesnay, fondateur du système physiocratique; accompagnées des éloges et d'autres travaux biographiques sur Quesnay par différents auteurs*, publiées avec une introduction et des notes par Auguste Oncken, Frankfurt: J. Baer.

Rabbeno, Ugo 1895, 'L'odierna crisi nella scienza economica', *Giornale degli economisti*, gennaio, 108–10.

Renner, Karl 1949, *The Institutions of Private Law: and Their Social Functions*, London: Routledge & Kegan Paul.

Ricardo, David 1821, *On the Principles of Political Economy and Taxation*, Third Edition, London: John Murray.

Ridgeway, William 1892, *The Origin of Metallic Currency and Weight Standards*, Cambridge: Cambridge University Press.

Rodbertus-Jagetzow, Carl 1851, *Dritter Brief an von Kirchmann von Rodbertus. Widerlegung der Ricardoschen Lehre von der Grundrente und Begründung einer neuen Rententheorie*, Berlin.

Rodbertus-Jagetzow, Carl 1884, *Das Kapital: Vierter socialer Brief an von Kirchmann*, herausgegeben und eingeleitet von Teophil Kozak, Beril: Puttkammer & Mühlbrecht.

Rokityanskii, Yakov G. 1994, 'Poslednie dni Professora I.I. Rubina', *Vestnik Rossiiskoi Akademii Nauk*, 64, No. 9, 828–34.

Rosenberg, Isaiah 1904, *Ricardo und Marx als Werttheoretiker. Eine Kritische Studie*, Wien: Ignaz Brand.

Roth, Regina et al. 2004, 'Einführung' zu Karl Marx, *Das Kapital. Kritik der politischen Ökonomie*, Dritter Band, MEGA, Berlin: Akademie Verlag.

Rubin, Isaak Illich 1924, 'Introduction' to I[saiah] Rosenberg, *Teoriya stoimosti u Ricardo i u Marksa: kriticheskii etyud*, Moscow: Moskovskii rabochii.

Rubin, Isaak Illich 1926, 'Avstriiskaya Shkola', *Bol'shaya Sovetskaya Entsiklopediya*, Moscow, First edition, 1, 244–54.

Rubin, Isaak Illich 1929, *Ocherki po teorii stoimosti Marksa*, Izdanie chetvertovo, Moscow-Leningrad: Gosudarstvennoe Izdatel'stvo.

Rubin, Isaak Illich 1929a, 'K istorii teksta pervoi glavy "Kapitala" K. Marksa', *Arkhiv K. Marksa i F. Engel'sa*, Vol. 4, 63–91.

Rubin, Isaak Illich 1929b, 'Dialekticheskoe razvitie kategorii v ekonomicheskoi sisteme Marksa: Ispravlennaya i dopolnennaya stenogramma doklada, prochitannovo 30 marta 1929 g. na dispute v Institute Krasnoi Professury', *Pod znamenem Marksizma*, No. 4 (April), 82–108, No. 5 (May), 51–82.

Rubin, Isaak Illich 1930, 'Uchenie Marksa o proizvodstve i potreblenii', *Arkhiv K. Marksa i F. Engel'sa*, Moscow: Gosudarstvennoe Izdael'stvo, 58–131.

Rubin, Isaak Illich 1979, *A History of Economic Thought*, translated and edited by Donald Filtzer, London: Ink Links.

Rubin, Isaak Illich 1990, *Essays on Marx's Theory of Value*, Montreal: Black Rose Books.

Rubin, Isaak Illich 2011, 'Ocherki po teorii deneg Marksa' (1926–8), in *Istoki: Sotsiokul'turnaya sreda ekonomicheskoi deyatel'nosti i ekonomicheskovo poznaniya*, edited by Ya.A. Kuz'minov et al., Moscow: Izdatel'skii dom Vysshei shkoly ekonomiki.

Ryazanov, David 1927, 'Ot "Reinskoi gazety" do "Svyatovo semeistva"', *Arkhiv K. Marksa i F. Engel'sa*, Moscow-Leningrad, Vol. III, 191–256.

Rykachev, A.M. 1910, *Den'gi i denezhnaya vlast: Opyt teoreticheskovo istol'kovaniya i opravdaniya kapitalizma*. Part I, St-Pg: M.M. Stayulevich.

Schmidt, Conrad 1889, *Die Durchschnittsprofitrate auf Grundlage des Marx'schen Werthgesetzes*, Stuttgart: J.H.W. Dietz.

Schmidt, Conrad 1890, *Soziale Frage und Bodenverstaatlichung*, Berliner Volkstribüne.

Schmidt, Conrad 1892, 'Die psychologische Richtung in der National-Oekonomie', *Die Neue Zeit*, 10, 2. Bd., H. 41, 421–9, 459–64.

Schmidt, Conrad 1893, 'Die Durchschnittsprofitrate und das Marx'sche Werthgesetz', *Die Neue Zeit*, 11, 1. Bd., H. 3, H. 4, 68–75, 112–24.

Schmidt, Conrad 1895, 'Der dritte Band des *Kapital*', *Sozialpolitisches Zentralblatt*, 25. Februar, 255–8. [Reprinted in Marchionatti, Roberto (ed.) 1998, *Karl Marx: Critical Responses*, Vol. II, London: Routlegde].

Schmidt, Conrad 1897, 'Grenznutzpsychologie und Marx'sche Werthlehre', *Der sozialistische Akademiker, Sozialistische Monatshefte*, 1–3, H. 1189701, S. 18–22.

Schmidt, Conrad 1898, 'Final Goal and Movement', *Vorwärts*, 20 February, in *Marxism and Social Democracy: The Revisionist Debate 1896–1898*, edited and translated by H. Tudor and J.M. Tudor, with an introduction by H. Tudor, Cambridge: Cambridge University Press, 1988.

Schmidt, Conrad 1899, 'Nachträgliche Bemerkungen zur Bernstein-Diskussion', *Sozialistische Monatshefte*, 3–5, 10, 493–9.

Schmidt, Conrad 1910, 'Positive Kritik des Marxschen Wertgesetzes', *Sozialistische Monatshefte*, 14–16, 10, 604–18.

Schüller, Richard 1895, *Die klassische Nationalökonomie und ihre Gegner*, Berlin: Carl Heymann Verlag.

Schüller, Richard 1899, *Die Wirthschaftspolitik der historischen Schule*, Berlin: Carl Heymann Verlag.

Schumpeter, Joseph Alois 1917, 'Das Sozialprodukt und die Rechenpfennige: Glossen und Beiträge zur Geldtheorie von heute', *Archiv für Sozialwissenschaft und Sozialpolitik*, Tübingen, Bd. 44, 627–715. [English version: Schumpeter, Joseph 1956, 'Money and the Social Product', *International Economic Papers*, 6, 148–211].

Schumpeter, Joseph Alois 1934, *The Theory of Economic Development: An Inquiry into Profits, Capital, Credit, Interest, and the Business Cycle*, London: Transaction Publishers.

Shionoya, Yuichi 2005, 'Rational Reconstruction of the German Historical School: An Overview', *The Soul of the German Historical School: Methodological Essays on Schmoller, Weber and Schumpeter*, New York: Springer.

Sieber, Nikolai Ivanovich 1871, 'Marx's Theory of Value and Money', translated by Rakhiya Mananova and James D. White, from Sieber 2001, *David Ricardo's Theory of Value and Capital in Connection with the Latest Contributions and Interpretations*, in *Marx's Capital and Capitalism: Markets in a Socialist Alternative (Research in Political Economy*, Vol. 19, 17–45), edited by Paul Zarembka.

Smith, Adam 1937, *An Inquiry into the Nature and Causes of the Wealth of Nations*, New York: Modern Library.

Smith, Adam 1976, *The Theory of Moral Sentiments*, Oxford: Clarendon Press.

Smith, Adam 1982, *Lectures on Jurisprudence*, Indianapolis: Liberty Fund.

Sombart, Werner 1892, 'Besprechung von: Julius Wolf, *Sozialismus und kapitalistische Gesellschaftsordnung*', *Archiv für soziale Gesetzgebung und Statistik*, 5, 487–98.

Sombart, Werner 1894, 'Zur Kritik des ökonomischen Systems von Karl Marx', *Archiv für soziale Gesetzgebung und Statistik*, Vol. 7, Berlin, 555–94.

Sombart, Werner 1899, 'Die gewerbliche Arbeit und ihre Organisation', *Brauns Archiv für soziale Gesetzgebung und Statistik*, Bd. XIV, 1–52 and 310–405.

Sombart, Werner 1902, *Der moderne Kapitalismus*, Leipzig: Duncker & Humblot. Bd. I. *Die Genesis des Kapitalismus*. Bd. II. *Die Theorie der kapitalistischen Entwicklung*.

Sombart, Werner 1906, *Warum gibt es in den Vereinigten Staaten keinen Sozialismus?*,

Tübingen: Verlag von J.C.B. Mohr (Paul Siebeck). [English version: *Why Is there No Socialism in the United States?*, Bristol: Macmillan, 1976].

Sombart, Werner 1913, *Die Zukunft der Juden*, Leipzig: Duncker & Humblot.

Stammler, Rudolf 1896, *Wirtschaft und Recht nach der materialistischen Geschichtsauffassung: Eine sozialphilosophische Untersuchung*, Leipzig: Veit Verlag.

Steinberg, James 1922, *Das Geldkapital*, Bonn, Leipzig: Schroeder.

Stepelevich, Lawrence S. (ed.) 1983, *The Young Hegelians: An Anthology*, London: Cambridge University Press.

Stephan, Cora 1974, 'Geld- und Staatstheorie in Hilferding's Finanzkapital: Zum Verhältnis von ökonomischer Theorie und politischer Strategie', *Gesellschaft: Beiträge zur Marxschen Theorie*, H. 2, 111–54.

Steuart, James 1767, *An Inquiry into the Principles of Political Oeconomy: Being an Essay on the Science of Domestic Policy in Free Nations. In which are particularly considered Population, Agriculture, Trade, Industry, Money, Coin, Interest, Circulation, Banks, Exchange, Public Credit, and Taxes*, 2 Vols, London: Printed for A. Millar and T. Cadell, in the Strand.

Steuart, James 1805, *The Works, Political, Metaphysical, and Chronological, of the Late Sir James Steuart of Coltness, Bart., Now First Collected by General Sir James Steuart, Bart., His Son, from His Father's Corrected Copies; to Which are Subjoined Anecdotes of the Author*, London: Printed for T. Cadell and W. Davies.

Svyatlovsky, V.V. 1923, *Proiskhozhdenie deneg i denezhnykh znakov*, Moscow/St. Petersburg.

Tawney, R.H. 1961, *Religion and the Rise of Capitalism*, Harmondsworth, Middlesex: Penguin.

Tönnies, Ferdinand 2001, *Community and Civil Society*, edited by Jose Harris, translated by Jose Harris and Margaret Hollis, Cambridge: Cambridge University Press.

Trakhtenberg, I.A. 1922, *Bumazhnye den'gi: Ocherki teorii deneg i denezhnovo obrashcheniya*, Moscow: Moskovskii rabochii.

Trotsky, Leon 1918, 'Gustav Eckstein', *Nashe Slovo*, No. 178 (August 3), reprinted in Trotsky, Leon 1972, *Political Profiles*, translated by R. Chappell, London: New Park.

Tucker, Robert C. 1978 (ed.), *The Marx-Engels Reader*, 2nd edition, New York: W.W. Norton.

Tudor, H. and J.M. Tudor (eds.) 1988, *Marxism and Social Democracy: The Revisionist Debate 1896–1898*, Cambridge: Cambridge University Press.

Tugan-Baranovsky, Mikhail I. 1917, *Osnovy politicheskoi ekonomii*, Petrograd: Pravo.

Vasina, Lyudmila L. and Yakov G. Rokityansky 1992, 'Stranitsy zhizni i tvorchestva ekonomista I.I. Rubina', *Vestnik Rossiiskoi akademii nauk*, No. 8, 129–44.

Waentig, Heinrich Eugen 1898, *Gewerbliche Mittelstandspolitik, eine rechtshistorisch-wirtschafts-politische Studie auf Grund österreichischer Quellen*, Leipzig: Duncker und Humblot.

Wagner, Adolph 1893, *Grundlegung der Politischen Ökonomie*. Teil 1: *Grundlagen der Volkswirtschaft*, 3. Auflage, Leipzig: C.F. Winter'sche Verlagshandlung.

Wagner, Adolph 1909, *Theoretische Sozialökonomik oder Allgemeine und theoretische Volkswirtschaftslehre: Grundriss tunlichst in prinzipieller Behandlungsweise*, Leipzig: C.F. Winter. Abt. 2. Bd. 2: *Sozialökonomische Theorie des Geldes und Geldwesens. Tunlichst in prinzipieller Behandlungsweise, zugleich in genauerer Ausführung.*

Weber, Max 1958, *The Protestant Ethic and the Spirit of Capitalism*, New York: Scribner.

Zeller, Eduard 1881, *A History of Greek Philosophy from the Earliest Period to the Time of Socrates*, London: Longmans, Green and Co.

Index

A Contribution to the Critique of Political Economy   2–3, 32, 39, 43, 103–106, 130, 163, 212, 216, 220, 225, 235, 266, 277, 282, 296–297, 450, 454–455, 460, 469, 473, 478–479, 538, 550, 552, 583, 587–602, 619, 635–637, 639, 641, 652n–653, 673–674n, 738n, 743, 756, 758, 760, 830
Abezgauz, G.   833n
Absolute Ground Rent   16, 182–183, 247–249, 255–260, 262, 270, 336
Abstract Labour   21, 31–32, 34–35, 85, 91, 114, 119, 129–131, 205, 219, 242, 264, 266, 350, 354–355, 363, 376, 387, 410, 412–413, 419, 443–444, 451n–452, 530–532, 536–540, 557, 561–567, 584, 611, 621–622, 624, 631n, 634–637, 639, 665, 667–669, 671–672, 674–681, 684, 691–695, 755, 757–758, 761, 765, 776, 793, 833
    See also: Concrete Labour
Accumulation of Capital   10n, 19, 35, 43–44, 48–50, 56, 84, 88–90, 93, 127, 132, 140, 157, 159, 174–176n, 214, 236, 247, 264, 269, 308, 314, 317, 329, 333, 337–338, 347–348, 351–352, 375, 390–393, 402, 406, 409, 418, 464, 472, 486, 489–490, 505–506, 508, 526–527, 625, 699, 703, 711–727, 744, 789, 791
Advanced Capital   143–150, 263
Adler, Max   11, 60n, 281–283n, 392n
Alienation   1, 36, 70, 74, 76–77, 82–83, 85–86, 91, 93, 164, 213, 308, 310, 449, 463, 730–731, 758, 764, 769, 775–783, 785, 787, 792, 795, 800, 805–806, 808, 810, 814–817
Alienation of Money from the Commodities   775–778, 785, 787, 810
Althusser, Louis   273–274
Amonn, Alfred   675
Anabaptists   41
Anderson, James   271
Antithesis between Commodities and Money   765, 770, 785–787, 797
    See also: Alienation of Money from the Commodities
Aquinas, Thomas   40–41
Aristotle   40, 341

Articles of Consumption
    See: Means of Consumption
Austrian School
    See: Subjective Theory of Value
Austro-Marxism   27, 29, 360n
Autonomisation (*Verselbständigung*) of Production Relations   768–769, 784, 786, 792, 794, 797, 800–801, 805, 808–810, 813–817
    See also: Detachment and Alienation of Production Relations
Average Rate of Profit   12, 20, 91, 144, 162, 164, 172–175, 178, 185, 192, 199–201, 210, 247–249, 253–258, 260, 262, 269, 290, 296, 298–301, 305–306, 311, 315, 323, 335, 350, 355, 364, 377, 405n, 412n–413n, 437, 443, 445, 447, 533–534, 540, 552, 555, 575–576, 579, 581, 621, 807, 809, 811–812, 815

Bailey, Samuel   33, 304, 306, 308, 335, 584–585, 587, 592, 602–618
Banking   168, 181, 713, 716, 718
Barton, John   271, 337
Bauer, Otto   5–7, 18–19 112–128, 282, 328–339
Bax, Belfort Ernest   11, 392n
Bernstein, Eduard   1, 5, 10, 59, 112–113, 129, 252n, 266n, 270n, 342n, 375n, 376n, 380, 389n, 405n
Bessonov, Sergei   728, 732, 735–736, 739, 742–748, 750–752, 833n
Blaug, Mark   406n, 444n, 447n
Böckh, August   658
Bogdanov, Alexander   739
Böhm-Bawerk, Eugen von   11, 22, 26–27, 186n, 197n, 207n–208n, 293n, 298, 312n, 348, 360n, 409n, 413n–417n, 423n, 430, 433n, 435–442, 543, 562, 629–630
Bolsheviks   92, 827
Bostaph, Samuel   407n
Bourgeois Mode of Production
    See: Capitalist Mode of Production
Bourgeoisie   24, 28, 57–58, 203, 220–221, 260n–261n, 272, 286–287, 330–331, 379–381, 384–385, 389, 429, 441, 464–465, 467, 537, 717
    See also: Capitalist Class

Bray, John Francis 384
Brentano, Lujo 22–23
Broadhurst, John 610
Bücher, Karl 22
Bukharin, Nikolai 27, 442, 828–829
Bund (*Allgemeine Jüdische Arbeiterbund*) 823
Business Cycle
  See: Crises
Buyers and Sellers of Commodities 134, 136n, 187, 267, 419, 422, 436, 551–552, 565, 627, 690, 695–696, 708, 712, 719–720, 725–726, 769–771, 785, 788
  See also: Purchase and Sale of Commodities

Calvin, John 41–45, 48, 52, 58, 99, 391
Capital
  Circulating: *See*: Circulating Capital
  Commodity: *See*: Commodity Capital
  Constant: *See*: Constant Capital
  Finance: *See*: Finance Capital
  Fixed: *See*: Fixed Capital
  Industrial: *See*: Industrial Capital
  Money: *See*: Money Capital
  Money-Dealing: *See*: Money-Dealing Capital
  Productive: *See*: Productive Capital
  Total Social: *See*: Total Social Capital
  Variable: *See*: Variable Capital
Capital, Book I 2–7, 32–35, 39, 44, 89, 101, 112–128, 131–132, 148–149, 218, 230, 299, 328, 348, 350, 363, 520, 552, 558, 582n–618, 639, 652n, 728, 730, 741, 757, 762, 764, 791, 804, 813
Capital, Book II 7–10, 39, 121, 129–161, 338n, 365, 412n, 452, 518, 552, 577, 728, 791, 798, 813
Capital, Book III 39, 95–96, 115, 121, 162–211, 143, 299, 350, 363, 391, 405n, 412n, 447, 499, 552, 579–580, 703n, 728, 798, 803, 807, 813
Capitalist Class 137, 179, 193, 298, 315, 331, 404, 505–506, 532, 577, 787, 800, 803
  See also: Bourgeoisie
Capitalist Commodity Production 26, 156, 235, 333, 378, 386–387, 411, 419, 421, 428, 440, 280, 462, 480, 483–485, 489–490, 496–500, 530–535, 543–545, 548–549, 551, 555, 561, 563, 578, 582n, 751
Capitalist Economy 18–19, 27–28, 30, 108, 232, 235, 241–242, 259, 265–266, 323, 330–331, 337, 343–345, 348, 352, 388, 393, 402, 422n, 438, 440–441, 452, 462–464, 466, 468, 472–473, 480–481, 483–485, 487–490, 498, 508–511, 527, 530–535, 550, 555, 563, 570, 572–573, 575, 577–581, 713, 719, 722, 733, 737, 740, 742–743, 747–751, 760, 768, 788–790, 792–794, 808–810, 814, 817
Capitalist Mode of Production 19, 31, 106, 136–141, 154–155, 176–177n, 184, 186, 203, 282, 313, 320–321, 331, 334, 339, 368, 374n, 386, 388
Capitalist Society 20–21, 31, 36–37, 39, 89, 109, 119–120, 150n, 214, 289, 291, 315, 338, 353–355, 362–363, 371, 375–376, 388, 396–397, 429, 439–441, 451, 454, 464–468, 472, 480, 488, 496–498, 500–501, 503–504, 507–510, 512, 520, 530, 538, 543–546, 548–550, 552, 555, 561, 571, 577, 579–580, 657, 715, 718, 726, 729, 732, 735, 747–748, 750, 754, 803, 806, 813–814
Carey, Henry Charles 260–261
Cartels 112n, 116
Cassel, Gustav 675, 739
Categories of Political Economy
  See: Economic Categories
Change of Form (of the Products of Labour under Commodity Production) 32, 452, 485, 514–515, 526, 584, 670–671, 684, 704–705, 721–722, 740, 752, 755, 758–760, 772–774, 779, 782
  See also: Metamorphosis of the Commodity
Cherbuliez, Antoine Elisée 310–311, 338, 503n
Chernyshevsky, Nikolay 503n
Child, Josiah 226
Circulating Capital 8, 21, 141–146, 248, 251–253, 264, 268n, 299, 305, 310, 323, 333, 337, 516, 553, 581, 796
Circulation Costs 144, 150–152, 194, 365–366
Circulation of Capital 6, 124, 133–161, 216–217, 251, 366, 789, 796–803, 805

Circulation of Commodities   33, 36, 110, 130, 133–134, 151, 158, 171, 178, 199, 216, 232, 268, 412, 419, 484–486, 514, 525, 529, 545, 620–621, 624–625, 638, 663, 670, 691, 694, 696–698, 700–704, 708, 710, 712, 718–719, 721, 725, 729, 768–769, 771, 773, 779, 781–783, 785, 787, 789–790, 810
Circulation of Money   134, 158, 216, 482–484, 525, 663–664, 694, 773–774, 779, 781, 787, 789, 799, 810
Civil Society   65–74, 82, 105, 378, 462, 625
Clark, John Bates   819
Class Antagonisms
  See: Class Struggle
Class Struggle   16, 24, 36–37, 72, 117–119, 140, 184, 212, 221, 244, 272, 277, 314, 322, 324, 333, 342, 385, 388, 403, 406, 441, 487, 501, 504, 731, 737, 792, 796, 807, 817
Classical Political Economy   21, 23–24, 28, 32–33, 137, 182, 226, 234, 239, 277, 310, 315, 322, 322–323, 330, 334–337, 343, 357n, 363, 367, 374n, 378–388, 397, 414, 421, 430–431, 440–441, 540–542, 565–567, 569–573n, 582, 585, 606n, 617–618, 640, 730, 738, 784, 799, 804, 814–815, 830, 832
Cohen, Hermann   118
Coins   464, 660, 663–665, 704, 713–714, 716, 718, 727, 780
  See also: Money
Colln, Friedrich von   383
Commercial Capital   134, 177–179, 203, 552, 733, 797–803, 811
  See also: Industrial Capital
  See also: Money Capital
Commercial Capitalist   551, 579n, 800–801
  See also: Industrial Capitalist
  See also: Money Capitalist
Commercial Profit   179, 199, 233, 552, 802–804, 811
Commodity Capital   6, 9, 124, 137–139, 142, 147, 177–178, 552, 797–799, 802
Commodity-Capitalist Economy/Society
  See: Capitalist Commodity Production
Commodity Circulation
  See: Circulation of Commodities
Commodity Economy   24, 31, 384, 386–388, 438, 440, 462–464, 472, 480–481, 483–485, 487–491, 495–496, 500, 509, 522–524, 530, 534–535, 535, 545, 547, 549, 552–553, 555–564, 566, 568, 575, 577–578, 580, 590, 594, 616, 624, 629, 633, 635, 637–638, 640–649, 652, 654, 656–657, 662, 665–667, 671–672, 680–682, 686, 691–692, 698, 701–703n, 706, 710–713, 716, 719, 723, 744, 747–750, 755–756, 760, 768, 788–795, 802, 809–810
Commodity Exchange
  See: Exchange of Commodities
Commodity Fetishim
  See: Fetishim of the Commodity
Commodity-Form (of the Products of Labour)   86, 156n, 374n, 376, 451, 485, 494, 523, 615, 626, 705–706, 720–721, 760, 778, 791, 794, 796, 798
  See also: Money-Form
  See also: Social Form (of the Products of Labour under Commodity Production)
  See also: Form of Value (of the Products of Labour under Commodity Production)
  See also: Change of Form (of the Products of Labour under Commodity Production)
Commodity Production
  See: Simple Commodity Production
  See: Capitalist Commodity Production
Commodity Society
  See: Commodity Economy
Communism   36–39, 41, 53, 77–80, 84, 93–99, 126n, 174n, 203–204, 209, 287, 298, 307, 327, 371, 495–496, 540, 556, 559, 656, 659, 731, 820
Competition   6, 11–12, 16, 49–51, 88, 120, 124, 164, 170, 172, 180, 184, 189, 198–200, 204, 206–207, 229–230, 247–248, 252–269, 300, 323, 350, 352, 378, 388, 391–395, 402–405, 419–420, 465, 552, 576, 579, 687, 692
Comte, Auguste   107, 229
Concentration of Capital   37, 88, 119n, 121, 311, 347, 351–352, 735, 794
Concrete Labour   6, 20–21, 31, 37, 72, 85, 124, 130, 190, 241–242, 266, 334, 354–355, 358–359, 363, 376, 387, 530–532, 536, 539–540, 558, 560–562, 565–567, 573, 634–637, 642–643, 667–674, 684, 693–696, 731, 755, 757–758, 761, 776, 793
  See also: Abstract Labour

INDEX   857

Conjuncture   413n, 504–506, 545, 555, 647,
    686, 718
Constant Capital   8, 87, 142–44, 156–158,
    171–179, 190n, 199, 224, 235–236, 248,
    251–268, 298, 302, 305, 310, 323, 333n–
    339, 407, 452, 508, 516–517, 551, 580,
    793–794
Consumption
    Individual   139–141, 154, 236, 411, 488, 507,
        528
    Industrial   236, 307
    Non-Productive   303, 464–465
    Personal   315, 344, 489, 505–508, 511–513,
        528, 647–648, 715–716, 780
    Productive   135, 137, 139, 153, 478, 507–
        508, 720n
    See also: Means of Consumption
Content of Value   31–32, 34, 190n, 540, 565,
    569, 583, 591–592, 599, 620, 622n, 636,
    640
    See also: Form of Value
Contradictory Character of Labour
    See also: Dual Character of Labour under
        Commodity Production
Contradictory Character of the Commodity
    See also: Dual Character of the Commodity
Costs of Production   90, 151, 173, 185–187,
    196, 223, 225, 229, 262, 265, 276, 290,
    303, 358, 404, 407, 409–410, 413, 417n,
    430, 434, 437, 447, 541, 555, 579, 621, 687,
    807
Cost-Prices
    See: Prices of Production
Credit   36, 41, 138, 141, 151, 152, 159, 168, 181,
    203, 254, 269, 278, 463n, 504–506,
    528–529, 551, 625n, 713–714, 719, 729,
    785–786, 795
Crises   4, 9, 23, 89–91, 132–133, 138, 140–141,
    145, 159, 181, 236, 264–269, 271–272, 276,
    322, 338, 341, 344, 509, 512, 529, 537, 543,
    786–787, 808–813, 819
Crystallisation of Social Forms   321, 387, 412,
    420, 560, 563, 634, 637n, 653–654, 661,
    677–678, 688, 725–727, 765–766, 770–
    774, 780, 782, 784–785, 795
    See also: Social Form (of the Products of
        Labour under Commodity Production)
    See also: Ossification of Production
        Relations

Cromwell, Oliver   220, 228
Cunow, Heinrich   14–15, 19–20, 212–245,
    340–352

Davenant, Charles   219–220
De Tracy, Destutt   243
Declining Tendency of the Rate of Profit
    See: Falling Tendency of the Rate of Profit
Demand, Effective
    See: Effective Demand
Demand, Solvent
    See: Effective Demand
Demand and Supply
    See: Supply and Demand
Detachment and Alienation of Production
    Relations under Capitalism   692–693,
    730–731, 766, 775, 792, 797–798, 800,
    800–817
    See also: Autonomisation (Verselbständi-
        gung) of Production Relations
Determination of Form or Determinations of
    Economic Form (Formbestimmtheit)   20,
    30, 36, 452, 514, 519, 521–522, 537, 550,
    553–554, 564, 581, 730, 772, 788, 796
    See also: Social Form (of the Products of
        Labour under Commodity Production)
Dialectical Method of Analysis   3, 5–7, 35–
    37, 39, 60–61, 80–84, 100–102, 114, 163,
    282, 341, 388–389, 392, 449, 455, 457,
    467, 485, 539n, 621, 625, 729, 731–732,
    753, 755, 772, 774
    See also: Law of the Unity of Opposites
    See also: Law of Negation
Dialectics
    See: Dialectical Method of Analysis
Dietzel, Heinrich   167n, 191n, 207n, 373, 417
Dietzgen, Peter Josef   117
Die Neue Zeit   4–5, 7, 10, 14, 26, 101, 112, 129,
    168, 212, 214, 246, 273, 300, 340, 353, 360,
    362, 378, 380, 405, 408
Differential Ground Rent   16, 168n, 182–183,
    246–248, 256, 259–270, 336, 572
Dilke, Charles Wentworth   308, 310, 332, 335
Dilthey, Wilhelm   122
Distribution of Labour (among the different
    Branches of Production)   21, 99, 338, 546,
    556–559, 562–564, 579–581, 633–634,
    637–638, 644, 667–669, 672, 681–683,
    692–694

Division of Labour   29, 37, 48–49, 64, 85, 94–97, 101, 111, 177–178, 205, 214, 283, 372, 387, 449, 454, 463, 472, 481, 545–546, 556, 579, 634, 641–643, 660, 671, 693–694, 698, 735, 741, 765, 768–769, 801, 808
Domestic Market   9n, 223, 237
Du Buat-Nançay, Louis-Gabriel, Comte   229
Dual Character of Labour under Commodity Production   31–32, 530, 536, 540, 561–562, 565–566, 624, 645, 731, 755–761, 793, 804
   See also: Abstract Labour
   See also: Concrete Labour
Dual Character of the Commodity   35, 451, 490, 494, 562, 624, 645, 649–650, 755–761
   See also: Use-Value
   See also: Exchange-Value
Dual Nature of the Commodity
   See: Dual Character of the Commodity
Dukor, G.   833n
Dvolaitsky, Sh.M.   822, 829, 832

Eckstein, Gustav   15–16, 27, 246–272, 275, 300n
Economic and Philosophic Manuscripts of 1844   1, 3, 29, 39, 76–86, 97–98, 114, 213, 449–452, 456–468, 523, 731, 817
Economic Categories   8, 18, 26, 28, 31, 35, 84, 129–130, 229, 249, 295–296, 323, 354n, 363, 375, 538–539, 544, 550–555, 563–565, 577, 581–582, 620, 625, 709, 726, 732, 738, 743–747, 752–753, 788, 791, 810, 833
   See also: Relations of Production
   See also: Social Form (of the Products of Labour under Commodity Production)
   See also: Social Form of the Production Process
   See also: Social Function (of the Labour Products under Commodity Production)
Economic Determination of Form
   See: Social Form
Economic Form
   See: Social Form
Economic Formation   343, 454, 479, 487n, 490, 532, 742, 746
   See also: Social Formation
   See also: Mode of Producion

Effective Demand   91n, 132, 140, 265, 425, 442, 445, 497–498, 503, 508, 510, 512, 515, 646, 650, 694
Engels, Friedrich   1–2, 9–14, 18, 22, 29, 37, 57–58, 87, 114–119, 130–131, 136n, 143, 148n, 162–163, 165–168, 172, 176, 184, 187n, 189n, 199n, 201, 209–212, 217, 277–279, 283, 386, 299, 328, 363, 390–191, 405, 408, 412n, 449–450n, 453–454, 460, 462, 464–465, 469, 470, 472, 495–496, 514, 519–520, 561, 577, 591–592, 615, 732, 738, 743, 755, 760, 777, 801–804, 807, 827, 829–832, 834
Equalisation of the Profit Rate
   See: Average Rate of Profit
Equivalent Form of Value   32, 583–584, 587, 597, 599, 601–602, 610, 651, 661, 666, 668, 670, 672, 677, 685, 698, 759, 763, 765, 767–768, 770, 780
   See also: Relative Form of Value
   See also: Functions or Forms of Money: Universal Equivalent
Exchange of Commodities   12–13, 20, 35, 87, 110, 166, 174, 188, 209–210, 232, 266, 347, 354, 370, 373, 378, 392, 412, 414, 419, 421, 451, 491, 494, 514, 521–526, 539n, 547, 588, 592, 613, 616, 622–627, 631, 634–639, 640–641, 644, 647, 652–654, 657, 659, 663–665, 669–679, 686, 688–691, 694–697, 702, 708, 710, 721–722, 729, 752, 758–759, 761, 765, 768, 771, 774, 780, 786, 800
Exchange Process
   See: Exchange of Commodities
Exchange-Value (Form of Value, Mode of Expression of Value)   9, 21, 29, 31–34, 43, 85, 90, 129, 131–132, 148, 205, 219, 222, 225, 227, 231, 233, 235–236, 242, 251, 283–284, 307–309, 350, 358, 363, 367, 374–376, 397, 406, 408, 414–440, 448–453, 463, 480–496, 509, 514, 520–527, 529n, 532, 535–536, 539, 560, 562, 567, 573, 583–618, 621–654, 659–666, 671–673, 684–685, 688–692, 698, 704–709, 720, 722, 725, 759, 764, 771–772, 774–775, 779, 782, 786, 788
   See also: Form of Value
Expanded Reproduction of Capital
   See: Accumulation of Capital

INDEX

Exploitation of the Workers   37, 39, 87–89, 91, 111, 117–119, 144, 203n, 205–206, 300–301, 323, 332–333, 376, 405n–406, 439, 464, 487, 509, 530, 532, 577, 812
  See also: Valorisation of Capital
Expression of Value   32–33, 187, 412, 583–585, 589, 593–597, 599–602, 605n, 609, 614–615, 617, 762, 765–767
  See also: Relation of Value

Falling Tendency of the Rate of Profit   15, 17, 20, 91–92, 112n, 175–176, 228, 247–248, 253–254, 258, 263, 314, 338, 314, 341, 348n, 794, 812
Fetishim of the Commodity   8, 17, 22, 39, 85, 92, 130, 276, 295, 307, 310, 323–324, 334, 363, 374, 391, 526, 539n, 544, 549, 562–563, 569, 588–589, 611–612, 635–636, 644, 672, 696, 705, 731, 750–751, 772, 796, 803, 805, 815–816
  See also: Social Properties of Things (of the Products of Labour under Commodity Production)
  See also: Reification of Production Relations under Commodity Production
Fetishisation of Production Relations between People   563, 772, 796, 803, 805
  See also: Reification of Production Relations under Commodity Production
Feudalism   106, 109, 221, 225n, 230, 244, 304, 344, 355, 379, 382–383, 393, 479, 483, 487n, 495, 506, 550n, 559, 565, 701–702, 711–712, 717, 750–751
Feuerbach, Ludwig   1, 39, 74–76, 78, 80, 83, 86, 213, 280, 286, 449–450, 455–458, 461
Fichte, Johann Gottlieb   280–281
Finance Capital   7, 14, 115, 132, 214, 278, 340n
Fireman, Peter   162
Fixed Capital   8, 25, 87, 90, 94, 97–98, 138, 141–147, 156–159, 248–249, 251–257, 263–264, 268n, 299, 302, 305, 310, 323, 337–339, 411, 516, 537, 553, 581, 688, 713–714, 766, 796
Forces of Production
  See: Productive Forces
Foreign Trade   3, 107, 220, 223–229, 237, 248, 330, 338, 704

Form of Value (of the Products of Labour under Commodity Production)   2, 32–34, 119n, 130, 347n, 374n, 486, 490, 494, 551, 553, 559–618, 620–622, 631n, 635–640, 651, 660, 666, 670–671, 683–685, 716, 743–744, 747, 757, 759–767, 770–771, 787
  See also: Equivalent Form of Value
  See also: Exchange-Value
  See also: Content of Value
  See also: Magnitude of Value
  See also: Relative Form of Value
  See also: Social Form (of the Products of Labour under Commodity Production)
Forms of Value, Development of (Simple, Expanded, General and Monetary Forms of Value)   32, 514, 583, 587, 597–599, 615, 617, 630n, 636–637, 658, 660, 683–385, 743, 755, 759–760, 762–763, 765–766, 770–771
Forms or Phases of Industrial Capital
  See: Money Capital
  See: Commodity Capital
  See: Productive Capital
Formal Use-Value   520–535
Franklin, Benjamin   134, 279, 291, 567
French Revolution   14, 55, 159, 214, 229, 330, 340n, 658
Friedrich Wilhelm IV, King of Prussia   386
Functions or Forms of Money   34–35, 485–486, 551, 553, 637–639, 657, 665, 675–678, 719, 743, 771–788, 810
  Hoard   35–36, 41, 43, 138–139, 333, 390n, 482, 485–489, 524–529, 534, 551, 625, 710–729, 780–788, 795
  Means of Circulation   35, 152, 266, 524–525, 527, 530, 534, 551, 740, 777–787
  Means of Payment   35, 135n, 269, 485–486, 489, 525, 528–529, 534, 551, 663–664, 680, 714, 726, 740, 780, 785–788, 810
  Measure of Value   35, 85, 269, 413, 656–657, 674–694, 706, 709–710, 767, 775–779, 784–787
  Medium of Circulation   268, 451n, 587, 674–679, 693–694, 702, 704, 709–710, 714, 718–719, 721, 723, 726–727
  Medium of Exchange   85, 232, 421, 425, 495, 661, 674–676, 678, 702
  Standard of Prices   777

Universal Equivalent   32, 36, 521–523, 551, 584, 599–600, 615, 651–653, 656–657, 661, 665, 670–672, 683, 685–686, 692, 695, 704, 724, 729, 759, 765–767, 771, 774–775, 786
World Money   35, 780

Ganilh, Charles   243
Garnier, Germain   243
Gascoine, Thomas   41
Generalised Equation of Commodities   34, 622, 626–629, 632–636, 638, 648, 651, 654, 665–668, 694
Gerlach, Otto   187–188
German Historical School
   See: Historical School, German
Gneisenau, Count Neidhardt von   382
Godwin, William   314
Goethe, Johann Wolfgang von   126n, 202n, 402n
Gold   41, 116, 118, 149, 151–152, 398, 464, 487n, 196, 522–526, 551, 555, 561, 590, 602, 607, 628, 640, 654, 661–669, 671–686, 692–696, 704–711, 716–718, 722–724, 727, 765–767, 769–770, 774–782, 785, 787
   See also: Precious Metals
Goldmann, Lucien   56
Gossen, Hermann Heinrich   430, 432
Gottl-Ottlilienfeld, Friedrich von   470n
Graunt, John   219
Gray, John   384
Graziadei, Antonio   687n
Ground Rent   10, 14n–16, 152, 154, 159, 181–184, 206, 219, 227, 229, 233–235, 240, 246–248, 249, 254–256, 258, 260–263, 270, 313–315, 322, 330–331, 333, 335–336, 375, 393, 412n, 414n, 501, 548, 566n, 578, 737, 754, 803–807, 811–812
   Differential: *See*: Differential Ground Rent
   Absolute Ground Rent: *See*: Absolute Ground Rent
Grundrisse   5, 39, 79, 82, 84–85, 87–89n, 93–98, 149n, 186n, 225n, 268n, 442, 447, 451
Guilds   174n, 215, 226, 379, 382n–384, 396, 565

Haller, Karl Ludwig von   383
Hammacher, Emil   453
Hardenberg, Karl August von   382

Harris, William   231
Hasbach, Wilhelm   207
Hegel, Georg Wilhelm Friedrich   1–7, 18, 28, 36, 39–40, 42–44, 46, 53, 59–107, 113–115, 123–127, 162–164, 186, 198, 213, 272–291, 324, 326, 329, 341, 348, 378, 406, 449, 451, 455–458, 462–463, 469, 477, 493, 538, 586, 606, 620, 623–625, 631, 641, 658, 728–729, 731, 743
   Encyclopaedia of the Philosophical Sciences   63, 107, 731
   Lectures on the History of Philosophy   18
   Phenomenology of Spirit   63, 83
   Science of Logic   5–6, 36, 62, 80–81, 114, 123–124, 164, 341, 451n, 493n–494n, 728–729, 731
   The Philosophy of History   42, 44, 64
   The Philosophy of Right   61, 65–72, 74, 78, 84, 87n, 126, 623, 625
Helfferich, Karl   660n–661, 674
Herschel, John   313
Hildebrand, Bruno   22, 379, 384
Hilferding, Rudolf   7, 16–18, 20–22, 24–25, 27, 353–377, 390–404, 442, 539, 542–543, 656–657, 674, 676, 738
   Finance Capital   7, 115, 132
Historical Materialism
   See: Materialist Conception of History
Historical School, German   11, 22–25, 107n, 121, 215–216, 312, 319, 356, 378–404, 429–430, 441, 537, 541
Historical-Social Determination
   See: Social Form
Historical-Social Form
   See: Social Form
Hoard
   See: Functions of Money
Hodgskin, Thomas   308–310, 332–333, 338
Home Market
   See: Domestic Market
Hume, David   219, 237, 330, 342

Imperialism   7, 9–10, 14, 72, 115, 132, 214, 340
Incomes   15–16, 30, 229–230, 241, 246, 276, 330–333, 336, 228, 407–408, 411, 418n, 425–427, 439, 452, 480, 499, 501, 503–505, 510, 512, 754, 803–808, 813, 815
Individual Labour
   See: Concrete Labour

INDEX   861

Industrial Capital   134–135, 137–139, 151, 158–
    159, 177–180, 194, 230, 239–240, 243,
    257–258, 269, 296, 298, 325, 419, 465–
    466, 468, 486, 532–534, 548, 550–552,
    575, 579–580, 724, 733, 794, 797–804
  See also: Money Capital
  See also: Commercial Capital
Industrial Capitalist   135, 137–139, 151, 158–
    159, 177–180n, 194, 229–230, 234, 239,
    243, 269, 314, 325n, 419, 465–468, 532–
    534, 548–552, 575, 579n–580, 724, 800
  See also: Money Capitalist
  See also: Commercial Capitalist
Intensity of Labour   353, 359, 579
Interest-Bearing Capital   179–180, 203n, 278
Interest on Loan Capital   26–27, 28n, 152–
    153, 179, 180, 203n, 219, 224, 229, 293n,
    321, 330, 332–333, 501, 533–534, 548,
    550, 552, 737, 739, 771, 803–807, 811, 815
Interest Rate
  See: Rate of Interest
Items of Consumption
  See: Means of Consumption

Jevons, William Stanley   25, 406, 408, 414,
    430, 820
Jones, Richard   14, 17–19, 276, 310–326, 334,
    537

Kabo, R.M.   830
Kant, Immanuel   5–7, 39–40, 50–70, 73, 77,
    86, 99, 113, 122–127n, 279–282, 288–289,
    342n–343n, 389, 399–400n, 405–406
Kaufman, Ilarion Ignat'evich   3–4, 100–111,
    162–163, 273, 728, 731, 821
Kautsky, Karl   1, 4–5, 7–10, 14–15, 18, 22–23,
    108, 115, 117, 129–161, 212, 215n–219, 225,
    246–247, 274, 277–278, 299, 322, 328–
    329, 334, 338n, 340n, 360, 390, 475, 587,
    607, 675–676
Knapp, Georg Friedrich   22, 664, 680
Knies, Karl   22, 379, 384
Kon, A.F.   833n
Krestinsky, N.N.   826
Kugelmann, Ludwig   3, 563n–564n, 576n

Labour
  Concrete: See: Concrete Labour
  Abstract: See: Abstract Labour

Labour Organisation
  See: Organisation of Labour
Labour Power   1–2, 6, 20, 87n, 89, 110–111,
    119n, 124, 134–138, 142–144, 148, 151,
    153, 157, 171, 175, 190n, 193, 195–196,
    229, 231–232, 235, 242, 256, 290, 302,
    305, 323, 335, 337–338, 355, 360, 395,
    411, 413–414, 452, 473–475, 501–502,
    505, 507, 511, 516, 519, 522, 530–534,
    550, 552, 577–578, 716, 789, 792–796,
    807
Labour Process   30, 142, 146–147, 152, 193n–
    194, 264, 323, 402, 452, 476, 513, 530, 543,
    564, 578, 582n, 709, 792
Labour Productivity
  See: Productivity of Labour
Labour Theory of Value   28, 31, 33, 112n,
    191n, 204–205, 219–220, 231–233, 248–
    255, 291–292, 296–299, 301, 303, 336,
    353, 357–358, 362–365, 387, 405n,
    412–413, 540–543, 557–558, 561, 567,
    572–574, 579–581, 584–587, 602, 604,
    608, 611, 613, 617, 669, 680–682, 686–
    687, 730
Labour Time   88n–89n, 91, 94–99, 119, 186n–
    187n, 192, 195, 205, 231, 235, 251, 259,
    265–266, 268n, 289–290, 306, 321, 350,
    419, 493, 515, 557, 589–590, 595, 609,
    611, 628, 631n, 650, 674, 692, 727n, 759,
    775
Labour Value
  See: Labour Theory of Value
Landé, Hugo   188–189
Landed Property   3, 107, 181–184, 193, 203,
    216, 229–230, 235, 248, 258, 298, 308,
    313–315, 321, 331–333, 806
Landlords   15–16, 37, 47, 56, 159, 221, 228–229,
    234, 243, 246–248, 258–260, 262, 272,
    276, 303–304, 314–316, 322, 330–332,
    337, 382, 393, 406, 419, 464–468, 552,
    578–579, 701, 711, 807
Landowners
  See: Landlords
Laplace, Pierre-Simon   249–250
Lassalle, Ferdinand   3–4, 281
Lauderdale, James Maitland, 8th Earl of   464
Law of Motion of Capitalist Society   21, 126–
    127, 189n, 206, 291, 322–323, 363, 368,
    370–371, 375, 377, 402, 448

Law of Negation   5, 65, 76–77, 79, 84, 123, 164, 186n, 388, 732, 753, 755, 766, 770, 774, 789–790
Law of the Unity of Opposites   36, 455, 477, 494n, 730, 732, 753, 755, 759, 766–770, 788, 790, 795–796, 799–803, 813
Law of Value   13, 85, 94–95, 99, 134, 143, 149, 162–166, 174, 188–192, 198–199, 205, 211n, 248–258, 261, 269–270, 290–292, 301, 303, 305–308, 335–336, 347, 350–351, 363, 375, 377, 405, 410–421, 428, 540, 557, 577, 579, 623–624, 749, 813
Left Hegelians   1
Lenin   9, 14n, 30, 35–36, 92, 110n, 132, 212n–213n, 247n–248n, 452, 510n–511n, 513, 539n, 566n, 728–729, 731, 736, 738–739, 742–743, 747, 750, 752, 760
Levin, Rahel   382
Levy, G.   830
Lexis, Wilhelm   148, 150, 153, 156, 162, 192n
Liebknecht, Wilhelm   20, 353–361, 830
Linguet, Simon-Nicholas Henri   15n
Loan Capital   550, 552, 805, 811
Locke, John   219–220, 257, 330, 336
Loria, Achille   162, 202n, 298, 350
Luden, Heinrich   383
Lukács, György   92n, 537–539n
Lunacharsky, Anatoly   825
Luther, Martin   41
Luxemburg, Rosa   5n, 9–11, 14, 22–24, 132, 140n, 214, 340n, 378–389, 392, 738

McCulloch, John Ramsay   17, 276, 306–307, 335
Mach, Ernst   17, 274–275, 288, 325
Magnitude of Value   144–145, 155, 374n, 563, 568–569, 572–575, 589, 610, 620, 631n, 651, 693, 806
See also: Form of Value
Malthus, Thomas   15, 17, 109, 197, 219, 243, 246, 256n, 261, 272, 276, 292, 296, 302–314, 322, 331–332, 335–337, 464–465
Marginal Utility Theory
See: Subjective Theory of Value
Marginalism
See: Subjective Theory of Value
Market Conjuncture
See: Conjuncture

Market Price   16, 48, 50, 88, 164, 174, 180, 183–184n, 186, 200, 219, 233, 247–248, 253, 258, 268, 350, 408, 431, 435–437, 443, 500, 555–557, 627, 669, 682, 685–686, 693–694
Market Value   174, 186, 200, 231, 252–253, 265, 336, 410, 428, 443, 500, 629
Markov, A.D.   830
Marshall, Alfred   409, 444, 819
Marwitz, Alexander von der   382
Material-Technical Process of Production
See: Production Process
Materialist Conception of History   1–2, 17–19, 39, 82, 104–107, 119, 160, 204, 213, 225, 275, 279, 288, 295, 312, 316, 322, 334, 390, 395, 399–400, 404, 453–454, 469, 471–472, 539, 543–544, 566, 721
Massie, Joseph   219
Mathematical School of Bourgeois Economics   26, 430–431, 444, 820
Mead, George Herbert   46
Means of Circulation
See: Functions of Money
Means of Consumption   1–2n, 20, 30, 72, 135n, 154–155, 157–158, 186, 193n, 195–196, 222, 224, 243, 261, 302–303, 310, 315, 333, 344, 355, 422–423, 427, 433–434, 452, 473, 483–408, 485, 487n, 499, 501–508, 510, 518–519, 522–528, 572, 576, 646, 698, 709, 711–716, 720, 754, 780–781, 786, 789, 794, 808, 812
Means of Payment
See: Functions of Money
Means of Production   16–17, 19–20, 29–30, 32, 36–37, 71, 79, 88, 90, 96–97, 119–120, 135, 138–139, 145, 151, 155–158, 172, 174, 176n, 193n, 199, 232, 234–236, 240, 247, 255, 258, 267–268, 307, 310, 315–316, 319, 323, 325n, 333–335, 338, 354, 371, 375, 402, 407, 409n, 413n, 417n, 429, 433–435, 438–439, 449–452, 471, 473, 484, 501, 505, 507–508, 511–513, 516–518, 527, 538, 540, 543, 545–552, 557, 570, 576–578, 643–646, 662, 689, 698, 701, 709, 712–716, 720, 731, 735, 748–751, 756, 791–793, 796, 803, 806
See also: Productive Forces

INDEX 863

Means of Subsistence
  See: Means of Consumption
Measure of Value
  See: Functions of Money
Medium of Exchange
  See: Functions of Money
Mehring, Franz   14, 214, 340n
Menger, Carl   22, 25–27, 207, 276, 305, 335, 371n, 406–409, 414–418, 425, 430–432, 441, 640, 674
Mensheviks   824, 828, 834–836
Menzhinsky, V.P.   825, 827, 834
Mercantilism   14–15, 29, 136–137, 214, 218–222, 227, 231–233, 236–237, 276, 296, 303, 329–330, 366–367, 378, 397, 527, 565, 737, 784, 799
Merchant's Capital   134, 177–179, 150, 204
Metamorphosis of the Commodity   131, 177–178, 230, 350, 515, 526, 528, 552, 669–671n, 673, 694–697, 699–701, 704–705, 710, 719, 721, 757–758, 778–781, 786–788, 809–810, 815
  See also: Change of Form (of the Products of Labour under Commodity Production)
Metternich, Klemens, Furst von   380–386
Mill, James   17, 276, 305, 335
Mill, John Stuart   29, 307, 338, 819
Mirabeau, Honoré Gabriel Riqueti, Count of   159
Mode of Production   4, 13, 15, 19, 21, 85, 89, 91, 96, 105–106, 110, 119–120, 136–139, 141, 145, 151, 154–155, 160–161, 171, 175–177, 180–181, 184, 186, 194–195, 198, 203, 211, 213, 282, 310–313, 320–321, 325, 331–334, 339, 352, 363, 368, 374, 377, 384, 386–388, 476, 483, 499, 506, 520, 536, 568
  See also: Social Formation
  See also: Capitalist Mode of Production
Molotov, Vyacheslav   835
Monetary Circulation   158, 216, 482, 525, 663–664
  See also: Circulation of Money
Monetary Exchange   110, 482, 636, 656, 682, 699, 710, 715
Money   2–3, 6, 9, 29, 31, 32–36, 42–44, 85, 87, 89, 124, 130, 133–136, 138, 140, 151–152, 180n, 232, 237, 267–268, 278, 285, 296, 323, 354, 411, 422, 425–426, 451, 482–487n, 494, 497, 514, 520–535, 548–551, 553, 555, 561, 568, 575, 584, 588, 602, 619–727, 729, 738, 743–744, 747, 750, 754–788, 791
  Direct Universal Exchangeability for any other Commodity   35, 624, 652–654, 657, 666, 761
  See also: Functions of Money
Money Capital   6, 124, 134–136, 138, 142–143, 152, 159, 177–178, 180n, 452, 486, 522, 532–535, 550, 552, 579, 733, 795, 797–803
  See also: Industrial Capital
  See also: Commercial Capital
Money Capitalist   135–136, 138, 180n, 533–534, 550, 552, 579n, 797, 803
  See also: Industrial Capitalist
  See also: Commercial Capitalist
Money Commodity   522, 671, 675–676, 680, 694
  See also: Gold
Money-Dealing Capital   177, 179, 801
Money-Form   267, 374n, 485, 487n, 494, 525, 551, 553, 568, 591, 615, 620, 636–637, 657, 661, 677, 692, 693, 705–707, 709, 721–722, 757, 765–767, 776, 778–782, 784–786, 790–791, 794, 799
  See also: Commodity-Form
  See also: Social Form (of the Products of Labour under Commodity Production)
  See also: Form of Value (of the Products of Labour under Commodity Production)
  See also: Change of Form (of the Products of Labour under Commodity Production)
Montesquieu, Charles-Louis de Secondat, Baron de La Brède et de   15n, 317
Müller, Adam Heinrich   383

Napoléon Bonaparte   282
Narodniks   9, 132n
Natural Economy   110, 257, 383, 431, 438, 480–485, 487n, 489–490, 496, 710–711
  See also: Simple Commodity Production
Necker, Jacques   229

Newton, Isaac 45
Neo-Kantianism 6, 58, 113, 122n, 125–126, 399n, 406
Non-Labour Revenues or Incomes 803–808, 812, 814–815
 See also: Profit of Enterprise
 See also: Interest on Loan Capital
 See also: Commercial Profit
 See also: Ground Rent
North, Dudley 219–220

Objectification of Production Relations
 See: Reification of Production Relations under Commodity Production
Oncken, August 226
Organic Composition of Capital 16–17, 19, 88, 90, 127, 171, 173, 199–200, 247–248, 252–259, 262, 264, 275, 290, 300–301, 323, 337–338, 504, 507, 510, 517, 580, 735, 794
 See also: Technical Composition of Capital
Organisation of Labour 369–372, 543–546, 559–560, 564–567, 582, 596, 633, 643, 695
Ossification (*Verknöcherung*) of Production Relations 765, 769–770, 782, 805, 814
 See also: Social Form (of the Products of Labour under Commodity Production)
 See also: Crystallisation of Social Forms
Overproduction 71–72, 90, 138, 140, 177n, 199, 248, 262, 264–265, 267, 276, 556, 643, 808

Paoletti, Ferdinando 229
Paris Commune 92
Parsons, Talcott 391n–392n, 395n
Parvus 14n, 26–27, 340n
Petry, Franz 630n, 971n
Petty, William 210, 219–220, 227, 231, 237, 279, 291, 329–330, 384, 642n
Physiocracy 14–15, 173, 214, 219–240, 246, 296, 298, 330, 336–337, 367, 799, 830
Plekhanov, Georgi 342n–343n, 405n, 738
Pokrovsky, Mikhail N. 828
Polanyi, Karl 379
Polarisation of Functions 36, 729, 753, 762–764, 775
 See also: Poles of the Expression of Value

Poles of the Expression of Value 32, 36, 583, 587, 593, 597, 599–602, 614–615, 651, 673, 729, 762–766, 775
 See: Relative Form of Value
 See: Equivalent Form of Value
Precious Metals 41, 296, 661–663, 702n, 711, 718
 See also: Gold
Preobrazhensky, Evgenii A. 662n
Prices of Production 10, 13, 16, 88n, 121, 164, 168n, 170–174, 179, 182n–184n, 189, 197, 247–248n, 251–258, 262, 268, 301–305, 323, 335–337, 410, 443–445, 447, 500, 552, 555, 575–576, 579–581, 807, 813
Primitive Accumulation of Capital 44–45, 393, 744, 791
Private Labour
 See: Concrete Labour
Private Property 15, 42, 55, 64, 72–74, 78–79, 117, 120, 203, 246, 322, 371n–372, 454, 545, 723, 790
Process of Production
 See: Production Process
Process of Reproduction
 See: Reproduction Process
Production Costs
 See: Costs of Production
Production Prices
 See: Prices of Production
Production Process 2, 8, 30–31, 37, 95–98, 101, 106, 130, 133–147, 153–159, 170–171, 181, 193n, 195, 203, 212, 216–217, 223–224, 232, 237, 240–242, 261, 264, 274n, 283–284, 306–307, 320–323, 330, 344, 365–369, 373, 400–402, 429, 440–441, 460–461, 468–471, 475–476, 480–499, 504–519, 527, 530, 532–536, 543–549, 552–555, 561–573, 582, 625, 637, 643–647, 653–655, 659, 672, 684, 687–692, 698–705, 709–710, 712, 715, 719–720, 722, 736–741, 746, 750, 752, 768, 772, 780, 787, 797, 799–800, 803–816
 See also: Reproduction Process
Production Relations
 See: Relations of Production
Production Time 142, 146–147
 See also: Working Period

INDEX 865

Production Relations
  See: Relations of Production
Productive Capital   6, 9, 124, 137, 142–143, 178, 260, 365, 533, 552, 797–798, 801, 803
Productive Forces of Labour   11, 19, 36, 86, 91, 93, 96–98, 105–106, 117, 127, 151, 176–177n, 225n, 282, 304, 308, 310, 320, 331–332, 334, 337–339, 355, 362, 368–369, 373, 410, 440–441, 498, 502, 512, 540, 543–544, 549, 554, 557, 559, 565–566, 570–571, 582, 682, 686–688, 715, 731–747, 750, 752, 755, 796, 808–809, 817
  See also: Productivity of Labour
  See also: Technology
Productive Labour   15, 150, 181, 190, 194, 203n, 205, 214, 219, 233, 236–244, 264, 307, 365, 478, 565, 567
  See also: Unproductive Labour
Productivity of Labour   12, 30, 88, 90–92, 98, 111, 120, 165, 175–176n, 190–191, 196–197, 205, 207, 209, 214, 222, 225, 242, 247, 266n, 310, 314, 316n, 365, 367, 439, 442–443, 445, 447, 452, 472, 499, 509–511, 517, 536, 549, 556–558, 563–565, 568–573, 578–580, 631, 669, 674, 684, 687, 715, 794, 813
  See also: Productive Forces of Labour
  See also: Technology
Profit   111, 130, 143–144, 147–148, 151, 154, 170–173, 185, 197, 203n, 207, 219, 222, 235, 239–240, 247, 255, 260, 265, 303, 307, 310, 313, 321, 329, 338, 366, 391, 393, 396, 414n, 429, 438–440, 496, 505–509, 513, 530, 532–533, 552, 566n, 570, 572, 576, 578, 581, 737, 739, 750, 754, 806
Profit of Enterprise   179–180, 203n, 333, 803–805
Profit Rate
  See: Rate of profit
Profit upon Alienation   223–231, 329, 333, 336
  See: Mercantiliam
Proletariat
  See: Working Class
Proudhon, Pierre-Joseph   1, 107, 154, 216, 342
Psychological School of Political Economy
  See: Subjective Theory of Value
Purchase and Sale of Commodities   1, 135n, 178, 268, 411, 418, 531, 547–548, 550–551, 559, 637–638, 656, 688, 697, 699–700, 702, 704, 727, 780–781, 783, 788, 809–810
  See also: Buyers and Sellers of Commodities

Quesnay, François   142, 159, 201, 207, 214, 226, 230, 233

Rabbeno, Ugo   202
Ramsay, George   17, 276, 310–311, 320–321, 334, 337, 339
Rate of Interest   180, 330
Rate of Profit   11–12, 15–17, 19–20, 88, 91–92, 111, 127, 144–145, 147, 150, 153–154, 162, 164, 170–178, 180n, 183, 185, 191n, 198–203n, 207, 210–211n, 247–249, 252–257, 259, 262–263, 276, 279, 290, 296, 298–300, 305, 311, 314, 323, 329, 332, 335, 337–339, 341, 350, 355, 364, 375, 377, 405n, 410, 413, 443, 445, 447n, 540, 552, 575, 578–579, 581, 621, 794, 807, 809, 811–812
  Average: See: Average Rate of Profit
  Declining Tendency: See: Falling Tendency of the Rate of Profit
Rate of Surplus Value   20, 88, 90, 127, 144, 147–148, 154, 157, 164, 170–171, 174, 191, 200, 207, 255, 263, 338–339, 355, 580, 794
Rau, Karl Heinrich   384
Ravenstone, Piercy   308, 310, 332
Raw Materials   87, 142–143, 147, 181, 224–225, 251, 256–257, 259, 262–263, 274, 300, 305, 310, 315, 333, 407, 439, 523
Reification of Production Relations under Commodity Production   31–32, 35–36, 84–85, 93, 192, 449, 537n, 539–540, 548–550, 555, 560, 562–563, 565, 568, 576, 582, 624, 644–645, 672–673, 677–678, 690, 694, 696, 707–709, 716, 730–731, 747–750, 753–755, 758, 769–773, 795–796, 803, 814–816
  See also: Social Properties of Things (of the Products of Labour under Commodity Production)
  See also: Fetishisation of Production Relations between People

Relation of Value   32, 155, 583, 593–594, 596, 601, 735, 762
   See also: Expression of Value
Relations of Production   17, 19, 21–22, 29, 31, 34–37, 58, 84, 105–106, 177, 204, 241, 308, 321, 334, 339, 346, 363, 368–369, 371–377, 397, 400, 449, 452, 498–499, 501, 504, 514, 519–521, 523, 529, 532–533, 536–537, 543–544, 546–555, 558–560, 562–568, 573, 575–576, 578–582, 621, 624, 626, 637, 641–641, 644–646, 648–650, 652–653, 656–657, 665, 671–673, 676–677, 688–690, 695–697, 700–702, 705, 709, 716, 719–723, 726–727, 729–755, 760, 768–773, 788, 791, 795–796, 802–803, 806, 808, 811, 813–817
   See also: Social Form of the Production Process
   See also: Social Form (of the Products of Labour under Commodity Production)
   See also: Social Function (of the Products of Labour under Commodity Production)
Relative Form of Value   32, 583–584, 587, 597, 599–602, 610, 651, 759, 763, 767–768
   See also: Equivalent Form of Value
Renner, Karl   372n, 374n
Reproduction of Capital
   See: Reproduction Process
Reproduction on an Expanded Scale
   See: Accumulation of Capital
   See also: Simple Reproduction
Reproduction Process   29–30, 37, 84, 89–90, 96, 137–140, 155, 159, 192, 203n, 268, 330, 338, 347, 448, 452–454, 466, 473–475, 478–479, 488–489, 508–509, 513, 515, 518–520, 558, 643, 684, 688–689, 698–702, 710, 795, 801, 811
   See also: Production Process
Reserve Army of Labour
   See: Unemployment
Reserve Fund   138, 712–714, 717–718, 783
Revenues   15, 37, 50, 158, 184, 240, 330, 337–339, 573n, 393, 402, 648, 715, 804–807, 811–814
Revisionism   5, 7, 10, 19, 112–113, 121, 214, 340, 342–343, 351, 389, 391, 405n, 408
Ricardian School   144, 148, 219, 276, 304–305, 321, 333, 460, 577

Ricardo, David   3, 15–18, 21, 30–33, 58, 67, 142–143, 149, 154, 173, 176n, 182, 191, 201, 207, 219, 225, 246–272, 275–277, 289–290, 296, 298–315, 321–323, 331–338, 357–358, 362–367, 374–378, 384, 386–388, 406, 409, 413, 428, 430, 443, 463–464, 536–582, 584–585, 587, 602–604, 611–614, 617, 625, 630–631, 730–731, 754, 784, 807, 829–830, 836
Rickert, Heinrich   122
Ridgeway, William   664
Rodbertus, Johann Karl   4, 15, 136, 143n, 167, 183, 207, 255–258, 270, 384, 405n, 819
Rokityansky, Yakov   819–836
Roscher, Wilhelm   22, 107, 379, 384–385
Rosenberg, Isaiah   21, 362–366, 536, 541–543, 567, 573, 575–577, 829–830
Rousseau, Jean-Jacques   342
Rubin, Isaak Il'ich   25–37, 429–836
Rubina, Polina Petrovna   826
Russian Revolution   92
Ryazanov, David   29, 74, 449–450, 454–455, 4457, 460, 463, 466, 469, 503n, 822, 827, 829–830n, 832, 834–836
Rykachev, Andrei   655–656
Rykov, A.I.   827, 829

Saint-Simon, Claude Henri de Rouvroy, comte de   167n, 820
Say, Jean-Baptiste   139n, 184, 243, 277, 384, 463n, 465
Schelling, Friedrich Wilhelm Joseph   280–281
Schmalz, Theodor   229
Schmidt, Conrad   12n, 13n, 26–27, 162, 165, 187n–189, 191, 369n, 405–429, 802n
Schmoller, Gustav von   22–23, 312n, 391, 394n
Scharnhorst, Gerhard von   382
Schüler, Richard   23–24, 378–389
Schumpeter, Joseph   439–441, 680n
Schweitzer, Jean Baptista von   117
Serfdom   70, 174n, 204, 382, 711
   See also: Feudalism
Shabs, S.   833n
Sieber, Nikolai Ivanovich   3
Simple Commodity Circulation   133, 216, 268, 789
Simple Commodity Economy
   See: Simple Commodity Production

INDEX 867

Simple Commodity Production   13, 163,
   165, 268, 280, 289, 291, 331, 392, 397,
   419–421, 428, 446, 449–452, 462–464,
   481, 483–490, 496, 509, 515, 524–527,
   530, 534–535, 547, 551, 555–558, 558,
   560, 563, 566, 577–578, 582n, 616,
   621, 681, 686, 703n, 713, 719, 726, 744,
   748–750, 771–788, 791–792, 794, 802,
   809–810
Simple Labour   20, 225, 353, 355, 359–360,
   611, 674
   See also: Skilled Labour
Simple Reproduction of Capital   402, 488–
   490, 703–704
   See also: Accumulation of Capital
Sismondi, Jean Charles Leonard Simonde de
   309, 311, 331, 384, 739
Skilled Labour   20, 353, 355, 358–360, 395,
   674
   See also: Simple Labour
Slavery   63, 66, 70, 77–78, 119n, 174n, 204, 482,
   487n, 660–661, 711
Smith, Adam   14–15, 24, 27, 40, 45–51, 54–55,
   58, 67, 75, 87, 89n, 93–94, 99, 129, 142,
   149–150n, 156, 173, 184, 191, 207, 210, 212,
   214–215, 219, 231–246, 249–254, 271, 289,
   296, 307, 326, 329–330, 335, 339, 354,
   359, 363, 366–367, 374, 378–389, 406,
   447, 462, 537, 541, 572, 581, 630, 642, 754,
   807, 819, 832
Social-Economic Form
   See: Social Form
Social Form (of the Products of Labour under
   Commodity Production)   20–21, 30–
   31, 34, 36, 142, 195, 241–242, 307, 311,
   354–355, 359, 362, 368, 375n, 440, 452,
   494–495, 513–515, 519–523, 525–527,
   535–537, 539–540, 543–544, 549, 550–
   551, 553–554, 559–575, 578, 581–582,
   590, 621, 629, 633–634, 644–645, 653,
   665, 669–672, 682, 684, 688–693, 695–
   697, 701–702, 706–707, 711, 715, 718,
   722, 725–727, 730, 737, 744–746, 748–
   750, 752, 756–758, 760–761, 765–766,
   769–770, 772, 774–775, 796, 803–805,
   808–809, 812–816
   See also: Social Function (of the Products
      of Labour under Commodity Production)

See also: Crystallisation of Social Forms
See also: Social Form of the Production
   Process
See also: Relations of Production
See also: Ossification of Production
   Relations
Social Form of the Production Process   452,
   535, 560, 566, 568, 571, 629, 633, 684,
   691, 715, 737–738
   See also: Mode of Production
Social Formation   2, 15, 37, 322, 343, 349,
   354–355, 365, 370–373, 454, 469, 479–
   481, 487n, 490, 532, 538, 540, 742,
   746–747, 751
   See also: Economic Formation
   See also: Mode of Production
Social Function (of the Labour Products
   under Commodity Production)   7, 20,
   34, 129, 142, 195, 242, 355, 359, 452,
   516, 521–524, 549, 551, 553–554, 621–
   622, 632–634, 644, 648–649, 653,
   656, 662, 672, 695, 718, 723, 765, 770–
   771
   See also: Social Form (of the Labour
      Products under Commodity Production)
   See also: Social Form of the Production
      Process
   See also: Relations of Production
Social Labour
   See: Abstract Labour
Social Properties of Things (of the Products of
   Labour under Commodity Production)
   548–550, 632, 634, 644, 648, 676, 688,
   691, 695, 758–759, 765–766, 772
   See also: Reification of Production Relations under Commodity Production
   See also: Fetishim of the Commodity
Social Structure of Commodity Economy
   544, 562, 633, 635, 641, 662, 696
   See also: Relations of Production
Social Structure of Production   30, 452, 513
   See also: Relations of Production
Social Structure of the Economy   544, 633,
   662
   See also: Relations of Production
Social Structure of the Reproduction Process
   30, 452, 519
   See also: Relations of Production

Socially Necessary Labour
　See: Abstract Labour
Soden, Friedrich Julius von 383
Sombart, Werner 10–13, 22–25, 144n, 162–211, 373, 390–404, 702n, 717n
Sorge, Friedrich 9
Sphere of Circulation 14, 148, 177, 199, 227, 251, 337, 528, 701, 703–707, 713–714, 717–718, 769, 782–783, 791, 794–797, 801–802, 811
Sphere of Production 14, 174, 182n, 199–200, 227, 301, 441, 448, 674, 791, 794, 796, 811
Stalin 29, 35, 37, 729, 834–835
Stalinism 92
Stammler, Rudolf 122, 372
Stein, Baron vom 382
Steinberg, James 723n
Steuart, James 15, 214, 220–228, 232, 311, 329
Stirner, Max 460
Stolzmann, Rudolf 831
Ströbel, Henrich 214
Subjective Labour Value
　See: Theory of Subjective Labour Value
Subjective Theory of Value 11–12, 22, 25–29, 33, 163, 201–202, 207–208, 270n, 312n, 336, 358, 363, 371, 376n, 405–449, 453, 460, 486, 496, 500n, 527, 536, 541, 544, 621–623, 640, 679–681, 754n
Substance of Value 569, 592, 599, 617, 620, 636
　See also: Content of Value
　See also: Form of Value
Supply and Demand 4, 27, 88n, 139, 149n, 153, 164, 174–175, 180, 187n, 224, 233, 265, 335, 344–345, 358, 410, 413n–414n, 424–425, 431, 437, 443n–445, 478, 500–501, 512, 647
Surplus Labour 91, 95–96, 98, 150, 192n–193n, 198, 204, 206, 223–224, 229, 242, 310, 315, 323, 330, 332, 339, 409, 487, 534, 582, 793, 805–806
Surplus Product 180n, 193n, 206, 214, 222–223, 227–229, 233, 238, 240, 306, 315, 330, 482, 489, 519, 534
Surplus Profit 181–182, 184n, 200n, 206, 248, 260, 314, 321, 333, 443
Surplus Value 8, 12, 16–17, 20–21, 87, 90–91, 111, 130, 134–135, 139, 142–144, 147–148, 151–160, 170–175, 178–180, 183, 191n–192n, 196–199, 203n, 205–206, 210, 217–221, 227, 238–241, 247–248, 252, 255–259, 300–303, 307, 310, 321, 329–331, 335, 338, 397, 406, 452, 464, 488, 519, 530–534, 550, 575–579, 581, 741, 788, 796, 803–808, 811, 814–815
Surplus Value Rate
　See: Rate of Surplus Value
Svyatlovsky, Vladimir V. 658n

Tawney, Richard Henry 44
Technical Composition of Capital 517, 735, 765
　See also: Organic Composition of Capital
Technique 395n, 443, 544, 549, 557, 684, 735–736, 740–741, 794, 808
　See also: Means of Production
　See also: Technology
　See also: Productive Forces of Labour
　See also: Productivity of Labour
Technology 90–91, 94–96, 112, 145, 191, 248n, 290, 302, 367–368, 371n, 394, 402, 443, 445, 447n, 517, 545, 549, 734, 736, 739, 740, 752
　See also: Means of Production
　See also: Technique
　See also: Productive Forces of Labour
　See also: Productivity of Labour
The German Ideology 1n, 29, 57, 213, 450, 454, 469, 471–472
The Holy Family 449, 454, 456, 461–462, 468–469, 471–472, 476–477, 510, 523
The Poverty of Philosophy 1, 7, 129, 136n, 467, 469, 498, 501, 503, 507, 738, 742
Theories of Surplus Value, Vol. I 3, 14–15, 39, 212–245, 328–339
Theories of Surplus Value, Vol. II 3, 15–16, 39, 246–272, 328–339, 611
Theories of Surplus Value, Vol. III 3, 16–18, 39, 273–339, 503, 573n, 604, 606, 608, 611–615
Theory of Labour Value
　See: Labour Theory of Value
Theory of Marginal Utility
　See: Subjective Theory of Value
Theory of Money 29, 33, 181, 278, 575, 587–588, 599, 619–727, 773, 775, 819, 831
Theory of Subjective Labour Value 541, 572, 680–681, 687

INDEX 869

Theory of Value   3, 7, 11–12n, 20, 25–28, 30–34, 112, 121, 129, 148, 152, 154, 160, 185–187, 191, 204–205, 217–220, 232–233, 248–249, 252, 275, 290–292, 296–304, 322, 335–336, 348, 353–366, 387, 410, 414, 421, 429–430, 442, 536–589, 599, 614, 619, 621–622, 625–641, 668–671, 680–681, 687, 689, 692, 729–733, 773, 804, 825–833
Thompson, William   367, 384
Thünen, Johann Heinrich von   384
Tönnies, Ferdinand   370n, 377
Tooke, Thomas   743
Torrens, Robert   306, 308, 335
Total Social Capital   9, 132, 154, 173, 236, 518, 703
Trakhtenberg, Iosif   680–681, 690n
Trotsky, Leon   15, 98n, 110n, 619n, 820
Trusts   112n, 116, 344
Tugan-Baranovsky, Mikhail   252n, 660, 821
Turgot, Anne Robert Jacques   207, 229, 329, 335
Turnover of Capital   90, 131, 142–150, 171, 235–236, 249n, 254, 295, 335, 718

Under-Consumption   140–141, 303, 344, 509–510
Unemployment   89, 96, 329, 337, 504, 510, 517, 735
Unity of Opposites
   See: Law of the Unity of Opposites
Universal Equivalent
   See: Functions of Money
Unpaid Labour   119, 180n, 223, 229, 234–235, 248, 251–252, 306, 321, 534, 582n, 790, 793
   See also: Surplus Labour
Unproductive Labour   15, 194n, 236–244, 264
   See also: Productive Labour
Unshlikht, I.S.   826
Use-Value   15, 21, 29–30, 32, 34, 87n, 90, 97, 132, 134, 155, 180n, 194, 196, 205, 222–223, 227, 229, 231, 236–238, 241–242, 264, 266, 307–309, 314, 323, 358, 362–363, 365, 367, 375n–376, 397, 406, 415, 425, 430–432, 435, 437, 448, 450–454, 463, 481–497, 509, 513–524, 527–536, 541, 548, 559, 562, 566, 574, 584, 589, 591–592, 594–597, 599–602, 605–606, 608–611, 621–622, 626, 628–630, 633, 635, 637, 641, 645–651, 659, 661, 663, 665–667, 671–673, 684, 691–692, 694, 703–706, 711, 717, 720–722, 757–760, 762–763, 776, 781–782, 787–788, 809
   Formal: *See*: Formal Use-Value
Use-Value of Labour Power   522, 530–532, 534

Valorisation of Capital   9, 133, 150, 155, 176n, 180n–183, 194n–196, 256, 271, 301, 323, 358, 484–486, 513, 516, 530, 582, 790–791, 794, 798
   See also: Exploitation of the Workers
Value   12–13, 16, 20–21, 26, 28, 32–33, 119, 129–130, 132, 134, 144n, 148–150, 152, 154–155, 159–160, 163–165, 170, 173, 179n, 181, 183, 187n, 192, 196–198, 205, 207, 209, 211, 221, 230, 234–235, 256–269, 283, 289–290, 300–302, 310, 323, 329, 332–333, 335, 353, 355, 358–359, 363, 365, 367, 375, 387, 406–407, 414–416, 429–432, 435–438, 465, 491, 500, 514, 517–519, 531–533, 539–581, 583–618, 673, 737–738, 741, 743, 747, 750, 754, 759–760, 763, 772–773, 776, 784, 788, 807, 816
   Law of: *See*: Law of Value
   See: Relation of Value
   See: Expression of Value
Value Expression
   See: Expression of Value
   See: Relation of Value
Value-Form
   See: Form of Value
Value of Labour Power   290, 335, 338, 502, 530, 793–794, 807
   See also: Variable Capital
Value Product   156, 192, 335
Value, Price and Profit   628, 634–635
Variable Capital   8, 16, 87, 142–144, 147–148, 156–157, 170–175, 185, 199, 203n, 235, 240, 248, 251–253, 256–258, 260, 262–264, 299, 302, 305, 310, 323, 333n, 337–339, 452, 516–519, 551–553, 793–794
   See also: Value of Labour Power
Vasina, Lyudmila   819–836
Vaughan, Rice   231
Verri, Pietro   229

Virgil   325n, 398n
Volgin, V.P.   824
Vulgar Economics   18, 27, 133–134, 142, 153, 162, 232, 243, 299, 300, 307, 324, 333, 342–352, 386, 388, 488, 516, 531, 544, 549, 573, 602, 738, 806–807, 814, 816, 831

Wage-Labour   3, 17, 20–21, 31, 37, 50, 72, 87, 101, 135–136, 142, 150, 179, 190n, 206, 216, 241, 262, 267, 283, 285, 308–309, 311, 315–316, 321, 323, 325, 354–355, 418n, 502, 511, 530, 532, 538–539, 553, 560, 578, 626, 722, 730, 791, 796, 807
Wage Labour and Capital   502, 511
Wage-Worker
   See: Wage-Labour
Wages   2, 49–50, 79, 87, 89, 92, 111, 136, 141, 147, 155–159, 171, 179–180n, 184, 191n, 195, 224–225, 231, 234–235, 238–240, 243, 246–247, 251, 253–256, 260, 262–263, 267, 290, 300, 303, 307, 314, 316, 319–320, 323, 330–335, 360, 365, 375, 405, 413n, 414n, 499, 501, 503–505, 513, 519, 570, 572, 578, 582, 631, 634, 713, 737, 750, 754, 806–807
Wages of Supervision and Management   180–181
Wagner, Adolph   22–23, 166–167, 207, 661, 675, 711–712, 831
Waentig, Heinrich   396

Walras, Léon   25–26, 406, 430, 820
Weber, Max   11, 22, 41, 43, 390–391n, 400, 717n
West, Edward   336
Whewell, William   311–312
Wieser, Friedrich von   26, 207, 414, 430, 433, 435, 439, 442
William of Orange   228
Windelband, Wilhelm   122, 126
Witzleben, Job von   382
Wolf, Julius   166–167n
Working Day   2, 4, 96, 111, 146, 251, 254, 264, 289, 487n, 579
Working Period   146–147
   See also: Production Time
World Market   3, 107, 176, 204, 216, 248, 283, 291, 507, 787
World Money
   See: Functions of Money
Working Class   4, 23, 37, 44, 91, 93, 116–118, 119–120, 128, 140–141, 160, 193, 215, 230, 261, 282, 287, 296, 304, 309, 316, 331–332, 337–338, 347, 391, 403, 501–505, 507, 510–511, 722, 737, 822, 827
Wundt, Wilhelm   126n

Zeller, Eduard   288, 293–295
Zheltenkov, V.V.   821
Zheltenkova, B.I.   827, 834–836
Zheltenkova, M.V.   821

CPSIA information can be obtained
at www.ICGtesting.com
Printed in the USA
LVHW010134281018
595009LV00001B/1/P